Casebook on Tort Law

CASEBOOK ON
TORT LAW

Kirsty Horsey & Erika Rackley

16th Edition

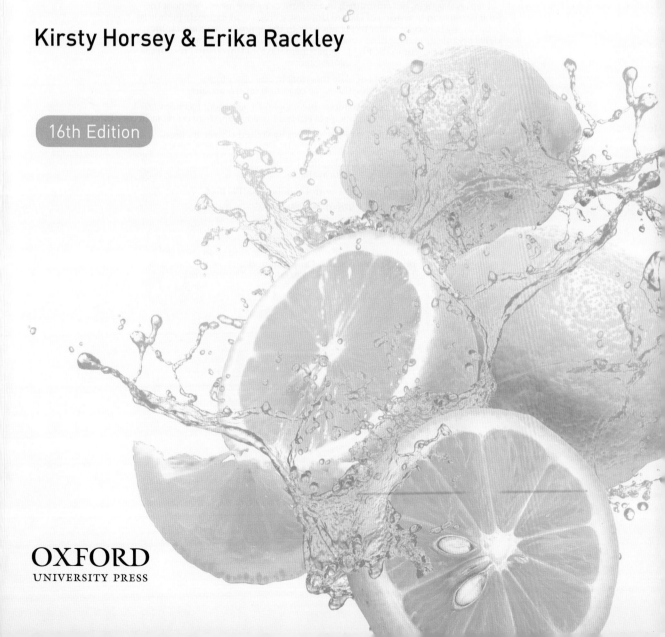

OXFORD
UNIVERSITY PRESS

OXFORD
UNIVERSITY PRESS

Great Clarendon Street, Oxford, OX2 6DP,
United Kingdom

Oxford University Press is a department of the University of Oxford.
It furthers the University's objective of excellence in research, scholarship,
and education by publishing worldwide. Oxford is a registered trade mark of
Oxford University Press in the UK and in certain other countries

Thirteenth edition 2015
Fourteenth edition 2017
Fifteenth edition 2019

Impression: 1

Public sector information reproduced under Open Government Licence v3.0
(http://www.nationalarchives.gov.uk/doc/open-government-licence/open-government-licence.htm)

Published in the United States of America by Oxford University Press
198 Madison Avenue, New York, NY 10016, United States of America

British Library Cataloguing in Publication Data
Data available

Library of Congress Control Number: 2021941846

ISBN 978–0–19–289365–9

Printed in Great Britain by
Bell & Bain Ltd., Glasgow

Kirsty Horsey

Kirsty Horsey is a Reader in Law at the University of Kent, teaching tort law to undergraduate students across all years. Her research interests lie in the overlap of medical, family and tort law. She is editor of a number of collections on the regulation of assisted reproduction (including, most recently, *Revisiting the Regulation of Human Fertilisation and Embryology* (Routledge, 2015)) and is a regular contributor to BioNews (bionews.org). She is co-author (with Erika Rackley) of *Tort Law* (7th edn, OUP, 2021). She tweets at @khorsey.

Erika Rackley

Erika Rackley is a Professor in the Law School at the University of Kent. She has taught tort law at a number of universities in the UK. Her research interests are broadly in the field of feminism, gender and law, particularly in relation to judicial diversity. She is author of *Women, Judging and the Judiciary: From Difference to Diversity* (Routledge, 2012), co-author (with Kirsty Horsey) of *Tort Law* (7th edn, OUP, 2021) and co-editor of *Feminist Judgments: From Theory to Practice* (Hart, 2010), *Feminist Perspectives on Tort Law* (Routledge, 2012) and *Women's Legal Landmarks: Celebrating the History of Women and Law in the UK and Ireland* (Hart, 2018). She tweets at @erikarackley.

Keep up to date with changes and developments at **@horseyrackley**.

Preface

Well, here we are again. Another two years have passed and we've found ourselves updating and revising this edition in circumstances we could never have imagined. As always, there are new cases and extracts and—excitingly—a new title. We've changed from 'torts' to 'tort law' to mirror the title of our companion textbook—*Tort Law* (also published by OUP). While each book stands alone, we hope that they will work well together as companion texts. Our aim continues to be that of Richard Kidner (the original author of this text): to write a casebook that provides 'within a small compass and at a relatively low cost, those cases which students will commonly be referred to in their courses' and which provide an insight into the legal issue at hand and are the best 'pegs on which to hang one's knowledge'.

As always, there are many further resources—as well as updates and commentary—on our **online resources** and via our Twitter account (@horseyrackley).

Finally, huge thanks to our colleagues and students past and present for their wisdom and insights, to Sarah Stephenson at OUP, to the wonderful Joy Ruskin-Tompkins and to Mike, Frank, Bill, Charlie, Enyo and Kasper.

We have done our best to state the law as of 31 March 2021.

Kirsty Horsey
Erika Rackley

New to this edition

The sixteenth edition has been thoroughly revised to reflect all recent developments in the law of torts since publication of the last edition, including new case extracts:

- *Poole Borough Council* v *GN* [2019] UKSC 25 (liability of public bodies)

- *Equitas Insurance Ltd* v *Municipal Mutual Insurance Ltd* [2019] EWCA Civ 718 (causation)

- *Henderson* v *Dorset Healthcare University NHS Foundation Trust* [2020] UKSC 43 (illegality defence)

- *Serafin* v *Malkiewicz and others* [2020] UKSC 23 (defamation)

- *R (on the application of Jalloh (formerly Jollah))* v *Secretary of State for the Home Department* [2020] UKSC 4 (false imprisonment)

- *Lachaux* v *Independent Print* [2019] UKSC 27 (defamation)

- *Stoffel & Co (Appellant)* v *Grondona* [2020] UKSC 42 (illegality defence)

- *Fearn and others* v *The Board of Trustees of the Tate Gallery* [2020] EWCA Civ 104 (nuisance; privacy)

- *WM Morrison Supermarkets plc* v *Various Claimants* [2020] UKSC 12 (vicarious liability)

- *Barclays Bank plc* v *Various Claimants* [2020] UKSC 13 (vicarious liability)

www.oup.com/uk/horsey_casebook16e/

Lecturer resources

Using the online resources saves you time by providing you with ready-made teaching and testing materials, while facilitating blended learning and enhancing the student experience. Lecturer resources are only available to lecturers who are adopting the book, to ensure that students cannot access material which could be used for assessment. Please visit www.oup.com/he/horsey-casebook16e if you have adopted or are thinking of adopting this book, for information on how to access the lecturer resources.

The test bank is a fully customisable resource containing ready-made assessments with which to test your students and aid their learning. Each answer is accompanied by feedback to explain to the student why their answer is correct or incorrect, and where in this book they can find further information.

Student resources

The online materials allow you to check your understanding, extend your knowledge and ensure you are up to date with the latest developments in the field. You can use them to consolidate your learning after each lecture, to prepare for seminars, as a starting point to research a coursework essay and of course during your revision. The student resources are completely open access, with no registration, meaning you can use them whenever and wherever.

Annotated web links

A selection of annotated web links, chosen by the authors and organised by chapter, direct you to video and audio clips of news reports and 'talking heads' with politicians, claimants and lawyers. The authors also include direct links to key cases on BAILII; with just one click you can access the full text of the case being discussed.

General guidance on how to answer problem questions and essays

The authors have provided essential guidance on how to approach both types of question you will encounter during your degree: essays and problem questions.

Annotated judgments and Acts

Further judgments annotated with explanatory notes and points for students to consider. This innovative resource will help you to develop the skills of reading and analysing judgments.

Twitter feed

Keep abreast of changes and developments in this fast-moving area of law with updates at @horseyrackley. Section references enable you to easily identify the relevant material in the book.

Acknowledgements

The publishers and authors would like to thank the following for permission to reproduce extracts from the publications listed below:

The Incorporated Council of Law Reporting for England and Wales—The Law Reports, The Weekly Law Reports and the Industrial Cases Reports.

Supreme Court of Canada, Canada Supreme Court Reports, reproduced with the permission of the Minister of Public Works and Government Services Canada.

Keith Stanton, *The Modern Law of Torts* (Sweet & Maxwell, 1994), pp 11–12, reproduced by permission of Thomson Reuters (Professional) UK Limited.

Extracts from the European Court of Justice © European Union, 1995–2021

Extracts from HUDOC © Council of Europe/European Court of Human Rights.

Every effort has been made to trace and contact copyright holders prior to publication. Where this has not proved possible, if notified, the publisher will undertake to rectify any errors or omissions at the earliest opportunity.

Contents in brief

TABLE OF CASES   xv

TABLE OF LEGISLATION   xxxii

1 Introduction   1

PART I The tort of negligence   11

2 Duty of care: basic principles   13

3 Special duty problems: omissions and acts of third parties   50

4 Special duty problems: psychiatric harm   62

5 Special duty problems: public bodies   96

6 Special duty problems: economic loss   132

7 Breach of duty: the standard of care   169

8 Causation and remoteness of damage   203

9 Defences to negligence   231

PART II Special liability regimes   259

10 Occupiers' liability   261

11 Product liability   298

12 Breach of statutory duty   316

PART III The personal torts   325

13 Intentional interferences with the person   327

14 Invasion of privacy   357

15 Defamation   391

PART IV The land torts   451

16 Trespass to land and nuisance   453

17 Actions under *Rylands* v *Fletcher*   488

PART V Liability, damages and limitations   503

18 Vicarious liability   505

19 Damages for death and personal injuries   533

INDEX   549

Contents in full

TABLE OF CASES   xv

TABLE OF LEGISLATION   xxxii

1 Introduction   1

1.1   The reach of tort law   1

1.2   The aims of the law of torts   4

      1.2.1 Deterrence   5

      1.2.2 Compensation   6

1.3   Studying tort law and reading cases   9

PART I The tort of negligence   11

2 Duty of care: basic principles   13

2.1   The rise and fall of the general duty of care   24

2.2   Reasonable foreseeability   34

2.3   Policy   40

3 Special duty problems: omissions and acts of third parties   50

3.1   No general duty for omissions   50

3.2   Exceptions to the rule   53

3.3   No general duty in respect of third party actions   55

4 Special duty problems: psychiatric harm   62

4.1   Primary victims   65

4.2   Secondary victims   76

4.3   Beyond primary and secondary victims   87

5 Special duty problems: public bodies   96

5.1   The fundamentals of the common law   96

5.2   Specific problematic areas: emergency services   111

5.3   The human rights effect   125

6   Special duty problems: economic loss   132

    6.1   'Pure' economic loss   132

    6.2   The *Hedley Byrne* exception   138
          6.2.1 Statements and advice   148
                 6.2.1.1 Assumption of responsibility   149
                 6.2.1.2 Reasonable reliance   154

    6.3   Liability to third parties   161

7   Breach of duty: the standard of care   169

    7.1   The level of reasonable risk—an objective standard   170

    7.2   The skill of the defendant   173
          7.2.1 The under-skilled   175
          7.2.2 Special skills and common practice   179
          7.2.3 Children   194

    7.3   Setting the standard of care   195
          7.3.1 Probability and seriousness of injury   197
          7.3.2 Cost of prevention   199
          7.3.3 Social value of the activity   201

8   Causation and remoteness of damage   203

    8.1   Causation   203
          8.1.1 An exception to the 'but for' rule—material increase in risk   212
          8.1.2 'Lost chance' claims   216

    8.2   Remoteness of damage   219
          8.2.1 The 'egg shell skull' rule   223
          8.2.2 The kind of damage   225

9   Defences to negligence   231

    9.1   Voluntarily assuming the risk   231
          9.1.1 Consent to a specific harm   232

    9.2   Illegality   234

    9.3   Contributory negligence   243

PART II Special liability regimes   259

10 Occupiers' liability   261

10.1   Occupiers' liability and negligence   265

10.2   Who is an occupier?   268

10.3   The status of the entrant: visitor or non-visitor?   270

10.4   The duty owed to visitors   278

10.5   The duty owed to non-visitors, including trespassers   282

10.6   Warnings and exclusions of liability   291

10.7   Defences   294

11 Product liability   298

11.1   Liability in negligence   298

11.2   Strict liability   301

12 Breach of statutory duty   316

12.1   Does the statute give rise to a claim in tort law and is a duty owed to the claimant?   316

12.2   Has the duty been breached and does the harm fall within the scope of the duty?   323

PART III The personal torts   325

13 Intentional interferences with the person   327

13.1   Trespass and negligence   327

13.2   Trespass to the person   330

    13.2.1 Battery and assault   330

    13.2.2 False imprisonment   334

    13.2.3 Defences   340

13.3   Intentional infliction of physical harm or distress   344

14 Invasion of privacy   357

14.1   Privacy and common law   357

14.2   The Human Rights Act and the reasonable expectation of privacy   359

14.3   Remedies   384

    14.3.1 Damages   384

    14.3.2 Injunctions   387

15	Defamation		391
	15.1	Who can sue?	392
	15.2	Who can be liable?	394
	15.3	The meaning of 'defamatory'	403
	15.4	Serious harm	405
	15.5	What do the words used mean?	413
	15.6	Do the words refer to the claimant?	423
	15.7	Truth	426
	15.8	Honest opinion	426
	15.9	Privilege	433
	15.10	Publication on a matter of public interest	436
	15.11	Offer of amends	444
	15.12	Damages	446

PART IV The land torts — 451

16	Trespass to land and nuisance		453
	16.1	Trespass to land	453
	16.2	Private nuisance	460
		16.2.1 Comparison with public nuisance	460
		16.2.2 Private nuisance: who can sue?	463
		16.2.3 Reasonable user	470
		16.2.3.1 Statutory authority and planning permission	472
		16.2.4 The effect of the Human Rights Act 1998	476
		16.2.5 Remedies	479

17	Actions under *Rylands* v *Fletcher*		488
	17.1	Merging *Rylands*, nuisance and negligence?	496

PART V Liability, damages and limitations — 503

18	Vicarious liability		505
	18.1	A relationship of, or akin to, employment	507
	18.2	The course of employment	516
	18.3	Liability for independent contractors	527

19   Damages for death and personal injuries   **533**

   19.1 Types of action for damages   533

   19.2 Calculation of loss of earnings and other losses   540

   19.3 Intangible losses   546

INDEX   549

Table of cases

Case names in **bold** indicate that the case features in a 'case box' (which can be found on the page numbers given in **bold**).

United Kingdom

8 Representative Claimants and others v MGN Ltd [2016] EWHC 855 (Ch) . . . 367

A v B plc [2002] EWCA Civ 337; [2003] QB 195 . . . 363, 364, 378

A v Essex County Council [2004] 1 WLR 1881 . . . 106

A v Hoare [2008] UKHL 6 . . . 330

A v National Blood Authority [2001] 3 All ER 289; [2001] Lloyd's Rep Med 187 (QBD) . . . **309–14**, 315

A-G see Attorney-General

AAA v Associated Newspapers [2013] EWCA Civ 554 . . . 374

AB v Leeds Teaching Hospital NHS Trust [2005] EWHC 644 (QB); [2005] QB 506 . . . 87

ABK v KDT & FGH [2013] EWHC 1192 (QB) . . . 354

Abouzaid v Mothercare (2001) *The Times*, 20 February . . . 315

Adam v Ward [1917] AC 309 (HL) . . . 434

Admiralty Commissioners v SS Volute [1922] 1 AC 129 . . . 196

Airedale NHS Trust v Bland [1993] AC 789 . . . 188

Al Saudi Banque v Clarke Pixley [1990] Ch 313 . . . 155

Al-Kandari v Brown [1988] QB 665 . . . 141

Alcock v Chief Constable of South Yorkshire [1992] 1 AC 310 (HL) . . . 1, 41, 46, 62, 63, 65, 67, 71, 73, 74, 75, 76, **77–81**, 82, 83, 88, 89, 90, 91, 92, 93, 94, 112

Aldred's Case (1610) 9 Co Rep 57b . . . 468

Ali and another v Channel 5 Broadcasting Ltd [2019] EWCA Civ 677 . . . 387

Aliakmon, The see Leigh and Sillavan Ltd v Aliakmon Shipping

Allen v Gulf Oil Refining Ltd [1980] QB 156 (CA) . . . 474

Allen v Gulf Oil Refining Ltd [1981] AC 1001 (HL) . . . 107, **472–3**, 474

Allied Maples Group Ltd v Simmons & Simmons [1995] 1 WLR 1602 (CA) . . . 218

American Cyanamid v Ethicon [1975] AC 396 . . . 479

Ames v The Spamhouse Project [2015] EWHC 127 (QB); [2015] 1 WLR 3409 . . . 408–9

Ancell v McDermot [1993] 4 All ER 355 . . . 112

Anchor Brewhouse v Berkley House [1987] 2 EGLR 172 (Ch) . . . **457–8**

Andrews v Hopkinson [1957] 1 QB 229 . . . 301

Andrews v Schooling [1991] 3 All ER 723 . . . 143

Anns v Merton LBC [1978] AC 728 (HL) . . . **27–8**, 30, 31, 32, 46, 98, 99, 107, 108, 109, 110, 144, 145, 146

Archer v Williams see Lady Archer v Williams

Armes v Nottinghamshire County Council [2017] UKSC 60 . . . 515, 528, 532

Arthur JS Hall & Co v Simons [2002] 1 AC 615 . . . 181

Ashley v Chief Constable of Sussex [2008] UKHL 25; [2008] 2 WLR 975 . . . 385

Askey v Golden Wine Co Ltd [1948] 2 All ER 35 . . . 235

Aswan Engineering v Lupdine Ltd [1987] 1 WLR 1 . . . 301

Atkinson v Newcastle Waterworks Co (1877) LR 2 Ex D 441 . . . 317, 322

Attorney-General v Guardian Newspapers Ltd (No 2) (Spycatcher) [1990] 1 AC 109 . . . 362

Attorney-General v PYA Quarries Ltd [1957] 2 QB 169 . . . 463

Attorney-General v Tod-Heatley [1897] 1 Ch 560 . . . 497

Attorney-General's Reference (No 6 of 1980) [1981] QB 715 . . . 342

Attorney-General's Reference (No 3 of 1994) [1998] AC 245 . . . 72

AXB v BXA [2018] EWHC 588 (QB) . . . 354

Bailey v Ministry of Defence [2007] EWHC 2913 (QB) . . . 211

Bailey v Ministry of Defence [2008] EWCA Civ 883 . . . 208, 211

Bailey and another v HSS Alarms (2000) *The Times*, 20 June (CA) . . . 51

Baker v Quantum Clothing [2011] UKSC 17; [2011] 4 All ER 273 . . . 181

Baker v TE Hopkins & Sons Ltd [1959] 1 WLR 966 (CA) . . . 38, 233

Baker v Willoughby [1970] AC 467 (HL) . . . 253, 255, 257

Bamford v Turnley (1862) 3 B & S 62 . . . 491

Banca Nazionale del Lavoro SPA v Playboy Club London Ltd [2018] UKSC 43 . . . 159

Banque Keyser SA v Skandia (UK) Insurance [1989] 3 WLR 25 (CA) . . . 141

Banque Keyser SA v Skandia (UK) Insurance [1990] 2 All ER 947 (HL) . . . 141

Barber v Somerset County Council [2004] UKHL 13; [2004] 1 WLR 1089 . . . 95

Barclays Bank v Various Claimants [2020] UKSC 13 . . . 527

Barings v Coopers and Lybrand [1997] 1 BCLC 427 . . . 158

Barker v Corus [2006] UKHL 20; [2006] 2 WLR 1027 . . . 215, 216

Barnett v Chelsea and Kensington Hospital Management Committee [1969] 1 QB 428 (QBD) . . . 2, 18, **203–4**

Barr and others v Biffa Waste Services Ltd [2012] EWCA Civ 312 . . . 476

Barrett v Enfield LBC [2001] 2 AC 550 (HL) . . . 32, 40, 102, 124, 530

Barrett v Ministry of Defence [1995] 1 WLR 1217 (CA) . . . **54–5**

Barron v Collins [2017] EWHC 162 (QB) . . . 411, 449

Barron v Vines [2016] EWHC 1226 (QB) . . . 408

Bartonshill Coal Co v McGuire (1858) 3 Macq 300 . . . 512

Basely v Clarkson (1682) 3 Lev 37 (Ct of Common Pleas) . . . 455

Baten's Case (1610) 9 Co Rep 536 . . . 459

Beach v Freeson [1971] 2 All ER 860 . . . 435

Beattie v Halliday (1982), unreported, 4 February . . . 254

Benham v Gambling [1941] AC 157 . . . 547

Benjamin v Storr (1874) LR 9 CP 400 . . . 321

Bennett v Tugwell [1971] QB 267 . . . 232

Bernstein v Skyviews and General Ltd [1978] QB 479 (QBD) . . . **455–7**, 458

Bilta (UK) Ltd v Nazir (No 2) [2015] UKSC 23 . . . 241

Birch v University College London Hospital NHS Foundation Trust [2008] EWHC 2237 (QB) . . . 186

Bird v Jones (1845) 7 QB 742 (Ct of Queen's Bench) . . . 2, 335, **336–7**

Blacker v Lake & Elliot (1912) Ld 106 LT 533 . . . 26

Blake v Galloway [2004] EWCA Civ 814; [2004] 1 WLR 2844 . . . 342

Blennerhasset v Novelty Sales Service (1933) 175 LTJo 393 . . . 425

Blyth v Proprietors of the Birmingham Waterworks (1856) 11 Ex 781 (Ex Ct) . . . **170–1**

Bocardo SA v Star Energy UK Onshore Ltd [2010] UKSC 35; [2010] 3 WLR 654 . . . 457

Bolam v Friern Hospital Management Committee [1957] 1 WLR 582 (QBD) . . . 113, 114, 178, **179–81**, 182, 183, 184, 185, 189, 190, 191, 193

Bolitho v City and Hackney Health Authority [1998] AC 232 . . . 181, 218

Bolton v Stone [1951] AC 850 (HL) . . . **197–8**, 199, 286

Bonnick v Morris [2002] UKPC 31; [2003] 1 AC 300 . . . 438, 439

Bonnington Castings Ltd v Wardlaw [1956] AC 613 (HL) . . . 204, 205, 206, 207, 208, 209, 210, 211, 214

Bookbinder v Tebbit (No 1) [1989] 1 WLR 640 . . . 394

Boston v Sandford (1691) 2 Salk 440 . . . 524

Bottomley v Bannister [1932] 1 KB 458 . . . 270

Bottomley v Todmorden Cricket Club [2003] EWCA Civ 1575 . . . 266

Bourhill v Young 1941 SC 395 . . . 79

Bourhill v Young [1943] AC 92 (HL) . . . **34–6**, 37, 62, 65, 66, 67, 77, 78, 172, 223

Boyce v Paddington Borough Council [1903] 1 Ch 109 . . . 321

Brannan v Airtours plc (1999) *The Times*, 1 February . . . 255

Branson v Bower [2001] EMLR 32 . . . 432

Brent Walker Group Plc v Time Out Ltd [1991] 2 QB 33 . . . 431

Brice v Brown [1984] 1 All ER 997 (QBD) . . . 68

Bridlington Relay Ltd v Yorkshire Electricity Board [1965] Ch 436 (Ch D) . . . 467, 469

Brink's Global Services v Igrox [2010] EWCA Civ 1207 . . . 508

Britannic Merthyr Coal Co v David [1910] AC 74 . . . 318

British Celanese v Hunt Capacitors [1969] 2 All ER 1253 . . . 134

British Chiropractic Association v Singh [2010] EWCA Civ 350; [2011] 1 WLR 133 . . . 432, 433

British Railways Board v Herrington [1972] AC 877 (HL) . . . 57, 272, 282, 286

Brooks v Commissioner of Police of the Metropolis [2005] UKHL 24; [2005] 1 WLR 1495 . . . 60, 116

Broom v Morgan [1953] 1 QB 597 . . . 512

Brown v Bower [2017] 4 WLR 197 . . . 433

Bryant v Lefever (1879) 4 CPD 172 . . . 468

Bull v Desporte [2019] EWHC 1650 (QB) . . . 374

Bunt v Tilley [2006] EWHC 407 (QB); [2006] 3 All ER 336 . . . 400

Burrell v Clifford [2016] EWHC 294 (Ch) . . . 387

Burstein v Times Newspapers Ltd [2001] 1 WLR 579 . . . 448

Burton v Islington Health Authority [1993] QB 204 . . . 71

Burton v Winters [1993] 1 WLR 1077 (CA) . . . 459–60

Bussey Law Firm PC and Timothy Raymond Bussey v Page [2015] EWHC 563 (QB) . . . 395–7

Butchart v Home Office [2006] EWCA Civ 239; [2006] 1 WLR 1155 . . . 87

Butler (or Black) v Fife Coal Co Ltd [1912] AC 149 . . . 321

Bybrook Barn Centre Ltd v Kent County Council [2001] BLR 55 (CA) . . . 502

Cairns v Modi [2012] EWCA Civ 1382; [2013] 1 WLR 1015 . . . 397, 449

Calgarth, The [1927] P 93 . . . 272, 275

Calvert v William Hill Credit Ltd [2008] EWCA Civ 888 . . . 87

Cambridge Water Co v Eastern Counties Leather plc [1994] 2 AC 264 (HL) . . . 471, 490, 492, 493, 494, 496

Campbell v MGN Ltd [2003] QB 633 (CA) . . . 358

Campbell v MGN Ltd [2004] UKHL 22; [2004] 2 AC 457 . . . 118, 357, 360, **362–5**, 367, 371, 372, 373, 374, 375, 377, 378

Campbell v MGN Ltd (No 2) [2005] UKHL 61; [2005] 4 All ER 793 . . . 367

Candler v Crane, Christmas & Co [1951] 2 KB 164 . . . 159

Candlewood Navigation v Mitsui OSK Lines (The Mineral Transporter) [1986] AC 1 (PC) . . . 46

Caparo Industries plc v Dickman [1989] QB 653 (CA) . . . 60

Caparo Industries plc v Dickman [1990] 2 AC 605 (HL) . . . 14, 16, 17, 23, **28–30**, 31, 32, 33, 34, 44, 46, 90, 98, 99, 100, 101, 102, 105, 124, 141, 149–50, 151, **154–7**, 158, 161, 163, 166, 167, 501, 530

Capital and Counties Bank Ltd v Henry & Sons (1882) 7 App Cas 741 . . . 419

Capital and Counties v Hampshire CC [1997] QB 1004 (CA) . . . 112–14

Carmarthenshire County Council v Lewis [1955] UKHL 2 . . . 51

Carstairs v Taylor (1871) LR 6 Ex 217 . . . 492, 493

Cattle v Stockton Waterworks (1875) LR 10 QBD 453 (Ct of Queen's Bench) . . . 132–3, 135

Cavalier v Pope [1906] AC 428 (HL) . . . 270

Central Motors (Glasgow) Ltd v Cessnock Garage & Motor Co 1925 SC 796 . . . 511

CG v Facebook Ireland Ltd and Joseph McCloskey [2015] NIQB 11 . . . 354

Chadwick v British Railways Board [1967] 1 WLR 912 (QBD) . . . 88, 91

Chaplin v Hicks [1911] 2 KB 786 . . . 217

Chase v Newsgroup Newspapers Ltd [2002] EWCA Civ 1772; [2003] EMLR 218 . . . 404, 426

Chatterton v Gerson [1981] QB 432 (QBD) . . . 341

Chester v Afshar [2004] UKHL 41; [2005] 1 AC 134 . . . 182, 186, 189, 385

Christian Brothers case see **Various Claimants v Catholic Child Welfare Society**

Christmas v Hampshire CC see **X (Minors) v Bedfordshire CC**

Church of Jesus Christ of Latter Day Saints (Great Britain) v West Yorkshire Fire and Civil Defence Authority see **Capital and Counties v Hampshire CC**

Clunis v Camden and Islington Health Authority [1998] QB 978 (CA) . . . 235, 236

Co-operative Group (CWS) Ltd v Pritchard [2011] EWCA Civ 329 . . . 245, 343

Cockroft v Smith (1705) 2 Salk 642 . . . 343

Coco v AN Clark (Engineers) Ltd [1968] FSR 415 (Ch D) . . . 360

Cole v Turner (1704) 87 ER 907 . . . 328, 331–2

Collier v Anglian Water Authority (2003) The Times, 26 March . . . 270

Collins v Wilcock [1984] 1 WLR 1172 (CA) . . . 330, 331, 332, 333

Colls v Home and Colonial Stores Limited [1904] AC 179 . . . 480, 485, 486

Commissioner of Police of the Metropolis v DSD and another [2018] UKSC 11 . . . 59, 122, 124, 131

Commissioner for Railways v McDermott [1967] 1 AC 169 . . . 288

Conarken v Network Rail Infrastructure [2011] EWCA Civ 644 . . . 135–7, 227

Cook v Swinfen [1967] 1 WLR 457 (CA) . . . 94

Cooke v MGN Ltd [2014] EWHC 2831 (QB) . . . 405–7

Cookson v Knowles [1979] AC 556 . . . 545

Corby Group Litigation v Corby Borough Council [2008] EWCA Civ 463; [2009] 2 WLR 609 . . . 469

Corr v IBC Vehicles Ltd [2006] EWCA Civ 331; [2008] 2 All ER 943 . . . 62

Corr v IBC Vehicles Ltd [2008] UKHL 13; [2008] 1 AC 884 . . . 228–9

Costello v Chief Constable of Northumbria Police [1999] 1 All ER 550 (CA) . . . 55

Coventry v Lawrence [2014] UKSC 13 . . . 458, 472, 476, 479, **484–6**

Coventry and others v Lawrence and another [2015] UKSC 50 . . . 487

Coventry and others v Lawrence and another (No 2) [2014] UKSC 46 . . . 487

Cox v Ministry of Justice [2016] UKSC 10 . . . 506, **510–14**, 515, 522, 523, 528

Crockfords Club (Fisher v CHT Ltd) [1965] 1 WLR 1093 . . . 269

Cross v Kirkby [2000] CA Transcript No 321 . . . 236

Crump v Lambert (1867) 3 Eq 409 . . . 462

Customs and Excise v Barclays Bank [2006] UKHL 28; [2007] 1 AC 181 . . . 31, **150–3**

Cutler v Wandsworth Stadium [1949] AC 398 . . . 320, 323

D v East Berkshire Community NHS Trust [2003] EWCA Civ 1151; [2004] QB 558 . . . 99, 102, 103, 104, 118, 119

D v East Berkshire Community NHS Trust [2005] UKHL 23; [2005] 2 AC 373 . . . 103, 106

D & F Estates Ltd v Church Commissioners for England [1989] AC 177 (HL) . . . 145, 146

Daborn v Bath Tramways Motor Co Ltd [1946] 2 All ER 333 . . . 201

Daiichi UK Ltd v Stop Huntington Animal Cruelty [2004] 1 WLR 1503 . . . 354

Dalton v Angus (1881) 6 App Cas 740 . . . 468

Dann v Hamilton [1939] 1 KB 509 . . . 176

Darby v National Trust [2001] PIQR 372 . . . 284, 285

Darnley v Croydon Health Services NHS Trust [2015] EWHC 2301 (QB) . . . 15

Darnley v Croydon Health Services NHS Trust [2018] QB 783 (CA) . . . 16, 20, 22

Darnley v Croydon Health Services NHS Trust [2018] UKSC 50 . . . 9, 13, **14–23**, 33, 34

Davies v Powell Duffryn Collieries Ltd [1942] AC 601 . . . 542

Davies v Swan Motor Co (Swansea) Ltd [1949] 2 KB 291 . . . 246, 247

Davis Contractors v Fareham Urban District Council [1956] AC 696 (HL) . . . 169

Delaware Mansions Ltd v Westminster City Council [2001] UKHL 55; [2002] 1 AC 321 . . . 502

Dennis v Ministry of Defence [2003] EWHC 198 (QB) . . . 479, 484

Department of Environment v T Bates Ltd [1990] 3 WLR 457 . . . 147

Derbyshire CC v Times Newspapers [1992] QB 770 (CA) . . . 392–4

Derbyshire CC v Times Newspapers [1993] AC 534 (HL) . . . 394

Derry v Peek (1889) 14 App Cas 337 . . . 140

Digital Equipment Co Ltd v Hampshire County Council and others *see* **Capital and Counties v Hampshire CC**

Dobson v Thames Water Utilities Ltd [2008] EWCA Civ 473 . . . 479

Doe d. Murray v Bridges (1831) 1 B & Ad 847 . . . 321

Donoghue v Folkestone Properties Ltd [2003] QB 1008; [2003] 2 WLR 1138 . . . 283, 286

Donoghue v Stevenson [1932] AC 562 (HL) . . . 24–7, 31, 35, 36, 51, 79, 105, 140, 144, 145, 146, 152, 156, 190, 196, 265, **298–300**

Dooley v Cammell Laird [1951] 1 Lloyd's Rep 271 . . . 88, 93

Dorset Yacht Co Ltd v Home Office *see* **Home Office v Dorset Yacht**

Doughty v Turner Manufacturing Co [1964] 1 QB 518 (CA) . . . 227–8

Douglas v Hello! Ltd [2001] QB 967 (CA) . . . 363, 375, 378

Douglas v Hello! Ltd (No 3) [2003] 3 All ER 996 (Ch) . . . 366, 378, 387

Douglas v Hello! Ltd (No 3) [2005] EWCA Civ 595; [2005] 4 All ER 128 . . . 366, 367

Dowson v Chief Constable of Northumbria Police [2010] EWHC 2612 (QB) . . . 352, 355

DPP v Smith [1961] AC 290 . . . 348

Dryden and others v Johnson Matthey plc [2018] UKSC 18 . . . 548

DSD v The Commissioner of Police for the Metropolis [2014] EWHC 436 (QB) . . . 119

Dubai Aluminium Co Ltd v Salaam [2002] UKHL 48; [2003] 2 AC 366 . . . 508, 511, 512, 513, 520, 525

Duce v Worcestershire Acute Hospitals NHS Trust [2018] EWCA Civ 1307 . . . 191

Duke of Brunswick v Harmer (1849) 14 QB 185; 117 ER 75 (QB) . . . 395

Dulieu v White & Sons [1901] 2 KB 669 . . . 35, 62, 65

Duncan v Findlater (1839) 6 Cl & Fin 894; (1839) MacL & Rob 911 . . . 512

Dunnage v Randall [2015] EWCA Civ 673 . . . 177

Dunne v North Western Gas Board [1964] 2 QB 806 . . . 492

Dutton v Bognor Regis Urban District Council [1972] 1 QB 373 . . . 145, 146

E v English Province of Our Lady of Charity [2012] EWCA Civ 938 . . . 513

E (a minor) v Dorset County Council *see* X (Minors) v Bedfordshire CC

Eagle v Chambers [2003] EWCA Civ 1107; [2004] RTR 115 . . . 253, 255, 256

East Suffolk Rivers Catchment Board v Kent [1941] AC 74 (HL) . . . 97, 108, 109, 110, 112

Economou v de Freitas [2018] EWCA Civ 2591 . . . 438–43

Edwards v London Borough of Sutton [2016] EWCA Civ 1005 . . . 267, 291, 294, 295, 296

EETPU v The Times [1980] QB 585 . . . 394

Ehrari v Curry [2007] EWCA Civ 120 . . . 256

Electrochrome v Welsh Plastics [1968] 2 All ER 205 . . . 133, 134

Elguzouli-Daf v Commissioner of Police [1995] 1 All ER 833; [1995] 2 WLR 173 . . . 42, 116

English Heritage v Taylor [2016] EWCA Civ 448 . . . 292–3

Entick v Carrington (1765) 2 Wils KB 275 . . . 97

Environment Agency (formerly National Rivers Authority) v Empress Car Co (Abertillery) Ltd [1999] 2 AC 22 . . . 492

Equitas Insurance Ltd v Municipal Mutual Insurance Ltd [2019] EWCA Civ 718 . . . 216

Esso Petroleum v Southport Corporation [1956] AC 218 . . . 454

Esterhuizen v Allied Dunbar Assurance plc [1998] 2 FLR 668 . . . 168

ETK v Newsgroup Newspapers [2011] EWCA Civ 439 . . . 374

Evans v Triplex Safety Glass Co Ltd [1936] 1 All ER 283 (KBD) . . . 301

F, Re [1990] 2 AC 1 (HL) . . . 333

Fairchild v Glenhaven Funeral Services Ltd [2002] 1 WLR 1052 (CA) . . . 213, 214, 266, 288

Fairchild v Glenhaven Funeral Services Ltd [2002] UKHL 22; [2003] 1 AC 32 . . . 208, 212–15, 216, 217, 218, 219

Farley v Skinner [2001] UKHL 49 . . . 159

FB (Suing by her Mother and Litigation Friend, WAC) v Princess Alexandra Hospital NHS Trust [2017] EWCA Civ 334 . . . 178

Fearn and others v The Board of Trustees of the Tate Gallery [2019] EWHC 246 (Ch) . . . 469, 471

Fearn and others v The Board of Trustees of the Tate Gallery [2020] EWCA Civ 104 . . . 470

Ferguson v British Gas Trading [2009] EWCA Civ 46 . . . 354, 355

Ferguson v Welsh [1987] 1 WLR 1553 (HL) . . . 265–6, 267

Fish v Kelly (1864) 144 ER 78 . . . 140

Fitzgerald v Lane and Patel [1989] AC 328 (HL) . . . 250–1

Fletcher v Rylands and Horrocks (1865) 3 H&C 774 . . . 491 *see also* **Rylands v Fletcher**

Flood v Times Newspapers Ltd [2012] UKSC 11; [2012] 2 AC 273 . . . 438, 439, 442

Flood v Times Newspapers Ltd [2014] EWCA Civ 1574 . . . 367

Flymenow Ltd v Quick Air Jet Charter GmbH [2016] EWHC 3197 (QB) . . . 447–8

Fowler v Lanning [1959] 1 QB 426 . . . 327, 329

Fraser v Evans [1969] 1 QB 349 . . . 375

French v Chief Constable of Sussex [2006] EWCA Civ 312 . . . 87

Froom v Butcher [1976] QB 286 (CA) . . . 2

Frost v Chief Constable of Yorkshire *see* **White v Chief Constable of South Yorkshire**

Fullam v Newcastle Chronicle & Journal Ltd [1977] 1 WLR 651 (CA) . . . 421

Fulton v Sunday Newspapers Ltd [2015] NIQB 100, appeal dismissed [2017] NICA 45 . . . 354

G v G (Minors: Custody Appeal) [1985] 1 WLR 647 . . . 254

Galli-Atkinson v Seghal [2003] EWCA Civ 697 . . . 82

Galoo v Bright Grahame Murray [1995] 1 All ER 16 . . . 158

Gardiner v Motherwell Machinery and Scrap Co Ltd [1961] 3 All ER 831; [1961] 1 WLR 1424 . . . 214

Garrett v London Borough of Camden [2001] EWCA Civ 395 . . . 94, 95

Geary v JD Wetherspoons plc [2011] EWHC 1506 (QB) . . . 294, 295, 296

Geddis v Proprietors of Bann Reservoir (1878) 3 App Cas 430 . . . 97, 472, 492

Gee and others v DePuy International Ltd [2018] EWHC 1208 (QB) . . . 314, 315

George v Skivington (1869) LR 5 Ex 1 . . . 26

Giggs (formerly known as CTB) v NGN Ltd and another [2012] EWHC 431 (QB) . . . 390

Gilbert v Stone (1647) Sty 72; 82 ER 539 . . . 455

Gillick v BBC (1995) *The Times*, 20 October . . . 420

Gillick v Brook Advisory Centres [2001] EWCA Civ 1263 . . . 416

Gillingham Borough Council v Medway
(Chatham) Dock Co Ltd [1993] QB 343
(QBD) . . . 472, 474

**Glasgow Corporation v Muir [1943] AC 448
(HL) . . . 171–2**, 175

**Godfrey v Demon Internet [2001] QB 201
(QBD) . . . 398–400**

Goldman v Hargrave [1967] 1 AC 645 (PC) . . . 52,
58, 499, 500, 501

Goldscheider v Royal Opera House Covent Garden
Foundation [2019] EWCA Civ 711 . . . 200, 227

Goldsmith v Bhoyrul [1998] 2 WLR 435 . . . 394

**Google Inc v Vidal-Hall and others [2015]
EWCA Civ 311** . . . 2, 357, 360, **377–9**

Gorham v BT [2000] 4 All ER 867 . . . 168

Gorringe v Calderdale MBC [2004] UKHL 15;
[2004] 2 All ER 326; [2004] 1 WLR 1057 . . . 98,
99, 104, 106, 111

Gorris v Scott (1874) LR 9 Ex 125 (Ex Ct) . . . 97,
318, **323**

Gough v Thorne [1966] 1 WLR 1387 (CA) . . .
194, 247

Gould v McAuliffe [1941] 2 All ER 527 . . . 276, 277

Governors of Peabody Donation Fund v
Sir Lindsay Parkinson & Co Ltd [1985] AC
210 . . . 28

Grant v Australian Knitting Mills Ltd [1936] AC 85
(PC) . . . 140, 156–7, 300, 301

**Gray v Thames Trains [2009] UKHL 33; [2009] 1
AC 1339 . . . 234–7**, 242

Greatorex v Greatorex [2000] EWHC 223 (QB) . . . 86

Grech v Odhams Press [1958] 2 QB 75 . . . 432

Green v Chelsea Waterworks Co (1894) 70 LT
547 . . . 492

Greene's case [1954] 2 QB 127 . . . 269

**Gregg v Scott [2005] UKHL 2; [2005] 2 AC
176 . . . 216–19**

**Gregory v Piper (1820) 9 B & C 591 (Ct of King's
Bench) . . . 453–4**

Grobbelaar v News Group Newspapers [2002]
UKHL 40; [2002] 1 WLR 3024 . . . 426

**Groves v Lord Wimborne [1898] 2 QB 402
(CA) . . . 316–18**, 319, 320

**Gul v McDonagh [2021] EWHC 97 (QB) . . .
247–9**

Gulati and others v MGN [2016] EWHC 1482
(Ch) . . . 387

Hale v Jennings Bros [1938] 1 All ER 579 . . . 493

Haley v London Electricity Board [1965] AC 778
(HL) . . . 37, 200

Hall v Brooklands Auto-Racing Club [1933] 1 KB
205 (CA) . . . 173, 196

**Halsey v Esso Petroleum [1961] 1 WLR 683
(QBD) . . . 461–3**, 470

Hambrook v Stokes Brothers [1925] 1 KB 141
(CA) . . . 62, 80

Hammersmith and City Railway Co v Brand
(1867) LR 2 QB 223 . . . 491

Hammersmith and City Railway Co v Brand
(1869) LR 4 HL 171 . . . 472, 492

Harrath v Stand for Peace Ltd [2017] EWHC 653
(QB) . . . 449

Harris v Birkenhead Corporation [1976] 1 All ER
279 . . . 270

Hartwell v Grayson, Rollo and Clover Docks Ltd
[1947] KB 901 . . . 269

Harvey v Plymouth City Council [2010] EWCA
Civ 860 . . . 277

Harvey v The Singer Manufacturing Co Ltd 1960
SC 155 . . . 226

Haseldine v CA Daw & Son Ltd [1941] 2 KB
343 . . . 174, 301

Hastings v Finsbury Orthopaedics Ltd and Stryker
UK Ltd [2019] CSOH 96 (Scotland) . . . 315

Hatton v Sutherland [2002] EWCA Civ 76 . . .
87, **93–5**

Hawley v Luminar Leisure Ltd [2006] EWCA
Civ 18 . . . 515

Hayes v Willoughby [2013] UKSC 17; [2013] 1
WLR 935 . . . 352, 356

Haynes v Harwood [1934] 2 KB 240 . . . 36

Haynes v Harwood [1935] 1 KB 146 (CA) . . . 35,
38, 39, 57, 59

Hays Plc v Hartley [2010] EWHC 1068 (QB) . . . 441

Hayward v Thompson [1982] QB 47 . . . 449

Healthcare at Home Ltd v The Common Services
Agency [2014] UKSC 49 . . . 404

Heasmans v Clarity Cleaning Co [1987] ICR
949 . . . 526

Heaton's Transport (St Helens) Ltd v Transport
and General Workers' Union [1973] AC
15 . . . 508

Heaven v Pender (1883) 11 QBD 503 . . . 25

**Hedley Byrne & Co Ltd v Heller & Partners Ltd
[1963] UKHL 4; [1964] AC 465** . . . 2–3, 27, 120,
121, **138–41**, 146, 148, 149, 150, 151, 153, 156,
160, 161, 162, 164, 165, 166, 167, 168

Henderson v Dorset Healthcare University
NHS Trust Foundation [2020] UKSC
43 . . . 242

Henderson v Henry E Jenkins & Sons [1970] AC
282 . . . 175–6

**Henderson v Merrett Syndicates [1995] 2 AC
145; [1994] 3 WLR 761 (HL)** . . . 101, 141,
149–50, 151, 152, 153

Herd v Weardale Steel, Coal and Coke Co [1913] 3 KB 771 (CA) . . . 338, 339, 340

Herd v Weardale Steel, Coal and Coke Co [1915] AC 67 (HL) . . . 338, 339

Herrington v British Railways Board *see* British Railways Board v Herrington

Hicks v Chief Constable of the South Yorkshire Police [1992] 2 All ER 65 . . . 467, 548

Hill v Chief Constable of West Yorkshire [1989] AC 53 (HL) . . . 28, 30, 32, 42, 60, 101, 105, 113, 114, **115**, 116, 117, 118, 122, 130

Hillen v ICI (Alkali) Ltd [1936] AC 65 . . . 272

Hinz v Berry [1970] 1 All ER 1084 . . . 64

Holbeck Hall Hotel v Scarborough BC [2000] QB 836 (CA) . . . **498–501**, 502

Hollywood Silver Fox Farm v Emmett [1936] 2 KB 468 (KBD) . . . 471

Holman v Johnson (1775) 1 Cowp 341 . . . 237

Holtby v Brigham & Cowan (Hull) Ltd [2000] 3 All ER 421 (CA) . . . 216

Home Office v Dorset Yacht [1970] UKHL 2; [1970] AC 1004 . . . 27, 30, 51, **55**, 97, 98, 101, 107, 146

Horrocks v Lowe [1975] AC 135 (HL) . . . 167

Hotson v East Berkshire Area Health Authority [1987] AC 750 (HL) . . . 210, 217, 218, 219

Hounga v Allen [2014] UKSC 47 . . . 241

Hourani v Thomson and others [2017] EWHC 432 (QB) . . . 354, 443

Howitt v Heads [1973] 1 QB 64 (QBD) . . . 539, **541–3**

Howmet Ltd v Economy Devices Ltd and others [2016] EWCA Civ 847 . . . 301

HRH Prince of Wales v Associated Newspapers [2006] EWCA Civ 1776 . . . 367

Hubbard v Pitt [1975] ICR 308 . . . 479

Hucks v Cole (1968) Times Law Reports, 9 May . . . 179

Hughes v Lord Advocate [1963] AC 837 (HL) . . . 224, **225–6**, 227, 229, 280

Hulton (E) & Co v Jones [1910] AC 20 (HL) . . . 424, 425

Hunt v Star Newspaper Co Ltd [1908] 2 KB 309 . . . 431

Hunter v British Coal [1998] 2 All ER 97 . . . 93

Hunter v Canary Wharf [1997] AC 655 (HL) . . . 2, 346, 358, 463, **464–9**, 476, 493

Hunter v Hanley 1955 SC 200; 1955 SLT 213 . . . 180, 182

Hussain v Lancaster City Council [1999] 4 All ER 125 . . . 502

Hutcheson (Formerly Known As 'KGM') v News Group Newspapers Ltd and others [2011] EWCA Civ 808 . . . 390

Ilkiw v Samuels [1963] 1 WLR 991 . . . 511, 518

Imperial Chemical Industries Ltd v Shatwell [1965] AC 656 . . . 233

Invercargill City Council v Hamlin [1996] 1 All ER 756; [1996] 2 WLR 367 (PC) . . . 110, 147

Iqbal v Dean Manson Solicitors [2011] EWCA Civ 123 . . . 355

Iqbal v Prison Officers Association [2009] EWCA Civ 1312; [2010] QB 732 . . . 329, **338–40**

Jackson v Murray [2015] UKSC 5 . . . **252–7**

Jaggard v Sawyer [1995] 2 All ER 189; [1995] 1 WLR 269 (CA) . . . 458, 485, 486

Jain v Trent SHA [2009] UKHL 4; [2009] 1 AC 853 . . . 111

Jameel v Dow Jones & Co [2005] EWCA Civ 75 . . . 406, 409

Jameel v Wall Street Journal Europe Sprl [2006] UKHL 44; [2007] 1 AC 359 . . . 375, 438, 439

James v Woodall Duckham Construction Co Ltd [1969] 1 WLR 903 (CA) . . . 63

James-Bowen and others v Commissioner of Police of the Metropolis [2016] EWCA Civ 1217 . . . 153

James-Bowen v Commissioner of Police of the Metropolis [2018] UKSC 40; [2018] 1 WLR 4021 . . . 18, 153

Janvier v Sweeney [1919] 2 KB 316 (CA) . . . 345, 348, 349, 350, 467

Jeynes v News Magazines Limited [2008] EWCA Civ 130 . . . 421

JGE v The Trustees of the Portsmouth Roman Catholic Diocesan Trust [2012] EWCA Civ 938 . . . **505–6**, 507, 508, 509, 521

JIH v News Group Newspapers [2010] EWHC 2818 (QB) . . . 390

JIH v News Group Newspapers [2011] EWCA Civ 42; [2011] 1 WLR 1645 . . . **388–90**

Jobling v Associated Dairies Ltd [1982] AC 794 (HL) . . . 235

John v MGN Ltd [1997] QB 586 (CA) . . . 385, 449

John Munroe (Acrylics) Ltd v London Fire and Civil Defence Authority [1996] 3 WLR 988 (QBD) . . . 113 *see also* **Capital and Counties v Hampshire CC**

Jolley v Sutton London Borough Council [2000] 3 All ER 409; [2000] 1 WLR 1082 (HL) . . . 227, **279–80**

Jones v Berkshire Area Health Authority (1986), unreported, 2 July . . . 45

Jones v Boyce (1816) 171 ER 540 . . . 249

Jones v Hulton & Co [1909] 2 KB 444 . . . 425

Jones v Livox Quarries Ltd [1952] 2 QB 608 (CA) . . . 245–6

Jones v Ruth [2011] EWCA Civ 804 . . . 356

Jones v Skelton [1963] 1 WLR 1362 . . . 420

Joseph v Spiller [2011] 1 AC 852 . . . 433

Joseph v Spiller [2012] EWHC 2958 (QB) . . . 448

Junior v McNicol (959) Times Law Reports, 26 March . . . 179

Junior Books Ltd v Veitchi Co Ltd [1983] 1 AC 520; [1982] 3 All ER 201 . . . 132, 157

K v Dewsbury Healthcare NHS Trust *see* D v East Berkshire Community NHS Trust [2013]

K v Oldham NHS Trust *see* D v East Berkshire Community NHS Trust [2013]

K v Secretary of State for the Home Department [2002] EWCA Civ 775 . . . 59

Kapfunde v Abbey National [1998] IRLR 583 . . . 168

Kay v Lambeth London Borough Council [2006] UKHL 10; [2006] 2 AC 465 . . . 104

Kaye v Robertson [1991] FSR 62 (CA) . . . 118, 357, 359

Keating v Bromley London Borough Council *see* **X (Minors) v Bedfordshire CC**

Kelly v Metropolitan Rly [1895] 1 QB 944 . . . 50

Kemsley v Foot [1952] AC 345 . . . 430, 431

Kennaway v Thompson [1981] QB 88 (CA) . . . 482–3, 484

Kennedy v Charity Commission [2014] UKSC 20; [2015] AC 435 . . . 336

Kent v Griffiths [2001] QB 36; [2000] 2 All ER 474 . . . 19, 114, 121, 124

Keown v Coventry Healthcare Trust [2006] EWCA Civ 39; [2006] 1 WLR 953 . . . 275, 291

Kerry v Carter [1969] 1 WLR 1372 . . . 255

Khorasandjian v Bush [1993] QB 727 . . . 358, 466, 467

Khuja (formerly known as PNM) v Times Newspapers [2017] UKSC 49 . . . 390

Kine v Jolly [1905] 1 CH 480 . . . 485

King v Phillips [1953] 1 QB 429 . . . 223

King v Sunday Newspapers Ltd [2010] NIQB 107, appeal dismissed [2011] NICA 8 . . . 354

Kirby v National Coal Board 1958 SC 514 . . . 519

Kirkham v Chief Constable of Manchester [1990] 2 QB 283 (CA) . . . 53, 233

Kitechnology BV v Unicor [1995] IL Pr 568 . . . 378

Knightley v Johns [1982] 1 WLR 349 (CA) . . . 59, 112, 116

Kolasa v Ealing Hospital NHS Trust [2015] EWHC 289 (QB) . . . 274, 277

Koutsogiannis v The Random House Group Ltd [2019] EWHC 48 (QB) . . . 432

Lachaux v Independent Print Ltd [2019] UKSC 27 . . . 412

Lady Archer v Williams [2003] EWHC 1670 (QB) . . . 387

Lady Archer v Williams [2003] EWHC 3048 (QB) . . . 387

Lagan Navigation Co v Lambeg Bleaching, Dyeing and Finishing Co Ltd [1927] AC 226 . . . 460

Lamb v Camden Borough Council [1981] QB 625 (CA) . . . 59

Lambert v Barratt Homes Ltd [2010] EWCA Civ 681 . . . 502

Lane v Capsey [1891] 3 Ch 411 . . . 460

Lane v Holloway [1968] 1 QB 379 (CA) . . . 342–3

Latimer v AEC Ltd [1952] 2 QB 701 (CA) . . . 199–200

Laugher v Pointer (1826) 5 B & C 547 . . . 515

Law Society v Kordowski [2011] EWHC 3185 (QB) . . . 354

Law Society v KPMG [2000] 4 All ER 540 . . . 158

Laws v Florinplace [1981] 1 All ER 659 (Ch D) . . . 479

Lawson v Glaves-Smith [2006] EWHC 2865 (QB) . . . 327

Le Lievre v Gould [1893] 1 QB 491 (CA) . . . 25

League Against Cruel Sports v Scott [1986] 1 QB 240 (QBD) . . . 454–5

Leakey v National Trust [1980] QB 485 (CA) . . . 498, 499, 500, 501

Leigh and Sillavan Ltd v Aliakmon Shipping (The Aliakmon) [1986] AC 785 (HL) . . . 138

Les Laboratoires Servier v Apotex Inc [2014] UKSC 55 . . . 238, 241

Letang v Cooper [1965] 1 QB 232 (CA) . . . 328–9, 330

Levi v Bates [2015] EWCA Civ 206 . . . 354

Lewis v Daily Telegraph [1964] AC 234 (HL) . . . 403, **418–19**, 420, 421

Lewis v Six Continents [2005] EWCA Civ 1805 . . . 296

Ley v Hamilton (1935) 153 LT 384 . . . 397

Lippiatt v South Gloucestershire Council [1999] 4 All ER 149 . . . 502

**Lister v Hesley Hall Ltd [2001] UKHL 22; [2002]
1 AC 215** . . . 506, 508, 511, 512, **516–19**, 520,
521, 523, 524, 525, 526

Lister v Romford Ice and Cold Storage Co Ltd
[1957] AC 555 . . . 114, 515

**Liverpool Women's Hospital NHS Foundation
Trust v Ronayne [2015] EWCA Civ 588** . . .
83–5, 86

Lloyd v Grace, Smith & Co [1912] AC 716 . . .
517, 524

LMS v East Lancashire Hospitals NHS Trust [2017]
(unreported) . . . 546

London Artists Ltd v Littler [1969] 2 QB
375 . . . 428

London Borough of Hackney v Persons Unknown
In London Fields, Hackney (The 'prescribed
Area') [2020] EWHC 1900 (QB) . . . 463

**Lonrho v Shell Petroleum (No 2) [1982] AC 173
(HL)** . . . 320, **321–2**

Loutchansky v The Times Newspapers (No 2)
[2001] EWCA Civ 1805; [2002] 2 QB
783 . . . 402, 438

Lowe v Associated Newspapers [2006] EWHC 320
(QB); [2007] QB 580 . . . 429, 432–3

Lumley v Gye (1853) 2 E & B 216 . . . 132

M (a minor) v Newham London Borough Council
see X **(Minors) v Bedfordshire CC**

McAlpine v Bercow [2013] EWHC 1342 (QB) . . .
394, **403–4**, 416, **420–3**

McCluskey v Wallace 1998 SC 711 . . . 253,
256, 257

McColl v Strathclyde Regional Council 1983 SC
225 . . . 188

McCrone v Riding [1938] 1 All ER 137 . . . 177

McCusker v Saveheat Cavity Wall Insulation Ltd
1987 SLT 24 . . . 254

McDonald (Deceased) v National Grid Electricity
Transmission plc [2014] UKSC 53 . . . 323

McFarlane v Scottish Borders Council 2005 SLT
39 . . . 255

**McFarlane v Tayside Health Board [1999] UKHL
50; [2000] 2 AC 59** . . . 33, 40, **45–7**, 48, 49

McGhee v National Coal Board [1973] 1 WLR 1
(HL) . . . 205, 206, 207, 208, 210, 213, 214, 215

McGuinn v Lewisham and Greenwich NHS Trust
[2017] EWHC 88 (QB) . . . 181

McHugh v Okai-Koi [2017] EWHC 710 (QB) . . .
243, 245

McKenna v British Aluminium [2002] Env LR 30
(Ch D) . . . 476, 479

McKennitt v Ash [2006] EWCA Civ 1714; [2007] 3
WLR 194 . . . 366, 373, 387

McKew v Holland & Hannen & Cubitts (Scotland)
Ltd [1969] 3 All ER 1621 (HL) . . . 79

McLoughlin v Grovers [2001] EWCA Civ
1743 . . . 94

McLoughlin v O'Brian [1983] 1 AC 410 (HL) . . .
65, 78, 79, 80, 84, 91

McWilliams v Sir William Arrol & Co [1962] 1
WLR 295 . . . 218

Maga v Birmingham Archdiocese of the Roman
Catholic Church [2010] EWCA Civ 256; [2010] 1
WLR 1441 . . . 505, 525

Maguire v Harland and Wolff [2005] EWCA
Civ 1 . . . 38

Majrowski v Guy's and St Thomas's NHS Hospital
Trust [2005] QB 848 (CA) . . . 528

Majrowski v Guy's and St Thomas's NHS Trust
[2006] UKHL 34; [2007] 1 AC 224 . . . 352, 354,
356, 506

Malcolm v Broadhurst [1970] 3 All ER 508 . . . 66,
67, 68

Malone v Laskey [1907] 2 KB 141 (CA) . . . 463,
465, 466

Mansfield v Weetabix [1998] 1 WLR 1263
(CA) . . . 177

Marc Rich & Co AG v Bishop Rock Marine (The
Nicholas H) [1994] 1 WLR 1071 (CA) . . . 43

**Marc Rich & Co AG v Bishop Rock Marine (The
Nicholas H) [1996] AC 211 (HL)** . . . 34, 40,
41–4, 113, 501

Marcic v Thames Water Utilities Ltd [2002] QB
929 (CA) . . . 477, 478

**Marcic v Thames Water Utilities Ltd [2003]
UKHL 66; [2004] 2 AC 42** . . . **476–9**

Marshall v Osmond [1983] QB 1034 . . . 112

Maynard v West Midlands Regional Health
Authority [1984] 1 WLR 634 (HL) . . .
182, 183

Mayor of Bradford v Pickles [1885] AC 587 . . . 471

MB (Caesarean Section), Re [1997] 2 FLR 426
(CA) . . . 2

Meering v Grahame-White Aviation Co Ltd (1920)
122 LT 44 (CA) . . . 337

Merchant Prince, The [1892] P 179 . . . 175

Merivale v Carson (1888) 20 QBD 275 . . . 428

Merlin Entertainments LPC, Chessington World
of Adventures Operations v Cave [2014] EWHC
3036 (QB) . . . 354

Mersey Docks and Harbour Board Trustees v Gibbs
(1866) LR 1 HL 93 . . . 97, 107

Mersey Docks and Harbour Board v Coggins &
Griffith (Liverpool) Ltd [1947] AC 1 (HL) . . . 515

Merthyr Tydfil County Borough Council v C
[2010] EWHC 62 (QB) . . . 106

Metropolitan Asylum District v Hill (1881) 6 App Cas 193 . . . 472

Michael v Chief Constable of South Wales Police [2015] UKSC 2; [2015] AC 1732 . . . 17, 19, 23, 31, 32, 34, 40, 50, 61, 99, 104, 105, 116, **117–21**, 131

Midland Bank Trust Co Ltd v Hett, Stubbs & Kemp [1979] Ch 384 (Ch D) . . . 150

Miller v Associated Newspapers [2016] EWHC 397 (QB) . . . 367

Miller v Jackson [1977] QB 966 (QB) . . . 483, 484

Miller v South of Scotland Electricity Board 1958 SC (HL) 20 . . . 40

Milne v Express Newspapers [2005] 1 All ER 1021 . . . 446

Mineral Transporter, The see Candlewood Navigation v Mitsui OSK Lines (The Mineral Transporter)

Ministry of Housing and Local Government v Sharp [1970] 2 QB 223 . . . 30, 152, 153

Mitchell v Glasgow City Council [2009] UKHL 11; [2009] 1 AC 874 . . . 50, 56, **59–61**, 99, 104, 105, 131

MNX v Khan [2017] EWHC 2990 (QB) . . . 48

Mohamud v WM Morrison Supermarkets plc [2016] UKSC 11 . . . 510, 511, 516, **522–4**, 526, 527

Monk v PC Harrington Ltd [2008] EWHC 1879 (QB) . . . 93

Monroe v Hopkins [2017] EWHC 433 (QB) . . . **407–11**, 412, 446

Monsanto v Tilly [2000] Env LR 313 (CA) . . . 453

Monson v Tussauds Ltd [1894] QB 671 (CA) . . . 392

Montgomery v Lanarkshire Health Board [2015] UKSC 11 . . . **182–93**, 342

Moore Stephens v Stone & Rolls Ltd [2009] UKHL 39 . . . 158

Morgan v Associated Newspapers Limited [2018] EWHC 1850 (QB) . . . 433

Morgan Crucible Co plc v Hill Samuel & Co Ltd [1991] Ch 295 . . . 152, 158, 161

Morris v CW Martin & Sons Ltd [1966] 1 QB 716 (CA) . . . 508, 517, 518

Morris v Murray [1991] 2 QB 6 (CA) . . . **232–3**

Morrison Sports Ltd v Scottish Power [2010] UKSC 37 . . . 322

Mosley v News Group Newspapers [2008] EWHC 1777 (QB) . . . 360, **374–7**, 384, **385–7**

Mullin v Richards [1998] 1 All ER 920; [1998] 1 WLR 1304 (CA) . . . 178, **194–5**

Murphy v Brentwood District Council [1991] 1 AC 398 (HL) . . . 28, 47, 98, 141, **144–7**, 148, 153

Murphy v Culhane [1977] QB 94 (CA) . . . 343

Murray v Big Pictures (UK) Ltd sub nom Murray v Express Newspapers [2008] EWCA Civ 446; [2008] 3 WLR 1360 . . . **371–3**, 374, 375

Murray v Ministry of Defence [1988] 1 WLR 692 (HL) . . . 337

Myroft v Sleight (1921) 37 TLR 646 . . . 404

Nail v News Group Newspapers [2005] 1 All ER 1040 . . . 446

Napier v Pressdram Ltd [2009] EWCA Civ 443; [2010] 1 WLR 934 . . . 347

National Coal Board v England [1954] AC 403 . . . 255

Nettleship v Weston [1971] 2 QB 691 (CA) . . . **175–7**, 178, 232

Network Rail Infrastructure Ltd v Williams and another [2018] EWCA Civ 1514 . . . 469

Network Rail Infrastructure v Morris [2004] EWCA Civ 172; [2004] Env LR 41 . . . 469, 471

Nevill v Fine Art & General Insurance Co Ltd [1897] AC 68 . . . 416, 419

Newstead v London Express Newspapers [1940] 1 KB 377 (CA) . . . **424–5**

Nicholas H, The see Marc Rich & Co AG v Bishop Rock Marine

Nichols v Marsland (1876) 2 Ex D 1 (CA) . . . 492

Nicholson v Atlas Steel Foundry and Engineering Co Ltd [1957] 1 WLR 613 . . . 206, 207, 210, 214

Nitrigin Eireann Teoranta v Inco Alloys [1992] 1 All ER 854 . . . 147

Nocton v Lord Ashburton [1914] AC 932 . . . 139, 162

North Glamorgan NHS Trust v Walters [2002] EWCA Civ 1792 . . . 82, 84, 85

OBG Ltd v Allan; Douglas v Hello! Ltd (No 3); Mainstream Properties Ltd v Young [2007] UKHL 21 . . . 366

Officer L, Re [2007] UKHL 36; [2007] 1 WLR 2135 . . . 129

Ogwo v Taylor [1988] AC 431 (HL) . . . 92

OLL Ltd v Secretary of State for Transport [1997] 3 All ER 897 . . . 120

OPO v MLA [2014] EWCA Civ 1277 . . . 327

Orange v Chief Constable of West Yorkshire Police [2001] EWCA Civ 611; [2002] QB 347 . . . 54

Orchard v Lee [2009] EWCA Civ 295 . . . 173

O'Rourke v Camden LBC [1998] AC 188 (HL) . . . 322

O'Shea v MGN [2001] EMLR 40 (QBD) . . . 425

Osman v Ferguson [1993] 4 All ER 344 (CA) . . . 112, 116, 122, 124

Overseas Tankship (UK) Ltd v Miller Steamship Co Pty Ltd (The Wagon Mound) (No 2) [1967] AC 617 (PC) . . . **199**, 223, 471, 490

Overseas Tankship (UK) Ltd v Morts Dock and Engineering Co Ltd (The Wagon Mound) (No 1) [1961] AC 388 (PC) . . . 69, 136, 199, **221–3**, 224, 225, 227

P Perl (Exporters) Ltd v Camden London Borough Council [1984] QB 342 . . . 30, 59

Page v Smith [1996] 1 AC 155 (HL) . . . 64, **65–8**, 69, 74, 75, 82, 87, 89, 91, 92, 94

Page v Smith (No 2) [1996] 1 WLR 855 (CA) . . . 69

Palmer v Tees Health Authority [1999] 2 LGLR 69 (CA) . . . 59

Pamplin v Express Newspapers Ltd (No 2) [1988] 1 WLR 116 (CA) . . . 448

Paris v Stepney Borough Council [1951] AC 367 (HL) . . . 200

Parkinson v St James Hospital [2001] 3 All ER 97 . . . 47

Pasley v Freeman (1789) 3 TR 51 . . . 140

Patel v Mirza [2016] UKSC 42 . . . 234, **237–41**, 242

Paul v Royal Wolverhampton NHS Trust [2020] EWHC 1415 (QB) . . . 82

Pearce v United Bristol Healthcare NHS Trust [1999] PIQR P 53 . . . 182, 185, 186, 189

Peires v Bickerton's Aerodromes Ltd [2016] EWHC 560 (Ch) . . . 486

Pepper v Hart [1993] AC 593 . . . 405, 406

Perrett v Collins [1998] Lloyd's Rep 255 (CA) . . . 44

Petch v Commissioners of Customs and Excise [1993] ICR 789 . . . 94

Phelps v Hillingdon London Borough Council [2001] 2 AC 619; [2000] 3 WLR 776 (HL) . . . 1, 102, 152

Philips v Whiteley Ltd [1938] 1 All ER 566 . . . 178

Phillips v Britannia Hygienic Laundry [1923] 1 KB 547 . . . 318

Phillips v Britannia Hygienic Laundry [1923] 2 KB 832 (CA) . . . **318–19**

Phillips v London and South Western Railway Co (1879) 4 QBD 406 . . . 547

Pitts v Hunt [1991] 1 QB 24 (CA) . . . 245

PJS v News Group Newspapers Ltd [2016] UKSC 26 . . . 374

Polemis and Furness, Withy & Co Ltd, Re [1921] 3 KB 560 (CA) . . . 2, **220–1**, 222, 246

Pollock v Cahill [2015] EWHC 2260 (QB) . . . 281

Polmear v Royal Cornwall Hospitals NHS Trust [2021] EWHC 196 (QB) . . . 82

Poole Borough Council v GN [2019] UKSC 25 . . . 23, 34, 56, **96–105**, 106, 111, 122

Port Swettenham Authority v TW Wu & Co (M) Sdn Bhd [1979] AC 580 (PC) . . . 517–18

Possfund Custodian Trustee v Diamond [1996] 2 All ER 774 . . . 158

Practice Statement (Judicial Precedent) [1966] 1 WLR 1234 . . . 545

Probert (A Child) v Moore [2012] EWHC 2324 (QB) . . . 246–7

Pullman v Hill & Co [1891] 1 QB 524 . . . 434

Quintas v National Smelting Co Ltd [1961] 1 WLR 401 . . . 255

R v Bournewood Mental Health Trust, ex p L [1999] 1 AC 458 . . . 335, 337

R v Brown [1994] 1 AC 212 (HL) . . . 342

R v Deputy Governor of Parkhurst Prison, ex p Hague [1992] 1 AC 58; [1991] 3 WLR 340 (HL) . . . 108, 319, 320

R v G [2003] UKHL 50; [2004] 1 AC 1034 . . . 348

R v Ireland [1996] 3 WLR 650 . . . 334

R v Meade & Belt (1823) 1 Lew CC 184 . . . 334

R v Smith [2012] EWCA Crim 2566; [2013] 1 WLR 1399 . . . 352

R v Sutton (Terrence) [1977] 1 WLR 182 (CA (Crim Div)) . . . 331

R (Binyam Mohamed) v Secretary of State for Foreign and Commonwealth Affairs [2010] EWCA Civ 65 . . . 388

R (Greenfield) v Secretary of State for the Home Department [2005] UKHL 14; [2005] 1 WLR 673 . . . 119

R (on the application of Jalloh (formerly Jollah)) v Secretary of State for the Home Department [2020] UKSC 4 . . . **334–6**

R (Lumba) v Secretary of State for the Home Department [2011] UKSC 12 . . . 327

Rabone and another v Pennine Care NHS Trust [2012] UKSC 2 . . . 54, 540

Ratcliff v McConnell [1999] 1 WLR 670 (CA) . . . 283, 284, 294

RE v Calderdale and Huddersfield NHS Foundation Trust [2017] EWHC 824 (QB) . . . 72, 86

Read v Coker (1853) 138 ER 1437 . . . 334

Read v J Lyons & Co Ltd [1947] AC 156 (HL) . . . 195, 461, 465, 492, 493

Reader v Molesworths [2007] 3 All ER 108 . . . 533

Rees v Darlington Memorial Hospital NHS Trust [2003] UKHL 52; [2003] 4 All ER 987 . . . 47, 192

Reeves v Commissioner of Police [1998] 2 All ER 381 (CA) . . . 245

Reeves v Commissioner of Police [2000] 1 AC 360 (HL) . . . **53–4**, 245, 286

Regan v Paul Properties [2006] EWCA Civ 1319; [2007] Ch 135 . . . **480–2**, 484, 485

Revill v Newbery [1996] QB 567 (CA) . . . 236, 237, 288

Reynolds v Clarke (1725) 93 ER 747 . . . 328

Reynolds v Times Newspapers Ltd [2001] 2 AC 127 (HL) . . . 391, 434, **436–8**, 439, 440, 441, 442, 443

Rhodes v OPO [2015] UKSC 32 . . . 327, **346–9**

Richard v The British Broadcasting Corporation (BBC) and another [2018] EWHC 1837 (Ch) . . . 387

Richardson v LRC Products [2000] Lloyd's Rep Med 280 . . . 314

Richley (Henderson) v Faull, Richley, Third Party [1965] 1 WLR 1454 . . . 175

Rickards v Lothian [1913] AC 263 (PC) . . . 492, 493, 494

Rigby v Chief Constable of Northamptonshire [1985] 1 WLR 1242 (QBD) . . . 112, 116

Robert Addie & Sons (Collieries) Ltd v Dumbreck [1929] AC 358 . . . 39–40, 282

Roberts v Ramsbottom [1980] 1 WLR 823 (QBD) . . . 177

Robinson v Balmain New Ferry [1910] AC 295 (PC) . . . 335, 337

Robinson v Chief Constable of West Yorkshire Police [2018] UKSC 4; [2018] 2 WLR 595 . . . 17, 18, 23, **32–3**, 34, 50, 53, 97, 99, 105, 106, 116

Robinson v Kilvert (1889) 41 ChD 88 (CA) . . . 471

Robinson v P E Jones (Contractors) [2011] EWCA Civ 9; [2011] 3 WLR 815 . . . 147

Robinson v Post Office [1974] 1 WLR 1176 (CA) . . . **223–4**

Roles v Nathan [1963] 1 WLR 1117 (CA) . . . **278–9**, 291

Rondel v Worsley [1969] 1 AC 191 . . . 30

Rose v Ford [1937] AC 826 . . . 547, 548

Rose v Plenty [1976] 1 WLR 141 (CA) . . . 518

Ross v Caunters [1980] Ch 297 (Ch D) . . . 30

Rothwell v Chemical & Insulating Co Ltd & Anor [2006] EWCA Civ 27 . . . 70

Rothwell v Chemical & Insulating Co Ltd [2007] UKHL 39; [2008] AC 281 . . . 64, 70, 548

Rowling v Takaro Properties Ltd [1988] AC 473 (PC) . . . 28

Rubber Improvements Ltd and Lewis v Daily Telegraph Ltd *see* Lewis v Daily Telegraph

Rufus v Elliott [2015] EWCA Civ 121 . . . 416

Rylands v Fletcher (1866) LR 1 Ex 265 (Ct of Ex Chamber) . . . **488–9**, 491, 492, 493, 495, 496

Rylands v Fletcher (1868) LR 3 HL 330 (HL) . . . **489–90**, 492, 493, 494

S (A Child) (identification: restrictions on publication), Re [2003] EWCA Civ 963; [2003] 3 WLR 1425 . . . 364, 365

S (A Child), Re [2004] UKHL 47; [2005] 1 AC 593 . . . 375

S (An Infant) v S [1972] AC 24 . . . 188

St Albans DC v ICL [1996] 4 All ER 481 . . . 307

St George v The Home Office [2008] EWCA Civ 1068 . . . 249

St George's Healthcare NHS Trust v S [1999] Fam 26 . . . 193

St Helen's Smelting Co v Tipping (1865) 11 HL Cas 642; 11 ER 1483 (HL) . . . 466, **470**

Salsbury v Woodland [1970] 1 QB 324 (CA) . . . 527

Saunders v Edwards [1987] 1 WLR 1116 . . . 237

Savage v South Essex NHS Foundation Trust [2008] UKHL 74; [2009] 2 WLR 115 . . . 54, 124, **125–8**, 130

Schneider v Eisovitch [1960] QB 430 . . . 68

SCM v Whittall [1971] 1 QB 337 . . . 136

Scout Association v Barnes [2010] EWCA Civ 1476 . . . 170, 202

Scullion v Bank of Scotland [2011] EWCA Civ 693 . . . 161

Secretary of State for the Home Department v JJ [2007] UKHL 45; [2008] AC 385 . . . 336

Sedleigh-Denfield v O'Callaghan [1940] AC 880 (HL) . . . **497–8**, 499

Selwood v Durham County Council & others [2012] EWCA Civ 979 . . . 61

Serafin v Malkiewicz [2020] UKSC 23 . . . 443

Shakil-Ur-Rahman v ARY Network Ltd [2016] EWHC 3110 (QB) . . . 449

Shakoor v Situ [2000] 4 All ER 181 . . . 178

Shelfer v City of London Lighting [1895] 1 Ch 287 (CA) . . . 458, 479, 480, 481, 482, 483, 484, 486

Shell UK v Total UK [2010] EWCA Civ 180; [2011] QB 86 . . . 137

Sheppard v Glossop Corporation [1921] 3 KB 132 . . . 97, 107, 108, 109

Sherratt v Chief Constable of Greater Manchester Police [2018] EWHC 1746 (QB) . . . 115, 122

Shiffman v St John of Jerusalem (Grand Priory in the British Realm of the Venerable Order of the Hospital) [1936] 1 All ER 557 . . . 493

Shorter v Surrey & Sussex Healthcare NHS Trust [2015] EWHC 614 (QB) . . . 83, 84, 85

Sidaway v Governors of the Bethlem Royal Hospital [1985] AC 871 (HL) . . . 182, 183, 184, 185, 186, 188, 189

Sienkiewicz v Greif (UK) Ltd [2011] 2 AC 229 . . . 209, 212

Sim v Stretch [1936] 2 All ER 1237 (HL) . . . 403, 406

Simkiss v Rhondda BC (1983) 81 LGR 460 (CA) . . . 281

Simmons v British Steel [2004] UKHL 20; [2004] ICR 585 . . . 69

Simmons v Castle [2012] EWCA Civ 1039 . . . 540

Slack v Leeds Industrial Co-operative Society Ltd [1924] 2 Ch 47 . . . 484

Slater v Clay Cross Co Ltd [1956] 2 QB 264 (CA) . . . 176, 268

Slipper v BBC [1991] QB 283 (CA) . . . 409

Smith v Chief Constable of Sussex Police [2008] UKHL 50; [2009] 1 AC 225 . . . 60, 99, 104, 116, 119, 122

Smith v Eric S Bush [1990] 1 AC 831 (HL) . . . 101, 149, 151, **159–60**, 161, 163

Smith v Lancashire Teaching Hospitals NHS Foundation Trust and others [2017] EWCA Civ 1916 . . . 539

Smith v Lancashire Teaching Hospitals NHS Trust and another [2016] EWHC 2208 (QB) . . . 539

Smith v Leech Brain & Co Ltd [1962] 2 QB 405 (QBD) . . . 224

Smith v Littlewoods Organisation Ltd [1987] AC 241 (HL) . . . 30, 52, **56–9**, 338, 339

Smith v London South Western Rly (1870) LR 6 CP 14 . . . 219

Smith v Stone (1647) Sty 65 . . . 455

Smith New Court Securities Ltd v Scrimgeour Vickers (Asset Management) Ltd [1997] AC 254 . . . 45

Sobrinho v Impresa Publishing SA [2016] EWHC 66 (QB); [2016] EMLR 12 . . . 408, 410

Spartan Steel & Alloys Ltd v Martin & Co (Contractors) Ltd [1973] QB 27 (CA) . . . **133–4**, 135

Spearman v Royal United Bath Hospitals NHS Foundation Trust [2017] EWHC 3027 (QB) . . . 247, **273–7**, **288–90**

Spiller v Joseph [2010] UKSC 53; [2011] 1 AC 852 . . . **427–32**

Spring v Guardian Assurance [1995] 2 AC 296 (HL) . . . 1, 121, 141, 150, 151, 152, **164–7**, 168

Standard Chartered Bank v Pakistan National Shipping Corp (No 2) [2003] 1 All ER 173 . . . 245

Stannard (t/a Wyvern Tyres) v Gore [2012] EWCA Civ 1248 . . . 496

Stansbie v Troman [1948] 2 KB 48 (CA) . . . 51, 57, 59

Staples v West Dorset District Council [1995] PIQR 439 . . . 284

Stapley v Gypsum Mines Ltd [1953] AC 663 . . . 177, 252, 255

Starr v Ward [2015] EWHC 1987 (QB) . . . 441

Steel and another v NRAM Ltd (formerly NRAM plc) (Scotland) [2018] UKSC 13 . . . 153

Stephens v Myers (1830) 172 ER 735 . . . 333

Stevenson Jordan & Harrison Ltd v McDonall & Evans [1952] 1 TLR 101 (CA) . . . 507

Stocker v Stocker [2019] UKSC 17 . . . **413–18**

Stoffel & Co v Grondona [2020] UKSC 42 . . . 242

Stovin v Wise [1996] AC 923 (HL) . . . **51–2**, 53, 96, 98, 99, 104, 106, **107–10**, 111

Stuart v Bell [1891] 2 QB 341 . . . 435

Stubbings v Webb [1993] AC 498 . . . 329–30

Sturges v Bridgman (1879) 11 ChD 852 (CA) . . . 470, 473, 484

Sube v News Group Newspapers Ltd [2020] EWHC 1125 (QB) . . . **351–4**

Sumner v Colborne Denbighshire County Council and The Welsh Ministers [2018] EWCA Civ 1006 . . . 111

Sutradhar v National Environmental Research Council [2006] UKHL 33; [2006] 4 All ER 490 . . . 53

Swift v Secretary of State for Justice [2013] EWCA Civ 193 . . . 539

Swinney v Chief Constable of Northumbria Police [1997] QB 464 (CA) . . . 59, 87

T (Adult: Refusal of Treatment), Re [1993] Fam 95 (CA) . . . 342

Tate and Lyle v Greater London Council [1983] 2 AC 509 (HL) . . . 463, 473

Taylor v Chief Constable of Hampshire Police [2013] EWCA Civ 496 . . . 227

Taylor v Novo [2013] EWCA Civ 194; [2014] QB 150 . . . 82, 83

Taylor v O'Connor [1971] AC 115 . . . 543

Telnikoff v Matusevitch [1992] 2 AC 343 . . . 430

Terry v Persons Unknown [2010] EWHC 119 (QB) . . . 390

Theaker v Richardson [1962] 1 WLR 151 (CA) . . . 394–5

Theedom v Nourish Training Ltd [2015] EWHC 3769 (QB); [2016] EMLR 10 . . . 409

Thomas v National Union of Mineworkers (South Wales Area) [1986] Ch 20 (Ch D) . . . 333, 508

Thomas v News Group Newspapers [2001] EWCA Civ 1233; [2002] EMLR 78 . . . 355

Thomas v News Group Newspapers Ltd [2001] EWCA Civ 1233; [2002] EMLR 4 . . . 352, 353, 354

Thompson v Price [1973] 2 All ER 846 . . . 539

Thompson v Smith Ship Repairers (North Shields) Ltd [1984] QB 405 (QBD) . . . 181

Thompson-Schwab v Costaki [1956] 1 WLR 335 (CA) . . . 2, 464, 470

Thornton v Daily Telegraph *see* Thornton v Telegraph Media Group Ltd

Thornton v Telegraph Media Group Ltd [2010] EWHC 1414 (QB); [2011] 1 WLR 1985 . . . 406

Times Newspapers Ltd and others v Flood and others [2017] UKSC 33 . . . 367

Tinkler v Ferguson [2018] EWHC 3563 (QB) . . . 433

Tinsley v Milligan [1994] 1 AC 340 (HL) . . . 238, 239, 242

Tomlinson v Congleton BC [2003] UKHL 47; [2004] AC 46 . . . 2, 169, 267, **271–2, 282–7**, 290, 294, 295, 296

Transco v Stockport Metropolitan Borough Council [2003] UKHL 61; [2004] 2 AC 1 . . . **490–5**, 496

Tremain v Pike [1969] 3 All ER 1303 . . . 219, 227

Trimingham v Associated Newspapers Ltd [2012] EWHC 1296 (QB) . . . 353, 354

Trotman v North Yorkshire County Council [1999] LGR 584 (CA) . . . 519

Tse Wai Chun Paul v Albert Cheng [2001] EMLR 777; [2000] HKCFA 35 . . . 428, 430

Tuberville v Savage (1669) 86 ER 684; 1 Mod 3 . . . 331, 332, 334

Turberville v Stampe (1698) 1 Ld Raym 264 . . . 512

Turner v Metro-Goldwyn-Mayer Pictures Ltd [1950] 1 All ER 449 . . . 428

United Australia Ltd v Barclays Bank Ltd [1941] AC 1 . . . 328

Vallejo v Wheeler (1774) 1 Cowp 143 . . . 240

Van Colle v Chief Constable of Hertfordshire [2008] UKHL 50; [2009] 1 AC 225; [2008] 3 WLR 593 . . . 60, 124, **128–9**, 130

Various Claimants v Catholic Child Welfare Society and Others [2012] UKSC 56; [2013] 2 AC 1 . . . 506, **507–10**, 511, 512, 513, 514, 515, 516, **520–2**, 523, 526, 528, 531

Vaughan v Taff Vale Ry Co (1860) 157 ER 1351 . . . 35

Veakins v Kier Islington Ltd [2009] EWCA Civ 1288 . . . 354

Vellino v Chief Constable of Greater Manchester [2002] EWCA Civ 1249; [2002] 1 WLR 218 . . . 236, 237

Vernon v Bosley (No 1) [1997] 1 All ER 577 . . . 77

Vernon Knight Associates v Cornwall Council [2013] EWCA Civ 950 . . . 502

Viasystems v Thermal Transfer Ltd [2005] EWCA Civ 1151; [2005] 4 All ER 1181 . . . 508, 515

Victorian Railways Commissioners v Coultas (1888) 13 App Cas 222 (PC) . . . 68, 345

Vidal-Hall and others v Google Inc [2014] EWHC 13 (QB) . . . 377

Videan v British Transport Commission [1963] 2 QB 640 (CA) . . . **38–9**, 40

W v Essex County Council [2001] 2 AC 592 . . . 106, 124

W Angliss and Co (Australia) Proprietary Ltd v Peninsular and Oriental Steam Navigation Co [1927] 2 KB 456 . . . 42

Wagon Mound, The (No 1) *see* **Overseas Tankship (UK) Ltd v Morts Dock and Engineering Co Ltd (The Wagon Mound) (No 1)**

Wagon Mound, The (No 2) *see* **Overseas Tankship (UK) Ltd v Miller Steamship Co Pty Ltd (The Wagon Mound) (No 2)**

Wainwright v Home Office [2002] QB 1334 (CA) . . . 346, 347

Wainwright v Home Office [2003] UKHL 53; [2004] 2 AC 406; [2007] 3 WLR 1137 . . . 3, **344–6**, 348, 357, **358–9**, 364, 378

Walker v Northumberland County Council [1995] 1 All ER 737 (QBD) . . . 87, 94, 95

Walter v Selfe (1851) 64 ER 849 . . . 462, 471

Wandsworth Board of Works v United Telephone Co Ltd (1884) 13 QBD 904 . . . 455

Wardlaw v Bonnington Castings Ltd 1955 SC 320 . . . 209

Warren v Henlys Ltd [1948] 2 All ER 935 . . . 524

Warriner v Warriner [2003] 3 All ER 447 . . . 546

Wasserman v Freilich [2016] EWHC 312 (QB) . . . 433

Watson v Buckley, Osborne Garrett & Co and Wyrovoys Products [1940] 1 All ER 174 . . . 301

Watson v Croft Promo-Sport [2009] EWCA Civ 15; [2009] 3 All ER 249 . . . 484, 485, 486

Watson v Thomas S. Whitney & Co Ltd [1966] 1 WLR 57 . . . 175

Watt v Hertfordshire County Council [1954] 1 WLR 835 (CA) . . . **201–2**

Watt v Longsdon [1930] 1 KB 130 (CA) . . . **434–5**

Webb v Beavan (1883) 11 QBD 609 . . . 392

Weld-Blundell v Stephens [1920] AC 956 (HL) . . . 57

Weller v Associated Newspapers Ltd [2015] EWCA 1176 . . . 374

Weller & Co v Foot and Mouth Disease Research Institute [1966] 1 QB 569 (QBD) . . . 133

Wells v Cooper [1958] 2 QB 265 (CA) . . . **173–4**

Wells v University Hospital Southampton NHS Foundation Trust [2015] EWHC 2376 (QB) . . . 72

Wells v Wells [1999] 1 AC 345 (HL) . . . **544–5**

West v Shepherd [1964] AC 326 (HL) . . . **547–8**

Wheat v E Lacon & Co Ltd [1966] AC 552 (HL) . . . **268–70**

Wheeler v Saunders [1996] Ch 19 (CA) . . . 472, **474–5**

White v Chief Constable of South Yorkshire [1998] UKHL 45; [1999] 2 AC 455; [1998] 3 WLR 1509 . . . 39, 46, **62–4**, 69, 70, 82, **87–92**, 94, 95, 214, 530

White v Jones [1995] 2 AC 207 (HL) . . . 101, 148, 150, 151, **161–4**, 168

White Lion Hotel v James [2021] EWCA Civ 31 . . . 231, **294–7**

Wild v Southend University Hospital NHS Foundation Trust [2014] EWHC 4053 (QB) . . . 71, 72, 83

Wildtree Hotels Ltd v Harrow London Borough Council [2001] 2 AC 1 . . . 491

Wilkes v DePuy International Ltd [2016] EWHC 3096 (QB) . . . 314, 315

Wilkinson v Downton [1897] 2 QB 57 (QBD) . . . 327, 334, **344**, 345, 346, 347, 348, 349, 350, 354, 467

Williams v A & W Hemphill Ltd 1966 SC (HL) 31 . . . 519

Williams v Natural Life Health Foods Ltd [1998] UKHL 17; [1998] 1 WLR 830 . . . 151, 153

Williams v Port of Liverpool Stevedoring Co Ltd [1956] 1 WLR 551 . . . 233

Williams v The Bermuda Hospitals Board (Bermuda) [2016] UKPC 4 . . . 208, **209–12**

Wilsher v Essex Area Health Authority [1987] QB 730 (CA) . . . 21, 178, 179, 207

Wilsher v Essex Area Health Authority [1988] AC 1074 (HL) . . . 178, **204–8**, 210, 211, 214, 217, 218, 219

Wilson v Pringle [1987] QB 237 (CA) . . . 329, **330–3**, 340

Wilsons & Clyde Coal Co Ltd v English [1937] UKHL 2; [1938] AC 57 . . . 93, 528

Wise v Kaye [1962] 1 QB 368 . . . 547

Wm Morrison Supermarkets plc v Various Claimants [2020] UKSC 12 . . . 516, 525, 526

Wong v Parkside Health Trust [2001] EWCA Civ 1721; [2003] 3 All ER 932 . . . 344, 345, 348

Wood v Commissioner of Police of the Metropolis [2009] EWCA Civ 414; [2010] 1 WLR 123 . . . 371

Wood v Law Society, The (1993) 143 NLJ 1475 . . . 323

Woodland v Essex County Council [2013] UKSC 66 . . . **528–31**

Woodland v Maxwell and Essex County Council [2015] EWHC 273 (QB) . . . 531

Woodland v Maxwell and Essex County Council [2015] EWHC 820 (QB) . . . 532

Woods v Martins Bank Ltd [1959] 1 QB 55 . . . 139, 140

Wooldridge v Sumner [1963] 2 QB 43 (CA) . . . **195–7**

Wright v Troy Lucas (a firm) and George Rusz [2019] EWHC 1098 (QB) . . . 175

Wyatt v Curtis [2003] EWCA Civ 1779 . . . 185

X (Minors) v Bedfordshire CC [1995] 2 AC 633 (HL) . . . 99, 100, 101, 102, 103, 104, 105, 106, 107, 112, 122, **320**

X & Y v London Borough of Hounslow [2009] EWCA Civ 286 . . . 61

YAH v Medway NHS Foundation Trust [2018] EWHC 2964 (QB) . . . **70–6**

Yeo v Times Newspapers Limited [2015] 1 WLR 971 . . . 433

Yuen Kun Yeu v Attorney-General of Hong Kong [1988] AC 175 (PC) . . . 28, 30, 50, 101

Zarb-Cousin v Association of British Bookmakers [2018] EWHC 2240 (QB) . . . 433

International Cases

Australia

Australian Safeway Stores v Zaluzna (1987) 162 CLR 479 . . . 263

Boral Bricks Pty Ltd v Cosmidis (No 2) [2014] NSWCA 139 . . . 257

Bryan v Maloney (1994) 128 ALR 163 (HC Australia) . . . 147

Burnie Port Authority v General Jones Pty Ltd (1994) 179 CLR 520 . . . 494, 496

Carroll v Purcell (1927) 35 ALJR 384 . . . 542

Fishenden v Higgs & Hill Ltd (1935) 153 LT 128 . . . 485, 486

Gardiner v Fairfax (1942) 42 SR (NSW) 171 . . . 428

Gill v Ethicon Sàrl (No 5) [2019] FCA 1905 (Australia) . . . 315

Goodger v Knapman [1924] SASR 347 . . . 542

Hackshaw v Shaw (1984) 155 CLR 614 . . . 263

Hargrave v Goldman (1963) 110 CLR 40 (HC Australia) . . . 51, 52

Insurance Commissioner v Joyce (1948) 77 CLR 39 . . . 176

Jaensch v Coffey (1984) 155 CLR 549 . . . 78

LJP Investments v Howard Chia Investments (1991) 24 NSWLR 499 . . . 458

McHale v Watson (1966) 115 CLR 199 . . . 194, 195

Myerson v Smith's Weekly (1923) 24 SR (NSW) 20 . . . 428

Rogers v Whitaker (1992) 175 CLR 479 . . . 189

Skelton v Collins (1966) 39 AJLR 480 . . . 548

Sutherland Shire Council v Heyman (1985) 60 ALR 1; 157 CLR 424 . . . 17, 29, 31, 109, 110, 156

Uren v John Fairfax (1967) 117 CLR 115 . . . 447

Usher v Williams (1955) 60 WALR 69 . . . 542

Walker v Turton-Sainsbury [1952] SASR 159 . . . 176

Canada

Bazley v Curry [1999] 2 SCR 53; (1999) 174 DLR (4th) 45 . . . 506, 518, 519, 520, 525

Canadian National Railway (CNR) v Norsk Pacific Hydro [1992] 1 SCR 1021 (Supreme Ct Canada) . . . 137

Car and General Insurance Co v Seymour and Maloney (1956) 2 DLR (2d) 369 . . . 176

Doe v Metropolitan Toronto (Municipality) Commissioners of Police [1998] 160 DLR (4th) 289 . . . 117

Grant v Torstar Corporation [2009] SCC 61 . . . 438

Hill v Hamilton-Wentworth Regional Police (2007) 285 DLR (4th) 620; 2007 SCC 41 . . . 116

Jacobi v Griffiths (1999) 174 DLR (4th) 71 . . . 518, 520

Laferrière v Lawson (1991) 78 DLR (4th) 609 . . . 218

McKinnon Industries Ltd v Walker [1951] 3 DLR 577 . . . 471

Nor-Video Services v Ontario Hydro (1978) 84 DLR (3d) 221 . . . 469

Nova Mink v Trans Canada Airlines [1951] 2 DLR 241 . . . 23

Queen, The v Saskatchewan Wheat Pool [1983] 1 SCR 205 . . . 324

Saadati v Moorhead [2017] 1 SCR 543 . . . 64

Star Village Tavern v Nield (1976) 71 DLR (3d) 439 . . . 1

Winnipeg Condominium Corporation v Bird Construction (1995) 121 DLR (4th) 193 . . . 147

Wright v Davidson (1992) 88 DLR (4th) 698 . . . 229

Court of Justice of the European Union

Commission of the European Communities v UK (Case C-300/95) ECLI:EU:C:1997:35 (Opinion of AG Tesauro) . . . 315

Commission of the European Communities v UK (Case C-300/95) ECLI:EU:C:1997:255; [1997] All ER (EC) 481 . . . 306, **307–8**, 311, 312, 313

eDate Advertising GmbH and Martinez v MGN (Joined Cases C-509/09 and C-161/10) ECLI:EU:C:2011:685 . . . 400

European Court of Human Rights

Armonienė v Lithuania (App no 36919/02) (2008) 48 EHRR 1252 . . . 382

Ashingdane v UK (App no 8225/78) [1985] ECHR 8 . . . 124

Dudgeon v UK (App no 7525/76) (1981) 4 EHRR 149 . . . 376

Earl Spencer v UK (App nos 28851/95 & 28852/95) (1998) 25 EHRR CD 105 . . . 363

Fressoz and Roire v France (App no 29183/95) (2001) 31 EHRR 2 . . . 353, 365

Glass v UK (App no 61827/00) (2004) 39 EHRR 15 . . . 188

Hatton v UK (App no 36022/97) (2003) 37 EHRR 28 . . . 476, 478, 479

HL v UK (App no 45508/99) (2005) 40 EHRR 32 . . . 335, 337

Jersild v Denmark (App no 15890/89) (1994) 19 EHRR 1 . . . 353, 365

K U v Finland (App no 2871/02) (2008), 2 December . . . 382

Keenan v UK (App no 27229/95) [2001] ECHR 239; (2001) 33 EHRR 38 . . . 54, 126, 127, 128

Leempoel v Belgium (App no 64772/01) (2006), 9 November . . . 377

Lingens v Austria (App no 9815/82) (1986) 8 EHRR 407 . . . 393

MGN v UK (App no 39401/04) [2011] ECHR 66 . . . 353, 367

Mosley v UK (App no 48009/08) (2011) 53 EHRR 30 2011 . . . 379–84

Nilsen and Johnsen v Norway (1999) 30 EHRR 878 . . . 353

Osman v UK (App no 23452/94) (1998) 29 EHRR 245 . . . 122, 125, 128, 129, 130, 131

Powell v UK (App no 45305/99) [2000] ECHR 703; (2000) 30 EHRR CD 362 . . . 126, 128

Renolde v France (App no 5608/05) [2008] ECHR 1085 . . . 54

Sunday Times, The v UK (App no 6538/74) (1979) 2 EHRR 245 . . . 393

Sunday Times, The v UK (App no 13166/87) (No 2) (1991) 14 EHRR 229 . . . 393

Tammer v Estonia (App no 41205/98) (2001) 37 EHRR 857 . . . 365

Tolstoy Miloslavsky v UK (App no 18139/91) (1995) 20 EHRR 442 . . . 385, 447

TP and KM v UK (App no 28945/95) [2001] ECHR 322 . . . 106

Tysiac v Poland (App no 5410/03) (2007) 45 EHRR 42 . . . 188

Von Hannover v Germany (App no 59320/00) (2005) 40 EHRR 1 . . . 357, **367–70**, 376, 382, 384

Wainwright v UK (App no 12350/04) (2007) 44 EHRR 809 . . . 359

X and Y v Netherlands (App no 8978/80) [1984] ECHR 4; (1985) 8 EHRR 235 . . . 382

X, Y and Z v UK (App no 3266/10) [2011] ECHR 1199 . . . 131

Z v Finland (App no 22009/93) (1997) 25 EHRR 371 . . . 365

Z and others v UK (App no 29392/95) [2001] ECHR 333 . . . 106, **122–4**, 130

India

Mehta v Union of India 1987 AIR (SC) 1086 . . . 496

New Zealand

Hosking v Runting [2003] 3 NZLR 385 . . . 364

Invercargill City Council v Hamlin [1994] 3 NZLR 513 . . . 110, 147, 148

Mainguard Packaging v Hilton Haulage [1990] 1 NZLR 360 . . . 135

New Zealand Forest Products v A-G [1986] 1 NZLR 14 . . . 134

United States

Bucheleres v Chicago Park District, 171 Ill 2d 435 (1996) . . . 287

Grimshaw v Ford Motor Co, 119 Cal App 3d 757 (1981) . . . 6

Moffett v Brewer, Iowa 1 Greene 348 (1848) . . . 460

Palsgraf v Long Island Railroad Co, 248 NY 339 (1928) . . . 37

Ultramares Corporation v Touche, 174 NE 441 (1931) . . . 154

US v Carroll Towing, 159 F 2d 169 (1947) . . . 171

Wagner v International Rly Co, 232 NY 176 (1921) . . . 39

Table of legislation

Legislation in **bold** indicates that the statute or part thereof is reproduced in the text at the page location indicated in **bold** type.

United Kingdom

Statutes

Administration of Justice Act 1982
  s 3 . . . 78

Banking Act 1979
  s 47 . . . 245

British Transport Commission Act 1949
  s 55 . . . 459

Building Act 1984 . . . 141

Children Act 1989 . . . 96, 97
  s 17 . . . 99
  s 31 . . . 99
  s 47 . . . 99

Civil Aviation Act 1949 . . . 457
  Pt II (ss 8–15) . . . 456
  s 40(1) . . . 456, 457
  s 40(2) . . . 456

Civil Aviation Act 1982
  s 39 . . . 459
  s 76(1) . . . 457

Civil Evidence Act 1995
  s 10 . . . 541

Civil Liability Act 2018 . . . 7, 8

Civil Liability (Contribution) Act 1978 . . . 251, 445
  s 1 . . . 445

Companies Act 1985 . . . 155, 157

Compensation Act 2006 . . . 169, 170
  s 1 . . . 170
  s 1(a) . . . 170
  s 1(b) . . . 170
  s 3 . . . 216

Congenital Disabilities (Civil Liability) Act 1976 . . . 72, 73

Consumer Protection Act 1987 . . . 298, 301, 302, 307, 309, 314, 315, 316
  Pt I (ss 1–9) . . . 302–5, 306
  s 1 . . . 302, 307
  ss 1–5 . . . 306
  s 1(1) . . . 302, 308
  s 1(2) . . . 302

  s 1(2)(a) . . . **302**
  s 1(2)(b) . . . **302**
  s 1(2)(c) . . . **302**
  s 1(3) . . . **302**
  s 2 . . . **302–3**, 304
  s 2(1) . . . **302**
  s 2(2) . . . **302**, 303, 304
  s 2(2)(a) . . . **302**
  s 2(2)(b) . . . **302**
  s 2(2)(c) . . . **302**, 307
  s 2(3) . . . **302–3**
  s 2(3)(a) . . . **303**
  s 2(3)(b) . . . **303**
  s 2(3)(c) . . . **303**
  s 2(4) . . . **303**
  s 2(5) . . . **303**
  s 2(6) . . . **303**
  s 3 . . . 302, **303**, 309, 314
  s 3(1) . . . **303**
  s 3(2) . . . **303**
  s 3(2)(a) . . . **303**
  s 3(2)(b) . . . **303**
  s 3(2)(c) . . . **303**
  s 4 . . . **303–4**, 306
  s 4(1) . . . **303**, 314
  s 4(1)(a) . . . **303**, 307
  s 4(1)(b) . . . **303**
  s 4(1)(c) . . . **303**
  s 4(1)(d) . . . **303**
  s 4(1)(e) . . . **303**, 306, 307, 308, 309, 313
  s 4(1)(f) . . . **304**
  s 4(2) . . . **304**
  s 4(2)(a) . . . **304**
  s 4(2)(b) . . . **304**
  s 5 . . . **304**
  s 5(1) . . . **304**
  s 5(2) . . . 301, **304**
  s 5(3) . . . **304**
  s 5(3)(a) . . . **304**
  s 5(3)(b) . . . **304**
  s 5(4) . . . **304**
  s 5(5) . . . **304**
  s 5(6) . . . **304**
  s 5(7) . . . **304**
  s 5(7)(a) . . . **304**
  s 5(7)(b) . . . **304**
  s 5(8) . . . **304**
  s 7 . . . **305**
  Pt III (ss 20–26) . . . 306

Pt V (ss 36–50) . . . **305–6**
s 41 . . . 316
s 45 . . . **305**
s 45(1) . . . **305**
s 46 . . . **305–6**
s 46(1) . . . **305**
s 46(1)(a) . . . **305**
s 46(1)(b) . . . **305**
s 46(1)(c) . . . **305**
s 46(1)(d) . . . **305**
s 46(1)(e) . . . **305**
s 46(1)(f) . . . **305**
s 46(2) . . . **305**
s 46(2)(a) . . . **305**
s 46(2)(b) . . . **305**
s 46(3) . . . **305–6**
s 46(4) . . . 305, **306**

Consumer Rights Act 2015 . . . 298, 307

Contracts (Rights of Third Parties) Act
1999 . . . 515
s 1 . . . 515

Copyright, Designs and Patents Act 1988
Pt I (ss 1–179) . . . 398

Countryside and Rights of Way Act 2000
Pt I (ss 1–46) . . . 264
s 2(1) . . . 262, 264, 265
s 13 . . . 282
s 16 . . . 264
s 20 . . . 265

County Courts Act 1984
s 66 . . . 404

Courts Act 2003 . . . 534

Criminal Damage Act 1971 . . . 348

Criminal Justice and Public Order Act 1994
s 61 . . . 459
s 68 . . . 459

Criminal Law Act 1977
s 6 . . . 459

Damages Act 1996 . . . 534, 546
s 1 . . . **546**
s 1(1) . . . **546**
s 1(2) . . . **546**
s 1(3) . . . 545, **546**
s 2 . . . **534**
s 2(1) . . . **534**
s 2(1)(a) . . . **534**
s 2(1)(b) . . . **534**
s 2(2) . . . **534**
s 2(3) . . . **534**
s 6 . . . 534

Damages (Scotland) Act 2011 . . . 302

Data Protection Act 1998 . . . 358, 382
s 4(4) . . . 527

Defamation Act 1952
s 2 . . . 392
s 5 . . . 417, 418, 426
s 6 . . . 427

Defamation Act 1996 . . . 444, 446
s 1 . . . 395, **397–8**, 399, 400
s 1(1) . . . **397**
s 1(1)(a) . . . **397**, 399
s 1(1)(b) . . . **397**, 399
s 1(1)(c) . . . **397**, 399
s 1(2) . . . **397**, 399
s 1(3) . . . 397, **398**, 399
s 1(3)(a) . . . **398**
s 1(3)(b) . . . **398**
s 1(3)(c) . . . **398**
s 1(3)(d) . . . **398**
s 1(3)(e) . . . **398**
s 1(4) . . . **398**
s 1(4)(a) . . . **398**
s 1(4)(b) . . . **398**
s 1(4)(c) . . . **398**
s 1(5) . . . **398**
s 2 . . . **444–5**
s 2(1) . . . **444**
s 2(2) . . . **444**
s 2(3) . . . **444**
s 2(3)(a) . . . **444**
s 2(3)(b) . . . **444**
s 2(3)(c) . . . **444**
s 2(4) . . . **444**
s 2(4)(a) . . . **444**
s 2(4)(b) . . . **444**
s 2(4)(c) . . . **444**
s 2(5) . . . **445**
s 2(6) . . . **445**
s 3 . . . **445**
s 3(1) . . . **445**
s 3(2) . . . **445**
s 3(3) . . . **445**
s 3(4) . . . **445**
s 3(4)(a) . . . **445**
s 3(4)(b) . . . **445**
s 3(5) . . . **445**, 446
s 3(6) . . . **445**
s 3(7) . . . **445**
s 3(8) . . . **445**
s 3(8)(a) . . . **445**
s 3(8)(b) . . . **445**
s 3(10) . . . **445**
s 4 . . . **445–6**
s 4(1) . . . **445**
s 4(2) . . . **445**
s 4(3) . . . **445**
s 4(3)(a) . . . **445**
s 4(3)(b) . . . **445**
s 4(4) . . . **446**
s 4(5) . . . **446**
s 14 . . . 427
s 15 . . . 427
s 17 . . . **398, 400**
s 17(1) . . . **398**

Defamation Act 2013 . . . 391, 392, 404, 405,
406, 427
Explanatory Notes . . . 406, 432, 439
s 1 . . . 392, **405**, 408, 409, 411, 412
s 1(1) . . . **404**, **405**, 406

s 1(2) . . . 404, **405**
s 2 . . . **426**
s 2(1) . . . **426**
s 2(2) . . . **426**
s 2(3) . . . **426**
s 2(4) . . . **426**
s 3 . . . 426, **427**
s 3(1) . . . **427**
s 3(2) . . . **427**
s 3(3) . . . **427**, 432
s 3(4) . . . **427**
s 3(4)(a) . . . **427**
s 3(4)(b) . . . **427**
s 3(5) . . . **427**
s 3(6) . . . **427**
s 3(7) . . . **427**
s 3(7)(a) . . . **427**
s 3(7)(b) . . . **427**
s 3(7)(c) . . . **427**
s 3(7)(d) . . . **427**
s 3(8) . . . **427**
s 4 . . . 427, 434, **436**, 439, 442, 444
s 4(1) . . . **436**
s 4(1)(a) . . . **436**
s 4(1)(b) . . . **436**, 442, 443
s 4(2) . . . **436**, 441, 442
s 4(3) . . . **436**, 442
s 4(4) . . . **436**, 438, 441
s 4(5) . . . **436**
s 4(6) . . . **436**, 439
s 5 . . . 395, **401**
s 5(1) . . . **401**
s 5(2) . . . **401**
s 5(3) . . . **401**
s 5(3)(a) . . . **401**
s 5(3)(b) . . . **401**
s 5(3)(c) . . . **401**
s 5(4) . . . **401**
s 5(5) . . . **401**
s 5(5)(a) . . . **401**
s 5(5)(b) . . . **401**
s 5(5)(c) . . . **401**
s 5(5)(d) . . . **401**
s 5(6) . . . **401**
s 5(7) . . . **401**
s 6 . . . 427, 432
s 8 . . . 395, **402**, 442
s 8(1) . . . **402**
s 8(1)(a) . . . **402**
s 8(1)(b) . . . **402**
s 8(2) . . . **402**
s 8(3) . . . **402**
s 8(4) . . . **402**
s 8(5) . . . **402**
s 8(5)(a) . . . **402**
s 8(5)(b) . . . **402**
s 8(6) . . . **402**
s 8(6)(a) . . . **402**
s 8(6)(b) . . . **402**
s 9 . . . 401
s 9(2) . . . 401
s 10 . . . 395, **398**

s 10(1) . . . **398**
s 10(2) . . . **398**
s 11 . . . 404, 415, 432, 447

Defective Premises Act 1972 . . . 141, 143, 146
s 1 . . . **142**, 143, 146, 147
s 1(1) . . . **142**
s 1(1)(a) . . . **142**
s 1(1)(b) . . . **142**
s 1(2) . . . **142**
s 1(3) . . . **142**
s 1(4) . . . **142**
s 1(4)(a) . . . **142**
s 1(4)(b) . . . **142**
s 2 . . . **142**, 146
s 2(1) . . . **142**
s 2(1)(a) . . . **142**
s 2(1)(b) . . . **142**
s 3 . . . **142–3**
s 3(1) . . . **142–3**
s 3(2) . . . **143**
s 3(2)(a) . . . **143**
s 3(2)(b) . . . **143**
s 3(2)(c) . . . **143**
s 4 . . . 270
s 6 . . . **143**
s 6(1) . . . **143**
s 6(1)(a) . . . **143**
s 6(1)(b) . . . **143**
s 6(1)(c) . . . **143**
s 6(2) . . . **143**
s 6(3) . . . **143**

Education Act 1996
s 7 . . . 530

Enterprise and Regulatory Reform Act 2013
s 69 . . . 319, 324
s 69(3) . . . 324

Environmental Protection Act 1990
s 73(6) . . . 495

Factories Acts . . . 321

Factory and Workshop Act 1878 . . . 317
s 5 . . . 316
s 82 . . . 317
s 87 . . . 317

Fatal Accidents Act 1976 . . . 302, 535, 538, 539,
540, 541, 542
s 1 . . . 533, **536**
s 1(1) . . . **536**
s 1(2) . . . **536**
s 1(3) . . . **536**, 539
s 1(3)(a) . . . **536**
s 1(3)(aa) . . . **536**
s 1(3)(b) . . . **536**, 538, 539
s 1(3)(c) . . . **536**
s 1(3)(d) . . . **536**
s 1(3)(e) . . . **536**
s 1(3)(f) . . . **536**
s 1(3)(fa) . . . **536**
s 1(3)(g) . . . **536**

s 1(4) . . . **536**
s 1(4A) . . . **536**
s 1(5) . . . **536**
s 1(5)(a) . . . **536**
s 1(5)(b) . . . **536**, 540
s 1(5)(g) . . . **536**
s 1(6) . . . **536**
s 1A . . . 78, 533, 535, **537**
s 1A(1) . . . **537**
s 1A(2) . . . 536, **537**
s 1A(2)(a) . . . **537**
s 1A(2)(aa) . . . **537**, 540
s 1A(2)(b) . . . **537**
s 1A(2A) . . . **537**, 540
s 1A(2A)(a) . . . **537**
s 1A(2A)(b) . . . **537**
s 1A(2A)(c) . . . **537**
s 1A(3) . . . **537**
s 1A(4) . . . **537**
s 1A(5) . . . **537**
s 2 . . . **537**
s 2(1) . . . **537**
s 2(2) . . . **537**
s 2(2)(a) . . . **537**
s 2(2)(b) . . . **537**
s 2(3) . . . **537**
s 2(4) . . . **537**
s 3 . . . **537–8**
s 3(1) . . . **537**
s 3(2) . . . **537**
s 3(3) . . . **537**, 539
s 3(4) . . . **538**
s 3(5) . . . **538**
s 3(6) . . . **538**
s 4 . . . **538**
s 5 . . . 243, **538**

Financial Services and Markets Act 2000
s 213 . . . 534

Gulf Oil Refining Act 1965 . . . 472, 473
s 5 . . . **473**

Health and Safety at Work Act 1974
s 47(2) . . . 324

Housing Act 1985 . . . 322
s 63(1) . . . 322

Human Fertilisation and Embryology Act 2008
s 43 . . . 536

Human Rights Act 1998 . . . 2, 96, 102, 104, 105,
111, 118, 119, 120, 122, 124, 128, 130, 188, 336,
357, 359, 360, 361, 363, 364, 366, 374, 376, 378,
391, 476, 477, 479, 540
s 2 . . . 366
s 3 . . . 366
s 6 . . . **360**, 363, 364, 366, 378, 477
s 6(1) . . . **360**, 361
s 6(2) . . . **360**
s 6(2)(a) . . . **360**
s 6(2)(b) . . . **360**
s 6(3) . . . **360**

s 6(3)(a) . . . **360**
s 6(3)(b) . . . **360**
s 6(4) . . . **360**
s 6(5) . . . **360**
s 6(6) . . . **360**
s 6(6)(a) . . . **360**
s 6(6)(b) . . . **360**
s 7 . . . **361**
s 7(1) . . . **361**
s 7(1)(a) . . . **361**
s 7(1)(b) . . . **361**
s 7(2) . . . **361**
s 7(3) . . . **361**
s 7(4) . . . **361**
s 7(5) . . . **361**
s 7(5)(a) . . . **361**
s 7(5)(b) . . . **361**
s 7(6) . . . **361**
s 7(6)(a) . . . **361**
s 7(6)(b) . . . **361**
s 7(7) . . . **361**
s 7(8) . . . **361**
s 8 . . . 102
s 12 . . . **361**, 366
s 12(1) . . . **361**
s 12(2) . . . **361–2**
s 12(2)(a) . . . **362**
s 12(2)(b) . . . **362**
s 12(3) . . . **362**
s 12(4) . . . 360, **362**
s 12(4)(a) . . . **362**
s 12(4)(b) . . . **362**

Immigration Act 1971 . . . 336

**Law Reform (Contributory Negligence) Act
1945** . . . 223, 244, 246, 250, 254, 255, 343, 538
s 1 . . . **244**, 245, 251
s 1(1) . . . **244**, 246, **247**, **252**, 254, 256, 538
s 4 . . . **244**

Law Reform (Limitation of Actions) Act 1954 . . . 328

Law Reform (Married Women and Tortfeasors)
Act 1935
s 6 . . . 251

**Law Reform (Miscellaneous Provisions) Act
1934** . . . 533, 535, 538
s 1 . . . **535**
s 1(1) . . . **535**
s 1(2) . . . **535**
s 1(3) . . . **535**
s 1(3)(a) . . . **535**
s 1(3)(b) . . . **535**
s 1(3)(c) . . . **535**
s 1(4) . . . **535**
s 1(5) . . . **535**
s 1(6) . . . **535**
s 1(7) . . . **535**

Law Reform (Miscellaneous Provisions)
Act 1971
s 4(1) . . . 542

Legal Aid, Sentencing and Punishment of
    Offenders Act 2012
    Pt 2 (ss 44–62) . . . 540

Limitation Act 1980 . . . 306
    s 2 . . . 329, 402
    s 4A . . . 402
    s 4A(a) . . . 402
    s 4A(b) . . . 402
    ss 11–14 . . . 329
    s 11A . . . 306
    s 11A(1) . . . 306
    s 11A(2) . . . 306
    s 11A(3) . . . 306
    s 11A(4) . . . 306
    s 11A(4)(a) . . . 306
    s 11A(4)(b) . . . 306
    s 11A(5) . . . 306
    s 32A . . . 402
    s 32A(1)(a) . . . 402
    s 33 . . . 329
    s 38(1) . . . 68

Lord Cairns' Act 1858 . . . 482, 483

Mental Capacity Act 2005 . . . 337, 342

Mental Health Act 1983 . . . 125, 337
    s 3 . . . 126, 127
    s 37 . . . 235
    s 41 . . . 235

Motor Car Acts . . . 318

National Health Service Act 1977 . . . 99

National Parks and Access to the Countryside Act
    1949 . . . 262

Nuclear Installations Act 1965 . . . 488
    s 7 . . . 495

Occupiers' Liability Act 1957 . . . 261, 263, 265,
    266, 268, 269, 270, 271, 272, 273, 274, 275, 277,
    278, 279, 282, 283, 284, 285, 288, 290, 295
    s 1 . . . 261–2, 270
    s 1(1) . . . 261, 288
    s 1(2) . . . 261, 268, 271, 280
    s 1(3) . . . 262
    s 1(3)(a) . . . 262
    s 1(3)(b) . . . 262
    s 1(4) . . . 261, **262**
    s 1(4)(a) . . . 262
    s 1(4)(b) . . . 262
    s 2 . . . 262, 264, 278, 288, 292, 293, 294, 295
    s 2(1) . . . 231, **262**, 291
    s 2(2) . . . **262**, 266, 271, 275, **280**, 285, 287, 295
    s 2(3) . . . **262**, 278, 280, 281, 296
    s 2(3)–(5) . . . 271
    s 2(3)(a) . . . 262
    s 2(3)(b) . . . 262, 278
    s 2(4) . . . 262, 278, 279, 291
    s 2(4)(a) . . . 262, 291
    s 2(4)(b) . . . 262, 266

    s 2(5) . . . **262**, 294, 295, 296, 297
    s 2(6) . . . 262
    s 3 . . . 263
    s 3(1) . . . 263
    s 3(2) . . . 263
    s 3(3) . . . 263
    s 3(4) . . . 263
    s 5 . . . 263
    s 5(1) . . . 263
    s 5(2) . . . 263
    s 5(3) . . . 263

Occupiers' Liability Act 1984 . . . 40, 261, 263,
    265, 268, 270, 272, 273, 274, 275, 276, 277, 282,
    283, 284, 285, 287, 288, 295
    s 1 . . . 264–5, 294
    s 1(1) . . . 264, 272
    s 1(1)(a) . . . 264, 272, 276
    s 1(1)(b) . . . 264, 272
    s 1(2) . . . 264
    s 1(2)(a) . . . 264
    s 1(2)(b) . . . 264
    s 1(3) . . . 264, 282, 284
    s 1(3)(a) . . . 264, 284
    s 1(3)(b) . . . 264, 284
    s 1(3)(c) . . . 264, 284, 287, 295
    s 1(4) . . . 264
    s 1(5) . . . 264, 294
    s 1(6) . . . 264, 294
    s 1(6A) . . . 264, 265, 282
    s 1(6A)(a) . . . 264
    s 1(6A)(b) . . . 264
    s 1(6AA) . . . 264
    s 1(6B) . . . 264
    s 1(6C) . . . 264, **265**
    s 1(6C)(a) . . . 265
    s 1(6C)(b) . . . 265
    s 1(7) . . . 265
    s 1(8) . . . 265
    s 1(9) . . . 265
    s 1A . . . 265
    s 1A(a) . . . 265
    s 1A(b) . . . 265
    s 1A(c) . . . 265

Occupiers' Liability (Scotland) Act 1960 . . . 263

Partnership Act 1890
    s 10 . . . 520

Police Act 1997
    Pt V (ss 112–127) . . . 521

Proceeds of Crime Act 2002 . . . 240

Protection from Harassment Act 1997 . . . 316,
    327, 334, 344, 345, 352, 353, 354–5, 356, 358,
    467, 506
    s 1 . . . 350–1, 354, 355, 356
    ss 1–3 . . . 352
    ss 1–5 . . . 351
    s 1(1) . . . 346, **350**, 351
    s 1(1)(a) . . . 350
    s 1(1)(b) . . . 350

s 1(1A) . . . 351
s 1(1A)(c) . . . 351
s 1(2) . . . **350**
s 1(2)(a) . . . **350**
s 1(2)(b) . . . **350**
s 1(2)(c) . . . **350**
s 1(3) . . . **350**, 355, 356
s 1(3)(a) . . . 356
s 1(4) . . . **351**
s 1(4)(a) . . . **351**
s 1(4)(b) . . . **351**
s 1(4)(c) . . . **351**
s 2 . . . 354, 356
s 2A(2)(c) . . . 350
s 3 . . . 316, **351**, 354, 356
s 3(1) . . . **351**, 354
s 3(2) . . . 346, **351**
s 3A . . . **351**
s 3A(1) . . . **351**
s 3A(2) . . . **351**
s 3A(2)(a) . . . **351**
s 3A(2)(b) . . . **351**
s 7 . . . **351**, 352
s 7(1) . . . **351**
s 7(2) . . . **351**, 352
s 7(3) . . . 346, **351**, 354
s 7(3)(a) . . . **351**
s 7(3)(b) . . . **351**
s 7(4) . . . **351**
s 7(5) . . . **351**

Railways Clauses Consolidation Act 1845
    s 47 . . . 318

Road Traffic Acts . . . 175

Road Traffic Act 1972 . . . 232

Road Traffic Act 1988
    s 149(3) . . . 234

Sale of Goods Act 1979 . . . 307

Senior Courts Act 1981 (formerly Supreme Court
    Act 1981)
    s 32A . . . **534**, 538
    s 32A(1) . . . 534
    s 32A(2) . . . 534
    s 32A(2)(a) . . . 534
    s 32A(2)(b) . . . 534
    s 32A(3) . . . 534
    s 32A(3)(a) . . . 534
    s 32A(3)(b) . . . 534
    s 32A(4) . . . 534
    s 69 . . . 404
    s 69(1) . . . 415

Social Action, Responsibility and Heroism Act
    2015 . . . 169, 170

Statute of Limitations . . . 329

Street Offences Act 1959 . . . 331

Supreme Court Act 1981 *see* **Senior Courts
    Act 1981**

Torts Act 1997
    s 11 . . . 245

Town and Country Planning Act 1947 . . . 468

Town and Country Planning Act 1971 . . . 468

Unfair Contract Terms Act 1977 . . . 150, 160, 231,
    291

Water Industry Act 1991 . . . 476, 477, 479
    s 209 . . . 495

Water Resources Act 1991
    s 85(1) . . . 492

Workmen's Compensation Act 1897 . . . 319

Statutory Instruments

Animals Order 1871 . . . 323
    s 75 . . . 323

Asbestos Industry Regulations 1931, SI 1930/1140
    . . . 323

Civil Procedure Rules 1998, SI 1998/3132
    Pt 25
    r 25.7 . . . 538
    Pt 55 . . . 459

Control of Noise at Work Regulations 2005, SI
    2005/1643 . . . 200
    r 6(1) . . . 200

Damages (Personal Injury) Order 2001, SI
    2001/230 . . . 546

Damages (Personal Injury) Order 2019, SI
    2019/1126 . . . 546

Damages (Variation of Periodical Payments) Order
    2005, SI 2005/841 . . . 534

Fatal Accidents Act 1976 (Remedial) Order 2020, SI
    2020/1023 . . . 540

Marriage (Same Sex Couples) Act 2013
    (Consequential and Contrary Provisions and
    Scotland) Order 2014, SI 2014/560 . . . 540

Motor Cars (Use and Construction) Order
    1904 . . . 318

Prison Rules 1964, SI 1964/388 . . . 319, 320, 344,
    359

Product Safety and Metrology etc (Amendment etc)
    (EU Exit) Regulations 2019, SI 2019/696 . . . 307

Southern Rhodesia (Petroleum) Order 1965, SI
    1965/2140 . . . 321, 322

Water Supply and Sewerage Services (Customer Service Standards) Regulations 1989, SI 1989/1159
reg 7B . . . 478

Water Supply and Sewerage Services (Customer Service Standards) (Amendment) Regulations 1993, SI 1993/500 . . . 478

Water Supply and Sewerage Services (Customer Service Standards) (Amendment) Regulations 2000, SI 2000/2301 . . . 478

International Legislation

Australia

New South Wales Civil Liability Act 2002
s 5R . . . 257

Germany

Copyright (Arts Domain) Act . . . 370
s 23(1) . . . 370

United States

Restatement (Second) of Torts
§402A . . . 301

European Legislation

Primary Legislation

European Community Treaty (EC Treaty)
Article 177 . . . 308
Article 189 . . . 308

Secondary Legislation

Council Regulation on jurisdiction 44/2001
Article 5(3) . . . 400

Directive 85/374/EEC Product Liability
Directive . . . 298, 302, 306, 307, 308, 309, 310, 311, 313, 314
Recital 16 . . . 312
Article 1 . . . 307
Article 4 . . . 312
Article 6 . . . 309, 310, 311, 312, 314
Article 7 . . . 314
Article 7(b) . . . 313
Article 7(e) . . . 306, 307, 308, 309, 310, 311, 312, 313, 314
Article 12 . . . 312
Article 15 . . . 312

International Instruments

Convention for the Protection of Human Rights and Dignity of the Human Being with regard to the Application of Biology and Medicine: Convention on Human Rights and Biomedicine 1997
Article 5 . . . 188

European Convention on Human Rights (ECHR)
. . . 104, 118, 119, 123, 124, 129, 130, 334, 336, 357, 359, 360, 362, 363, 364, 365, 366, 369, 370, 374, 375, 377, 378, 380, 384, 391, 394, 476, 478
Article 1 . . . 130
Article 2 . . . 54, 117, 119, 120, 122, **125**, 126, 127, 128, 129, 130, 131, 540
Article 2(1) . . . **125**, 126, 127, **128**, 130
Article 2(2) . . . **125**
Article 2(2)(a) . . . **125**
Article 2(2)(b) . . . **125**
Article 2(2)(c) . . . **125**
Article 3 . . . 102, 106, 117, 119, 120, 122, 124, 131
Article 5 . . . 334, 336
Article 6 . . . 111, 122, 123, 124, 130, 388, 487
Article 6(1) . . . 123, 124
Article 8 . . . 102, 106, 118, 119, 120, 123, 188, 353, 357, 359, 360, **361**, 362, 363, 364, 365, 366, 367, 368, 369, 370, 371, 372, 373, 374, 376, 377, 378, 379, 380, 381, 382, 384, 385, 389, 476, 477, 478, 479, 539, 540
Article 8(1) . . . **361**, 365, 371, 476
Article 8(2) . . . **361**, 365, 371, 372, 373, 376, 476
Article 10 . . . 353, 364, 365, 366, 367, 368, 371, 372, 373, 375, 378, 379, 380, 381, 384, 389, 393, 425, 447
Article 10(1) . . . 365, 393
Article 10(2) . . . 365, 368, 393, 394, 441
Article 13 . . . 122, 124, 359
Article 14 . . . 540
Article 34 . . . 361
Protocol 1 . . . 476
Article 1 . . . 111, 123, 477

Hague Rules . . . 41, 42, 44

Hague-Visby Rules . . . 42, 44

Lugano Convention . . . 401

1

Introduction

What is tort law? One answer is that a 'tort' is a civil 'wrong' for which the law provides a remedy. Tort law is, therefore, the name given to a diverse collection of these wrongs. Beyond this, however, there is no general agreement as to what defines or distinguishes a 'tort' and, by extension, tort law. What we do know is that it covers a wide range of activities and many different types of loss. Learner drivers driving into lamp posts, oil spills, people falling down stairs, toilet cisterns falling off walls, police negligence, Twitter 'spats', itchy underpants, celebrities trying to hide affairs, image-based sexual abuse and defrosting lobsters, *this* is the stuff of tort law. And it is these, and other cases, which are covered in this book. Which leads us nicely to perhaps the best definition what tort is: '[t]ort is what is in the tort books, and the only thing holding it together is the binding' (Tony Weir *An Introduction to Tort Law* (OUP, 2006), p ix).

1.1 The reach of tort law

This book begins with the tort of negligence. This relatively recent introduction to tort law covers a wide and varied range of human activity including personal injury, property damage and economic loss. As such, negligence (and tort law more generally) often negotiates a difficult balance between tricky and complex legal and social issues, of what might be expected, and in turn one should tolerate, as part of everyday life and what is so out of the ordinary that an action should be allowed.

While recovery for a negligently caused road accident is straightforward (though we might query whether tort is the most effective mechanism of compensation in such cases), to what extent should someone be protected from psychiatric injury, as in the Hillsborough Stadium disaster case (**Alcock v Chief Constable of South Yorkshire Police** [1992] 1 AC 310), where people claimed for psychiatric illnesses arising from seeing or hearing of the death of a relative? What about economic interests? Should you be able to sue for a negligently written reference which meant you didn't get a job (**Spring v Guardian Assurance** [1995] 2 AC 296)? Or if your employment prospects are damaged by your school's failure to identify your dyslexia (*Phelps* v *Hillingdon London Borough Council* [2001] 2 AC 619)? What about protection of profits? Should a pub owner be able to sue for lost profits if a lorry damages a bridge between a village and its pub so that people are unable to get to it? Or is that simply one of the risks of being in business (*Star Village Tavern* v *Nield* (1976) 71 DLR (3d) 439)?

Other issues concern the occupiers of land. For example, should they be required to treat trespassers in the same way as those who have permission to visit, or are trespassers less deserving? If a person in a public park ignores a notice saying 'Dangerous Water. No Swimming', should they be able to sue if they dive in and hurt their head on a rock? Or should people be responsible for the consequences of their own choices (*Tomlinson* v *Congleton Borough Council* [2003] UKHL 47)?

Moreover, even if an interest is protected other issues may arise. What should happen when a claimant is partially at fault for his own injury, for example by not wearing a seat belt when involved in a road accident (*Froom v Butcher* [1976] QB 286)? What if the injury appears to have been caused by more than one event or act—how do we separate a legally relevant act from one which is merely the background to the event (*Barnett v Chelsea and Kensington Hospital Management Committee* [1969] 1 QB 428)? And should a defendant be liable for all the consequences of his act or for only some of them? If a stevedore carelessly drops a plank into the hold of a ship we might expect it to dent the hold, but what if the hold unexpectedly contains petrol fumes and the ship blows up? Should they be liable for the total loss of the ship or just the (notional) dent (*Re Polemis and Furness, Withy & Co Ltd* [1921] 3 KB 560)?

Despite its apparently ever-expanding reach, negligence is, of course, not the only tort to deal with personal and property interest. The tort of nuisance, for example, deals with rights between neighbouring landowners. This can cover not only direct interference such as overhanging trees or encroaching roots, but also things which interfere with the use of the property such as noise, smoke or obnoxious smells. This raises the issue of what rights ownership of land gives to a landowner—are they entitled to be free from interference with their television reception (*Hunter v Canary Wharf Ltd* [1997] AC 655), or be free from prostitutes perambulating outside their premises (*Thompson-Schwab v Costaki* [1956] 1 WLR 335)?

Tort law also covers intentional wrongs through the torts of trespass to the person (assault, battery and false imprisonment), to land or to goods, though the aim here is typically to protect the right itself rather than to provide compensation. These intentional torts also raise questions about what interests are being protected. For example, false imprisonment raises issues about the powers of the police and the liberty of the individual as well as freedom of movement more generally—but is a person 'imprisoned' if they cannot take their preferred route, and are free to go back the way they came (*Bird v Jones* (1845) 7 QB 742)? Similarly, while battery protects a person against any unwarranted contact, does a pregnant woman have the right to refuse medical treatment even if it will harm the foetus (*Re MB (Caesarean Section)* [1997] 2 FLR 426)? And what about our online presence—do we have the right to prevent others from tracking and collecting information relating to our internet usage (*Google Inc v Vidal-Hall and others* [2015] EWCA Civ 311)?

The issues in tort law, then, coalesce around two broad questions. The first asks 'what interests should be protected?' While the courts have been fairly clear that a person should be protected against personal injury or damage to goods, they are less sure, for example, about how far a person's interest in their reputation or private life should be protected. Here a balance has to be struck between freedom of speech and freedom from interference. Unsurprisingly, the Human Rights Act 1998 has played a central role in the determination and development of the law in this context, which has been one of the liveliest areas of tort law in recent years. Other interests that are less well protected by tort law include economic interests in situations where the claimant loses money but suffers no physical damage (*Hedley Byrne & Co*

Ltd v *Heller and Partners* [1963] UKHL 4) or where an individual is significantly distressed by an individual's one-off act (*Wainwright* v *Home Office* [2003] UKHL 53).

The second question inquires into the mind of the defendant and asks what is the level of protection required? Should liability be limited to *intentional* acts? Or is *negligence* or fault sufficient? If so, what do we mean by this? What counts as unreasonable behaviour? What is the level of safety from the acts of others that we are entitled expect? Or are there, for example, activities that are so dangerous that a person who engages in them should be strictly liable for any damage caused by the activity even if they are not at fault?

However, even once liability is established this still leaves a further—vital—question: who should pay? One way tort has dealt with this is to identify a defendant (who may or may not be the tortfeasor; that is, the person who committed the tort) with sufficient money to pay the damages. The doctrine of vicarious liability, whereby an employer is liable for the torts of their employee (or someone who is akin to an employee) if they are committed in the course of their employment, is one example of this. A system of insurance is another. Sometimes the law requires a person engaging in an activity to acquire compulsory insurance, as in the case of motor or employers' liability insurance, on other occasions individuals will voluntarily insure themselves against liability, as is the case in relation to home and contents insurance.

While the existence of insurance is essential to the operation of the tort system (for without it defendants would be unable to pay and claimants would go uncompensated), in practice it works to undercut the corrective justice purposes of tort law. Rather than the claimant's loss being shifted onto the careless defendant, it is spread across those who were not careless, but who insured against the risk of being so (Joanne Conaghan and Wade Mansell *The Wrongs of Tort* (2nd edn, Pluto Press, 1999), p 12). At the same time there are increasing concerns about the financial and social costs of insurance, and tort liability more generally, having an overly restrictive and inhibiting effect on business and other organisations such as the NHS. While opinion is divided on the extent to which these concerns are justified, without doubt the *perception* of the existence of a 'compensation culture' is making its presence felt on tort law.

Magna Carta and the compensation culture
Lord Dyson MR, High Sheriff's Law Lecture, Oxford, 13 October 2015

17. There is nothing new about the idea that the law requires the payment of fair compensation for harm which results from civil wrongs. It is long established. It is one of the hallmarks of the rule of law and the law of our land. But what is compensation culture and how does it fit in to all of this? Lord Falconer, who was Lord Chancellor at the time, gave an apt definition in 2005. He put it this way: '"Compensation culture" is a catch-all expression . . . It's the idea that for every accident someone is at fault. For every injury, someone is to blame. And, perhaps most damaging, for every accident, there is someone to pay'. . . .

19. One consequence of this is the view that as a society we have undergone a cultural shift. . . . To borrow from Tony Weir we have become 'a wondrously unstoical and whinging society' in which, rather than 'grin and bear it', we 'grit (our) teeth and sue'. . . .

38. [T]he reality of what goes on in our courts does not match [this] perception. . . .

39. [However,] a perception that the law requires compensation for any accident regardless of the circumstances is likely to lead to individuals, businesses and governments to act on the basis that

the perception is true. This might have the consequence that nobody apologises for bumping into another person in case that is taken as an acknowledgement that an accident has occurred which attracts legal liability. Another consequence might be that schools ban certain activities as a result of their misperception of the law. More significantly perhaps, . . . [it] might lead to threat of litigation and then to settlements that would not have been made if the law had been properly understood. . . .

41. [J]ust as the [Magna Carta] barons demanded their right to receive justice according to the law of the land, we should remind ourselves of what the law actually requires and do what we can to explode the false perception of the compensation culture.

Notes

1. See further on the compensation culture: Stephen Sedley 'Mischief Wrought' London Review of Books, 4 March 2021; Alan Saggerson 'Something Must Be Done: Recent Legislative Contributions to the Common Law' Lecture at Lincoln's Inn, 30 October 2018; Richard Lewis 'Compensation Culture Reviewed: Incentives to Claim and Damages Levels' [2014] JPIL 20; Lord Dyson 'Compensation Culture: Fact of Fantasy?' Holdsworth Club Lecture, 15 March 2013.

1.2 The aims of the law of torts

Keith Stanton, in *The Modern Law of Tort* (Sweet & Maxwell, 1994), pp 11–12, explains the aims of the tort system.

Considerable effort has been expended in attempts to identify the aims of the law of tort. A justification ought to exist for the existence of a system which consumes resources in transferring money from one person (the injurer) to another (the victim). However, the range of interests protected by the law of tort makes any search for a single aim underlying the law a difficult one. Actions for wrongful interference with goods or trespasses to land serve fundamentally different ends from an action seeking compensation for a personal injury. In practice much of the discussion concerning the aims of the law of tort has concentrated on accidents and compensation for personal injuries.

The different aims which have been suggested seem to be capable of classification under a number of heads. Those who have studied tort from the perspective of economic theory have tended to favour the 'deterrent' aim of tort. This sees tort as a system which is designed to reduce the frequency and the severity of accidents. Fear of legal liability and the resulting awards of damages provides an incentive to persons, both injurers and potential victims, to indulge in safer conduct, both by avoiding hazardous activities and by increasing the level of safety precautions they provide. In practice, the 'deterrent' approach will choose to sacrifice the interests of the victim in favour of those of the defendant by leaving injured plaintiffs to bear their own losses if the damage could not have been avoided by the use of cost-justified precautions.

In contrast, the 'compensation' aim, which became very dominant among academic lawyers in the 1970s, sees the primary aim of tort as being to reduce the disruption which accidents cause to the lifestyles of victims and those dependent upon them. Victims may lose their income and may require expensive nursing care. An award of compensation alleviates this disruption and any attendant social problems. The whole thrust of the compensation aim is the protection of victims: the defendant is merely an agent by which this is achieved.

Additionally, the tort system can be seen as a mechanism for retribution and the appeasement of the injured person's feelings, as providing a mechanism for the protection of rights and as a technique whereby society is able to express judgment on the injurer's conduct. Recent practice, particularly in the context of 'disaster' litigation seems to have brought this judgmental role of tort back to prominence, even if it has failed to attract academic support.

A subsidiary aim to those already mentioned is that any compensation system should be efficient in the sense of providing an effective mechanism for distributing the money paid into it to the victims of accidents. A large percentage of this money should not be consumed by the operating costs of the system.

The difficulty presented by the law of tort is that it has developed with only limited reference to these aims and that it may fail to achieve any of them properly. In addition, the deterrence and compensation aims are almost certainly incompatible with each other.

Tort law is typically understood as being grounded in the principle of corrective justice. As such, it is built on two key elements—fault and causation. A defendant is liable to make good a claimant's losses because they (a) factually caused the claimant to suffer those losses and (b) were to blame (at fault) in so acting. This is typically achieved by requiring the defendant to *compensate* (pay damages to) the claimant for the losses they have caused them. Though it is worth noting here that corrective justice is only, in fact, 'done' where the defendant, and not for example an insurance company, pays the compensation. Moreover, as Stanton suggests, there are times when the compensatory function of tort pulls against its other purposes, usually its function as a deterrent. We may want to award compensation to a deserving claimant and yet not want to deter people from engaging in the same activity. As Lord Dyson notes in the extract in section 1.1, there is a real risk that people become *over-cautious* for fear of liability and as a result abandon activities which, though risky, also bring societal benefits—school trips are cancelled, footpaths are closed and candy floss, kettles in hotel rooms, knives in sandwich shops, full-fat milk and hanging baskets are 'banned'.

Notes

1. See further on the aims of tort law: Jonathan Morgan 'Abolishing Personal Injuries Law? A Response to Lord Sumption' [2018] Prof Neg 122; Peter Cane *Atiyah's Accidents, Compensation and the Law* (7th edn, CUP, 2006); Carol Harlow *Understanding Tort Law* (Sweet & Maxwell, 2005), Ch 2; Kirsty Horsey and Erika Rackley *Tort Law* (5th edn, OUP, 2017), Ch 1; Glanville Williams 'The Aims of the Law of Tort' (1951) 4 CLP 137; Richard Lewis and Ann Morris 'Tort Law Culture: Image and Reality' (2012) 39 J L & Soc 577.

1.2.1 Deterrence

While tort law has an important role in *deterring* people from engaging in tortious activities, it is essential, then, that we not only know what actions are wrongful, but that our response to them encourage neither over- nor under-deterrence.

While over-deterrence may result where the perception of the chance of liability is exaggerated, under-deterrence arises where either the chances of someone suing to enforce their rights are small, such as where the matter may be one of principle and the damage is slight, or where the consequences to the individual tortfeasor are slight. How, for example, is a car driver who negligently causes an accident deterred *by tort law* when (apart from a rise in premiums) it will be his insurance company who pays and not him? The fact that most of us do, at least try to, drive carefully is not evidence of the deterrent effect of tort law. Rather, it is because the *criminal* law sets a standard which, as ordinary members of society, we accept and adhere to. The wearing of seat belts by car passengers is a case in point. It was only once the failure to wear one became subject to a fine under the Highway Code that wearing seat belts became commonplace (Carol Harlow *Understanding Tort Law* (Sweet & Maxwell, 2005) p 38).

So how effective is tort law as a means of accident prevention? Well, it depends where you are looking. Certainly, it is more likely to have success when appealing to the economic interests of commercial enterprises than individuals. This is most likely because general commercial enterprises which cause damage have to compete with those which do not, and accordingly market forces will drive the accident-causing companies out of business because having to pay compensation will make them less competitive. However, this will only work, where risks are covered by insurance, if the insurance company distinguishes sufficiently between 'negligent' and 'non-negligent' companies. For example, if an insurer demands the same premium from all car manufacturers because this is administratively easier than to examine the accident record of each, then the 'negligent' manufacturer will not be less competitive. Even if a distinction is made, it is unlikely that insurance premiums would be such a large proportion of costs as to make a competitive difference. Furthermore, even if a higher premium is charged it may still be more profitable to pay that higher premium and continue to 'cut corners' (see e.g. the US case of *Grimshaw* v *Ford Motor Co*, 119 Cal App 3d 757 (1981)).

This raises a further question about the kind of conduct that we want to encourage or restrict. While it is open to debate as to whether legislation is the better vehicle for a change in the law, tort law has the advantage that it can take an incremental approach to new developments and can engage the public in considering how to handle change. Consider, for example, debates concerning the validity of 'advance directives' given by a person about how they want to be treated if they are no longer able to decide for themselves or the non-consensual posting of private sexual images on the internet—might tort law provide a better response to these alongside, or in place of, legislation?

1.2.2 Compensation

The corrective justice underpinnings of tort law require that the victim's (claimant's) loss is 'transferred' to the defendant, usually by the defendant himself compensating the victim (usually financially). However, more often than not, it is not the defendant himself who pays, but rather his (or his employer's) insurer. Thus, no one suffers too great a penalty but rather the loss is spread or distributed amongst all the premium payers. If the insurance fund is large enough, the cost to each premium payer will be minimal. And tort law moves from being a mechanism of loss-shifting to one of loss-distribution.

One consequence of this is that the focus of tort law has also shifted. The question is no longer one of who of the claimant or defendant should bear the loss but rather whether the claimant *deserves* compensation. This, in turn, has led to the expansion of liability and is one of the things that has fuelled the 'compensation culture' discussed earlier. The need for there to be a justification for requiring the payment of damages seems to have been lost or minimised. Thus, the perception is that a person should be compensated for an injury whether it was caused by fault or was a 'pure' accident, or even caused by the victim himself. This has led to questions being asked about whether the economy as a whole can afford this level of compensation and whether it is an efficient way of dealing with personal injuries.

In fact, the compensation culture critique may be better understood as a reworking of a perennial criticism of tort law as a mechanism of compensation: that it acts as a 'lottery' (PS Atiyah *The Damages Lottery* (Hart, 2007)). While some claimants receive large sums in damages, many people get nothing at all—with the result that the (ever-decreasing) social security system is left to provide a floor of support for those who fall outside the tort system. Without doubt, the tort law system delivers slow and expensive justice, hampered by the combined weight of increasing claims, high legal costs and its commitment to proving fault.

But what are the alternatives? One is the introduction of 'no-fault' systems. These have been introduced, primarily (but not only) for motor vehicle accidents in a number of jurisdictions including the United States, Japan, Ireland and New Zealand. The system is simple. Every car driver (or employer or doctor) pays a premium (usually via the road tax system or similar), and every person injured by a motor vehicle (or at work or in a medical context) is compensated regardless of the fault of the driver. (There are usually limits on the amounts recovered and the amounts insured, and potential victims or defendants can take out additional private insurance to cover these.) Without doubt, non-adversarial administrative systems are significantly more efficient, cheaper and quicker than litigation. They avoid the associated costs with needing to attribute blame, level the playing field between those injured as a result of someone's 'fault' and those who are not, who suffer the same injury as the result of 'bad luck' and challenge the assumption that compensation should be 'full' (i.e. seeking to put the claimant in the same position as had the tort not occurred) as opposed to 'real' (i.e. a smaller realistic amount that the claimant can live on). The New Zealand Accident Compensation Scheme, which has been running since 1972, for example,

pays out 'real' rather than 'full' compensation. Because of its focus on rehabilitation, a decision on coverage is made on average within 1.1 days of a claim and payment is made within 8.3 days. Two thirds of claimants return to work within 70 days and the administrative costs are 8% (Per Land 'Book Review of Sonia Macleod and Christopher Hodges (ed) *Redress Schemes for Personal Injuries*' (2018) 25 Eur J Health Law 469 at 471)

In so doing, compensation (albeit at a lower level) is more widely available.

However, in the UK despite some limited reforms relating to whiplash injuries in the recent Civil Liability Act 2018 and around some clinical negligence claims, there appears to be minimal appetite at present for more wholesale reform. As Lord Sumption noted in a recent speech while 'law of tort is an extraordinarily clumsy and inefficient way of dealing with serious cases of personal injury. It often misses the target, or hits the wrong target. It makes us no safer, while producing undesirable side effects. What is more, it does all of these things at disproportionate cost and with altogether excessive delay . . . I have no doubt it will survive' (Lord Sumption, 'Abolishing Personal Injuries Law—A Project' Personal Injuries Bar Association Annual Lecture, London, 16 November 2017).

'Abolishing Personal Injuries Law—A Project'
Lord Sumption, Personal Injuries Bar Association Annual Lecture, London, 16 November 2017

In the first place the only obvious alternative is a system of fault-free compensation funded either from taxation or by compulsory insurance. This would be a great deal less wasteful, because it would reduce the proportion of the cost of settling personal injury claims represented by investigatory and legal costs. But the additional coverage involved in dispensing with fault would enormously increase the overall cost. The New Zealand example is said to have been accepted by public opinion there, but it has not been adopted in a single other common law country. The second reason why fault will survive as the essential criterion for compensation is the phenomenon so familiar to economists of concentrated benefits but diffused costs. The hardships and costs associated with grave disabilities are visible and for those affected catastrophic; while the costs are subtle, indirect and thinly spread across the whole population. The one area where the public feels the cost directly is motor accidents. Annual motor premiums are a significant item in family budgets and we all notice when they have gone up. That no doubt accounts for the fact that government initiatives in this area have been concentrated in the motor sector. The third and perhaps most significant reason why it will survive is that it responds to widespread public notions about personal responsibility and the proper function of law. I do not myself share these notions, but I am in a minority on this. It is fundamental to my conception of the judicial function, that I do not sit just to give effect to my personal moral preferences.

My prediction would be that fault will remain the touchstone of our law of personal injuries, but that the principle will be eroded at the edges by statutory intervention from one end and judicial hindsight from the other. The result will be to increase the overall cost of personal injury claims and, I suspect to provoke a legislative reaction as mounting insurance premiums and pressures on the NHS budget lead to calls to control the costs. The outcome is likely to be the abolition of the principle of full indemnity and its replacement by a statutory measure of damages with a view to achieving a better balance between public and private interests.

I would expect this to take two forms. One is the imposition of value thresholds on personal injury claims, with a view to eliminating small claims. Small claims account for the great majority of claims and are disproportionately costly and cumbersome to administer. The second will be the capping or abolition of certain heads of loss. There is a case for abolishing damages for non-pecuniary losses, or at least limiting it to long-term pain and suffering and loss of amenity. There is a case for limiting damages for loss of earnings to the amount necessary to support a reasonable standard of living, rather than the superior standard of living which the richest accident victims might have expected if they had not been injured. To some extent these things are already happening. Successive decisions of the Supreme Court of Canada have limited the scope for large awards of non-pecuniary loss. The same trend is observable in the Judicial College guidelines in this country. In New South Wales liability thresholds and caps on awards for loss of earnings were adopted for motor accidents by legislation enacted in 1999, and extended to other personal injury claims in 2002. The British Government's current proposals [now the Civil Liability Act 2018] appear to envisage a rather similar system of thresholds and caps for whiplash injuries. It is I think significant, and indicative of the direction of travel, that the New South Wales legislation followed large and unpopular increases in insurance premiums. But it is also right to point out that it was accompanied by other measures making altogether more generous statutory provision for certain categories of victim than anything that has so far been contemplated in the United Kingdom. The statutory damages scheme for motor accidents extends in New South Wales to personal injuries occurring without fault. Moreover, since 2006 there has been a generous statutory scheme for compensating those suffering from personal injuries involving long-term care. Looking after the principal losers may be the price to be paid for limiting the generality of accident claims.

What all of this means is that the officers of this association can rest easy in their seats. It is likely to be needed for a considerable time to come.

Notes

1. In January 2021, the government announced further delays to the implementation of the 'whiplash reform programme'. It is now due to go 'live' in May 2021. John Hyde 'Whiplash reforms delayed another month' *Law Society Gazette* 11 January 2021.

2. Another alternative is the wider use of first-party insurance. One criticism of these no-fault accident compensation schemes (and indeed of tort law) is that it raises the question of why we should compensate for accidents but not for naturally acquired diseases. After all, there is no difference in need between an individual who is born blind, who becomes blind as a result of a disease or who is blinded through the defendant's negligence. Why should only the latter be able to claim compensation? One response is to suggest that the onus of responsibility of insuring oneself against being injured or developing a particular condition be shifted on to the potential *victim*. However, while this would address some of the expense and time-consuming criticisms made of the present system, arguments for the systematic use of first-party insurance are not popular—not least because it is likely that inequalities between claimants would simply be replicated as the wealthy would be able to afford better protection with the result that it would 'simply substitute one system of arbitrary and fortuitous distribution for another' (Joanne Conaghan and Wade Mansell 'From the Permissive to the Dismissive Society: Patrick Atiyah's Accidents, Compensation and the Market' (1998) 25 J L & Soc 284, 291).

3. See further Sonia Macleod and Christopher Hodges (eds) *Redress Schemes for Personal Injuries* (Hart, 2017); Per Lang 'Book Review of Sonia Macleod and Christopher Hodges (ed) *Redress Schemes for Personal Injuries*' (2018) 25 Eur J Health Law 469; Jonathan Morgan 'Abolishing Personal Injuries Law? A Response to Lord Sumption' [2018] Prof Neg 122.

1.3 Studying tort law and reading cases

While no one doubts that torts play an essential role in regulating the conduct of people in society, human activity means that there will inevitably be losses and tort tries to determine whether the victim or the person who caused the damage should bear the loss. However, as we've seen, this eminently sensible objective is much more complicated than appears at first sight. The rest of this book attempts to illustrate the rules we use to achieve this aim, although it should always be asked whether that is the right objective and how well it is being achieved. But before we start, a tip.

Cases are everything! Tort law is almost wholly a case-driven subject and therefore a good knowledge of the cases and what they stand for is essential. A textbook can *describe* the law, but the law itself is in the cases and their interpretation. Nothing can beat reading a well-written judgment in order to get a clear overview of the development of the law and exposition of a particular issue. To this end, we've annotated **Darnley v Croydon Health Services NHS Trust** [2018] UKSC 50—in the next chapter (see Figure 2.1). This not only offers an introduction to the tort of negligence, but also gives you an idea as to how to go about reading a judgment.

We think this book is best used alongside a textbook that provides a structure for the law and explains what is going on—but remember, though the job of a textbook author is to find a way of explaining the cases in as straightforward a way as possible, often the law is not coherent and may even be contradictory. Different authors have different ideas about how to make sense of the muddle, and so not only will the titles and contents of chapters in a tort textbook perhaps be different, but also cases may be placed in different chapters. The seventh edition of *Tort Law* by Horsey and Rackley is designed to be used in conjunction with this book, though we hope that you'll find this casebook a useful companion whichever textbook you are using.

There are three steps to reading and understanding cases. The first is analytical and is common to most subjects. Your first task is to identify what is relevant *for your purposes* about the case. What information is background and what is material? How does this case differ from previous cases? What is the essential element in the decision? This will usually involve a good understanding of the facts, but may involve a reinterpretation of previous cases. That is why some exam questions ask 'Would it make any difference if . . .?' This is aimed to test analytical ability in identifying the crucial elements of a case.

The second step is to understand the history of the development of tort. No one would sit down and invent the law as we have it today. The present law is a jumble of earlier competing ideas and compromises, and these need to be unravelled. A good example of this is the rules around liability for psychiatric harm, discussed in Chapter 4. It is impossible to understand the present position—let alone be able to make predictions as to how it might develop—without knowing how we got there, how the tort developed and what compromises have been made along the way.

see online resources

This leads to the final point. Tort is not a purely abstract subject. Decisions matter, not only to the individuals concerned, but also in the wider social, economic and political context. Accordingly, it is necessary, certainly at the appellate level, to understand what each decision is trying to achieve and how it fits in with the aims of tort described in section 1.2. The courts are now much more willing to discuss these issues, and recent House of Lords and Supreme Court judgments often contain references about the social and economic factors behind the decision.

With all this in mind, it's time to get started.

The tort of negligence

PART I

2   Duty of care: basic principles
     2.1   The rise and fall of the general duty of care
     2.2   Reasonable foreseeability
     2.3   Policy

3   Special duty problems: omissions and acts of third parties
     3.1   No general duty for omissions
     3.2   Exceptions to the rule
     3.3   No general duty in respect of third party actions

4   Special duty problems: psychiatric harm
     4.1   Primary victims
     4.2   Secondary victims
     4.3   Beyond primary and secondary victims

5   Special duty problems: public bodies
     5.1   The fundamentals of the common law
     5.2   Specific problematic areas: emergency services
     5.3   The human rights effect

6   Special duty problems: economic loss
     6.1   'Pure' economic loss
     6.2   The *Hedley Byrne* exception
     6.3   Liability to third parties

7   Breach of duty: the standard of care
     7.1   The level of reasonable risk—an objective standard
     7.2   The skill of the defendant
     7.3   Setting the standard of care

8   Causation and remoteness of damage
    8.1   Causation
    8.2   Remoteness of damage

9   Defences to negligence
    9.1   Voluntarily assuming the risk
    9.2   Illegality
    9.3   Contributory negligence

2

Duty of care: basic principles

The tort of negligence is a large and amorphous subject. According to Percy H Winfield's enduring definition, the tort of negligence is 'the breach of a legal duty to take care by an inadvertent act or omission that injures another' (Percy H Winfield 'The History of Negligence in the Law of Torts' (1926) 42 LQR 184, 184). This threefold presentation neatly encapsulates the three essential elements of the tort. In other words, in order to establish a claim in the tort of negligence three things need to be established:

(1) the defendant owes the claimant a *duty of care*; and

(2) the defendant *breached this duty* by falling below the required standard of care in the circumstances of the case; and

(3) the defendant's breach of their duty is both the factual and legal *cause* of the claimant's injury.

To which we might also add:

(4) the defendant is unable to raise any partial or full *defences* to the claimant's action.

In this chapter we shall begin our examination of the tort of negligence through analysis of the first of these elements: the duty of care. Before we do, however, it might help to see an example of what a negligence claim looks like, by looking at a recent judgment of the Supreme Court (see Figure 2.1). This will offer an initial taster of what sorts of problems negligence addresses and show how the various elements of a negligence claim work together.

For the remainder of the chapter, our focus will be on the first element of a claim in negligence—the element which receives the greatest attention in **Darnley**—the duty of care. In this chapter we shall introduce the basic concept of a duty of care and some of the general themes and questions which arise out of the case law. Particular duty problems, for example those concerning negligence liability for psychiatric injuries or for pure economic loss, will be discussed in later chapters.

In essence, duty is about relationships. It must be shown that the particular defendant stood in the required relationship to the claimant such that they came under an obligation to use care towards them. If the defendant does not owe a duty of care to the claimant, then the defendant will not be liable regardless of how carelessly they acted and how much loss they caused to the claimant. Moreover, the duty of care must be owed *in respect of the particular type of harm (or injury) suffered*—a defendant may owe the claimant a duty of care in respect of one type of loss and none in respect of another.

The question then as to when a defendant owes such a duty is crucial. In the great majority of cases, establishing whether a duty of care is owed is straightforward. The case law and statutes establish a range of situations in which we owe duties of care to one another. However, on occasion, cases will arise for which there is no existing precedent which settles whether a duty of care is owed. In these 'novel' duty situations, the court must work out for itself whether such a duty should be recognised. The trouble the courts have had is in identifying a test which they can use in these novel cases. The leading case is the House of Lords' decision in ***Caparo Industries plc* v *Dickman*** [1990] AC 605.

FIGURE 2.1 Case example: *Darnley* v *Croydon Health Services NHS Trust* [2018] UKSC 50

Darnley v Croydon Health Services NHS Trust [2018] UKSC 50

LORD LLOYD-JONES (with whom LADY HALE, LORD REED, LORD KERR and LORD HODGE agree)

> Lord Lloyd-Jones begins with a detailed account of the facts of the case.

1. The appellant, Michael Mark Junior Darnley, who was then aged 26, was assaulted in the late afternoon of 17 May 2010 when he was struck on the head by an unknown assailant in south London. He later telephoned his friend Robert Tubman. The appellant told Mr Tubman about the assault and complained that he had a headache and that it was getting worse. Mr Tubman was sufficiently concerned that he drove the appellant to the Accident and Emergency Department ('A & E department') at Mayday Hospital, Croydon which was managed by the respondent NHS Trust. It was noted in the clerking record that the appellant attended at 20:26 on 17 May 2010.

> Note the date—it has taken eight years for this case to reach the UK Supreme Court.

> The timing of events is crucial in this case.

2. Mr Tubman accompanied the appellant at the A & E department and was a witness to the conversation with the female A & E receptionist. The trial judge accepted Mr Tubman's account of the conversation which took place. The appellant provided his personal details. He informed the receptionist that he had been assaulted by being struck over the back of the head and he thought that he had a head injury, that he was feeling very unwell and that his head was hurting. The receptionist did not have a helpful attitude and was more concerned about how the injury occurred. She asked the appellant if the Police were involved. The appellant and Mr Tubman both told the receptionist that the appellant was really unwell and they were worried that he had a head injury and needed urgent attention. The receptionist told the appellant that he would have to go and sit down and that he would have to wait up to four to five hours before somebody looked at him. The appellant told the receptionist that he could not wait that long as he felt as if he was about to collapse. The receptionist replied that if the appellant did collapse he would be treated as an emergency.

> This is an interesting aside. Why do you think that Lord Lloyd-Jones included this in his judgment? This gives an indication as to how he's going to decide the case.

3. The identity of the A & E receptionist who spoke to the appellant and Mr Tubman is not known, save that it must have been one of the two receptionists on duty at that time, namely Valerie Ashley or Susan Reeves-Bristow. Neither had any recollection of the conversation that took place and each was able to give evidence only of her usual practice.

4. The appellant sat down with Mr Tubman in the waiting area of the A & E department. However, the appellant decided to leave because he felt too unwell to remain and he wanted to go home to take some paracetamol.

→

➡

The judge found that the appellant and Mr Tubman left after 19 minutes at 20:45. Neither informed the receptionist or told anyone else that they were leaving. However, Mrs Reeves-Bristow and Mrs Ashley noticed that they had left and they told the receptionist taking over on the next shift to look out for the appellant because they were concerned that a patient with a reported head injury had left the A & E department.

5. Mrs Ashley and Mrs Reeves-Bristow gave evidence as to their usual practice when a person with a head injury asked about waiting times. Mrs Ashley said that she would tell them that they could expect to be seen by a triage nurse within 30 minutes of arrival and it would be quite incorrect to tell them that they would have to wait up to four to five hours before being seen. Mrs Reeves-Bristow stated that she would tell them that the triage nurse would be informed and they would be seen as soon as possible.

6. Mr Tubman drove the appellant to his mother's house, some 13 minutes' drive away, arriving shortly after 21:10. The appellant went to bed. At about 21:30 that evening the appellant became distressed and attracted the attention of his sister by banging on the wall of his bedroom. An ambulance was called at 21:44. The ambulance was re-routed and a second ambulance was called arriving at his mother's home at 22:05. The appellant was taken by ambulance back to the A & E department at Mayday Hospital. During the journey he became hypertensive, his GCS was recorded as 9/15 and he projectile vomited. He arrived at the Mayday Hospital A & E department at 22:38. A CT scan (reported at 00:15 on 18 May 2010) identified a large extra-dural haematoma overlying the left temporal lobe and inferior parietal lobe with a marked midline shift. The appellant was intubated and ventilated and transferred from Mayday Hospital by ambulance into the care of neurosurgeons at St George's Hospital, Tooting arriving at 00:55. He was transferred to the operating theatre at 01:00 and underwent an operation for the evacuation of the haematoma.

7. Unfortunately, the appellant has suffered permanent brain damage in the form of a severe and very disabling left hemiplegia.

> Paralysis on one side of the body.

> Lord Lloyd-Jones goes on to consider what the courts below have decided.

Trial

8. The appellant brought proceedings against the respondent NHS Trust. His pleaded case included an allegation of breach of duty by the non-clinical reception staff concerning the information he was given about the time he would have to wait before being seen by a clinician and also a failure to assess the appellant for priority triage.

9. The trial took place on 25–27 April 2015 before HHJ Robinson, sitting as a judge of the High Court. He gave judgment on 31 July 2015: [2015] EWHC 2301 (QB).

10. The judge made the following findings of fact and came to the following conclusions of law.

(1) The appellant did not fall into the category of patients who should have been fast tracked under the priority triage system. His presentation was not such as to have alerted the reception staff to the presence of a condition so serious that it was immediately necessary to bring it to the attention of the nurse.

(2) The fact that the appellant was not seen by a triage nurse during the 19 minutes he was present at the hospital did not amount to a breach of duty or cause any loss.

> The NHS Trust may be liable either *directly*, for breach of a duty of care it owed to Darnley, or *vicariously*, for the receptionist's breach of a duty she owed to Darnley. On vicarious liability, see Chapter 18.

➡

➡

(3) If the appellant had been told that he would be seen within 30 minutes he would have stayed and would have been seen before he left. He would have been admitted or told to wait. He would have waited and his later collapse would have occurred within a hospital setting.

(4) The appellant's decision to leave the A & E department was, in part at least, made on the basis of information provided by the receptionist which was inaccurate or incomplete.

(5) It was reasonably foreseeable that some patients do leave A & E departments without being seen or treated and that, in such cases, harm may result. It is reasonably foreseeable that someone who believes it may be four or five hours before they will be seen by a doctor may decide to leave, in circumstances where they would have stayed if they believed they would be seen much sooner by a triage nurse.

(6) Had the appellant suffered the collapse at around 21:30 whilst at the Mayday Hospital he would have been transferred to St George's Hospital and would have undergone the surgery earlier. In those circumstances he would have made a very near full recovery.

(7) Receptionists in A & E departments are not under a duty to guard patients against harm caused by failure to wait to be seen, even if such harm could, as a matter of fact in the individual case, be prevented by the provision of full and accurate information about waiting times.

(8) The harm suffered in this case was outside the scope of any duty or obligation owed by the respondent by its reception staff.

(9) It would not be fair, just and reasonable to impose liability upon the respondent for harm arising as a result of the failure by the receptionist staff to inform the appellant of the likely waiting time to be seen by a triage nurse.

(10) The connection between the alleged inadequacies of the information provided and the harm suffered was broken because the decision to leave was one that was ultimately the decision of the appellant.

Court of Appeal

11. The appellant appealed to the Court of Appeal (Jackson, McCombe and Sales LJJ): [2018] QB 783. The appeal was dismissed by a majority (McCombe LJ dissenting) on the ground that neither the receptionist nor the health trust acting by the receptionist owed any duty to advise about waiting times, alternatively the damage was outside the scope of any duty owed, alternatively there was no causal link between any breach of duty and the injury. Jackson LJ considered that the giving of incorrect information by the receptionist was not an actionable mis-statement. When she told the appellant that he would have to wait for up to four or five hours, she was not assuming responsibility to the appellant for the catastrophic consequences which he might suffer if he simply walked out of the hospital. Nor did he consider that it was fair, just and reasonable to impose upon the receptionist, or the trust acting by the receptionist, a duty not to provide inaccurate information about waiting times. To do so would add a new layer of responsibility to clerical staff and a new head of liability for NHS health trusts (at para 53). Moreover, even if the receptionist were in breach of duty by giving incorrect information to the appellant, the scope of that duty could not extend to liability for the consequences of a patient walking out without

---

The judge is using the language of **Caparo v Dickman** to justify not imposing liability. See further section 3.3.

The judge goes on to hold that, even if the receptionist had owed a duty of care to Darnley, her conduct in breaching that duty should not be treated as a legal cause of Darnley's injuries. Darnley's decision to leave the hospital 'broke the chain of causation' between the breach and the harm.

Now Lord Sales.

See further on the assumption of responsibility in the context of misstatements, section 6.2.1.

The judge took the view that, for the defendant NHS Trust to be liable in negligence, *the receptionist* needs to owe the claimant, Darnley, a duty of care. [Compare McCombe LJ at [13] below.] The judge concluded that the receptionist was not under a duty to *accurately inform a patient of the likely waiting time to see a triage nurse*. If there was no duty, there could be no breach of duty and so no liability in negligence.

Darnley loses.

Moreover, even if the receptionist had been in breach of her duty of care, the chain of causation was broken when the appellant left the hospital—i.e. it became too remote.

The majority of the Court of Appeal deny Darnley's claim on the same basis as the trial judge.

➡

→

What do you think about this? Why do you think the judge added this point?

telling staff that he was about to leave (at paras 56–57). The appellant should accept responsibility for his own actions.

12. In a concurring judgment, Sales LJ considered that, whether what had occurred was a failure to provide information or the provision of inaccurate information, no relevant duty of care would arise (at para 83). In his view, the fair, just and reasonable view was that information as to likely waiting times was provided as a matter of courtesy and out of a general spirit of trying to be helpful to the public (at para 88). Both judges in the majority pointed to undesirable social consequences which would follow if such a duty of care were imposed (at paras 55, 84, 87, 88).

Duty here is framed much wider. The hospital has a duty not to provide misinformation to patient (generally, i.e. not limited to waiting time), whichever member of staff is providing it.

The key issue here is the possibility of an increasing number of claims against the NHS. With this in mind, in Sale LJ's view 'the fair, just and reasonable view is that such information is provided as a matter of courtesy and out of a general spirit of trying to be helpful to the public, as the judge held, and that its provision is not subject to a duty of care in law such that compensation must bepaid if a mistake is made. Imposition of such a duty would be likely to lead to defensive practices on the part of NHS trusts to forbid their receptionists to provide any information about likely waiting times'. (at [88])

13. In his dissenting judgment, McCombe LJ considered that, on the particular facts found by the judge, the respondent was in breach of a duty of care owed to the appellant. The information provided could only have given the false impression that the appellant would not be seen or assessed by anyone sooner than the indicated period of up to four or five hours, short of something like a collapse (at para 68). Moreover, he rejected the suggestion that the functions of a hospital can be divided into those of receptionists and those of medical staff; it is the duty of the hospital not to provide misinformation to patients, whether it is provided by reception staff or medical staff (at para 71). Incomplete and inaccurate information had been provided negligently. The failure to impart the reality of the triage system to the appellant on his arrival was, on the facts of this case, a breach of duty by the hospital (at para 77). Furthermore, that breach of duty was causative of the appellant's injury (at para 79).

Not only did the hospital owe Darnley a duty of care, the receptionist's actions meant that they were in breach and that this breach had caused his injury.

Duty of care

14. I consider that the approach of the majority in the Court of Appeal to the issue of duty of care is flawed in a number of respects.

15. First, we are not here concerned with the imposition of a duty of care in a novel situation. The common law in this jurisdiction has abandoned the search for a general principle capable of providing a practical test applicable in every situation in order to determine whether a duty of care is owed and, if so, what is its scope. (*Caparo Industries plc v Dickman* [1990] 2 AC 605 per Lord Bridge at p 617; *Michael v Chief Constable of South Wales Police (Refuge intervening)* [2015] AC 1732 per Lord Toulson at para 106; *Robinson v Chief Constable of West Yorkshire Police* [2018] 2 WLR 595 per Lord Reed at para 24). In the absence of such a universal touchstone, it has taken as a starting point established categories of specific situations where a duty of care is recognised and it has been willing to move beyond those situations on an incremental basis, accepting or rejecting a duty of care in novel situations by analogy with established categories (*Caparo* per Lord Bridge at p 618 citing Brennan J in the High Court of Australia in *Sutherland Shire Council v Heyman* (1985) 60 ALR 1, at pp 43–44). The familiar statement of principle by Lord Bridge in *Caparo* at pp 617–618 in which he refers to the ingredients of foreseeability of damage, proximity and fairness does not require a re-evaluation of whether those criteria are satisfied on every occasion on which an established category of duty is applied. In particular, as Lord Reed demonstrated in his judgment in *Robinson* (at paras 26, 27), where the existence of a duty of care has previously been established, a consideration of justice and reasonableness has already been taken into account in arriving at the relevant principles and it is, normally, only in cases where the court is asked to go beyond the established categories of duty of care that it will be necessary to

This is where Lord Lloyd-Jones begins his analysis.

An excellent summary of the 'incremental by analogy' approach.

This is important—if it is not a novel duty situation then this case will fall within a hospital's general duty of care.

That is, you DO NOT need to turn to *Caparo* on every occasion. This is true when answering problem questions too.

THIS is when a court needs to turn to *Caparo.*

→

consider whether it would be fair, just and reasonable to impose such a duty. The recent decision of the Supreme Court in *James-Bowen v Comr of Police of the Metropolis* [2018] 1 WLR 4021 was such a case and it was necessary for the court on that occasion to consider whether extension by analogy of established categories of duty was justified and the policy implications of such an extension. By contrast, ***Robinson*** itself involved no more than the application of a well-established category of duty of care and all that was required was the application to particular circumstances of established principles.

See case extract in section 2.1.

16.   In the present case Jackson LJ observed (at para 53) that to hold the respondent responsible would create 'a new head of liability for NHS health trusts'. To my mind, however, the present case falls squarely within an established category of duty of care. It has long been established that such a duty is owed by those who provide and run a casualty department to persons presenting themselves complaining of illness or injury and before they are treated or received into care in the hospital's wards. The duty is one to take reasonable care not to cause physical injury to the patient (***Barnett v Chelsea and Kensington Hospital Management Committee*** [1969] 1 QB 428, per Nield J at pp 435–436). In the present case, as soon as the appellant had attended at the respondent's A & E department seeking medical attention for the injury he had sustained, had provided the information requested by the receptionist and had been 'booked in', he was accepted into the system and entered into a relationship with the respondent of patient and health care provider. The damage complained of is physical injury and not economic loss. This is a distinct and recognisable situation in which the law imposes a duty of care. Moreover, the scope of the duty to take reasonable care not to act in such a way as foreseeably to cause such a patient to sustain physical injury clearly extends to a duty to take reasonable care not to provide misleading information which may foreseeably cause physical injury. While it is correct that no authority has been cited in these proceedings which deals specifically with misleading information provided by a receptionist in an A & E department causing physical injury, it is not necessary to address, in every instance where the precise factual situation has not previously been the subject of a reported judicial decision, whether it would be fair, just and reasonable to impose a duty of care. It is sufficient that the case falls within an established category in which the law imposes a duty of care.

17.   Secondly, this duty of care is owed by the hospital trust and it is not appropriate to distinguish, in this regard, between medical and non-medical staff. In the specific context of this case, where misleading information was provided as to the time within which medical attention might be available, it is not appropriate to distinguish between medically qualified professionals and administrative staff in determining whether there was a duty of care. That distinction may well be highly relevant in deciding whether there was a negligent breach of duty; there the degree of skill which can reasonably be expected of a person will be likely to depend on the responsibility with which he or she is charged. In the present circumstances, however, questions as to the existence and scope of a duty of care owed by the trust should not depend on whether the misleading information was provided by a person who was or was not medically qualified. The respondent had charged its non-medically qualified staff with the role of being the first point of contact with persons seeking medical assistance and, as a result, with the responsibility for providing accurate information as to its availability.

And so, arguments against establishing 'a new head of liability' fall away.

Note the much wider understanding of the substance of the hospital's duty.

Here Lord Lloyd-Jones is saying that the relevant duty of care is owed by the hospital. Hospital receptionists act for the hospital no less than the doctors and nurses. So the fact that the information was provided by a receptionist does not mean that it falls outside the hospital's duty. He does, however, say here that the fact that the misleading information was provided by a receptionist rather than a medical professional may make a difference to whether that duty was breached, since the skill and care one might expect of a receptionist is likely to be less than that of a doctor.

It is not necessary for there to be an earlier case dealing specifically with the same circumstances in the case at hand. This makes sense—otherwise it would be impossible for the law to develop. It is simply a new factual example of the well-established duty owed by hospitals.

18. In *Kent v Griffiths* [2001] QB 36 the London Ambulance Service was held liable in negligence for its delay in responding to an emergency call as a result of which the claimant suffered brain damage. The Court of Appeal upheld the judge's decision on the ground that the ambulance had not arrived in a reasonable time. However, it also founded liability on the alternative basis that the call handler had given misleading assurances that an ambulance would be arriving shortly. (See the reference to *Kent v Griffiths* by Lord Toulson in **Michael v Chief Constable of South Wales Police** at para 138.) In *Kent v Griffiths* Lord Woolf MR, with whom Aldous and Laws LJJ agreed, observed with regard to the existence of a duty of care (at para 45) that what was being provided was a health service and he asked rhetorically why the position of the ambulance staff should be different from that of doctors or nurses. More specifically, he stated (at para 49) that the acceptance of the emergency call established a duty of care and that, if wrong information had not been given about the arrival of the ambulance, other means of transport could have been used.

19. On this point, therefore, I find myself in total agreement with the observations of McCombe LJ in his dissenting judgment. The duty of the respondent trust must be considered in the round. While it is not the function of reception staff to give wider advice or information in general to patients, it is the duty of the NHS Trust to take care not to provide misinformation to patients and that duty is not avoided by the misinformation having been provided by reception staff as opposed to medical staff. In this regard, it is simply not appropriate to distinguish between medical and non-medical staff in the manner proposed by the respondent.

20. It is convenient to observe at this point that *Kent v Griffiths* is also relevant in another sense. For the reasons explained earlier in this judgment, in deciding whether a duty of care is owed in the present circumstances it is not necessary to proceed incrementally by analogy with decided cases because no extension of an established category of duty is called for here. Nevertheless, I note the close analogy between the present case and the alternative basis of decision in *Kent v Griffiths*. In both cases, as a result of the provision of inaccurate information by non-medically qualified staff, there was a delay in the provision of urgently required medical attention with the result that serious physical injury was suffered.

> Here Lord Lloyd-Jones offers a secondary line of reasoning on the duty question: even if this were to be treated as a novel duty situation, falling outside all of the established situations in which a duty of care is owed, the imposition of such a duty would nonetheless be justified on the incremental and by analogy approach.

21. Thirdly, I consider that the judgments of the majority in the Court of Appeal elide issues of the existence of a duty of care and negligent breach of duty. They place emphasis on what a reasonable person would have done and could reasonably be expected to have done in the context of a busy A & E department. Thus Jackson LJ draws attention to the difficult conditions in which staff at such departments often have to work, observing (at para 54) that A & E department waiting areas are not always havens of tranquillity. Similarly, Sales LJ considers (at paras 84–87) that if there is a duty to provide 'precise and accurate information' about the length of time before a patient might be seen by a triage nurse, it is difficult to see why it does not extend to an obligation to correct such information as changing pressures on resources arise. He observes (at paras 85, 87) that it would not be fair, just or reasonable to impose 'a duty of fine-grained perfection' regarding the information provided and that 'it is not as a matter of legal duty incumbent on a receptionist and the employing NHS trust to provide minute-perfect or hour-perfect information about how long the wait might be'. These observations

> A useful warning to keep questions of duty and breach distinct (and rejoinder to those who claim that the various elements of a claim in negligence are effectively interchangeable).

→ seem to me to be directed at false targets; it is not suggested that receptionists in an A & E department should act in this way. The question under consideration is whether the respondent owes a duty to take reasonable care when providing, by its receptionists, information as to the period of time within which medical attention is likely to be available. More fundamentally, however, these observations are really concerned not with the existence of a duty of care but with the question whether there has been a negligent breach of duty as a result of a failure to meet the standard reasonably expected.

22. For these reasons, I consider that the submissions of Mr Havers QC on behalf of the respondent and the observations by the majority in the Court of Appeal (at paras 55 and 88) on the social cost of imposing such a duty of care are misplaced. This is not a new head of liability for NHS health trusts. In any event, I consider that what are said to be the undesirable consequences of imposing the duty in question are considerably over-stated. Jackson LJ considered (at para 55) that litigation about who said what to whom in the waiting rooms of A & E departments could become a fertile area for claimants and their representatives. Alternatively, in his view, health care providers could close down this area of risk altogether by instructing reception staff to say nothing to patients apart from asking for their details. In the same way, Sales LJ considered (at para 88) that the imposition of such a duty could lead to defensive practices on the part of NHS Trusts resulting in the withdrawal of information which is generally helpful to the public. There is no reason to suppose that the factual context of an A & E department is likely to give rise to any unusual evidential difficulties. The burden of proof of the provision of misleading information will be on the claimant. Hospital staff will be able to give evidence as to their usual practice. So far as substantive liability is concerned, the requirements of negligence and causation will remain effective control factors. It is undoubtedly the fact that Hospital A & E departments operate in very difficult circumstances and under colossal pressure. This is a consideration which may well prove highly influential in many cases when assessing whether there has been a negligent breach of duty.

23. Finally in this regard, I should record that in considering the issue of duty of care I have been greatly assisted by a case note on the decision of the Court of Appeal in the present case by Professor James Goudkamp ([2017] CLJ 481). He considers that the parties were within an established duty category and that the only question, relevantly, was whether the defendant breached that duty. He observes that discussion as to what the reasonable person would have done in the circumstances in question indicates that the dispute is about the breach element, that being the only element of the cause of action in negligence that is concerned with the satisfactoriness of the defendant's conduct.

He concludes:

Accordingly, on traditional principles, **Darnley** is not, in fact, a duty of care case at all. Rather, properly understood, the issue was whether the defendant had breached its duty in giving, by its receptionist, inaccurate information to the claimant. (at p 482)

I agree with his analysis. It is to that question of negligent breach of duty that I now turn.

→

Side note (left):

Case notes are an excellent way of understanding a case. This is particularly true when the case is new and so not covered by your textbooks. Case notes are usually relatively short (4–5 pages) and offer a focused discussion of the facts, argument and decision of a given case. There are excellent case note sections in the *Law Quarterly Review* and *Cambridge Law Journal.*

Side note (right):

The Court of Appeal was concerned about the burden a duty of care would place on hospitals and those working at hospitals. Lord Lloyd-Jones isn't dissenting from those concerns. But he thinks they go only to the question of whether a duty has been breached not whether such a duty arises in the first place.

Is he right? Can you think of any downsides for treating all these concerns as matters of the standard of care?

Negligent breach of duty

→

24. The reception desk at the A & E department was the first point of contact between the respondent trust and members of the public seeking medical assistance. It has not been suggested that the respondent was in any way at fault in allocating this responsibility to receptionists who were not medically qualified. Moreover, it has not been suggested that the receptionists should have provided accurate information to each patient on arrival as to precisely when he or she would be seen by a medically qualified member of staff. Anyone who has any experience of A & E departments will know that this would be impossible. The pressures on medical staff are enormous, the demand for attention is constantly fluctuating and priorities are likely to change. However, it is not unreasonable to require receptionists to take reasonable care not to provide misleading information as to the likely availability of medical assistance.

25. The particular role performed by the individual concerned will be likely to have an important bearing on the question of breach of the duty of care. As Mustill LJ explained in **Wilsher v Essex Area Health Authority** [1987] QB 730, 750–751, the legitimate expectation of the patient is that he will receive from each person concerned with his care a degree of skill appropriate to the task which he or she undertakes. A receptionist in an A & E department cannot, of course, be expected to give medical advice or information but he or she can be expected to take reasonable care not to provide misleading advice as to the availability of medical assistance. The standard required is that of an averagely competent and well-informed person performing the function of a receptionist at a department providing emergency medical care.

26. Responding to requests for information as to the usual system of operation of the A & E department was well within the area of responsibility of the receptionists. The two receptionists on duty at the material time were both aware that the standard procedure was that anyone complaining of a head injury would be seen by a triage nurse and they accepted that the usual practice was that such a patient would be told that they would be seen by a triage nurse within 30 minutes of arrival (Mrs Ashley) or as soon as possible (Mrs Reeves-Bristow). No reason has been suggested as to why the appellant was not told of the standard procedure. The hospital was operating within the acceptable range of triage timing agreed by the experts and the actual position was that the appellant, had he remained, would have been seen by a triage nurse within 30 minutes because he was complaining of a head injury. It is not unreasonable to require that patients in the position of the appellant should be provided on arrival, whether orally by a receptionist, by leaflet or prominent notice, with accurate information that they would normally be seen by a triage nurse within 30 minutes.

27. However, instead the appellant was simply told that he would have to wait for up to four or five hours to see a doctor. That information was incomplete and misleading. The Chief Executive of the respondent described it in his letter to the appellant dated 23 March 2011 as 'completely incorrect'. The appellant was misinformed as to the true position and, as a result, misled as to the availability of medical assistance. The trial judge made the critical finding that it was reasonably foreseeable that a person who believes that it

---

Remember, in order for there to be an actionable claim in negligence the claimant needs to establish that the defendant
(1) Owed them a *duty of care*
(2) Which they *breached*
(3) Which in turn *caused their injury.*

This is the standard of care expected of a hospital receptionist— the question for the court is whether the receptionists in this case fell below this standard.

Darnley was not told this, and left after 19 minutes (at [4]).

Again Lord Lloyd-Jones accepts the burdens and difficulties hospital workers face. But he considers that these concerns can be accommodated within the standard of care: i.e. they can be factored in when working out how *much* care we can reasonably expect of a given worker. While receptionists will not be expected to offer the same information as, e.g., doctors, they can be expected to take reasonable care to provide accurate information as to when the patient is likely to be seen.

While the NHS Trust offered plenty of arguments as to why hospitals, and hospital receptionists, should owe no duty of care, this reveals that they could not offer any good reason why this particular receptionist had given misleading information to Darnley. With the court having already concluded that there was a duty of care extending to the receptionist's provision of such information, this makes it almost inevitable that the Trust will be held to have breached this duty.

→

→

Lord Lloyd-Jones concludes that the hospital was in breach of its duty of care.

may be four or five hours before he will be seen by a doctor may decide to leave. In the light of that finding I have no doubt that the provision of such misleading information by a receptionist as to the time within which medical assistance might be available was negligent.

Causation

Finally, Darnley needs to establish that the defendant's breach of its duty of care caused his injuries.

28. The appellant remained in the waiting area of the A & E department for only 19 minutes before deciding to leave because he felt too unwell to remain. He failed to tell any member of staff of his departure. In the Court of Appeal Jackson LJ concluded, in the alternative, (at para 56) that if he was wrong in his view that the receptionist or the respondent acting by the receptionist was in breach of a duty of care owed to the appellant by giving incorrect information, the claim could still not succeed because the scope of that duty could not extend to liability for the consequences of a patient walking out without telling the staff that he was about to leave. In his view, echoing that of the trial judge, the appellant should accept responsibility for his own actions. Sales LJ agreed with this alternative reason for dismissing the appeal.

Lawyers talk of a 'break in the chain of causation' (or 'novus actus interveniens', where someone—it may be the claimant or a third party—does something which should be treated as the true or operative cause of the harm. Here the idea is that it is Darnley's own decision to leave the hospital which should be regarded as what caused his injuries, not the misleading information which the hospital gave him.

29. This reasoning, however, fails to take account of the effect of the misleading information with which the appellant was provided and of three critical findings of fact made by the trial judge. First, the judge found that, if the appellant had been told that he would be seen within 30 minutes, he would have stayed in the waiting area and would have been seen before he left. He would then have been admitted or told to wait. He would have waited and his later collapse would have occurred within a hospital setting. Secondly, the judge found that the appellant's decision to leave was made, in part at least, on the basis of information provided to him by the receptionist which was inaccurate or incomplete. Thirdly, the judge found that it was reasonably foreseeable that a person who believes that it may be four or five hours before he will be seen by a doctor may decide to leave, in circumstances where that person would have stayed if he believed he would be seen much sooner by a triage nurse. The conclusion of the majority of the Court of Appeal on this point seems to me to be inconsistent with these findings of fact. Far from constituting a break in the chain of causation, the appellant's decision to leave was reasonably foreseeable and was made, at least in part, on the basis of the misleading information that he would have to wait for up to four or five hours before being seen by a doctor. In this regard it is also relevant that the appellant had just sustained what was later discovered to be a very grave head injury. Both the appellant and Mr Tubman had told the receptionist that the appellant was really unwell and needed urgent attention. The appellant told her that he felt as if he was about to collapse. He was in a particularly vulnerable condition and did, in fact, collapse as a result of his injury within an hour of leaving the hospital. In these circumstances, one can readily appreciate how the judge came to his conclusion that the appellant's departure was reasonably foreseeable.

Here Lord Lloyd-Jones explains why Darnley's decision to leave shouldn't be treated as breaking the chain of causation between the hospital's breach and his resulting injuries. Not only was Darnley's decision based on the very misinformation the hospital provided, he was also in a very vulnerable state because of the injury he had already suffered. As such, it would be unreasonable to treat Darnley's injuries as solely the result of his own actions.

30. The trial judge made a further finding of fact that had the appellant suffered the collapse at around 21:30 whilst at the Mayday Hospital, he would have been transferred to St George's Hospital and would have undergone surgery earlier with the result that he would have made a very near full recovery.

→

→

31. In these circumstances, the case that the appellant's unannounced departure from the A & E department broke the chain of causation is simply not made out.

Conclusion

32. For these reasons I would allow the appeal and remit the case to the Queen's Bench Division for the assessment of damages.

33. Finally, the court would like to express its appreciation of the clarity and economy of the written and oral submissions of both parties in this case. They were a model of what can be achieved and without any loss of depth or substance.

This was, for some time, seen as setting down a three-stage 'test', whereby a duty of care will be owed only if (1) it was reasonably foreseeable that someone in the claimant's position would be harmed if the defendant did not take care, (2) the parties were in a relationship of proximity, and (3) it is fair, just and reasonable to impose such a duty. However, the central message of *Caparo* was that it was, in fact, *impossible* to set down any single test to identify those situations in which a duty of care is owed:

I think that it has to be recognised that to search for any single formula which will serve as a general test of liability is to pursue a will-o'-the wisp. The fact is that once one discards, as it is now clear one must, the concept of foreseeability of harm as the single exclusive test, even a *prima facie* test, of the existence of the duty of care, the attempt to state some general principle which will determine liability in an infinite variety of circumstances serves not to clarify the law but merely to bedevil its development in a way which corresponds with practicality and common sense. (Lord Oliver, Caparo at 632)

This message has now been re-emphasised in a series of recent Supreme Court decisions: see **Michael v Chief Constable of South Wales** [2015] UKSC 2, at [106] (Lord Toulson); **Robinson v Chief Constable of West Yorkshire Police** [2018] UKSC 4, at [21] (Lord Reed); **Darnley v Croydon Health Services NHS Trust** [2018] UKSC 50, at [15] (Lord Lloyd-Jones); **Poole Borough Council v GN** [2019] UKSC 25, at [30], [64] (Lord Reed).

So, if no test tells us when a duty of care should arise in novel circumstances, what can? The standard answer here is 'policy', which, in this context, tends to mean any and every factor which might bear on the appropriateness of imposing such a duty. This point was well expressed by McDonald J in the Canadian case of *Nova Mink v Trans Canada Airlines* [1951] 2 DLR 241 when he said:

When upon analysis of the circumstances and application of the appropriate formula, a court holds that the defendant was under a duty of care, the court is stating as a conclusion of law what is really a conclusion of policy as to responsibility for conduct involving unreasonable risk. It is saying that such circumstances presented such an appreciable risk of harm to others as to entitle them to protection against unreasonable conduct by the actor. It is declaring also that a cause of action can exist in other situations of the same type, and *pro tanto* is moving in the direction of establishing further categories of human relationships entailing recognised duties of care. . . . Accordingly there is always a large element of judicial policy and social expediency involved in the determination of the duty problem, however it may be obscured by the use of the traditional formulae.

Notes

1. For a general overview of the tort of negligence as well as discussion of its function see Kirsty Horsey and Erika Rackley *Tort Law* (7th edn, OUP, 2021), Ch 2; Joanne Conaghan and Wade Mansell *The Wrongs of Tort* (2nd edn, Pluto Press, 1999), Chs 4 and 5; Steve Hedley 'Making Sense of Negligence' (2016) 36 Legal Studies 491; Peter Cane *Atiyah's Accidents, Compensation and the Law* (7th edn, CUP, 2006), Chs 2 and 3; Andrew Robertson 'On the Function of the Law of Negligence' (2013) 33 OJLS 31; and Tony Weir 'The Staggering March of Negligence' in Peter Cane and Jane Stapleton (eds) *The Law of Obligations: Essays in Honour of John Fleming* (OUP, 1988), p 97.

2. On the development and purpose of duty of care see Nicholas McBride 'Duties of Care—Do They Really Exist?' (2004) 24 OJLS 417; and David Howarth 'Many Duties of Care—Or A Duty of Care? Notes from the Underground' (2006) 26 OJLS 449.

2.1 The rise and fall of the general duty of care

Donoghue v Stevenson is a—perhaps even *the*—landmark decision in the law of torts. What has become known as Lord Atkin's 'neighbour principle'—the idea that an individual must take reasonable care to avoid injuring those who they can (or should) reasonably foresee will be injured if they do not take such care—provided the foundation for the modern law of negligence.

Donoghue v Stevenson
House of Lords [1932] AC 562

At about 8.50 pm on 26 August 1928, Mrs Donoghue met a friend in a café owned by Francis Minchella in Wellmeadow Road, Paisley. Her friend bought a bottle of ginger beer and an ice-cream. The bottle was made of opaque glass. Minchella poured part of the contents into a tumbler containing the ice-cream. Donoghue drank some of this and the friend then poured the remainder of the ginger beer into the glass. It was said that a decomposed snail floated out of the bottle and Donoghue claimed that—as a result—she suffered shock and gastroenteritis, and asked for £500 damages from the manufacturer of the ginger beer, Stevenson. The defendant argued that there could be no liability, as there was no contract between himself and Donoghue. Held: by majority, that such a defendant could be liable to such a claimant in negligence.

LORD ATKIN: We are solely concerned with the question whether, as a matter of law in the circum-stances alleged, the defender owed any duty to the pursuer [Mrs Donoghue] to take care.

It is remarkable how difficult it is to find in the English authorities statements of general application defining the relations between parties that give rise to the duty. The Courts are concerned with the particular relations which come before them in actual litigation, and it is sufficient to say whether the duty exists in those circumstances. The result is that the Courts have been engaged upon an elabo-rate classification of duties as they exist in respect of property, whether real or personal, with further divisions as to ownership, occupation or control, and distinctions based on the particular relations of the one side or the other, whether manufacturer, salesman or landlord, customer, tenant, stranger, and so on. In this way it can be ascertained at any time whether the law recognizes a duty, but only where the case can be referred to some particular species which has been examined and classi-fied. And yet the duty which is common to all the cases where liability is established must logically be based upon some element common to the cases where it is found to exist. To seek a complete logical definition of the general principle is probably to go beyond the function of the judge, for the more general the definition the more likely it is to omit essentials or to introduce non-essentials. The attempt was made by Brett MR in *Heaven v Pender* (1883) 11 QBD 503, 509, in a definition to which I will later refer. As framed, it was demonstrably too wide, though it appears to me, if properly limited, to be capable of affording a valuable practical guide.

At present I content myself with pointing out that in English law there must be, and is, some general conception of relations giving rise to a duty of care, of which the particular cases found in the books are but instances. The liability for negligence, whether you style it such or treat it as in other systems as a species of 'culpa,' is no doubt based upon a general public sentiment of moral wrongdoing for which the offender must pay. But acts or omissions which any moral code would censure cannot in a practical world be treated so as to give a right to every person injured by them to demand relief. In this way rules of law arise which limit the range of complainants and the extent of their remedy. The rule that you are to love your neighbour becomes in law, you must not injure your neighbour; and the lawyer's question, Who is my neighbour? receives a restricted reply. You must take reasonable care to avoid acts or omissions which you can reasonably foresee would be likely to injure your neighbour. Who, then, in law is my neighbour? The answer seems to be—persons who are so closely and di-rectly affected by my act that I ought reasonably to have them in contemplation as being so affected when I am directing my mind to the acts or omissions which are called in question. This appears to me to be the doctrine of *Heaven v Pender*, as laid down by Lord Esher (then Brett MR) when it is lim-ited by the notion of proximity introduced by Lord Esher himself and AL Smith LJ in *Le Lievre v Gould* [1893] 1 QB 491. Lord Esher says: 'That case established that, under certain circumstances, one man may owe a duty to another, even though there is no contract between them. If one man is near to another, or is near to the property of another, a duty lies upon him not to do that which may cause a personal injury to that other, or may injure his property.' So AL Smith LJ: 'The decision of *Heaven v Pender* 11 QBD 503, 509 was founded upon the principle, that a duty to take due care did arise when the person or property of one was in such proximity to the person or property of another that, if due care was not taken, damage might be done by the one to the other.' I think that this sufficiently states the truth if proximity be not confined to mere physical proximity, but be used, as I think it was intended, to extend to such close and direct relations that the act complained of directly affects a person whom the person alleged to be bound to take care would know would be directly affected by his careless act. . . .

. . . I venture to say that in the branch of the law which deals with civil wrongs, dependent in England at any rate entirely upon the application by judges of general principles also formulated by judges, it is of particular importance to guard against the danger of stating propositions of law in wider terms than is necessary, lest essential factors be omitted in the wider survey and the inherent adaptability of English law be unduly restricted. For this reason it is very necessary in considering reported cases in the law of torts that the actual decision alone should carry authority, proper weight, of course, being given to the dicta of the judges. . . .

LORD MACMILLAN: It humbly appears to me that the diversity of view which is exhibited in such cases as *George v Skivington* LR 5 Ex 1 on the one hand and *Blacker v Lake & Elliot, Ld* 106 LT 533, on the other hand—to take two extreme instances—is explained by the fact that in the discussion of the topic which now engages your Lordships' attention two rival principles of the law find a meeting place where each has contended for supremacy. On the one hand, there is the well established principle that no one other than a party to a contract can complain of a breach of that contract. On the other hand, there is the equally well established doctrine that negligence apart from contract gives a right of action to the party injured by that negligence—and here I use the term negligence, of course, in its technical legal sense, implying a duty owed and neglected. The fact that there is a contractual relationship between the parties which may give rise to an action for breach of contract, does not exclude the co-existence of a right of action founded on negligence as between the same parties, independently of the contract, though arising out of the relationship in fact brought about by the contract. Of this the best illustration is the right of the injured railway passenger to sue the railway company either for breach of the contract of safe carriage or for negligence in carrying him. And there is no reason why the same set of facts should not give one person a right of action in contract and another person a right of action in tort. . . .

Where, as in cases like the present, so much depends upon the avenue of approach to the question, it is very easy to take the wrong turning. If you begin with the sale by the manufacturer to the retail dealer, then the consumer who purchases from the retailer is at once seen to be a stranger to the contract between the retailer and the manufacturer and so disentitled to sue upon it. There is no contractual relation between the manufacturer and the consumer; and thus the plaintiff, if he is to succeed, is driven to try to bring himself within one or other of the exceptional cases where the strictness of the rule that none but a party to a contract can found on a breach of that contract has been mitigated in the public interest, as it has been in the case of a person who issues a chattel which is inherently dangerous or which he knows to be in a dangerous condition. If, on the other hand, you disregard the fact that the circumstances of the case at one stage include the existence of a contract of sale between the manufacturer and the retailer, and approach the question by asking whether there is evidence of carelessness on the part of the manufacturer, and whether he owed a duty to be careful in a question with the party who has been injured in consequence of his want of care, the circumstance that the injured party was not a party to the incidental contract of sale becomes irrelevant, and his title to sue the manufacturer is unaffected by that circumstance . . .

. . . Having regard to the inconclusive state of the authorities in the Courts below and to the fact that the important question involved is now before your Lordships for the first time, I think it desirable to consider the matter from the point of view of the principles applicable to this branch of law which are admittedly common to both English and Scottish jurisprudence.

The law takes no cognizance of carelessness in the abstract. It concerns itself with careless-ness only where there is a duty to take care and where failure in that duty has caused damage. In such circumstances carelessness assumes the legal quality of negligence and entails the con-sequences in law of negligence. What, then, are the circumstances which give rise to this duty to take care? In the daily contacts of social and business life human beings are thrown into, or place themselves in, an infinite variety of relations with their fellows; and the law can refer only to the standards of the reasonable man in order to determine whether any particular relation gives rise to a duty to take care as between those who stand in that relation to each other. The grounds of ac-tion may be as various and manifold as human errancy; and the conception of legal responsibility may develop in adaptation to altering social conditions and standards. The criterion of judgment must adjust and adapt itself to the changing circumstances of life. The categories of negligence are never closed. The cardinal principle of liability is that the party complained of should owe to the party complaining a duty to take care, and that the party complaining should be able to prove that he has suffered damage in consequence of a breach of that duty. Where there is room for di-versity of view, it is in determining what circumstances will establish such a relationship between the parties as to give rise, on the one side, to a duty to take care, and on the other side to a right to have care taken.

Notes

1. The ruling of the House of Lords was on a point of law only, on the assumption that the facts alleged were true. The trial of the actual action was set down for 10 January 1932, but by then Stevenson had died and the case was settled for £200. This means that it was never established whether there was, in fact, a snail in the bottle of ginger beer. For the family history of Donoghue and other interesting points about the case, see Lord Rodger 'Mrs Donoghue and Alfenus Varus' (1988) 41 CLP 1 and William McBryde, '*Donoghue* v *Stevenson*: The Story of the Snail in the Bottle Case' in A Gamble (ed) *Obligations in Context* (W Green, 1990), p 17.

Anns v Merton London Borough Council
House of Lords [1978] AC 728

Following **Donoghue** there was relatively little development of the duty concept. However, eventually the inevitable expansion came, reaching its highpoint in **Home Office v Dorset Yacht Co Ltd** [1970] UKHL 2 (where it was suggested that a duty should exist whenever damage was foreseeable) and **Anns v Merton London Borough Council** [1978] (which in-troduced an additional 'policy' restriction). A retreat swiftly followed. The remarks of Lord Wilberforce are reproduced here for ease of reference because this passage is often referred to in later cases, but this idea has now been abandoned and the dictum has been disapproved.

LORD WILBERFORCE: Through the trilogy of cases in this House—*Donoghue v Stevenson* [1932] AC 562, *Hedley Byrne & Co Ltd v Heller & Partners Ltd* [1964] AC 465, and *Dorset Yacht Co Ltd v Home Office* [1970] AC 1004, the position has now been reached that in order to establish that a duty of care arises in a particular situation, it is not necessary to bring the facts of that situation within those of previous situations in which a duty of care has been held to exist. Rather the question has to be approached in two stages. First one has to ask whether, as between the alleged wrongdoer and the person who has suffered damage there is a sufficient relationship of proximity or neighbourhood such that, in the reasonable contemplation of the former, carelessness on his part may be likely to cause damage to the latter—in which case a prima facie duty of care arises. Secondly, if the first question is answered affirmatively, it is necessary to consider whether there are any considerations which ought to negative, or to reduce or limit the scope of the duty or the class of person to whom it is owed or the damages to which a breach of it may give rise. (at 751–2)

Notes

1. *Anns* itself concerned the potential liability of a local authority towards a lessee of a building for failure to ensure that the building complied with deposited plans, particularly in relation to the depth of the foundations. It was overruled in **Murphy v Brentwood District Council** [1991] 1 AC 398 (see section 6.2).

2. For discussion of the retreat from the Anns principle see Richard Kidner 'Resiling From the *Anns* Principle: The Variable Nature of Proximity in Negligence' (1987) 7 LS 319.

Caparo Industries plc v Dickman is the leading case on establishing novel duties of care. As noted at the start of the chapter, it is typically seen as setting down two approaches that courts should adopt when seeking to determine whether, on the facts of a particular case, a duty of care is owed: the three-stage 'test' and the 'incremental and by analogy' approach.

> ### *Caparo Industries plc v Dickman*
> House of Lords [1990] 2 AC 605

This case concerned the liability of auditors for negligent misstatement, and the substantive issues are dealt with in section 6.2.1.2. The following extracts deal with general issues as to duty of care in which the House of Lords sought to reassert the limits that were traditionally placed on liability.

LORD BRIDGE: . . . [S]ince the *Anns* case a series of decisions of the Privy Council and of your Lordships' House, notably in judgments and speeches delivered by Lord Keith of Kinkel, have emphasised the inability of any single general principle to provide a practical test which can be applied to every situation to determine whether a duty of care is owed and, if so what is its scope: see *Governors of Peabody Donation Fund v Sir Lindsay Parkinson & Co Ltd* [1985] AC 210, 239F–241C, *Yuen Kun Yeu v Attorney-General of Hong Kong* [1988] AC 175, 190E–194F; *Rowling v Takaro Properties Ltd* [1988] AC 473, 501D–G; *Hill v Chief Constable of West Yorkshire* [1989] AC 53, 60B–D. What emerges is that, in addition to the foreseeability of damage, necessary ingredients in any situation giving rise to a duty of care are that there should exist between the party owing the duty and the party to whom it is owed a relationship characterised by the law as one of 'proximity' or 'neighbourhood' and that the situation should be one in which the court considers it fair, just and reasonable that the law should impose a duty of a given scope upon the one party for the benefit of the other. But it is implicit in the passages referred to that the concepts of proximity and fairness embodied in these additional ingredients are not susceptible of any such precise definition as would be necessary to give them utility as practical tests, but amount in effect to little more than convenient labels to attach to the features of different specific situations which, on a detailed examination of all the circumstances, the law recognises pragmatically as giving rise to a duty of care of a given scope. Whilst recognising, of course, the importance of the underlying general principles common to the whole field of negligence, I think the law has now moved in the direction of attaching greater significance to the more traditional categorisation of distinct and recognisable situations as guides to the existence, the scope and the limits of the varied duties of care which the law imposes. We must now, I think, recognise the wisdom of the words of Brennan J in the High Court of Australia in *Sutherland Shire Council v Heyman* (1985) 60 ALR 1, 43–44, where he said:

> It is preferable, in my view, that the law should develop novel categories of negligence incrementally and by analogy with established categories, rather than by a massive extension of a prima facie duty of care restrained only by indefinable 'considerations which ought to negative, or to reduce or limit the scope of the duty or the class of person to whom it is owed'.

One of the most important distinctions always to be observed lies in the law's essentially different approach to the different kinds of damage which one party may have suffered in consequence of the acts or omissions of another. It is one thing to owe a duty of care to avoid causing injury to the person or property of others. It is quite another to avoid causing others to suffer purely economic loss. . . .

LORD ROSKILL: . . . I agree with your Lordships that it has now to be accepted that there is no simple formula or touchstone to which recourse can be had in order to provide in every case a ready answer to the questions whether, given certain facts, the law will or will not impose liability for negligence or in cases where such liability can be shown to exist, determine the extent of that liability. Phrases such as 'foreseeability,' 'proximity,' 'neighbourhood,' 'just and reasonable,' 'fairness,' 'voluntary acceptance of risk,' or 'voluntary assumption of responsibility' will be found used from time to time in the different cases. But, as your Lordships have said, such phrases are not precise definitions. At best they are but labels or phrases descriptive of the very different factual situations which can exist in particular cases and which must be carefully examined in each case before it can be pragmatically determined whether a duty of care exists and, if so, what is the scope and extent of that duty. If this conclusion involves a return to the traditional categorisation of cases as pointing to the existence and scope of any duty of care, as my noble and learned friend Lord Bridge of Harwich, suggests, I think this is infinitely preferable to recourse to somewhat wide generalisations which leave their practical application matters of difficulty and uncertainty. This conclusion finds strong support from the judgment of Brennan J in *Sutherland Shire Council v Heyman*, 60 ALR 1, 43–44 in the High Court of Australia in the passage cited by my noble and learned friends.

LORD OLIVER: . . . Thus the postulate of a simple duty to avoid any harm that is, with hindsight, reasonably capable of being foreseen becomes untenable without the imposition of some intelligible limits to keep the law of negligence within the bounds of common sense and practicality. Those limits have been found by the requirement of what has been called a 'relationship of proximity' between plaintiff and defendant and by the imposition of a further requirement that the attachment of liability for harm which has occurred be 'just and reasonable.' But although the cases in which the courts have imposed or withheld liability are capable of an approximate categorisation, one looks in vain for some common denominator by which the existence of the essential relationship can be tested. Indeed it is difficult to resist a conclusion that what have been treated as three separate requirements are, at least in most cases, in fact merely facets of the same thing, for in some cases the degree of foreseeability is such that it is from that alone that the requisite proximity can be deduced, whilst in others the absence of that essential relationship can most rationally be attributed simply to the court's view that it would not be fair and reasonable to hold the defendant responsible. 'Proximity' is, no doubt, a convenient expression so long as it is realised that it is no more than a label which embraces not a definable concept but merely a description of circumstances from which, pragmatically, the courts conclude that a duty of care exists.

There are, of course, cases where, in any ordinary meaning of the words, a relationship of proximity (in the literal sense of 'closeness') exists but where the law, whilst recognising the fact of the relationship, nevertheless denies a remedy to the injured party on the ground of public policy. *Rondel v Worsley* [1969] 1 AC 191 was such a case, as was *Hill v Chief Constable of West Yorkshire* [1989] AC 53, so far as concerns the alternative ground of that decision. But such cases do nothing to assist in the identification of those features from which the law will deduce the essential relationship on which liability depends . . .

Perhaps, therefore, the most that can be attempted is a broad categorisation of the decided cases according to the type of situation in which liability has been established in the past in order to found an argument by analogy. Thus, for instance, cases can be classified according to whether what is complained of is the failure to prevent the infliction of damage by the act of the third party (such as *Dorset Yacht Co Ltd v Home Office* [1970] AC 1004, *P Perl (Exporters) Ltd v Camden London Borough Council* [1984] QB 342, *Smith v Littlewoods Organisation Ltd* [1987] AC 241 and, indeed, *Anns v Merton London Borough Council* [1978] AC 728 itself), in failure to perform properly a statutory duty claimed to have been imposed for the protection of the plaintiff either as a member of a class or as a member of the public (such as the *Anns* case, *Ministry of Housing and Local Government v Sharp* [1970] 2 QB 223, *Yuen Kun Yeu v Attorney-General of Hong Kong* [1988] AC 175) or in the making by the defendant of some statement or advice which has been communicated, directly or indirectly, to the plaintiff and upon which he has relied. Such categories are not, of course, exhaustive. Sometimes they overlap as in the *Anns* case, and there are cases which do not readily fit into easily definable categories (such as *Ross v Caunters* [1980] Ch 297). Nevertheless, it is, I think, permissible to regard negligent statements or advice as a separate category displaying common features from which it is possible to find at least guidelines by which a test for the existence of the relationship which is essential to ground liability can be deduced.

Notes

1. As noted earlier, it was until recently thought that, in these passages, the House of Lords was proposing a new 'three-stage test' for establishing duties of care. However, the key message of **Caparo** is that there is *no* general test for determining when duties of care arise, or at least no general test which will provide satisfactory answers. Accordingly, the aim of the House of Lords was not to offer a new and improved test, or indeed any concrete guidance at all to courts faced with answering such questions. So what is the point of the House of Lords' references to 'proximity' and the need to be satisfied that the imposition of a duty is 'fair, just and reasonable'? The answer is that they help mark a clean break from the approach in **Anns** whereby foreseeability of harm is the only positive reason needed for the recognition of such a duty: under **Anns**, once foreseeability of harm was established, there was, in effect, a presumption that a duty will be owed. Not so under **Caparo**. Even if harm is foreseeable, we need to go on to ask if the relationship between the parties is sufficiently proximate *and* whether such a duty would be fair, just and reasonable, before we come to even a provisional conclusion that a duty of care is owed. That these additional elements have no fixed or easily discernible content is, therefore, secondary to the basic message that courts have been finding duties of care too readily and that they should slow down.

2. That the elements of 'proximity' and 'fairness, justice and reasonableness' have no fixed or easily discerned content does not mean that we can say nothing in general terms about them. One thing that is clear is that proximity here is not limited to geographical proximity—Donoghue was many miles away from Stevenson at the time she was injured. Moreover, in contrast to how the term was used in *Anns*, it is clear from the context that proximity is something additional to the reasonable foreseeability of harm. Having said that, in cases of personal injury or damage to property caused by a defendant's positive actions, it seems that proximity is established whenever the defendant ought reasonably to have foreseen damage to the claimant. In other cases, however, such as those involving pure psychiatric injury or pure economic loss, something more than mere foresight will be required.

3. As we shall see, the real guidance which *Caparo* offers to courts faced with novel duty situations is to be found not in the three-stage 'test' but in the 'incremental and by analogy' approach Lord Bridge borrows from Brennan J in the High Court of Australia's decision in *Sutherland Shire Council* v *Heyman*. How useful, or reliable, this approach is, is a matter of dispute. In *Customs and Excise* v *Barclays Bank* [2006] UKHL 28, the House of Lords warned against taking this approach too literally or regarding it as an infallible guide to liability. Lord Bingham said:

> I incline to agree with the view . . . that the incremental test is of little value as a test in itself, and is only helpful when used in combination with a test or principle which identifies the legally significant features of a situation. The closer the facts of the case in issue to those of a case in which a duty of care has been held to exist, the readier a court will be, on the approach of Brennan J adopted in *Caparo* v *Dickman*, to find that there has been an assumption of responsibility or that the proximity and policy conditions of the threefold test are satisfied. The converse is also true. (at [7])

Later he said:

> It seems to me that the outcomes (or majority outcomes) of the leading cases cited above are in every or almost every instance sensible and just, irrespective of the test applied to achieve that outcome. This is not to disparage the value of and need for a test of liability in tortious negligence, which any law of tort must propound if it is not to become a morass of single instances. But it does in my opinion concentrate attention on the detailed circumstances of the particular case and the particular relationship between the parties in the context of their legal and factual situation as a whole. (at [8])

This raises the very difficult question of the balance between principle and strict precedent; an issue which was at the forefront of *Donoghue* itself.

4. More recently, in *Michael* v *Chief Constable of South Wales Police* [2015] UKSC 2, Lord Toulson commented:

> In *Caparo Plc* v *Dickman* [1990] 2 AC 605 Lord Bridge (with whom Lords Roskill, Ackner and Oliver of Aylmerton agreed) emphasised the inability of any single general principle to provide a practical test which could be applied to every situation to determine whether a duty of care is owed and, if so, what is its scope. He said . . . that there must be not only foreseeability of damage, but there must also exist between the party owing the duty and the party to whom it is owed a relationship characterised by the law as one of 'proximity' or 'neighbourhood', and the situation should be one in which the court considers it fair, just and reasonable that the court should impose a duty of a given scope on one party for the benefit of the other. He added that the concepts both of 'proximity' and 'fairness' were not susceptible of any definition which would make them useful as practical tests, but were little more than labels to attach to features of situations which the law recognised as giving rise to a duty of care. Paradoxically, this passage in Lord Bridge's speech has sometimes come to be treated as a blueprint for deciding cases, despite the pains which the author took to make clear that it was not intended to be any such thing. (at [106])

> ### *Robinson v Chief Constable of West Yorkshire Police*
> Supreme Court [2018] UKSC 4

The claimant, an elderly woman, was knocked to the ground and injured when two police officers attempted to arrest a suspected drug dealer. Her claim for damages was dismissed at trial on the basis that the police had an immunity against claims in negligence. The Court of Appeal rejected her appeal on the grounds that the police generally owe no duty of care to members of the public and that, on the facts, there was no proximity between the parties and it would not be fair, just and reasonable to impose such a duty. Held: the Supreme Court allowed the claimant's appeal and held that the defendants owed and breached a duty of care to the claimant.

LORD REED:

21. The proposition that there is a *Caparo* test which applies to all claims in the modern law of negligence, and that in consequence the court will only impose a duty of care where it considers it fair, just and reasonable to do so on the particular facts, is mistaken. As Lord Toulson JSC pointed out in his landmark judgment in *Michael* v *Chief Constable of Wales* [2015] UKSC 2, para 106, that understanding of the case mistakes the whole point of the *Caparo* case, which was to repudiate the idea that there is a single test which can be applied in all cases in order to determine whether a duty of care exists, and instead to adopt an approach based, in the manner characteristic of the common law, on precedent, and on the development of the law incrementally and by analogy with established authorities.

24. In the *Caparo* case [1990] 2 AC 605, Lord Bridge of Harwich noted that, since the *Anns* case, a series of decisions of the Privy Council and the House of Lords, notably in judgments and speeches delivered by Lord Keith of Kinkel (including his speech in *Hill* v *Chief Constable of West Yorkshire* [1989] AC 53), had emphasised 'the inability of any single general principle to provide a practical test which can be applied to every situation to determine whether a duty of care is owed and, if so, what is its scope': p 617. It is ironic that the immediately following passage in Lord Bridge's speech has been treated as laying down such a test, despite, as Lord Toulson JSC remarked in *Michael's* case, the pains which he took, at pp 617–618, to make clear that it was not intended to be any such thing.

25. . . . It was [the incremental and by analogy] approach, and not a supposed tripartite test, which Lord Bridge then proceeded to apply to the facts before him.

26. Applying the approach adopted in the *Caparo* case, there are many situations in which it has been clearly established that a duty of care is or is not owed: for example, by motorists to other road users, by manufacturers to consumers, by employers to their employees, and by doctors to their patients. As Lord Browne-Wilkinson explained in *Barrett* v *Enfield London Borough Council* [2001] 2 AC 550, 559–560:

> Once the decision is taken that, say, company auditors though liable to shareholders for negligent auditing are not liable to those proposing to invest in the company . . . that decision will apply to all future cases of the same kind.

Where the existence or non-existence of a duty of care has been established, a consideration of justice and reasonableness forms part of the basis on which the law has arrived at the relevant principles. It is therefore unnecessary and inappropriate to reconsider whether the existence of the duty is fair, just and reasonable (subject to the possibility that this court may be invited to depart from an established line of authority). Nor, a fortiori, can justice and reasonableness constitute a basis for discarding established principles and deciding each case according to what the court may regard as its broader merits. Such an approach would be a recipe for inconsistency and uncertainty.

27. It is normally only in a novel type of case, where established principles do not provide an answer, that the courts need to go beyond those principles in order to decide whether a duty of care should be recognised. Following the *Caparo* case, the characteristic approach of the common law in such situations is to develop incrementally and by analogy with established authority. The drawing of an analogy depends on identifying the legally significant features of the situations with which the earlier authorities were concerned. The courts also have to exercise judgement when deciding whether a duty of care should be recognised in a novel type of case. It is the exercise of judgement in those circumstances that involves consideration of what is 'fair, just and reasonable'. As Lord Millett observed in *McFarlane v Tayside Health Board* [2000] 2 AC 59, 108, the court is concerned to maintain the coherence of the law and the avoidance of inappropriate distinctions if injustice is to be avoided in other cases. But it is also 'engaged in a search for justice, and this demands that the dispute be resolved in a way which is fair and reasonable and accords with ordinary notions of what is fit and proper'.

29. Properly understood, the *Caparo* case thus achieves a balance between legal certainty and justice. In the ordinary run of cases, courts consider what has been decided previously and follow the precedents (unless it is necessary to consider whether the precedents should be departed from). In cases where the question whether a duty of care arises has not previously been decided, the courts will consider the closest analogies in the existing law, with a view to maintaining the coherence of the law and the avoidance of inappropriate distinctions. They will also weigh up the reasons for and against imposing liability, in order to decide whether the existence of a duty of care would be just and reasonable. In the present case, however, the court is not required to consider an extension of the law of negligence. All that is required is the application to particular circumstances of established principles governing liability for personal injuries.

Notes

1. *Robinson* is important not only for what it says about duties of care generally but also for what it tells us about duties of care owed by public authorities and by the police in particular. For further discussion of these issues, see Chapter 5.

2. The Supreme Court confirms that, where a case falls within an established duty category, we can determine that a duty of care is owed without appeal to *Caparo* and without asking whether it would fair and just to do so: that question has already been answered in the cases in which the category was established. But it may not always be clear whether a given case does fall within such an established category. Take, for example, *Darnley v Croydon Health Services NHS Trust*. As we have seen, that case involved a claimant who went to hospital with a serious head injury and who was incorrectly told by a receptionist that he would have to wait four to five hours for treatment. The claimant went home rather than wait, where his condition deteriorated. By the time he returned to hospital, it was too late to save him from permanent brain damage. In the Court of Appeal, the case was seen as raising a novel duty question: do hospital receptionists owe a duty of care to patients concerning waiting times? The court concluded, by a majority, that it would not be fair, just and reasonable to do so. On appeal, however, the Supreme Court considered that this was not a novel duty case at all:

   [T]he present case falls squarely within an established category of duty of care. It has long been established that such a duty is owed by those who provide and run a casualty department to persons presenting themselves complaining of illness or injury and before they are treated or received into care in the hospital's wards. The duty is one to take reasonable care not to cause physical injury to the patient. (Lord Lloyd-Jones at [16])

3. **Robinson** is one of a series of recent Supreme Court decisions in which the court has downplayed, or indeed simply rejected, Caparo's three-stage test and has given greater prominence to its incremental and by analogy approach (see too **Michael v Chief Constable of South Wales Police** [2015] UKSC 2 at [102], Darnley at [15], **Poole Borough Council v GN** [2019] UKSC 25 at [64]). Hitherto, the incremental approach had been largely marginalised, even ignored. One reason for this is that it might be thought to operate unjustly. The implication of the incremental approach, as presented by Brennan J, was not simply that the courts can recognise novel duty situations by incremental development from analogous existing categories, but that this is the *only* way novel duty situations should be recognised. But, if this is true, it means that some claimants will lose out simply because there is no existing case sufficiently analogous to theirs. This means novel claims being dismissed not on their merits but simply by virtue of their novelty. As such, it is not surprising that, faced with truly novel claims, the courts had set the incremental approach to one side and endeavoured to 'apply' the three-stage 'test' instead (for a good example of this, see **The Nicholas H**, discussed in section 2.3). So what should we make of the Supreme Court placing greater emphasis on the incremental approach? Neither **Robinson** nor **Darnley** were novel duty cases, so the court did not need to put this approach into action. Nonetheless, from what Lord Reed says in **Robinson**, it is clear that the Supreme Court is not suggesting that truly novel claims fail on their novelty alone. Rather, Lord Reed offers a different understanding of the incremental approach, whereby courts faced with novel claims still have, in the end, to make a judgement of justness and reasonableness. But this judgement is to be made not by straight appeal to high principle but via a consideration of whatever analogous cases we can find (remembering that analogy is a matter of degree) and the more fact-specific considerations these cases identify.

2.2 Reasonable foreseeability

The duty of care might be said to operate on two levels. There is the question of whether, in the class of case in issue, there is a legal duty or not (e.g. whether there is a duty not to make careless statements). There is also the question which arises in every case of negligence of whether *this particular defendant* owes a duty to *this particular claimant*—the 'unforeseeable claimant' problem. That is, while it is clear that the law imposes a general obligation to take care in the given situation, the question is whether, on this particular occasion, there is a sufficient relationship between the defendant and the claimant for that defendant to owe a duty to that claimant.

> ### Bourhill v Young
> House of Lords [1943] AC 92

Mrs Bourhill, who was eight months pregnant, was travelling by tram along Colinton Road in Edinburgh. When she reached her stop, she left the tram and walked round the nearside and front of the tramcar to pick up her fish basket. John Young, a motorcyclist, passed the tram on the nearside, and about 15 metres further on crashed into a car. He sustained injuries from which he died. Young was negligent in that he was travelling too fast. The claimant saw nothing of the cyclist until hearing the noise of the accident. After Young's body had been removed Bourhill approached the site and saw the blood on the road. It was accepted that the claimant had suffered 'nervous shock' as a result of the accident, though there was some dispute as to whether this had contributed to the stillbirth of her child about a month later. Assuming Young would have been liable to the owner of the car into which he crashed, the question for the court was whether he was also liable to Bourhill. The case is relevant for two points: (a) whether the claimant was a foreseeable claimant, and (b) the extent to which psychiatric damage is recoverable (see section 4.2). Held: no duty was owed to the claimant, she was not a foreseeable victim.

LORD RUSSELL: A man is not liable for negligence in the air. The liability only arises 'where there is a duty to take care and where failure in that duty has caused damage': see per Lord Macmillan in *Donoghue* v *Stevenson*. In my opinion, such a duty only arises towards those individuals of whom it may be reasonably anticipated that they will be affected by the act which constitutes the alleged breach.

Can it be said that John Young could reasonably have anticipated that a person, situated as was the appellant, would be affected by his proceeding towards Colinton at the speed at which he was travelling? I think not. His road was clear of pedestrians. The appellant was not within his vision, but was standing behind the solid barrier of the tramcar. His speed in no way endangered her. In these circumstances I am unable to see how he could reasonably anticipate that, if he came into collision with a vehicle coming across the tramcar into Glenlockhart Road, the resultant noise would cause physical injury by shock to a person standing behind the tramcar. In my opinion, he owed no duty to the appellant, and was, therefore, not guilty of any negligence in relation to her. . . .

LORD WRIGHT: My Lords, that damage by mental shock may give a cause of action is now well established and it not disputed in this case, but as Phillimore J pointed out in his admirable judgment in *Dulieu* v *White & Sons* [1901] 2 KB 669, the real difficulty in questions of this kind is to decide whether there has been a wrongful act or breach of duty on the part of the defendant vis-à-vis the plaintiff. That being the prior question, if it is answered against the plaintiff the matter is concluded. I shall, therefore, consider that issue in the first place.

This general concept of reasonable foresight as the criterion of negligence or breach of duty (strict or otherwise) may be criticized as too vague, but negligence is a fluid principle, which has to be applied to the most diverse conditions and problems of human life. It is a concrete, not an abstract, idea. It has to be fitted to the facts of the particular case. Willes J defined it as absence of care according to the circumstances: *Vaughan* v *Taff Vale Ry Co* (1860) 157 ER 1351. It is also always relative to the individual affected. This raises a serious additional difficulty in the cases where it has to be determined, not merely whether the act itself is negligent against someone, but whether it is negligent vis-à-vis the plaintiff. This is a crucial point in cases of nervous shock. Thus, in the present case John Young was certainly negligent in an issue between himself and the owner of the car which he ran into, but it is another question whether he was negligent vis-à-vis the appellant. In such cases terms like 'derivative' and 'original' and 'primary' and 'secondary' have been applied to define and distinguish the type of the negligence. If, however, the appellant has a cause of action it is because of a wrong to herself. She cannot build on a wrong to someone else. Her interest, which was in her own bodily security was of a different order from the interest of the owner of the car. That this is so is also illustrated by cases such as have been called in the United States 'rescue' or 'search' cases. This type has been recently examined and explained in the Court of Appeal in *Haynes* v *Harwood* [1935] 1 KB 146, where the plaintiff, a police constable, was injured in stopping runaway horses in a crowded street in which were many children. His act was due to his mental reaction, whether instinctive or deliberate, to the spectacle of others' peril. Maugham LJ in the Court of Appeal approved the language used by the trial judge, Finaly J ([1934] 2 KB 240, 247), when he held that to leave the horses unattended was a breach of duty not only to any person injured by being run over (in fact, no one was so injured), but also to the constable. Finlay J's words were: 'It seems to me that if horses run away it must be quite obviously contemplated that people are likely to be knocked down. It must also, I think, be contemplated that persons will attempt to stop the horses and try to prevent injury to life or limb.' . . . This again shows how the ambit of the persons affected by negligence or misconduct may extend beyond persons who are actually subject to physical impact . . . There is no dispute about the facts. Upon these facts, can it be said that a duty is made out, and breach of that duty, so that the damage which is found is recoverable? I think not. The appellant was completely outside the range of the collision. She merely heard a noise, which upset her, without her having any definite idea at all. As she said: 'I just got into a pack of nerves and I did not know whether I was going to get it or not.' She saw nothing of the actual accident, or, indeed, any marks of blood until later. I cannot accept that John Young could reasonably have foreseen, or, more correctly, the reasonable hypothetical observer could reasonably have foreseen, the likelihood that anyone placed as the appellant was, could be affected in the manner in which she was. In my opinion, John Young was guilty of no breach of duty to the appellant, and was not in law responsible for the hurt she sustained. I may add that the issue of duty or no duty is, indeed, a question for the court, but it depends on the view taken of the facts. In the present case both courts below have taken the view that the appellant has, on the facts of the case, no redress, and I agree with their view. . . .

LORD PORTER: In the case of a civil action there is no such thing as negligence in the abstract. There must be neglect of the use of care towards a person towards whom the defendant owes the duty of observing care, and I am content to take the statement of Lord Atkin in *Donoghue v Stevenson* [1932] AC 562, 580, as indicating the extent of the duty. 'You must take,' he said, 'reasonable care to avoid acts or omissions which you can reasonably foresee would be likely to injure your neighbour. Who, then, in law is my neighbour? The answer seems to be—persons who are so closely and directly affected by my act that I ought reasonably to have them in contemplation as being so affected when I am directing my mind to the acts or omissions which are called in question.' Is the result of this view that all persons in or near the street down which the negligent driver is progressing are potential victims of his negligence? Though from their position it is quite impossible that any injury should happen to them and though they have no relatives or even friends who might be endangered, is a duty of care to them owed and broken because they might have been but were not in a spot exposed to the errant driving of the peccant car? I cannot think so. The duty is not to the world at large. It must be tested by asking with reference to each several complainant: Was a duty owed to him or her? If no one of them was in such a position that direct physical injury could reasonably be anticipated to them or their relations or friends normally I think no duty would be owed, and if, in addition, no shock was reasonably to be anticipated to them as a result of the defender's negligence, the defender might, indeed, be guilty of actionable negligence to others but not of negligence towards them. In the present case the appellant was never herself in any bodily danger nor reasonably in fear of danger either for herself or others. She was merely a person who, as a result of the action, was emotionally disturbed and rendered physically ill by that emotional disturbance. The question whether emotional disturbance or shock, which a defender ought reasonably to have anticipated as likely to follow from his reckless driving, can ever form the basis of a claim is not in issue.

Notes

1. Foresight of damage (or foreseeability) is a necessary ingredient in all cases of negligence. The claimant must fall within a class of individuals put at *foreseeable risk* by the defendant's action—the defendant does not owe a duty of care to the world at large. Lord Wright continued:

> Does the criterion of reasonable foresight extend beyond people of ordinary health or susceptibility, or does it take into account the peculiar susceptibilities or infirmities of those affected which the defendant neither knew of nor could reasonably be taken to have foreseen? . . . One who suffers from the terrible tendency to bleed on slight contact, which is denoted by the term 'a bleeder,' cannot complain if he mixes with the crowd and suffers severely, perhaps fatally, from being merely brushed against. There is no wrong done there. A blind or deaf man who crosses the traffic on a busy street cannot complain if he is run over by a careful driver who does not know of and could not be expected to observe and guard against the man's infirmity. (***Bourhill*** at 109)

This should be read in light of the decision in *Haley* v *London Electricity Board* [1965] AC 778. The claimant, who was blind, tripped over a hammer which had been placed on the pavement by the defendant to prevent pedestrians from walking along the pavement as they carried out their work. As a result of the fall the claimant became almost totally deaf. The House of Lords, finding for the claimant, held that the defendant's duty to take reasonable care not to act in a way that endangered others extended to all those who might reasonably be expected to walk along the pavement—including blind pedestrians:

> I should have thought with respect that the example of a blind or deaf man run over in the street by a careful driver ignorant of the victim's infirmity is not altogether satisfactory . . . Having regard to the large number of blind persons using the streets in this country, the figure of 107,000 registered blind persons being given, it must be reasonably foreseeable that blind persons will pass along a pavement in the ordinary course using proper precautions for their own safety in so doing . . . In deciding what is reasonably foreseeable one must have regard to common knowledge . . . No doubt there are many places open to the public where for one reason or another one would be surprised to see a blind person walking alone, but a city pavement is not one of them. (Lord Reid at 803–4)

Given this, do you think the facts of ***Bourhill*** would be decided differently today?

2. Many of the early psychiatric harm cases involved miscarriage or stillbirth as a way of demonstrating a physical injury associated with the negligently caused shock prior to the time when there were psychiatric experts available to the courts (see Martha Chamallas and Linda Kerber 'Women, Mothers, and the Law of Fright: A History' (1990) 88 Mich L Rev 814).

3. A good example of the unforeseeable claimant rule is the US cases of *Palsgraf* v *Long Island Railroad Co*, 248 NY 339 (1928). The claimant, Helen Palsgraf, was waiting on a platform for a train to Rockaway Beach. Another train stopped and two men ran to get it, and a guard pushed one of them from behind to help him in. In doing so he dislodged a parcel, which turned out to contain fireworks. The fireworks exploded when they fell, and this was alleged to have upset some scales some distance away which fell upon the claimant. It is unlikely that this fantastic scenario actually occurred, but, even assuming the facts to be true, it was said that while a duty may have been owed to the two men in the train, no duty was owed to the claimant. Cardozo CJ quoted *Pollock on Torts*, saying 'Proof of negligence in the air so to speak will not do.' He pointed out that a claimant must have an original and primary duty owed to her, and not one simply derived from a wrong to someone else, and that the orbit of the danger as disclosed to the eye of reasonable vigilance is the orbit of the duty. 'Negligence, like risk, is thus a term of relation.' In other words, the fact that a duty was owed by the guard to the men he was pushing onto the train, did not necessarily mean that a duty was owed to Palsgraf. She was outside the orbit of the risk, and therefore was an unforeseeable claimant. See further William L Prosser '*Palsgraf* Revisited' (1953) 52 Mich L Rev 1.

4. A more recent example of the unforeseeable claimant rule is *Maguire v Harland and Wolff* [2005] EWCA Civ 1 where the wife of a man who worked for the defendants and who came into contact with asbestos, sued when she contracted mesothelioma as a result of washing (without the aid of a washing machine) his work clothes which had been contaminated. It was held that even though a duty was owed to the husband (who fortunately had not become ill), no duty was owed to the claimant as at the time (in the 1960s) it was not foreseeable that anyone could contract the disease from such low-level exposure to 'secondary' contact with asbestos. Accordingly, she was not a foreseeable claimant.

> ### *Videan v British Transport Commission*
> Court of Appeal [1963] 2 QB 640

North Tawton is a small railway station on the edge of Dartmoor on the ex-London South Western Railway line to Plymouth. On 26 July 1959 the stationmaster, Dennis Videan, was about to embark on a family outing to Exeter when he realised that his son Richard, aged 2, was missing. He was seen sitting on the railway line, and at the same time a motorised trolley, driven by Souness, was approaching. Souness did not see the child until very late, and in an effort to save his son, Videan threw himself in front of the trolley and was killed. His son was saved, but injured. Held: while the son, as a trespasser, was an unforeseeable victim his father was not, and so a duty of care was owed to him.

LORD DENNING MR: I turn now to the widow's claim in respect of the death of her husband. In order to establish it, the widow must prove that Souness owed a duty of care to the stationmaster, that he broke that duty, and that, in consequence of the breach, the stationmaster was killed. Mr Fox-Andrews [counsel for the defendant] says that the widow can prove none of these things. All depends, he says, on the test of foreseeability; and, applying that test, he puts the following dilemma: If Souness could not reasonably be expected to foresee the presence of the child, he could not reasonably be expected to foresee the presence of the father. He could not foresee that a trespasser would be on the line. So how could he be expected to foresee that anyone would be attempting to rescue him? Mr Fox-Andrews points out that, in all the rescue cases that have hitherto come before the courts, such as *Haynes v Harwood & Son* [1935] 1 KB 146, and *Baker v TE Hopkins & Sons Ltd* [1959] 1 WLR 966, the conduct of the defendant was a wrong to the victim or the potential victim. How can he be liable to the rescuer when he is not liable to the rescued?

I cannot accept this view. The right of the rescuer is an independent right and is not derived from that of the victim. The victim may have been guilty of contributory negligence—or his right may be excluded by contractual stipulation—but still the rescuer can sue. So also the victim may, as here, be a trespasser and excluded on that ground, but still the rescuer can sue. Foreseeability is necessary, but not foreseeability of the particular emergency that arose. Suffice it that he ought reasonably to foresee that, if he did not take care, some emergency or other might arise, and that someone or other might be impelled to expose himself to danger in order to effect a rescue. Such is the case here. Souness ought to have anticipated that some emergency or other might arise. His trolley was not like an express train which is heralded by signals and whistles and shouts of 'Keep clear.' His trolley came silently and swiftly upon the unsuspecting quietude of a country station. He should have realised that someone or other might be put in peril if he came too fast or did not keep a proper look-out; and if anyone was put in peril, then someone would come to the rescue. As it happened, it was the stationmaster trying to rescue his child; but it would be the same if it had been a passer-by.

Whoever comes to the rescue, the law should see that he does not suffer for it. It seems to me that, if a person by his fault creates a situation of peril, he must answer for it to any person who attempts to rescue the person who is in danger. He owes a duty to such a person above all others. The rescuer may act instinctively out of humanity or deliberately out of courage. But whichever it is, so long as it is not wanton interference, if the rescuer is killed or injured in the attempt, he can recover damages from the one whose fault has been the cause of it. . . .

PEARSON LJ: I now come to the appeal of the widow, who claims damages for the death of her husband caused, as she contends, by the negligence of Souness acting as the servant of the defendant Commission. It is clear from the evidence and the judge's findings that Souness in his approach to the station was acting negligently in relation to anyone to whom he owed a duty of care, and that the conduct of Souness in this respect caused the accident. The only disputable question is whether Souness owed any relevant duty of care to the deceased. The Commission's argument, evidently accepted by the judge, has been that the position of the rescuer could not be any better than the position of the person rescued, and that, as the infant plaintiff's trespass was unforeseeable, so the act of his father in trying to rescue him was unforeseeable, and therefore both the infant plaintiff and his father were outside the zone of reasonable contemplation and the scope of duty. That would no doubt have been a formidable argument if the deceased had been only a father rescuing his son. But the deceased was the stationmaster, having a general responsibility for dealing with any emergency that might arise at the station. It was foreseeable by Souness that if he drove his vehicle carelessly into the station he might imperil the stationmaster, as the stationmaster might well have some proper occasion for going on the track in the performance of his duties. For this purpose it is not necessary that the particular accident which happened should have been foreseeable. It is enough that it was foreseeable that some situation requiring the stationmaster to go on the line might arise, and if any such situation did arise, a careless approach to the station by Souness with his vehicle would be dangerous to the stationmaster. On that ground I hold that Souness's careless approach to the station was a breach of a duty owing by him to the deceased as stationmaster, and it caused the accident, and consequently the Commission is liable to the widow and her appeal should be allowed.

Notes

1. It is clear that where a defendant's negligence creates a situation where another needs to be rescued, the rescuer will not be an unforeseeable victim. It is foreseeable that when a person puts another (or himself) in a position of peril, someone will attempt a rescue. As US judge Cardozo CJ famously put it: 'Danger invites rescue' (*Wagner* v *International Rly Co*, 232 NY 176 (1921)). So, for example, in *Haynes* v *Harwood* [1935] 1 KB 146, the defendant was found to owe a duty of care to a police officer who was injured attempting to stop runaway horses after a horse van was negligently left unattended and the horses bolted. However, following **White v Chief Constable of South Yorkshire Police** [1998] UKHL 45, the duty owed to rescuers does not extend to cases where their injuries are purely psychiatric. See further discussion in section 4.2.

2. Traditionally the law relating to trespassers has been very strict. Occupiers were simply under an obligation not to deliberately or recklessly cause them harm (*Addie & Sons (Collieries) Ltd* v

Dumbreck [1929] AC 358). This was particularly harsh, especially in relation to young children as noted by Lord Denning MR in **Videan**:

> It has commonly been supposed that the occupier of land owes no duty towards a trespasser to take care for his protection. To make the occupier liable, said Lord Hailsham in *Robert Addie & Sons (Collieries) Ltd v Dumbreck*, 'There must be some act done with the deliberate intention of doing harm to the trespasser, or at least some act done with reckless disregard of the presence of the trespasser'. This rule seems fair enough if you put all trespassers in the same bag as burglars or poachers and treat them all alike. But as soon as you realise that a trespasser may be innocent of any wicked intent—he may be a child too young to do wrong or a grown-up who has lost his way—you find that the rule works most unfairly. Hence the shifts to which generations of judges have been put to escape the rule . . . The true principle is this: In the ordinary way the duty to use reasonable care extends to all persons lawfully on the land, but it does not extend to trespassers, for the simple reason that he cannot ordinarily be expected to foresee the presence of a trespasser. But the circumstances may be such that he ought to foresee even the presence of a trespasser: and then the duty of care extends to the trespasser also. Children's cases afford a good illustration. As I said in *Miller's* case: 'He ought to have children in contemplation if he knows that they are in the vicinity or are likely—then or later—to be attracted to the spot'. . . . [In this case] It could not reasonably be foreseen that a trespasser would be there. Not even a child trespasser could be foreseen, for there is no evidence that children were in the habit of trespassing there at all. . . . [The defendant] could not reasonably be expected to foresee that a child was there . . . I hold, therefore, that the child's claim fails. (at 663–8)

This has now been addressed by the Occupiers' Liability Act 1984 (see further section 10.5).

2.3 Policy

Policy factors have always been present in the formulation of the duty issue but have been variously expressed. Clearly, in determining the level of proximity required to establish a duty, policy elements will be present, often in the form of a desire to prevent a 'flood' of claims. In addition, overt policy arguments can be used to deny liability by determining whether it is 'fair, just and reasonable' that a duty should be imposed. ***Marc Rich & Co AG v Bishop Rock Marine Co Ltd (The Nicholas H)*** [1996] 1 AC 211 and ***McFarlane v Tayside Health Board*** [1999] UKHL 50 are good examples of this approach. Inevitably, there is overlap with other factors considered by the court when establishing whether there is a duty of care, most notably proximity, as was recognised by Lord Kerr in ***Michael v Chief Constable of South Wales Police*** [2015] UKSC 2 (see section 5.2).

LORD KERR:

159. As to what is 'fair, just and reasonable', Lord Browne-Wilkinson in *Barrett* v *Enfield London Borough Council* [2001] 2 AC 550, 559 explained:

> In English law the decision as to whether it is fair, just and reasonable to impose a liability in negligence on a particular class of would-be defendants depends on weighing in the balance the total detriment to the public interest in all cases from holding such class liable in negligence as against the total loss to all would-be plaintiffs if they are not to have a cause of action in respect of the loss they have individually suffered.

160. This passage clearly contemplates that, in deciding what is 'fair, just and reasonable', courts are called on to make judgments that are informed by what they consider to be preponderant policy considerations. Some assessment has to be made of what a judge considers the public interest to be; what detriment would be caused to that interest if liability were held to exist; and what harm would be done to claimants if they are denied a remedy for the loss that they have suffered. These calculations are not conducted according to fixed principle. They will frequently, if not indeed usually, be made without empirical evidence. For the most part, they will be instinctual reactions to any given set of circumstances.

161. Similar value judgments are required for decisions on proximity. In *Alcock v Chief Constable of South Yorkshire Police* [1992] 1 AC 310, 411 Lord Oliver stated that 'the concept of "proximity" is an artificial one which depends more upon the court's perception of what is the reasonable area for the imposition of liability than upon any logical process of analogical deduction'. Again these are value judgments, based essentially on what the court considers to be right for the particular circumstances of the case at the time that the appraisal is being made. It is, I believe, important to be alive to the true nature of these decisions, especially when one comes to consider the precedent value of earlier cases in which such judgments have been made. A decision based on what is considered to be correct legal principle cannot be lightly set aside in subsequent cases where the same legal principle is in play. By contrast, a decision which is not the product of, in the words of Lord Oliver, 'any logical process of analogical deduction' holds less sway, particularly if it does not accord with what the subsequent decision-maker considers to be the correct instinctive reaction to contemporaneous standards and conditions. Put bluntly, what one group of judges felt was the correct policy answer in 2009, should not bind another group of judges, even as little as five years later.

> ### *Marc Rich & Co AG v Bishop Rock Marine Co Ltd (The Nicholas H)*
> House of Lords [1996] 1 AC 211

The *Nicholas H* was on a voyage from Chile to Italy when cracks developed in her hull and she put into San Juan in Puerto Rico. Mr Ducat was employed by NKK, a classification society, whose role is to certify ships as fit for sea for the purposes of insurance. Such societies are independent non-profit-making organisations. Initially, Ducat recommended permanent repairs but the shipowners objected and he was finally persuaded to allow temporary repairs. After the ship put to sea the temporary welds cracked and the ship sank with total loss of the cargo. The contract between the shipowners and the cargo owners incorporated the Hague Rules, an international convention which limited the liability of the shipowners. The claim by the cargo owners against the shipowners was settled for the amount of the limited liability ($500,000), and the cargo owners then sued NKK for the remainder of their loss ($5.7 million) on the assumption that Ducat was negligent in allowing temporary repairs. Held: by majority, Ducat owed no duty of care to the claimants, and so NKK was not liable.

LORD STEYN: . . . The dealings between shipowners and cargo owners are based on a contractual structure, the Hague Rules, and tonnage limitation, on which the insurance of international trade depends: Dr Malcolm Clarke, 'Misdelivery and Time Bars' [1990] LMCLQ 314. Underlying it is the system of double or overlapping insurance of cargo. Cargo owners take out direct insurance in respect of the cargo. Shipowners take out liability risks insurance in respect of breaches of their duties of care in respect of the cargo. The insurance system is structured on the basis that the potential liability of shipowners to cargo owners is limited under the Hague Rules and by virtue of tonnage limitation provisions. And insurance premiums payable by owners obviously reflect such limitations on the shipowners' exposure.

If a duty of care by classification societies to cargo owners is recognised in this case, it must have a substantial impact on international trade. In his article Mr Cane described the likely effect of imposing such duty of care as follows [1994] LMCLQ 363, 375:

> Societies would be forced to buy appropriate liability insurance unless they could bargain with shipowners for an indemnity. To the extent that societies were successful in securing indemnities from shipowners in respect of loss suffered by cargo owners, the limitation of the liability of shipowners to cargo owners under the Hague–Visby Rules would effectively be destroyed. Shipowners would need to increase their insurance cover in respect of losses suffered by cargo owners; but at the same time, cargo owners would still need to insure against losses above the Hague–Visby recovery limit which did not result from actionable negligence on the part of a classification society. At least if classification societies are immune from non-contractual liability, they can confidently go without insurance in respect of third-party losses, leaving third parties to insure themselves in respect of losses for which they could not recover from shipowners.

Counsel for the cargo owners challenged this analysis. On instructions he said that classification societies already carry liability risks insurance. That is no doubt right since classification societies do not have a blanket immunity from all tortious liability. On the other hand, if a duty of care is held to exist in this case, the potential exposure of classification societies to claims by cargo owners will be large. That greater exposure is likely to lead to an increase in the cost to classification societies of obtaining appropriate liability risks insurance. Given their role in maritime trade classification societies are likely to seek to pass on the higher cost to owners. Moreover, it is readily predictable that classification societies will require owners to give appropriate indemnities. Ultimately, shipowners will pay.

The result of a recognition of a duty of care in this case will be to enable cargo owners, or rather their insurers, to disturb the balance created by the Hague Rules and Hague–Visby Rules as well as by tonnage limitation provisions, by enabling cargo owners to recover in tort against a peripheral party to the prejudice of the protection of shipowners under the existing system. For these reasons I would hold that the international trade system tends to militate against the recognition of the claim in tort put forward by the cargo owners against the classification society.

. . .

The position and role of NKK

The fact that a defendant acts for the collective welfare is a matter to be taken into consideration when considering whether it is fair, just and reasonable to impose a duty of care: *Hill* v *Chief Constable of West Yorkshire* [1989] AC 53; *Elguzouli-Daf v Commissioner of Police of the Metropolis* [1995] 2 WLR 173.

Even if such a body has no general immunity from liability in tort, the question may arise whether it owes a duty of care to aggrieved persons, and, if so, in what classes of case, eg only in cases involving the direct infliction of physical harm or on a wider basis.

In *W Angliss and Co (Australia) Proprietary Ltd v Peninsular and Oriental Steam Navigation Co* [1927] 2 KB 456, 462, Wright J (later to become Lord Wright)—a great judge with special expertise in maritime law and practice—described classification societies, such as Lloyd's, as occupying 'a public and quasi-judicial position.' There is a refrain of this idea to be found in Singh & Colinvaux, (*British Shipping Laws*), (1967), vol 13, pp 167–169, paras 391–394, where the editors describe a classification society as an impartial critic and arbiter (as opposed to arbitrator). These observations are helpful but not definitive. Nowadays one would not describe classification societies as carrying on quasi-judicial functions. But it is still the case that (apart from their statutory duties) they act in the public interest. The reality is simply that NKK—and I am deliberately reverting to the evidence about NKK—is an independent and non-profit-making entity, created and operating for the sole purpose of promoting the collective welfare, namely the safety of lives and ships at sea. In common with other classification societies NKK fulfils a role which in its absence would have to be fulfilled by states. And the question is whether NKK, and other classification societies, would be able to carry out their functions as efficiently if they become the ready alternative target of cargo owners, who already have contractual claims against shipowners. In my judgment there must be some apprehension that the classification societies would adopt, to the detriment of their traditional role, a more defensive position.

Policy factors

Counsel for the cargo owners argued that a decision that a duty of care existed in this case would not involve wide ranging exposure for NKK and other classification societies to claims in tort. That is an unrealistic position. If a duty is recognised in this case there is no reason why it should not extend to annual surveys, docking surveys, intermediate surveys, special surveys, boiler surveys, and so forth. And the scale of NKK's potential liability is shown by the fact that NKK conducted an average of 14,500 surveys per year over the last five years.

At present the system of settling cargo claims against shipowners is a relatively simple one. The claims are settled between the two sets of insurers. If the claims are not settled, they are resolved in arbitration or court proceedings. If a duty is held to exist in this case as between the classification society and cargo owners, classification societies would become potential defendants in many cases. An extra layer of insurance would become involved. The settlement process would inevitably become more complicated and expensive. Arbitration proceedings and court proceedings would often involve an additional party. And often similar issues would have to be canvassed in separate proceedings since the classification societies would not be bound by arbitration clauses in the contracts of carriage. If such a duty is recognised, there is a risk that classification societies might be unwilling from time to time to survey the very vessels which most urgently require independent examination. It will also divert men and resources from the prime function of classification societies, namely to save life and ships at sea. These factors are, by themselves, far from decisive. But in an overall assessment of the case they merit consideration.

Is the imposition of a duty of care fair, just and reasonable?

Like Mann LJ in the Court of Appeal [1994] 1 WLR 1071, 1085H, I am willing to assume (without deciding) that there was a sufficient degree of proximity in this case to fulfil that requirement for the existence of a duty of care. The critical question is therefore whether it would be fair, just and reasonable to impose such a duty. For my part I am satisfied that the factors and arguments advanced on behalf of cargo owners are decisively outweighed by the cumulative effect, if a duty is recognised, of the matters discussed in paragraphs [above] ie the outflanking of the bargain between shipowners and cargo owners; the negative effect on the public role of NKK; and the other considerations of policy. By way of summary, I look at the matter from the point of view of the three parties concerned. I conclude that the recognition of a duty would be unfair, unjust and unreasonable as against the shipowners who would ultimately have to bear the cost of holding classification societies liable, such consequence being at variance with the bargain between shipowners and cargo owners based on an internationally agreed contractual structure. It would also be unfair, unjust and unreasonable towards classification societies, notably because they act for the collective welfare and unlike ship-owners they would not have the benefit of any limitation provisions. Looking at the matter from the point of view of cargo owners, the existing system provides them with the protection of the Hague Rules or Hague–Visby Rules. But that protection is limited under such Rules and by tonnage limitation provisions. Under the existing system any shortfall is readily insurable. In my judgment the lesser injustice is done by not recognising a duty of care. It follows that I would reject the primary way in which counsel for the cargo owners put his case.

Notes

1. The decision in **The Nicholas H** is an example of the 'pragmatic' approach the House of Lords had in mind in **Caparo**. In effect, Lord Steyn assumes (without deciding) that there was sufficient proximity and decides the case on the basis of policy considerations, of analysing the reasons for and against the recognition of a duty and deciding whether, on balance, a duty ought to be recognised.

2. There was a vigorous dissent by Lord Lloyd. He argued: (a) that the existence of the Hague Rules in the contract between the shipowners and the cargo owners was irrelevant as it would be nonsense if NKK were liable if the Rules were not incorporated but not liable if they were; further, the Hague Rules are purely a matter between shipowners and cargo owners and have nothing to do with the potential liability of third parties; (b) there was no evidence that, if liable, classification societies would pass on the cost to shipowners; and (c) the fact that classification societies are charitable non-profit-making organisations was irrelevant—he pointed out that hospitals are charitable non-profit-making organisations but are often held liable in tort.

3. The essential point about **The Nicholas H** was that there was a 'self-contained' system whereby everyone knew where they stood. The shipowners and the cargo owners knew the limits of their liability and could avoid the consequences in advance by insuring themselves against their own loss. Accordingly, the principle would not apply to someone outside the system, such as a member of the crew. Compare *Perrett v Collins* [1998] Lloyd's Rep 255, in which the first defendant constructed a light kit plane substituting a different gearbox but failed to change the propeller to suit. The second defendant certified the aircraft as airworthy. It was held that the second defendant owed a duty to the claimant, who was a passenger injured when the plane crashed. **The Nicholas H** was distinguished on the grounds that it does not apply to personal injury cases and a passenger was entitled to rely on careful certification; and the defendant had undertaken a statutory duty for the protection of the public, rather than simply for the purposes of the insurance industry.

4. It seems clear that not all lawyers mean the same thing by 'policy'. For some, 'policy' covers any and every argument that might be offered for or against the imposition of a duty of care. For others, however, 'policy' captures only some of these arguments. We see this where policy is contrasted with 'principle', and those who draw this distinction are more likely to contend that courts should refrain from appeals to policy and decide on the basis of principle alone. Whether this is a sound proposal cannot be assessed until we have some understanding of where the divide between principle and policy lies. But this is a question the courts have, by and large, ignored. What we can say is while the courts readily accept that there are certain *questions* which they should not answer (questions which, e.g., should be left for Parliament), there is little sign that they consider that there are certain arguments, or a certain class of arguments, which they should not consider.

see online resources

For more information go to the **online resources**.

McFarlane v *Tayside Health Board*
House of Lords [1999] UKHL 5

Mr McFarlane had undergone a vasectomy, which he was negligently told was successful. His wife later became pregnant with their fifth child, Catherine. At issue was the extent of a doctor's liability: should the doctor be responsible for the full costs of the child's upkeep or should the parents be expected to bear the financial burden of bringing up a child they had taken positive steps to ensure they would not have. Held: while Mrs McFarlane could claim for the pain and suffering during pregnancy and in giving birth, the parents could not claim for the cost of bringing up the child. It would not be fair, just and reasonable to impose a duty of care in such cases.

LORD STEYN: . . . It is possible to view the case simply from the perspective of corrective justice. It requires somebody who has harmed another without justification to indemnify the other. On this approach the parents' claim for the cost of bringing up Catherine must succeed. But one may also approach the case from the vantage point of distributive justice. It requires a focus on the just distribution of burdens and losses among members of a society. If the matter is approached in this way, it may become relevant to ask commuters on the Underground the following question: Should the parents of an unwanted but healthy child be able to sue the doctor or hospital for compensation equivalent to the cost of bringing up the child for the years of his or her minority, ie until about 18 years? My Lords, I am firmly of the view that an overwhelming number of ordinary men and women would answer the question with an emphatic 'No'. And the reason for such a response would be an inarticulate premise as to what is morally acceptable and what is not. Like Ognall J in *Jones v Berkshire Area Health Authority* (unreported) 2 July 1986 they will have in mind that many couples cannot have children and others have the sorrow and burden of looking after a disabled child. The realisation that compensation for financial loss in respect of the upbringing of a child would necessarily have to discriminate between rich and poor would surely appear unseemly to them. It would also worry them that parents may be put in a position of arguing in court that the unwanted child, which they accepted and care for, is more trouble than it is worth. Instinctively, the traveller on the Underground would consider that the law of tort has no business to provide legal remedies consequent upon the birth of a healthy child, which all of us regard as a valuable and good thing.

My Lords, to explain decisions denying a remedy for the cost of bringing up an unwanted child by saying that there is no loss, no foreseeable loss, no causative link or no ground reasonable restitution is to resort to unrealistic and formalistic propositions which mask the real reasons for the decisions. And judges ought to strive to give the real reasons for their decision. It is my firm conviction that where courts of law have denied a remedy for the cost of bringing up an unwanted child the real reasons have been grounds of distributive justice. That is, of course, a moral theory. It may be objected that the House must act like a court of law and not like a court of morals. That would only be partly right. The court must apply positive law. But judges' sense of the moral answer to a question, or the justice of the case, has been one of the great shaping forces of the common law. What may count in a situation of difficulty and uncertainty is not the subjective view of the judge but what he reasonably believes that the ordinary citizen would regard as right. Two recent illustrations of the relevance of the moral dimension in the development of the law illustrate the point. In *Smith New Court Securities Ltd v Scrimgeour Vickers (Asset Management) Ltd* [1997] AC 254 the House differentiated between the measure of damages for fraudulent and negligent misrepresentation. Pointing out that tort law and morality are inextricably interwoven I said (with the agreement of Lord Keith of Kinkel and Lord

Jauncey of Tullichettle) that as between the fraudster and the innocent party, moral considerations militate in favour of requiring the fraudster to bear the risk of misfortunes directly caused by the fraud: . . . In *Frost [also known as White] v Chief Constable of South Yorkshire Police* [1998] 3 WLR 1509 the police officers claimed compensation for psychiatric loss they sustained as a result of the Hillsborough disaster. By a majority the House ruled against the claim. The principal theme of the judgments of the majority was based on considerations of distributive justice. In separate judgments Lord Hoffmann and I reasoned that it would be morally unacceptable if the law denied a remedy to bereaved relatives as happened in *Alcock v Chief Constable of South Yorkshire Police* [1992] 1 AC 310 but granted it to police officers who were on duty. Lord Hoffmann expressly invoked considerations of distributive justice . . . Lord Browne-Wilkinson and I expressed agreement with this reasoning. In my judgment I observed . . . 'The claim of the police officers on our sympathy, and the justice of their case, is great but not as great as that of others to whom the law denies redress'. That is the language of distributive justice. The truth is that tort law is a mosaic in which the principles of corrective justice and distributive justice are interwoven. And in situations of uncertainty and difficulty a choice sometimes has to be made between the two approaches.

In my view it is legitimate in the present case to take into account considerations of distributive justice. That does not mean that I would decide the case on grounds of public policy. On the contrary, I would avoid those quick sands. Relying on principles of distributive justice I am persuaded that our tort law does not permit parents of a healthy unwanted child to claim the costs of bringing up the child from a health authority or a doctor. If it were necessary to do so, I would say that the claim does not satisfy the requirement of being fair, just and reasonable.

LORD HOPE: . . . There must be a relationship of proximity between the negligence and the loss which is said to have been caused by it and the attachment of liability for the harm must be fair, just and reasonable. The mere fact that it was reasonably foreseeable that the pursuers would have to pay for the costs of rearing their child does not mean that they have incurred a loss of the kind which is recoverable.

In *Candlewood Navigation Corporation Ltd v Mitsui OSK Lines Ltd* [1986] AC 1, 25 Lord Fraser of Tullybelton, delivering the judgment of the Board, said:

> Their Lordships consider that some limit or control mechanism has to be imposed upon the liability of a wrongdoer towards those who have suffered economic damage in consequence of his negligence.

This theme was developed and applied in *Caparo Industries Plc v Dickman* [1990] 2 AC 605. In that case Lord Bridge of Harwich said . . . after referring to a series of cases since *Anns v Merton London Borough Council* [1978] AC 728:

> What emerges is that, in addition to the foreseeability of damage, necessary ingredients in any situation giving rise to a duty of care are that there should exist between the party owing the duty and the party to whom it is owed a relationship characterised by the law as one of 'proximity' or 'neighbourhood' and that the situation should be one in which the court considers it fair, just and reasonable that the law should impose a duty of a given scope upon the one party for the benefit of the other.

Lord Oliver of Aylmerton made the same point in his speech . . . [and] he offered this further guidance:

> . . . 'proximity' in cases such as this is an expression used not necessarily as indicating literally 'closeness' in a physical or metaphorical sense but merely as a convenient label to

describe circumstances from which the law will attribute a duty of care. It has to be borne in mind that the duty of care is inseparable from the damage which the plaintiff claims to have suffered from its breach. It is not a duty to take care in the abstract but a duty to avoid causing to the particular plaintiff damage of the particular kind which he has in fact sustained.

These observations were taken a step further in *Murphy v Brentwood District Council* [1991] 1 AC 398. In the course of his discussion of the relevant principles Lord Oliver said this . . .:

In the straightforward case of the direct infliction of physical injury by the act of the plaintiff there is, indeed, no need to look beyond the foreseeability by the defendant of the result in order to establish that he is in a 'proximate' relationship with the plaintiff. . .. The infliction of physical injury to the person or property of another universally requires to be justified. The causing of economic loss does not. If it is to be categorised as wrongful it is necessary to find some factor beyond the mere occurrence of the loss and the fact that its occurrence could be foreseen. Thus the categorisation of damage as economic serves at least the useful purpose of indicating that something more is required. . . .

. . .

How is one to apply these very general, and necessarily imprecise, principles to the present case? . . .

There must be a relationship of proximity, and the attachment of liability for the harm must be just, fair and reasonable.

I do not wish to place undue emphasis on the fact that the pursuers chose to keep the child. The fact is, as Mrs Smith so ably demonstrated, they had no other choice. The law is not so harsh as to drive parents, in the very difficult situation in which the pursuers found themselves, to the alternatives of abortion or placing for adoption, which, for obvious reasons, they would have found quite unacceptable. Nevertheless they are now bringing the child up within the family. There are benefits in this arrangement as well as costs. In the short term there is the pleasure which a child gives in return for the love and care which she receives during infancy. In the longer term there is the mutual relationship of support and affection which will continue well beyond the ending of the period of her childhood.

In my opinion it would not be fair, just or reasonable, in any assessment of the loss caused by the birth of the child, to leave these benefits out of account. Otherwise the pursuers would be paid far too much. They would be relieved of the cost of rearing the child. They would not be giving anything back to the wrongdoer for the benefits. But the value which is to be attached to these benefits is incalculable. The costs can be calculated but the benefits, which in fairness must be set against them, cannot. The logical conclusion, as a matter of law, is that the costs to the pursuers of meeting their obligations to the child during her childhood are not recoverable as damages. It cannot be established that, overall and in the long run, these costs will exceed the value of the benefits. This is economic loss of a kind which must be held to fall outside the ambit of the duty of care which was owed to the pursuers by the persons who carried out the procedures in the hospital and the laboratory.

Notes

1. **McFarlane** was distinguished by the Court of Appeal in *Parkinson* v *St James Hospital* [2001] 3 All ER 97 which held that where a *disabled* child was born, damages would be awarded to cover the additional costs arising from the disability but not the full maintenance of the child.

2. The issue returned to the House of Lords just four years after **McFarlane** in *Rees* v *Darlington Memorial Hospital NHS Trust* [2003] 4 All ER 987 where the majority of the House of Lords upheld

the decision and principle in **McFarlane** but added a 'gloss' in the form of a modest conventional award (over and above pain and suffering) recognising that the parent has suffered a legal wrong. (In this case the award was £15,000.) Lord Nicholls put it thus:

> Judges of course do not have, and do not claim to have, any special insight into what contemporary society regards as fair and reasonable, although their legal expertise enables them to promote a desirable degree of consistency from one case or type of case to the next, and to avoid other pitfalls. But, however controversial and difficult the subject matter, judges are required to decide the cases brought before the courts. Where necessary, therefore, they must form a view on what are the requirements of fairness and reasonableness in a novel type of case.
>
> In **McFarlane v Tayside Health Board** [2000] 2 AC 59, your Lordships' House held unanimously that a negligent doctor is not required to meet the cost of bringing up a healthy child born in these circumstances. The language, and to some extent the legal reasoning, employed by each of their Lordships differed. But, however expressed, the underlying perception of all their Lordships was that fairness and reasonableness do not require that the damages payable by a negligent doctor should extend so far. The approach usually adopted in measuring recoverable financial loss is not appropriate when the subject of the legal wrong is the birth of an unintended healthy child and the head of claim is the cost of the whole of the child's upbringing.
>
> I have heard nothing in the submissions advanced on the present appeal to persuade me that this decision by the House was wrong and ought to be revisited. On the contrary, that the negligent doctor or, in most cases, the National Health Service should pay all the costs of bringing up the child seems to me a disproportionate response to the doctor's wrong. It would accord ill with the values society attaches to human life and to parenthood. The birth of a child should not be treated as comparable to a parent suffering a personal injury, with the cost of rearing the child being treated as special damages akin to the financially adverse consequences flowing from the onset of a chronic medical condition.
>
> But this is not to say it is fair and reasonable there should be no award at all except in respect of stress and trauma and costs associated with the pregnancy and the birth itself. An award of some amount should be made to recognise that in respect of birth of the child the parent has suffered a legal wrong, a legal wrong having a far-reaching effect on the lives of the parent and any family she may already have. The amount of such an award will inevitably have an arbitrary character. I do not dissent from the sum of £15,000 suggested by my noble and learned friend Lord Bingham of Cornhill in this regard. To this limited extent I agree that your Lordships' House should add a gloss to the decision in **McFarlane v Tayside Health Board** [2000] 2 AC 59. (at [14]–[17])

See further on this issue, Nicky Priaulx *The Harm Paradox: Tort Law and the Unwanted Child in an Era of Choice* (Routledge-Cavendish, 2007) and, on the role played by Lady Hale in the development of this area of law, see Erika Rackley *Women, Judging and the Judiciary: From Difference to Diversity* (Routledge, 2013), pp 180–5.

3. More recently, in *MNX v Khan* [2017] EWHC 2990 (QB) the claimant had consulted her doctor to establish whether she had the faulty gene for haemophilia. Her nephew had the condition (being the aunt of an affected male is an indication of carrier status) and she wished to avoid having a child with haemophilia. Relying solely on the results of a blood test (which only confirmed that the claimant herself was not a haemophilic, and not whether she was a carrier), she was led to believe by her GP that any children she may have would not be affected by haemophilia. Unfortunately, this was not the case. Her son had both haemophilia and—unrelatedly—autism. The claimant argued that had she been referred for the correct testing prior to becoming pregnant she would have been aware of her carrier status and had foetal testing and terminated the pregnancy. The parties agreed that she was entitled to damages in relation to her child's haemophilia (estimated at £1,400,000) and her prolonged pregnancy. But what of his autism? This was

unrelated to his autism. The haemophilia did not cause his autism, though it made the management of it more difficult. Could the claimant, therefore, recover the much larger sum (estimated at £9,000,000) in relation to this? Yip J held that she could:

> 53. As a matter of simple 'but for' causation, FGN would not have been born but for the defendant's negligence. The claimant therefore would not have had a child with the combined problems of haemophilia and autism. Had she known she was a carrier, she would have undergone foetal testing and would then have terminated this particular pregnancy. The other risks associated with that pregnancy would no longer have existed.

Yip J continued:

> 66. Asking whether it was fair, just and reasonable to impose a duty in respect of the autism costs and considering principles of distributive justice may give rise to difficult questions as to where to draw any line. As Lord Steyn said in **McFarlane**, principles of distributive justice: 'require a focus on the just distribution of burdens and losses among members of a society'.
>
> 67. In my view, this is an area where opinions may differ. The distribution of burdens and losses between innocent patients and NHS doctors is generally a controversial topic. The sensitivities of this case perhaps give rise to even more ground for debate. However, I do not accept the defendant's suggestion that imposing liability here would mean that doctors would be under increased pressure to advise in relation to all potential consequences of pregnancy and birth when advising on one particular risk. Nor do I think the defendant's reference to the need for other professionals to purchase cover for coincidental loss is relevant. The rising cost of professional indemnity for general practitioners is a matter of legitimate public concern. However, allowing recovery of the autism costs in this case will not open the floodgates to numerous other claims. The circumstances of this case, with the coexistence of two disabilities, will be rare.

Do you agree?

3

Special duty problems: omissions and acts of third parties

3.1 No general duty for omissions

The common law has long taken the view that it would be too great a burden to impose liability upon people for 'mere' omissions. The law cannot require a person to love his neighbour, but can only ask that they should avoid injuring them, so there is, for example, no liability for failing to prevent someone walking over a cliff (see *Yuen Kun Yeu* v *Attorney General of Hong Kong* [1987] AC 175). The use of the word 'mere' here is a deliberate judicial technique, though as will be seen from the case law, some omissions can result in more than 'mere' consequences (see e.g. **Mitchell v Glasgow City Council** [2009] UKHL 11, or **Michael v Chief Constable of South Wales Police** [2015] UKSC 2).

Even though it is the courts' general position that mere inaction does not give rise to liability, duties in this respect can in fact be imposed by interpreting an omission as a negligent act. Most omissions take place in the context of wider action or activity. Thus, in *Kelly* v *Metropolitan Rly* [1895] 1 QB 944, the claimant was injured in a railway accident where a train was driven into a wall at Baker Street station. The defendants argued that the engine driver had merely omitted to turn off the steam. However, the court found that the driver had committed the positive act of driving the train negligently. There is often a blurred distinction between the two, as illustrated by much of the case law. Indeed, in **Robinson v Chief Constable of West Yorkshire Police** [2018] UKSC 4, Lord Hughes said that there

> . . . is no firm line capable of determination between a case of omission and of commission. . . the great majority of cases can be analysed in terms of either. *Michael* could be said to be a case of omission to respond adequately to the 999 call. But it was argued for the claimant as a case of a series of positive acts, such as, for example, misreporting the complaint when passing it from one police force to another (at [117]).

A duty of care may also be imposed where there is a *pre*-tort relationship between the claimant and the defendant. A duty in respect of omissions can come about either via the defendant 'assuming responsibility', which induces reliance by the claimant, or by reliance which comes out of a relationship of responsibility between the parties (e.g. parent–child (see *Carmarthenshire County Council* v *Lewis* [1955] UKHL 2), teacher–pupil, solicitor–client, and so on). Further, contractual relationships (see *Stansbie* v *Troman* [1948] 2 KB 48 and *Bailey and another* v *HSS Alarms* The Times, 20 June 2000) and some relationships governed by statute (e.g. that between occupiers of premises and their visitors, considered in Chapter 10) may mean that a duty of care arises.

There has been much academic criticism of the rule but its application was clearly restated by the House of Lords in **Stovin v Wise**.

Stovin v Wise
House of Lords [1996] AC 923

The facts and decision in this case are outlined in Chapter 5. The extract below deals specifically with the general issue of liability for omissions.

LORD HOFFMANN:

4. Acts and omissions

The judge made no express mention of the fact that the complaint against the council was not about anything which it had done to make the highway dangerous but about its omission to make it safer. Omissions, like economic loss, are notoriously a category of conduct in which Lord Atkin's generalisation in **Donoghue v Stevenson** [1932] AC 562 offers limited help. In the High Court of Australia in *Hargrave v Goldman* (1963) 110 CLR 40, 66, Windeyer J drew attention to the irony in Lord Atkin's allusion, in formulating his 'neighbour' test, to the parable of the Good Samaritan [1932] AC 562, 580:

> The priest and the Levite, when they saw the wounded man by the road, passed by on the other side. He obviously was a person whom they had in contemplation and who was closely and directly affected by their action. Yet the common law does not require a man to act as the Samaritan did.

A similar point was made by Lord Diplock in **Dorset Yacht Co Ltd v Home Office** [1970] AC 1004, 1060. There are sound reasons why omissions require different treatment from positive conduct. It is one thing for the law to say that a person who undertakes some activity shall take reasonable care not to cause damage to others. It is another thing for the law to require that a person who is doing nothing in particular shall take steps to prevent another from suffering harm from the acts of third parties [like Mrs Wise] or from natural causes. One can put the matter in political, moral or economic terms. In political terms it is less of an invasion of an individual's freedom for the law to require him to consider the safety of others in his actions than to impose upon him a duty to rescue or protect.

A moral version of this point may be called the 'why pick on me?' argument. A duty to prevent harm to others or to render assistance to a person in danger or distress may apply to a large and indeterminate class of people who happen to be able to do something. Why should one be held liable rather than another? In economic terms, the efficient allocation of resources usually requires an activity should bear its own costs. If it benefits from being able to impose some of its costs on other people (what economists call 'externalities,') the market is distorted because the activity appears cheaper than it really is. So liability to pay compensation for loss caused by negligent conduct acts as a deterrent against increasing the cost of the activity to the community and reduces externalities. But there is no similar justification for requiring a person who is not doing anything to spend money on behalf of someone else. Except in special cases (such as marine salvage) English law does not reward someone who voluntarily confers a benefit on another. So there must be some special reason why he should have to put his hand in his pocket.

In *Hargrave v Goldman*, 110 CLR 40, 66, Windeyer J said:

> The trend of judicial development in the law of negligence has been . . . to found a duty to take care either in some task undertaken, or in the ownership, occupation, or use of land or chattels.

There may be a duty to act if one has undertaken to do so or induced a person to rely upon one doing so. Or the ownership or occupation of land may give rise to a duty to take positive steps for the benefit of those who come upon the land and sometimes for the benefit of neighbours. In *Hargrave v Goldman* the High Court of Australia held that the owner and occupier of a 600-acre grazing property in Western Australia had a duty to take reasonable steps to extinguish a fire, which had been started by lightning striking a tree on his land, so as to prevent it from spreading to his neighbour's land. This is a case in which the limited class of persons who owe the duty (neighbours) is easily identified and the political, moral and economic arguments which I have mentioned are countered by the fact that the duties are mutual. One cannot tell where the lightning may strike and it is therefore both fair and efficient to impose upon each landowner a duty to have regard to the interests of his neighbour. In giving the advice of the Privy Council affirming the decision (*Goldman v Hargrave* [1967] 1 AC 645) Lord Wilberforce underlined the exceptional nature of the liability when he pointed out that the question of whether the landowner had acted reasonably should be judged by reference to the resources he actually had at his disposal and not by some general or objective standard. This is quite different from the duty owed by a person who undertakes a positive activity which carries the risk of causing damage to others. If he does not have the resources to take such steps as are objectively reasonable to prevent such damage, he should not undertake that activity at all.

Notes

1. On the general issue see also **Smith v Littlewoods Organisation Ltd** [1987] AC 241 (parts of which are extracted in section 3.3), where Lord Goff stated that 'the common law does not impose liability for what are called pure omissions' (at 271). He also said that the general proposition of there being no duty for omissions may one day need to be reconsidered as it is said to provoke an invidious comparison with affirmative duties of good-neighbourliness in most countries outside the common law orbit. However, if that were to be done there would need to be strict limits on any such affirmative duty (note, in any case, that this was prior to **Stovin v Wise**. Further exploration of the 'good neighbour' point can be seen in Allen Linden 'Toward Tort Liability For Bad Samaritans' (2016) 53 Alberta L Rev 837.

2. In **Stovin v Wise**, Lord Nicholls refers to people who do not go to the aid of others (in the absence of a pre-tort relationship that would impose a duty to do so) as 'callous bystander[s]' (at 931). He says that the law requires there to be something more than just being present—something additional must make it 'fair and reasonable' to impose a positive obligation to assist.

3. Ten years after *Stovin v Wise*, Lord Hoffmann again reiterated the principle that there can be no duty of care in respect of omissions in the context of a case where the British Geological Survey (BGS), agents of the British Government, omitted to test irrigation wells in Bangladesh for the specific presence of arsenic, resulting in many people, including the claimant, being poisoned by arsenic. People 'can only be liable for the things they did . . . not for what they did not do' (*Sutradhar* v *National Environmental Research Council* [2006] UKHL 33 at [27]). The principle has recently been reaffirmed in *Robinson* v *Chief Constable of West Yorkshire Police* [2018] UKSC 4.

3.2 Exceptions to the rule

As indicated earlier, there are some exceptions to the general rule that no duty of care is owed in respect of omissions, largely in the context of a consideration of the pre-tort relationship between claimant and defendant. Duty may be imposed, for example, where a defendant has express responsibility for (or control over) the claimant, or has assumed responsibility for them in some way.

Reeves v Commissioner of Police for the Metropolis
House of Lords [2000] 1 AC 360

The partner of a man who committed suicide while in police custody claimed that the police had owed him a duty of care to prevent him from taking his own life, which they had breached by failing to take reasonable steps to assess him as a suicide risk. The defendants argued that though they owed a duty not to physically harm him, they owed him no duty in respect of his suicide, even though the opportunity only arose from their own carelessness.

LORD HOFFMANN: Morritt LJ [in the Court of Appeal] drew a distinction between a prisoner who was of sound mind and one who was not. He said, at p 190, that when a prisoner was of sound mind, 'I find it hard to see how there is any material increase in the risk in any causative sense.' In *Kirkham v Chief Constable of the Greater Manchester Police* [1990] 2 QB 283, 289–290 Lloyd LJ said much the same. It seems to me, however, they were really saying that the police should not owe a person of sound mind a duty to take reasonable care to prevent him from committing suicide. If he wants to take his life, that is his business. He is a responsible human being and should accept the intended consequences of his acts without blaming anyone else. *Volenti non fit injuria*. The police might owe a general moral duty not to provide any prisoner with the means of committing suicide, whether he is sound mind or not. Such a duty might even be enforceable by disciplinary measures. But the police did not owe Mr Lynch, a person of sound mind, a duty of care so as to enable him or his widow to bring an action in damages for its breach.

My Lords, I can understand this argument, although I do not agree with it. It is not, however, the position taken by the commissioner. He accepts that he owed a duty of care to Mr Lynch to take reasonable care to prevent him from committing suicide. Mr Lynch could not rely on a duty owed to some other hypothetical prisoner who was of unsound mind. The commissioner does not seek to withdraw this concession on the ground that Mr Lynch has been found to have been of sound mind. For my part, I think that the commissioner is right not to make this distinction. The difference between being of sound and unsound mind, while appealing to lawyers who like clear-cut rules, seems to me inadequate to deal with the complexities of human psychology in the context of the stresses caused by imprisonment. The duty, as I have said, is a very unusual one, arising from the complete control which the police or prison authorities have over the prisoner, combined with the special danger of people in prison taking their own lives. (at 368)

Notes

1. See also *Orange* v *Chief Constable of West Yorkshire Police* [2001] EWCA Civ 611, in which it was clarified that the duty is to take reasonable care to assess whether prisoners are a suicide risk. If there is no real reason to believe this, no duty in respect of omissions can arise (later confirmed by the European Court of Human Rights in *Keenan* v *UK* (Application no 27229/95) [2001] ECHR 239).

2. Health authorities also have a duty to protect psychiatric patients detained or voluntarily in their care, including from harming themselves: *Savage* v *South Essex Partnership NHS Trust* [2008] UKHL 74, *Renolde* v *France* (Application no 5608/05) [2008] ECHR 1085. Slightly different issues arise with voluntary inpatients, though in *Rabone* v *Pennine Care NHS Trust* [2012] UKSC 2 the Supreme Court found that the state has an obligation under Article 2 European Convention on Human Rights to protect such patients from suicide, when there was a clear risk.

Barrett v *Ministry of Defence* [1995]
Court of Appeal [1995] 1 WLR 1217

A duty officer on a Norwegian naval base ordered that an extremely drunken naval airman (Barrett) be taken back to his bed. However, he omitted to order that someone should stay to watch over him. Later, Barrett choked to death on his own vomit. Held: the duty officer was liable (and the Ministry of Defence vicariously) for his failure to have someone stay with Barrett. By taking the deceased to his bed, responsibility for his safety had been assumed.

BELDAM LJ: In the present case I would reverse the judge's finding that the defendant was under a duty to take reasonable care to prevent the deceased from abusing alcohol to the extent he did. Until he collapsed, I would hold that the deceased was in law alone responsible for his condition. Thereafter, when the defendant assumed responsibility for him, it accepts that the measures taken fell short of the standard reasonably to be expected. It did not summon medical assistance and its supervision of him was inadequate.

The final question is how far the deceased should be regarded as responsible for his death . . .

The immediate cause of the deceased's death was suffocation due to inhalation of vomit. The amount of alcohol he had consumed not only caused him to vomit, it deprived him of the spontaneous ability to protect his air passages after he had vomited. His fault was therefore a continuing and direct cause of his death. Moreover his lack of self-control in his own interest caused the defendant to have to assume responsibility for him. But for his fault, it would not have had to do so. How far in such circumstances is it just and equitable to regard the deceased as the author of his misfortune? The deceased involved the defendant in a situation in which it had to assume responsibility for his care and I would not regard it as just and equitable in such circumstances to be unduly critical of the defendant's fault. I consider a greater share of blame should rest upon the deceased than on the defendant and I would reduce the amount of the damages recoverable by the plaintiff by two-thirds, holding the defendant one-third to blame. (at 1225–6)

Notes

1. Although the assumption of responsibility in **Barrett v Ministry of Defence** led to a finding that a duty of care was owed in respect of the duty officer's omission and ultimately to a finding of liability, the claimant did not recover in full due to the principle of contributory negligence (discussed in section 9.3).

2. In *Costello v Chief Constable of Northumbria Police* [1999] 1 All ER 550, a female police officer was attacked by a prisoner in a custody cell. A nearby (male) police inspector had heard her screams, but did not come to her aid. For public policy reasons the police (as vicariously liable for the inspector) were found to owe each other a duty of care to come to one another's aid.

3.3 No general duty in respect of third party actions

In a similar way to the law regarding omissions (and indeed there is a great deal of overlap), the common law adheres to the general principle that it is too burdensome on individuals to impose a duty on them in relation to the actions of others (third parties). However, here too there are exceptions, which follow similar ideas to the exceptions to the omissions rule as outlined in section 3.1. Pre-tort relationships are also important here, as are the familiar ideas of control and assumed responsibility. The content, or scope, of the duty is important—often if it can be framed as a duty to prevent a third party acting in a certain way, or to protect some-one against something particular happening, liability may follow. The greater the degree of foreseeability and proximity of relationship, the more likely it is that a duty can be imposed.

> ### Home Office v Dorset Yacht Co Ltd
> House of Lords [1970] UKHL 2

The defendants (for whom the Home Office was vicariously liable) were guards in charge of boys detained in an institution for young offenders on an island off the south coast of England. The guards' negligence allowed some of the boys to escape, later vandalising yachts belonging to the claimant. Held: the supervisory relationship and position of re-sponsibility of the guards, as well as it being highly likely that the boys would try to escape, was enough to establish a duty of care in respect of the actions of the boys.

LORD PEARSON: In my opinion, this case falls under the exception and not the rule, because there was a special relation. The Borstal boys were under the control of the defendants' officers, and con-trol imports responsibility. The boys' interference with the boats appears to have been a direct result of the defendants' officers' failure to exercise proper control and supervision. Problems may arise in other cases as to the responsibility of the defendants' officers for acts done by Borstal boys when they have completed their escape from control and are fully at large and acting independently. No such problem faces the plaintiffs in this case. (at 25)

Notes

1. Compare **Mitchell v Glasgow City Council** [2009] UKHL 11, discussed later in this section, where no such duty was found in the context of a murder, where the city council landlord was aware that its tenant had received death threats from another tenant, whom the council had threatened to evict. Lord Hope said that a 'duty to warn another person that he is at risk of loss, injury or damage as the result of the criminal act of a third party will only arise where the person who is said to be under that duty has by his words or conduct assumed responsibility for the safety of the person who is at risk' (at [29]). See also **Poole Borough Council v GN** [2019] UKSC 25, where the council failed to protect vulnerable children in its housing from the violent harassing actions of a neighbouring family, despite its knowledge of the ongoing situation. The Supreme Court found that the council had no common law duty to protect the children from harm.

2. These cases are also discussed in the context of duties owed by public bodies (Chapter 5): they are examples of cases that illustrate how difficult it is for claimants to establish, even where there is what seems to be a proximate relationship in which some responsibility might be assumed, a duty owed to them by a public body in respect of its mismanagement of a situation which creates an opportunity for third parties to cause harm.

Smith v Littlewoods Organisation Ltd
House of Lords [1987] AC 241

An empty cinema owned by the Littlewoods Organisation started being regularly broken into and damaged. On one occasion a small fire had been started. Contractors employed by Littlewoods knew about the vandalism but Littlewoods did not. One night a fire was deliberately started by vandals inside the cinema, which spread to two other properties. It was alleged that Littlewoods should have prevented the vandals gaining access to the cinema. Held: dismissing the appeal, the defenders were not liable as they were unaware of the earlier acts of vandalism and thus owed no duty to the pursuers.

LORD GOFF: My Lords, the Lord President founded his judgment on the proposition that the defenders, who were both owners and occupiers of the cinema, were under a general duty to take reasonable care for the safety of premises in the neighbourhood.

Now if this proposition is understood as relating to a general duty to take reasonable care *not to cause damage* to premises in the neighbourhood (as I believe that the Lord President intended it to be understood) then it is unexceptionable. But it must not be overlooked that a problem arises when the pursuer is seeking to hold the defender responsible for having failed to *prevent* a third party from causing damage to the pursuer or his property by the third party's own deliberate wrongdoing. In such a case, it is not possible to invoke a general duty of care: for it is well recognised that there is no *general* duty of care to prevent third parties from causing such damage. The point is expressed very clearly in *Hart and Honoré, Causation in the Law*, 2nd ed (1985), when the authors state, at pp 196–197:

> The law might acknowledge a general principle that, whenever the harmful conduct of another is reasonably foreseeable, it is our duty to take precautions against it . . . But, up to now, no legal system has gone so far as this . . .

The same point is made in *Fleming The Law of Torts*, 6th ed (1983), where it is said, at p 200: 'there is certainly no *general* duty to protect others against theft or loss.' I wish to add that no such general duty exists even between those who are neighbours in the sense of being occupiers of adjoining premises. There is no general duty upon a householder that he should act as a watchdog, or that his house should act as a bastion, to protect his neighbour's house . . .

Another statement of principle, which has been much quoted, is the observation of Lord Sumner in *Weld-Blundell v Stephens* [1920] AC 956, when he said, at p 986: 'In general . . . even though A is in fault he is not responsible for injury to C which B, a stranger to him, deliberately chooses to do.' This dictum may be read as expressing the general idea that the voluntary act of another, independent of the defender's fault, is regarded as a novus actus interveniens which, to use the old metaphor, 'breaks the chain of causation.' But it also expresses a general perception that we ought not to be held responsible in law for the deliberate wrongdoing of others. Of course, if a duty of care is imposed to guard against deliberate wrongdoing by others, it can hardly be said that the harmful effects of such wrongdoing are not caused by such breach of duty. We are therefore thrown back to the duty of care. But one thing is clear, and that is that liability in negligence for harm caused by the deliberate wrongdoing of others cannot be founded simply upon foreseeability that the pursuer will suffer loss or damage by reason of such wrongdoing. There is no such general principle. We have therefore to identify the circumstances in which such liability may be imposed.

That there are special circumstances in which a defender may be held responsible in law for injuries suffered by the pursuer through a third party's deliberate wrongdoing is not in doubt. For example, a duty of care may arise from a relationship between the parties, which gives rise to an imposition or assumption of responsibility upon or by the defender, as in *Stansbie v Troman* [1948] 2 KB 48, where such responsibility was held to arise from a contract. In that case a decorator, left alone on the premises by the householder's wife, was held liable when he went out leaving the door on the latch, and a thief entered the house and stole property. Such responsibility might well be held to exist in other cases where there is no contract, as for example where a person left alone in a house has entered as a licensee of the occupier. . . .

These are all special cases. But there is a more general circumstance in which a defender may be held liable in negligence to the pursuer although the immediate cause of the damage suffered by the pursuer is the deliberate wrongdoing of another. This may occur where the defender negligently causes or permits to be created a source of danger, and it is reasonably foreseeable that third parties may interfere with it and, sparking off the danger, thereby cause damage to persons in the position of the pursuer. The classic example of such a case is, perhaps, *Haynes v Harwood* [1935] 1 KB 146, where the defendant's carter left a horse-drawn van unattended in a crowded street, and the horses bolted when a boy threw a stone at them. A police officer who suffered injury in stopping the horses before they injured a woman and children was held to be entitled to recover damages from the defendant. There, of course, the defendant's servant had created a source of danger by leaving his horses unattended in a busy street. Many different things might have caused them to bolt—a sudden noise or movement, for example, or, as happened, the deliberate action of a mischievous boy. But all such events were examples of the very sort of thing which the defendant's servant ought reasonably to have foreseen and to have guarded against by taking appropriate precautions. In such a case, Lord Sumner's dictum (*Weld-Blundell v Stephens* [1920] AC 956, 986) can have no application to exclude liability.

Haynes v Harwood was a case concerned with the creation of a source of danger in a public place. We are concerned in the present case with an allegation that the defenders should be held liable for the consequences of deliberate wrongdoing by others who were trespassers on the defenders' property. In such a case it may be said that the defenders are entitled to use their property as their own and so should not be held liable if, for example, trespassers interfere with dangerous things on their land. But this is, I consider, too sweeping a proposition. It is well established that an occupier of land may be liable to a trespasser who has suffered injury on his land; though in *Herrington v British Railways Board* [1972] AC 877, in which the nature and scope of such liability was reconsidered by your Lordships' House, the standard of care so imposed on occupiers was drawn narrowly so as to take proper account of the rights of occupiers to enjoy the use of their land. It is, in my opinion, consistent with the existence of such liability that an occupier who negligently causes or permits a source of danger to be created on his land, and can reasonably foresee that third parties may trespass on his land and, interfering with the source of danger, may spark it off, thereby causing damage to the person or property of those in the vicinity, should be held liable to such a person for damage so caused to him. It is useful to take the example of a fire hazard, not only because that is the relevant hazard which is alleged to have existed in the present case, but also because of the intrinsically dangerous nature of fire hazards as regards neighbouring property. Let me give an example of circumstances in which an occupier of land might be held liable for damage so caused. Suppose that a person is deputed to buy a substantial quantity of fireworks for a village fireworks display on Guy Fawkes night. He stores them, as usual, in an unlocked garden shed abutting onto a neighbouring house. It is well known that he does this. Mischievous boys from the village enter as trespassers and, playing with the fireworks, cause a serious fire which spreads to and burns down the neighbouring house. Liability might well be imposed in such a case; for, having regard to the dangerous and tempting nature of fireworks, interference by naughty children was the very thing which, in the circumstances, the purchaser of the fireworks ought to have guarded against.

But liability should only be imposed under this principle in cases where the defender has negligently caused or permitted the creation of a source of danger on his land, and where it is foreseeable that third parties may trespass on his land and spark it off, thereby damaging the pursuer or his property. Moreover it is not to be forgotten that, in ordinary households in this country, there are nowadays many things which might be described as possible sources of fire if interfered with by third parties, ranging from matches and firelighters to electric irons and gas cookers and even oil-fired central heating systems. These are commonplaces of modern life; and it would be quite wrong if householders were to be held liable in negligence for acting in a socially acceptable manner. No doubt the question whether liability should be imposed on defenders in a case where a source of danger on his land has been sparked off by the deliberate wrongdoing of a third party is a question to be decided on the facts of each case, and it would, I think, be wrong for your Lordships' House to anticipate the manner in which the law may develop: but I cannot help thinking that cases where liability will be so imposed are likely to be very rare.

There is another basis upon which a defender may be held liable for damage to neighbouring property caused by a fire started on his (the defender's) property by the deliberate wrongdoing of a third party. This arises where he has knowledge or means of knowledge that a third party has created or is creating a risk of fire, or indeed has started a fire, on his premises, and then fails to take such steps as are reasonably open to him (in the limited sense explained by Lord Wilberforce in *Goldman v Hargrave* [1967] 1 AC 645, 663–664) to prevent any such fire from damaging neighbouring property. If, for example, an occupier of property has knowledge, or means of knowledge, that intruders are in the habit of trespassing upon his property and starting fires there, thereby creating a risk that fire may spread to and damage neighbouring property, a duty to take reasonable steps to prevent such damage may be held to fall upon him. He could, for example, take reasonable steps to keep the intruders out. He could also inform the police; or he could warn his neighbours and invite their assistance. If the defender is a person of substantial means, for example a large public company, he might even be expected to employ some agency to keep a watch on the premises. What is reasonably required would, of course, depend on the particular facts of the case. I observe that, in *Goldman v Hargrave*, such liability was held to sound in nuisance; but it is difficult to believe that, in this respect, there can be any material distinction between liability in nuisance and liability in negligence. . . .

I wish to emphasise that I do not think that the problem in these cases can be solved simply through the mechanism of foreseeability. When a duty *is* cast upon a person to take precautions against the wrongdoing of third parties, the ordinary standard of foreseeability applies and so the possibility of such wrongdoing does not have to be very great before liability is imposed. I do not myself subscribe to the opinion that liability for the wrongdoing of others is limited because of the unpredictability of human conduct. So, for example, in *Haynes v Harwood* [1935] 1 KB 146, liability was imposed although it cannot have been at all likely that a small boy would throw a stone at the horses left unattended in the public road; and in *Stansbie v Troman* [1948] 2 KB 48, liability was imposed although it cannot have been at all likely that a thief would take advantage of the fact that the defendant left the door on the latch while he was out. Per contra, there is at present no general duty at common law to prevent persons from harming others by their deliberate wrongdoing, however foreseeable such harm may be if the defender does not take steps to prevent it.

Notes

1. Lord Goff suggests that a duty in respect of third parties' actions can arise in four circumstances: a special relationship either between claimant and defendant or between the defendant and the third party (e.g. a relationship of responsibility or control); creation of a source of danger, or failure to take steps to abate a known danger.

2. In *Stansbie* v *Troman* [1948] 2 KB 48, mentioned in the extract above, a decorator (Stansbie) was working alone in Troman's house. He left, leaving the door unlocked, despite having been specifically asked to lock up. A thief entered the property and stole £334. The decorator was held liable on the basis that he had accepted the duty under their contractual relationship.

3. There have been a number of cases on this problem of liability for the act of a third party. On property damage, see *Lamb* v *Camden Borough Council* [1981] QB 625 and *P Perl (Exporters) Ltd* v *Camden London Borough Council* [1984] QB 342. On potential liability of the police for third party actions, see *Knightley* v *Johns* [1982] 1 WLR 349 and *Swinney* v *Chief Constable of Northumbria Police* [1997] QB 464 and consider the implication of *Commissioner of Police of the Metropolis (Appellant) v DSD and another (Respondents)* [2018] UKSC 11.

4. Problematic questions arise in the context of the release from detention of mentally ill patients, or violent criminals, who go on to harm others. See, for example, *Palmer* v *Tees Health Authority* [1999] 2 LGLR 69 and *K v Secretary of State for the Home Department* [2002] EWCA Civ 775.

Mitchell v Glasgow City Council
House of Lords [2009] UKHL 11

The claimant, a 72-year-old tenant of the council, had complained on multiple occasions about the violent and anti-social behaviour of his neighbour, Drummond, another tenant. The council had warned Drummond about this many times. A further 'serious incident' led them to call him in for a meeting, at which they threatened to evict him. They neither warned Mitchell that this meeting was taking place, nor that he might be at real and serious risk of injury after the meeting had ended. Upon returning home from the meeting, Drummond attacked Mitchell, who later died of his injuries. Held: the council owed Mitchell no duty of care.

LORD HOPE:

27. The assertion that there was a duty to warn is deceptively simple. But the implications of saying that there was a duty to warn in this case are complex and far reaching. This, it may be said, is a clear case where there had been threats to kill and Drummond's behaviour suggested that, if provoked, he might give effect to them. But if there was a duty to warn in this case, must it not follow that there is a duty to warn in every case where a social landlord has reason to suspect that his tenant may react to steps to address his anti-social behaviour by attacking the person or property of anyone he suspects of informing against him? And if social landlords are under such a duty, must social workers and private landlords not be under the same duty too? In this case it is said that the duty was owed to the deceased. But others in the neighbourhood had complained to the defenders about Drummond's behaviour. Was the duty to warn not owed to them also? It is said that there was a duty to keep the deceased informed of the steps that they proposed to take against Drummond, and in particular to warn him that a meeting had been arranged for 31 July. This suggests that the defenders would have had to determine, step by step at each stage, whether or not the actions that they proposed to take in fulfilment of their responsibilities as landlords required a warning to be given, and to whom. And they would have had to defer taking that step until the warning had been received by everyone and an opportunity given for it to be acted on. The more attentive they were to their ordinary duties as landlords the more onerous the duty to warn would become.

28. These problems suggest that to impose a duty to warn, together with the risk that action would be taken against them by anybody who suffered loss, injury or damage if they had received no warning, would deter social landlords from intervening to reduce the incidence of anti-social behaviour. The progress of events in this case shows that the defenders were doing their best to persuade Drummond to stop abusing his neighbours. These attempts might have worked, as no doubt they have done in other cases. Far better that attempts should be made to cure these problems than leave them unsolved or to be dealt with, inevitably after the event, by the police. As in the case of the police, it is desirable too that social landlords, social workers and others who seek to address the many behavioural problems that arise in local authority housing estates and elsewhere, often in very difficult circumstances, should be safeguarded from legal proceedings arising from an alleged failure to warn those who might be at risk of a criminal attack in response to their activities. Such proceedings, whether meritorious or otherwise, would involve them in a great deal of time, trouble and expense which would be more usefully devoted to their primary functions in their respective capacities: see Lord Brown of Eaton-under-Heywood's observations in *Van Colle v Chief Constable of the Hertfordshire Police* [2008] 3 WLR 593, para 133. There are other considerations too. Defensive measures against the risk of legal proceedings would be likely to create a practice of giving warnings as a matter of routine. Many of them would be for no good purpose, while others would risk causing undue alarm or reveal the taking of steps that would be best kept confidential.

29. As I have already noted, in *Caparo Industries plc v Dickman* [1989] QB 653, 703, Taylor LJ summed the matter up by saying that fairness and public policy were the tests. Public policy was at the root of the decision in *Hill v Chief Constable of West Yorkshire* [1989] AC 53 about the scope of the duty owed by the police which the House followed in *Brooks v Commissioner of Police of the Metropolis* [2005] UKHL 24; [2005] 1 WLR 1495 and again in *Smith v Chief Constable of Sussex Police*: see *Van Colle v Chief Constable of the Hertfordshire Police* [2008] 3 WLR 593. I would take the same approach to this case. The situation would have been different if there had been a basis for saying that the defenders had assumed a responsibility to advise the deceased of the steps that they were taking, or in some other way had induced the deceased to rely on them to do so. It would then have been possible to say not only that there was a relationship of proximity but that a duty to warn

was within the scope of that relationship. But it is not suggested in this case that this ever happened, and Mr McEachran very properly accepted that he could not present his argument on this basis. I would conclude therefore that it would not be fair, just or reasonable to hold that the defenders were under a duty to warn the deceased of the steps that they were taking, and that the common law case that is made against them is irrelevant. I would also hold, as a general rule, that a duty to warn another person that he is at risk of loss, injury or damage as the result of the criminal act of a third party will arise only where the person who is said to be under that duty has by his words or conduct assumed responsibility for the safety of the person who is at risk.

Notes

1. See also *X & Y v London Borough of Hounslow* [2009] EWCA Civ 286. Compare *Selwood v Durham County Council and others* [2012] EWCA Civ 979, where the council was found to have owed a duty of care to a social worker, who was stabbed by a psychiatric patient at a case conference. He had previously repeatedly threatened to kill her, but she had not been warned of this fact.

2. In **Michael v Chief Constable of South Wales Police** [2015] UKSC 2 (extracted and discussed in section 5.2), the assumption of responsibility argument was rejected, in the context of a woman murdered by her ex-boyfriend. She had called 999 following threats by the man and a physical attack on her then boyfriend, had been heard to scream, and been given assurances the police would attend. Despite her reliance on the police operator's statements, the police were found not to have assumed responsibility and to have owed her no duty of care (though the Supreme Court Justices unanimously refused to strike out the human rights claim against the police).

4

Special duty problems: psychiatric harm

When can a person who has suffered psychiatric injury as a result of the act of the defendant claim in negligence? Initially, a claimant could only succeed if they were also within the range of physical impact (*Dulieu* v *White* [1901] 2 KB 669). In other words, only the 'primary' victim could sue; that is, the person who would foreseeably suffer physical damage. Liability was later extended to 'secondary' victims; that is, where the claimant was not at risk of physical injury, but saw or heard the accident which caused the shock with his or her own unaided senses (*Hambrook* v *Stokes* [1925] 1 KB 141). Later still, in ***Bourhill*** v ***Young*** [1943] AC 92, the appropriate test became foreseeability of injury by shock, but this leaves open the question as to when this is foreseeable. It is suggested that the courts in effect created 'sub-rules' or guidelines which indicated the kind of case where proximity in the legal sense would exist. In ***Alcock*** v ***Chief Constable of South Yorkshire Police*** [1992] 1 AC 310, a compromise position seems to have been adopted whereby the test is one of 'foresight' but one where foresight has a coded meaning. Thus, where the claimant has suffered psychiatric damage, the test of proximity required to establish a duty of care is foresight, as determined in light of the relevant guidelines.

But why should there be special rules at all? Why is negligently caused psychiatric injury treated differently to similarly caused physical injury? The first thing to note is that these rules only apply in relation to 'pure' psychiatric injuries, that is where the claimant *only* suffers psychiatric injury. Where the claimant receives such injuries as a result of physical injuries negligently inflicted by the defendant, recovery is straightforward (*Corr* v *IBC Vehicles Ltd* [2006] EWCA Civ 331). The key arguments for restricting compensation in relation to negligently inflicted psychiatric harm were summarised by Lord Steyn in ***White*** v ***Chief Constable of South Yorkshire Police*** (the facts and decision in ***White*** are extracted in section 4.3).

> ***White* v *Chief Constable of South Yorkshire Police***
> House of Lords [1998] UKHL 45

LORD STEYN:

Policy Considerations and Psychiatric Harm

Policy considerations have undoubtedly played a role in shaping the law governing recovery for pure psychiatric harm. The common law imposes different rules for the recovery of compensation for physical injury and psychiatric harm. Thus it is settled law that bystanders at tragic events, even if they suffer foreseeable psychiatric harm, are not entitled to recover damages: *Alcock v Chief Constable of South Yorkshire Police* [1992] 1 AC 310. The courts have regarded the policy reasons against admitting such claims as compelling.

It seems to me useful to ask why such different rules have been created for the recovery of the two kinds of damage. In his *Casebook on Tort*, 7th ed, Weir gives the following account (at 88):

> . . . there is equally no doubt that the public . . . draws a distinction between the neurotic and the cripple, between the man who loses his concentration and the man who loses his leg. It is widely felt that being frightened is less than being struck, that trauma to the mind is less than lesion to the body. Many people would consequently say that the duty to avoid injuring strangers is greater than the duty not to upset them. The law has reflected this distinction as one would expect, not only by refusing damages for grief altogether, but by granting recovery for other psychical harm only late and grudgingly, and then only in very clear cases. In tort, clear means close—close to the victim, close to the accident, close to the defendant.

I do not doubt that public perception has played a substantial role in the development of this branch of the law. But nowadays we must accept the medical reality that psychiatric harm may be more serious than physical harm. It is therefore necessary to consider whether there are other objective policy considerations which may justify different rules for the recovery of compensation for physical injury and psychiatric harm. And in my view it would be insufficient to proceed on the basis that there are unspecified policy considerations at stake. If, as I believe, there are such policy considerations it is necessary to explain what the policy considerations are so that the validity of my assumptions can be critically examined by others.

My impression is that there are at least four distinctive features of claims for psychiatric harm which in combination may account for the differential treatment. Firstly, there is the complexity of drawing the line between acute grief and psychiatric harm: see Hedley, Nervous Shock: Wider Still and Wider, 1997 CLJ 254. The symptoms may be the same. But there is greater diagnostic uncertainty in psychiatric injury cases than in physical injury cases. The classification of emotional injury is often controversial. In order to establish psychiatric harm expert evidence is required. That involves the calling of consultant psychiatrists on both sides. It is a costly and time consuming exercise. If claims for psychiatric harm were to be treated as generally on a par with physical injury it would have implications for the administration of justice. On its own this factor may not be entitled to great weight and may not outweigh the considerations of justice supporting genuine claims in respect of pure psychiatric injury. Secondly, there is the effect of the expansion of the availability of compensation on potential claimants who have witnessed gruesome events. I do not have in mind fraudulent or bogus claims. In general it ought to be possible for the administration of justice to expose such claims. But I do have in mind the *unconscious* effect of the prospect of compensation on potential claimants. Where there is generally no prospect of recovery, such as in the case of injuries sustained in sport, psychiatric harm appears not to obtrude often. On the other hand, in the case of industrial accidents, where there is often a prospect of recovery of compensation, psychiatric harm is repeatedly encountered and often endures until the process of claiming compensation comes to an end: see *James v Woodall Duckham Construction Co Ltd* [1969] 1 WLR 903 (CA). The litigation is sometimes an unconscious disincentive to rehabilitation. It is true that this factor is already present in cases of physical injuries with concomitant mental suffering. But it may play a larger role in cases of pure psychiatric harm, particularly if the categories of potential recovery are enlarged. For my part this factor cannot be dismissed.

The third factor is important. The abolition or a relaxation of the special rules governing the recovery of damages for psychiatric harm would greatly increase the class of persons who can recover damages in tort. It is true that compensation is routinely awarded for psychiatric harm where the plaintiff has suffered some physical harm. It is also well established that psychiatric harm resulting from the apprehension of physical harm is enough: *Page v Smith* [1996] AC 155. These two principles are not surprising. In built in such situations are restrictions on the classes of plaintiff who can sue: the requirement of the infliction of some physical injury or apprehension of it introduces an element of immediacy which restricts the category of potential plaintiffs. But in cases of pure psychiatric harm there is potentially a wide class of plaintiffs involved. Fourthly, the imposition of liability for pure psychiatric harm in a wide range of situations may result in a burden of liability on defendants which may be disproportionate to tortious conduct involving perhaps momentary lapses of concentration, eg in a motor car accident.

The wide scope of potential liability for pure psychiatric harm is not only illustrated by the rather unique events of Hillsborough but also by accidents involving trains, coaches and buses, and the everyday occurrence of serious collisions of vehicles all of which may result in gruesome scenes. In such cases there may be many claims for psychiatric harm by those who have witnessed and in some ways assisted at the scenes of the tragic events. Moreover, protagonists of very wide theories of liability for pure psychiatric loss have suggested that 'workplace claims loom large as the next growth area of psychiatric injury law', the paradigm case being no doubt a workman who has witnessed a tragic accident to an employee . . .

Notes

1. **White** is one of many cases arising from the Hillsborough Stadium disaster in 1989. Ninety-six people died and over 400 people were injured as a result of overcrowding at the Hillsborough Stadium at the FA Cup semi-final between Liverpool and Nottingham Forest football clubs. In 2016, an inquest ruled that they were unlawfully killed and a catalogue of failings by police and the ambulance services contributed to their deaths (**David Conn 'Hillsborough inquests jury rules 96 victims were unlawfully killed' *The Guardian* 26 April 2016**).

2. As Lord Steyn noted in **White**, 'the law [of negligence] cannot compensate for all emotional suffering even if it is acute and truly debilitating' (at 491). The claimant (whether a primary or secondary victim) must, therefore, be suffering from a recognisable psychiatric illness—mere grief and sorrow (*Hinz v Berry* [1970] 1 All ER 1084), or anxiety (*Rothwell v Chemical and Insulating Co Ltd* [2007] UKHL 39) is not enough.

see online resources

3. Despite eye-catching headlines suggesting that the court had removed the need for claimants to have suffered a recognisable psychiatric illness, the Supreme Court of Canada in *Saadati v Moorhead* [2017] 1 SCR 543 confined its reasoning to the much narrower basis that the claimant need not *adduce expert evidence or other proof* that they are suffering from a recognisable psychiatric illness. It also reaffirmed that in order to be recoverable the psychiatric injury must 'transcend ordinary emotional upset or distress'. Recognising that mental injury is often not as 'readily determinable' as physical injury (at [37]) and medical evidence may assist in determining it (at [38]), Brown J also noted that 'no cogent basis has been offered to this Court for erecting distinct rules which operate to preclude liability in cases of mental injury, but not in cases of physical injury' (at [35]):

36. It follows that requiring claimants who allege one form of personal injury (mental) to prove that their condition meets the threshold of 'recognizable psychiatric illness', while not imposing a corresponding requirement upon claimants alleging another form of personal injury (physical) to show that their condition carries a certain classificatory label, is inconsistent with prior statements of this Court, among others. It accords unequal—that is, less—protection to victims of mental injury. And it does so for no principled reason (Beever [Allan *Rediscovering the Law of Negligence* (Hart, 2007)], at p. 410). I would not endorse it.

4.1 Primary victims

If a person has or might foreseeably have suffered physical damage, the question is whether a duty must be shown to have existed in relation to the psychiatric damage separate from the duty owed in relation to the physical damage or whether it is sufficient that if the duty can be shown to exist in relation to actual or potential physical damage, then damages for psychiatric injury can also be recovered. In *Dulieu* v *White* [1901] 2 KB 669, the court allowed recovery for the claimant when a horse van burst into the pub where she was working, even though she suffered no actual physical injury but was in the range of potential impact. This was affirmed in *Page* v *Smith*.

Page v *Smith*
House of Lords [1996] 1 AC 155

The claimant was involved in a car accident negligently caused by the defendant. Although the claimant was physically unhurt, the accident caused him to suffer a revival of a psychiatric injury which he had suffered from some years before. The Court of Appeal held that the defendant was not liable as the illness was not foreseeable independently from the potential physical injury. Held: allowing the appeal, that the defendant was liable for the psychiatric illness.

LORD LLOYD:

Introduction

This is the fourth occasion on which the House has been called on to consider 'nervous shock'. On the three previous occasions, *Bourhill v Young* [1943] AC 92, *McLoughlin v O'Brian* [1983] AC 410 and *Alcock v Chief Constable of South Yorkshire Police* [1992] 1 AC 310, the plaintiffs were, in each case, outside the range of foreseeable physical injury.

In all these cases the plaintiff was the secondary victim of the defendant's negligence. He or she was in the position of a spectator or bystander. In the present case, by contrast, the plaintiff was a participant. He was himself directly involved in the accident, and well within the range of foreseeable physical injury. He was the primary victim. This is thus the first occasion on which your Lordships have had to decide whether, in such a case, the foreseeability of physical injury is enough to enable the plaintiff to recover damages for nervous shock.

The factual distinction between primary and secondary victims of an accident is obvious and of long-standing. It was recognised by Lord Russell of Killowen in *Bourhill v Young*, when he pointed out that Mrs Bourhill was not physically involved in the collision . . . In [*Alcock*] Lord Oliver of Aylmerton said . . . of cases in which damages are claimed for nervous shock:

Broadly they divide into two categories, that is to say, those cases in which the injured plaintiff was involved, either mediately, or immediately, as a participant, and those in which the plaintiff was no more than the passive and unwilling witness of injury caused to others.

Later in the same speech . . . he referred to those who are involved in an accident as the primary victims, and to those who are not directly involved, but who suffer from what they see or hear, as the secondary victims. This is, in my opinion, the most convenient and appropriate terminology.

. . .

The correct approach

. . . Otton J [at first instance] adopted the same line of reasoning:

Once it is established that CFS exists and that a relapse or recrudescence can be triggered by the trauma of an accident and that nervous shock was suffered by the plaintiff who is actually involved in the accident, it becomes a foreseeable consequence. The nervous shock cases relied on by Mr Priest, in my judgment, have no relevance. The plaintiff was not a spectator of the accident who suffered shock from what he witnessed happening to another. He was directly involved and suffered the shock directly from experiencing the accident. The remoteness argument, therefore, must be rejected.

Since physical injury to the plaintiff was clearly foreseeable, although it did not in the event occur, the judge did not consider, as a separate question, whether the defendant should have foreseen injury by nervous shock.

. . .

If as *in Malcolm v Broadhurst* [1970] 3 All ER 508, the plaintiff had suffered a head injury or a broken leg, or significant bruising, with consequential psychiatric illness, it is very doubtful whether the case would ever have reached the Court of Appeal at all. It would be like many other personal injury cases which are tried or settled every day in the High Court and the County Courts. Of course, it would have been necessary to prove that the psychiatric illness was genuine, and that it was caused by the accident. But nobody would have stopped to consider the foreseeability of nervous [shock]. Nobody would have referred to *Bourhill v Young* [1943] AC 92. We now know that the plaintiff escaped without external injury. Can it be the law that this makes all the difference? Can it be the law that the fortuitous absence of foreseeable physical injury means that a different test has to be applied? Is it to become necessary, in ordinary personal injury claims, where the plaintiff is the primary victim, for the court to concern itself with different 'kinds' of injury?

Suppose, in the present case, the plaintiff had been accompanied by his wife, just recovering from a depressive illness, and that she had suffered a cracked rib, followed by an onset of psychiatric illness. Clearly, she would have recovered damages, including damages for her illness, since it is conceded that the defendant owed the occupants of the car a duty not to cause physical harm. Why should it be necessary to ask a different question, or apply a different test, in the case of the plaintiff? Why should it make any difference that the physical illness that the plaintiff undoubtedly suffered as a result of the accident operated through the medium of the mind, or of the nervous system, without physical injury? If he had suffered a heart attack, it cannot be doubted that he would have recovered damages for pain and suffering, even though he suffered no broken bones. It would have been no answer that he had a weak heart.

. . .

Foreseeability of psychiatric injury remains a crucial ingredient when the plaintiff is the secondary victim, for the very reason that the secondary victim is almost always outside the area of physical impact, and therefore outside the range of foreseeable physical injury. But where the plaintiff is the primary victim of the defendant's negligence, the nervous shock cases, by which I mean the cases following on from *Bourhill v Young*, are not in point. Since the defendant was admittedly under a duty of care not to cause the plaintiff foreseeable physical injury, it was unnecessary to ask whether he was under a *separate* duty of care not to cause foreseeable psychiatric injury.

. . .

In an age when medical knowledge is expanding fast, and psychiatric knowledge with it, it would not be sensible to commit the law to a distinction between physical and psychiatric injury, which may already seem somewhat artificial, and may soon be altogether outmoded. Nothing will be gained by treating them as different 'kinds' of personal injury, so as to require the application of different tests in law.

. . .

Are there any disadvantages in taking the simple approach adopted by Otton J? It may be said that it would open the door too wide, and encourage bogus claims. As for opening the door, this is a very important consideration in claims by secondary victims. It is for this reason that the courts have, as a matter of policy, rightly insisted on a number of control mechanisms. Otherwise, a negligent defendant might find himself being made liable to all the world. Thus in the case of secondary victims, foreseeability of injury by shock is not enough. The law also requires a degree of proximity: see *Alcock's* case [1992] 1 AC 310 *per* Lord Keith of Kinkel, at p 396 . . . This means not only proximity to the event in time and space, but also proximity of relationship between the primary victim and the secondary victim. A further control mechanism is that the secondary victim will only recover damages for nervous shock if the defendant should have foreseen injury by shock to a person of normal fortitude or 'ordinary phlegm'.

None of these mechanisms are required in the case of a primary victim. Since liability depends on foreseeability of physical injury, there could be no question of the defendant finding himself liable to all the world. Proximity of relationship cannot arise, and proximity in time and space goes without saying.

Nor in the case of a primary victim is it appropriate to ask whether he is a person of 'ordinary phlegm.' In the case of physical injury there is no such requirement. The negligent defendant, or more usually his insurer, takes his victim as he finds him. The same should apply in the case of psychiatric injury. There is no difference in principle, as Geoffrey Lane J pointed out in *Malcolm v Broadhurst* [1970] 3 All ER 508, between an eggshell skull and an eggshell personality. Since the number of potential claimants is limited by the nature of the case, there is no need to impose any further limit by reference to a person of ordinary phlegm. Nor can I see any justification for doing so.

As for bogus claims, it is sometimes said that if the law were such as I believe it to be, the plaintiff would be able to recover damages for a fright. This is not so. Shock by itself is not the subject of compensation, any more than fear or grief or any other human emotion occasioned by the defendant's negligent conduct. It is only when shock is followed by recognisable psychiatric illness that the defendant may be held liable.

There is another limiting factor. Before a defendant can be held liable for psychiatric injury suffered by a primary victim, he must at least have foreseen the risk of physical injury. So that if, to take the example given by my noble and learned friend, Lord Jauncey of Tullichettle, the defendant bumped his neighbour's car while parking in the street, in circumstances in which he could not reasonably foresee that the occupant would suffer any physical injury at all, or suffer injury so trivial as not to found an action in tort, there could be no question of his being held liable for the onset of hysteria. Since he could not reasonably foresee any injury, physical or psychiatric, he would owe the plaintiff no duty of care. That example is, however, very far removed from the present.

So I do not foresee any great increase in unmeritorious claims. The court will, as ever, have to be vigilant to discern genuine shock resulting in recognised psychiatric illness. But there is nothing new in that. The floodgates argument has made regular appearances in this field, ever since it first appeared in *Victorian Railways Commissioners v Coultas* (1888) 13 App Cas 222. I do not regard it as a serious obstacle here.

My provisional conclusion, therefore, is that Otton J's approach was correct. The test in every case ought to be whether the defendant can reasonably foresee that his conduct will expose the plaintiff to risk of personal injury. If so, then he comes under a duty of care to that plaintiff. If a working definition of 'personal injury' is needed, it can be found in section 38(1) of the Limitation Act 1980: '"personal injuries" includes any disease and any impairment of a person's physical or mental condition . . .' There are numerous other statutory definitions to the same effect. In the case of a secondary victim, the question will usually turn on whether the foreseeable injury is psychiatric, for the reasons already explained. In the case of a primary victim the question will almost always turn on whether the foreseeable injury is physical. But it is the same test in both cases, with different applications. There is no justification for regarding physical and psychiatric injury as different 'kinds' of injury. Once it is established that the defendant is under a duty of care to avoid causing personal injury to the plaintiff, it matters not whether the injury in fact sustained is physical, psychiatric or both. The utility of a single test is most apparent in those cases such as *Schneider v Eisovitch* [1960] QB 430, *Malcolm v Broadhurst* [1970] 3 All ER 508 and *Brice v Brown* [1984] 1 All ER 997, where the plaintiff is both primary and secondary victim of the same accident.

Applying that test in the present case, it was enough to ask whether the defendant should have reasonably foreseen that the plaintiff might suffer physical injury as a result of the defendant's negligence, so as to bring him within the range of the defendant's duty of care. It was unnecessary to ask, as a separate question, whether the defendant should reasonably have foreseen injury by shock; and it is irrelevant that the plaintiff did not, in fact, suffer any external physical injury.

. . .

In conclusion, the following propositions can be supported. **1.** In cases involving nervous shock, it is essential to distinguish between the primary victim and secondary victims. **2.** In claims by secondary victims the law insists on certain control mechanisms, in order as a matter of policy to limit the number of potential claimants. Thus, the defendant will not be liable unless psychiatric injury is foreseeable in a person of normal fortitude. These control mechanisms have no place where the plaintiff is the primary victim. **3.** In claims by secondary victims, it may be legitimate to use hindsight in order to be able to apply the test of reasonable foreseeability at all. Hindsight, however, has no part to play where the plaintiff is the primary victim. **4.** Subject to the above qualifications, the approach in all cases should be the same, namely, whether the defendant can reasonably foresee that his conduct will expose the plaintiff to the risk of personal injury, whether physical or psychiatric. If the answer is yes, then the duty of care is established, even though physical injury does not, in fact, occur. There is no justification for regarding physical and psychiatric injury as different 'kinds of damage'. **5.** A defendant who is under a duty of care to the plaintiff, whether as primary or secondary victim, is not liable for damages for nervous shock unless the shock results in some recognised psychiatric illness. It is no answer that the plaintiff was predisposed to psychiatric illness. Nor is it relevant that the illness takes a rare form or is of unusual severity. The defendant must take his victim as he finds him.

Notes

1. The claimant in *Page* spent a long time in court. The accident occurred in July 1987 and he finally succeeded in March 1996 after ten judgments had been delivered in the case (see *Page v Smith (No 2)* [1996] 1 WLR 855).

2. *Page* establishes that where the claimant is in the zone of physical danger they are able to recover for psychiatric harm notwithstanding the fact that (a) no physical harm is in fact suffered and (b) the psychiatric injury itself is not reasonably foreseeable. The majority argued that there was no distinction between direct physical injury and psychiatric illness—they were the same 'kind of damage'—and so all that needed to be foreseen was one or the other.

3. In dissent, Lord Keith argued that the defendant should only be liable if the hypothetical reasonable man in his position should have foreseen that the claimant, regarded as a man of normal fortitude, might suffer nervous shock leading to an identifiable illness. He thought that, on the facts of *Page*, nervous shock was not foreseeable and the fact that the claimant might have suffered direct personal injury was irrelevant. Similarly, Lord Jauncey, also in dissent, noted that there should be foreseeability of the kind of damage that actually occurred, not that which *might* have occurred.

4. The case also raises difficulties in relation to duty of care and remoteness. It might be thought that if a different level of proximity is required in relation to different interests, then where two such interests arise out of one event the requisite level of proximity should be established in relation to each interest. However, the House of Lords in *Page* said this is not the case. This could cause injustice as between a claimant who happens to be a foreseeable claimant in relation to some damage (which did not actually occur) and one who is not. This is the kind of thing *Overseas Tankship (UK) Ltd v Morts Dock and Engineering Co (The Wagon Mound) (No 1)* [1961] AC 388 was supposed to prevent. This criticism was also voiced by Lord Goff in *White v Chief Constable of South Yorkshire Police*, where he pointed out that in *The Wagon Mound (No 1)* a 'common sense' distinction had been made between damage by fire and other possible damage and it would equally be a matter of common sense to say that physical injury was different from psychiatric injury. Accordingly, Lord Goff criticises *Page* for abandoning foresight of psychiatric damage as a necessary requirement and the unifying link in all such cases.

5. Indeed, one consequence of *Page* is that psychiatric injury following physical injury will rarely be too remote. In *Simmons v British Steel* [2004] UKHL 20, the pursuer fell and banged his head. The impact was severe, but as the claimant was wearing protective headgear the injury was not as serious as it could have been. Alongside headaches and blurred vision, the claimant also experienced an exacerbation of a pre-existing skin condition, and developed a change in his personality which resulted in a severe depressive illness (he had not returned to work since the accident). The employer was held liable for all the consequences of the injury. Lord Rodger said:

> Since the pursuer in the present case actually suffered physical injuries as a result of the defenders' fault and negligence, the starting point is that he is a primary victim in terms of Lord Lloyd's classification. Mr Smith argued [counsel for the defendant], however, that the pursuer's psoriasis and his depressive illness sprang not from the accident itself, but from his anger at the happening of the accident. Hence he could not recover damages. I see no reason to give effect to such a distinction, even supposing that it can be realistically drawn in a given case. Regret, fear for the future, frustration at the slow pace of recovery and anger are all emotions that are likely to arise, unbidden, in the minds of those who suffer injuries in an accident such as befell the pursuer. If, alone or in combination with other factors, any of these emotions results in stress so intense that the victim develops a recognised mental illness, there is no reason in principle why he should not recover damages for that illness. On Lord Lloyd's approach, all that matters is that the defenders were in breach of their duty of care not to expose the pursuer to the risk of personal injury and that, as a result of the

breach, the pursuer suffered both physical and psychiatric injuries. The defenders are liable in damages for both types of injury and, in particular, for the exacerbation of the pursuer's psoriasis and for the depressive illness which followed—even if those developments were not reasonably foreseeable. (at [55]–[56])

6. Lord Lloyd's restrictive definition of a primary victim as a party who is *necessarily* within the zone of physical danger has been widely criticised (see e.g. Lord Goff in **White**). Opinions differ over whether Lord Lloyd intended to limit the primary victim category to those claimants who were in physical danger, and it remains unclear as to when a claimant *who is not in peril* will be recognised as a primary victim. This was considered, but not resolved, by the House of Lords in *Rothwell* v *Chemical and Insulating Co Ltd* [2007] UKHL 39. In this case, the House of Lords was invited to depart from **Page** and return to the rule that psychiatric injury must be foreseeable in all cases. Lord Hope said that 'attractive though that argument is, I would prefer to leave it for another day' (at [52]). However, he distinguished **Page** saying:

> The category of primary victim should be confined to persons who suffer psychiatric injury caused by fear or distress resulting from involvement in an accident caused by the defendant's negligence or its immediate aftermath. A person like [the claimant] who suffers psychiatric injury because of something that he may experience in the future as a result of the defendant's past negligence is in an entirely different category. (at [54])

In *Rothwell* several claimants were exposed to asbestos and developed pleural plaques. It was claimed that this *might* lead to an asbestos-related disease and also that the claimants suffered anxiety because of that possibility. The Court of Appeal said that there was no liability for causing 'anxiety', even in primary victim cases, saying 'anxiety is a form of psychiatric prejudice that is less serious than one of the recognised forms of psychiatric injury. The law does not recognise a duty to take reasonable care not to cause anxiety' (Lord Phillips, *Rothwell* [2006] EWCA Civ 27 at [63]). This was approved by the House of Lords.

One situation where the courts have recognised a claimant as a primary victim where there has not been an accident of the kind envisaged by Lord Hope in *Rothwell* is in the context of negligent treatment of pregnant women during childbirth.

YAH v Medway NHS Foundation Trust
Queen's Bench Division [2018] EWHC 2964 (QB)

The claimant suffered psychiatric harm following the negligent and traumatic delivery of her daughter XAS. XAS was later diagnosed with cerebral palsy (for which the defendant admitted liability). Held: she was entitled to damages as a primary victim.

MRS JUSTICE WHIPPLE:

ISSUES

5. The central issues going to liability are:
    (1) Whether the claimant is, properly classified, a primary victim in law (the 'primary victim' issue).
    (2) If she is a primary victim, whether she must show that her psychiatric injury was caused by shock in order to recover damages (the 'shock' issue).
    (3) If she is a primary victim, whether the psychiatric damage that she suffered is too remote from the defendant's admitted negligence to permit recovery of damages (the 'remoteness' issue).
    (4) Whether she has an alternative claim as a secondary victim (the 'secondary victim' issue).
6. If liability is established as either a primary or secondary victim, I must determine the value of damages due to her ('quantum').

LIABILITY ISSUES

1. Primary Victim

15. The claimant has always maintained that she is a primary victim. The defendant has asserted, by way of denial of her claim, that she is a secondary victim, although the defendant's skeleton suggests that the distinction is unimportant.

16. It is well established in law that a secondary victim must bring him or herself within the criteria which were established in *Alcock v Chief Constable of South Yorkshire* [1992] 1 AC 310, including the requirement that the claimant's psychiatric illness must be caused by shock, defined by Lord Ackner in the following way at p 401F:

'Shock', in the context of this cause of action, involves the sudden appreciation by sight or sound of a horrifying event, which violently agitates the mind. It has yet to include psychiatric illness caused by the accumulation over a period of time of more gradual assaults on the nervous system.

By contrast, a primary victim does not have to satisfy the *Alcock* criteria (or the *Alcock* 'control mechanisms', as they are sometimes called). Specifically, a primary victim does not have to demonstrate that his or her psychiatric illness has been caused by witnessing the sort of shocking event described by Lord Ackner.

17. I accept Mr Booth's [counsel for the claimant] submission that it is important to identify, at the outset, whether the claimant is a primary or a secondary victim. The two categories of claim are governed by different rules. I reject Mr Bishop's [counsel for the defendant] submission that categorisation does not matter.

18. Mr Booth submits that the claimant is, quite plainly, a primary victim. XAS was unborn at the time of the negligence; as a matter of law, mother and daughter were at that time one and the same legal person. Mr Booth reminds me of a passage in *Wild v Southend University Hospital NHS Foundation Trust* [2014] EWHC 4053 (QB), where I was counsel for the father who was suing as a secondary victim for psychiatric damage consequent on witnessing the stillbirth of his child, Matthew. The defendant hospital argued that the father could not recover because his concern was for the baby, not the mother, and the baby could not be the primary victim in relation to whom the father was the 'secondary victim' because the baby had no separate legal personality at that time. The Judge (Michael Kent QC, sitting as a deputy high court judge) rejected that argument, in the following passage:

20. [. . .] The law regards the mother and the foetus as one legal person and, in the words of the editors of Grubb and Kennedy Principles of Medical Law (Third edition) paragraph 5.167, '*a court will inevitably conclude that one who, in the eyes of the law, has never become a "person", cannot be said to have obtained life, and therefore cannot be said to have suffered death*'. Mr Bagot [counsel for the defendant] accepts the latter proposition and builds on it to say that, for that reasons, there is no primary victim in this case. [. . .] He says that the [father's] case and the psychiatric opinion are based upon [the father's] reaction to the death of his son, yet Matthew is neither said to be the primary victim nor could he be the primary victim.

21. Miss Whipple's response is to say that one must not confuse legal with factual analysis. As a matter of law there is no distinction between Matthew in the womb and his mother. As a matter of fact, however, the circumstances that gave rise to the psychological injury related to the death of Matthew in the womb, but because he was considered in law part of his mother, [the mother] was properly described as the primary victim. The law does not fail to give legal protection to the foetus. A child negligently injured in utero but born alive has a claim for damages (*Burton v Islington Health Authority* [1993] QB 204) and the perpetrator of an assault on a pregnant woman may be convicted of manslaughter if the child is born alive but dies as a result of the injury in the womb: *Attorney-General's Reference (No. 3 of 1994)* [1998] AC 245. Therefore, although the [father] cannot as a matter of law treat Matthew as the primary victim, for the purposes of a claim such as this, his potential for separate existence cannot be ignored either on the facts or as a matter of law.

22. I think Miss Whipple is right on this point: in such cases the only proper way to characterise the situation is to say that the mother is a primary victim. She indeed has a claim whether or not she has suffered psychiatric illness as a result of the events leading to the still-birth. Even though the alleged secondary victim's shock-induced psychiatric illness may be more to do with his concern for the unborn child than for the mother, nevertheless his shock is a consequence of the injury or threatened injury to the mother in that her foetus is damaged or destroyed by the relevant negligent act. [. . .]

19. Mr Booth took me to two recent cases where the analysis in *Wild* has been accepted: *Wells v University Hospital Southampton NHS Foundation Trust* [2015] EWHC 2376 (QB) at [82]–[83] (Dingemans J) and *RE v Calderdale and Huddersfield NHS Foundation Trust* [2017] EWHC 824 (QB) at [40] (Goss J). In both of these cases the mother sued for psychiatric injury consequent on obstetric negligence and in both the court concluded that the mother was a primary victim (although I accept that in *Wells,* the conclusion was *obiter* because no breach of duty was established; and in *RE* the mother was entitled to damages for psychiatric injury as primary and alternatively as secondary victim).

20. In answer, Mr Bishop submits that *Wild* is to be distinguished because in that case the issue of primary victim arose in a different context (namely, to deal with one aspect of the defendant's challenge to the father's secondary victim claim) and the judge's conclusion that the mother was the primary victim does not transpose to this case where the mother is bringing her own claim. Mr Bishop also submitted, in arguments not presaged in his skeleton argument or elsewhere in advance of trial, so far as I am aware, that the effect of the Congenital Disabilities (Civil Liability) Act 1976, which gives a child the right to sue for damages resulting from negligence before the child's birth, modifies the common law position so that where the child survives and can sue independently pursuant to the 1976 Act, the mother is to be understood as losing her status as the primary victim; he also suggested (again, in an unheralded argument) that the status of the mother alters at the time a baby is born so that she becomes at that moment a secondary victim.

21. I answer Mr Bishop's various submissions in the following ways. First, it is settled law that a baby is part of its mother until birth; there is, up to that point, a single legal person. Each of the three cases to which I was referred (*Wild, Wells* and *RE*) illustrate this principle. There is, of course, a much larger body of case law and commentary which establishes the principle—the deputy judge touched on some of it at [21] of *Wild.*

22. It flows from that principle that the mother is a primary victim in so far as she suffers personal injury consequent on negligence which occurs before the baby is born. I believe this also to be settled law. Certainly, it is endorsed in the three cases to which I was referred.

23. As to the effect of the 1976 Act, Mr Bishop is right to point out that if the baby lives, he or she may sue for damages for events which occurred before birth. The Act thus confers on the baby a right which he or she would not otherwise have, to sue for injuries caused by events occurring before birth (at which point the baby lacked a separate legal personality). But I do not accept Mr Bishop's submission that the effect of the statute is to deprive the mother of the co-existing right to sue as primary victim. The Act does not, on its face, interfere with any of the mother's rights; specifically, it does not remove rights from the mother to sue for injuries sustained as a result of those same acts. If that was what was intended by the Act, clear words would be required, and there are none. Further,

if Mr Bishop is right, the Act creates an exception to the general common law rule that a person who sustains personal injury as a consequence of the negligence of another can sue for compensatory damages. Mr Bishop did not explain how such an exception was justified and for my part, I fail to see what legitimate policy objective it would promote; specifically, the policy objective cannot be the avoidance of double recovery because the compensatory principle would prevent either mother or baby from recovering the same loss twice.

24. Mr Bishop did not press his third argument at the hearing, preferring to re-cast it as an aspect of his remoteness argument (to which I shall come). But it is important to be clear that the claimant did not cease to be a primary victim at the moment XAS was born. The fact that the claimant's psychiatric damage became manifest later in time, after XAS was born, does not change the claimant's status. She was and is a primary victim, in so far as she suffered personal injury caused by negligence which occurred before XAS was born.

25. The claimant is a primary victim. Accordingly, this claim falls to be determined according to the ordinary rules governing personal injury claims in negligence. It does not fall to be determined by reference to the *Alcock* criteria, which attach only to secondary victim claims.

2. Shock: is it a component of a primary victim claim?

26. There is a dispute between the parties as to what the ordinary rules for personal injury claims require. Mr Bishop draws a distinction between personal injury claims which are for physical injury with or without a claim for psychiatric harm, on the one hand; and 'pure' psychiatric injury claims where the claim is only for psychiatric injury and includes no claim for any physical injury at all, on the other. In relation to the first category, he accepts a claimant can in principle recover damages for any recognised psychiatric condition which results from the defendant's negligence, regardless of its precise trigger. So, he accepts that it is not necessary in that sort of a case for a claimant to show that the recognised psychiatric condition was caused by shock (in the *Alcock* sense or in any sense); any form of psychiatric illness, which falls into a recognised diagnostic category, can be the subject of a claim. However, he argues, the position is different for the separate category of 'pure' psychiatric injury claims, which he says can only succeed if the claimant can demonstrate that the injury has been caused by 'shock'.

27. For this submission, Mr Bishop takes *Alcock* as his starting point. There are a number of references in that case to nervous shock claims, which he argued encompassed both participant claims, where the claimant is the primary victim, and witness claims, where the claimant is a secondary victim. So, as examples, he points to Lord Ackner's statement at 400E that '*it is now generally accepted that an analysis of the reported cases of nervous shock establishes that it is a type of claim in a category of its own*', and Lord Oliver's statement at p 407 C–E:

It is customary to classify cases in which damages are claimed for injury occasioned in this way under a single generic label as cases of 'liability for nervous shock.' This may be convenient but in fact the label is misleading if and to the extent that it is assumed to lead to a conclusion that they have more in common than the factual similarity of the medium through which the injury is sustained—that of an assault upon the nervous system of the plaintiff through witnessing or taking part in an event—and that they will, on account of this factor, provide a single common test for the circumstances which give rise to a duty of care. Broadly they divide into two categories, that is to say, those cases in which the injured plaintiff was involved, either mediately or immediately, as a participant, and those in which the plaintiff was no more than the passive and unwilling witness of injury caused to others. In the context of the instant appeals the cases of the former type are not particularly helpful, except to the extent that they yield a number of illuminating dicta, for they illustrate only a directness of relationship (and thus a duty) which is almost self-evident from a mere recital of the facts.

28. In anticipation of Mr Booth's submissions based on *Page v Smith* [1996] 1 AC 155, Mr Bishop submitted that that case is authority for the proposition that there is no separate test of foreseeability for pure psychiatric claims, but that is all; *Page v Smith* did not eradicate the requirement established by *Alcock* for the claimant to demonstrate that the psychiatric illness was caused by shock. Mr Bishop submitted that *Page v Smith* modified the test of 'shock' as it applied to primary victim claims for pure psychiatric damage, to include a subjective component which would reflect the legal principle that the tortfeasor must take his victim as he finds him—with an egg-shell skull if that is what the victim has—as well as an objective component which would remain faithful to the *Alcock* approach which requires the victim to be judged by the standards of a person of 'ordinary phlegm'. But Mr Bishop could not be more specific about the test of shock which on his case applied to this or other similar claims, he said he could find no help on the point from *Page v Smith* and could not show me any other authority on the point beyond *Alcock*.

29. Mr Booth disagreed with Mr Bishop's analysis, which he said was misconceived in law. Mr Booth starts with *Alcock*, and suggests that the House of Lords in that case drew a very clear distinction between primary victims and secondary victims, and applied the 'shock' criterion only to the latter category of cases. In passing, Mr Booth noted that the language used in *Alcock* and other cases of that vintage was rather old-fashioned, with the term 'nervous shock' being used in places to describe what would now be called, simply, psychiatric injury or psychiatric illness—the point being that medicine has moved on and psychiatrists now recognise that mental illness comes in many different forms and can be triggered by many different factors, not all of which fit under the umbrella term of 'nervous shock'.

30. Mr Booth argues that, whatever the position following *Alcock*, the matter has been clarified by the House of Lords in *Page v Smith*. In that case, the majority (Lords Ackner, Browne-Wilkinson and Lloyd) upheld the trial judge's conclusion in favour of Mr Page. Mr Booth reminded me that the accident in which Mr Page was involved fell a long way short of the sort of shocking event envisaged in *Alcock*—it was a low impact collision in which no one was hurt. By allowing the appeal, the House of Lords necessarily accepted that shock as described in *Alcock* was not a necessary component of Mr Page's claim. Mr Booth submitted that shock, however it is defined, is not a necessary component in law for any ordinary (primary victim) claim for damages for personal injury, whether the claim is for physical injury or psychiatric injury or a combination of both. To make good that submission, he took me to Lord Lloyd's leading speech, where the distinction between primary and secondary victims was confirmed as having important legal consequences (p 184 F); Lord Lloyd then posed the rhetorical question at p 187 B:

Can it be the law that the fortuitous absence of actual physical injury means that a different test has to be applied? Is it to become necessary, in ordinary personal injury claims, where the plaintiff is the primary victim, for the court to concern itself with different 'kinds' of injury?

31. Lord Lloyd's answer was no and no. He said at p 188 F:

In an age when medical knowledge is expanding fast, and psychiatric knowledge with it, it would not be sensible to commit the law to a distinction between physical and psychiatric injury, which may already seem somewhat artificial, and may soon be altogether outmoded. Nothing will be gained by treating them as different 'kinds' of personal injury, so as to require the application of different tests in law.

Lord Lloyd confirmed that the *Alcock* control mechanisms were not required in the case of a primary victim (p 189 D); nor was it necessary to ask whether the plaintiff was of 'ordinary phlegm' because in the case of physical injury there is no such requirement and the negligent defendant must take his victim as he finds him (p 189 E); there was no justification for regarding physical and psychiatric injury as different kinds of injury, once established that the defendant is under a duty of care to avoid causing personal injury to a person, it matters not whether the injury in fact sustained is physical, psychiatric or both, a single test applies (p 190 E).

32. Mr Booth also took me to Lord Browne-Wilkinson's speech in agreement with Lord Lloyd. Lord Browne-Wilkinson said that it was irrelevant that Mr Page had suffered no physical injury because he had, on the judge's findings, suffered personal injury in the form of psychiatric harm (p 181 E). The question was whether the defendant in such a case should reasonably foresee that a person may suffer psychiatric injury 'of some kind', whether or not accompanied by physical injury (p 181 F). The defendant owed a duty of care to prevent foreseeable damage which included psychiatric damage (p 182 G). There was a danger in the Court drawing distinctions between physical illness and psychiatric illness; the time had come for the law to accept that the same criteria should apply for both types of claim (p 183 B).

33. Mr Booth finally drew my attention to the absurdity of Mr Bishop's argument on the facts of this case, where on any view the claimant had endured a longer and more stressful birth than she should have done, by virtue of the defendant's negligence. She therefore had a claim for physical injury (in the form of additional pain and suffering), if she had wished to bring it. If she had included a claim for physical injury of that sort, and whether or not she succeeded on that aspect of her claim, Mr Bishop accepted that she would not have to demonstrate that shock was the trigger for the psychiatric element of her claim: that made a nonsense of Mr Bishop's distinction.

34. I accept Mr Booth's submissions and reject those of Mr Bishop on this issue. *Page v Smith* establishes the approach in personal injury claims, whether the injuries consist of physical or psychiatric injuries or both. There is no requirement for a primary victim who brings a claim for 'pure' psychiatric injury to show that the injury was caused by shock. To return to Lord Ackner's axiom, old-fashioned though it is, a primary victim *can* in principle claim for psychiatric injury which has been caused not by shock, but by 'the accumulation over a period of time of more gradual assaults on the nervous system', which have given rise to a recognised psychiatric condition.

3. Remoteness

Outline of arguments

35. Having clarified the legal basis on which this claim proceeds, I turn to the mainstay of Mr Bishop's case (at least as presented at trial) which is that the damage sustained by the claimant is too remote from the defendant's negligence to sound in damages.

36. This issue ultimately turns on the evidence of fact and expert evidence. There is no dispute that the claimant has suffered psychiatric illness (in the form of a recognised psychiatric condition), nor that her psychiatric illness was caused or materially contributed to by the defendant's negligence: . . . What is in dispute is the precise trigger for the claimant's psychiatric problems, which itself leads to differing views on the correct diagnosis. Those points build up to the divergent overarching submissions on remoteness.

37. The claimant's case is that the claimant's mental disorder was caused by a number of factors associated with XAS's birth, including (i) a difficult labour culminating in an emergency caesarean section and (ii) the worry immediately after XAS was born in not knowing whether XAS would survive; and (iii) the strain of looking after XAS. Each factor has made a material contribution to the psychiatric

injury; and the psychiatric injury, however diagnosed, is a single and indivisible injury. The first two factors go back to the events of 9 July 2012 when XAS was born and the days immediately following XAS's birth. Thus, the psychiatric injury is closely related in time to the defendant's negligence and is sufficiently proximate to sound in damages. I did not understand Mr Bishop to dispute her entitlement to damages if she made out her case on the cause of her mental health problems, accepting on that case that the damage was not too remote.

38. The defendant's case is that the claimant's psychiatric illness was caused predominantly by the stress of having to care for a disabled child. The defendant challenges the assertion that the claimant's difficult labour contributed at all, and suggests that the claimant's distress in the first few days after having XAS did not go beyond 'normal' upset and distress that any parent would suffer in these circumstances and so was not causative of the claimant's problems, which came later in time once she knew the likely extent of XAS's brain injury.

[The judge reviewed the fact and expert evidence.]

Conclusion

81. In line with Dr Tattersall's [expert evidence for the claimant] evidence, I therefore conclude that the claimant suffered an anxiety disorder shortly after she had XAS as a response to her experience at XAS's birth and afterwards. The depression came later, triggered in large part by a recognition of the extent of XAS's brain damage. The conditions combined to form a single indivisible mental disorder which has varied in intensity over time and which is ongoing, currently resurgent with the stress of the trial, and with fluctuations likely in future.

82. It follows that I also accept that the difficulties experienced by the claimant during labour, and the worry immediately afterwards of not knowing whether XAS would survive, were contributors to the mental disorder. . . .

83. I find that the contribution of all of those causes was material to the outcome.

84. In light of the established causation of the claimant's mental disorder, I reject Mr Bishop's submission that the claimant's damage is too remote. . . . The claimant's mental disorder is inexorably bound up with the claimant's experiences in the delivery room and with her worry about XAS's likelihood of survival in the first few hours and days of XAS's life. The causes of the mental disorder are closely linked to the defendant's obstetric negligence just before XAS was born. The first factor is directly contemporaneous with that negligence, because the difficult labour was the reflection and direct consequence of the failure to deliver XAS earlier.

85. The claimant therefore establishes her claim for damages as a primary victim.

4. Secondary victim

86. Although the claimant's experiences during the delivery of XAS and afterwards were shocking and traumatic, using those terms in the ordinary way, they do not constitute 'shock' in an *Alcock* sense. Thus, the claimant would not, if she was a secondary victim, have been entitled to recover damages.

4.2 Secondary victims

It is generally agreed that where the claimant is a secondary victim, someone who suffers psychiatric illness as a result of witnessing injury or the risk of injury to another, special rules of proximity apply. The test is still one of foreseeability, but judges have set out guidelines as to when such liability will arise: in effect saying when such damage is or is not foreseeable. As often happens in the law of negligence, the issue largely turns on what we can be expected to tolerate. Seeing one's daughter run over by a car is different from seeing a stranger run over. In **Bourhill v Young** [1943] AC 92, Lord Parker said:

> the driver of a car or vehicle even though careless is entitled to assume that the ordinary frequenter of the streets has sufficient fortitude to endure such incidents as may from time to time be expected to occur in them . . . and is not to be considered negligent towards one who does not possess the customary phlegm.

If, therefore, a secondary victim suffers psychiatric harm in circumstances where the ordinarily courageous person would not, the defendant will owe no duty of care—even if a severe psychological reaction results. Though, of course, it may be difficult to say when only grief, rather than psychiatric illness, is foreseeable (*Vernon v Bosley (No 1)* [1997] 1 All ER 577).

Alcock v *Chief Constable of South Yorkshire Police*
House of Lords [1992] 1 AC 310

This case arose out of the facts of the Hillsborough Stadium disaster. It was a test case involving friends and family members of victims of the disaster who had suffered psychiatric injury as a result of the disaster. They fell into various groups. Some were present at the match (but not in the vicinity of the disaster), some saw the events on television and some heard about them on the radio. In most cases the person with whom the claimant was concerned was killed, in other cases that person was injured, and in one case they were uninjured. Held: the defendant was not liable to any of the claimants.

LORD ACKNER: My Lords, if sympathy alone were to be the determining factor in these claims, then they would never have been contested. It has been stressed throughout the judgments in the courts below and I would emphasise it yet again in your Lordships' House that the human tragedy which occurred on the afternoon of 15 April 1989 at the Hillsborough Stadium when 95 people were killed and more than 400 others received injuries from being crushed necessitating hospital treatment, remains an utterly appalling one.

It is, however, trite law that the defendant, the Chief Constable of South Yorkshire, is not an insurer against psychiatric illness occasioned by the shock sustained by the relatives or friends of those who died or were injured, or were believed to have died or to have been injured. This is, of course, fully recognised by the appellants, the plaintiffs in these actions, whose claims for damages to compensate them for their psychiatric illnesses are based upon the allegation that it was the defendant's negligence, that is to say his breach of his duty of care owed to them as well as to those who died or were injured in controlling the crowds at the stadium, which caused them to suffer their illnesses. The defendant, for the purposes of these actions, has admitted that he owed a duty of care only to those who died or were injured and that he was in breach of only that duty. He has further accepted that each of the plaintiffs has suffered some psychiatric illness. Moreover for the purpose of deciding whether the defendant is liable to pay damages to the plaintiffs in respect of their illnesses, the trial judge, Hidden J, made the assumption that the illnesses were caused by the shocks sustained by the plaintiffs by reason of their awareness of the events at Hillsborough. The defendant has throughout contested liability on the ground that, in all the circumstances, he was not in breach of any duty of care owed to the plaintiffs.

Since the decision of your Lordships' House in *McLoughlin v O'Brian* [1983] 1 AC 410, if not earlier, it is established law that (1) a claim for damages for psychiatric illness resulting from shock caused by negligence can be made without the necessity of the plaintiff establishing that he was himself injured or was in fear of personal injury; (2) a claim for damages for such illness can be made when the shock results: (a) from death or injury to the plaintiff's spouse or child or the fear of such death or injury and (b) the shock has come about through the sight or hearing of the event, or its immediate aftermath.

To succeed in the present appeals the plaintiffs seek to extend the boundaries of this cause of action by: (1) removing any restrictions on the categories of persons who may sue; (2) extending the means by which the shock is caused, so that it includes viewing the simultaneous broadcast on television of the incident which caused the shock; (3) modifying the present requirement that the aftermath must be 'immediate.'

. . .

THE NATURE OF THE CAUSE OF ACTION

In *Bourhill v Young* [1943] AC 92, 103, Lord Macmillan said:

> in the case of mental shock there are elements of greater subtlety than in the case of an ordinary physical injury and these elements may give rise to debate as to the precise scope of the legal liability.

It is now generally accepted that an analysis of the reported cases of nervous shock establishes that it is a type of claim in a category of its own. Shock is no longer a variant of physical injury but a separate kind of damage. Whatever may be the pattern of the future development of the law in relation to this cause of action, the following propositions illustrate that the application simpliciter of the reasonable foreseeability test is, today, far from being operative.

(1) Even where the risk is reasonably foreseeable, the law gives no damages if the psychiatric injury was not induced by shock. Psychiatric illnesses caused in other ways, such as from the experience of having to cope with the deprivation consequent upon the death of a loved one, attracts no damages. Brennan J in *Jaensch v Coffey*, 155 CLR 549, 569 [an Australian case], gave as examples, the spouse who has been worn down by caring for a tortiously injured husband or wife and who suffers psychiatric illness as a result, but who, nevertheless, goes without compensation; a parent made distraught by the wayward conduct of a brain-damaged child and who suffers psychiatric illness as a result also has no claim against the tortfeasor liable to the child.

(2) Even where the nervous shock and the subsequent psychiatric illness caused by it could both have been reasonably foreseen, it has been generally accepted that damages for merely being informed of, or reading, or hearing about the accident are not recoverable. In *Bourhill v Young* [1943] AC 92, 103, Lord Macmillan only recognised the action lying where the injury by shock was sustained 'through the medium of the eye or the ear without direct contact.' . . .

(3) Mere mental suffering, although reasonably foreseeable, if unaccompanied by physical injury, is not a basis for a claim for damages. To fill this gap in the law a very limited category of relatives are given a statutory right by the Administration of Justice Act 1982, section 3 inserting a new section 1A into the Fatal Accidents Act 1976, to bring an action claiming damages for bereavement.

(4) As yet there is no authority establishing that there is liability on the part of the injured person, his or her estate, for mere psychiatric injury which was sustained by another by reason of shock, as a result of a self-inflicted death, injury or peril of the negligent person, in circumstances where the risk of such psychiatric injury was reasonably foreseeable. On the basis that there must be a limit at some reasonable point to the extent of the duty of care owed to third parties which rests upon everyone in all his actions, Lord Robertson, the Lord Ordinary, in his judgment in the *Bourhill* case, 1941 SC 395, 399, did not view with favour the suggestion that a negligent window-cleaner who loses his grip and falls from a height, impaling himself on spiked railings, would be liable for the shock-induced psychiatric illness occasioned to a pregnant woman looking out of the window of a house situated on the opposite side of the street.

(5) 'Shock', in the context of this cause of action, involves the sudden appreciation by sight or sound of a horrifying event, which violently agitates the mind. It has yet to include psychiatric illness caused by the accumulation over a period of time of more gradual assaults on the nervous system.

I do not find it surprising that in this particular area of the tort of negligence, the reasonable foreseeability test is not given a free rein. As Lord Reid said in *McKew v Holland & Hannen & Cubitts (Scotland) Ltd* [1969] 3 All ER 1621, 1623:

A defender is not liable for a consequence of a kind which is not foreseeable. But it does not follow that he is liable for every consequence which a reasonable man could foresee.

. . .

Although it is a vital step towards the establishment of liability, the satisfaction of the test of reasonable foreseeability does not, in my judgment, ipso facto satisfy Lord Atkin's well known neighbourhood principle enunciated in *Donoghue v Stevenson* [1932] AC 562, 580. For him to have been reasonably in contemplation by a defendant he must be:

so closely and directly affected by my act that I ought reasonably to have them in contemplation as being so affected when I am directing my mind to the acts or omissions which are called in question.

The requirement contained in the words 'so closely and directly affected . . . that' constitutes a control upon the test of reasonable foreseeability of injury. Lord Atkin was at pains to stress, at pp 580–582, that the formulation of a duty of care, merely in the general terms of reasonable foreseeability, would be too wide unless it were 'limited by the notion of proximity' which was embodied in the restriction of the duty of care to one's 'neighbour.'

THE THREE ELEMENTS

Because 'shock' in its nature is capable of affecting such a wide range of persons, Lord Wilberforce in *McLoughlin v O'Brian* [1983] 1 AC 410, 422, concluded that there was a real need for the law to place some limitation upon the extent of admissible claims and in this context he considered that there were three elements inherent in any claim. It is common ground that such elements do exist and are required to be considered in connection with all these claims. The fundamental difference in approach is that on behalf of the plaintiffs it is contended that the consideration of these three elements is merely part of the process of deciding whether, as a matter of fact, the reasonable foreseeability test has been satisfied. On behalf of the defendant it is contended that these elements operate as a control of limitation on the mere application of the reasonable foreseeability test. They introduce the requirement of 'proximity' as conditioning the duty of care.

The three elements are (1) the class of persons whose claims should be recognised; (2) the proximity of such persons to the accident—in time and space; (3) the means by which the shock has been caused . . .

(1) The class of persons whose claim should be recognised

When dealing with the possible range of the class of persons who might sue, Lord Wilberforce in *McLoughlin v O'Brian* [1983] 1 AC 410 contrasted the closest of family ties—parent and child and husband and wife—with that of the ordinary bystander. He said that while existing law recognised the claims of the first, it denied that of the second, either on the basis that such persons must be assumed to be possessed with fortitude sufficient to enable them to endure the calamities of modern life, or that defendants cannot be expected to compensate the world at large. He considered that these positions were justified, that other cases involving less close relationships must be very carefully considered, adding, at p 422:

> The closer the tie (not merely in relationship, but in care) the greater the claim for consideration. The claim, in any case, has to be judged in the light of the other factors, such as proximity to the scene in time and place, and the nature of the accident.

I respectfully share the difficulty expressed by Atkin LJ in *Hambrook v Stokes Brothers* [1925] 1 KB 141, 158–159—how do you explain why the duty is confined to the case of parent or guardian and child and does not extend to other relations of life also involving intimate associations; and why does it not eventually extend to bystanders? As regards the latter category, while it may be very difficult to envisage a case of a stranger, who is not actively and foreseeably involved in a disaster or its aftermath, other than in the role of rescuer, suffering shock-induced psychiatric injury by the mere observation of apprehended or actual injury of a third person in circumstances that could be considered reasonably foreseeable, I see no reason in principle why he should not, if in the circumstances, a reasonably strong-nerved person would have been so shocked. In the course of argument your Lordships were given, by way of an example, that of a petrol tanker careering out of control into a school in session and bursting into flames. I would not be prepared to rule out a potential claim by a passer-by so shocked by the scene as to suffer psychiatric illness.

As regards claims by those in the close family relationships referred to by Lord Wilberforce, the justification for admitting such claims is the presumption, which I would accept as being rebuttable, that the love and affection normally associated with persons in those relationships is such that a defendant ought reasonably to contemplate that they may be so closely and directly affected by his conduct as to suffer shock resulting in psychiatric illness. While as a generalisation more remote relatives and, *a fortiori*, friends, can reasonably be expected not to suffer illness from the shock, there can well be relatives and friends whose relationship is so close and intimate that their love and affection for the victim is comparable to that of the normal parent, spouse or child of the victim and should for the purpose of this cause of action be so treated. . . .

(2) The proximity of the plaintiff to the accident

It is accepted that the proximity to the accident must be close both in time and space. Direct and immediate sight or hearing of the accident is not required. It is reasonably foreseeable that injury by shock can be caused to a plaintiff, not only through the sight or hearing of the event, but of its immediate aftermath.

Only two of the plaintiffs before us were at the ground. However, it is clear from *McLoughlin v O'Brian* [1963] 1 AC 410 that there may be liability where subsequent identification can be regarded as part of the 'immediate aftermath' of the accident. Mr Alcock identified his brother-in-law in a bad condition in the mortuary at about midnight, that is some eight hours after the accident. This was the earliest of the identification cases. Even if this identification could be described as part of the 'aftermath,' it could not in my judgment be described as part of the *immediate* aftermath. *McLoughlin's* case was described by Lord Wilberforce as being upon the margin of what the process of logical progression from case to case would allow. Mrs McLoughlin had arrived at the hospital within an hour or so after the accident. Accordingly in the post-accident identification cases before your Lordships there was not sufficient proximity in time and space to the accident.

(3) The means by which the shock is caused

Lord Wilberforce concluded that the shock must come through sight or hearing of the event or its immediate aftermath but specifically left for later consideration whether some equivalent of sight or hearing, e.g. through simultaneous television, would suffice. . . . Of course it is common ground that it was clearly foreseeable by the defendant that the scenes at Hillsborough would be broadcast live and that amongst those who would be watching would be parents and spouses and other relatives and friends of those in the pens behind the goal at the Leppings Lane end. However he would also know of the code of ethics which the television authorities televising this event could be expected to follow, namely that they would not show pictures of suffering by recognisable individuals. Had they done so, Mr Hytner accepted that this would have been a '*novus actus*' breaking the chain of causation between the defendant's alleged breach of duty and the psychiatric illness. As the defendant was reasonably entitled to expect to be the case, there were no such pictures. Although the television pictures certainly gave rise to feelings of the deepest anxiety and distress, in the circumstances of this case the simultaneous television broadcasts of what occurred cannot be equated with the 'sight or hearing of the event or its immediate aftermath.' Accordingly shocks sustained by reason of these broadcasts cannot found a claim. I agree, however, with Nolan LJ [in the Court of Appeal] that simultaneous broadcasts of a disaster cannot in all cases by ruled out as providing the equivalent of the actual sight or hearing of the event or its immediate aftermath. Nolan LJ gave . . . an example of a situation where it was reasonable to anticipate that the television cameras, whilst filming and transmitting pictures of a special event of children travelling in a balloon, in which there was media interest, particularly amongst the parents, showed the balloon suddenly bursting into flames. Many other such situations could be imagined where the impact of the simultaneous television pictures would be as great, if not greater, than the actual sight of the accident.

CONCLUSION

Only one of the plaintiffs, who succeeded before [the first instance judge], namely Brian Harrison, was at the ground. His relatives who died were his two brothers. The quality of brotherly love is well known to differ widely—from Cain and Abel to David and Jonathan. I assume that Mr Harrison's relationship with his brothers was not an abnormal one. His claim was not presented upon the basis that there was such a close and intimate relationship between them, as gave rise to that very special bond of affection which would make his shock-induced psychiatric illness reasonably foreseeable by the defendant. Accordingly, the judge did not carry out the requisite close scrutiny of their relationship. Thus there was no evidence to establish the necessary proximity which would make his claim reasonably foreseeable and, subject to the other factors, to which I have referred, a valid one. The other plaintiff who was present at the ground, Robert Alcock, lost a brother-in-law. He was not, in my judgment, reasonably foreseeable as a potential sufferer from shock-induced psychiatric illness, in default of very special facts and none was established. Accordingly their claims must fail, as must those of the other plaintiffs who only learned of the disaster by watching simultaneous television.

Notes

1. Compare the different ways in which the judges conceptualise the relationship between physical and psychiatric injury. In *Alcock*, for example, Lord Ackner says that 'shock is no longer a variant of physical injury but a separate kind of damage'. In *Page* v *Smith* Lord Lloyd argues that there is 'no justification for regarding physical and psychiatric injury as different kinds of injury'. While in *White* Lord Steyn said that while there may be no qualitative differences between physical and psychiatric harm, nevertheless they are treated differently by the law on policy grounds as the contours of tort law are profoundly affected by distinctions between different kinds of damage. Which view do you find most persuasive?

2. The so-called '*Alcock*' control mechanisms have been subject to trenchant criticism (compare Jane Stapleton 'In Restraint of Tort' in Peter Birks (ed) *The Frontiers of Liability: Volume 2* (OUP, 1994), p 95 and Donal Nolan '*Alcock* v *Chief Constable of South Yorkshire Police* (1991)' in Charles Mitchell and Paul Mitchell (eds) *Landmark Cases in the Law of Tort* (Hart, 2010), p 273). For a while it seemed that the courts were seeking to avoid their more restrictive effects. For example, in *Galli-Atkinson* v *Seghal* [2003] EWCA Civ 697, the 'immediate aftermath' of an event was interpreted generously so that it was understood as being made up of different component parts, in particular the mother's visit to the scene of the accident and the hospital morgue to allow a mother's claim for psychiatric harm following the death of her daughter in a road traffic accident. Similarly, in *North Glamorgan NHS Trust* v *Walters* [2002] EWCA Civ 1792 the court held that a shocking event need not be confined to a single moment in time—allowing a mother to recover as a secondary victim for psychiatric harm she suffered as a result of events over a 36-hour period leading to the death of her baby son.

3. The courts later adopted a more restrictive approach. In *Taylor* v *Novo* [2013] EWCA Civ 194 the Court of Appeal confirmed the existing rules on liability for psychiatric injury and reiterated that there should be no extension of liability. The mother of the claimant was negligently injured at work and died suddenly three weeks later in front of her daughter. In bringing her claim against her mother's employers, the claimant sought to establish proximity by arguing that there were, in fact, two 'events'—the accident and her mother's collapse and death—and that, as the cause of her injuries, the latter was the 'operative' or relevant event in determining proximity. This was rejected by the Court of Appeal:

   > In reality there was a single accident or event . . . which had two consequences. The first was the injuries to [the mother's] head and arm; and the second (three weeks later) was her death . . . if [the claimant] had been in physical proximity to her mother at the time of the accident and had suffered shock and psychiatric illness as a result of seeing the accident and the injuries sustained by her mother, she would have qualified as a secondary victim on established principles. But in my view, to allow [the claimant] to recover as a secondary victim on the facts of the present case would be to go too far . . . [I]f . . . right, [she] would have been able to recover damages for psychiatric illness even if her mother's death had occurred months, and possibly years, after the accident (subject, of course, to proving causation). This suggests that the concept of proximity to a secondary victim cannot reasonably be stretched this far. (Lord Dyson MR at [29]–[30])

4. However, there are recent signs of a potential relaxation in this kind of case. In *Paul* v *Royal Wolverhampton NHS Trust* [2020] EWHC 1415 (QB), a father collapsed and died in front of his two young daughters while on a shopping trip, 14 months after receiving negligent medical care. At first instance, Master Cooke found that the death occurred so long after the negligence, it could not be the 'event' required to establish a claim. This was overturned on appeal, Chamberlain J concluding that there had only been one 'event' caused by the negligence, which was the heart attack, and that *Taylor* v *Novo* did not preclude liability (at [75]). *Paul* and another similar case (*Polmear* v *Royal Cornwall Hospitals NHS Trust* [2021] EWHC 196 (QB)) are due to be heard by the Court of Appeal.

5. The question of what *kind* of 'event' a secondary victim needs to have witnessed was considered in a clinical negligence context in *Wild v Southend Hospital NHS Trust* [2014] EWHC 4053 (QB) and soon after by the Court of Appeal in **Liverpool Women's Hospital NHS Foundation Trust v Ronayne** [2015] EWCA Civ 588.

> ### *Liverpool Women's Hospital NHS Foundation Trust v Ronayne*
> Court of Appeal [2015] EWCA Civ 588

The claimant's wife suffered a series of complications after undergoing a hysterectomy at the defendant's hospital (it was common ground that this was as a result of the defendant's negligence). The claimant suffered psychiatric injury as a result of the 'shock' of his wife's rapid deterioration over the course of 36 hours and in particular seeing her connected to various machines, including drips and monitors, and seeing her appearance. The claimant clearly had a close tie of love and affection to the immediate victim (his wife), proximity in time and space and had seen the condition of his wife deteriorate through his own unaided senses. The question for the court was whether his illness had been caused by a shocking (or horrifying) event. Held: it had not.

TOMLINSON LJ:

11. It is unnecessary on this appeal to revisit the 'control mechanisms' which regulate recovery in this field, which can be said to be both arbitrary and pragmatic but which are well-understood, binding on us, and which were considered only recently by this court in *Taylor v Novo* [2014] QB 150.

12. In *Alcock*, Lord Ackner said, at page 401F:-

'Shock' in the context of this cause of action, involves the sudden appreciation by sight or sound of a horrifying event, which violently agitates the mind. It has yet to include psychiatric illness caused by the accumulation over a period of time of more gradual assaults on the nervous system.

13. In *Shorter v Surrey & Sussex Healthcare NHS Trust* [2015] EWHC 614 QB Swift J, who also has enormous experience in this field, was concerned with a claimant who saw her sister in undeniably distressing circumstances in hospital. It was suggested that the claimant's professional background—she was a radiographer—gave her an unusual degree of insight into her sister's medical condition and that, as a result, she would have been more sensitive to events at the hospital and therefore more likely to find them 'horrifying'. Swift J said this, at paragraph 214:-

... it seems to me that it is necessary to be cautious in finding that the claimant's professional expertise made the sight of Mrs Sharma more 'horrifying' than it would have been to a person without that knowledge. I consider that the 'event' must be one which would be recognised as 'horrifying' by a person of ordinary susceptibility; in other words, by objective standards. After all, certain people would find it *more* frightening to have no medical knowledge and *not* to know what was going on; they may feel helpless and isolated. Others may have armed themselves in advance with medical information from the internet which leads them to feel far greater fear than is in fact justified. It would be unfortunate if secondary victims' claims were to become embroiled in debates about an individual claimant's level of medical knowledge and its effects upon whether an 'event' should be classified as 'horrifying'.

I respectfully agree with those observations, and in particular with the judge's view that the question whether an event is for these purposes to be recognised as in the relevant sense 'horrifying' must be judged by objective standards and by reference to persons of ordinary susceptibility.

. . .

33. I do not for a moment doubt the profound distress which the claimant must have suffered in consequence of the appalling sequence of events which unfolded after the initial realisation that his wife was not recovering as expected from the surgery which she underwent on 8 July. Anyone would have the most profound sympathy for a loving husband and father who has in consequence suffered psychiatric illness. Nonetheless, the circumstances with which the claimant was confronted in my judgment fall far short of those which have been recognised by the law as founding secondary victim liability.

34. There is some confusion in the [trial] judge's paragraphs 10, 19 and 21 as to the precise dates involved, but it is I think clear that the judge treated as the relevant event here the period beginning with 'the sight of the sudden shocking state and condition of his wife' when he first saw her at about 1700 on 18 July prior to surgery connected to drips, monitors etc through to the first moment when he saw her in her post-operative swollen condition, connected to life support systems.

35. In my judgment the judge was wrong to regard the events of this period of probably about 36 hours as, for present purposes, one event. It was not, like *Walters*, 'a seamless tale with an obvious beginning and an equally obvious end.' In *Walters* the obvious beginning was the mother awakening to see her baby rigid and choking after a convulsion, with blood pouring out of his mouth. The obvious end was the tragic death of the baby in the mother's arms. The working out of the tragedy, with the raising of hopes, the journey up the motorway to London following in the wake of the ambulance, and the dashing of hopes and then their final destruction was almost Sophoclean in its seamlessness.

36. The present case is in my judgment not comparable, just as Swift J found the facts in *Shorter* not comparable. As there, so here, there was in my judgment a series of events over a period of time. There was no 'inexorable progression' and the claimant's perception of what he saw on the two critical occasions was in each case conditioned or informed by the information which he had received in advance and by way of preparation.

37. In the first place, I do not regard the sight of his wife at about 1700 on 18 July as the obvious beginning of a distinct event. It is nothing like the 'assault upon the senses' to which Mrs Walters awoke which Ward LJ equiparated with the mother seeing her child bleeding in a seat after a road traffic accident, and compare also the facts in *McLoughlin v O'Brian*. The claimant knew from his time at the hospital earlier in the morning that abnormalities had been found, a shadow on his wife's lower lung and abnormalities in the blood. Before he saw her later in the day he knew that, as a result of a CT scan, a mass had been found in her abdomen which the doctors could not identify. He knew before seeing her that she was to go into theatre for immediate surgery, and he knew that that meant that her condition, whatever it was, was, in his own words, 'deadly serious.' In these circumstances I regard it as artificial to regard the sight of his wife in her pre-operative condition as constituting the beginning of an event distinct from what had gone before.

38. Equally I regard it as wholly artificial to describe the sight of his wife in her post-operative condition as the end of a distinct event. It was all part of a continuum. Thankfully it was very different in nature from the death which occurred in *Walters*. The claimant knew that the next 24 hours were critical, and that the story was far from over. As it turned out, the story had many weeks and months to run.

39. Furthermore this sequence of events was far from seamless. The claimant went home whilst his wife underwent surgery. At 11.30 that evening the claimant was told that things had gone well and that there was no point in his returning to hospital as his wife was unconscious. He was told to visit the next day. Before next seeing his wife it was explained to him that the mass on the CT scan had been discovered to be 'bad peritonitis' and it was further explained to him that she was being treated with a cocktail of antibiotics, but that the next 24 hours were critical. In other words, it was explained

to him that her life was in danger. It was explained to him that a suture had been found in her colon which had permitted bacteria to leak into the abdominal wall and had poisoned her blood. The claimant deduced, if it was not explained, that a mistake had been made in carrying out the hysterectomy. He was overwhelmed by anger.

40. It follows that this was not in my judgment a case in which there was a sudden appreciation of an event. As Swift J found in *Shorter*, there was a series of events which gave rise to an accumulation during that period of gradual assaults on the claimant's mind. Ward LJ in *Walters* contrasted what there occurred with a 'gradual dawning of realisation that her child's life had been put in danger by the defendant's negligence,' which would not have amounted to a sudden and unexpected assault on her mind. That in my judgment is an apt description of what here occurred—a gradual realisation by the claimant that his wife's life was in danger in consequence of a mistake made in carrying out the initial operation. At each stage in this sequence of events the claimant was conditioned for what he was about to perceive. Before first seeing his wife connected to drips, monitors etc he knew, of course, that she was in hospital, and that that was because she was not recovering as expected from her operation and was running a high temperature. He knew that abnormalities had been found and that she was to undergo immediate exploratory surgery. There was in these circumstances nothing sudden or unexpected about being ushered in to see her and finding her connected to medical equipment as she was. Similarly the next day. One important purpose of the doctor wishing to have a word with Mr Ronayne before he visited his wife for the first time after the operation was no doubt to prepare him for the condition in which he would find her. There is no evidence that the doctor warned of her swollen appearance, and I will assume that he did not, but he did warn that she was gravely ill. The really bad news, that her life was in real danger, was imparted orally. Further, it was the explanation of the mistake which had led to this state of affairs which induced in the claimant extreme anger *before* the second of the incidents said to be part of the shocking event, the sight of his swollen wife on life support. Having been told of the severity of his wife's condition and that she was being administered a cocktail of antibiotics, it cannot in my judgment be said that what thereafter occurred had the necessary element of suddenness.

41. Furthermore what the claimant saw on these two occasions was not in my judgment horrifying by objective standards. Both on the first occasion and on the second the appearance of the claimant's wife was as would ordinarily be expected of a person in hospital in the circumstances in which she found herself. What is required in order to found liability is something which is exceptional in nature. On the first occasion she was connected to monitors and drips. The reaction of most people of ordinary robustness to that sight, given the circumstances in which she had been taken into the A. and E. Department, and the knowledge that abnormalities had been found, including a shadow over the lung, necessitating immediate exploratory surgery, would surely be one of relief that the matter was in the hands of the medical professionals, with perhaps a grateful nod to the ready availability of modern medical equipment. The same is more or less true of her swollen appearance on the second occasion. There is I think a danger of the 'Michelin Man' epithet acquiring a significance greater than it deserves. The claimant was conditioned to see someone from whom a litre of abscess had been drained and whose life was in grave danger. The pressure pads, routine medical equipment, no doubt contributed to the swollen appearance. I can readily accept that the appearance of Mrs Ronayne on this occasion must have been both alarming and distressing to the claimant, but it was not in context exceptional and it was not I think horrifying in the sense in which that word has been used in the authorities. Certainly however it did not lead to a sudden violent agitation of the mind, because the claimant was prepared to witness a person in a desperate condition and was moreover already extremely angry.

42. In my judgment therefore the claim fails at the first hurdle.

Notes

1. While the decision in **Ronayne** was welcomed by those who think it important to prevent 'flood-gates' of liability putting an uncontrollable and unwarranted drain on limited NHS resources (see Joanne Hughes 'Husband not entitled to damages as a secondary victim as sight of his wife in hospital was not sufficiently "horrifying"' *Lexology* 18 June 2015), others have suggested that 'it is hard to resist the conclusion that the need for a sudden shocking event is an unnecessary and arbitrary restriction' (Andrew S Burrows and John H Burrows 'A Shocking Requirement in the Law of Negligence Liability for Psychiatric Illness: *Liverpool Women's Hospital NHS Foundation Trust* **v** *Ronayne* [2015] EWCA Civ 588' (2016) 24 Med L Rev 278, 284). Either way, it is clear that the chances of successfully bringing a claim in such circumstances appeared— until recently—very slim indeed. However, in *RE and others v Calderdale and Huddersfield NHS Foundation Trust* [2017] EWHC 824 (QB) a grandmother was able to recover as a secondary victim for the psychiatric harm she suffered after witnessing the traumatic and chaotic birth of her granddaughter:

   > She was present throughout the birth and witnessed the aftermath. She, too, was convinced that RE [her granddaughter] was dead. There is agreement between the Consultant Psychiatrists that she has suffered PTSD as a result of observing the events of RE's birth. I am satisfied that her first-hand observation of the first 15 minutes of life, that is the period immediately following her birth, was the triggering event for PTSD. She has and had a very close relationship with . . . [her daughter, RE's mother]. It is not suggested on behalf of the defendant that she was not sufficiently close in terms of relationship to RE and to the event to be capable of being a secondary victim. The only issue is whether the event was sufficiently horrifying to establish a claim. As in the case of the Second Claimant [RE's mother], I find that the event was sufficiently sudden, shocking and objectively horrifying to reach the conclusion that the Fourth Claimant's [the grandmother] claim for damages for nervous shock is established. (Goss J at [48])

   Commenting on *RE*, Jaime Lindsey suggests the case:

   > raises important questions that need to be asked in light of well-publicised financial constraints on the NHS. These difficult birth injury cases usually only turn on a matter of minutes where difficult judgements are made under high-pressure circumstances. Of course, healthcare professionals should be and are trained to deal with those situations. However, if costs do noticeably increase and litigation has a detrimental impact on those already under strain NHS employees, we could reach a situation where NHS hospitals feel they have no choice but to prevent friends and family from being present with a patient to avoid potential liability. This is clearly an extreme scenario which is not yet close to materialising, but the unintended consequences of any expansion of liability in this context need to be taken seriously. ('Psychiatric Injury Claims and Pregnancy: *RE (a Minor) and Others v Calderdale & Huddersfield NHS Foundation Trust* [2017] EWHC 824' (2018) 26 Med L Rev 117 at 123–4)

   Do you agree?

2. If a person carelessly injures himself, that person owes no duty, even to close relatives, in relation to any psychiatric harm suffered. In *Greatorex v Greatorex* [2000] EWHC 223 (QB), the defendant carelessly caused a road accident in which he was severely injured. Coincidentally, his father, as a fire fighter, attended the scene and subsequently suffered post-traumatic stress disorder. It was held that the son owed no duty to the father, as to do so would 'curtail the right to self determination and liberty of the individual' (Cazelet J at [69]) and would open up the possibility of undesirable litigation within the family. Do you agree? Does this ignore the prevalence of liability insurance (the defendant was uninsured and so any compensation award would have been met by the Motor Insurers' Bureau)?

4.3 Beyond primary and secondary victims

The primary and secondary victim distinction makes the most sense in the context of accidents caused by the defendant's careless acts: primary victims are those involved in, and endangered by, the accident; secondary victims those who were not involved but witnessed, or later learned of, what happened to the immediate victims. It is clear, however, that psychiatric harms can be suffered in other ways. Though the courts have, on occasion, sought to fit all psychiatric injury claims within the framework of primary and secondary victims, the better approach is to acknowledge with Lord Phillips CJ that 'there is no magic in this terminology' (in *French* v *Chief Constable of Sussex* [2006] EWCA Civ 312 at [31]). 'Primary' and 'secondary' victim are best seen as terms of art, and there are some claimants who suffer (pure) psychiatric harm *other than* through being involved in or witnessing an accident who fall outside such classification. The question then is in what other circumstances does the law recognise victims of psychiatric harms as having a claim in negligence?

We know from **White** that no special status is conferred simply by virtue of being a rescuer or employer. However, a claimant will be able to establish that the defendant owes a duty of care not to cause them psychiatric harm where the defendant has 'assumed responsibility' to ensure that the claimant avoids reasonably foreseeable psychiatric injury. Examples of relationships in which such an assumption of responsibility has been found include bookmaker and gambler (*Calvert* v *William Hill Credit Ltd* [2008] EWCA Civ 888); doctor and patient (*AB* v *Leeds Teaching Hospital NHS Trust* [2005] EWHC 644 (QB)); police and police informant (*Swinney* v *Chief Constable of Northumbria Police* [1997] QB 464); prison officer and prisoners (*Butchart* v *Home Office* [2006] EWCA Civ 239) and employer and employee in the so-called 'stress at work' cases (*Walker* v *Northumberland County Council* [1995] 1 All ER 737; **Hatton** v **Sutherland** [2002] EWCA Civ 76).

White v Chief Constable of South Yorkshire Police
House of Lords [1999] 2 AC 455

This case also arose out of the Hillsborough Stadium disaster. The claimants were police officers who had been on duty during the incident and who had suffered psychiatric harm as a result. They sought to avoid the restrictions of the primary or secondary victim distinction, which defeated their claims, and argued for recovery on the basis that they were either rescuers or employees. Held: the defendant was not liable; neither rescuers nor employees are placed in any special position in relation to recovery for psychiatric harm by virtue of being so defined. NOTE: this case was known as *Frost* v *Chief Constable of South Yorkshire Police* in the Court of Appeal.

LORD GOFF (in dissent):

A NEW CONTROL MECHANISM?

. . . [It has been submitted] relying on certain passages in the opinion of Lord Lloyd in *Page v Smith* [1996] 1 AC 155, . . . that it was a prerequisite of the right of recovery by primary victims in respect of psychiatric injury suffered by them that they should have been within the range of foreseeable physical injury. I have already expressed the opinion that no such conclusion can be drawn from Lord Lloyd's opinion in *Page v Smith*. I understand however that, even if my view on that point is accepted as correct, some of your Lordships nevertheless consider that a new control mechanism to the same effect should now be introduced and imposed by this House as a matter of policy.

I am compelled to say that I am unable to accept this suggestion because in my opinion (1) the proposal is contrary to well-established authority; (2) the proposed control mechanism would erect an artificial barrier against recovery in respect of foreseeable psychiatric injury and as such is undesirable; and (3) the underlying concern is misconceived. . . .

(1) The proposal is contrary to well-established authority

I have here in mind the cases . . . concerned (a) with rescuers, and (b) with those who have, as a result of another's negligence, been put in the position of being, or of thinking that they are, the involuntary cause of another's death or injury. . . . [T]he most relevant cases concerned with the first category (rescuers) are *Chadwick* [1967] 1 W.L.R. 912 (in which the trial judge treated the fact that there was some danger of physical injury as irrelevant) . . . As to the second category, the most relevant case is *Dooley* [1971] 1 Lloyd's Rep. 271 in which, as in other cases of this kind, the plaintiff was never in any personal danger. Furthermore, both categories of case were stated by Lord Oliver in *Alcock* . . . to be examples of primary victims, in the case of which he plainly did not consider that there was any applicable control mechanism, for example any requirement that the plaintiff should have been within the range of foreseeable physical injury. Having regard in particular to the prominence now given to Lord Oliver's opinion in *Alcock* in segregating cases of secondary victims as those cases to which special control mechanisms apply, it would be a remarkable departure from existing authority now to create a new control mechanism, viz. that the plaintiff must have been exposed to the risk of physical injury, and to hold that this mechanism is applicable in the case of primary victims. What is here at issue therefore is not whether we should *extend* liability for psychiatric injury to primary victims who do not come within the range of foreseeable physical injury. The question is whether, having regard to existing authority, we should *restrict* liability for psychiatric injury to primary victims who are within the range of such injury.

(2) The proposed control mechanism would erect a new artificial barrier against recovery in respect of foreseeable psychiatric injury and as such is undesirable

The control mechanisms now in force are those established in *Alcock* to be applicable in the case of secondary victims, viz. (a) a close tie of love and affection to the immediate victim, (b) proximity in time and space to the incident or its aftermath, and (c) perception by sight or hearing, or its equivalent, of the event or its aftermath. These rules, being arbitrary in nature, are widely perceived to create unjust and unacceptable distinctions . . . To introduce the control mechanism now proposed in the case of primary victims would in the same way create distinctions regarded as unjust and unacceptable.

To illustrate the point, let me take the always useful extreme example. Suppose that there was a terrible train crash and that there were two Chadwick brothers living nearby, both of them small and agile window cleaners distinguished by their courage and humanity. Mr. A. Chadwick worked on the front half of the train, and Mr. B. Chadwick on the rear half. It so happened that, although there was some physical danger present in the front half of the train, there was none in the rear. Both worked for 12 hours or so bringing aid and comfort to the victims. Both suffered P.T.S.D. in consequence of the general horror of the situation. On the new control mechanism now proposed, Mr. A would recover but Mr. B would not. To make things worse, the same conclusion must follow even if Mr. A was unaware of the existence of the physical danger present in his half of the train. This is surely unacceptable. May I stress that, although I have taken an extreme example, the contrast I have drawn could well arise in real life; and the new control mechanism now proposed could provoke criticisms of the same kind as those which have been made of the mechanisms recognised in *Alcock*.

(3) The underlying concern is misconceived

I sense that the underlying concern, which has prompted a desire to introduce this new control mechanism, is that it is thought that, without it, the policemen who are plaintiffs in the present case would be 'better off' than the relatives in *Alcock* who failed in their claims, and that such a result would be undesirable. To this, there are at least three answers. First, the control mechanisms which excluded recovery by the relatives in *Alcock* would, in my opinion, have been equally applicable to the policemen in the present case if on the facts they had (like the relatives) been no more than witnesses of the consequences of the tragedy. Second, the question whether any of the relatives might be able to recover because he fell within the broad category of rescuer is still undecided; and, strangely, the control mechanism now proposed to exclude the claims of the policemen in the present case would likewise exclude the claims of relatives if advanced on the basis that they were rescuers. Third, however, it is in any event misleading to think in terms of one class of plaintiffs being 'better off' than another. Tort liability is concerned not only with compensating plaintiffs, but with awarding such compensation against a defendant who is responsible in law for the plaintiff's injury. It may well be that one plaintiff will succeed on the basis that he can establish such responsibility, whereas another plaintiff who has suffered the same injury will not succeed because he is unable to do so. In such a case, the first plaintiff will be 'better off' than the second, but it does not follow that the result is unjust or that an artificial barrier should be erected to prevent those in the position of the first plaintiff from succeeding in their claims. The true requirement is that the claim of each plaintiff should be judged by reference to the same legal principles.

LORD STEYN:

DIFFERENT KINDS OF HARM

. . . In an ideal world all those who have suffered as a result of the negligence ought to be compensated. But we do not live in Utopia: we live in a practical world where the tort system imposes limits to the classes of claims that rank for consideration as well as to the heads of recoverable damages. This results, of course, in imperfect justice but it is by and large the best that the common law can do. The application of the requirement of reasonable foreseeability was sufficient for the disposal of the resulting claims for death and physical injury. But the common law regards reasonable foreseeability as an inadequate tool for the disposal of claims in respect of emotional injury.

The law divides those who were mentally scarred by the events of Hillsborough in different categories. There are those whose mental suffering was a concomitant of physical injury. This type of mental suffering is routinely recovered as 'pain and suffering'. Next, there are those who did not suffer any physical injuries but sustained mental suffering . . .

The four police officers were actively helping to deal with the human consequences of the tragedy and as a result suffered from post traumatic stress disorder. The police officers put in the forefront of their case that they suffered harm as a result of a tort and that justice demands that they should be compensated. A constant theme of the argument of counsel for the police officers was that there is no justification for regarding physical and psychiatric injury as different kinds of damage, and in so arguing he was repeating an observation of Lord Lloyd of Berwick in *Page v Smith* [1996] AC 155 . . . It is of some importance to examine this proposition. Courts of law must act on the best medical insight of the day. Nowadays courts accept that there is no rigid distinction between body and mind. Courts accept that a recognizable psychiatric illness results from an impact on the central nervous system. In this sense therefore there is no qualitative difference between physical harm and psychiatric harm. And psychiatric harm may be far more debilitating than physical harm.

It would, however, be an altogether different proposition to say that no distinction is made or ought to be made between principles governing the recovery of damages in tort for physical injury and psychiatric harm. The contours of tort law are profoundly affected by distinctions between different kinds of damage or harm: see *Caparo Industries Plc v Dickman* [1990] 2 AC 605 . . . The analogy of the relatively liberal approach to recovery of compensation for physical damage and the more restrictive approach to the recovery for economic loss springs to mind. [See extract of Lord Steyn's discussion of 'Policy Considerations and Psychiatric Harm' at the beginning of the chapter.]

. . .

THE POLICE OFFICERS['] CLAIMS

In the present case, the police officers were more than mere bystanders. They were all on duty at the stadium. They were all involved in assisting in the course of their duties in the aftermath of the terrible events. And they have suffered debilitating psychiatric harm. The police officers therefore argue, and are entitled to argue, that the law ought to provide compensation for the wrong which caused them harm. This argument cannot be lightly dismissed. But I am persuaded that a recognition of their claims would substantially expand the existing categories in which compensation can be recovered for pure psychiatric harm. Moreover, as the majority in the Court of Appeal was uncomfortably aware, the awarding of damages to these police officers sits uneasily with the denial of the claims of bereaved relatives by the decision of the House of Lords in *Alcock*. The decision of the Court of Appeal has introduced an imbalance in the law of tort which might perplex the man on the Underground. Since the answer may be that there should be compensation in all these categories I must pursue the matter further.

THE EMPLOYMENT ARGUMENT

The majority in the Court of Appeal upheld the argument of counsel for two police officers that they fall into a special category . . . it became obvious that there were two separate themes to the argument. The first rested on the duty of an employer to care for the safety of his employees and to take reasonable steps to safeguard them from harm. When analysed this argument breaks down. It is a non sequitur to say that because an employer is under a duty to an employee not to cause him physical injury, the employer should as a necessary consequence of that duty (of which there is no breach) be under a duty not to cause the employee psychiatric injury . . . The rules to be applied when an employee brings an action against his employer for harm suffered at his workplace are the rules of tort. One is therefore thrown back to the ordinary rules of the law of tort which contain restrictions on the recovery of compensation for psychiatric harm. This way of putting the case does not therefore advance the case of the police officers. . . .

The second theme is on analysis an argument as to where the justice lay on this occasion. One is considering the claims of police officers who sustained serious psychiatric harm in the course of performing and assisting their duties in harrowing circumstances. That is, a weighty moral argument: the police perform their duties for the benefit of us all. The difficulty is, however, twofold. First, the pragmatic rules governing the recovery of damages for pure psychiatric harm do not at present include police officers who sustain such injuries while on duty. If such a category were to be created by judicial decision, the new principle would be available in many different situations, e.g. doctors and hospital workers who are exposed to the sight of grievous injuries and suffering. Secondly, it is common ground that police officers who are traumatized by something they encounter in their work have the benefit of statutory schemes which permit them to retire on pension. In this sense they are already better off than bereaved relatives who were not allowed to recover in *Alcock*. The claim of the police officers on our sympathy, and the justice of the case, is great but not as great as that of others to whom the law denies redress.

THE RESCUE ARGUMENT

The majority in the Court of Appeal held that three of the police officers could be classed as rescuers because they actively gave assistance in the aftermath of the tragedy: the majority used the concept of rescuer in an undefined but very wide sense . . .

The law has long recognized the moral imperative of encouraging citizens to rescue persons in peril. Those who altruistically expose themselves to danger in an emergency to save others are favoured by the law. A rescue attempt to save someone from danger will be regarded as foreseeable. A duty of care to a rescuer may arise even if the defendant owed no duty to the primary victim, for example, because the latter was a trespasser. If a rescuer is injured in a rescue attempt, a plea of *volenti non fit injuria* will not avail a wrongdoer. A plea of contributory negligence will usually receive short shrift. A rescuer's act in endangering himself will not be treated as a *novus actus interveniens*. The meaning given to the concept of a rescuer in these situations is of no assistance in solving the concrete case before the House. Here the question is: who may recover in respect of pure psychiatric harm sustained as a rescuer?

Counsel for the appellant is invoking the concept of a rescuer as an exception to the limitations recognized by the House of Lords in *Alcock* and *Page v Smith*. The restrictive rules, and the underlying policy considerations, of the decisions of the House are germane. The specific difficulty counsel faces is that it is common ground that none of the four police officers were at any time exposed to personal danger and none thought that they were so exposed. Counsel submitted that this is not a requirement. He sought comfort in the general observations in *Alcock* of Lord Oliver about the category of 'participants' . . . None of the other Law Lords in *Alcock* discussed this category. Moreover, the issue of rescuers entitlement to recover for psychiatric harm was not before the House on that occasion and Lord Oliver was not considering the competing arguments presently before the House. The explanation of Lord Oliver's observations has been the subject of much debate. It was also vigorously contested at the bar. In my view counsel for the appellant has tried to extract too much from general observations not directed to the issue now before the House . . . Counsel was only able to cite one English decision in support of his argument namely the first instance judgment in *Chadwick v British Railways Board* [1967] 1. Q.B. 912. Mr Chadwick had entered a wrecked railway carriage to help and work among the injured. There was clearly a risk that the carriage might collapse. Waller J. (later Lord Justice Waller) said (at 918A):

> although there was clearly an element of personal danger in what Mr. Chadwick was doing, I think I must deal with this case on the basis that it was the horror of the whole experience which caused his reaction.

On the judge's findings the rescuer had passed the threshold of being in personal danger but his psychiatric injury was caused by 'the full horror of his experience' when he was presumably not always in personal danger. This decision has been cited with approval: see *McLoughlin v O'Brian* [[1983] 1 AC 410] . . . and in *Alcock* . . . I too would accept that *Chadwick* was correctly decided. But it is not authority for the proposition that a person who never exposed himself to any personal danger and never thought that he was in personal danger can recover pure psychiatric injury as a rescuer. In order to recover compensation for pure psychiatric harm as rescuer it is not necessary to establish that his psychiatric condition was *caused* by the perception of personal danger. And Waller J rightly so held. But in order to contain the concept of rescuer in reasonable bounds for the purposes of the recovery of compensation for pure psychiatric harm the plaintiff must at least satisfy the threshold requirement that he objectively exposed himself to danger or reasonably believed that he was doing so. Without such limitation one would have the unedifying spectacle that, while bereaved relatives are not allowed to recover as in *Alcock*, ghoulishly curious spectators, who assisted in some peripheral way in the aftermath of a disaster, might recover. For my part the limitation of actual or apprehended dangers is what proximity in this special situation means. In my judgment it would be an unwarranted extension of the law to uphold the claims of the police officers. I would dismiss the argument under this heading.

THUS FAR AND NO FURTHER

My Lords, the law on the recovery of compensation for pure psychiatric harm is a patchwork quilt of distinctions which are difficult to justify. There are two theoretical solutions. The first is to wipe out recovery in tort for pure psychiatric injury. The case for such a course has been argued by Professor Stapleton. But that would be contrary to precedent and, in any event, highly controversial. Only Parliament could take such a step. The second solution is to abolish all the special limiting rules applicable to psychiatric harm. That appears to be the course advocated by *Mullany and Handford, Tort Liability for Psychiatric Damage: The Law of Nervous Shock*, (1993). They would allow claims for pure psychiatric damage by mere bystanders: see (1997) 113 L.Q.R. 410 . . . Precedent rules out this course and, in any event, there are cogent policy considerations against such a bold innovation. In my view the only sensible general strategy for the courts is to say thus far and no further. The only prudent course is to treat the pragmatic categories as reflected in authoritative decisions such as *Alcock* and *Page v Smith* as settled for the time being but by and large to leave any expansion or development in this corner of the law to Parliament. In reality there are no refined analytical tools which will enable the courts to draw lines by way of compromise solution in a way which is coherent and morally defensible. It must be left to Parliament to undertake the task of radical law reform.

see online resources

Explore the case further with an annotated version of **White** available from the **online resources.**

Notes

1. Lord Goff's opinion appears before Lord Steyn's in **White**, despite his being in the minority, because of the practice of listing the opinions of the law lords in order of seniority.

2. Following **White**, rescuers can only be 'primary victims' if they are, or believe themselves to be, exposed to physical danger. If this is not the case then they will be treated as secondary victims and will only be able to recover if they meet the **Alcock** criteria. But should police officers and other professional rescuers be treated differently from other members of the public because they are more used to witnessing harrowing scenes? In **White**, Lord Hoffmann rejected any automatic rule to this end (see *Ogwo* v *Taylor* [1988] AC 431) but said that 'it is legitimate to take into account the fact that in the nature of things many [rescuers] will be from occupations in which they are trained and required to run such risks and which provide for appropriate benefits if they should suffer such injuries'.

3. In **White** it was generally accepted that the law on psychiatric harm had taken a 'wrong turn'. As Lord Hoffmann noted:

   It may be said that the common law should not pay attention to these feelings about the relative merits of different classes of claimants. It should stick to principle and not concern itself with distributive justice. An extension of liability to rescuers and helpers would be a modest incremental development in the common law tradition and, as between these plaintiffs and these defendants, produce a just result. My Lords, I disagree. It seems to me that in this area of the law, the search for principle was called off in *Alcock v Chief Constable of South Yorkshire* [1992] 1 AC 310. No one can pretend that the existing law, which your Lordships have to accept, is founded upon principle. I agree with Jane Stapleton's remark that: (see *The Frontiers of Liability* ed Peter Birks, OUP (1994) Volume 2, p 87[)]?

> once the law has taken a wrong turning or otherwise fallen into an unsatisfactory internal state in relation to a particular case of action, incrementalism cannot provide the answer.

Consequently your Lordships are now engaged, not in the bold development of principle, but in a practical attempt, under adverse conditions, to preserve the general perception of the law as system of rules which is fair between one citizen and another.

Responsibility for addressing any injustice was placed firmly at the feet of Parliament. However, over the years Parliament has demonstrated a remarkable—but unsurprising—lack of appetite to tackle the issue. Most recently, a Private Member's Bill which among other things extended the list of relationships which had a 'close tie of love and affection' (Negligence and Damages Bill 2015) failed to make it past its first reading.

4. Another category of claimants who do not readily fit the primary and secondary victim distinction are so-called unwilling participants or unwitting agents. These are claimants who believe that they were in some way 'responsible' for the death or injury of another. In *Dooley v Cammell Laird* [1951] 1 Lloyd's Rep 271, for example, a rope on a crane broke causing the load to plunge into the ship's hold. The crane driver felt responsible and was allowed to recover damages for psychiatric injury. However, in *Hunter v British Coal* [1998] 2 All ER 97 it was held that this applies only when the claimant is present when the injury occurs. The claimant had accidentally knocked a water hydrant (which was badly sited) in a coal mine: when he was some 30 metres away the hydrant 'exploded' and around ten minutes after that he was told that his co-worker was dead. The defendants were not liable as the claimant was not present at the time of the injury and so was not a primary victim. Nor could he claim as a secondary victim as his reaction was regarded as 'abnormal'. For a more recent application, see *Monk v PC Harrington Ltd* [2008] EWHC 1879 (QB).

Hatton v Sutherland
Court of Appeal [2002] EWCA Civ 76

The case involved four appeals from claimants (two teachers, an administrative assistant and a factory worker) suffering stress-induced psychiatric illness. In each case the judge at first instance had awarded damages for negligence against the claimants' employers. Held: an employer owes a duty of care to their employees in respect of psychiatric harm, though, on the facts, there had been no breach.

HALE LJ:

Duty

19. The existence of a duty of care can be taken for granted. All employers have a duty to take reasonable care for the safety of their employees: to see that reasonable care is taken to provide them with a safe place of work, safe tools and equipment, and a safe system of working: see *Wilsons & Clyde Coal Co Ltd v English* [1938] AC 57. However, where psychiatric harm is suffered, the law distinguishes between 'primary' and 'secondary' victims. A primary victim is usually someone within

the zone of foreseeable physical harm should the defendant fail to take reasonable care: see *Page v Smith* [1996] AC 155. A secondary victim is usually someone outside that zone: typically such a victim foreseeably suffers psychiatric harm through seeing, hearing or learning of physical harm tortiously inflicted upon others. There are additional control mechanisms to keep liability towards such people strictly within bounds: see *Alcock v Chief Constable of South Yorkshire Police* [1992] 1 AC 310. In *Frost v Chief Constable of South Yorkshire Police [White]* [1999] 2 AC 455, the House of Lords applied that distinction to police officers (and others) who were not themselves within the zone of physical danger caused by the defendant's negligence, but had to deal with the consequences of catastrophic harm to others in the course of their duties. Lord Steyn observed . . . that

> . . . the rules to be applied when an employee brings an action against his employer for harm suffered at his workplace are the rules of the law of tort. One is therefore thrown back to the ordinary rules of the law of tort which contain restrictions on the recovery of compensation for psychiatric harm. . . . The duty of an employer to safeguard his employees from harm could also be formulated in contract . . . But such a term could not be wider than the duty imposed by the law of tort.

Taken to its logical conclusion this would apply the same distinction between those inside and those outside the zone of foreseeable risk of physical harm to the employer's general duty of care to his employees.

20. We have not been invited to go down that road, no doubt because it is not open to us. . . . In the landmark case of *Walker v Northumberland County Council* [1995] 1 All ER 737, Colman J applied those same principles in upholding the claim. Both have recently been cited with approval in this Court in *Garrett v London Borough of Camden* [2001] EWCA Civ 395. Also in *Frost*, Lord Hoffmann stated . . . that

> The control mechanisms were plainly never intended to apply to all cases of psychiatric injury. They contemplate that the injury has been caused in consequence of death or injury suffered (or apprehended to have been suffered or as likely to be suffered) by someone else.

As to *Walker*, he commented, at p 506A, that:

> the employee . . . was in no sense a secondary victim. His mental breakdown was caused by the strain of doing the work which his employer had required him to do.

21. In summary, therefore, claims for psychiatric injury fall into four different categories:

(1) tortious claims by primary victims: usually those within the foreseeable scope of physical injury, for example, the road accident victim in *Page v Smith* [1996] AC 155; some primary victims may not be at risk of physical harm, but at risk of foreseeable psychiatric harm because the circumstances are akin to those of primary victims in contract (see (3) below);

(2) tortious claims by secondary victims: those outside that zone who suffer as a result of harm to others, for example, the witnesses of the Hillsborough disaster in *Alcock v Chief Constable of South Yorkshire Police* [1992] 1 AC 310;

(3) contractual claims by primary victims: where the harm is the reasonably foreseeable product of specific breaches of a contractual duty of care towards a victim whose identity is known in advance, for example, the solicitors' clients in *Cook v Swinfen* [1967] 1 WLR 457, CA, *McLoughlin v Grovers* [2001] EWCA Civ 1743, or the employees in *Petch v Commissioners of Customs and Excise* [1993] ICR 789, *Walker v Northumberland County Council* [1995] 1 All ER 737, *Garrett v London Borough of Camden* [2001] EWCA Civ 395, and in all the cases before us;

(4) contractual claims by secondary victims: where the harm is suffered as a result of harm to others, in the same way as secondary victims in tort, but there is also a contractual relationship with the defendant, as with the police officers in *Frost v Chief Constable of South Yorkshire Police* [1999] 2 AC 455.

22. There are, therefore, no special control mechanisms applying to claims for psychiatric (or physical) injury or illness arising from the stress of doing the work which the employee is required to do. But these claims do require particular care in determination, because they give rise to some difficult issues of foreseeability and causation and, we would add, identifying a relevant breach of duty. As Simon Brown LJ pithily put it in *Garrett*, at para 63:

> Many, alas, suffer breakdowns and depressive illnesses and a significant proportion could doubtless ascribe some at least of their problems to the strains and stresses of their work situation: be it simply overworking, the tensions of difficult relationships, career prospect worries, fears or feelings of discrimination or harassment, to take just some examples. *Unless, however, there was a real risk of breakdown which the claimant's employers ought reasonably to have foreseen and which they ought properly to have averted, there can be no liability.* (Emphasis supplied)

Notes

1. Hale LJ went on to articulate 16 'practical propositions' on the issues relating to breach of duty (at [34]). These were unanimously approved by the House of Lords (*Barber* v *Somerset County Council* [2004] UKHL 13 at [10]), though the law lords disagreed with Hale LJ on the facts of the appeal.

2. In **White** Lord Hoffmann sought to distinguish the earlier case of *Walker* v *Northumberland County Council* [1995] 1 All ER 737 in which an employer was found liable for the workplace stress of their employee on the basis that in *Walker* the claimant's psychiatric harm 'was caused by the strain of doing the work which his employer had required him to do' (at 506), whereas in **White** the police officers' injures stemmed from their *witnessing* of the death and injury of others. Do you find this distinction persuasive?

5

Special duty problems: public bodies

Public bodies have extensive powers to act for the public benefit but often have limited resources. Difficult decisions must be made, and if those decisions are wholly unreasonable they may be corrected by judicial review, or via claims under the Human Rights Act 1998—that is, by *public law* remedies. It is more difficult to establish when negligence by a public body provides a *private law* right of action to someone harmed. While the general principles of duty of care apply, there are several other limitations on the liability of public bodies in negligence. Often this comes down to the question whether the public body concerned was involved in the exercise of a statutory *power* (discretionary), rather than a statutory *duty*. In relation to the exercise of statutory powers Lord Hoffmann said in **Stovin v Wise** [1996] AC 923 that in addition to the decision of the public body being unreasonable, there must be 'exceptional grounds for holding that the policy of the statute requires compensation to be paid to persons who suffer loss because the power was not exercised' (at 953).

This chapter discusses first the fundamental common law principles applicable to the exercise of discretion by public bodies and then the effect of jurisprudence from the European Court of Human Rights and the passage of the Human Rights Act 1998 in establishing obligations owed directly by the state.

5.1 The fundamentals of the common law

> **Poole Borough Council v GN & another**
> Supreme Court [2019] UKSC 25

This case involved two brothers who had been housed, with their mother, by the defendant council, on an estate. They suffered ongoing abuse and harassment from a local family, which the council was aware of, leading to them suffering physical and psychological harm. Their claim was that the council was negligent in its failure to exercise its powers under the Children Act 1989 to protect them from this abuse. Both boys were classified as children in need under the statute. Their claim failed at first instance but was allowed by the Court of Appeal. The council appealed to the Supreme Court. Held: no duty of care was owed to the claimants.

LORD REED: . . .

Relevant developments in the law of negligence

25. It is accepted that the provisions of the 1989 Act which impose duties on local authorities do not create a statutory cause of action. The question is whether local authorities may instead be liable at common law for breach of a duty of care in relation to the performance of their functions under the Act. In order to answer that question, it will be necessary to consider a number of authorities decided over the period between about 1995 and the present day. Before doing so, it may be helpful to begin with an overview, necessarily stated in general and simplified terms, of how legal thinking about the liabilities of public authorities in negligence developed over that period. As will become apparent, the period has been marked by shifting approaches by the highest court. In its recent case law this court has attempted to establish a clearer framework.

26. As was explained in *Robinson v Chief Constable of West Yorkshire Police* [2018] UKSC 4; [2018] AC 736, paras 31–42, public authorities other than the Crown were traditionally understood to be subject to the same general principles of the law of tort, at common law, as private individuals and bodies: see, for example, *Entick v Carrington* (1765) 2 Wils KB 275 and *Mersey Docks and Harbour Board v Gibbs* (1866) LR 1 HL 93. That position might be altered by statute, by imposing duties whose breach gave rise to a statutory liability in tort towards private individuals, or by excluding liability for conduct which would otherwise be tortious at common law: see respectively *Gorris v Scott* (1874) LR 9 Ex 125 and *Geddis v Proprietors of Bann Reservoir* (1878) 3 App Cas 430.

27. In particular, as Lord Reid explained in *Dorset Yacht Co Ltd v Home Office* [1970] AC 1004, 1030, a person performing a statutory duty was liable for an act which, but for the statute, would be actionable at common law, if he performed the act carelessly so as to cause needless damage. His liability arose because the defence which the statute provided extended only to the careful performance of the act. The rationale, Lord Reid explained, was that:

> Parliament deems it to be in the public interest that things otherwise unjustifiable should be done, and that those who do such things with due care should be immune from liability to persons who may suffer thereby. But Parliament cannot reasonably be supposed to have licensed those who do such things to act negligently in disregard of the interests of others so as to cause them needless damage.

Lord Reid added at p 1031 that the position was not the same where Parliament conferred a discretion. If the discretion was exercised lawfully, then the act in question would be authorised by Parliament:

> But there must come a stage when the discretion is exercised so carelessly or unreasonably that there has been no real exercise of the discretion which Parliament has conferred. The person purporting to exercise his discretion has acted in abuse or excess of his power. Parliament cannot be supposed to have granted immunity to persons who do that.

28. Like private individuals, public bodies did not generally owe a duty of care to confer benefits on individuals, for example by protecting them from harm: see, for example, *Sheppard v Glossop Corpn* [1921] 3 KB 132 and *East Suffolk Rivers Catchment Board v Kent* [1941] AC 74. In this context I am intentionally drawing a distinction between causing harm (making things worse) and failing to confer a benefit (not making things better), rather than the more traditional distinction between acts and omissions, partly because the former language better conveys the rationale of the distinction drawn in the authorities, and partly because the distinction between acts and omissions seems to be found difficult to apply. As in the case of private individuals, however, a duty to protect from harm, or to

confer some other benefit, might arise in particular circumstances, as for example where the public body had created the source of danger or had assumed responsibility to protect the claimant from harm: see, for example, *Dorset Yacht Co Ltd v Home Office*, as explained in *Gorringe v Calderdale Metropolitan Borough Council* [2004] UKHL 15; [2004] 1 WLR 1057, para 39.

29. This traditional understanding was departed from in *Anns v Merton London Borough Council* [1978] AC 728, where Lord Wilberforce laid down a new approach to determining the existence of a duty of care. It had two stages. First, it was necessary to decide whether there was a prima facie duty of care, based on the foreseeability of harm. Secondly, in order to place limits on the breadth of the first stage, it was necessary to consider whether there were reasons of public policy for excluding or restricting any such prima facie duty. These included, in the case of public authorities exercising discretionary powers, the supposed non-justiciability of decisions falling into the category of policy as opposed to operations. That two-stage approach had major implications for public authorities, as they have a multitude of functions designed to protect members of the public from foreseeable harm of one kind or another, with the consequence that the first stage inquiry was readily satisfied, and the only limits to liability became public policy, including the distinction between policy and operations.

30. The *Anns* decision led to a period during which the courts struggled to contain liability, particularly for 'pure' economic loss (ie, economic loss which was not the result of physical damage or personal injury) and for the failures of public authorities to perform their statutory functions with reasonable care. Clarification of the general approach to establishing a duty of care in novel situations was provided by *Caparo Industries plc v Dickman* [1990] 2 AC 605, but the decision was widely misunderstood as establishing a general tripartite test which amounted to little more than an elaboration of the *Anns* approach, basing a prima facie duty on the foreseeability of harm and 'proximity', and establishing a requirement that the imposition of a duty of care should also be fair, just and reasonable: a requirement that in practice led to evaluations of public policy which the courts were not well equipped to conduct in a convincing fashion.

31. Although the decision in *Anns* was departed from in *Murphy v Brentwood District Council* [1991] 1 AC 398, its reasoning in relation to the liabilities of public authorities remained influential until *Stovin v Wise* [1996] AC 923, where a majority of the House of Lords reasserted the importance of the distinction in the law of negligence between harming the claimant and failing to confer a benefit on him or her, typically by protecting him or her from harm. The distinction between policy and operations was also rejected. The resultant position, as explained by Lord Hoffmann in a speech with which the other members of the majority agreed, was that '[in] the case of positive acts, therefore, the liability of a public authority in tort is in principle the same as that of a private person but may be *restricted* by its statutory powers and duties' (p 947: emphasis in original). In relation to failures to perform a statutory duty, Lord Hoffmann stated at p 952 that '[i]f such a duty does not give rise to a private right to sue for breach, it would be unusual if it nevertheless gave rise to a duty of care at common law which made the public authority liable to pay compensation for foreseeable loss caused by the duty not being performed'.

32. Further clarification was provided by the decision in *Gorringe v Calderdale Metropolitan Borough Council*. In a speech with which the other members of the Appellate Committee agreed, Lord Hoffmann reiterated at para 17 the importance of the distinction between causing harm and failing to protect from harm, in the context of a highway authority's alleged duty of care to provide warning signs on the road:

> It is not sufficient that it might reasonably have foreseen that in the absence of such warnings, some road users might injure themselves or others. Reasonable foreseeability of physical injury is the standard criterion for determining the duty of care owed by people who

undertake an activity which carries a risk of injury to others. But it is insufficient to justify the imposition of liability upon someone who simply does nothing: who neither creates the risk nor undertakes to do anything to avert it.

Lord Hoffmann also emphasised the difficulty of finding that a statutory duty or power generated a common law duty of care, observing at para 32 that it was 'difficult to imagine a case in which a common law duty can be founded simply upon the failure (however irrational) to provide some benefit which a public authority has power (or a public law duty) to provide'.

33. Lord Hoffmann stressed at para 38 that the House was 'not concerned with cases in which public authorities have actually done acts or entered into relationships or undertaken responsibilities which give rise to a common law duty of care'. For example, '[a] hospital trust provides medical treatment pursuant to the public law duty in the [National Health Service Act 1977], but the existence of its common law duty is based simply upon its acceptance of a professional relationship with the patient no different from that which would be accepted by a doctor in private practice.' The duty in such a case 'rests upon a solid, orthodox common law foundation and the question is not whether it is created by the statute but whether the terms of the statute (for example, in requiring a particular thing to be done or conferring a discretion) are sufficient to exclude it'.

34. It took time for the significance of *Stovin v Wise* and *Gorringe* to be fully appreciated: they were not cited, for example, in *Smith v Chief Constable of Sussex Police* [2008] UKHL 50; [2009] AC 225. Confusion also persisted concerning the effect of *Caparo* until clarification was provided in *Michael* and *Robinson*. The long shadow cast by *Anns* and the misunderstanding of *Caparo* have to be borne in mind when considering the reasoning of decisions concerned with the liabilities of public authorities in negligence which date from the intervening period. Although the decisions themselves are generally consistent with the principles explained in *Gorringe* and later cases and can be rationalised on that basis, their reasoning has in some cases, and to varying degrees, been superseded by those later developments.

35. For the purposes of the present case, it is necessary to consider a number of decisions of the House of Lords concerned with local authorities' duties of care to children affected by their discharge of their statutory functions, together with some other cases in which the Court of Appeal's decision in *D v East Berkshire* was considered, and the decisions in *Mitchell*, *Michael* and *Robinson*.

X (Minors) v Bedfordshire County Council

36. The first authority which is germane to the present case is *X (Minors) v Bedfordshire County Council*, decided by the House of Lords in 1995. The case concerned a number of claims against local authorities, some relating to their functions under child care legislation and others to their functions as education authorities. All of the claims had been struck out as disclosing no cause of action.

37. In one of the child care appeals, the *Bedfordshire* case itself, five children brought claims for damages against the council for failing to exercise its statutory powers and duties (including those conferred or imposed by sections 17, 31 and 47 of the 1989 Act, and similar provisions in earlier legislation) so as to protect them from harm at the hands of their parents. In the other child care appeal, *M (A Minor) v Newham London Borough Council*, a child and her mother brought claims for damages against the council, the area health authority and a consultant psychiatrist employed by the latter. The case against the council was based on vicarious liability for the negligence of a social worker in its employment. It was alleged that he and the psychiatrist had been negligent when investigating allegations of child abuse. They interviewed the child without taking a full history of the mother's domestic circumstances, with the consequence that they mistakenly assumed, when the child referred to her abuser by his first name, that she was referring to the mother's partner, rather than to another

man with the same first name who had previously lived at the mother's address. They then told the mother that her partner was the abuser, leading her to exclude her partner from her home. On the basis of the psychiatrist's and social worker's conclusion that the mother would be unable to protect the child from her partner, the child was taken into compulsory care and placed with foster parents, where she remained for almost a year. Eventually the mother obtained sight of a transcript of the interview, from which it was apparent that the child had not identified her partner as the abuser. She then informed the local authority, and the child was returned to her care.

38. It should be noted at the outset that the *Bedfordshire* and *Newham* cases were radically different from one another. In the former case, the allegation was that the council had failed to protect the children from harm inflicted by third parties. The question therefore arose whether there were circumstances, such as an assumption of responsibility to protect the children from harm, which placed the council under a common law duty to protect them. That question did not arise in the *Newham* case. There, the allegation was that the council's employee had himself harmed the child, by negligently causing her to be removed from her home and detained against her will, with the result that she suffered a psychiatric disorder. Unlike in the *Bedfordshire* case, there was no need to establish an assumption of responsibility towards the child: that is not a necessary ingredient either of the tort of wrongfully depriving a person of her liberty, or of the tort of negligently inflicting a psychiatric injury. No such distinction was however drawn between the two claims.

39. Lord Browne-Wilkinson gave the leading speech, with which Lord Jauncey of Tullichettle, Lord Lane and Lord Ackner agreed. He began by dispelling confusion about some aspects of the law governing the liability of public authorities, concluding at pp 734–735 that 'in order to found a cause of action flowing from the careless exercise of statutory powers or duties, the plaintiff has to show that the circumstances are such as to raise a duty of care at common law. The mere assertion of the careless exercise of a statutory power or duty is not sufficient.' He went on to explain at p 736 that the exercise of a statutory discretion could not be impugned unless it was so unreasonable as to fall outside the ambit of the discretion conferred:

> It is clear both in principle and from the decided cases that the local authority cannot be liable in damages for doing that which Parliament has authorised. Therefore if the decisions complained of fall within the ambit of such statutory discretion they cannot be actionable in common law. However if the decision complained of is so unreasonable that it falls outside the ambit of the discretion conferred upon the local authority, there is no a priori reason for excluding all common law liability.

In these respects, Lord Browne-Wilkinson's approach accords with more recent authorities, as well as the older authorities to which he referred.

40. In relation to the *Bedfordshire* case, Lord Browne-Wilkinson convincingly rejected the contention that the statutory provisions created a cause of action for breach of statutory duty. In considering whether the circumstances were such as to impose a duty of care on the council at common law, Lord Browne-Wilkinson considered that questions arising from the policy/operational distinction could not be resolved at that preliminary stage. Nor could the question whether the council had acted in the reasonable exercise of its discretion. There remained the three issues mentioned in *Caparo*: whether the defendants could reasonably foresee that the claimants might be injured, whether their relationship with the claimants had the necessary quality of proximity, and whether it was in all the circumstances just and reasonable that a duty of care should be imposed. The first two of these issues were conceded. The only question which required to be decided was whether it was just and reasonable to impose a duty of care.

41. In that regard, Lord Browne-Wilkinson concluded at pp 749–751 that there were a number of reasons of public policy for denying liability: the multi-disciplinary nature of the system of decision-making, the delicacy and difficulty of the decisions involved, the risk that local authorities would respond to the imposition of liability by adopting a defensive approach to decision-making, the risk of vexatious and costly litigation, and the availability of administrative complaints procedures. Lord Browne-Wilkinson also noted that *Caparo* required that, in deciding whether to develop novel categories of negligence, the court should proceed incrementally and by analogy with decided categories. The nearest analogies, in his view, were the cases where a common law duty of care had been sought to be imposed upon the police, in relation to the protection of members of the public, and upon statutory regulators of financial dealings, in relation to the protection of investors. In neither of those situations had it been thought appropriate to impose a common law duty of care: *Hill v Chief Constable of West Yorkshire* and *Yuen Kun Yeu v Attorney General of Hong Kong* [1988] AC 175.

42. No claim was made in the *Newham* case on the basis of direct liability. In relation to the question of vicarious liability raised by that case, and also potentially by the *Bedfordshire* case, Lord Browne-Wilkinson accepted at p 752 that the social worker and the psychiatrist exercised professional skills, and that in general a professional duty of care is owed irrespective of contract and can arise even where the professional 'assumes to act for the plaintiff' pursuant to a contract with a third party, as in *Henderson v Merrett Syndicates Ltd* [1995] 2 AC 145 and *White v Jones* [1995] 2 AC 207. The social worker and the psychiatrist had not, however, assumed any responsibility towards the claimants. Although the carrying out of their duties involved contact with or a relationship with the claimants, they were nevertheless employed or retained to advise the local authority and the health authority respectively, not to advise or treat the claimants. The position was not the same as in *Smith v Eric S Bush* [1990] 1 AC 831, where the purchaser of a house had foreseeably relied on the advice given by the surveyor to the building society which was going to lend money on the security of the property. Even if the advice tendered by the social worker to the local authority came to the knowledge of the child or his parents, they would not regulate their conduct in reliance on the report. The effect of the report would be reflected in the way the local authority acted. Nor was the position the same as in *Henderson v Merrett Syndicates*, where the duty of care to the claimants was imposed by the terms of the defendants' contract with a third party; so also in *White v Jones*. Lord Browne-Wilkinson concluded at p 753:

> In my judgment in the present cases, the social workers and the psychiatrist did not, by accepting the instructions of the local authority, assume any general professional duty of care to the plaintiff children. The professionals were employed or retained to advise the local authority in relation to the well-being of the plaintiffs but not to advise or treat the plaintiffs.

Lord Browne-Wilkinson added that in any event, the same policy considerations which led to the view that no direct duty of care was owed by the local authority applied with at least equal force to the question whether it would be just and reasonable to impose a duty of care on the social worker and the psychiatrist. The psychiatrist also benefited from witness immunity.

43. The fundamental problem with this reasoning, so far as relating to an assumption of responsibility, is that as explained in para 38 above, the liability of the social worker and the psychiatrist in the *Newham* case did not depend on whether they had assumed a responsibility towards the child.

44. Lord Browne-Wilkinson's conclusion that there was no assumption of responsibility in the child abuse cases can be contrasted with his conclusion in the education cases, which concerned failures to diagnose and address special educational needs. He concluded in the first of those cases (the *Dorset* case) that a direct claim could lie against the local authority on the basis that it was offering a service to the public, namely the provision of psychological advice, which the claimant had accepted. By holding itself out as offering a service, it came under a duty of care to those using the service, in the same way as a health authority conducting a hospital under statutory powers was under a duty of care to those whom it admitted. There could also be vicarious liability for negligence on the part of the educational psychologists which the local authority employed to provide the service, and on whose professional advice the claimant's parents were said to have relied.

45. The position was similar in the second education case (the *Hampshire* case), which was based on vicarious liability for the negligence of a headmaster and an advisory teacher. Lord Browne-Wilkinson concluded that, whether it was operated privately or under statutory powers, a school which accepted a pupil assumed responsibility for his educational needs. The education of the pupil was the very purpose for which the child went to the school. The head teacher, being responsible for the school, came under a duty of care to exercise the reasonable skills of a headmaster in relation to such educational needs. The position was the same where an advisory teacher was brought in to advise on the educational needs of a specific pupil, whether he was consulted privately or was provided by the local authority. If he knew that his advice would be communicated to the pupil's parents, he must foresee that they would rely on such advice. Therefore, in giving that advice, he owed a duty to the child to exercise the skill and care of a reasonable advisory teacher.

. . .

D v East Berkshire Community NHS Trust

52. The case of *D v East Berkshire Community NHS Trust,* decided by the Court of Appeal in 2003, involved three appeals which were heard together. In the first appeal ('*East Berkshire*'), a mother claimed damages in respect of psychiatric injury alleged to have been suffered as a result of being falsely accused by doctors of suffering from Munchausen syndrome by proxy. In the second appeal ('*Dewsbury*'), a father and his daughter claimed for psychiatric injury and financial loss resulting from unfounded allegations by doctors and social workers of sexual abuse, which led to the father and daughter being prevented from seeing one another for about a fortnight. The daughter's claim was thus analogous to that of the child in the *Newham* case considered in *X (Minors) v Bedfordshire*. In the third appeal ('*Oldham*'), parents claimed in respect of psychological distress suffered as a result of unfounded allegations by doctors of having inflicted injuries on their daughter, which led to the child being separated from her parents for almost a year. The *Dewsbury* appeal was thus the only case which concerned social workers and the local authority which employed them. The claims in the three appeals were brought against the local authority in the *Dewsbury* case, and the health authorities in the other two cases, on the basis of vicarious liability. In each case, the court of first instance had determined as a preliminary issue that no duty of care was owed. It was common ground in the appeals that the critical issue was whether the third element of the tripartite test understood to have been adopted in *Caparo*, that the imposition of a duty of care was fair, just and reasonable, was satisfied.

53. In that regard, the Court of Appeal noted that several of the policy factors which Lord Browne-Wilkinson relied on, in *X (Minors) v Bedfordshire*, had been questioned in *Barrett v Enfield* and *Phelps v Hillingdon*. Furthermore, the Human Rights Act 1998 had come into force since *X (Minors) v Bedfordshire* was decided. The effect of section 8 was to impose a potential liability on local authorities to compensate children where there was a failure to protect them from ill-treatment and neglect which infringed their rights under article 3 of the European Convention on Human Rights, and to compensate children and their parents where the children were taken into care, or prevented from having contact with a parent, in circumstances which violated their rights under article 8. Litigation of a kind which in *X (Minors) v Bedfordshire* the House of Lords had considered it important to avoid as a matter of public policy had therefore become, under statute, a potential consequence of the conduct of

those involved in taking decisions in child abuse cases. In those circumstances, the court stated at para 81, 'the reasons of policy that led the House of Lords to hold that no duty of care towards a child arises, in so far as those reasons have not already been discredited by the subsequent decisions of the House of Lords, will largely cease to apply'. It concluded at para 84:

> It follows that it will no longer be legitimate to rule that, as a matter of law, no common law duty of care is owed to a child in relation to the investigation of suspected child abuse and the initiation and pursuit of care proceedings. It is possible that there will be factual situations where it is not fair, just or reasonable to impose a duty of care, but each case will fall to be determined on its individual facts.

54. Although a duty of care might be owed to the child, the court considered that the position of the parents was different. In view of the potential conflict between the best interests of the child and the interests of the parents, there were in the court's view cogent reasons of public policy for concluding that, where child care decisions were being taken, no common law duty of care should be owed to the parents. Another way of expressing the point would have been to say that the imposition of a common law duty of care towards the parents would be inconsistent with the statutory framework, since it would interfere with the performance by the authority of its statutory powers and duties in the manner intended by Parliament.

55. Applying those conclusions to the facts of the individual appeals, the court concluded that no duty of care was owed to the mother in the *East Berkshire* case, the father in the *Dewsbury* case, or the parents in the *Oldham* case. On the other hand, *X (Minors) v Bedfordshire* could no longer be regarded as precluding the claim by the child in the *Dewsbury* case against the local authority for negligence in the manner in which its employees contributed to the child protection investigation. The court did not need to consider whether there had been an assumption of responsibility towards the child, since the doctors and social workers were alleged to have harmed her, rather than to have failed to protect her from harm.

56. The Court of Appeal's reasoning effectively knocked away the public policy objection to liability. It did not, however, undermine some other aspects of the reasoning in *X (Minors) v Bedfordshire*. It remained the position that, where a decision under challenge was taken in the exercise of a statutory discretion, it was necessary to establish that the decision fell outside the ambit of the discretion and was not, therefore, authorised by Parliament. It also remained necessary, in circumstances where a duty of care depended on an assumption of responsibility, to establish that there had been such an assumption of responsibility, and that the duty contended for fell within its scope.

57. The parents in *D v East Berkshire* appealed to the House of Lords. Their appeals were dismissed: [2005] UKHL 23; [2005] 2 AC 373. No issue was taken with the Court of Appeal's decision concerning the child in the *Dewsbury* appeal, and it was conceded that the doctors in the other appeals owed a duty of care to the children. Like the Court of Appeal, the House of Lords considered that the duty of care admittedly owed to the child in any case of suspected abuse would be compromised by the imposition of a concurrent duty of care towards the parents, since the interests of the parents might conflict with those of the child. In those circumstances, no duty of care could be owed to the parents.

58. Lord Nicholls, in a speech with which Lord Steyn, Lord Rodger of Earlsferry and Lord Brown of Eaton-under-Heywood agreed, observed at para 82 that the law had moved on since the decision in *X (Minors) v Bedfordshire*:

> There the House held it was not just and equitable to impose a common law duty on local authorities in respect of their performance of their statutory duties to protect children. Later

cases mentioned by my noble and learned friend, Lord Bingham of Cornhill, have shown that this proposition is stated too broadly. Local authorities may owe common law duties to children in the exercise of their child protection duties.

The latter sentence made it clear that the House of Lords accepted that a duty of care could be owed to the child.

Later authorities

59. The case of *Kay v Lambeth London Borough Council* [2006] UKHL 10; [2006] 2 AC 465 was not concerned with social services, but it raised a question as to whether there were circumstances in which lower courts might not be bound by decisions of the House of Lords, in the light of contrary decisions of the European Court of Human Rights. In a speech with which the other members of the committee expressed agreement on that aspect of the case, Lord Bingham concluded that lower courts should normally follow precedents which are binding on them under the domestic principles of stare decisis. He admitted one partial exception to that rule. Explaining that there were a number of considerations which made *X v Bedfordshire* a very exceptional case, he stated at para 45 that on these extreme facts 'the Court of Appeal was entitled to hold, as it did in para 83 of its judgment in *D* [*v East Berkshire*], that the decision of the House in *X v Bedfordshire*, in relation to children, could not survive the 1998 Act'.

60. The case of *Mitchell v Glasgow City Council*, decided by the House of Lords in 2009, [2009] UKHL 11, concerned the question whether a local authority owed a duty of care to warn one of its tenants that he might be in danger when it responded to previous violent behaviour towards him by his neighbour by inviting the neighbour to a meeting and telling him that continued anti-social behaviour could result in his eviction. Following the traditional approach re-established in *Stovin v Wise* and *Gorringe*, the local authority was held not to be under a duty of care to protect its tenant from harm inflicted by a third party. It was accepted that there were particular situations where a duty of care could arise, such as where the defendant had created the source of the danger, or where the third party was under the defendant's supervision or control, or where the defendant had assumed a responsibility to the claimant which lay within the scope of the duty alleged, but no such circumstances existed in the case at hand. No reference was made to the decision of the Court of Appeal in *D v East Berkshire*.

61. The case of *Michael v Chief Constable of South Wales Police*, decided by this court in 2015, concerned the question whether the police owed a duty of care to a person who made an emergency call reporting threats of violence by a third party. Following essentially the same approach as in *Stovin v Wise*, *Gorringe* and *Mitchell*, this court decided by a majority that no duty of care was owed. It was recognised that liability for harm caused by a third party could arise in certain situations, such as where the wrongdoer was under the defendant's control, or where the defendant had assumed a responsibility towards the claimant to protect her, but the situation in the case at hand was not considered to be of that kind.

62. In *Michael*, the decision of the Court of Appeal in *D v East Berkshire* was relied on in support of an argument that the common law should be developed in harmony with the obligations of public authorities under the Human Rights Act. That argument was however rejected by Lord Toulson, who observed that the same argument had also been rejected by the House of Lords in *Smith v Chief Constable of Sussex Police*. The majority of the court agreed. As explained earlier, the reasoning of the Court of Appeal in the *East Berkshire* case was not that, because the European Court of Human Rights had found violations of the Convention, it followed that British courts should follow suit under the law of tort. Rather, the reasoning was that, since claims could be brought under the Convention, it followed that claims could also be brought under the Human Rights Act: a possibility which pulled the rug from under some of the policy-based reasoning in *X (Minors) v Bedfordshire*.

63. Most recently, the decision of this court in 2018 in the case of *Robinson v Chief Constable of West Yorkshire Police* drew together several strands in the previous case law. The case concerned the question whether police officers owed a duty to take reasonable care for the safety of an elderly pedestrian when they attempted to arrest a suspect who was standing beside her and was likely to attempt to escape. The court held that, since it was reasonably foreseeable that the claimant would suffer personal injury as a result of the officers' conduct unless reasonable care was taken, a duty of care arose in accordance with the principle in *Donoghue v Stevenson* [1932] AC 562. Such a duty might be excluded by statute or the common law if it was incompatible with the performance of the officers' functions, but no such incompatibility existed on the facts of the case. The court distinguished between a duty to take reasonable care not to cause injury and a duty to take reasonable care to protect against injury caused by a third party. A duty of care of the latter kind would not normally arise at common law in the absence of special circumstances, such as where the police had created the source of danger or had assumed a responsibility to protect the claimant against it. The decision in *Hill v Chief Constable of West Yorkshire* was explained as an example of the absence of a duty of care to protect against harm caused by a third party, in the absence of special circumstances. It did not lay down a general rule that, for reasons of public policy, the police could never owe a duty of care to members of the public.

64. *Robinson* did not lay down any new principle of law, but three matters in particular were clarified. First, the decision explained, as *Michael* had previously done, that *Caparo* did not impose a universal tripartite test for the existence of a duty of care, but recommended an incremental approach to novel situations, based on the use of established categories of liability as guides, by analogy, to the existence and scope of a duty of care in cases which fall outside them. The question whether the imposition of a duty of care would be fair, just and reasonable forms part of the assessment of whether such an incremental step ought to be taken. It follows that, in the ordinary run of cases, courts should apply established principles of law, rather than basing their decisions on their assessment of the requirements of public policy. Secondly, the decision re-affirmed the significance of the distinction between harming the claimant and failing to protect the claimant from harm (including harm caused by third parties), which was also emphasised in *Mitchell* and *Michael*. Thirdly, the decision confirmed, following *Michael* and numerous older authorities, that public authorities are generally subject to the same general principles of the law of negligence as private individuals and bodies, except to the extent that legislation requires a departure from those principles. That is the basic premise of the consequent framework for determining the existence or non-existence of a duty of care on the part of a public authority.

65. It follows (1) that public authorities may owe a duty of care in circumstances where the principles applicable to private individuals would impose such a duty, unless such a duty would be inconsistent with, and is therefore excluded by, the legislation from which their powers or duties are derived; (2) that public authorities do not owe a duty of care at common law merely because they have statutory powers or duties, even if, by exercising their statutory functions, they could prevent a person from suffering harm; and (3) that public authorities can come under a common law duty to protect from harm in circumstances where the principles applicable to private individuals or bodies would impose such a duty, as for example where the authority has created the source of danger or has assumed a responsibility to protect the claimant from harm, unless the imposition of such a duty would be inconsistent with the relevant legislation.

Notes

1. One valuable point is the separation of public and private law. The question is whether the decision is properly within the discretion of the public body, but there can be liability if the decision is so unreasonable as to take it outside the ambit of that discretion as long as there are other exceptional circumstances justifying a private right of action.

2. The abuse cases from *X v Bedfordshire* (mentioned in the extract) later reached the European Court of Human Rights, where they became *Z and others v UK* (Application no 29392/95) [2001] ECHR 333 (discussed in section 5.2) and *TP and KM v UK* (Application no 28945/95) [2001] ECHR 322 respectively. In *Z*, the Article 3 rights of the children were held to have been violated; in *TP and KM*, it was the Article 8 rights of mother and daughter.

3. In *D v East Berkshire Community NHS Trust* [2005] UKHL 23, also mentioned in the extract, the assumed facts were that a doctor had misdiagnosed a child's illness, wrongly concluding that the cause was abuse by the parents. The action was brought by the parents for psychiatric injury to them and the child caused by this wrongful allegation. It was held that a duty was owed to the child but not to the parents, as to have both would produce a conflict of interest. Lord Rodger said:

   > The duty to the children is simply to exercise reasonable care and skill in diagnosing and treating any condition from which they may be suffering. In carrying out that duty the doctors have regard only to the interests of the children. Suppose, however, that they were also under a duty to the parents not to cause them psychiatric harm by concluding that they might have abused their child. Then, in deciding how to proceed, the doctors would always have to vtake account of the risk that they might harm the parents in this way. There would be not one but two sets of interests to be considered. Acting on, or persisting in, a suspicion of abuse might well be reasonable when only the child's interests were engaged, but unreasonable if the interests of the parents had also to be taken into account. Of its very nature, therefore, this kind of duty of care to the parents would cut across the duty of care to the children (at [110]).

4. A duty of care *can* be owed to parents. In *A v Essex County Council* [2004] 1 WLR 1881, the claimants adopted a child who proved to be very aggressive. They had told the council that they could only cope with a child with no more than mild behaviour problems. It was said that there was no duty to the adopting parents on the part of the professionals involved in compiling reports on the child, although there would be a duty to the child. The adopters were in fact found to be owed a duty of care as it was intended that they should receive various reports which due to an administrative error were not passed on to them. (See also *W v Essex County Council* [2001] 2 AC 592.)

5. The conflict of interest idea from *D v East Berkshire Community NHS Trust* [2005] UKHL 23 has since been refined. It is not the case that no duty can arise towards *parents* of children suspected of being abused: it is anyone *suspected of or being investigated for* the abuse to whom a duty cannot arise (*Merthyr Tydfil County Borough Council v C* [2010] EWHC 62 (QB)).

6. *Poole* (alongside *Robinson v Chief Constable of West Yorkshire Police* [2018] UKSC 4, where the lead judgment was also given by Lord Reed) can now be taken as giving the definitive answer to the question of when a public body might owe a private law duty of care (see [65] in particular, for a summary). The decision in *Stovin* was approved, alongside *Gorringe*, Lord Reed saying the significance of those cases had been underestimated (see [34]).

> ## Stovin v Wise
> House of Lords [1996] AC 923

Norfolk County Council was aware that a road junction was dangerous and in January 1988 it wrote to British Rail, the owner of the land, suggesting that at their expense part of a bank of earth should be removed to improve visibility. British Rail agreed to seek internal approval but nothing further was done by either party. The defendants were under no statutory obligation to exercise their powers. In December 1988 the claimant was involved in a road accident at the junction which would not have happened if the work had been done. Held: the county council owed no duty of care to the claimant.

LORD HOFFMANN:. . .

Negligent conduct in the exercise of statutory powers

Since *Mersey Docks and Harbour Board Trustees v Gibbs* (1866) LR 1 HL 93 it has been clear law that in the absence of express statutory authority, a public body is in principle liable for torts in the same way as a private person. But its statutory powers or duties may restrict its liability. For example, it may be authorised to do something which necessarily involves committing what would otherwise be a tort. In such a case it will not be liable: *Allen v Gulf Oil Refining Ltd* [1981] AC 1001. Or it may have discretionary powers which enable it to do things to achieve a statutory purpose notwithstanding that they involve a foreseeable risk of damage to others. In such a case, a bona fide exercise of the discretion will not attract liability: *X (Minors) v Bedfordshire County Council* [1995] 2 AC 633 and *Dorset Yacht Co Ltd v Home Office* [1970] AC 1004.

In the case of positive acts, therefore, the liability of a public authority in tort is in principle the same as that of a private person but may be *restricted* by its statutory powers and duties. The argument in the present case, however, is that whereas a private person would have owed no duty of care in respect of an omission to remove the hazard at the junction, the duty of the highway authority is *enlarged* by virtue of its statutory powers. The existence of the statutory powers is said to create a 'proximity' between the highway authority and the highway user which would not otherwise exist.

Negligent omission to use statutory powers

Until the decision of this House in *Anns v Merton London Borough Council* [1978] AC 728, there was no authority for treating a statutory power as giving rise to a common law duty of care. Two cases in particular were thought to be against it. In *Sheppard v Glossop Corporation* [1921] 3 KB 132 the council had power to light the streets of Glossop. But their policy was to turn off the lamps at 9 pm. The plaintiff was injured when he fell over a retaining wall in the dark after the lamps had been extinguished. He sued the council for negligence. The Court of Appeal said that the council owed him no duty of care. Atkin LJ said, at p 150:

> [The local authority] is under no legal duty to act reasonably in deciding whether it shall exercise its statutory powers or not, or in deciding to what extent, over what particular area, or for what particular time, it shall exercise its powers. . . . The real complaint of the plaintiff is not that they caused the danger, but that, the danger being there, if they had lighted it he would have seen and avoided it.

In *East Suffolk Rivers Catchment Board v Kent* [1941] AC 74, 102 the facts of which are too well known to need repetition [see note 1 following this extract], Lord Romer cited *Sheppard v Glossop Corporation* and stated the principle which he said it laid down, at p 102:

> Where a statutory authority is entrusted with a mere power it cannot be made liable for any damage sustained by a member of the public by reason of a failure to exercise that power.

...

Anns v Merton London Borough Council

... Lord Wilberforce had to deal with an argument by the council which was based upon two propositions. The first was that if the council owed no duty to inspect in the first place, it could be under no liability for having done so negligently. The second relied upon Lord Romer's principle in the *East Suffolk* case [1941] AC 74, 97: a public authority which has a mere statutory power cannot on that account owe a duty at common law to exercise the power. Lord Wilberforce did not deny the first proposition. This, if I may respectfully say so, seems to me to be right. If the public authority was under no duty to act, either by virtue of its statutory powers or on any other basis, it cannot be liable because it has acted but negligently failed to confer a benefit on the plaintiff or to protect him from loss. The position is of course different if the negligent action of the public authority has left the plaintiff in a worse position than he would have been in if the authority had not acted at all. Lord Wilberforce did however deny the council's second proposition.

... Upon what principles can one say of a public authority that not only did it have a duty in public law to consider the exercise of the power but that it would thereupon have been under a duty in private law to act, giving rise to a claim in compensation against public funds for its failure to do so? Or as Lord Wilberforce puts it in the *Anns* case [1978] AC 728, 754:

> The problem which this kind of action creates, is to define the circumstances in which the law should impose, over and above, or perhaps alongside, these public law powers and duties, a duty in private law towards individuals such that they may sue for damages in a civil court.

The only tool which the *Anns* case provides for defining these circumstances is the distinction between policy and operations. . .

The *East Suffolk* case [1941] AC 74 and *Sheppard v Glossop Corporation* [1921] 3 KB 132 were distinguished as involving questions of policy or discretion. The inspection of foundations, on the other hand, was 'heavily operational' and the power to inspect could therefore give rise to a duty of care. Lord Romer's statement of principle in *East Suffolk* was limited to cases in which the exercise of the power involved a policy decision.

Policy and operations

Whether a statutory duty gives rise to a private cause of action is a question of construction: see *R v Deputy Governor of Parkhurst Prison, ex parte Hague* [1992] 1 AC 58. It requires an examination of the policy of the statute to decide whether it was intended to confer a right to compensation for breach. Whether it can be relied upon to support the existence of a common law duty of care is not exactly a question of construction, because the cause of action does not arise out of the statute itself. But the policy of the statute is nevertheless a crucial factor in the decision. . . .

The same is true of omission to perform a statutory duty. If such a duty does not give rise to a private right to sue for breach, it would be unusual if it nevertheless gave rise to a duty of care at common law which made the public authority liable to pay compensation for foreseeable loss caused by the duty not being performed. It will often be foreseeable that loss will result if, for example, a benefit or service is not provided. If the policy of the act is not to create a statutory liability to pay compensation, the same policy should ordinarily exclude the existence of a common law duty of care.

In the case of a mere statutory power, there is the further point that the legislature has chosen to confer a discretion rather than create a duty. Of course there may be cases in which Parliament has chosen to confer a power because the subject matter did not permit a duty to be stated with sufficient precision. It may nevertheless have contemplated that in circumstances in which it would be irrational not to exercise the power, a person who suffered loss because it had not been exercised, or not properly exercised, would be entitled to compensation. I therefore do not say that a statutory 'may' can never give rise to a common law duty of care. I prefer to leave open the question of whether the *Anns* case was wrong to create any exception to Lord Romer's statement of principle in the *East Suffolk* case and I shall go on to consider the circumstances (such as 'general reliance') in which it has been suggested that such a duty might arise. But the fact that Parliament has conferred a discretion must be some indication that the policy of the act conferring the power was not to create a right to compensation. The need to have regard to the policy of the statute therefore means that exceptions will be rare.

In summary, therefore, I think that the minimum preconditions for basing a duty of care upon the existence of a statutory power, if it can be done at all, are, first, that it would in the circumstances have been irrational not to have exercised the power, so that there was in effect a public law duty to act, and secondly, that there are exceptional grounds for holding that the policy of the statute requires compensation to be paid to persons who suffer loss because the power was not exercised.

Particular and general reliance

In *Sutherland Shire Council v Heyman* 157 CLR 424, 483, Brennan J, as I have mentioned, thought that a statutory power could never generate a common law duty of care unless the public authority had created an expectation that the power would be used and the plaintiff had suffered damage from reliance on that expectation. A common example is the lighthouse authority which, by the exercise of its power to build and maintain a lighthouse, creates in mariners an expectation that the light will warn them of danger. In such circumstances, the authority (unlike the Glossop Corporation in *Sheppard v Glossop Corporation* [1921] 3 KB 132) owes a duty of care which requires it not to extinguish the light without giving reasonable notice. This form of liability, based upon representation and reliance, does not depend upon the public nature of the authority's powers and causes no problems.

In the same case, however, Mason J suggested a different basis upon which public powers might give rise to a duty of care. He said, at p 464:

> [T]here will be cases in which the plaintiff's reasonable reliance will arise out of a general dependence on an authority's performance of its function with due care, without the need for contributing conduct on the part of a defendant or action to his detriment on the part of a plaintiff. Reliance or dependence in this sense is in general the product of the grant (and exercise) of powers designed to prevent or minimise a risk of personal injury or disability, recognised by the legislature as being of such magnitude or complexity that individuals cannot, or may not, take adequate steps for their own protection. This situation generates on one side (the individual) a general expectation that the power will be exercised and on the other side (the authority) a realisation that there is a general reliance or dependence on its exercise of the power. . . . The control of air traffic, the safety inspection of aircraft and the fighting of a fire in a building by a fire authority. . . may well be examples of this type of function.

This ground for imposing a duty of care has been called 'general reliance.' It has little in common with the ordinary doctrine of reliance; the plaintiff does not need to have relied upon the expectation that the power would be used or even known that it existed. It appears rather to refer to general expectations in the community, which the individual plaintiff may or may not have shared. A widespread assumption that a statutory power will be exercised may affect the general pattern of economic and social behaviour. For example, insurance premiums may take into account the expectation that statutory powers of inspection or accident prevention will ordinarily prevent certain kinds of risk from materialising. Thus the doctrine of general reliance requires an inquiry into the role of a given statutory power in the behaviour of members of the general public, of which an outstanding example is the judgment of Richardson J in *Invercargill City Council v Hamlin* [1994] 3 NZLR 513, 526.

It appears to be essential to the doctrine of general reliance that the benefit or service provided under statutory powers should be of a uniform and routine nature, so that one can describe exactly what the public authority was supposed to do. Powers of inspection for defects clearly fall into this category. Another way of looking at the matter is to say that if a particular service is provided as a matter of routine, it would be irrational for a public authority to provide it in one case and arbitrarily withhold it in another. This was obviously the main ground upon which this House in the *Anns* case considered that the power of the local authority to inspect foundations should give rise to a duty of care.

But the fact that it would be irrational not to exercise the power is, as I have said, only one of the conditions which has to be satisfied. It is also necessary to discern a policy which confers a right to financial compensation if the power has not been exercised. Mason J thought in *Sutherland Shire Council v Heyman* 157 CLR 424, 464, that such a policy might be inferred if the power was intended to protect members of the public from risks against which they could not guard themselves. In the *Invercargill* case, as I have said, the New Zealand Court of Appeal [1994] 3 NZLR 513 and the Privy Council [1996] 2 WLR 367 found it in general patterns of socio-economic behaviour. I do not propose to explore further the doctrine of general reliance because, for reasons which I shall explain, I think that there are no grounds upon which the present case can be brought within it. I will only note in passing that its application may require some very careful analysis of the role which the expected exercise of the statutory power plays in community behaviour. For example, in one sense it is true that the fire brigade is there to protect people in situations in which they could not be expected to be able to protect themselves. On the other hand, they can and do protect themselves by insurance against the risk of fire. It is not obvious that there should be a right to compensation from a negligent fire authority which will ordinarily insure by right of subrogation to an insurance company. The only reason would be to provide a general deterrent against inefficiency. But there must be better ways of doing this than by compensating insurance companies out of public funds. And while premiums no doubt take into account the existence of the fire brigade and the likelihood that it will arrive swiftly upon the scene, it is not clear that they would be very different merely because no compensation was paid in the rare cases in which the fire authority negligently failed to perform its public duty.

Notes

1. In *East Suffolk Rivers Catchment Board v Kent* [1941] AC 74 the defendants had *power* under statute to repair river banks. In 1936 a combination of a gale and a spring tide breached the river bank causing flooding of the claimant's land. Three times the defendants tried to dam the breach, without success. The breach was finally repaired by an alternative method 178 days after starting work. It should have been done in 14 days. Although the defendants only had a power to repair the bank

and were under no *duty* to do so, the claimant claimed that they were liable because they had voluntarily undertaken the work and by their negligence had taken too long to repair the damage. The House of Lords held that the defendants were not liable. They could be liable only if their negligence had made the situation worse than it would have been without their intervention.

2. In *Gorringe* v *Calderdale MBC* [2004] UKHL 15, the claimant collided with a bus which was obscured by a sharp crest in the road. In the past there had been a 'SLOW' warning sign painted on the road but this had disappeared when the road was resurfaced. The claimant sued the council for failing to warn her of the danger, but the House of Lords dismissed her claim, relying on **Stovin**. One point to emerge is a potential distinction between cases where the public body has merely failed to provide a benefit, as in **Stovin**, and cases where a relationship (albeit created by a statutory duty) exists between the parties. In *Gorringe* Lord Hoffmann said 'I find it difficult to imagine a case in which a common law duty can be founded simply upon the failure (however irrational) to provide some benefit which a public authority has power (or a public duty) to provide' (at [32]). See also *Sumner* v *Colborne Denbighshire County Council and The Welsh Ministers* [2018] EWCA Civ 1006.

3. Lord Hoffmann was clearly cautious about general reliance being the foundation of claims, as was Lord Nicholls—for he pointed out that if reliance means only that the public can expect that the authority will act as a reasonable authority, that is not enough to provide liability (at [938]). Lord Nicholls and Lord Slynn dissented on the ground that there were sufficient special circumstances over and above the reasonableness or otherwise of the decision to bring about proximity.

4. Limitations on the liability of public bodies were once again illustrated by *Jain* v *Trent SHA* [2009] UKHL 4, this time in relation to the bringing of legal action by regulatory bodies. In that case the claimants owned a nursing home and without giving them any notice the defendant health authority made an *ex parte* application to the magistrates' court to cancel the home's registration. This resulted in the home's immediate closure. The claimants' appeal was heard five months later and was successful, and the tribunal was highly critical of the authority's actions, but by then the business had been destroyed. The House of Lords regretted that the common law was unable to provide a remedy, although the House noted that the Human Rights Act 1998 (which was not applicable at the time of the events in this case) would now provide an action under Article 1 First Protocol to the European Convention on Human Rights (ECHR) (right to peaceful enjoyment of possessions) and Article 6 ECHR (right to a fair hearing). Lord Scott said that:

> where action is taken by a state authority under statutory powers designed for the benefit or protection of a particular class of persons, a tortious duty of care will not be held to be owed by the State authority to others whose interests may be adversely affected by an exercise of the statutory power. The reason is that the imposition of such a duty would or might inhibit the exercise of the statutory powers and be potentially adverse to the interests of the class of persons the powers were designed to benefit or protect, thereby putting at risk the achievement of their statutory purpose. (at [28])

However, could it not be argued that the claimants could expect (and rely upon) the expeditious hearing of their case?

5.2 Specific problematic areas: emergency services

Claims against the emergency services are illustrative of how claims against public bodies create a 'special duty problem'. The same is true of claims against the armed forces. Also see many of the 'omissions' cases outlined in Chapter 3 (one problem with public bodies is that it is often an omission on their part which leads to an allegation of negligence, so there is a great deal of overlap). Public policy has loomed large in the context of whether a duty should be imposed, especially in 'novel' situations with no previous analogous case (see section 2.3, though now see comments in **Poole** about the relevance of public policy arguments).

> ### *Capital and Counties plc v Hampshire County Council*
> Court of Appeal [1997] QB 1004

A number of cases concerning fire brigades were heard together. In one (*London Fire Brigade*), the defendants attended a fire but failed to check a neighbouring property where the fire later spread. It was held that there was insufficient proximity and so no duty to have done so. In another case (*Hampshire*) a fire officer ordered the sprinkler system to be turned off and, because he had made the situation worse than it would otherwise have been, there was sufficient proximity and thus liability. The extracts below deal only with the subsequent question of whether, assuming there is sufficient proximity, it would be 'fair and reasonable' to impose liability.

STUART-SMITH LJ: . . . We consider first, therefore, whether there is any reason of policy why the Hampshire Fire Authority should not be liable. The starting point is that 'the public policy consideration which has first claim on the loyalty of the law is that wrongs should be remedied, and that very potent considerations are required to override that policy': *per* Lord Browne-Wilkinson in *X (Minors) v Bedfordshire County Council* [1995] 2 AC 633, 749.

. . .

In the *East Suffolk* case, it is clear that the board would have been liable if through their negligence they had added to the damage the plaintiff would otherwise have suffered. The dividing line between liability and non-liability is thus defined and there is no need to pray in aid any concept of public policy. We agree with Mr Sumption that the courts should not grant immunity from suit to fire brigades simply because the judge may have what he describes as a visceral dislike for allowing possibly worthless claims to be made against public authorities, whose activities involve the laudable operation of rescuing the person or property of others in conditions often of great danger. Such claims may indeed be motivated by what is sometimes perceived to be the current attitude to litigation: 'If you have suffered loss and can see a solvent target, sue it.' None the less, if a defendant is to be immune from suit such immunity must be based upon principle.

It seems to us that in those cases where the courts have granted immunity or refused to impose a duty of care it is usually possible to discern a recognition that such a duty would be inconsistent with some wider object of the law or interest of the particular parties. Thus, if the existence of a duty of care would impede the careful performance of the relevant function, or if investigation of the allegedly negligent conduct would itself be undesirable and open to abuse by those bearing grudges, the law will not impose a duty. Some cases on either side of the line illustrate this.

. . .

In *Ancell v McDermot[t]* [1993] 4 All ER 355 it was held that the imposition of a duty of care on the police to protect road users from hazards caused by others would be so extensive as to divert the police from the proper functions of detecting and preventing crime. And in *Osman v Ferguson* [1993] 4 All ER 344, although the majority of the court considered that it was arguable that there was sufficient proximity between the plaintiff's family and investigating police officers, the imposition of a duty of care towards a potential victim might result in the significant diversion of police resources from the investigation and suppression of crime and was therefore contrary to public policy.

On the other hand liability has been imposed when, in the course of carrying out their duties, the police have themselves created the danger: see *Rigby v Chief Constable of Northamptonshire* [1985] 1 WLR 1242; *Knightley v Johns* [1982] 1 WLR 349; *Alcock v Chief Constable of South Yorkshire* [1992] 1 AC 310 and *Marshall v Osmond* [1983] QB 1034.

In our judgment there is no doubt on which side of the line a case such as the *Hampshire* case falls. It is one where the defendants, by their action in turning off the sprinklers, created or increased the danger. There is no ground for giving immunity in such a case.

Rougier J in the *London Fire Brigade* case, after citing from the speeches of Lord Keith of Kinkel and Lord Templeman in *Hill's* case [1989] AC 53, set out a number of reasons why in his judgment it was not appropriate to impose a common law duty to take care on fire brigades. He said [1996] 3 WLR 988, 1003:

> I think that as regards the fire brigade many of these considerations are applicable and militate on grounds of public policy against the imposition of any common law duty. In particular, I would single out the following. (1) I do not think that any extra standard of care would be achieved. (2) Rather the reverse, if a common law duty of care can lead to defensive policing, by the same token it can lead to defensive fire-fighting. Fearful of being accused of leaving the scene too early, the officer in charge might well commit his resources when they would have been better employed elsewhere. He would be open to criticism every time there was a balance to be struck or that sort of operational choice to be made. (3) If the efficiency of the emergency services is to be tested, it should be done not in private litigation but by an inquiry instituted by national or local authorities who are responsible to the electorate. This follows the reasoning of Lord Templeman in *Hill's* case [1989] AC 53. (4) *Marc Rich & Co AG v Bishop Rock Marine Co Ltd* [1996] AC 211 suggests that the fact that a defendant in the position of the fire brigade acts for the collective welfare is one that should be taken into account. (5) Last, and to my mind by far the most important consideration, is what is sometimes referred to as the 'floodgates' argument.

Judge Crawford QC in the *West Yorkshire* case added a number of others—we continue the numbering from that set out in the passage above. (6) The distraction that court cases would involve from the proper task of fire-fighting. (7) It might create massive claims which would be an unreasonable burden on the taxpayer. (8) It is for the individual to insure against fire risks.

These reasons have been subjected to considerable criticism by counsel for the plaintiffs on the following lines.

(1) and (2): No improvement in standard of care; defensive fire-fighting

It seems hardly realistic that a fire officer who has to make a split second decision as to the manner in which fire-fighting operations are to be conducted will be looking over his shoulder at the possibility of his employers being made vicariously liable for his negligence. If there can be liability for negligence, it is better to have a high threshold of negligence established in the *Bolam* test and for judges to remind themselves that fire officers who make difficult decisions in difficult circumstances should be given considerable latitude before being held guilty of negligence. It is not readily apparent why the imposition of a duty of care should divert the fire brigade resources from other fire-fighting duties.

(3): Private litigation unsuitable for discovering failures of service

As to this reason, counsel for the plaintiffs in the *Hampshire* case pointed out that, although there was a very extensive internal inquiry in that case starting on the day of the fire, it was only the litigation that uncovered the serious shortcomings of the service.

(4): Undesirability of actions against authorities operating for collective welfare

It was said that the fact that the defendant is a public authority acting for the collective welfare of the community such as the National Health Service has never been regarded as a ground for immunity; in any event the benefit is also for the individual householder.

(5): Floodgates

Having regard to the extreme paucity of recorded cases against fire brigades in spite of the fact that for over 40 years *Halsbury's Laws of England* have indicated that an action would lie, this argument should be disregarded. Again, the *Bolam* test should afford sufficient protection.

(6): Distraction from fire-fighting

In any action against a public authority officers and employees will be distracted from their ordinary duties; that should not be regarded as a valid ground for granting immunity.

(7): Massive claims against the taxpayer

This is ultimately an argument for the immunity from suit of government departments and all public authorities.

(8): Insurance

The general rule in English law is that in determining the rights inter se of A and B, the fact that one of them is insured is to be disregarded: see *per* Viscount Simonds in *Lister v Romford Ice and Cold Storage Co Ltd* [1957] AC 555, 576, 577. Insurance premiums are calculated having regard to the existence and likely response of the fire brigade; very substantial reductions in premiums are granted where buildings are protected by sprinklers; there may be underinsurances and absence of insurance, particularly in the lower end of the property market. Further, it would be unusual for there to be effective insurance against personal injury. Finally, there is nothing to prevent fire brigades insuring against their liability. Indeed the London and West Yorkshire brigades are insured.

In our judgment there is considerable force in the criticisms made. If we had found a sufficient relationship of proximity in the *London Fire Brigade* and *West Yorkshire* cases, we do not think that we would have found the arguments for excluding a duty of care on the ground that it would not be just, fair and reasonable convincing. The analogy with the police exercising their functions of investigating and suppressing crime is not close. The floodgates argument is not persuasive; nor is that based on insurance. Many of the other arguments are equally applicable to other public services, for example, the National Health Service. We do not think that the principles which underlie those decisions where immunity has been granted can be sufficiently identified in the case of fire brigades.

Notes

1. This is a complicated set of decisions and the case is much bound up with issues which relate to all public bodies. There now seems to be some confusion between factors which limit proximity and those which will be relevant for the incremental development test. It is suggested that policy will be relevant for proximity insofar as the court is trying to set a rule for a category of case such as negligent misstatement or economic loss, and the main part of *Capital and Counties* may be regarded as limiting proximity in cases where a public body has a power but not a duty to act.

2. *Capital and Counties* was distinguished in *Kent v Griffiths* [2000] 2 All ER 474 in a claim against an ambulance service. The claimant suffered an asthma attack and her doctor ordered an ambulance which took 40 minutes to arrive. She had a respiratory arrest. No explanation was given for the delay. In holding the defendants liable, it was said that the ambulance service was part of the health service and not like the police or fire services whose function was to protect the public generally. There was no conflict between the interests of the public at large and the claimant, and no issue of allocation of resources or a conflict of priorities, thus a duty of care arose, in particular as the ambulance was responding to a named individual. If there had been a more urgent case needing attention that would have been different, but that would have been a matter of the

standard of care (responding in a reasonable time in the circumstances) rather than a question of whether a duty was owed.

3. A duty was found on similar grounds against the police, who had failed to respond promptly to a 999 call, despite assurances that they would do so and that the caller could leave it with them, in *Sherratt* v *Chief Constable of Greater Manchester Police* [2018] EWHC 1746 (QB).

Hill v Chief Constable of West Yorkshire
House of Lords [1989] AC 53

Between 1975 and 1980 a serial killer known as 'the Yorkshire Ripper' was active in the West Yorkshire area. The mother of his last victim, Jacqueline Hill, sued the police on behalf of the estate of her daughter for alleged negligence in failing to catch him earlier than they did. Held: no duty was owed as there was insufficient proximity, but the House also held (*obiter*) that the action would be barred for public policy reasons.

LORD KEITH: . . . [T]here is another reason why an action for damages in negligence should not lie against the police in circumstances such as those of the present case, and that is public policy. . . . Potential existence of such liability may in many instances be in the general public interest, as tending towards the observance of a higher standard of care in the carrying on of various different types of activity. I do not, however, consider that this can be said of police activities. The general sense of public duty which motivates police forces is unlikely to be appreciably reinforced by the imposition of such liability so far as concerns their function in the investigation and suppression of crime. From time to time they make mistakes in the exercise of that function, but it is not to be doubted that they apply their best endeavours to the performance of it. In some instances the imposition of liability may lead to the exercise of a function being carried on in a detrimentally defensive frame of mind. The possibility of this happening in relation to the investigative operations of the police cannot be excluded. Further it would be reasonable to expect that if potential liability were to be imposed it would be not uncommon for actions to be raised against police forces on the ground that they had failed to catch some criminal as soon as they might have done, with the result that he went on to commit further crimes. While some such actions might involve allegations of a simple and straightforward type of failure—for example that a police officer negligently tripped and fell while pursuing a burglar—others would be likely to enter deeply into the general nature of a police investigation, as indeed the present action would seek to do. The manner of conduct of such an investigation must necessarily involve a variety of decisions to be made on matters of policy and discretion, for example as to which particular line of inquiry is most advantageously to be pursued and what is the most advantageous way to deploy the available resources. Many such decisions would not be regarded by the courts as appropriate to be called in question, yet elaborate investigation of the facts might be necessary to ascertain whether or not this was so. A great deal of police time, trouble and expense might be expected to have to be put into the preparation of the defence to the action and the attendance of witnesses at the trial. The result would be a significant diversion of police manpower and attention from their most important function, that of the suppression of crime. Closed investigations would require to be reopened and retraversed, not with the object of bringing any criminal to justice but to ascertain whether or not they had been competently conducted.

Notes

1. *Hill* was applied in *Osman* v *Ferguson* [1993] 4 All ER 344 and again confirmed in *Brooks* v *Commissioner of Police of the Metropolis* [2005] 1 WLR 1495. In that case Duwayne Brooks was a witness to the racist murder in 1993 of his friend Stephen Lawrence. The subsequent investigation was badly conducted and the claimant suffered post-traumatic stress disorder (the actions of the police were later roundly condemned in Sir William Macpherson's *Report on the Stephen Lawrence Inquiry* (Cm 4262-I, 1999). Lord Steyn supported *Hill* (although Lord Bingham had doubts about its extent) and accordingly *Hill* was used to prevent duty of care to a *witness* where the alleged breaches of duty were inextricably bound up with the investigation of the case.

2. In *Smith* v *Chief Constable of Sussex* [2008] UKHL 50, the House of Lords again affirmed *Hill*, in a case where a man complained to the police about threats made by his ex-partner and was subsequently attacked, after the police had done little or nothing to investigate his claims. Lord Carswell said:

   > I am satisfied nevertheless that the reasons underlying the acceptance of the general rule that a duty of care is not imposed upon police officers in cases such as the present remain valid. . . The factor of paramount importance is to give the police sufficient freedom to exercise their judgment in pursuit of their objects in work in the public interest, without being trammelled by the need to devote excessive time and attention to complaints or being constantly under the shadow of threatened litigation. Over-reaction to complaints, resulting from defensive policing, is to be avoided just as much as failure to react with sufficient speed and effectiveness. That said, one must also express the hope that police officers will make good use of this freedom, with wisdom and discretion in judging the risks, investigating complaints and taking appropriate action to minimise or remove the risk of threats being carried out. . . It remains to be considered whether there are any exceptions to the generality of the rule. (at [108]–[109])

   Lord Bingham dissented, arguing that 'if a member of the public (A) furnishes a police officer (B) with apparently credible evidence that a third party whose identity and whereabouts are known presents a specific and imminent threat to his life or physical safety, B owes A a duty to take reasonable steps to assess such threat and, if appropriate, take reasonable steps to prevent it being executed' (at [44]). As yet, there have been no 'exceptions to the generality of the rule', as potentially envisaged by Lord Carswell in *Smith* (see further **Michael v Chief Constable of South Wales Police** [2015] UKSC 2 in the following extract).

3. In *Elguzouli-Daf* v *Commissioner of Police* [1995] 1 All ER 833, the claimant had been held in custody for 85 days before the Crown Prosecution Service (CPS) dropped the charges. It was held that the CPS owed no duty to the claimant, as such a duty would lead prosecutors to take a defensive attitude and the welfare of the community amounted to sufficient policy reason to preclude a duty.

4. As with other public bodies, the police can be found liable in relation to direct and positive acts (see e.g. *Rigby* v *Chief Constable of Northampton* [1985] 1 WLR 1242; *Knightley* v *Johns* [1982] 1 WLR 349). The principle was strongly reaffirmed in **Robinson v Chief Constable of West Yorkshire Police** in which the Supreme Court (overturning the Court of Appeal) found police officers owed a duty of care to an elderly woman who was knocked to the ground and injured during the arrest of a drug dealer on a Huddersfield street.

5. The Supreme Court of Canada has held that the police *can* be liable for negligent investigation of a case, for example where an innocent person is wrongly convicted: see *Hill* v *Hamilton-Wentworth Regional Police* (2007) 285 DLR (4th) 620; 2007 SCC 41 (although there was no liability on the facts). McLachlin CJ said that no compelling distinction lies between the exercise of professional discretion by police and others, and that on the 'chilling effect' of potential liability, 'the record does not support the conclusion that recognising potential liability in tort significantly

changes the behaviour of police', thus rejecting the notion of defensive policing. See also *Doe* v *Metropolitan Toronto (Municipality) Commissioners of Police* [1998] 160 DLR (4th) 289.

6. For a discussion of the issues in **Hill**, see Hanna Wilberg 'Defensive Practice or Conflict of Duties? Policy Concerns in Public Authority Negligence Claims' (2010) 126 LQR 420; Claire McIvor 'Getting Defensive About Police Negligence: The *Hill* Principle, the Human Rights Act 1998 and the House of Lords' [2010] CLJ 133; Kirsty Horsey 'Trust in the Police? Police Negligence, Invisible Immunity and Disadvantaged Claimants' in Janice Richardson and Erika Rackley (eds) *Feminist Perspectives on Tort Law* (Routledge, 2012).

Michael v Chief Constable of South Wales Police
Supreme Court [2015] UKSC 2

A woman phoned 999, reporting that her former partner was threatening her life, and had already violently dragged away her current boyfriend. The police call handler failed to properly categorise the call, and there was no immediate response. The woman called back, at which point the operator heard screaming, which then stopped. The police then responded immediately but upon arrival at the woman's house, found that she had been stabbed to death. At first instance, a claim in negligence on her behalf was allowed to proceed. The Court of Appeal found in favour of the defendants, on the basis of **Hill**, and issued summary judgment for the defendants. Held: the majority held that the police owed her no duty of care (Lord Kerr and Lady Hale dissenting).

LORD TOULSON:

Issues 1 and 2: did the police owe a duty of care to Ms Michael on receiving her 999 call?

115. The refusal of the courts to impose a private law duty on the police to exercise reasonable care to safeguard victims or potential victims of crime, except in cases where there has been a representation and reliance, does not involve giving special treatment to the police. It is consistent with the way in which the common law has been applied to other authorities vested with powers or duties as a matter of public law for the protection of the public. . . .

116. The question is therefore not whether the police should have a special immunity, but whether an exception should be made to the ordinary application of common law principles which would cover the facts of the present case.

117. Ms Monaghan [counsel for the intervenors] has advanced essentially two arguments in support of the interveners' liability principle. The first is that the nature and scale of the problem of domestic violence is such that the courts ought to introduce such a principle to provide protection for victims and a spur to the police to respond to the problem more effectively. The second is that the common law should be extended in harmony with the obligations of the police under articles 2 and 3 of the Convention.

118. I recognise fully that the statistics about the incidence of domestic violence and the facts of individual cases such as the present are shocking. I recognise also that the court has been presented with fresh material on the subject. However, I am not persuaded that they should cause the court to create a new category of duty of care for several reasons.

119. If the foundation of a duty of care is the public law duty of the police for the preservation of the Queen's peace, it is hard to see why the duty should be confined to potential victims of a particular kind of breach of the peace. Would a duty of care be owed to a person who reported a credible threat

to burn down his house? Would it be owed to a company which reported a credible threat by animal rights extremists to its premises? If not, why not?

120. It is also hard to see why it should be limited to particular potential victims. If the police fail through lack of care to catch a criminal before he shoots and injures his intended victim and also a bystander (or if he misses his intended target and hits someone else), is it right that one should be entitled to compensation but not the other, when the duty of the police is a general duty for the preservation of the Queen's peace? Similarly if the intelligence service fails to respond appropriately to intelligence that a terrorist group is intending to bring down an airliner, is it right that the service should be liable to the dependants of the victims on the plane but not the victims on the ground? Such a distinction would be understandable if the duty is founded on a representation to, and reliance by, a particular individual but that is not the basis of the interveners' liability principle. These questions underline the fact that the duty of the police for the preservation of the peace is owed to members of the public at large, and does not involve the kind of close or special relationship ('proximity' or 'neighbourhood') necessary for the imposition of a private law duty of care.

121. As to the argument that imposition of the interveners' liability principle should improve the performance of the police in dealing with cases of actual or threatened domestic violence, the court has no way of judging the likely operational consequences of changing the law of negligence in the way that is proposed. Mr Bowen [counsel for the appellants] and Ms Monaghan were critical of statements in *Hill* and other cases that the imposition of a duty of care would inevitably lead to an unduly defensive attitude by the police. Those criticisms have force. But the court would risk falling into equal error if it were to accept the proposition, on the basis of intuition, that a change in the civil law would lead to a reduction of domestic violence or an improvement in its investigation. Failures in the proper investigation of reports of violence or threatened violence can have disciplinary consequences (as there were in the present case), and it is speculative whether the addition of potential liability at common law would make a practical difference at an individual level to the conduct of police officers and support staff. At an institutional level, it is possible to imagine that it might lead to police forces changing their priorities by applying more resources to reports of violence or threatened violence, but if so, it is hard to see that it would be in the public interest for the determination of police priorities to be affected by the risk of being sued.

122. The only consequence of which one can be sure is that the imposition of liability on the police to compensate victims of violence on the basis that the police should have prevented it would have potentially significant financial implications. The payment of compensation and the costs of dealing with claims, whether successful or unsuccessful, would have to come either from the police budget, with a corresponding reduction of spending on other services, or from an increased burden on the public or from a combination of the two.

123. In support of the argument that the court should develop the common law to encompass the duties of the police under the Convention, Mr Bowen and Ms Monaghan submitted that consistency between the common law and the Convention should be encouraged and relied in particular on observations of the Court of Appeal in *D v East Berkshire NHS Trust* [2003] EWCA Civ 1151, [2004] QB 558, paras 79–85.

124. There are certainly areas where the Convention has had an influence on the common law. Possibly the most striking example is in the law of confidentiality, which the courts have developed to include a partial law of privacy in response to the requirements of article 8 (*Campbell v MGN Ltd* [2004] 2 AC 457). But two points should be noted about that. First, the common law had long been regarded as defective. It was heavily criticised by Bingham LJ in *Kaye v Robertson* [1991] FSR 62, but the Court of Appeal held with regret that only Parliament could cure it. The Human Rights Act 1998

provided the means for reform. In debates on the bill Lord Irvine of Lairg, LC made it clear that in his view the Act would open the way to the courts developing rights of privacy through article 8, and so it did. Secondly, development of the law was necessary to comply with article 8, as interpreted by the Strasbourg court.

125. The circumstances of the present case are different. The suggested development of the law of negligence is not necessary to comply with articles 2 and 3. On orthodox common law principles I cannot see a legal basis for fashioning a duty of care limited in scope to that of articles 2 and 3, or for gold plating the claimant's Convention rights by providing compensation on a different basis from the claim under the Human Rights Act 1998. Nor do I see a principled legal basis for introducing a wider duty in negligence than would arise either under orthodox common law principles or under the Convention.

126. The same argument, that the common law should be developed in harmony with the obligations of public bodies including the police under the Human Rights Act 1998 and articles 2 and 3 of the Convention, was advanced in *Smith* [v *Chief Constable of Sussex*] as a ground for holding that the police owed a duty of care to the deceased after he reported receiving threats. Reliance was similarly placed on the approach of the Court of Appeal *in D v East Berkshire NHS Trust* (as noted by Lord Phillips MR, who had delivered the judgment of the Court of Appeal in that case). Counsel for Mr Smith relied particularly on the analysis of the effect of the Human Rights Act in *D v East Bedfordshire NHS Trust* at paras 55 to 87: see the reported argument at [2009] 1 AC 225, 240. The argument by analogy with that case which presently commends itself to Lady Hale is therefore not a new argument, but one which failed to persuade the majority in *Smith*.

127. The argument was rejected by the House of Lords for reasons given by Lord Hope (paras 81–82), Lord Phillips (paras 98–99) and most fully by Lord Brown (paras 136–139). Lord Brown did not consider that the possibility of a Human Rights Act claim was a good reason for creating a parallel common law claim, still less for creating a wider duty of care. He observed that Convention claims had different objectives from civil actions, as Lord Bingham pointed out in *R (Greenfield) v Secretary of State for the Home Department* [2005] 1 WLR 673. Whereas civil actions are designed essentially to compensate claimants for losses, Convention claims are intended to uphold minimum human rights standards and to vindicate those rights. The difference in purpose has led to different time limits and different approaches to damages and causation. Lord Brown recognised that the violation of a fundamental right is a very serious thing, but he saw no sound reason for matching the Convention claim with a common law claim. To do so would in his view neither add to the vindication of the right, nor be likely to deter the police from the action or inaction which risked violating it in the first place.

128. It is unnecessary for the purposes of this appeal to decide questions about the scope of article 3 and I would not wish to influence the Court of Appeal's consideration of the judgment in *DSD v Commissioner of Police of the Metropolis*. It does not alter the essence of the argument which was considered and rejected by the House of Lords in *Smith*. I am not persuaded that it would be right for the court to depart from that decision, which itself was consistent with a line of previous authorities.

129. In support of the narrower liability principle proposed by Lord Bingham in *Smith*, Mr Bowen submitted that limitation of a duty of care to A to cases where A has provided the police with apparently credible evidence that she or he is under a specific and imminent threat to their life or personal safety from a person whose identity and whereabouts are known would satisfy the requirement of closeness or 'proximity'. But the majority in *Smith* rejected Lord Bingham's formula for reasons which remain cogent. It would be unsatisfactory to draw dividing lines according to whether the threat is reported by A or by someone else (for example, in the present case by the man driven home by Ms Michael's murderer before he returned and killed her); or whether the threat is credible and imminent

or credible but not imminent; or whether the whereabouts of the person making the threat are known or unknown; or whether the threatened violence was to A's person or property or both. As to the first of those distinctions (whether the threat was reported by A or someone else), Lord Bingham's own position was ambiguous because his formula confined the duty to a case where the threat was reported by A, but he also disapproved the decision in *OLL Ltd v Secretary of State for Transport*, in which the concerns about the safety of the children and adults at sea were raised by other people.

130. More generally, I would reject the narrower liability principle advocated by the claimants for the same reasons as the broader liability principle advocated by the interveners. If it is thought that there should be public compensation for victims of certain types of crime, above that which is provided under the criminal injuries compensation scheme, in cases of pure omission by the police to perform their duty for the prevention of violence, it should be for Parliament to determine whether there should be such a scheme and, if so, what should be its scope as to the types of crime, types of loss and any financial limits. By introducing the Human Rights Act 1998 a cause of action has been created in the limited circumstances where the police have acted in breach of articles 2 and 3 (or article 8). There are good reasons why the positive obligations of the state under those articles are limited. The creation of such a statutory cause of action does not itself provide a sufficient reason for the common law to duplicate or extend it.

131. So far I have been addressing the appellants' and the interveners' arguments. Lord Kerr advances an alternative liability principle which he puts in a broader and a narrower form. He acknowledges (at para 144) that for a duty of care to arise it is necessary to identify a feature (or combination of features) which creates (or create) a sufficient proximity of relationship between the claimant and the defendant. The question 'Is there a sufficient proximity of relationship?' is a shorthand way of putting the question posed by Lord Devlin in *Hedley Byrne* [1964] AC 465 at p 525 'Is the relationship between the parties in this case such that it can be brought within a category giving rise to a special duty?' As Lord Devlin observed, the first step in such an inquiry is to see how far the authorities have gone, for new categories in the law do not spring into existence overnight. In the earlier part of this judgment I have examined how far the authorities presently go and have considered whether there should be a new exception to the general principle about omissions to prevent harm being caused by a third party who is not under the defendant's control.

132. Lord Kerr's broader proposal (at para 144) is that 'proximity of relationship' in the present context should comprise these elements: (i) a closeness of association between the claimant and the defendant, which can but need not necessarily arise from information communicated to the defendant; (ii) the information should convey to the defendant that serious harm is likely to befall the intended victim if urgent action is not taken; (iii) the defendant is a person or agency who might reasonably be expected to provide protection in those circumstances; and (iv) he should be able to provide for the intended victim's protection without unnecessary danger to himself.

133. Lord Kerr notes that this suggested principle might at first sight appear similar to Lord Bingham's liability principle, but he observes that his principle, unlike Lord Bingham's, has the ingredient of proximity built into it as part of what has to be established. This is in my respectful opinion a serious flaw. Whereas Lord Bingham identified the factors which he considered should give rise to duty of care in law, Lord Kerr's proposition requires it to be established that the relationship has sufficient closeness (proximity) to amount to proximity. In this respect it is circular. It leaves the question of closeness or proximity open ended. It amounts to saying that there is a relationship of proximity if the relationship is sufficiently close for there to be proximity.

134. Lord Kerr says (at para 163) that the nature of the interaction between the parties is critical to the question whether the necessary proximity exists. He goes on to say (at para 166) that this

depends on the facts of the particular case and that for this reason his proposition at para 144 is loosely drawn (or, as I would say, circular). It provides no yardstick for answering the question which it poses.

135. Lord Kerr says that any narrower test would run the risk of producing anomalous results such as the example which he gives at para 165. In that paragraph he posits the case of a person who through the negligence of the police is given a false impression that an assurance of timeous assistance has been given, on which the person relies. If a person is negligently misled by the police into believing that help is at hand, and acts on what she has negligently been led falsely to believe, she would have a potential claim under the *Hedley Byrne* principle. Whether that was so in this case is the subject of issue 3. There is, however, nothing anomalous in the *Hedley Byrne* principle itself or in its limitation. The principle established by *Hedley Byrne* is that a careless misrepresentation may give rise to a relationship akin to contract under which there is a positive duty to act. Lord Devlin spoke of 'an assumption of responsibility in circumstances in which, but for the absence of consideration, there would be a contract' and he said that 'wherever there is a relationship equivalent to contract, there is a duty of care' (pp 529–530). To extend the principle to a case in which the core ingredients were absent would be to cut its moorings.

136. However, Lord Kerr goes on to advance a narrower liability principle (at para 168). His narrower proposition is that whether a relationship of proximity exists should depend on whether sufficient information has been conveyed or is available to the police to alert them to the urgent need to take action which it is within their power to take; the information must be specific; and the threat must be imminent. It is critical, he says, that the police know of an imminent threat to a particular individual, and the duty is personalised to the intended victim.

137. Lord Kerr's narrower liability principle closely resembles Lord Bingham's liability principle, which was rejected by a majority of the House of Lords. It presents most of the problems to which I have referred, such as why a duty should be owed to the intended victim of a drive-by shooting but not to an injured bystander; why the threat should have to be imminent; and why the victim of a threatened arson attack should be owed a duty of protection against consequential personal injury, but not the burning down of his home. Lord Kerr rightly says (at para 181) that the police have been empowered to protect the public from harm. They have indeed a duty to keep the peace and to protect property, which applies to all potential victims of crime. Lord Kerr does not subscribe to the interveners' liability principle, and I cannot see a proper basis for holding there is a private law duty of care within the terms of Lord Kerr's narrower alternative.

Issue 3: should the police be held to have assumed responsibility to take reasonable care for Ms Michael's safety?

138. Mr Bowen submitted that what was said by the Gwent call handler who received Ms Michael's 999 call was arguably sufficient to give rise to an assumption of responsibility on the *Hedley Byrne* principle as amplified in *Spring v Guardian Assurance Plc*. I agree with the Court of Appeal that the argument is not tenable. The only assurance which the call handler gave to Ms Michael was that she would pass on the call to the South Wales Police. She gave no promise how quickly they would respond. She told Ms Michael that they would want to call her back and asked her to keep her phone free, but this did not amount to advising or instructing her to remain in her house, as was suggested. Ms Michael's call was made on her mobile phone. Nor did the call handler's inquiry whether Ms Michael could lock the house amount to advising or instructing her to remain there. The case is very different from *Kent v Griffiths* where the call handler gave misleading assurances that an ambulance would be arriving shortly.

Notes

1. All was not lost for the claimants, as the seven-member Supreme Court unanimously found that the case could go to trial on the ground that the police's (in)actions had potentially violated Ms Michael's Article 2 right to life (at [139]). Human rights claims are discussed in section 5.3.

2. In dissent, Lady Hale agreed with Lord Kerr, as well as identifying potential policy reasons that may militate against those expounded in *Hill* and subsequently relied on in the cases outlined above. She said:

   > [I]n developing the law it is wise to proceed on a case by case basis, and the formulation offered by Lord Kerr would be sufficient to enable this claim to go to trial at common law as well as under the Human Rights Act 1998. It is difficult indeed to see how recognising the possibility of such claims could make the task of policing any more difficult than it already is. It might conceivably, however, lead to some much-needed improvements in their response to threats of serious domestic abuse. This continues to be a source of concern to Her Majesty's Inspectorate of Constabulary: see *Everyone's Business: Improving the Police Response to Domestic Abuse* (2014). I very much regret to say that some of the attitudes which have led to the inadequacies revealed in that report may also have crept into the policy considerations discussed in *Smith* (by Lord Carswell at para 107 and Lord Hope at para 76). If the imposition of liability in negligence can help to counter such attitudes, so much the better. But the principles suggested here should apply to all specific threats of imminent injury to individuals which the police are in a position to prevent, whatever their source. (at [198])

   The fact that cracks are beginning to show in support at the highest level for *Hill*, perhaps shows that the door is not firmly closed against this type of claim, where there is a clearer assumption of responsibility. See, for example, *Sherratt* v *Chief Constable of Greater Manchester Police* [2018] EWHC 1746 (QB).

3. In *Commissioner of Police of the Metropolis* v *DSD and another* [2018] UKSC 11 (the Court of Appeal deliberations on which were mentioned in the extract above at [128]) the Supreme Court upheld a finding that the failings of the police, this time in their investigations into John Worboys, the 'Black Cab Rapist', engaged the claimant's rights under Article 3 ECHR, placing a positive duty on the police. It is hard to see that a corresponding private law duty should not arise in such a situation.

4. In *Osman* v *UK* (2000) 29 EHRR 245, the European Court of Human Rights found that the application of the *Hill* 'immunity' for the police was a breach of Article 6 which requires that in the determination of their civil rights everyone is entitled to a fair hearing. The court said that the application of a blanket immunity in *Osman* v *Ferguson* was an unjustifiable restriction on the applicant's right to have a determination of the merits of the claim. The argument was that the public policy in restricting claims against the police must be balanced against the interests of the *particular* claimant, whereas the common law was balancing the interests of the police against potential claimants as a whole, and this amounted to a blanket immunity. However, the European Court reconsidered its view in *Z*.

Z and others v *UK*
European Court of Human Rights (Application no 29392/95) [2001] ECHR 333

This case arose out of *X* v *Bedfordshire* (discussed in the *Poole* extract from [36]), in particular from the fact that the defendants had failed to prevent abuse of the applicants. The House of Lords had struck out the claim, finding that it was not fair and reasonable to impose a duty. Held: this was *not* a breach of Article 6, which requires that in the determination of civil rights everyone is entitled to a fair hearing, but that there *had* been a violation of Articles 3 and 13.

THE COURT:

94. It is contended by the applicants in this case that the decision of the House of Lords, finding that the local authority owed no duty of care, deprived them of access to a court as it was effectively an exclusionary rule, or an immunity from liability, which prevented their claims from being decided on the facts.

95. The Court observes, firstly, that the applicants were not prevented in any practical manner from bringing their claims before the domestic courts. Indeed, the case was litigated with vigour up to the House of Lords, the applicants being provided with legal aid for that purpose. Nor is it that any procedural rules or limitation periods had been relied on. The domestic courts were concerned with the application brought by the defendants to have the case struck out as disclosing no reasonable cause of action. This involved the pre-trial determination of whether, assuming the facts of the applicants' case as pleaded were true, there was a sustainable claim in law. The arguments before the courts were, therefore, concentrated on the legal issues, primarily whether a duty of care in negligence was owed to the applicants by the local authority.

96. Moreover, the Court is not persuaded that the House of Lords' decision that, as a matter of law, there was no duty of care in the applicants' case may be characterised as either an exclusionary rule or an immunity which deprived them of access to a court. As Lord Browne-Wilkinson explained in his leading speech, the House of Lords was concerned with the issue whether a novel category of negligence, that is a category of cases in which a duty of care had not previously been held to exist, should be developed by the courts in their law-making role under the common law (see paragraph 46 above). The House of Lords, after weighing in the balance the competing considerations of public policy, decided not to extend liability in negligence into a new area. In so doing, it circumscribed the range of liability under tort law.

97. That decision did end the case, without the factual matters being determined on the evidence. However, if as a matter of law, there was no basis for the claim, the hearing of evidence would have been an expensive and time-consuming process which would not have provided the applicants with any remedy at its conclusion. There is no reason to consider the striking-out procedure which rules on the existence of sustainable causes of action as *per se* offending the principle of access to a court. In such a procedure, the plaintiff is generally able to submit to the court the arguments supporting his or her claims on the law and the court will rule on those issues at the conclusion of an adversarial procedure (see paragraphs 66–68 above).

98. Nor is the Court persuaded by the suggestion that, irrespective of the position in domestic law, the decision disclosed an immunity in fact or practical effect due to its allegedly sweeping or blanket nature. That decision concerned only one aspect of the exercise of local authorities' powers and duties and cannot be regarded as an arbitrary removal of the courts' jurisdiction to determine a whole range of civil claims. . . . As it has recalled above in paragraph 87, it is a principle of Convention case-law that Article 6 does not in itself guarantee any particular content for civil rights and obligations in national law, although other Articles such as those protecting the right to respect for family life (Article 8) and the right to property (Article 1 of Protocol No 1) may do so. It is not enough to bring Article 6 §1 into play that the non-existence of a cause of action under domestic law may be described as having the same effect as an immunity, in the sense of not enabling the applicant to sue for a given category of harm.

99. Furthermore, it cannot be said that the House of Lords came to its conclusion without carefully balancing the policy reasons for and against the imposition of liability on the local authority in the circumstances of the applicants' case. Lord Browne-Wilkinson, in his leading judgment in the House of Lords, acknowledged that the public policy principle that wrongs should be remedied required very potent counter-considerations to be overridden (see paragraph 46 above). He weighed that principle against the other public policy concerns in reaching the conclusion that it was not fair, just or reasonable to impose a duty of care on the local authority in the applicants' case. It may be noted that in subsequent cases the domestic courts have further defined this area of law concerning the liability of local authorities in child-care matters, holding that a duty of care may arise in other factual situations, where, for example, a child has suffered harm once in local authority care, or a foster family has suffered harm as a result of the placement in their home by the local authority of an adolescent with a history of abusing younger children (see *W and Others v Essex County Council* and *Barrett*, both cited above, paragraphs 62–65 above).

100. The applicants, and the Commission in its report, relied on *Osman* (cited above) as indicating that the exclusion of liability in negligence, in that case concerning the acts or omissions of the police in the investigation and prevention of crime, acted as a restriction on access to a court. The Court considers that its reasoning in *Osman* was based on an understanding of the law of negligence (see, in particular, *Osman*, cited above,. . . [paras] 138–39) which has to be reviewed in the light of the clarifications subsequently made by the domestic courts and notably by the House of Lords. The Court is satisfied that the law of negligence as developed in the domestic courts since the case of *Caparo Industries plc* (cited above) and as recently analysed in the case of *Barrett* . . . includes the fair, just and reasonable criterion as an intrinsic element of the duty of care and that the ruling of law concerning that element in this case does not disclose the operation of an immunity. In the present case, the Court is led to the conclusion that the inability of the applicants to sue the local authority flowed not from an immunity but from the applicable principles governing the substantive right of action in domestic law. There was no restriction on access to a court of the kind contemplated in *Ashingdane* [v *the UK* (Application no 8225/78) [1985] ECHR 8].

101. The applicants may not, therefore, claim that they were deprived of any right to a determination on the merits of their negligence claims. Their claims were properly and fairly examined in light of the applicable domestic legal principles concerning the tort of negligence. Once the House of Lords had ruled on the arguable legal issues that brought into play the applicability of Article 6 §1 of the Convention (see paragraphs 87–89 above), the applicants could no longer claim any entitlement under Article 6 §1 to obtain any hearing concerning the facts. As pointed out above, such a hearing would have served no purpose, unless a duty of care in negligence had been held to exist in their case. It is not for this Court to find that this should have been the outcome of the striking-out proceedings since this would effectively involve substituting its own views as to the proper interpretation and content of domestic law.

Notes

1. The court in **Z** accepted that the striking-out procedure is not a breach of Article 6. (On this see Lord Woolf in *Kent* v *Griffiths* [2000] 2 All ER 474 at 485.) Despite the ruling on Article 6, the Court held that there was a breach of Article 3 (no one shall be subjected to torture or degrading treatment or punishment) and of Article 13 (everyone shall have an effective remedy before a national authority for violation of the Convention). On this point it is argued that the Human Rights Act 1998 now provides an effective remedy, even where (as here) the extrajudicial remedies were inadequate. This appears to be confirmed in *Commissioner of Police of the Metropolis* v *DSD and another* [2018] UKSC 11.

2. The Human Rights Act 1998 provides a direct right of action where the state or its organs have been in breach of the European Convention on Human Rights. For discussion of this form of liability, see **Savage v South Essex NHS Foundation Trust** [2008] UKHL 74 and **Van Colle v Chief Constable of Hertfordshire** [2008] UKHL 50, both extracted in the following section.

5.3 The human rights effect

European Convention on Human Rights—Article 2: Right to Life

1. Everyone's right to life shall be protected by law. No one shall be deprived of his life intentionally save in the execution of a sentence of a court following his conviction of a crime for which this penalty is provided by law.

2. Deprivation of life shall not be regarded as inflicted in contravention of this Article when it results from the use of force which is no more than absolutely necessary:

   (a) in defence of any person from unlawful violence;

   (b) in order to effect a lawful arrest or to prevent the escape of a person lawfully detained;

   (c) in action lawfully taken for the purpose of quelling a riot or insurrection.

At first sight it might seem odd that this Article could apply to the civil liability of a public body, but over recent years there has been considerable jurisprudence establishing that Article 2 requires a state to have in place a structure which will help to protect life; in other words there is a need to take appropriate steps to safeguard the lives of those under the jurisdiction of the state.

Attempts have been made to hold public bodies liable for violation of Article 2 for failing to prevent the infliction of harm by others, for example where police have been warned of threats to the claimant by a third party, or where hospitals have failed to safeguard patients' interests, resulting in loss of life. Although theoretically possible (see the following cases), such cases have not yet succeeded against the police, though they have in respect of mental health patients.

The test is, first, whether there was a 'real and immediate risk' to life (confirmed in *Osman v UK*), then whether the public body, such as the police, a prison or a hospital, had done enough to safeguard those in its care against that risk. As with public body liability in negligence, it is hard to meet these thresholds. (However, the result can be that whereas the public body itself has done enough (and thus will not be liable under Article 2), the institution may nevertheless be vicariously liable if an individual employee has been negligent in the performance of his or her individual obligations.)

Savage v South Essex NHS Foundation Trust
House of Lords [2008] UKHL 74

In July 2004 Carol Savage, who was suffering from paranoid schizophrenia, absconded from the hospital where she was being treated as a detained patient (under the Mental Health Act 1983) in an open acute psychiatric ward. She committed suicide by throwing herself in front of a train. Her adult daughter brought the action alleging that the South Essex NHS Foundation Trust violated her mother's Article 2 right to life by allowing her to escape from the hospital and kill herself. The law lords did not strike out the claim, instead referring the matter to trial.

LORD SCOTT:

8. The other line of Strasbourg authority stems, particularly, from *Powell v United Kingdom* (2000) 30 EHRR CD 362 . . . *Powell* was a case of alleged medical negligence in which a young boy had died in an NHS hospital. His parents said that his death had been caused by the negligence of the hospital and that therefore it 'must be concluded that there was a breach of the State's obligation to protect life.' The Strasbourg court rejected that conclusion, at p 364:

> . . . it cannot accept that matters such as error of judgment on the part of a health professional or negligent co-ordination among health professionals in the treatment of a particular patient are sufficient of themselves to call a Contracting State to account from the standpoint of its positive obligations under Article 2 of the Convention to protect life.

9. *Powell*, therefore, is authority for the proposition that, in the context of care of patients in hospitals, something more will be required to establish a breach of the article 2(1) positive obligation to protect life than, simply, a failure on the part of the hospital to meet the standard of care of the patient required by the common law duty of care. *Keenan*, on the other hand, and the other 'custody' cases referred to by my noble and learned friend, show that where individuals are in custody and are, or ought to be, known to pose a 'real and immediate' suicide risk, the article 2(1) positive obligation requires the authorities to take 'reasonable steps' to avert that risk. My Lords, I do not accept the starkness of the contrast between these two lines of authority on which the submissions that have been presented to your Lordships appear to be based. The standard of care required by our domestic law to be shown in order to discharge the common law duty of care is a flexible one dependent upon the circumstances of each individual case. The same must be true of the standard of protection required by article 2(1) to be extended by the State and State agents to individuals within the State's jurisdiction whose lives are in danger. That circumstances alter cases is as true, in my opinion, of the State's article 2(1) positive obligation as it is of the standard of care required by the common law duty.

10. Every patient who enters hospital knows that he or she may be at risk of medical error. We know that these things happen. Sometimes the error constitutes medical negligence, sometimes it does not. *Powell* shows that provided that there is no serious systemic fault and provided, in the event of death, that there is a proper investigation of the causes, a negligent medical error will not necessarily be enough to constitute a breach of the article 2(1) positive obligation. The case would, in my opinion, be no different if the patient who had died were an inmate in a prison hospital or a mentally ill patient who had been sectioned under section 3 and transferred to the hospital wing of the mental hospital on account of some medical condition. If, however, the conditions in the prison hospital or the hospital wing had been markedly inferior to those in an ordinary hospital and had contributed to the patient's death, the article 2(1) positive obligation might well be engaged.

11. As to persons known to be a suicide risk, the State has no general obligation, in my opinion, either at common law or under article 2(1), to place obstacles in the way of persons desirous of taking their own life. The positive obligation under section 2(1) to protect life could not, for example, justify the removal of passport facilities from persons proposing to travel to Switzerland with suicidal intent. Children may need to be protected from themselves, so, too, may mentally ill persons but adults in general do not. Their personal autonomy is entitled to respect subject only to whatever proportionate limitations may be placed by the law on that autonomy in the public interest. The prevention of suicide, no longer a criminal act, is not among those limitations.

12. Persons in police custody or in prison are in a different situation. Their personal autonomy has been lawfully restricted by action taken against them by the State. The restrictions imposed may, for some, bring about depression, feelings of hopelessness and thoughts of suicide. Such a state of mind, if apparent to those who have charge of the person concerned, would constitute, in my opinion, a circumstance highly relevant to the standard of protection required by the positive obligation under article 2(1). The *Keenan* test refers to a 'real and immediate' risk of self-harm known, or that ought to be known, to the custodial authorities. Such a knowledge would plainly constitute a very significant circumstance.

13. Mentally ill patients detained under section 3 are in a position in some respects similar to, but in other respects very different from, the position of those in police custody or in prison. Their position is similar in that they are detained by law. Some sectioned mental patients may be content with their lot but others will not be. It appears from the number of times Mrs Savage attempted to abscond that she fell into the latter class. Their position is dissimilar in that they are detained, as Baroness Hale has said, for their protection and not as a punishment. This is a distinction that some mentally ill patients may be unable to appreciate but it has an important consequence in the attitude to these patients to be expected of the hospitals or institutions in which they find themselves. The patients will be there for their protection, not as a punishment, and, unless protection of the public from them is one of the reasons for their having been sectioned, it would behove the hospital or institution to respect their personal autonomy and to impose restrictions on them to the minimum extent of strictness consistent with the need to protect them from themselves. Runwell Hospital could have kept Mrs Savage in a locked ward, instead of an open acute ward, could have subjected her to checks on her whereabouts every 15 minutes instead of the 30 minute checks that were prescribed at the time of her fatal absconding on 5 July 2004, and, no doubt, could have imposed other restrictions that would have made it virtually impossible for her to abscond. However the hospital were, in my opinion, entitled, and perhaps bound, to allow Mrs Savage a degree of unsupervised freedom that did carry with it some risk that she might succeed in absconding. They were entitled to place a value on her quality of life in the Hospital and accord a degree of respect to her personal autonomy above that to which prisoners in custody could expect.

14. The question whether there was on 5 July 200[4] a 'real and immediate' risk of Mrs Savage committing suicide that was known, or ought to have been known, to the Hospital must be decided at a trial. The hurdle is a stiff one particularly in the absence of evidence of any previous suicide attempt by Mrs Savage. If there was such a risk, the question whether the 'reasonable steps' that the Hospital should have taken to protect her included placing further restrictions on her freedom and personal autonomy than were in place on 5 July must be decided at a trial. So, too, must be the question whether the respondent has *locus standi* to maintain this action. . . .

LORD RODGER:

67. It may be useful to summarise the relevant obligations of health authorities like the Trust and to note the way they relate to one another.

68. In terms of article 2, health authorities are under an over-arching obligation to protect the lives of patients in their hospitals. In order to fulfil that obligation, and depending on the circumstances, they may require to fulfil a number of complementary obligations.

69. In the first place, the duty to protect the lives of patients requires health authorities to ensure that the hospitals for which they are responsible employ competent staff and that they are trained to a high professional standard. In addition, the authorities must ensure that the hospitals adopt systems of work which will protect the lives of patients. Failure to perform these general obligations may result

in a violation of article 2. If, for example, a health authority fails to ensure that a hospital puts in place a proper system for supervising mentally ill patients and, as a result, a patient is able to commit suicide, the health authority will have violated the patient's right to life under article 2.

70. Even though a health authority employed competent staff and ensured that they were trained to a high professional standard, a doctor, for example, might still treat a patient negligently and the patient might die as a result. In that situation, there would be no violation of article 2 since the health authority would have done all that the article required of it to protect the patient's life. Nevertheless, the doctor would be personally liable in damages for the death and the health authority would be vicariously liable for her negligence. This is the situation envisaged by *Powell*.

71. The same approach would apply if a mental hospital had established an appropriate system for supervising patients and all that happened was that, on a particular occasion, a nurse negligently left his post and a patient took the opportunity to commit suicide. There would be no violation of any obligation under article 2, since the health authority would have done all that the article required of it. But, again, the nurse would be personally liable in damages for the death and the health authority would be vicariously liable too. Again, this is just an application of *Powell*.

72. Finally, article 2 imposes a further 'operational' obligation on health authorities and their hospital staff. This obligation is distinct from, and additional to, the authorities' more general obligations. The operational obligation arises only if members of staff know or ought to know that a particular patient presents a 'real and immediate' risk of suicide. In these circumstances article 2 requires them to do all that can reasonably be expected to prevent the patient from committing suicide. If they fail to do this, not only will they and the health authorities be liable in negligence, but there will also be a violation of the operational obligation under article 2 to protect the patient's life. This is comparable to the position in *Osman* and *Keenan*. As the present case shows, if no other remedy is available, proceedings for an alleged breach of the obligation can be taken under the Human Rights Act 1998.

Van Colle v *Chief Constable of Hertfordshire*
House of Lords [2008] UKHL 50

Van Colle was due to give evidence against Brougham on a charge of theft. Brougham threatened Van Colle saying, 'If you don't drop the charge you will be in danger'. The police were informed of the threats, but the responsible officer took no action to protect the witness and ultimately Brougham shot Van Colle dead. Held: the police were not liable as they could not reasonably have apprehended violence against Van Colle in view of the minor nature of the charge. There was no 'real and immediate' risk to life that would engage Article 2.

LORD BINGHAM:

28. Article 2 of the European Convention provides, in paragraph 1:

Everyone's right to life shall be protected by law. No one shall be deprived of his life intentionally. . .

According to what has become a conventional analysis, this provision enjoins each member state not only to refrain from the intentional and unlawful taking of life ('Thou shalt not kill') but also to take appropriate steps to safeguard the lives of those within its jurisdiction: *Osman v United Kingdom* (1998) [(2000)] 29 EHRR 245, para 115. The state's duty in this respect (as this para of the judgment of the Strasbourg court in *Osman* makes clear) includes but extends beyond its primary duty to secure the right to life by putting in place effective criminal law provisions to deter the commission of offences against the person backed up by law enforcement machinery for the prevention, suppression and sanctioning of breaches of such provisions. Article 2 may also, 'in certain well-defined circumstances', imply a positive obligation on national authorities to take preventative measures to protect an individual whose life is at risk from the criminal acts of another. The scope of this last obligation was the subject of dispute in *Osman*, and lies at the heart of this appeal.

29. In *Osman*, para 116, the court defined the circumstances in which the obligation arises:

> . . . it must be established to [the court's] satisfaction that the authorities knew or ought to have known at the time of the existence of a real and immediate risk to the life of an identified individual or individuals from the criminal acts of a third party and that they failed to take measures within the scope of their powers which, judged reasonably, might have been expected to avoid that risk.

Every ingredient of this carefully drafted ruling is, I think, of importance.

30. The appellant Chief Constable, and the Secretary of State, relied on the ruling of my noble and learned friend Lord Carswell in *In re Officer L* [2007] UKHL 36, [2007] 1 WLR 2135, para 20, that the test of real and immediate risk is one not easily satisfied, the threshold being high, and I would for my part accept that a court should not lightly find that a public authority has violated one of an individual's fundamental rights or freedoms, thereby ruling, as such a finding necessarily does, that the United Kingdom has violated an important international convention. But I see force in the submission of Mr Owen QC, for the Equality and Human Rights Commission, that the test formulated by the Strasbourg court in *Osman* and cited on many occasions since is clear and calls for no judicial exegesis. It is moreover clear that the Strasbourg court in *Osman*, para 116, roundly rejected the submission of Her Majesty's Government that the failure to perceive the risk to life in the circumstances known at the time or to take preventative measures to avoid that risk must be tantamount to gross negligence or wilful disregard of the duty to protect life. Such a rigid standard would be incompatible with the obligation of member states to secure the practical and effective protection of the right laid down in article 2. That article protected a right fundamental in the scheme of the Convention and it was sufficient for an applicant to show that the authorities did not do all that could reasonably be expected of them to avoid a real and immediate risk to life of which they had or ought to have had knowledge.

31. It is plain from *Osman* and later cases that article 2 may be invoked where there has been a systemic failure by member states to enact laws or provide procedures reasonably needed to protect the right to life. But the article may also be invoked where, although there has been no systemic failure of that kind, a real and immediate risk to life is demonstrated and individual agents of the state have reprehensibly failed to exercise the powers available to them for the purpose of protecting life. . .

32. In its formulation of the 'real and immediate risk' test the Strasbourg court, in para 116 of its *Osman* judgment, laid emphasis on what the authorities knew or ought to have known 'at the time'. This is a crucial part of the test, since where (as here) a tragic killing has occurred it is all too easy to interpret the events which preceded it in the light of that knowledge and not as they appeared at the time. In the present case the Court of Appeal expressly warned itself against the dangers of hindsight (in para 13 of their judgment) but I do not think that the judge, in the course of her lengthy judgment, did so. Mr Faulks QC, for the Chief Constable, was in my view right to submit that the court should endeavour to place itself in the chair of DC Ridley and assess events as they unfolded through his eyes. But the application of the test depends not only on what the authorities knew, but also on what they ought to have known. Thus stupidity, lack of imagination and inertia do not afford an excuse to a national authority which reasonably ought, in the light of what it knew or was told, to make further enquiries or investigations: it is then to be treated as knowing what such further enquiries or investigations would have elicited.

Notes

1. The Convention (including via the Human Rights Act 1998) protects against systemic failures by public bodies which bring about harm to citizens. It would have clearly applied if, for example, in *Savage* there were no systems in place to check whether a person was a suicide risk (see Lord Rodger at [72]). More difficult to determine is whether the existence of 'a real and immediate risk' becomes a 'systemic' failure. The speeches in *Van Colle* seem to veer away from the need for an 'organisational' failure towards a liability based on the fault of an individual. The fault of an individual could be organisational if there is no system for discovering or preventing negligence by an employee. However, in *Van Colle*, the police officer was not a senior official and the appropriate supervisory procedures were in place.

2. *Osman* v *UK* (2000) 29 EHRR 245 was also a case of failure of the police to protect someone from harm. Here the police were warned about the activities of Paget-Lewis and they interviewed him a number of times. Eventually Paget-Lewis shot and killed Osman and injured his teenage son. The police were not liable in negligence, following the principles laid down in *Hill*, which allowed a duty of care to be denied. On appeal to the European Court of Human Rights, liability under Article 2 was also denied, as the Court found that the police had no reason to suspect that Paget-Lewis was likely to kill Osman: there was no 'real and immediate risk' to his life. Note, however, that the case was much concerned with Article 6 (right to a trial) as the (negligence) case had been rejected on the 'fair, just and reasonable' principle without a full trial. On this see *Z*. On the question of Article 2 (right to life), the European Court of Human Rights said:

> The Court notes that the first sentence of Article 2 § 1 enjoins the State not only to refrain from the intentional and unlawful taking of life, but also to take appropriate steps to safeguard the lives of those within its jurisdiction. . . It is common ground that the State's obligation in this respect extends beyond its primary duty to secure the right to life by putting in place effective criminal-law provisions to deter the commission of offences against the person backed up by law-enforcement machinery for the prevention, suppression and sanctioning of breaches of such provisions. It is thus accepted by those appearing before the Court that Article 2 of the Convention may also imply in certain well-defined circumstances a positive obligation on the authorities to take preventive operational measures to protect an individual whose life is at risk from the criminal acts of another individual. The scope of this obligation is a matter of dispute between the parties. (at [115])

On that question the Court said:

> In the opinion of the Court where there is an allegation that the authorities have violated their positive obligation to protect the right to life in the context of their above-mentioned duty to prevent and suppress offences against the person, it must be established to its satisfaction that the authorities knew or ought to have known at the time of the existence of a real and immediate risk to the life of an identified individual or individuals from the criminal acts of a third party and that they failed to take measures within the scope of their powers which, judged reasonably, might have been expected to avoid that risk. The Court does not accept the Government's view that the failure to perceive the risk to life in the circumstances known at the time or to take preventive measures to avoid that risk must be tantamount to gross negligence or wilful disregard of the duty to protect life. Such a rigid standard must be considered to be incompatible with the requirements of Article 1 of the Convention and the obligations of Contracting States under that Article to secure the practical and effective protection of the rights and freedoms laid down therein, including Article 2. For the Court, and having regard to the nature of the right protected by Article 2, a right fundamental in the scheme of the Convention, it is sufficient for an applicant to show that the authorities did not do all that could be reasonably expected of them to avoid a real and immediate risk to life of which they have or ought to have knowledge. This is a question which can only be answered in the light of all the circumstances of any particular case. (at [116])

3. A claim similar to that in *Osman* was also rejected by the House of Lords in **Mitchell v Glasgow City Council** [2009] UKHL 11 (warnings to a housing authority about the activities of a neighbour). On the applicability of Article 2, Lord Rodger said:

> I therefore see nothing in the relationship of landlord and secure tenant to give rise to any positive Article 2 obligation on the part of the Council to protect Mr Mitchell's life. The public authority with the positive duty to protect Mr Mitchell from criminal assaults by Drummond was Strathclyde Police, not the Council.
>
> . . .
>
> Councils and housing associations etc do not have, and are not meant to have, the resources, staff or powers to take effective steps to prevent such crimes. On the contrary, they are resourced on the basis that they are landlords operating within a society where the responsibility for preventing violent crime lies with the police, who, in their turn, are given the resources, training and powers to do the job. Costly duplication of the work of the police is neither necessary nor indeed desirable. (at [69]–[70])

   This is like the common law test of what it is reasonable to expect a public body to do, and the resources available will be a factor. Also consider the potential implications of *X, Y and Z v UK* (Application no 32666/10) [2011] ECHR 1199.

4. For a discussion of the issues in this section, see François du Bois, 'Human Rights and the Tort Liability of Public Bodies' (2011) 127 LQR 589.

5. More insight may be provided by the Supreme Court in **Michael v Chief Constable of South Wales Police** [2015] UKSC 2 (discussed earlier in the context of the negligence claim). There, claims in negligence and under Article 2 were allowed to proceed at first instance. The Court of Appeal ruled out the negligence claim but not the Article 2 claim. The Supreme Court considered both issues, finding that the claim under Article 2 should be allowed to proceed to trial.

6. *Commissioner of Police of the Metropolis v DSD and another* [2018] UKSC 11 also illustrates the potential of a human rights claim as an alternative to negligence. Here, a human rights duty under Article 3 (freedom from inhumane and degrading treatment) was imposed on the Metropolitan Police in the context of their failure to protect victims of a notorious serial rapist. Systemic failures by the police in the investigation of more than 100 rapes and sexual assaults perpetrated by 'the Black cab rapist' over a period of years violated the victims' Article 3 rights.

see online resources

6

Special duty problems: economic loss

This chapter deals with negligence that causes 'pure' economic loss (i.e. financial losses not consequent on another harm or loss). As will be seen, whether or not a duty of care can be established in this context depends on whether the loss stems from a negligent statement or advice, or from a negligent activity.

The basic rule is that a person may sue for negligently caused economic loss which is consequent on physical loss already suffered, but no duty of care is owed if they suffer only economic loss ('pure' economic loss). There are exceptions to this general rule where sufficient proximity exists between the parties, and one element in this is usually reliance by one on the other, in the context of an assumption of responsibility. However, despite the large number of cases on this subject at a very high level, as yet no case spells out definitively what degree of proximity is necessary. What is clear is that no claimant has succeeded in claiming activity-related pure economic loss, except possibly in one anomalous case which has been explained away and subsequently ignored (*Junior Books* v *Veitchi* [1982] 3 All ER 201).

6.1 'Pure' economic loss

> ### *Cattle* v *Stockton Waterworks*
> Court of Queen's Bench (1875) LR 10 QBD 453

The claimant was a contractor employed to dig a tunnel under a road, through ground that belonged to a private individual. Unfortunately, a water main belonging to the defendants was defective and caused flooding of the works, and this meant that the claimant lost money on his contract. Held: the defendants were not liable.

BLACKBURN J: . . . as was pointed out by Coleridge J, in *Lumley v Gye* (1853) 2 E & B 216, at p 252, Courts of Justice should not 'allow themselves, in the pursuit of perfectly complete remedies for all wrongful acts, to transgress the bounds, which our law, in a wise consciousness as I conceive of its limited powers, has imposed on itself, of redressing only the proximate and direct consequence of wrongful acts.' In this we quite agree. No authority in favour of the plaintiff's right to sue was cited, and, as far as our knowledge goes, there was none that could have been cited. . . .

In the present case there is no pretence for saying that the defendants were malicious or had any intention to injure anyone. They were, at most, guilty of a neglect of duty, which occasioned injury to the property of Knight, but which did not injure any property of the plaintiff. The plaintiff's claim is to recover the damage which he has sustained by his contract with Knight becoming less profitable, or, it may be, a losing contract, in consequence of this injury to Knight's property. We think this does not give him any right of action.

Notes

1. This case encapsulates the problems which the courts have experienced with economic loss. Such claims tended to fail partly because of the 'floodgates' argument and partly because of the realisation that foreseeability is not by itself a sufficient limitation on the range of potential claimants. If Cattle could sue, could his workers who were temporarily laid off also claim? What about local shopkeepers and pub owners, who would have taken less money while the workers were laid off?

Spartan Steel v Martin & Co
Court of Appeal [1973] QB 27

The defendants negligently cut a power cable supplying electricity to the claimants, who manufactured steel alloys. At the time of the power cut there was a 'melt' in progress, and in order to stop the steel solidifying the claimants had to add oxygen to it and pour it off. This reduced its value, and subsequently caused a lost profit on that melt. The claimants claimed these sums, as well as the profit they would have made on melts they could have processed during the time when the power was cut off. Held: the claimants could recover for the physical damage to the melt in progress, plus loss of profit on that melt, but not for the profits they had expected to make while the power was off.

LORD DENNING MR: At bottom I think the question of recovering economic loss is one of policy. Whenever the courts draw a line to mark out the bounds of *duty*, they do it as matter of policy so as to limit the responsibility of the defendant. Whenever the courts set bounds to the *damages* recoverable—saying that they are, or are not, too remote—they do it as matter of policy so as to limit the liability of the defendant.

The more I think about these cases, the more difficult I find it to put each into its proper pigeonhole. Sometimes I say: 'There was no duty.' In others I say: 'The damage was too remote.' So much so that I think the time has come to discard those tests which have proved so elusive. It seems to me better to consider the particular relationship in hand, and see whether or not, as a matter of policy, economic loss should be recoverable, or not. Thus in *Weller & Co v Foot and Mouth Disease Research Institute* [1966] 1 QB 569 it was plain that the loss suffered by the auctioneers was not recoverable, no matter whether it is put on the ground that there was no duty or that the damage was too remote. Again in *Electrochrome Ltd v Welsh Plastics Ltd* [1968] 2 All ER 205, it is plain that the economic loss suffered by the plaintiffs' factory (due to the damage to the fire hydrant) was not recoverable, whether because there was no duty or that it was too remote.

So I turn to the relationship in the present case. It is of common occurrence. . . .

The first consideration is the position of the statutory undertakers. If the board do not keep up the voltage or pressure of electricity, gas or water—or, likewise, if they shut it off for repairs—and thereby cause economic loss to their consumers, they are not liable in damages, not even if the cause of it is due to their own negligence. The only remedy (which is hardly ever pursued) is to prosecute the board before the magistrates. . . .

The second consideration is the nature of the hazard, namely, the cutting of the supply of electricity. This is a hazard which we all run. It may be due to a short circuit, to a flash of lightning, to a tree falling on the wires, to an accidental cutting of the cable, or even to the negligence of someone or other. And when it does happen, it affects a multitude of persons: not as a rule by way of physical damage to them or their property, but by putting them to inconvenience, and sometimes to economic loss. The supply is usually restored in a few hours, so the economic loss is not very large. Such a hazard is regarded by most people as a thing they must put up with—without seeking compensation from anyone. Some there are who install a stand-by system. Others seek refuge by taking out an insurance policy against breakdown in the supply. But most people are content to take the risk on themselves. When the supply is cut off, they do not go running round to their solicitor. They do not try to find out whether it was anyone's fault. They just put up with it. They try to make up the economic loss by doing more work next day. This is a healthy attitude which the law should encourage.

The third consideration is this: if claims for economic loss were permitted for this particular hazard, there would be no end of claims. Some might be genuine, but many might be inflated, or even false. A machine might not have been in use anyway, but it would be easy to put it down to the cut in supply. It would be well-nigh impossible to check the claims. If there was economic loss on one day, did the claimant do his best to mitigate it by working harder next day? And so forth. Rather than expose claimants to such temptation and defendants to such hard labour—on comparatively small claims—it is better to disallow economic loss altogether, at any rate when it stands alone, independent of any physical damage.

The fourth consideration is that, in such a hazard as this, the risk of economic loss should be suffered by the whole community who suffer the losses—usually many but comparatively small losses—rather than on the one pair of shoulders, that is, on the contractor on whom the total of them, all added together, might be very heavy.

The fifth consideration is that the law provides for deserving cases. If the defendant is guilty of negligence which cuts off the electricity supply and causes actual physical damage to person or property, that physical damage can be recovered. . . .

These considerations lead me to the conclusion that the plaintiffs should recover for the physical damage to the one melt (£368), and the loss of profit on that melt consequent thereon (£400): but not for the loss of profit on the four melts (£1,767), because that was economic loss independent of the physical damage. I would, therefore, allow the appeal and reduce the damages to £768.

Notes

1. Similarly, in *British Celanese v Hunt Capacitors* [1969] 2 All ER 1253, strips of metal foil escaped from the defendants' premises and struck an electricity sub-station, causing a power cut. The claimants made synthetic yarn, and material in their machines solidified. They were able to recover damages for their physical loss, together with consequent economic loss. Compare *Electrochrome v Welsh Plastics* [1968] 2 All ER 205, where the defendants struck a fire hydrant (not owned by the claimants) which caused the water supply to the claimants' factory to be cut off for some hours. The claimants were engaged in electroplating hardware, and the factory was closed for a day as the process depended on the supply of water. However, as they suffered no physical damage they were unable to sue.

2. The **Spartan Steel** decision was rejected in similar circumstances in New Zealand. In *New Zealand Forest Products v A-G* [1986] 1 NZLR 14, an electricity cable which supplied only the claimant (as

in *Spartan Steel*) was cut by the negligence of the defendants, causing the claimants' mill to cease operation. The claimants were able to recover all their loss of profit even though no physical damage had been caused. It seems to have been significant that the defendants knew that the cable supplied only the claimants. However, this factor was not regarded as decisive in *Mainguard Packaging v Hilton Haulage* [1990] 1 NZLR 360, where liability was imposed because the defendants should have realised that the damage to the relevant cable would cut off the claimants, among others.

3. For discussion of this difficult topic see Patrick Atiyah 'Negligence and Economic Loss' (1967) 83 LQR 248 and Christian Witting 'Distinguishing Between Property Damage and Pure Economic Loss in Negligence' (2001) 21 LS 481.

Conarken Group v *Network Rail Infrastructure*
Court of Appeal [2011] EWCA Civ 644

The defendants were employers of drivers of heavy goods vehicles who damaged railway property: in one case, a bridge and in another, electrical equipment at a level crossing. It was agreed that they were liable for the cost of repairs to Network Rail's property, but the issue was whether they were also liable for the amounts of compensation that Network Rail was obliged to pay (Schedule 8 payments) to the train-operating companies (TOCs), which were unable to run their services because of the damage to the track. Held: the defendants were liable for the consequential economic losses—that is, the amounts that Network Rail had to pay to the TOCs.

MOORE-BICK LJ:

95. As the authorities to which the judge referred show, the law has long been concerned to ensure that a reasonable limit is placed on the extent of the consequences of a wrongful act for which the perpetrator can be held liable. That is partly because it has recognised that the consequences of an act or omission may be very far-reaching and that it is unreasonable to hold a person responsible for those that he could not reasonably have been expected to guard against. As Lord Hoffmann observed, the scope of the duty in each case depends upon the purpose of the rule imposing the duty and the purpose of the rule that one must take reasonable care not to cause harm to other people or their property is to impose responsibility on people for governing their actions in a way that prevents reasonably foreseeable harm. However, in this context 'pure' economic loss, that is, financial loss suffered otherwise than as a consequence of damage to the person or property of the claimant, poses particular difficulties because of the broad network of economic links that exist in any developed society. The dangers inherent in allowing a claimant to recover in respect of pure economic loss were recognised in the latter part of the nineteenth century and lie at the root of the decision in *Cattle v The Stockton Waterworks Company* (1875) LR 10 QB 453 and many later decisions. Such claims have been rejected, except in those cases in which financial loss is in the most immediate contemplation of the wrongdoer, for reasons of policy rather than principle.

96. However, this is not a case in which the claimant is seeking to recover in respect of economic loss divorced from physical damage to property. The appellants accept that they caused damage to Network Rail's property and that its unavailability for use by TOCs gave rise to a liability to make Schedule 8 payments under the Track Access Agreements. The only question is whether the loss represented by that liability is recoverable from those who caused the physical damage which put the track out of use.

97. Mr Bartlett put his argument in a number of ways, but at the root of them all lay the submission that Network Rail is not entitled to recover in respect of the kind of losses that the Schedule 8 payments

represent, namely, a future loss of revenue resulting from a decline in passenger confidence and an obligation to make payments under the franchise agreements in respect of poor performance. In effect, he sought to treat the losses in respect of which the TOCs were entitled to be compensated as if they were Network Rail's own losses. Indeed, one of his submissions was that Network Rail would not be entitled to recover in respect of a future loss of business if it were operating rail services for its own account, especially if that were based on a rather speculative assessment of a reduction in public confidence in the reliability of the railways. It should therefore not be better placed simply because it is providing the infrastructure which enables the TOCs to do so. He also relied on the fact that since, as was common ground, the TOCs could not themselves have recovered damages in respect of pure economic loss of that kind, it would not be right to enable Network Rail to render such a loss recoverable simply by entering into contracts with the TOCs to indemnify them. . . .

99. In my view it is wrong to approach the question that arises in this case through an analysis of the Schedule 8 payments, as if the claimants in these cases were the TOCs (who have suffered no damage to their property), rather than Network Rail (which has). The judge was right, therefore, to hold in paragraph 62 of his judgment that the way in which the Schedule 8 payments have been calculated is irrelevant. All that matters for present purposes is that they represent a genuine and reasonable attempt to assess the damage caused to the TOCs by the closure of the lines and the consequent disruption to services. It was not in dispute that economic loss resulting from physical damage is recoverable and in any event that is well established by existing authorities. This court accepted as much in *SCM v Whittall* and subsequent cases, despite its insistence on the irrecoverability of 'pure' economic loss. In my view the judge was right, therefore, to approach the case by asking himself whether a loss in the form of a liability to make Schedule 8 payments to the TOCs under the Track Access Agreements was within the scope of the appellants' duty and not too remote in law to be recoverable.

100. Any asset of a commercial nature is capable of being used to generate revenue, either by being put to use directly by the owner or by being made available for use by others in return for payment. Buildings, lorries, ships and aircraft are just examples of a type whose variety is endless. That is part of everyday experience. Whether an ordinary member of the public can be taken to be aware of the particular arrangements established for the use of the rail network is in my view immaterial, since he can certainly be expected to be aware that the rail network is a commercial asset which can be used to generate revenue for its owner in one way or another. It might be by running its own services, or by allowing others to do so for a fee, or a combination of the two. Under the current arrangements Network Rail generates revenue by making the network available to the TOCs for a fee and any payment it is liable to make to the TOCs in respect of periods when the network is unavailable represents a net loss of revenue. It is immaterial for these purposes whether the fee is reduced or suspended in respect of periods during which the track is unavailable, whether part of it has to be refunded or whether payments have to be made under provisions broadly similar to a liquidated damages clause. In each case it suffers a net loss of revenue.

101. I think it is clear, therefore, that two types of loss flow naturally from any damage to the infrastructure that renders the track itself unavailable for use: the cost of repair and the loss of revenue attributable to the loss of availability of the track itself. Both are in my view within the scope of the duty of the motorist, or indeed anyone else, to exercise reasonable care not to cause physical damage to the infrastructure. Subject to the limitations imposed by the rules relating to remoteness, therefore, all such loss is in principle recoverable from the person who caused the damage. The rules concerning remoteness of damage confine the scope of the tortfeasor's liability to that which was reasonably foreseeable as the consequence of his wrongful act: *Overseas Tankship (UK) Ltd v Morts Docks & Engineering Co Ltd, The 'Wagon Mound' (No 1)* [1961] AC 388.

JACKSON LJ:

145. The common law rules and principles which regulate the recoverability and assessment of damages form a vast and rippling skein, to which many judges and jurists have contributed over the last two centuries. I would not presume to offer a comprehensive review of that skein. I do, however, suggest that four principles relevant to the present appeal can be discerned from the authorities:

i)   Economic loss which flows directly and foreseeably from physical damage to property may be recoverable. The threshold test of foreseeability does not require the tortfeasor to have any detailed knowledge of the claimant's business affairs or financial circumstances, so long as the general nature of the claimant's loss is foreseeable.

ii) One of the recognised categories of recoverable economic loss is loss of income following damage to revenue generating property.

iii) Loss of future business as a result of damage to property is a head of damage which lies on the outer fringe of recoverability. Whether the claimant can recover for such economic loss depends upon the circumstances of the case and the relationship between the parties.

iv) In choosing the appropriate measure of damages for the purposes of assessing recoverable economic loss, the court seeks to arrive at an assessment which is fair and reasonable as between the claimant and the defendant.

Notes

1. It was said (at [97]) to be common ground that the TOCs could not have sued because their loss was purely economic: they had no property interest in any of the damaged assets. However, in a similar Canadian case, parties in the same position as the TOCs were able to sue. In *Canadian National Railway Co* v *Norsk Pacific* [1992] 1 SCR 1021, a railway bridge spanning a river was damaged by the defendant's barge. The bridge was owned by the Canadian Government and was used by four different railway companies. The claimants had to reroute their trains for several weeks and successfully sued for the additional cost involved, even though they had no property interest in the bridge and their loss was purely economic loss. McLachlan J said that pure economic loss is recoverable where there is sufficient proximity and that here there was, because the government and the railway companies could be regarded as being engaged in a joint venture in relation to the bridge.

2. A variant of the problem in *Conarken* occurred in *Shell UK* v *Total UK* [2010] EWCA Civ 180, which involved the devastating fire at the Buncefield Oil Terminal in 2005, caused by the negligence of a person for whom Total was responsible. Shell sued for loss of profits because, with the plant destroyed, it was no longer able to supply its customers with fuel. The problem was that the relevant tanks and pipelines were not owned by the claimants, but rather by a company that held them on trust for Shell. Due to the contractual arrangements, Shell had neither possession nor the right to possession of the equipment. The Court of Appeal held that a person who holds equitable title under a trust may sue for the economic loss resulting from damage to the property held in trust as long as the legal owner is also joined in the action to prevent double recovery. The court said:

   This shows that there are cases where a trustee can sue for economic loss which, not he, but his beneficiary has suffered provided only that he is a party to the action so that there is no question of double recovery. We . . . would be prepared to hold that a duty of care is owed to a beneficial owner of property (just as much as to a legal owner of property) by a defendant, such as Total, who can reasonably foresee that his negligent actions will damage that property. If, therefore, such property is, in breach of duty, damaged by the defendant, that defendant will be liable not merely for the physical loss of that property but also for the foreseeable consequences of that loss, such as the extra expenditure to which the beneficial owner is put or the loss of profit which he incurs. Provided that the beneficial owner can join the legal owner in the proceedings, it does not matter that the beneficial owner is not himself in possession of the property. (at [141])

For a discussion of this case, see Kelvin Low 'Equitable Title and Economic Loss' (2010) 126 LQR 507.

3. A similar conclusion was reached in *Leigh and Sillavan Ltd* v *Aliakmon Shipping (The Aliakmon)* [1986] AC 785, one of many cases dealing with the problem where goods are damaged which do not belong to the claimant, but for which he has to bear the risk of damage. In that case the claimants were buyers of steel coil which was damaged on its voyage in the 'Aliakmon'. The contract stipulated that the sellers reserved title to (i.e. owned) the steel, but the buyers had to take the risk of its being damaged. The House of Lords held that the buyers could not sue for the loss, since it was purely economic loss. Lord Brandon said:

[T]here is a long line of authority for the principle that, in order to enable a person to claim in negligence for loss caused to him by reason of loss of or damage to property, he must have had either the legal ownership of or a possessory title to the property concerned at the time when the loss or damage occurred, and it is not enough for him to have only had contractual rights in relation to such property which have been adversely affected by the loss or damage to it. (at 809)

The result is that the sellers could sue, but would not bother to do so because they have received full price from the buyers. The buyers have paid the full price for damaged steel, but are unable to recover from the person who damaged it. However, as the House of Lords pointed out, the buyers could have ordered their contractual arrangements so as to avoid this result, and the best solution to the problem probably lies in contract rather than tort.

6.2 The *Hedley Byrne* exception

Limited exceptions to the rules on pure economic loss caused by negligence stem from a case about a negligently conducted credit check of an advertising company. In that case, the House of Lords found that, in the absence of a disclaimer of liability, a duty of care in respect of pure economic losses could arise in such situations, providing certain conditions were met.

Hedley Byrne & Co Ltd v *Heller and Partners*
House of Lords [1963] UKHL 4

The claimants, Hedley Byrne & Co, were advertising agents who intended to engage in an advertising programme for Easipower Ltd which would cost about £100,000. They asked their own bankers, National Provincial Bank Ltd, to obtain a reference about Easipower, and National Provincial wrote to the defendants, Heller and Partners, who were Easipower's bankers. In a letter clearly stating that it was for 'private use and without responsibility on the part of the bank or its officials' Heller replied that Easipower was a 'respectably constituted company, considered good for its ordinary business engagements. Your figures are larger than we are accustomed to see.' Easipower went into liquidation, and the claimants lost £17,000. Held: a duty in respect of pure economic loss could arise in relation to carelessly made statements, which were relied on. However, in the circumstances, the disclaimer in the letter prevented such a duty arising; the defendants were not liable.

LORD REID: A reasonable man, knowing that he was being trusted or that his skill and judgment were being relied on, would, I think, have three courses open to him. He could keep silent or decline to give the information or advice sought: or he could give an answer with a clear qualification that he accepted no responsibility for it or that it was given without that reflection or enquiry which a careful answer would require: or he could simply answer without any such qualification. If he chooses to adopt the last course he must, I think, be held to have accepted some responsibility for his answer being given carefully, or to have accepted a relationship with the enquirer which requires him to exercise such care as the circumstances require. . . .

LORD MORRIS: My Lords, I consider that it follows and that it should now be regarded as settled that if someone possessed of a special skill undertakes, quite irrespective of contract, to apply that skill for the assistance of another person who relies upon such skill, a duty of care will arise. The fact that the service is to be given by means of or by the instrumentality of words can make no difference. Furthermore, if in a sphere in which a person is so placed that others could reasonably rely upon his judgment or his skill or upon his ability to make careful inquiry, a person takes it upon himself to give information or advice to, or allows his information or advice to be passed on to, another person who, as he knows or should know, will place reliance upon it, then a duty of care will arise . . .

LORD DEVLIN: I think, therefore, that there is ample authority to justify your Lordships in saying now that the categories of special relationships which may give rise to a duty to take care in word as well as in deed are not limited to contractual relationships or to relationships of fiduciary duty, but include also relationships which in the words of Lord Shaw in *Nocton* v *Lord Ashburton* at page 972 are 'equivalent to contract' that is, where there is an assumption of responsibility in circumstances in which, but for the absence of consideration, there would be a contract. Where there is an express undertaking, an express warranty as distinct from mere representation, there can be little difficulty. The difficulty arises in discerning those cases in which the undertaking is to be implied. In this respect the absence of consideration is not irrelevant. Payment for information or advice is very good evidence that it is being relied upon and that the informer or adviser knows that it is. Where there is no consideration, it will be necessary to exercise greater care in distinguishing between social and professional relationships and between those which are of a contractual character and those which are not. It may often be material to consider whether the adviser is acting purely out of good nature or whether he is getting his reward in some indirect form. The service that a bank performs in giving a reference is not done simply out of a desire to assist commerce. It would discourage the customers of the bank if their deals fell through because the bank had refused to testify to their credit when it was good. . . .

I shall therefore content myself with the proposition that wherever there is a relationship equivalent to contract, there is a duty of care. Such a relationship may be either general or particular. Examples of a general relationship are those of solicitor and client and of banker and customer. For the former *Nocton* v *Lord Ashburton* has long stood as the authority and for the latter there is the decision of Salmon, J in *Woods* v *Martins Bank* which I respectfully approve. There may well be others yet to be established. Where there is a general relationship of this sort it is unnecessary to do more than prove its existence and the duty follows. Where, as in the present case, what is relied on is a particular relationship created *ad hoc*, it will be necessary to examine the particular facts to see whether there is an express or implied undertaking of responsibility.

I regard this proposition as an application of the general conception of proximity. Cases may arise in the future in which a new and wider proposition, quite independent of any notion of contract, will be needed. There may, for example, be cases in which a statement is not supplied for the use of any particular person, any more than in *Donoghue* v *Stevenson* the ginger beer was supplied for consumption by any particular person; and it will then be necessary to return to the general conception of proximity and to see whether there can be evolved from it, as was done in *Donoghue* v *Stevenson*, a specific proposition to fit the case. . . .

LORD PEARCE: The law of negligence has been deliberately limited in its range by the Courts' insistence that there can be no actionable negligence *in vacuo* without the existence of some duty to the plaintiff. For it would be impracticable to grant relief to everybody who suffers damage through the carelessness of another.

The reason for some divergence between the law of negligence in word and that of negligence in act is clear. Negligence in word creates problems different from those of negligence in act. Words are more volatile than deeds. They travel fast and far afield. They are used without being expended and take effect in combination with innumerable facts and other words. Yet they are dangerous and can cause vast financial damage. How far they are relied on unchecked (by analogy with there being no probability of intermediate inspection—See *Grant* v *Australian Knitting Mills Ltd* [1936] AC 85) must in many cases be a matter of doubt and difficulty. If the mere hearing or reading of words were held to create proximity, there might be no limit to the persons to whom the speaker or writer could be liable. Damage by negligent acts to persons or property on the other hand is more visible and obvious; its limits are more easily defined, and it is with this damage that the earlier cases were more concerned. It was not until 1789 that *Pasley and Another* v *Freeman*, 3 TR 51, recognised and laid down a duty of honesty in words to the world at large—thus creating a remedy designed to protect the economic as opposed to the physical interests of the community. Any attempts to extend this remedy by imposing a duty of care as well as a duty of honesty in representations by word were curbed by *Derry* v *Peek* (14 App Cas 337).

. . . There is also, in my opinion, a duty of care created by special relationships which though not fiduciary give rise to an assumption that care as well as honesty is demanded.

Was there such a special relationship in the present case as to impose on the defendants a duty of care to the plaintiffs as the undisclosed principals for whom the National Provincial Bank was making the enquiry? The answer to that question depends on the circumstances of the transaction. If, for instance, they disclosed a casual social approach to the enquiry no such special relationship or duty of care would be assumed (see *Fish* v *Kelly* 144 ER 78, 83). To import such a duty the representation must normally, I think, concern a business or professional transaction whose nature makes clear the gravity of the enquiry and the importance and influence attached to the answer. It is conceded that Salmon J rightly found a duty of care in *Woods* v *Martins Bank Ltd* [1959] 1 QB 55, but the facts in that case were wholly different from those in the present case. A most important circumstance is the form of the enquiry and of the answer. Both were here plainly stated to be without liability. Mr Gardiner argues that those words are not sufficiently precise to exclude liability for negligence. Nothing, however, except negligence could, in the facts of this case, create a liability (apart from fraud to which they cannot have been intended to refer and against which the words would be no protection since they would be part of the fraud). I do not, therefore, accept that even if the parties were already in contractual or other special relationship the words would give no immunity to a negligent answer. But in any event they clearly prevent a special relationship from arising. They are part of the material from which one deduces whether a duty of care and a liability for negligence was assumed. If both parties say expressly (in a case where neither is deliberately taking advantage of the other) that there shall be no liability, I do not find it possible to say that a liability was assumed.

Notes

1. In *Caparo Industries plc v Dickman* [1990] 2 AC 605 (section 6.2.1.2), Lord Oliver viewed 'voluntary assumption of responsibility' as a convenient phrase, but not sufficient as a test for the existence of the duty, it meaning no more than that the defendant's act was voluntary and the law attributes to it an assumption of responsibility. Later, in *Spring v Guardian Assurance* [1995], Lord Goff spoke of an assumption or undertaking of responsibility coupled with reliance by the claimant.

2. According to Slade LJ in *Banque Keyser SA v Skandia (UK) Insurance* [1989] 3 WLR 25, even silence can be a breach of duty. He says, 'Can a mere failure to speak ever give rise to liability in negligence under *Hedley Byrne* principles? In our view it can, subject to the all-important proviso that there has been on the facts a voluntary assumption of responsibility in the relevant sense and reliance on that assumption' (at 101). He cites *Al-Kandari v Brown* [1988] QB 665 as a possible example, and gives the hypothetical example of a father employing an estate agent to advise his son about a proposed house purchase, where the agent negligently fails to tell the son that a motorway is to be built nearby. The son could sue. 'To draw a distinction on those particular facts between misinformation and a failure to inform would be to perpetuate the sort of nonsense in the law which Lord Devlin condemned in *Hedley Byrne v Heller*.' The point was not discussed on appeal ([1990] 2 All ER 947), where Lord Templeman merely said 'that there was no negligent misstatement and the silence of [A] did not amount to an assertion that [B] was trustworthy and the banks did not rely on the silence of [A]' (at 955). See also *Henderson v Merrett Syndicates* [1995] 2 AC 145.

Hedley Byrne allowed courts to begin to expand the kinds of situations in which defendants could be found liable for causing pure economic loss. In the years following, liability extended beyond economic loss caused by relied-upon statements to include some activities. As we shall see, however, this expansion was reversed with the House of Lords' judgment in *Murphy v Brentwood District Council* [1991] 1 AC 398, and since then the general position is that economic loss caused by reliance on negligently made statements, advice or similar (in the appropriate circumstances) can be recoverable, whereas that based on a negligently performed activity will not be. The particular problem was well illustrated by a series of cases concerning defective buildings. Where a defect in a building (caused by negligence— e.g. of a builder, surveyor, inspector or architect) results in physical injury, there is usually no problem establishing liability in negligence (and/or the statutory liability that may arise from the Defective Premises Act 1972 or the Building Act 1984). By far the most difficult question has been the liability of builders, inspectors and others where the defect is one of quality which, though causing *physical* defects to the building, affects only the *economic* value of the building itself. Other issues relate to whether there can be liability where one part of a building damages another part (because there can be liability only if the defective part damages 'other' property).

DEFECTIVE PREMISES ACT 1972

1. Duty to build dwellings properly

(1) A person taking on work for or in connection with the provision of a dwelling (whether the dwelling is provided by the erection or by the conversion or enlargement of a building) owes a duty—

(a) if the dwelling is provided to the order of any person, to that person; and

(b) without prejudice to paragraph (a) above, to every person who acquires an interest (whether legal or equitable) in the dwelling;

to see that the work which he takes on is done in a workmanlike or, as the case may be, professional manner, with proper materials and so that as regards that work the dwelling will be fit for habitation when completed.

(2) A person who takes on any such work for another on terms that he is to do it in accordance with instructions given by or on behalf of that other shall, to the extent to which he does it properly in accordance with those instructions, be treated for the purposes of this section as discharging the duty imposed on him by subsection (1) above except where he owes a duty to that other to warn him of any defects in the instructions and fails to discharge that duty.

(3) A person shall not be treated for the purposes of subsection (2) above as having given instructions for the doing of work merely because he has agreed to the work being done in a specified manner, with specified materials or to a specified design.

(4) A person who—

(a) in the course of a business which consists of or includes providing or arranging for the provision of dwellings or installations in dwellings; or

(b) in the exercise of a power of making such provision or arrangements conferred by or by virtue of any enactment;

arranges for another to take on work for or in connection with the provision of a dwelling shall be treated for the purposes of this section as included among the persons who have taken on the work.

. . .

2. Cases excluded from the remedy under section 1

(1) Where—

(a) in connection with the provision of a dwelling or its first sale or letting for habitation any rights in respect of defects in the state of the dwelling are conferred by an approved scheme to which this section applies on a person having or acquiring an interest in the dwelling; and

(b) it is stated in a document of a type approved for the purposes of this section that the requirements as to design or construction imposed by or under the scheme have, or appear to have, been substantially complied with in relation to the dwelling;

no action shall be brought by any person having or acquiring an interest in the dwelling for breach of the duty imposed by section 1 above in relation to the dwelling.

. . .

3. Duty of care with respect to work done on premises not abated by disposal of premises

(1) Where work of construction, repair, maintenance or demolition or any other work is done on or in relation to premises, any duty of care owed, because of the doing of the work, to persons who

might reasonably be expected to be affected by defects in the state of the premises created by the doing of the work shall not be abated by the subsequent disposal of the premises by the person who owed the duty.

(2) This section does not apply—

(a) in the case of premises which are let, where the relevant tenancy of the premises commenced, or the relevant tenancy agreement of the premises was entered into, before the commencement of this Act;

(b) in the case of premises disposed of in any other way, when the disposal of the premises was completed, or a contract for their disposal was entered into, before the commencement of this Act; or

(c) in either case, where the relevant transaction disposing of the premises is entered into in pursuance of an enforceable option by which the consideration for the disposal was fixed before the commencement of this Act.. . .

6. Supplemental

(1) In this Act—

'disposal', in relation to premises, includes a letting, and an assignment or surrender of a tenancy, of the premises and the creation by contract of any other right to occupy the premises, and 'dispose' shall be construed accordingly;

'personal injury' includes any disease and any impairment of a person's physical or mental condition;

'tenancy' means—

(a) a tenancy created either immediately or derivatively out of the freehold, whether by a lease or underlease, by an agreement for a lease or underlease or by a tenancy agreement, but not including a mortgage term or any interest arising in favour of a mortgagor by his attorning tenant to his mortgagee; or

(b) a tenancy at will or a tenancy on sufferance; or

(c) a tenancy, whether or not constituting a tenancy at common law, created by or in pursuance of any enactment;

and cognate expressions shall be construed accordingly.

(2) Any duty imposed by or enforceable by virtue of any provision of this Act is in addition to any duty a person may owe apart from that provision.

(3) Any term of an agreement which purports to exclude or restrict, or has the effect of excluding or restricting, the operation of any of the provisions of this Act, or any liability arising by virtue of any such provision, shall be void.

Notes

1. In *Andrews* v *Schooling* [1991] 3 All ER 723, the defendants converted two houses into flats and granted a long lease of a ground-floor flat to the claimant. The defendants did no work to the cellar, and because they failed to put in a damp-proofing system, damp entered the claimant's flat from the cellar. The claimant sought damages but the defendants claimed that section 1 of the 1972 Act did not apply to omissions. The Court of Appeal held that the Act applied both to carrying out work badly and to a failure to carry out necessary work.

2. The 1972 Act is also relevant in the context of occupiers' liability—see section 10.2.

> ### *Murphy* v *Brentwood District Council*
> House of Lords [1991] 1 AC 398

In 1970, the claimant purchased a house that had been built by ABC Homes and was constructed on a concrete raft foundation over an infilled site. The raft design was submitted to the defendant council for approval and, after advice from consulting engineers was received, was approved. From 1981 cracks began appearing in the internal walls of the house and it was found that the concrete raft had subsided. This also caused breakage of soil and gas pipes. The claimant eventually sold the house for £35,000 less than its value in good condition and sued the council as being responsible for the negligent approval of the design by the consulting engineers. Held (overruling *Anns* v *Merton London Borough Council* [1978] AC 728): the council owed no duty of care in respect of Murphy's economic losses.

LORD BRIDGE: If a manufacturer negligently puts into circulation a chattel containing a latent defect which renders it dangerous to persons or property, the manufacturer, on the well known principles established by *Donoghue* v *Stevenson* [1932] AC 562, will be liable in tort for injury to persons or damage to property which the chattel causes. But if a manufacturer produces and sells a chattel which is merely defective in quality, even to the extent that it is valueless for the purpose for which it is intended, the manufacturer's liability at common law arises only under and by reference to the terms of any contract to which he is a party in relation to the chattel; the common law does not impose on him any liability in tort to persons to whom he owes no duty in contract but who, having acquired the chattel, suffer economic loss because the chattel is defective in quality. If a dangerous defect in a chattel is discovered before it causes any personal injury or damage to property, because the danger is now known and the chattel cannot safely be used unless the defect is repaired, the defect becomes merely a defect in quality. The chattel is either capable of repair at economic cost or it is worthless and must be scrapped. In either case the loss sustained by the owner or hirer of the chattel is purely economic. It is recoverable against any party who owes the loser a relevant contractual duty. But it is not recoverable in tort in the absence of a special relationship of proximity imposing on the tortfeasor a duty of care to safeguard the plaintiff from economic loss. There is no such special relationship between the manufacturer of a chattel and a remote owner or hirer.

I believe that these principles are equally applicable to buildings. If a builder erects a structure containing a latent defect which renders it dangerous to persons or property, he will be liable in tort for injury to persons or damage to property resulting from that dangerous defect. But if the defect becomes apparent before any injury or damage has been caused, the loss sustained by the building owner is purely economic. If the defect can be repaired at economic cost, that is the measure of the loss. If the building cannot be repaired, it may have to be abandoned as unfit for occupation and therefore valueless. These economic losses are recoverable if they flow from breach of a relevant contractual duty, but, here again, in the absence of a special relationship of proximity they are not recoverable in tort. The only qualification I would make to this is that, if a building stands so close to the boundary of the building owner's land that after discovery of the dangerous defect it remains a potential source of injury to persons or property on neighbouring land or on the highway, the building owner ought, in principle, to be entitled to recover in tort from the negligent builder the cost of obviating the danger, whether by repair or by demolition, so far as that cost is necessarily incurred in order to protect himself from potential liability to third parties.

The fallacy which, in my opinion, vitiates the judgments of Lord Denning MR and Sachs LJ in *Dutton* [1972] 1 QB 373 is that they brush these distinctions aside as of no consequence . . . Stamp LJ on the other hand, fully understood and appreciated them and his statement of the applicable principles as between the building owner and the builder . . . seems to me unexceptionable. He rested his decision in favour of the plaintiff against the local authority on a wholly distinct principle which will require separate examination.

The complex structure theory

In my speech in *D & F Estates* [1989] AC 177, 206G–207H I mooted the possibility that in complex structures or complex chattels one part of a structure or chattel might, when it caused damage to another part of the same structure or chattel, be regarded in the law of tort as having caused damage to 'other property' for the purpose of the application of ***Donoghue* v *Stevenson*** principles. I expressed no opinion as to the validity of this theory, but put it forward for consideration as a possible ground on which the facts considered in ***Anns*** [1978] AC 728 might be distinguishable from the facts which had to be considered in *D & F Estates* itself. I shall call this for convenience 'the complex structure theory' and it is, so far as I can see, only if and to the extent that this theory can be affirmed and applied that there can be any escape from the conclusions I have indicated above under the rubric 'Dangerous defects and defects of quality.'

. . . The reality is that the structural elements in any building form a single indivisible unit of which the different parts are essentially interdependent. To the extent that there is any defect in one part of the structure it must to a greater or lesser degree necessarily affect all other parts of the structure. Therefore any defect in the structure is a defect in the quality of the whole and it is quite artificial, in order to impose a legal liability which the law would not otherwise impose, to treat a defect in an integral structure, so far as it weakens the structure, as a dangerous defect liable to cause damage to 'other property.'

A critical distinction must be drawn here between some part of a complex structure which is said to be a 'danger' only because it does not perform its proper function in sustaining the other parts and some distinct item incorporated in the structure which positively malfunctions so as to inflict positive damage on the structure in which it is incorporated. Thus, if a defective central heating boiler explodes and damages a house or a defective electrical installation malfunctions and sets the house on fire, I see no reason to doubt that the owner of the house, if he can prove that the damage was due to the negligence of the boiler manufacturer in the one case or the electrical contractor in the other, can recover damages in tort on ***Donoghue* v *Stevenson*** [1932] AC 562 principles. But the position in law is entirely different where, by reason of the inadequacy of the foundations of the building to support the weight of the superstructure, differential settlement and consequent cracking occurs. Here, once the first cracks appear, the structure as a whole is seen to be defective and the nature of the defect is known. Even if, contrary to my view, the initial damage could be regarded as damage to other property caused by a latent defect, once the defect is known the situation of the building owner is analogous to that of the car owner who discovers that the car has faulty brakes. He may have a house which, until repairs are effected, is unfit for habitation, but, subject to the reservation I have expressed with respect to ruinous buildings at or near the boundary of the owner's property, the building no longer represents a source of danger and as it deteriorates will only damage itself.

For these reasons the complex structure theory offers no escape from the conclusion that damage to a house itself which is attributable to a defect in the structure of the house is not recoverable in tort on *Donoghue* v *Stevenson* principles, but represents purely economic loss which is only recoverable in contract or in tort by reason of some special relationship of proximity which imposes on the tortfeasor a duty of care to protect against economic loss.

The relative positions of the builder and the local authority

I have so far been considering the potential liability of a builder for negligent defects in the structure of a building to persons to whom he owes no contractual duty. Since the relevant statutory function of the local authority is directed to no other purpose than securing compliance with building byelaws or regulations by the builder, I agree with the view expressed in *Anns* [1978] AC 728 and by the majority of the Court of Appeal in *Dutton* [1972] 1 QB 373 that a negligent performance of that function can attract no greater liability than attaches to the negligence of the builder whose fault was the primary tort giving rise to any relevant damage. I am content for present purposes to assume, though I am by no means satisfied that the assumption is correct, that where the local authority, as in this case or in *Dutton*, have in fact approved the defective plans or inspected the defective foundations and negligently failed to discover the defect, their potential liability in tort is coextensive with that of the builder.

Only Stamp LJ in *Dutton* was prepared to hold that the law imposed on the local authority a duty of care going beyond that imposed on the builder and extending to protection of the building owner from purely economic loss. I must return later to consider the question of liability for economic loss more generally, but here I need only say that I cannot find *in Hedley Byrne & Co Ltd* v *Heller & Partners Ltd* [1964] AC 465 or *Dorset Yacht Co Ltd* v *Home Office* [1970] AC 1004 any principle applicable to the circumstances of *Dutton* or the present case that provides support for the conclusion which Stamp LJ sought to derive from those authorities. . . .

Liability for economic loss

All these considerations lead inevitably to the conclusion that a building owner can only recover the cost of repairing a defective building on the ground of the authority's negligence in performing its statutory function of approving plans or inspecting buildings in the course of construction if the scope of the authority's duty of care is wide enough to embrace purely economic loss. The House has already held in *D & F Estates* that a builder, in the absence of any contractual duty or of a special relationship of proximity introducing the *Hedley Byrne* principle of reliance, owes no duty of care in tort in respect of the quality of his work. As I pointed out in *D & F Estates*, to hold that the builder owed such a duty of care to any person acquiring an interest in the product of the builder's work would be to impose upon him the obligations of an indefinitely transmissible warranty of quality.

By section 1 of the Defective Premises Act 1972 Parliament has in fact imposed on builders and others undertaking work in the provision of dwellings the obligations of a transmissible warranty of the quality of their work and of the fitness for habitation of the completed dwelling. But besides being limited to dwellings, liability under the Act is subject to a limitation period of six years from the completion of the work and to the exclusion provided for by section 2. It would be remarkable to find that similar obligations in the nature of a transmissible warranty of quality, applicable to buildings of every kind and subject to no such limitations or exclusions as are imposed by the Act of 1972, could be derived from the builder's common law duty of care or from the duty imposed by building byelaws or regulations. In *Anns* Lord Wilberforce expressed the opinion that a builder could be held liable for a breach of statutory duty in respect of buildings which do not comply with the byelaws. But he cannot, I think, have meant that the statutory obligation to build in conformity with the byelaws by itself gives rise to obligations in the nature of transmissible warranties of quality. If he did mean that, I must respectfully disagree. I find it impossible to suppose that anything less than clear express language such as is used in section 1 of the Act of 1972 would suffice to impose such a statutory obligation.

As I have already said, since the function of a local authority in approving plans or inspecting buildings in course of construction is directed to ensuring that the builder complies with building byelaws or regulations, I cannot see how, in principle, the scope of the liability of the authority for a negligent failure to ensure compliance can exceed that of the liability of the builder for his negligent failure to comply.

There may, of course, be situations where, even in the absence of contract, there is a special relationship of proximity between builder and building owner which is sufficiently akin to contract to introduce the element of reliance so that the scope of the duty of care owed by the builder to the owner is wide enough to embrace purely economic loss.

Notes

1. **Murphy** was applied in *Department of Environment* v *Bates Ltd* [1990] 3 WLR 457. The claim-ants were sub-lessees of the buildings built by the defendants and discovered that some of the concrete in the buildings was soft. They sued the builder for the cost of the remedial work and the cost of alternative (office) accommodation while the work was carried out. The House of Lords held that there was no liability, since the buildings were not unsafe but rather suffered a defect of quality in that they could not be loaded to their designed capacity unless repaired. The loss resulted from the quality of the building itself and was therefore pure economic loss and irrecoverable.

2. The line between liability and non-liability is illustrated by *Nitrigin Eireann Teoranta* v *Inco Alloys* [1992] 1 All ER 854, where the claimants operated a chemical factory. In 1983 they discovered a crack in a steel pipe supplied by the defendants. The pipe was repaired but it was held that no cause of action arose as the pipe had merely damaged itself and the loss was economic loss. However, in 1984 the pipe burst, and this caused damage to surrounding parts of the factory. This did give rise to a cause of action as 'other' property was damaged.

3. See also *Robinson* v *PE Jones (Contractors)* [2011] EWCA Civ 9. The defendant built two defective flues, but liability in contract was limited. It was held that, at least in manufacturing and building contracts, no greater duty was owed in tort than in contract. Stanley Burnton LJ said that:

   [I]t must now be regarded as settled law that the builder/vendor of a building does not by reason of his contract to construct or to complete the building assume any liability in the tort of negligence in relation to defects in the building giving rise to purely economic loss. The same applies to a builder who is not the vendor, and to the seller or manufacturer of a chattel . . . Thus the crucial distinction is between a person who supplies something which is defective and a person who supplies something (whether a building, goods or a service) which, because of its defects, causes loss or damage to something else. (at [92])

4. **Murphy** has been rejected in most Commonwealth countries. In *Bryan* v *Maloney* (1994) 128 ALR 163, the High Court of Australia held that there was sufficient proximity between a builder and subsequent purchasers because the house was a permanent structure intended to be used indefinitely. In *Invercargill City Council* v *Hamlin* [1996] 1 All ER 756, the Privy Council accepted that New Zealand law was different, saying that policy conditions were such as to lead to liability, without casting doubt on the correctness of **Murphy** in England and Wales. The New Zealand Court of Appeal ([1994] NZLR 513 (CA)) had said that house buyers rely on building inspectors to ensure compliance by builders with building regulations. Accordingly, the council was liable for negligent inspection of foundations when subsidence later occurred. In Canada the Supreme Court held in *Winnipeg Condominium Corporation* v *Bird Construction* (1995) 121 DLR (4th) 193,

that builders or architects could be liable where negligence caused the building to be dangerous. Liability was limited to the cost of making the building safe.

5. The rejection of **Murphy** has led to a loosening of the bonds of the common law. In *Invercargill City Council* (see note 4, in the NZ Court of Appeal) Cooke P said, 'While the disharmony may be regrettable, it is inevitable now that the Commonwealth jurisdictions have gone on their own paths without taking English decisions as the invariable starting point. The ideal of a uniform Common-law has proved as unattainable as any ideal of a uniform law. It could not survive the independence of the United States; constitutional evolution in the Commonwealth has done the rest. What of course is both desirable and feasible . . . is to take account and learn from decisions in other jurisdictions' (at 523).

6. The effect of **Murphy** on the liability of builders and others is discussed in Duncan Wallace '*Anns Beyond Repair*' (1991) 107 LQR 230 and Carl Stychin 'Dangerous Liaisons: New Developments in the Law of Defective Premises' (1996) 16 LS 387.

6.2.1 Statements and advice

The harmful effects of a statement can sometimes carry further than the effects of an act, and it is often easier to make a careless statement than commit a negligent act. Fairly stringent limitations have therefore been placed on the notion of proximity, so that it is said that there must be 'a special relationship' between the parties before a duty of care can arise. After **Hedley Byrne**, the range of liability steadily expanded, although the ever-increasing complexity and interrelation of communications—particularly in an increasingly digital world—means that new problems are always presenting themselves.

The traditional view of **Hedley Byrne** liability is that it depends upon a voluntary assumption of responsibility by the defendant when giving advice or exercising skills, and the claimant's reliance on that advice or skill. Liability extends to 'tripartite' cases where the advice is not given to the claimant but rather to a third party who acts to the detriment of the claimant (section 6.3). Also, there may be cases where reliance is not necessary at all because the defendant assumes a responsibility analogous to a fiduciary obligation (**White v Jones** [1995] 2 AC 207). If a defendant is liable for a negligent statement, the claimant may recover their losses, even though these may be purely economic. The extent to which a person who suffers pure economic loss as the result of an activity may recover is determined by **Murphy**, though sometimes the line between statements and activities is quite blurred.

The particular issues which need to be addressed each time statement/advice claims are considered are the following.

(1) When is a person under a duty to be careful in making a statement?

(2) To whom is that duty owed?

(3) When can there be liability to a third party, that is, to a person who is not a recipient of the information but who suffers damage because of the act of a person who is?

(4) To what extent can a person absolve themselves of responsibility?

It would be too onerous a burden to hold a person responsible whenever they carelessly make a statement which turns out to be wrong and someone else has suffered loss as a result. This would mean, for example, a person could be liable for even a casual statement made at a party. The courts have established that special rules of proximity apply in this area, so that a 'special relationship' must be established between the parties, and to a large extent this depends on the defendant knowing that the claimant is justifiably relying upon them for their special skill, expertise or knowledge.

6.2.1.1 Assumption of responsibility

> ### *Henderson v Merrett Syndicates*
> House of Lords [1995] 2 AC 145

The case concerned Lloyd's underwriters and the main issue was whether there could be concurrent liability in contract and tort. The extract below deals only with the discussion of the *Hedley Byrne* principle.

LORD GOFF: . . . From these statements, and from their application in *Hedley Byrne*, we can derive some understanding of the breadth of the principle underlying the case. We can see that it rests upon a relationship between the parties, which may be general or specific to the particular transaction, and which may or may not be contractual in nature. All of their Lordships spoke in terms of one party having assumed or undertaken a responsibility towards the other. On this point, Lord Devlin spoke in particularly clear terms in both passages from his speech which I have quoted above. Further, Lord Morris spoke of that party being possessed of a 'special skill' which he undertakes to 'apply for the assistance of another who relies upon such skill.' But the facts of *Hedley Byrne* itself, which was concerned with the liability of a banker to the recipient for negligence in the provision of a reference gratuitously supplied, show that the concept of a 'special skill' must be understood broadly, certainly broadly enough to include special knowledge. Again, though *Hedley Byrne* was concerned with the provision of information and advice, the example given by Lord Devlin of the relationship between solicitor and client, and his and Lord Morris's statements of principle, show that the principle extends beyond the provision of information and advice to include the performance of other services. It follows, of course, that although, in the case of the provision of information and advice, reliance upon it by the other party will be necessary to establish a cause of action (because otherwise the negligence will have no causative effect), nevertheless there may be other circumstances in which there will be the necessary reliance to give rise to the application of the principle. In particular, as cases concerned with solicitor and client demonstrate, where the plaintiff entrusts the defendant with the conduct of his affairs, in general or in particular, he may be held to have relied on the defendant to exercise due skill and care in such conduct.

In subsequent cases concerned with liability under the *Hedley Byrne* principle in respect of negligent misstatements, the question has frequently arisen whether the plaintiff falls within the category of persons, to whom the maker of the statement owes a duty of care. In seeking to contain that category of persons within reasonable bounds, there has been some tendency on the part of the courts to criticise the concept of 'assumption of responsibility' as being 'unlikely to be a helpful or realistic test in most cases' (see *Smith v Eric S Bush* [1990] 1 AC 831, 864–865, *per* Lord Griffiths; and see also *Caparo Industries plc v Dickman* [1990] 2 AC 605, 628, *per* Lord Roskill). However, at least in cases such as the present, in which the same problem does not arise, there seems to be no reason why recourse should not be had to the concept, which appears after all to have been adopted, in one form or another, by all of their Lordships in *Hedley Byrne* [1964] AC 465 (see, eg, Lord Reid, at pp 483, 486 and 487. Lord Morris (with whom Lord Hodson agreed), at p 494; Lord Devlin, at pp 529 and 531; and Lord Pearce at p 538). Furthermore, especially in a context concerned with a liability which may arise under a contract or in a situation 'equivalent to contract,' it must be expected that an objective test will be applied when asking the question whether, in a particular case, responsibility should be held to have been assumed by the defendant to the plaintiff: see *Caparo Industries plc v*

Dickman [1990] 2 AC 605, 637, *per* Lord Oliver of Aylmerton. In addition, the concept provides its own explanation why there is no problem in cases of this kind about liability for pure economic loss; for if a person assumes responsibility to another in respect of certain services, there is no reason why he should not be liable in damages for that other in respect of economic loss which flows from the negligent performance of those services. It follows that, once the case is identified as falling within the *Hedley Byrne* principle, there should be no need to embark upon any further enquiry whether it is 'fair, just and reasonable' to impose liability for economic loss—a point which is, I consider, of some importance in the present case. The concept indicates too that in some circumstances, for example where the undertaking to furnish the relevant service is given on an informal occasion, there may be no assumption of responsibility; and likewise that an assumption of responsibility may be negatived by an appropriate disclaimer. I wish to add in parenthesis that, as Oliver J recognised in *Midland Bank Trust Co Ltd v Hett, Stubbs & Kemp* [1979] Ch 384, 416F–G, (a case concerned with concurrent liability of solicitors in tort and contract, to which I will have to refer in a moment) an assumption of responsibility by, for example, a professional man may give rise to liability in respect of negligent omissions as much as negligent acts of commission, as for example when a solicitor assumes responsibility for business on behalf of his client and omits to take a certain step, such as the service of a document, which falls within the responsibility so assumed by him.

Notes

1. Lord Goff concentrates more on the 'undertaking of responsibility' and less on reliance. This leads him to suggest that the principle applies equally to the provision of services and can include omissions. The test of whether responsibility has been undertaken is objective and is then imposed by law, although a disclaimer may be effective (subject to the Unfair Contract Terms Act 1977). Does this principle explain cases such as *Spring* v *Guardian Assurance* and *White* v *Jones*? In the former there was no reliance by the claimant on any statement made by the defendant, although he did rely on the defendant doing his job properly. In the latter case there was no reliance at all. The issue of 'mutuality' (i.e. reliance by the claimant upon the defendant) did not arise in *Henderson*, and therefore it might be asked whether (as Lord Goff says) there is one broad *Hedley Byrne* principle, or two separate principles, one relating to reliance and the other (as in *White* v *Jones*) to a 'quasi-fiduciary' obligation to protect the interests of someone who would obviously be affected by failing to perform a duty owed to another.

> ### *Customs and Excise Commissioners* v *Barclays Bank*
> House of Lords [2006] UKHL 28

Customs and Excise obtained orders freezing the accounts of two companies at the defendant bank. The bank mistakenly paid money out of the accounts and Customs claimed damages for negligence on the basis that they had relied on the bank to observe the orders. Held: the bank was not liable.

LORD BINGHAM:

14. I do not think that the notion of assumption of responsibility, even on an objective approach, can aptly be applied to the situation which arose between the Commissioners and the Bank on notification to it of the orders. Of course it was bound by law to comply. But it had no choice. It did not

assume any responsibility towards the Commissioners as the giver of references in *Hedley Byrne* (but for the disclaimer) and *Spring*, the valuers in *Smith v Bush*, the solicitors in *White v Jones* and the agents in *Henderson v Merrett* may plausibly be said to have done towards the recipient or subject of the references, the purchasers, the beneficiaries and the Lloyd's Names. Save for the notification of the order . . . nothing crossed the line between the Commissioners and the Bank (see *Williams v Natural Life Health Foods Ltd*, p 835). Nor do I think that the Commissioners can be said in any meaningful sense to have relied on the Bank. The Commissioners, having obtained their orders and notified them to the Bank, were no doubt confident that the Bank would act promptly and effectively to comply. But reliance in the law is usually taken to mean that if A had not relied on B he would have acted differently. Here the Commissioners could not have acted differently, since they had availed themselves of the only remedy which the law provided. Mr Sales suggested, although only as a fall-back argument, that the relationship between the Commissioners and the Bank was, in Lord Shaw's words adopted by Lord Devlin in *Hedley Byrne* (p 529), 'equivalent to contract'. But the essence of any contract is voluntariness, and the Bank's position was wholly involuntary. . . .

LORD HOFFMANN:

35. There is a tendency, which has been remarked upon by many judges, for phrases like 'proximate', 'fair, just and reasonable' and 'assumption of responsibility' to be used as slogans rather than practical guides to whether a duty should exist or not. These phrases are often illuminating but discrimination is needed to identify the factual situations in which they provide useful guidance. For example, in a case in which A provides information to C which he knows will be relied upon by D, it is useful to ask whether A assumed responsibility to D: *Hedley Byrne & Co Ltd v Heller & Partners Ltd* [1964] AC 465: *Smith v Eric S Bush* [1990] 1 AC 831. Likewise, in a case in which A provides information on behalf of B to C for the purpose of being relied upon by C, it is useful to ask whether A assumed responsibility to C for the information or was only discharging his duty to B: *Williams v Natural Life Health Foods Ltd* [1998] 1 WLR 830. Or in a case in which A provided information to B for the purpose of enabling him to make one kind of decision, it may be useful to ask whether he assumed responsibility for its use for a different kind of decision: *Caparo Industries plc v Dickman* [1990] 2 AC 605. In these cases in which the loss has been caused by the claimant's reliance on information provided by the defendant, it is critical to decide whether the defendant (rather than someone else) assumed responsibility for the accuracy of the information to the claimant (rather than to someone else) or for its use by the claimant for one purpose (rather than another). The answer does not depend upon what the defendant intended but, as in the case of contractual liability, upon what would reasonably be inferred from his conduct against the background of all the circumstances of the case. The purpose of the inquiry is to establish whether there was, in relation to the loss in question, the necessary relationship (or 'proximity') between the parties and, as Lord Goff of Chieveley pointed out in *Henderson v Merrett Syndicates Ltd* [1995] 2 AC 145, 181, the existence of that relationship and the foreseeability of economic loss will make it unnecessary to undertake any further inquiry into whether it would be fair, just and reasonable to impose liability. In truth, the case is one in which, but for the alleged absence of the necessary relationship, there would be no dispute that a duty to take care existed and the relationship is what makes it fair, just and reasonable to impose the duty.

36. It is equally true to say that a sufficient relationship will be held to exist when it is fair, just and reasonable to do so. Because the question of whether a defendant has assumed responsibility is a legal inference to be drawn from his conduct against the background of all the circumstances of the case, it is by no means a simple question of fact. Questions of fairness and policy will enter into the decision and it may be more useful to try to identify these questions than simply to bandy terms like 'assumption of responsibility' and 'fair, just and reasonable'. In *Morgan Crucible Co plc v Hill Samuel & Co Ltd* [1991] Ch 295, 300–303 I tried to identify some of these considerations in order to encourage the evolution of lower-level principles which could be more useful than the high abstractions commonly used in such debates.

37. In *Henderson v Merrett Syndicates Ltd* itself, the House used the concept of assumption of responsibility in a situation which did not involve reliance upon information but where, once again, the issue was whether the necessary relationship between claimant and defendant existed. The issues in that case were whether the managing agents of a Lloyd's syndicate owed a duty of care in respect of their underwriting to Names with whom they had no contractual relationship and whether they owed a separate duty in tort to Names with whom they did have a contractual relationship. In fact, the arguments in *Henderson*'s case were a rerun of *Donoghue v Stevenson* in a claim for economic loss. In that case, as it seems to me, the use of the concept of assumption of responsibility, while perfectly legitimate, was less illuminating. The question was not whether the defendant had assumed responsibility for the accuracy of a particular statement but a much more general responsibility for the consequences of their conduct of the underwriting. To say that the managing agents assumed a responsibility to the Names to take care not to accept unreasonable risks is little different from saying that a manufacturer of ginger beer assumes a responsibility to consumers to take care to keep snails out of his bottles.

38. Even in this context, however, the notion of assumption of responsibility serves a different, weaker, but nevertheless useful purpose in drawing attention to the fact that a duty of care is ordinarily generated by something which the defendant has decided to *do*: giving a reference, supplying a report, managing a syndicate, making ginger beer. It does not much matter why he decided to do it; it may be that he thought it would be profitable or it may be that he was providing a service pursuant to some statutory duty, as in *Phelps v Hillingdon London Borough Council* [2001] 2 AC 619 and *Ministry of Housing and Local Government v Sharp* [1970] 2 QB 223. In the present case, however, the duty is not alleged to arise from anything which the bank was doing. It is true that the bank was carrying on the business of banking, handling money on behalf of its customers. But that is not alleged to have been either necessary or sufficient to generate the duty in this case. Not necessary, because if such a duty is created by notice of the freezing order, it must apply to anyone who has possession or control of the defendant's assets: the garage holding his car, the stockbroker nominee company holding his shares, his grandmother holding a drawer-full of his bank notes. On being given notice of the order, they would all be under an obligation to take reasonable care to ensure that the defendant did not get his hands on the assets. Not sufficient, because there is no suggestion that, apart from the freezing order, the bank in carrying on its ordinary business would be under any duty to protect the position of the Commissioners. . . .

LORD RODGER:

52. Therefore it is not surprising that there are cases in the books—notably *Ministry of Housing and Local Government v Sharp* [1970] 2 QB 223, approved by Lord Slynn of Hadley in *Spring v Guardian Assurance plc* [1995] 2 AC 296 . . . which do not readily yield to analysis in terms of a voluntary assumption of responsibility, but where liability has none the less been held to exist. I see no reason to treat these cases as exceptions to some over-arching rule that there must be a voluntary assumption of responsibility before the law recognises a duty of care. Such a rule would inevitably lead to the

concept of voluntary assumption of responsibility being stretched beyond its natural limits—which would in the long run undermine the very real value of the concept as a criterion of liability in the many cases where it is an appropriate guide. In any event, as the words which I have quoted from his speech in **Merrett Syndicates** make clear, Lord Goff himself recognised that, although it may be decisive in many situations, the presence or absence of a voluntary assumption of responsibility does not necessarily provide the answer in all cases. Indeed in **Hedley Byrne** Lord Reid saw it as only one possible basis, the other being where the defendant has 'accepted a relationship with the inquirer which requires him to exercise such care as the circumstances require': [1964] AC 465, 486.

Notes

1. The decision in **Customs and Excise** appears to suggest that in some appropriate cases (usually where information or advice is provided) the assumption of responsibility test will be sufficient, but in general terms the question is always whether there is a 'sufficient' relationship between the parties, and that can be established by a variety of means. This is perhaps part of a movement away from legal principles of a high level of abstraction and a reminder that attention must be paid to the specific issues in the case.

2. The principal reason for this decision is that the bank did not 'voluntarily' assume responsibility as it had no choice but to obey the freezing order. Thus the ability to choose a course of action seems important. However, there have been cases where a defendant has been liable even though they were obliged by law to provide the relevant information. In *Ministry of Housing* v *Sharp* [1970] 2 QB 223 a registrar of local land charges mistakenly stated that there were no charges on a piece of land, causing loss to the claimants. The registrar was obliged to answer the question but was held liable. Lord Denning said that it was not a matter of assumption of responsibility but only of foresight of loss. However, that is far too wide a view and in **Murphy** it was recast as a case of reliance. Presumably the registrar was being relied on to give the right answer (albeit to a third party) and this suggests he may not have been liable if he had simply failed to answer the question at all (for that would merely have been a breach of his statutory duty with its own remedy). Indeed in **Customs and Excise** Lord Hoffmann said, 'The order carries its own remedies and its reach does not extend any further' (at [39]), meaning that it did not create a duty of care in and of itself.

3. In *James-Bowen and others* v *Commissioner of Police for the Metropolis* [2016] EWCA Civ 1217 a claim for economic loss based on assumption of responsibility was rejected, in relation to lost earnings suffered after a poorly conducted internal investigation into the claimant's (a police officer) conduct during an arrest. However, the claim was not struck out in full as a duty of care might arguably have been found on ordinary principles. The Supreme Court later unanimously allowed the Commissioner's appeal, finding that the duty contended for was novel and therefore the court had to proceed incrementally and by analogy with previous decisions (*James-Bowen and others* v *Commissioner of Police of the Metropolis* [2018] UKSC 40, see Lord Lloyd-Jones at [23]). It was ultimately not persuaded that the law should be extended.

4. There has been vacillation on the importance of the 'assumption of responsibility' concept in the years since **Hedley Byrne**. Lord Steyn, in *Williams* v *Natural Life Health Foods Ltd* [1998] UKHL 17, said that 'there [is] no better rationalisation for liability in tort for negligent misrepresentation than the concept of an assumption of responsibility' (at 837). However, after **Customs & Excise** it was deemed something to be determined 'flexibly' in line with the facts of a particular case. Lord Rodger said: 'the presence or absence of a voluntary assumption of responsibility does not necessarily provide the answer in all cases' (at [20]). Nevertheless, in later years it appears to have been reinstated as a touchstone of liability. Lord Wilson, in *Steel and another* v *NRAM Ltd (formerly NRAM plc) (Scotland)* [2018] UKSC 13 remarked that it has 'become clear that, although it may require cautious incremental development in order to fit cases to which it does not readily apply, this concept remains the foundation of the liability' (at [24]).

6.2.1.2 Reasonable reliance

Information can spread far beyond the person to whom it is given, inevitably extending the range of potential claimants. While ordinarily in negligence the question of who one might become liable to is answered by the foreseeable claimant rule, this is not sufficient in an area where more stringent proximity is required. Therefore, the question is: who can be deemed to be within a 'special relationship' with the defendant, so as to be justified in relying on them (especially in cases where the information is not strictly addressed to the claimant)?

> ### *Caparo Industries plc v Dickman*
> House of Lords [1990] 2 AC 605

The claimants were shareholders in Fidelity plc and after the accounts for 1984 (which were audited by the defendants) were published they purchased further shares, ultimately making a successful takeover bid. They alleged that they had suffered loss by relying on the 1984 accounts which should have shown a loss of £465,000 rather than a profit of £1.3 million. Held: the defendant auditors owed no duty to the claimants.

LORD BRIDGE: The salient feature of all these cases is that the defendant giving advice or information was fully aware of the nature of the transaction which the plaintiff had in contemplation, knew that the advice or information would be communicated to him directly or indirectly and knew that it was very likely that the plaintiff would rely on that advice or information in deciding whether or not to engage in the transaction in contemplation. In these circumstances the defendant could clearly be expected, subject always to the effect of any disclaimer of responsibility, specifically to anticipate that the plaintiff would rely on the advice or information given by the defendant for the very purpose for which he did in the event rely on it. So also the plaintiff, subject again to the effect of any disclaimer, would in that situation reasonably suppose that he was entitled to rely on the advice or information communicated to him for the very purpose for which he required it. The situation is entirely different where a statement is put into more or less general circulation and may foreseeably be relied on by strangers to the maker of the statement for any one of a variety of different purposes which the maker of the statement has no specific reason to anticipate. To hold the maker of the statement to be under a duty of care in respect of the accuracy of the statement to all and sundry for any purpose for which they may choose to rely on it is not only to subject him, in the classic words of Cardozo CJ to 'liability in an indeterminate amount for an indeterminate time to an indeterminate class': see *Ultramares Corporation v Touche* (1931) 174 NE 441, 444; it is also to confer on the world at large a quite unwarranted entitlement to appropriate for their own purposes the benefit of the expert knowledge or professional expertise attributed to the maker of the statement. Hence, looking only at the circumstances of these decided cases where a duty of care in respect of negligent statements has been held to exist, I should expect to find that the 'limit or control mechanism . . . imposed upon the liability of a wrongdoer towards those who have suffered economic damage in consequence of his negligence' rested in the necessity to prove, in this category of the tort of negligence, as an essential ingredient of the 'proximity' between the plaintiff and the defendant, that the defendant knew that his statement would be communicated to the plaintiff, either as an individual or as a member of an identifiable class, specifically in connection with a particular transaction or transactions of a particular kind (eg in a prospectus inviting investment) and that the plaintiff would be very likely to rely on it for the purpose of deciding whether or not to enter upon that transaction or upon a transaction of that kind. . . .

These considerations amply justify the conclusion that auditors of a public company's accounts owe no duty of care to members of the public at large who rely upon the accounts in deciding to buy shares in the company. If a duty of care were owed so widely, it is difficult to see any reason why it should not equally extend to all who rely on the accounts in relation to other dealings with a company as lenders or merchants extending credit to the company. A claim that such a duty was owed by auditors to a bank lending to a company was emphatically and convincingly rejected by Millett J in *Al Saudi Banque v Clarke Pixley* [1990] Ch 313. The only support for an unlimited duty of care owed by auditors for the accuracy of their accounts to all who may foreseeably rely upon them is to be found in some jurisdictions in the United States of America where there are striking differences in the law in different states. In this jurisdiction I have no doubt that the creation of such an unlimited duty would be a legislative step which it would be for Parliament, not the courts, to take . . .

No doubt these provisions [of the Companies Act 1985] establish a relationship between the auditors and the shareholders of a company on which the shareholder is entitled to rely for the protection of his interest. But the crucial question concerns the extent of the shareholder's interest which the auditor has a duty to protect. The shareholders of a company have a collective interest in the company's proper management and in so far as a negligent failure of the auditor to report accurately on the state of the company's finances deprives the shareholders of the opportunity to exercise their powers in general meeting to call the directors to book and to ensure that errors in management are corrected, the shareholders ought to be entitled to a remedy. But in practice no problem arises in this regard since the interest of the shareholders in the proper management of the company's affairs is indistinguishable from the interest of the company itself and any loss suffered by the shareholders, eg by the negligent failure of the auditor to discover and expose a misappropriation of funds by a director of the company, will be recouped by a claim against the auditors in the name of the company, not by individual shareholders.

I find it difficult to visualise a situation arising in the real world in which the individual shareholder could claim to have sustained a loss in respect of his existing shareholding referable to the negligence of the auditor which could not be recouped by the company. But on this part of the case your Lordships were much pressed with the argument that such a loss might occur by a negligent undervaluation of the company's assets in the auditor's report relied on by the individual shareholder in deciding to sell his shares at an undervalue. The argument then runs thus. The shareholder, qua shareholder, is entitled to rely on the auditor's report as the basis of his investment decision to sell his existing shareholding. If he sells at an undervalue he is entitled to recover the loss from the auditor. There can be no distinction in law between the shareholder's investment decision to sell the shares he has or to buy additional shares. It follows, therefore, that the scope of the duty of care owed to him by the auditor extends to cover any loss sustained consequent on the purchase of additional shares in reliance on the auditor's negligent report.

I believe this argument to be fallacious. Assuming without deciding that a claim by a shareholder to recover a loss suffered by selling his shares at an undervalue attributable to an undervaluation of the company's assets in the auditor's report could be sustained at all, it would not be by reason of any reliance by the shareholder on the auditor's report in deciding to sell; the loss would be referable to the depreciatory effect of the report on the market value of the shares before ever the decision of the shareholder to sell was taken. A claim to recoup a loss alleged to flow from the purchase of overvalued shares, on the other hand, can only be sustained on the basis of the purchaser's reliance on the report. The specious equation of 'investment decisions' to sell or to buy as giving rise to parallel claims thus appears to me to be untenable. Moreover, the loss in the case of the sale would be of a loss of part of the value of the shareholder's existing holding, which, assuming a duty of care owed to individual shareholders, it might sensibly lie within the scope of the auditor's duty to protect. A loss, on the other hand, resulting from the purchase of additional shares would result from a wholly independent transaction having no connection with the existing shareholding.

I believe it is this last distinction which is of critical importance and which demonstrates the unsoundness of the conclusion reached by the majority of the Court of Appeal. It is never sufficient to ask simply whether A owes B a duty of care. It is always necessary to determine the scope of the duty by reference to the kind of damage from which A must take care to save B harmless. 'The question is always whether the defendant was under a duty to avoid or prevent that damage, but the actual nature of the damage suffered is relevant to the existence and extent of any duty to avoid or prevent it': see *Sutherland Shire Council v Heyman*, 60 ALR 1, 48, *per* Brennan J. Assuming for the purpose of the argument that the relationship between the auditor of a company and individual shareholders is of sufficient proximity to give rise to a duty of care, I do not understand how the scope of that duty can possibly extend beyond the protection of any individual shareholder from losses in the value of the shares which he holds. As a purchaser of additional shares in reliance on the auditor's report, he stands in no different position from any other investing member of the public to whom the auditor owes no duty. . . .

LORD OLIVER: . . . What can be deduced from the **Hedley Byrne** case, therefore, is that the necessary relationship between the maker of a statement or giver of advice ('the adviser') and the recipient who acts in reliance upon it ('the advisee') may typically be held to exist where (1) the advice is required for a purpose, whether particularly specified or generally described, which is made known, either actually or inferentially, to the adviser at the time when the advice is given; (2) the adviser knows, either actually or inferentially, that his advice will be communicated to the advisee, either specifically or as a member of an ascertainable class, in order that it should be used by the advisee for that purpose; (3) it is known either actually or inferentially, that the advice so communicated is likely to be acted upon by the advisee for that purpose without independent inquiry, and (4) it is so acted upon by the advisee to his detriment. That is not, of course, to suggest that these conditions are either conclusive or exclusive, but merely that the actual decision in the case does not warrant any broader propositions. . . .

In seeking to ascertain whether there should be imposed on the adviser a duty to avoid the occurrence of the kind of damage which the advisee claims to have suffered it is not, I think, sufficient to ask simply whether there existed a 'closeness' between them in the sense that the advisee had a legal entitlement to receive the information upon the basis of which he has acted or in the sense that the information was intended to serve his interest or to protect him. One must, I think, go further and ask, in what capacity was his interest to be served and from what was he intended to be protected? A company's annual accounts are capable of being utilised for a number of purposes and if one thinks about it it is entirely foreseeable that they may be so employed. But many of such purposes have absolutely no connection with the recipient's status or capacity, whether as a shareholder, voting or non-voting, or as a debenture-holder. Before it can be concluded that the duty is imposed to protect the recipient against harm which he suffers by reason of the particular use that he chooses to make of the information which he receives, one must, I think, first ascertain the purpose for which the information is required to be given. Indeed the paradigmatic **Donoghue v Stevenson** case of a manufactured article requires, as an essential ingredient of liability, that the article has been used by the consumer in the manner in which it was intended to be used: see *Grant v Australian Knitting*

Mills Ltd [1936] AC 85, 104 and *Junior Books Ltd v Veitchi Co Ltd* [1983] 1 AC 520, 549, 552. I entirely follow that if the conclusion is reached that the very purpose of providing the information is to serve as the basis for making investment decisions or giving investment advice, it is not difficult then to conclude also that the duty imposed upon the adviser extends to protecting the recipient against loss occasioned by an unfortunate investment decision which is based on carelessly inaccurate information. . . . I do not believe and I see no grounds for believing that, in enacting the statutory provisions [of the Companies Act 1985], Parliament had in mind the provision of information for the assistance of purchasers of shares or debentures in the market, whether they be already the holders of shares or other securities or persons having no previous proprietary interest in the company. It is unnecessary to decide the point on this appeal, but I can see more force in the contention that one purpose of providing the statutory information might be to enable the recipient to exercise whatever rights he has in relation to his proprietary interest by virtue of which he receives it, by way, for instance, of disposing of that interest. I can, however, see no ground for supposing that the legislature was intending to foster a market for the existing holders of shares or debentures by providing information for the purpose of enabling them to acquire such securities from other holders who might be minded to sell.

For my part, I think that the position as regards the auditor's statutory duty was correctly summarised by O'Connor LJ, in his dissenting judgment when he said, at p 714:

> The statutory duty owed by auditors to shareholders is, I think, a duty owed to them as a body. I appreciate that it is difficult to see how the over-statement of the accounts can cause damage to the shareholders as a body; it will be the underlying reasons for the overstatement which cause damage, for example fraudulent abstraction of assets by directors or servants, but such loss is recoverable by the company. I am anxious to limit the present case to deciding whether the statutory duty operates to protect the individual shareholders as a potential buyer of further shares. If I am wrong in thinking that under the statute no duty is owed to shareholders as individuals, then I think the duty must be confined to transactions in which the shareholder can only participate because he is a shareholder. The Companies Act 1985 imposes a duty to shareholders as a class and the duty should not extend to an individual save as a member of the class in respect of some class activity. Buying shares in a company is not such an activity.

In my judgment, accordingly, the purpose for which the auditors' certificate is made and published is that of providing those entitled to receive the report with information to enable them to exercise in conjunction those powers which their respective proprietary interests confer upon them and not for the purposes of individual speculation with a view to profit. The same considerations as limit the existence of a duty of care also, in my judgment, limit the scope of the duty and I agree with O'Connor LJ that the duty of care is one owed to the shareholders as a body and not to individual shareholders.

To widen the scope of the duty to include loss caused to an individual by reliance upon the accounts for a purpose for which they were not supplied and were not intended would be to extend it beyond the limits which are so far deducible from the decisions of this House. It is not, as I think, an extension which either logic requires or policy dictates and I, for my part, am not prepared to follow the majority of the Court of Appeal in making it. In relation to the purchase of shares of other shareholders in a company, whether in the open market or as a result of an offer made to all or a majority of the existing shareholders, I can see no sensible distinction, so far as a duty of care is concerned, between a potential purchaser who is, vis-à-vis the company, a total outsider and one who is already the holder of one or more shares.

Notes

1. There were two grounds for this decision: first, there was not sufficient proximity between the claimants and the defendants and, secondly, the accounts were produced for the purpose of informing the members (the shareholders) of the company in order to assist them in directing the company, and not for the purpose of advising *individual* shareholders as to further speculation.

2. Compare *Galoo* v *Bright Grahame Murray* [1995] 1 All ER 16. The defendants audited the accounts of a company (Gamine) which was purchased by Hillsdown Holdings. The auditors failed to detect that Gamine was insolvent. The terms of the agreement to sell Gamine were that the price would be 5.2 times the net profits for 1986. The defendants knew that the price was to be fixed this way and were to deliver a set of the audited completion accounts direct to Hillsdown. Accordingly, it was held that as there was sufficient proximity on the special facts, the claim would not be struck out.

3. Note also *Moore Stephens* v *Stone & Rolls Ltd* [2009] UKHL 39 where the House of Lords confirmed the **Caparo** principle, pointing out that no duty is owed to shareholders *individually*, nor directly to creditors of an audited company. This difficult case involved the question whether auditors could be liable to a company for failing to detect fraud by the company when that fraud was carried out by the owner and sole shareholder. The point of the action was for the liquidators of the now bankrupt company to sue the auditors in order to reimburse the banks who were the victims of the fraud. It was agreed that the auditors were in breach of their duty to the company, but by a majority it was held that no action applied as the action was based on the company's own illegality.

4. A potential ground of liability was exposed in *Morgan Crucible* v *Hill Samuel* [1991] Ch 295. The claimant was engaged in a hostile takeover bid for a company. The defendants were the directors and financial advisors of the company, who publicly issued a number of statements. It was said that *if* the object of these statements was to encourage the claimants to increase their bid, a duty of care could be owed to them. The intention of the defendants (objectively determined) to influence the claimants is significant. Thus, in *Possfund Custodian Trustee* v *Diamond* [1996] 2 All ER 774 it was argued that a prospectus issued in pursuance of a flotation on the unlisted securities market may be directed not only to the recipients of the prospectus but may also be designed 'to inform and encourage after-market purchasers' (at 788). Accordingly, an action by a subsequent purchaser of shares based on negligent misrepresentations in the prospectus was not struck out.

5. In *The Law Society* v *KPMG* [2000] 4 All ER 540, a firm of solicitors engaged the defendant accountants to prepare a report to be submitted to the Law Society to the effect that the solicitors had complied with the Society's accounts rules. The accountants failed to detect that the solicitors had engaged in fraud and the Law Society successfully sued for the amount they had to pay to the firm's defrauded clients through a no-fault compensation scheme. Although the contract was with the solicitors, the accountants knew that the purpose was to alert the Society to the need to exercise its powers of intervention, and it was foreseeable that if the Society was not so alerted a loss would fall on its compensation fund. Accordingly, the **Caparo** requirements were met.

6. In most of these cases the issue is the liability of the *auditor* for a negligent audit of the accounts which have been drawn up by someone else. The question is: have the defendants negligently failed to detect *other people's* fraud or mistakes? In *Barings* v *Coopers and Lybrand* [1997] 1 BCLC 427 Leggatt LJ said that 'the primary responsibility for safeguarding a company's assets and preventing errors and defalcations rests with the directors. But material irregularities, and *a fortiori* fraud, will normally be brought to light by sound audit procedures, one of which is the practice of pointing out weaknesses in internal controls. An auditor's task is so to conduct the audit as to make it probable that material misstatements in financial documents will be detected' (at 435).

7. In the recent case *Banca Nazionale del Lavoro SPA* v *Playboy Club London Ltd* [2018] UKSC 43, it was held that a casino could not have been considered to have reasonably relied on a credit reference of one of its customers provided to an intermediate organisation, despite the fact that (as it later transpired) the customer's bank had provided negligent advice and the customer had wrongly profited at the expense of the casino. The Playboy Club was, however, later allowed, after more evidence had been uncovered, to reframe its claim in the tort of deceit.

8. The following case demonstrates that if a house surveyor realises that their report will be relied on by purchasers of a house (even though they are not their clients), the surveyor may be liable if the report is negligently prepared (*Farley* v *Skinner* [2001] UKHL 49). Yet even if an auditor realises that accounts that they have audited may be relied on by the purchasers of the company, the auditor will not be liable. What do you think explains this distinction?

> ### Smith v Eric S Bush
> House of Lords [1990] 1 AC 831

Smith wanted to buy a house and approached her building society for a mortgage, who asked the defendants, Bush, to value the property. The valuation was negligently carried out, and damage was later caused to the property when the chimney collapsed. The contract for the valuation was between the building society and the defendant, although the claimant was obliged to reimburse the building society for the fee. The purpose of the valuation was to protect the security of the building society, not to advise the claimant on the value of the house, although it was foreseeable that she would rely on it. Held: the surveyors owed the claimant a duty.

LORD TEMPLEMAN: The common law imposes on a person who contracts to carry out an operation an obligation to exercise reasonable skill and care. A plumber who mends a burst pipe is liable for his incompetence or negligence whether or not he has been expressly required to be careful. The law implies a term in the contract which requires the plumber to exercise reasonable skill and care in his calling. The common law also imposes on a person who carries out an operation an obligation to exercise reasonable skill and care where there is no contract. Where the relationship between the operator and a person who suffers injury or damage is sufficiently proximate and where the operator should have foreseen that carelessness on his part might cause harm to the injured person, the operator is liable in the tort of negligence. . . .

These two appeals are based on allegations of negligence in circumstances which are akin to contract. . . . Mrs Smith paid £36.89 to the Abbey National for a report and valuation and the Abbey National paid the appellants for the report and valuation. . . . the valuer knew or ought to have known that the purchaser would only contract to purchase the house if the valuation was satisfactory and that the purchaser might suffer injury or damage or both if the valuer did not exercise reasonable skill and care. In these circumstances I would expect the law to impose on the valuer a duty owed to the purchaser to exercise reasonable skill and care in carrying out the valuation.

A valuer who values property as a security for a mortgage is liable either in contract or in tort to the mortgagee for any failure on the part of the valuer to exercise reasonable skill and care in the valuation. The valuer is liable in contract if he receives instructions from and is paid by the mortgagee. The valuer is liable in tort if he receives instruction from and is paid by the mortgagor but knows that the valuation is for the purpose of a mortgage and will be relied upon by the mortgagee. . . .

In *Candler v Crane, Christmas & Co* [1951] 2 KB 164, the accountants of a company showed their draft accounts to and discussed them with an investor who, in reliance on the accounts, subscribed for shares in the company. Denning LJ, whose dissenting judgment was subsequently approved in the *Hedley Byrne* case [1964] AC 465, found that the accountants owed a duty to the investor to exercise reasonable skill and care in preparing the draft accounts. Denning LJ said, at p 176:

> If the matter were free from authority, I should have said that they clearly did owe a duty of care to him. They were professional accountants who prepared and put before him these accounts, knowing that he was going to be guided by them in making an investment in the company. On the faith of those accounts he did make the investment, whereas if the accounts had been carefully prepared, he would not have made the investment at all. The result is that he has lost his money.

Denning LJ, at pp 178–179 rejected the argument that:

> a duty to take care only arose where the result of a failure to take care will cause physical damage to person or property. . . . I can understand that in some cases of financial loss there may not be a sufficiently proximate relationship to give rise to a duty of care; but, if once the duty exists, I cannot think that liability depends on the nature of the damage.

The duty of professional men 'is not merely a duty to use care in their reports. They have also a duty to use care in their work which results in their reports,' p 179. The duty of an accountant is owed:

> to any third person to whom they themselves show the accounts, or to whom they know their employer is going to show the accounts, so as to induce him to invest money or take some other action on them. But I do not think the duty can be extended still further so as to include strangers of whom they have heard nothing and to whom their employer, without their knowledge may choose to show their accounts. . . . The test of proximity in these cases is: did the accountants know that the accounts were required for submission to the plaintiff and use by him?: pp 180–181.

Subject to the effect of any disclaimer of liability, these considerations appear to apply to the valuers in the present appeals.

. . . I agree that by obtaining and disclosing a valuation, a mortgagee does not assume responsibility to the purchaser for that valuation. But in my opinion the valuer assumes responsibility to both mortgagee and purchaser by agreeing to carry out a valuation for mortgage purposes knowing that the valuation fee has been paid by the purchaser and knowing that the valuation will probably be relied upon by the purchaser in order to decide whether or not to enter into a contract to purchase the house. The valuer can escape the responsibility to exercise reasonable skill and care by an express exclusion clause, provided the exclusion clause does not fall foul of the Unfair Contract Terms Act 1977. . . .

. . . The contractual duty of a valuer to value a house for the Abbey National did not prevent the valuer coming under a tortious duty to Mrs Smith who was furnished with a report of the valuer and relied on the report.

In general I am of the opinion that in the absence of a disclaimer of liability the valuer who values a house for the purpose of a mortgage, knowing that the mortgagee will rely and the mortgagor will probably rely on the valuation, knowing that the purchaser mortgagor has in effect paid for the valuation, is under a duty to exercise reasonable skill and care and that duty is owed to both parties to the mortgage for which the valuation is made. Indeed, in both the appeals now under consideration the existence of such a dual duty is tacitly accepted and acknowledged because notices excluding liability for breach of the duty owed to the purchaser were drafted by the mortgagee and imposed on the purchaser.

Notes

1. The issue of reliance was similarly raised in *Scullion* v *Bank of Scotland* [2011] EWCA Civ 693. The claimant alleged that he was misled by a valuation provided to the mortgage lenders and shown to him. However, it was held that no duty was owed because there was no proximity, nor would it be fair, just and reasonable to impose one. The difference was that this was a 'buy to let' transaction and therefore classed as a commercial venture. Lord Neuberger MR pointed out that the purchaser's main interest would have been in the rent that could be obtained on the property rather than in its capital value, whereas the mortgagee's interest was solely in the capital value in order to protect its loan. Accordingly, he held that the purchaser of a 'buy to let' property could be expected to obtain his own valuation (concentrating on rental value) and that therefore no duty was owed to them by the mortgagee's valuer.

2. In **Smith v Bush** the survey was directed to the building society to advise them whether the house was good security for the loan. Was this the same purpose as advising the purchaser as to the value of the house? In *Morgan Crucible* v *Hill Samuel* [1991] Ch 295, the Court of Appeal pointed out that at first instance the judge had distinguished **Smith v Bush** on the ground of 'the different economic relationships between the parties and the nature of the markets', but went on to say that 'we would not think it right by reference to economic considerations to dismiss as unarguable an otherwise arguable case' (at 302, 319). Does this mean that the fact that Mrs Smith paid for the survey and was a 'consumer' is not the distinguishing feature?

6.3 Liability to third parties

This section deals with the situation where one party makes a statement to B but damage is caused to C (usually by B acting on A's statement). Can there be liability to C when no statement was made to them directly? If so, how should 'proximity' be defined? **Hedley Byrne** is said largely to depend on 'reliance'. It is true that in this situation C relies on A making a non-negligent statement to B, but he does not *act* in reliance on the statement. Despite these conceptual problems, liability has in fact been extended into this area, making it difficult to establish the true basis of **Hedley Byrne** liability.

> **White v Jones**
> House of Lords [1995] 2 AC 207

In 1986 the testator cut his daughters out of his will, but he later relented and instructed the defendant solicitors to draw up a new will giving the daughters £9,000 each. The new will had negligently not been drawn up by the time the testator died. The daughters sued the solicitors. Held: the defendants were liable.

LORD BROWNE-WILKINSON: . . . I agree that your Lordships should hold that the defendant solicitors were under a duty of care to the plaintiffs arising from an extension of the principle of assumption of responsibility explored in *Hedley Byrne and Co Ltd v Heller & Partners Ltd* [1964] AC 465. In my view, although the present case is not directly covered by the decided cases, it is legitimate to extend the law to the limited extent proposed using the incremental approach by way of analogy advocated in *Caparo Industries plc v Dickman* [1990] 2 AC 605. To explain my reasons requires me to attempt an analysis of what is meant by 'assumption of responsibility' in the law of negligence.

To avoid misunderstanding I must emphasise that I am considering only whether some duty of care exists, not with the extent of that duty which will vary according to the circumstances.

Far from that concept having been invented by your Lordships' House in *Hedley Byrne*, its genesis is to be found in *Nocton v Lord Ashburton* [1914] AC 932. It is impossible to analyse what is meant by 'assumption of responsibility' or 'the *Hedley Byrne* principle' without first having regard to *Nocton's* case. . . .

In my judgment, there are three points relevant to the present case which should be gathered from *Nocton's* case. First, there can be special relationships between the parties which give rise to the law treating the defendant as having assumed a duty to be careful in circumstances where, apart from such relationship, no duty of care would exist. Second, a fiduciary relationship is one of those special relationships. Third, a fiduciary relationship is not the only such special relationship: other relationships may be held to give rise to the same duty.

The second of those propositions merits further consideration, since if we can understand the nature of one 'special relationship' it may cast light on when, by analogy, it is appropriate for the law to treat other relationships as being 'special.' The paradigm of the circumstances in which equity will find a fiduciary relationship is where one party, A, has assumed to act in relation to the property or affairs of another, B. A, having assumed responsibility, pro tanto, for B's affairs, is taken to have assumed certain duties in relation to the conduct of those affairs, including normally a duty of care. Thus, a trustee assumes responsibility for the management of the property of the beneficiary, a company director for the affairs of the company and an agent for those of his principal. By so assuming to act in B's affairs, A comes under fiduciary duties to B. Although the extent of those fiduciary duties (including duties of care) will vary from case to case some duties (including a duty of care) arise in each case. The importance of these considerations for present purposes is that the special relationship (ie a fiduciary relationship) giving rise to the assumption of responsibility held to exist in *Nocton's* case does not depend on any mutual dealing between A and B, let alone on any relationship akin to contract. Although such factors may be present, equity imposes the obligation because A has assumed to act in B's affairs. Thus, a trustee is under a duty of care to his beneficiary whether or not he has had any dealing with him: indeed he may be as yet unborn or unascertained and therefore any direct dealing would be impossible.

Moreover, this lack of mutuality in the typical fiduciary relationship indicates that it is not a necessary feature of all such special relationships that B must in fact rely on A's actions. If B is unaware of the fact that A has assumed to act in B's affairs (eg in the case of B being an unascertained beneficiary) B cannot possibly have relied on A. What is important is not that A knows that B is consciously relying on A, but A knows that B's economic well being is dependent upon A's careful conduct of B's affairs. Thus, in my judgment *Nocton* demonstrates that there is at least one special relationship giving rise to the imposition of a duty of care that is dependent neither upon mutuality of dealing nor upon actual reliance by the plaintiff on the defendant's actions.

I turn then to consider the *Hedley Byrne* case [1964] AC 465. In that case this House had to consider the circumstances in which there could be liability for negligent misstatement in the absence of either a contract or a fiduciary relationship between the parties. The first, and for present purposes perhaps the most important, point is that there is nothing in the *Hedley Byrne* case to cast doubt on the decision in *Nocton's* case. On the contrary, each of their Lordships treated *Nocton's* case as their starting point and asked the question 'in the absence of any contractual or fiduciary duty, what circumstances give rise to a special relationship between the plaintiff and the defendant sufficient to justify the imposition of the duty of care in the making of statements?' The House was seeking to define a further special relationship in addition to, not in substitution for, fiduciary relationships: see *per* Lord Reid, at p 486; *per* Lord Morris of Borth-y-Gest, at p 502; *per* Lord Hodson, at p 511; *per* Lord Devlin, at p 523; *per* Lord Pearce, at p 539.

Second, since this House was concerned with cases of negligent misstatement or advice, it was inevitable that any test laid down required both that the plaintiff should rely on the statement or advice and that the defendant could reasonably foresee that he would do so. In the case of claims based on negligent statements (as opposed to negligent actions) the plaintiff will have no cause of action at all unless he can show damage and he can only have suffered damage if he has relied on the negligent statement. Nor will a defendant be shown to have satisfied the requirement that he should foresee damage to the plaintiff unless he foresees such reliance by the plaintiff as to give rise to the damage. Therefore although reliance by the plaintiff is an essential ingredient in a case based on negligent misstatement or advice, it does not follow that in all cases based on negligent action or inaction by the defendant it is necessary in order to demonstrate a special relationship that the plaintiff has in fact relied on the defendant or the defendant has foreseen such reliance. If in such a case careless conduct can be foreseen as likely to cause and does in fact cause damage to the plaintiff that should be sufficient to found liability.

Third, it is clear that the basis on which (apart from the disclaimer) the majority would have held the bank liable for negligently giving the reference was that, were it not for the disclaimer, the bank would have assumed responsibility for such reference. Although there are passages in the speeches which may point the other way, the reasoning of the majority in my judgment points clearly to the fact that the crucial element was that, by choosing to answer the enquiry, the bank had assumed to act, and thereby created the special relationship on which the necessary duty of care was founded. Thus Lord Reid, at p 486, pointed out that a reasonable man knowing that he was being trusted, had three possible courses open to him: to refuse to answer, to answer but with a disclaimer of responsibility, or simply to answer without such disclaimer. . . .

Just as in the case of fiduciary duties, the assumption of responsibility referred to is the defendants' assumption of responsibility for the task not the assumption of legal liability. Even in cases of ad hoc relationships, it is the undertaking to answer the question posed which creates the relationship. If the responsibility for the task is assumed by the defendant he thereby creates a special relationship between himself and the plaintiff in relation to which the law (not the defendant) attaches a duty to carry out carefully the task so assumed. If this be the right view, it does much to allay the doubts about the utility of the concept of assumption of responsibility voiced by Lord Griffiths in *Smith v Eric S Bush* [1990] 1 AC 831, 862 and by Lord Roskill in *Caparo Industries plc v Dickman* [1990] 2 AC 605, 628: see also Kit Barker in 'Unreliable Assumptions in the Modern Law of Negligence' (1993) 109 LQR 461. As I read those judicial criticisms they proceed on the footing that the phrase 'assumption of responsibility' refers to the defendant having assumed legal responsibility. I doubt whether the same criticisms would have been directed at the phrase if the words had been understood, as I think they should be, as referring to a conscious assumption of responsibility for the task rather than a conscious assumption of legal liability to the plaintiff for its careful performance. Certainly, the decision in both cases is consistent with the view I take. . . .

Let me now seek to bring together these various strands so far as is necessary for the purposes of this case: I am not purporting to give any comprehensive statement of this aspect of the law. The law of England does not impose any general duty of care to avoid negligent misstatements or to avoid causing pure economic loss even if economic damage to the plaintiff was foreseeable. However, such a duty of care will arise if there is a special relationship between the parties. Although the categories of cases in which such special relationship can be held to exist are not closed, as yet only two categories have been identified, viz. (1) where there is a fiduciary relationship and (2) where the defendant has voluntarily answered a question or tenders skilled advice or services in circumstances where he knows or ought to know that an identified plaintiff will rely on his answers or advice. In both these categories the special relationship is created by the defendant voluntarily assuming to act in the matter by involving himself in the plaintiff's affairs or by choosing to speak. If he does so assume to act or speak he is said to have assumed responsibility for carrying through the matter he has entered upon. In the words of Lord Reid in *Hedley Byrne* [1964] AC 465, 486 he has 'accepted a relationship . . . which requires him to exercise such care as the circumstances require,' ie although the extent of the duty will vary from category to category, *some* duty of care arises from the special relationship. Such relationship can arise even though the defendant has acted in the plaintiff's affairs pursuant to a contract with a third party. . . .

The solicitor who accepts instructions to draw a will knows that the future economic welfare of the intended beneficiary is dependent upon his careful execution of the task. It is true that the intended beneficiary (being ignorant of the instructions) may not rely on the particular solicitor's actions. But, as I have sought to demonstrate, in the case of a duty of care flowing from a fiduciary relationship liability is not dependent upon actual reliance by the plaintiff on the defendant's actions but on the fact that, as the fiduciary is well aware, the plaintiff's economic wellbeing is dependent upon the proper discharge by the fiduciary of his duty. Second, the solicitor by accepting the instructions has entered upon, and therefore assumed responsibility for, the task of procuring the execution of a skilfully drawn will knowing that the beneficiary is wholly dependent upon his carefully carrying out his function. That assumption of responsibility for the task is a feature of both the two categories of special relationship so far identified in the authorities. It is not to the point that the solicitor only entered on the task pursuant to a contract with the third party (ie the testator). There are therefore present many of the features which in the other categories of special relationship have been treated as sufficient to create a special relationship to which the law attaches a duty of care. In my judgment the analogy is close.

Spring v *Guardian Assurance*
House of Lords [1995] 2 AC 296

Spring was employed by a company which was taken over by Guardian Assurance and he was subsequently made redundant. He tried but was unable to get a new, similar job, because the defendants had negligently written a very unfavourable reference about him. Held: the defendants were liable.

LORD GOFF: . . . The wide scope of the principle recognised in *Hedley Byrne* is reflected in the broad statements of principle which I have quoted. All the members of the Appellate Committee in this case spoke in terms of the principle resting upon an assumption or undertaking of responsibility by the defendant towards the plaintiff, coupled with reliance by the plaintiff on the exercise by the defendant of due care and skill. Lord Devlin, in particular, stressed that the principle rested upon an assumption of responsibility when he said, at p 531, that 'the essence of the matter in the present case and in others of the same type is the acceptance of responsibility.' For the purpose of the case now before your Lordships it is, I consider, legitimate to proceed on the same basis. Furthermore, although *Hedley Byrne* itself was concerned with the provision of information and advice, it is clear that the principle in the case is not so limited and extends to include the performance of other services, as for example the professional services rendered by a solicitor to his client (see in particular, Lord Devlin, at pp 529–530). Accordingly where the plaintiff entrusts the defendant with the conduct of his affairs, in general or in particular, the defendant may be held to have assumed responsibility to the plaintiff, and the plaintiff to have relied on the defendant to exercise due skill and care, in respect of such conduct.

For present purposes, I wish also to refer to the nature of the 'special skill' to which Lord Morris referred in his statement of principle. It is, I consider, clear from the facts of *Hedley Byrne* itself that the expression 'special skill' is to be understood in a broad sense, certainly broad enough to embrace special knowledge. Furthermore Lord Morris himself, when speaking of the provision of a statement in the form of information or advice, referred to the defendant's judgment or skill or ability to make careful inquiry, from which it appears that the principle may apply in a case in which the defendant has access to information and fails to exercise due care (and skill, to the extent that this is relevant) in drawing on that source of information for the purposes of communicating it to another.

The fact that the inquiry in *Hedley Byrne* itself was directed, in a case concerned with liability in respect of a negligent misstatement (in fact a reference), to whether the maker of the statement was liable to a recipient of it who had acted in reliance upon it, may have given the impression that this is the only way in which liability can arise under the principle in respect of a misstatement. But, having regard to the breadth of the principle as stated in *Hedley Byrne* itself, I cannot see why this should be so. Take the case of the relationship between a solicitor and his client, treated implicitly by Lord Morris and expressly by Lord Devlin as an example of a relationship to which the principle may apply. I can see no reason why a solicitor should not be under a duty to his client to exercise due care and skill when making statements to third parties, so that if he fails in that duty and his client suffers damage in consequence, he may be liable to his client in damages. The question whether a person who gives a reference to a third party may, if the reference is negligently prepared be liable in damages not to the recipient but to the subject of the reference, did not arise in *Hedley Byrne* and so was not addressed in that case. That is the central question with which we are concerned in the present case; and I propose first to consider it in the context of an ordinary relationship between employer and employee, and then to turn to apply the relevant principles to the more complex relationships which existed in the present case.

Prima facie (ie, subject to the point on defamation, which I will have to consider later), it is my opinion that an employer who provides a reference in respect of one of his employees to a prospective future employer will ordinarily owe a duty of care to his employee in respect of the preparation of the reference. The employer is possessed of special knowledge, derived from his experience of the employee's character, skill and diligence in the performance of his duties while working for the employer. Moreover, when the employer provides a reference to a third party in respect of his employee, he does so not only for the assistance of the third party, but also, for what it is worth, for the assistance of the employee. Indeed, nowadays it must often be very difficult for an employee to obtain fresh employment without the benefit of a reference from his present or a previous employer. It is for this reason that, in ordinary life, it may be the employee, rather than a prospective future employer, who asks the employer to provide the reference; and even where the approach comes from the prospective future employer, it will (apart from special circumstances) be made with either the express or the tacit authority of the employee. The provision of such references is a service regularly provided by employers to their employees; indeed, references are part of the currency of the modern employment market. Furthermore, when such a reference is provided by an employer, it is plain that the employee relies upon him to exercise due skill and care in the preparation of the reference before making it available to the third party. In these circumstances, it seems to me that all the elements requisite for the application of the *Hedley Byrne* [1964] AC 465 principle are present. . . .

I wish however to add that, in considering the duty of care owed by the employer to the employee, although it can and should be expressed in broad terms, nevertheless the central requirement is that reasonable care and skill should be exercised by the employer in ensuring the accuracy of any facts which either (1) are communicated to the recipient of the reference from which he may form an adverse opinion of the employee, or (2) are the basis of an adverse opinion expressed by the employer himself about the employee. I wish further to add that it does not necessarily follow that, because the employer owes such a duty of care to his employee, he also owes a duty of care to the recipient of the reference. The relationship of the employer with the recipient is by no means the same as that with his employee; and whether, in a case such as this, there should be held (as was prima facie held to be so on the facts of the *Hedley Byrne* case itself) a duty of care owed by the maker of the reference to the recipient is a point on which I do not propose to express an opinion, and which may depend on the facts of the particular case before the court.

It had been argued that the appropriate tort for a misleading reference was the tort of defamation, and that there would have been no liability in defamation because the reference would have attracted qualified privilege, which meant there could be no liability unless the writer was in law malicious. The Court of Appeal had agreed that if there was no liability in defamation there should not be in negligence, for otherwise the defence of qualified privilege would be subverted. This issue is dealt with by Lord Slynn:

LORD SLYNN: . . . It seems to me that on the basis of these authorities two questions therefore arise. The first is whether the nature of the tort of defamation and the tort of injurious falsehood is such that it would be wrong to recognise the possibility of a duty of care in negligence for a false statement. The second question is whether, independently of the existence of the other two torts, and taking the tests adopted by Lord Bridge of Harwich in *Caparo Industries plc v Dickman* [1990] 2 AC 605, a duty of care can in any event arise in relation to the giving of a reference. If the answer to the first is 'No,' and to the second 'Yes' then it remains to consider whether in all the circumstances such a duty of care was owed in this case by an employer to an ex-employee.

As to the first question the starting-point in my view is that the suggested claim in negligence and the torts of defamation and injurious and malicious falsehood do not cover the same ground, as Mr Tony Weir shows in his note in [1993] CLJ 376. They are separate torts, defamation not requiring a proof by the plaintiff that the statement was untrue (though justification may be a defence) or that he suffered economic damage, but being subject to defences quite different from those in negligence, such as the defence of qualified privilege which makes it necessary to prove malice. Malicious falsehood requires proof that the statement is false, that harm has resulted and that there was express malice. Neither of these involves the concept of a duty of care. The essence of a claim in defamation is that a person's reputation has been damaged; it may or not involve the loss of a job or economic loss. A claim that a reference has been given negligently is essentially based on the fact, not so much that reputation has been damaged, as that a job, or an opportunity, has been lost. A statement carelessly made may not be defamatory—a statement that a labourer is 'lame,' a secretary 'very arthritic' when neither statement is true, though they were true of some other employee mistakenly confused with the person named.

I do not consider that the existence of either of these two heads of claim, defamation and injurious falsehood, a priori prevents the recognition of a duty of care where, but for the existence of the other two torts, it would be fair, just and reasonable to recognise it in a situation where the giver of a reference has said or written what is untrue and where he has acted unreasonably and carelessly in what he has said.

The policy reasons underlying the requirement that the defence of qualified privilege is only dislodged if express malice is established do not necessarily apply in regard to a claim in negligence. There may be other policy reasons in particular situations which should prevail. Thus, in relation to a reference given by an employer in respect of a former employee or a departing employee (and assuming no contractual obligation to take care in giving a reference) it is relevant to consider the changes which have taken place in the employer-employee relationship, with far greater duties imposed on the employer than in the past, whether by statute or by judicial decision, to care for the physical, financial and even psychological welfare of the employee.

As to the second question it is a relevant circumstance that in many cases an employee will stand no chance of getting another job, let alone a better job, unless he is given a reference. There is at least a moral obligation on the employer to give it. This is not necessarily true when the claim is laid in defamation even if on an occasion of qualified privilege. In the case of an employee or ex-employee the damage is clearly foreseeable if a careless reference is given; there is as obvious a proximity of relationship in this context as can be imagined. The sole question therefore, in my view, is whether balancing all the factors (*per* Lord Bridge of Harwich in *Caparo Industries plc v Dickman* [1990] 2 AC 605, 618):

> the situation should be one in which the court considers it fair, just and reasonable that the law should impose a duty of a given scope upon the one party for the benefit of the other.

Hedley Byrne & Co Ltd v Heller & Partners Ltd [1964] AC 465 does not decide the present case, but I find it unacceptable that the person to whom a reference is given about an employee X should be able to sue for negligence if he relies on the statement (and, for example, employs X who proves to be inadequate for the job) as it appears to be assumed that he can; but that X who is refused employment because the recipient relies on a reference negligently given should have no recourse unless he can prove express malice as defined by Lord Diplock in *Horrocks v Lowe* [1975] AC 135, 149–151. . . .

I do not accept the *in terrorem* arguments that to allow a claim in negligence will constitute a restriction on freedom of speech or that in the employment sphere employers will refuse to give references or will only give such bland or adulatory ones as is forecast. They should be and are capable of being sufficiently robust as to express frank and honest views after taking reasonable care both as to the factual content and as to the opinion expressed. They will not shrink from the duty of taking reasonable care when they realise the importance of the reference both to the recipient (to whom it is assumed that a duty of care exists) and to the employee (to whom it is contended on existing authority there is no such duty). They are not being asked to warrant absolutely the accuracy of the facts or the incontrovertible validity of the opinions expressed but to take reasonable care in compiling or giving the reference and in verifying the information on which it is based. The courts can be trusted to set a standard which is not higher than the law of negligence demands. Even if it is right that the number of references given will be reduced, the quality and value will be greater and it is by no means certain that to have more references is more in the public interest than to have more careful references.

Those giving such references can make it clear what are the parameters within which the reference is given such as stating their limited acquaintance with the individual either as to time or as to situation. This issue does not arise in the present case but it may be that employers can make it clear to the subject of the reference that they will only give one if he accepts that there will be a disclaimer of liability to him and to the recipient of the reference.

Notes

1. Lord Goff bases **Hedley Byrne** liability on voluntary assumption of responsibility and reliance, but does not link the two. In **Hedley Byrne** the claimant was both the person to whom the statement was made as a result of the assumption of responsibility, and the person who acted on it to his detriment. However, Lord Goff said that **Hedley Byrne** can extend to cases where there is (a) an assumption of responsibility by the defendant to the claimant, and (b) the claimant 'relies' on the defendant not being negligent, even if the statement is made to someone else who then acts to the detriment of the claimant. In what sense did the claimant 'rely' on the defendant? Presumably Spring had no choice but to use the defendant as a referee but no doubt was entitled to expect him to act without negligence. A different explanation of this type of liability occurs in **White v Jones**.

2. It may be that a duty of care arises only when there is an existing relationship. In *Kapfunde* v *Abbey National* [1998] IRLR 583, a doctor retained by the defendants was not liable to a job applicant who was refused employment on the doctor's advice. It was said that **White v Jones** was not helpful as that had not radically extended the law. Does this mean that a referee other than the current employer would not be liable?

3. Lord Browne-Wilkinson admits that **White v Jones** did not fit in with traditional interpretations of **Hedley Byrne** liability. As **Spring v Guardian Assurance** showed, there is a problem in these cases with 'reliance'. His lordship neatly avoided this problem by suggesting that there may be cases where reliance is not necessary, by analogy with fiduciary duties where that element of 'mutuality' is not required. **White v Jones** was not a case of an actual fiduciary obligation, but was close enough to it (see also *Esterhuizen* v *Allied Dunbar Assurance plc* [1998] 2 FLR 668). Accordingly, if the views of Lord Browne-Wilkinson are followed, a new category of **Hedley Byrne** liability exists which has not yet been fully defined, but which places an obligation upon a person who voluntarily undertakes a task knowing that another will be directly affected if they fail to exercise proper skill and there is no other way the loss can be avoided.

4. The principle in **White v Jones** extends to financial advisors. In *Gorham* v *BT* [2000] 4 All ER 867, Mr Gorham bought a personal pension but the defendants failed to advise him that he and his dependants would be better off joining their occupational pension scheme. After his death his wife successfully claimed for the benefits she would have received had her husband been properly advised.

5. For a discussion of **White v Jones** and other cases, see Nicholas McBride and Andrew Hughes 'Hedley Byrne in the House of Lords' (1996) 15 LS 376.

7

Breach of duty: the standard of care

Once it has been established that there is a sufficient relationship between the parties to establish a duty, the question then arises whether the defendant has been in breach of this duty. This involves a number of issues, many of which are obscured by resort to the judgment of the 'reasonable man'. A fictitious—and gendered—being that is no more than the 'anthropomorphic conception of justice' (Lord Radcliffe, *Davis Contractors* v *Fareham Urban District Council* [1956] at 728), and justice is a complicated concept. The 'reasonable man' may give the impression of certainty where there is none, for whether it is reasonable to take a certain risk involves questions of economic and social policy which are rarely expressed in the law reports.

Of course, we cannot be protected by the law against all risks: we must accept the so-called 'vicissitudes of life' and can only expect to be compensated for damage caused by unreasonable activities. The issue of the standard of care can be put in two ways: either we ask whether the defendant created an unreasonable risk, or we can ask what level of safety a potential claimant is entitled to expect. These are two sides of the same coin and will usually, but not always, lead to the same result. However, we also know that damage is going to occur as a result of human activity, and who should bear the risk of that damage is an important matter of social policy. To a great extent that question is answered by the fact that we have a fault rather than a no-fault system of compensation, but even within the fault system, how losses are distributed is to some extent governed by our understanding of what risks are unreasonable.

In recent years there has been much debate about the existence of a so-called compensation culture. The suggestion is that we have become more 'risk averse' which, coupled with an increasing unwillingness to take personal responsibility for our actions, means that we are turning to the law for redress in respect of quite ordinary risks and that, as a result, many worthwhile activities, such as school trips, village fetes and so on are curtailed for fear of legal action.

While the jury remains out as to whether there is sufficient evidence of such a shift in attitudes, there is general agreement that the *perception* of a compensation culture is 'a bad thing': 'the pursuit of an unrestrained culture of blame and compensation has many evil consequences and one is certainly the interference with the liberty of the citizen' (Lord Hobhouse, **Tomlinson** v **Congleton Borough Council** [2004] UKHL 47 at [81]). The government attempted to stem the growth of such a culture through the largely unnecessary Compensation Act 2006 and even more redundant Social Action, Responsibility and Heroism Act 2015.

COMPENSATION ACT 2006

1. Deterrent effect of potential liability

A court considering a claim in negligence may, in determining whether the defendant should have taken particular steps to meet the standard of care (whether by taking precautions against a risk or otherwise), have regard to whether a requirement to take those steps might—

    (a) prevent a desirable activity from being undertaken at all, to a particular extent or in a particular way, or

    (b) discourage persons from undertaking functions in connection with a desirable activity.

Notes

1. The Compensation Act 2006 was intended to 'send the message' that people should not be deterred from participating in socially useful events and pursuits—so-called 'good risky activities'. This is nothing new. As Jackson LJ noted in *Scout Association* v *Barnes* [2010] EWCA Civ 1476:

   > It is the function of the law of tort to deter negligent conduct and to compensate those who are the victims of such conduct. It is not the function of the law of tort to eliminate every iota of risk or to stamp out socially desirable activities . . . This principle is now enshrined in section 1 of the Compensation Act 2006 . . . [it] has always been part of the common law. (at [34])

   The Social Action, Responsibility and Heroism Act 2015 adds even less to understandings of the tort of negligence and is yet to be cited in a reported case.
2. See further James Goudkamp 'Restating the Common Law? The Social Action, Responsibility and Heroism Act 2015' (2017) 37 LS 577.

7.1 The level of reasonable risk—an objective standard

The standard which the law requires a person to attain must be objectively determined. A person will (usually) be regarded as negligent if they fail to act according to that standard, even if it is more difficult for them to do so than for others. The reason is that we are all entitled to expect a certain level of protection from the acts of others. The concept of the 'reasonable man' does two things: it judges whether the defendant was careless and defines the level of safety a claimant is entitled to expect.

> **Blyth v Proprietors of the Birmingham Waterworks**
> Court of Exchequer (1856) 11 Ex 781

The claimant's house was flooded, after the defendants' water main burst following an unusually severe frost. Held: the defendants were not negligent.

ALDERSON B: . . . The case turns upon the question, whether the facts proved show that the defendants were guilty of negligence. Negligence is the omission to do something which a reasonable man, guided upon those considerations which ordinarily regulate the conduct of human affairs, would do, or doing something which a prudent and reasonable man would not do. The defendants might have been liable for negligence, if, unintentionally, they omitted to do that which a reasonable person would have done, or did that which a person taking reasonable precautions would not have done. A reasonable man would act with reference to the average circumstances of the temperature in ordinary years. The defendants had provided against such frosts as experience would have led men, acting prudently, to provide against; and they are not guilty of negligence, because their precautions proved insufficient against the effects of the extreme severity of the frost of 1855, which penetrated to a greater depth than any which ordinarily occurs south of the polar regions. Such a state of circumstances constitutes a contingency against which no reasonable man can provide. The result was an accident, for which the defendants cannot be held liable.

Notes

1. This case introduces an interesting and important issue. If the defendants had buried the mains lower they might have escaped the effects of the frost, but that would have been more expensive. Hence, setting the 'standard of care' can involve difficult economic issues: how much should be paid for safety? At what level of cost is a potential defendant entitled to say that the proposed safety measure is too expensive? In *US v Carroll Towing*, 159 F 2d 169 (1947), Judge Learned Hand said that if the probability of the damage occurring is called P, the extent of the potential damage (i.e. the liability) is called L and the cost of preventing the damage (i.e. the burden) is called B, then liability depends on whether B is less than L multiplied by P: that is, whether $B < PL$. While this may be a useful guide in some cases, it is rather simplistic. Other values may also be relevant. For example, could the formula be used on its own to justify the possibility of cancer being contracted by workers in a chemical factory?

Glasgow Corporation v Muir
House of Lords [1943] AC 448

The defendants, Glasgow Corporation, owned an old mansion in King's Park, Glasgow, in which there were tea rooms managed by Alexander and a shop for the sale of sweets and ices. One wet afternoon, Alexander allowed a picnic party of 30–40 people to shelter in the old mansion and eat their tea there. A large, heavy tea urn was carried into the building along a narrow passage. Unfortunately, one of the men carrying the urn (McDonald) inexplicably dropped his side of the urn and six children (including Eleanor Muir) who had been waiting in the passage to buy sweets were scalded by the hot tea. Held: Alexander was not negligent in allowing the urn to be carried into the tea room.

LORD MACMILLAN: My Lords, the degree of care for the safety of others which the law requires human beings to observe in the conduct of their affairs varies according to the circumstances. There is no absolute standard, but it may be said generally that the degree of care required varies directly with the risk involved. Those who engage in operations inherently dangerous must take precautions which are not required of persons engaged in the ordinary routine of daily life. It is, no doubt, true that in every act which an individual performs there is present a potentiality of injury to others. All things are possible, and, indeed, it has become proverbial that the unexpected always happens, but, while the precept *alterum non laedere* requires us to abstain from intentionally injuring others, it does not impose liability for every injury which our conduct may occasion. . . . Legal liability is limited to those consequences of our acts which a reasonable man of ordinary intelligence and experience so acting would have in contemplation. 'The duty to take care,' as I essayed to formulate it in *Bourhill* v *Young* ([1943] AC 92, 104), 'is the duty to avoid doing or omitting to do anything the doing or omitting to do which may have as its reasonable and probable consequence injury to others, and the duty is owed to those to whom injury may reasonably and probably be anticipated if the duty is not observed.' . . . The standard of foresight of the reasonable man is, in one sense, an impersonal test. It eliminates the personal equation and is independent of the idiosyncrasies of the particular person whose conduct is in question. Some persons are by nature unduly timorous and imagine every path beset with lions. Others, of more robust temperament, fail to foresee or nonchalantly disregard even the most obvious dangers. The reasonable man is presumed to be free both from over-apprehension and from over-confidence, but there is a sense in which the standard of care of the reasonable man involves in its application a subjective element. It is still left to the judge to decide what, in the circumstances of the particular case, the reasonable man would have had in contemplation, and what, accordingly, the party sought to be made liable ought to have foreseen. Here there is room for diversity of view, as, indeed, is well illustrated in the present case. What to one judge may seem far-fetched may seem to another both natural and probable.

With these considerations in mind I turn to the facts of the occurrence on which your Lordships have to adjudicate. . . . The question, as I see it, is whether Mrs Alexander, when she was asked to allow a tea urn to be brought into the premises under her charge, ought to have had in mind that it would require to be carried through a narrow passage in which there were a number of children and that there would be a risk of the contents of the urn being spilt and scalding some of the children. If, as a reasonable person, she ought to have had these considerations in mind, was it her duty to require that she should be informed of the arrival of the urn, and, before allowing it to be carried through the narrow passage, to clear all the children out of it in case they might be splashed with scalding water? . . .

In my opinion, Mrs Alexander had no reason to anticipate that such an event would happen as a consequence of granting permission for a tea urn to be carried through the passage way where the children were congregated, and, consequently, there was no duty incumbent on her to take precautions against the occurrence of such an event. I think that she was entitled to assume that the urn would be in charge of responsible persons (as it was) who would have regard for the safety of the children in the passage (as they did have regard), and that the urn would be carried with ordinary care, in which case its transit would occasion no danger to bystanders. The pursuers have left quite unexplained the actual cause of the accident. The immediate cause was not the carrying of the urn through the passage, but McDonald's losing grip of his handle. How he came to do so is entirely a matter of speculation. He may have stumbled or he may have suffered a temporary muscular failure. We do not know, and the pursuers have not chosen to enlighten us by calling McDonald as a witness. Yet it is argued that Mrs Alexander ought to have foreseen the possibility, nay, the reasonable probability of an occurrence the nature of which is unascertained. Suppose that McDonald let go his handle through carelessness. Was Mrs Alexander bound to foresee this as reasonably probable and to take precautions against the possible consequences? I do not think so.

Notes

1. The reasonable man has been variously described as 'the man on the Clapham omnibus' and 'the man who in the evening pushes his lawnmower in his shirtsleeves' (Lord Greer, *Hall v Brooklands Auto-Racing Club* [1933] 1 KB 205 at 224). AP Herbert in *Uncommon Law* (Methuen, 1935) described him as follows:

   All solid virtues are his, save only that peculiar quality by which the affection of other men is won. . . . Devoid in short of any human weakness, with not one single saving vice, sans prejudice, procrastination, ill nature, avarice, and absence of mind, as careful for his own safety as he is for that of others, this excellent but odious character stands like a monument in our Courts of Justice, vainly appealing to his fellow citizens to order their lives after his own example.

2. The truth of the matter is, of course, that there is no such individual as the reasonable man. The reasonable man is a judicial construct—or shorthand—through which the judges seek to determine what was reasonable conduct in the circumstances of the particular case.

3. Feminist and other legal scholars have argued that, despite claims to gender-neutrality, the standard of the reasonable man in fact embodies a male point of view. As such, it holds women to a standard devised without them in mind. On this view, it may well be 'dangerously misleading' to adopt the now commonplace rebranding 'reasonable person'—since it attributes a 'false universality to what is in fact a partial and loaded standard' (Joanne Conaghan 'Tort Law and the Feminist Critique of Reason' in Anne Bottomley (ed) *Feminist Perspectives on the Foundational Subjects of Law* (Cavendish, 1996), p 47 at 58).

7.2 The skill of the defendant

People have varying degrees of skill. Thus while the test of liability is objective, the degree of skill which a potential claimant is entitled to expect from a potential defendant will not necessarily be that of the 'ordinary man', but rather the skill of the reasonable example of that kind of person. For example, doctors must conform to the level of skill of the 'reasonable doctor' and not that of the 'man on the Clapham omnibus', while the standard expected of a child is scaled according to what can be 'objectively expected' of a child of that age (*Orchard v Lee* [2009] EWCA Civ 295 at [9]).

Wells v Cooper
Court of Appeal [1958] 2 QB 265

The claimant, Wells, was delivering fish to the defendant's house. As he was leaving he pulled the back door to close it and the door handle came away in his hand, and he lost his balance and fell. The handle had been fixed to the door by the defendant, who had some experience as an amateur carpenter, a few months earlier, and consisted of a lever-type handle fixed by a base plate which was held to the door by four three-quarter inch screws. The claimant argued that the defendant ought to have used longer screws and that, had the defendant done so, he would not have been injured. Held: the defendant had not fallen below the standard of care expected of him.

JENKINS LJ: As above related, the defendant did the work himself. We do not think the mere fact that he did it himself instead of employing a professional carpenter to do it constituted a breach of his duty of care. No doubt some kinds of work involve such highly specialized skill and knowledge, and create such serious dangers if not properly done, that an ordinary occupier owing a duty of care to others in regard to the safety of premises would fail in that duty if he undertook such work himself instead of employing experts to do it for him. See *Haseldine v C A Daw & Son Ltd, per* Scott LJ, [1941] 2 KB 343. But the work here in question was not of that order. It was a trifling domestic replacement well within the competence of a householder accustomed to doing small carpentering jobs about his home, and of a kind which must be done every day by hundreds of householders up and down the country.

Accordingly, we think that the defendant did nothing unreasonable in undertaking the work himself. But it behoved him, if he was to discharge his duty of care to persons such as the plaintiff, to do the work with reasonable care and skill, and we think the degree of care and skill required of him must be measured not by reference to the degree of competence in such matters which he personally happened to possess, but by reference to the degree of care and skill which a reasonably competent carpenter might be expected to apply to the work in question. Otherwise, the extent of the protection that an invitee could claim in relation to work done by the invitor himself would vary according to the capacity of the invitor, who could free himself from liability merely by showing that he had done the best of which he was capable, however good, bad or indifferent that best might be.

Accordingly, we think the standard of care and skill to be demanded of the defendant in order to discharge his duty of care to the plaintiff in the fixing of the new handle in the present case must be the degree of care and skill to be expected of a reasonably competent carpenter doing the work in question. This does not mean that the degree of care and skill required is to be measured by reference to the contractual obligations as to the quality of his work assumed by a professional carpenter working for reward, which would, in our view, set the standard too high. The question is simply what steps would a reasonably competent carpenter wishing to fix a handle such as this securely to a door such as this have taken with a view to achieving that object.

In fact the only complaint made by the plaintiff in regard to the way in which the defendant fixed the new handle is that three-quarter inch screws were inadequate and that one inch screws should have been used. The question may, therefore, be stated more narrowly as being whether a reasonably competent carpenter fixing this handle would have appreciated that three-quarter inch screws such as those used by the defendant would not be adequate to fix it securely and would accordingly have used one inch screws instead. . . .

In relation to a trifling and perfectly simple operation such as the fixing of the new handle we think that the defendant's experience of domestic carpentry is sufficient to justify his inclusion in the category of reasonably competent carpenters. The matter then stands thus. The defendant, a reasonably competent carpenter, used three-quarter inch screws, believing them to be adequate for the purpose of fixing the handle. There is no doubt that he was doing his best to make the handle secure and believed that he had done so. Accordingly, he must be taken to have discharged his duty of reasonable care, unless the belief that three-quarter inch screws would be adequate was one which no reasonably competent carpenter could reasonably entertain, or, in other words, an obvious blunder which should at once have been apparent to him as a reasonably competent carpenter. The evidence adduced on the plaintiff's side failed, in the judge's view, to make that out. He saw and heard the witnesses, and had demonstrated to him the strength of attachment provided by three-quarter inch screws. We see no sufficient reason for differing from his conclusion. Indeed, the fact that the handle remained secure during the period of four or five months between the time it was fixed and the date of the accident, although no doubt in constant use throughout that period, makes it very difficult to accept the view that the inadequacy of the three-quarter inch screws should have been obvious to the defendant at the time when he decided to use them.

Notes

1. In *Wright v Troy Lucas (a firm) and George Rusz* [2019] EWHC 1098 (QB), the defendant, who had no professional legal qualifications, ran a legal firm and held himself out as having 'extensive experience' of clinical negligence claims and offering advice which was 'as good as, if not better, than any solicitor or barrister' (at [18]). He was found to be in breach of his duty of care in relation to his negligent mishandling of the claimant's case against the NHS:

   on the most charitable view, the defendants were out of their depth and simply had no idea how to carry out the work they had undertaken to provide. . . . Whatever the motivation, however, it is apparent that the defendants acted in breach of the duty of care arising from the relationship they had assumed. . . . I have no hesitation in finding that the defendants should be held to the duty and standard of care that they had chosen to assume when holding themselves out as competent to carry out legal services for the claimant in his clinical negligence litigation. (Eady J at [84], [82])

7.2.1 The under-skilled

> #### *Nettleship* v *Weston*
> Court of Appeal [1971] 2 QB 691

The claimant, Nettleship, was teaching a friend of his, Weston, to drive. She negligently hit a lamp post and the claimant suffered a broken kneecap. Held: that the defendant was liable (though the claimant's damages were reduced by 50 per cent for contributory negligence). (Note: the extract below deals only with the issue of standard of care. The case also raised the issue whether the claimant consented to the risk of injury, and it was held that he did not.)

LORD DENNING MR:

The Responsibility of the Learner Driver towards Persons on or near the Highway

Mrs Weston is clearly liable for the damage to the lamp post. In the civil law if a driver goes off the road on to the pavement and injures a pedestrian, or damages property, he is prima facie liable. Likewise if he goes on to the wrong side of the road. It is no answer for him to say: 'I was a learner driver under instruction. I was doing my best and could not help it.' The civil law permits no such excuse. It requires of him the same standard of care as of any other driver. 'It eliminates the personal equation and is independent of the idiosyncrasies of the particular person whose conduct is in question': see *Glasgow Corporation v Muir* [1943] AC 448, 457 by Lord Macmillan. The learner driver may be doing his best, but his incompetent best is not good enough. He must drive in as good a manner as a driver of skill, experience and care, who is sound in mind and limb, who makes no errors of judgment, has good eyesight and hearing, and is free from any infirmity: see *Richley (Henderson) v Faull, Richley, Third Party* [1965] 1 WLR 1454 and *Watson v Thomas S. Whitney & Co Ltd* [1966] 1 WLR 57.

The high standard thus imposed by the judges is, I believe, largely the result of the policy of the Road Traffic Acts. Parliament requires every driver to be insured against third party risks. The reason is so that a person injured by a motor car should not be left to bear the loss on his own, but should be compensated out of the insurance fund. The fund is better able to bear it than he can. But the injured person is only able to recover if the driver is liable in law. So the judges see to it that he is liable, unless he can prove care and skill of a high standard: see *The Merchant Prince* [1892] P 179 and *Henderson v Henry E. Jenkins & Sons* [1970] AC 282. Thus we are, in this branch of the law, moving away from the concept: 'No liability without fault.' We are beginning to apply the test: 'On whom should the risk fall?' Morally the learner driver is not at fault; but legally she is liable to be because she is insured and the risk should fall on her.

The Responsibility of the Learner Driver towards Passengers in the Car

Mrs Weston took her son with her in the car. We do not know his age. He may have been 21 and have known that his mother was learning to drive. He was not injured. But if he had been injured, would he have had a cause of action?

I take it to be clear that if a driver has a passenger in the car he owes a duty of care to him. But what is the standard of care required of the driver? Is it a lower standard than he or she owes towards a pedestrian on the pavement? I should have thought not. But, suppose that the driver has never driven a car before, or has taken too much to drink or has poor eyesight or hearing: and, furthermore, that the passenger *knows* it and yet accepts a lift from him. Does that make any difference? Dixon J thought it did. In *The Insurance Commissioner v Joyce* (1948) 77 CLR 39, 56, he said:

> If a man accepts a lift from a car driver whom he knows to have lost a limb or an eye or to be deaf, he cannot complain if he does not exhibit the skill and competence of a driver who suffers from no defect. . . . If he knowingly accepts the voluntary services of a driver affected by drink, he cannot complain of improper driving caused by his condition, because it involved no breach of duty.

That view of Dixon J seems to have been followed in South Australia: see *Walker v Turton-Sainsbury* [1952] SASR 159; but in the Supreme Court of Canada Rand J did not agree with it: see *Car and General Insurance Co v Seymour and Maloney* (1956) 2 DLR (2d) 369, 375.

We have all the greatest respect for Sir Owen Dixon, but for once I cannot agree with him. The driver owes a duty of care to every passenger in the car, just as he does to every pedestrian on the road: and he must attain the same standard of care in respect of each. If the driver were to be excused according to the knowledge of the passenger, it would result in endless confusion and injustice. One of the passengers may know that the learner driver is a mere novice. Another passenger may believe him to be entirely competent. One of the passengers may believe the driver to have had only two drinks. Another passenger may know that he has had a dozen. Is the one passenger to recover and the other not? Rather than embark on such inquiries, the law holds that the driver must attain the same standard of care for passengers as for pedestrians. The knowledge of the passenger may go to show that he was guilty of contributory negligence in ever accepting the lift—and thus reduce his damages—but it does not take away the duty of care, nor does it diminish the standard of care which the law requires of the driver: see *Dann v Hamilton* [1939] 1 KB 509 and *Slater v Clay Cross Co Ltd* [1956] 2 QB 264, 270.

The Responsibility of a Learner Driver towards his Instructor

The special factor in this case is that Mr Nettleship was not a mere passenger in the car. He was an instructor teaching Mrs Weston to drive.

Seeing that the law lays down, for all drivers of motor cars, a standard of care to which all must conform, I think that even a learner driver, so long as he is the sole driver, must attain the same standard towards all passengers in the car, including an instructor. But the instructor may be debarred from claiming for a reason peculiar to himself. He may be debarred because he has voluntarily agreed to waive any claim for any injury that may befall him. Otherwise he is not debarred. He may, of course, be guilty of contributory negligence and have his damages reduced on that account. He may, for instance, have let the learner take control too soon, he may not have been quick enough to correct his errors, or he may have participated in the negligent act himself: see *Stapley v Gypsum Mines Ltd* [1953] AC 663. But, apart from contributory negligence, he is not excluded unless it be that he has voluntarily agreed to incur the risk.

Notes

1. The decision in **Nettleship v Weston** is a majority decision. Salmon LJ dissented on following basis:

    Any driver normally owes exactly the same duty to a passenger in his car as he does to the general public, namely to drive with reasonable care and skill in all the relevant circumstances. As a rule, the driver's personal idiosyncrasy is not a relevant circumstance. In the absence of a special relationship what is reasonable care and skill is measured by the standard of competence usually achieved by the ordinary driver. In my judgment, however, there may be special facts creating a special relationship which displaces this standard or even negatives any duty, although the onus would certainly be upon the driver to establish such facts . . . [T]he learner-driver and his instructor are jointly in charge of the car. The instructor is entitled to expect the learner to pay attention to what he is told, perhaps to take exceptional care, and certainly to do his best. The instructor, in most cases as the present, knows, however, that the learner has practically no driving experience or skill and that, for the lack of this experience and skill, the learner will almost certainly make mistakes which may well injure the instructor unless he takes adequate steps to correct them. To my mind, therefore, the relationship is usually such that the beginner does not owe the instructor a duty to drive with the skill and competence to be expected of an experienced driver. The instructor knows that the learner does not possess such skill and competence. (at 703)

    Which line of reasoning do you find most persuasive?

2. Prior to the civil case, Weston had been convicted of driving without due care and attention. As in relation to the civil law claim, it is no defence in criminal law for a learner driver to say that they were 'doing their inexperienced best' (*McCrone* v *Riding* [1938] 1 All ER 137)—though it might reduce the sentence imposed. A criminal conviction is admissible in civil proceedings as prima facie evidence of negligence.

3. A person will not be liable in negligence if they are suffering from impaired ability but are unaware of that fact. In *Mansfield* v *Weetabix* [1998] 1 WLR 1263, the defendant driver suffered from starvation of glucose which meant that his brain did not function properly and he crashed into the claimant's shop. The Court of Appeal held that he was not at fault and distinguished **Nettleship v Weston** [1971] 2 QB 691 on the ground that that case did not deal with the situation where the actor was unaware of his disability. But was the learner driver in **Nettleship** any more to blame than the defendant here? The court thought that to impose liability in *Mansfield* would amount to strict liability, but are not the public entitled to expect that they will not be injured by erratic driving whatever the cause? If the defendant had been aware of his condition he would have been liable: *Roberts* v *Ramsbottom* [1980] 1 WLR 823.

4. Compare the recent case of *Dunnage* v *Randall* [2015] EWCA Civ 673 in which the claimant, an undiagnosed paranoid schizophrenic, set himself on fire injuring his nephew (who was attempting to prevent the accident). Randall, who died as a result of his injuries, was found to have fallen below the standard of care of a reasonable man. Rejecting the application of *Mansfield v Weetabix*, the Court of Appeal held that '[u]nless a defendant can establish that his condition entirely eliminates responsibility . . . he remains vulnerable to liability if he does not meet the objective standard of care. It is the entirety of the elimination which drives this conclusion, and once that entirety is eroded or diminished, he is fixed with the standard. The evidence was that [the defendant's] . . . responsibility came very close to complete elimination, but the experts stopped short of finding that it was complete' (Rafferty LJ at [114]).

5. In *Philips* v *Whiteley Ltd* [1938] 1 All ER 566, the claimant had her ears pierced by a jeweller and subsequently suffered an infection. It was decided that the infection was probably not due to the ear piercing, but, even if it were, the jeweller would not have been liable as he had taken all reasonable precautions that a jeweller would take and could not be expected to conform to the standards of a surgeon. See also *Shakoor* v *Situ* [2000] 4 All ER 181 where it was held that a practitioner of Chinese herbal medicine was not to be judged by the standard of the reasonable GP but rather by the reasonable practitioner of that art. The defendant had not held himself out as skilled in orthodox medicine and the claimant had chosen to use the 'alternative' medical system.

6. In contrast, where the defendant *is* holding themselves out as occupying a particular post, their actual rank or experience is irrelevant—their conduct is assessed according to the standard reasonably expected of a reasonably competent person occupying that post. In the Court of Appeal in *Wilsher* v *Essex Area Health Authority* [1987] QB 730 at 750, it was argued that a junior inexperienced doctor owed a lower duty of care: Mustill LJ rejected this, saying:

> This notion of a duty tailored to the actor, rather than to the act which he elects to perform, has no place in the law of tort. . . . To my mind it would be a false step to subordinate the legitimate expectation of the patient that he will receive from each person concerned with his care a degree of skill appropriate to the task which he undertakes to an understandable wish to minimise the psychological and financial pressures on hard pressed young doctors.

(The case was reversed on appeal on a different point: [1988] AC 1074.)

7. More recently, in *FB (Suing by her Mother and Litigation Friend, WAC)* v *Princess Alexandra Hospital NHS Trust* [2017] EWCA Civ 334 involving the negligence of Senior House Officer (SHO), Dr Rushd, in respect of the treatment of a young child, Jackson LJ had this to say:

1. The general law of negligence

54. The issue arising in this case is part of a wider problem with which the courts have wrestled for over a century, namely to what extent are the personal attributes and experience of the defendant relevant in determining whether he/she was negligent? The general rule is that the courts disregard them. Nevertheless, there are some characteristics of a person which the law cannot ignore, for example the fact that she was a child. In **Mullins** [sic] **v Richards** [1998] 1 All ER 820 the court judged the conduct of the defendant by the standard of 'an ordinarily prudent and reasonable 15-year-old schoolgirl'.

56. From the defendant's point of view, it is harsh to disregard their limitations and to hold them liable for doing that which they could not help doing or for failing to achieve that which they could not achieve. But a claimant is entitled to expect that those whom he or she encounters in the ordinary transactions of life will adhere to certain general standards. Thus in **Nettleship v Weston** [1971] QB 691 the Court of Appeal held that a learner driver should be judged by the standards of a competent and experienced driver. In effect, the law of tort achieves a compromise. It takes account of those characteristics which cannot be ignored (for example that the defendant was a child or was blind), but subject to that it imposes a general duty of care upon all members of society, which is not tailored to their individual strengths and weaknesses. . . .

2. Professional negligence

57. In the context of professional negligence litigation, the foundational twentieth century authority setting the required standard of skill and care is of course **Bolam v Friern Hospital Management Committee** [1957] 1 WLR 582. The defendant is required to exercise the skill and care of a reasonably competent member of his/her profession. The defendant's obligation to exercise that degree of skill and care is sometimes contractual, sometimes tortious and sometimes both. In the present case, there was no contract between the parties. So Dr Rushd's duty to exercise reasonable skill and care in assessing the claimant was a duty imposed by the law of tort.

58. In some of the earlier professional negligence cases, the courts focused upon the individual experience of the defendant in determining what constituted a reasonable degree of skill and care. In *Junior v McNicol* (Times Law Reports, March 26, 1959) the court took into account that the defendant house surgeon was 'a comparative beginner'. In *Hucks v Cole* (Times Law Reports, May 9, 1968) the Court of Appeal held that the defendant was to be judged by the standard of 'a general practitioner with a diploma in obstetrics'.

59. In *Wilsher v Essex AHA* [1987] 1 QB 730 the Court of Appeal for the first time gave detailed consideration to the standard of care required of a junior doctor. (This issue did not arise in the subsequent appeal to the House of Lords). The majority of the court held that a hospital doctor should be judged by the standard of skill and care appropriate to the post which he or she was fulfilling, for example the post of junior houseman in a specialised unit. That involves leaving out of account the particular experience of the doctor or their length of service. This analysis works in the context of a hospital, where there is a clear hierarchy with consultants at the top, then registrars and below them various levels of junior doctors. Whether doctors are performing their normal role or 'acting up', they are judged by reference to the post which they are fulfilling at the material time. The health authority or health trust is liable if the doctor whom it puts into a particular position does not possess (and therefore does not exercise) the requisite degree of skill for the task in hand.

60. Thus in professional negligence, as in the general law of negligence, the standard of care which the law requires is an imperfect compromise. It achieves a balance between the interests of society and fairness to the individual practitioner.

3. The present case

63. The conduct of Dr Rushd in the present case must be judged by the standard of a reasonably competent SHO in an accident and emergency department. The fact that Dr Rushd was aged 25 and 'relatively inexperienced' (witness statement paragraph 5) does not diminish the required standard of skill and care. On the other hand, the fact that she had spent six months in a paediatric department does not elevate the required standard. Other SHOs in A&E departments will have different backgrounds and experience, but they are all judged by the same standard.

64. I agree with Thirlwall LJ [who gave the leading judgment] that history taking is a basic skill which hospital doctors at all levels are expected to possess. The fact that FB's [the claimant] eyes had been rolling and uncoordinated was the event that precipitated the hospital visit. The ambulance staff picked this up. I do not accept the judge's conclusion that only a doctor more senior than Dr Rushd can reasonably have been expected to elicit this important fact. Therefore the judge's decision cannot stand.

65. Before parting with this case, I must acknowledge that junior hospital doctors work long hours under considerable pressure. They are often involved in life and death decisions. The pressures can be even greater when they are working all night, as Dr Rushd was here. If mistakes are made, it is devastating for the patient and it is expensive for the NHS trust. Doctors, however, are human. Even good and conscientious doctors may, from time to time, fall short. That is not a reason to lose heart or (even worse) to abandon medical practice. Those who have learnt from past mistakes often have even more to offer.

7.2.2 Special skills and common practice

> ### *Bolam v Friern Hospital Management Committee*
> Queen's Bench Division [1957] 1 WLR 582

The claimant suffered a fracture of the pelvis while he was undergoing electroconvulsive therapy. The issue was whether the doctor was negligent in failing to give a relaxant drug before the treatment, or in failing to provide means of restraint during it. Evidence was given of the practices of various doctors in this regard, and the extracts below deal with the appropriate test to be applied in assessing the conduct of the defendant. Held: the defendants were not liable.

MCNAIR J (addressing the jury): Before I turn to that, I must tell you what in law we mean by 'negligence.' In the ordinary case which does not involve any special skill, negligence in law means a failure to do some act which a reasonable man in the circumstances would do, or the doing of some act which a reasonable man in the circumstances would not do; and if that failure or the doing of that act results in injury, then there is a cause of action. How do you test whether this act or failure is negligent? In an ordinary case it is generally said you judge it by the action of the man in the street. He is the ordinary man. In one case it has been said you judge it by the conduct of the man on the top of a Clapham omnibus. He is the ordinary man. But where you get a situation which involves the use of some special skill or competence, then the test as to whether there has been negligence or not is not the test of the man on the top of a Clapham omnibus, because he has not got this special skill. The test is the standard of the ordinary skilled man exercising and professing to have that special skill. A man need not possess the highest expert skill; it is well established law that it is sufficient if he exercises the ordinary skill of an ordinary competent man exercising that particular art. I do not think that I quarrel much with any of the submissions in law which have been put before you by counsel. Mr Fox-Andrews put it in this way, that in the case of a medical man, negligence means failure to act in accordance with the standards of reasonably competent medical men at the time. That is a perfectly accurate statement, as long as it is remembered that there may be one or more perfectly proper standards; and if he conforms with one of those proper standards, then he is not negligent. Mr Fox-Andrews also was quite right, in my judgment, in saying that a mere personal belief that a particular technique is best is no defence unless that belief is based on reasonable grounds. That again is unexceptionable. But the emphasis which is laid by the defence is on this aspect of negligence, that the real question you have to make up your minds about on each of the three major topics is whether the defendants, in acting in the way they did, were acting in accordance with a practice of competent respected professional opinion. Mr Stirling submitted that if you are satisfied that they were acting in accordance with a practice of a competent body of professional opinion, then it would be wrong for you to hold that negligence was established. In a recent Scottish case, *Hunter v Hanley*, 1955 SLT 213, Lord President Clyde [at 217] said:

> In the realm of diagnosis and treatment there is ample scope for genuine difference of opinion and one man clearly is not negligent merely because his conclusion differs from that of other professional men, nor because he has displayed less skill or knowledge than others would have shown. The true test for establishing negligence in diagnosis or treatment on the part of a doctor is whether he has been proved to be guilty of such failure as no doctor of ordinary skill would be guilty of, if acting with ordinary care.

If that statement of the true test is qualified by the words 'in all the circumstances,' Mr Fox-Andrews would not seek to say that that expression of opinion does not accord with the English law. It is just a question of expression. I myself would prefer to put it this way, that he is not guilty of negligence if he has acted in accordance with a practice accepted as proper by a responsible body of medical men skilled in that particular art. I do not think there is much difference in sense. It is just a different way of expressing the same thought. Putting it the other way round, a man is not negligent, if he is acting in accordance with such a practice, merely because there is a body of opinion who would take a contrary view. At the same time, that does not mean that a medical man can obstinately and pigheadedly carry on with some old technique if it has been proved to be contrary to what is really substantially the whole of informed medical opinion. Otherwise you might get men today saying: 'I do not believe in anaesthetics. I do not believe in antiseptics. I am going to continue to do my surgery in the way it was done in the eighteenth century.' That clearly would be wrong.

Before I get to the details of the case, it is right to say this, that it is not essential for you to decide which of two practices is the better practice, as long as you accept that what the defendants did was in accordance with a practice accepted by responsible persons; if the result of the evidence is that you are satisfied that this practice is better than the practice spoken of on the other side, then it is really a stronger case. Finally, bear this in mind, that you are now considering whether it was negligent for certain action to be taken in August, 1954, not in February, 1957; and in one of the well-known cases on this topic it has been said you must not look with 1957 spectacles at what happened in 1954.

Notes

1. The **Bolam** test applies outside the medical context to *all* professionals exercising a special skill or competence (see e.g. *Arthur JS Hall & Co v Simons* [2002] 1 AC 615).

2. Although **Bolam** gives wide latitude to professionals acting in their professional capacity to determine the standards by which they are to be judged, a defendant cannot escape liability in negligence simply by arguing that they are following common practice.

   There is no rule of law that a relevant code of practice or other official or regulatory instrument necessarily sets the standard of care for the purpose of the tort of negligence. The classic statements by Swanwick J in *Stokes* and Mustill J in *Thompson v Smiths Shiprepairers* . . . remain good law. What they say about the relevance of the reasonable and prudent employer following a 'recognised and general practice' applies equally to following a code of practice which sets out practice that is officially required or recommended. Thus to follow a relevant code of practice or regulatory instrument will often afford a defence to a claim in negligence. But there are circumstances where it does not do so. For example, it may be shown that the code of practice or regulatory instrument is compromised because the standards that it requires have been lowered as a result of heavy lobbying by interested parties; or because it covers a field in which apathy and fatalism has prevailed amongst workers, trade unions, employers and legislators; or because the instrument has failed to keep abreast of the latest technology and scientific understanding. (Lord Dyson in *Baker v Quantum Clothing* [2011] UKSC 17 at [101])

3. Following **Bolam**, a doctor will not have fallen below the standard of care expected of a reasonable doctor, if they have acted in accordance with a respectable body of the medical profession (even if it is a minority viewpoint). However, this is qualified by a 'gloss' applied by the House of Lords in *Bolitho v City and Hackney Health Authority* [1998] AC 232 which established that in rare cases a doctor could be held to be negligent even if the treatment was sanctioned by a body of professional opinion. Lord Browne-Wilkinson noted that McNair J had referred to a *responsible* body of medical men and that the practice should be regarded as proper by a competent *reasonable* body of opinion, and said that expert evidence could be ignored if it could not be shown that such opinion had a logical basis, or if the experts had not reached a defensible opinion. See further Rachael Mulheron 'Trumping *Bolam*: A Critical Legal Analysis of *Bolitho*'s "Gloss"' [2010] CLJ 609.

4. *Bolitho* was followed in *McGuinn v Lewisham and Greenwich NHS Trust* [2017] EWHC 88 (QB). The claimant sued the hospital for damages for the 'wrongful birth' of her daughter, Matilda, on the basis that the doctors treating her should have been aware that the foetus was at risk of suffering from microcephaly and referred the claimant for further investigations. The claimant claimed that had she been aware of this risk, she would have elected to terminate her pregnancy. The judge held that the defendants' actions 'lacked a sufficiently logical and rational basis' (at [175]) and as a result fell below the standard expected of a reasonable doctor.

The **Bolam** test was applied in *Sidaway* v *Governors of the Bethlem Royal Hospital* [1985] AC 871 to the question of whether a patient should be informed of the risk as it does to diagnosis and treatment. Rejecting the doctrine of informed consent, the majority of the House of Lords held that the doctor was not liable for failing to inform the patient of a known small risk of paralysis. The decision in *Sidaway* was widely and severely criticised. In *Chester* v *Afshar* [2005] 1 AC 134, for example, Lord Steyn noted that '[i]n modern law medical paternalism no longer rules and a patient has a prima facie right to be informed by a surgeon of a small but well established risk of serious injury as a result of surgery' (at [16]). (See further José Miola 'The Standard of Care in Medical Negligence—Still Reasonably Troublesome?' in Janice Richardson and Erika Rackley (eds) *Feminist Perspectives on Tort Law* (Routledge, 2012), p 163.) Over the years, the courts have tacitly departed from it in favour of Lord Woolf MR's test in *Pearce* v *United Bristol Healthcare NHS Trust* [1999] PIQR P 53 and *Sidaway* itself was overruled in **Montgomery v Lanarkshire Health Board**.

Montgomery v Lanarkshire Health Board
Supreme Court [2015] UKSC 11

In 1999, the claimant gave birth to a baby boy. As a result of complications during the birth, during which the baby was starved of oxygen, the baby was born with significant disabilities. The claimant sued in negligence (on behalf of her son). The claimant was a relatively small woman and diabetic. Women with diabetes are more likely to have large babies and there is a 9–10 per cent risk of shoulder dystocia during vaginal delivery (the baby's shoulders being too wide to pass through the mother's pelvis). The claimant was told that she was having a larger than usual baby; however, she was not told about the risks of her experiencing mechanical problems during labour. Her doctor accepted that there was a high risk of shoulder dystocia, but despite this she said that her practice was not to spend a lot of time, or indeed any time at all, discussing it with the patient. The primary question for the court was whether, in failing to warn the claimant of the risk, the doctor was in breach of her duty of care towards the claimant. Held: patients have a right to make their own decisions and to be given sufficient information to do so. Doctors, therefore, have a corresponding duty to take reasonable care to ensure that a patient is aware of material risks inherent in treatment, and of any alternatives except in circumstances where 'he reasonably considers that its disclosure would be seriously detrimental to the patient's health' (at [88]).

LORD KERR AND LORD REED:

Sidaway

39. In *Maynard v West Midlands Regional Health Authority* [1984] 1 WLR 634 . . . the House of Lords approved the dictum of Lord President Clyde in *Hunter v Hanley* 1955 SC 200 . . . that the true test for establishing negligence in diagnosis or treatment on the part of a doctor is whether she has been proved to be guilty of such failure as no doctor of ordinary skill would be guilty of if acting with ordinary care. Lord Scarman, in a speech with which the other members of the House agreed, stated . . .:

A case which is based on an allegation that a fully considered decision of two consultants in the field of their special skill was negligent clearly presents certain difficulties of proof. It is not enough to show that there is a body of competent professional opinion which considers that theirs was a wrong decision, if there also exists a body of professional opinion, equally competent, which supports the decision as reasonable in the circumstances. It is not enough to show that subsequent events show that the operation need never have been performed, if at the time the decision to operate was taken it was reasonable in the sense that a responsible body of medical opinion would have accepted it as proper.

40. In that part of his speech, Lord Scarman followed the approach adopted in *Bolam v Friern Hospital Management Committee* [1957] 1 WLR 582, a case concerned with advice as well as with diagnosis and treatment, where McNair J directed the jury that a doctor was not guilty of negligence if she had acted in accordance with a practice accepted as proper by a responsible body of medical practitioners skilled in that particular art. The question whether the same approach should be applied (as it had been, in *Bolam* itself) in relation to a failure to advise a patient of risks involved in treatment was considered by the House of Lords in *Sidaway v Board of Governors of the Bethlem Royal Hospital and the Maudsley Hospital* which was, of course, decided in 1985, two years after the *Maynard* decision.

41. In *Sidaway's* case this question was approached by the members of the House in different ways, but with a measure of overlap. At one end of the spectrum was Lord Diplock, who considered that any alleged breach of a doctor's duty of care towards his patient, whether it related to diagnosis, treatment or advice, should be determined by applying the *Bolam* test:

The merit of the *Bolam* test is that the criterion of the duty of care owed by a doctor to his patient is whether he has acted in accordance with a practice accepted as proper by a body of responsible and skilled medical opinion . . . To decide what risks the existence of which a patient should be voluntarily warned and the terms in which such warning, if any, should be given, having regard to the effect that the warning may have, is as much an exercise of professional skill and judgment as any other part of the doctor's comprehensive duty of care to the individual patient, and expert medical evidence on this matter should be treated in just the same way. The *Bolam* test should be applied. . . .

42. Lord Diplock provided some reassurance to members of the judiciary:

But when it comes to warning about risks, the kind of training and experience that a judge will have undergone at the Bar makes it natural for him to say (correctly) it is my right to decide whether any particular thing is done to my body, and I want to be fully informed of any risks there may be involved of which I am not already aware from my general knowledge as a highly educated man of experience, so that I may form my own judgment as to whether to refuse the advised treatment or not.

No doubt if the patient in fact manifested this attitude by means of questioning, the doctor would tell him whatever it was the patient wanted to know. . . .

There was on the other hand no obligation to provide patients with unsolicited information about risks:

The only effect that mention of risks can have on the patient's mind, if it has any at all, can be in the direction of deterring the patient from undergoing the treatment which in the expert opinion of the doctor it is in the patient's interest to undergo. . . .

43. At the other end of the spectrum was the speech of Lord Scarman, who took as his starting point 'the patient's right to make his own decision, which may be seen as a basic human right protected by the common law' . . . From that starting point, he inferred:

If, therefore, the failure to warn a patient of the risks inherent in the operation which is recommended does constitute a failure to respect the patient's right to make his own decision, I can see no reason in principle why, if the risk materialises and injury or damage is caused, the law should not recognise and enforce a right in the patient to compensation by way of damages. . . .

44. In other words, if (1) the patient suffers damage, (2) as a result of an undisclosed risk, (3) which would have been disclosed by a doctor exercising reasonable care to respect her patient's right to decide whether to incur the risk, and (4) the patient would have avoided the injury if the risk had been disclosed, then the patient will in principle have a cause of action based on negligence.

45. Lord Scarman pointed out that the decision whether to consent to the treatment proposed did not depend solely on medical considerations:

> The doctor's concern is with health and the relief of pain. These are the medical objectives. But a patient may well have in mind circumstances, objectives, and values which he may reasonably not make known to the doctor but which may lead him to a different decision from that suggested by a purely medical opinion. . . .

46. This is an important point. The relative importance attached by patients to quality as against length of life, or to physical appearance or bodily integrity as against the relief of pain, will vary from one patient to another. Countless other examples could be given of the ways in which the views or circumstances of an individual patient may affect their attitude towards a proposed form of treatment and the reasonable alternatives. The doctor cannot form an objective, 'medical' view of these matters, and is therefore not in a position to take the 'right' decision as a matter of clinical judgment.

47. In Lord Scarman's view, if one considered the scope of the doctor's duty by beginning with the right of the patient to make her own decision whether she would or would not undergo the treatment proposed, it followed that the doctor was under a duty to inform the patient of the material risks inherent in the treatment. A risk was material, for these purposes, if a reasonably prudent patient in the situation of the patient would think it significant. The doctor could however avoid liability for injury resulting from the occurrence of an undisclosed risk if she could show that she reasonably believed that communication to the patient of the existence of the risk would be detrimental to the health (including the mental health) of her patient.

48. It followed from that approach that medical evidence would normally be required in order to establish the magnitude of a risk and the seriousness of the possible injury if it should occur. Medical evidence would also be necessary to assist the court to decide whether a doctor who withheld information because of a concern about its effect upon the patient's health was justified in that assessment. The determination of the scope of the doctor's duty, and the question whether she had acted in breach of her duty, were however ultimately legal rather than medical in character.

49. Lord Scarman summarised his conclusions as follows . . . :

> To the extent that I have indicated I think that English law must recognise a duty of the doctor to warn his patient of risk inherent in the treatment which he is proposing: and especially so, if the treatment be surgery. The critical limitation is that the duty is confined to material risk. The test of materiality is whether in the circumstances of the particular case the court is satisfied that a reasonable person in the patient's position would be likely to attach significance to the risk. Even if the risk be material, the doctor will not be liable if upon a reasonable assessment of his patient's condition he takes the view that a warning would be detrimental to his patient's health.

57. It would therefore be wrong to regard *Sidaway* as an unqualified endorsement of the application of the *Bolam* test to the giving of advice about treatment. Only Lord Diplock adopted that position. On his approach, the only situation, other than one covered by the *Bolam* test, in which a doctor

would be under a duty to provide information to a patient would be in response to questioning by the patient.

The subsequent case law

63. In the present case, as in earlier cases, the Court of Session applied the *Bolam* test, subject to the qualifications derived from Lord Bridge's speech. In England and Wales, on the other hand, although *Sidaway's* case remains binding, lower courts have tacitly ceased to apply the *Bolam* test in relation to the advice given by doctors to their patients, and have effectively adopted the approach of Lord Scarman.

64. The case of *Pearce v United Bristol Healthcare NHS Trust* [1999] PIQR P 53 is particularly significant in this context. The case concerned an expectant mother whose baby had gone over term. Her consultant obstetrician took the view that the appropriate course was for her to have a normal delivery when nature took its course, rather than a caesarean section at an earlier date, and advised her accordingly. In the event, the baby died *in utero*. The question was whether the mother ought to have been warned of that risk. In a judgment with which Roch and Mummery LJJ agreed, Lord Woolf MR said . . . :

> In a case where it is being alleged that a plaintiff has been deprived of the opportunity to make a proper decision as to what course he or she should take in relation to treatment, it seems to me to be the law, as indicated in the cases to which I have just referred, that if there is a significant risk which would affect the judgment of a reasonable patient, then in the normal course it is the responsibility of a doctor to inform the patient of that significant risk, if the information is needed so that the patient can determine for him or herself as to what course he or she should adopt.

65. In support of that approach, the Master of the Rolls referred in particular to the passage from Lord Bridge's speech in *Sidaway* . . . In Lord Bridge's formulation . . . the question for the judge was whether disclosure of a risk was so obviously necessary to an informed choice on the part of the patient that no doctor who recognised and respected his patient's right of decision and was exercising reasonable care would fail to make it. In our view, the Master of the Rolls was correct to consider that 'a significant risk which would affect the judgment of a reasonable patient' would meet that test. Lord Woolf's approach is also consistent with that adopted in *Sidaway* by Lord Templeman ('information which is adequate to enable the patient to reach a balanced judgment'), as well as with the test favoured by Lord Scarman ('that a reasonable person in the patient's position would be likely to attach significance to the risk'). It does not, on the other hand, have anything to do with the *Bolam* test.

66. The Extra Division [a Division of the Inner House of the Scottish Court of Session] correctly pointed out in the present case that Lord Woolf spoke of a 'significant' risk, whereas Lord Bridge, when describing the kind of case he had in mind, had referred to a 'substantial' risk. In so far as 'significant' and 'substantial' have different shades of meaning, 'significant' is the more apt adjective. Lord Bridge accepted that a risk had to be disclosed where it was 'obviously necessary to an informed choice'; and the relevance of a risk to the patient's decision does not depend solely upon its magnitude, or upon a medical assessment of its significance.

67. The point is illustrated by the case of *Wyatt v Curtis* [2003] EWCA Civ 1779, which concerned the risk of around 1% that chickenpox during pregnancy might result in significant brain damage. The Court of Appeal applied the law as stated in *Pearce*, observing that it was no less binding on the court than *Sidaway*. Sedley LJ stated:

> Lord Woolf's formulation refines Lord Bridge's test by recognising that what is substantial and what is grave are questions on which the doctor's and the patient's perception may differ, and in relation to which the doctor must therefore have regard to what may be the patient's

perception. To the doctor, a chance in a hundred that the patient's chickenpox may produce an abnormality in the foetus may well be an insubstantial chance, and an abnormality may in any case not be grave. To the patient, a new risk which (as I read the judge's appraisal of the expert evidence) doubles, or at least enhances, the background risk of a potentially catastrophic abnormality may well be both substantial and grave, or at least sufficiently real for her to want to make an informed decision about it. . . .

68. It is also relevant to note the judgments in *Chester v Afshar*. The case was concerned with causation, but it contains relevant observations in relation to the duty of a doctor to advise a patient of risks involved in proposed treatment. Lord Bingham of Cornhill said that the doctor in question had been under a duty to warn the patient of a small (1%–2%) risk that the proposed operation might lead to a seriously adverse result. The rationale of the duty, he said, was 'to enable adult patients of sound mind to make for themselves decisions intimately affecting their own lives and bodies' (para 5). Lord Steyn cited with approval para 21 of Lord Woolf MR's judgment in *Pearce*. Lord Walker of Gestingthorpe referred to a duty to advise the patient, a warning of risks being an aspect of the advice . . . He also observed at para 92 that during the 20 years which had elapsed since *Sidaway's* case, the importance of personal autonomy had been more and more widely recognised. He added at para 98 that, in making a decision which might have a profound effect on her health and well-being, a patient was entitled to information and advice about possible alternative or variant treatments.

69. In more recent case law the English courts have generally treated Lord Woolf MR's statement in *Pearce* as the standard formulation of the duty to disclose information to patients, although some unease has on occasion been expressed about the difficulty of reconciling that approach with the speeches of Lord Diplock and Lord Bridge in *Sidaway's* case (see, for example, *Birch v University College London Hospital NHS Foundation Trust* [2008] EWHC 2237 (QB)). Significantly, the guidance issued by the Department of Health and the General Medical Council has treated *Chester v Afshar* as the leading authority.

Conclusions on the duty of disclosure

74. The Hippocratic Corpus advises physicians to reveal nothing to the patient of her present or future condition, 'for many patients through this cause have taken a turn for the worse' (*Decorum*, XVI). Around two millennia later, in *Sidaway's* case Lord Templeman said that 'the provision of too much information may prejudice the attainment of the objective of restoring the patient's health' . . .; and similar observations were made by Lord Diplock and Lord Bridge. On that view, if the optimisation of the patient's health is treated as an overriding objective, then it is unsurprising that the disclosure of information to a patient should be regarded as an aspect of medical care, and that the extent to which disclosure is appropriate should therefore be treated as a matter of clinical judgment, the appropriate standards being set by the medical profession.

75. Since *Sidaway*, however, it has become increasingly clear that the paradigm of the doctor–patient relationship implicit in the speeches in that case has ceased to reflect the reality and complexity of the way in which healthcare services are provided, or the way in which the providers and recipients of such services view their relationship. One development which is particularly significant in the present context is that patients are now widely regarded as persons holding rights, rather than as the passive recipients of the care of the medical profession. They are also widely treated as consumers exercising choices: a viewpoint which has underpinned some of the developments in the provision of healthcare services. In addition, a wider range of healthcare professionals now provide treatment and advice of one kind or another to members of the public, either as individuals, or as members of a team drawn from different professional backgrounds (with the consequence that, although this judgment is concerned particularly with doctors, it is also relevant, *mutatis mutandis*, to other healthcare providers). The treatment which they can offer is now understood to depend not only upon their clinical judgment, but upon bureaucratic decisions as to such matters as resource allocation, cost-containment and hospital administration: decisions which are taken by non-medical professionals. Such decisions are generally understood within a framework of institutional rather than personal responsibilities, and are in principle susceptible to challenge under public law rather than, or in addition to, the law of delict or tort.

76. Other changes in society, and in the provision of healthcare services, should also be borne in mind. One which is particularly relevant in the present context is that it has become far easier, and far more common, for members of the public to obtain information about symptoms, investigations, treatment options, risks and side-effects via such media as the internet (where, although the information available is of variable quality, reliable sources of information can readily be found), patient support groups, and leaflets issued by healthcare institutions. The labelling of pharmaceutical products and the provision of information sheets is a further example, which is of particular significance because it is required by laws premised on the ability of the citizen to comprehend the information provided. It would therefore be a mistake to view patients as uninformed, incapable of understanding medical matters, or wholly dependent upon a flow of information from doctors. The idea that patients were medically uninformed and incapable of understanding medical matters was always a questionable generalisation, as Lord Diplock implicitly acknowledged by making an exception for highly educated men of experience. To make it the default assumption on which the law is to be based is now manifestly untenable.

77. These developments in society are reflected in professional practice. The court has been referred in particular to the guidance given to doctors by the General Medical Council, who participated as interveners in the present appeal. One of the documents currently in force (*Good Medical Practice* (2013)) states, under the heading 'The duties of a doctor registered with the General Medical Council':

> Work in partnership with patients. Listen to, and respond to, their concerns and preferences. Give patients the information they want or need in a way they can understand. Respect patients' right to reach decisions with you about their treatment and care.

78. Another current document (*Consent: patients and doctors making decisions together* (2008)) describes a basic model of partnership between doctor and patient:

> The doctor explains the options to the patient, setting out the potential benefits, risks, burdens and side effects of each option, including the option to have no treatment. The doctor may recommend a particular option which they believe to be best for the patient, but they must not put pressure on the patient to accept their advice. The patient weighs up the potential benefits, risks and burdens of the various options as well as any non-clinical issues that are relevant to them. The patient decides whether to accept any of the options and, if so, which one. . . .

In relation to risks, in particular, the document advises that the doctor must tell patients if treatment might result in a serious adverse outcome, even if the risk is very small, and should also tell patients about less serious complications if they occur frequently . . . The submissions on behalf of the General Medical Council acknowledged, in relation to these documents, that an approach based upon the informed involvement of patients in their treatment, rather than their being passive and potentially reluctant recipients, can have therapeutic benefits, and is regarded as an integral aspect of professionalism in treatment.

79. Earlier editions of these documents (*Good Medical Practice* (1998), and *Seeking patients' consent: The ethical considerations* (1998)), in force at the time of the events with which this case is concerned, were broadly to similar effect. No reference was made to them however in the proceedings before the Court of Session.

80. In addition to these developments in society and in medical practice, there have also been developments in the law. Under the stimulus of the Human Rights Act 1998, the courts have become increasingly conscious of the extent to which the common law reflects fundamental values. As Lord Scarman pointed out in *Sidaway's* case, these include the value of self-determination (see, for example, *S (An Infant) v S* [1972] AC 24 . . .; *McColl v Strathclyde Regional Council* 1983 SC 225 . . .; *Airedale NHS Trust v Bland* [1993] AC 789 . . .). As well as underlying aspects of the common law, that value also underlies the right to respect for private life protected by article 8 of the European Convention on Human Rights. The resulting duty to involve the patient in decisions relating to her treatment has been recognised in judgments of the European Court of Human Rights, such as *Glass v United Kingdom* (2004) 39 EHRR 15 and *Tysiac v Poland* (2007) 45 EHRR 42, as well as in a number of decisions of courts in the United Kingdom. The same value is also reflected more specifically in other international instruments: see, in particular, article 5 of the Convention for the Protection of Human Rights and Dignity of the Human Being with regard to the Application of Biology and Medicine: Convention on Human Rights and Biomedicine, concluded by the member states of the Council of Europe, other states and the European Community at Oviedo on 4 April 1997.

81. The social and legal developments which we have mentioned point away from a model of the relationship between the doctor and the patient based upon medical paternalism. They also point away from a model based upon a view of the patient as being entirely dependent on information provided by the doctor. What they point towards is an approach to the law which, instead of treating patients as placing themselves in the hands of their doctors (and then being prone to sue their doctors in the event of a disappointing outcome), treats them so far as possible as adults who are capable of understanding that medical treatment is uncertain of success and may involve risks, accepting responsibility for the taking of risks affecting their own lives, and living with the consequences of their choices.

82. In the law of negligence, this approach entails a duty on the part of doctors to take reasonable care to ensure that a patient is aware of material risks of injury that are inherent in treatment. This can be understood, within the traditional framework of negligence, as a duty of care to avoid exposing a person to a risk of injury which she would otherwise have avoided, but it is also the counterpart of the patient's entitlement to decide whether or not to incur that risk. The existence of that entitlement, and the fact that its exercise does not depend exclusively on medical considerations, are important. They point to a fundamental distinction between, on the one hand, the doctor's role when considering possible investigatory or treatment options and, on the other, her role in discussing with the patient any recommended treatment and possible alternatives, and the risks of injury which may be involved.

83. The former role is an exercise of professional skill and judgment: what risks of injury are involved in an operation, for example, is a matter falling within the expertise of members of the medical profession. But it is a *non sequitur* to conclude that the question whether a risk of injury, or the availability of an alternative form of treatment, ought to be discussed with the patient is also a matter of purely professional judgment. The doctor's advisory role cannot be regarded as solely an exercise of medical skill without leaving out of account the patient's entitlement to decide on the risks to her health which she is willing to run (a decision which may be influenced by non-medical considerations). Responsibility for determining the nature and extent of a person's rights rests with the courts, not with the medical professions.

84. Furthermore, because the extent to which a doctor may be inclined to discuss risks with a patient is not determined by medical learning or experience, the application of the *Bolam* test to this question is liable to result in the sanctioning of differences in practice which are attributable not to divergent schools of thought in medical science, but merely to divergent attitudes among doctors as to the degree of respect owed to their patients.

85. A person can of course decide that she does not wish to be informed of risks of injury (just as a person may choose to ignore the information leaflet enclosed with her medicine); and a doctor is not obliged to discuss the risks inherent in treatment with a person who makes it clear that she would prefer not to discuss the matter. Deciding whether a person is so disinclined may involve the doctor making a judgment; but it is not a judgment which is dependent on medical expertise. It is also true that the doctor must necessarily make a judgment as to how best to explain the risks to the patient, and that providing an effective explanation may require skill. But the skill and judgment required are not of the kind with which the *Bolam* test is concerned; and the need for that kind of skill and judgment does not entail that the question whether to explain the risks at all is normally a matter for the judgment of the doctor. That is not to say that the doctor is required to make disclosures to her patient if, in the reasonable exercise of medical judgment, she considers that it would be detrimental to the health of her patient to do so; but the 'therapeutic exception', as it has been called, cannot provide the basis of the general rule.

86. It follows that the analysis of the law by the majority in *Sidaway* is unsatisfactory, in so far as it treated the doctor's duty to advise her patient of the risks of proposed treatment as falling within the scope of the *Bolam* test, subject to two qualifications of that general principle, neither of which is fundamentally consistent with that test. It is unsurprising that courts have found difficulty in the subsequent application of *Sidaway*, and that the courts in England and Wales have in reality departed from it; a position which was effectively endorsed, particularly by Lord Steyn, in *Chester v Afshar*. There is no reason to perpetuate the application of the *Bolam* test in this context any longer.

87. The correct position, in relation to the risks of injury involved in treatment, can now be seen to be substantially that adopted in *Sidaway* by Lord Scarman, and by Lord Woolf MR in *Pearce*, subject to the refinement made by the High Court of Australia in *Rogers v Whitaker* . . . An adult person of sound mind is entitled to decide which, if any, of the available forms of treatment to undergo, and her consent must be obtained before treatment interfering with her bodily integrity is undertaken. The doctor is therefore under a duty to take reasonable care to ensure that the patient is aware of any material risks involved in any recommended treatment, and of any reasonable alternative or variant treatments. The test of materiality is whether, in the circumstances of the particular case, a reasonable person in the patient's position would be likely to attach significance to the risk, or the doctor is or should reasonably be aware that the particular patient would be likely to attach significance to it.

88. The doctor is however entitled to withhold from the patient information as to a risk if he reasonably considers that its disclosure would be seriously detrimental to the patient's health. The doctor is also excused from conferring with the patient in circumstances of necessity, as for example where the patient requires treatment urgently but is unconscious or otherwise unable to make a decision. It is unnecessary for the purposes of this case to consider in detail the scope of those exceptions.

89. Three further points should be made. First, it follows from this approach that the assessment of whether a risk is material cannot be reduced to percentages. The significance of a given risk is likely to reflect a variety of factors besides its magnitude: for example, the nature of the risk, the effect which its occurrence would have upon the life of the patient, the importance to the patient of the benefits sought to be achieved by the treatment, the alternatives available, and the risks involved in those alternatives. The assessment is therefore fact-sensitive, and sensitive also to the characteristics of the patient.

90. Secondly, the doctor's advisory role involves dialogue, the aim of which is to ensure that the patient understands the seriousness of her condition, and the anticipated benefits and risks of the proposed treatment and any reasonable alternatives, so that she is then in a position to make an informed decision. This role will only be performed effectively if the information provided is comprehensible. The doctor's duty is not therefore fulfilled by bombarding the patient with technical information which she cannot reasonably be expected to grasp, let alone by routinely demanding her signature on a consent form.

91. Thirdly, it is important that the therapeutic exception should not be abused. It is a limited exception to the general principle that the patient should make the decision whether to undergo a proposed course of treatment: it is not intended to subvert that principle by enabling the doctor to prevent the patient from making an informed choice where she is liable to make a choice which the doctor considers to be contrary to her best interests.

92. There are, of course, arguments which can be advanced against this approach: for example, that some patients would rather trust their doctors than be informed of all the ways in which their treatment might go wrong; that it is impossible to discuss the risks associated with a medical procedure within the time typically available for a healthcare consultation; that the requirements imposed are liable to result in defensive practices and an increase in litigation; and that the outcome of such litigation may be less predictable.

93. The first of these points has been addressed in para 85 above. In relation to the second, the guidance issued by the General Medical Council has long required a broadly similar approach. It is nevertheless necessary to impose legal obligations, so that even those doctors who have less skill or inclination for communication, or who are more hurried, are obliged to pause and engage in the discussion which the law requires. This may not be welcomed by some healthcare providers; but the reasoning of the House of Lords in *Donoghue v Stevenson* [1932] AC 562 was no doubt received in a similar way by the manufacturers of bottled drinks. The approach which we have described has long been operated in other jurisdictions, where healthcare practice presumably adjusted to its requirements. In relation to the third point, in so far as the law contributes to the incidence of litigation, an approach which results in patients being aware that the outcome of treatment is uncertain and potentially dangerous, and in their taking responsibility for the ultimate choice to undergo that treatment, may be less likely to encourage recriminations and litigation, in the event of an adverse outcome, than an approach which requires patients to rely on their doctors to determine whether a risk inherent in a particular form of treatment should be incurred. In relation to the fourth point, we would accept that a departure from the *Bolam* test will reduce the predictability of the outcome of litigation, given the difficulty of overcoming that test in contested proceedings. It appears to us however that a degree of unpredictability can be tolerated as the consequence of protecting patients from exposure to risks of injury which they would otherwise have chosen to avoid. The more fundamental response to such points, however, is that respect for the dignity of patients requires no less.

The disclosure of risks in the present case

94. Approaching the present case on this basis, there can be no doubt that it was incumbent on Dr McLellan [the consultant obstetrician and gynaecologist employed by Lanarkshire Health Board] to advise Mrs Montgomery [the claimant] of the risk of shoulder dystocia if she were to have her baby by vaginal delivery, and to discuss with her the alternative of delivery by caesarean section. The Court of Session focused upon the consequent risk that the baby might suffer a grave injury, a risk which was relatively small. The risk of shoulder dystocia, on the other hand, was substantial: on the

evidence, around 9–10%. Applying the approach which we have described, the exercise of reasonable care undoubtedly required that it should be disclosed. Quite apart from the risk of injury to the baby (a risk of about 1 in 500 of a brachial plexus injury, and a much smaller risk of a more severe injury, such as cerebral palsy, or death), it is apparent from the evidence . . . that shoulder dystocia is itself a major obstetric emergency, requiring procedures which may be traumatic for the mother, and involving significant risks to her health. No woman would, for example, be likely to face the possibility of a fourth degree tear, a Zavanelli manoeuvre or a symphysiotomy with equanimity. The contrast of the risk involved in an elective caesarean section, for the mother extremely small and for the baby virtually non-existent, is stark and illustrates clearly the need for Mrs Montgomery to be advised of the possibility, because of her particular circumstances, of shoulder dystocia. This conclusion is reinforced by Dr McLellan's own evidence . . . that she was aware that the risk of shoulder dystocia was likely to affect the decision of a patient in Mrs Montgomery's position, and that Mrs Montgomery herself was anxious about her ability to deliver the baby vaginally.

95. There is no question in this case of Dr McLellan's being entitled to withhold information about the risk because its disclosure would be harmful to her patient's health. Although her evidence indicates that it was her policy to withhold information about the risk of shoulder dystocia from her patients because they would otherwise request caesarean sections, the 'therapeutic exception' is not intended to enable doctors to prevent their patients from taking an informed decision. Rather, it is the doctor's responsibility to explain to her patient why she considers that one of the available treatment options is medically preferable to the others, having taken care to ensure that her patient is aware of the considerations for and against each of them.

Notes

1. **Montgomery** is a landmark decision. Informed consent is now 'firmly part of English law' (Lady Hale at [107]).

2. In *Duce* v *Worcestershire Acute Hospitals NHS Trust* [2018] EWCA Civ 1307, Hamblen LJ suggested that there were two stages to the **Montgomery** test (the paragraph numbers refer to **Montgomery**):

   32. The nature of the duty was held at [87] to be:
      a duty to take reasonable care to ensure that the patient is aware of any material risks involved in any recommended treatment, and of any reasonable alternative or variant treatments.
   33. In the light of the differing roles identified this involves a twofold test:
      (1) What risks associated with an operation were or should have been known to the medical professional in question. That is a matter falling within the expertise of medical professionals [83].
      (2) Whether the patient should have been told about such risks by reference to whether they were material. That is a matter for the Court to determine [83]. This issue is not therefore the subject of the **Bolam** test and not something that can be determined by reference to expert evidence alone [84–85].
   34. The test of materiality is:
      . . . whether, in the circumstances of the particular case, a reasonable person in the patient's position would be likely to attach significance to the risk, or the doctor is or should reasonably be aware that the particular patient would be likely to attach significance to it. [87]
   35. Factors of relevance to determining materiality may include: the odds of the risk materialising; the nature of the risk; the effect its occurrence would have on the life of the patient;

the importance to the patient of the benefits sought to be achieved by the treatment; the alternatives available and the risks associated with them.

3. One consequence of **Montgomery** is that a substantial sum of the Lanarkshire NHS Board's budget has been taken out of the collective pot. Maternity claims already represent the highest value, and the second highest number, of all NHS claims (though these represent just 0.1 per cent of all births). However, while Lords Reed and Kerr acknowledged that the decision *could* lead to an increase in defensive practices, as well as in claims from women claiming that they had not been adequately advised, they did not expect this to be the case—do you agree?

Lady Hale in **Montgomery** offered a timely and important recognition of patient autonomy—and, in particular, women's choice in the context of pregnancy and childbirth—in her 'footnote' to the main judgment.

Montgomery v *Lanarkshire Health Board*
Supreme Court [2015] UKSC 11

LADY HALE:

108. It is now well recognised that the interest which the law of negligence protects is a person's interest in their own physical and psychiatric integrity, an important feature of which is their autonomy, their freedom to decide what shall and shall not be done with their body (the unwanted pregnancy cases are an example: see *Rees v Darlington Memorial Hospital NHS Trust* [2003] UKHL 52 . . .) Thus, as Jonathan Herring puts it in *Medical Law and Ethics* (2012), 4th ed, p 170, 'the issue is not whether enough information was given to ensure consent to the procedure, but whether there was enough information given so that the doctor was not acting negligently and giving due protection to the patient's right of autonomy'.

109. An important consequence of this is that it is not possible to consider a particular medical procedure in isolation from its alternatives. Most decisions about medical care are not simple yes/no answers. There are choices to be made, arguments for and against each of the options to be considered, and sufficient information must be given so that this can be done: see the approach of the General Medical Council in *Consent: patients and doctors making decisions together* (2008), para 5 . . .

110. Pregnancy is a particularly powerful illustration. Once a woman is pregnant, the foetus has somehow to be delivered. Leaving it inside her is not an option. The principal choice is between vaginal delivery and caesarean section. One is, of course, the normal and 'natural' way of giving birth; the other used to be a way of saving the baby's life at the expense of the mother's. Now, the risks to both mother and child from a caesarean section are so low that the National Institute for Health and Clinical Excellence (NICE clinical guideline 132, [new 2011] [para 1.2.9.5]) clearly states that 'For women requesting a CS, if after discussion and offer of support (including perinatal mental health support for women with anxiety about childbirth), a vaginal birth is still not an acceptable option, offer a planned CS'.

111. That is not necessarily to say that the doctors have to volunteer the pros and cons of each option in every case, but they clearly should do so in any case where either the mother or the child is at heightened risk from a vaginal delivery. In this day and age, we are not only concerned about risks to the baby. We are equally, if not more, concerned about risks to the mother. And those include the risks associated with giving birth, as well as any after-effects. One of the problems in this case was that for too long the focus was on the risks to the baby, without also taking into account what the mother might face in the process of giving birth.

112. It was well recognised in 1999 that an insulin-dependent diabetic mother could have a larger than average baby. This brings with it a 9 to 10% risk of 'mechanical problems' in labour, either that the baby's head will fail to descend or, worse still, that it will descend but the baby's shoulders will be too broad to follow the head through the birth canal and will therefore get stuck. Desperate manoeuvres are then required to deliver the baby. As the Royal College of Obstetricians and Gynaecologists state in their Guideline No 42 on *Shoulder Dystocia* (2005),

> There can be a high perinatal mortality and morbidity associated with the condition, even when it is managed appropriately. Maternal morbidity is also increased, particularly post-partum haemorrhage (11%) and fourth-degree perineal tears (3.8%), and their incidence remains unchanged by the manoeuvres required to effect delivery.

No-one suggests that this was not equally well known in 1999. The risk of permanent injury to the baby is less than the risk of injury to the mother, but it includes a very small risk of catastrophic injury resulting from the deprivation of oxygen during delivery, as occurred in this case.

113. These are risks which any reasonable mother would wish to take into account in deciding whether to opt for a vaginal delivery or a caesarean section. No doubt in doing so she would take serious account of her doctor's estimation of the likelihood of these risks emerging in her case. But it is not difficult to understand why the medical evidence in this case was that, if offered a caesarean section, any insulin dependent pregnant woman would take it. What could be the benefits of vaginal delivery which would outweigh avoiding the risks to both mother and child?

114. We do not have a full transcript of the evidence, but in the extracts we do have Dr McLellan referred to explaining to a mother who requested a caesarean section 'why it may not be in the mother's best interest' and later expressed the view that 'it's not in the maternal interests for women to have caesarean sections'. Whatever Dr McLellan may have had in mind, this does not look like a purely medical judgment. It looks like a judgment that vaginal delivery is in some way morally preferable to a caesarean section: so much so that it justifies depriving the pregnant woman of the information needed for her to make a free choice in the matter. Giving birth vaginally is indeed a unique and wonderful experience, but it has not been suggested that it inevitably leads to a closer and better relationship between mother and child than does a caesarean section.

115. In any event, once the argument departs from purely medical considerations and involves value judgments of this sort, it becomes clear, as Lord Kerr and Lord Reed conclude at para 85, that the *Bolam* test, of conduct supported by a responsible body of medical opinion, becomes quite inapposite. A patient is entitled to take into account her own values, her own assessment of the comparative merits of giving birth in the 'natural' and traditional way and of giving birth by caesarean section, whatever medical opinion may say, alongside the medical evaluation of the risks to herself and her baby. She may place great value on giving birth in the natural way and be prepared to take the risks to herself and her baby which this entails. The medical profession must respect her choice, unless she lacks the legal capacity to decide (*St George's Healthcare NHS Trust v S* [1999] Fam 26). There is no good reason why the same should not apply in reverse, if she is prepared to forgo the joys of natural childbirth in order to avoid some not insignificant risks to herself or her baby. She cannot force her doctor to offer treatment which he or she considers futile or inappropriate. But she is at least entitled to the information which will enable her to take a proper part in that decision.

116. As NICE (2011) puts it, 'Pregnant women should be offered evidence-based information and support to enable them to make informed decisions about their care and treatment' (para 1.1.1.1). Gone are the days when it was thought that, on becoming pregnant, a woman lost, not only her capacity, but also her right to act as a genuinely autonomous human being.

7.2.3 Children

> **Mullin v Richards**
> Court of Appeal [1998] 1 WLR 1304

The claimant and defendant, both 15-year-old schoolgirls, were fighting with plastic rulers, using them as swords, when one of the rulers broke and a fragment of plastic entered the claimant's eye. Held: the defendant was not liable.

HUTCHISON LJ: . . . The test of foreseeability is an objective one; but the fact that the first defendant was at the time a 15-year-old schoolgirl is not irrelevant. The question for the judge is not whether the actions of the defendant were such as an ordinarily prudent and reasonable adult in the defendant's situation would have realised gave rise to a risk of injury, it is whether an ordinarily prudent and reasonable 15-year-old schoolgirl in the defendant's situation would have realised as much. In that connection both counsel referred us to, and relied upon, the Australian decision in *McHale v Watson* (1966) 115 CLR 199 and in particular, the passage in the judgment of Kitto J, at pp 213–214. I cite a portion of the passage I have referred to, all of which was cited to us by Mr Lee on behalf of the appellant, and which Mr Stephens has adopted as epitomising the correct approach:

> The standard of care being objective, it is no answer for him [that is a child], any more than it is for an adult, to say that the harm he caused was due to his being abnormally slow-witted, quick-tempered, absent-minded or inexperienced. But it does not follow that he cannot rely in his defence upon a limitation upon the capacity for foresight or prudence, not as being personal to himself, but as being characteristic of humanity at his stage of development and in that sense normal. By doing so he appeals to a standard of ordinariness, to an objective and not a subjective standard.

Mr Stephens also cited to us a passage in the judgment of Owen J at p 234:

> . . . the standard by which his conduct is to be measured is not that to be expected of a reasonable adult but that reasonably to be expected of a child of the same age, intelligence and experience.

I venture to question the word 'intelligence' in that sentence, but I understand Owen J to be making the same point essentially as was made by Kitto J It is perhaps also material to have in mind the words of Salmon LJ in *Gough v Thorne* [1966] 1 WLR 1387, 1391, which is cited also by Mr Stephens, where he said:

> The question as to whether the plaintiff can be said to have been guilty of contributory negligence depends on whether any ordinary child of 13½ can be expected to have done any more than this child did. I say 'any ordinary child'. I do not mean a paragon of prudence; nor do I mean a scatter-brained child; but the ordinary girl of 13½.

I need say no more about that principle as to the way in which age affects the assessment of negligence because counsel are agreed upon it and, despite the fact that we have been told that there has been a good deal of controversy in other jurisdictions and that there is no direct authority in this jurisdiction, the approach in *McHale v Watson* seems to me to have the advantage of obvious, indeed irrefutable, logic . . .

BUTLER-SLOSS LJ: I agree with both judgments and since there has been little authority on the proper approach to the standard of care to be applied to a child, I would like to underline the observations of Hutchison LJ and rely upon two further passages in the persuasive judgment of Kitto J in the High Court of Australia in *McHale v Watson* (1966) 115 CLR 199 starting at p 213:

> In regard to the things which pertain to foresight and prudence, experience, understanding of causes and effects, balance of judgment, thoughtfulness—it is absurd, indeed it is a misuse of language, to speak of normality in relation to persons of all ages taken together. In those things normality is, for children, something different from what normality is for adults; the very concept of normality is a concept of rising levels until 'years of discretion' are attained. The law does not arbitrarily fix upon any particular age for this purpose, and tribunals of fact may well give effect to different views as to the age at which normal adult foresight and prudence are reasonably to be expected in relation to particular sets of circumstances. But up to that stage the normal capacity to exercise those two qualities necessarily means the capacity which is normal for a child of the relevant age; and it seems to me that it would be contrary to the fundamental principle that a person is liable for harm that he causes by falling short of an objective criterion of 'propriety' in his conduct—propriety, that is to say, as determined by a comparison with the standard of care reasonably to be expected in the circumstances from the normal person—to hold that where a child's liability is in question the normal person to be considered is someone other than a child of corresponding age.

I would respectfully endorse those observations as entirely appropriate to English law and I would like to conclude with another passage of Kitto J particularly relevant to today, at p 216:

> . . . in the absence of relevant statutory provision, children, like everyone else, must accept as they go about in society the risks from which ordinary care on the part of others will not suffice to save them. One such risk is that boys of twelve may behave as boys of twelve . . .

—and I would say that girls of 15 playing together may play as somewhat irresponsible girls of 15. I too would allow this appeal.

7.3 Setting the standard of care

The standard of care does not exist in the abstract: 'The law in all cases exacts a degree of care commensurate with the risk' (Lord Macmillan, *Read* v *Lyons Co Ltd* [1947] AC 156 at 173). Whether a defendant is in breach of duty requires a decision whether a reasonable man would foresee the danger and regard the risk as unreasonable. This can be a complicated and difficult question, which involves balancing a number of factors including the circumstances of the situation in which the accident or injury occurred.

> *Wooldridge v Sumner*
> Court of Appeal [1963] 2 QB 43

The claimant, Wooldridge, was a photographer who was attending the National Horse Show at White City. The perimeter of the arena was marked by a line of tubs with shrubs in them, and the claimant was standing just behind these. The defendant owned a horse called 'Work of Art' which was ridden by Holladay. The judge found that in attempting to take a corner the horse was going too fast, and it plunged through the line of tubs, injuring the claimant. Held: that the defendant was not liable as, in the heat of the moment, Holladay had merely made an error of judgement and was not negligent.

DIPLOCK LJ: . . .To treat Lord Atkin's statement 'You must take reasonable care to avoid acts or omissions which you can reasonably foresee would be likely to injure your neighbour', [1932] AC 562, 580, as a complete exposition of the law of negligence is to mistake aphorism for exegesis. It does not purport to define what is reasonable care and was directed to identifying the persons to whom the duty to take reasonable care is owed. What is reasonable care in a particular circumstance is a jury question and where, as in a case like this, there is no direct guidance or hindrance from authority it may be answered by inquiring whether the ordinary reasonable man would say that in all the circumstances the defendant's conduct was blameworthy.

The matter has to be looked at from the point of view of the reasonable spectator as well as the reasonable participant; not because of the maxim *volenti non fit injuria*, but because what a reasonable spectator would expect a participant to do without regarding it as blameworthy is as relevant to what is reasonable care as what a reasonable participant would think was blameworthy conduct in himself. The same idea was expressed by Scrutton LJ in *Hall v Brooklands* [1933] 1 KB 205, 214: 'What is reasonable care would depend upon the perils which might be reasonably expected to occur, *and the extent to which the ordinary spectator might be expected to appreciate and take the risk of such perils.*'

A reasonable spectator attending voluntarily to witness any game or competition knows and presumably desires that a reasonable participant will concentrate his attention upon winning, and if the game or competition is a fast-moving one, will have to exercise his judgment and attempt to exert his skill in what, in the analogous context of contributory negligence, is sometimes called 'the agony of the moment.' If the participant does so concentrate his attention and consequently does exercise his judgment and attempt to exert his skill in circumstances of this kind which are inherent in the game or competition in which he is taking part, the question whether any mistake he makes amounts to a breach of duty to take reasonable care must take account of those circumstances.

The law of negligence has always recognised that the standard of care which a reasonable man will exercise depends upon the conditions under which the decision to avoid the act or omission relied upon as negligence has to be taken. The case of the workman engaged on repetitive work in the noise and bustle of the factory is a familiar example. More apposite for present purposes are the collision cases, where a decision has to be made upon the spur of the moment. 'A's negligence makes collision so threatening that though by the appropriate measure B could avoid it, B has not really time to think and by mistake takes the wrong measure. B is not to be held guilty of any negligence and A wholly fails.' (*Admiralty Commissioners v S S Volute*, [1922] 1 AC 129, 136) A fails not because of his own negligence; there never has been any contributory negligence rule in *Admiralty*. He fails because B has exercised such care as is reasonable in circumstances in which he has not really time to think. No doubt if he has got into those circumstances as a result of a breach of duty of care which he owes to A, A can succeed upon this antecedent negligence; but a participant in a game or competition gets into the circumstances in which he has no time or very little time to think by his decision to take part in the game or competition at all. It cannot be suggested that the participant, at any rate if he has some modicum of skill, is, by the mere act of participating, in breach of his duty of care to a spectator who is present for the very purpose of watching him do so. If, therefore, in the course of the game or competition, at a moment when he really has not time to think, a participant by mistake takes a wrong measure, he is not, in my view, to be held guilty of any negligence.

Furthermore, the duty which he owes is a duty of care, not a duty of skill. Save where a consensual relationship exists between a plaintiff and a defendant by which the defendant impliedly warrants his skill, a man owes no duty to his neighbour to exercise any special skill beyond that which an ordinary reasonable man would acquire before indulging in the activity in which he is engaged at the relevant time. It may well be that a participant in a game or competition would be guilty of negligence to a spectator if he took part in it when he knew or ought to have known that his lack of skill was such that even if he exerted it to the utmost he was likely to cause injury to a spectator watching him. No question of this arises in the present case. It was common ground that Mr Holladay was an exceptionally skilful and experienced horseman.

The practical result of this analysis of the application of the common law of negligence to participant and spectator would, I think, be expressed by the common man in some such terms as these: 'A person attending a game or competition takes the risk of any damage caused to him by any act of a participant done in the course of and for the purposes of the game or competition notwithstanding that such act may involve an error of judgment or a lapse of skill, unless the participants' conduct is such as to evince a reckless disregard of the spectator's safety.'

7.3.1 Probability and seriousness of injury

> ### *Bolton v Stone*
> House of Lords [1951] AC 850

The claimant, Stone, was struck by a cricket ball hit out of a cricket ground at Cheetham Hill, Manchester. The ground was surrounded by a fence the top of which, due to the slope of the ground, was 17 feet above the level of the pitch. The fence was 78 yards from the striker, and the claimant, when hit, was 100 yards away. One member of the club said that he thought that about six balls had been hit out of the ground in 28 years, none causing any injury. Held: the club was not negligent.

LORD REID: . . . Counsel for the respondent in this case had to put his case so high as to say that, at least as soon as one ball had been driven into the road in the ordinary course of a match, the appellants could and should have realized that that might happen again and that, if it did, someone might be injured; and that that was enough to put on the appellants a duty to take steps to prevent such an occurrence. If the true test is foreseeability alone I think that must be so. Once a ball has been driven on to a road without there being anything extraordinary to account for the fact, there is clearly a risk that another will follow, and if it does there is clearly a chance, small though it may be, that someone may be injured. On the theory that it is foreseeability alone that matters it would be irrelevant to consider how often a ball might be expected to land in the road and it would not matter whether the road was the busiest street, or the quietest country lane; the only difference between these cases is in the degree of risk.

It would take a good deal to make me believe that the law has departed so far from the standards which guide ordinary careful people in ordinary life. In the crowded conditions of modern life even the most careful person cannot avoid creating some risks and accepting others. What a man must not do, and what I think a careful man tries not to do, is to create a risk which is substantial. . . . In my judgment the test to be applied here is whether the risk of damage to a person on the road was so small that a reasonable man in the position of the appellants, considering the matter from the point of view of safety, would have thought it right to refrain from taking steps to prevent the danger.

In considering that matter I think that it would be right to take into account not only how remote is the chance that a person might be struck but also how serious the consequences are likely to be if a person is struck; but I do not think that it would be right to take into account the difficulty of remedial measures. If cricket cannot be played on a ground without creating a substantial risk, then it should not be played there at all. I think that this is in substance the test which Oliver J applied in this case. He considered whether the appellants' ground was large enough to be safe for all practical purposes and held that it was. This is a question not of law but of fact and degree. It is not an easy question and it is one on which opinions may well differ. I can only say that having given the whole matter repeated and anxious consideration I find myself unable to decide this question in favour of the respondent. But I think that this case is not far from the borderline. If this appeal is allowed, that does not in my judgment mean that in every case where cricket has been played on a ground for a number of years without accident or complaint those who organize matches there are safe to go on in reliance on past immunity. I would have reached a different conclusion if I had thought that the risk there had been other than extremely small, because I do not think that a reasonable man considering the matter from the point of view of safety would or should disregard any risk unless it is extremely small. . . .

LORD RADCLIFFE: My Lords, I agree that this appeal must be allowed. I agree with regret, because I have much sympathy with the decision that commended itself to the majority of the members of the Court of Appeal. I can see nothing unfair in the appellants being required to compensate the respondent for the serious injury that she has received as a result of the sport that they have organised on their cricket ground at Cheetham Hill. But the law of negligence is concerned less with what is fair than with what is culpable, and I cannot persuade myself that the appellants have been guilty of any culpable act or omission in this case.

I think that the case is in some respects a peculiar one, not easily related to the general rules that govern liability for negligence. If the test whether there has been a breach of duty were to depend merely on the answer to the question whether this accident was a reasonably foreseeable risk, I think that there would have been a breach of duty, for that such an accident might take place some time or other might very reasonably have been present to the minds of the appellants. It was quite foreseeable, and there would have been nothing unreasonable in allowing the imagination to dwell on the possibility of its occurring. But there was only a remote, perhaps I ought to say only a very remote, chance of the accident taking place at any particular time, for, if it was to happen, not only had a ball to carry the fence round the ground but it had also to coincide in its arrival with the presence of some person on what does not look like a crowded thoroughfare and actually to strike that person in some way that would cause sensible injury.

Those being the facts, a breach of duty has taken place if they show the appellants guilty of a failure to take reasonable care to prevent the accident. One may phrase it as 'reasonable care' or 'ordinary care' or 'proper care'—all these phrases are to be found in decisions of authority—but the fact remains that, unless there has been something which a reasonable man would blame as falling beneath the standard of conduct that he would set for himself and require of his neighbour, there has been no breach of legal duty. And here, I think, the respondent's case breaks down. It seems to me that a reasonable man, taking account of the chances against an accident happening, would not have felt himself called upon either to abandon the use of the ground for cricket or to increase the height of his surrounding fences. He would have done what the appellants did: in other words, he would have done nothing. Whether, if the unlikely event of an accident did occur and his play turn to another's hurt, he would have thought it equally proper to offer no more consolation to his victim than the reflection that a social being is not immune from social risks, I do not say, for I do not think that that is a consideration which is relevant to legal liability.

> ### Overseas Tankship (UK) Ltd v Miller Steamship Co Pty Ltd (The Wagon Mound) (No 2)
> Privy Council [1967] AC 617

The defendants carelessly transferred furnace oil from a nearby wharf onto a vessel, *The Wagon Mound* which was moored in Sydney Harbour, causing a large quantity of the oil to spill into the harbour where it accumulated around the wharf and the claimants' vessels. The owners of the wharf were carrying out repairs on the claimants' ships which caused pieces of hot metal to fly off and into the wharf. On one such occasion it is thought that the metal fell onto an object supporting a piece of inflammable material in the oil-covered water, which subsequently ignited. This caused the oil to catch alight and the ensuing fire quickly destroyed the wharf and the claimants' vessels. Held: the oil spill was negligent.

LORD REID: . . . [I]t does not follow that, no matter what the circumstances may be, it is justifiable to neglect a risk of such a small magnitude, A reasonable man would only neglect such a risk if he had some valid reason for doing so: eg, that it would involve considerable expense to eliminate the risk, He would weigh the risk against the difficulty of eliminating it. If the activity which caused the injury to Miss Stone had been an unlawful activity there can be little doubt but that **Bolton v Stone** would have been decided differently. In their Lordships' judgment **Bolton v Stone** did not alter the general principle that a person must be regarded as negligent if he does not take steps to eliminate a risk which he knows or ought to know is a real risk and not a mere possibility which would never influence the mind of a reasonable man. What that decision did was to recognise and give effect to the qualification that it is justifiable not to take steps to eliminate a real risk if it is small and if the circumstances are such that a reasonable man, careful of the safety of his neighbour, would think it right to neglect it.

In the present case there was no justification whatever for discharging the oil into Sydney Harbour. Not only was it an offence to do so but it involved considerable loss financially. If the ship's engineer had thought about the matter there could have been no question of balancing the advantages and disadvantages. From every point of view it was both his duty and his interest to stop the discharge immediately . . . If a real risk is one which would occur to the mind of a reasonable man in the position of the defendant's servant and which he would not brush aside as far-fetched and if the criterion is to be what that reasonable man would have done in the circumstances, then surely he would not neglect such a risk if action to eliminate it presented no difficulty, involved no disadvantage, and required no expense.

Notes

1. This is the second of **The Wagon Mound** cases. The first case, **Overseas Tankship (UK) Ltd v Morts Dock and Engineering Co (The Wagon Mound) (No 1)** [1961] AC 388 was brought by the owners of the wharf on the issue of remoteness. It is discussed in Chapter 8.

7.3.2 Cost of prevention

> ### Latimer v AEC Ltd
> Court of Appeal [1952] 2 QB 701

Following a heavy rainstorm, the defendants' factory was flooded. When the flood subsided the whole floor was covered with a thin film of the oily mixture caused by the rainwater mixing with an oily liquid which usually flowed in channels in the factory floor. The defendants put sawdust down on most, but not all, of the floor. The claimant slipped and fell on an untreated part of the floor. It was argued that the defendants should have closed the factory. Held: the defendants were not liable as they had acted as a reasonable employer would have acted.

> DENNING LJ: . . . [I]t seems to me that [Pilcher J] has fallen into error by assuming it would be sufficient to constitute negligence that there was a foreseeable risk which the defendants could have avoided by some measure or other, however extreme. That is not the law. It is always necessary to consider what measures the defendant ought to have taken, and to say whether they could reasonably be expected of him. In a converse case, for example, a brave man tries to stop a runaway horse. It is a known risk and a serious risk, but no one would suggest that he could reasonably be expected to stand idly by. It is not negligence on his part to run the risk. So here the employers knew that the floor was slippery and that there was some risk in letting the men work on it; but, still, they could not reasonably be expected to shut down the whole works and send all the men home. In every case of foreseeable risk, it is a matter of balancing the risk against the measures necessary to eliminate it. It is only negligence if, on balance, the defendant did something which he ought not to have done, or omitted to do something which he ought to have done. In this case, in the circumstances of this torrential flood, it is quite clear the defendants did everything they could reasonably be expected to do. It would be quite unreasonable, it seems to me, to expect them to send all the men home. I agree, therefore, that there was no negligence at common law.

Notes

1. A risk of greater damage than normal may increase the obligations of a potential defendant. In *Paris* v *Stepney Borough Council* [1951] AC 367, the claimant was a garage hand with only one eye, who was struck in his only eye by a splinter from a bolt. He was not wearing goggles. The House of Lords, by a majority, held that although the disability did not increase the risk of injury, it did increase the risk of the injury being more serious (i.e. becoming blind rather than one-eyed), and therefore the employers should have supplied him with goggles, even though they need not have done so for a person with two eyes.

2. An increased risk of injury to particular individuals may also be relevant: for example, if children are likely to be present, special precautions may be necessary. In *Haley* v *London Electricity Board* [1965] AC 778, the defendants had dug a trench along a pavement, and as a barrier had placed a hammer across it with one end resting on the ground and the other about two feet above it. The claimant was blind and his stick failed to touch the barrier, and he fell and was rendered deaf. The House of Lords held that the presence of blind persons was foreseeable, and the increased likelihood of injury to them obliged the defendants to take precautions which would not be necessary in the case of sighted persons.

3. In *Goldscheider* v *Royal Opera House Covent Garden Foundation* [2019] EWCA Civ 711, the claimant, a viola player in the orchestra of the Royal Opera House (ROH) in Covent Garden, London, was able to recover for the damage caused to his hearing as a result by being placed too close to the trumpet section in the orchestra 'pit' in breach of the Control of Noise at Work Regulations 2005. Regulation 6(1) states '(1) The employer shall ensure that risk from the exposure of his employees to noise is either eliminated at source or, where this is not reasonably practicable, reduced to as low a level as is reasonably practicable'. McCombe and Bean LJJ in the Court of Appeal, rejecting the ROH's appeal, held that despite undertaking a risk assessment and providing performers with ear plugs and training, it had failed to take 'all reasonably practical steps' to protect the claimant's hearing. They continued:

one might have expected evidence on the following lines. Firstly, it might have been shown that a level of 91–92dB(A) is regularly reached in public performances of Wagner operas at the ROH whatever the configuration of the pit, whatever the number of brass instruments used and whoever is conducting. Secondly, evidence might have been led to show that to keep within the upper EAV [exposure action value] would mean that Wagner could not be performed at all at the ROH, or that his works could be performed only in a way which would compromise artistic standards to an unacceptable extent. Thirdly, the Defendant might have attempted to prove that the only way in which the rehearsals could have been scheduled is on the basis of six hours rehearsal per day on consecutive days, with no consideration being given to whether it was essential for the loudest passages to be played again and again throughout the day at full volume. It is in our judgment particularly significant that the pit was reconfigured after 1 September with the brass instruments being split up. There is no evidence that this caused an unacceptable reduction (or indeed any reduction at all) in the artistic standards of the *Ring* Cycle [the Wagner opera the claimant was performing] when it came to be performed in public. Alterations made by defendants after a workplace accident do not necessarily demonstrate liability retrospectively, but they do make it very difficult for the defendant to prove that all reasonably practicable steps had already been taken. (at [41]–[42])

7.3.3 Social value of the activity

> ### *Watt* v *Hertfordshire County Council*
> Court of Appeal [1954] 1 WLR 835

The case concerned an accident close to a fire station in which a woman was trapped under a heavy lorry. The fire station had a heavy jack for lifting, but the vehicle which was equipped to carry it was elsewhere. Instead the jack was loaded onto a lorry which had no means of securing the jack. On the way to the accident the lorry had to brake suddenly and the jack moved forward, injuring the claimant's ankle. Held: the defendants were not negligent in sending out the jack unsecured.

SINGLETON LJ: . . . Would the reasonably careful head of the station have done anything other than that which the sub-officer did? I think not. Can it be said, then, that there is a duty on the employers here to have a vehicle built and fitted to carry this jack at all times, or if they have not, not to use the jack for a short journey of 200 or 300 yards? I do not think that that will do.

Asquith LJ, in *Daborn v Bath Tramways Motor Co Ltd*, said, [1946] 2 All ER 333, 336:

> In determining whether a party is negligent, the standard of reasonable care is that which is reasonably to be demanded in the circumstances. A relevant circumstance to take into account may be the importance of the end to be served by behaving in this way or in that. As has often been pointed out, if all the trains in this country were restricted to a speed of five miles an hour, there would be fewer accidents, but our national life would be intolerably slowed down. The purpose to be served, if sufficiently important, justifies the assumption of abnormal risk.

The purpose to be served in this case was the saving of life. The men were prepared to take that risk. They were not, in my view, called on to take any risk other than that which normally might be encountered in this service. I agree with Barry J that on the whole of the evidence it would not be right to find that the employers were guilty of any failure of the duty which they owed to their workmen. In my opinion the appeal should be dismissed.

DENNING LJ: It is well settled that in measuring due care you must balance the risk against the measures necessary to eliminate the risk. To that proposition there ought to be added this: you must balance the risk against the end to be achieved. If this accident had occurred in a commercial enterprise without any emergency there could be no doubt that the servant would succeed. But the commercial end to make profit is very different from the human end to save life or limb. The saving of life or limb justifies taking considerable risk, and I am glad to say that there have never been wanting in this country men of courage ready to take those risks, notably in the fire service.

In this case the risk involved in sending out the lorry was not so great as to prohibit the attempt to save life. I quite agree that fire engines, ambulances and doctors' cars should not shoot past the traffic lights when they show a red light. That is because the risk is too great to warrant the incurring of the danger. It is always a question of balancing the risk against the end. I agree that this appeal should be dismissed.

Notes

1. This does not mean that all socially valuable activities are immune from claims in negligence. In *Scout Association* v *Barnes* [2010] EWCA Civ 1486, the claimant was injured while playing a game in the dark at a scout meeting. Finding for the claimant, Smith LJ stated:

   Every one accepts, including the [trial] judge, that scouting activities will often properly include an element of risk. However, that cannot mean that any scouting activity, however risky, is acceptable just because scouting is a very good thing. The social value of the particular activity must be taken into account in assessing whether the activity was reasonably safe. It was common ground before the judge that the game played in the light was reasonably safe, although plainly there were some inherent risks. The judge held, as he was entitled to do, that playing in the dark significantly increased those risks. It was also common ground that the game had some social value; it was a good active competitive game to keep boys occupied on long winter evenings. But, on the evidence, the judge was bound to form the view that the particular justification for playing this game in the dark was only that it added excitement. The darkness did not add any other social or educative value but it did significantly increase the risk of injury. I think that the judge's attitude towards social value was clear from the passages I have quoted above. I think it is clear that he thought that the added excitement of playing the game in the dark, which might well encourage boys to attend scouts—a desirable objective—did not justify the increased foreseeable risk. (at [46])

8

Causation and remoteness of damage

Causation and remoteness of damage are separate but related topics. Once it has been shown that a defendant owed the claimant a duty of care and was in breach of that duty, liability can still be avoided if it can be shown that the breach did not cause the damage (often referred to as the 'cause in fact' test). Similarly, if the damage was too remote a consequence of the breach or that there was a break in the chain of causation ('cause in law'), there will be no liability.

Causation problems usually occur when we see that the damage was actually caused by a number of different factors. Putting it another way, a number of factors may have combined together to bring about the damage. The problem is determining which, if any, factors were legally relevant, so as to be able to say that the person responsible for that factor should be liable, perhaps (but not always) to the exclusion of those responsible for other factors.

A remoteness problem arises where the claimant's harm has *in fact* been caused by the defendant's act, but the damage is unpredictable in nature.

8.1 **Causation**

No simple formula can test whether an act or event is a legally relevant cause of damage, and many books and cases content themselves with asking whether the act was a 'substantial' factor in bringing about the harm. The solution is pragmatic rather than theoretical, and is founded as much on policy as on logic. However, the test that is the starting point in all cases (though it doesn't solve them all, as we shall see) is the 'but for' test.

Barnett v Chelsea and Kensington Hospital Management Committee
Queen's Bench Division [1969] 1 QB 428

The claimant, Barnett, was a nightwatchman. At 5 am one morning, he drank some tea and about 20 minutes later began vomiting. At 8 am he went to the defendant hospital and was seen by a nurse who telephoned the doctor on duty, who said he should go to bed, then call his own doctors. The man returned to work but continued to feel ill, and by 2 pm was dead. It was shown that he had been poisoned with arsenic (a coroner's verdict of murder by persons unknown was returned). His widow claimed against the hospital for failing to treat her husband. Held: the hospital was not liable.

NIELD J: Without doubt the casualty officer should have seen and examined the deceased. His failure to do either cannot be described as an excusable error as has been submitted. It was neg-ligence. It is unfortunate that he was himself at the time a tired and unwell doctor, but there was no one else to do that which it was his duty to do. Having examined the deceased I think the first and provisional diagnosis would have been one of food poisoning. . . .

It remains to consider whether it is shown that the deceased's death was caused by that negli-gence or whether, as the defendants have said, the deceased must have died in any event. In his concluding submission Mr Pain submitted that the casualty officer should have examined the de-ceased and had he done so he would have caused tests to be made which would have indicated the treatment required and that, since the defendants were at fault in these respects, therefore the onus of proof passed to the defendants to show that the appropriate treatment would have failed, and authorities were cited to me. I find myself unable to accept that argument, and I am of the view that the onus of proof remains upon the plaintiff, and I have in mind (without quoting it) the decision cited by Mr Wilmers in *Bonnington Castings Ltd v Wardlaw* [1956] AC 613. However, were it otherwise and the onus did pass to the defendants, then I would find that they have discharged it, as I would proceed to show.

There has been put before me a timetable which I think is of much importance. The deceased attended at the casualty department at five or 10 minutes past eight in the morning. If the casualty officer had got up and dressed and come to see the three men and examined them and decided to admit them, the deceased (and Dr Lockett agreed with this) could not have been in bed in a ward before 11 am. I accept Dr Goulding's evidence that an intravenous drip would not have been set up before 12 noon, and if potassium loss was suspected it could not have been discovered until 12.30 pm. Dr Lockett, dealing with this, said: 'If this man had not been treated until after 12 noon the chances of survival were not good.' . . .

For those reasons, I find that the plaintiff has failed to establish, on the balance of probabilities, that the defendants' negligence caused the death of the deceased.

Notes

1. The 'but for' formulation relies on a balance of probabilities test. However, that test does not solve all problems. John Fleming (*Law of Torts* (9th edn, Sweet & Maxwell, 1998)) puts the case of two people carrying candles independently and simultaneously approaching a leaking gas pipe, causing an explosion. Each is 50 per cent likely to have been *the* cause, therefore each could claim that the explosion would have happened anyway, even if they had not been there, and escape liability.

Wilsher v Essex Area Health Authority
House of Lords [1988] AC 1074

The claimant was born prematurely and developed a retinal condition which left him almost totally blind. Experts listed a number of possible causes, mostly 'innocent' (non-negligent) and attributable to his prematurity. One potential cause, however, was that a junior doc-tor had misplaced a catheter in the claimant's arm which gave too low a reading of oxygen in the blood with the result that the claimant was given too much oxygen, known to be a possible cause of the condition. The trial judge found the defendants liable, relying on *McGhee v National Coal Board* [1973] 1 WLR 1, which he said amounted to the proposition that 'where there is a situation in which a general duty of care arises and there is a failure to take a precaution, and that very damage occurs against which the precaution is designed to be a protection, then the burden lies on the defendant to show that he was not in breach of duty as well as to show that the damage did not result from his breach of duty'. The House of Lords discussed this principle at length, ultimately rejecting it.

LORD BRIDGE: The starting point for any consideration of the relevant law of causation is the decision of this House in *Bonnington Castings Ltd v Wardlaw* [1956] AC 613. This was the case of a pursuer who, in the course of his employment by the defenders, contracted pneumoconiosis over a period of years by the inhalation of invisible particles of silica dust from two sources. One of these (pneumatic hammers) was an 'innocent' source, in the sense that the pursuer could not complain that his exposure to it involved any breach of duty on the part of his employers. The other source, however, (swing grinders) arose from a breach of statutory duty by the employer. Delivering the leading speech in the House Lord Reid said at pp 619–20:

> It would seem obvious in principle that a pursuer or plaintiff must prove not only negligence or breach of duty but also that such fault caused or materially contributed to his injury, and there is ample authority for that proposition both in Scotland and in England. I can find neither reason nor authority for the rule being different where there is breach of a statutory duty. The fact that Parliament imposes a duty for the protection of employees has been held to entitle an employee to sue if he is injured as a result of a breach of that duty, but it would be going a great deal farther to hold that it can be inferred from the enactment of a duty that Parliament intended that any employee suffering injury can sue his employer merely because there was a breach of duty and it is shown to be possible that his injury may have been caused by it. In my judgment, the employee must in all cases prove his case by the ordinary standard of proof in civil actions; he must make it appear at least that on a balance of probabilities the breach of duty caused or materially contributed to his injury.

Their Lordships concluded, however, from the evidence that the inhalation of dust to which the pursuer was exposed by the defenders' breach of statutory duty had made a material contribution to his pneumoconiosis which was sufficient to discharge the onus on the pursuer of proving that his damage was caused by the defenders' tort.

In *McGhee v National Coal Board* [1973] 1 WLR 1 the pursuer worked in a brick kiln in hot and dusty conditions in which brick dust adhered to his sweaty skin. No breach of duty by his employers, the defenders, was established in respect of his working conditions. However, the employers were held to be negligent in failing to provide adequate washing facilities which resulted in the pursuer having to bicycle home after work with his body still caked in brick dust. The pursuer contracted dermatitis and the evidence that this was caused by the brick dust was accepted. Brick dust adhering to the skin was a recognised cause of industrial dermatitis and the provision of showers to remove it after work was a usual precaution to minimise the risk of the disease. The precise mechanism of causation of the disease, however, was not known and the furthest the doctors called for the pursuer were able to go was to say that the provision of showers would have materially reduced the risk of dermatitis. They were unable to say that it would probably have prevented the disease.

The pursuer failed before the Lord Ordinary and the First Division of the Court of Session on the ground that he had not discharged the burden of proof of causation. He succeeded on appeal to the

House of Lords. Much of the academic discussion to which this decision has given rise has focused on the speech of Lord Wilberforce, particularly on two paragraphs. He said at p 6:

> But the question remains whether a pursuer must necessarily fail if, after he has shown a breach of duty, involving an increase of risk of disease, he cannot positively prove that this increase of risk caused or materially contributed to the disease while his employers cannot positively prove the contrary. In this intermediate case there is an appearance of logic in the view that the pursuer, on whom the onus lies, should fail—a logic which dictated the following judgments. The question is whether we should be satisfied in factual situations like the present, with this logical approach. In my opinion, there are further considerations of importance. First, it is a sound principle that where a person has, by breach of a duty of care, created a risk, and injury occurs within the area of that risk, the loss should be borne by him *unless he shows that it had some other cause*. Secondly, from the evidential point of view, one may ask, why should a man who is able to show that his employer should have taken certain precautions, because without them there is a risk, or an added risk, of injury or disease, and who in fact sustains exactly that injury or disease, have to assume the burden of proving more; namely, that it was the addition to the risk, caused by the breach of duty, which caused or materially contributed to the injury? In many cases, of which the present is typical, this is impossible to prove, just because honest medical opinion cannot segregate the causes of an illness between compound causes. And if one asks which of the parties, the workman or the employers should suffer from this inherent evidential difficulty, the answer as a matter in policy or justice should be that it is the creator of the risk who, ex hypothesi must be taken to have foreseen the possibility of damage, who should bear its consequences.

He then referred to the cases of *Bonnington Castings Ltd v Wardlaw* [1956] AC 613 and *Nicholson v Atlas Steel Foundry and Engineering Co Ltd* [1957] 1 WLR 613 and added at p 7:

> The present factual situation has its differences: the default here consisted not in adding a material quantity to the accumulation of injurious particles but by failure to take a step which materially increased the risk that the dust already present would cause injury. And I must say that, at least in the present case, to bridge the evidential gap by inference seems to me something of a fiction, since it was precisely this inference which the medical expert declined to make. But I find in the cases quoted an analogy which suggests the conclusion that, *in the absence of proof that the culpable addition had, in the result, no effect*, the employers should be liable for an injury, squarely within the risk which they created and that they, not the pursuer, should suffer the consequence of the impossibility, foreseeably inherent in the nature of his injury, of segregating the precise consequence of their default.

(I have added the emphasis in both these two passages.)

My Lords, it seems to me that both these paragraphs, particularly in the words I have emphasised, amount to saying that, in the circumstances, the burden of proof of causation is reversed and thereby to run counter to the unanimous and emphatic opinions expressed in *Bonnington Castings Ltd v Wardlaw* [1956] AC 613 to the contrary effect. I find no support in any of the other speeches for the view that the burden of proof is reversed and, in this respect, I think Lord Wilberforce's reasoning must be regarded as expressing a minority opinion.

A distinction is, of course, apparent between the facts of *Bonnington Castings Ltd v Wardlaw*, where the 'innocent' and 'guilty' silica dust particles which together caused the pursuer's lung disease were inhaled concurrently and the facts of *McGhee v National Coal Board* [1973] 1 WLR 1 where the 'innocent' and 'guilty' brick dust was present on the pursuer's body for consecutive periods. In the one case the concurrent inhalation of 'innocent' and 'guilty' dust must both have contributed to the cause of the disease. In the other case the consecutive periods when 'innocent' and 'guilty' brick dust was present on the pursuer's body may both have contributed to the cause of the disease or, theoretically at least, one or other may have been the sole cause. But where the layman is told by the doctors that the longer the brick dust remains on the body, the greater the risk of dermatitis, although the doctors cannot identify the process of causation scientifically, there seems to be nothing irrational in drawing the inference, as a matter of common sense, that the consecutive periods when brick dust remained on the body probably contributed cumulatively to the causation of the dermatitis. I believe that a process of inferential reasoning on these general lines underlies the decision of the majority in *McGhee*'s case.

Lord Simon of Glaisdale said at p 8:

> But *Bonnington Castings Ltd v Wardlaw* [1956] AC 613 and *Nicholson v Atlas Steel Foundry Engineering Co Ltd* [1957] 1 WLR 613 establish, in my view, that where an injury is caused by two (or more) factors operating cumulatively, one (or more) of which factors is a breach of duty and one (or more) is not so, in such a way that it is impossible to ascertain the proportion in which the factors were effective in producing the injury or which factor was decisive, the law does not require a pursuer or plaintiff to prove the impossible, but holds that he is entitled to damages for the injury if he proves on a balance of probabilities that the breach or breaches of duty contributed substantially to causing the injury. If such factors so operate cumulatively, it is, in my judgment, immaterial whether they do so concurrently or successively.

The conclusion I draw from these passages is that *McGhee v National Coal Board* [1973] 1 WLR 1 laid down no new principle of law whatever. On the contrary, it affirmed the principle that the onus of proving causation lies on the pursuer or plaintiff. Adopting a robust and pragmatic approach to the undisputed primary facts of the case, the majority concluded that it was a legitimate inference of fact that the defenders' negligence had materially contributed to the pursuer's injury. The decision, in my opinion, is of no greater significance than that and the attempt to extract from it some esoteric principle which in some way modifies, as a matter of law, the nature of the burden of proof of causation which a plaintiff or pursuer must discharge once he has established a relevant breach of duty is a fruitless one.

In the Court of Appeal in the instant case Sir Nicolas Browne-Wilkinson VC, being in a minority, expressed his view on causation with understandable caution. But I am quite unable to find any fault with the following passage in his dissenting judgment [1987] QB 730, 779:

> To apply the principle in *McGhee v National Coal Board* [1973] 1 WLR 1 to the present case would constitute an extension of that principle. In the *McGhee* case there was no doubt that the pursuer's dermatitis was physically caused by brick dust: the only question was whether the continued presence of such brick dust on the pursuer's skin after the time when he should have been provided with a shower caused or materially contributed to the dermatitis which he contracted. There was only one possible agent which could have caused the dermatitis, viz brick dust, and there was no doubt that the dermatitis from which he suffered was caused by that brick dust.

In the present case the question is different. There are a number of different agents which could have caused the RLF [retrolental fibroplasia]. Excess oxygen was one of them. The defendants failed to take reasonable precautions to prevent one of the possible causative agents (eg excess oxygen) from causing RLF. But no one can tell in this case whether excess oxygen did or did not cause or contribute to the RLF suffered by the plaintiff. The plaintiff's RLF may have been caused by some completely different agent or agents, eg hypercarbia, intraventricular haemorrhage, apnoea or *patent ductus arteriosus*. In addition to oxygen, each of those conditions has been implicated as a possible cause of RLF. This baby suffered from each of those conditions at various times in the first two months of his life. There is no satisfactory evidence that excess oxygen is more likely than any of those other five candidates to have caused RLF in this baby. To my mind, the occurrence of RLF following a failure to take a necessary precaution to prevent excess oxygen causing RLF provides no evidence and raises no presumption that it was excess oxygen rather than one or more of the five other possible agents which caused or contributed to RLF in this case.

The position, to my mind, is wholly different from that in the *McGhee* case where there was only one candidate (brick dust) which could have caused the dermatitis and failure to take a precaution against brick dust causing dermatitis was followed by dermatitis caused by brick dust. In such a case, I can see the common sense, if not the logic, of holding that, in the absence of any other evidence, the failure to take the precaution caused or contributed to the dermatitis. To the extent that certain members of the House of Lords decided the question on inference from evidence or presumptions, I do not consider that the present case falls within their reasoning. A failure to take preventative measures against one out of six possible causes is no evidence as to which of those six caused the injury.

Notes

1. This case and those cited in it have always caused controversy and have been further discussed by the courts in many subsequent cases, as well as in other jurisdictions. In **Fairchild** (extracted in section 8.1.1) Lord Bingham said that the passage in **Wilsher** beginning 'The conclusion I draw from these passages is that *McGhee* laid down no new principle of law whatever' should no longer be regarded as authoritative (at [22]).

2. The problem in *McGhee* was whether the provision of washing facilities would have prevented the claimant's disease. (That is, could the claimant show that it was their absence which 'caused' the disease?) It was also possible that he could have contracted the disease solely from normal exposure while he was working rather than from his prolonged exposure because he could not wash the dust off. The existence of the dust was 'innocent', in the sense that its presence was not anyone's fault, hence the only claim in negligence could be the failure to remove it at the earliest opportunity. Therefore, one cause (the presence of the dust) was 'innocent' and the other (the failure to provide washing facilities) was 'guilty'.

3. **Wilsher**'s effect could be defined as where the defendant's failure (in *McGhee* not providing washing facilities) materially increases a risk of harm which already exists (dermatitis from brick dust), the defendant can be held liable. But where the failure creates only a *new risk*, it is not possible to infer that that caused the damage.

4. Possibly in contradiction to **Wilsher**, in *Bailey* v *Ministry of Defence* [2008] EWCA Civ 883 two potential causes of the claimant's cardiac arrest and brain damage—one negligent and one 'natural'—were treated by the Court of Appeal as *cumulative* causes, following *Bonnington*. This resulted in a finding that the negligent treatment made a 'material contribution' to the claimant's harm, sufficient to establish liability. Despite being controversial for a number of years, the case was affirmed by the Privy Council (**Williams v The Bermuda Hospitals Board (Bermuda)** [2016] UKPC 4).

> ## Williams v The Bermuda Hospitals Board (Bermuda)
> Privy Council [2016] UKPC 4

Williams attended a hospital emergency department with severe abdominal pain. He was examined by a doctor, who thought he might have appendicitis and a CT scan was ordered. The scan did not take place for another 4–5 hours. Williams's appendix ruptured in this time. The resulting sepsis was instrumental in his later suffering myocardial ischaemia and requiring life support treatment in intensive care. Williams could not establish that on the balance of probabilities the delay in diagnosis and treatment at the hospital was the cause of the later injuries, as there was a possibility that the appendix had begun to rupture anyway upon his arrival at hospital. The appeal court found that the negligent delay in his treatment had materially contributed to the injury.

The Privy Council upheld this finding, Lord Toulson applying *Bonnington*, finding that the myocardial ischaemia resulted from the cumulative effect of both 'innocent' and 'guilty' (attributable to the delay) sepsis. The hospital's negligence had materially contributed to Williams's harm and they should be liable for it.

LORD TOULSON:

32. In *Bonnington* there was no suggestion that the pneumoconiosis was 'divisible', meaning that the severity of the disease depended on the quantity of dust inhaled. Lord Reid interpreted the medical evidence as meaning that the particles from the swing grinders were a cause of the entire disease. True, they were only part of the cause, but they were a partial cause of the entire injury, as distinct from being a cause of only part of the injury. Lord Reid's approach was understandable in view of the way in which the case was argued. The Lord Ordinary recorded in his opinion that it was conceded by the employers' counsel that the claimant had contracted pneumoconiosis arising out of and in the course of his employment, although 'there was reserved for argument the question of which part of the process was the probable source of infection', and that the employers argued that 'on the balance of probabilities the source of the infection was the silica dust which was discharged during the dressing process involving the use of the pneumatic tools, and nothing else': 1955 SC 320, 321, 324. It was not argued by the employers that the dust from the swing grinders could be linked, at most, to only a small part of the severity of his disease and that any damages should reflect the limited injury thereby caused.[1]

33. On Lord Reid's interpretation of the medical evidence, the question posed by the Lord President was the wrong question because it involved a false 'either or' premise. Since the disease was caused by the totality of the toxic material inhaled, the relevant question was whether the particles from the swing grinders made any material contribution to the whole.

34. Lord Tucker and Lord Keith of Avonholm both saw it as a matter of inference that the dust from the swing grinders was a contributory cause of the disease. Lord Tucker said, at p 623, that the inference to be drawn from the known facts was that 'the silica dust discharged from the swing grinders contributed to the harmful condition of the atmosphere, which admittedly resulted in the pursuer

---

[1] In later cases it has been the accepted view that pneumoconiosis is a 'divisible' disease, its severity being dependent on the quantity of dust inhaled; and, therefore, where there has been more than one source of toxic material, the extent of the liability of a defendant responsible for part of the exposure should reflect the degree of injury suffered by the claimant as a result of that exposure. See the judgment of Lord Phillips of Worth Matravers in *Sienkiewicz v Greif (UK) Ltd* [2011] 2 AC 229, para 90: 'Where the disease is indivisible, such as lung cancer, a defendant who has tortiously contributed to the cause of the disease will be liable in full. Where the disease is divisible, such as asbestosis, the tortfeasor will be liable in respect of the share of the disease for which he is responsible.'

contracting pneumoconiosis, and was therefore a contributory cause of the disease'. Lord Keith said, at p 626, that the claimant had proved enough to support the inference that the employers' fault had materially contributed to his illness, because prima facie the particles inhaled were acting cumulatively and that the natural inference was that, had it not been for the cumulative effect, he would not have developed pneumoconiosis when he did.

35. The parallel with the present case is obvious. The Board is not persuaded by Ms Harrison's argument that *Bonnington* is distinguishable because in that case the inhalation from two sources was simultaneous, whereas in the present case the sepsis attributable to the hospital's negligence developed after sepsis had already begun to develop.

36. In considering that argument, it is instructive to compare and contrast *Hotson v East Berkshire Health Authority* [1987] AC 750. The claimant fell from a tree and fractured his left femoral epiphysis. He was taken to hospital, where for several days his injury was not properly diagnosed or treated. He suffered avascular necrosis of the epiphysis, leaving him with a permanent disability. The House of Lords held that on proper analysis of the evidence the avascular necrosis must have been caused in one or other of two ways. Either it was caused by irreparable rupture of the blood vessels to the epiphysis at the moment of the fall, or it was caused by later pressure within the joint from bruising or internal bleeding. There was no room for finding that the avascular necrosis was caused by a combination of the two factors. The trial judge's findings were to the effect that on the balance of probabilities the cause was the original traumatic injury. The claim therefore failed.

37. Lord Bridge said, at p 782, that unless the claimant proved on a balance of probabilities that the delay in treatment was at least a contributory cause of the avascular necrosis, he failed on causation, and that the judge's findings amounted to a finding of fact that the fall was the sole cause of the avascular necrosis. He added, at p 783:

> But if the plaintiff had proved on a balance of probabilities that the authority's negligent failure to diagnose and treat his injury promptly had materially contributed to the development of avascular necrosis, I know of no principle of English law which would have entitled the authority to a discount from the full measure of damage to reflect the chance that, even given prompt treatment, avascular necrosis might well still have developed.

That passage runs counter to Ms Harrison's submission that in principle the 'material contribution' approach is confined to cases in which the timing of origin of the contributory causes is simultaneous.

38. The distinction drawn by Ms Harrison is also inconsistent with the opinion of Lord Simon of Glaisdale in *McGhee v National Coal Board* [1973] 1 WLR 1, 8. Referring to *Bonnington* and to *Nicholson v Atlas Steel Foundry and Engineering Co Ltd* [1957] 1 WLR 613, Lord Simon said that where on the balance of probabilities an injury is caused by two (or more) factors operating cumulatively, one (or more) of which is a breach of duty, it is immaterial whether the cumulative factors operate concurrently or successively.

39. The sequence of events may be highly relevant in considering as a matter of fact whether a later event has made a material contribution to the outcome (as *Hotson* illustrates), or conversely whether an earlier event has been so overtaken by later events as not to have made a material contribution to the outcome. But those are evidential considerations. As a matter of principle, successive events are capable of each making a material contribution to the subsequent outcome.

40. A claim will fail if the most that can be said is that the claimant's injury is likely to have been caused by one or more of a number of disparate factors, one of which was attributable to a wrongful act or omission of the defendant: *Wilsher v Essex Area Health Authority* [1988] AC 1074. In such a case the claimant will not have shown as a matter of probability that the factor attributable to the defendant caused the injury, or was one of two or more factors which operated cumulatively to cause

it. In *Wilsher* the injury was a condition known as retrolental fibroplasia or RLF, to which premature babies are vulnerable. The condition may be caused by various factors, one of which is an oversupply of oxygen. The claimant was born prematurely and as a result of clinical negligence he was given too much oxygen. He developed RLF, but it was held by the House of Lords that it was not enough to show that the defendant's negligence added to the list of risk factors to which he was exposed. The fact that the administration of excess oxygen was negligent did not warrant an inference that it was a more likely cause of the RLF than the various other known possible causes. The House of Lords distinguished the case from *Bonnington* in which the injury was caused by a single known process (the inhalation of dust).

41. In the present case the judge found that injury to the heart and lungs was caused by a single known agent, sepsis from the ruptured appendix. The sepsis developed incrementally over a period of approximately six hours, progressively causing myocardial ischaemia. (The greater the accumulation of sepsis, the greater the oxygen requirement.) The sepsis was not divided into separate components causing separate damage to the heart and lungs. Its development and effect on the heart and lungs was a single continuous process, during which the sufficiency of the supply of oxygen to the heart steadily reduced.

42. On the trial judge's findings, that process continued for a minimum period of two hours 20 minutes longer than it should have done. In the judgment of the Board, it is right to infer on the balance of probabilities that the hospital board's negligence materially contributed to the process, and therefore materially contributed to the injury to the heart and lungs.

43. That conclusion means that it is unnecessary for the Board to address in further detail the rival arguments about the way in which the Court of Appeal dealt (or did not deal) with the judge's finding about the length of culpable delay. Although the Court of Appeal was critical in some respects about the judge's finding (notably about the time of ordering the CT scan), it made no clear finding about when the operation should have begun. However, no useful purpose would be served at this stage in going into that aspect of the matter further, since it makes no difference to the outcome of the appeal, the purpose of which has been to determine a question of principle about the proper approach to causation in the circumstances of this case.

44. Although not strictly necessary, it may be helpful to comment by way of postscript on two matters which were raised in argument. First, Ms Harrison was critical of the decision, and more particularly the reasoning, of the Court of Appeal in *Bailey*. The starting point is Foskett J's findings of fact, which were set out in close detail in his judgment: [2007] EWHC 2913 (QB).

45. The claimant was admitted to hospital suffering from a gall stone requiring surgical removal. There was a delay in diagnosis but that was not itself a significant matter. On 11 January 2001 she underwent an endoscopic procedure known as an ERCP. Her treatment in the aftermath of the ERCP was negligent. As a result, she had to undergo further major procedures over the following days which should not have been necessary and which led to her being in a weakened state. In addition, she developed pancreatitis, which was an unfortunate, but non-negligent, complication of the ERCP. For 12 days she was in the ITU [intensive care unit] until she was transferred to the renal unit on 26 January. There she vomited in her sleep and aspirated the vomit, causing her to suffer a cardiac arrest and hypoxic brain damage.

46. The judge found on the strength of medical evidence that 'the claimant's generally weakened and debilitated condition on 26 January caused her not to be able to respond naturally and effectively to the emergence of vomit from her gut with the consequence that she inhaled it' (para 54). The question was whether this was too remote a consequence of her negligent treatment following the ERCP, having regard to the fact that her weakened state was partly due to the pancreatitis for which the hospital was not responsible. The judge's critical finding was at para 60:

I do not think it can be doubted that there were two components to the weakness of the claimant as at 26 January, both very closely interlinked and having their foundation in the ERCP carried out on 11 January. One component was the weakness engendered by the pancreatitis, the other was the weakness engendered by the consequence of the negligence on 11–12 January which led to a very stormy passage for the claimant ending (purely from a surgical point of view) on 19 January when the packing of the liver was removed. Even leaving out of account the independent effect of the pancreatitis, it defies all common sense to say that she had recovered from the effects of all that by 26 January. I am satisfied, on the balance of probabilities, that she had not and that she was weakened as a result. I cannot say whether the contribution made by this component was more or less than that made by the pancreatitis and it follows that I cannot say whether the contribution made by the pancreatitis was greater or smaller than the contribution of the other component. All I can say is that the natural inference is that each contributed materially to the overall weakness and it was the overall weakness that caused the aspiration.

47. In the view of the Board, on those findings of primary fact Foskett J was right to hold the hospital responsible in law for the consequences of the aspiration. As to the parallel weakness of the claimant due to her pancreatitis, the case may be seen as an example of the well known principle that a tortfeasor takes his victim as he finds her. The Board does not share the view of the Court of Appeal that the case involved a departure from the 'but-for' test. The judge concluded that the totality of the claimant's weakened condition caused the harm. If so, 'but-for' causation was established. The fact that her vulnerability was heightened by her pancreatitis no more assisted the hospital's case than if she had an egg shell skull.

48. Finally, reference was made during the argument to the 'doubling of risk' test which has sometimes been used or advocated as a tool used in deciding questions of causation. The Board would counsel caution in its use. As Baroness Hale of Richmond said in *Sienkiewicz* at para 170, evaluation of risk can be important in making choices about future action. This is particularly so in the medical field, where a practitioner will owe a duty to the patient to see that the patient is properly informed about the potential risks of different forms of treatment (or non-treatment). Use of such evidence, for example epidemiological evidence, to determine questions of past fact is rather different. That is not to deny that it may sometimes be very helpful. If it is a known fact that a particular type of act (or omission) is likely to have a particular effect, proof that the defendant was responsible for such an act (or omission) and that the claimant had what is the usual effect will be powerful evidence from which to infer causation, without necessarily requiring a detailed scientific explanation for the link. But inferring causation from proof of heightened risk is never an exercise to apply mechanistically. A doubled tiny risk will still be very small.

49. The Board will humbly advise Her Majesty that the appeal should be dismissed with costs.

8.1.1 An exception to the 'but for' rule—material increase in risk

Fairchild v *Glenhaven Funeral Services*
House of Lords [2002] UKHL 22

The claimants developed mesothelioma (a fatal lung cancer) by negligent exposure to asbestos dust. The disease could be caused by exposure to even a small number of asbestos fibres. The claimants had worked for a number of negligent employers successively and were unable to prove during which employment the disease had been contracted. Held: each employer had materially increased *the risk* of contracting the disease and all were jointly and severally liable.

LORD BINGHAM:

2. The essential question underlying the appeals may be accurately expressed in this way. If

(1) C was employed at different times and for differing periods by both A and B, and

(2) A and B were both subject to a duty to take reasonable care or to take all practicable measures to prevent C inhaling asbestos dust because of the known risk that asbestos dust (if inhaled) might cause a mesothelioma, and

(3) both A and B were in breach of that duty in relation to C during the periods of C's employment by each of them with the result that during both periods C inhaled excessive quantities of asbestos dust, and

(4) C is found to be suffering from a mesothelioma, and

(5) any cause of C's mesothelioma other than the inhalation of asbestos dust at work can be effectively discounted, but

(6) C cannot (because of the current limits of human science) prove, on the balance of probabilities, that his mesothelioma was the result of his inhaling asbestos dust during his employment by A or during his employment by B or during his employment by A and B taken together,

is C entitled to recover damages against either A or B or against both A and B? To this question (not formulated in these terms) the Court of Appeal (Brooke, Latham and Kay LJJ), in a reserved judgment of the court reported at [2002] 1 WLR 1052, gave a negative answer. It did so because, applying the conventional 'but for' test of tortious liability, it could not be held that C had proved against A that his mesothelioma would probably not have occurred but for the breach of duty by A, nor against B that his mesothelioma would probably not have occurred but for the breach of duty by B, nor against A and B that his mesothelioma would probably not have occurred but for the breach of duty by both A and B together. So C failed against both A and B. The crucial issue on appeal is whether, in the special circumstances of such a case, principle, authority or policy requires or justifies a modified approach to proof of causation.

21. This detailed review of *McGhee* permits certain conclusions to be drawn. First, the House was deciding a question of law. Lord Reid expressly said so (p 3). The other opinions, save perhaps that of Lord Kilbrandon, cannot be read as decisions of fact or as orthodox applications of settled law. Secondly, the question of law was whether, on the facts of the case as found, a pursuer who could not show that the defender's breach had probably caused the damage of which he complained could nonetheless succeed. Thirdly, it was not open to the House to draw a factual inference that the breach probably had caused the damage: such an inference was expressly contradicted by the medical experts on both sides; and once that evidence had been given the crux of the argument before the Lord Ordinary and the First Division and the House was whether, since the pursuer could not prove that the breach had probably made a material contribution to his contracting dermatitis, it was enough to show that the breach had increased the risk of his contracting it. Fourthly, it was expressly held by three members of the House (Lord Reid at p 5, Lord Simon at p 8 and Lord Salmon at pp 12–13) that in the circumstances no distinction was to be drawn between making a material contribution to causing the disease and materially increasing the risk of the pursuer contracting it. Thus the proposition expressly rejected by the Lord Ordinary, the Lord President and Lord Migdale was expressly accepted by a majority of the House and must be taken to represent the ratio of the decision, closely tied though it was to the special facts on which it was based. Fifthly, recognising

that the pursuer faced an insuperable problem of proof if the orthodox test of causation was applied, but regarding the case as one in which justice demanded a remedy for the pursuer, a majority of the House adapted the orthodox test to meet the particular case. The authority is of obvious importance in the present appeal since the medical evidence left open the possibility, as Lord Reid pointed out at p 4, that the pursuer's dermatitis could have begun with a single abrasion, which might have been caused when he was cycling home, but might equally have been caused when he was working in the brick kiln; in the latter event, the failure to provide showers would have made no difference. In *McGhee*, however, unlike the present appeals, the case was not complicated by the existence of additional or alternative wrongdoers.

33. The present appeals raise an obvious and inescapable clash of policy considerations. On the one hand are the considerations powerfully put by the Court of Appeal ([2002] 1 WLR 1052 at 1080, para 103) which considered the claimants' argument to be not only illogical but

> also susceptible of unjust results. It may impose liability for the whole of an insidious disease on an employer with whom the claimant was employed for quite a short time in a long work-ing life, when the claimant is wholly unable to prove on the balance of probabilities that that period of employment had any causative relationship with the inception of the disease. This is far too weighty an edifice to build on the slender foundations of *McGhee v National Coal Board* [1973] 1 WLR 1, and Lord Bridge has told us in *Wilsher v Essex Area Health Authority* [1988] AC 1074 that *McGhee* established no new principle of law at all. If we were to accede to the claimants' arguments, we would be distorting the law to accommodate the exigencies of a very hard case. We would be yielding to a contention that all those who have suffered injury after being exposed to a risk of that injury from which someone else should have pro-tected them should be able to recover compensation even when they are quite unable to prove who was the culprit. In a quite different context Lord Steyn has recently said in *Frost v Chief Constable of Yorkshire* [1999] 2 AC 455, 491 that our tort system sometimes results in imperfect justice, but it is the best the common law can do.

The Court of Appeal had in mind that in each of the cases discussed in paras 14–21 above (*Wardlaw, Nicholson, Gardiner, McGhee*) there was only one employer involved. Thus there was a risk that the defendant might be held liable for acts for which he should not be held legally liable but no risk that he would be held liable for damage which (whether legally liable or not) he had not caused. The crux of cases such as the present, if the appellants' argument is upheld, is that an employer may be held liable for damage he has not caused. The risk is the greater where all the employers potentially liable are not before the court. This is so on the facts of each of the three appeals before the House, and is always likely to be so given the long latency of this condition and the likelihood that some employers potentially liable will have gone out of business or disappeared during that period. It can properly be said to be unjust to impose liability on a party who has not been shown, even on a balance of probabilities, to have caused the damage complained of. On the other hand, there is a strong policy argument in favour of compensating those who have suffered grave harm, at the expense of their employers who owed them a duty to protect them against that very harm and failed to do so, when the harm can only have been caused by breach of that duty and when science does not permit the victim accurately to attribute, as between several employers, the precise responsibility for the harm he has suffered. I am of opinion that such injustice as may be involved in imposing liability on a duty-breaking employer in these circumstances is heavily outweighed by the injustice of denying redress to a victim. Were the law otherwise, an employer exposing his employee to asbestos dust could obtain complete immunity against mesothelioma (but not asbestosis) claims by employing only those who had previously been exposed to excessive quantities of asbestos dust. Such a result would reflect no credit on the law. It seems to me, as it did to Lord Wilberforce in *McGhee* [1973] 1 WLR 1 at 7, that

> the employers should be liable for an injury, squarely within the risk which they created and that they, not the pursuer, should suffer the consequence of the impossibility, foreseeably inherent in the nature of his injury, of segregating the precise consequence of their default.

Conclusion

34. To the question posed in paragraph 2 of this opinion I would answer that where conditions (1)–(6) are satisfied C is entitled to recover against both A and B. That conclusion is in my opinion consistent with principle, and also with authority (properly understood). Where those conditions are satisfied, it seems to me just and in accordance with common sense to treat the conduct of A and B in exposing C to a risk to which he should not have been exposed as making a material contribution to the contracting by C of a condition against which it was the duty of A and B to protect him. I consider that this conclusion is fortified by the wider jurisprudence reviewed above. Policy considerations weigh in favour of such a conclusion. It is a conclusion which follows even if either A or B is not before the court. It was not suggested in argument that C's entitlement against either A or B should be for any sum less than the full compensation to which C is entitled, although A and B could of course seek contribution against each other or any other employer liable in respect of the same damage in the ordinary way. No argument on apportionment was addressed to the House. I would in conclusion emphasise that my opinion is directed to cases in which each of the conditions specified in (1)–(6) of paragraph 2 above is satisfied and to no other case. . ..

Notes

1. For a discussion of this area, see Jane Stapleton 'Lords a'Leaping Evidentiary Gaps' (2002) 10 Torts LJ 276.

2. *Fairchild* inevitably means that although only one defendant did actually cause the injury, all are liable. The occasions when this is justified are very rare (see at [34] in the above extract). As Lord Nicholls pointed out (at [43]) considerable restraint is called for in any relaxation of the threshold: it certainly does not apply merely because a claimant has difficulty in surmounting the burden of proof. It is a matter of policy—here the point was that all defendants were in breach of their duty to the claimant and it would be unjust if all were exonerated because of the claimant's inability to prove who was the real cause, even though one of the negligent parties evidently did injure the claimant.

3. In *Barker* v *Corus UK Ltd* [2006] UKHL 20, two issues arose which had not in *Fairchild*. In *Barker*, the claimant had three separate exposures to asbestos. The first was for a short period employed by one company, the second for about six months when employed by another company (Corus) and the third was for periods of self-employment. The first employer was insolvent, so if Corus were to be liable for the whole damage, following *Fairchild*, it would not be able to claim a contribution.

   There were two issues. In *Fairchild* each exposure involved a breach of duty. In *Barker* the question arose whether there could be liability on one employer if some of the other exposures were either non-tortious or caused by the claimant. The law lords held that the *Fairchild* rule would still apply, so the employer in breach of duty and who may (or may not) have actually caused the damage would be liable. Lord Hoffmann said:

   > The purpose of the *Fairchild* exception is to provide a cause of action against a defendant who has materially increased the risk that the claimant will suffer damage and may have

caused that damage, but cannot be proved to have done so because it is impossible to show, on a balance of probability, that some other exposure to the same risk may not have caused it instead. For this purpose, it should be irrelevant whether the other exposure was tortious or non-tortious, by natural causes or human agency or by the claimant himself. These distinctions may be relevant to whether and to whom responsibility can also be attributed, but from the point of view of satisfying the requirement of a sufficient causal link between the defendant's conduct and the claimant's injury, they should not matter. (at [17])

The second issue was whether a defendant so held liable could be required to pay for the whole loss or only in proportion to the risk he created (as is the case for material contribution to harm since *Holtby* v *Brigham & Cowan (Hull) Ltd* [2000] 3 All ER 421). Lord Hoffmann said that

the attribution of liability according to the relative degree of contribution to the chance of the disease being contracted would smooth the roughness of the justice which a rule of joint and several liability creates . . . fairness suggests that if more than one person may have been responsible, liability should be divided according to the probability that one or other caused the harm. (at [43])

On the question of how the proportion of risk was to be quantified, Lord Hoffmann said:

It may be that the most practical method of apportionment will be according to the time of exposure for which each defendant is responsible, but allowance may have to be made for the intensity of exposure and the type of asbestos. (at [48])

4. The apportionment effect of *Barker* was reversed by section 3 of the Compensation Act 2006, which provides that where the conditions for applying **Fairchild** are met, each defendant remains liable for the whole loss.

5. The principle has caused much subsequent confusion in the law, which has arguably been rendered incoherent by **Fairchild** and later decisions. In *Equitas Insurance Ltd* v *Municipal Mutual Insurance Ltd* [2019] EWCA Civ 718, Males LJ commented: 'once the courts can be confident that the objective of ensuring victim protection has been achieved, it is desirable that the anomalies should be corrected and that the law should return to the fundamental principles of the common law. Put shortly, once unorthodoxy has served its purpose, we should revert to orthodoxy' (at [91]). Do you agree?

8.1.2 'Lost chance' claims

Here we look at another case where it was argued (ultimately unsuccessfully) that the 'but for' causation rule should be relaxed in favour of the claimant.

Gregg v *Scott*
House of Lords [2005] UKHL 2

The claimant consulted Scott about a lump under his arm, which he (negligently) failed to diagnose as non-Hodgkin's lymphoma (a cancer). The claimant argued that the misdiagnosis had delayed his treatment by nine months. Expert evidence showed that the effect of the delay was to reduce his chances of surviving for more than ten years from 42 per cent to 25 per cent. The defendant argued that even if there had been no delay the probability was that the claimant would not have survived anyway. The claimant tried to succeed on different grounds—that the doctor's negligence had caused him to lose the chance of survival. Held: the defendant was not liable as the claimant was unable to show that on a balance of probabilities he would have been cured had the doctor not been negligent.

LORD HOFFMANN:

Loss of a chance

72. The alternative submission was that reduction in the prospect of a favourable outcome ('loss of a chance') should be a recoverable head of damage. There are certainly cases in which it is. *Chaplin v Hicks* [1911] 2 KB 786 is a well-known example. The question is whether the principle of that case can apply to a case of clinical negligence such as this.

73. The answer can be derived from three cases in the House of Lords: *Hotson v East Berkshire Area Health Authority* [1987] AC 750, *Wilsher v Essex Area Health Authority* [1988] AC 1074 and *Fairchild v Glenhaven Funeral Services Ltd* [2003] 1 AC 32.

74. In *Hotson* the claimant was a boy who broke his hip when he fell out of a tree. The hospital negligently failed to diagnose the fracture for five days. The hip joint was irreparably damaged by the loss of blood supply to its cartilage. The judge found that the rupture of the blood vessels caused by the fall had probably made the damage inevitable but there was a 25% chance that enough had remained intact to save the joint if the fracture had been diagnosed at the time. He and the Court of Appeal awarded the claimant damages for loss of the 25% chance of a favourable outcome.

75. The House of Lords unanimously reversed this decision. They said that the claimant had not lost a chance because, on the finding of fact, nothing could have been done to save the joint. The outcome had been determined by what happened when he fell out of the tree. Either he had enough surviving blood vessels or he did not. That question had to be decided on a balance of probability and had been decided adversely to the claimant.

76. In *Wilsher* a junior doctor in a special care baby unit negligently put a catheter in the wrong place so that a monitor failed to register that a premature baby was receiving too much oxygen. The baby suffered rentrolental [sic] fibroplasia ('RLF'), a condition of the eyes which resulted in blindness. The excessive oxygen was a possible cause of the condition and had increased the chances that it would develop but there were other possible causes: statistics showed a correlation between RLF and various conditions present in the Wilsher baby. But the causal mechanism linking them to RLF was unknown.

77. The Court of Appeal awarded damages for the reduction in the chance of a favourable outcome. Again this was reversed by the House of Lords. The baby's RLF was caused by lack of oxygen or by something else or a combination of causes. The defendant was liable only if the lack of oxygen caused or substantially contributed to the injury. That had to be proved on a balance of probability.

78. In *Fairchild*, the claimant had contracted mesothelioma by exposure to asbestos. The medical evidence was that the condition was probably the result of a cell mutation caused by a single fibre. The claimant had worked with asbestos for more than one employer and could not prove whose fibre had caused his disease. The Court of Appeal said that the cause of the disease was not indeterminate. It had either been caused by the defendant's fibre or it had not. It was for the claimant to prove causation on a balance of probability. The House of Lords accepted that the disease had a determinate cause in one fibre or other but constructed a special rule imposing liability for conduct which only increased the chances of the employee contracting the disease. That rule was restrictively defined in terms which make it inapplicable in this case.

79. What these cases show is that, as Helen Reece points out in an illuminating article ('Losses of Chances in the Law' (1996) 59 MLR 188) the law regards the world as in principle bound by laws of causality. Everything has a determinate cause, even if we do not know what it is. The blood-starved hip joint in *Hotson*, the blindness in *Wilsher*, the mesothelioma in *Fairchild*; each had its cause and it was for the plaintiff to prove that it was an act or omission for which the defendant was responsible.

The narrow terms of the exception made to this principle in *Fairchild* only serves to emphasise the strength of the rule. The fact that proof is rendered difficult or impossible because no examination was made at the time, as in *Hotson*, or because medical science cannot provide the answer, as in *Wilsher*, makes no difference. There is no inherent uncertainty about what caused something to happen in the past or about whether something which happened in the past will cause something to happen in the future. Everything is determined by causality. What we lack is knowledge and the law deals with lack of knowledge by the concept of the burden of proof.

80. Similarly in the present case, the progress of Mr Gregg's disease had a determinate cause. It may have been inherent in his genetic make-up at the time when he saw Mr Scott, as Hotson's fate was determined by what happened to his thigh when he fell out of the tree. Or it may, as Mance LJ suggests, have been affected by subsequent events and behaviour for which Dr Scott was not responsible. Medical science does not enable us to say. But the outcome was not random; it was governed by laws of causality and, in the absence of a special rule as in *Fairchild*, inability to establish that delay in diagnosis caused the reduction in expectation in life cannot be remedied by treating the outcome as having been somehow indeterminate.

81. This was the view of the Supreme Court of Canada in *Laferrière v Lawson* (1991) 78 DLR (4th) 609, a case very like the present. A doctor negligently failed in 1971 to tell a patient that a biopsy had revealed a lump in her breast to be cancerous. She first learned of the cancer in 1975, when the cancer had spread to other parts of the body and she died in 1978 at the age of 56. The judge found that earlier treatment would have increased the chances of a favourable outcome but was not satisfied on a balance of probability that it would have prolonged her life. Gonthier J said that although the progress of the cancer was not fully understood, the outcome was determined. It was either something capable of successful treatment or it was not.

> Even though our understanding of medical matters is often limited, I am not prepared to conclude that particular medical conditions should be treated for purposes of causation as the equivalent of diffuse elements of pure chance, analogous to the non-specific factors of fate or fortune which influence the outcome of a lottery. (p 656)

82. One striking exception to the assumption that everything is determined by impersonal laws of causality is the actions of human beings. The law treats human beings as having free will and the ability to choose between different courses of action, however strong may be the reasons for them to choose one course rather than another. This may provide part of the explanation for why in some cases damages are awarded for the loss of a chance of gaining an advantage or avoiding a disadvantage which depends upon the independent action of another person: see *Allied Maples Group Ltd v Simmons & Simmons* [1995] 1 WLR 1602 and the cases there cited.

83. But the true basis of these cases is a good deal more complex. The fact that one cannot prove as a matter of necessary causation that someone would have done something is no reason why one should not prove that he was more likely than not to have done it. So, for example, the law distinguishes between cases in which the outcome depends upon what the claimant himself (*McWilliams v Sir William Arrol & Co* [1962] 1 WLR 295) or someone for whom the defendant is responsible (*Bolitho v City and Hackney Health Authority* [1998] AC 232) would have done, and cases in which it depends upon what some third party would have done. In the first class of cases the claimant must prove on a balance of probability that he or the defendant would have acted so as to produce a favourable outcome. In the latter class, he may recover for loss of the chance that the third party would have so acted. This apparently arbitrary distinction obviously rests on grounds of policy. In addition, most of the cases in which there has been recovery for loss of a chance have involved

financial loss, where the chance can itself plausibly be characterised as an item of property, like a lottery ticket. It is however unnecessary to discuss these decisions because they obviously do not cover the present case.

84. . . . In the present case it is urged that Mr Gregg has suffered a wrong and ought to have a remedy. Living for more than 10 years is something of great value to him and he should be compensated for the possibility that the delay in diagnosis may have reduced his chances of doing so. In effect, the appellant submits that the exceptional rule in *Fairchild* should be generalised and damages awarded in all cases in which the defendant may have caused an injury and has increased the likelihood of the injury being suffered. In the present case, it is alleged that Dr Scott may have caused a reduction in Mr Gregg's expectation of life and that he increased the likelihood that his life would be shortened by the disease.

85. It should first be noted that adopting such a rule would involve abandoning a good deal of authority. The rule which the House is asked to adopt is the very rule which it rejected in *Wilsher*'s case [1988] AC 1074. Yet *Wilsher*'s case was expressly approved by the House in *Fairchild* [2003] 1 AC 32. *Hotson* [1987] AC 750 too would have to be overruled. Furthermore, the House would be dismantling all the qualifications and restrictions with which it so recently hedged the *Fairchild* exception. There seem to me to be no new arguments or change of circumstances which could justify such a radical departure from precedent.

Notes

1. Lord Nicholls dissented (as did Lord Hope), accepting the 'loss of a chance' argument. He said:

   In order to achieve a just result in such cases the law defines the claimant's actionable damage more narrowly by reference to the *opportunity* the claimant lost, rather than by reference to the loss of the desired *outcome* which was never within his control. In adopting this approach the law does not depart from the principle that the claimant must prove actionable damage on the balance of probability. The law adheres to this principle but defines actionable damage in different, more appropriate terms. The law treats the claimant's loss of his opportunity or chance as itself actionable damage. The claimant must prove this loss on balance of probability. The court will then measure this loss as best it may. (at [17])

2. For a comment on this case, see Jane Stapleton 'Loss of a Chance of Cure from Cancer' (2005) 68 MLR 996.

8.2 Remoteness of damage

Even if the defendant's act caused the damage, liability can still be excluded if the damage was too remote; that is, if the *kind* of damage was an unforeseeable consequence of the act.

One problem is the relationship between this concept and duty of care, for some cases can be decided by application of either concept (e.g. *Tremain* v *Pike* [1969] 3 All ER 1303), and a number of economic loss and psychiatric harm cases were once regarded as remoteness cases, whereas now they are seen as raising duty issues. One way to illustrate the difference is by the facts (but not the decision) in *Smith* v *London South Western Rly* (1870) LR 6 CP 14. The defendant's employees had cut some hedge trimmings which were laid in heaps alongside a railway line, and a passing train set fire to one of the heaps. The fire spread across a stubble field 200 yards wide, across a road, and finally burnt the claimant's cottage. If we assume that the fire at the cottage was unforeseeable, for example because the road would have acted as a firebreak, the position is this: if the claimant did *not* own the field there is no liability because no duty was owed to him since he was not a foreseeable claimant, having no property that was likely to be damaged. But if he *did* own the field he becomes a foreseeable claimant, and the question becomes one of remoteness: for how much damage can he recover?

Polemis and Furness, Withy & Co Ltd, Re (Re Polemis)
Court of Appeal [1921] 3 KB 560

Polemis chartered a ship to Furness, Withy & Co. Its cargo included a number of drums of petrol, some of which leaked into the hold. Some stevedores negligently dislodged a plank which fell into the hold, causing a spark which ignited the petrol vapour. A fire started, which ultimately destroyed the ship. The arbitrators found that 'the causing of the spark could not reasonably have been anticipated from the falling of the board, though some damage to the ship might reasonably have been anticipated'. Held: the charterers (as employers of the stevedores) were liable.

BANKES LJ: In the present case the arbitrators have found as a fact that the falling of the plank was due to the negligence of the defendants' servants. The fire appears to me to have been directly caused by the falling of the plank. Under these circumstances I consider that it is immaterial that the causing of the spark by the falling of the plank could not have been reasonably anticipated. The appellants' junior counsel sought to draw a distinction between the anticipation of the extent of damage resulting from a negligent act, and the anticipation of the type of damage resulting from such an act. He admitted that it could not lie in the mouth of a person whose negligent act had caused damage to say that he could not reasonably have foreseen the extent of the damage, but he contended that the negligent person was entitled to rely upon the fact that he could not reasonably have anticipated the type of damage which resulted from his negligent act. I do not think that the distinction can be admitted. Given the breach of duty which constitutes the negligence, and given the damage as a direct result of that negligence, the anticipations of the person whose negligent act has produced the damage appear to me to be irrelevant. I consider that the damages claimed are not too remote . . .

SCRUTTON LJ: The second defence is that the damage is too remote from the negligence, as it could not be reasonably foreseen as a consequence. On this head we were referred to a number of well known cases in which vague language, which I cannot think to be really helpful, has been used in an attempt to define the point at which damage becomes too remote from, or not sufficiently directly caused by, the breach of duty, which is the original cause of action, to be recoverable. For instance, I cannot think it useful to say the damage must be the natural and probable result. This suggests that there are results which are natural but not probable, and other results which are probable but not natural. I am not sure what either adjective means in this connection; if they mean the same thing, two need not be used; if they mean different things, the difference between them should be defined. And as to many cases of fact in which the distinction has been drawn, it is difficult to see why one case should be decided one way and one another . . . To determine whether an act is negligent, it is relevant to determine whether any reasonable person would foresee that the act would cause damage; if he would not, the act is not negligent. But if the act would or might probably cause damage, the fact that the damage it in fact causes is not the exact kind of damage one would expect is immaterial, so long as the damage is in fact directly traceable to the negligent act, and not due to the operation of independent causes having no connection with the negligent act, except that they could not avoid its results. Once the act is negligent, the fact that its exact operation was not foreseen is immaterial. . . . In the present case it was negligent in discharging cargo to knock down the planks of the temporary staging, for they might easily cause some damage either to workmen, or cargo, or the ship. The fact that they did directly produce an unexpected result, a spark in an atmosphere of petrol vapour which caused a fire, does not relieve the person who was negligent from the damage which his negligent act directly caused.

Notes

1. This case is no longer regarded as good law following the decision in *The Wagon Mound (No 1)*, in the following extract, but it is useful to know because of the extensive debate on the subject of remoteness and the various tests which have been adopted. For a discussion of the *Polemis* rule, see Martin Davies 'The Road from Morocco' (1982) 45 MLR 534.

2. The test required *some* damage to be foreseeable and to have actually occurred, for otherwise there would be no duty or breach of duty. Thus, the charterers were at least liable for the dent in the steel plating in the hold when the plank fell, but the question was whether they were liable for more. It would not have applied if the claimants had suffered no foreseeable damage at all.

Overseas Tankship (UK) Ltd v *Morts Dock and Engineering Co (The Wagon Mound) (No 1)*
Privy Council [1961] AC 388

The defendants were charterers of *The Wagon Mound*, which was moored at a wharf in Sydney Harbour. They negligently allowed some oil to spill into the harbour and some of this drifted to another wharf, owned by the claimants. The manager of the claimants' wharf asked whether it was safe to continue welding operations and was told that the flammability of oil in seawater was very low. However, later that day a fire broke out at the wharf, apparently caused by molten metal from the welding falling on some cotton waste lying on a piece of floating debris, which ignited and set fire to the surrounding oil. The claimants suffered loss caused by the oil congealing on their slipways, as well as fire damage. The trial judge found that the defendant could not reasonably be expected to have known that the oil was capable of burning when spread on water and therefore the defendants were liable only for the slipway damage caused by the oil. The Privy Council agreed, finding that the fire damage was not reasonably foreseeable.

VISCOUNT SIMONDS: Enough has been said to show that the authority of *Polemis* has been severely shaken though lip-service has from time to time been paid to it. In their Lordships' opinion it should no longer be regarded as good law. It is not probable that many cases will for that reason have a different result, though it is hoped that the law will be thereby simplified, and that in some cases, at least, palpable injustice will be avoided. For it does not seem consonant with current ideas of justice or morality that for an act of negligence, however slight or venial, which results in some trivial foreseeable damage the actor should be liable for all consequences however unforeseeable and however grave, so long as they can be said to be 'direct.' It is a principle of civil liability, subject only to qualifications which have no present relevance that a man must be considered to be responsible for the probable consequences of his act. To demand more of him is too harsh a rule, to demand less is to ignore that civilised order requires the observance of a minimum standard of behaviour.

This concept applied to the slowly developing law of negligence has led to a great variety of expressions which can, as it appears to their Lordships, be harmonised with little difficulty with the single exception of the so-called rule in *Polemis*. For, if it is asked why a man should be responsible for the natural or necessary or probable consequences of his act (or any other similar description of them) the answer is that it is not because they are natural or necessary or probable, but because, since they have this quality, it is judged by the standard of the reasonable man that he ought to have foreseen them. Thus it is that over and over again it has happened that in different judgments in the same case, and sometimes in a single judgment, liability for a consequence has been imposed on the ground that it was reasonably foreseeable or, alternatively, on the ground that it was natural or necessary or probable. The two grounds have been treated as conterminous, and so they largely are. But, where they are not, the question arises to which the wrong answer was given in *Polemis*. For, if some limitation must be imposed upon the consequences for which the negligent actor is to be held responsible—and all are agreed that some limitation there must be—why should that test (reasonable foreseeability) be rejected which, since he is judged by what the reasonable man ought to foresee, corresponds with the common conscience of mankind, and a test (the 'direct' conse-quence) be substituted which leads to nowhere but the never-ending and insoluble problems of cau-sation. 'The lawyer,' said Sir Frederick Pollock, 'cannot afford to adventure himself with philosophers in the logical and metaphysical controversies that beset the idea of cause.' Yet this is just what he has most unfortunately done and must continue to do if the rule in *Polemis* is to prevail. A conspicuous example occurs when the actor seeks to escape liability on the ground that the 'chain of causation' is broken by a '*nova causa*' or '*novus actus interveniens*.' . . .

It is, no doubt, proper when considering tortious liability for negligence to analyse its elements and to say that the plaintiff must prove a duty owed to him by the defendant, a breach of that duty by the defendant, and consequent damage. But there can be no liability until the damage has been done. It is not the act but the consequences on which tortious liability is founded. Just as (as it has been said) there is no such thing as negligence in the air, so there is no such thing as liability in the air. Suppose an action brought by A for damage caused by the carelessness (a neutral word) of B, for example, a fire caused by the careless spillage of oil. It may, of course, become relevant to know what duty B owed to A, but the only liability that is in question is the liability for damage by fire. It is vain to isolate the liability from its context and to say that B is or is not liable, and then to ask for what damage he is liable. For his liability is in respect of that damage and no other. If, as admittedly it is, B's liability (culpability) depends on the reasonable foreseeability of the consequent damage, how is that to be determined except by the foreseeability of the damage which in fact happened—the damage in suit? And, if that damage is unforeseeable so as to displace liability at large, how can the liability be restored so as to make compensation payable?

But, it is said, a different position arises if B's careless act has been shown to be negligent and has caused some foreseeable damage to A. Their Lordships have already observed that to hold B liable for consequences however unforeseeable of a careless act, if, but only if, he is at the same time liable for some other damage however trivial, appears to be neither logical nor just. This be-comes more clear if it is supposed that similar unforeseeable damage is suffered by A and C but other foreseeable damage, for which B is liable, by A only. A system of law which would hold B liable to A but not to C for the similar damage suffered by each of them could not easily be defended. Fortunately, the attempt is not necessary. For the same fallacy is at the root of the proposition. It is irrelevant to the question whether B is liable for unforeseeable damage that he is liable for foreseeable damage, as irrelevant as would the fact that he had trespassed on Whiteacre be to the question whether he has trespassed on Blackacre. Again, suppose a claim by A for damage by fire by the careless act of B. Of what relevance is it to that claim that he has another claim arising out of the same careless act? It would surely not prejudice his claim if that other claim failed: it cannot assist it if it succeeds. Each of them rests on its own bottom, and will fail if it can be established that the damage could not reasonably be foreseen. We have come back to the plain common sense stated by Lord Russell of Killowen in *Bourhill v Young* [1943] AC 92, 101. As Denning LJ said in *King v Phillips* [1953] 1 QB 429: 'there can be no doubt since *Bourhill v Young* that the test of *liability for shock* is foreseeability of *injury by shock*.' Their Lordships substitute the word 'fire' for 'shock' and endorse this statement of the law.

Notes

1. For a discussion of this case, see Marc Stauch 'Risk and Remoteness of Damage in Negligence' (2001) 64 MLR 191.

2. In *The Wagon Mound (No 2)*, heard later, evidence showed that it was *possible* (though still unlikely) for the oil to have ignited in these circumstances. Therefore, the issue became one of breach—as the damage was now foreseeable, would a reasonable person have taken steps to prevent it? (See section 7.3.1.)

3. The reason for the different evidence and findings of fact between the two Wagon Mound cases may be that when *The Wagon Mound (No 1)* was decided the contributory negligence rules in New South Wales meant that if a claimant was contributorily negligent at all the claimant lost their case *entirely* (note: this changed with the Law Reform (Contributory Negligence) Act 1945, see section 9.3). Naturally, therefore, the claimants would have been wary of saying that the fire was foreseeable. By the time of *The Wagon Mound (No 2)* the rules had changed, so that in a case of contributory negligence the damages could be apportioned between the parties, thus providing less risk to the claimant.

8.2.1 The 'egg shell skull' rule

The Wagon Mound (No 1) changed the theory of remoteness of damage, but did it make any practical difference? One area where this question arose was the so-called 'egg shell skull' rule, whereby, in personal injury cases at least, you take your victims as you find them—that is, if the claimant has a 'thin skull' and therefore suffers greater damage than might be expected, a defendant is liable for the whole loss and not just for the damage which might have been expected to occur to a 'normal' person.

> *Robinson v Post Office*
> Court of Appeal [1974] 1 WLR 1176

The claimant slipped on an oily ladder and cut his shin. He went to a doctor who gave him an anti-tetanus injection. The claimant was allergic to the serum and contracted encephalitis. Held: the defendants were liable for the entire damage.

ORR LJ: Mr Newey's main argument, however, was that the onset of encephalitis was not reasonably foreseeable and that on the basis of the decision of the Privy Council in *Overseas Tankship (UK) Ltd v Morts Dock and Engineering Co Ltd (The Wagon Mound)* [1961] AC 388, the Post Office should not be held liable for that consequence of the injury. In answer to this argument the plaintiff relied on the judgment of Lord Parker C J in *Smith v Leech Brain & Co Ltd* [1962] 2 QB 405. In that case an employee already suffering from premalignant changes had, as a result of his employers' negligence, sustained a burn which the judge found to have been the promoting agent in the development of cancer from which the employee died, and in a fatal accident claim by his widow it was argued for the defendant employers that the development of cancer was unforeseeable and that on the basis of *The Wagon Mound* decision the claim should be dismissed. Lord Parker CJ, however, rejected this argument in the following passages from his judgment, at pp 414–415, which are quoted in the judgment now under appeal:

> For my part, I am quite satisfied that the Judicial Committee in *The Wagon Mound* case did not have what I may call, loosely, the thin-skull cases in mind. It has always been the law of this country that a tortfeasor takes his victim as he finds him . . . The test is not whether these employers could reasonably have foreseen that a burn would cause cancer and that he would die. The question is whether these employers could reasonably foresee the type of injury he suffered, namely, the burn. What, in the particular case, is the amount of damage which he suffers as a result of that burn, depends upon the characteristics and constitution of the victim.

It is to be noted, as pointed out in the judgment under appeal, that the last of these passages is supported by very similar language used by Lord Reid in the later case of *Hughes v Lord Advocate* [1963] AC 837, 845.

On this appeal Mr Newey did not challenge the correctness of Lord Parker CJ's reasoning and conclusion in the *Leech Brain* case and accepted that some at least of the subsequent decisions fell within the same principle, but he claimed that an essential link which was missing in the present case was that it was not foreseeable that administration of a form of anti-tetanus prophylaxis would itself give rise to a rare serious illness. In our judgment, however, there was no missing link and the case is governed by the principle that the Post Office had to take their victim as they found him, in this case with an allergy to a second dose of ATS [anti-tetanus serum] . . . In our judgment the principle that a defendant must take the plaintiff as he finds him involves that if a wrongdoer ought reasonably to foresee that as a result of his wrongful act the victim may require medical treatment he is, subject to the principle of *novus actus interveniens*, liable for the consequences of the treatment applied although he could not reasonably foresee those consequences or that they could be serious.

Notes

1. *Robinson* v *Post Office* is also a good example of the application of the 'but for' test of causation. The claimant also sued the doctor. When the claimant saw the doctor he was given a test to see if there would be an adverse reaction to the serum. The doctor was supposed to wait half an hour, but in fact waited only half a minute to see if there was a reaction. Thus, although negligent, the doctor was not liable because the reaction did not become apparent for nine days. The test, even if performed properly, would have made no difference.

8.2.2 The kind of damage

In *The Wagon Mound (No 1)* Viscount Simonds said that 'the essential factor in determining liability is whether the damage is of such a kind as the reasonable man should have foreseen'. Obviously, the answer to such a question will depend on how broadly the 'kind of damage' is interpreted.

> ### Hughes v Lord Advocate
> House of Lords [1963] AC 837

Post Office employees had erected a shelter tent over a utility hole where they were working. They left the tent unattended, but surrounded by four red paraffin lamps, one at each corner, and removed the ladder from the hole. A boy picked up one of the paraffin lamps and took it and the ladder into the shelter to go into the hole. The lamp was knocked over and there was an explosion, causing flames to reach 30 feet. The boy fell back into the hole and was badly burnt. The question for the court was whether this was so unlikely as to be unforeseeable. Held: the defendant was liable.

LORD REID: This accident was caused by a known source of danger, but caused in a way which could not have been foreseen, and, in my judgment, that affords no defence. I would therefore allow the appeal.

LORD JENKINS: It is true that the duty of care expected in cases of this sort is confined to reasonably foreseeable dangers, but it does not necessarily follow that liability is escaped because the danger actually materialising is not identical with the danger reasonably foreseen and guarded against. Each case much depends on its own particular facts. For example (as pointed out in the opinions), in the present case the paraffin did the mischief by exploding, not burning, and it is said that while a paraffin fire (caused, for example, by the upsetting of the lighted lamp or otherwise allowing its contents to leak out) was a reasonably foreseeable risk so soon as the pursuer got access to the lamp, an explosion was not.

　To my mind, the distinction drawn between burning and explosion is too fine to warrant acceptance. Supposing the pursuer had on the day in question gone to the site and taken one of the lamps, and upset it over himself, thus setting his clothes alight, the person to be considered responsible for protecting children from the dangers to be found there would presumably have been liable. On the other hand, if the lamp, when the boy upset it, exploded in his face, he would have had no remedy because the explosion was an event which could not reasonably be foreseen. This does not seem to me to be right.

LORD MORRIS: My Lords, in my view, there was a duty owed by the defenders to safeguard the pursuer against the type or kind of occurrence which in fact happened and which resulted in his injuries, and the defenders are not absolved from liability because they did not envisage 'the precise concatenation of circumstances which led up to the accident.' . . .

LORD GUEST: In dismissing the appellant's claim the Lord Ordinary and the majority of the judges of the First Division reached the conclusion that the accident which happened was not reasonably foreseeable. In order to establish a coherent chain of causation it is not necessary that the precise details leading up to the accident should have been reasonably foreseeable; it is sufficient if the accident which occurred is of a type which should have been foreseeable by a reasonably careful person . . . or as Lord Mackintosh expressed it in the *Harvey* case, 1960 SC 155, the precise concatenation of circumstances need not be envisaged. Concentration has been placed in the courts below on the explosion which, it was said, could not have been foreseen because it was caused in a unique fashion by the paraffin forming into vapour and being ignited by the naked flame of the wick. But this, in my opinion, is to concentrate on what is really a non-essential element in the dangerous situation created by the allurement. The test might better be put thus: Was the igniting of paraffin outside the lamp by the flame a foreseeable consequence of the breach of duty? In the circumstances, there was a combination of potentially dangerous circumstances against which the Post Office had to protect the appellant. If these formed an allurement to children it might have been foreseen that they would play with the lamp, that it might tip over, that it might be broken, and that when broken the paraffin might spill and be ignited by the flame. All these steps in the chain of causation seem to have been accepted by all the judges in the courts below as foreseeable. But because the explosion was the agent which caused the burning and was unforeseeable, therefore the accident, according to them, was not reasonably foreseeable. In my opinion, this reasoning is fallacious. An explosion is only one way in which burning can be caused. Burning can also be caused by the contact between liquid paraffin and a naked flame. In the one case paraffin vapour and in the other case liquid paraffin is ignited by fire. I cannot see that these are two different types of accident. They are both burning accidents and in both cases the injuries would be burning injuries. Upon this view the explosion was an immaterial event in the chain of causation. It was simply one way in which burning might be caused by the potentially dangerous paraffin lamp. . . .

LORD PEARCE: The obvious risks were burning and conflagration and a fall. All these in fact occurred, but unexpectedly the mishandled lamp instead of causing an ordinary conflagration produced a violent explosion. Did the explosion create an accident and damage of a different type from the misadventure and damage that could be foreseen? In my judgment it did not. The accident was but a variant of the foreseeable.

Notes

1. *Hughes* raises interesting questions as to what needs to be foreseeable:
    (a) Damage by paraffin—in which case would the defendants have been liable if the boys had drunk the paraffin?
    (b) Damage by lamp—in which case would the defendants have been liable if the claimant had dropped the lamp on his foot?
    (c) Damage by burning—how was the claimant supposed to have burnt himself? If it is supposed that there was a risk that the boy might touch the lamp and burn himself (how badly?), is that a variant of being sucked into the hole by an unforeseeable explosion?

2. **Hughes** is not inconsistent with the theory in **The Wagon Mound (No 1)**; that is, that remoteness should be tested by probability rather than by cause—nevertheless, it is based on probability of result rather than probability of the method of bringing about the result.

3. In **Jolley v Sutton London Borough Council** [2000] 3 All ER 409, an old boat had been left for some time on land belonging to the defendants. The claimant (aged 14) and a friend decided to try to repair it and raised it up by using a jack. About six weeks later the boat collapsed, injuring the claimant who was underneath it. The Court of Appeal found that the defendants were not liable as even though interference by children was foreseeable, it was not foreseeable that a child would try to jack the boat up. They said that this was not a foreseeable kind of *accident* and **Hughes** was distinguished. However, the House of Lords held the defendants liable saying that the appropriate risk was that of children meddling with the boat and being harmed and that risk had materialised.

4. In *Tremain* v *Pike* [1969] 3 All ER 1303, the defendant operated a farm which was infested by rats. The claimant, a herdsman employed by the defendant, contracted a rare disease, Weil's disease, from contact with rats' urine. Payne J held that this was different from foreseeable damage such as injury by rat bites, and therefore it was too remote. Injury by rat bites is foreseeable; injury by rats' urine is not. But if the test was injury by rats the result might have been different.

5. It seems, therefore, that it is foreseeability of the *type* of damage, not the *extent* or the exact way in which it was caused, that must be foreseeable. This has been confirmed by the Court of Appeal in **Conarken Group Ltd v Network Rail Infrastructure Ltd** [2011] EWCA Civ 644, *Taylor* v *Chief Constable of Hampshire Police* [2013] EWCA Civ 496 and most recently in *Goldscheider* v *Royal Opera House Covent Garden Foundation* [2019] EWCA Civ 711.

> ### Doughty v Turner Manufacturing Co
> Court of Appeal [1964] 1 QB 518

The defendants had two cauldrons containing sodium cyanide powder, which became liquid when heated to 800°C. Each cauldron had a cover made of an asbestos compound. What was not known was that the compound, when heated above 500°C underwent a chemical change and emitted steam. Due to negligence, one of the covers slid into the liquid, which then erupted, injuring the claimant who was standing nearby. Held: the defendants were not liable.

HARMAN LJ: The plaintiff's argument most persuasively urged by Mr James rested, as I understood it, on admissions made that, if this lid had been dropped into the cauldron with sufficient force to cause the molten material to splash over the edge, that would have been an act of negligence or carelessness for which the defendants might be vicariously responsible. Reliance was put upon **Hughes v Lord Advocate** [1963] AC 837, where the exact consequences of the lamp overturning were not foreseen, but it was foreseeable that, if the manhole were left unguarded, boys would enter and tamper with the lamp, and it was not unlikely that serious burns might ensue for the boys. Their Lordships' House distinguished **The Wagon Mound** case [1961] AC 388 on the ground that the damage which ensued, though differing in degree, was the same in kind as that which was foreseeable. So it is said here that a splash causing burns was foreseeable and that this explosion was really only a magnified splash which also caused burns and that, therefore, we ought to follow **Hughes v Lord Advocate** and hold the defendants liable. I cannot accept this. In my opinion, the damage here was of an entirely different kind from the foreseeable splash.

Indeed, the evidence showed that any disturbance of the material resulting from the immersion of the hard-board was past an appreciable time before the explosion happened. This latter was caused by the disintegration of the hard-board under the great heat to which it was subjected and the consequent release of the moisture enclosed within it. This had nothing to do with the agitation caused by the dropping of the board into the cyanide. I am of opinion that it would be wrong on these facts to make another inroad on the doctrine of foreseeability which seems to me to be a satisfactory solvent of this type of difficulty.

Notes

1. If an explosion is a variant of fire, why is an eruption not a variant of a splash?
2. A better solution to this case is that taken by Diplock LJ, and is based on duty. The foreseeable risk was burning people by splashing if the cover was dropped from a height into the bath. However, as the chemical change in the cover was unknown, there was no duty to prevent the cover being *in* the bath: thus, if the cover slides in gently, the defendants are not in breach of any duty. Note also that if the claimant had been outside the range of potential splashing (said to be about one foot) he would have been an unforeseeable claimant anyway.

Corr v IBC Vehicles
House of Lords [2008] UKHL 13

The claimant's husband suffered severe head injuries in June 1996 due to the negligence of the defendant employers. As a result of his injury he became severely depressed and in May 2002 (almost six years after the accident) he committed suicide. Held: the defendants were liable for financial losses attributable to the claimant's suicide.

LORD BINGHAM:

The foreseeability issue

11. . . . [I]t is now accepted that there can be no recovery for damage which was not reasonably foreseeable. This appeal does not invite consideration of the corollary that damage may be irrecoverable although reasonably foreseeable. It is accepted for present purposes that foreseeability is to be judged by the standards of the reasonable employer, as of the date of the accident and with reference to the very accident which occurred, but with reference not to the actual victim but to a hypothetical employee. In this way effect is given to the principle that the tortfeasor must take his victim as he finds him. Mr Cousins submits that while psychological trauma and depression were a foreseeable result of the accident (and thus of the employer's breach), Mr Corr's conduct in taking his own life was not.

13. I have some sympathy with the feeling, expressed by Ward LJ in paragraph 61 of his judgment, that 'suicide does make a difference'. It is a feeling which perhaps derives from recognition of the finality and irrevocability of suicide, possibly fortified by religious prohibition of self-slaughter and recognition that suicide was, until relatively recently, a crime. But a feeling of this kind cannot absolve the court from the duty of applying established principles to the facts of the case before it. Here, the inescapable fact is that depression, possibly severe, possibly very severe, was a foreseeable consequence of this breach. The Court of Appeal majority were right to uphold the claimant's submission that it was not incumbent on her to show that suicide itself was foreseeable. But, as Lord

Pearce observed in *Hughes v Lord Advocate* [1963] AC 837, 857, 'to demand too great precision in the test of foreseeability would be unfair to the pursuer since the facets of misadventure are innumerable'. That was factually a very different case from the present, but the principle that a tortfeasor who reasonably foresees the occurrence of some damage need not foresee the precise form which the damage may take in my view applies. I can readily accept that some manifestations of severe depression could properly be held to be so unusual and unpredictable as to be outside the bounds of what is reasonably foreseeable, but suicide cannot be so regarded. While it is not, happily, a usual manifestation, it is one that, as Sedley LJ put it, is not uncommon. That is enough for the claimant to succeed. But if it were necessary for the claimant in this case to have established the reasonable foreseeability by the employer of suicide, I think the employer would have had difficulty escaping an adverse finding: considering the possible effect of this accident on a hypothetical employee, a reasonable employer would, I think, have recognised the possibility not only of acute depression but also of such depression culminating in a way in which, in a significant minority of cases, it unhappily does.

The *novus actus* issue

15. The rationale of the principle that a *novus actus interveniens* breaks the chain of causation is fairness. It is not fair to hold a tortfeasor liable, however gross his breach of duty may be, for damage caused to the claimant not by the tortfeasor's breach of duty but by some independent, supervening cause (which may or may not be tortious) for which the tortfeasor is not responsible. This is not the less so where the independent, supervening cause is a voluntary, informed decision taken by the victim as an adult of sound mind making and giving effect to a personal decision about his own future. Thus I respectfully think that the British Columbia Court of Appeal (McEachern CJBC, Legg and Hollinrake JJA) were right to hold that the suicide of a road accident victim was a *novus actus* in the light of its conclusion that when the victim took her life 'she made a conscious decision, there being no evidence of disabling mental illness to lead to the conclusion that she had an incapacity in her faculty of volition': *Wright v Davidson* (1992) 88 DLR (4th) 698, 705. In such circumstances it is usual to describe the chain of causation being broken but it is perhaps equally accurate to say that the victim's independent act forms no part of a chain of causation beginning with the tortfeasor's breach of duty.

16. In the present case Mr Corr's suicide was not a voluntary, informed decision taken by him as an adult of sound mind making and giving effect to a personal decision about his future. It was the response of a man suffering from a severely depressive illness which impaired his capacity to make reasoned and informed judgments about his future, such illness being, as is accepted, a consequence of the employer's tort. It is in no way unfair to hold the employer responsible for this dire consequence of its breach of duty, although it could well be thought unfair to the victim not to do so.

Notes

1. *Corr v IBC* is another example of how remoteness and causation rarely act as a break on recovery in personal injury actions once a breach of duty relating to *some* damage has been established. Nevertheless, one must beware of the incremental problem. Lord Bingham stressed that the test of substantive liability is whether *at the time of the accident* a reasonable employer could reasonably have foreseen the kind of consequences. Lord Neuberger said, 'I accept that it can often be dangerous to deduce that, if each step in a chain was foreseeable from the immediately preceding step, then the final step must have been foreseeable from the start'. However, he continued,

'nonetheless, once it is accepted that Mr Corr's severe depression is properly the liability of the employer, I find it hard to see why . . . Mr Corr's suicide should not equally be the liability of the employer. It is notorious that severely depressed people not infrequently try to kill themselves: indeed, the evidence before us suggests that the chances are higher than 10%' (at [56]). Thus the argument seems to be that depression is a foreseeable result of physical injury and suicide is a common consequence of depression, and hence not too remote.

2. The defendants also argued that Corr should be held partially responsible for his act, thus allowing for the reduction of his damages by way of contributory negligence. In the event the House of Lords did not reduce the damages, but Lords Scott, Mance and Neuberger thought it might be appropriate if the person's mind was not wholly impaired, and they thought the issue was one of degrees of responsibility for one's own actions.

9

Defences to negligence

Even if the elements of a claim in negligence are established, the defendant may be able to raise a defence. This may work to defeat the claim entirely or simply reduce the amount of damages payable. What the defendant is effectively saying is 'though I did carelessly injure the claimant, there is nonetheless a good reason why the law should not hold me responsible'. The defendant might, for example, argue that the claimant had voluntarily accepted the risk occurring (*volenti non fit injuria*) or that an award of damages would be inappropriate on the basis that the claimant was injured while they were engaged in an illegal, or inherently risky, activity (illegality). Alternatively, they may argue that the claimant was partly to blame for their injuries (contributory negligence).

9.1 Voluntarily assuming the risk

The defence of *volenti non fit injuria* provides a complete defence to an action. The defence is based on the view that a person cannot sue if she *consents* to the risk of damage. Typically the case law refers to 'consent' in the context of intentional torts and '*volenti*' or voluntary assumption of risk in relation to negligence. The defence can arise in two ways. First, where the claimant consents to the specific harm caused by the defendant and (sometimes) where they have consented to the risk of that harm. Secondly, where the claimant consents (or, at least, is *to be treated as* consenting) to the defendant excluding their liability for any injuries they may cause—most straightforwardly in cases of occupier's liability. While an occupier owes a duty of care to those they allow onto their premises, they may limit or avoid liability associated with this by putting up a notice along the lines that they 'exclude liability for any injuries visitors may suffer on the premises'. Here the claimant's consent is not to any particular factual harm or danger but rather to the defendant's exclusion or waiver of liability. The claimant is effectively saying not 'I accept that what I am doing is dangerous' but rather 'I accept that I cannot sue you if I end up injured'. If a visitor sees such a notice and enters the premises nonetheless—or indeed even if they do not see it but the occupier is held to have taken 'reasonable steps' to bring it to the visitor's attention—their claim for any injuries they then suffer (subject to the provisions of the Unfair Contract Terms Act 1977) will be defeated (see Occupiers' Liability Act 1957, s 2(1); **White Lion Hotel v James** [2021] EWCA Civ 31). We shall look at this in more detail in Chapter 10, for now we shall concentrate on the first application of the defence.

9.1.1 Consent to a specific harm

In order for the defence to be established the defendant must show that the claimant either agreed to, or voluntarily took the risk of, the specific harm that materialised. The test is a subjective one; it is not enough that a reasonable person might have been aware of the risk—the particular claimant must know and agree to it.

> **Morris v Murray**
> Court of Appeal [1991] 2 QB 6

The claimant and defendant had spent the afternoon drinking, during which time the defendant consumed the equivalent of 17 whiskies; the alcohol concentration in his blood was more than three times that permitted for a car driver. The defendant suggested that they go for a flight in his light aircraft for which he held a pilot's licence. The flight was 'short and chaotic' and the plane crashed shortly after take-off, killing the defendant and seriously injuring the claimant. Held: the defendant was not liable as the claimant had consented to the risk.

FOX LJ: . . . Lord Denning [in **Nettleship v Weston** [1971] 2 QB 691] said, at p 701:

> Knowledge of the risk of injury is not enough. . . . Nothing will suffice short of an agreement to waive any claim for negligence. The plaintiff must agree, expressly or impliedly, to waive any claim for any injury that may befall him due to the lack of reasonable care by the defendant: or, more accurately, due to the failure by the defendant to measure up to the standard of care which the law requires of him.

Salmon LJ, at p 704, adopted, in a dissenting judgment, a different approach. He said that if, to the knowledge of the passenger, the driver was so drunk as to be incapable of driving safely, a passenger having accepted a lift could not expect the driver to drive other than dangerously. The duty of care, he said, sprang from relationship. The relationship which the passenger has created in accepting a lift in such circumstances cannot entitle him to expect the driver to discharge a duty of care which the passenger knows that he is incapable of discharging. The result is that no duty is owed by the driver to the passenger to drive safely. The difficulty about this analysis is that it may tend to equate '*sciens*' [knowing of a risk] with '*volens*' [wanting, accepting a risk] which is not the law. However, there must be cases where the facts are so strong that '*volens*' is the only sensible conclusion. Salmon LJ said that, alternatively, if there is a duty owed to the passenger to drive safely, the passenger by accepting the lift clearly assumed the risk of the driver failing to discharge that duty.

I doubt whether the gap between Lord Denning MR's approach and that of Salmon LJ is a very wide one. On the one hand, you may have an implicit waiver of any claims by reason of an exhibited notice as to the assumption of risk: see *Bennett v Tugwell* [1971] QB 267, which was decided before the Road Traffic Act 1972. On the other hand, if it is evident to the passenger from the first that the driver is so drunk that he is incapable of driving safely, the passenger must have accepted the obvious risk of injury. You may say that he is *volens* or that he has impliedly waived the right to claim or that the driver is impliedly discharged from the normal duty of care. In general, I think that the volenti doctrine can apply to the tort of negligence, though it must depend upon the extent of the risk, the passenger's knowledge of it and what can be inferred as to his acceptance of it. The passenger cannot be *volens* (in the absence of some form of express disclaimer) in respect of acts of negligence which he had no reason to anticipate and he must be free from compulsion. Lord Pearce in *Imperial Chemical Industries Ltd v Shatwell* [1965] AC 656, 687–688, said:

> as concerns common law negligence, the defence of volenti non fit injuria is clearly appli-
> cable if there was a genuine full agreement, free from any kind of pressure, to assume the
> risk of loss. In *Williams v Port of Liverpool Stevedoring Co Ltd* [1956] 1 WLR 551 Lynskey J
> rejected the defence where one stevedore was injured by the deliberate negligence of the
> whole gang (to which the plaintiff gave 'tacit consent') in adopting a dangerous system of
> unloading. There was an overall duty on the master to provide a safe system of work, and it is
> difficult for one man to stand out against his gang. In such circumstances one may not have
> that deliberate free assumption of risk which is essential to the plea and which makes it as
> a rule unsuitable in master and servant cases owing to the possible existence of indefinable
> social and economic pressure. If the plaintiff had been shown to be a moving spirit in the
> decision to unload in the wrong manner it would be different. But these matters are questions
> of fact and degree.

. . . I think that in embarking upon the flight the plaintiff had implicitly waived his rights in the event of injury consequent on Mr Murray's failure to fly with reasonable care. . . .

Considerations of policy do not lead me to any different conclusion. Volenti as a defence has, perhaps, been in retreat during this century—certainly in relation to master and servant cases. It might be said that the merits could be adequately dealt with by the application of the contributory negligence rules. The judge held that the plaintiff was only 20 per cent to blame (which seems to me to be too low) but if that were increased to 50 per cent so that the plaintiff's damages were reduced by half, both sides would be substantially penalised for their conduct. It seems to me, however, that the wild irresponsibility of the venture is such that the law should not intervene to award damages and should leave the loss where it falls. Flying is intrinsically dangerous and flying with a drunken pilot is great folly.

Notes

1. On the facts of **Morris v Murray** the claimant, though intoxicated, was capable of understanding the risks. But what about a claimant who is incapable of doing so? One consequence of **Morris v Murray** is that a claimant who is so intoxicated that they are unable to understand the risks, is better protected than someone who is sober or only slightly tipsy. See further *Kirkham v Chief Constable of Manchester* [1990] 2 QB 283 in which the claimant committed suicide while on remand. Rejecting the application of *volenti*, Lloyd LJ held:

   > Where a man of sound mind injures himself in an unsuccessful suicide attempt, it is difficult
   > to see why he should not be met by a plea of *volenti non fit injuria*. He has not only courted
   > the risk of injury by another; he has inflicted the injury himself . . . But in the present case
   > Mr Kirkham was not of sound mind . . . True, he was sane in the legal sense. His suicide was
   > a deliberate and conscious act . . . But in the end I have been persuaded . . . that, even so, he
   > was not truly *volens*. Having regard to his mental state, he cannot, by his act, be said to have
   > waived or abandoned any claim arising out of his suicide. So I would reject the defence of
   > *volenti non fit injuria*. (at 290)

2. Rescuers do not consent to the risks that their rescue involves. In *Baker v TE Hopkins & Son Ltd* [1959] 1 WLR 966, the defendant company had been engaged to clean out a well. In so doing, they adopted a dangerous system of working involving lowering a petrol engine which emitted poisonous fumes. Two workers were overcome by fumes, and the claimant, a doctor, volunteered to go down the well to rescue them, knowing of the existence of fumes. He too was overcome,

and he could not be pulled out of the well because the rope which was tied to his waist became caught. Tragically, all three men died. The defendants were liable and unable to rely on the defence of *volenti*. Morris LJ said:

> If C, activated by an impulsive desire to save life, acts bravely and promptly and subjugates any timorous over-concern for his own well being or comfort, I cannot think it would be either rational or seemly to say that he freely and voluntarily agreed to incur the risks of the situation which had been created by A's negligence. (at 976)

3. Section 149(3) of the Road Traffic Act 1988 prevents the defence of *volenti* operating in relation to motor vehicles where compulsory insurance is required:

> (3) The fact that a person so carried has willingly accepted as his the risk of negligence on the part of the user shall not be treated as negativing any such liability of the user.

It does not prevent the operation of the defence of illegality.

9.2 Illegality

In ***Gray* v *Thames Trains Ltd*** [2009] UKHL 33 Lord Hoffmann suggested that '[t]he maxim *ex turpi causa* [*non oritur actio* (literally: no action may be founded on an illegal act)] expresses not so much a principle as a policy. Furthermore that policy is not based upon a single justification but on a group of reasons, which vary in different situations' (at [30]). The key difficulty with the illegality defence is how to distinguish between those unlawful acts which do and those which do not preclude recovery by the victim. Different tests have been suggested. The early test of whether the claim would offend the 'public conscience' is out of favour. Recent years have seen the courts split between what has been termed a 'range of factors' approach—whereby the court must weigh up the various policy arguments for and against barring the claim—and a 'rule-based approach', which holds that illegality will provide a defence where but only where the claimant has to rely on their unlawful conduct to make out their claim. In ***Patel* v *Mirza*** [2016] UKSC 42 the Supreme Court, by majority, endorsed the former approach.

Gray v Thames Trains
House of Lords [2009] UKHL 33

The claimant was injured in the Ladbroke Grove rail crash in October 1999 which was caused by the negligence of the defendant. He suffered post-traumatic stress disorder and while undergoing the effects of this condition he stabbed and killed a pedestrian, Mr Boultwood. He was convicted of manslaughter on the grounds of diminished responsibility and was ordered to be detained in a secure hospital indefinitely. He claimed for loss of earnings, damages for his detention and for his loss of reputation, and also an indemnity against any claims by dependants of the person he killed. Held: that while the defendant was liable to the claimant, that liability was limited and excluded any loss (e.g. loss of earnings after the conviction or the indemnity) which flowed from his killing of the pedestrian.

LORD HOFFMANN . . .

32. The particular rule for which the appellants contend may, as I said, be stated in a wider or a narrower form. The wider and simpler version is that which was applied by Flaux J: you cannot recover for damage which is the consequence of your own criminal act. In its narrower form, it is that you cannot recover for damage which is the consequence of a sentence imposed upon you for a criminal act. I make this distinction between the wider and narrower version of the rule because there is a particular justification for the narrower rule which does not necessarily apply to the wider version.

33. I shall deal first with the narrower version, which was stated in general terms by Denning J in *Askey v Golden Wine Co Ltd* [1948] 2 All ER 35, 38:

> It is, I think, a principle of our law that the punishment inflicted by a criminal court is personal to the offender, and that the civil courts will not entertain an action by the offender to recover an indemnity against the consequences of that punishment.

34. The leading English authority is the decision of the Court of Appeal in *Clunis v Camden and Islington Health Authority* [1998] QB 978, in which the plaintiff had been detained in hospital for treatment of a mental disorder. On 24 September 1992 the hospital discharged him and on 17 December 1992 he stabbed a man to death. He pleaded guilty to manslaughter on the grounds of diminished responsibility and was sentenced, as in this case, to be detained in hospital pursuant to section 37 of the Mental Health Act 1983 with an indefinite restriction order under section 41.

35. The plaintiff sued the Health Authority, alleging that it had been negligent in discharging him and not providing adequate after care and claiming damages for his loss of liberty. The Health Authority applied to strike out the action on the ground that, even assuming that it had been negligent and that the plaintiff would not otherwise have committed manslaughter, damages could not be recovered for the consequences of the plaintiff's own unlawful act. In other words, the Health Authority relied upon the wider version of the rule. Beldam LJ, who gave the judgment of the Court, accepted this submission. He said (at pp 989–990):

> In the present case the plaintiff has been convicted of a serious criminal offence. In such a case public policy would in our judgment preclude the court from entertaining the plaintiff's claim unless it could be said that he did not know the nature and quality of his act or that what he was doing was wrong. The offence of murder was reduced to one of manslaughter by reason of the plaintiff's mental disorder but his mental state did not justify a verdict of not guilty by reason of insanity. Consequently, though his responsibility for killing Mr. Zito is diminished, he must be taken to have known what he was doing and that it was wrong. A plea of diminished responsibility accepts that the accused's mental responsibility is substantially impaired but it does not remove liability for his criminal act . . . The court ought not to allow itself to be made an instrument to enforce obligations alleged to arise out of the plaintiff's own criminal act and we would therefore allow the appeal on this ground. . . .

49. It is true that even if Mr Gray had not committed manslaughter, his earning capacity would have been impaired by the post-traumatic stress disorder caused by the defendants' negligence. But liability on this counter-factual basis is in my opinion precluded by the decision of this House in *Jobling v Associated Dairies Ltd* [1982] AC 794. In that case, the plaintiff suffered an injury caused by his employer's breach of statutory duty. It caused him partial disablement which reduced his earning capacity. Three years later he was found to be suffering from unrelated illness which was wholly disabling. The question was whether he could claim for the disablement which hypothetically he would have continued to suffer if it had not been overtaken by the effects of the supervening illness. The answer was that he could not. The fact that he would in any event have been disabled from earning could not be disregarded. Likewise in this case, in assessing the damages for the effect of the stress disorder upon Mr Gray's earning capacity, the fact that he would have been unable to earn anything after arrest because he had committed manslaughter cannot be disregarded.

50. My Lords, that is in my opinion sufficient to dispose of most of the claims which are the subject of this appeal. Mr Gray's claims for loss of earnings after his arrest and for general damages for his detention, conviction and damage to reputation are all claims for damage caused by the lawful sentence imposed upon him for manslaughter and therefore fall within the narrower version of the rule which I would invite your Lordships to affirm. But there are some additional claims which may be more difficult to bring within this rule, such as the claim for an indemnity against any claims which might be brought by dependants of the dead pedestrian and the claim for general damages for feelings of guilt and remorse consequent upon the killing. Neither of these was a consequence of the sentence of the criminal court.

51. I must therefore examine a wider version of the rule, which was applied by Flaux J. This has the support of the reasoning of the Court of Appeal in *Clunis's* case [1998] QB 978 as well as other authorities. It differs from the narrower version in at least two respects: first, it cannot, as it seems to me, be justified on the grounds of inconsistency in the same way as the narrower rule. Instead, the wider rule has to be justified on the ground that it is offensive to public notions of the fair distribution of resources that a claimant should be compensated (usually out of public funds) for the consequences of his own criminal conduct. Secondly, the wider rule may raise problems of causation which cannot arise in connection with the narrower rule. The sentence of the court is plainly a consequence of the criminality for which the claimant was responsible. But other forms of damage may give rise to questions about whether they can properly be said to have been caused by his criminal conduct.

52. The wider principle was applied by the Court of Appeal in *Vellino v Chief Constable of the Greater Manchester Police* [2002] 1 WLR 218. The claimant was injured in consequence of jumping from a second-floor window to escape from the custody of the police. He sued the police for damages, claiming that they had not taken reasonable care to prevent him from escaping. Attempting to escape from lawful custody is a criminal offence. The Court of Appeal (Schiemann LJ and Sir Murray Stuart-Smith; Sedley LJ dissenting) held that, assuming the police to have been negligent, recovery was precluded because the injury was the consequence of the plaintiff's unlawful act.

53. This decision seems to me based upon sound common sense. The question, as suggested in the dissenting judgment of Sedley LJ, is how the case should be distinguished from one in which the injury is a consequence of the plaintiff's unlawful act only in the sense that it would not have happened if he had not been committing an unlawful act. An extreme example would be the car which is damaged while unlawfully parked. Sir Murray Stuart-Smith, at para 70, described the distinction:

> The operation of the principle arises where the claimant's claim is founded upon his own criminal or immoral act. The facts which give rise to the claim must be inextricably linked with the criminal activity. It is not sufficient if the criminal activity merely gives occasion for tortious conduct of the defendant.

54. This distinction, between causing something and merely providing the occasion for someone else to cause something, is one with which we are very familiar in the law of torts. It is the same principle by which the law normally holds that even though damage would not have occurred but for a tortious act, the defendant is not liable if the immediate cause was the deliberate act of another individual. Examples of cases falling on one side of the line or the other are given in the judgment of Judge LJ in *Cross v Kirkby* [2000] CA Transcript No 321. It was Judge LJ, at para 103, who formulated the test of 'inextricably linked' which was afterwards adopted by Sir Murray Stuart-Smith LJ in *Vellino v Chief Constable of the Greater Manchester Police* [2002] 1 WLR 218. Other expressions which he approved, at paras 100 and 104, were 'an integral part or a necessarily direct consequence' of the unlawful act (Rougier J: see *Revill v Newbery* [1996] QB 567, 571) and 'arises directly *ex turpi* *causa*' (Bingham LJ in *Saunders v Edwards* [1987] 1 WLR 1116, 1134.) It might be better to avoid metaphors like 'inextricably linked' or 'integral part' and to treat the question as simply one of causation. Can one say that, although the damage would not have happened but for the tortious conduct of the defendant, it was caused by the criminal act of the claimant? (*Vellino v Chief Constable of the Greater Manchester Police* [2002] 1 WLR 218). Or is the position that although the damage would not have happened without the criminal act of the claimant, it was caused by the tortious act of the defendant? (*Revill v Newbery* [1996] QB 567).

55. However the test is expressed, the wider rule seems to me to cover the remaining heads of damage in this case. Mr Gray's liability to compensate the dependants of the dead pedestrian was an immediate 'inextricable' consequence of his having intentionally killed him. The same is true of his feelings of guilt and remorse. I therefore think that Flaux J was right and I would allow the appeal and restore his judgment.

Notes

1. This case produces all sorts of puzzles. Presumably the defence of illegality applied because the claimant had *some* responsibility for what he did. But equally he wouldn't have done it but for the negligent acts of the defendant. The result is that he gets *some* damages (loss of earnings up to the conviction) but not all. This seems to be a bit of a fudge. Moreover, he receives no compensation for the undoubted wrong he suffered. This is, perhaps, more straightforward. It would be inconsistent to imprison someone on the ground that he was responsible for a serious offence and then compensate him for his detention. Do you agree?

2. And what about the dependants of Mr Boultwood? Presumably they wouldn't be able to sue Thames Trains because, in relation to the rail accident, they are unforeseeable claimants. Thus they have to rely on the claimant's money—but he hasn't got any because he has been deprived of compensation because he killed Mr Boultwood.

Patel v Mirza
Supreme Court [2016] UKSC 42

The claimant entered into an agreement with the defendant under which the claimant was to pay money to the defendant, which the defendant would then use to bet on the price movement of shares on the basis of inside information. Investing on the back of such information is criminal and the contract was void for illegality. The defendant did not obtain the inside information he had expected to receive, so the agreement could not be carried out. The claimant sued to recover the money he had paid to the defendant. Held: the claimant was entitled to recover the money and his illegality provided no defence.

LORD TOULSON:

Introduction

1. 'No court will lend its aid to a man who founds his cause of action upon an immoral or an illegal act.' So spoke Lord Mansfield in *Holman v Johnson* (1775) 1 Cowp 341, 343, ushering in two centuries and more of case law about the extent and effect of this maxim. He stated that the reason was one of public policy:

If, from the plaintiff's own stating or otherwise, the cause of action appears to arise ex turpi causa, or the transgression of a positive law of this country, there the court says he has no right to be assisted. It is upon that ground the court goes; not for the sake of the defendant, but because they will not lend their aid to such a plaintiff. So if the plaintiff and defendant were to change sides, and the defendant was to bring his action against the plaintiff, the latter would then have the advantage of it; for where both are equally in fault, potior est conditio defendentis.

2. Illegality has the potential to provide a defence to civil claims of all sorts, whether relating to contract, property, tort or unjust enrichment, and in a wide variety of circumstances.

3. Take the law of contract. A contract may be prohibited by a statute; or it may be entered into for an illegal or immoral purpose, which may be that of one or both parties; or performance according to its terms may involve the commission of an offence; or it may be intended by one or both parties to be performed in a way which will involve the commission of an offence; or an unlawful act may be committed in the course of its performance. The application of the doctrine of illegality to each of these different situations has caused a good deal of uncertainty, complexity and sometimes inconsistency.

The law at a crossroads

82. In his *Restatement of the English Law of Contract* (Oxford University Press, 2016), pp 221–222, Professor Andrew Burrows explained the difficulty of attempting to state the law in relation to illegality:

Leaving aside the law on what one can loosely label 'statutory illegality' [cases where a statute makes a contract or a contract term unenforceable by either or one party] the law on the effect of illegality in contract (which one may loosely refer to as 'the common law of illegality') is in a state of flux . . .

Traditionally, two Latin maxims have often been referred to without greatly illuminating the legal position: ex turpi causa non oritur actio ('no action arises from a disgraceful cause') and in pari delicto potior est conditio defendentis ('where both parties are equally in the wrong the position of the defendant is the stronger'). As previously understood, illegality in the law of contract—as developed from those Latin maxims—was governed by a series of rules which tended to distinguish, for example, between illegality in formation and illegality in performance. Unfortunately, commentators and courts have found it very difficult to state those rules with confidence and precision. Hence the textbook treatments not only differ from each other but are characterised by long-winded attempts to explain the law. Sharp propositions when offered by the courts or the books have to be qualified by reference to cases or hypothetical examples that do not fit those rules; and convincing justifications of those rules have proved elusive. More recently, therefore, and in line with a similar trend in respect of illegality as a defence in tort, some courts have favoured greater flexibility culminating in a 'range of factors' approach aimed at achieving a proportionate response to contractual illegality in preference to the traditional rule-based approach.

83. Since the law was at a crossroads, Professor Burrows set out alternative possible formulations of a 'rule-based approach' and a 'range of factors approach'.

84. One possible version of a rule-based approach, at p 224, which *Tinsley v Milligan* and *Les Laboratoires Servier v Apotex Inc* could be interpreted as supporting, would be a single master rule based on reliance:

If the formation, purpose or performance of a contract involves conduct that is illegal (such as a crime) or contrary to public policy (such as a restraint of trade), a party cannot enforce the contract if it has to rely on that conduct to establish its claim.

85. An alternative rule-based formulation, at p 225, saw the reliance rule as only one of a number of rules and essentially confined to the creation of property rights. On this approach a formulation of the rules might be:

Rule 1. A contract which has as its purpose, or is intended to be performed in a manner that involves, conduct that is illegal (such as a crime) or contrary to public policy (such as a restraint of trade) is unenforceable (a) by either party if both parties knew of that purpose or intention; or (b) by one party if only that party knew of that purpose or intention.

Rule 2. If rule 1 is inapplicable because it is only the performance of a contract that involves conduct that is illegal or contrary to public policy, the contract is unenforceable by the party who performed in that objectionable way but is enforceable by the other party unless that party knew of, and participated in, that objectionable performance.

Rule 3. Proprietary rights created by a contract that involves conduct that is illegal or contrary to public policy will not be recognised unless the claimant can establish the proprietary rights without reliance on that conduct.

. . .

93. If a 'range of factors' approach were preferred, Professor Burrows suggested, at pp 229–230, that a possible formulation would read as follows:

If the formation, purpose or performance of a contract involves conduct that is illegal (such as a crime) or contrary to public policy (such as a restraint of trade), the contract is unenforceable by one or either party if to deny enforcement would be an appropriate response to that conduct, taking into account where relevant—

(a) how seriously illegal or contrary to public policy the conduct was;

(b) whether the party seeking enforcement knew of, or intended, the conduct;

(c) how central to the contract or its performance the conduct was;

(d) how serious a sanction the denial of enforcement is for the party seeking enforcement;

(e) whether denying enforcement will further the purpose of the rule which the conduct has infringed;

(f) whether denying enforcement will act as a deterrent to conduct that is illegal or contrary to public policy;

(g) whether denying enforcement will ensure that the party seeking enforcement does not profit from the conduct;

(h) whether denying enforcement will avoid inconsistency in the law thereby maintaining the integrity of the legal system.

Professor Burrows noted that the final factor is capable of a wider or narrower approach, depending on what one understands by inconsistency.

94. The reference to what is an 'appropriate response' brings to the surface the moral dimension underlying the doctrine of illegality, which inevitably influences the minds of judges and peeps out in their judgments from time to time. *Tinsley v Milligan* caused disquiet to Lord Goff and others precisely because its reasoning jarred with their sense of what was just and appropriate.

. . .

99. . . . . [T]here are two broad discernible policy reasons for the common law doctrine of illegality as a defence to a civil claim. One is that a person should not be allowed to profit from his own wrongdoing. The other, linked, consideration is that the law should be coherent and not self-defeating, condoning illegality by giving with the left hand what it takes with the right hand.

. . .

101. . . . . [O]ne cannot judge whether allowing a claim which is in some way tainted by illegality would be contrary to the public interest, because it would be harmful to the integrity of the legal system, without a) considering the underlying purpose of the prohibition which has been transgressed, b) considering conversely any other relevant public policies which may be rendered ineffective or less effective by denial of the claim, and c) keeping in mind the possibility of overkill unless the law is applied with a due sense of proportionality. We are, after all, in the area of public policy. That trio of necessary considerations can be found in the case law.

. . .

107. In considering whether it would be disproportionate to refuse relief to which the claimant would otherwise be entitled, as a matter of public policy, various factors may be relevant. Professor Burrows' list is helpful but I would not attempt to lay down a prescriptive or definitive list because of the infinite possible variety of cases. Potentially relevant factors include the seriousness of the conduct, its centrality to the contract, whether it was intentional and whether there was marked disparity in the parties' respective culpability.

108. The integrity and harmony of the law permit—and I would say require—such flexibility. Part of the harmony of the law is its division of responsibility between the criminal and civil courts and tribunals. Punishment for wrongdoing is the responsibility of the criminal courts and, in some instances, statutory regulators. It should also be noted that under the Proceeds of Crime Act 2002 the state has wide powers to confiscate proceeds of crime, whether on a conviction or without a conviction. Punishment is not generally the function of the civil courts, which are concerned with determining private rights and obligations. The broad principle is not in doubt that the public interest requires that the civil courts should not undermine the effectiveness of the criminal law; but nor should they impose what would amount in substance to an additional penalty disproportionate to the nature and seriousness of any wrongdoing. . . .

109. The courts must obviously abide by the terms of any statute, but I conclude that it is right for a court which is considering the application of the common law doctrine of illegality to have regard to the policy factors involved and to the nature and circumstances of the illegal conduct in determining whether the public interest in preserving the integrity of the justice system should result in denial of the relief claimed. I put it in that way rather than whether the contract should be regarded as tainted by illegality, because the question is whether the relief claimed should be granted.

. . .

113. Critics of the 'range of factors' approach say that it would create unacceptable uncertainty. I would make three points in reply. First, one of the principal criticisms of the law has been its uncertainty and unpredictability. Doctrinally it is riven with uncertainties: see, for example, paras 4–8 above. There is also uncertainty how a court will in practice steer its way in order to reach what appears to be a just and reasonable result. Second, I am not aware of evidence that uncertainty has been a source of serious problems in those jurisdictions which have taken a relatively flexible approach. Third, there are areas in which certainty is particularly important. Ordinary citizens and businesses enter into all sorts of everyday lawful activities which are governed by well understood rules of law. Lord Mansfield said in *Vallejo v Wheeler* (1774) 1 Cowp 143, 153:

> In all mercantile transactions the great object should be certainty: and therefore, it is of more consequence that a rule should be certain, than whether the rule is established one way or the other. Because speculators in trade then know what ground to go upon.

The same considerations do not apply in the same way to people contemplating unlawful activity. . . .

Summary and disposal

120. The essential rationale of the illegality doctrine is that it would be contrary to the public interest to enforce a claim if to do so would be harmful to the integrity of the legal system (or, possibly, certain aspects of public morality, the boundaries of which have never been made entirely clear and which do not arise for consideration in this case). In assessing whether the public interest would be harmed in that way, it is necessary a) to consider the underlying purpose of the prohibition which has been transgressed and whether that purpose will be enhanced by denial of the claim, b) to consider any other relevant public policy on which the denial of the claim may have an impact and c) to consider whether denial of the claim would be a proportionate response to the illegality, bearing in mind that punishment is a matter for the criminal courts. Within that framework, various factors may be relevant, but it would be a mistake to suggest that the court is free to decide a case in an undisciplined way. The public interest is best served by a principled and transparent assessment of the considerations identified, rather by than the application of a formal approach capable of producing results which may appear arbitrary, unjust or disproportionate.

Notes

1. *Patel* was not itself a tort case. The claimant's allegation was not that the defendant had wronged him; rather he simply claimed that the defendant should not be entitled to retain the money that the claimant had paid him, since the contract under which that money was paid was void and the purpose of the payment (to bet on share price movements) had failed. As such, the claim did not fall within the domain of tort law but instead belongs to the law of unjust enrichment. Nonetheless, the court made clear that the approach courts should take to the illegality defence should be, in broad terms, the same whether the claimant is looking to enforce a contract, recover compensation for a tort, claim an item of property or seeking restitution of an unjust enrichment.

2. This was the fourth time the Supreme Court had ruled on the illegality defence in the previous three years. The three earlier decisions—*Hounga* v *Allen* [2014] UKSC 47, *Les Laboratoires Servier* v *Apotex Inc* [2014] UKSC 55 and *Bilta (UK) Ltd* v *Nazir (No 2)* [2015] UKSC 23—had seen the court split between the 'range of factors' and 'rule-based' approaches. This prompted Lord Neuberger in *Bilta* to say 'the proper approach to the defence of illegality needs to be addressed by this court (certainly with a panel of seven and conceivably with a panel of nine Justices) as soon as appropriately possible' (at [15]). *Patel* provided that opportunity and a panel of nine Supreme Court Justices was convened to hear the appeal.

3. Though the court was unanimous in holding that the illegality defence did not bar Mr Patel's claim, it was once more split on the question of what approach should be adopted when determining the applicability of the defence. The lead judgment given by Lord Toulson had the agreement of Lady Hale, Lord Kerr, Lord Wilson and Lord Hodge, while Lord Neuberger gave a judgment adopting a broadly similar approach. Lord Mance, Lord Clarke and Lord Sumption, however, favoured the 'rule-based' approach. However, given that the object of convening the nine-justice panel was to resolve the disagreement as to the proper approach to be employed when dealing with the illegality defence, we might expect *Patel* to be treated as having settled this question by opting decisively for a 'range of factors' approach.

4. The main argument against the 'range of factors' approach is that it creates too much uncertainty. This approach requires the court to weigh up the policies behind the illegality defence—principally, ensuring that the law is consistent and that wrongdoers do not benefit from their wrongdoing—alongside the policies underlying the relevant rules of law which render the claimant's conduct unlawful, to determine whether, all things considered, it would be against public

policy to allow the claimant's claim. But how these policy considerations are to be weighed will vary from case to case, meaning that it will often be uncertain whether or not the defence will be successfully raised. It was this concern which was the principal driver for the minority's rejection of the 'range of factors' approach in favour of (what they took to be) the more certain 'rule-based' approach. Lord Toulson addresses this concern at [109] in the extract above.

5. The rule the minority preferred would make the defence available only where the claimant is obliged to rely on his own illegal act in making his claim. This principle had been applied by the House of Lords in *Tinsley* v *Milligan* [1994] 1 AC 340. Again, this was not a tort case but a dispute about property ownership. Tinsley and Milligan bought a house in which to live together as a couple and on the understanding that they would be beneficial co-owners. Legal title to the house was, however, put in Tinsley's name alone, to enable Milligan, with Tinsley's knowledge and consent, to make fraudulent claims for social security benefits. Later, the couple fell out and Tinsley tried to evict Milligan. Milligan counterclaimed for an order that the house be sold and the proceeds split between them. The court held Milligan could not rely on her own unlawful conduct when seeking to establish her co-ownership of the house. However, if Milligan could make her case without having to rely on that unlawful conduct, her claim would not be barred by her illegality. This is what Milligan was able to do. There is a rule of property law that says that if you pay for an item of property which is put into someone else's name, you are nonetheless to be treated as the beneficial owner of that property. This was the case here: Milligan had paid part of the purchase price for the house put in Tinsley's name, so this rule of property law meant that she became a beneficial co-owner of the house. Importantly, pleading this rule meant that Milligan did not need to say anything about why she had contributed to the price of the property or why it had then been registered in Tinsley's name alone. In **Patel**, the majority rejected this reliance rule on the basis that it operated arbitrarily—after all, the court in *Tinsley* knew full well of Milligan's unlawful conduct, so why was the court free to ignore it if, but only if, she was able to make her claim without mentioning it—and that it did not in fact provide any greater certainty than the 'range of factors' approach, since the courts were often uncertain about whether claimants were or were not 'relying' on their illegality when bringing their claims.

6. In 2020, illegality once again returned to the Supreme Court in *Henderson* v *Dorset Healthcare University NHS Trust Foundation* [2020] UKSC 43 and *Stoffel & Co* v *Grondona* [2020] UKSC 42. Both cases affirmed the centrality of **Patel** as providing a test for the illegality defence across all areas of law. In *Henderson* v *Dorset Healthcare University NHS Trust Foundation* the claimant, who was under the care of the defendant's community mental health team, had killed her mother while experiencing a serious psychotic episode. She was later convicted of manslaughter by reason of diminished responsibility. The NHS Trust admitted it had negligently failed to return the claimant to hospital following a deterioration of her condition and that, had it done so, the tragic events would not have taken place. However, they argued that the claimant's claim for damages for the losses she had suffered as a result of her actions was barred on the basis of illegality because the damages she claims resulted from: (a) the sentence imposed on her by the criminal court; and/or (b) her own criminal act of manslaughter. A key question for the court was whether, following **Patel**, they were still bound by the House of Lords' opinion in **Gray**. Rejecting the claimant's claim, the court unanimously agreed that **Gray** remained good law and compatible with the approach set out in **Patel**. The application of the illegality defence was justified on two public policy considerations: consistency between the criminal law and tort law and the need to maintain public confidence in the legal system:

> For one branch of the law to enable a person to profit from behaviour which another branch of the law treats as being criminal or otherwise unlawful would tend to produce inconsistency and disharmony in the law, and so cause damage to the integrity of the legal system . . . the decision in **Gray** should be affirmed as being '**Patel** compliant'—it is how **Patel** 'plays out in that particular type of case'. The clearly stated public policy based rules set out in **Gray** should be applied and followed in comparable cases. (Lord Hamblen at [119], [145])

7. An example of the application of Lord Toulson's approach is the first instance decision in *McHugh v Okai-Koi* [2017] EWHC 710 (QB). The defendant had been convicted of causing death by careless driving after the deceased, who had climbed onto the car's bonnet in order to prevent the defendant from driving away during a serious 'road rage' incident, slipped from the bonnet hitting her head on a Belisha beacon.

> 19. As to Lord Toulson's first consideration, I have already found that Mr and Mrs McHugh's behavio[u]r was highly culpable, but I do not consider that the denial of the claim, on the grounds of public interest, would be enhanced in circumstances where Mrs Okai-Koi was also convicted by a jury of causing death by careless driving. Mrs Okai-Koi sought to defend the charge of causing death by dangerous driving in the criminal proceedings on the basis that her actions were motivated by necessity. The jury acquitted her of that charge but convicted her of causing death by careless driving, thereby rejecting the defence of necessity in respect of that charge. As I have already said it was a fateful misjudgment on her part that she moved off, knowing that Mrs McHugh was on the bonnet. The jury were clearly satisfied, to the requisite standard of proof, that Mrs Okai-Koi's driving fell below that of a reasonable competent, prudent and careful driver, notwithstanding the circumstances in which she found herself. There were in my view, two causes of Mrs McHugh's accident, her own and her husband's criminal conduct and Mrs Okai-Koi's decision to move off with Mrs McHugh on the bonnet.
>
> 21. As to Lord Toulson's second consideration, I reject Mr Katrak's (counsel for the claimant) submission that a relevant public policy issue in this case is that the denial of the claim would deprive Mr and Mrs McHugh's children of damages, as dependents [sic], because of circumstances for which they were not responsible. In my view that submission is inconsistent with section 5 of the Fatal Accidents Act 1976 which permits me to make a reduction in the award of damages for contributory negligence.
>
> 22. As to Lord Toulson's third consideration, I do not consider that the denial of the claim would be proportionate in the circumstances where Mrs Okai-Koi has been convicted of causing death by careless driving and where Mrs McHugh's actions were not the sole cause of the accident.

8. *McHugh v Okai-Koi* is also an example of the extent to which contributory negligence can be used to significantly reduce the claimant's award, without having to use the 'all or nothing' approach of illegality. David Pittaway QC (sitting as a High Court Judge) continued:

> 24. In my view, the highly exceptional circumstances of this tragic accident lead me to the conclusion that Mrs McHugh's share of the responsibility is considerably greater than that of Mrs Okai-Koi. I have concluded that Mrs McHugh behaved in a highly culpable manner as the protagonist of the altercation that took place because she was very intoxicated. For the reasons outlined above, I have concluded that Mrs Okai-Koi should not have moved off when she knew that Mrs McHugh was on the bonnet but she did so in extraordinary circumstances. In these circumstances, I consider that a just and equitable division of responsibility is 75/25 in favour of Mrs Okai-Koi.

9.3 Contributory negligence

The principle of contributory negligence is that the damages awarded to a claimant who themselves were at fault should be reduced to the extent that their fault contributed to the accident or the damage. It might seem logical that if a defendant is to be held responsible for their fault, then so should a claimant. However, the effect of a finding of contributory negligence on the part of the claimant is entirely different from a finding of fault on the part of the defendant. At least in personal injury cases, a defendant will usually be insured or distribute their loss in some other way. Thus, a defendant who is made liable will not often bear the burden themselves. But where a *claimant* is held to be contributorily negligent and their damages are reduced, they will almost always bear the burden themselves:

> To find a defendant guilty of negligence shifts the loss away from the claimant and typically spreads it by means of insurance . . . A finding of contributory negligence usually has precisely the opposite effect, which is to leave part or all of the loss on the claimant, who will typically be without insurance. Thus, reduction of damages for contributory negligence falls much more heavily on the claimant than liability for negligence bears on the defendant. (Peter Cane *Atiyah's Accidents, Compensation and the Law* (7th edn, CUP, 2006), p 56)

Why should we deliberately under-compensate people in this way? It is doubtful whether the doctrine has any deterrent effect: for example, the threat of contributory negligence did little to encourage people to wear seat belts; this only became commonplace once it was a criminal offence. Rather it seems to adhere to a rough sense of 'justice'. Where the claimant is also responsible for their loss, the defendant should not in addition—to that extent—be held responsible for it.

The rules for establishing contributory negligence on the part of the claimant are not the same as the rules for establishing liability for negligence on the part of the defendant. Since 1945, these have been placed on a statutory footing. The Law Reform (Contributory Negligence) Act 1945 removed the bar which prevented the claimant from recovering *anything* where there had been a finding of contributory negligence allowing for damages to be reduced to the extent that 'the court thinks just and equitable having regard to the claimant's share in the responsibility for the damage'. In order to establish whether the claimant is contributorily negligent, the court asks two questions:

(1) has the claimant taken reasonable care for his own safety;

(2) *and*, if not, whether their failure to take reasonable care contributed to their injury: that is, was the act of the claimant merely the background against which the negligence of the defendant operated, or did it causally contribute to the accident?

LAW REFORM (CONTRIBUTORY NEGLIGENCE) ACT 1945

1. **Apportionment of liability in case of contributory negligence**

(1) Where any person suffers damage as the result partly of his own fault and partly of the fault of any other person or persons, a claim in respect of that damage shall not be defeated by reason of the fault of the person suffering the damage, but the damages recoverable in respect thereof shall be reduced to such extent as the court thinks just and equitable having regard to the claimant's share in the responsibility for the damage . . .

4. **Interpretation**

The following expressions have the meanings hereby respectively assigned to them, that is to say—

'court' means, in relation to any claim, the court or arbitrator by or before whom the claim falls to be determined;

'damage' includes loss of life and personal injury;

. . .

'fault' means negligence, breach of statutory duty or other act or omission which gives rise to a liability in tort or would apart from this Act, give rise to the defence of contributory negligence.

Notes

1. Despite some views to the contrary (see e.g. Morritt LJ's dissent in the Court of Appeal in *Reeves v Commissioner of Police for the Metropolis* [1998] 2 All ER 381), the wording of the Act suggests that it is not possible for a claimant to be 100 per cent contributorily negligent. Indeed, in *Pitts v Hunt* [1991] 1 QB 24, Balcombe LJ suggested such a view was logically unsupportable:

   > Section 1 begins with the premise that the person 'suffers damage as the result partly of his own fault and partly of the fault of any other person or persons . . .' Thus before the section comes into operation, the court must be satisfied that there is fault on the part of both parties which has caused damage. It is then expressly provided that the claim 'shall not be defeated by reason of the fault of the person suffering the damage . . .' To hold that he is himself entirely responsible for the damage effectively defeats his claim. It is then provided that 'the damages recoverable in respect thereof'—that is, the damage suffered partly as a result of his own fault and partly the fault of any other person—'shall be reduced . . .' It therefore presupposes that the person suffering the damage will recover some damages.

   However, the proportion by which the claimant's damages are reduced can be very high. See further *McHugh v Okai-Koi* [2017] EWHC 710 (QB) discussed in section 9.2.

2. Similarly, although there have been suggestions to the contrary (see e.g. Lord Hope's citation with approval in *Reeves v Commissioner of Police for the Metropolis* [2000] 1 AC 360, that 'one should not be unduly inhibited by the use of the word "negligence" in the expression "contributory negligence"' (at 383)), it now seems that contributory negligence is confined to the tort of negligence. In *Standard Chartered Bank v Pakistan National Shipping Corp (No 2)* [2003] 1 All ER 173, for example, the court held that contributory negligence is no defence to deceit, nor is it a defence to conversion or intentional trespass to goods (Torts Act 1997, s 11) except for conversion of a cheque (Banking Act 1979, s 47). Nor can it be a defence to assault or battery: *Co-operative Group (CWS) Ltd v Pritchard* [2011] EWCA Civ 329.

3. Contributory negligence can, however, be used even where the responsibility of the claimant for her own damage was the very thing which it was the duty of the defendant to prevent. In *Reeves* the claimant committed suicide when it was the duty of the police to prevent that happening. The House of Lords held that in exceptional circumstances contributory negligence can apply where a claimant intends to injure himself and a deduction of 50 per cent was made. *Volenti* was not applicable, because that would have negatived the duty of the police to prevent the suicide.

Jones v Livox Quarries Ltd
Court of Appeal [1952] 2 QB 608

The claimant worked in a quarry and was injured when riding on the back of a slow-moving vehicle (a traxcavator)—'in the position in which a footman stood at the back of an eighteenth century carriage'—when it was run into from behind by a dumper truck. Held: the claimant was contributorily negligent.

DENNING LJ: . . . Although contributory negligence does not depend on a duty of care, it does depend on foreseeability. Just as actionable negligence requires the foreseeability of harm to others, so contributory negligence requires the foreseeability of harm to oneself. A person is guilty of contributory negligence if he ought reasonably to have foreseen that, if he did not act as a reasonable, prudent man, he might be hurt himself; and in his reckonings he must take into account the possibility of others being careless.

Once negligence is proved, then no matter whether it is actionable negligence or contributory negligence, the person who is guilty of it must bear his proper share of responsibility for the consequences. The consequences do not depend on foreseeability, but on causation. The question in every case is: What faults were there which caused the damage? Was his fault one of them? The necessity of causation is shown by the word 'result' in section 1(1) of the Act of 1945, and it was accepted by this court in *Davies v Swan Motor Co (Swansea) Ltd.*

There is no clear guidance to be found in the books about causation. All that can be said is that causes are different from the circumstances in which, or on which, they operate. The line between the two depends on the facts of each case. It is a matter of common sense more than anything else. In the present case, as the argument of Mr Arthian Davies [counsel for the appellant] proceeded, it seemed to me that he sought to make foreseeability the decisive test of causation. He relied on the trial judge's statement that a man who rode on the towbar of the traxcavator 'ran the risk of being thrown off and no other risk.' That is, I think, equivalent to saying that such a man could reasonably foresee that he might be thrown off the traxcavator, but not that he might be crushed between it and another vehicle.

In my opinion, however, foreseeability is not the decisive test of causation. It is often a relevant factor, but it is not decisive. Even though the plaintiff did not foresee the possibility of being crushed, nevertheless in the ordinary plain common sense of this business the injury suffered by the plaintiff was due in part to the fact that he chose to ride on the towbar to lunch instead of walking down on his feet. If he had been thrown off in the collision, Mr Arthian Davies admits that his injury would be partly due to his own negligence in riding on the towbar; but he says that, because he was crushed, and not thrown off, his injury is in no way due to it. That is too fine a distinction for me. I cannot believe that that purely fortuitous circumstance can make all the difference to the case. As Scrutton LJ said in *In re Polemis and Another and Furness, Withy & Co Ltd* [1921] 3 KB 560, 577 'Once the act is negligent, the fact that its exact operation was not foreseen is immaterial.'

In order to illustrate this question of causation, I may say that if the plaintiff, whilst he was riding on the towbar, had been hit in the eye by a shot from a negligent sportsman, I should have thought that the plaintiff's negligence would in no way be a cause of his injury. It would only be the circumstance in which the cause operated. It would only be part of the history. But I cannot say that in the present case. The man's negligence here was so much mixed up with his injury that it cannot be dismissed as mere history. His dangerous position on the vehicle was one of the causes of his damage just as it was in *Davies v Swan Motor Co (Swansea) Ltd.*

The present case is a good illustration of the practical effect of the Act of 1945. In the course of the argument my Lord suggested that before the Act of 1945 he would have regarded this case as one where the plaintiff should recover in full. That would be because the negligence of the dumper driver would then have been regarded as the predominant cause. Now, since the Act, we have regard to all the causes, and one of them undoubtedly was the plaintiff's negligence in riding on the towbar of the traxcavator. His share in the responsibility was not great—the trial judge assessed it at one-fifth—but, nevertheless, it was his share, and he must bear it himself.

Notes

1. When determining whether the claimant has taken reasonable care for their own safety, an objective standard is applied. In other words, the question is: what would a reasonable person in the claimant's position have done to avoid being hurt? However, the law does allow for some modification of this objective standard, for example in relation to children (*Probert (A Child) v Moore*

[2012] EWHC 2324 (QB)) where 'the person's state of mind is such that, whether temporarily or permanently, they do not appreciate that they are putting themselves in danger and it cannot be said that they should have so appreciated'; *Spearman v Royal United Bath Hospitals NHS Foundation Trust* [2017] EWHC 3027 (QB) at [74]; *Gul v McDonagh* [2021] EWHC 97 (QB)).

> ### Gul v McDonagh
> Queen's Bench Division [2021] EWHC 97 (QB)

The claimant—a 13-year-old boy—suffered 'catastrophic injuries' when he was hit by a car which was being driven at over twice the 20 mph speed limit (the defendant was later convicted for dangerous driving). Held: even allowing for his age, the claimant's failure to recognise that the car was being driven much faster than usual and failing to adjust his actions accordingly amounted to contributory negligence.

GARGAN J:

The law: basic principles

8. The starting point is section 1(1) of the Law Reform (Contributory Negligence) Act 1945 which provides:

> Where any person suffers damage as the result partly of his own fault and partly of the fault of any other person or persons, a claim in respect of that damage shall not be defeated by reason of the fault of the person suffering the damage, but the damages recoverable in respect thereof shall be reduced to such extent as the court thinks just and equitable having regard to the claimant's share in the responsibility for the damage.

9. Whether and, if so, to what extent a finding of contributory negligence should be made involves a balance of blameworthiness and causative potency: see *Davies v Swan Motor Co* [1949] 2 KB 291:

> Whilst causation is the decisive factor in determining whether there should be a reduced amount payable to the plaintiff, nevertheless, the amount of the reduction does not depend solely on the degree of causation. The amount of the reduction is such an amount as may be found by the court to be 'just and equitable', having regard to the claimant's 'share in the responsibility' for the damage. This involves a consideration, not only of the causative potency of a particular factor, but also of its blameworthiness.

10. The test for negligence is objective. Where the court is asked to assess whether to make a finding of contributory negligence against a child the court does not apply the same standards as it would apply to an adult. The most helpful guidance as to the approach the court should take is set out in *Gough v Thorne* [1966] 1 WLR 1387:

10.1 Lord Denning at p.1390:

> A very young child cannot be guilty of contributory negligence. An older child maybe. But it depends on the circumstances. A judge should only find a child guilty of contributory negligence if he or she is of such an age to be expected to take precautions for his or her safety: and then he or she is only to be found guilty if blame should be attached to him or her. A child has not the road sense or experience of his or her elders. He or she is not to be found guilty unless he or she is blameworthy.

10.2 Lord Salmon LJ at p.1391:

> The question as to whether the plaintiff can be said to have been guilty of contributory negligence depends on whether an ordinary child of 13 could be expected to have done more

than this child did. I did say 'ordinary child'. I did not mean a paragon of prudence; nor do I mean a scatter-brained child; but the ordinary child of 13.

11. There is no hard and fast rule as to the age at which a child may be held to be guilty of contributory negligence—although counsel could find no reported cases in which a finding has been made against a child under the age of 8. When judging the actions of a child, the standard of care is to be measured by that reasonably to be expected of a child of the same age, intelligence and experience.

12. The claimant in this case was 13 and would have just started Year 9 at secondary school. He can properly be expected to have a degree of road sense—not as much road sense as an adult but considerably more than an 8 year old.

83. The central question is whether, given his clear view of the Focus [the defendant's car] when it was about 42m away, the claimant should have appreciated that it represented a potential danger to him if he crossed.

84. Mr Rose QC points out that, when he appeared before the Crown Court for sentence, the first defendant accepted that he was wholly to blame for the accident. Whilst this is obviously helpful for the claimant it is not determinative. The admission must be placed in context. The first defendant was seeking to express remorse for his conduct in the hope of a more lenient sentence. An allegation that the claimant was partially to blame was unlikely to help him. His comment at the sentencing hearing can be contrasted with the self-serving statement presented in interview where he sought to deflect blame by saying '*I admit that I did knock the young lad down but this was an accident. I was not driving dangerously. The pedestrian stepped off the path in front of me*'. Ultimately, the first defendant's views are not persuasive and I must apply my own judgment to the facts.

89. The witnesses who saw the Focus comment upon how badly and how fast it was being driven. In my judgment that should have been apparent to a reasonable adult who had made an appropriate assessment of the dangers he faced in crossing the road. I then have to consider whether a reasonable 13 year old with the claimant's experience should be expected to have made the same judgment. I accept that many children cannot judge how fast vehicles are going or how far away they are. However, at 13, I consider it likely that the claimant would have experience of crossing roads on his own, even roads where traffic might be going at 40mph. It would be wholly wrong to expect the claimant to have been able to estimate the precise speed of the Focus. However, in my judgment a reasonable 13 year old making a careful assessment would have realised that the Focus was being driven much faster than usual. Further, although the claimant did not have far to go, I consider that a reasonable 13 year old would have considered that the Focus represented a source of potential danger and would have waited for the Focus to pass. Further, even if a reasonable 13 year old had set off, I consider that they would have kept the Ford Focus under observation so that, if necessary, they could hurry across the very short distance. . . .

95. . . . I conclude that a reasonably careful 13 year old would and should have waited for the Focus to pass. Further, even if they did [set] off, I consider that a reasonable 13 year old, realising that the Focus was travelling unusually quickly, would and should have kept his eye on it as he crossed.

96. In my judgment the claimant should have waited for the vehicle to pass. Further, if he elected to cross he should have kept his eye on the vehicle as he did so. If the claimant had adopted either of these courses the accident would have been avoided either because he would have remained on the southern pavement or because, having started to cross, he would have been able to accelerate and reach safety as the Focus approached.

What if any reduction should be made?

97. In determining what reduction it is just and equitable to make on account of the claimant's contributory negligence, it is necessary to evaluate the relative degree of blameworthiness and

causative effect of the acts and omissions which constitute negligence on the part of the claimant and the first defendant respectively.

98. It is generally expected that a court will impose a high burden on drivers of cars to reflect the fact that a car is potentially a dangerous weapon. The first defendant's driving in this case was particularly egregious. His speed excessive, the risk of injury obvious and his motivation the desire to avoid arrest. Insofar as the claimant could see the defendant so too the defendant could see the claimant and could and should have slowed down. It would not have taken much adjustment on the part of the defendant to allow the claimant to complete that final 30cm across the road. The causative potency of all these factors is extremely high and must weigh heavily against the first defendant.

99. Mr Rose QC argues that even if the claimant's conduct was culpable the first defendant's conduct was so extreme that it is not just and equitable to make any reduction in the claimant's compensation. Mr Horlock QC suggested a reduction of 25% in his skeleton argument. However, in his oral submissions he accepted that such a deduction was too great on the facts of this case and suggested that the appropriate bracket was in the region of 10% to 20%.

100. Whilst deeply sympathetic to the claimant, I do not think his culpable misjudgment can be wholly ignored. However, when balanced against the conduct of the first defendant it falls very much at the lowest end of the scale suggested by the second defendant. I consider that the just and equitable reduction in all the circumstances of this case is 10%.

Notes

1. A claimant will not be contributorily negligent if they have acted reasonably. In *Jones* v *Boyce* (1816) 171 ER 540, the claimant was a passenger on the defendant's coach. A defective coupling rein broke while the coach was going downhill and the claimant, fearing a crash, threw himself from the coach breaking his leg. Had he stayed where he was he would have been safe. Lord Ellenborough held that the claimant was not contributorily negligent:

   The question is, whether he was placed in such a situation as to render what he did a prudent precaution, for the purpose of self-preservation. . . . Therefore it is for your consideration, whether the plaintiff's act was the measure of an unreasonably alarmed mind, or such as a reasonable and prudent mind would have adopted . . . A coach proprietor certainly is not to be responsible for the rashness and imprudence of a passenger; it must appear that there existed a reasonable cause for alarm. (at 541)

2. In *St George* v *The Home Office* [2008] EWCA Civ 1068 the claimant, a 29-year-old man, had been sentenced to four months in prison. Since the age of 16 he had been addicted to drugs and alcohol, and he told the prison on reception that he tended to suffer epileptic fits when withdrawing from his addiction. Nevertheless, he was placed on a top bunk in a dormitory. He suffered seizures and fell from the bunk. The prison was clearly in breach of its duty to the claimant, but they argued that the claimant was contributorily negligent. The trial judge agreed, reducing his damages by 15 per cent to reflect his 'lifestyle decisions'. Fortunately, on appeal, the court held that the 'fault' was not a 'potent' cause of his injury as it was too remote in time and was not connected to the negligence of the prison staff.

   In my judgment, the claimant's fault in becoming addicted to drugs and alcohol in his mid-teens was not a potent cause of the status and the consequent brain injury which were triggered by his fall on 3 November 1997. It was too remote in time, place and circumstance and was not sufficiently connected with the negligence of the prison staff or, to use Lord Birkenhead's words, was not sufficiently 'mixed up with the state of things brought about' by the prison staff . . . to be properly regarded as a cause of the injury . . . [T]he claimant's addiction was no more than part of the history which had led to his being a person whose medical and psychological conditions were as they were when he was admitted to Brixton prison. (Dyson LJ at [56])

Dyson LJ went on to consider the trial judge's analogy of the claimant's fault with the liability of an intoxicated man who walks out in front of a car.

The judge recognised that the analogy . . . of a person wandering abroad in a drug-induced state of intoxication walking into the path of a negligently driven car was very far from being perfect. I respectfully consider that this is not a good analogy at all. In my judgment, the fault of such a person (negligently walking into the path of a car) is a potent cause of the injury which he sustains in the accident. The fault (walking in the road in a drug-induced state of intoxication) is closely connected in time and place with the accident which is caused then and there by a combination of the negligence of the claimant and the defendant. There is a far closer analogy with the case of a claimant who seeks medical treatment for a condition from which he is suffering as a result of his own fault and sustains injury as a result of negligent treatment. Examples of such a condition are lung cancer caused by smoking or cirrhosis of the liver caused by excessive consumption of alcohol. Mr Kent [counsel for the appellant] accepts that in such cases it would be wrong to reduce a successful claimant's damages under the 1945 Act, although it is his fault that he is suffering from the medical condition for which he is being treated and, but for that condition, he would not have required medical treatment in the first place. One of the reasons why I consider Mr Kent is right to make this concession is that the claimant's fault in smoking or consuming excessive alcohol over a period of time is not a potent cause of the injury suffered as a result of the negligent medical treatment. The fault is not sufficiently closely connected with the defendant's negligence. Rather, the fault is part of the claimant's history which has led to his being a man who is suffering from a particular medical condition. (Dyson LJ at [57]–[58])

This has to be correct. The point here is not that the claimant's addictions were not a cause of his injuries. In all successful cases of contributory negligence there will be more than one cause of the claimant's injuries—that is, both the claimant and defendant will have contributed to the accident. Even where the claimant's carelessness was a 'but for' cause of their own injuries the defence will not be available if the injuries they suffered arose from some risk or danger of which they were not aware and against which they could not have been expected to take precautions. By way of completeness, the court also held that even if the doctrine applied, it would not be just and equitable to reduce the damages.

Fitzgerald v *Lane*
House of Lords [1989] AC 328

The claimant was a pedestrian who carelessly stepped into the road and was hit by a car driven by the first defendant. This propelled him further into the road and he was struck again by a car driven by the second defendant. The trial judge determined that all three were equally to blame, and gave judgment for the claimant for two-thirds of his damages. Held: in light of the trial judge's finding, the claimant should only receive 50 per cent of his damages.

LORD ACKNER: . . .

The correct approach to the determination of contributory negligence, apportionment and contribution

It is axiomatic that whether the plaintiff is suing one or more defendants, for damages for personal injuries, the first question which the judge has to determine is whether the plaintiff has established liability against one or other or all the defendants, ie that they, or one or more of them, were negligent (or in breach of statutory duty) and that the negligence (or breach of statutory duty) caused or materially contributed to his injuries. The next step, of course, once liability has been established, is to assess what is the total of the damage that the plaintiff has sustained as a result of the established negligence. It is only after these two decisions have been made that the next question arises, namely, whether the defendant or defendants have established (for the onus is upon them) that the plaintiff, by his own negligence, contributed to the damage which he suffered. If, and only if, contributory negligence is established does the court then have to decide, pursuant to section 1 of the Law Reform (Contributory Negligence) Act 1945, to what extent it is just and equitable to reduce the damages which would otherwise be recoverable by the plaintiff, having regard to his 'share in the responsibility for the damage.'

All the decisions referred to above are made in the main action. Apportionment of liability in a case of contributory negligence between plaintiff and defendants must be kept separate from apportionment of *contribution between the defendants inter se*. Although the defendants are each liable to the plaintiff for the whole amount for which he has obtained judgment, the proportions in which, as between themselves, the defendants must meet the plaintiff's claim, do not have any direct relationship to the extent to which the total damages have been reduced by the contributory negligence, although the facts of any given case may justify the proportions being the same.

Once the questions referred to above in the main action have been determined in favour of the plaintiff to the extent that he has obtained a judgment against two or more defendants, then and only then should the court focus its attention on the claims which may be made between those defendants for contribution pursuant to the Civil Liability (Contribution) Act 1978, re-enacting and extending the court's powers under section 6 of the Law Reform (Married Women and Tortfeasors) Act 1935. In the contribution proceedings, whether or not they are heard during the trial of the main action or by separate proceedings, the court is concerned to discover what contribution is just and equitable, having regard to the responsibility between the tortfeasors inter se, for the damage which the plaintiff has been adjudged entitled to recover. That damage may, of course, have been subject to a reduction as a result of the decision in the main action that the plaintiff, by his own negligence, contributed to the damage which he sustained.

Thus, where the plaintiff successfully sues more than one defendant for damages for personal injuries, and there is a claim between co-defendants for contribution, there are two distinct and different stages in the decision-making process—the one in the main action and the other in the contribution proceedings.

The trial judge's error

Mr Stewart [counsel for the claimant] accepts that the judge telescoped or elided the two separate stages referred to above into one when he said: 'I find that it is impossible to say that one of the parties is more or less to blame than the other and hold that the responsibility should be borne equally by all three.' The judge, in my judgment, misdirected himself by thinking in tripartite terms, instead of pursuing separately the two stages—phase 1: was the plaintiff guilty of contributory negligence and, if so, to what extent should the recoverable damages be reduced, issues which concerned the plaintiff on the one hand and the defendants jointly on the other hand; and phase 2: the amount of the contribution recoverable between the two defendants having regard to the extent of their responsibility for the damage recovered by the plaintiff—an issue which affected only the defendants *inter se* and in no way involved the plaintiff.

Notes

1. This case makes clear that one should first assess the degree of responsibility of the claimant for his own loss in relation to the totality of the actions of the defendants, and only at a later stage should one assess the responsibility of the defendants as between themselves. This solves one version of the 'relativities' problem, in that a claimant is no better off being injured by two defendants than by one. However, other problems remain. The difficulty arises from the fact that the claimant's responsibility is assessed relative to that of the defendant, so that a claimant is better off if he is injured by a grossly negligent defendant. For example, a claimant acts carelessly: this carelessness will have a lower relative value in relation to a very negligent defendant than in relation to a slightly negligent defendant. Thus, the *same* conduct by the claimant will be assessed at, say, 50 per cent in relation to a slightly negligent defendant, but at only 25 per cent in relation to a very negligent defendant. Does this seem fair? How might this problem be solved?

Jackson v Murray
Supreme Court [2015] UKSC 5

The claimant, a 13-year-old child, was seriously injured after being hit by a car when she ran into the road after alighting from her school bus. The Lord Ordinary (the trial judge) found the claimant to be contributorily negligent reducing her damages by 90 per cent, reduced to 70 per cent on appeal. Held: by majority, the parties were 'at least equally as blameworthy' and the claimant's award was increased to 50 per cent of the agreed damages.

LORD REED:

1. A school minibus draws up on a country road on a winter's evening. Two children get off. One of the children tries to cross the road. She steps out from behind the minibus, into the path of an oncoming car. The driver is driving too fast: he has seen the bus, but has made no allowance for the possibility that a child might attempt to cross in front of him. He is not keeping a proper look-out, and does not see her, but he is going too fast to have stopped in time even if he had seen her. His car hits the child, causing her to sustain severe injuries. If he had been driving at a reasonable speed, and had been keeping a proper look-out, he would not have hit her.

Apportionment

19. Section 1(1) of the Law Reform (Contributory Negligence) Act 1945 provides:

Where any person suffers damage as the result partly of his own fault and partly of the fault of any other person or persons, a claim in respect of that damage shall not be defeated by reason of the fault of the person suffering the damage, but the damages recoverable in respect thereof shall be reduced to such extent as the court thinks just and equitable having regard to the claimant's share in the responsibility for the damage.

20. Section 1(1) does not specify how responsibility is to be apportioned, beyond requiring the damages to be reduced to such extent as the court thinks just and equitable having regard to the claimant's share in the responsibility for the damage (not, it is to be noted, responsibility for the accident). Further guidance can however be found in the decided cases. In particular, in *Stapley v Gypsum Mines Ltd* [1953] AC 663, 682, Lord Reid stated:

A court must deal broadly with the problem of apportionment and in considering what is just and equitable must have regard to the blameworthiness of each party, but 'the claimant's share in the responsibility for the damage' cannot, I think, be assessed without considering the relative importance of his acts in causing the damage apart from his blameworthiness.

21. That approach is illustrated by its application to the facts of that case, where the deceased and a co-worker had been instructed by their employer to bring down a dangerous roof, and not to work beneath it in the meantime. In disobedience of the instruction, they had given up their attempts to bring down the roof, and the deceased had then proceeded to work beneath it. It collapsed and killed him. Although there was held to have been negligence on the part of the co-worker, for which the employer was responsible, the deceased's conduct had contributed much more immediately to the accident than anything that the co-worker did or failed to do: both men were at fault up to the stage when the deceased entered the area in question, but he alone was at fault in working beneath the dangerous roof. The House of Lords therefore assessed the contributory negligence of the deceased at 80%, altering the 50% apportionment made by the trial judge.

22. A further illustration is provided by *Baker v Willoughby* [1970] AC 467. The case was one in which the plaintiff was a pedestrian who had been struck by the defendant's car while crossing the road. The plaintiff had negligently failed to see the defendant's car approaching. The defendant had a clear view of the plaintiff prior to the collision, but was driving at an excessive speed or failing to keep a proper look-out or both. The judge found that the plaintiff was 25% to blame. On appeal, the Court of Appeal increased that apportionment to 50%. The House of Lords restored the judge's assessment.

23. Lord Reid, with the agreement of the other members of the House, made some general observations about apportionment in cases of this kind at p 490:

> The Court of Appeal recognised that the trial judge's assessment ought not to be varied unless 'some error in the judge's approach is clearly discernible.' But they appear to have thought it impossible to differentiate when both parties had a clear view of each other for 200 yards prior to impact and neither did anything about it. I am unable to agree. There are two elements in an assessment of liability, causation and blameworthiness. I need not consider whether in such circumstances the causative factors must necessarily be equal, because in my view there is not even a presumption to that effect as regards blameworthiness.
>
> A pedestrian has to look to both sides as well as forwards. He is going at perhaps three miles an hour and at that speed he is rarely a danger to anyone else. The motorist has not got to look sideways though he may have to observe over a wide angle ahead: and if he is going at a considerable speed he must not relax his observation, for the consequences may be disastrous . . . In my opinion it is quite possible that the motorist may be very much more to blame than the pedestrian.

24. That dictum was applied by the Second Division in *McCluskey v Wallace* 1998 SC 711, a case in which a child aged 10 had crossed the road without taking reasonable care to check whether traffic was coming. She was struck by a driver who was driving at an appropriate speed but had failed to notice her, and could have avoided her if he had been paying proper attention. An assessment of the child's contributory negligence at 20% was upheld.

25. A similar approach to the assessment of blameworthiness, in cases concerning motorists who drive negligently and hit careless pedestrians, can be seen in the judgment of the Court of Appeal, delivered by Hale LJ, in *Eagle v Chambers* [2003] EWCA Civ 1107; [2004] RTR 115. The claimant had been walking down the middle of a well-lit road, late at night, while in an emotional state. The defendant motorist would have seen and avoided her if he had been driving with reasonable care. He had however failed to see her. His ability to drive safely was impaired by alcohol. The trial judge reduced the claimant's damages by 60%. On appeal, that apportionment was reduced to 40%.

26. Hale LJ noted that there were two aspects to apportioning liability between claimant and defendant, namely the respective causative potency of what they had done, and their respective blameworthiness. In relation to the former, it was accepted that the defendant's causative potency was much greater than the claimant's on the facts of the case. In relation to blameworthiness, the defendant was equally if not more blameworthy. In that regard, Hale LJ noted that a car could do much more damage to a person than a person could usually do to a car, and that the potential 'destructive disparity' between the parties could be taken into account as an aspect of blameworthiness. The court had consistently imposed a high burden upon the drivers of cars, to reflect the potentially dangerous nature of driving. In the circumstances of the case, the judge's apportionment had been plainly wrong.

Review of apportionment

27. It is not possible for a court to arrive at an apportionment which is demonstrably correct. The problem is not merely that the factors which the court is required to consider are incapable of precise measurement. More fundamentally, the blameworthiness of the pursuer and the defender are incommensurable. The defender has acted in breach of a duty (not necessarily a duty of care) which was owed to the pursuer; the pursuer, on the other hand, has acted with a want of regard for her own interests. The word 'fault' in section 1(1), as applied to 'the person suffering the damage' on the one hand, and the 'other person or persons' on the other hand, is therefore being used in two different senses. The court is not comparing like with like.

28. It follows that the apportionment of responsibility is inevitably a somewhat rough and ready exercise (a feature reflected in the judicial preference for round figures), and that a variety of possible answers can legitimately be given. That is consistent with the requirement under section 1(1) to arrive at a result which the court considers 'just and equitable'. Since different judges may legitimately take different views of what would be just and equitable in particular circumstances, it follows that those differing views should be respected, within the limits of reasonable disagreement.

31. Given the broad nature of the judgment which has to be made, and the consequent impossibility of determining a right answer to the question of apportionment, one can say in this context, as Lord Fraser of Tullybelton said in relation to an exercise of judgment of a different kind in *G v G (Minors: Custody Appeal)* [1985] 1 WLR 647, 651:

> It is comparatively seldom that the Court of Appeal, even if it would itself have preferred a different answer, can say that the judge's decision was wrong, and unless it can say so, it will leave his decision undisturbed.

32. As one would expect, given that section 1(1) applies throughout the United Kingdom, the same approach has been followed in Scotland. In *McCusker v Saveheat Cavity Wall Insulation Ltd* 1987 SLT 24, 29, Lord Justice-Clerk Ross cited the dictum of Lord Justice-Clerk Wheatley in the unreported case of *Beattie v Halliday*, 4 February 1982:

> An appeal court will not lightly interfere with an apportionment fixed by the judge of first instance. It will only do so if it appears that he has manifestly and to a substantial degree gone wrong.

The case of *Beattie* concerned contribution between joint wrongdoers, where the court is concerned with the comparative responsibility of persons who are both liable for the damage. The dictum would apply *a fortiori* to apportionment under the 1945 Act, where the difficulties are more acute, . . .

35. The question, therefore, is whether the court below went wrong. In the absence of an identifiable error, such as an error of law, or the taking into account of an irrelevant matter, or the failure to take

account of a relevant matter, it is only a difference of view as to the apportionment of responsibility which exceeds the ambit of reasonable disagreement that warrants the conclusion that the court below has gone wrong. In other words, in the absence of an identifiable error, the appellate court must be satisfied that the apportionment made by the court below was not one which was reasonably open to it.

36. There may be cases of apportionment under the 1945 Act where the appellate court can identify an error on the part of the court below. In the case of *Stapley*, for example, although Lord Reid observed at p 682 that 'normally one would not disturb such an award', the trial judge appeared to have left out of account a material fact, namely that the deceased deliberately and culpably entered the area of danger. Similarly, in the present case, the Extra Division [the Scottish appeal court] identified an error on the part of the Lord Ordinary in categorising the pursuer's conduct as reckless.

37. Even in the absence of an identifiable error, a wide difference of view as to the apportionment which is just and equitable, going beyond what Lord Fraser described as the generous ambit within which a reasonable disagreement is possible, can in itself justify the conclusion that the court below has gone wrong. The point is illustrated by the case of *National Coal Board v England* [1954] AC 403, in which the trial judge considered a 50% apportionment to be appropriate, on the basis that the plaintiff and the defendant's employee were equally to blame. The House of Lords held that the damages should be reduced by only 25%. Lord Reid observed at p 427 that it was not right to disturb the trial judge's apportionment lightly, but that 'the difference between holding the parties equally to blame and holding the one's share of responsibility to be three times that of the other is so substantial that we should give effect to it'. Lord Porter, with whom Lord Oaksey agreed, similarly considered that, as in *Stapley*, 'the wide difference between [the House's] view and that held in the court of first instance warranted a variation in the proportional amount awarded' (p 420).

38. The need for the appellate court to be satisfied, in the absence of an identifiable error, that the apportionment made by the court below was outside the range of reasonable determinations is reflected in the fact that apportionments are not altered by appellate courts merely on the basis of a disagreement as to the precise figure. In *Kerry v Carter*, as I have explained, the appellate court disagreed with the trial judge as to which party bore the greater share of responsibility. In *Quintas v National Smelting Co Ltd* [1961] 1 WLR 401, *Brannan v Airtours Plc*, *The Times*, February 1, 1999 and *McFarlane v Scottish Borders Council*, as in *Stapley v Gypsum Mines Ltd*, *National Coal Board v England* and *Baker v Willoughby*, the appellate court intervened on the basis of a difference of view as to whether the parties bore equal responsibility or one party bore much greater responsibility than the other. The same is true of *Eagle v Chambers*, where Hale LJ observed that a finding as to which of the parties, if either, was the more responsible for the damage was different from a finding as to the precise extent of a less than 50% contribution. There was a qualitative difference between a finding of 60% contribution and a finding of 40% which was not so apparent in the quantitative difference between 40% and 20%.

The present case

39. Having explained the reasons for their conclusion that the Lord Ordinary's apportionment of 90% of the responsibility for the accident to the pursuer was too high, the Extra Division provided only a very brief explanation of their own apportionment of 70% of the responsibility to the pursuer, at para 28:

> We nevertheless recognize that the major share of responsibility must be attributed to the pursuer, because her negligence was both seriously blameworthy and of major causative significance.

The Extra Division had however already stated, at para 27, that 'the defender's behaviour was culpable to a substantial degree'. They had also stated, at para 28, that 'the defender's excessive speed was causally significant' and that 'the attribution of causative potency to the driver must be greater than that to the pedestrian'. It would appear to follow that it could be said of the defender, as well as the pursuer, that his 'negligence was both seriously blameworthy and of major causative significance'. Why then did the Extra Division conclude that 'the major share of responsibility must be attributed to the pursuer'?

40. As the Extra Division recognised, it is necessary when applying section 1(1) of the 1945 Act to take account both of the blameworthiness of the parties and the causative potency of their acts. In relation to causation, the Extra Division based its view that 'the attribution of causative potency to the driver must be greater than that to the pedestrian' on the fact that 'a car is potentially a dangerous weapon'. Like the Court of Appeal in *Eagle v Chambers*, I would take the potentially dangerous nature of a car being driven at speed into account when assessing blameworthiness; but the overall assessment of responsibility should not be affected by the heading under which that factor is taken into account. Even leaving out of account the potentially dangerous nature of a car being driven at speed, I would not have assessed the causative potency of the conduct of the defender as being any less than that of the pursuer. This is not a case, such as *Ehrari v Curry* [2007] EWCA Civ 120; [2007] RTR 521 (where contributory negligence was assessed at 70%), in which a pedestrian steps directly into the path of a car which is travelling at a reasonable speed, and the driver fails to take avoiding action as promptly as he ought to have done. In such a case, the more direct and immediate cause of the damage can be said to be the conduct of the pedestrian, which interrupted a situation in which an accident would not otherwise have occurred. Nor is it a case, such as *Eagle v Chambers* (in which contributory negligence was assessed at 40%) or *McCluskey v Wallace* (where the contributory negligence of a child was assessed at 20%), in which a driver ploughs into a pedestrian who has been careless of her own safety but has been in his line of vision for long enough for him easily to have avoided her. In the present case, the causation of the injury depended upon the combination of the pursuer's attempting to cross the road when she did, and the defender's driving at an excessive speed and without keeping a proper look-out. If the pursuer had waited until the defender had passed, he would not have collided with her. Equally, if he had slowed to a reasonable speed in the circumstances and had kept a proper look-out, he would have avoided her.

41. Given the Extra Division's conclusion that the causative potency of the defender's conduct was greater than that of the pursuer's, their conclusion that 'the major share of the responsibility must be attributed to the pursuer', to the extent of 70%, can only be explained on the basis that the pursuer was considered to be far more blameworthy than the defender. I find that difficult to understand, given the factors which their Lordships identified. As I have explained, they rightly considered that the pursuer did not take reasonable care for her own safety: either she did not look to her left within a reasonable time before stepping out, or she failed to make a reasonable judgment as to the risk posed by the defender's car. On the other hand, as the Extra Division recognised, regard has to be had to the circumstances of the pursuer. As they pointed out, she was only 13 at the time, and a 13 year old will not necessarily have the same level of judgment and self-control as an adult. As they also pointed out, she had to take account of the defender's car approaching at speed, in very poor light conditions, with its headlights on. As they recognised, the assessment of speed in those circumstances is far from easy, even for an adult, and even more so for a 13 year old. It is also necessary to bear in mind that the situation of a pedestrian attempting to cross a relatively major road with a 60 mph speed limit, after dusk and without street lighting, is not straightforward, even for an adult.

42. On the other hand, the Extra Division considered that the defender's behaviour was 'culpable to a substantial agree'. I would agree with that assessment. He had to observe the road ahead and keep a proper look-out, adjusting his speed in the event that a potential hazard presented itself. As the Extra Division noted, he was found to have been driving at an excessive speed and not to have modified his speed to take account of the potential danger presented by the minibus. The danger was obvious, because the minibus had its hazard lights on. Notwithstanding that danger, he continued driving at 50 mph. As the Lord Ordinary noted, the Highway Code advises drivers that 'at 40 mph your vehicle will probably kill any pedestrians it hits'. As in *Baker v Willoughby* and *McCluskey v Wallace*, that level of danger points to a very considerable degree of blameworthiness on the part of a driver who fails to take reasonable care while driving at speed.

43. In these circumstances, I cannot discern in the reasoning of the Extra Division any satisfactory explanation of their conclusion that the major share of the responsibility must be attributed to the pursuer: a conclusion which, as I have explained, appears to depend on the view that the pursuer's conduct was far more blameworthy than that of the defender. As it appears to me, the defender's conduct played at least an equal role to that of the pursuer in causing the damage and was at least equally blameworthy.

44. The view that parties are equally responsible for the damage suffered by the pursuer is substantially different from the view that one party is much more responsible than the other. Such a wide difference of view exceeds the ambit of reasonable disagreement, and warrants the conclusion that the court below has gone wrong. I would accordingly allow the appeal and award 50% of the agreed damages to the pursuer.

Notes

1. In dissent, Lord Hodge disagreed on the application of the principles to the facts of the case. Unlike the decision of the Lord Ordinary, the Extra Division's assessment of apportionment was not open to criticism, even if the court would have favoured an alternative assessment:

   On the Lord Ordinary's unchallenged findings, there was no reason for the pursuer [claimant] not to have seen the approaching car. Either she did not look or . . . 'she failed to identify and react sensibly to the presence of the defender's car in close proximity'. I construe the latter possibility as meaning that she saw the car and took the risk of running in front of it. Not to look or knowingly to run into the path of the car displayed a very high degree of carelessness. The Extra Division were entitled to view her behaviour as both very seriously blameworthy and of major causative significance and also, because of the extent of her blameworthiness, to attribute to her the major share of responsibility. As I have said, the opinion of the Extra Division must be read with the Lord Ordinary's findings of fact. On those findings I might have concluded that the defender was one-third responsible and the pursuer two-thirds. But that is not the role of an appellate court, which cannot substitute its judgment for that of a court below unless that court is plainly wrong. Nobody has submitted that the Extra Division failed to take into account any material fact or misunderstood the evidence. Thus their assessment is one of broad judgment in which there is ample room for reasonable disagreement. As I am not persuaded that the Extra Division's determination was outside the generous limits of reasonable disagreement, I would have dismissed the appeal. (at [57]–[59])

2. For a comparative consideration of 'a car as a potentially dangerous weapon' in cases involving a pedestrian, see the discussion of section 5R of the Civil Liability Act in the New South Wales Court of Appeal case of *Boral Bricks Pty Ltd* v *Cosmidis (No 2)* [2014] NSWCA 139 (7 May 2014) in which it was held that 'no distinction is made between the fact that from one perspective the driver is in control of a vehicle that could cause serious harm to a pedestrian, whilst from the perspective of the pedestrian, it was the likelihood of serious harm which was to be considered . . . if each were equally careless, liability should be shared equally' (Beaton JA at [99]).

Special liability regimes

PART II

10 Occupiers' liability

    10.1 Occupiers' liability and negligence

    10.2 Who is an occupier?

    10.3 The status of the entrant: visitor or non-visitor?

    10.4 The duty owed to visitors

    10.5 The duty owed to non-visitors, including trespassers

    10.6 Warnings and exclusions of liability

    10.7 Defences

11 Product liability

    11.1 Liability in negligence

    11.2 Strict liability

12 Breach of statutory duty

    12.1 Does the statute give rise to a claim in tort law and is a duty owed to the claimant?

    12.2 Has the duty been breached and does the harm fall within the scope of the duty?

Occupiers' liability

This chapter deals with the liability of an occupier to persons who are injured on their premises. The basis of liability is fault, and, to visitors at least, the duty differs little from the requirements of negligence, but there are sufficient differences to make it subject to a special chapter—not least that the common law has been put on a statutory footing through the enactment of the Occupiers' Liability Acts 1957 and 1984. These differences arise partly for historical reasons, but also because of the need to balance the rights of the occupier to deal with their property as they wish and the need to protect those who enter their property (whether invited or otherwise) from injury.

Although draconian rules relating to trespassers have been ameliorated, and the duty owed is now flexible enough to distinguish between kinds of trespassers, for example the burglar and the wandering child, a clear distinction continues to be made between lawful and unlawful visitors. It is important therefore to identify from the outset which category the person who has been injured falls into as this will determine which of the Occupiers' Liability Acts applies.

- The Occupiers' Liability Act 1957 ('the 1957 Act')—covers lawful visitors (including invitees and licensees at common law and contractual visitors).
- The Occupiers' Liability Act 1984 ('the 1984 Act')—covers unlawful visitors (typically trespassers).

OCCUPIERS' LIABILITY ACT 1957

1. Preliminary

(1) The rules enacted by the two next following sections shall have effect, in place of the rules of the common law, to regulate the duty which an occupier of premises owes to his visitors in respect of dangers due to the state of the premises or to things done or omitted to be done on them.

(2) The rules so enacted shall regulate the nature of the duty imposed by law in consequence of a person's occupation or control of premises and of any invitation or permission he gives (or is to be treated as giving) to another to enter or use the premises, but they shall not alter the rules of the common law as to the persons on whom a duty is so imposed or to whom it is owed; and accordingly for the purpose of the rules so enacted the persons who are to be treated as an occupier and as his visitors are the same (subject to subsection (4) of this section) as the persons who would at common law be treated as an occupier and as his invitees or licensees.

(3) The rules so enacted in relation to an occupier of premises and his visitors shall also apply, in like manner and to the like extent as the principles applicable at common law to an occupier of premises and his invitees or licensees would apply, to regulate—

(a) the obligations of a person occupying or having control over any fixed or moveable structure, including any vessel, vehicle or aircraft; and

(b) the obligations of a person occupying or having control over any premises or structure in respect of damage to property, including the property of persons who are not themselves his visitors.

(4) A person entering any premises in exercise of rights conferred by virtue of—

(a) section 2(1) of the Countryside and Rights of Way Act 2000, or

(b) an access agreement or order under the National Parks and Access to the Countryside Act 1949,

is not, for the purposes of this Act, a visitor of the occupier of the premises.

2. Extent of occupier's ordinary duty

(1) An occupier of premises owes the same duty, the 'common duty of care', to all his visitors, except in so far as he is free to and does extend, restrict, modify or exclude his duty to any visitor or visitors by agreement or otherwise.

(2) The common duty of care is a duty to take such care as in all the circumstances of the case is reasonable to see that the visitor will be reasonably safe in using the premises for the purposes for which he is invited or permitted by the occupier to be there.

(3) The circumstances relevant for the present purpose include the degree of care, and of want of care, which would ordinarily be looked for in such a visitor, so that (for example) in proper cases—

(a) an occupier must be prepared for children to be less careful than adults; and

(b) an occupier may expect that a person, in the exercise of his calling, will appreciate and guard against any special risks ordinarily incident to it, so far as the occupier leaves him free to do so.

(4) In determining whether the occupier of premises has discharged the common duty of care to a visitor, regard is to be had to all the circumstances, so that (for example)—

(a) where damage is caused to a visitor by a danger of which he had been warned by the occupier, the warning is not to be treated without more as absolving the occupier from liability, unless in all the circumstances it was enough to enable the visitor to be reasonably safe; and

(b) where damage is caused to a visitor by a danger due to the faulty execution of any work of construction, maintenance or repair by an independent contractor employed by the occupier, the occupier is not to be treated without more as answerable for the danger if in all the circumstances he had acted reasonably in entrusting the work to an independent contractor and had taken such steps (if any) as he reasonably ought in order to satisfy himself that the contractor was competent and that the work had been properly done.

(5) The common duty of care does not impose on an occupier any obligation to a visitor in respect of risks willingly accepted as his by the visitor (the question whether a risk was so accepted to be decided on the same principles as in other cases in which one person owes a duty of care to another).

(6) For the purposes of this section, persons who enter premises for any purpose in the exercise of a right conferred by law are to be treated as permitted by the occupier to be there for that purpose, whether they in fact have his permission or not.

3. Effect of contract on occupier's liability to third party

(1) Where an occupier of premises is bound by contract to permit persons who are strangers to the contract to enter or use the premises, the duty of care which he owes to them as his visitors cannot be restricted or excluded by that contract, but (subject to any provision of the contract to the contrary) shall include the duty to perform his obligations under the contract, whether undertaken for their protection or not, in so far as those obligations go beyond the obligations otherwise involved in that duty.

(2) A contract shall not by virtue of this section have the effect, unless it expressly so provides, of making an occupier who has taken all reasonable care answerable to strangers to the contract for dangers due to the faulty execution of any work of construction, maintenance or repair or other like operation by persons other than himself, his servants and persons acting under his direction and control.

(3) In this section 'stranger to the contract' means a person not for the time being entitled to the benefit of the contract as a party to it or as the successor by assignment or otherwise of a party to it, and accordingly includes a party to the contract who has ceased to be so entitled.

(4) Where by the terms or conditions governing any tenancy (including a statutory tenancy which does not in law amount to a tenancy) either the landlord or the tenant is bound, though not by contract, to permit persons to enter or use premises of which he is the occupier, this section shall apply as if the tenancy were a contract between the landlord and the tenant. . . .

5. Implied term in contracts

(1) Where persons enter or use, or bring or send goods to, any premises in exercise of a right conferred by contract with a person occupying or having control of the premises, the duty he owes them in respect of dangers due to the state of the premises, or to things done or omitted to be done on them, in so far as the duty depends on a term to be implied in the contract by reason of its conferring that right, shall be the common duty of care.

(2) The foregoing subsection shall apply to fixed and moveable structures as it applies to premises.

(3) This section does not affect the obligations imposed on a person by or by virtue of any contract for the hire of, or for the carriage for reward of persons or goods in, any vehicle, vessel, aircraft or other means of transport, or by virtue of any contract of bailment.

You may find it helpful to look at the annotated version of the 1957 Act or the Occupiers' Liability Acts 'at a glance' table. These can be downloaded from the **online resources**.

see online
resources

Notes

1. Some jurisdictions have abandoned distinctions based on the status of the entrant. The Occupiers' Liability (Scotland) Act 1960, for example, makes no distinction between trespassers and visitors. This seems sensible, especially given that the 1957 and 1984 Acts will often lead to the same result (the difference being whether the case fails on the basis that there has been no breach of duty (under the 1957 Act) or that no duty arises in the first place (under the 1984 Act)). Australia has gone even further and abandoned the separate rules of occupiers' liability altogether (see *Australian Safeway Stores* v *Zaluzna* (1987) 162 CLR 479, approving the view of Deane J in *Hackshaw* v *Shaw* (1984) 155 CLR 614).

OCCUPIERS' LIABILITY ACT 1984

1. Duty of occupier to persons other than his visitors

(1) The rules enacted by this section shall have effect, in place of the rules of the common law, to determine—

    (a) whether any duty is owed by a person as occupier of premises to persons other than his visitors in respect of any risk of their suffering injury on the premises by reason of any danger due to the state of the premises or to things done or omitted to be done on them; and

    (b) if so, what that duty is.

(2) For the purposes of this section, the persons who are to be treated respectively as an occupier of any premises (which, for those purposes, include any fixed or movable structure) and as his visitors are—

    (a) any person who owes in relation to the premises the duty referred to in section 2 of the Occupiers' Liability Act 1957 (the common duty of care), and

    (b) those who are his visitors for the purposes of that duty.

(3) An occupier of premises owes a duty to another (not being his visitor) in respect of any such risk as is referred to in subsection (1) above if—

    (a) he is aware of the danger or has reasonable grounds to believe that it exists;

    (b) he knows or has reasonable grounds to believe that the other is in the vicinity of the danger concerned or that he may come into the vicinity of the danger (in either case, whether the other has lawful authority for being in that vicinity or not); and

    (c) the risk is one against which, in all the circumstances of the case, he may reasonably be expected to offer the other some protection.

(4) Where, by virtue of this section, an occupier of premises owes a duty to another in respect of such a risk, the duty is to take such care as is reasonable in all the circumstances of the case to see that he does not suffer injury on the premises by reason of the danger concerned.

(5) Any duty owed by virtue of this section in respect of a risk may, in an appropriate case, be discharged by taking such steps as are reasonable in all the circumstances of the case to give warning of the danger concerned or to discourage persons from incurring the risk.

(6) No duty is owed by virtue of this section to any person in respect of risks willingly accepted as his by that person (the question whether a risk was so accepted to be decided on the same principles as in other cases in which one person owes a duty of care to another).

(6A) At any time when the right conferred by section 2(1) of the Countryside and Rights of Way Act 2000 is exercisable in relation to land which is access land for the purposes of Part I of that Act, an occupier of the land owes (subject to subsection (6C) below) no duty by virtue of this section to any person in respect of—

    (a) a risk resulting from the existence of any natural feature of the landscape, or any river, stream, ditch or pond whether or not a natural feature, or

    (b) a risk of that person suffering injury when passing over, under or through any wall, fence or gate, except by proper use of the gate or of a stile.

(6AA) Where the land is coastal margin for the purposes of Part 1 of that Act (including any land treated as coastal margin by virtue of section 16 of that Act), subsection (6A) has effect as if for paragraphs (a) and (b) of that subsection there were substituted 'a risk resulting from the existence of any physical feature (whether of the landscape or otherwise)'.

(6B) For the purposes of subsection (6A) above, any plant, shrub or tree, of whatever origin, is to be regarded as a natural feature of the landscape.

(6C) Subsection (6A) does not prevent an occupier from owing a duty by virtue of this section in respect of any risk where the danger concerned is due to anything done by the occupier—

 (a) with the intention of creating that risk, or

 (b) being reckless as to whether that risk is created.

(7) No duty is owed by virtue of this section to persons using the highway, and this section does not affect any duty owed to such persons.

(8) Where a person owes a duty by virtue of this section, he does not, by reason of any breach of the duty, incur any liability in respect of any loss of or damage to property.

(9) In this section—

'highway' means any part of a highway other than a ferry or waterway; 'injury' means anything resulting in death or personal injury, including any disease and any impairment of physical or mental condition; and 'movable structure' includes any vessel, vehicle or aircraft.

1A. Special considerations relating to access land

In determining whether any, and if so what, duty is owed by virtue of section 1 by an occupier of land at any time when the right conferred by section 2(1) of the Countryside and Rights of Way Act 2000 is exercisable in relation to the land, regard is to be had, in particular, to—

 (a) the fact that the existence of that right ought not to place an undue burden (whether financial or otherwise) on the occupier,

 (b) the importance of maintaining the character of the countryside, including features of historic, traditional or archaeological interest, and

 (c) any relevant guidance given under section 20 of that Act.

You may find it helpful to look at the annotated version of the 1984 Act or the Occupiers' Liability Acts 'at a glance' table. These can be downloaded from the **online resources**.

see online resources

10.1 Occupiers' liability and negligence

One consequence of adopting duties based on the status of the entrant is the need to distinguish between a person's duty under the ***Donoghue* v *Stevenson*** principle not to injure another and his duties under either of the Occupiers' Liability Acts. In practice, the problem does not matter very much as the two duties are very similar. However, the usual view is that so-called 'activity duties' are dealt with by the rules of ordinary negligence and 'occupancy duties' by the special rules of occupiers' liability. While the distinction between the two is not always clear, it is usually determined by asking whether the premises themselves have been rendered unsafe.

> ### *Ferguson v Welsh*
> House of Lords [1987] 1 WLR 1553

The claimant, Ferguson, was partially paralysed as a result of an accident while he was engaged on demolition work on a building owned by the council. The council had contracted with another, Spence, who, in breach of an express provision, had engaged the

Welsh brothers who, in turn, had employed the unsafe system of work which had caused the injury to the claimant. The claimant's claim against the Welsh brothers was successful at first instance. On appeal, the Court of Appeal ordered a retrial against Spence and so, by the time the case reached the House of Lords, only the liability of the council was at issue. Held: the claimant had no claim against the council either under the 1957 Act or at common law.

> LORD GOFF:. . . [I]n my judgment Mr Ferguson's action against the council must fail because I cannot see how the council could be held liable to him, in particular under the Occupiers' Liability Act 1957.
>
> On the assumption that Mr Ferguson was the lawful visitor of the council on the land, the council owed to him the common duty of care, ie a duty 'to take such care as in all the circumstances of the case is reasonable to see that the visitor will be reasonably safe in using the premises for the purposes for which he is invited or permitted by the occupier to be there:' see section 2(2) of the Act. I have emphasised the words 'in using the premises' because it seems to me that the key to the problem in the present case lies in those words. I can see no basis, even on the evidence now available, for holding that Mr Ferguson's injury arose from any breach by the council of that duty. There can, no doubt, be cases in which an independent contractor does work on premises which result in such premises becoming unsafe for a lawful visitor coming upon them, as when a brick falls from a building under repair onto the head of a postman delivering the mail. In such circumstances the occupier may be held liable to the postman, though in considering whether he is in breach of the common duty of care there would have to be considered, inter alia, the circumstances specified in section 2(4)(b) of the Act. But if I ask myself, in relation to the facts of the present case, whether it can be said that Mr Ferguson's injury arose from a failure by the council to take reasonable care to see that persons in his position would be reasonably safe in using the premises for the relevant purposes, the answer must, I think, be no. There is no question as, I see it, of Mr Ferguson's injury arising from any such failure; for it arose not from his use of the premises but from the manner in which he carried out his work on the premises. For this simple reason, I do not consider that the Occupiers' Liability Act 1957 has anything to do with the present case.

Notes

1. The distinction between occupancy and activity duties—that is, between duties arising from the dangerous condition of premises and those arising from dangerous activities carried out on the premises—was affirmed by the Court of Appeal in *Fairchild* v *Glenhaven Funeral Services* [2002] 1 WLR 1052. However, this does not mean that a defendant will never be liable for injuries caused by activities carried out on their land. In *Bottomley* v *Todmorden Cricket Club* [2003] EWCA Civ 1575, for example, the Court of Appeal held that the 1957 Act does not apply to an occupier's so-called 'activity duty'. The claimant was injured while he was helping to set up a fireworks display. Dismissing the (occupier) defendant's appeal, Brooke LJ suggested:

   > 42. It appears . . . that some confusion lingers over the effect of the decision of this court in ***Fairchild v Glenhaven Services Ltd***. Of course, there may be many occasions when an

occupier may be legally liable in negligence in respect of the activities which he permits or encourages on his land. This liability stems from his 'activity duty'. He may also be legally liable for the state of his premises, and this liability stems from his 'occupancy duty' . . .

48. On the facts of the present case the club ought to have taken reasonable care in its selection of a suitable 'contractor' to conduct this dangerous pyrotechnics display on its land, and it failed to do so. . . .

49. Occupiers usually escape liability in a case like this because they can show they have taken reasonable care to select competent and safe contractors, and in those cases an injured employee or agent can look no further than his own employer or principal for redress. But as the House of Lords acknowledged in *Ferguson v Welsh*, there may be circumstances in which the occupier of the land who wishes something dangerous to be done on his land for his benefit may be liable, too, and this in my judgment is one of those cases. If this result is tested by applying the range of tests for identifying a legal duty of care which the House of Lords has developed in the years that followed *Ferguson v Welsh*, the result is in my judgment the same. The injuries suffered by Mr Bottomley were foreseeable if there was no proper safety plan: there was the requisite proximity between the club and Mr Bottomley who was lawfully on their premises that evening; and it is fair, just and reasonable to impose liability on the club because it did not do what it ought to have done before it allowed this dangerous event to take place on its land.

However, the case law is not consistent on this. Compare, for example, *Tomlinson v Congleton Borough Council* [2003] UKHL 47 in which 'dangers due to things done or omitted to be done on the premises' was interpreted by Lord Hobhouse to include activities taking place on the premises: '[I]f shooting is taking place on the premises, a danger to visitors may arise from that fact. If speedboats are allowed to go into an area where swimmers are, the safety of the swimmers may be endangered' (at [69]) and *Edwards* v *London Borough of Sutton* [2016] EWCA Civ 1005 in which McCombe LJ suggested that a small ornamental bridge might present a danger from the 'state of the premises'.

42. One can see that an unfenced bridge or a bridge with low parapets will present more danger of a fall than would a bridge with high guard rails. There are, of course, many such unprotected bridges up and down the country in all sorts of locations. In argument, we discussed golf courses, where plank bridges, with no side rails, crossing over ditches are common and have to be negotiated by golfers with trolleys. Ornamental bridges with low walls, together with water features, are likely to be common features of decoration in public gardens. Any structure of this type presents the risk that the user may fall from it. Unlike natural land features, such as steep slopes or difficult terrain or cliffs close to coastal paths, which Lord Hobhouse in *Tomlinson* said could hardly be described as part of the 'state of the premises', it seems to me that a bridge with no sides or only low ones may present a danger from the 'state of the premises' such as to give rise to the common duty of care. However, while I am prepared to assume that there was objectively a 'danger' arising from the state of the premises in this respect here, does this mean that, in order to discharge the common duty of care, arising from that objective possibility of danger, no such bridges must be left open to visitors or must not be left open to visitors without guard rails or express warnings? In my judgment, the answer to this question is a clear 'no'.

Edwards, who had been rendered paraplegic and wheelchair-dependent after falling from a small ornamental bridge in Beddington Park, lost in the Court of Appeal:

61. Mr Edwards has suffered injury which can evoke nothing but the most enormous sympathy. However, . . . not every accident (even if it has serious consequences) has to have been the fault of another; and an occupier is not an insurer against injuries sustained on his premises.

10.2 Who is an occupier?

Liability is imposed on the *occupier* who may also—but need not be—the owner of the land or premises. The principal test is one of control. This ensures that the person who may be found to be liable is the person who is in a position to prevent the damage. The test is the same whether the claim is brought under the 1957 or 1984 Act. It is possible for two people to be occupiers of either the same, or different parts of, the premises at the same time.

Wheat v E Lacon & Co Ltd
House of Lords [1966] AC 552

Lacon & Co, a brewery company, owned 'The Golfer's Arms' public house at Great Yarmouth and employed Mr Richardson as their manager. He and his wife lived on the upper floor and rented out rooms to paying guests, including, on this occasion, to the claimant and his family. Wheat was killed when he hit his head on a concrete floor after falling down some stairs in the dark. The handrail on the stairs ended just above the third step from the bottom and there was no knob on the end of it. At the top of the stairs was a light fitting but it had no bulb and the stairs were dark. Held: while the brewery owed the claimant a duty of care as occupiers of the stairs, on the facts it was in breach of that duty. (A claim in the tort of negligence against Mr and Mrs Richardson had already failed.)

LORD DENNING: The case raises this point of law: did the brewery company owe any duty to Mr Wheat to see that the handrail was safe to use or to see that the stairs were properly lighted? That depends on whether the brewery company was 'an occupier' of the private portion of the 'Golfer's Arms,' and Mr Wheat its 'visitor' within the Occupiers' Liability Act, 1957: for, if so, the brewery company owed him the 'common duty of care.'

In order to determine this question we must have resort to the law before the Act: for it is expressly enacted [in section 1(2)] that the Act

> shall not alter the rules of the common law as to the persons on whom a duty is so imposed or to whom it is owed; and accordingly. . . the persons who are to be treated as an occupier and as his visitors are the same. . . as the persons who would at common law be treated as an occupier and as his invitees or licensees.

At the outset, I would say that no guidance is to be obtained from the use of the word 'occupier' in other branches of the law: for its meaning varies according to the subject-matter.

In the Occupiers' Liability Act, 1957, the word 'occupier' is used in the same sense as it was used in the common law cases on occupiers' liability for dangerous premises. It was simply a convenient word to denote a person who had a sufficient degree of control over premises to put him under a duty of care towards those who came lawfully on to the premises. Those persons were divided into two categories, invitees and licensees: and a higher duty was owed to invitees than to licensees. But by the year 1956 the distinction between invitees and licensees had been reduced to vanishing point. The duty of the occupier had become simply a duty to take reasonable care to see that the premises were reasonably safe for people coming lawfully on to them: and it made no difference whether they were invitees or licensees: see *Slater v Clay Cross Co Ltd* [1956] 2 QB 264. The Act of 1957 confirmed the process. It did away, once and for all, with invitees and licensees and classed them all as 'visitors', and it put upon the occupier the same duty to all of them, namely, the common duty of care. This duty is simply a particular instance of the general duty of care which each man owes to his 'neighbour'. . . . Translating this general principle into its particular application to dangerous premises, it becomes simply this: wherever a person has a sufficient degree of control over premises that he ought to realise that any failure on his part to use care may result in injury to a person coming lawfully there, then he is an 'occupier' and the person coming lawfully there is his 'visitor': and the 'occupier' is under a duty to his 'visitor' to use reasonable care. In order to be an 'occupier' it is not necessary for a person to have entire control over the premises. He need not have exclusive occupation. Suffice it that he has some degree of control. He may share the control with others. Two or more may be 'occupiers.' And whenever this happens, each is under a duty to use care towards persons coming lawfully on to the premises, dependent on his degree of control. If each fails in his duty, each is liable to a visitor who is injured in consequence of his failure, but each may have a claim to contribution from the other.

In *Salmond on Torts*, 14th ed (1965), p 372, it is said that an 'occupier' is 'he who has the immediate supervision and control and the power of permitting or prohibiting the entry of other persons.' This definition was adopted by Roxburgh J in *Hartwell v Grayson, Rollo and Clover Docks Ltd*, [1947] KB 901, and by Diplock LJ in the present case. There is no doubt that a person who fulfils that test is an 'occupier.' He is the person who says 'come in.' But I think that test is too narrow by far. There are other people who are 'occupiers,' even though they do not say 'come in.' If a person has any degree of control over the state of the premises it is enough.

. . . I ask myself whether the brewery company had a sufficient degree of control over the premises to put them under a duty to a visitor. Obviously they had complete control over the ground floor and were 'occupiers' of it. But I think that they had also sufficient control over the private portion. They had not let it out to Mr Richardson by a demise. They had only granted him a licence to occupy it, having a right themselves to do repairs. That left them with a residuary degree of control which was equivalent to that retained by the Chelsea Corporation in *Greene's* case [1954] 2 QB 127. They were in my opinion 'an occupier' within the Act of 1957. Mr Richardson, who had a licence to occupy, had also a considerable degree of control. So had Mrs Richardson, who catered for summer guests. All three of them were, in my opinion, 'occupiers' of the private portion of the 'Golfer's Arms.' There is no difficulty in having more than one occupier at one and the same time, each of whom is under a duty of care to visitors. The Court of Appeal so held in the recent case of *Crockfords Club (Fisher v CHT Ltd)* [1965] 1 WLR 1093.

What did the common duty of care demand of each of these occupiers towards their visitors? Each was under a duty to take such care as 'in all the circumstances of the case' is reasonable to see that the visitor will be reasonably safe. So far as the brewery company are concerned, the circumstances demanded that on the ground floor they should, by their servants, take care not only of the structure of the building, but also the furniture, the state of the floors and lighting, and so forth, at all hours of day or night when the premises were open. But in regard to the private portion, the circumstances did not demand so much of the brewery company. They ought to see that the structure was reasonably safe, including the handrail, and that the system of lighting was efficient. But I doubt whether they were bound to see that the lights were properly switched on or the rugs laid safely on the floor. The brewery company were entitled to leave those day-to-day matters to Mr and Mrs Richardson. They, too, were occupiers. The circumstances of the case demanded that Mr and Mrs Richardson should take care of those matters in the private portion of the house. And of other matters, too. If they had realised the handrail was dangerous, they should have reported it to the brewery company.

We are not concerned here with Mr and Mrs Richardson. The judge has absolved them from any negligence and there is no appeal. We are only concerned with the brewery company. They were, in my opinion, occupiers and under a duty of care. In this respect I agree with Sellers LJ and Winn J [in the courts below], but I come to a different conclusion on the facts. I can see no evidence of any breach of duty by the brewery company. So far as the handrail was concerned, the evidence was overwhelming that no one had any reason before this accident to suppose that it was in the least dangerous. So far as the light was concerned, the proper inference was that it was removed by some stranger shortly before Mr Wheat went down the staircase. Neither the brewery company nor Mr and Mrs Richardson could be blamed for the act of a stranger.

Notes

1. It may not be necessary for a person to have property rights over the land at all. In *Collier* v *Anglian Water Authority* The Times, 26 March 1983, the claimant tripped over an uneven paving slab on the promenade at Mablethorpe owned by the local authority who kept it clean and granted leases to shop owners on it, but did no repair work on it. The repairs were conducted by the water authority (who appeared to have no property interest in the promenade) as part of their duty to maintain adequate sea defences. It was held that both the local authority and the water authority were occupiers, the latter because, by maintaining the promenade as part of their statutory duty, they exercised control over it.

2. Conversely, if a person has the right to occupy the land they may be considered to be the occupier even if they have never set foot on it. In *Harris* v *Birkenhead Corporation* [1976] 1 All ER 279, the defendants were held to be occupiers, even though they had never visited or exercised control over the property. The defendants compulsorily purchased a house. When the tenant left without telling the defendants, the house became derelict. The claimant, aged 4, entered the house and was seriously injured when she fell from a second-floor window. The defendants were held to be occupiers, even though they had never entered the property, because the compulsory purchase order gave them the immediate right to enter.

3. Typically, a landlord who has leased out premises will not have retained sufficient control to be treated as an occupier for the purposes of the Occupiers' Liability Acts. In such situations, a tenant who suffers an injury as a result of a defect in the premises they are renting will have no claim under the Acts; there is no 'occupier' (other than themselves) to sue. Nor does the common law offer much protection in such circumstances (*Cavalier* v *Pope* [1906] AC 428; *Bottomley* v *Bannister* [1932] 1 KB 458). This gap is addressed by section 4 of the Defective Premises Act 1972.

10.3 The status of the entrant: visitor or non-visitor?

Section 1 of the Occupiers' Liability Act 1957 defines a visitor as a person who could have been either an 'invitee' or a 'licensee' at common law. An invitee was a person you asked to come onto your land for your purposes, and a licensee was a person you permitted to enter. It is no longer necessary to distinguish between an invitee or licensee, but it is still necessary to define the outer limits of the two categories as anyone who falls outside these categories is classed as a 'non-visitor' and, as such, falls within the remit of the Occupiers' Liability Act 1984 instead.

The key question is: did the claimant have express, or implied, permission to be on the premises? Such permission is rarely unlimited. If a visitor goes beyond what they have been invited or given permission to do, they will cease to be treated as a visitor. Thus, a person may be at the same time a visitor for some purposes and not for others depending on the scope of the permission granted by the occupier.

Tomlinson v Congleton Borough Council
House of Lords [2003] UKHL 47

The council owned the Brereton Heath Country Park near Congleton in Cheshire. In the park is a 14-acre lake with sandy beaches. After sunbathing, the claimant ran and dived into the water, striking his head on the sandy bottom and breaking his neck. He became tetraplegic. Notices around the lake stated 'Dangerous Water. No Swimming' but the council knew that these were often ignored and had planned, for a number of years, to plant vegetation on the 'beach' areas to prevent people from entering the water. They had not yet done this for financial reasons. The claimant conceded that he was a trespasser when he entered the water, but claimed that the defendants had failed to prevent him encountering danger. Held: the council was not liable. The claimant's injuries were not caused by the state of the premises or activities thereon. In any event, though the defendants were aware of the danger and had reasonable grounds to believe that people were in the vicinity of it, the risk was not one against which they could be reasonably expected to offer protection. (Note: this extract relates to the discussion as to the status of the claimant—see section 10.5 for discussion of the duty aspects of the case).

LORD HOFFMANN:. . .

Visitor or trespasser?

6. The 1957 Act was passed to amend and codify the common law duties of occupiers to certain persons who came upon their land. The common law had distinguished between invitees, in whose visit the occupier had some material interest, and licensees, who came simply by express or implied permission. Different duties were owed to each class. The Act, on the recommendation of the Law Reform Committee (*Third Report: Occupiers' Liability to Invitees, Licensees and Trespassers* (1954) (Cmd 9305)), amalgamated (without redefining) the two common law categories, designated the combined class 'visitors' (section 1(2)) and provided that (subject to contrary agreement) all visitors should be owed a 'common duty of care'. That duty is set out in section 2(2), as refined by subsections (3) to (5). . .

7. At first Mr Tomlinson claimed that the council was in breach of its common duty of care under section 2(2). His complaint was that the premises were not reasonably safe because diving into the water was dangerous and the council had not given adequate warning of this fact or taken sufficient steps to prevent or discourage him from doing it. But then a difficulty emerged. The county council, as manager of the park, had for many years pursued a policy of prohibiting swimming or the use of inflatable dinghies or mattresses. Canoeing and windsurfing were allowed in one area of the lake and angling in another. But not swimming; except, I suppose, by capsized canoeists or windsurfers. Notices had been erected at the entrance and elsewhere saying 'DANGEROUS WATER. NO SWIMMING'. The policy had not been altogether effective because many people, particularly rowdy teenagers, ignored the notices. They were sometimes rude to the Rangers who tried to get them out of the water. Nevertheless, it was hard to say that swimming or diving was, in the language of section 2(2), one of the purposes 'for which [Mr Tomlinson was] invited or permitted by the occupier to

be there'. The council went further and said that once he entered the lake to swim, he was no longer a 'visitor' at all. He became a trespasser, to whom no duty under the 1957 Act is owed. The council cited a famous bon mot of Scrutton LJ in *The Carlgarth* [1927] P 93, 110: 'When you invite a person into your house to use the staircase, you do not invite him to slide down the banisters'. This quip was used by Lord Atkin in *Hillen v ICI (Alkali) Ltd* [1936] AC 65, 69 to explain why stevedores who were lawfully on a barge for the purpose of discharging it nevertheless became trespassers when they went on to an inadequately supported hatch cover in order to unload some of the cargo. They knew, said Lord Atkin, at pp 69–70, that they ought not to use the covered hatch for this purpose; 'for them for such a purpose it was out of bounds; they were trespassers'. So the stevedores could not complain that the barge owners should have warned them that the hatch cover was not adequately supported. Similarly, says the council, Mr Tomlinson became a trespasser and took himself outside the 1957 Act when he entered the water to swim.

8. Mr Tomlinson's advisers, having reflected on the matter, decided to concede that he was indeed a trespasser when he went into the water. Although that took him outside the 1957 Act, it did not necessarily mean that the council owed him no duty. At common law the only duty to trespassers was not to cause them deliberate or reckless injury, but after an inconclusive attempt by the House of Lords to modify this rule in *Herrington v British Railways Board* [1972] AC 877, the Law Commission recommended the creation of a statutory duty to trespassers: see its *Report on Liability for Damage or Injury to Trespassers and Related Questions of Occupiers' Liability* (1976) (Law Com No 75) (Cmnd 6428). The recommendation was given effect by the 1984 Act. Section 1(1) describes the purpose of the Act:

> The rules enacted by this section shall have effect, in place of the rules of the common law, to determine—(a) whether any duty is owed by a person as occupier of premises to persons other than his visitors in respect of any risk of their suffering injury on the premises by reason of any danger due to the state of the premises or to things done or omitted to be done on them; and (b) if so, what that duty is.

11. . . . . On one analysis, this is a rather odd hypothesis. Mr Tomlinson's complaint is that he should have been prevented or discouraged from going into the water, that is to say, from turning himself into a trespasser. Logically, it can be said, that duty must have been owed to him (if at all) while he was still a lawful visitor. Once he had become a trespasser, it could not have meaningful effect. In the Court of Appeal, ante, p 63f–g, para 52, Longmore LJ was puzzled by this paradox:

> At what point does he become a trespasser? When he starts to paddle, intending thereafter to swim? There was no evidence that Mr Tomlinson in fact swam at all. He dived from a position in which swimming was difficult, if not impossible. I would be troubled if the defendants' duty of care differed depending on the precise moment when a swim could be said to have begun.

. . .

15. I would certainly agree with Longmore LJ that the incidence and content of the duty should not depend on the precise moment at which Mr Tomlinson crossed the line between the status of lawful visitor and that of trespasser. But there is no dispute that the act in respect of which Mr Tomlinson says that he was owed a duty, namely, diving into the water, was to his knowledge prohibited by the terms upon which he had been admitted to the park. It is, I think, for this reason that the council owed him no duty under the 1957 Act and that the incidence and content of any duty they may have owed was governed by the 1984 Act.

> ### Spearman v Royal United Bath Hospitals NHS Foundation Trust
> Queen's Bench Division [2017] EWHC 3027 (QB)

The claimant suffered serious injuries after either falling or jumping from a flat roof while a patient at the Royal United Hospital in Bath. Held: the hospital was liable for his injuries as it had failed to take reasonable steps to ensure that the premises were reasonably safe.

(Note: this extract relates to the discussion as to the status of the claimant—see section 10.5 for discussion of the duty aspects of the case.)

MARTIN SPENCER J: . . .

2. The issue which I have to decide is whether this accident occurred as a result of the breach of duty of the defendant whether owed to the claimant under the Occupiers Liability Act 1957 and/or the Occupiers Liability Act 1984 or at Common Law, or whether the claimant was the author of his own misfortune. . . .

HISTORY

[The claimant had developed Type 1 diabetes as a child, which he controlled by injecting himself with insulin. In his early 20s, he had been involved in a car accident which had left him with a brain injury and—importantly in the context of the case—a phobia of hospitals.]

THE INCIDENT IN QUESTION

12. On the evening of 5 May 2011, the claimant suffered a particularly bad hypoglycaemic attack. [By the time the ambulance arrived] James was virtually comatose. [Despite some improvement following the administering of glucose], the ambulance personnel decided to take the claimant to hospital. This decision was supported by Andrew Spearman [the claimant's brother], despite his brother's dislike of hospitals and reluctance to go. . . .

14. Andrew Spearman believed that, once James had fully recovered his consciousness he would very likely be very cross about being in hospital . . . He warned the paramedics that his brother would continue to be difficult about going into hospital and would not want to stay, as was also apparent from his behaviour.

15. The ambulance arrived at the hospital at 22.00. [By this time, the claimant still had a low Glasgow Coma Score and was not fully obeying commands for movement but was able to initiate 'purposeful movement to painful stimulus'. He was signed over to the hospital at 22.10.] . . .

17. Miss Thompson went to fetch the forms that she would need to complete when carrying out her initial assessment of the claimant which meant leaving the claimant for about 1 minute whilst she went to the main nursing station, a very short distance away. In that time, it appears that the claimant got off the trolley. The trolley had its sides raised up. The claimant removed the drip bag from the drip stand attached to the trolley, slid down the bed to get off of the trolley and then walked away. He found his way through several sets of doors and down a corridor until eventually he reached a door which has been referred to during the trial as 'door 1'. Behind this was a locker for storing lost property and, more importantly, a flight of stairs leading up to a door going past Victoria Ward and then further flights of stairs leading up to another door ('door 2') and out onto a flat roof. On the far side of the flat roof was a door ('door 3') leading to Marlborough Ward which was a general medical ward.

18. It is necessary to describe the situation on the flat roof. This is relatively high up from ground level, and on one side affords a view of a cricket ground from where, in the summer, it is possible to watch the cricket. On the other side, there is a courtyard which used to be a car park for the

consultants. Originally, there was an external fire escape leading down to the consultants' car park. However, in 2003 the internal fire escape was constructed leading down to the emergency department and it was therefore this internal fire escape which formed the flight of stairs up which the claimant went to gain access to the flat roof. On both sides of the roof, there is fencing 1.4m high and, for the most part, the fencing bends inwards from halfway up to prevent anyone from climbing onto it and over it. It general, it may be assumed that this was an effective safety measure. It appears that the flat roof was used by staff (and also, sometimes, patients) from Marlborough Ward as an area to take the sun or spend breaks during the summer and also, contrary to hospital policy, for smoking breaks. To this end, some benches and plastic chairs had been taken out and put on the flat roof. Although it is a matter of conjecture, it appears to be a reasonable assumption, and is my finding, that the claimant used the furniture to climb up and over the fencing and he then fell into the courtyard below. The position where the claimant was eventually found was directly below the position where the chairs were stacked on the bench. [Evidence suggests the timing of the accident was 22.13.] . . .

21. In the accident, the claimant suffered a severe traumatic brain injury and multiple fractures including fractures to his lower limbs, sternum, ribs, lumbar spine and left wrist. This has required extensive treatment and neuro-rehabilitation and he remains an in-patient at Park House Neurological Rehabilitation Centre, Redford. He has been left with profound problems with all aspects of cognitive functioning affecting memory and executive function, and dyspraxia. He is no longer able to care for himself or live independently and he is dependant [sic] on others for care and assistance with all activities of daily living including personal hygiene and dressing, cooking, cleaning and the taking of medication.

Issue 2: was the claimant a 'visitor' or a trespasser at the time of the accident?

49. It is the defendant's case that, by leaving the Emergency Department and going up the stairs onto the flat roof, the claimant became a trespasser and that the duty owed to him by the hospital was only the duty imposed by the Occupiers Liability Act 1984. For the claimant, it is argued that there was dual duty: first, the 'common duty of care' owed under the Occupiers Liability Act 1957 on the basis that, at all material times, the claimant remained a 'visitor' for the purposes of the Act and was not a trespasser (or at least, the very earliest time he was a trespasser was when he went over the barrier on the flat roof); secondly, a duty owed at common law by the hospital to its patients which is an enhanced duty which takes into account the fact that some patients will be 'vulnerable', including those that are confused and/or mentally unstable.

50. It was submitted on behalf of the defendant that the claimant became a trespasser when he left the Emergency Department and went through door 1 and up the staircase. It is argued that he was no longer in a location in the hospital where he was authorised to be and, as such, was a trespasser. It was further submitted that whether a person is or is not a trespasser is simply a question of objective fact: it is not governed by the state of mind of the person in question. Lord Faulks QC [counsel for the defendant] concedes that sometimes the line between being (or remaining) a visitor and being a trespasser is 'not bright' and may be made brighter by, for example, putting up a 'no entry' notice. However, he submits that such a notice is not required and objectively the staircase was no longer part of the Emergency Department and was therefore no longer an authorised location.

51. In support of his submission, Lord Faulks QC relies upon a number of previous decisions or authorities. The first is *Kolasa v Ealing Hospital NHS Trust* [2015] EWHC 289 (QB) . . . In that case, the claimant had been assaulted, robbed and rendered unconscious on his way home from work.

Before setting off for home he had been drinking with three colleagues and was intoxicated. He was taken to North Ealing Hospital where he was assessed by a triage nurse as not suffering from serious injury and he was asked to wait. He said that he had felt unwell and gone outside where there were ramps for ambulances leading up and down, to and from the Accident and Emergency Department ('A&E') to the road, A&E being some thirty feet above ground level. There were walls on either side of the ramps. The claimant was seen to climb onto one of the walls but he fell and sustained injury. . . . [T]he learned Judge said this:

42. I also make the finding of fact that, although when the claimant was brought to the hospital and was put to wait in A&E he was a visitor to the hospital and was owed the common duty of care under section 2(2) of the 1957 Act, his act of climbing over the wall was not an act covered by his general permission to be on the site as a patient nor was it part of the permission given by the defendant to patients leaving the site after, or even without, treatment. He was, therefore, no longer an invitee or visitor but a trespasser.

43. To use the famous example of Lord Justice Scrutton in *The Calgarth* [1927] P 93 at page 110:

When you invite a person into your house to use the staircase, you do not invite him to slide down the banisters—you invite him to use the staircase in the ordinary way in which it is used.

44. Mr. Norris' primary submission to me is that the protection extended both to visitors and to trespassers under the 1957 and 1984 Acts respectively is from danger caused by the state of the premises, an 'occupancy duty' rather than a more general obligation to protect the visitor/trespasser from danger he may face while on the premises. That is clear from the discussion of the law at paragraph 12-04 of the current edition of *Clerk and Lindsell on Torts*. I accept that submission.

52. Having thus found that Mr Kolasa was a trespasser for the purposes of the law, the learned Judge found that there was nothing dangerous about the state of the premises where the claimant fell, the wall being of an adequate safe height. He found that the provision of an additional handrail after a later accident to another patient was 'the reaction of a risk adverse defendant to the circumstances of this particular accident, which involved someone sitting on the part of a first floor perimeter wall an area known to be used for recreational purposes, and, thus falling to his death.' He found that the defendant had acted on the specific recommendation of health and safety experts but could not have been criticised if they had not erected the rail. He found that, in truth, the accident to Mr Kolasa was nothing to do with the state of the premises and was, instead, the entire fault of the claimant himself given his state of intoxication.

53. In giving his judgment, [the judge] referred to the authority of the Court of Appeal decision in *Keown v Coventry Healthcare NHS Trust* [2006] 1 WLR 953 a further authority upon which Lord Faulks QC relies. There, the 11-year-old claimant had climbed the underside of an external metal fire escape of an accommodation block and day clinic in the grounds of a hospital owned by the defendant and fell from a height of about 30 feet, severely injuring himself. There was evidence in that case that the hospital grounds were known as a place where children liked to play. The claim was brought under the 1984 Act on the basis that the fire escape constituted a material danger and allurement to children. The claimant accepted he appreciated that climbing the underside of the fire escape was dangerous and that he should not be doing it. The Court of Appeal held that—

The threshold requirement posed by section 1(1)(a) of the Occupiers' Liability Act 1984 was not whether there was a risk of suffering injury by reason of the state of the premises, but whether there was a risk of injury by reason of any danger due to the state of the premises; that a fire escape was not inherently dangerous, so that, if a person chose to create danger by climbing it improperly knowing that it was dangerous to do so, any danger was due to such person's activity and not the state of the premises; that, in general, the age of the trespasser was not relevant, but it was a question of fact and degree whether premises which were not dangerous from the point of view of an adult could be dangerous for a child; that the claimant had been aware not only that there was a risk of falling but also that his actions were dangerous and he should not have been climbing the exterior of the fire escape; and that, accordingly, no risk arose out of the state of the fire escape there being no element of disrepair or structural deficiency

If, therefore, I find that, at the material time, the claimant was a trespasser and no longer a visitor, this case establishes the test to be applied under the 1984 Act and that the investigation will be concerned with whether the flat roof was dangerous because of, for example, disrepair or structural deficiency.

54. For the claimant, Mr Hopkins QC argues first that there is no direct evidence that the claimant was intent upon discharging himself but, even if he had formed an intention to discharge himself, this did not convert him into a trespasser and he remained a lawful visitor on the premises until he left. He uses the example of a patient who, having formed an intention to discharge himself, decides first to use the lavatory or visit a café on the premises. Such a person remains a 'visitor' until he leaves the hospital premises. He relies upon the lack of any sign prohibiting access such as to convert the claimant into a trespasser, whether over door 1 or over door 2, the lack of a sign saying that the staircase was a fire escape only and the lack of any physical barrier such as a functioning lock. He argues that there was nothing to inform the claimant that he should not pass through door 1 to the staircase or through door 2 to the roof space and nothing to make him a trespasser on the roof space.

55. In support of his argument, Mr Hopkins QC relies upon the case of *Gould v McAuliffe* [1941] 2 All ER 527. There, the plaintiff had gone to a public house to meet her husband and while waiting for him had occasion to look for a lavatory. She did not enquire where she could find one but went through a garden at the side of the public house. Some years before there had indeed been a lavatory there and the plaintiff had used it but it had since been removed. Not finding this lavatory, the plaintiff passed to the other side of the garden and went through a gate which was open at the time into a yard. She was then immediately attacked and injured by a dog belonging to the licensee of the premises, the defendant. It was argued on behalf of the defendant that, in the place where she was attacked the plaintiff was a trespasser. The Court of Appeal held that the defendant was an invitee not only when she went into the garden but also when she went through the gate into the yard where she was bitten. Scott LJ stated:

> In the court below it was contended that the plaintiff became a trespasser when she passed through the gate because the licensee of the house did not intend the public to use the yard. The gate was not locked, nor was there any notice on it that the yard was private, or that trespassers were forbidden, or that there was a dangerous dog there. Singleton LJ held that the plaintiff was acting quite reasonably. In my view the facts constitute an invitation by the defendant to persons on his premises. The plaintiff was, therefore, an invitee not only to enter the garden, but also to use the gate leading, as she mistakenly thought, to a lavatory. In the view of the court that disposes of the whole case.

Discussion

56. Although the case of *Gould v McAuliffe* was decided before either of the Occupier Liability Acts had been passed and at a time when the law treated trespassers harshly, nevertheless it informs the issue which I need to decide. Firstly, in my judgment whether a person is or is not a trespasser is not solely determined by whether the place where they are is or is not an 'authorised' place. A person's state of mind and intention is an important additional factor. If a patient, who is a lawful visitor to a hospital (whether the Emergency Department or any other department) has finished his or her treatment and is leaving, he or she does not cease to be a visitor in general until they leave the hospital premises. The position may be different if they deliberately enter an area marked 'no entry', or 'private' or know that they are entering a part of the hospital where they have no right to be. But if the patient simply makes a mistake and goes the wrong way, it could not possibly be suggested that such a person was now a trespasser. So here, intending to leave the Emergency Department, Mr Spearman, in his confused state of mind, thought (wrongly but honestly) that he needed to go upstairs to get out and, indeed, go over the barrier to get out. His belief meant that he remained a lawful visitor and, in my judgment, he did not become a trespasser at any time material to this case. Just as, for Goddard LJ in *Gould's* case, it was determinative that 'there was nothing to show that an invitee to this garden ought not to go through the gate in question', so here, the lack of any notice over door 1 and the lack of any lock on door 1 had the same effect. With respect to His Honour Judge Bidder QC [in *Kolasa*], the suggestion that the mere act of climbing over the wall, not being an act covered by the general permission to be on the site as a patient nor being part of the permission given by the defendant to patients leaving the site after treatment, was enough to convert the claimant in that case from being an invitee or visitor to being a trespasser is too simplistic as it fails to take account of the state of mind of the claimant. I have no doubt that the decision in that case was correct because the claimant could not rely upon his own self-induced intoxication in asserting that he was doing something which he thought he was authorised to do and the claim never seems to have been argued that way. The present case is wholly different where, as I have found, the claimant was mentally disturbed and did what he did as a result of a genuine and honest mistake, made in his state of confusion, it being wholly foreseeable that confused and mentally unstable patients would be part of [the] cohort of visitors to the department.

Notes

1. Under the 1957 Act, the question is not whether the presence of the claimant was foreseeable, but rather whether it was impliedly permitted. In *Harvey* v *Plymouth City Council* [2010] EWCA Civ 860, the claimant had been drinking all evening and, in an attempt to escape paying a taxi fare in the early hours of the morning, ran across land belonging to the council at which point he fell down an unprotected steep slope. The land was commonly used for informal recreational purposes. It was not in dispute that an owner of land may confer an implied licence by conduct. However, even if there were an implied licence for general recreational activity, it would not mean that there was a licence for any kind of activity:

   In deciding whether the claimant was a licensee, the question was, not whether his activity or similar activities might have been foreseen, but whether they had been impliedly assented to by the Council. In my view there was no evidence to support such a finding. When a council licenses the public to use its land for recreational purposes, it is consenting to normal recreational activities, carrying normal risks. An implied licence for general recreational activity cannot, in my view, be stretched to cover any form of activity, however reckless. (Carnwath LJ at [27])

10.4 The duty owed to visitors

The nature of the duty owed by an occupier to his visitors is dealt with in section 2 of the Occupiers' Liability Act 1957, and has generally been equated with the ordinary rules of negligence, subject to the particular conditions in section 2(3) and (4), which relate to children and to skilled entrants and to the role of warnings. It should be noted that the statute does not require the premises themselves to be safe, but rather that the visitor is enabled to be safe. As discussed in section 10.6, this can be achieved either by making sure the premises are safe and/or by warning the entrant of dangers or otherwise enabling the visitor to avoid them. Children invited onto premises are owed a common duty of care like all other visitors, however, the occupier may need to do more to ensure that they are kept *reasonably* safe; conversely skilled visitors—that is, those visiting 'in the exercise of a calling'—are expected to guard against special risks associated with their profession (s 2(3)(b)).

> ### Roles v Nathan
> Court of Appeal [1963] 1 WLR 1117

Donald and Joseph Roles were chimney sweeps who were working on the flues of the Manchester Assembly Rooms. There was a boiler with lengthy flues and, the fire being difficult to light, a boiler engineer was consulted. He advised that two vent holes should be sealed up, and warned the Roles brothers of the dangers of working on the flues with the fires lit and of the risk of carbon monoxide poisoning. One day the men were working on the flue (with the fire lit) in the presence of the engineer and the manager. The work had not been finished and the two returned later that evening to complete it. They died of carbon monoxide poisoning, and at first instance the judge held the occupier liable for not having the fire drawn or at least damped down. Held: the majority of the Court of Appeal found the occupier was not liable.

LORD DENNING MR: The occupier now appeals and says that it is not a case of negligence and contributory negligence, but that, on the true application of the Occupiers' Liability Act, 1957, the occupier was not liable at all. This is the first time we have had to consider that Act. It has been very beneficial. It has rid us of those two unpleasant characters, the invitee and the licensee, who haunted the courts for years, and it has replaced them by the attractive figure of a visitor, who has so far given no trouble at all. The Act has now been in force six years, and hardly any case has come before the courts in which its interpretation has had to be considered. The draftsman expressed the hope that 'the Act would replace a principle of the common law with a new principle *of the common law*, instead of having the judgment of Willes J construed as if it were a statute, one is to have a statute which can be construed as if it were a judgment of Willes J.' It seems that his hopes are being fulfilled. All the fine distinctions about traps have been thrown aside and replaced by the common duty of care.

'The common duty of care,' the Act says, 'is a duty to take such care as in all the circumstances of the case is reasonable to see that the visitor'—note the visitor, not the premises—'will be reasonably safe in using the premises for the purposes for which he is invited or permitted by the occupier to be there.' That is comprehensive. All the circumstances have to be considered. But the Act goes on to give examples of the circumstances that are relevant. The particular one in question here is in subsection (3) of section 2:

The circumstances relevant for the present purpose include the degree of care, and of want of care, which would ordinarily be looked for in such a visitor, so that (for example) in proper cases. . . (b) an occupier may expect that a person, in the exercise of his calling, will appreciate and guard against any special risks ordinarily incident to it, so far as the occupier leaves him free to do so.

. . . Likewise in the case of a chimney sweep who comes to sweep the chimneys or to seal up a sweep-hole. The householder can reasonably expect the sweep to take care of himself so far as any dangers from the flues are concerned. These chimney sweeps ought to have known that there might be dangerous fumes about and ought to have taken steps to guard against them. They ought to have known that they should not attempt to seal up a sweep-hole whilst the fire was still alight. They ought to have had the fire withdrawn before they attempted to seal it up, or at any rate they ought not to have stayed in the alcove too long when there might be dangerous fumes about. All this was known to these two sweeps; they were repeatedly warned about it, and it was for them to guard against the danger. It was not for the occupier to do it, even though he was present and heard the warnings. When a householder calls in a specialist to deal with a defective installation on his premises, he can reasonably expect the specialist to appreciate and guard against the dangers arising from the defect. The householder is not bound to watch over him to see that he comes to no harm. I would hold, therefore, that the occupier here was under no duty of care to these sweeps, at any rate in regard to the dangers which caused their deaths. If it had been a different danger, as for instance if the stairs leading to the cellar gave way, the occupier might no doubt be responsible, but not for these dangers which were special risks ordinarily incidental to their calling.

Even if I am wrong about this point, and the occupier was under a duty of care to these chimney sweeps, the question arises whether the duty was discharged by the warning that was given to them. This brings us to subsection (4) which states:

In determining whether the occupier of premises has discharged the common duty of care to a visitor, regard is to be had to all the circumstances, so that (for example)—(a) where damage is caused to a visitor by a danger of which he had been warned by the occupier, the warning is not to be treated without more as absolving the occupier from liability, unless in all the circumstances it was enough to enable the visitor to be reasonably safe.

Apply subsection (4) to this case. I am quite clear that the warnings which were given to the sweeps were enough to enable them to be reasonably safe. The sweeps would have been quite safe if they had heeded these warnings. They should not have come back that evening and attempted to seal up the sweep-hole while the fire was still alight. They ought to have waited till next morning, and then they should have seen that the fire was out before they attempted to seal up the sweep-hole. In any case they should not have stayed too long in the sweep-hole. In short, it was entirely their own fault. The judge held that it was contributory negligence. I would go further and say that under the Act the occupier has, by the warnings, discharged his duty.

Jolley v Sutton London Borough Council
House of Lords [2000] 1 WLR 1082

The claimant, a 14-year-old boy, was crushed when an abandoned boat fell on him and caused serious spinal injuries which left him paralysed. The boat had been abandoned for at least two years on land owned by the defendant. Although it appeared to be in relatively good condition, it was in fact rotten. Held: though the boat was not likely to pose a danger to adults, it was reasonably foreseeable that children may approach the boat and be tempted to climb onto it and, accordingly, the council was liable for the claimant's injuries (reduced by 25 per cent for contributory negligence).

LORD HOFFMANN:. . . The issue in this appeal is a very narrow one. The council admits that it was the occupier of the grassed area near the flats where the plaintiff lived, that the plaintiff was allowed to play there and that he was accordingly a 'visitor' upon its land within the meaning of the Occupier's Liability Act 1957: see section 1(2). The council therefore owed the plaintiff the 'common duty of care' defined in section 2(2) of the Act:

> a duty to take such care as in all the circumstances of the case is reasonable to see that the visitor will be reasonably safe in using the premises for the purposes for which he is invited or permitted by the occupier to be there.

By way of further explanation, section 2(3) says that the relevant circumstances will include 'the degree of care, and want of care, which would ordinarily be looked for in such a visitor' so that, for example, in proper cases: 'an occupier must be prepared for children to be less careful than adults'.

It is also agreed that the plaintiff must show that the injury which he suffered fell within the scope of the council's duty and that in cases of physical injury, the scope of the duty is determined by whether or not the injury fell within a description which could be said to have been reasonably foreseeable.. . .

It is also agreed that what must have been foreseen is not the precise injury which occurred but injury of a given description. The foreseeability is not as to the particulars but the genus. And the description is formulated by reference to the nature of the risk which ought to have been foreseen. So, in *Hughes v Lord Advocate* [1963] AC 837 the foreseeable risk was that a child would be injured by falling in the hole or being burned by a lamp or by a combination of both. The House of Lords decided that the injury which actually materialised fell within this description, notwithstanding that it involved an unanticipated explosion of the lamp and consequent injuries of unexpected severity. . . .

In the present case, the rotten condition of the boat had a significance beyond the particular danger it created. It proclaimed the boat and its trailer as abandoned, *res nullius*, there for the taking, to make of them whatever use the rich fantasy life of children might suggest.

In the Court of Appeal, Lord Woolf MR observed, at p 1553, that there seemed to be no case of which counsel were aware 'where want of care on the part of a defendant was established but a plaintiff, who was a child, had failed to succeed because the circumstances of the accident were not foreseeable'. I would suggest that this is for a combination of three reasons: first, because a finding or admission of want of care on the part of the defendant establishes that it would have cost the defendant no more trouble to avoid the injury which happened than he should in any case have taken; secondly, because in such circumstances the defendants will be liable for the materialisation of even relatively small risks of a different kind, and thirdly, because it has been repeatedly said in cases about children that their ingenuity in finding unexpected ways of doing mischief to themselves and others should never be underestimated. For these reasons, I think that the judge's broad description of the risk as being that children would 'meddle with the boat at the risk of some physical injury' was the correct one to adopt on the facts of this case. The actual injury fell within that description and I would therefore allow the appeal.

Notes

1. An occupier is entitled to assume that parents will take reasonable care of young children. In *Simkiss v Rhondda Borough Council* (1983) 81 LGR 460, Catherine Simkiss, aged 7, and a friend, aged 10, went to picnic on a hillside occupied by the defendants. They came there as visitors, and the picnic spot was visible from Catherine's parents' flat. After the picnic the children walked up the mountain intending to slide down a 'bluff' (a very steep almost vertical slope of grass with some boulders on it) on a blanket. On the way down, they slid out of control and the claimant was seriously injured, including a fractured femur and skull. The defendants were not liable because (a) the occupiers were entitled to assume that parents would have warned their children of the dangers, and (b) the standard applicable to the occupier was that of a reasonably prudent parent, and they could not be expected to fence off every natural hazard which provided an opportunity for children to injure themselves:

   > [I]t never entered [the plaintiff's father's] head, so far as I can see from his evidence, that this little girl would try to slide down this slope on a blanket, and it seems to me from the photographs that the slope was only dangerous if somebody tried to effect to toboggan down it. I see no reason why the Borough Council should be required to exercise a higher standard of care than that of a reasonably prudent parent. If the exercise of reasonable care required the Borough Council to fence off this bluff, it seems to me it would also require them to fence every natural hazard in the Rhondda Valley which was adjacent to housing estates. The Borough Council are in no special position compared with other occupiers. There are many parts of the country with open spaces adjacent to houses where children play unattended, and this is to be encouraged. It is not unreasonable, in my judgment, for such occupiers to assume that the parents of children have warned them of the dangers of natural hazards, and would not allow them to play round such places unless the children appreciated the dangers. (Dunn LJ)

   But what if the child does not have 'a reasonably prudent parent' and so has not been warned of the danger. Should the fact that the claimant's parents fail to give sufficient regard to their child's safety entitle occupiers to escape liability for their own neglect?

2. Where the occupier is aware of a particular vulnerability of the visitor, they will be expected to take steps to ensure the visitor is safe. In *Pollock v Cahill* [2015] EWHC 2260 (QB), the defendants were liable after the claimant, who was blind, sustained serious brain and spinal injuries after falling out of an open second-floor window while staying at the defendants' house.

   51. [T]he reference to 'such a visitor' [in section 2(3) of the Occupiers' Liability Act 1957] requires the occupier to have regard to any known vulnerability . . . If [the claimant] had been a sighted person, the open window would not have rendered the premises unsafe. It was the fact that he was blind that made them so. . . .

   53. Obviously the window was not dangerous per se although the sill was lower than many sills in the domestic setting. However, an open window did create an obvious risk for a blind person, particularly when it was on the second storey of the house with nothing to prevent a fall to the ground below. As is admitted in the Defence it was reasonably foreseeable that a person who fell from the window might sustain serious injury. Mr Pollock [the claimant] was and is an adventurous and resourceful man. But he was a blind man. His adventure activities [among other things, he was the first blind man to reach the South Pole] were carried out after very careful risk assessments and always with the assistance of others. The fact that he was a resourceful blind person was irrelevant to the risk created by an open window. The evidence of Mrs Cahill [one of the defendants] as the person who opened the window was that she did not think of it as a risk and that she had no concern about the safety of an open

window in the room. She did understand that Mr Pollock required particular care because she was concerned about the stairs. If it is a fact that she did not think of the open window as a risk, she was wrong to take that view. It is of note that she accepted that she would not have allowed a child to be unattended in the bedroom with an open window. . . . The parallel drawn with Mr Pollock's behaviour at hotels when he would ask a member of hotel staff to explain the windows in his room to him is false. When Mr Pollock was at a hotel, he was a stranger and the hotel would not know he was blind. Mrs Cahill was fully aware of his position. I am satisfied that the Cahills failed to discharge the common duty of care they owed as occupiers. The open window was a real risk to Mr Pollock. They created that risk. They ought to have appreciated the risk and taken steps to prevent it by keeping the window closed or by warning Mr Pollock about it with particular reference as to the extent of the drop from the window. (Davis J)

see online resources

Explore the case further with the **online resources**.

10.5 The duty owed to non-visitors, including trespassers

The issue of the level of duty which should be owed to trespassers has had a turbulent history. Traditionally, the law relating to trespassers has been very strict. Trespassers went onto premises at their own risk and occupiers were simply under an obligation not to deliberately or recklessly cause them harm (*Addie & Sons (Collieries) Ltd v Dumbreck* [1929] AC 358). However, even before the passing of the 1984 Act attitudes towards trespassers—especially when they were children—were beginning to soften (see *British Railways Board v Herrington*) [1972] AC 877, though they continue to be treated differently to their lawful counterparts. The position now is as follows:

(1) The Occupiers' Liability Act 1984 applies to personal injuries incurred by trespassers and other non-visitors, including people exercising a private right of way and ramblers *lawfully* exercising a public right of way by using a footpath across private land (subject to some exclusions) (s 1(6A) as inserted the Countryside and Rights of Way Act 2000, s 13).

(2) Property damage to all non-visitors is covered, if at all, by the common law, as expressed in *British Railways Board v Herrington* [1972] AC 877.

A crucial difference between the 1957 Act and the 1984 Act is that while an occupier will *always* owe a duty of care to a visitor, this is not the case in relation to a non-visitor. In order for a duty to be owed under the 1984 Act the three conditions, set out in section 1(3), need to be met.

> **Tomlinson v Congleton Borough Council**
> House of Lords [2003] UKHL 47

The facts are set out in section 10.3.

LORD HOFFMANN:

4. It is a terrible tragedy to suffer such dreadful injury in consequence of a relatively minor act of carelessness. It came nowhere near the stupidity of Luke Ratcliff, a student who climbed a fence at 2.30 am on a December morning to take a running dive into the shallow end of a swimming pool

(see *Ratcliff v McConnell* [1999] 1 WLR 670) or John Donoghue, who dived into Folkestone Harbour from a slipway at midnight on 27 December after an evening in the pub: *Donoghue v Folkestone Properties Ltd* [2003] QB 1008. John Tomlinson's mind must often recur to that hot day which irretrievably changed his life. He may feel, not unreasonably, that fate has dealt with him unfairly. And so in these proceedings he seeks financial compensation: for the loss of his earning capacity, for the expense of the care he will need, for the loss of the ability to lead an ordinary life. But the law does not provide such compensation simply on the basis that the injury was disproportionately severe in relation to one's own fault or even not one's own fault at all. Perhaps it should, but society might not be able to afford to compensate everyone on that principle, certainly at the level at which such compensation is now paid. The law provides compensation only when the injury was someone else's fault. In order to succeed in his claim, that is what Mr Tomlinson has to prove. . . .

A DANGER 'DUE TO THE STATE OF THE PREMISES'

26. The first question, therefore, is whether there was a risk within the scope of the statute; a danger 'due to the state of the premises or to things done or omitted to be done on them'. The judge found that there was 'nothing about the mere at Brereton Heath which made it any more dangerous than any other ordinary stretch of open water in England'. There was nothing special about its configuration; there were no hidden dangers. It was shallow in some places and deep in others, but that is the nature of lakes. Nor was the Council doing or permitting anything to be done which created a danger to persons who came to the lake. No power boats or jet skis threatened the safety of either lawful windsurfers or unlawful swimmers. So the Council submits that there was no danger attributable to the state of premises or things done or omitted on them. In *Donoghue v Folkestone Properties Ltd* [2003] 2 WLR 1138, 1153 Lord Phillips of Worth Matravers MR expressed the same opinion. He said that he had been unable to identify the 'state of the premises' which carried with it the risk of the injury suffered by Mr Tomlinson:

> It seems to me that Mr Tomlinson suffered his injury because he chose to indulge in an activity which had inherent dangers, not because the premises were in a dangerous state.

27. In making this comment, the Master of the Rolls was identifying a point which is in my opinion central to this appeal. It is relevant at a number of points in the analysis of the duties under the 1957 and 1984 Acts. Mr Tomlinson was a person of full capacity who voluntarily and without any pressure or inducement engaged in an activity which had inherent risk. The risk was that he might not execute his dive properly and so sustain injury. Likewise, a person who goes mountaineering incurs the risk that he might stumble or misjudge where to put his weight. In neither case can the risk be attributed to the state of the premises. Otherwise any premises can be said to be dangerous to someone who chooses to use them for some dangerous activity. In the present case, Mr Tomlinson knew the lake well and even if he had not, the judge's finding was that it contained no dangers which one would not have expected. So the only risk arose out of what he chose to do and not out of the state of the premises.

28. Mr Braithwaite was inclined to accept the difficulty of establishing that the risk was due to the state of the premises. He therefore contended that it was due to 'things done or omitted to be done' on the premises. When asked what these might be, he said that they consisted in the attraction of the lake and the Council's inadequate attempts to keep people out of the water. The Council, he said, were 'luring people into a deathtrap'. Ward LJ said that the water was 'a siren call strong enough to turn stout men's minds'. In my opinion this is gross hyperbole. The trouble with the island of the Sirens was not the state of the premises. It was that the Sirens held mariners spellbound until they died of hunger. The beach, give or take a fringe of human bones, was an ordinary Mediterranean beach. If

Odysseus had gone ashore and accidentally drowned himself having a swim, Penelope would have had no action against the Sirens for luring him there with their songs. Likewise in this case, the water was perfectly safe for all normal activities. In my opinion 'things done or omitted to be done' means activities or the lack of precautions which cause risk, like allowing speedboats among the swimmers. It is a mere circularity to say that a failure to stop people getting into the water was an omission which gave rise to a duty to take steps to stop people from getting into the water.

29. It follows that in my opinion, there was no risk to Mr Tomlinson due to the state of the premises or anything done or omitted upon the premises. That means that there was no risk of a kind which gave rise to a duty under the 1957 or 1984 Acts. I shall nevertheless go on to consider the matter on the assumption that there was.

THE CONDITIONS FOR THE EXISTENCE OF A DUTY

(i) Knowledge or foresight of the danger

30. Section 1(3) has three conditions which must be satisfied. First, under paragraph (a), the occupier must be aware of the danger or have reasonable grounds to believe that it exists. For this purpose, it is necessary to say what the relevant danger was. . . I accept that the Council must have known that there was a possibility that some boisterous teenager would injure himself by horseplay in the shallows and I would not disturb the concurrent findings that this was sufficient to satisfy paragraph (a). But the chances of such an accident were small. I shall return later, in connection with condition (c), to the relevance of where the risk comes on the scale of probability.

(ii) Knowledge or foresight of the presence of the trespasser

31. Once it is found that the risk of a swimmer injuring himself by diving was something of which the Council knew or which they had reasonable grounds to believe to exist, paragraph (b) presents no difficulty. The Council plainly knew that swimmers came to the lake and Mr Tomlinson fell within that class.

(iii) Reasonable to expect protection

32. That leaves paragraph (c). Was the risk one against which the Council might reasonably be expected to offer the claimant some protection? The judge found that 'the danger and risk of injury from diving in the lake where it was shallow were obvious.' In such a case the judge held, both as a matter of common sense and following consistent authority (*Staples v West Dorset District Council* [1995] PIQR 439; *Ratcliff v McConnell* [1999] 1 WLR 670; *Darby v National Trust* [2001] PIQR 372), that there was no duty to warn against the danger. A warning would not tell a swimmer anything he did not already know. Nor was it necessary to do anything else. 'I do not think', said the judge, 'that the defendants' legal duty to the claimant in the circumstances required them to take the extreme measures which were completed after the accident'. Even if Mr Tomlinson had been owed a duty under the 1957 Act as a lawful visitor, the Council would not have been obliged to do more than they did.

33. The Court of Appeal disagreed. Ward LJ said that the Council was obliged to do something more. The gravity of the risk, the number of people who regularly incurred it and the attractiveness of the beach created a duty. The prohibition on swimming was obviously ineffectual and therefore it was necessary to take additional steps to prevent or discourage people from getting into the water. Sedley LJ said: 'It is only where the risk is so obvious that the occupier can safely assume that nobody will take it that there will be no liability.' Longmore LJ dissented. The majority reduced the damages by two-thirds to reflect Mr Tomlinson's contributory negligence, although Ward LJ said that he would have been inclined to reduce them only by half. The Council appeals against the finding

of liability and Mr Tomlinson appeals against the apportionment, which he says should have been in accordance with the view of Ward LJ.

THE BALANCE OF RISK, GRAVITY OF INJURY, COST AND SOCIAL VALUE

34. My Lords, the majority of the Court of Appeal appear to have proceeded on the basis that if there was a foreseeable risk of serious injury, the Council was under a duty to do what was necessary to prevent it. But this in my opinion is an oversimplification. Even in the case of the duty owed to a lawful visitor under section 2(2) of the 1957 Act and even if the risk had been attributable to the state of the premises rather than the acts of Mr Tomlinson, the question of what amounts to 'such care as in all the circumstances of the case is reasonable' depends upon assessing, as in the case of common law negligence, not only the likelihood that someone may be injured and the seriousness of the injury which may occur, but also the social value of the activity which gives rise to the risk and the cost of preventative measures. These factors have to be balanced against each other. . . .

THE 1957 AND 1984 ACTS CONTRASTED

38. In the case of the 1984 Act, there is the additional consideration that unless in all the circumstances it is reasonable to expect the occupier to do something, that is to say, to 'offer the other some protection', there is no duty at all. One may ask what difference there is between the case in which the claimant is a lawful visitor and there is in principle a duty under the 1957 Act but on the particular facts no duty to do anything, and the case in which he is a trespasser and there is on the particular facts no duty under the 1984 Act. Of course in such a case the result is the same. But Parliament has made it clear that in the case of a lawful visitor, one starts from the assumption that there is a duty whereas in the case of a trespasser one starts from the assumption that there is none.

THE BALANCE UNDER THE 1957 ACT

39. My Lords, it will in the circumstances be convenient to consider first the question of what the position would have been if Mr Tomlinson had been a lawful visitor owed a duty under section 2(2) of the 1957 Act. Assume, therefore, that there had been no prohibition on swimming. What was the risk of serious injury? To some extent this depends upon what one regards as the relevant risk. As I have mentioned, the judge thought it was the risk of injury through diving while the Court of Appeal thought it was any kind of injury which could happen to people in the water. Although, as I have said, I am inclined to agree with the judge, I do not want to put the basis of my decision too narrowly. So I accept that we are concerned with the steps, if any, which should have been taken to prevent any kind of water accident. According to the Royal Society for the Prevention of Accidents, about 450 people drown while swimming in the United Kingdom every year (see *Darby v National Trust* [2001] PIQR 372, 374). About 25–35 break their necks diving and no doubt others sustain less serious injuries. So there is obviously some degree of risk in swimming and diving, as there is in climbing, cycling, fell walking and many other such activities.

40. I turn then to the cost of taking preventative measures. Ward LJ described it (£5,000) as 'not excessive'. Perhaps it was not, although the outlay has to be seen in the context of the other items (rated 'essential' and 'highly desirable') in the Borough Council budget which had taken precedence over the destruction of the beaches for the previous two years.

41. I do not however regard the financial cost as a significant item in the balancing exercise which the court has to undertake. There are two other related considerations which are far more important. The first is the social value of the activities which would have to be prohibited in order to reduce or eliminate the risk from swimming. And the second is the question of whether the Council should be entitled to allow people of full capacity to decide for themselves whether to take the risk.

42. The Court of Appeal made no reference at all to the social value of the activities which were to be prohibited. The majority of people who went to the beaches to sunbathe, paddle and play with their children were enjoying themselves in a way which gave them pleasure and caused no risk to themselves or anyone else. This must be something to be taken into account in deciding whether it was reasonable to expect the Council to destroy the beaches. . . .

FREE WILL

44. The second consideration, namely the question of whether people should accept responsibility for the risks they choose to run, is the point made by Lord Phillips of Worth Matravers MR in *Donoghue v Folkestone Properties Ltd* [2003] 2 WLR 1138, 1153 and which I said was central to this appeal. Mr Tomlinson was freely and voluntarily undertaking an activity which inherently involved some risk. By contrast, Miss Bessie Stone, to whom the House of Lords held that no duty was owed, was innocently standing on the pavement outside her garden gate at 10 Beckenham Road, Cheetham when she was struck by a ball hit for 6 out of the Cheetham Cricket Club ground. She was certainly not engaging in any activity which involved an inherent risk of such injury. So compared with *Bolton v Stone*, this is an a fortiori case.

45. I think it will be extremely rare for an occupier of land to be under a duty to prevent people from taking risks which are inherent in the activities they freely choose to undertake upon the land. If people want to climb mountains, go hang gliding or swim or dive in ponds or lakes, that is their affair. Of course the landowner may for his own reasons wish to prohibit such activities. He maybe think[s] that they are a danger or inconvenience to himself or others. Or he may take a paternalist view and prefer people not to undertake risky activities on his land. He is entitled to impose such conditions, as the Council did by prohibiting swimming. But the law does not require him to do so.

46. My Lords, as will be clear from what I have just said, I think that there is an important question of freedom at stake. It is unjust that the harmless recreation of responsible parents and children with buckets and spades on the beaches should be prohibited in order to comply with what is thought to be a legal duty to safeguard irresponsible visitors against dangers which are perfectly obvious. The fact that such people take no notice of warnings cannot create a duty to take other steps to protect them. I find it difficult to express with appropriate moderation my disagreement with the proposition of Sedley LJ (at para. 45) that it is 'only where the risk is so obvious that the occupier can safely assume that nobody will take it that there will be no liability'. A duty to protect against obvious risks or self-inflicted harm exists only in cases in which there is no genuine and informed choice, as in the case of employees, or some lack of capacity, such as the inability of children to recognise danger (*British Railways Board v Herrington* [1972] AC 877) or the despair of prisoners which may lead them to inflict injury on themselves (*Reeves v Commissioner of Police* [2000] 1 AC 360).

47. It is of course understandable that organisations like the Royal Society for the Prevention of Accidents should favour policies which require people to be prevented from taking risks. Their function is to prevent accidents and that is one way of doing so. But they do not have to consider the cost, not only in money but also in deprivation of liberty, which such restrictions entail. The courts will naturally respect the technical expertise of such organisations in drawing attention to what can be done to prevent accidents. But the balance between risk on the one hand and individual autonomy on the other is not a matter of expert opinion. It is a judgment which the courts must make and which in England reflects the individualist values of the common law.

48. As for the Council officers, they were obvious[ly] motivated by the view that it was necessary to take defensive measures to prevent the Council from being held liable to pay compensation. The Borough Leisure Officer said that he regretted the need to destroy the beaches but saw no alternative if the Council was not to be held liable for an accident to a swimmer. So this appeal gives your Lordships the opportunity to say clearly that local authorities and other occupiers of land are ordinarily under no duty to incur such social and financial costs to protect a minority (or even a majority) against obvious dangers. On the other hand, if the decision of the Court of Appeal were left standing, every such occupier would feel obliged to take similar defensive measures. Sedley LJ was able to say that if the logic of the Court of Appeal's decision was that other public lakes and ponds required similar precautions, 'so be it'. But I cannot view this prospect with the same equanimity. In my opinion it would damage the quality of many people's lives.

49. In the particular case of diving injuries, there is little evidence that such defensive measures have had much effect. Dr Penny, the Council's expert, said that over the past decade there had been little change in the rate of serious diving accidents. Each year, as I have mentioned, there are about 25–35 fracture-dislocations of the neck. Almost all those affected are males and their average age is consistently around 25 years. In spite of greatly increased safety measures, particularly in swimming pools, the numbers (when Dr Penny gave evidence) had remained the same for a decade:

> This is probably because of the sudden, unpredictable nature of these dangerous dives, undertaken mostly by boisterous young men. . . hence the common description the 'Macho Male Diving Syndrome.'

50. My Lords, for these reasons I consider that even if swimming had not been prohibited and the Council had owed a duty under section 2(2) of the 1957 [Act], that duty would not have required them to take any steps to prevent Mr Tomlinson from diving or warning him against dangers which were perfectly obvious. If that is the case, then plainly there can have been no duty under the 1984 Act. The risk was not one against which he was entitled under section 1(3)(c) to protection. I would therefore allow the appeal and restore the decision of Jack J. It follows that the cross-appeal against the apportionment of damages must be dismissed. . . .

LORD HOBHOUSE:

81. The fourth point, one to which I know that your Lordships attach importance, is the fact that it is not, and should never be, the policy of the law to require the protection of the foolhardy or reckless few to deprive, or interfere with, the enjoyment by the remainder of society of the liberties and amenities to which they are rightly entitled. Does the law require that all trees be cut down because some youths may climb them and fall? Does the law require the coast line and other beauty spots to be lined with warning notices? Does the law require that attractive water side picnic spots be destroyed because of a few foolhardy individuals who choose to ignore warning notices and indulge in activities dangerous only to themselves? The answer to all these questions is, of course, no. But this is the road down which your Lordships, like other courts before, have been invited to travel and which the councils in the present case found so inviting. In truth, the arguments for the claimant have involved an attack upon the liberties of the citizen which should not be countenanced. They attack the liberty of the individual to engage in dangerous, but otherwise harmless, pastimes at his own risk and the liberty of citizens as a whole fully to enjoy the variety and quality of the landscape of this country. The pursuit of an unrestrained culture of blame and compensation has many evil consequences and one is certainly the interference with the liberty of the citizen. The discussion of social utility in the Illinois Supreme Court is to the same effect: *Bucheleres v Chicago Park District* 171 Ill 2d 435, at 457–8.

> ### *Spearman* v *Royal United Bath Hospitals NHS Foundation Trust*
> Queen's Bench Division [2017] EWHC 3027 (QB)

The facts are set out in section 10.3.

Issue 3: What was the nature of the duty owed?

57. Whether a visitor for the purposes of the 1957 Act or a trespasser for the purposes of the 1984 Act, it is argued on behalf of the defendant that the duty owed is purely statutory and there is no room for a superimposed duty at common law. . . .

58. For the claimant, Mr Hopkins QC argued that the statutory obligation under the 1957 Act is confined to 'occupancy' duties and that those duties may be concurrent with other common law duties such as activity duties. In support, I was referred to *Clark and Lindsell on Torts* (21st Edition) at paragraphs 12-04 to 12-05 where it is stated:

> 'It could be argued that these words [ie section 1(1)] are wide enough for the Act to apply to all injuries on land due to the negligence of the occupier, thus erasing the common law distinction. But it now seems clear that this is not the correct interpretation, and the specific reference to the "state of the premises" limits the effect of the Act to occupancy duties', making reference to a number of cases including *Revill v Newberry* [1996] QB 567 at 574 etc and *Fairchild v Glenhaven Funeral Services Limited* [2002] 1 WLR 1052 (in the Court of Appeal).

Clerk and Lindsell then continue:

> '12-05 There is no doubt that liability under the Act (like occupiers liability at common law) may co-exist with the duties owed in some other capacity, for example as a school, hospital authority, employer or event organiser, in such a case the claimant can rely on whichever cause of action is more advantageous to him. Occupation of premises is a ground of liability and is not a ground of exemption from liability' (quoting from *Commissioner for Railways v McDermott* [1967] 1 AC 169 at 186)

59. In my judgment, Mr Hopkins QC is correct. In many cases it may make little difference whether the duty is expressed to be that under section 2 of the Occupiers Liability Act 1957 or a common law duty owed by a hospital to patients and other visitors. The reason is that the statute makes it clear that the duty is owed by reference to 'all the circumstances of the case' and that those circumstances include the nature of the visitors so that, as specifically stated in the statute, an occupier must be prepared for children to be less careful than adults. So too a hospital must anticipate that patients attending or being brought into the hospital will include vulnerable patients who are confused and mentally unstable and may therefore be expected to act in an unpredictable way. . . .

60. In my judgment, this is not to impose an intolerably high burden on the hospital.

Issue 4: Breach of duty

62. In a sense, breach of duty is one of the easier issues for the court to decide. If, as I have decided, the defendant was under an obligation to carry out a risk assessment in order to identify and assess the risks to patients, and to take reasonable measures to prevent such risks, it did not do so. In my judgment, this duty included identification and assessment of the risk of vulnerable patients getting to the roof space from the Accident and Emergency Department unaccompanied and causing themselves injury. However, no risk assessment was carried out at all.

. . .

63. It is, of course, true that a defendant is not to be found to have been in breach of duty merely by reference to the fact that, an accident having occurred, remedial steps are taken to prevent a repeat

of the accident. Were this to imply liability, it would potentially have a 'chilling effe
employers and a wide range of other bodies in relation to taking steps to make
visitors etc safer if they were thereby thought to be admitting liability. However, eq
remedial steps may in some cases also be a recognition that there was a lack o
previously gone unobserved: that would be the position where for example, premi
that it was 'an accident waiting to happen'. In my opinion, any competent Health and Safety a
informed that there were confused and mentally unstable patients in the Emergency Department,
that there was a door allowing free entry to a staircase leading to a flat roof and that there was furniture on the flat roof allowing a safety barrier to be scaled or surmounted would agree that this was a
potentially toxic combination which together meant that the premises were not reasonably safe for
those patients.

64. . . . In my judgment the defendant in this case was in breach of duty in the following respects:

1) In failing to secure door 1 so that it only allowed free access from the stair side and not from
the Emergency Department: this would have been a simple and relatively cheap step to take
and it was in fact quickly taken after Mr Spearman's accident;

2) In failing to remove furniture from the roof space and in allowing furniture to be left so as to
provide a means of surmounting the barrier relatively easily;

3) In failing to carry out a proper and suitable risk assessment which encompassed and considered the risk to vulnerable patients should they access the flat roof space via the internal
fire escape staircase. . . .

Issue 5: Was this accident reasonably foreseeable?

65. It is argued on behalf of the defendant that it was not reasonably foreseeable that the claimant
would do what he did, namely enter the roof area from the A&E department, get over the barrier and
fall to the courtyard below. In this regard, I was told that there had never been an example of any
patient doing such a thing before . . .

66. For the claimant, it is submitted that it was reasonably foreseeable that vulnerable patients
might come to harm on the roof space by climbing over the barrier. Reliance is placed upon the
curved design of the barrier itself giving rise to the inference that the defendant had foreseen the
risk of patients climbing over the barrier, the design being intended to deter or mitigate this risk. . . .

69. In my judgment, it was clearly reasonably foreseeable that an accident of this kind might
happen. First, it was reasonably foreseeable that, without door 1 being locked, patients who were
confused might go through that door, up the stairs to the roof space. . . . Second, it was reasonably
foreseeable that a confused or vulnerable patient on the roof might go over the edge. As Mr Hopkins
QC submitted, the erection of the fence was in itself a clear recognition of this risk.

70. Mr Gubb says that whilst the accident might have been reasonably foreseeable had the protective fencing not been there, it was not reasonably foreseeable with the fencing in place. However,
he then has to contend with the presence of the furniture. . . . The risk assessment needs to include
the assessment of the risk that furniture may enable service users to climb over barriers. I do not consider that Mr Gubb was right in suggesting that the erection of the barrier meant that an accident of
this kind was not reasonably foreseeable, but, in in [sic] any event, once the presence of the furniture
is put into the equation, an accident becomes eminently reasonably foreseeable.

Issue 5 [sic]: Causation

71. Had it been my finding that the defendant was only in breach of duty in relation to the furniture
on the roof, then it would have been necessary to decide whether the claimant would have got over

the barrier even if the furniture had not been there. In fact, I would have found that he probably would not have done. He was not a particularly athletic man and, from looking at the pictures of the barrier, it seems to me that it would have been quite substantially difficult for somebody to climb over the barrier, certainly at the point where the claimant went over where it was curved inwards at the top. However, my finding that door 1 should have been secured makes the issue of causation extremely straight forward. Had that door been secure, Mr Spearman would never have got to the roof space in the first place and the accident would never have occurred. Causation is clearly established.

CONCLUSION

75. In conclusion, I consider that the defendant owed Mr Spearman a duty pursuant to the Occupiers Liability Act 1957 to take reasonable steps to ensure that the premises were reasonably safe for him as a vulnerable patient who was confused and mentally unstable at the time that he was in the Emergency Department of the hospital. I further consider that the hospital owed Mr Spearman a superimposed duty at common law which encompassed his reasonable safety not merely by reference to the state of the premises but also by reference to the overall operation of the enterprise which included supervision of patients, flow and management of patients and restriction of access to areas where patients did not need to go. These duties complement each other so that whilst, for much of the time, supervision will be adequate, there will also be times when it is not possible for the defendant to maintain constant supervision of a patient and, at those times, other duties step in to fill the breach by restricting access to dangerous or unauthorised areas and by taking reasonable steps to see that areas to which vulnerable patients might gain access are reasonably safe. The best way to address these duties is through risk assessments, there being well established risk assessment tools which assist a hospital in identifying and assessing appropriate risks and taking reasonable steps to mitigate or avoid them. In breach of duty, the defendant failed to carry out a suitable risk assessment with a result that there was the potential for an unsafe environment to arise. Then, like the lining up of the holes in a swiss [sic] cheese, the different points at which the accident would or could have been prevented failed. Thus, first, there was a short period when the patient was left on his own. This was not a breach of duty but was the first hole in the swiss [sic] cheese. Then, the patient found his way through door 1 which was not secured. Then he found his way through door 2, equally unsecured and onto the roof. Then there was furniture on the roof which enabled him to surmount or scale the barrier. Finally, the claimant's confused state of mind meant that he failed to see or recognise the danger that he was in but, fixated upon the need to leave the premises, got over the barrier and fell to the courtyard below sustaining the injuries which he did. This was an accident which could and should have been prevented and there shall be judgment for the claimant accordingly.

Notes

1. The opinions in **Tomlinson** contain some unusually strong judicial language attacking the so-called 'compensation culture'. Lords Hobhouse and Hoffmann are at pains to stress the dangers of becoming too risk-averse and to reverse this trend. As noted in Chapter 1, while views vary widely on whether such a culture exists, the *perception* of a compensation culture is very real. And, given the very real effect this is having on lawyers, judges, politicians, policy-makers and members of the public alike, it is this that we should be seeking to address. See further, Lord Dyson MR 'Compensation Culture: Fact or Fantasy?' Holdsworth Club Lecture, 15 March 2013 and other references listed in section 1.1.

2. In determining whether it is reasonable to expect the occupier to offer protection, the courts must engage in a balancing exercise similar to that which they embark upon when determining

whether a duty of care has been breached. This includes taking into account the
ing the occupier to take steps to make the premises safer. In *Keown v Coventry H*
[2006] EWCA Civ 39, for example, the 11-year-old claimant fell from a fire escape.
Court of Appeal held that the claimant's injuries were caused by his activity (in cli
underside of a fire escape) rather than the state of the premises (that is, the fire esc
went on to comment that the NHS could not be expected to guard against such a ri

> It would not be reasonable to expect a National Health Service trust to offer prot.....on from
> such a risk. If it had to offer protection from the risk of falling from a normal fire escape, it
> would presumably have to offer the same protection from falling from drain pipes, balco-
> nies, roofs. . . windows and even trees in the grounds. This seems to me to be going too far. I
> say this for two reasons. First, the resources of a National Health Service trust are much more
> sensibly utilised in the treatment and care of patients together with the proper remuneration
> of nurses and doctors rather than catering for the contingency (one hopes infrequent) that
> children will climb where they know they should not go. Secondly, if the courts say that
> such protection should be afforded, it will not just be a matter of putting a fence round a fire-
> escape or hiring an extra security guard. It is more likely that what will happen will be what,
> in due course, the judge found happened in this case. The Trust has now built a perimeter
> fence round the entire site; there is only one entrance; anyone coming in is asked their busi-
> ness; children are turned away. . . It is not unfair to say, however, that the hospital ground
> is becoming a bit like a fortress. The amenity which local people had of passing through the
> grounds to the neighbouring streets and which children had of harmlessly playing in the
> grounds has now been lost. It is not reasonable to expect that this should happen to avoid
> the occasional injury, however sad it is when such injury occurs. (Longmore LJ at [17])

3. Similarly, in *Edwards v London Borough of Sutton* [2016] EWCA Civ 1005, McCombe LJ, allowing
   the council's appeal, noted that 'not every accident (even if it has serious consequences) has to
   have been the fault of another; and an occupier is not an insurer against injuries sustained on his
   premise' (at [61]).

10.6 Warnings and exclusions of liability

Section 2(1) of the Occupiers' Liability Act 1957 allows an occupier to exclude liability 'in
so far as he is free to and does extend, restrict, modify or exclude his duty to any visitor
or visitors by agreement or otherwise', subject to the restrictions imposed by the Unfair
Contract Terms Act 1977. It is necessary to distinguish between an exclusion notice, which
is subject to the Unfair Contract Terms Act, and a warning notice, which is subject to the
test of adequacy in section 2(4) of the Occupiers' Liability Act 1957. A warning will only be
sufficient to discharge an occupier's duty to a particular visitor if, in all the circumstances, it
is enough to enable that visitor to be reasonably safe. Lord Denning MR in **Roles v Nathan**
used the following example:

> Supposing, for instance, that there was only one way of getting into and out of premises, and it was
> by a footbridge over a stream which was rotten and dangerous. . . [previously] the occupier could
> escape all liability to any visitor by putting up a notice: 'This bridge is dangerous', even though there
> was no other way by which the visitor could get in or out, and he had no option but to go over the
> bridge. In such a case, s 2(4)(a) [of the 1957 Act] makes it clear that the occupier would nowadays
> be liable. But if there were two footbridges, one of which was rotten, and the other safe a hundred
> yards away, the occupier could still escape liability, even today, by putting up a notice: 'Do not use
> this footbridge. It is dangerous. There is a safe one further upstream'. Such a warning is sufficient
> because it does enable the visitor to be reasonably safe. (at 1124)

English Heritage v Taylor
Court of Appeal [2016] EWCA Civ 448

The claimant, Taylor, suffered a serious head injury after falling over a sheer drop while at a day out with his grandchildren at Carisbrooke Castle. Upholding the finding of the trial judge, the Court of Appeal found that the drop was not obvious and, as such, the defendant was in breach of its duty of care in failing to provide a warning sign. Taylor was, however, found to be 50 per cent contributorily negligent.

ETHERTON MR:

3. The castle fortifications comprise various stone and earth works. They include an outer bastion which comprises not only the outer bastion wall, but also ramparts, ditches or moats and angled corner bastions. The outer bastion is open to the public who can gain access without entering the site through the entrance shop at its western end. There are and at the material time were two designated walks, one of which is known as the 'Bastion Walk'. The Bastion Walk runs round the tower fortifications and an area known as the 'Bowling Green'. It is approximately 10–12 feet wide. Just north east of the Bowling Green, there is an elevated firing platform known as the north-east bastion where two cannons are sited. I shall refer to this as 'the platform'.

4. The platform is flat and surrounded by a low bank and stands at least 25 feet above the outer bastion. Directly below the platform (at the base of a steep slope) is a grass pathway running along part of the top of the outer bastion wall. I shall refer to this as 'the grass pathway'. At the point beneath the platform, the grass pathway is approximately 10 feet wide. On the side of the grass pathway away from and below the platform there is a dry moat.

5. The slope from the platform down to the grass pathway is very steep. There was also at the material time an informal path down the steep slope from the platform to the grass pathway. The grass and other vegetation on the slope had been worn away in places by the feet of visitors who had opted to access the grass pathway by the most direct route from the platform. The Recorder found that the defendant's employees must have been aware of the use of this route by visitors.

6. On the day of the accident, the claimant, his wife and their grandchildren were on the platform. The children were playing on the cannons. The claimant left the others and went down the steep informal path in the direction of the grass pathway. Although he had no recollection of what happened next, it is clear that he must have attempted to walk down the informal path (rather than sliding down on his bottom) and must have lost his footing and been propelled across the grass pathway and over the sheer face of the bastion wall into the moat.

7. A central issue in this case is whether anyone on the platform who was contemplating going down the steep slope to the grass pathway could have seen that there was a sheer drop from the pathway into the moat such that going down the steep slope was an obvious danger from which there was no reasonable need for the defendant to protect its visitors. . . .

8. The Recorder had the benefit of a site visit. . . .

11. . . . He then explained why he considered that the defendant had been in breach of section 2 of the [1957] Act. He said:

> 30. The fact that the sheer drop beside the bastion path, beside the path along the Bastion Walk was and is a danger to visitors and that they need to be made specifically aware of it is and was recognised by the defendant. This is evidenced by the sign which was placed at the commencement of the designated Bastion Walk. Objectively it is clear, and I find as a fact, that that sheer drop represents a danger to persons on the bastion path unless visitors are clearly warned of its presence.

12. [The Recorder] continued: . . .

34. . . . as stated, in my judgment, the defendant failed to comply with its duty under the Occupier's Liability Act, Section 2, and failing to provide additional signage of warning of the sheer drop just beyond the bastion path, in particular in failing to put such a signage on the artillery platform, or on the pathway below but large enough for it to be visible from that platform, so that someone standing on the firing platform and looking east would see the warning. The existence of the informal path was an indication that that was a point at which visitors might be accessing the bastion path, and indeed were actually doing so. The defendant should have been alive to the possibility that visitors following the same route as the Taylors [the claimants] or a similar route, may not have been aware of the existence of the bastion wall at all, or if they were aware of it might not be aware of how close it was to the artillery platform, or of the fact that it incorporated a sheer drop. . . .

28. Mr O'Sullivan [counsel for English Heritage] says that the Recorder's finding against the defendant is extremely important. He says that, as with many public organisations which have large areas of land and premises open to the public, it has acted (as an occupier) in a way consistent with the principle that adult visitors do not require warnings of obvious risks except in cases where they do not have a genuine and informed choice. He also says that, if we dismiss this appeal, organisations like English Heritage will be under pressure to adopt an unduly defensive approach to their guardianship of historic sites which are part of our precious heritage and this will lead to an unwelcome proliferation of unsightly warning signs. This is contrary to the public interest. The courts should be astute to avoid such a consequence. Moreover, a decision in favour of the claimant in the present case will fuel the popular conception that this country is in the grip of a compensation culture.

29. I do not accept these *in terrorem* arguments. First, the decision that I have reached in this case is a straightforward application of the principle to which I have referred at para 28 above. There is no basis for interfering with the Recorder's finding that the sheer drop from the grass pathway into the moat was not an obvious danger.

30. Secondly, I accept that questions of whether a danger is obvious may not always be easy to resolve. In some cases, this may present an occupier of land with a difficulty. But there are many areas of life in which difficult borderline judgments have to be made. This is well understood by the courts and is taken into account in deciding whether negligence or a breach of section 2 of the Act has been established. In this context, it is highly relevant that the common duty of care is to take such care 'as in all the circumstances is reasonable' to see that the visitor is 'reasonably' safe in using the premises for the purpose for which he is invited or permitted by the occupier to be there. The court is, therefore, required to consider all the circumstances. These will include how obvious the danger is and, in an appropriate case, aesthetic matters. If an occupier is in doubt as to whether a danger is obvious, it may be well advised to take reasonable measures to reduce or eliminate the danger. But the steps need be no more than reasonable steps. That is why the decision in this case should not be interpreted as requiring occupiers like English Heritage to place unsightly warning signs in prominent positions all over sensitive historic sites. They are required to do no more than take reasonable steps. The Recorder found the existence of a breach of the common duty of care on a very specific basis, namely the failure to provide a sign warning of a sheer drop which was not obvious.

Explore the case further with the **online resources**.

see online resources

Notes

1. Under the 1984 Act an occupier may discharge their duty by giving a warning or by discouraging people from entering the premises (e.g. a locked gate) as long as the occupier has taken reasonable steps to bring the danger to the claimant's attention (s 1(5)).

10.7 Defences

No duty is owed by the occupier under either of the Occupiers' Liability Acts in respect of risks willingly accepted by the entrant (1957 Act, s 2(5); 1984 Act, s 1(6)). In *Ratcliff* v *McConnell* [1999] 1 WLR 670, for example, the Court of Appeal held that no duty was owed to a claimant who accepted the risk of serious injury from diving into water of an unknown depth when he climbed over a fence surrounding his college's open-air swimming pool on his way home after a night out. Nor they will not be fully liable where the claimant's own negligence has contributed to the injuries they have suffered.

> ### *White Lion Hotel* v *James*
> Court of Appeal [2021] EWCA Civ 31

Christopher James had died after falling from a second floor window while staying at the White Lion Hotel. At first instance, the judge found that the owners of the hotel had failed to take reasonable care for the safety of the deceased in using the room (as required by the 1957 Act, s 2), but made a finding of 60 per cent contributory negligence. There was no appeal against these findings. Rather, the appeal was on a point of law: the judge—having found that the deceased had chosen to sit on the window sill, partly out of the window, and thereby had recognised and accepted the risk of falling from the window due to leaning too far out or losing his balance—had failed to apply the principle, found in section 2(5) of the 1957 Act, and applied in *Tomlinson*, *Edwards* v *London Borough of Sutton* and *Geary* v *JD Wetherspoons plc* [2011] EWHC 1506, that 'a person of full age and capacity who chooses to run an obvious risk cannot found an action against a defendant on the basis that the latter has either permitted him to do so, or not prevented him from so doing' (at [5]). Held: the Court of Appeal found that such a principle was not 'absolute' and that the defence in section 2(5) had not been made out.

DAVIS LJ:

76. The appellant's primary ground of appeal, namely that a person of full age and capacity who chooses to run an obvious risk cannot found an action against a defendant on the basis that the latter has either permitted him to do so, or not prevented him from so doing, is derived from what is said to be the ratio of *Tomlinson*, *Edwards* and *Geary*.

77. In my judgment, consideration of these authorities does not provide unequivocal support for the proposition contended for by the appellant.

Tomlinson

78. The claim in *Tomlinson* was brought pursuant to section 1 of the Occupiers' Liability Act 1984 as the claimant was a trespasser. . . . It is only if those three conditions are met that the duty arises. As was stated . . . by Lord Hoffmann: in the case of a lawful visitor one starts with the assumption that

there is a duty whereas in the case of a trespasser one starts with the assumption that there is none. On the facts in *Tomlinson* the claimant did not meet the requirements of section 1(3)(c), thus there was no assumption of duty.

79. Lord Hoffmann then went on to consider what the position would have been if there had been a duty under either the 1984 or the 1957 Act. However, given the finding on the facts that there was no duty, Lord Hoffmann's consideration of the 1957 Act cannot properly be described as the ratio of the case. Further, in assessing the duty under section 2(2) Lord Hoffman[n] made no reference to section 2(5). The focus was upon the council's hypothetical duty under section 2(2) of the 1957 Act. . . . Lord Hoffman[n] appears to be placing the principle relating to a claimant's acceptance of the obviousness of a danger as one element in a balancing exercise going to the reasonableness assessment pursuant to section 2(2) of the 1957 Act. He is balancing the obviousness of the danger against the social and financial cost of precautions. I do not read it as representing an absolute defence, rather he is identifying or considering the circumstances under which it would be reasonable to hold an occupier liable in respect of obvious dangers or risks. Lord Hoffman[n] regarded Mr Tomlinson's exercise of free will in voluntarily choosing to run an obvious risk as an important consideration, but identified other considerations of which account should be taken, including the social value which would be lost by the preventative measures under consideration, namely destroying beaches.

81. In *Edwards* at [47] McCombe LJ identified the potential for injury which must have been obvious such that any user of the bridge would appreciate the need to take care and any user limiting the width of the bridge's track, by pushing a bicycle to his side, would see the need to take extra care, as being a 'particularly forceful consideration' militating against a duty to take protective steps. . . . he attached weight to the fact that the addition of side barriers would have altered the character of the bridge significantly, to an extent out of proportion to a remote risk which had never materialised in its known history. Notwithstanding the somewhat broad assertion of what is described as 'principle' . . . McCombe LJ noted the obviousness of the danger and . . . conducted the proportionality assessment relevant to section 2(2). In McCombe LJ's reasoning, the obviousness of the danger did not operate as an absolute defence, but as one element of a balancing exercise. . . .

83. For the reasons given, I do not read *Tomlinson* or *Edwards* as being authority for a principle which displaces the normal analysis required by section 2 of the 1957 Act: ... What a claimant knew, and should reasonably have appreciated, about any risk he was running is relevant to that analysis and, in cases such as *Edwards* and *Tomlinson*, may be decisive. In other cases, a conscious decision by a claimant to run an obvious risk may, nevertheless, not outweigh other factors: the lack of social utility of the particular state of the premises from which the risk arises (the ability to open the lower sash window); the low cost of remedial measures to eliminate the risk (£7 or £8 per window); and the real, even if relatively low, risk of an accident recognised by the guilty plea. This was a risk which was not only foreseeable, it was likely to materialise as part of the normal activity of a visitor staying in the bedroom.

84. Separate from the considerations above, there are a number of factual features which distinguish this case from those of *Edwards*, *Tomlinson* and *Geary*:

  i)   The lower sash window was defective. No defect was present in the ornamental bridge in *Edwards*, the body of water in *Tomlinson*, nor the bannister in *Geary*;

  ii) In this case the judge found that a risk assessment would have made a critical difference. In *Edwards* McCombe LJ found that a risk assessment would have done no more than state the obvious;

  iii) The risk of injury was foreseeable. In *Edwards* the risk was remote and had never previously materialised;

iv) The social value lost by taking preventative measures was low given that the top sash window could still be opened. In *Edwards* side barriers would have significantly altered the character of the ornamental bridge, in *Tomlinson* destroying the beaches would have been at huge social cost;

v) The financial costs of fitting the window restrictors was negligible (£7 or £8 per window). The same cannot be said of the preventative measures in *Edwards* or *Tomlinson*;

85. A further and material distinction as between this case and the authorities relied upon by the appellant is the fact that the deceased was a guest at the appellant's hotel. In *Lewis* [v *Six Continents* [2005] EWCA Civ 1805] the claimant returned to his hotel room at around 10pm having consumed alcohol. He later fell from the window. Sedley LJ noted that the common duty of care is owed not in the abstract but by a particular occupier here, a medium sized hotel, to a particular visitor, a young man with nothing to distinguish him from the hotel's other adult guests. This observation reflects the provisions of section 2(3) of the 1957 Act and the references to 'want of care' of a visitor. The formulation of the duty encompasses the recognition that visitors are not always careful.

86. In my judgment, there is a material difference between a visitor to a park, even a pub, and a guest in a hotel. During the time the guest is in the hotel room it is a 'home from home'. The guest in the room may be tired, off-guard, relaxing and may well have had more than a little to drink. Despite notices to the contrary he may be tempted to smoke out of the window and in hot weather the guest will want fresh air, particularly, as in this case, in a room with no air conditioning. As the judge observed, these are 'facts of life' for any hotelier. These are normal activities.

87. Contrast these facts with the 'activities' contemplated in *Tomlinson*. Lord Hoffman[n] . . . observed that 'it will be extremely rare for an occupier of land to be under a duty to prevent people from taking risks which are inherent in the activities they freely choose to undertake upon the land. If people want to climb mountains, go hang gliding or swim or dive in ponds or lakes, that is their affair.' These activities go far beyond those involved in the ordinary occupation of a hotel room.

88. For the reasons given, I do not accept the appellant's primary contention. There is no absolute principle that a visitor of full age and capacity who chooses to run an obvious risk cannot found an action against an occupier on the basis that the latter has either permitted him so to do, or not prevented him from so doing.

Section 2(5)

89. The defence of *volenti non fit injuria* was always a defence available to the occupier of the property and section 2(5) expressly preserves it. The editors of *Clerk & Lindsell on Torts*, 23rd Edition, 11-43 recognise this. At [36] of *Geary*, Coulson J accepted that the statutory offence has been confirmed to be indistinguishable from the common law defence of *volenti*.

92. If the defence is to succeed it must be shown that the deceased was fully aware of the relevant danger and consequent risk. . . .

94. . . . [I]n making a finding of contributory negligence, the judge found that the deceased consciously adopted a precarious position, he could foresee the danger of falling, if not the precise manner, and very considerable care was required if he was to sit on the sill. Any lapse of concentration and he might fall. He concluded that 'in choosing to act as he did he was guilty of a blameworthy failure to take reasonable care for his own safety.' Upon that basis the judge made the unappealed finding of 60 per cent contributory negligence.

95. The deceased fell in the early hours of the morning. He had attended a wedding, drunk alcohol, when he returned to the room it is likely that he was hot and tired. He was unable to sleep and felt the need for, at least, fresh air. In assessing his actions and the knowledge of any risk and its consequences, account can properly be taken of the condition of the deceased and his ability to fully appreciate what he was doing and the consequences of it, such as to meet the stringent requirements of the test of *volenti*.

96. It is pertinent to observe that the appellant, who owned and managed the hotel, did not appreciate the risk prior to the accident. In the circumstances, to make a finding that the deceased, a visitor, should possess greater knowledge than the occupier of the premises is a considerable step to take.

97. The findings of the judge . . . represent knowledge of the general risk which the deceased faced. There is no finding that the deceased was aware of, and expressly or impliedly accepted, that the risk had been created by the appellant's breach of duty and by his actions he was deliberately absolving or forgiving the appellant for creating the risk. There is no finding that in sitting as he did the deceased was waiving his legal right to sue. In my judgment these are findings which provide a basis for the determination of contributory negligence. They do not go sufficiently far to meet the requirements of section 2(5). . . .

106. . . . [T]he determination made by the judge that there should be judgment for the respondent subject to a reduction of 60% contributory negligence is upheld.

11

Product liability

This chapter deals with damage caused by defective products. In tort law, the topic is covered by two separate legal regimes. The first is the ordinary law of negligence (with some qualifications) and the second is the system of strict liability introduced by the Consumer Protection Act 1987, as required by a European Directive. The latter is limited to personal injuries and to some damage to private property, and there are still a number of cases where a claimant has to rely on negligence—for example, where there is damage to goods used for commercial purposes. Also, the Act applies only to certain kinds of defendants (mainly 'producers'), and a claimant will need to use negligence if, for example, they are injured by a defectively repaired product.

One important point is that *both* systems apply only to damage to things other than the defective product and not to damage which the defective product causes to itself: that is a matter solely for the law of contract.

For those who need to refresh their memory on this, or those who have yet to study contract law, we have included a basic overview of the liabilities that may arise in contract in relation to defective products, including under the Consumer Rights Act 2015, on our **online resources.**

see online
resources

11.1 **Liability in negligence**

Donoghue v *Stevenson* [1932] AC 562 not only established a general concept of duty of care in negligence (the wide rule) but also laid down the qualifications of that broad concept when applied to liability for damage caused by a defective product (the narrow rule). The relevant passages are reproduced below.

Donoghue v *Stevenson*
House of Lords [1932] AC 562

The facts are given in section 2.1. Held: a manufacturer owes a duty of care to the end-consumer of a product which they have produced negligently, even though there is no contractual relationship between them.

LORD ATKIN: There will no doubt arise cases where it will be difficult to determine whether the contemplated relationship is so close that the duty arises. But in the class of case now before the Court I cannot conceive any difficulty to arise. A manufacturer puts up an article of food in a container which he knows will be opened by the actual consumer. There can be no inspection by any purchaser and no reasonable preliminary inspection by the consumer. Negligently, in the course of preparation, he allows the contents to be mixed with poison. It is said that the law of England and Scotland is that the poisoned consumer has no remedy against the negligent manufacturer. If this were the result of the authorities, I should consider the result a grave defect in the law, and so contrary to principle that I should hesitate long before following any decision to that effect which had not the authority of this House. I would point out that, in the assumed state of the authorities, not only would the consumer have no remedy against the manufacturer, he would have none against any one else, for in the circumstances alleged there would be no evidence of negligence against any one other than the manufacturer; and, except in the case of a consumer who was also a purchaser, no contract and no warranty of fitness, and in the case of the purchase of a specific article under its patent or trade name, which might well be the case in the purchase of some articles of food or drink, no warranty protecting even the purchaser-consumer. There are other instances than of articles of food and drink where goods are sold intended to be used immediately by the consumer, such as many forms of goods sold for cleaning purposes, where the same liability must exist. The doctrine supported by the decision below would not only deny a remedy to the consumer who was injured by consuming bottled beer or chocolates poisoned by the negligence of the manufacturer, but also to the user of what should be a harmless proprietary medicine, an ointment, a soap, a cleaning fluid or cleaning powder. I confine myself to articles of common household use, where every one, including the manufacturer, knows that the articles will be used by other persons than the actual ultimate purchaser—namely, by members of his family and his servants, and in some cases his guests. I do not think so ill of our jurisprudence as to suppose that its principles are so remote from the ordinary needs of civilized society and the ordinary claims it makes upon its members as to deny a legal remedy where there is so obviously a social wrong.

It will be found, I think, on examination that there is no case in which the circumstances have been such as I have just suggested where the liability has been negatived. There are numerous cases, where the relations were much more remote, where the duty has been held not to exist. There are also dicta in such cases which go further than was necessary for the determination of the particular issues, which have caused the difficulty experienced by the Courts below. I venture to say that in the branch of the law which deals with civil wrongs, dependent in England at any rate entirely upon the application by judges of general principles also formulated by judges, it is of particular importance to guard against the danger of stating propositions of law in wider terms than is necessary, lest essential factors be omitted in the wider survey and the inherent adaptability of English law be unduly restricted. For this reason it is very necessary in considering reported cases in the law of torts that the actual decision alone should carry authority, proper weight, of course, being given to the dicta of the judges.

In my opinion several decided cases support the view that in such a case as the present the manufacturer owes a duty to the consumer to be careful . . .

My Lords, if your Lordships accept the view that this pleading discloses a relevant cause of action you will be affirming the proposition that by Scots and English law alike a manufacturer of products, which he sells in such a form as to show that he intends them to reach the ultimate consumer in the form in which they left him with no reasonable possibility of intermediate examination, and with the knowledge that the absence of reasonable care in the preparation or putting up of the products will result in an injury to the consumer's life or property, owes a duty to the consumer to take that reasonable care.

LORD MACMILLAN: . . . The question is: Does he owe a duty to take care, and to whom does he owe that duty? Now I have no hesitation in affirming that a person who for gain engages in the business of manufacturing articles of food and drink intended for consumption by members of the public in the form in which he issues them is under a duty to take care in the manufacture of these articles. That duty, in my opinion, he owes to those whom he intends to consume his products. He manufactures his commodities for human consumption; he intends and contemplates that they shall be consumed. By reason of that very fact he places himself in a relationship with all the potential consumers of his commodities, and that relationship which he assumes and desires for his own ends imposes upon him a duty to take care to avoid injuring them. He owes them a duty not to convert by his own carelessness an article which he issues to them as wholesome and innocent into an article which is dangerous to life and health. It is sometimes said that liability can only arise where a reasonable man would have foreseen and could have avoided the consequences of his act or omission. In the present case the respondent, when he manufactured his ginger-beer, had directly in contemplation that it would be consumed by members of the public. Can it be said that he could not be expected as a reasonable man to foresee that if he conducted his process of manufacture carelessly he might injure those whom he expected and desired to consume his ginger-beer? The possibility of injury so arising seems to me in no sense so remote as to excuse him from foreseeing it. Suppose that a baker, through carelessness, allows a large quantity of arsenic to be mixed with a batch of his bread, with the result that those who subsequently eat it are poisoned, could he be heard to say that he owed no duty to the consumers of his bread to take care that it was free from poison, and that, as he did not know that any poison had got into it, his only liability was for breach of warranty under his contract of sale to those who actually bought the poisoned bread from him? Observe that I have said 'through carelessness,' and thus excluded the case of a pure accident such as may happen where every care is taken. I cannot believe, and I do not believe, that neither in the law of England nor in the law of Scotland is there redress for such a case . . . It must always be a question of circumstances whether the carelessness amounts to negligence, and whether the injury is not too remote from the careless-ness. I can readily conceive that where a manufacturer has parted with his product and it has passed into other hands it may well be exposed to vicissitudes which may render it defective or noxious, for which the manufacturer could not in any view be held to be to blame. It may be a good general rule to regard responsibility as ceasing when control ceases. So, also, where between the manufacturer and the user there is interposed a party who has the means and opportunity of examining the manu-facturer's product before he re-issues it to the actual user. But where, as in the present case, the ar-ticle of consumption is so prepared as to be intended to reach the consumer in the condition in which it leaves the manufacturer, and the manufacturer takes steps to ensure this by sealing or otherwise closing the container so that the contents cannot be tampered with, I regard his control as remaining effective until the article reaches the consumer and the container is opened by him. The intervention of any exterior agency is intended to be excluded, and was in fact in the present case excluded.

Notes

1. The above principle was applied in *Grant v Australian Knitting Mills Ltd* [1936] AC 85, where the claimant contracted dermatitis from wearing woollen underpants manufactured by the defen-dants, which contained sulphur residues. It was pointed out that the use of the word 'control' by Lord Macmillan was misleading ('I regard his control as remaining effective until the article reaches the consumer'). According to the Privy Council, all that was meant was that 'the con-sumer must use the article exactly as it left the maker, that is in all material features, and use it as it was intended to be used' (Lord Wright at 104).

In *Grant*, the harm could have been avoided if the underpants had been washed before use, but Lord Wright forthrightly pointed out that 'it was not contemplated that they should first be washed' (at 105). What if the packet said 'Warning: wash before use'? If the claimant had not done so, would that have been a complete defence, or merely contributory negligence on their part?

2. The principle has been extended to repairers of goods (*Haseldine* v *Daw* [1941] 2 KB 343), and also to distributors where they might be expected to test a product before passing it on. Thus, in *Watson* v *Buckley, Osborne Garrett & Co and Wyrovoys Products* [1940] 1 All ER 174 the claimant's hair was dyed by Buckley with dye that she obtained from the distributors, Osborne Garrett & Co, who had bought it from Wyrovoys Products. The dye was packaged by Osborne Garrett. Stable J held Buckley liable in contract and Osborne Garrett in tort (Wyrovoys Products had ceased to exist). Liability was based on the fact that by packaging the dye the defendants had entered a relationship with the ultimate consumer. However, the principle is not limited to situations where the defendant packages the goods as their own, for it will extend to cases where the goods remain in the same form, but where it is expected that the distributor or retailer will have tested them. Thus, in *Andrews* v *Hopkinson* [1957] 1 QB 229 it was held that a commercial seller of a second-hand car was liable in negligence for not testing the car for safety before selling it. See also *Evans* v *Triplex Safety Glass Co Ltd* [1936] 1 All ER 283 (KBD) where a fault with a car windscreen was found more likely to be attributable to the fitters than the manufacturer.

3. A defendant is liable only if the defective product damages property other than itself. The problem is defining what 'other property' is. In *Aswan Engineering* v *Lupdine Ltd* [1987] 1 WLR 1, the claimants bought a quantity of waterproofing compound from the first defendants, Lupdine Ltd. The compound was packed in buckets which had been manufactured by the second defendants. The compound was exported to Kuwait where the buckets were stacked five high on the quayside in full sunshine, subsequently collapsing in the heat. The whole consignment was lost. It was held that there was no liability on the sellers in contract as the buckets were of satisfactory quality, and no liability in tort because the type of damage was unforeseeable. One issue was whether the product had merely damaged itself, or whether the buckets (assuming they were defective, which they were not) had damaged 'other property' (the compound) of the claimants. It was thought, *obiter*, by Lloyd LJ that the contents of the buckets were 'other property'.

   A similar problem arises under section 5(2) of the Consumer Protection Act 1987 (section 11.2), which says that there is no liability under the Act for damage to the product itself or to the whole or any part of any product which has been supplied with the product in question comprised in it.

4. A defendant will escape liability if it can be shown that the claimant had actual or constructive knowledge of the defect but continued to use the product (*Howmet Ltd* v *Economy Devices Ltd and others* [2016] EWCA Civ 847).

5. Another problem arises in respect of defects that occur in the *design* (rather than manufacturing) process of goods. Design defects may potentially affect consumers on a much larger scale, are more difficult to discover and the link from design defect to harm (causation) is often harder to establish. It is here that we see the limitations of the tort of negligence's protection of people from harms caused by defective products, though some of these limits ought to be ameliorated by the introduction of a strict liability regime in relation to defective products, as the next section discusses.

11.2 Strict liability

Strict liability for products—liability without the need to establish fault—has long been accepted in the United States (see *Restatement (Second) of Torts*, s 402A), and there were numerous recommendations over time, both in Britain and in Europe, for its adoption. Eventually, in 1985, a European Directive (85/374/EEC) was issued on liability for defective products. As a result of the mandatory nature of the Directive, strict liability was finally adopted in the UK by Part 1 of the Consumer Protection Act 1987. (There will be some minor changes to the text of the Act as presented here following the UK's exit from the European Union.)

The route to success under the Act is to establish that harm was caused by a 'defect in a product' (s 2(1)), with the key concept of 'defect' being defined in section 3 and further elucidated in case law.

CONSUMER PROTECTION ACT 1987

PART I PRODUCT LIABILITY

1. Purpose and construction of Part I

(1) This Part shall have effect for the purpose of making such provision as is necessary in order to comply with the product liability Directive and shall be construed accordingly.

(2) In this Part, except in so far as the context otherwise requires—

'dependant' and 'relative' have the same meaning as they have in, respectively, the Fatal Accidents Act 1976 and the Damages (Scotland) Act 2011;

'producer', in relation to a product, means—

    (a) the person who manufactured it;

    (b) in the case of a substance which has not been manufactured but has been won or abstracted, the person who won or abstracted it;

    (c) in the case of a product which has not been manufactured, won or abstracted but essential characteristics of which are attributable to an industrial or other process having been carried out (for example, in relation to agricultural produce), the person who carried out that process;

'product' means any goods or electricity and (subject to subsection (3) below) includes a product which is comprised in another product, whether by virtue of being a component part or raw material or otherwise; and 'the product liability Directive' means the Directive of the Council of the European Communities, dated 25th July 1985, (No 85/374/EEC) on the approximation of the laws, regulations and administrative provisions of the member States concerning liability for defective products.

(3) For the purposes of this Part a person who supplies any product in which products are comprised, whether by virtue of being component parts or raw materials or otherwise, shall not be treated by reason only of his supply of that product as supplying any of the products so comprised.

2. Liability for defective products

(1) Subject to the following provisions of this Part, where any damage is caused wholly or partly by a defect in a product, every person to whom subsection (2) below applies shall be liable for the damage.

(2) This subsection applies to—

    (a) the producer of the product;

    (b) any person who, by putting his name on the product or using a trade mark or other distinguishing mark in relation to the product, has held himself out to be the producer of the product;

    (c) any person who has imported the product into a member State from a place outside the member States in order, in the course of any business of his, to supply it to another.

(3) Subject as aforesaid, where any damage is caused wholly or partly by a defect in a product, any person who supplied the product (whether to the person who suffered the damage, to the

producer of any product in which the product in question is comprised or to any other person) shall be liable for the damage if—

    (a) the person who suffered the damage requests the supplier to identify one or more of the persons (whether still in existence or not) to whom subsection (2) above applies in relation to the product;

    (b) that request is made within a reasonable period after the damage occurs and at a time when it is not reasonably practicable for the person making the request to identify all those persons; and

    (c) the supplier fails, within a reasonable period after receiving the request, either to comply with the request or to identify the person who supplied the product to him.

(4) [Repealed]

(5) Where two or more persons are liable by virtue of this Part for the same damage, their liability shall be joint and several.

(6) This section shall be without prejudice to any liability arising otherwise than by virtue of this Part.

3. Meaning of 'defect'

(1) Subject to the following provisions of this section, there is a defect in a product for the purposes of this Part if the safety of the product is not such as persons generally are entitled to expect; and for those purposes 'safety', in relation to a product, shall include safety with respect to products comprised in that product and safety in the context of risks of damage to property, as well as in the context of risks of death or personal injury.

(2) In determining for the purposes of subsection (1) above what persons generally are entitled to expect in relation to a product all the circumstances shall be taken into account, including—

    (a) the manner in which, and purposes for which, the product has been marketed, its get-up, the use of any mark in relation to the product and any instructions for, or warnings with respect to, doing or refraining from doing anything with or in relation to the product;

    (b) what might reasonably be expected to be done with or in relation to the product; and

    (c) the time when the product was supplied by its producer to another;

    and nothing in this section shall require a defect to be inferred from the fact alone that the safety of a product which is supplied after that time is greater than the safety of the product in question.

4. Defences

(1) In any civil proceedings by virtue of this Part against any person ('the person proceeded against') in respect of a defect in a product it shall be a defence for him to show—

    (a) that the defect is attributable to compliance with any requirement imposed by or under any enactment or with any Community obligation; or

    (b) that the person proceeded against did not at any time supply the product to another; or

    (c) that the following conditions are satisfied, that is to say—

        (i) that the only supply of the product to another by the person proceeded against was otherwise than in the course of a business of that person's; and

        (ii) that section 2(2) above does not apply to that person or applies to him by virtue only of things done otherwise than with a view to profit; or

    (d) that the defect did not exist in the product at the relevant time; or

    (e) that the state of scientific and technical knowledge at the relevant time was not such that a producer of products of the same description as the product in question might be expected to have discovered the defect if it had existed in his products while they were under his control; or

(f) that the defect—
    (i) constituted a defect in a product ('the subsequent product') in which the product in question had been comprised; and
    (ii) was wholly attributable to the design of the subsequent product or to compliance by the producer of the product in question with instructions given by the producer of the subsequent product.

(2) In this section 'the relevant time', in relation to electricity, means the time at which it was generated, being a time before it was transmitted or distributed, and in relation to any other product, means—

(a) if the person proceeded against is a person to whom subsection (2) of section 2 above applies in relation to the product, the time when he supplied the product to another;

(b) if that subsection does not apply to that person in relation to the product, the time when the product was last supplied by a person to whom that subsection does apply in relation to the product.

5. Damage giving rise to liability

(1) Subject to the following provisions of this section, in this Part 'damage' means death or personal injury or any loss of or damage to any property (including land).

(2) A person shall not be liable under section 2 above in respect of any defect in a product for the loss of or any damage to the product itself or for the loss of or any damage to the whole or any part of any product which has been supplied with the product in question comprised in it.

(3) A person shall not be liable under section 2 above for any loss of or damage to any property which, at the time it is lost or damaged, is not—

(a) of a description of property ordinarily intended for private use, occupation or consumption; and

(b) intended by the person suffering the loss or damage mainly for his own private use, occupation or consumption.

(4) No damages shall be awarded to any person by virtue of this Part in respect of any loss of or damage to any property if the amount which would fall to be so awarded to that person, apart from this subsection and any liability for interest, does not exceed £275.

(5) In determining for the purposes of this Part who has suffered any loss of or damage to property and when any such loss or damage occurred, the loss or damage shall be regarded as having occurred at the earliest time at which a person with an interest in the property had knowledge of the material facts about the loss or damage.

(6) For the purposes of subsection (5) above the material facts about any loss of or damage to any property are such facts about the loss or damage as would lead a reasonable person with an interest in the property to consider the loss or damage sufficiently serious to justify his instituting proceedings for damages against a defendant who did not dispute liability and was able to satisfy a judgment.

(7) For the purposes of subsection (5) above a person's knowledge includes knowledge which he might reasonably have been expected to acquire—

(a) from facts observable or ascertainable by him; or

(b) from facts ascertainable by him with the help of appropriate expert advice which it is reasonable for him to seek;
    but a person shall not be taken by virtue of this subsection to have knowledge of a fact ascertainable by him only with the help of expert advice unless he has failed to take all reasonable steps to obtain (and, where appropriate, to act on) that advice.

(8) Subsections (5) to (7) above shall not extend to Scotland.

6.

...

7. Prohibition on exclusions from liability

The liability of a person by virtue of this Part to a person who has suffered damage caused wholly or partly by a defect in a product, or to a dependant or relative of such a person, shall not be limited or excluded by any contract term, by any notice or by any other provision.

PART V

45. Interpretation

(1) In this Act, except in so far as the context otherwise requires—

'aircraft' includes gliders, balloons and hovercraft;

'business' includes a trade or profession and the activities of a professional or trade association or of a local authority or other public authority;

'goods' includes substances, growing crops and things comprised in land by virtue of being attached to it and any ship, aircraft or vehicle;

'personal injury' includes any disease and any other impairment of a person's physical or mental condition;

'ship' includes any boat and any other description of vessel used in navigation;

'substance' means any natural or artificial substance, whether in solid, liquid or gaseous form or in the form of a vapour, and includes substances that are comprised in or mixed with other goods.

46. Meaning of 'supply'

(1) Subject to the following provisions of this section, references in this Act to supplying goods shall be construed as references to doing any of the following, whether as principal or agent, that is to say—

    (a) selling, hiring out or lending the goods;

    (b) entering into a hire-purchase agreement to furnish the goods;

    (c) the performance of any contract for work and materials to furnish the goods;

    (d) providing the goods in exchange for any consideration (including trading stamps) other than money;

    (e) providing the goods in or in connection with the performance of any statutory function; or

    (f) giving the goods as a prize or otherwise making a gift of the goods; and, in relation to gas or water, those references shall be construed as including references to providing the service by which the gas or water is made available for use.

(2) For the purposes of any reference in this Act to supplying goods, where a person ('the ostensible supplier') supplies to another person ('the customer') under a hire-purchase agreement, conditional sale agreement or credit-sale agreement or under an agreement for the hiring of goods (other than a hire-purchase agreement) and the ostensible supplier—

    (a) carries on the business of financing the provision of goods for others by means of such agreements; and

    (b) in the course of that business acquired his interest in the goods supplied to the customer as a means of financing the provision of them for the customer by a further person ('the effective supplier'),

    the effective supplier and not the ostensible supplier shall be treated as supplying the goods to the customer.

(3) Subject to subsection (4) below, the performance of any contract by the erection of any building or structure on any land or by the carrying out of any other building works shall be treated for the

purposes of this Act as a supply of goods in so far as, but only in so far as, it involves the provision of any goods to any person by means of their incorporation into the building, structure or works.

(4) Except for the purposes of, and in relation to, notices to warn or any provision made by or under Part III of this Act, references in this Act to supplying goods shall not include references to supplying goods comprised in land where the supply is effected by the creation or disposal of an interest in the land.

You may find it helpful to look at the annotated version of sections 1–5 of the Act which can be found on the **online resources**.

see online resources

LIMITATION ACT 1980

11A. Actions in respect of defective products

(1) This section shall apply to an action for damages by virtue of any provision of Part I of the Consumer Protection Act 1987.

(2) None of the time limits given in the preceding provisions of this Act shall apply to an action to which this section applies.

(3) An action to which this section applies shall not be brought after the expiration of the period of ten years from the relevant time, within the meaning of section 4 of the said Act of 1987; and this subsection shall operate to extinguish a right of action and shall do so whether or not that right of action had accrued, or time under the following provisions of this Act had begun to run, at the end of the said period of ten years.

(4) Subject to subsection (5) below, an action to which this section applies in which the damages claimed by the plaintiff consist of or include damages in respect of personal injuries to the plaintiff or any other person or loss of or damage to any property, shall not be brought after the expiration of the period of three years from whichever is the later of—

(a) the date on which the cause of action accrued; and

(b) the date of knowledge of the injured person or, in the case of loss of or damage to property, the date of knowledge of the plaintiff or (if earlier) of any person in whom his cause of action was previously vested.

Notes

1. In relation to section 4(1)(e) of the Consumer Protection Act, the so-called 'developments risk' or 'state of the art' defence, the European Commission instituted an action against the UK on the ground that this section did not comply with Article 7(e) of the Directive (***Commission of the European Communities* v *UK*** (Case C-300/95), EU:C:1997:255) but this was rejected (see the following extract).

2. The European Commission launched a public consultation in January 2017 to evaluate how the Directive continues to perform, considering whether it meets its objectives and also the needs of consumers and producers, particularly in an increasingly digitised age and with emerging technologies (European Commission 'Public Consultation on the rules on liability of the producer for damage caused by a defective product' 10 January 2017). The resultant fifth report on the Product Liability Directive for the period 2011–15 was published in 2018. It concluded that

the Directive continues to be fit for purpose despite products having increased in complexity over time, though some legal terms (including 'defect' and 'product') may need better definition (especially in light of new types of product).

3. It is uncertain whether computer software is 'goods' for the purposes of the Act. Note, however, that the Directive speaks of 'movables', which may be wider than 'goods', and the European Commission is clearly of the view that the Directive applies to software. If defective software is incorporated into a machine it should be possible to regard the whole machine as defective. This at least will protect anyone injured by the machine and will leave the software manufacturer and the machine assembler to sort out liability between themselves on a contractual basis. For the purposes of the Sale of Goods Act 1979, software by itself is not goods but a disk containing it is (*St Albans District Council* v *ICL* [1996] 4 All ER 481). If the same applied to the Consumer Protection Act 1987, it would mean that if you download software from the internet there would be no liability on the producer, but if you pick up a free software disk there would be. As software will normally be on something, that something will be goods, and so the problem will arise only where software is downloaded. However, the Consumer Rights Act 2015 now gives formalised rights under contract to consumers in respect of 'digital goods', so it would be a surprise if a similar principle did not extend. In such a situation the Directive probably does apply, but note that economic loss is not covered; neither is damage to things used by a business.

4. In light of the UK's exit from the European Union, changes (not yet in effect at the time of writing) will be made to small parts of the wording of the Consumer Protection Act 1987. Section 1 will be put into the past tense; the Act will cover importers into the UK rather than member states (s 2(2)(c)); s 4(1)(a) will refer to 'retained requirements' of Community obligations (Product Safety and Metrology etc (Amendment etc) (EU Exit) Regulations 2019, SI 2019/696).

Commission of the European Communities v *UK (EC v UK)*
European Court of Justice (Case C-300/95) EU:C:1997:255

The European Commission alleged that section 4(1)(e) of the 1987 Act (the 'development risks defence') was not in compliance with the requirements of Article 7(e) of the Directive. Article 7(e) had stated that: 'The producer shall not be liable . . . if he proves . . . that the state of scientific and technical knowledge at the time when he put the product into circulation was not such as to enable the existence of the defect to be discovered . . .'

JUDGMENT OF THE COURT:

16. In its application, the Commission argues that the United Kingdom legislature has broadened the defence under Article 7(e) of the Directive to a considerable degree and converted the strict liability imposed by Article 1 of the Directive into mere liability for negligence. . . .

23. In order to determine whether the national implementing provision at issue is clearly contrary to Article 7(e) as the Commission argues, the scope of the Community provision which it purports to implement must first be considered. . . .

25. Several observations can be made as to the wording of Article 7(e) of the Directive.

26. First. . . that provision refers to 'scientific and technical knowledge at the time when [the producer] put the product into circulation', Article 7(e) is not specifically directed at the practices and safety standards in use in the industrial sector in which the producer is operating, but, unreservedly, at the state of scientific and technical knowledge, including the most advanced level of such knowledge, at the time when the product in question was put into circulation.

27. Second, the clause providing for the defence in question does not contemplate the state of knowledge of which the producer in question actually or subjectively was or could have been

apprised, but the objective state of scientific and technical knowledge of which the producer is presumed to have been informed.

28. However, it is implicit in the wording of Article 7(e) that the relevant scientific and technical knowledge must have been accessible at the time when the product in question was put into circulation.

29. It follows that, in order to have a defence under Article 7(e) of the Directive, the producer of a defective product must prove that the objective state of scientific and technical knowledge, including the most advanced level of such knowledge, at the time when the product in question was put into circulation was not such as to enable the existence of the defect to be discovered. Further, in order for the relevant scientific and technical knowledge to be successfully pleaded as against the producer, that knowledge must have been accessible at the time when the product in question was put into circulation. On this last point, Article 7(e) of the Directive, contrary to what the Commission seems to consider, raises difficulties of interpretation which, in the event of litigation, the national courts will have to resolve, having recourse, if necessary, to Article 177 of the EC Treaty.

30. For the present, it is the heads of claim raised by the Commission in support of its application that have to be considered. . . .

32. The Commission takes the view that inasmuch as section 4(1)(e) of the Act refers to what may be expected of a producer of products of the same description as the product in question, its wording clearly conflicts with Article 7(e) of the Directive in that it permits account to be taken of the subjective knowledge of a producer taking reasonable care, having regard to the standard precautions taken in the industrial sector in question.

33. That argument must be rejected in so far as it selectively stresses particular terms used in section 4(1)(e) without demonstrating that the general legal context of the provision at issue fails effectively to secure full application of the Directive. Taking that context into account, the Commission has failed to make out its claim that the result intended by Article 7(e) of the Directive would clearly not be achieved in the domestic legal order. . . .

37. . . . . [T]he Court has consistently held that the scope of national laws, regulations or administrative provisions must be assessed in the light of the interpretation given to them by national courts. . . Yet in this case the Commission has not referred in support of its application to any national judicial decision which, in its view, interprets the domestic provision at issue inconsistently with the Directive.

38. Lastly, there is nothing in the material produced to the Court to suggest that the courts in the United Kingdom, if called upon to interpret section 4(1)(e), would not do so in the light of the wording and the purpose of the Directive so as to achieve the result which it has in view and thereby comply with the third paragraph of Article 189 of the Treaty. . . Moreover, section 1(1) of the Act expressly imposes such an obligation on the national courts.

Notes

1. The test is objective and 'knowledge' includes knowledge even at an advanced level. However, the Court also notes that the knowledge must be *accessible*, and presumably one way of establishing this is to show that other producers were or ought to have been aware of the knowledge. But that would not be the only way of showing that the knowledge was accessible. Following *EC v UK*, section 4(1)(e) of the Act should be interpreted as meaning that the defence will apply only when the knowledge of the potential defect was not accessible and one way of showing that is to show that other producers would not be expected to have known of the problem, but the defendant may also need to show that there was no other way that the knowledge could be regarded as accessible.

> ### A v National Blood Authority
> Queen's Bench Division [2001] EWHC QB 446; [2001] 3 All ER 289

The claimants contracted Hepatitis C by transfusions of blood taken from infected donors. The claim was made under the Consumer Protection Act 1987 (it was conceded that blood was a 'product' and that its preparation involved an 'industrial process'). At the relevant time the risk of infection was known but it was not possible to test for the presence of the Hepatitis C virus in the blood of donors, and thus the risk of infection could not be avoided. Accordingly, one issue was whether 'unavoidability' was a relevant circumstance in determining whether a product was defective. Another issue was whether an unavoidable but known risk qualified for the 'development risks defence' (Consumer Protection Act, s 4(1)(e)); that is, that the state of scientific knowledge at the time was not such as to enable the existence of the defect to be discovered. Held: the defendants were liable and could not rely on the defence. (Note: because the Act implements the European Directive, the judgment generally refers to the terms of the Directive, hence 'Article 6' (which corresponds with section 3 of the Act, extracted earlier) and 'Article 7(e)' as outlining the defence in question (s 4(1)(e) of the Act.)

BURTON J:

32. Having set out what is common ground, I now summarise briefly the difference between the two parties, some of which is already apparent from my setting in context of the factual common ground:

    (i) As to Article 6, the Claimants assert that, with the need for proof of negligence eliminated, consideration of the conduct of the producer, or of a reasonable or legitimately expectable producer, is inadmissible or irrelevant. Therefore questions of avoidability cannot and do not arise: what the Defendants could or should have done differently: whether there were any steps or precautions reasonably available: whether it was impossible to take any steps by way of prevention or avoidance, or impracticable or economically unreasonable. Such are not 'circumstances' falling to be considered within Article 6. Insofar as the risk was known to blood producers and the medical profession, it was not known to the public at large (save for those few patients who might ask their doctor, or read the occasional article about blood in a newspaper) and no risk that any percentage of transfused blood would be infected was accepted by them.

    (ii) The Defendants assert that the risk was known to those who mattered, namely the medical profession, through whom blood was supplied. Avoiding the risk was impossible and unattainable, and it is not and cannot be legitimate to expect the unattainable. Avoidability or unavoidability is a circumstance to be taken into account within Article 6. The public did not and/or was not entitled to expect 100% clean blood. The most they could legitimately expect was that all legitimately expectable (reasonably available) precautions—or in this case tests—had been taken or carried out . . .

    (iii) The Claimants respond that Article 7(e) does not apply to risks which are known before the supply of the product, whether or not the defect can be identified in the particular product; and there are a number of other issues between the parties in respect of Article 7(e) to which I shall return later. . . .

All Circumstances

35. The dispute therefore is as to what further, if anything, falls to be considered within 'all circumstances'. There is no dispute between the parties, as set out in paragraph 31(i) and (ii)

above, that consideration of the fault of the producer is excluded; but does consideration of 'all circumstances' include consideration of the conduct to be expected from the producer, the level of safety to be expected from a producer of that product? The parties agree that the starting point is the particular product with the harmful characteristic, and if its inherent nature and intended use (e.g., poison) are dangerous, then there may not need to be any further consideration, provided that the injury resulted from that known danger. However, if the product was not intended to be dangerous, that is the harmful characteristic was not intended, by virtue of the intended use of the product, then there must be consideration of whether it was safe and the level of safety to be legitimately expected. At this stage, the Defendants assert that part of the investigation consists of what steps could have been taken by a producer to avoid that harmful characteristic. The Defendants assert that conduct is to be considered not by reference to identifying the individual producer's negligence, but by identifying and specifying the safety precautions that the public would or could reasonably expect from a producer of the product. The exercise is referred to as a balancing act; the more difficult it is to make safe, and the more beneficial the product, the less is expected and vice versa, an issue being whether a producer has complied with the safety precautions reasonably to be expected . . .

Non-Standard Products

36. In any event, however, the Claimants make a separate case in relation to the blood products here in issue: namely that they are what is called in the United States 'rogue products' or 'lemons', and in Germany '*Ausreisser*'—'escapees' or 'off the road' products. These are products which are isolated or rare specimens which are different from the other products of a similar series, different from the products as intended or desired by the producer. In the course of Mr Forrester QC's [counsel for the claimant] submissions, other more attractive or suitable descriptions were canvassed, and I have firmly settled on what I clearly prefer, namely the 'non-standard' product. Thus a *standard* product is one which is and performs as the producer intends. A *non-standard* product is one which is different, obviously because it is deficient or inferior in terms of safety, from the standard product: and where it is the harmful characteristic or characteristics present in the non-standard product, but not in the standard product, which has or have caused the material injury or damage. Some Community jurisdictions in implementing the Directive have specifically provided that there will be liability for 'non-standard' products, i.e., that such will automatically be defective within Article 6: Italy and Spain have done so by express legislation, and Dr Weber, in *Produkthaftung im Belgischen Recht* 1988 at 219–20, considers that that is now the position in Belgium also as a result of the implementation of the Directive. . . .

38. In a jurisdiction where, unlike Spain and Italy, and perhaps Belgium, no legislative distinction has been drawn between standard and non-standard products, the distinction, even if I were to conclude that the blood bags in this case are non-standard products, would not be absolute. Non-standard products would not be automatically defective. A product may be unsafe because it differs from the standard product, or because the standard product itself is unsafe, or at risk of being unsafe. It may however be easier to prove defectiveness if the product differs from the standard product. . . .

Article 7(e)

47. I repeat, for the sake of convenience at this stage, Article 7(e):

> The producer shall not be liable as a result of this Directive if he proves . . . that the state of scientific and technical knowledge at the time when he put the product into circulation was not such as to enable the existence of the defect to be discovered.

. . .

The Issues Between the Parties

50. Must the producer prove that the defect had not been and could not be discovered in the product in question, as the Defendants contend, or must the producer prove that the defect had not been and could not be discovered generally, i.e., in the population of products? If it be the latter, it is common ground here that the existence of the defect in blood generally, i.e., of the infection of blood in some cases by hepatitis virus notwithstanding screening, was known, and indeed known to the Defendants. The question is thus whether, in order to take advantage of the escape clause, the producer must show that no objectively assessable scientific or technical information existed anywhere in the world which had identified, and thus put producers potentially on notice of, the problem; or whether it is enough for the producer to show that, although the existence of the defect in such product was or should have been known, there was no objectively accessible information available anywhere in the world which would have enabled a producer to discover the existence of that known defect in the particular product in question . . .

Conclusions on Article 6

55. I do not consider it to be arguable that the consumer had an actual expectation that blood being supplied to him was not 100% clean, nor do I conclude that he had knowledge that it was, or was likely to be, infected with Hepatitis C. It is not seriously argued by the Defendants, notwithstanding some few newspaper cuttings which were referred to, that there was any public understanding or acceptance of the infection of transfused blood by Hepatitis C. Doctors and surgeons knew, but did not tell their patients unless asked, and were very rarely asked. It was certainly, in my judgment, not known and accepted by society that there was such a risk . . .

56. I do not consider that the legitimate expectation of the public at large is that legitimately expectable tests will have been carried out or precautions adopted. Their legitimate expectation is as to the safeness of the product (or not) . . .

57. In this context I turn to consider what is intended to be included within 'all circumstances' in Article 6. I am satisfied that this means all relevant circumstances. It is quite plain to me that (albeit that Professor [Jane] Stapleton has been pessimistic about its success) the Directive was intended to eliminate proof of fault or negligence. I am satisfied that this was not simply a legal consequence, but that it was also intended to make it easier for claimants to prove their case, such that not only would a consumer not have to prove that the producer did not take reasonable steps, or all reasonable steps, to comply with his duty of care, but also that the producer did not take all legitimately expectable steps either. In this regard I note paragraph 16 of the Advocate General's Opinion in *Commission v UK* [[1997] All ER (EC) 481] where, in setting out the background to the Directive, he pointed out that:

> Albeit injured by a defective product, consumers were in fact and too often deprived of an effective remedy, since it proved very difficult procedurally to prove negligence on the part of the producer, that is to say, that he failed to take all appropriate steps to avoid the defect arising. . . .

63. I conclude therefore that *avoidability* is not one of the *circumstances* to be taken into account within Article 6. I am satisfied that it is not a relevant circumstance, because it is outwith the purpose of the Directive, and indeed that, had it been intended that it would be included as a derogation from, or at any rate a palliation of, its purpose, then it would certainly have been mentioned; for it would have been an important circumstance, and I am clear that, irrespective of the absence of any word such as *notamment* in the English language version of the Directive, it was intended that the most significant circumstances were those listed.

64. This brings me to a consideration of Article 7(e) in the context of consideration of Article 6. Article 7(e) provides a very restricted escape route, and producers are, as emphasised in

Commission v UK [[1997] All ER (EC) 481] unable to take advantage of it, unless they come within its very restricted conditions, whereby a producer who has taken all possible precautions (certainly all legitimately expectable precautions, if the terms of Article 6, as construed by Mr Underhill QC [counsel for the defendants], are to be cross-referred) remains liable unless that producer can show that 'the state of scientific and technical knowledge [anywhere and anyone's in the world, provided reasonably accessible] was not such as to enable the existence of the defect to be discovered'. The significance seems to be as follows. Article 7(e) is the escape route (if available at all) for the producer who has done all he could reasonably be expected to do (and more); and yet that route is emphatically very restricted, because of the purpose and effect of the Directive (see particularly paragraphs 26, 36 and 38 of the European Court's judgment). This must suggest a similarly restricted view of Article 6, indeed one that is even more restricted, given the availability of the (restricted) Article 7(e) escape route. If that were not the case, then if the Article 7(e) defence were excluded, an option permitted (and indeed taken up, in the case of Luxembourg and Finland) for those Member States who wish to delete this 'exonerating circumstance' as 'unduly restricting the protection of the consumer' (Recital 16 and Article 15), then, on the Defendants' case, an even less restrictive 'exonerating circumstance', and one available even in the case of risks known to the producer, would remain in Article 6; and indeed one where the onus does not even rest on the Defendant, but firmly on the Claimant.

65. Further, in my judgment, the infected bags of blood were non-standard products. I have already recorded that it does not seem to me to matter whether they would be categorised in US tort law as manufacturing or design defects. They were in any event different from the norm which the producer intended for use by the public . . .

But I am satisfied, as I have stated above, that the problem was not *known* to the consumer. However, in any event, I do not accept that the consumer expected, or was entitled to expect, that his bag of blood was defective even if (which I have concluded was not the case) he had any knowledge of any problem. I do not consider, as Mr Forrester QC put it, that he was expecting or entitled to expect a form of Russian roulette. That would only arise if, contrary to my conclusion, the public took that as socially acceptable (*sozialadäquat*). For such knowledge and acceptance there would need to be at the very least publicity and probably express warnings, and even that might not, in the light of the no-waiver provision in Article 12 set out above, be sufficient. . . .

67. The first step must be to identify the harmful characteristic which caused the injury (Article 4). In order to establish that there is a defect in Article 6, the next step will be to conclude whether the product is standard or non-standard. This will be done (in the absence of admission by the producer) most easily by comparing the offending product with other products of the same type or series produced by that producer. If the respect in which it differs from the series includes the harmful characteristic, then it is, for the purpose of Article 6, non-standard. If it does not differ, or if the respect in which it differs does not include the harmful characteristic, but all the other products, albeit different, share the harmful characteristic, then it is to be treated as a standard product.

Non-standard Products

68. The circumstances specified in Article 6 may obviously be relevant—the product may be a second—as well as the circumstances of the supply. But it seems to me that the primary issue in relation to a non-standard product may be whether the public at large accepted the non-standard nature of the product—i.e., they accept that a proportion of the products is defective (as I have concluded they do not in this case). That, as discussed, is not of course the end of it, because the question is of *legitimate* expectation, and the Court may conclude that the expectation of the public is too high

or too low. But manifestly questions such as warnings and presentations will be in the forefront. However I conclude that the following are not relevant:

(i) Avoidability of the harmful characteristic—i.e., impossibility or unavoidability in relation to precautionary measures.

(ii) The impracticality, cost or difficulty of taking such measures.

(iii) The benefit to society or utility of the product: (except in the context of whether—with full information and proper knowledge—the public does and ought to accept the risk). . . .

Standard Products

71. If a standard product is unsafe, it is likely to be so as a result of alleged error in design, or at any rate as a result of an allegedly flawed system. The harmful characteristic must be identified, if necessary with the assistance of experts. The question of presentation/time/circumstances of supply/social acceptability etc. will arise as above. The sole question will be safety for the foreseeable use. If there are any comparable products on the market, then it will obviously be relevant to compare the offending product with those other products, so as to identify, compare and contrast the relevant features. There will obviously need to be a full understanding of how the product works—particularly if it is a new product, such as a scrid [an imaginary product], so as to assess its safety for such use. Price is obviously a significant factor in legitimate expectation, and may well be material in the comparative process. But again it seems to me there is no room in the basket for:

(i) what the producer could have done differently:

(ii) whether the producer could or could not have done the same as the others did.. . .

Conclusions on Article 7(e)

74. As to construction:

(i) I note (without resolving the question) the force of the argument that the *defect* in Article 7(b) falls to be construed as the defect in the particular product; but I do not consider that to be determinative of the construction of Article 7(e), and indeed I am firmly of the view that such is not the case in Article 7(e).

(ii) The analysis of Article 7(e), with the guidance of *Commission v UK* [[1997] All ER (EC) 481], seems to me to be entirely clear. If there is a known risk, i.e., the existence of the defect is known or should have been known in the light of non-Manchurianly accessible information, then the producer continues to produce and supply at his own risk. It would, in my judgment, be inconsistent with the purpose of the Directive if a producer, in the case of a known risk, continues to supply products simply because, and despite the fact that, he is unable to identify in which if any of his products that defect will occur or recur, or, more relevantly in a case such as this, where the producer is obliged to supply, continues to supply without accepting the responsibility for any injuries resulting, by insurance or otherwise.

(iii) *The existence of the defect* is in my judgment clearly generic. Once the *existence of the defect* is known, then there is then the *risk* of that defect materialising in any particular product. . . .

76. The purpose of Article 7(e) was plainly not to discourage innovation, and to exclude development risks from the Directive, and it succeeds in its objective, subject to the very considerable restrictions that are clarified by *Commission v UK*: namely that the risk ceases to be a development risk and becomes a known risk not if and when the producer in question (or, as the CPA inappropriately sought to enact in Section 4(1)(e) 'a producer of products of the same description as the product in question') had the requisite knowledge, but if and when such knowledge were accessible anywhere in the world outside Manchuria. Hence it protects the producer in respect of the unknown (*inconnu*).

But the consequence of acceptance of the Defendants' submissions would be that protection would also be given in respect of the known.

77. The effect is, it seems to me . . . that non-standard products are incapable of coming within Article 7(e). Non-standard products may qualify once—i.e., if the problem which leads to an occasional defective product is (unlike the present case) not known: this may perhaps be more unusual than in relation to a problem with a standard product, but does not seem to me to be an impossible scenario. However once the problem is known by virtue of accessible information, then the non-standard product can no longer qualify for protection under Article 7(e).

The Result in Law on Issue I

78. Unknown risks are unlikely to qualify by way of defence within Article 6. They may however qualify for Article 7(e). Known risks do not qualify within Article 7(e), even if unavoidable in the particular product. They may qualify within Article 6 if fully known and socially acceptable.

79. The blood products in this case were non-standard products, and were unsafe by virtue of the harmful characteristics which they had and which the standard products did not have.

80. They were not *ipso facto* defective (an expression used from time to time by the Claimants) but were defective because I am satisfied that the public at large was entitled to expect that the blood transfused to them would be free from infection. There were no warnings and no material publicity, certainly none officially initiated by or for the benefit of the Defendants, and the knowledge of the medical profession, not materially or at all shared with the consumer, is of no relevance. It is not material to consider whether any steps or any further steps could have been taken to avoid or palliate the risk that the blood would be infected.

Notes

1. This case is important not only for its interpretation of Articles 6 ('what is a defect?') and 7 (defences) of the Directive (Consumer Protection Act, ss 3 and 4(1)), but also because Burton J stresses the no-fault nature of product liability under the Directive/Act. The question is not whether it is unfair to impose liability on a defendant who cannot avoid the loss but, given that some losses will occur, which of the two parties should bear the cost, or perhaps which of the two should insure against the risk. The purpose of the Directive was to prefer the consumer in this situation, and to impose strict liability, reflecting a more general international move towards consumer protectionism in this area of law as well as many others.

2. When does a risk become 'socially acceptable' (Burton J at [65])? In other words, when is it generally agreed that not every example of a product will be perfect? In *Richardson* v *LRC Products* [2000] Lloyd's Rep Med 280, the claimant became pregnant after her husband used one of the defendant's condoms, which fractured during sex. The cause of the fracture was unexplained. The judge seems to have assumed that there was no defect in the condom when it left the factory, but even if there was he said it would not be defective within the Act. He pointed out that while the expectation is that the condom will not fail, no method of contraception is 100 per cent effective and there will always be inexplicable failures. Thus, he seems to have thought that so long as the testing procedures were rigorous, that was all the public was entitled to expect. In *A v National Blood Authority*, Burton J thought this case was unclear, but in general the question is whether the public generally accept that condoms sometimes burst. Given the warnings placed on packaging, it is likely that we should be able to assume that this is the case.

3. The latest cases to consider the concept of defects and what is (or is not) socially acceptable relate to metal-on-metal hip replacements (*Wilkes* v *DePuy International Ltd* [2016] EWHC 3096 (QB); *Gee and others* v *DePuy International Ltd* [2018] EWHC 1208 (QB)). In *Wilkes*, Hickinbottom J ruled

that consumers were not entitled to expect that medicinal products would be risk-free. In *Gee*, 312 individuals affected by 'adverse reaction to metal debris' following their hip replacements which used products from DePuy, claimed damages under the Consumer Protection Act 1987 in respect of tissue damage, pain, swelling and numbness, and removal and replacement of the joint with further corrective surgery. Mrs Justice Andrews DBE said that the cost of rectification, avoidability of harm and public benefit were relevant concepts in assessing what the public generally is entitled to expect. Given that when the products were used (around 2002), artificial hip producers only had the knowledge available at that time, she found that the claimants could not establish that the safety of the product did not meet the standard that the public generally were entitled to expect. The correct test, she said, is whether the product had an abnormal tendency to result in damage or harm, compared with comparable products on the market at that time. This seems to result in a stricter test than that envisaged by Burton J in *A v National Blood Authority*.

Which test will be followed in the future is a matter of speculation. In *Gill v Ethicon Sàrl (No 5)* [2019] FCA 1905 (Australia), Katzmann J found producers of transvaginal mesh implants used in reconstructive surgery liable for the pain and other symptoms that many women had subsequently been left with. She held that defectiveness and warnings given or not given were intertwined in the question of what consumers can legitimately expect. As there had been no clear instruction or warning, consumers were entitled to expect that their doctors would be using safe products. In *Hastings v Finsbury Orthopaedics Ltd and Stryker UK Ltd* [2019] CSOH 96 (Scotland), *Wilkes* and *Gee* were considered, though the claimant's case that consumer expectation would be based on products being at least as good as comparable alternatives was favoured over the defendant's reliance on *Gee*.

4. What is technical knowledge? In *Abouzaid* v *Mothercare* The Times, 20 February 2001, the teenage claimant's eye was injured when an elastic strap on one of the defendants' products sprang back. The claimant's case relied on the Department of Trade database which did not reveal any similar accidents having happened before and said that without such information it was not possible to have discovered the defect. The Court of Appeal thought that such accident records were probably not 'technical knowledge' and found the defendants liable.

5. Burton J mentions 'Manchuria' (at [76]). This relates to the accessibility of the technical knowledge—see *Commission v UK* (Case 300/95), EU:C:1997:35, Opinion of AG Tesauro at [23], where the example of an article published only in Manchuria and written in Chinese was given. The argument is that it would be unrealistic to expect manufacturers in general to know of research which is not reasonably likely to circulate. Now that much global research is available on the internet, this example is probably a little outdated. Burton J's alternative analogy—unpublished research results held within a company (at [49])—is probably more illustrative.

For further reading see Christopher Newdick 'The Development Risks Defence of the Consumer Protection Act 1987' [1988] CLJ 455 and more generally Jane Stapleton *Product Liability* (Butterworths, 1994). On the possible change of emphasis following *Wilkes*, see Jacob Eisler 'One Step Forward and Two Steps Back in Product Liability: The Search for Clarity in the Identification of Defects' [2017] CLJ 233 and Donal Nolan 'Strict Product Liability for Design Defects' (2018) 134 LQR 176.

12

Breach of statutory duty

The tort of breach of statutory duty enables a claimant in certain circumstances to recover compensation for losses caused by a defendant's failure to comply with a statutory obligation. It is separate to and distinct from claims arising directly as a result of a breach of a statutorily imposed duty, such as those arising out of the Consumer Protection Act 1987 (which make it an offence to supply goods which contravene the safety regulations, and, in s 41, expressly states that a person contravening the regulations will also be liable to pay compensation to a person harmed by the breach) or the Protection from Harassment Act 1997 (s 3 of which allows a claimant who has been unreasonably subjected to a course of conduct that the defendant knows, or ought to know, amounts to harassment to sue the defendant for damages).

Most statutes, however, make no mention of potential civil liability and it is here that the tort of breach of statutory duty may provide a remedy. In essence, liability may be imposed if the court believes that Parliament intended there to be a remedy. However, 'divining' the will of Parliament is rarely straightforward. Moreover, there are differing views as to the role and function of the tort of breach of statutory duty, largely depending on the context in which it arises.

For the tort of breach of statutory duty, the following need to be established (in addition to the usual requirements relating to causation and defences):

(1) the statute gives rise to a claim in tort law;

(2) a duty is owed to the claimant;

(3) the defendant has breached their duty; and

(4) the claimant's loss or injury falls within the scope of the duty.

12.1 Does the statute give rise to a claim in tort law and is a duty owed to the claimant?

> ### Groves v Lord Wimborne
> Court of Appeal [1898] 2 QB 402

The claimant, a young boy, was seriously injured while working in the defendant's iron works. He caught his arm in a steam winch. His forearm was later amputated. The machinery had been left unfenced contrary to section 5 of the Factory and Workshop Act 1878, which imposed an absolute duty on the employer to ensure that certain dangerous machinery was fenced. Held: in allowing the machinery to be and remain unfenced, the employer was in breach of his statutory duty to the claimant.

VAUGHAN WRIGHT LJ: . . . In the result I entertain no doubt that upon the proper construction of the Factory and Workshop Act, 1878, the Legislature did not intend the remedy or benefit which may be given under section 82 through the intervention of the Secretary of State to a person injured through a breach of the provisions of the Act with regard to fencing machinery to be the only remedy open to a person so injured. . . .

With regard to the first point it cannot be doubted that, where a statute provides for the performance by certain persons of a particular duty, and some one belonging to a class of persons for whose benefit and protection the statute imposes the duty is injured by failure to perform it, *prima facie*, and, if there be nothing to the contrary, an action by the person so injured will lie against the person who has so failed to perform the duty. I have equally no doubt that, where in a statute of this kind a remedy is provided in cases of non-performance of the statutory duty, that is a matter to be taken into consideration for the purpose of determining whether an action will lie for injury caused by non-performance of that duty, or whether the Legislature intended that there should be no other remedy than the statutory remedy; but it is by no means conclusive or the only matter to be taken into consideration for that purpose. If it be found that the remedy so provided by the statute is to enure for the benefit of the person injured by the breach of the statutory duty, that is an additional matter which ought to be taken into consideration in dealing with the question whether the Legislature intended the statutory remedy to be the only remedy. But again, the fact that the Legislature has provided that that remedy shall enure, or under some circumstances shall enure, for the benefit of the person injured, is not conclusive of the question, and, although it may be a cogent and weighty consideration, other matters also have to be considered. In such a case as this one must, as Lord Cairns said in *Atkinson v Newcastle Waterworks Co* [[1877] 2 Ex D 441], look at the general scope of the Act and the nature of the statutory duty; and in addition one must look at the nature of the injuries likely to arise from a breach of that duty, the amount of the penalty imposed for a breach of it, and the kind of person upon whom it is imposed, before one can come to a proper conclusion as to whether the Legislature intended the statutory remedy to be the only remedy for breach of the statutory duty. I can add nothing to the observations of my brother AL Smith [also sitting in the Court of Appeal] with regard to the provisions of section 87, which in certain cases substitute a fellow-servant for the occupier of the factory as the person upon whom the penalty is to be imposed, or to the observations of my brother Rigby [also sitting in the Court of Appeal] as to the improbability of the Legislature having intended that the 100/fine should be the only remedy for a breach of duty which might lead to the death or serious injury of a person of the class intended to be benefited or protected by the Act. I entirely agree in the conclusion that upon the true construction of the Act the penalty provided by section 82 is not intended to be the only remedy for breach of the statutory duty created by the Act. But, although in the result I arrive at this conclusion without any doubt, I think that the question raised at the trial was one which at first sight was by no means free from difficulty. So far as I am aware, there is no instance up to the present time in which it has been held that, where a statute in terms provides that a penalty imposed by the Act shall go to the person injured by breach of the statutory duty, there is a civil remedy by action besides the statutory remedy. We have not, however, to decide that point, because section 82 does not say that the penalty shall go to the person injured, or give him or any person power to recover it. All it does is to enable the Secretary of State, if he thinks fit under the circumstances of the case, to say that the penalty imposed or part of it shall be applied for the benefit of the person injured. In making these observations on the particular case I do not wish to be considered as going back in the slightest degree from the general proposition that no hard and fast line can be drawn as to what provisions in an Act will indicate that the intention of the Legislature was that the remedy provided by the statute should be the only remedy. In each case one must look at the whole of the statute, and gather from all its provisions the answer to the question whether that was the intention.

Phillips v Britannia Hygienic Laundry
Court of Appeal [1923] 2 KB 832

The axle of a lorry owned by the defendants was defective and broke. As a result, one of its wheels came off and damaged the claimant's van. The Motor Cars (Use and Construction) Order 1904 stated that 'the motor car and all the fittings thereof shall be in such a condition as not to cause, or to be likely to cause, danger to any person in the motor car or on any highway'. Held: the regulations did not give rise to civil liability.

ATKIN LJ: . . . This is an important question, and I have felt some doubt upon it, because it is clear that these regulations are in part designed to promote the safety of the public using highways. The question is whether they were intended to be enforced only by the special penalty attached to them in the Act. In my opinion, when an Act imposes a duty of commission or omission, the question whether a person aggrieved by a breach of the duty has a right of action depends on the intention of the Act. Was it intended to make the duty one which was owed to the party aggrieved as well as to the State, or was it a public duty only? That depends on the construction of the Act and the circumstances in which it was made and to which it relates. One question to be considered is, does the Act contain reference to a remedy for breach of it? Prima facie if it does that is the only remedy. But that is not conclusive. The intention as disclosed by its scope and wording must still be regarded, and it may still be that, though the statute creates the duty and provides a penalty, the duty is nevertheless owed to individuals. Instances of this are *Groves v Lord Wimborne* [1898] 2 QB 402, and *Britannic Merthyr Coal Co v David* [1910] AC 74. To my mind, and in this respect I differ from McCardie J [the first instance judge], the question is not to be solved by considering whether or not the person aggrieved can bring himself within some special class of the community or whether he is some designated individual. The duty may be of such paramount importance that it is owed to all the public. It would be strange if a less important duty, which is owed to a section of the public, may be enforced by an action, while a more important duty owed to the public at large cannot. The right of action does not depend on whether a statutory commandment or prohibition is pronounced for the benefit of the public or for the benefit of a class. It may be conferred on any one who can bring himself within the benefit of the Act, including one who cannot be otherwise specified than as a person using the highway. Therefore I think McCardie J is applying too strict a test when he says ([1923] 1 KB 547):

> The Motor Car Acts and Regulations were not enacted for the benefit of any particular class of folk. They are provisions for the benefit of the whole public, whether pedestrians or vehicle users, whether aliens or British citizens, and whether working or walking or standing upon the highway.

Kelly CB in stating the argument for the defendant in *Gorris v Scott* LR 9 Ex 125, refers to the obligation imposed upon railway companies by section 47 of the Railways Clauses Consolidation Act, 1845, to erect gates across public carriage roads crossed by the railway on the level, and to keep the gates closed except when the crossing is being actually and properly used, under the penalty of 40s for every default. It was never doubted that if a member of the public crossing the railway were injured by the railway company's breach of duty, either in not erecting a gate or in not keeping it closed, he would have a right of action. Therefore the question is whether these regulations, viewed in the circumstances in which they were made and to which they relate, were intended to impose a duty which is a public duty only or whether they were intended, in addition to the public duty, to impose a duty enforceable by an individual aggrieved. I have come to the conclusion that the duty they were intended to impose was not a duty enforceable by individuals injured, but a public duty only, the sole remedy for which is the remedy provided by way of a fine. They impose obligations of various kinds, some are concerned more with the maintenance of the highway than with the safety of passengers; and they are of varying degrees of importance; yet for breach of any regulation a fine not exceeding 10/- is the penalty. It is not likely that the Legislature, in empowering a department to make regulations for the use and construction of motor cars, permitted the department to impose new duties in favour of individuals and new causes of action for breach of them in addition to the obligations already well provided for and regulated by the common law of those who bring vehicles upon highways. In particular it is not likely that the Legislature intended by these means to impose on the owners of vehicles an absolute obligation to have them roadworthy in all events even in the absence of negligence.

Notes

1. While there is no general rule by which to determine whether a statute gives rise to civil liability, it is clear that there are a number of 'indicators'. These include whether the duty was imposed for the protection of a limited class of the public; the existence of alternative means of enforcing the duty; other remedies provided for by the statute; the extent to which the statute's scope is limited and specific or general and administrative; as well as various, ubiquitous, policy considerations.

2. The decision in **Phillips v Britannia Hygienic Laundry** may seem surprising—after all, surely the regulation was to protect other road users? However, at the time the control of motor cars was a highly contentious and political issue, and so it may be that the court felt inhibited from entering such an arena especially given that compulsory insurance had not yet been introduced.

3. Similarly, in **Groves v Lord Wimborne**, timing was everything. Just a year earlier Parliament had enacted the Workmen's Compensation Act 1897 which imposed, for the first time, liability on employers in relation to 'accidents arising out of and in the course of employment'. **Groves** continued this trend, shifting responsibility for the safety of the workforce from the employee (who could do little about it) to the employer (who could). In the process, it dealt another blow to the 'unholy trinity' (comprising the doctrine of common employment and the (complete) defences of contributory negligence and *volenti*). It remained unscathed for 155 years until the pendulum swung the other way with the enactment of section 69 of the Enterprise and Regulatory Reform Act 2013 (see section 12.2).

4. In *R v Deputy Governor of Parkhurst, ex p Hague* [1991] 3 WLR 340, Lord Jauncey said, in relation to breach of statutory duty, that:

   > it must always be a matter for consideration whether the legislature intended that private law rights of action should be conferred upon individuals in respect of breaches of the relevant statutory provision. The fact that a particular provision was intended to protect certain individuals is not of itself sufficient to confer private law rights of action upon them. Something more is required to show that the legislature intended such conferment. (at 170–1)

   The 'more' that is required is the intention of the legislature to provide a right of action, and according to Lord Bridge, in the same case, that is a matter of statutory construction like any other (at 159). But how can that be when the problem arises only because the statute says nothing about the issue? In *Hague* itself it was held that the Prison Rules were administrative only and gave rise to no right of action (the claimant had claimed that segregation in breach of the Prison Rules gave him an action in private law). The shift away from the reasoning in *Groves* (where the question was whether the statute was intended to confer a *benefit* on the claimant) and focus on the provision of a *right of action* has significantly limited the scope of the tort of breach of statutory duty (see e.g. Lord Browne-Wilkinson in *X v Bedfordshire County Council*).

X v *Bedfordshire County Council*
House of Lords [1995] 2 AC 633

The facts are set out in section 5.1.

LORD BROWNE-WILKINSON:

(A) Breach of statutory duty *simpliciter*

The principles applicable in determining whether such statutory cause of action exists are now well established, although the application of those principles in any particular case remains difficult. The basic proposition is that in the ordinary case a breach of statutory duty does not, by itself, give rise to any private law cause of action. However a private law cause of action will arise if it can be shown, as a matter of construction of the statute, that the statutory duty was imposed for the protection of a limited class of the public and that Parliament intended to confer on members of that class a private right of action for breach of the duty. There is no general rule by reference to which it can be decided whether a statute does create such a right of action but there are a number of indicators. If the statute provides no other remedy for its breach and the Parliamentary intention to protect a limited class is shown, that indicates that there may be a private right of action since otherwise there is no method of securing the protection the statute was intended to confer. If the statute does provide some other means of enforcing the duty that will normally indicate that the statutory right was intended to be enforceable by those means and not by private right of action: *Cutler v Wandsworth Stadium Ltd* [1949] AC 398; *Lonrho Ltd v Shell Petroleum Co Ltd (No 2)* [1982] AC 173. However, the mere existence of some other statutory remedy is not necessarily decisive. It is still possible to show that on the true construction of the statute the protected class was intended by Parliament to have a private remedy. Thus the specific duties imposed on employers in relation to factory premises are enforceable by an action for damages, notwithstanding the imposition by the statutes of criminal penalties for any breach: see *Groves v Wimborne (Lord)* [1898] 2 QB 402.

Although the question is one of statutory construction and therefore each case turns on the provisions in the relevant statute, it is significant that your Lordships were not referred to any case where it had been held that statutory provisions establishing a regulatory system or a scheme of social welfare for the benefit of the public at large had been held to give rise to a private right of action for damages for breach of statutory duty. Although regulatory or welfare legislation affecting a particular area of activity does in fact provide protection to those individuals particularly affected by that activity, the legislation is not to be treated as being passed for the benefit of those individuals but for the benefit of society in general. Thus legislation regulating the conduct of betting or prisons did not give rise to a statutory right of action vested in those adversely affected by the breach of the statutory provisions, ie bookmakers and prisoners: see *Cutler*'s case [1949] AC 398; *Reg v Deputy Governor of Parkhurst Prison, Ex parte Hague* [1992] 1 AC 58. The cases where a private right of action for breach of statutory duty have been held to arise are all cases in which the statutory duty has been very limited and specific as opposed to general administrative functions imposed on public bodies and involving the exercise of administrative discretions.

> ### Lonrho Ltd v Shell Petroleum Co Ltd (No 2)
> House of Lords [1982] AC 173

After the unilateral declaration of independence by the government of Southern Rhodesia, Parliament passed the Southern Rhodesia (Petroleum) Order 1965, which prohibited the supply of oil to Southern Rhodesia. Lonrho owned a pipeline from Mozambique to Rhodesia, which was thereupon closed. They alleged that the defendants and others had maintained the supply of oil to Rhodesia, thereby prolonging the period of unconstitutional government and lengthening the period of closure of the claimant's pipeline. One of the arguments related to liability for the breach of statutory duty arising from the Order. Held: the Order did not give rise to civil liability.

LORD DIPLOCK: The sanctions Order thus creates a statutory prohibition upon the doing of certain classes of acts and provides the means of enforcing the prohibition by prosecution for a criminal offence which is subject to heavy penalties including imprisonment. So one starts with the presumption laid down originally by Lord Tenterden CJ in *Doe d Murray v Bridges* (1831) 1 B & Ad 847, 859, where he spoke of the 'general rule' that 'where an Act creates an obligation, and enforces the performance in a specified manner . . . that performance cannot be enforced in any other manner'—a statement that has frequently been cited with approval ever since, including on several occasions in speeches in this House. Where the only manner of enforcing performance for which the Act provides is prosecution for the criminal offence of failure to perform the statutory obligation or for contravening the statutory prohibition which the Act creates, there are two classes of exception to this general rule.

The first is where upon the true construction of the Act it is apparent that the obligation or prohibition was imposed for the benefit or protection of a particular class of individuals, as in the case of the Factories Acts and similar legislation. As Lord Kinnear put it in *Butler (or Black) v Fife Coal Co Ltd* [1912] AC 149, 165, in the case of such a statute:

> There is no reasonable ground for maintaining that a proceeding by way of penalty is the only remedy allowed by the statute . . . We are to consider the scope and purpose of the statute and in particular for whose benefit it is intended. Now the object of the present statute is plain. It was intended to compel mine owners to make due provision for the safety of the men working in their mines, and the persons for whose benefit all these rules are to be enforced are the persons exposed to danger. But when a duty of this kind is imposed for the benefit of particular persons there arises at common law a correlative right in those persons who may be injured by its contravention.

The second exception is where the statute creates a public right (ie a right to be enjoyed by all those of Her Majesty's subjects who wish to avail themselves of it) and a particular member of the public suffers what Brett J in *Benjamin v Storr* (1874) LR 9 CP 400, 407, described as 'particular, direct, and substantial' damage 'other and different from that which was common to all the rest of the public.' Most of the authorities about this second exception deal not with public rights created by statute but with public rights existing at common law, particularly in respect of use of highways. *Boyce v Paddington Borough Council* [1903] 1 Ch 109 is one of the comparatively few cases about a right conferred upon the general public by statute. It is in relation to that class of statute only that Buckley J's oft-cited statement at p 114 as to the two cases in which a plaintiff, without joining the Attorney-General, could himself sue in private law for interference with that public right, must be understood. The two cases he said were: . . . first, where the interference with the public right is such as that some private right of his is at the same time interfered with . . . and, secondly, where no private right is interfered with, but the plaintiff, in respect of his public right, suffers special damage peculiar to himself from the interference with the public right.' The first case would not appear to depend upon the existence of a public right in addition to the private one; while to come within the second case at all it has first to be shown that the statute, having regard to its scope and language, does fall within that class of statutes which creates a legal right to be enjoyed by all of Her Majesty's subjects who wish to avail themselves of it. A mere prohibition upon members of the public generally from doing what it would otherwise be lawful for them to do, is not enough.

In agreement with all those present and former members of the judiciary who have considered the matter I can see no ground on which contraventions by Shell and BP of the sanctions Order though not amounting to any breach of their contract with Lonrho, nevertheless constituted a tort for which Lonrho could recover in a civil suit any loss caused to them by such contraventions.

Notes

1. Lord Browne-Wilkinson's approach was affirmed by the Supreme Court in *Morrison Sports Ltd* v *Scottish Power* [2010] UKSC 37 in which the court concluded that there was 'no basis whatever for thinking that the drafter of the provision intended to introduce a civil right of action but—somehow—botched that comparatively straightforward task and came up with the words in the subsection which are so singularly ill suited to the supposed purpose' (Lord Rodger at [16]). Rather the wording of the relevant subsection was to allow for both the payment of a criminal fine and a civil remedy, if so provided for by the Secretary of State (at [27]).

2. Another example of welfare legislation not providing a private right is *O'Rourke* v *Camden LBC* [1998] AC 188 which involved the duty to house the homeless under section 63(1) of the Housing Act 1985:

   Furthermore, there are certain contra-indications which make it unlikely that Parliament intended to create private law rights of action.

   The first is that the Act is a scheme of social welfare, intended to confer benefits at the public expense on grounds of public policy. Public money is spent on housing the homeless not merely for the private benefit of people who find themselves homeless but on grounds of general public interest: because, for example, proper housing means that people will be less likely to suffer illness, turn to crime or require the attention of other social services. The expenditure interacts with expenditure on other public services such as education, the National Health Service and even the police. It is not simply a private matter between the claimant and the housing authority. Accordingly, the fact that Parliament has provided for the expenditure of public money on benefits in kind such as housing the homeless does not necessarily mean that it intended cash payments to be made by way of damages to persons who, in breach of the housing authority's statutory duty, have unfortunately not received the benefits which they should have done . . . (Lord Hoffmann at 194)

   Lord Hoffmann went on to suggest that further contra-indications included the fact that provision of a benefit under the Act involved 'a good deal of judgment on the part of the housing authority' and that an adequate public law remedy was available.

3. Other cases where a statutory duty has not given rise to a civil right of action include *Atkinson* v *Newcastle Waterworks Co* (1877) LR 2 Ex D 441 in which a requirement to fix and maintain fire plugs and to maintain water in the mains at a certain pressure, did not give a right of action to

the claimant whose house burnt down because of insufficient supply of water. Similarly, in *Cutler v Wandsworth Stadium* [1949] AC 398 a duty on racetrack owners, so long as a 'totalisator' is being operated, to allow bookmakers onto the course, did not give rise to a claim for the claimant bookmaker who was excluded. Nor did an obligation on the Law Society to consider complaints by individuals against the conduct of solicitors provide a basis for a civil claim from a person who alleged that the Law Society failed to investigate her complaint adequately (*Wood* v *The Law Society* (1993) 143 NLJ 1475).

4. However, in *McDonald (Deceased)* v *National Grid Electricity Transmission plc* [2014] UKSC 53, the court allowed the claim (by majority), relying on the Asbestos Industry Regulations 1931, of a lorry driver who—though not employed by the defendants—came into contact with asbestos dust when he attended Battersea Power Station between 1954 and 1959 to collect pulverised fuel ash as part of his work. The duty imposed by the regulations to 'persons employed' was not limited to any particular employment (at [103]).

12.2 Has the duty been breached and does the harm fall within the scope of the duty?

> ### *Gorris* v *Scott*
> Court of Exchequer (1874) LR 9 Exch 125

The defendant owned a ship called *The Hastings*, on which he carried the claimant's sheep from Hamburg to Newcastle. On the voyage some of the sheep were washed overboard. The Animals Order 1871 required sheep and cattle to be kept in pens. If they had been, which they had not, they would not have been lost. Held: the defendants were not liable as the duty was imposed in order to prevent disease and so the claimant's loss did not fall within the scope of the duty.

PIGOTT B: . . . I am of opinion that the declaration shews no cause of action. It is necessary to see what was the object of the legislature in this enactment, and it is set forth clearly in the preamble as being 'to prevent the introduction into Great Britain of contagious or infectious diseases among cattle, sheep, or other animals,' and the 'spread of such diseases in Great Britain.' The purposes enumerated in section 75 are in harmony with this preamble, and it is in furtherance of that section that the order in question was made. The object, then, of the regulations which have been broken was, not to prevent cattle from being washed overboard, but to protect them against contagious disease. The legislature never contemplated altering the relations between the owners and carriers of cattle, except for the purposes pointed out in the Act; and if the Privy Council had gone out of their way and made provisions to prevent cattle from being washed overboard, their act would have been *ultra vires*. If, indeed, by reason of the neglect complained of, the cattle had contracted a contagious disease, the case would have been different. But as the case stands on this declaration, the answer to the action is this: Admit there has been a breach of duty; admit there has been a consequent injury; still the legislature was not legislating to protect against such an injury, but for an altogether different purpose; its object was not to regulate the duty of the carrier for all purposes, but only for one particular purpose.

Notes

1. The question at the centre of the tort of breach of statutory duty—that is, the intention of Parliament in respect of a particular statute—has been widely criticised. It has been likened to searching for a 'will o' the wisp'.

   > It is capricious and arbitrary, 'judicial legislation' at its very worst.
   >
   > Not only does it involve an unnecessary fiction, but it may lead to decisions being made on the basis of insignificant details of phraseology instead of matters of substance. If the question whether a person injured by breach of a statutory obligation is to have a right of action for damages is in truth a question to be decided by the court, let it be acknowledged as such and some useful principles of law developed (Winfield & Jolowicz, [*Tort* (11th edn, 1979)] at p 159). (Dickson J, *The Queen* v *Saskatchewan Wheat Pool* [1983] at 216)

   As long ago as 1969 the Law Commission recommended that rather than courts trying to answer the impossible, it should be presumed, unless stated to the contrary, that any statute which imposes a duty is intended to give rise to a civil remedy (*The Interpretation of Statutes*, Law Com No 21). This was never implemented. Although until relatively recently section 47(2) of the Health and Safety at Work Act 1974 operated to this effect in the context of health and safety legislation. It provided that a 'breach of a duty imposed by health and safety regulations shall, so far as it causes damage, be actionable except in so far as the regulations provide otherwise'. This presumption was reversed by section 69 of the Enterprise and Regulatory Reform Act 2013 which states that 'breach of a duty imposed by a statutory instrument containing (whether alone or with other provision) health and safety regulations shall not be actionable except to the extent that regulations under this section so provide' (s 69(3)). See further Nigel Tomkins 'Civil Health and Safety Law after the Enterprise and Regulatory Reform Act 2013' [2013] JPIL 203.

2. In *The Queen* v *Saskatchewan Wheat Pool* [1983] 1 SCR 205, the Supreme Court of Canada after an extensive survey of the British, US and Canadian approach to the tort of breach of statutory duty, rejected the British position of, to use Glanville Williams's phrase, 'looking for what is not there' (in 'The Effect of Penal Legislation in the Law of Tort' (1960) 23 MLR 233, 244): 'the legislature has imposed a penalty on a strictly admonitory basis and there seems little justification to add civil liability when such liability would tend to produce liability without fault' (Dickson J at 224). Dickson J also suggested that the tort should be subsumed within negligence, although the statutory formulation of the duty may afford a specific and useful standard of reasonable conduct (at 227). See further MH Matthews 'Negligence and Breach of Statutory Duty' (1984) 4 OJLS 429.

The personal torts

PART III

13 Intentional inferences with the person
    13.1 Trespass and negligence
    13.2 Trespass to the person
    13.3 Intentional infliction of physical harm or distress

14 Invasion of privacy
    14.1 Privacy and common law
    14.2 The Human Rights Act and the reasonable expectation of privacy
    14.3 Remedies

15 Defamation
    15.1 Who can sue?
    15.2 Who can be liable?
    15.3 The meaning of 'defamatory'
    15.4 Serious harm
    15.5 What do the words used mean?
    15.6 Do the words refer to the claimant?
    15.7 Truth
    15.8 Honest opinion
    15.9 Privilege
    15.10 Publication on a matter of public interest
    15.11 Offer of amends
    15.12 Damages

13

Intentional interferences with the person

This chapter covers a number of actions which seek to protect an individual's right to be free from unwanted interference with their personal or bodily integrity—namely the torts of assault, battery and false imprisonment, which together comprise the 'trespass to the person torts', the tort in **Wilkinson v Downton** and under the Protection from Harassment Act 1997.

The law of trespass today reveals much of its origins in the criminal law, and to some extent this is borne out by the fact that its function is often as a deterrent rather than compensatory. Unlike negligence, an action will lie in trespass even if the claimant has suffered no damage or physical injury. It is the right itself which is protected, rather than the freedom from resulting damage, and as such trespass forms the basis of many of our civil liberties today. For example, false imprisonment has been used to establish whether a detention was lawful (*R (on the application of Lumba)* v *Secretary of State for the Home Department* [2011] UKSC 12), while civil claims for battery have been brought after unsuccessful criminal prosecutions for rape (*Lawson* v *Glaves-Smith* [2006] EWHC 2865 (QB)).

While much of the language and subject matter of the trespass to the person torts will be familiar, the tort in **Wilkinson v Downton**—which provides a remedy for those injured *indirectly* by the defendant's intentional act—has for much of its 124-year existence been rather obscure. In fact, following the establishment of a statutory tort of harassment in the Protection from Harassment Act 1997, it was thought it would disappear altogether. Its somewhat surprising—and happily short-lived—resurrection by the Court of Appeal in the so-called 'banned memoir case' (*OPO* v *MLA* [2014] EWCA Civ 1277) towards the end of 2014 (overturned by the Supreme Court a year later (in **Rhodes v OPO** [2015] UKSC 32)), pitted it in direct opposition to one of our most fundamental civil liberties: freedom of expression.

13.1 Trespass and negligence

Although at one point it was thought that a trespass could be committed negligently (*Fowler* v *Lanning* [1959] 1 QB 426), the distinction between trespass and negligence is now well established.

> ### *Letang v Cooper*
> Court of Appeal [1965] 1 QB 232

The claimant, Letang, was sunbathing in the grounds of the Ponsmere Hotel at Perranporth in Cornwall when the defendant negligently drove over her legs with his Jaguar. When she attempted to sue more than three years later, as action in negligence was time-barred under the Law Reform (Limitation of Actions) Act 1954, she attempted to sue for trespass (for which the general limitation period is six years). Held: denying her claim, the Court of Appeal held that where the injury is caused negligently the only cause of action is in negligence, not trespass.

LORD DENNING MR: The argument, as it was developed before us, became a direct invitation to this court to go back to the old forms of action and to decide this case by reference to them. The statute bars an action on the case [now called an action for negligence], it is said, after three years, whereas trespass to the person is not barred for six years. The argument was supported by reference to text-writers, such as *Salmond on Torts*, 13th ed (1961), p 790. I must say that if we are, at this distance of time, to revive the distinction between trespass and case, we should get into the most utter confusion. The old common lawyers tied themselves in knots over it, and we should do the same. Let me tell you some of their contortions. Under the old law, whenever one man injured another by the direct and immediate application of force, the plaintiff could sue the defendant in trespass to the person, without alleging negligence . . . whereas if the injury was only consequential, he had to sue in case. You will remember the illustration given by Fortescue J in *Reynolds v Clarke* (1725) 93 ER 747: 'If a man throws a log into the highway, and in that act it hits me, I may maintain trespass because it is an immediate wrong; but if as it lies there I tumble over it, and receive an injury, I must bring an action upon the case; because it is only prejudicial in consequence.' Nowadays, if a man carelessly throws a piece of wood from a house into a roadway, then whether it hits the plaintiff or he tumbles over it the next moment, the action would not be trespass or case, but simply negligence. . . .

I must decline, therefore, to go back to the old forms of action in order to construe this statute. I know that in the last century Maitland said 'the forms of action we have buried, but they still rule us from their graves' (see Maitland, *Forms of Action* (1909), p 296), but we have in this century shaken off their trammels. These forms of action have served their day. They did at one time form a guide to substantive rights; but they do so no longer. Lord Atkin, in *United Australia Ltd v Barclays Bank Ltd* [1941] AC 1, told us what to do about them: 'When these ghosts of the past stand in the path of justice clanking their mediaeval chains the proper course for the judge is to pass through them undeterred'.

The truth is that the distinction between trespass and case is obsolete. We have a different sub-division altogether. Instead of dividing actions for personal injuries into trespass (direct damage) or case (consequential damage), we divide the causes of action now according as the defendant did the injury intentionally or unintentionally. If one man intentionally applies force directly to another, the plaintiff has a cause of action in assault and battery, or, if you so please to describe it, in trespass to the person. 'The least touching of another in anger is a battery', *per* Holt CJ in *Cole v Turner* (1704) 87 ER 907. If he does not inflict injury intentionally, but only unintentionally, the plaintiff has no cause of action today in trespass. His only cause of action is in negligence, and then only on proof of want of reasonable care. If the plaintiff cannot prove want of reasonable care, he may have no cause of action at all. Thus, it is not enough nowadays for the plaintiff to plead that 'the defendant shot the plaintiff'. He must also allege that he did it intentionally or negligently. If intentional, it is the tort of assault and battery. If negligent and causing damage, it is the tort of negligence.

The modern law on this subject was well expounded by Diplock J in *Fowler v Lanning* [1959] 1 QB 426, with which I fully agree. But I would go this one step further: when the injury is not inflicted intentionally, but negligently, I would say that the only cause of action is negligence and not trespass. If it were trespass, it would be actionable without proof of damage; and that is not the law today.

In my judgment, therefore, the only cause of action in the present case, where the injury was unintentional, is negligence and is barred by reason of the express provision of the statute. . . .

I come, therefore, to the clear conclusion that the plaintiff's cause of action here is barred by the Statute of Limitations. Her only cause of action here, in my judgment, where the damage was unintentional, was negligence and not trespass to the person. It is therefore barred by the word 'negligence' in the statute.

Notes

1. Despite Croom-Johnson LJ's reference to an 'unintentional trespass' in **Wilson v Pringle** [1987] QB 237 he continued: 'It is the act and not the injury which must be intentional. An intention to injure is not essential to an action for trespass to the person. It is the mere trespass by itself which is the offence' (at 249). For all practical purposes, therefore, it can be said that trespass deals with direct intentional acts, and negligence with careless or indirect acts. This was endorsed by Smith LJ in **Iqbal v Prison Officers Association** [2009] EWCA Civ 1312, who held that 'it is well established that all forms of trespass require an intentional act. An act of negligence will not suffice' (at [71]).

2. But what counts as an 'intentional act'? It is clear that this extends beyond the situations where the defendant intended the actual harm that materialised but also to subjective recklessness; that is, where the defendant *foresees* that their actions will have the relevant consequences:

   > There is no need to prove an intention to cause harm. However, it seems to me that it could be said that false imprisonment is different from battery. In battery, the tort is complete without any harm being caused; the mere deliberate touching is enough. So it would be immaterial whether the harm were intentional or not. However, with false imprisonment, the loss of liberty is the essence of the tort and, in my view, the claimant must show not merely an intentional act or omission (to the extent that an omission will suffice—see above) but also an intention to deprive the claimant of his liberty. I can illustrate the point as follows. If a security guard in an office block locks the door to the claimant's room believing that the claimant has gone home for the night and not realising that he is in fact still inside the room, he has committed a deliberate act. However, he did not intend to confine the claimant. He may well be guilty of negligence because he did not check whether the room was empty but he would not be guilty of the intentional tort of false imprisonment. (Smith LJ, *Iqbal* at [72])

3. One area where the distinction between trespass and negligence has caused problems is in relation to limitation periods; that is, the period within which the claimant must begin an action. This issue has become important in cases where sexual abuse occurred many years ago. The general rule in section 2 of the Limitation Act 1980 is that an action must be initiated within a *fixed* period of six years of the act complained of. However, sections 11–14 create a different regime for actions for 'damages for negligence, nuisance or breach of duty' in personal injury cases. In such cases the limitation period is three years from either the date when the cause of action accrued or the 'date of knowledge', whichever is the later. In addition, the court (by s 33) has a *discretion* to extend this period when it appears that it would be equitable to do so. In **Letang v Cooper** Lord Denning held that a trespass could be a 'breach of duty' and accordingly the more flexible period of three years with discretion applied. This was rejected by the House of Lords in *Stubbings*

v *Webb* [1993] AC 498 where the claimant sued many years after the event, saying that she had been sexually abused by her father. The House said that this could only be trespass and was not a breach of duty, so the six-year period applied and her action was out of time. However, in *A v Hoare* [2008] UKHL 6, the House changed its mind and decided that Lord Denning's view in **Letang** was correct, and so the more flexible period once again applies to cases of trespass to the person. In *A v Hoare* the claimant was raped in 1989 but did not bring a civil action, presumably because the defendant was not worth suing. However, in 2004, while in prison, he won £7 million on the lottery and the action was begun. It was held that the discretionary period applied. See further Nikki Godden 'Sexual Abuse and Claims in Tort: Limitation Periods After *A v Hoare* and other appeals (2008) and *AB and others v Nugent Care Society; GR v Wirral MBC (2009)'* (2010) 18 FLS 179.

13.2 Trespass to the person

The trespass torts are conventionally described as sharing the same characteristics: (a) an intentional act; (b) direct and immediate harm; and (c) are actionable without loss. The three torts—battery, assault and false imprisonment—were defined by Goff LJ in **Collins v Wilcock**.

Collins v Wilcock
Court of Appeal [1984] 1 WLR 1172

The facts are set out in the extract of Croom-Johnson LJ in **Wilson v Pringle** [1987] QB 237 (see section 13.2.1).

GOFF LJ: The law draws a distinction, in terms more easily understood by philologists than by ordinary citizens, between an assault and a battery. An assault is an act which causes another person to apprehend the infliction of immediate, unlawful, force on his person; a battery is the actual infliction of unlawful force on another person. Both assault and battery are forms of trespass to the person. Another form of trespass to the person is false imprisonment, which is the unlawful imposition of constraint upon another's freedom of movement from a particular place.

13.2.1 Battery and assault

Wilson v Pringle
Court of Appeal [1987] QB 237

Wilson, the claimant, and Pringle, the defendant, were pupils at Great Wyrley High School, Walsall. They were both aged 13. It was agreed (the case proceeded on a strike-out basis) that while in a corridor the claimant was carrying a handgrip-type of bag, holding it over his shoulder with his right hand. The defendant admitted that as an act of ordinary horseplay he pulled the bag off the claimant's shoulder, and this caused the claimant to fall and injure his hip. The question for the court was whether this amounted to a battery. Held: in order for there to be an actionable battery, there needed to be some 'hostile intent' and so the defendant had an arguable case, and the case was remitted for trial. (Important note: the view of Lord Goff in **Collins v Wilcock** rejecting the need for 'hostile intent' (discussed in the extract below) is now the preferred view in this area.)

CROOM-JOHNSON LJ: The first distinction between the two causes of action where there is personal injury is the element of contact between the plaintiff and defendant: that is, a touching of some sort. In the action for negligence the physical contact (where it takes place at all) is normally though by no means always unintended. In the action for trespass, to constitute a battery, it is deliberate. Even so it is not every intended contact which is tortious. Apart from special justifications (such as acting in self-defence) there are many examples in everyday life where an intended contact or touch is not actionable as a trespass. These are not necessarily those (such as shaking hands) where consent is actual or to be implied. They may amount to one of the instances had in mind in *Tuberville v Savage*, 1 Mod 3 which take place in innocence. A modern instance is the batsman walking up the pavilion steps at Lord's after making a century. He receives hearty slaps of congratulation on his back. He may not want them. Some of them may be too heavy for comfort. No one seeks his permission, or can assume he would give it if it were asked. But would an action for trespass to the person lie?

Another ingredient in the tort of trespass to the person is that of hostility. The references to anger sufficing to turn a touch into a battery (*Cole v Turner*, (1704) 87 ER 907) and the lack of an intention to assault which prevents a gesture from being an assault are instances of this. If there is hostile intent, that will by itself be cogent evidence of hostility. But the hostility may be demonstrated in other ways.

The defendant in the present case has sought to add to the list of necessary ingredients. He has submitted that before trespass to the person will lie it is not only the touching that must be deliberate but the infliction of injury. The plaintiff's counsel, on the other hand, contends that it is not the injury to the person which must be intentional, but the act of touching or battery which precedes it: as he put it, what must be intentional is the application of force and not the injury. . . .

In our view, the submission made by counsel for the plaintiff is correct. It is the act and not the injury which must be intentional. An intention to injure is not essential to an action for trespass to the person. It is the mere trespass by itself which is the offence. . . .

What, then, turns a friendly touching (which is not actionable) into an unfriendly one (which is)? We have been referred to two criminal cases. *Reg v Sutton (Terrence)* [1977] 1 WLR 182 was decided in the Court of Appeal (Criminal Division). It was a case concerning alleged indecent assault on boys who consented in fact although in law they were too young to do so. They were asked to pose for photographs. The only touching of the boys by the appellant was to get them to stand in poses. It was touching on the hands, arms, legs or torso but only for the purpose of indicating how he wanted them to pose; it was not hostile or threatening. The court which was presided over by Lord Widgery CJ held these were therefore not assaults.

A more recent authority is **Collins v Wilcock** [1984] 1 WLR 1172. The case was not cited to the judge. It had not been reported at the time of the hearing of the Order 14 appeal. The facts were that a woman police officer, suspecting that a woman was soliciting contrary to the Street Offences Act 1959, tried to question her. The woman walked away, and was followed by the police officer. The officer took hold of her arm in order to restrain her. The woman scratched the officer's arm. She was arrested, charged with assaulting a police officer in the execution of her duty, and convicted. On appeal by case stated, the appeal was allowed, on the ground that the officer had gone beyond the scope of her duty in detaining the woman in circumstances short of arresting her. The officer had accordingly committed a battery.

The judgment of the Divisional Court was given by Robert Goff LJ. It is necessary to give a long quotation to do full justice to it. He said, at pp 1177–1178:

> We are here concerned primarily with battery. The fundamental principle, plain and incontest-
> able, is that every person's body is inviolate. It has long been established that any touching
> of another person, however slight, may amount to a battery. So Holt CJ held in *Cole v Turner*

(1704) 87 ER 907 that 'the least touching of another in anger is a battery.' The breadth of the principle reflects the fundamental nature of the interest so protected. As Blackstone wrote in his *Commentaries*, 17th ed. (1830), vol 3, p 120: 'the law cannot draw the line between different degrees of violence, and therefore totally prohibits the first and lowest stage of it; every man's person being sacred, and no other having a right to meddle with it, in any the slightest manner.' The effect is that everybody is protected not only against physical injury but against any form of physical molestation.

But so widely drawn a principle must inevitably be subject to exceptions. For example, children may be subjected to reasonable punishment; people may be subjected to the lawful exercise of the power of arrest; and reasonable force may be used in self-defence or for the prevention of crime. But, apart from these special instances where the control or constraint is lawful, a broader exception has been created to allow for the exigencies of everyday life. Generally speaking, consent is a defence to battery; and most of the physical contacts of ordinary life are not actionable because they are impliedly consented to by all who move in society and so expose themselves to the risk of bodily contact. So nobody can complain of the jostling which is inevitable from his presence in, for example, a supermarket, an underground station or a busy street; nor can a person who attends a party complain if his hand is seized in friendship, or even if his back is, within reason, slapped: see *Tuberville v Savage* (1669) 86 ER 684. Although such cases are regarded as examples of implied consent, it is more common nowadays to treat them as falling within a general exception embracing all physical contact which is generally acceptable in the ordinary conduct of daily life. We observe that, although in the past it has sometimes been stated that a battery is only committed where the action is 'angry, revengeful, rude, or insolent' (see Hawkins, *Pleas of the Crown*, 8th ed (1824), vol 1, c 15, section 2), we think that nowadays it is more realistic, and indeed more accurate, to state the broad underlying principle, subject to the broad exception.

Among such forms of conduct, long held to be acceptable, is touching a person for the purpose of engaging his attention, though of course using no greater degree of physical contact than is reasonably necessary in the circumstances for that purpose . . .

It still remains to indicate what is to be proved by a plaintiff who brings an action for battery. Robert Goff LJ's judgment is illustrative of the considerations which underlie such an action, but it is not practicable to define a battery as 'physical contact which is not generally acceptable in the ordinary conduct of daily life'. [Note: this is now the accepted definition of a battery.]

In our view, the authorities lead one to the conclusion that in a battery there must be an intentional touching or contact in one form or another of the plaintiff by the defendant. That touching must be proved to be a hostile touching. That still leaves unanswered the question 'when is a touching to be called hostile?' Hostility cannot be equated with ill-will or malevolence. It cannot be governed by the obvious intention shown in acts like punching, stabbing or shooting. It cannot be solely governed by an expressed intention, although that may be strong evidence. But the element of hostility, in the sense in which it is now to be considered, must be a question of fact for the tribunal of fact. It may be imported from the circumstances. Take the example of the police officer in *Collins* v *Wilcock* [1984] 1 WLR 1172. She touched the woman deliberately, but without an intention to do more than restrain her temporarily. Nevertheless, she was acting unlawfully and in that way was acting with hostility. She was acting contrary to the woman's legal right not to be physically restrained. We see no more difficulty in establishing what she intended by means of questions and answer, or by inference from the surrounding circumstances, than there is in establishing whether an apparently playful blow was struck in anger. The rules of law governing the legality of arrest may require strict application to the facts of appropriate cases, but in the ordinary give and take of everyday life the tribunal of fact should find no difficulty in answering the question 'was this, or was it not, a battery?' Where the immediate act of touching does not itself demonstrate hostility, the plaintiff should plead the facts which are said to do so.

Although we are all entitled to protection from physical molestation, we live in a crowded world in which people must be considered as taking on themselves some risk of injury (where it occurs) from the acts of others which are not in themselves unlawful. If negligence cannot be proved, it may be that an injured plaintiff who is also unable to prove a battery, will be without redress.

Notes

1. In *Re F* [1990] 2 AC 1, Lord Goff doubted the correctness of the decision in **Wilson v Pringle** and restated his view in **Collins v Wilcock**:

   > There are also specific cases where physical interference without consent may not be unlawful—chastisement of children, lawful arrest, self-defence, the prevention of crime, and so on. As I pointed out in **Collins v Wilcock**, a broader exception has been created to allow for the exigencies of everyday life—jostling in a street or some other crowded place, social contact at parties, and such like. This exception has been said to be founded on implied consent, since those who go about in public places, or go to parties, may be taken to have impliedly consented to bodily contact of this kind. Today this rationalisation can be regarded as artificial; and in particular, it is difficult to impute consent to those who, by reason of their youth or mental disorder, are unable to give their consent. For this reason, I consider it more appropriate to regard such cases as falling within a general exception embracing all physical contact which is generally acceptable in the ordinary conduct of everyday life.
   >
   > In the old days it used to be said that, for a touching of another's person to amount to a battery, it had to be a touching 'in anger' . . . and it has recently been said that the touching must be 'hostile' to have that effect (see **Wilson v Pringle** . . .) I respectfully doubt whether that is correct. A prank that gets out of hand; an over-friendly slap on the back; surgical treatment by a surgeon who mistakenly thinks that the patient has consented to it—all these things may transcend the bounds of lawfulness, without being characterised as hostile. Indeed the suggested qualification is difficult to reconcile with the principle that any touching of another's body is, in the absence of lawful excuse, capable of amounting to a battery and a trespass. (at 73)

   It is now clear that what needs to be established is that the touching is that 'which is not generally acceptable in the ordinary conduct of daily life'. There is no need for the defendant to have a hostile intent.

2. An 'assault' occurs where the claimant apprehends imminent physical contact (*Stephens v Myers* (1830) 172 ER 735); but if the defendant is actually unable to deliver the blow, there is no assault (at least if the claimant should have realised that the attack was impossible). In *Thomas v National Union of Miners (South Wales Area)* [1986] Ch 20, striking miners gathered outside a number of collieries in South Wales during the 1984–5 miners' strike. They were verbally abusive as working miners were taken inside by bus. Dismissing the claimant's application for an injunction against the striking miners, Scott J continued:

   > [Counsel for the claimant] submitted that the picketing complained of was tortious under a number of heads. It represented, he said, the tort of assault in that the miners going to work were put in fear of violence. I cannot accept this. Assault is defined in *Clerk & Lindsell on Torts*, 15th ed (1982), para 14-10 as 'an overt act indicating an immediate intention to commit a battery, coupled with the capacity to carry that intention into effect.' The tort of

assault is not, in my view, committed, unless the capacity in question is present at the time the overt act is committed. Since the working miners are in vehicles and the pickets are held back from the vehicles, I do not understand how even the most violent of threats or gestures could be said to constitute an assault. (at 62)

3. Traditionally words have not by themselves amounted to an assault (*R v Meade v Belt* [1823] 1 Lew CC 184). A reason may be that an assault must be a threat of an *immediate* battery, and words, if delivered from a distance, do not do that, but rather give the recipient the chance to avoid the future battery. Nevertheless, it is clear that words by themselves can induce fear and in *R v Ireland* [1996] 3 WLR 650, the House of Lords recognised this. Lord Steyn said that words, even if not accompanied by any actions, could cause apprehension of immediate contact. It is unlikely, however, that threats of a *future* battery would amount to an assault—though there may be a claim in the tort of **Wilkinson v Downton** or, if repeated, under the Protection from Harassment Act 1997.

4. It is also clear that words may qualify an otherwise innocent act so as to make it intimidatory, or qualify an intimidatory act, so as to make it innocent. In *Read v Coker* (1853) 138 ER 1437, the defendant's workers committed an assault when they gathered around the claimant, rolling up their sleeves and threatening to break the claimant's neck if he did not leave. The words characterised the otherwise innocent act as one threatening imminent contact. On the other hand, in *Tuberville v Savage* (1669) 86 ER 684, Tuberville put his hand on his sword and said, 'If it were not assize time [that is when judges from the King's Bench were visiting], I would not take such language from you.' As in effect he was saying that he would not strike as the judges were in town, this rendered the act innocent. There was no assault.

see online
resources

13.2.2 **False imprisonment**

> ### *R (on the application of Jalloh (formerly Jollah)) v Secretary of State for the Home Department*
> Supreme Court [2020] UKSC 4

The claimant, a Liberian national named Ibrahima Jalloh, had been placed under an unlawful curfew after being released from an immigration detention centre on bail. These included a requirement to live at a specified address in Sunderland, to submit to electronic tagging and to stay at home each night between the hours of 11 pm and 7 am. This had lasted a total of 891 days. He sought damages for false imprisonment, arguing that he had been confined to his house without any legal basis for long periods of time. Held: the claimant had been falsely imprisoned for the period of time he had been confined to his house.

LADY HALE:

1. The right to physical liberty was highly prized and protected by the common law long before the United Kingdom became party to the European Convention on Human Rights ('ECHR'). A person who was unlawfully imprisoned could, and can, secure his release through the writ of habeas corpus. He could, and can, also secure damages for the tort of false imprisonment. This case is about the meaning of imprisonment at common law and whether it should, or should not, now be aligned with the concept of deprivation of liberty in article 5 of the ECHR. . . .

20. Ms Dinah Rose QC, for the claimant, derives the following propositions . . .

21. First, imprisonment is the imposition of restraint upon a person's liberty so that he is compelled at the will of a third person to stay within a defined boundary. Second, the restraint must be complete, in the sense that he is required to stay within a defined area. There is no imprisonment if movement is blocked in one direction but he remains free to depart in a different direction. Third, it is imprisonment no matter how short the period—a few seconds is sufficient. Fourth, the restraint must be immediate and not conditional. Fifth, complete restraint does not mean that there must be physical barriers such as locks or guards to prevent him leaving. Nor does it mean that it must be physically impossible to leave. He is imprisoned if he is made to stay by intimidation or threats, fear of the consequences, or submission to apparent legal authority. Sixth, it is also imprisonment if he is made to stay by the threat of imprisonment if he leaves, including the threat of arrest or prosecution. Seventh, the threat does not have to be a threat to return him to the same place of confinement. Eighth, it is also imprisonment if he is only able to leave the defined area by an unreasonable means or route, for example, by jumping out of a first-floor window or risking prosecution by doing so.

22. An obvious illustration of the reasonableness principle is the true story told by Eric Williams in his 1949 novel, *The Wooden Horse*. Prisoners of war escaped from their prison camp by concealing their tunnelling under a wooden vaulting horse: their will was never overborne because they always intended to escape and it did prove physically possible for them to do so but they clearly were imprisoned while they were in the camp. . . .

23. The most problematic case from the claimant's point of view is the *Bournewood* decision in the House of Lords. But, argues Ms Rose, it has no bearing because if a person is not actually confined at the moment, the fact that he might be confined if he tries to leave does not make it imprisonment. This is different from being actually confined by fear of the consequences if one leaves. In any event, she points out that the case might well be decided differently today. The Court of Appeal were unanimous in holding that the patient was imprisoned. The House of Lords decided otherwise by a narrow majority and it is not easy to grasp their rationale. And the European Court of Human Rights held that he *had* been deprived of his liberty: *HL v United Kingdom* (2005) 40 EHRR 32. So far as is known, this is the only example of a deprivation of liberty which did not amount to imprisonment at common law: generally speaking, one may well be imprisoned without being deprived of one's liberty, but the other way round is harder to envisage.

Discussion on the first issue

24. As it is put in *Street on Torts*, 15th ed (2018), by Christian Witting, p 259, 'False imprisonment involves an act of the defendant which directly and intentionally (or possibly negligently) causes the confinement of the claimant within an area delimited by the defendant.' The essence of imprisonment is being made to stay in a particular place by another person. The methods which might be used to keep a person there are many and various. They could be physical barriers, such as locks and bars. They could be physical people, such as guards who would physically prevent the person leaving if he tried to do so. They could also be threats, whether of force or of legal process. . . .

25. In this case there is no doubt that the defendant defined the place where the claimant was to stay between the hours of 11.00 pm and 7.00 am. There was no suggestion that he could go somewhere else during those hours without the defendant's permission. This is not a case like *Bird v Jones* where the claimant could cross the bridge by another route or *Robinson v Balmain New Ferry Co Ltd* where he had agreed to go onto the wharf on terms that he could only get out if he paid a penny.

26. The fact that the claimant did from time to time ignore his curfew for reasons that seemed good to him makes no difference to his situation while he was obeying it. Like the prisoner who goes absent from his open prison, or the tunneller who gets out of the prison camp, he is not imprisoned while he is away. But he is imprisoned while he is where the defendant wants him to be.

27. There is, of course, a crucial difference between voluntary compliance with an instruction and enforced compliance with that instruction. The Court of Appeal held that this was a case of enforced not voluntary compliance and I agree. . . . There can be no doubt that the claimant's compliance was enforced. He was wearing an electronic tag which meant that leaving his address would be detected. The monitoring company would then telephone him to find out where he was. He was warned in the clearest possible terms that breaking the curfew could lead to a £5,000 fine or imprisonment for up to six months or both. He was well aware that it could also lead to his being detained again under the 1971 Act. All of this was backed up by the full authority of the State, which was claiming to have the power to do this. The idea that the claimant was a free agent, able to come and go as he pleased, is completely unreal.

28. For what it is worth, in the case of *Secretary of State for the Home Department v JJ* [2007] UKHL 45; [2008] AC 385, it was taken for granted that a curfew enforced by electronic tagging, clocking in and clocking out, and arrest or imprisonment for breach was a 'classic detention or confinement' (para 59).

Notes

1. The court also rejected the Home Office's second argument: that the concept of imprisonment for the purpose of the tort of false imprisonment should be aligned with the concept of deprivation of liberty within the meaning of Article 5 ECHR:

   It is, of course, the case that the common law is capable of being developed to meet the changing needs of society. In Lord Toulson's famous words in *Kennedy v Charity Commission* [2014] UKSC 20; [2015] AC 435, para 133, 'it was not the purpose of the Human Rights Act that the common law should become an ossuary'. Sometimes those developments will bring it closer to the ECHR and sometimes they will not. But what Mr Tam [counsel for the defendant] is asking this Court to do is not to develop the law but to make it take a retrograde step: to restrict the classic understanding of imprisonment at common law to the very different and much more nuanced concept of deprivation of liberty under the ECHR. The Strasbourg court has adopted this approach because of the need to draw a distinction between the deprivation and the restriction of physical liberty. There is no need for the common law to draw such a distinction and every reason for the common law to continue to protect those whom is has protected for centuries against unlawful imprisonment, whether by the State or private persons. (Lady Hale at [33])

Bird v Jones
Court of Queen's Bench (1845) 7 QB 742

In August 1843 the Hammersmith Bridge Company cordoned off part of their bridge, placed seats on it and charged spectators for viewing a regatta. The claimant objected to this and forced his way into the enclosure, where he was stopped by two police officers. He was prevented from proceeding across the bridge, but was allowed to go back the way he came. He refused, and in the course of proceedings for his arrest the question arose whether he had been imprisoned on the bridge. Held: he had not been; his movements were not completely restrained as he could go another way.

COLERIDGE J: And I am of opinion that there was no imprisonment. To call it so appears to me to confound partial obstruction and disturbance with total obstruction and detention. A prison may have its boundary large or narrow, visible and tangible, or, though real, still in the conception only; it may itself be moveable or fixed: but a boundary it must have; and that boundary the party imprisoned must be prevented from passing; he must be prevented from leaving that place, within the ambit of which the party imprisoning would confine him, except by prison-breach. Some confusion seems to me to arise from confounding imprisonment of the body with mere loss of freedom: it is one part of the definition of freedom to be able to go whither-soever one pleases; but imprisonment is something more than the mere loss of this power; it includes the notion of restraint within some limits defined by a will or power exterior to our own . . .

Notes

1. A defendant will not be liable for false imprisonment if the claimant can move in another direction or if there is a reasonable means of escape. Much turns, of course, on what is considered a reasonable means of escape or a reasonable condition for release. In *Robinson v Balmain New Ferry* [1910] AC 295, the payment of a penny to leave the defendant's premises was held to be a reasonable condition. The defendants operated a ferry from Sydney to Balmain. There were turnstiles on the Sydney side which collected payment for the journey in either direction, whether or not the visitor had, in fact, travelled on the ferry. The claimant entered on the Sydney side, paying a penny. Finding that no ferry was due to cross for 20 minutes, he decided to leave the wharf, whereupon he was asked to pay a further penny. He refused and for a short time was prevented from leaving. His claim for false imprisonment failed: 'the payment of a penny was a quite fair condition, and if he did not choose to comply with it the defendants were not bound to let him through. He could proceed on the journey he had contracted for' (Lord Lorebourn LC at 299–300). See further Mark Lunney 'False Imprisonment, Fare Dodging and Federation: Mr Robertson's Evening Out' (2009) 31 Sydney L Rev 537.

   Though it is necessary to show a complete restriction of the claimant's freedom of movement, the claimant need not be aware of the restriction. Nor does the claimant need to have suffered any additional harm (beyond the restriction of their movements) from his false imprisonment:

   > it appears to me that a person could be imprisoned without his knowing it. I think a person can be imprisoned while he is asleep, while he is in a state of drunkenness, while he is unconscious, and while he is a lunatic . . . Of course the damages might be diminished and would be affected by the question whether he was conscious of it or not. (Atkin LJ, *Meering* v *Grahame-White Aviation* (1920) 122 LT 44 at 53–4)

2. This was confirmed *obiter* by the House of Lords in *Murray* v *Ministry of Defence* [1988] 1 WLR 692 (though in that case the claimant knew her freedom of movement was restricted): 'the law attaches supreme importance to the liberty of the individual and if he suffers a wrongful interference with that liberty it should remain actionable even without proof of special damage' (at 529).

3. As Lady Hale notes in *Jalloh* (at [23]), the only example of a deprivation of liberty which did not amount to imprisonment at common law is *R v Bournewood Mental Health Trust, ex p L* [1999] 1 AC 458 in which a mentally ill patient was voluntarily held in an unlocked hospital ward, though the staff at the hospital had agreed that should he try to leave he would be detained compulsorily under the Mental Health Act 1983. This is indeed what happened. The majority of the House of Lords held that *potential* deprivation of a claimant's liberty was not sufficient to ground a claim. This is unlikely to be followed today. The claimant was successful in the European Court of Human Rights in *HL* v *UK* (Application no 45508/99) (2005) 40 EHRR 32. The facts of *Bournewood* would now fall within the remit of the Mental Capacity Act 2005.

> ### *Iqbal v Prison Officers Association*
> Court of Appeal [2009] EWCA Civ 1312

A prisoner sued the defendant trade union which had called an unlawful strike resulting in very few prison officers turning up for work. As a result, the claimant was not allowed to leave his cell—as usual—for exercise and recreation. Held: rejecting his claim for false imprisonment, the tort could only be established on the basis of an omission if the claimant was owed a positive duty of care, and since the prison officers' duty was to the prison governor and not the prisoner there could be no claim.

LORD NEUBERGER MR:

No liability for a pure omission

15. In *Smith v Littlewoods Organisation Ltd* [1987] AC 241, 271 Lord Goff of Chieveley said that 'the common law does not impose liability for what are called pure omissions'. Specifically in relation to the tort of false imprisonment, it seems to me that this proposition derives support from *Herd v Weardale Steel, Coal and Coke Co Ltd* [1913] 3 KB 771, affirmed [1915] AC 67. In that case the Court of Appeal, by a majority (Buckley and Hamilton LJJ), reversed Pickford J's upholding of a false imprisonment claim by an employee of a coal-mining company, whose complaint was based on his employers' refusal to comply with his request to take him to the surface, after he had wrongfully refused to do work, until more than two hours after his request had been made.

16. Buckley LJ . . . then turned to the claim in false imprisonment, and said, at p 787:

> What kept [the plaintiff] from getting to the surface was not any act which the defendants did, but the fact that he was at the bottom of a deep shaft, and that there were no means of getting out other than the particular means which belonged to his employers and over which the plaintiff had contractual rights which at that moment were not in operation.

17. At p 789 Buckley LJ considered what the position would have been if there had been an hour's delay in conveying an employee to the surface at the end of his shift, merely on the grounds of the employer's convenience. He said that in such a case, in his opinion, the employee 'would be entitled to damages for breach of contract', and then asked 'would there be any false imprisonment?' He answered that question:

> In my opinion there would not. The master has not imprisoned the man. He has not enabled him to get out as under the contract he ought to have done, but he has done no act compelling him to remain there.

A little later, he added 'to my mind [the employers] did not imprison [the employee], because they did not keep him [in the mine]; they only abstained from giving him facilities for getting away'. . . .

19. In dismissing the plaintiff's appeal the House of Lords [1915] AC 67 seems largely to have relied on the proposition that the existence of a contractual relationship between the parties, including an implied obligation on the defendants to take the plaintiff up to the surface at the end of his shift, left no room for a claim in tort: see pp 73, 76. However, there were observations which seem to me to be consistent with the notion that no claim for false imprisonment can be based on a defendant's refusal to act, as opposed to his positive act. At p 71 Viscount Haldane LC said that

> If a man chooses to go [to] the bottom of a mine, from which by the nature of physical circumstances he cannot escape, it does not follow . . . that he can compel the owner to bring him up out of it.

He then explained that, depending on the circumstances, 'The owner may or may not be under a duty . . . on broad grounds the neglect of which may possibly involve him in a criminal charge or a civil liability'. However, he thought it unnecessary to discuss those aspects, 'because they have . . . nothing to do with false imprisonment'. . . .

20. It might be said that the plaintiff went down the mine voluntarily in that case, whereas in this case the claimant was originally placed in his cell against his will. But it is hard to see how that can affect the point of principle, at least unless there is no statutory, or other special, duty owed by the prison officers to the claimant. Anyway, once the plaintiff in the *Herd case* [1913] 3 KB 771 had entered into his contract of employment, his going down the mine was, at least in a sense, not voluntary, as he was contractually obliged to do it. Indeed, in some ways the unsuccessful plaintiff's case in the *Herd case* [1913] 3 KB 771 was stronger than the claimant's case here: he was free to leave the mine at any time, but merely lacked the means to do so, whereas the claimant was not free to leave his cell unless the governor decided he could do so.

21. It seems to me that the reasoning in the *Herd case* supports the first proposition advanced by Mr Beloff [counsel for the defendant], which is also reflected in *Street on Torts*, 12th ed (2007), p 250, where there is this: 'A false imprisonment will *normally* result from some positive act' (emphasis added). I would put the point in these terms. At least as a general principle, defendants are not to be held liable in tort for the results of their inaction, in the absence of a specific duty to act, a duty which would normally arise out of the particular relationship between the claimant and the defendant. Such a hard and fast distinction between action and inaction may seem arbitrary to some people, but it is not unprincipled, and, while it may lead to apparent injustice in particular cases, it does help to ensure a degree of clarity and certainty in the law. However, a general rule such as that propounded by Lord Goff in the *Smith case* [1987] AC 241, 271 and applied by the majority of the Court of Appeal in the *Herd case* [1913] 3 KB 771, can often, perhaps inevitably, be said to beg the question at issue when it is relied on in a particular case.

. . .

Conclusions on the issue of liability for false imprisonment

34. While readily acknowledging the force of the argument to the contrary, which is powerfully advanced by Sullivan LJ [in dissent], I am of the view that the judge was wrong to hold that any prison officers, and hence the POA [Prison Officers Association], were liable for the tort of false imprisonment in this case. I rest my reasoning primarily on the arguments that (a) the mere failure of the prison officers to work at the prison, while it may have been a breach of their employment contracts, involved no positive action on their part, and (b) that failure was not the direct cause of the claimant being confined to his cell throughout 29 August 2007. The fact that there was what might be characterised as a generalised state of inaction, in the form of a withdrawal of labour, on the part of the prison officers, directed at no prisoner, is a thread which connects these two points.

35. It may be that there could be circumstances in which a failure to act could give rise to a claim for false imprisonment, but I suspect that those circumstances would, at least normally, be such that there would be a breach of an independent duty to the claimant, i.e., a duty arising under contract (as explained by Buckley LJ in the *Herd case* . . .) or pursuant to a different tort (as alluded to by Viscount Haldane LC in the *Herd case* . . .). However, even if a defendant's failure to act can of itself exceptionally give rise to a claim for false imprisonment, I am of the view that it did not do so in the present case. Additionally, the case law makes it clear that a defendant can only be liable for false imprisonment if he is directly responsible for the imprisonment, and, in my opinion, the strike by the officers at the prison cannot fairly be characterised as a direct cause of the claimant's confinement in his cell throughout 29 August. . . .

40. The rights of prisoners should certainly be acknowledged: indeed according and respecting rights are one of the hallmarks of a civilised society. Further, it can fairly be said that every moment out of his cell is valuable to a prisoner. However, I think that the court should be reluctant to reach a conclusion whose implications could lead to many small private law damages claims arising from what may often be little more than poor timekeeping by prison officers, and whose outcome may often turn on issues such as whether an officer in an undermanned prison could better have organised his working day to ensure that a prisoner was let out of his cell at precisely the time stipulated by the governor.

Notes

1. It is difficult not to notice the power imbalance between the claimants and defendants in *Iqbal* and *Herd*: prisoners pitted against the prison officers' trade union; miners against their employers. Historically, the trespass torts have been used to highlight discrepancies in, and abuses of, power. And, in any dispute the weaker party will often bear the brunt of the disruption. Of course, any view on the fairness or otherwise of these decisions will depend on one's views of the different interests of the parties but it may be, in this case, that Sullivan LJ's final paragraph in his dissenting judgment in *Iqbal* hits the nail on the head:

   It is in the nature of a prison officer's employment that the third parties who will suffer if he goes on strike action will be those who have been imprisoned, and that the manner in which they will probably suffer will be the loss of such measure of liberty as is permitted to them by the governor under the prison regime. In my judgment, in so far as there is a conflict between the prisoners' right not to be deprived of that liberty by persons, including prison officers, acting otherwise than in accordance with the prison governor's authority, and the right of prison officers (absent any statutory prohibition) to strike, the former right must take precedence over the latter. While the right to strike is important, the right not to be falsely imprisoned is of fundamental importance. (at [103])

13.2.3 Defences

A common element of all the trespass to the person torts is that the defendant must have acted without 'lawful justification or excuse'. This usually arises as a defence. Here we consider the most common defence in this area—consent—as well as the ineffective defence of provocation.

As we have seen from **Wilson v Pringle**, consent is not strictly a 'defence' to trespass to the person, but rather a denial that any tort was committed in the first place. This is so because if a trespass is defined as an offensive contact, a touching cannot be offensive to a person who has consented to it. Consent may be express or implied, so that, for example, a rugby player consents to contacts within the rules during a game. Difficulties can arise in the context of medical treatment. Certainly, where a patient consents to a particular treatment, the doctor will not commit a battery when acting on this. But this simply prompts a further question: when is (a patient's) consent valid?

Chatterton v Gerson
Queen's Bench Division [1981] QB 432

During an operation for a hernia the claimant's ileo-inguinal nerve was trapped and this caused her great pain. The defendant, a specialist in chronic intractable pain, injected the claimant in an attempt to block the pain. Unfortunately, this was unsuccessful and rendered her right leg numb meaning that she could only move with a stick. The claimant sued in trespass (on the ground that her consent to the injection was invalid as she had not been informed of the potential consequences) and negligence (on the ground that the defendant owed her a duty to warn her of the risks). Held: rejecting both claims, the judge held that her consent was valid as she understood the general nature of the operation.

BRISTOW J: It is clear law that in any context in which consent of the injured party is a defence to what would otherwise be a crime or a civil wrong, the consent must be real. Where for example a woman's consent to sexual intercourse is obtained by fraud, her apparent consent is no defence to a charge of rape. It is not difficult to state the principle or to appreciate its good sense. As so often, the problem lies in its application.

In my judgment what the court has to do in each case is to look at all the circumstances and say 'Was there a real consent?' I think justice requires that in order to vitiate the reality of consent there must be a greater failure of communication between doctor and patient than that involved in a breach of duty if the claim is based on negligence. When the claim is based on negligence the plaintiff must prove not only the breach of duty to inform, but that had the duty not been broken she would not have chosen to have the operation. Where the claim is based on trespass to the person, once it is shown that the consent is unreal, then what the plaintiff would have decided if she had been given the information which would have prevented vitiation of the reality of her consent is irrelevant.

In my judgment once the patient is informed in broad terms of the nature of the procedure which is intended, and gives her consent, that consent is real, and the cause of the action on which to base a claim for failure to go into risks and implications is negligence, not trespass. Of course if information is withheld in bad faith, the consent will be vitiated by fraud. Of course if by some accident, as in a case in the 1940's in the Salford Hundred Court where a boy was admitted to hospital for tonsilectomy [sic] and due to administrative error was circumcised instead, trespass would be the appropriate cause of action against the doctor, though he was as much the victim of the error as the boy. But in my judgment it would be very much against the interests of justice if actions which are really based on a failure by the doctor to perform his duty adequately to inform were pleaded in trespass.

In this case in my judgment even taking the plaintiff's evidence at its face value she was under no illusion as to the general nature of what an intrathecal injection of phenol solution nerve block would be, and in the case of each injection her consent was not unreal. I should add that getting the patient to sign a pro forma expressing consent to undergo the operation 'the effect and nature of which have been explained to me,' as was done here in each case, should be a valuable reminder to everyone of the need for explanation and consent. But it would be no defence to an action based on trespass to the person if no explanation had in fact been given. The consent would have been expressed in form only, not in reality.

Notes

1. The issue in trespass is whether the patient knew *what* was being done, and the issue in negligence is whether she ought to have been informed of the risks. The courts have adopted a more patient-friendly approach to a doctor's failure to warn of risks in the context of negligence—see further ***Montgomery* v *Lanarkshire Health Board*** [2015] UKSC 11.

   In *Blake* v *Galloway* [2004] EWCA Civ 814, a group of 15-year-olds were engaging in horseplay by throwing twigs and bark at each other. The defendant threw a piece of bark which struck the claimant in the eye. The Court of Appeal held that there was no battery as the claimant must be taken to have consented to any missile being thrown more or less in accordance with the tacit understandings or conventions of the game. Nor was there liability in negligence as there was no failure to take reasonable care in the circumstances of the horseplay in which they were engaged. There would only be liability if there was recklessness.

2. There are limits to what one can consent to (***Lane* v *Holloway*** [1968] 1 QB 379). Consent will not be valid when it is to actions which are deemed contrary to public policy (see *AG's Reference (No 6 of 1980)* [1981] QB 715 and *R* v *Brown* [1994] 1 AC 212).

3. If an individual is able to consent to what would otherwise be a battery, surely it follows that there is a corresponding ability to refuse consent to such actions? The law is clear that an individual has an absolute right to the inviolability of their body:

   > an adult patient who . . . suffers from no mental incapacity has an absolute right to choose whether to consent to medical treatment, to refuse it, or to choose one rather than another of the treatments being offered. This right of choice is not limited to decisions which others might regard as sensible. (Lord Donaldson MR, *Re T (Adult: Refusal of Treatment)* [1993] Fam 95 at 102)

   Of course, this simply prompts yet another question as to when someone has capacity to refuse (or indeed consent) to medical treatment. The common law test of capacity has been enshrined in statute (for those over 16) in the Mental Capacity Act 2005. (See further Emma Cave, 'Protecting Patients from their Bad Decisions: Rebalancing Rights, Relationships, and Risk' (2017) 25 Med L Rev 527.)

Lane v *Holloway*
Court of Appeal [1968] 1 QB 379

Relations were strained between the claimant, Lane, who was a retired gardener aged 64, and the defendant, his 23-year-old neighbour, Holloway. One night Lane came back from the pub and was talking to a neighbour. Mrs Holloway called out, 'You bloody lot'. Lane replied, 'Shut up, you monkey faced tart'. Holloway sprang up and said, 'What did you say to my wife?' Lane replied, 'I want to see you on your own', and he later threw a light punch at Holloway, whereupon the younger man punched him in the eye. The wound needed 19 stitches. Held: the defendant was liable and no deduction from damages should be made for Lane's provocation.

LORD DENNING MR: The first question is: Was there an assault by Mr. Holloway for which damages are recoverable in a civil court? I am quite clearly of opinion that there was. It has been argued before us that no action lies because this was an unlawful fight: that both of them were concerned in illegality; and therefore there can be no cause of action in respect of it. *Ex turpi causa oritur non actio.* To that I entirely demur. Even if the fight started by being unlawful, I think that one of them can sue the other for damages for a subsequent injury if it was inflicted by a weapon or savage blow out of all proportion to the occasion. I agree that in an ordinary fight with fists there is no cause of action to either of them for any injury suffered. The reason is that each of the participants in a fight voluntarily takes upon himself the risk of incidental injuries to himself. *Volenti non fit injuria.* But he does not take on himself the risk of a savage blow out of all proportion to the occasion. The man who strikes a blow of such severity is liable in damages unless he can prove accident or self-defence.

In this case the Judge found that

> with a young man of 23 and a man of 64, whom he knows to be somewhat infirm, the young man cannot plead a challenge seriously: nor is he entitled to go and strike him because of an insult hurled at his wife.

I quite agree. Mr Holloway in anger went much too far. He gave a blow out of proportion to the occasion for which he must answer in damages. . . .

The defendant has done a civil wrong and should pay compensation for the physical damage done by it. Provocation by the plaintiff can properly be used to take away any element of aggravation. But not to reduce the real damages. . . .

On the evidence this young man went much too far in striking a blow out of all proportion to the occasion. It must have been a savage blow to produce these consequences. I think the damages ought to be increased from £75 to £300 and I would allow the appeal accordingly.

Notes

1. *Lane* **v** *Holloway* establishes that illegality and consent are both effective defences to claims in trespass to the person (though not applicable in the case). It also establishes that provocation is not a defence to any tort, including battery—it merely reduces the claimant's entitlement to exemplary and, possibly, compensatory damages (compare *Lane* **v** *Holloway* and *Murphy* v *Culhane* [1977] QB 94) and confirms *Cockroft* v *Smith* (1705) 2 Salk 642, that in order to rely on the defence of self-defence, the defendant's actions must be proportionate to the force exerted on them.

2. Following *Lane* **v** *Holloway* it was suggested that if a person genuinely shows a lack of regard for his own safety (which on the facts was the case in *Lane* **v** *Holloway*), damages might be reduced for contributory negligence. However, it has since been established that contributory negligence is not a defence to assault or battery. In *Co-operative Group (CWS) Ltd* v *Pritchard* [2011] EWCA Civ 329, there was a scuffle at the claimant's workplace and she sued for assault. The defendants alleged that the claimant had been abusive and so was contributorily negligent, but the court held that this defence was not available. Aikens LJ said:

> There is no case before the 1945 Act which holds that there was such a defence in the case of an 'intentional tort' such as assault and battery. There are many pointers indicating that there was no such defence. Insofar as there are cases since the 1945 Act that suggest that the Act can be used to reduce damages awarded for the torts of assault or battery in a case where it is found that the claimant was 'contributorily negligent' they are unsatisfactory and cannot stand with statements of principle made in two subsequent House of Lords decisions. I would conclude that the 1945 Act cannot, in principle, be used to reduce damages in cases where claims are based on assault and battery . . .

For a discussion of this case, see James Goudkamp 'Contributory Negligence and Trespass to the Person' (2011) 127 LQR 519.

13.3 Intentional infliction of physical harm or distress

Unlike the trespass torts which provide a remedy for direct actual or potential physical infringements of the claimant's person, the tort in *Wilkinson v Downton* covers intentional acts that cause injury *indirectly*, without physically interfering (or threatening to physically interfere) with the claimant or their movements. Although, it had (and still has) great potential, for many years it was rarely used. Most notably, in *Wong v Parkside Health Trust* [2003] 3 All ER 932 the Court of Appeal declined to use it to develop a general tort of harassment and, following *Wainwright v Home Office* [2004] 2 AC 406 and the enactment of the Protection from Harassment Act 1997, it seemed destined for obscurity. However, in autumn 2014 everyone seemed to be talking about it. Could this obscure little tort take on the giant of freedom of expression? (Spoiler: no.)

Wilkinson v *Downton*
Queen's Bench Division [1897] 2 QB 57

The claimant's husband had gone for a day at the races. The defendant came to her house and, as a practical joke, falsely told her that her husband had had an accident. The claimant later suffered severe physical and psychological reactions. Held: the defendant was liable for the injuries caused.

WRIGHT J: The defendant has, as I assume for the moment, wilfully done an act calculated to cause physical harm to the plaintiff—that is to say, to infringe her legal right to personal safety, and has in fact thereby caused physical harm to her. That proposition without more appears to me to state a good cause of action, there being no justification alleged for the act. This wilful injuria is in law malicious, although no malicious purpose to cause the harm which was caused nor any motive of spite is imputed to the defendant.

It remains to consider whether the assumptions involved in the proposition are made out. One question is whether the defendant's act was so plainly calculated to produce some effect of the kind which was produced that an intention to produce it ought to be imputed to the defendant, regard being had to the fact that the effect was produced on a person proved to be in an ordinary state of health and mind. I think that it was. It is difficult to imagine that such a statement, made suddenly and with apparent seriousness, could fail to produce grave effects under the circumstances upon any but an exceptionally indifferent person, and therefore an intention to produce such an effect must be imputed, and it is no answer in law to say that more harm was done than was anticipated, for that is commonly the case with all wrongs. The other question is whether the effect was, to use the ordinary phrase, too remote to be in law regarded as a consequence for which the defendant is answerable. Apart from authority, I should give the same answer and on the same ground as the last question, and say that it was not too remote.

Wainwright v *Home Office*
House of Lords [2003] UKHL 53

Mrs Wainwright and her son went to Armley Prison, Leeds, to visit another son, where they were strip-searched in a procedure which breached the Prison Rules—invalidating their consent. They relied on the tort in **Wilkinson v Downton** and privacy in order to ground a claim for the anxiety and distress they had suffered as a result of the prison officers' actions. Held: the defendants were not liable as they had not intended to cause the claimants harm. (Note: the privacy aspects of this case are discussed in Chapter 14.)

LORD HOFFMANN:

36. I turn next to the alternative argument based upon *Wilkinson v Downton* [1897] 2 QB 57. This is a case which has been far more often discussed than applied. Thomas Wilkinson, landlord of the Albion public house in Limehouse, went by train to the races at Harlow, leaving his wife Lavinia behind the bar. Downton was a customer who decided to play what he would no doubt have described as a practical joke on Mrs Wilkinson. He went into the Albion and told her that her husband had decided to return in a horse-drawn vehicle which had been involved in an accident in which he had been seriously injured. The story was completely false and Mr Wilkinson returned safely by train later that evening. But the effect on Mrs Wilkinson was dramatic. Her hair turned white and she became so ill that for some time her life was thought in danger. The jury awarded her £100 for nervous shock and the question for the judge on further consideration was whether she had a cause of action.

37. The difficulty in the judge's way was the decision of the Privy Council in *Victorian Railway Comrs v Coultas* (1888) 13 App Cas 222, in which it had been said that nervous shock was too remote a consequence of a negligent act (in that case, putting the plaintiff in imminent fear of being run down by a train) to be a recoverable head of damages. RS Wright J distinguished the case on the ground that Downton was not merely negligent but had intended to cause injury. Quite what the judge meant by this is not altogether clear; Downton obviously did not intend to cause any kind of injury but merely to give Mrs Wilkinson a fright. The judge said, however, at p 59, that as what he said could not fail to produce grave effects 'upon any but an exceptionally indifferent person', an intention to cause such effects should be 'imputed' to him. . . .

41. Commentators and counsel have nevertheless been unwilling to allow *Wilkinson v Downton* to disappear beneath the surface of the law of negligence. Although, in cases of actual psychiatric injury, there is no point in arguing about whether the injury was in some sense intentional if negligence will do just as well, it has been suggested (as the claimants submit in this case) that damages for distress falling short of psychiatric injury can be recovered if there was an intention to cause it. This submission was squarely put to the Court of Appeal in *Wong v Parkside Health NHS Trust* [2001] EWCA Civ 1721; [2003] 3 All ER 932 and rejected. Hale LJ said that before the passing of the Protection from Harassment Act 1997 there was no tort of intentional harassment which gave a remedy for anything less than physical or psychiatric injury. That leaves *Wilkinson v Downton* with no leading role in the modern law. . . .

44. I do not resile from the proposition that the policy considerations which limit the heads of recoverable damage in negligence do not apply equally to torts of intention. If someone actually intends to cause harm by a wrongful act and does so, there is ordinarily no reason why he should not have to pay compensation. But I think that if you adopt such a principle, you have to be very careful about what you mean by intend. In *Wilkinson v Downton* RS Wright J wanted to water down the concept of intention as much as possible. He clearly thought, as the Court of Appeal did afterwards in *Janvier v Sweeney* [1919] 2 KB 316, that the plaintiff should succeed whether the conduct of the defendant was intentional or negligent. But the *Victorian Railway Comrs* case 13 App Cas 222 prevented him from saying so. So he devised a concept of imputed intention which sailed as close to negligence as he felt he could go.

45. If, on the other hand, one is going to draw a principled distinction which justifies abandoning the rule that damages for mere distress are not recoverable, imputed intention will not do. The defendant must actually have acted in a way which he knew to be unjustifiable and intended to cause harm or at least acted without caring whether he caused harm or not. Lord Woolf CJ, as I read his judgment, at [2002] QB 1334, 1350, paras 50–51, might have been inclined to accept such a principle. But the facts did not support a claim on this basis. The judge made no finding that the prison officers intended to cause distress or realized that they were acting without justification in asking the Wainwrights to strip. He said, at paragraph 83, that they had acted in good faith and, at paragraph 121, that:

> The deviations from the procedure laid down for strip-searches were, in my judgment, not intended to increase the humiliation necessarily involved but merely sloppiness.

46. Even on the basis of a genuine intention to cause distress, I would wish, as in *Hunter's* case [1997] AC 655, to reserve my opinion on whether compensation should be recoverable. In institutions and workplaces all over the country, people constantly do and say things with the intention of causing distress and humiliation to others. This shows lack of consideration and appalling manners but I am not sure that the right way to deal with it is always by litigation. The Protection from Harassment Act 1997 defines harassment in section 1(1) as a 'course of conduct' amounting to harassment and provides by section 7(3) that a course of conduct must involve conduct on at least two occasions. If these requirements are satisfied, the claimant may pursue a civil remedy for damages for anxiety: section 3(2). The requirement of a course of conduct shows that Parliament was conscious that it might not be in the public interest to allow the law to be set in motion for one boorish incident. It may be that any development of the common law should show similar caution.

47. In my opinion, therefore, the claimants can build nothing on *Wilkinson v Downton* [1897] 2 QB 57. It does not provide a remedy for distress which does not amount to recognized psychiatric injury and so far as there may a tort of intention under which such damage is recoverable, the necessary intention was not established. I am also in complete agreement with Buxton LJ, at [2002] QB 1334, 1355–1356, paras 67–72, that *Wilkinson v Downton* has nothing to do with trespass to the person.

More recently, in **Rhodes v OPO** [2015] UKSC 32, the Supreme Court was asked to consider the scope of the tort in **Wilkinson v Downton** and whether it could ever be used to prevent a person publishing true information about himself.

Rhodes v OPO
Supreme Court [2015] UKSC 32

The case involved the publication of a well-known performing artist's memoirs in which he recounted the sexual abuse he suffered while at school and his subsequent mental health issues. The claim was brought on behalf of his son, OPO (who suffers from a number of conditions including attention deficit hyperactivity disorder, Asperger's, dysgraphia and dyspraxia) and sought to prevent the publication of the book, on the basis that it would cause him significant distress. This was unanimously rejected by the Supreme Court.

LADY HALE AND LORD TOULSON (with whom LORD CLARKE and LORD WILSON agreed):
  [The Justices reviewed the previous case law.]
  72. The order made by the Court of Appeal [in this case] was novel in two respects. The material which the appellant was banned from publishing was not deceptive or intimidatory but

autobiographical; and the ban was principally directed, not to the substance of the autobiographical material, but to the vivid form of language used to communicate it. The appeal therefore raises important questions about freedom of speech and about the nature and limits of liability under *Wilkinson v Downton*.

73. In *Wilkinson v Downton* Wright J recognised that wilful infringement of the right to personal safety was a tort. It has three elements: a conduct element, a mental element and a consequence element. The issues in this case relate to the first and second elements. It is common ground that the consequence required for liability is physical harm or recognised psychiatric illness. In *Wainwright v Home Office* Lord Hoffmann discussed and left open (with expressions of caution) the question whether intentional causation of severe distress might be actionable, but no one in this case has suggested that it is.

74. The conduct element requires words or conduct directed towards the claimant for which there is no justification or reasonable excuse, and the burden of proof is on the claimant. We are concerned in this case with the curtailment of freedom of speech, which gives rise to its own particular considerations. We agree with the approach of the Court of Appeal in regarding the tort as confined to those towards whom the relevant words or conduct were directed, but they may be a group. A person who shouts 'fire' in a cinema, when there is no fire, is addressing himself to the audience. In the present case the Court of Appeal treated the publication of the book as conduct directed towards the claimant and considered that the question of justification had therefore to be judged vis-à-vis him. In this respect we consider that they erred.

75. The book is for a wide audience and the question of justification has to be considered accordingly, not in relation to the claimant in isolation. In point of fact, the father's case is that although the book is dedicated to the claimant, he would not expect him to see it until he is much older. Arden LJ [in the Court of Appeal] said that the father could not be heard to say that he did not intend the book to reach the child, since it was dedicated to him and some parts of it are addressed to him. We have only found one passage addressed to him, which is in the acknowledgments, but more fundamentally we do not understand why the appellant may not be heard to say that the book is not intended for his eyes at this stage of his life. Arden LJ also held that there could be no justification for the publication if it was likely to cause psychiatric harm to him. That approach excluded consideration of the wider question of justification based on the legitimate interest of the defendant in telling his story to the world at large in the way in which he wishes to tell it, and the corresponding interest of the public in hearing his story.

76. When those factors are taken into account, as they must be, the only proper conclusion is that there is every justification for the publication. A person who has suffered in the way that the appellant has suffered, and has struggled to cope with the consequences of his suffering in the way that he has struggled, has the right to tell the world about it. And there is a corresponding public interest in others being able to listen to his life story in all its searing detail. Of course vulnerable children need to be protected as far as reasonably practicable from exposure to material which would harm them, but the right way of doing so is not to expand *Wilkinson v Downton* to ban the publication of a work of general interest. But in pointing out the general interest attaching to this publication, we do not mean to suggest that there needs to be some identifiable general interest in the subject matter of a publication for it to be justified within the meaning of *Wilkinson v Downton*.

77. Freedom to report the truth is a basic right to which the law gives a very high level of protection. (See, for example, *Napier v Pressdram Ltd* [2009] EWCA Civ 443, [2010] 1 WLR 934, para 42.) It is difficult to envisage any circumstances in which speech which is not deceptive, threatening or possibly abusive, could give rise to liability in tort for wilful infringement of another's right to personal

safety. The right to report the truth is justification in itself. That is not to say that the right of disclosure is absolute, for a person may owe a duty to treat information as private or confidential. But there is no general law prohibiting the publication of facts which will cause distress to another, even if that is the person's intention. The question whether (and, if so, in what circumstances) liability under *Wilkinson v Downton* might arise from words which are not deceptive or threatening, but are abusive, has not so far arisen and does not arise for consideration in this case.

. . .

80. Our conclusion that the publication of the appellant's book is not within the scope of the conduct element of the tort is enough to decide this case. However, the issue of the mental element required for the tort has been argued before us and it is right that we should address it. The Court of Appeal found that the necessary intention could be imputed to the appellant. The court cannot be criticised for doing so, since it was bound by previous decisions of the court which upheld that approach (in particular, *Janvier v Sweeney* and *Wong v Parkside Health NHS Trust*).

81. There is a critical difference, not always recognised in the authorities, between imputing the existence of an intention as a matter of law and inferring the existence of an intention as a matter of fact. Imputation of an intention by operation of a rule of law is a vestige of a previous age and has no proper role in the modern law of tort. It is unsound in principle. It was abolished in the criminal law nearly 50 years ago and its continued survival in the tort of wilful infringement of the right to personal safety is unjustifiable. It required the intervention of Parliament to expunge it from the criminal law, but that was only because of the retrograde decision in *DPP v Smith*. The doctrine was created by the courts and it is high time now for this court to declare its demise.

82. The abolition of imputed intent clears the way to proper consideration of two important questions about the mental element of this particular tort.

83. First, where a recognised psychiatric illness is the product of severe mental or emotional distress, a) is it necessary that the defendant should have intended to cause illness or b) is it sufficient that he intended to cause severe distress which in fact results in recognisable illness? Option b) is close to the version stated by *Salmond & Heuston* which attracted Lord Woolf in *Wainwright v Home Office*.

84. Secondly, is recklessness sufficient and, if so, how is recklessness to be defined for this purpose? Recklessness is a word capable of different shades of meaning. In everyday usage it may include thoughtlessness about the likely consequences in circumstances where there is an obvious high risk, or in other words gross negligence. In *R v G* [2003] UKHL 50, [2004] 1 AC 1034, the House of Lords construed 'recklessly' in the Criminal Damage Act 1971 as meaning that 'A person acts recklessly . . . with respect to . . . a result when he is aware of a risk that it will occur; and it is, in the circumstances known to him, unreasonable to take the risk'. The House of Lords based its interpretation on the definition proposed by the Law Commission in clause 18(c) of the Criminal Code Bill annexed to its Report on Criminal Law: A Criminal Code for England and Wales and Draft Criminal Code Bill, Vol 1 (Law Com No 177, 1989). A similar definition of recklessness was included in a draft Bill for reforming the law of offences against the person, which the Government published in 1998 but did not take forward. The Law Commission has repeated its proposal in a scoping consultation paper on Reform of Offences against the Person (LCCP 217, 2015). The exact wording of its proposed definition is:

> A person acts recklessly with respect to a result if he is aware of a risk that it will occur and it is unreasonable to take that risk having regard to the circumstances as he knows or believes them to be.

85. In thinking about these questions it is pertinent to consider the practical implications. Suppose that a hostage taker demands money from the family of the hostage (H) for his safe release, or that a blackmailer threatens harm to a person unless the family of the victim (V) meets his demands. The wife or parent of H or V suffers severe distress causing them to develop a recognised psychiatric illness. We doubt that anyone would dispute that in those circumstances the hostage taker or blackmailer ought to be held liable for the consequences of his evil conduct. There would be no difficulty in inferring as a matter of fact that he intended to cause severe distress to the claimant; it was the means of trying to achieve his demand. But the wrongdoer may not have had the intention to cause psychiatric illness, and he may well have given no thought to its likelihood.

86. Compare that scenario with an example at the other end of the spectrum. The defendant has a dispute with his neighbour. Tempers become flared and he makes a deliberately insulting remark. He intends it to be upsetting, but he does not anticipate or intend that the neighbour will suffer severe emotional distress. Unfortunately the episode and in particular the insult have that effect, and the distress leads to a recognised form of psychiatric illness. It would be disproportionate to hold the defendant liable when he never intended to cause the neighbour to be seriously upset.

87. Our answer to the first question is that of option (b) (para 83 above). Our answer to the second question is not to include recklessness in the definition of the mental element. To hold that the necessary mental element is intention to cause physical harm or severe mental or emotional distress strikes a just balance. It would lead to liability in the examples in para 85 but not in the example in para 86. It means that a person who actually intends to cause another to suffer severe mental or emotional distress (which should not be understated) bears the risk of legal liability if the deliberately inflicted severe distress causes the other to suffer a recognised psychiatric illness. A loose analogy may be drawn with the 'egg shell skull' doctrine, which has an established place in the law of tort. This formulation of the mental element is preferable to including recklessness as an alternative to intention. Recklessness was not a term used in *Wilkinson v Downton* or *Janvier v Sweeney* and it presents problems of definition. The Law Commission's definition would be clear, but it would not cover the example of the hostage taker or the blackmailer, because it would require proof of actual foresight of the risk of the claimant suffering psychiatric illness.

88. It would be possible to limit liability for the tort to cases in which the defendant's conduct was 'extreme, flagrant or outrageous', as in Canada. But this argument has not so far been advanced in this country, and, although Arden LJ adverted to it as a possibility, the appellant has not sought to pursue it. We are inclined to the view, which is necessarily obiter, that the tort is sufficiently contained by the combination of a) the conduct element requiring words or conduct directed at the claimant for which there is no justification or excuse, b) the mental element requiring an intention to cause at least severe mental or emotional distress, and c) the consequence element requiring physical harm or recognised psychiatric illness.

89. In the present case there is no basis for supposing that the appellant has an actual intention to cause psychiatric harm or severe mental or emotional distress to the claimant.

90. We conclude that there is no arguable case that the publication of the book would constitute the requisite conduct element of the tort or that the appellant has the requisite mental element. On both grounds the appeal must be allowed.

**see online
resources**

Notes

1. Lady Hale and Lord Toulson suggested that it was 'common ground' that the necessary consequence for liability was physical harm or a recognised psychiatric illness, leaving open the question as to whether intentionally causing severe distress might be actionable (at [73]). Lord Neuberger, in a short concurring judgment, suggested it should be:

   > As I see it, therefore, there is plainly a powerful case for saying that, in relation to the instant tort, liability for distressing statements, where intent to cause distress is an essential ingredient, it should be enough for the claimant to establish that he suffered significant distress as a result of the defendant's statement. It is not entirely easy to see why, if an intention to cause the claimant significant distress is an ingredient of the tort and is enough to establish the tort in principle, the claimant should have to establish that he suffered something more serious than significant distress before he can recover any compensation. Further, the narrow restrictions on the tort should ensure that it is rarely invoked anyway. (at [119]).

2. So where does this leave the tort in **Wilkinson v Downton**? While the court was keen to rein in the application of the tort (as expanded by the Court of Appeal), there is no suggestion that it should 'disappear'. Lord Neuberger identified five points to aid decisions as to when an action may arise:

   > In order to decide when a statement, which is not otherwise tortious, and which causes a claimant distress, should be capable of founding a cause of action . . . First, that there must be circumstances in which such a cause of action should exist: the facts of **Wilkinson** and *Janvier* make that point good. Secondly, given the importance of freedom of expression, which includes the need to avoid constraining ordinary (even much offensive) discourse, it is vital that the boundaries of the cause of action are relatively narrow. Thirdly, because of the importance of legal certainty, particularly in the area of what people can say, the tort should be defined as clearly as possible. Fourthly, in the light of the almost literally infinite permutations of possible human interactions, it is realistic to proceed on the basis that it may well be that no set of parameters can be devised which would cater for absolutely every possibility. Fifthly, given all these factors, there will almost inevitably be aspects of the parameters on which it would be wrong to express a concluded view, and to let the law develop in a characteristic common law way, namely on a case by case basis. (at [104])

PROTECTION FROM HARASSMENT ACT 1997

1. Prohibition of harassment

(1) A person must not pursue a course of conduct—
   (a) which amounts to harassment of another, and
   (b) which he knows or ought to know amounts to harassment of the other.

(2) A person must not pursue a course of conduct—
   (a) which involves harassment of two or more persons, and
   (b) which he knows or ought to know involves harassment of those persons, and
   (c) by which he intends to persuade any person (whether or not one of those mentioned above)—

   not to do something that he is entitled or required to do, or

   to do something that he is not under any obligation to do.

(3) For the purposes of this section, or section 2A(2)(c), the person whose course of conduct is in question ought to know that it amounts to or involves harassment of another if a reasonable person in possession of the same information would think the course of conduct amounted to or involved harassment of the other.

(4) Subsection (1) or (1A) does not apply to a course of conduct if the person who pursued it shows—

    (a) that it was pursued for the purpose of preventing or detecting crime,

    (b) that it was pursued under any enactment or rule of law or to comply with any condition or requirement imposed by any person under any enactment, or

    (c) that in the particular circumstances the pursuit of the course of conduct was reasonable.

3. Civil remedy

(1) An actual or apprehended breach of section 1(1) may be the subject of a claim in civil proceedings by the person who is or may be the victim of the course of conduct in question.

(2) On such a claim, damages may be awarded for (among other things) any anxiety caused by the harassment and any financial loss resulting from the harassment.

. . .

3A. Injunctions to protect persons from harassment within section 1(1A)

(1) This section applies where there is an actual or apprehended breach of section 1(1A) by any person ('the relevant person').

(2) In such a case—

    (a) any person who is or may be a victim of the course of conduct in question, or

    (b) any person who is or may be a person falling within section 1(1A)(c),

may apply to the High Court or a county court for an injunction restraining the relevant person from pursuing any conduct which amounts to harassment in relation to any person or persons mentioned or described in the injunction.

. . .

7. Interpretation of this group of sections

(1) This section applies for the interpretation of sections 1 to 5.

(2) References to harassing a person include alarming the person or causing the person distress.

(3) A 'course of conduct' must involve—

    (a) in the case of conduct in relation to a single person (see section 1(1)), conduct on at least two occasions in relation to that person, or

    (b) in the case of conduct in relation to two or more persons (see section 1(1A)), conduct on at least one occasion in relation to each of those persons.

(4) 'Conduct' includes speech.

(5) References to a person, in the context of the harassment of a person, are references to a person who is an individual.

Sube v News Group Newspapers Ltd
Queen's Bench Division [2020] EWHC 1125 (QB)

A married couple with nine children had been the subject of a series of newspaper articles detailing their dissatisfaction with their social housing offered by Luton Borough Council. Although the couple had originally approached the press (hoping to put pressure on the council), they were unhappy with the 'indignant tone' of the articles, published under headlines such as 'Jobless dad whines about £15k-a-year council home—and turns down five bedroom house'. Following an unsuccessful claim for defamation, they brought claims against two newspaper publishers, for damages and an injunction in respect of alleged harassment contrary to the Protection from Harassment Act (PHA) 1997. Held: the court rejected their claim, holding that 'nothing short of conscious or negligent abuse of media freedom will justify a finding of harassment' (at [68]).

WARBY J:

65. The overall approach which the Court should take to the interpretation and application of these provisions [PHA 1997, sections 1–3 and 7] is well-established.

(1) A person who causes another alarm and distress is not by that token guilty of harassing them:

> It does not follow [t]hat because references to harassing a person include alarming a person or causing a person distress (section 7(2)), any course of conduct which causes alarm or distress therefore amounts to harassment. . . So to reason would be illogical and would produce perverse results . . .

R v Smith [2012] EWCA Crim 2566 [2013] 1 WLR 1399 [24].

(2) Harassment is a more nuanced and specific concept. Harassment is

> . . . an ordinary English word with a well understood meaning. Harassment is a persistent and deliberate course of unreasonable and oppressive conduct, targeted at another person, which is calculated to and does cause that person alarm, fear or distress.

Hayes v Willoughby [2013] UKSC 17 [2013] 1 WLR 935 [1] (Lord Sumption SC).

(3) In order to establish a civil claim for harassment the claimant must prove conduct on at least two occasions which is, from an objective standpoint, calculated to cause alarm or distress and oppressive, and unacceptable to such a degree that it would sustain criminal liability: see *Dowson v Chief Constable of Northumbria Police* [2010] EWHC 2612 (QB) [142] (Simon J).

(4) The last point reflects the fact that the conduct prohibited by s 1 is not only a tort but also a crime. Hence:-

> [Where] the quality of the conduct said to constitute harassment is being examined, courts will have in mind that irritations, annoyances, even a measure of upset, arise at times in everybody's day-to-day dealings with other people. Courts are well able to recognise the boundary between conduct which is unattractive, even unreasonable, and conduct which is oppressive and unacceptable. To cross the boundary from the regrettable to the unacceptable the gravity of the misconduct must be of an order which would sustain criminal liability under section 2.

Majrowski v Guy's and St Thomas's NHS Trust [2006] UKHL 34 [2007] 1 AC 224 [30] (Lord Nicholls).

66. This is a claim for harassment by publication. That is clearly legitimate, as a matter of principle. Although the PHA was primarily aimed at the problem of 'stalking', it has been clear for some time that the tort and the crime encompass harassment by publication. Indeed, much harassment does involve the persistent publication of embarrassing or otherwise unwelcome statements, true or false, on the internet or on social media. But the tort and the crime can be committed by a course of conduct consisting of publication in or by the conventional news media. The Court of Appeal addressed the point in *Thomas v News Group Newspapers Ltd* [2001] EWCA Civ 1233 [2002] EMLR 78, declining to strike out a claim under the PHA in respect of a series of articles in *The Sun* which were said to constitute harassment by reference to the claimant's colour.

67. When presented with a claim of this kind, the Court must be especially mindful of the threshold of gravity required before a finding of harassment can be made; and it must be careful to ensure that its approach is compatible with the human rights engaged by the particular facts of the case. In this case, as in all or most cases of alleged harassment by publication, there is a tension. On the one hand, the claimants have Article 8 rights to respect for their private and family life and their home. On the other side are the publishers' Article 10 rights to convey information and ideas, and the rights of the public at large to receive such information and ideas. The PHA must be interpreted and applied in a way that upholds the Article 8 rights but avoids undue interference with Article 10 rights.

68. These points emerge from the authorities:

(1) It is for the claimant to demonstrate that the conduct complained of is unreasonable, to the degree required by the authorities cited above; and it is not a question of assessing the reasonableness of any opinions expressed in the publications complained of:-

> Whether conduct is reasonable will depend upon the circumstances of the particular case. When considering whether the conduct of the press in publishing articles is reasonable for the purposes of the 1997 Act, the answer does not turn upon whether opinions expressed in the article are reasonably held. The question must be answered by reference to the right of the press to freedom of expression which has been so emphatically recognised by the jurisprudence both of Strasbourg and this country.

Thomas v News Group [32] (Lord Phillips MR).

(2) The Court must test the '*necessity*' of any interference with freedom of expression by using the well-known three-part test:

> The test of 'necessity in a democratic society' requires the Court to determine whether the 'interference' corresponded to a 'pressing social need', whether it was proportionate to the legitimate aim pursued and whether the reasons given . . . to justify it are relevant and sufficient.

Nilsen and Johnsen v Norway (1999) 30 EHRR 878 [43].

(3) In general, the techniques of reporting, including the tone and editorial decisions about content, are matters for the media and not the Court to determine: see, for instance, *Jersild v Denmark* (1995) 19 EHRR 1 [31], *Fressoz & Roire v France* (1999) 31 EHRR 2 [52], *MGN Ltd v United Kingdom* [2011] 53 EHRR 66 [145], *Trimingham v Associated Newspapers Ltd* [2012] EWHC 1296 (QB) [85] (Tugendhat J).

(4) The court's assessment of the harmful tendency of the statements complained of must always be objective, and not swayed by the subjective feelings of the claimant:

> [i]t would be a serious interference with freedom of expression if those wishing to express their own views could be silenced by, or threatened with, claims for harassment based on subjective claims by individuals that they feel offended or insulted:

Trimingham [267] (Tugendhat J).

(5) Applied to the tort of harassment, these principles mean that nothing short of a conscious or negligent abuse of media freedom will justify a finding of harassment:-

> . . . the test [of reasonableness] requires the publisher to consider whether a proposed series of articles, which is likely to cause distress to an individual, will constitute an abuse of the freedom of press which the pressing social needs of a democratic society require should be curbed.

Thomas v News Group [50] (Lord Phillips MR).

(6) It will be a rare or exceptional case in which these criteria are satisfied, in relation to media publication.

34. In general, press criticism, even if robust, does not constitute unreasonable conduct and does not fall within the natural meaning of harassment. . . .

35. . . . before press publications are capable of constituting harassment, they must be attended by some exceptional circumstance which justifies sanctions and the restriction on the freedom of expression that they involve. . . . such circumstances will be rare. . .

Thomas v News Group (Lord Phillips MR).

69. Those observations appear to be borne out by history to date. *Trimingham* was the first claim for harassment by a media publisher to come to trial in England and Wales. It related to the content of 65 articles referring to the claimant's sexual orientation in what were said to be disparaging terms, 152 reader comments, said to taunt and lampoon her over her sexuality and appearance, and the conduct of journalists in gathering information for publication. The claim was dismissed. In the 8 years since then there have been cases, such as *Hourani v Thomson* [2017] EWHC 432 (QB), involving campaigns of harassment using a variety of media. But no other case of harassment by a media organisation appears to have come to trial in this jurisdiction. Two such cases have been brought unsuccessfully in Northern Ireland, relating to series of articles alleging involvement in serious criminal activity: *King v Sunday Newspapers Ltd* ([2010] NIQB 107, appeal dismissed [2011] NICA 8) and *Fulton v Sunday Newspapers Ltd* [2015] NIQB 100 (appeal dismissed, [2017] NICA 45).

Notes

1. The Act introduces a civil remedy for harassment (s 3) as well as a criminal offence of harassment (s 2).

2. The Protection from Harassment Act 1997 has an extremely wide remit. It has been used in response to the publication of victimising newspaper articles (*Thomas v News Group Newspapers Ltd* [2001] EWCA Civ 1233; *Trimingham v Associated Newspapers Ltd* [2012] EWHC 1296 (QB); cf **Sube v News Group Newspapers Ltd** [2020] EWHC 1125 (QB)), sending mass emails and setting up websites (*Merlin Entertainments LPC, Chessington World of Adventures Operations v Cave* [2014] EWHC 3036 (QB)), a Facebook page revealing the identity and whereabouts of a convicted sex offender (*CG v Facebook Ireland Ltd and Joseph McCloskey* [2015] NIQB 11), unjustified bills and threats of legal action (*Ferguson v British Gas* [2009] EWCA Civ 46), paparazzi photographers (News: 'Harry Styles harassment case, photographers consent to permanent injunctions' Inforrm's blog, 11 March 2014; Natalie Peck 'Harassment and injunctions: Cheryl Cole' Inforrm's blog, 7 July 2011), bullying in the workplace (*Majrowski* and *Veakins v Kier Islington Ltd* [2009] EWCA Civ 1288), intimidating public demonstrations (*Daiichi UK Ltd v Stop Huntington Animal Cruelty* [2004] 1 WLR 1503) and in cases of so-called 'revenge porn' and other forms of image-based sexual abuse (*ABK v KDT & FGH* [2013] EWHC 1192 (QB); *AXB v BXA* [2018] EWHC 588 (QB) and generally Kirsty Horsey and Erika Rackley 'Tort Law' in Rosemary Auchmuty (ed) *Great Debates on Law and Gender* (Palgrave, 2018)).

3. There must be a 'course of conduct', which means (s 7(3)) conduct on at least two occasions. It does not, therefore, cover one-off incidents, such as the practical joke in **Wilkinson v Downton**, however serious. Nevertheless, a single publication of a harassing statement or image online will amount to a 'course of conduct' where the defendant does so 'in the knowledge that such publications will inevitably come to [the claimant's] attention on more than one occasion and on each occasion cause them alarm and distress constitutes harassment under the PHA' (Tugendhat J, *Law Society v Kordowski* [2011] EWHC 3185 (QB) at [61]). A victim who fears that a single incident of harassing conduct *might* in the future *become* a course of conduct may be able to claim under section 3(1) which provides a remedy for the 'apprehension' of a breach of section 1.

4. In *Levi v Bates* [2015] EWCA Civ 206 the Court of Appeal considered whether, if at all, a person who has been harmed (or who anticipates harm) from harassment aimed at someone else (the target) can avail herself of the protection of the civil remedies afforded under the Protection from

Harassment Act 1997. The defendant, Mr Bates, had been engaged in a smear campaign against Mr Levi following the financial collapse of Leeds United Football Club. He published a number of derogatory accusations and even suggested that fans might put questions directly to Bates, alongside his home address. Mrs Bates claimed to have suffered distress as a result of the threats involving potential violence at her home. Finding for the claimants, Longmore LJ, in a concurring judgment, stated:

54. The [trial] judge held that Mrs Levi could not recover damages (or obtain an injunction) in respect of incidents (d) and (e) because the harassing conduct was aimed at her husband and not at her. For this purpose he relied on a dictum of Simon J in *Dowson v Chief Constable of Northumbria* [2010] EWHC 2612 (QB) that there must be conduct which occurs on at least two occasions which is targeted at the claimant, which itself appears to derive from a dictum of Lord Phillips MR in *Thomas v News Group Newspapers* [2001] EWCA Civ 1233; [2002] EMLR 78 para 30 that the harassing conduct must be targeted at an individual.

55. It is right that, for the statutory tort of harassment to occur, there must be a course of conduct which is aimed (or targeted) at an individual since that is inherent in the term 'harassment'. But I see no reason why it should be only that individual who can sue, if the defendant knows or ought to know that his conduct will amount to harassment of another individual. The tort (and crime) of harassment does not require an intent to harass any one individual; section 1 of the Act is clear that the question whether conduct is harassing conduct is an objective question for the fact-finder. If therefore a defendant knows or ought to know that his conduct amounts to harassment, he should be liable to the person harassed, even if the conduct is aimed at another person. A defendant is always entitled to show, pursuant to section 1(3) of the Act, that in the particular circumstances, his pursuit of the course of conduct was reasonable.

56. It may not be often that a person who is not the target of the harassing conduct will, in fact, be harassed. But a wife, or other close family member, may well suffer a feeling of harassment if a defendant publishes her and her husband's address with a view to encouraging members of the public to visit that address in an aggressive or hostile manner. The same applies to publication of a telephone number or a reminder to the public that what is her telephone number (as well as her husband's) can be found in the telephone book. If it is reasonable for one private individual to publish such information about another private individual, there will be no tort; but publication of such information in pursuance of a private grudge may well not be reasonable at all and was not reasonable in this case.

5. It is not necessary, however, that each event itself should amount to harassment, for it is the course of conduct that is the harassment. Thus two events, when combined, can amount to harassment even though each event taken separately would not do so. In *Iqbal v Dean Manson Solicitors* [2011] EWCA Civ 123, Rix LJ said:

[T]he Act is concerned with courses of conduct which amount to harassment, rather than with individual instances of harassment. Of course, it is the individual instances which will make up the course of conduct, but it still remains the position that it is the course of conduct which has to have the quality of amounting to harassment, rather than individual instances of conduct . . . The reason why the statute is drafted in this way is not hard to understand. Take the typical case of stalking, or of malicious phone calls. When a defendant, D, walks past a claimant C's door, or calls C's telephone but puts the phone down without speaking, the single act by itself is neutral, or may be. But if that act is repeated on a number of occasions, the course of conduct may well amount to harassment. That conclusion can only be arrived at by looking at the individual acts complained of as a whole. (at [45])

6. The Act was applied in *Ferguson v British Gas Trading* [2009] EWCA Civ 46. In this case the claimant had switched her supply of gas from British Gas to nPower in May 2006. However, from August 2006 to early 2007 British Gas sent her a number of bills and letters which threatened to cut off her supply of gas, to start legal proceedings and to report her to credit-rating agencies. She wasted a lot of time in trying to sort this out and suffered considerable anxiety. Jacobs LJ held

that it was strongly arguable that the conduct of British Gas was a breach of the Act. On the issue of the gravity of the conduct, he quoted Lord Nicholls in *Majrowski* v *Guy's and St Thomas' NHS Trust* [2006] UKHL 34 who said that where 'the quality of the conduct said to constitute harassment is being examined, courts will have in mind that irritations, annoyances, even a measure of upset, arise at times in everybody's day-to-day dealings with other people. Courts are well able to recognise the boundary between conduct which is unattractive, even unreasonable, and conduct which is oppressive and unacceptable' (at [30]). In *Majrowski*, Lord Nicholls also said that 'to cross the boundary from the regrettable to the unacceptable the gravity of the misconduct must be of an order which would sustain criminal liability under section 2' (at [30]).

7. The question whether damage needs to be foreseeable arose in *Jones* v *Ruth* [2011] EWCA Civ 804 where the claimants were subjected to aggressive and intimidatory conduct by the defendants, causing them anxiety and depression. The trial judge rejected their claim under the Protection from Harassment Act on the ground that their injury was not foreseeable. However, the claim was allowed by the Court of Appeal which said that foreseeability of damage was not a relevant issue under the Act:

> I am not persuaded that foreseeability of the injury or loss sustained by a claimant in a case of harassment is an essential element in the cause of action . . . Conduct of the kind described in s 1 is actionable under s 3 in respect of anxiety or injury caused by the harassment and any financial loss resulting from the harassment. There is nothing in the statutory language to import an additional requirement of foreseeability. Nor is the foreseeability of damage the gist of the tort. Section 1 is concerned with deliberate conduct of a kind which the defendant knows or ought to know will amount to harassment of the claimant. Once that is proved the defendant is responsible in damages for the injury and loss which flow from that conduct. (at [32])

8. Section 1(3) excludes certain conduct from the remit of the Act, including activity for the purpose of detecting or preventing crime (s 1(3)(a)). In *Hayes* v *Willoughby* [2013] UKSC 17, the Supreme Court held that where a harasser claims that he was pursuing his course of conduct for the purpose of preventing or detecting crime within section 1(3)(a) he must show that he was acting rationally:

> He must have thought rationally about the material suggesting the possibility of criminality and formed the view that the conduct said to constitute harassment was appropriate for the purpose of preventing or detecting it. If he has done these things, then he has the relevant purpose. The court will not test his conclusions by reference to the view which a hypothetical reasonable man in his position would have formed. (Lord Sumption at [15])

14

Invasion of privacy

The protection of privacy has long been a problem for the common law, partly because it has not been possible to agree a definition of the interests which deserve to be protected and partly because of the need to protect the conflicting right to freedom of speech (see **Wainwright v Home Office** [2003] UKHL 53). This chapter details how some privacy interests are now protected by tort law with the development of the equitable action of breach of confidence and the emergence from that of a tort of misuse of private information (**Google Inc v Vidal-Hall and others** [2015] EWCA Civ 311). This is a common law right to protection from invasion of privacy, existing mainly in relation to the protection of personal information (including photographs) and a 'reasonable expectation of privacy' in specific situations. The development of the law in this area shows the influence of the Human Rights Act (HRA) 1998 and the European Convention on Human Rights (ECHR) on private law. It has also been the subject of some controversy, especially in relation to the protection of celebrity privacy.

14.1 Privacy and common law

As was clear from *Kaye v Robertson* [1991] FSR 62, there is no general tort to protect privacy. Additionally, the courts were long resolute in the idea that no common law action for protection of privacy could be developed, Parliament refused to create one, and the Calcutt Committee on Privacy recommended against a statutory tort relating to privacy in 1990.

There are two kinds of privacy problem: the first relates to invasion of the claimant's space either physically or mentally (the classic right to be left alone) and the other is the dissemination of information about the claimant that they would rather keep to themselves. This is now protected in tort via the development of the equitable action for breach of confidence (stemming from **Campbell v MGN** [2004] UKHL 22) into the tort of misuse of private information, confirmed in **Google Inc v Vidal-Hall and others**. It is also clear that the HRA provides a right against the state for failing to protect citizens against privacy invasions under the terms (and limitations) of Article 8 ECHR (**Von Hannover v Germany** (Application no 59320/00) (2005) 40 EHRR 1), and also has led to the development of 'horizontal' claims against private individuals or organisations, as acknowledged in **Campbell v MGN** and subsequent cases.

> ### Wainwright v Home Office
> House of Lords [2003] UKHL 53

The facts are stated in section 13.3.

LORD HOFFMANN:

15. My Lords, let us first consider the proposed tort of invasion of privacy. Since the famous article by Warren and Brandeis (*The Right to Privacy* (1890) 4 Harvard LR 193) the question of whether such a tort exists, or should exist, has been much debated in common law jurisdictions. Warren and Brandeis suggested that one could generalise certain cases on defamation, breach of copyright in unpublished letters, trade secrets and breach of confidence as all based upon the protection of a common value which they called privacy or, following Judge Cooley (*Cooley on Torts*, 2nd ed (1888), p 29) the right to be let alone. They said that identifying this common element should enable the courts to declare the existence of a general principle which protected a person's appearance, sayings, acts and personal relations from being exposed in public.

16. Courts in the United States were receptive to this proposal and a jurisprudence of privacy began to develop. It became apparent, however, that the developments could not be contained within a single principle; not, at any rate, one with greater explanatory power than the proposition that it was based upon the protection of a value which could be described as privacy. Dean Prosser, in his work on *The Law of Torts,* 4th ed (1971), p 804, said that:

> What has emerged is no very simple matter . . . it is not one tort, but a complex of four. To date the law of privacy comprises four distinct kinds of invasion of four different interests of the plaintiff, which are tied together by the common name, but otherwise have almost nothing in common except that each represents an interference with the right of the plaintiff 'to be let alone'.

17. Dean Prosser's taxonomy divided the subject into (1) intrusion upon the plaintiff's physical solitude or seclusion (including unlawful searches, telephone tapping, long-distance photography and telephone harassment) (2) public disclosure of private facts and (3) publicity putting the plaintiff in a false light and (4) appropriation, for the defendant's advantage, of the plaintiff's name or likeness. These, he said, at p 814, had different elements and were subject to different defences.

18. The need in the United States to break down the concept of 'invasion of privacy' into a number of loosely-linked torts must cast doubt upon the value of any high-level generalisation which can perform a useful function in enabling one to deduce the rule to be applied in a concrete case. English law has so far been unwilling, perhaps unable, to formulate any such high-level principle. There are a number of common law and statutory remedies of which it may be said that one at least of the underlying values they protect is a right of privacy. Sir Brian Neill's well known article 'Privacy: a challenge for the next century' in *Protecting Privacy* (ed B Markesinis, 1999) contains a survey. Common law torts include trespass, nuisance, defamation and malicious falsehood; there is the equitable action for breach of confidence and statutory remedies under the Protection from Harassment Act 1997 and the Data Protection Act 1998. There are also extra-legal remedies under Codes of Practice applicable to broadcasters and newspapers. But there are gaps; cases in which the courts have considered that an invasion of privacy deserves a remedy which the existing law does not offer. Sometimes the perceived gap can be filled by judicious development of an existing principle. The law of breach of confidence has in recent years undergone such a process: see in particular the judgment of Lord Phillips of Worth Matravers MR in *Campbell v MGN Ltd* [2003] QB 633. On the other hand, an attempt to create a tort of telephone harassment by a radical change in the basis of the action for private nuisance in *Khorasandjian v Bush* [1993] QB 727 was held by the House of Lords in **Hunter v Canary Wharf Ltd** [1997] AC 655 to be a step too far. The gap was filled by the 1997 Act.

19. What the courts have so far refused to do is to formulate a general principle of 'invasion of privacy' (I use the quotation marks to signify doubt about what in such a context the expression would mean) from which the conditions of liability in the particular case can be deduced. . . .

23. The absence of any general cause of action for invasion of privacy was again acknowledged by the Court of Appeal in *Kaye v Robertson* [1991] FSR 62, in which a newspaper reporter and photographer invaded the plaintiff's hospital bedroom, purported to interview him and took photographs. The law of trespass provided no remedy because the plaintiff was not owner or occupier of the room and his body had not been touched. Publication of the interview was restrained by interlocutory injunction on the ground that it was arguably a malicious falsehood to represent that the plaintiff had consented to it. But no other remedy was available. At the time of the judgment (16 March 1990) a Committee under the chairmanship of Sir David Calcutt QC was considering whether individual privacy required statutory protection against intrusion by the press. Glidewell LJ said, at p 66:

> The facts of the present case are a graphic illustration of the desirability of Parliament considering whether and in what circumstances statutory provision can be made to protect the privacy of individuals.

Notes

1. Lord Hoffmann comprehensively rejected a general right of privacy at common law. While there had been considerable sympathy for such a right, problems of definition and the balance of privacy against freedom of expression had in the past suggested that judicial development of such a tort was inappropriate. Neither was statutory protection forthcoming—in 1990 the Calcutt Committee on Privacy (Cm 1102) recommended against any statutory tort of infringement of privacy, preferring to rely on a system of self-regulation.

2. The HRA 1998 was not in force at the time of the events in **Wainwright**. Had it been, the claimants would have been able to sue as they suffered at the hands of a public authority. In *Wainwright* v *UK* (Application no 12350/04) (2007) 44 EHRR 809, the European Court of Human Rights declared that there were breaches of the ECHR. Although the Court ordered damages of €3,000 for each applicant, the grounds of the decision are quite limited. In considering Article 8 ECHR (respect for family and private life) the Court said in relation to the strip-searches that such a highly invasive and potentially debasing procedure must be conducted with rigorous adherence to procedures and due respect to human dignity. The defendants in this case had not properly complied with the Prison Rules and the searches were not proportionate to the legitimate aim of fighting drugs in prisons in the manner in which they were carried out. The Court also held that the fact that the prison officers could not be liable for their actions was a violation of Article 13 (right to an effective remedy). It therefore seems that the Court has determined that the state must remedy disproportionate invasions of privacy effected by officials of the state. This is more like wrongful use of state power and, while evidently useful, the decision may be thought to have little effect on invasions of privacy by individuals or corporations.

14.2 The Human Rights Act and the reasonable expectation of privacy

How does the law protect what can be considered to be private *information* and when can it be expected that such information will not be made public? Initial protection emerged from the equitable principle of breach of confidence, whereby information arising out of a confidential relationship should not be disclosed—not a common law tort at all. However, the law has now developed way beyond that. Since **Campbell**, it is clear that there is no need for a pre-existing confidential relationship to have existed, as once was the case (*Coco v AN Clark (Engineers) Ltd* [1968] FSR 415). Latterly, the main driver of the content of the obligation is Article 8 ECHR. There is now a general obligation to protect information where there is a 'reasonable expectation' of privacy attached, subject to the countervailing public interest in the freedom of speech (see HRA, s 12(4)).

There are two main issues: first, when is information to be regarded as sufficiently 'private' for the obligation to arise (i.e. when is there a 'reasonable expectation of privacy?') and, secondly, how is the balance between confidentiality and freedom of speech to be achieved? But there is also a theoretical problem. The stricter view is that the law is still based on the equitable obligation of confidence, albeit as 'informed' by the HRA—or one could say that the equitable obligation 'absorbed' the principles in the Act. An alternative, more radical, view was that espoused by Eady J in **Mosley v News Group Newspapers** [2008] EWHC 1777 (QB) (extracted later in this section), where he talked of 'the new methodology' that, in effect, permits the HRA to have direct ('horizontal') effect between individuals. This is difficult because, in theory, the Act can create rights only between individuals and public bodies, so there needs to be a source of the obligation of privacy other than the Act itself. There is no reason why equity cannot provide this theoretical basis because it in no way inhibits the content of the obligation as drawn from the ECHR. As we will see, such theoretical musings over principle are probably now redundant in light of judicial confirmation of the existence of a 'tort of misuse of private information' (**Google Inc v Vidal-Hall and others**).

HUMAN RIGHTS ACT 1998

6. Acts of public authorities

(1) It is unlawful for a public authority to act in a way which is incompatible with a Convention right.

(2) Subsection (1) does not apply to an act if—

(a) as the result of one or more provisions of primary legislation, the authority could not have acted differently; or

(b) in the case of one or more provisions of, or made under, primary legislation which cannot be read or given effect in a way which is compatible with the Convention rights, the authority was acting so as to give effect to or enforce those provisions.

(3) In this section 'public authority' includes—

(a) a court or tribunal, and

(b) any person certain of whose functions are functions of a public nature, but does not include either House of Parliament or a person exercising functions in connection with proceedings in Parliament.

(4) [Repealed]

(5) In relation to a particular act, a person is not a public authority by virtue only of subsection (3)

(b) if the nature of the act is private.

(6) 'An act' includes a failure to act but does not include a failure to—

(a) introduce in, or lay before, Parliament a proposal for legislation; or

(b) make any primary legislation or remedial order.

7. Proceedings

(1) A person who claims that a public authority has acted (or proposes to act) in a way which is made unlawful by section 6(1) may—

    (a) bring proceedings against the authority under this Act in the appropriate court or tribunal, or

    (b) rely on the Convention right or rights concerned in any legal proceedings, but only if he is (or would be) a victim of the unlawful act.

(2) In subsection (1)(a) 'appropriate court or tribunal' means such court or tribunal as may be determined in accordance with rules; and proceedings against an authority include a counterclaim or similar proceeding.

(3) If the proceedings are brought on an application for judicial review, the applicant is to be taken to have a sufficient interest in relation to the unlawful act only if he is, or would be, a victim of that act.

(4) If the proceedings are made by way of a petition for judicial review in Scotland, the applicant shall be taken to have title and interest to sue in relation to the unlawful act only if he is, or would be, a victim of that act.

(5) Proceedings under subsection (1)(a) must be brought before the end of—

    (a) the period of one year beginning with the date on which the act complained of took place; or

    (b) such longer period as the court or tribunal considers equitable having regard to all the circumstances, but that is subject to any rule imposing a stricter time limit in relation to the procedure in question.

(6) In subsection (1)(b) 'legal proceedings' includes—

    (a) proceedings brought by or at the instigation of a public authority; and

    (b) an appeal against the decision of a court or tribunal.

(7) For the purposes of this section, a person is a victim of an unlawful act only if he would be a victim for the purposes of Article 34 of the Convention if proceedings were brought in the European Court of Human Rights in respect of that act.

(8) Nothing in this Act creates a criminal offence.

. . .

THE EUROPEAN CONVENTION ON HUMAN RIGHTS

Article 8

Right to respect for private and family life

1. Everyone has the right to respect for his private and family life, his home and his correspondence.

2. There shall be no interference by a public authority with the exercise of this right except such as is in accordance with the law and is necessary in a democratic society in the interests of national security, public safety or the economic well-being of the country, for the prevention of disorder or crime, for the protection of health or morals, or for the protection of the rights and freedoms of others.

HUMAN RIGHTS ACT 1998

12. Freedom of expression

(1) This section applies if a court is considering whether to grant any relief which, if granted, might affect the exercise of the Convention right to freedom of expression.

(2) If the person against whom the application for relief is made ('the respondent') is neither present nor represented, no such relief is to be granted unless the court is satisfied—

(a) that the applicant has taken all practicable steps to notify the respondent; or

(b) that there are compelling reasons why the respondent should not be notified.

(3) No such relief is to be granted so as to restrain publication before trial unless the court is satisfied that the applicant is likely to establish that publication should not be allowed.

(4) The court must have particular regard to the importance of the Convention right to freedom of expression and, where the proceedings relate to material which the respondent claims, or which appears to the court, to be journalistic, literary or artistic material (or to conduct connected with such material), to—

(a) the extent to which—

the material has, or is about to, become available to the public; or

it is, or would be, in the public interest for the material to be published;

(b) any relevant privacy code.

Campbell v MGN Ltd
House of Lords [2004] UKHL 22

The *Daily Mirror* published an article about the model Naomi Campbell detailing the fact that she was a drug addict receiving treatment at Narcotics Anonymous (NA). It also gave some details of the treatment—including for how long, how frequently and at what times of day she received it. The article was accompanied by photographs of her leaving the place where the treatment had taken place. Held (Lords Nicholls and Hoffmann dissenting): the defendant was liable for publishing confidential information about which Ms Campbell might have a reasonable expectation of privacy (the photos and the treatment details, but not the news item itself). Publication would have caused substantial offence to a person of ordinary sensibilities in the claimant's position. The claimant was awarded £3,500. (Note: although the judges differed as to how the competing interests of privacy and free speech should be balanced on the facts of this case, Lord Hoffmann stated that they were unanimous on the general principles.)

LORD HOFFMANN (dissenting):

46. In recent years, however, there have been two developments of the law of confidence, typical of the capacity of the common law to adapt itself to the needs of contemporary life. One has been an acknowledgement of the artificiality of distinguishing between confidential information obtained through the violation of a confidential relationship and similar information obtained in some other way. The second has been the acceptance, under the influence of human rights instruments such as article 8 of the European Convention, of the privacy of personal information as something worthy of protection in its own right.

47. The first development is generally associated with the speech of Lord Goff of Chieveley in *Attorney-General v Guardian Newspapers Ltd (No 2)* [1990] 1 AC 109, 281, where he gave, as illustrations of cases in which it would be illogical to insist upon violation of a confidential relationship, the 'obviously confidential document . . . wafted by an electric fan out of a window into a crowded street' and the 'private diary . . . dropped in a public place'. He therefore formulated the principle as being that

a duty of confidence arises when confidential information comes to the knowledge of a person . . . in circumstances where he has notice, or is held to have agreed, that the information is confidential, with the effect that it would be just in all the circumstances that he should be precluded from disclosing the information to others.

48. This statement of principle, which omits the requirement of a prior confidential relationship, was accepted as representing current English law by the European Court of Human Rights in *Earl Spencer v United Kingdom* (1998) 25 EHRR CD 105 and was applied by the Court of Appeal in *A v B plc* [2003] QB 195, 207. It is now firmly established.

49. The second development has been rather more subtle. Until the Human Rights Act 1998 came into force, there was no equivalent in English domestic law of article 8 the European Convention or the equivalent articles in other international human rights instruments which guarantee rights of privacy. So the courts of the United Kingdom did not have to decide what such guarantees meant. Even now that the equivalent of article 8 has been enacted as part of English law, it is not directly concerned with the protection of privacy against private persons or corporations. It is, by virtue of section 6 of the 1998 Act, a guarantee of privacy only against public authorities. Although the Convention, as an international instrument, may impose upon the United Kingdom an obligation to take some steps (whether by statute or otherwise) to protect rights of privacy against invasion by private individuals, it does not follow that such an obligation would have any counterpart in domestic law.

50. What human rights law has done is to identify private information as something worth protecting as an aspect of human autonomy and dignity. And this recognition has raised inescapably the question of why it should be worth protecting against the state but not against a private person. There may of course be justifications for the publication of private information by private persons which would not be available to the state—I have particularly in mind the position of the media, to which I shall return in a moment—but I can see no logical ground for saying that a person should have less protection against a private individual than he would have against the state for the publication of personal information for which there is no justification. Nor, it appears, have any of the other judges who have considered the matter.

51. The result of these developments has been a shift in the centre of gravity of the action for breach of confidence when it is used as a remedy for the unjustified publication of personal information. It recognises that the incremental changes to which I have referred do not merely extend the duties arising traditionally from a relationship of trust and confidence to a wider range of people. As Sedley LJ observed in a perceptive passage in his judgment in *Douglas v Hello! Ltd* [2001] QB 967, 1001, the new approach takes a different view of the underlying value which the law protects. Instead of the cause of action being based upon the duty of good faith applicable to confidential personal information and trade secrets alike, it focuses upon the protection of human autonomy and dignity—the right to control the dissemination of information about one's private life and the right to the esteem and respect of other people.

52. These changes have implications for the future development of the law. They must influence the approach of the courts to the kind of information which is regarded as entitled to protection, the extent and form of publication which attracts a remedy and the circumstances in which publication can be justified.

BARONESS HALE:

132. Neither party to this appeal has challenged the basic principles which have emerged from the Court of Appeal in the wake of the Human Rights Act 1998. The 1998 Act does not create any new cause of action between private persons. But if there is a relevant cause of action applicable, the court as a public authority must act compatibly with both parties' Convention rights. In a case such

as this, the relevant vehicle will usually be the action for breach of confidence, as Lord Woolf CJ held in *A v B plc* [2002] EWCA Civ 337, [2003] QB 195, 202, para 4:

> [Articles 8 and 10] have provided new parameters within which the court will decide, in an action for breach of confidence, whether a person is entitled to have his privacy protected by the court or whether the restriction of freedom of expression which such protection involves cannot be justified. The court's approach to the issues which the applications raise has been modified because, under section 6 of the 1998 Act, the court, as a public authority, is required not to 'act in a way which is incompatible with a Convention right'. The court is able to achieve this by absorbing the rights which Articles 8 and 10 protect into the long-established action for breach of confidence. This involves giving a new strength and breadth to the action so that it accommodates the requirements of these articles.

133. The action for breach of confidence is not the only relevant cause of action: the inherent jurisdiction of the High Court to protect the children for whom it is responsible is another example: see *In re S (a child) (identification: restrictions on publication)* [2003] EWCA Civ 963, [2003] 3 WLR 1425. But the courts will not invent a new cause of action to cover types of activity which were not previously covered: see *Wainwright v Home Office* [2003] 3 WLR 1137. Mrs Wainwright and her disabled son suffered a gross invasion of their privacy when they were strip-searched before visiting another son in prison. The common law in this country is powerless to protect them. As they suffered at the hands of a public authority, the Human Rights Act would have given them a remedy if it had been in force at the time, but it was not. That case indicates that our law cannot, even if it wanted to, develop a general tort of invasion of privacy. But where existing remedies are available, the court not only can but must balance the competing Convention rights of the parties.

134. This begs the question of how far the Convention balancing exercise is premissed on the scope of the existing cause of action. Clearly outside its scope is the sort of intrusion into what ought to be private which took place in *Wainwright*. Inside its scope is what has been termed the protection of the individual's 'informational autonomy' by prohibiting the publication of confidential information. How does the scope of the action for breach of confidence accommodate the Article 8 rights of individuals? As Randerson J summed it up in *Hosking v Runting* [2003] 3 NZLR 385, 403, para 83 at p 403:

> [The English courts] have chosen to develop the claim for breach of confidence on a case by case basis. In doing so, it has been recognised that no pre-existing relationship is required in order to establish a cause of action and that an obligation of confidence may arise from the nature of the material or may be inferred from the circumstances in which it has been obtained.

The position we have reached is that the exercise of balancing article 8 and article 10 may begin when the person publishing the information knows or ought to know that there is a reasonable expectation that the information in question will be kept confidential. . . .

137. It should be emphasised that the 'reasonable expectation of privacy' is a threshold test which brings the balancing exercise into play. It is not the end of the story. Once the information is identified as 'private' in this way, the court must balance the claimant's interest in keeping the information private against the countervailing interest of the recipient in publishing it. Very often, it can be expected that the countervailing rights of the recipient will prevail.

138. The parties agree that neither right takes precedence over the other. This is consistent with Resolution 1165 (1998) of the Parliamentary Assembly of the Council of Europe, para 10:

> The Assembly reaffirms the importance of everyone's right to privacy, and of the right to freedom of expression, as fundamental to a democratic society. These rights are neither absolute nor in any hierarchical order, since they are of equal value.

139. Each right has the same structure. Article 8(1) states that 'everyone has the right to respect for his private and family life, his home and his correspondence'. Article 10(1) states that 'Everyone has the right to freedom of expression. This right shall include freedom to hold opinions and to receive and impart information and ideas without interference by public authorities and regardless of frontiers. . . .' Unlike the article 8 right, however, it is accepted in article 10(2) that the exercise of this right 'carries with it duties and responsibilities.' Both rights are qualified. They may respectively be interfered with or restricted provided that three conditions are fulfilled:

(a) The interference or restriction must be 'in accordance with the law'; it must have a basis in national law which conforms to the Convention standards of legality.

(b) It must pursue one of the legitimate aims set out in each article. Article 8(2) provides for 'the protection of the rights and freedoms of others'. Article 10(2) provides for 'the protection of the reputation or rights of others' and for 'preventing the disclosure of information received in confidence'. The rights referred to may either be rights protected under the national law or, as in this case, other Convention rights.

(c) Above all, the interference or restriction must be 'necessary in a democratic society'; it must meet a 'pressing social need' and be no greater than is proportionate to the legitimate aim pursued; the reasons given for it must be both 'relevant' and 'sufficient' for this purpose.

140. The application of the proportionality test is more straightforward when only one Convention right is in play: the question then is whether the private right claimed offers sufficient justification for the degree of interference with the fundamental right. It is much less straightforward when two Convention rights are in play, and the proportionality of interfering with one has to be balanced against the proportionality of restricting the other. As each is a fundamental right, there is evidently a 'pressing social need' to protect it. The Convention jurisprudence offers us little help with this. The European Court of Human Rights has been concerned with whether the state's interference with privacy (as, for example, in *Z v Finland* (1997) 25 EHRR 371) or a restriction on freedom of expression (as, for example, in *Jersild v Denmark* (1994) 19 EHRR 1, *Fressoz and Roire v France* (2001) 31 EHRR 2, and *Tammer v Estonia* (2001) 37 EHRR 857) could be justified in the particular case. In the national court, the problem of balancing two rights of equal importance arises most acutely in the context of disputes between private persons.

141. Both parties accepted the basic approach of the Court of Appeal in *In re S* [2003] 3 WLR 1425, 1451–2, at paras 54–60. This involves looking first at the comparative importance of the actual rights being claimed in the individual case; then at the justifications for interfering with or restricting each of those rights; and applying the proportionality test to each. The parties in this case differed about whether the trial judge or the Court of Appeal had done this, the appellant arguing that the Court of Appeal had assumed primacy for the Article 10 right while the respondent argued that the trial judge had assumed primacy for the Article 8 right.

Notes

1. As to the balancing of the interests it was generally agreed that the newspaper could publish the fact that the claimant had taken drugs, but there was a difference of opinion concerning the information about the *treatment* and the publication of the photographs. On the latter issue Baroness Hale said, 'But here the accompanying text made it plain that these photographs were different. They showed her coming either to or from the NA meeting. They showed her in the company of others, some of whom were undoubtedly part of the group. They showed the place where the meeting was taking place, which will have been entirely recognisable to anyone who knew the locality. A picture is "worth a thousand words" because it adds to the impact of what the words convey; but it also adds to the information given in those words. If nothing else, it tells the reader what everyone looked like; in this case it also told the reader what the place looked like. In context, it also added to the potential harm, by making her think that she was being followed or betrayed, and deterring her from going back to the same place again' (at [155]).

2. This case takes a fairly conservative line on the role of the HRA, declaring that it has no direct effect and thus does not itself create a right of action, although the ECHR will 'inform' the issue of what is to be regarded as private and how confidentiality and freedom of speech are to be balanced. For a more radical view on the role of the ECHR, see *McKennitt* v *Ash* [2007] 2 WLR 194 (discussed later in this section).

3. In *Douglas* v *Hello! Ltd (No 3)* [2005] EWCA Civ 595, Michael Douglas and Catherine Zeta-Jones contracted with *OK!* magazine (for £1 million) for the exclusive rights to photographs of their wedding in New York. Guests were told that no photographs were to be taken. The wedding reception was infiltrated by a paparazzo who sold six photographs (for £125,000) to *Hello!* magazine. It was assumed that *Hello!* must have known of the arrangement with *OK!* At first instance (*Douglas* v *Hello!* [2003] 3 All ER 996) the defendants were held liable and the claimants were awarded damages of £3,750 each for personal distress.

   In the Court of Appeal the claimants held on to their claim for liability but lost their appeal on damages. The result seems to be as follows.

   (a) Photographs of the wedding fell within the protection of the law of confidentiality as now extended to cover private or personal information. On the relevance of the ECHR Lord Phillips MR said: 'We conclude that, in so far as private information is concerned, we are required to adopt, as the vehicle for performing such duty as falls on the courts in relation to Convention rights, the cause of action formerly described as breach of confidence. As to the nature of that duty, it seems to us that sections 2, 3, 6 and 12 of the Human Rights Act all point in the same direction. The court should, insofar as it can, develop the action for breach of confidence in such a manner as will give effect to both Article 8 and Article 10 rights. In considering the nature of those rights, account should be taken of the Strasbourg jurisprudence. In particular, when considering what information should be protected as private pursuant to Article 8, it is right to have regard to the decisions of the ECtHR' (at [53]). There was no appeal from the award of £3,750 for distress, but the court said that even though the damages were low the claimants should have been granted an interlocutory injunction to prevent publication.

   (b) The Douglases' commercial rights were infringed. Lord Phillips said: 'Where an individual ("the owner") has at his disposal information which he has created or which is private or personal and to which he can properly deny access to third parties, and he reasonably intends to profit commercially by using or publishing that information, then a third party who is, or ought to be, aware of these matters and who has knowingly obtained the information without authority, will be in breach of duty if he uses or publishes the information to the detriment of the owner' (at [118]). However, the court rejected the idea that damages should be based on a notional licence fee—that is, what the claimants might have charged *Hello!* to use the photographs.

   The Douglases were not parties to the appeal to the House of Lords ([2007] UKHL 21), where *OK!* successfully claimed breach of confidence and gained damages of £1,026,706 from *Hello!*

4. Both **Campbell** and *Douglas* are important as they consolidated (the then) recent developments of this equitable principle. The essential point is that the wrong will protect 'personal information', but it is difficult to decide when a person has a 'reasonable expectation' of privacy. Why, for example, could the press disclose that Naomi Campbell was a drug addict but not that she was being treated by Narcotics Anonymous? How are pictures different from other forms of information?

5. In *Prince of Wales v Associated Newspapers* [2006] EWCA Civ 1776, the Court of Appeal agreed that publication of the prince's journal detailing a visit to Hong Kong was a breach of confidence and would have been so even if the source had not been an employee of the prince, for example if the journal had been found in the street. The court repeated its view in *Douglas v Hello! (No 3)* [2005] EWCA Civ 595 that information is confidential if 'it is available to one person (or a group of persons) and not generally available to others, provided that the person (or group) who possesses the information does not intend that it shall become available to others' and that 'it must include information that is personal to the person who possesses it and that he does not intend shall be imparted to the general public. The nature of the information, or the form in which it is kept, may suffice to make it plain that the information satisfies these criteria' (at [33]). The court viewed this as compatible with the principle in **Campbell** that the question was whether a person had a reasonable expectation of privacy.

6. Costs are a serious problem in defamation and privacy cases. The risk of having to pay huge costs can have a 'chilling' effect and inhibit a person from saying what they are entitled to, and thus can act as a bar to freedom of speech. On the other hand, conditional fee agreements (CFAs) (no win, no fee) are a means by which the impecunious may pursue the protection of their reputation. Campbell's claimed costs from the defendants amounted to £1,086,295. The defendants failed in their claim before the House of Lords (*Campbell v MGN (No 2)* [2005] UKHL 61) that they should not have to pay the 'success fee' of the appeal to the House which was conducted under a CFA (this was £279,981 and almost doubled the actual cost). They argued that the threat of large fees was contrary to their freedom of expression under Article 10 ECHR, but this was rejected. Nevertheless, Lord Hoffmann did say that finding ways of moderating costs would be in the interests of all and that legislation may be necessary to find a way of complying with Article 10. In *MGN Ltd v UK* (Application no 39401/04) [2011] ECHR 66, the European Court of Human Rights upheld MGN's claim. (Note: Lord Justice Jackson's *Review of Civil Litigation Costs: Final Report* (TSO, 2010) abolished recoverable success fees in CFAs.)

7. In relation to the 'phone-hacking' scandal at the *Mirror* newspapers, Mann J awarded damages to multiple affected claimants in *8 Representative Claimants and others v MGN Ltd* [2016] EWHC 855 (Ch), also finding that the regime permitting the recovery of success fees attached to CFAs is not incompatible with freedom of expression (see also *Miller v Associated Newspapers* [2016] EWHC 397 (QB)). The defendants were given permission to 'leapfrog' the Court of Appeal and have their appeal heard by the Supreme Court alongside that in *Flood v Times Newspapers* [2014] EWCA Civ 1574 (a defamation case raising similar costs issues) in January 2017. In April 2017 the Supreme Court unanimously dismissed all three appeals (*Times Newspapers Ltd and others v Flood and others* [2017] UKSC 33).

Von Hannover v Germany

European Court of Human Rights (Application no 59320/00) (2005) 40 EHRR 1

Princess Caroline of Monaco complained of the publication of photographs of her in her daily life, albeit in public places, such as when out walking or leaving a restaurant. The German courts had refused a remedy on the grounds of freedom of the press and the public interest in knowing how she behaved outside her official functions. The European Court of Human Rights, however, found a violation of Article 8.

THE COURT:

56. In the present case the applicant did not complain of an action by the State, but rather of the lack of adequate State protection of her private life and her image.

57. The Court reiterates that although the object of Article 8 is essentially that of protecting the individual against arbitrary interference by the public authorities, it does not merely compel the State to abstain from such interference: in addition to this primarily negative undertaking, there may be positive obligations inherent in an effective respect for private or family life. These obligations may involve the adoption of measures designed to secure respect for private life even in the sphere of the relations of individuals between themselves . . . That also applies to the protection of a person's picture against abuse by others.

The boundary between the State's positive and negative obligations under this provision does not lend itself to precise definition. The applicable principles are, nonetheless, similar. In both contexts regard must be had to the fair balance that has to be struck between the competing interests of the individual and of the community as a whole; and in both contexts the State enjoys a certain margin of appreciation . . .

58. That protection of private life has to be balanced against the freedom of expression guaranteed by Article 10 of the Convention. In that context the Court reiterates that the freedom of expression constitutes one of the essential foundations of a democratic society. Subject to paragraph 2 of Article 10, it is applicable not only to 'information' or 'ideas' that are favourably received or regarded as inoffensive or as a matter of indifference, but also to those that offend, shock or disturb. Such are the demands of that pluralism, tolerance and broadmindedness without which there is no 'democratic society' . . .

In that connection the press plays an essential role in a democratic society. Although it must not overstep certain bounds, in particular in respect of the reputation and rights of others, its duty is nevertheless to impart—in a manner consistent with its obligations and responsibilities—information and ideas on all matters of public interest . . . Journalistic freedom also covers possible recourse to a degree of exaggeration, or even provocation . . .

59. Although freedom of expression also extends to the publication of photos, this is an area in which the protection of the rights and reputation of others takes on particular importance. The present case does not concern the dissemination of 'ideas', but of images containing very personal or even intimate 'information' about an individual. Furthermore, photos appearing in the tabloid press are often taken in a climate of continual harassment which induces in the person concerned a very strong sense of intrusion into their private life or even of persecution.

60. In the cases in which the Court has had to balance the protection of private life against the freedom of expression it has always stressed the contribution made by photos or articles in the press to a debate of general interest . . .

c. Application of these general principles by the Court

61. The Court points out at the outset that in the present case the photos of the applicant in the various German magazines show her in scenes from her daily life, thus engaged in activities of a purely private nature such as practising sport, out walking, leaving a restaurant or on holiday. The photos, in which the applicant appears sometimes alone and sometimes in company, illustrate a series of articles with such anodyne titles as 'Pure happiness', 'Caroline . . . a woman returning to life', 'Out and about with Princess Caroline in Paris' and 'The kiss. Or: they are not hiding anymore . . .'. . . .

62. The Court also notes that the applicant, as a member of the Prince of Monaco's family, represents the ruling family at certain cultural or charitable events. However, she does not exercise any function within or on behalf of the State of Monaco or one of its institutions . . .

63. The Court considers that a fundamental distinction needs to be made between reporting facts—even controversial ones—capable of contributing to a debate in a democratic society relating to politicians in the exercise of their functions, for example, and reporting details of the private life of an individual who, moreover, as in this case, does not exercise official functions. While in the former case the press exercises its vital role of 'watchdog' in a democracy by contributing to 'impart[ing] information and ideas on matters of public interest' it does not do so in the latter case.

64. Similarly, although the public has a right to be informed, which is an essential right in a democratic society that, in certain special circumstances, can even extend to aspects of the private life of public figures, particularly where politicians are concerned, this is not the case here. The situation here does not come within the sphere of any political or public debate because the published photos and accompanying commentaries relate exclusively to details of the applicant's private life.

65. As in other similar cases it has examined, the Court considers that the publication of the photos and articles in question, of which the sole purpose was to satisfy the curiosity of a particular readership regarding the details of the applicant's private life, cannot be deemed to contribute to any debate of general interest to society despite the applicant being known to the public . . .

66. In these conditions freedom of expression calls for a narrower interpretation . . .

67. In that connection the Court also takes account of the resolution of the Parliamentary Assembly of the Council of Europe on the right to privacy, which stresses the 'one-sided interpretation of the right to freedom of expression' by certain media which attempt to justify an infringement of the rights protected by Article 8 of the Convention by claiming that 'their readers are entitled to know everything about public figures' . . .

68. The Court finds another point to be of importance: even though, strictly speaking, the present application concerns only the publication of the photos and articles by various German magazines, the context in which these photos were taken—without the applicant's knowledge or consent—and the harassment endured by many public figures in their daily lives cannot be fully disregarded . . .

In the present case this point is illustrated in particularly striking fashion by the photos taken of the applicant at the Monte Carlo Beach Club tripping over an obstacle and falling down . . . It appears that these photos were taken secretly at a distance of several hundred metres, probably from a neighbouring house, whereas journalists and photographers' access to the club was strictly regulated . . .

69. The Court reiterates the fundamental importance of protecting private life from the point of view of the development of every human being's personality. That protection—as stated above—extends beyond the private family circle and also includes a social dimension. The Court considers that anyone, even if they are known to the general public, must be able to enjoy a 'legitimate expectation' of protection of and respect for their private life . . .

70. Furthermore, increased vigilance in protecting private life is necessary to contend with new communication technologies which make it possible to store and reproduce personal data . . . This also applies to the systematic taking of specific photos and their dissemination to a broad section of the public.

71. Lastly, the Court reiterates that the Convention is intended to guarantee not rights that are theoretical or illusory but rights that are practical and effective . . .

72. The Court has difficulty in agreeing with the domestic courts' interpretation of section 23(1) of the Copyright (Arts Domain) Act, which consists in describing a person as such as a figure of contemporary society '*par excellence*'. Since that definition affords the person very limited protection of their private life or the right to control the use of their image, it could conceivably be appropriate for politicians exercising official functions. However, it cannot be justified for a 'private' individual, such as the applicant, in whom the interest of the general public and the press is based solely on her membership of a reigning family whereas she herself does not exercise any official functions.

In any event the Court considers that, in these conditions, the Act has to be interpreted narrowly to ensure that the State complies with its positive obligation under the Convention to protect private life and the right to control the use of one's image.

73. Lastly, the distinction drawn between figures of contemporary society '*par excellence*' and 'relatively' public figures has to be clear and obvious so that, in a state governed by the rule of law, the individual has precise indications as to the behaviour he or she should adopt. Above all, they need to know exactly when and where they are in a protected sphere or, on the contrary, in a sphere in which they must expect interference from others, especially the tabloid press.

74. The Court therefore considers that the criteria on which the domestic courts based their decisions were not sufficient to protect the applicant's private life effectively. As a figure of contemporary society '*par excellence*' she cannot—in the name of freedom of the press and the public interest—rely on protection of her private life unless she is in a secluded place out of the public eye and, moreover, succeeds in proving it (which can be difficult). Where that is not the case, she has to accept that she might be photographed at almost any time, systematically, and that the photos are then very widely disseminated even if, as was the case here, the photos and accompanying articles relate exclusively to details of her private life.

75. In the Court's view, the criterion of spatial isolation, although apposite in theory, is in reality too vague and difficult for the person concerned to determine in advance. In the present case merely classifying the applicant as a figure of contemporary society '*par excellence*' does not suffice to justify such an intrusion into her private life.

d. Conclusion

76. As the Court has stated above, it considers that the decisive factor in balancing the protection of private life against freedom of expression should lie in the contribution that the published photos and articles make to a debate of general interest. It is clear in the instant case that they made no such contribution since the applicant exercises no official function and the photos and articles related exclusively to details of her private life.

77. Furthermore, the Court considers that the public does not have a legitimate interest in knowing where the applicant is and how she behaves generally in her private life even if she appears in places that cannot always be described as secluded and despite the fact that she is well known to the public.

Even if such a public interest exists, as does a commercial interest of the magazines in publishing these photos and these articles, in the instant case those interests must, in the Court's view, yield to the applicant's right to the effective protection of her private life.

78. Lastly, in the Court's opinion the criteria established by the domestic courts were not sufficient to ensure the effective protection of the applicant's private life and she should, in the circumstances of the case, have had a 'legitimate expectation' of protection of her private life.

79. Having regard to all the foregoing factors, and despite the margin of appreciation afforded to the State in this area, the Court considers that the German courts did not strike a fair balance between the competing interests.

80. There has therefore been a breach of Article 8 of the Convention.

Notes

1. This decision is fairly restrictive as it seems to take the view that freedom of expression would normally be limited to the role of the press as a 'watchdog' in protecting the public interest (at [63]). The Court noted that the princess did not exercise any official function on behalf of Monaco and that details of her daily life contributed nothing to debates of general interest to society despite her being a public figure. However, in a concurring opinion, Judge Cabral Barreto said that 'the applicant is a public figure and the public does have a right to be informed about her life' (at [1]) and that the test is whether a person has a 'legitimate expectation' of being safe from media intrusion. Perhaps the answer is that those who seek publicity can only expect limited protection and cannot always choose the nature of that publicity, but a person who has no official position and who seeks privacy will be better protected at least in relation to places and functions where they would not expect to be exposed to the press.

2. Princess Caroline was awarded £7,000 against the German Government for its failure to protect her interests.

3. In *Wood v Commissioner of Police of the Metropolis* [2009] EWCA Civ 414, the police photographed the claimant (a protestor) in the street after he had attended a meeting of a company indirectly involved in the arms trade. There was no disturbance at the meeting and the claimant had never been arrested for his campaigning activities. The Court of Appeal held that the taking of the photographs violated Article 8. Laws LJ said that the mere act of taking a photograph of a person in a public place would not violate Article 8, but that the *retention* of photographs by a state authority would, because the police action was:

   > unexplained at the time it happened and carrying as it did the implication that the images would be kept and used, is a sufficient intrusion by the state into the individual's own space, his integrity, as to amount to a prima facie violation of Article 8(1). It attains a sufficient level of seriousness and in the circumstances the claimant enjoyed a reasonable expectation that his privacy would not be thus invaded. (at [46])

   The majority (Laws LJ dissenting) held that the action of the police could not be justified under Article 8(2).

Murray v Big Pictures (UK) Ltd
Court of Appeal [2008] EWCA Civ 446 (*sub nom Murray v Express Newspapers*)

The claimant was David Murray, the 19-month-old son of Dr and Mrs Murray (otherwise known as JK Rowling, the author of the *Harry Potter* books). Covert photographs were taken of the family walking from their flat to a local café. Mrs Murray was shown alongside the buggy. David's face in profile was visible, as were the clothes he was wearing, his size, the style and colour of his hair and the colour of his skin. This picture was subsequently published in the *Sunday Express*. Held: David's privacy action should not have been struck out: he had a reasonable expectation of privacy.

SIR ANTHONY CLARKE MR:
24. The principles stated by Lord Nicholls [in *Campbell*] can we think be summarised in this way:
    (i) The right to freedom of expression enshrined in article 10 of the Convention and the right to respect for a person's privacy enshrined in article 8 are vitally important rights. Both lie at the heart of liberty in a modern state and neither has precedence over the other: see [12].
    (ii) Although the origin of the cause of action relied upon is breach of confidence, since information about an individual's private life would not, in ordinary usage, be called 'confidential', the more natural description of the position today is that such information is private and the essence of the tort is better encapsulated now as misuse of private information: see [14].

(iii) The values enshrined in articles 8 and 10 are now part of the cause of action and should be treated as of general application and as being as much applicable to disputes between individuals as to disputes between individuals and a public authority: see [17].

(iv) Essentially the touchstone of private life is whether in respect of the disclosed facts the person in question had a reasonable expectation of privacy: see [21].

(v) In deciding whether there is in principle an invasion of privacy, it is important to distinguish between that question, which seems to us to be the question which is often described as whether article 8 is engaged, and the subsequent question whether, if it is, the individual's rights are nevertheless not infringed because of the combined effect of article 8(2) and article 10: see [22]. . . .

35. In these circumstances, so far as the relevant principles to be derived from *Campbell* are concerned, they can we think be summarised in this way. The first question is whether there is a reasonable expectation of privacy. This is of course an objective question. The nature of the question was discussed in *Campbell*. Lord Hope emphasised that the reasonable expectation was that of the person who is affected by the publicity. He said at [99]:

> The question is what a reasonable person of ordinary sensibilities would feel if she was placed in the same position as the claimant and faced with the same publicity.

We do not detect any difference between Lord Hope's opinion in this regard and the opinions expressed by the other members of the appellate committee.

36. As we see it, the question whether there is a reasonable expectation of privacy is a broad one, which takes account of all the circumstances of the case. They include the attributes of the claimant, the nature of the activity in which the claimant was engaged, the place at which it was happening, the nature and purpose of the intrusion, the absence of consent and whether it was known or could be inferred, the effect on the claimant and the circumstances in which and the purposes for which the information came into the hands of the publisher.

37. In the case of a child the position is somewhat different from that of an adult. The judge recognised this in [23] of his judgment, where he said this, albeit in the context of a somewhat differently formulated test discussed by Lord Hope at [100] in *Campbell*:

> This test cannot, of course, be applied to a child of the Claimant's age who has no obvious sensitivity to any invasion of his privacy which does not involve some direct physical intrusion into his personal space. A literal application of Lord Hope's words would lead to a rejection of any claim by an infant unless it related to harassment of an extreme kind. A proper consideration of the degree of protection to which a child is entitled under Art. 8 has, I think, for the reasons which I gave earlier to be considered in a wider context by taking into account not only the circumstances in which the photograph was taken and its actual impact on the child, but also the position of the child's parents and the way in which the child's life as part of that family has been conducted. This merely reinforces my view about the artificiality of bringing the claim in the name of the child. The question whether a child in any particular circumstances has a reasonable expectation for privacy must be determined by the Court taking an objective view of the matter including the reasonable expectations of his parents in those same circumstances as to whether their children's lives in a public place should remain private. Ultimately it will be a matter of judgment for the Court with every case depending upon its own facts. The point that needs to be emphasized is that the assessment of the impact of the taking and the subsequent publication of the photograph on the child cannot be limited by whether the child was physically aware of the photograph being taken or published or personally affected by it. The Court can attribute to the child reasonable expectations about his private life based on matters such as how it has in fact been conducted by those responsible for his welfare and upbringing.

38. Subject to the point we made earlier that we do not share the judge's view that the proceedings are artificial, we agree with the approach suggested by the judge in that paragraph. Thus, for example, if the parents of a child courted publicity by procuring the publication of photographs of the child in order to promote their own interests, the position would or might be quite different from a case like this, where the parents have taken care to keep their children out of the public gaze.

39. As applied in this case, which, unlike *McKennitt v Ash*, is not a case in which there was a pre-existing relationship between the parties, the first question at any trial of the action would be whether article 8 was in principle engaged; that is whether David had a reasonable expectation of privacy in the sense that a reasonable person in his position would feel that the Photograph should not be published. On Lord Nicholls' analysis, that is a lower test than would be involved if the question were whether a reasonable person in his position would regard publication as either offensive or highly offensive. That question would or might be relevant at the second, balancing stage, assuming article 8 to be engaged on the footing that David had a reasonable expectation that commercial picture agencies like BPL would not set out to photograph him with a view to selling those photographs for money without his consent, which would of course have to be given through his parents.

40. At a trial, if the answer to the first question were yes, the next question would be how the balance should be struck as between the individual's right to privacy on the one hand and the publisher's right to publish on the other. If the balance were struck in favour of the individual, publication would be an infringement of his or her article 8 rights, whereas if the balance were struck in favour of the publisher, there would be no such infringement by reason of a combination of articles 8(2) and 10 of the Convention.

41. At each stage, the questions to be determined are essentially questions of fact. The question whether there was a reasonable expectation [of] privacy is a question of fact. If there was, the next question involves determining the relevant factors and balancing them. As Baroness Hale put it at [157], the weight to be attached to the various considerations is a matter of fact and degree. That is essentially a matter for the trial judge.

57. It seems to us that, subject to the facts of the particular case, the law should indeed protect children from intrusive media attention, at any rate to the extent of holding that a child has a reasonable expectation that he or she will not be targeted in order to obtain photographs in a public place for publication which the person who took or procured the taking of the photographs knew would be objected to on behalf of the child. That is the context in which the photographs of David were taken.

58. It is important to note that so to hold does not mean that the child will have, as the judge puts it in [66], a guarantee of privacy. To hold that the child has a reasonable expectation of privacy is only the first step. Then comes the balance which must be struck between the child's rights to respect for his or her private life under article 8 and the publisher's rights to freedom of expression under article 10. This approach does not seem to us to be inconsistent with that in *Campbell*, which was not considering the case of a child.

Notes

1. The Court of Appeal stressed that the appeal was being brought on behalf of David and *not* his parents: 'We do not think that the reality is that the parents seek through their son to establish a right to personal privacy for themselves and their children when engaged in ordinary family activities. The positions of parents on the one hand and children on the other hand are distinct' (at [14]). This suggests that had JK Rowling herself been claiming, she would have been unsuccessful.

2. It is generally accepted that one should be very wary of portraying children in the media, and often when such pictures are published the face is pixelated to prevent identity. Would this picture have been acceptable if the child's face had been obscured, or would that have been just as problematic as it would be obvious who the child was? The Independent Press Standards Organisation (IPSO) Editors' Code states that 'Editors must not use the fame, notoriety or position of the parent or guardian as sole justification for publishing details of a child's private life' (at 6(v)). However, the Code also indicates that the mere publication of a child's image cannot breach the Code when it is taken in a public place and is unaccompanied by any private details or materials which might embarrass or inconvenience the child. This may have been based on the view in **Campbell** that there would have been no action if the photograph had simply depicted Campbell on a more banal errand such as a shopping trip (see Baroness Hale at [154]). In its section on whether the 'Public Interest' may justify publishing the information, para 5 states that in 'cases involving children under 16, editors must demonstrate an exceptional public interest to over-ride the normally paramount interests of the child'.

3. On the 'reasonable expectation of privacy' question, the issue must be looked at from the point of view of the child for it is *their* expectations that are considered. One question is whether similar photographs would be taken and published if the subject is the child of 'ordinary' parents. Thus, presumably, the inclusion of a picture of a child in a general street scene would not be actionable, but it was noted that in **Murray** the child was 'targeted' for particular reasons. It was also noted that the situation might be different if the parents courted publicity by arranging for the publication of photographs of the child in order to promote their own interests.

4. Though children do not have an inalienable right to privacy, *ETK v Newsgroup Newspapers* [2011] EWCA Civ 439 confirmed that courts should give particular weight to the Article 8 rights of children likely to be affected by a publication. Recent cases show that decisions about photographs of children can go either way: compare, for example, *AAA v Associated Newspapers* [2013] EWCA Civ 554 and *Weller and others* v *Associated Newspapers Ltd* [2015] EWCA Civ 1176. On 'non-celebrity' children, see *Bull v Desporte* [2019] EWHC 1650 (QB).

5. The impact of an invasion of adults' privacy *on* their children may also be a factor taken into account in a case (*ETK v Newsgroup Newspapers*). In reinstating an injunction temporarily overturned by a Court of Appeal decision, in a case brought about by a celebrity's extramarital sexual activities, the Supreme Court in *PJS v News Group Newspapers Ltd* [2016] UKSC 26 found that the Court of Appeal had not adequately considered the impact that the publication of the information would have on the children of the celebrity concerned.

Mosley v News Group Newspapers
Queen's Bench Division [2008] EWHC 1777 (QB)

The *News of the World* published an article about the claimant—then president of the Fédération Internationale de l'Automobile (FIA), and thus responsible for F1 motor racing—under the headline 'F1 boss has sick Nazi orgy with five hookers'. The article described, alongside covertly taken photographs, the claimant's participation in sadomasochistic activities with a number of women, all of whom consented to what happened. Held: the claimant was awarded damages of £60,000 for breach of privacy.

EADY J:

The 'new methodology'

7. Although the law of 'old-fashioned breach of confidence' has been well established for many years, and derives historically from equitable principles, these have been extended in recent years under the stimulus of the Human Rights Act 1998 and the content of the Convention itself. The law now

affords protection to information in respect of which there is a reasonable expectation of privacy, even in circumstances where there is no pre-existing relationship giving rise of itself to an enforceable duty of confidence. That is because the law is concerned to prevent the violation of a citizen's autonomy, dignity and self-esteem. It is not simply a matter of 'unaccountable' judges running amok. Parliament enacted the 1998 statute which requires these values to be acknowledged and enforced by the courts. In any event, the courts had been increasingly taking them into account because of the need to interpret domestic law consistently with the United Kingdom's international obligations. It will be recalled that the United Kingdom government signed up to the Convention more than 50 years ago.

10. . . . If the first hurdle can be overcome, by demonstrating a reasonable expectation of privacy, it is now clear that the court is required to carry out the next step of weighing the relevant competing Convention rights in the light of an 'intense focus' upon the individual facts of the case: see eg *Campbell* and *Re S (A Child)* [2005] 1 AC 593. It was expressly recognised that no one Convention right takes automatic precedence over another. In the present context, for example, it has to be accepted that any rights of free expression, as protected by Article 10, whether on the part of Woman E or the journalists working for the *News of the World*, must no longer be regarded as simply 'trumping' any privacy rights that may be established on the part of the Claimant. Language of that kind is no longer used. Nor can it be said, without qualification, that there is a 'public interest that the truth should out': cf. *Fraser v Evans* [1969] 1 QB 349, 360F–G, per Lord Denning MR.

11. In order to determine which should take precedence, in the particular circumstances, it is necessary to examine the facts closely as revealed in the evidence at trial and to decide whether (assuming a reasonable expectation of privacy to have been established) some countervailing consideration of public interest may be said to justify any intrusion which has taken place. This is integral to what has been called 'the new methodology': *Re S (A Child)* at [23].

12. This modern approach of applying an 'intense focus' is thus obviously incompatible with making broad generalisations of the kind to which the media often resorted in the past such as, for example, 'Public figures must expect to have less privacy' or 'People in positions of responsibility must be seen as "role models" and set us all an example of how to live upstanding lives'. Sometimes factors of this kind may have a legitimate role to play when the 'ultimate balancing exercise' comes to be carried out, but generalisations can never be determinative. In every case 'it all depends' (ie upon what is revealed by the intense focus on the individual circumstances).

14. . . . This 'ultimate balancing test' has been recognised as turning to a large extent upon proportionality: see eg Sedley LJ in *Douglas v Hello! Ltd* [2001] QB 967 at [137]. The judge will often have to ask whether the intrusion, or perhaps the degree of the intrusion, into the claimant's privacy was proportionate to the public interest supposedly being served by it.

15. One of the more striking developments over the last few years of judicial analysis, both here and in Strasbourg, is the acknowledgment that the balancing process which has to be carried out by individual judges on the facts before them necessarily involves an evaluation of the use to which the relevant defendant has put, or intends to put, his or her right to freedom of expression. That is inevitable when one is weighing up the relative worth of one person's rights against those of another. It has been accepted, for example, in the House of Lords that generally speaking 'political speech' would be accorded greater value than gossip or 'tittle tattle': see eg *Campbell* at [148] and also *Jameel (Mohammed) v Wall Street Journal Europe Sprl* [2007] 1 AC 359 at [147].

Was there a reasonable expectation of privacy or a duty of confidence?

98. In deciding whether there was at stage one a reasonable expectation of privacy generalisations are perhaps best avoided, just as at stage two, and the question must be addressed in the light of all the circumstances of the particular case: see eg *Murray v Big Pictures* [2008] EWCA Civ

446 at [35]–[39]. Nevertheless, one is usually on safe ground in concluding that anyone indulging in sexual activity is entitled to a degree of privacy—especially if it is on private property and between consenting adults (paid or unpaid).

99. There is now a considerable body of jurisprudence in Strasbourg and elsewhere which recognises that sexual activity engages the rights protected by Article 8. As was noted long ago in *Dudgeon v UK* (1981) 4 EHRR 149, there must exist particularly serious reasons before interferences on the part of public authorities can be legitimate for the purposes of Article 8(2) because sexual behaviour 'concerns a most intimate aspect of private life'. That case concerned the criminal law in the context of buggery and gross indecency (in Northern Ireland). It was said at [60] that Article 8 rights protect in this respect 'an essentially private materialisation of the human personality'.

100. There are many statements to similar effect, the more lofty of which do not necessarily withstand rigorous analysis. The precise meaning is not always apparent. Nevertheless, the underlying sentiments are readily understood in everyday language; namely, that people's sex lives are to be regarded as essentially their own business—provided at least that the participants are genuinely consenting adults and there is no question of exploiting the young or vulnerable.

104. . . . . In the light of these two strands of authority, it becomes fairly obvious that the clandestine recording of sexual activity on private property must be taken to engage Article 8. What requires closer examination is the extent to which such intrusive behaviour could be justified by reference to a countervailing public interest; that is to say, at the stage of carrying out the ultimate balancing test. I will focus on those arguments shortly.

Was there a public interest to justify the intrusion? My own conclusions

131. When the courts identify an infringement of a person's Article 8 rights, and in particular in the context of his freedom to conduct his sex life and personal relationships as he wishes, it is right to afford a remedy and to vindicate that right. The only permitted exception is where there is a countervailing public interest which in the particular circumstances is strong enough to outweigh it; that is to say, because one at least of the established 'limiting principles' comes into play. Was it necessary and proportionate for the intrusion to take place, for example, in order to expose illegal activity or to prevent the public from being significantly misled by public claims hitherto made by the individual concerned (as with Naomi Campbell's public denials of drug-taking)? Or was it necessary because the information, in the words of the Strasbourg court in *Von Hannover* at [60] and [76], would make a contribution to 'a debate of general interest'? That is, of course, a very high test. It is yet to be determined how far that doctrine will be taken in the courts of this jurisdiction in relation to photography in public places. If taken literally, it would mean a very significant change in what is permitted. It would have a profound effect on the tabloid and celebrity culture to which we have become accustomed in recent years.

132. The facts of this case are far removed from those in *Von Hannover*. There can be little doubt that intimate photographs or recording of private sexual activity, however unconventional, would be extremely difficult to justify at all by Strasbourg standards: see eg *Dudgeon v UK* (cited above) at [49]–[53]. It is those to which we are now required by the Human Rights Act to have regard. Obviously, titillation for its own sake could never be justified. Yet it is reasonable to suppose that it was this which led so many thousands of people to accept the *News of the World*'s invitation on 30 March to 'See the shocking video at notw.co.uk'. It would be quite unrealistic to think that these visits were prompted by a desire to participate in a 'debate of general interest' of the kind contemplated in *Von Hannover*.

133. More recently the principles have been affirmed in Strasbourg in the case of *Leempoel v Belgium*, App No 64772/01, 9 November 2006:

> In matters relating to striking a balance between protecting private life and the freedom of expression that the Court had had to rule upon, it has always emphasised . . . the requirement that the publication of information, documents or photographs in the press should serve the public interest and make a contribution to the debate of general interest . . . Whilst the right for the public to be informed, a fundamental right in a democratic society that under particular circumstances may even relate to aspects of the private life of public persons, particularly where political personalities are involved . . . publications whose sole aim is to satisfy the curiosity of a certain public as to the details of the private life of a person, whatever their fame, should not be regarded as contributing to any debate of general interest to society.

In the light of the strict criteria I am required to apply, in the modern climate, I could not hold that any of the visual images, whether published in the newspaper or on the website, can be justified in the public interest. Nor can it be said in this case that even the information conveyed in the verbal descriptions would qualify.

Notes

1. Eady J clearly wished to leave behind the equitable origins of breach of confidence and to establish 'the new methodology' on the basis of the ECHR. The difficulty in theory is that the Convention creates rights only between individuals and public bodies, but Article 8 ECHR seems to be treated rather differently from the other Articles and subsequent cases show that Eady J appears to have been right.

2. Eady J noted that had the 'Nazi theme' alleged by the *News of the World* been proved, the conclusion may have been different, as then there may have been a public interest in the publication. (The claimant, who died in 2021, was the son of Oswald Mosley, founder of the British Union of Fascists.)

3. Discussion about the nature of the claim in privacy is now less important since the explicit recognition of a *tort* of misuse of private information, first by Tugendhat J in *Vidal-Hall and others* v *Google Inc* [2014] EWHC 13 (QB) (at [70], echoing an expression first used by Lord Nicholls in **Campbell**) and later affirmed by the Court of Appeal (**Google Inc v Vidal-Hall and others** [2015]). This tort exists separately, and alongside, the equitable action for breach of confidence.

Google Inc v Vidal-Hall and others
Court of Appeal [2015] EWCA Civ 311

LORD DYSON MR AND LADY JUSTICE SHARP:

1. The appeal in this case raises two important issues of law. The first is whether the cause of action for misuse of private information is a tort, specifically for the purposes of the rules providing for service of proceedings out of the jurisdiction.

2. The claimants are three individuals who used Apple computers between the summer of 2011 and about 17 February 2012. Each of them accessed the internet using their Apple Safari browser.

3. The case concerns the operation of what has become known as the 'Safari workaround'. The essence of the complaint is that the defendant collected private information about the claimants'

internet usage via their Apple Safari browser (the Browser-Generated Information, or 'BGI') without the claimants' knowledge and consent, by using a small string of text saved on the user's device ('cookies'). This allowed the defendant to recognise the browser sending the BGI. The BGI was then aggregated and used by the defendant as part of its commercial offering to advertisers via its 'doubleclick' advertising service. This meant advertisers could select advertisements targeted or tailored to the claimants' interests, as deduced from the collected BGI, which could be and were displayed on the screens of the claimants' computer devices. This revealed private information about the claimants, which was or might have been seen by third parties. The tracking and collation of the claimants' BGI was contrary to the defendant's publicly stated position that such activity could not be conducted for Safari users unless they had expressly allowed it to happen.

4. The issue of classification or nomenclature has been the subject of some discussion in the cases, and amongst academics. So far as we are aware however—with the possible exception, on the defendant's case, of *Douglas v Hello! (No 3)*—this is the first case in which the 'classification' question has made a difference. Put shortly, if a claim for misuse of information is not a tort for the purposes of service out of the jurisdiction, but is classified as a claim for breach of confidence, then on the authority of *Kitechnology BV v Unicor*, which is binding on us, the claimants will not be able to serve their claims for misuse of private information on the defendant.

5. Although the issue as framed in this appeal in one sense is a narrow one, it is nonetheless appropriate to look at it in the broader context. Fifteen years have passed since the coming into force of the Human Rights Act 1998 (the HRA) in October 2000, which incorporates into our domestic law the European Convention for the Protection of Human Rights and Fundamental Freedoms (the Convention). And it is a decade now since the seminal decision of the House of Lords in *Campbell v MGN* [2004] 2 AC 457. The problem the courts have had to grapple with during this period has been how to afford appropriate protection to 'privacy rights' under article 8 of the Convention, in the absence (as was affirmed by the House of Lords in *Wainwright v Home Office* [2004] 2 AC 406) of a common law tort of invasion of privacy.

6. We were taken to a number of cases by Mr White to establish what is in fact an uncontroversial proposition—that the gap was bridged by developing and adapting the law of confidentiality to protect one aspect of invasion of privacy, the misuse of private information. This addressed the tension between the requirement to give appropriate effect to the right to respect for private and family life set out in article 8 of the Convention and the common law's perennial need (for the best of reasons, that of legal certainty) to appear not to be doing anything for the first time (to which Sedley LJ pointed in one of the earliest cases in which this issue was addressed: *Douglas v Hello! Limited* [2001] QB 967 (*Douglas v Hello (No 1)*) para 111).

7. Thus, in *A v B plc* [2003] QB 195 at para 4, Lord Woolf CJ, giving the judgment of the court, said that articles 8 and 10 of the Convention provided new parameters within which the courts would decide actions for breach of confidence, and that the court could act in a way that was compatible with Convention rights, as it was required to do under section 6 of the HRA 1998, by 'absorbing the rights which articles 8 and 10 protect into the long-established action for breach of confidence.'

8. However, a number of things need to be said. First, there are problems with an analysis which fails to distinguish between a breach of confidentiality and an infringement of privacy rights protected by article 8, not least because the concepts of confidence and privacy are not the same and protect different interests. Secondly, as has been consistently emphasised by the courts, we are concerned with a developing area of the law. Although the process may have started as one of 'absorption' (*per* Lord Woolf) it is clear that, contrary to the submissions of the defendant, there are now two separate and distinct causes of action: an action for breach of confidence; and one for misuse

of private information. Thirdly, it is also the case that the action for misuse of private information has been referred to as a tort by the courts.

9. . . . [W]e cannot find any satisfactory or principled answer to the question why misuse of private information should not be categorised as a tort for the purposes of service out of the jurisdiction. Misuse of private information is a civil wrong without any equitable characteristics. We do not need to attempt to define a tort here. But if one puts aside the circumstances of its 'birth', there is nothing in the nature of the claim itself to suggest that the more natural classification of it as a tort is wrong.

10. We come back then to the question we have to decide. Against the background we have described, and in the absence of any sound reasons of policy or principle to suggest otherwise, we have concluded in agreement with the judge that misuse of private information should now be recognised as a tort for the purposes of service out the jurisdiction. This does not create a new cause of action. In our view, it simply gives the correct legal label to one that already exists. We are conscious of the fact that there may be broader implications from our conclusions, for example as to remedies, limitation and vicarious liability, but these were not the subject of submissions, and such points will need to be considered as and when they arise.

> ### Mosley v UK
> European Court of Human Rights (Application no 48009/08) (2011) 53 EHRR 30

The late Max Mosley subsequently asked the European Court of Human Rights to affirm that the UK had failed to impose a legal duty on newspapers to notify victims in advance in order to allow them the opportunity to seek an interim injunction to prevent publication of material that amounted to a breach of privacy. The claim was rejected.

THE COURT:

105. The Court further notes that as far as the balancing act in the circumstances of the applicant's particular case was concerned, the domestic court firmly found in favour of his right to respect for private life and ordered the payment to the applicant of substantial monetary compensation. The assessment which the Court must undertake in the present proceedings relates not to the specific facts of the applicant's case but to the general framework for balancing rights of privacy and freedom of expression in the domestic legal order. The Court must therefore have regard to the general principles governing the application of Article 8 and Article 10, before examining whether there has been a violation of Article 8 as a result of the absence of a legally binding pre-notification requirement in the United Kingdom.

A. GENERAL PRINCIPLES

i. Article 8

106. It is clear that the words 'the right to respect for . . . private . . . life' which appear in Article 8 require not only that the State refrain from interfering with private life but also entail certain positive obligations on the State to ensure effective enjoyment of this right by those within its jurisdiction . . . Such an obligation may require the adoption of positive measures designed to secure effective respect for private life even in the sphere of the relations of individuals between themselves . . .

107. The Court emphasises the importance of a prudent approach to the State's positive obligations to protect private life in general and of the need to recognise the diversity of possible methods to secure its respect. The choice of measures designed to secure compliance with that obligation in

the sphere of the relations of individuals between themselves in principle falls within the Contracting States' margin of appreciation. . . .

108. The Court recalls that a number of factors must be taken into account when determining the breadth of the margin of appreciation to be accorded to the State in a case in which Article 8 of the Convention is engaged. First, the Court reiterates that the notion of 'respect' in Article 8 is not clear-cut, especially as far as the positive obligations inherent in that concept are concerned: bearing in mind the diversity of the practices followed and the situations obtaining in the Contracting States, the notion's requirements will vary considerably from case to case . . . Thus Contracting Parties enjoy a wide margin of appreciation in determining the steps to be taken to ensure compliance with the Convention . . . In this regard, the Court recalls that by reason of their direct and continuous contact with the vital forces of their countries, the State authorities are, in principle, in a better position than the international judge to give an opinion on how best to secure the right to respect for private life within the domestic legal order . . .

109. Second, the nature of the activities involved affects the scope of the margin of appreciation. The Court has previously noted that a serious interference with private life can arise where the state of domestic law conflicts with an important aspect of personal identity . . . Thus, in cases concerning Article 8, where a particularly important facet of an individual's existence or identity is at stake, the margin allowed to the State is correspondingly narrowed . . . The same is true where the activities at stake involve a most intimate aspect of private life . . .

110. Third, the existence or absence of a consensus across the Member States of the Council of Europe, either as to the relative importance of the interest at stake or as to the best means of protecting it, is also relevant to the extent of the margin of appreciation: where no consensus exists, the margin of appreciation afforded to States is generally a wide one . . . Similarly, any standards set out in applicable international instruments and reports are relevant to the interpretation of the guarantees of the Convention and in particular to the identification of any common European standard in the field . . .

111. Finally, in cases where measures which an applicant claims are required pursuant to positive obligations under Article 8 would have an impact on freedom of expression, regard must be had to the fair balance that has to be struck between the competing rights and interests arising under Article 8 and Article 10 . . .

ii. Article 10

112. The Court emphasises the pre-eminent role of the press in informing the public and imparting information and ideas on matters of public interest in a State governed by the rule of law . . . Not only does the press have the task of imparting such information and ideas but the public also has a right to receive them. Were it otherwise, the press would be unable to play its vital role of 'public watchdog' . . .

113. It is to be recalled that methods of objective and balanced reporting may vary considerably and that it is therefore not for this Court to substitute its own views for those of the press as to what technique of reporting should be adopted . . . However, editorial discretion is not unbounded. The press must not overstep the bounds set for, among other things, 'the protection of . . . the rights of others', including the requirements of acting in good faith and on an accurate factual basis and of providing 'reliable and precise' information in accordance with the ethics of journalism . . .

114. The Court also reiterates that there is a distinction to be drawn between reporting facts—even if controversial—capable of contributing to a debate of general public interest in a democratic society, and making tawdry allegations about an individual's private life . . . In respect of the former,

the pre-eminent role of the press in a democracy and its duty to act as a 'public watchdog' are important considerations in favour of a narrow construction of any limitations on freedom of expression. However, different considerations apply to press reports concentrating on sensational and, at times, lurid news, intended to titillate and entertain, which are aimed at satisfying the curiosity of a particular readership regarding aspects of a person's strictly private life . . . Such reporting does not attract the robust protection of Article 10 afforded to the press. As a consequence, in such cases, freedom of expression requires a more narrow interpretation . . . While confirming the Article 10 right of members of the public to have access to a wide range of publications covering a variety of fields, the Court stresses that in assessing in the context of a particular publication whether there is a public interest which justifies an interference with the right to respect for private life, the focus must be on whether the publication is in the interest of the public and not whether the public might be interested in reading it.

115. It is commonly acknowledged that the audiovisual media have often a much more immediate and powerful effect than the print media . . . Accordingly, although freedom of expression also extends to the publication of photographs, the Court recalls that this is an area in which the protection of the rights of others takes on particular importance, especially where the images contain very personal and intimate 'information' about an individual or where they are taken on private premises and clandestinely through the use of secret recording devices . . . Factors relevant to the assessment of where the balance between the competing interests lies include the additional contribution made by the publication of the photos to a debate of general interest as well as the content of the photographs . . .

116. The Court recalls that the nature and severity of any sanction imposed on the press in respect of a publication are relevant to any assessment of the proportionality of an interference with the right to freedom of expression . . . Thus the Court must exercise the utmost caution where measures taken or sanctions imposed by the national authorities are such as to dissuade the press from taking part in the discussion of matters of legitimate public concern . . .

117. Finally, the Court has emphasised that while Article 10 does not prohibit the imposition of prior restraints on publication, the dangers inherent in prior restraints are such that they call for the most careful scrutiny on the part of the Court. This is especially so as far as the press is concerned, for news is a perishable commodity and to delay its publication, even for a short period, may well deprive it of all its value and interest . . . The Court would, however, observe that prior restraints may be more readily justified in cases which demonstrate no pressing need for immediate publication and in which there is no obvious contribution to a debate of general public interest.

B. APPLICATION OF THE GENERAL PRINCIPLES TO THE FACTS OF THE CASE

118. As noted above (see paragraph 106), it is clear that a positive obligation arises under Article 8 in order to ensure the effective protection of the right to respect for private life. The question for consideration in the present case is whether the specific measure called for by the applicant, namely a legally binding pre-notification rule, is required in order to discharge that obligation.

119. The Court observes at the outset that this is not a case where there are no measures in place to ensure protection of Article 8 rights. A system of self-regulation of the press has been established in the United Kingdom, with guidance provided in the Editors' Code and Codebook and oversight of journalists' and editors' conduct by the PCC [now IPSO]. This system reflects the 1970 declaration, the 1998 resolution and the 2008 resolution of the Parliamentary Assembly of the Council of Europe (see paragraphs 55 and 58–59 above). While the PCC itself has no power to award damages, an individual may commence civil proceedings in respect of any alleged violation of the right to respect

for private life which, if successful, can lead to a damages award in his favour. In the applicant's case, for example, the newspaper was required to pay GBP 60,000 damages, approximately GBP 420,000 in respect of the applicant's costs and an unspecified sum in respect of its own legal costs in defending the claim. The Court is of the view that such awards can reasonably be expected to have a salutary effect on journalistic practices. Further, if an individual is aware of a pending publication relating to his private life, he is entitled to seek an interim injunction preventing publication of the material. Again, the Court notes that the availability of civil proceedings and interim injunctions is fully in line with the provisions of the Parliamentary Assembly's 1998 resolution . . . Further protection for individuals is provided by the Data Protection Act 1998, which sets out the right to have unlawfully collected or inaccurate data destroyed or rectified . . .

120. The Court further observes that, in its examination to date of the measures in place at domestic level to protect Article 8 rights in the context of freedom of expression, it has implicitly accepted that *ex post facto* damages provide an adequate remedy for violations of Article 8 rights arising from the publication by a newspaper of private information. Thus in **Von Hannover**, cited above, the Court's analysis focused on whether the judgment of the domestic courts in civil proceedings brought following publication of private material struck a fair balance between the competing interests. In *Armoniene*, cited above, a complaint about the disclosure of the applicant's husband's HIV-positive status focused on the 'derisory sum' of damages available in the subsequent civil proceedings for the serious violation of privacy. While the Court has on occasion required more than civil law damages in order to satisfy the positive obligation arising under Article 8, the nature of the Article 8 violation in the case was of particular importance. Thus in *X and Y v the Netherlands*, 26 March 1985, the Court insisted on the need for criminal law provisions to achieve deterrence in a case which involved forced sexual intercourse with a sixteen year old mentally handicapped girl. In *K U v Finland*, 2 December 2008, the availability of civil law damages from an Internet service provider was inadequate where there was no possibility of identifying the person who had posted an advert in the name of the applicant, at the time only twelve years old, on a dating website, thus putting him at risk of sexual abuse.

121. In the present case the Court must consider whether, notwithstanding its past approach in cases concerning violations of the right to respect for private life by the press, Article 8 requires a pre-notification rule in order to ensure effective protection of the right to respect for private life. In doing so, the Court will have regard, first, to the margin of appreciation available to the respondent State in this field (see paragraphs 108–110 above) and, second, to the clarity and potential effectiveness of the rule called for by the applicant. While the specific facts of the applicant's case provide a backdrop to the Court's consideration of this question, the implications of any pre-notification requirement are necessarily far wider. However meritorious the applicant's own case may be, the Court must bear in mind the general nature of the duty called for. In particular, its implications for freedom of expression are not limited to the sensationalist reporting at issue in this case but extend to political reporting and serious investigative journalism. The Court recalls that the introduction of restrictions on the latter type of journalism requires careful scrutiny.

i. **The margin of appreciation**

122. The Court recalls, first, that the applicant's claim relates to the positive obligation under Article 8 and that the State in principle enjoys a wide margin of appreciation (see paragraph 108 above). It is therefore relevant that the respondent State has chosen to put in place a system for balancing the competing rights and interests which excludes a pre notification requirement. It is also relevant that a parliamentary committee recently held an inquiry on privacy issues during which written and oral

evidence was taken from a number of stakeholders, including the applicant and newspaper editors. In its subsequent report, the Select Committee rejected the argument that a pre-notification requirement was necessary in order to ensure effective protection of respect for private life . . .

123. Second, the Court notes that the applicant's case concerned the publication of intimate details of his sexual activities, which would normally result in a narrowing of the margin of appreciation (see paragraph 109 above). However, the highly personal nature of the information disclosed in the applicant's case can have no significant bearing on the margin of appreciation afforded to the State in this area given that, as noted above (see paragraph 121 above), any pre-notification requirement would have an impact beyond the circumstances of the applicant's own case.

124. Third, the Court highlights the diversity of practice among member States as to how to balance the competing interests of respect for private life and freedom of expression . . . Indeed the applicant has not cited a single jurisdiction in which a pre-notification requirement as such is imposed. In so far as any common consensus can be identified, it therefore appears that such consensus is against a pre-notification requirement rather than in favour of it. The Court recognises that a number of member States require the consent of the subject before private material is disclosed. However, it is not persuaded that the need for consent in some States can be taken to constitute evidence of a European consensus as far as a pre-notification requirement is concerned. Nor has the applicant pointed to any international instruments which require States to put in place a pre-notification requirement. Indeed, as the Court has noted above (see paragraph 119), the current system in the United Kingdom fully reflects the resolutions of the Parliamentary Assembly of the Council of Europe . . . The Court therefore concludes that the respondent State's margin of appreciation in the present case is a wide one.

ii. The clarity and effectiveness of a pre-notification requirement

126. . . . . However, the Court is persuaded that concerns regarding the effectiveness of a pre- notification duty in practice are not unjustified. Two considerations arise. First, it is generally accepted that any pre notification obligation would require some form of 'public interest' exception . . . Thus a newspaper could opt not to notify a subject if it believed that it could subsequently defend its decision on the basis of the public interest. The Court considers that in order to prevent a serious chilling effect on freedom of expression, a reasonable belief that there was a 'public interest' at stake would have to be sufficient to justify non-notification, even if it were subsequently held that no such 'public interest' arose. The parties' submissions appeared to differ on whether 'public interest' should be limited to a specific public interest in not notifying (for example, where there was a risk of destruction of evidence) or extend to a more general public interest in publication of the material. The Court would observe that a narrowly defined public interest exception would increase the chilling effect of any pre-notification duty.

128. Second, and more importantly, any pre-notification requirement would only be as strong as the sanctions imposed for failing to observe it. A regulatory or civil fine, unless set at a punitively high level, would be unlikely to deter newspapers from publishing private material without pre-notification. In the applicant's case, there is no doubt that one of the main reasons, if not the only reason, for failing to seek his comments was to avoid the possibility of an injunction being sought and granted . . . Thus the *News of the World* chose to run the risk that the applicant would commence civil proceedings after publication and that it might, as a result of those proceedings, be required to pay damages. In any future case to which a pre-notification requirement applied, the newspaper in question could choose to run the same risk and decline to notify, preferring instead to incur an ex post facto fine.

129. Although punitive fines or criminal sanctions could be effective in encouraging compliance with any pre-notification requirement, the Court considers that these would run the risk of being incompatible with the requirements of Article 10 of the Convention. It reiterates in this regard the need to take particular care when examining restraints which might operate as a form of censorship prior to publication. It is satisfied that the threat of criminal sanctions or punitive fines would create a chilling effect which would be felt in the spheres of political reporting and investigative journalism, both of which attract a high level of protection under the Convention.

iii. Conclusion

132. . . . However, the Court has consistently emphasised the need to look beyond the facts of the present case and to consider the broader impact of a pre-notification requirement. The limited scope under Article 10 for restrictions on the freedom of the press to publish material which contributes to debate on matters of general public interest must be borne in mind. Thus, having regard to the chilling effect to which a pre-notification requirement risks giving rise, to the significant doubts as to the effectiveness of any pre-notification requirement and to the wide margin of appreciation in this area, the Court is of the view that Article 8 does not require a legally binding pre-notification requirement. Accordingly, the Court concludes that there has been no violation of Article 8 of the Convention by the absence of such a requirement in domestic law.

Notes

1. The Court approves the view of Eady J that there was no justification for the invasion of privacy, but nevertheless notes that each jurisdiction has a wide 'margin of appreciation' within which to frame the reasonable expectation of privacy and the public interest in publication. This margin allows individual courts and jurisdictions an element of choice based on local values and culture, but this discretion will be diminished if there is wide consensus across the jurisdictions as to where the limits should be placed.

2. On the particular point at issue, the question of a 'pre-notification' rule, the Court considered that such a rule would have too great a 'chilling effect' so as to limit freedom of speech. It would also be ineffective because large media companies would regard any fine as merely one of the costs of being in the newspaper business. However, this problem is also bound up with the question of remedies—notably the 'super-injunction', which prevents not only publication of information but also anyone knowing that an injunction has been issued. If there is no justification for pre-notification, how can a super-injunction be justified? This is discussed further in section 14.3.2.

14.3 Remedies

14.3.1 Damages

The level of damages in privacy cases has been relatively modest, having been guided by the European Court of Human Rights in **Von Hannover**. The amounts have been, for example, nowhere near those awarded in defamation cases (see section 15.12). The relevant principles are discussed by Eady J in **Mosley**.

> ### *Mosley v News Group Newspapers*
> Queen's Bench Division [2008] EWHC 1777 (QB)

The facts are given in section 14.2 and this extract deals solely with the issue of compensatory damages. Eady J had already decided that exemplary damages—designed to make an example of the defendant—were not allowable because 'there is no existing authority (whether statutory or at common law) to justify such an extension and, indeed, it would fail the tests of necessity and proportionality' (at [197]).

EADY J:

The nature of compensatory damages in privacy cases

214. Because both libel and breach of privacy are concerned with compensating for infringements of Article 8, there is clearly some scope for analogy. On the other hand, it is important to remember that this case is not directly concerned with compensating for, or vindicating, injury to reputation. The claim was not brought in libel. The distinctive functions of a defamation claim do not arise. The purpose of damages, therefore, must be to address the specific public policy factors in play when there has been 'an old fashioned breach of confidence' and/or an unauthorised revelation of personal information. It would seem that the law is concerned to protect such matters as personal dignity, autonomy and integrity.

216. Thus it is reasonable to suppose that damages for such an infringement may include distress, hurt feelings and loss of dignity. The scale of the distress and indignity in this case is difficult to comprehend. It is probably unprecedented. Apart from distress, there is another factor which probably has to be taken into account of a less tangible nature. It is accepted in recent jurisprudence that a legitimate consideration is that of vindication to mark the infringement of a right: see eg *Ashley v Chief Constable of Sussex* [2008] 2 WLR 975 at [21]–[22] and *Chester v Afshar* [2005] 1 AC 134 at [87]. Again, it should be stressed that this is different from vindication of reputation (long recognised as a proper factor in the award of libel damages). It is simply to mark the fact that either the state or a relevant individual has taken away or undermined the right of another—in this case taken away a person's dignity and struck at the core of his personality. It is a relevant factor, but the underlying policy is to ensure that an infringed right is met with 'an adequate remedy'. If other factors mean that significant damages are to be awarded, in any event, the element of vindication does not need to be reflected in an even higher award. As Lord Scott observed in *Ashley*, ibid, '. . . there is no reason why an award of compensatory damages should not also fulfil a vindicatory purpose'.

217. If the objective is to provide an adequate remedy for the infringement of a right, it would not be served effectively if the court were merely to award nominal damages out of distaste for what the newspaper had revealed. As I have said, that should not be the court's concern. It would demonstrate that the judge had been distracted from the main task. The danger would be that the more unconventional the taste, and the greater the embarrassment caused by the revelation, the less effective would be the vindication. The easier it would be for the media to hound minorities.

218. These are the elements which need to be recognised in an award of damages in this field but, of course, they must be proportionate and not open to the criticism of arbitrariness: see eg *Tolstoy Miloslavsky v UK* (1995) 20 EHRR 442. It has been recognised since the Court of Appeal decision in *John v MGN Ltd* [1997] QB 586 that there must be a readily identifiable scale in the field of defamation so as to avoid, as far as possible, the vices pointed out in Strasbourg. The guidance there provided can to that extent be transferred to the present environment. Thus, it will be legitimate, in

particular, to pay some attention to the current levels of personal injury awards in order to help maintain a sense of proportion.

222. It must be recognised that it may be appropriate to take into account any aggravating conduct in privacy cases on the part of the defendant which increases the hurt to the claimant's feelings or 'rubs salt in the wound' . . .

224. So too, it may be appropriate that a claimant's conduct should be taken into account (as it is in libel cases). Logically, it may be said, a claimant's conduct has nothing to do with whether or not his privacy has been invaded or the impact upon his feelings caused by such an intrusion. There is no doctrine of contributory negligence. On the other hand, the extent to which his own conduct has contributed to the nature and scale of the distress might be a relevant factor on causation. Has he, for example, put himself in a predicament by his own choice which contributed to his distress and loss of dignity?

225. To what extent is he the author of his own misfortune? Many would think that if a prominent man puts himself, year after year, into the hands (literally and metaphorically) of prostitutes (or even professional dominatrices) he is gambling in placing so much trust in them. There is a risk of exposure or blackmail inherent in such a course of conduct . . .

226. To a casual observer, therefore, and especially with the benefit of hindsight, it might seem that the Claimant's behaviour was reckless and almost self-destructive. This does not excuse the intrusion into his privacy but it might be a relevant factor to take into account when assessing causal responsibility for what happened. It could be thought unreasonable to absolve him of all responsibility for placing himself and his family in the predicament in which they now find themselves. It is part and parcel of human dignity that one must take at least some responsibility for one's own actions . . .

227. An issue to which attention was directed in counsel's submissions was that of deterrence. Passing reference has been made in the authorities from time to time to this concept, but it seems at least questionable whether deterrence should have a distinct (as opposed to a merely incidental) role to play in the award of compensatory damages. It is a notion more naturally associated with punishment. It often comes into the court's assessment of an appropriate punishment for prevalent criminal offences. There is also the anomaly to be considered, already mentioned in the context of exemplary damages; namely, that if damages are paid to an individual for the purpose of deterring the defendant (or others) it would naturally be seen as an undeserved windfall.

228. Furthermore, if deterrence is to have any prospect of success it would be necessary to take into account (as with exemplary damages) the means of the relevant defendant (often a newspaper group). Any award against the present Defendant would have to be so large that it would fail the test of proportionality when seen as fulfilling a compensatory function. There is also a concomitant danger in including a large element of deterrence by way of 'chilling effect'.

230. I am conscious naturally that the analogy with defamation can only be pressed so far. I have already emphasised that injury to reputation is not a directly relevant factor, but it is also to be remembered that libel damages can achieve one objective that is impossible in privacy cases. Whereas reputation can be vindicated by an award of damages, in the sense that the claimant can be restored to the esteem in which he was previously held, that is not possible where embarrassing personal information has been released for general publication. As the media are well aware, once privacy has been infringed, the damage is done and the embarrassment is only augmented by pursuing a court action. Claimants with the degree of resolve (and financial resources) of Mr Max Mosley are likely to be few and far between. Thus, if journalists successfully avoid the grant of an interlocutory injunction, they can usually relax in the knowledge that intrusive coverage of someone's sex life will carry no adverse consequences for them and (as Mr Thurlbeck [author of the original article] put it in his 2 April email) that the news agenda will move on.

231. Notwithstanding all this, it has to be accepted that an infringement of privacy cannot ever be effectively compensated by a monetary award. Judges cannot achieve what is, in the nature of things, impossible. That unpalatable fact cannot be mitigated by simply adding a few noughts to the number first thought of. Accordingly, it seems to me that the only realistic course is to select a figure which marks the fact that an unlawful intrusion has taken place while affording some degree of solatium to the injured party. That is all that can be done in circumstances where the traditional object of restitutio is not available. At the same time, the figure selected should not be such that it could be interpreted as minimising the scale of the wrong done or the damage it has caused.

Notes

1. Mosley was awarded £60,000 plus costs of £420,000. He also sued in Germany, where he negotiated a settlement of €250,000. He was also awarded €7,000 in France.

2. The damages in **Mosley** were considerably higher than in previous privacy cases. Was this because of the allegations of the Nazi connotations of the proceedings, or perhaps because of the secret filming of what went on and the publication of the video on the internet?

3. Compare other awards: in *Douglas*, the claimants were awarded £3,750 each for unauthorised publication of wedding photographs; in *McKennitt* v *Ash* [2007] 2 WLR 194, the claimant was awarded £5,000 for stories about her personal and sexual relationships; in *Lady Archer* v *Williams* [2003] EWHC 1670 (QB), the claimant was awarded £2,500 for stories by her personal assistant. (Note here also the risks of litigation: Lady Archer was awarded costs, but was unable to recoup them from the defendant. She then sued her lawyers for wasting costs and lost that action too: see [2003] EWHC 3048 (QB).) In *Burrell* v *Clifford* [2016] EWHC 294 (Ch) Paul Burrell (former royal butler) was awarded £5,000 (plus costs, despite the defendant—publicist Max Clifford—arguing against these) for the publication of information contained in a personal letter to the defendant. In *Ali and another* v *Channel 5 Broadcasting Ltd* [2019] EWCA Civ 677, the Court of Appeal confirmed awards of £10,000 to two claimants whose eviction from their privately rented property had been shown on Channel 5's *Can't Pay? We'll Take it Away*.

4. In *Gulati and others* v *MGN* [2016] EWHC 1482 (Ch), multiple claimants received significant damages payments ranging from £72,500 to £260,250 (amounting to a total of some £1.2 million) in the phone-hacking cases. The size and extent of the awards can probably be said to represent the repeated invasions of privacy suffered by the claimants and the criminal nature by which the information was obtained.

5. Where there is significant harm, both general and aggravated damages may be awarded. In *Richard* v *The British Broadcasting Corporation (BBC) and another* [2018] EWHC 1837 (Ch)), the entertainer Sir Cliff Richard was awarded £210,000 general and aggravated damages, with additional special damages to be later determined, after the BBC had filmed and sensationally broadcast footage of police entering one of his properties as part of an investigation into an allegation of historic child sexual abuse (for which Richard was never charged).

14.3.2 Injunctions

There has been much controversy and confusion in recent years about the granting of so-called 'super-injunctions' in privacy cases—so much so that a special committee chaired by the Master of the Rolls was set up to discuss the issue (see *The Report of the Committee on Super Injunctions: Super Injunctions, Anonymised Injunctions and Open Justice* 20 May 2011).

There has been much confusion about terminology. The Committee distinguished between 'anonymised inunctions' and 'super-injunctions' as follows:

> a super-injunction can properly be defined as follows: an interim injunction which restrains a person from: (i) publishing information which concerns the applicant and is said to be confidential or private; and, (ii) publicising or informing others of the existence of the order and the proceedings (the 'super' element of the order).
>
> This is to be contrasted with an anonymised injunction, which is: an interim injunction which restrains a person from publishing information which concerns the applicant and is said to be confidential or private where the names of either or both of the parties to the proceedings are not stated. (at [2.14])

The Committee also noted that super-injunctions are now extremely rare and are granted only when there is a danger of a 'tip-off'—that is, when the defendant or his associates could frustrate the purpose of the order if he or they were to become aware of it in advance; for example, in fraud cases in which the assets could be hidden before the order takes effect. That said, a new super-injunction, taken against the *Sunday Times* by a famous person to prevent any information about them—even their gender—being published, was reported in February 2017. The *Sunday Times* is said to have issued legal proceedings to have the injunction overturned, though such action may be redundant given that the identity of the celebrity concerned was leaked by overseas media outlets and then reported in the UK press.

The Committee also said that the correct approach to anonymised injunctions is that taken in *JIH v News Group Newspapers*. It also recommended that official guidance should be issued and that a standard form of injunction should be drafted for interim non-disclosure orders; this has been done.

JIH v *News Group Newspapers*
Court of Appeal [2011] EWCA Civ 42

The claimant, known for these purposes as 'JIH', was a well-known sportsman, who had been in a long-term and conventional relationship with 'X'. He sought to prevent publication of an alleged sexual encounter that he had in 2010 with 'Z'. In August 2010, JIH discovered that the defendants had been told by 'Z' of this alleged encounter. JIH began proceedings without revealing his identity in the publicly available court papers. Held: JIH was granted anonymity.

THE MASTER OF THE ROLLS (LORD NEUBERGER): The cardinal importance of open justice is demonstrated by what is stated in Article 6 of the Convention. But it has long been a feature of the common law . . . The point was perhaps most pithily made by Lord Atkinson when he said 'in public trial is to be found, on the whole, the best security for the pure, impartial, and efficient administration of justice, the best means for winning for it public confidence and respect.' For a more recent affirmation of the principle, see *R (Binyam Mohamed) v Secretary of State for Foreign and Commonwealth Affairs* [2010] EWCA Civ 65, paras 38–42, per Lord Judge CJ.

However, as with almost all fundamental principles, the open justice rule is not absolute: as is clear from Article 6, there will be individual cases, even types of cases, where it has to be qualified. In a case involving the grant of an injunction to restrain the publication of allegedly private information, it is, as I have indicated, rightly common ground that, where the court concludes that it is right to grant an injunction (whether on an interim or final basis) restraining the publication of private information, the court may then have to consider how far it is necessary to impose restrictions on the reporting of the proceedings in order not to deprive the injunction of its effect.

In a case such as this, where the protection sought by the claimant is an anonymity order or other restraint on publication of details of a case which are normally in the public domain, certain principles were identified by the Judge, and which, together with principles contained in valuable written observations to which I have referred, I would summarise as follows:

(1) The general rule is that the names of the parties to an action are included in orders and judgments of the court.

(2) There is no general exception for cases where private matters are in issue.

(3) An order for anonymity or any other order restraining the publication of the normally reportable details of a case is a derogation from the principle of open justice and an interference with the Article 10 rights of the public at large.

(4) Accordingly, where the court is asked to make any such order, it should only do so after closely scrutinising the application, and considering whether a degree of restraint on publication is necessary, and, if it is, whether there is any less restrictive or more acceptable alternative than that which is sought.

(5) Where the court is asked to restrain the publication of the names of the parties and/or the subject matter of the claim, on the ground that such restraint is necessary under Article 8, the question is whether there is sufficient general, public interest in publishing a report of the proceedings which identifies a party and/or the normally reportable details to justify any resulting curtailment of his right and his family's right to respect for their private and family life.

(6) On any such application, no special treatment should be accorded to public figures or celebrities: in principle, they are entitled to the same protection as others, no more and no less.

(7) An order for anonymity or for reporting restrictions should not be made simply because the parties consent: parties cannot waive the rights of the public.

(8) An anonymity order or any other order restraining publication made by a Judge at an interlocutory stage of an injunction application does not last for the duration of the proceedings but must be reviewed at the return date.

(9) Whether or not an anonymity order or an order restraining publication of normally reportable details is made, then, at least where a judgment is or would normally be given, a publicly available judgment should normally be given, and a copy of the consequential court order should also be publicly available, although some editing of the judgment or order may be necessary.

(10) Notice of any hearing should be given to the defendant unless there is a good reason not to do so, in which case the court should be told of the absence of notice and the reason for it, and should be satisfied that the reason is a good one.

Where, as here, the basis for any claimed restriction on publication ultimately rests on a judicial assessment, it is therefore essential that (a) the judge is first satisfied that the facts and circumstances of the case are sufficiently strong to justify encroaching on the open justice rule by restricting the extent to which the proceedings can be reported, and (b) if so, the judge ensures that the restrictions on publication are fashioned so as to satisfy the need for the encroachment in a way which minimises the extent of any restrictions.

In the present case, as in many cases where the court grants an injunction restraining publication of information, the claimant's case as to why there is a need for restraints on publication of aspects of the proceedings themselves which can normally be published is simple and cogent. If the media could publish the name of the claimant and the substance of the information which he is seeking to exclude from the public domain (ie what would normally be information of absolutely central significance in any story about the case—who is seeking what), then the whole purpose of the injunction would be undermined, and the claimant's private life may be unlawfully exposed.

In the course of his judgment, at [2010] EWHC 2818 (QB), paras 8 and 9, Tugendhat J accepted the proposition advanced before him by Mr Tomlinson for JIH that:

> Where the court has accepted that the publication of private information should be restrained, if the court is to avoid disclosing the information in question it must proceed in one of two alternative ways:
>
> (1) If its public judgment or order directly or indirectly discloses the nature of the information in question then it should be anonymised;
> (2) If the claimant is named in the public judgment or order then the information should not be directly or indirectly identified.

While that is not an unfair assessment in the present case, in other cases the position will sometimes be a little less stark. However, in any case, it is plainly correct that, where the court permits the identity of the claimant to be revealed, it is hard to envisage circumstances where that would not mean that significantly less other information about the proceedings could be published than if the proceedings were anonymised. Thus, if the identity of JIH could be published in the context of the present proceedings, it would not be appropriate to permit the publication of even the relatively exiguous information contained in paras 7–9 above. As the Judge went on to say, the obvious corollary is that, if the claimant is accorded anonymisation, it will almost always be appropriate to permit more details of the proceedings to be published than if the claimant is identified.

Notes

1. Guidance on anonymised injunctions was later issued. See Master of the Rolls (2011) *Practice Guidance: Interim Non-Disclosure Orders* (available at **www.judiciary.gov.uk**). The Ministry of Justice also now publishes information about how often such orders are made.

2. Commenting on the 'tipping-off' point in *Terry v Persons Unknown* [2010] EWHC 119 (QB), Tugendhat J said:

   > The reason why, on some occasions, applicants wish for there to be an order restricting reports of the fact that injunction has been granted is in order to prevent the alleged wrong-doer from being tipped off about the proceedings before an injunction could be applied for, or made against him, or before he can be served. In the interval between learning of the intention of the applicant to bring proceedings, and the receipt by the alleged wrongdoer of an injunction binding upon him, the alleged wrongdoer might consider that he or she could disclose the information, and hope to avoid the risk of being in contempt of court. Alternatively, in some cases, the alleged wrongdoer may destroy any evidence which may be needed in order to identify him as the source of the leak. Tipping off of the alleged wrong-doer can thus defeat the purpose of the order. (at [138])

3. Anonymity orders can be varied (so a once anonymous claimant may not stay that way)—see, for examples, *Hutcheson (Formerly Known As 'KGM') v News Group Newspapers Ltd and others* [2011] EWCA Civ 808; *Giggs (formerly known as CTB) v NGN Ltd and another* [2012] EWHC 431 (QB); *Khuja (formerly known as PNM) v Times Newspapers* [2017] UKSC 49.

15

Defamation

Defamation protects a person's reputation. It enables an individual (or, more controversially, a company) to prevent the publication of, or recover damages for, public statements which make, or are likely to make, people think less of them. At its heart is a balance between freedom of speech (protected under the European Convention on Human Rights and the Human Rights Act 1998) and the interests of an individual in the protection of their reputation. For many years, this balance appeared to be 'off'. The UK was dubbed 'the libel capital of the world' for the ease with which actions could be brought here. The Defamation Act 2013, which came into force on 1 January 2014, sought to 'rebalance' the law of defamation. It codifies and changes much of the common law, the main results of which are as follows:

(1) In order to be defamatory the publication of the statement must have caused, or be likely to cause, 'serious harm' to the reputation of the claimant. In the case of a company or corporation (or any other 'bodies for profit'), this must include financial loss.

(2) 'New' defences of 'truth' and 'honest opinion' replacing the common law defences of justification and honest comment.

(3) Introduction of a new 'publication on a matter of public interest' defence, replacing the so-called **Reynolds** defence.

(4) A new category of privilege to protect scientists and academics publishing in peer-reviewed journals.

(5) Reform of the single publication rule, limiting the number of claims that may be brought in relation to a particular statement.

(6) Restrictions on so-called 'libel tourism'.

(7) Further protection for 'secondary' publishers, including operators of websites.

(8) Abolition of trial by jury, unless a court orders otherwise.

(9) Repeal of outdated provisions on slander relating to the chastity of women and contagious diseases.

(10) New powers allowing a court to order a defamatory statement to be removed or for the distribution of that statement to be stopped.

The tort of defamation comes in two forms: libel and slander. A distinction is drawn at common law between libel (a defamatory statement in permanent form, typically writing, but also including, for example, 'a statue, a caricature, an effigy, chalk marks on a wall, signs, or pictures' (*Monson* v *Tussauds Ltd* [1894] QB 671 at 692)) and slander (i.e. statements that are temporary or transitory, usually speech but also mimicry, gestures and sign language). However the test is one of 'permanence' rather than form. The distinction between the torts of libel and slander has been criticised, however the Defamation Act 2013 does not abolish it and applies in *all* cases of defamation (i.e. both libel and slander). In both cases, the claimant needs to demonstrate that the publication of the defamatory statement has 'caused or is likely to cause serious harm'—or injury—'to the reputation of the claimant'. On top of this, the Act mirrors the common law position by requiring in cases of slander that the claimant demonstrate some sort of material *loss* flowing from this, for example by losing money as a result of being shunned by business clients. There are now just two exceptions to this: where the statement imputed criminal conduct (*Webb* v *Beavan* (1883) 11 QBD 609) and incompetence in business dealings (as clarified by the Defamation Act 1952, s 2).

While the Defamation Act 2013 has changed the *substance* of the law, it has not changed the *structure* of defamation claims. In order to establish a claim in the tort of defamation, four questions need to be addressed.

(1) Is the statement defamatory?

(2) Does the statement refer to the claimant?

(3) Has the statement been published or communicated to a third party?

(4) Are there any applicable defences?

see online resources

You may find it helpful to explore the Defamation Act further with an annotated version available from the **online resources**.

Notes

1. For a general overview of the 2013 Act as well as discussion of the function of defamation, see David Howarth 'Libel: Its Purpose and Reform' (2011) 74 MLR 845; Alastair Mullis and Andrew Scott 'Tilting at Windmills: The Defamation Act 2013' (2014) 77 MLR 87; James Price and Felicity McMahon (eds) *Blackstone's Guide to the Defamation Act 2013* (OUP, 2013); and the many interesting and informative posts on the Inforrm blog (www.inforrm.wordpress.com).

15.1 Who can sue?

Individuals can sue for the protection of their reputation, as can corporations. The question has arisen whether public bodies and political parties should also be able to bring a claim for defamation. In all cases, claims are now limited by the serious harm requirement introduced by section 1 of the Defamation Act 2013.

> ### *Derbyshire County Council* v *Times Newspapers*
> Court of Appeal [1992] QB 770

The defendants published an article questioning the propriety of certain investments made by the council of money in its superannuation fund. The council claimed that it had been injured in its credit and reputation and had been brought into public contempt. This raised the question whether a local authority could claim for libel in respect of its administrative or governing reputation. Held: the local authority could not sue as it would unduly inhibit free speech.

BUTLER-SLOSS LJ: . . . The European Court of Human Rights has considered the application of article 10 to contempt of court in *The Sunday Times v United Kingdom* (1979) 2 EHRR 245; to criminal defamation in *Lingens v Austria* (1986) 8 EHRR 407 and to breach of confidential information in *The Sunday Times v United Kingdom (No 2)* (1991) 14 EHRR 229. In each case the court considered whether the interference complained of was necessary in a democratic society. In the *Lingens* case it said, at p 418:

> **39**. The adjective 'necessary,' within the meaning of article 10(2), implies the existence of a 'pressing social need'. . . . The contracting states have a certain margin of appreciation in assessing whether such a need exists. . . but it goes hand in hand with a European supervision, embracing both the legislation and the decisions applying it, even those given by an independent court. . . . **40**. . . . The court must determine whether the interference at issue was 'proportionate to the legitimate aim pursued' and whether the reasons adduced by the Austrian courts to justify it are 'relevant and sufficient'. . . . **41**. In this connection, the court has to recall that freedom of expression, as secured in paragraph 1 of article 10, constitutes one of the essential foundations of a democratic society and one of the basic conditions for its progress and for each individual's self-fulfilment. Subject to paragraph 2, it is applicable not only to 'information' or 'ideas' that are favourably received or regarded as inoffensive or as a matter of indifference, but also to those that offend, shock or disturb. Such are the demands of that pluralism, tolerance and broadmindedness without which there is no 'democratic society'. . . . These principles are of particular importance as far as the press is concerned. Whilst the press must not overstep the bounds set, *inter alia*, for the 'protection of the reputation of others', it is nevertheless incumbent on it to impart information and ideas on political issues just as on those in other areas of public interest. Not only does the press have the task of imparting such information and ideas: the public also has a right to receive them. . . .

. . .

I also believe that the application of article 10 to local authorities is right in principle. A local authority is a corporation. It is also an elected body, elected in local elections and often run in council on party political lines, as is this council. Elected councillors are politicians in the public domain. They are and expect to be exposed to criticism and comment from many quarters within their sphere of activity. Such comment may, and no doubt does, from time to time overstep boundaries acceptable to the individual or local authority so criticised. Although this appeal is only the third case ever brought by a local authority to come before the courts, not only are there numerous local authorities, we were also provided with a list of government departments which happen to be bodies corporate and would, on the argument of Mr Newman for the council, equally have the right to sue for libel. In *The Sunday Times v United Kingdom (No 2)*, 14 EHRR 229, 241 the European Court of Human Rights, following its decision in *Lingens* (1986) 8 EHRR 407, set out the principles enshrined in article 10:

(a) . . . Freedom of expression, as enshrined in article 10, is subject to a number of exceptions which, however, must be narrowly interpreted and the necessity for any restrictions must be convincingly established. (b) . . . Not only does the press have the task of imparting such information and ideas: the public also has a right to receive them. Were it otherwise, the press would be unable to play its vital role of 'public watchdog'.

. . .

Before turning to the competing interests and engaging in the balancing exercise, it is necessary to consider who is the public authority who may be seen to be exercising the interference referred to in article 10(1). Mr Newman has urged us to treat the Derbyshire County Council as the public authority and leave it to the court in each individual libel action to undertake the balancing exercise of the competing interests. It is true that the Derbyshire County Council is a public authority and it is engaged in an attempt to discourage a national newspaper from critical comment about its affairs by an action for damages. But Mr Lester raises a more fundamental argument, with which I agree, that the effect of this court declaring the law in such a way as to enable the local authority to sue in libel, would be interference by a judicial authority with the right of freedom of expression of the press. Such a judicial interference is unacceptable unless it falls within the exceptions set out in article 10(2), which are to be narrowly interpreted and the necessity for any restrictions convincingly established. This issue involves a question of principle as to whether a local authority can sue for libel and not a decision to be made in respect of each individual action.

This court has to balance the competing interests of the freedom of the press to provide informa-tion, to comment, criticise, offend, shock or disturb, against the right of a governmental corporation to be protected against the false, or seriously inaccurate, or unjust accounts of its activities. I have already set out the dangers of allowing a governmental authority to have the right to sue. But in doing the balancing act it is necessary also to consider whether an injustice will be perpetrated if a local authority does not have the right to protect its governing reputation by an action for libel, and whether such an action, if available to a local authority, would be proportionate to the legitimate aim pursued. If a local authority was unable to sue in libel it would not, however, be without recourse to the courts. There seem to me to be three possible remedies: (1) an action for malicious falsehood; (2) a prosecution, with leave of the judge for criminal libel; and (3) an action for libel by an individual within the local authority.

. . .

In my view, the existing available protection is adequate and gives to a governmental body all such rights as are necessary in a democratic society for the protection of its governing reputation. To give it more would be out of proportion to the need shown and would entail too high a risk of unjustifiable interference with the freedom of expression of the press and public. In carrying out the balancing exercise I, for my part, come down in favour of the freedom of speech even though it may go beyond generally acceptable limits, since there is adequate alternative protection available to a council.

Notes

1. This decision was affirmed by the House of Lords without recourse to the European Convention: [1993] AC 534.
2. The **Derbyshire** principle was extended to political parties. In *Goldsmith* v *Bhoyrul* [1998] 2 WLR 435, it was held that the Referendum Party was unable to bring an action for defamation. Buckley J said that 'the public interest in free speech and criticism in respect of those bodies putting themselves forward for office or to govern is also sufficiently strong to justify withholding the right to sue' (at 463). A trade union is also unable to sue: *EETPU* v *The Times* [1980] QB 585. However, individual politicians are able to bring claims (*Bookbinder* v *Tebbit (No 1)* [1989] 1 WLR 640; *McAlpine* v *Bercow* [2013] EWHC 1342 (QB)).

15.2 Who can be liable?

In order for it to be actionable the defamatory statement must have been published. The term 'published' may be misleading here. Rather, the requirement is one of communication; that is, the statement must have been communicated to a third party (*Theaker* v *Richardson*

[1962] 1 WLR 151). At common law any person who distributes a defamatory statement could be liable, and this includes not only the author but also the printer, the publisher, the wholesaler and the retailer, even if they were unaware that the statement was defamatory. Moreover, at common law a new cause of action arose every time the defamatory material was repeated or 'published' (*Duke of Brunswick* v *Harmer* [1849]). Thus a single statement may have a number of different 'publishers'. Section 8 of the Defamation Act 2013 introduces an exception to this through a single publication rule which stops actions being brought in relation to publication of the *same material* by the *same publisher* after a one-year limitation period from the date of the first publication of that material to the public or a section of the public.

Section 1 of the Defamation Act 1996 had previously introduced a defence of 'innocent dissemination' for those other than authors, editors or publishers who are only involved in distribution of material as long as they have shown reasonable care, and a further layer of protection for so-called 'secondary' publishers was added by section 10 of the 2013 Act and for website operators by section 5 of the same Act.

> ### Bussey Law Firm PC and Timothy Raymond Bussey v Page
> Queen's Bench Division [2015] EWHC 563 (QB)

The defendant was sued by a US law firm in respect of a defamatory post on Google Maps (which had been traced to his account). It stated:

> A Google User received 10 months ago
> Overall Poor to fair
> Scumbag Tim Bussey, pays for false reviews, loses 80% of his cases.
> Not a happy camper
> 3 out of 3 found this review helpful

The defendant argued that his Google account had been 'hacked' and that the hacker had posted the words complained of. Held: rejecting the 'unknown hacker defence', the defendant was ordered to pay £50,000 in damages and £50,000 on account of costs.

EADY J:

2. The central issue on liability was whether the Claimants could prove to the required standard that [the defendant] Mr Page was responsible for the original posting on 27 January 2012. He admitted that the posting had been made from his Google account. He could hardly do otherwise. This fact was originally established, at no doubt considerable expense, by Mr Bussey who had instructed a firm of California lawyers to obtain a subpoena in respect of Google's records. Mr Page's response was to advance certain hypothetical explanations as to how an unidentified third party might have posted the allegations via his account but without his knowledge. I will briefly address those theories shortly, but I must remember that I am concerned with what is the most likely explanation on a balance of probabilities.

3. After the commencement of proceedings, the posting was voluntarily removed about a year later. (There has never been any suggestion that the allegations were true.) . . .

5. It was suggested in Mr Page's recently served witness statement that a third party must have hacked into his Google account in order to post the offending review. Naturally, one asks why anyone should take that step. If the objective were merely to hide the hacker's identity from the Claimants, there would be the simpler option of setting up an anonymous Google account. This would in itself render the would-be publisher untraceable, and especially if it were done from a public computer.

6. If such a hacker wished, nevertheless, to use someone else's account, it is not easy to see why he would choose that of the Defendant. He is based in England and it would make more sense, surely, to choose someone in or near Colorado Springs, where the Claimants practise. This would present a rather more credible scenario, if the account were traced, since their clients or potential clients are more likely to be found within easy reach.

7. It is necessary to have in mind how challenging it would be to hack into the Defendant's account. It is accepted that he had adopted especially sophisticated password and security arrangements. It would require great dedication and skill to circumvent them. Even if they could be overcome there is, as I have noted already, no ready explanation as to why such a hacker would need or wish to take such a difficult route.

8. Mr Page's primary suggestion is rather intricate. He has put forward the idea that he must himself have been the hacker's real target. The theory is that he or she *might* have been seeking retribution for some decision or action taken by Mr Page in his capacity as moderator of 'sub-reddits' on the www.reddit.com website. In other words, this could provide an explanation why the third party wanted Mr Page to take the blame for the attack on the Claimants. This plan would still, of course, involve the third party successfully hacking into Mr Page's account in the first place and then making the (very big) assumption that the target (ie the Claimants) would actually go to the trouble and expense of identifying Mr Page and thereafter of pursuing him in a foreign jurisdiction. When one comes to assess the competing possibilities, it is fair to say that this somewhat obscure explanation defies probability.

10. The Claimants established that Mr Page advertised on Twitter as being willing to post 'feedback' or 'testimonial' (a description which corresponds to the posting complained of here) for $5 via the Fiver.com website. This would at least provide a possible motive for his targeting the Claimants, of whom he had no personal knowledge or experience. Indeed, it is difficult to know why else he would have done so. He says, however, that he was never in fact paid for any such transaction, although his Paypal records disclose substantial dollar payments between November 2011 and March 2012. He put in late supplementary evidence to show the extent of his Fiver.com activity, but after enlargement it emerged that there was an unexplained gap (an apparent deletion) covering the period between 24 January and 10 February 2012 (ie the period embracing the date of the relevant posting).

11. I have to come to a conclusion in the light of the probabilities. The likelihood is, in the absence of any convincing explanation to the contrary, that the posting from Mr Page's account was authored or authorised by him. It is extremely improbable that anyone successfully hacked into that account on 27 January 2012 with a view to posting the words complained of. There is no evidence that anyone did so on that date and, moreover, no reason why anyone with a grudge against the Claimants should attempt to go down that route in any event. Why Mr Page should himself choose to attack the Claimants is also unclear, but the most likely explanation would appear to be a purely financial one. I do not need, however, to come to a conclusion on motive since it is not essential to the Claimants' cause of action. All I need say is that the overwhelming probability is that he is responsible for the posting from his account on the date in question and for its remaining accessible thereafter. There is simply no other reasonable explanation.

12. The publication was calculated to cause serious harm to the Claimants and, in particular, to Mr Bussey's personal reputation and to his legal practice. It is likely to have been read by a significant number of searchers and, in particular, by potential clients checking them out. It is noted that three people are supposed to have found the comment 'helpful'. One cannot, however, attach too much significance to that and it is certainly *possible* that one person using different accounts made all three entries (as Mr Page pointed out).

13. It is well known that the purpose of compensatory general damages is threefold. The court must compensate (1) for hurt feelings and distress, and (2) for injury to reputation, as well as bearing in mind (3) the need to award a sum which will serve as an outward and visible sign of vindication. There is no doubt that the allegation caused Mr Bussey considerable anxiety and distress, as it reflected upon his personal integrity and his professional competence throughout the period of ready access. His evidence about the impact upon him was unchallenged. I need to take account also of the stress of having to pursue litigation both in the United States and in a foreign jurisdiction. There is also some evidence of a decline in income at the relevant time which could be, at least in part, attributable to that publication. Yet I am primarily concerned in Mr Bussey's case with the impact upon him personally and the need for clear vindication. I would assess the damages in his case at £45,000.

14. In so far as the firm has sued separately in its own name, I am concerned not with hurt feelings but primarily with the need to compensate for injury to reputation and for convincing vindication. I have little doubt that the posting would have adversely impacted on the practice, including financially, and I should also take into account to some extent the 'grapevine effect' of such allegations: see eg *Cairns v Modi* [2013] 1 WLR 1015, at [26]; *Ley v Hamilton* (1935) 153 LT 384, 386. I would assess the award, conservatively, at £25,000 for the first Claimant.

15. The claim for damages has been capped at £50,000 and that must therefore represent the total sum to be recovered by the Claimants.

17. I would grant an injunction if I thought it likely that Mr Page would republish the defamatory allegations or any similar words defamatory of the Claimants, but I do not believe in the light of the evidence he has given that he will do so.

DEFAMATION ACT 1996

1. Responsibility for publication

(1) In defamation proceedings a person has a defence if he shows that—

   (a) he was not the author, editor or publisher of the statement complained of,

   (b) he took reasonable care in relation to its publication, and

   (c) he did not know, and had no reason to believe, that what he did caused or contributed to the publication of a defamatory statement.

(2) For this purpose 'author', 'editor' and 'publisher' have the following meanings, which are further explained in subsection (3)—

'author' means the originator of the statement, but does not include a person who did not intend that his statement be published at all;

'editor' means a person having editorial or equivalent responsibility for the content of the statement or the decision to publish it; and

'publisher' means a commercial publisher, that is, a person whose business is issuing material to the public, or a section of the public, who issues material containing the statement in the course of that business.

(3) A person shall not be considered the author, editor or publisher of a statement if he is only involved—

(a) in printing, producing, distributing or selling printed material containing the statement;

(b) in processing, making copies of, distributing, exhibiting or selling a film or sound recording (as defined in Part I of the Copyright, Designs and Patents Act 1988) containing the statement;

(c) in processing, making copies of, distributing or selling any electronic medium in or on which the statement is recorded, or in operating or providing any equipment system or service by means of which the statement is retrieved, copied, distributed or made available in electronic form;

(d) as the broadcaster of a live programme containing the statement in circumstances in which he has no effective control over the maker of the statement;

(e) as the operator of or provider of access to a communications system by means of which the statement is transmitted, or made available, by a person over whom he has no effective control. In a case not within paragraphs (a) to (e) the court may have regard to those provisions by way of analogy in deciding whether a person is to be considered the author, editor or publisher of a statement. . . .

(4) In determining for the purposes of this section whether a person took reasonable care, or had reason to believe that what he did caused or contributed to the publication of a defamatory statement, regard shall be had to—

(a) the extent of his responsibility for the content of the statement or the decision to publish it,

(b) the nature or circumstances of the publication, and

(c) the previous conduct or character of the author, editor or publisher.

(5) This section does not apply to any cause of action which arose before the section came into force.

17. Interpretation

(1) In this Act—

'publication' and 'publish', in relation to a statement, have the meaning they have for the purposes of the law of defamation generally, but 'publisher' is specially defined for the purposes of section 1;

'statement' means words, pictures, visual images, gestures or any other method of signifying meaning; . . .

DEFAMATION ACT 2013

10. Action against a person who was not the author, editor etc

(1) A court does not have jurisdiction to hear and determine an action for defamation brought against a person who was not the author, editor or publisher of the statement complained of unless the court is satisfied that it is not reasonably practicable for an action to be brought against the author, editor or publisher.

(2) In this section 'author', 'editor' and 'publisher' have the same meaning as in section 1 of the Defamation Act 1996.

Godfrey v Demon Internet
Queen's Bench Division [2001] QB 201

The defendant Internet Service Provider (ISP) carried a newsgroup called 'soc.culture.thai'. On 13 January 1997, an unknown person made a posting on that site from the United States which purported to have been posted by the claimant, but it was a forgery and defamatory of the claimant. It followed a path from the American ISP to the defendant's news server in England. On 17 January the claimant sent a fax to the defendant informing it of the forgery and requesting its removal. However, it was not removed and expired naturally on 27 January. Held: the defendant ISP was liable for losses arising after 17 January, the date the defendant was informed of the libel.

MORLAND J: . . . The governing statute is the Defamation Act 1996. Section 1 is headed 'Responsibility for Publication'.

In my judgment the Defendants were clearly not the publisher of the posting defamatory of the Plaintiff within the meaning of Section 1(2) and 1(3) and incontrovertibly can avail themselves of Section 1(1)(a).

However the difficulty facing the Defendants is Section 1(1)(b) and 1(1)(c). After the 17th January 1997 after receipt of the Plaintiff's fax the Defendants knew of the defamatory posting but chose not to remove it from their Usenet news servers. In my judgment this places the Defendants in an insuperable difficulty so that they cannot avail themselves of the defence provided by Section 1.

I am fortified in this conclusion by the contents of the Consultation Document issued by the Lord Chancellor's Department in July 1995 and the words of Lord Mackay LC during debate on the Defamation Bill on the 2nd April 1996 (see Hansard Col 214).

In the Consultation Document it is said:—

2.4 The defence of innocent dissemination has never provided an absolute immunity for distributors, however mechanical their contribution. It does not protect those who knew that the material they were handling was defamatory, or who ought to have known of its nature. Those safeguards are preserved, so that the defence is not available to a defendant who knew that his act involved or contributed to publication defamatory of the plaintiff. It is available only if, having taken all reasonable care, the defendant had no reason to suspect that his act had that effect. Sub-sections (5) and (6) describe factors which will be taken into account in determining whether the defendant took all reasonable care.

2.5 Although it has been suggested that the defence should always apply unless the plaintiff is able to show that the defendant did indeed have the disqualifying knowledge or cause for suspicion, only the defendant knows exactly what care he has taken. Accordingly, as in most defences, it is for the defendant to show that the defence applies to him.

Lord Mackay LC said in moving rejection of an amendment of Lord Lester of Herne Hill:—

Clause 1 is intended to provide a defence for those who have unwittingly provided a conduit which has enabled another person to publish defamatory material. It is intended to provide a modern equivalent of the common law defence of innocent dissemination, recognising that there may be circumstances in which the unwitting contributor to the process of publication may have had no idea of the defamatory nature of the material he has handled or processed.

The amendment proposed by the noble Lord would, in effect, create an entirely new defence. It would give a defence to a person who was indeed aware, or on notice that he was contributing to a defamatory publication, but nevertheless chose to do so. . . .

It is imperative that we do not lose sight of the effect on plaintiffs of giving a defence to those who have in fact been instrumental in bringing material which has defamed the plaintiff to its audience. . . .

But in my submission it would not be right to deprive a plaintiff of his cause of action against a defendant who was aware that he might be wronging the plaintiff and misjudged the plaintiff's chances of succeeding in a defamation action.

Mr Barca, for the Defendants, submitted that at Common Law the Defendants did not publish the defamatory posting and there was no publication.

Section 17 of the 1996 Act reads:—

> 'Publication' and 'publish', in relation to a statement, have the meaning they have for the purposes of the law of defamation generally, but 'publisher' is specially defined for the purposes of section 1.

At Common Law liability for the publication of defamatory material was strict. There was still publication even if the publisher was ignorant of the defamatory material within the document. Once publication was established the publisher was guilty of publishing the libel unless he could establish, and the onus was upon him, that he was an innocent disseminator.

In my judgment the Defendants, whenever they transmit and whenever there is transmitted from the storage of their news server a defamatory posting, publish that posting to any subscriber to their ISP who accesses the newsgroup containing that posting. Thus every time one of the Defendants' customers accesses 'soc.culture.thai' and sees that posting defamatory of the Plaintiff there is a publication to that customer.

I do not accept Mr Barca's argument that the Defendants were merely owners of an electronic device through which postings were transmitted. The Defendants chose to store 'soc.culture.thai' postings within their computers. Such postings could be accessed on that newsgroup. The Defendants could obliterate and indeed did so about a fortnight after receipt.

Notes

1. The important point in *Godfrey* is that the defendants hosted the site where the material appeared and had the power to remove it. They were liable because they had been made aware of the existence of the defamatory material but had failed to delete it. Section 1 of the Defamation Act 1996 only protects those who have taken reasonable care and who have no reason to suspect that the material is defamatory.

2. In *Bunt* v *Tilley* [2006] EWHC 407 (QB), the claimant sued not only the authors of the defamatory statements that appeared on various websites, but also the ISPs (AOL, Tiscali and BT), which facilitated their appearance. Eady J concluded that he would not attribute liability at common law to a telephone company or other passive medium of communication, such as an ISP.

3. Internet cases pose interesting jurisdictional problems. If the defendant is domiciled in a European state, Article 5(3) of the Council Regulation on jurisdiction (Regulation No 44/2001) states: 'A person domiciled in a Member State may, in another Member State, be sued in matters relating to tort . . . in the courts for the place where the harmful event occurred or may occur.' In *eDate Advertising GmbH and Martinez* v *MGN* (Joined Cases C-509/09 and C-161/10), EU:C:2011:685, the Grand Chamber of the European Court of Justice said that the expression 'place where the harmful event occurred' is intended to cover both the place where the damage occurred and the place of the event giving rise to it (at [41]). In relation to the application of those two criteria to defamation, the Court has held that, in the case of a newspaper article distributed in several states, the victim may bring an action for damages against the publisher either before the courts of the place in which the publisher of the defamatory publication is established, which have jurisdiction to award damages for all of the harm caused by the defamation, or before the courts of each state in which the publication was distributed and in which the victim claims to have suffered injury to his reputation, which have jurisdiction to rule solely in respect of the harm caused in that state. In the case of an alleged infringement of personality rights on an Internet website, the claimant has the option of bringing an action for liability, in respect of all of the

damage caused, either before the courts of the member state in which the publisher of that content is established or before the courts of the member state in which the centre of his interests is based. Or he may bring an action before the courts of the territory in which the content has been accessible. Those courts have jurisdiction only in respect of the damage caused in that country. Thus, the claimant was able to sue in France for damage caused to him in France by publication in England of a false allegation that 'Kylie Minogue is back with Olivier Martinez', with details of their meeting.

4. Section 9 of the Defamation Act 2013 creates a new 'threshold test' for acceptance of jurisdiction in defamation cases by courts in England and Wales in cases against non-domiciled persons (i.e. persons not living in the UK, EU or in a Lugano Convention state). In such cases, courts in England and Wales lack jurisdiction unless they are 'satisfied that, of all the places in the world in which the statement complained of has been published, England and Wales is clearly the most appropriate place in which to bring an action in respect of the statement' (s 9(2)).

DEFAMATION ACT 2013

5. Operators of websites

(1) This section applies where an action for defamation is brought against the operator of a website in respect of a statement posted on the website.

(2) It is a defence for the operator to show that it was not the operator who posted the statement on the website.

(3) The defence is defeated if the claimant shows that—

    (a) it was not possible for the claimant to identify the person who posted the statement,

    (b) the claimant gave the operator a notice of complaint in relation to the statement, and

    (c) the operator failed to respond to the notice of complaint in accordance with any provision contained in regulations.

(4) For the purposes of subsection (3)(a), it is possible for a claimant to 'identify' a person only if the claimant has sufficient information to bring proceedings against the person.

(5) Regulations may—

    (a) make provision as to the action required to be taken by an operator of a website in response to a notice of complaint (which may in particular include action relating to the identity or contact details of the person who posted the statement and action relating to its removal);

    (b) make provision specifying a time limit for the taking of any such action;

    (c) make provision conferring on the court a discretion to treat action taken after the expiry of a time limit as having been taken before the expiry;

    (d) make any other provision for the purposes of this section.. . .

(6) The defence under this section is defeated if the claimant shows that the operator of the website has acted with malice in relation to the posting of the statement concerned.

(7) The defence under this section is not defeated by reason only of the fact that the operator of the website moderates the statements posted on it by others.

Notes

1. While the effect of this defence means that website operators will not be automatically liable in defamation (even if they moderate comments), they may become liable if they do not act in accordance with the regulations and where users use pseudonyms (thus preventing the claimant from identifying the poster directly).

DEFAMATION ACT 2013

8. Single publication rule

(1) This section applies if a person—

    (a) publishes a statement to the public ('the first publication'), and

    (b) subsequently publishes (whether or not to the public) that statement or a statement which is substantially the same.

(2) In subsection (1) 'publication to the public' includes publication to a section of the public.

(3) For the purposes of section 4A of the Limitation Act 1980 (time limit for actions for defamation etc) any cause of action against the person for defamation in respect of the subsequent publication is to be treated as having accrued on the date of the first publication.

(4) This section does not apply in relation to the subsequent publication if the manner of that publication is materially different from the manner of the first publication.

(5) In determining whether the manner of a subsequent publication is materially different from the manner of the first publication, the matters to which the court may have regard include (amongst other matters)—

    (a) the level of prominence that a statement is given;

    (b) the extent of the subsequent publication.

(6) Where this section applies—

    (a) it does not affect the court's discretion under section 32A of the Limitation Act 1980 (discretionary exclusion of time limit for actions for defamation etc), and

    (b) the reference in subsection (1)(a) of that section to the operation of section 4A of that Act is a reference to the operation of section 4A together with this section.

LIMITATION ACT 1980

4A. Limit for actions for defamation or malicious falsehood

The time limit under section 2 of this Act shall not apply to an action for—

    (a) libel or slander, or

    (b) slander of title, slander of goods or other malicious falsehood,

but no such action shall be brought after the expiration of one year from the date on which the cause of action accrued.

Notes

1. Section 2 of the Limitation Act 1980 states that an action founded on tort shall not be brought after the expiration of six years from the date on which the cause of action arose.

2. Section 8 of the Defamation Act 2013 reverses *Loutchansky v The Times Newspapers (No 2)* [2002] 2 QB 783 (in which it was established that the time began to run every time a web archive was accessed). The new 'single publication rule' only applies to material that has been published to the public, or section of the public, and does not apply when the defamatory material is republished in a substantially different form to the original, or is published in a different manner (e.g. if it is moved from an obscure part of a website to the front page) or by someone else.

15.3 The meaning of 'defamatory'

It is now generally accepted that a statement will be considered defamatory if it is likely to 'lower the claimant in the estimation of right-thinking members of society in general' (*Sim v Stretch* [1936] 2 All ER 1237).

> ### *McAlpine v Bercow*
> Queen's Bench Division [2013] EWHC 1342 (QB)

A BBC *Newsnight* report included a serious allegation of child abuse and references to 'a leading Conservative politician from the Thatcher years' and 'a prominent Tory politician at the time'. Following the broadcast there was intense media speculation as to the politician's identity, as well as on Twitter, which led to the name of Lord McAlpine, former Deputy Chairman and Treasurer of the Conservative Party, 'trending'. In response to this, Sally Bercow, the wife of the speaker of the House of Commons, tweeted: 'Why is Lord McAlpine trending? *Innocent face*'. At the time, Bercow had over 56,000 followers. Unfortunately, it was a case of mistaken identity: it was quickly accepted that Lord McAlpine was entirely innocent. Held: the tweet was defamatory on its natural and ordinary meaning, or by virtue of innuendo. The case was eventually settled for £15,000, which Lord McAlpine donated to a children's charity.

TUGENDHAT J:

What Does The Law Mean by Defamatory?

36. The applicable law is well established and not in dispute. As a matter of law, words are defamatory of a claimant if (1) they refer to that claimant and (2) they substantially affect in an adverse manner the attitude of other people towards the claimant, or have a tendency so to do.

37. There is no dispute that the Tweet refers to the Claimant, because it names him. The issue here is what the Tweet means, and whether it defames him.

38. If the Tweet does mean that the Claimant abused children, then there is obviously no dispute that that is one of the most seriously defamatory allegations which it is possible to make against a person.

39. In libel actions there is often room for argument as to what a statement means. Even if it is defamatory, there can be argument as to whether the allegation is a very serious one, or some less serious one.

40. A classic example is *Rubber Improvements Ltd* and **Lewis v Daily Telegraph Ltd** [1964] AC 234. In that case *The Daily Telegraph* had published an article headed 'Inquiry on Firm by City Police' and the *Daily Mail* had published an article headed 'Fraud Squad Probe Firm'. The plaintiffs claimed that those articles meant that they were guilty of fraud. The defendants admitted that the articles were defamatory, but they maintained that the articles did not go so far as to include actual guilt of fraud, but something less. The House of Lords held that the articles could not mean that the plaintiffs were guilty of fraud. As Lord Devlin put it at p 286:

> If the ordinary sensible man was capable of thinking that wherever there was a police inquiry there was guilt, it would be almost impossible to give accurate information about anything . . .

41. More recently three different levels of possible defamatory meaning have been explained by the Court of Appeal in *Chase* v *Newsgroup Newspapers Ltd* [2003] EMLR 218, [2002] EWCA Civ 1772 at 45:

> The sting of a libel may be capable of meaning that a claimant has in fact committed some serious act, such as murder. Alternatively it may be suggested that the words mean that there are reasonable grounds to suspect that he/she has committed such an act. A third possibility is that they may mean that there are grounds for investigating whether he/she has been responsible for such an act.

42. The court is not bound to choose between the contentions of the parties as to what the Tweet means. I must make up my own mind.

. . .

Notes

1. Of course, like the reasonable man, a 'right-thinking member of society' is a legal fiction who joins the reasonable man on the Clapham omnibus, to allow the court to come to its own conclusion as to whether a statement is defamatory:

   > The Clapham omnibus has many passengers. The most venerable is the reasonable man, who was born during the reign of Victoria but remains in vigorous health. Amongst the other passengers are the right-thinking member of society, familiar from the law of defamation, the officious bystander, the reasonable parent, the reasonable landlord, and the fair-minded and informed observer, all of whom have had season tickets for many years. (Lord Reed, *Healthcare at Home Ltd* v *The Common Services Agency* [2014] UKSC 49 at [1])

2. Section 11 of the Defamation Act 2013 abolishes the presumption in favour of a jury trial. Under section 69 of the Senior Courts Act 1981 and section 66 of the County Courts Act 1984 there was a presumption in favour of a jury trial, 'unless the court is of the opinion that the trial requires any prolonged examination of documents or accounts or any scientific or local investigation which cannot be conveniently made with a jury'. The 2013 Act leaves the courts a residual discretion to order a jury trial, but gives no guidance on when it might be appropriate to so order.

3. Opinion may be sharply divided on whether a person has acted reprehensibly. For example, is it defamatory to say of a trade union member that he has refused to support an official strike? While some trade unionists may regard it as disloyal, others—such as their employer, for example—might applaud the action. In *Myroft* v *Sleight* (1921) 37 TLR 646, McCardie J thought it would not be defamatory, for it would merely be alleging 'independence of thought or courage of opinion or speech or manliness of action' although he did decide that it would be defamatory to say that a person who had voted for the strike had refused to leave work, for that would be to allege hypocrisy or underhand disloyalty.

4. Section 1(1) of the Defamation Act 2013 adds a seriousness requirement to this common law test, to ensure that only the most egregious cases are brought. In addition, where a company, corporation or some other 'body for profit', wishes to bring a claim they have to demonstrate that the harm caused to their reputation by the defamatory statement caused, or is likely to cause, serious financial loss (s 1(2)).

15.4 **Serious harm**

DEFAMATION ACT 2013

1. Serious harm

(1) A statement is not defamatory unless its publication has caused or is likely to cause serious harm to the reputation of the claimant.

(2) For the purposes of this section, harm to the reputation of a body that trades for profit is not 'serious harm' unless it has caused or is likely to cause the body serious financial loss.

Cooke v MGN Ltd
Queen's Bench Division [2014] EWHC 2831 (QB)

The *Sunday Mirror* published an article with a front page headline 'MILLIONAIRE TORY CASHES IN ON TV BENEFITS STREET' referring to the owner of a number of properties on the street which featured in Channel 4's programme *Benefits Street*. The article extended over a number of pages and suggested that the houses were kept in a poor state of repair. The claimants, a housing association and its chief executive who owned three houses on the street, argued that the article was defamatory. Held: the claimants had not been able to prove that there had been serious harm to their reputation and so their claim failed.

BEAN J:

The Defamation Act 2013

27. Section 1 of the Defamation Act 2013, under the heading 'Requirement of serious harm', provides:-

(1) A statement is not defamatory unless its publication has caused or is likely to cause serious harm to the reputation of the claimant.

(2) For the purposes of this section harm to the reputation of a body that trades for profit is not 'serious harm' unless it has caused or is likely to cause the body serious financial loss.

28. The Act only applies to defamation claims where the cause of action has arisen since the beginning of 2014. Mr Tomlinson and Mr Price [counsel in the case] tell me this is the first case in which the interpretation of the Act has come before the courts. . . .

30. It is common ground that s 1(1) requires a claimant to show that serious harm has been caused or is likely to be caused to his reputation. It is not enough to show that the publication has caused or is likely to cause serious distress or injury to feelings. . . .

34. The 2013 Act was the product of extensive parliamentary scrutiny. A draft Bill was produced in March 2011 for public consultation and pre-legislative scrutiny by a Joint Committee of both Houses. The Joint Committee reported on the draft Bill on 19th October 2011. The Defamation Bill itself was then presented to the House of Commons on 20th May 2012 and after detailed consideration in both Houses received Royal Assent on 25th April 2013.

35. Both Mr Tomlinson and Mr Price have sought to refer to *Hansard* to cite remarks made in the course of the Bill's passage through Parliament, relying on *Pepper v Hart* [1993] AC 593. I consider

that it is proper to refer to the Ministerial foreword to the draft Bill, to the Joint Committee's report on the draft Bill, and to the Explanatory Notes to the Act, to identify the mischief at which it was aimed. I also consider that the parliamentary history, and in particular any respect in which the Act differs from the original draft Bill, may be highly illuminating. It is also proper to refer to statements made by the promoters of the Bill (that is to say the sponsoring minister in each House or the proposer of any successful amendment) in order to resolve a genuine ambiguity in the Act.

36. The Explanatory Notes to the Act, referring to s 1(1), state:—

The section builds on the consideration given by the courts in a series of cases to the question of what is sufficient to establish that a statement is defamatory. A recent example is *Thornton v Telegraph Media Group Ltd* in which a decision of the House of Lords in *Sim v Stretch* was identified as authority for the existence of a 'threshold of seriousness' in what is defamatory. There is also currently potential for trivial cases to be struck out on the basis that they are an abuse of process because so little is at stake. In *Jameel v Dow Jones & Co* it was established that there needs to be a real and substantial tort. The section raises the bar for bringing a claim so that only cases involving serious harm to the claimant's reputation can be brought.

37. The original draft Bill had provided in Clause 1(1) that:—

A statement is not defamatory unless its publication has caused or is likely to cause substantial harm to the reputation of the claimant.

The Joint Committee on the draft Bill recommended replacing 'substantial harm' with 'serious and substantial harm'. In the event the Bill introduced by the Government in 2012 used the phrase 'serious harm'. It is obvious, without the necessity of referring to *Hansard*, that 'serious harm' involves a higher threshold than 'substantial harm' would have done; and also that as the Explanatory Notes put it, it 'raises the bar' over which a claimant must jump.

38. This much is not controversial. Mr Tomlinson, however, sought to rely on an observation made by Lord McNally, the Minister of State in charge of the Bill, in the House of Lords Grand Committee debate of 17th December 2012, when he said [emphasis added]:—

Our view is that the serious harm test would raise the bar *to a modest extent* above the requirement of the current law.

39. I do not consider that this statement is admissible as an aid to construction of the phrase 'serious harm'. To use it for that purpose would be to allow legislation by speech. If a Minister taking part in a debate on a Bill or on a particular clause of a Bill says that he intends it to make a modest change (or, conversely, a major change), it is difficult to see what other parliamentarians are supposed to do about it. This point is given added significance by the fact that the Minister of State's observations were made in the second House. When the Bill had been before the House of Commons, up to and including its third reading on 12th September 2012, there was no definition in it of 'serious harm'. Any Member of Parliament who thought about it was entitled to assume that by using the word 'serious' and not defining it the draftsman was leaving it to judges in contested claims to say whether on the facts of the case the serious harm test was satisfied. 'Serious' is an ordinary word in common usage and I do not consider that it creates an ambiguity so as to bring *Pepper v Hart* into play.

How can serious harm ... be proved?

. . .

43. I do not accept that in every case evidence will be required to satisfy the serious harm test. Some statements are so obviously likely to cause serious harm to a person's reputation that this likelihood can be inferred. If a national newspaper with a large circulation wrongly accuses someone of

being a terrorist or a paedophile, then in either case (putting to one side for the moment the question of a prompt and prominent apology) the likelihood of serious harm to reputation is plain, even if the individual's family and friends knew the allegation to be untrue. In such a case the matter would be taken no further by requiring the claimant to incur the expense of commissioning an opinion poll survey, or to produce a selection of comments from the blogosphere which might in any event be unrepresentative of the population of 'right thinking people' generally. But I do not consider that the Article in the present case, with the meaning relating to the claimants which I have held it to have, comes anywhere near that type of case.

44. In assessing the likelihood of serious harm being caused to the claimants' reputation in the present case I attach significance to the apology. I have already held that the apology was sufficient to eradicate or at least minimise any unfavourable impression created by the original article in the mind of the hypothetical reasonable reader who read both. That leaves a residual class of readers of the original article who did not read the apology. As for them, it is important to note that the apology is now far more accessible on internet searches than the original Article. Mr Price observes, and I agree, that 'only somebody actively trying to find the unamended Article may come across it, if they try hard enough. But there is no reason for anyone to do so other than for the purposes of this claim'.

Monroe v Hopkins
Queen's Bench Division [2017] EWHC 433 (QB)

Daily Mail columnist Katie Hopkins sent two tweets referring to food blogger and writer Jack Monroe accusing her of vandalising a war memorial and desecrating the memory of those who fought for her freedom, or of approving or condoning such behaviour. Held: the tweets were defamatory and had caused Monroe 'real and substantial distress' and 'harm to her reputation which was serious, albeit not "very serious" or "grave"' (at [82]).

WARBY J:

Serious harm

63. The evidence has convinced me that Ms Monroe was very upset by the First and Second Tweets [which read '@MsJackMonroe scrawled on any memorials recently? Vandalised the memory of those who fought for your freedom. Grandma got any more medals?' and 'Can someone explain to me—in 10 words or less—the difference between irritant @PennyRed and social anthrax @Jack Monroe' respectively]. This is apparent from her angry reaction to the First Tweet [she tweeted 'I have NEVER "scrawled on a memorial". Brother in the RAF. Dad was a Para in the Falklands. You're a piece of shit' (with a screenshot of the first tweet)]. Some of what she tweeted afterwards to her own followers could be read as making light of what had been said, and as mocking Ms Hopkins and revelling in the prospect of suing her [after being blocked by Hopkins, Monroe tweeted, 'BA_DA_BOOM! It lies! It smears! It's wrong! It panics! It blocks! It's @KTHopkins everyone!' (with six pictures of a chicken) followed by a further tweet saying 'Gin o clock. Cheers. God isn't it good sweet justice when a poisonous bully gets shown up for what it is and runs runs runs away.'] But the case for the defence, that this was the true overall picture, is not made out. People can react in a variety of ways when wounded. This individual, in this situation, wrote some things that turned out to be unhelpful to her case in this action. But they were written in the heat of the moment. Generally speaking, I accept Ms Monroe's evidence about how things were for her that evening.

64. Her initial reaction was to be 'completely horrified, both that people would think that I had vandalised a war memorial, and at the incoming storm that would be heading my way from the many people I believed would accept that what the Defendant had said was true.' Ms Monroe thought the accusation was being targeted at her personally. Believing Ms Hopkins had a massive following on Twitter she anticipated that she would start to receive abuse as a result. Ms Monroe's evidence is that she received abusive tweets from people who had read those complained of. I shall come back to the evidence about the 'torrent of abuse', which is hotly disputed. But I accept her evidence that she felt anxious and upset, and had difficulty sleeping.

65. I also accept the claimant's evidence about her reaction to the Second Tweet, and her feelings at the way that Ms Hopkins has behaved since publication, and how she has conducted the defence of the proceedings. Ms Monroe found it very upsetting and frustrating that rather than say the First Tweet had been false and express some regret about posting it, she just 'switched her line of attack' and made what Ms Monroe saw as a 'deliberate call to arms'. There has been no apology, and I accept that this has allowed the claimant's injured feelings to remain raw.

66. It is said that Ms Hopkins acted maliciously in sending the Second Tweet, knowing it was untrue to suggest that Ms Monroe had vandalised or condoned the vandalisation of a war memorial. I do not know what Ms Hopkins' actual state of mind was, as she has not given evidence, nor has she explained her position otherwise than through her lawyers. If she had done so, and persuasively rebutted what Ms Monroe says about these matters, I might have disregarded this part of the claimant's evidence. But in the absence of any rebuttal I conclude that Ms Monroe's response was and remains a reasonable one. I remain of the view I expressed in *Barron v Vines* [2016] EWHC 1226 (QB) [22], that when malice is alleged in aggravation of damages,

> . . . the issue is not the actual state of mind of the defendant. It is whether the claimants have suffered additional injury to feelings as a result of the defendant's outward behaviour. If the defendant has behaved in a way which leads the claimants reasonably to believe he acted maliciously that is enough.

67. All of this, however, is about injury to feelings, and the issue I have to address at this stage is whether serious harm to reputation has been proved. As Dingemans J noted in *Sobrinho v Impresa Publishing SA* [2016] EWHC 66 (QB), [2016] EMLR 12 [46], unless serious harm to reputation can be established an injury to feelings alone, however grave, will not be sufficient.

68. In *Sobrinho* at [46]–[50] Dingemans J identified a number of other uncontroversial propositions about the Serious Harm requirement:

> 46. . . . 'Serious' is an ordinary word in common usage. Section 1 requires the claimant to prove as a fact, on the balance of probabilities, that the statement complained of has caused or will probably cause serious harm to the claimant's reputation. . . .
>
> 47. Secondly it is open to the claimant to call evidence in support of his case on serious harm and it is open to the defendant to call evidence to demonstrate that no serious harm has occurred or is likely to do so. However a Court determining the issue of serious harm is, as in all cases, entitled to draw inferences based on the admitted evidence. Mass media publications of very serious defamatory allegations are likely to render the need for evidence of serious harm unnecessary. This does not mean that the issue of serious harm is a 'numbers game'. Reported cases have shown that very serious harm to a reputation can be caused by the publication of a defamatory statement to one person.
>
> 48. Thirdly there are obvious difficulties in getting witnesses to say that they read the words and thought badly of the claimant, compare *Ames v The Spamhouse* [sic] *Project* [2015]

EWHC 127 (QB) at paragraph 55. This is because the claimant will have an understandable desire not to spread the contents of the article complained of by asking persons if they have read it and what they think of the claimant, and because persons who think badly of the claimant are not likely to co-operate in providing evidence.

49. Fourthly, where there are publications about the same subject matter which are not the subject of complaint . . . there can be difficult points of causation which arise. . .

50. Fifthly, as Bingham LJ stated in *Slipper v BBC* [1991] QB 283 at 300, the law would part company with the realities of life if it held that the damage caused by publication of a libel began and ended with publication to the original publishee. Defamatory statements are objectionable not least because of their propensity 'to percolate through underground channels and contaminate hidden springs' through what has sometimes been called 'the grapevine effect'. However it must also be noted that Bingham LJ continued and said 'Usually, in fairness to a defendant, such effects must be discounted or ignored for lack of proof' before going on to deal with further publications which had been proved to be natural, provable and perhaps even intentional results of the publication sued upon.

69. Where an allegation has a seriously defamatory tendency and is widely published a claimant may choose to rely on those facts alone, perhaps in conjunction with evidence as to the identity of the publishees, as the basis for an inference that serious harm was actually caused. That, at one stage at least, was the primary position adopted on behalf of Ms Monroe. In some cases it may be enough. It is certainly not necessary in every case to engage in a detailed forensic examination of the precise factual picture, in order to determine whether the Serious Harm requirement is satisfied. Often, the factors relevant whether serious harm has been caused will be 'the same as those which come into play when assessing whether a tort is real and substantial for *Jameel* purposes' or an abuse of process: *Ames v Spamhaus Project Ltd* [2015] EWHC 127 (QB), [2015] 1 WLR 3409 [52]. As pointed out by HHJ Moloney QC (sitting as a Judge of the High Court) in *Theedom v Nourish Training Ltd* [2015] EWHC 3769 (QB) [2016] EMLR 10 [15](h),

> it is important to bear in mind that s 1 is essentially a threshold requirement, intended by Parliament to weed out those undeserving libel claims otherwise technically viable, but which do not involve actual serious harm to reputation or likely serious harm to reputation in the future.

70. In this case, however, the issues on serious harm have developed, and the evidence and argument has spawned a reasonably complex set of interlocking or overlapping sub-issues. This is mainly due to the way that the case for Ms Hopkins has been pleaded and pursued. There are no less than 11 main issues. I have reached the clear conclusion that the Serious Harm requirement is satisfied, on the straightforward basis that the tweets complained of have a tendency to cause harm to this claimant's reputation in the eyes of third parties, of a kind that would be serious for her. In the light of that conclusion I do not believe it is necessary for present purposes to examine in exhaustive detail all the sub-issues. Nor do I think it necessary for the purposes of arriving at a fair and reasonable conclusion on the extent of harm, and the appropriate sum in damages. I therefore do not think that I do an injustice to the considerable skill and effort that has been devoted to these issues if I identify and address them in turn, in fairly summary form.

71. The main points, and my conclusions on them, are these:—

> (1) The extent of publication. Reliance is placed on the allegedly limited extent of publication of the First Tweet, and its deletion 'around two hours' after first publication. I have dealt with and rejected Ms Hopkins' case on these points.

(2) Transience. It is true that the First Tweet was transient. The Second Tweet less so, although any tweet disappears from the reader's view as time goes on. But this is a weak point. What matters, when considering transience, is not the period of time for which a person is exposed to the message but the impact the message has. It is a commonplace of experience that live broadcasts can have a powerful impact, even if the viewer sees them once only. Print copies of newspapers are not often read more than once.

(3) The credibility of the publisher in the eyes of publishees. This is clearly a relevant question. Skilfully treading a somewhat delicate line, Mr Price [counsel for the defendant] submits that Twitter is the 'Wild West' of social media, and not as authoritative as (for instance) The Sun or the Daily Mail, which are established institutions, subject to regulation, that employ lawyers to check copy. On the facts of this case, I do not find this submission persuasive. I shall come to the question of whether Ms Hopkins' mistake was or would have been obvious to all. But there is no good reason to conclude that a reader would discount the allegation because of who Ms Hopkins is, or the fact that she published on Twitter. She is a well-known figure. She made clear at the time she was a Sun columnist.

(4) The absence of evidence that the allegation was believed. There is a dearth of such evidence, but this is a commonplace of litigation in this field and understandable for reasons identified by Dingemans J in *Sobrinho*. It is said to be remarkable, bearing in mind how uninhibited people are on Twitter, that there is nothing indicating that a person changed their position in respect of Ms Monroe as a result of the tweets. I think this submission lacks a sound evidential basis. I am not persuaded that the absence of evidence of this kind is evidence of a lack of harm.

(5) Evidence that 'no harm was done' to Ms Monroe['s] reputation. This is said to be 'obvious' from contemporaneous social media activity. I reject this. There is some evidence of social media activity suggesting that some people paid little attention to what had been said. But this represents only a fraction of the readership, and there is no sound basis on which to infer that it is representative of the whole. Certainly, some people realised that Ms Hopkins had mistaken Ms Monroe for Ms Penny [in the first tweet], and did so before the half-hearted early morning tweet of 2 June [the tweet read: '@MsJackMonroe I was confused about identity. I got it wrong']. But the evidence does not persuade me that this was a universal realisation. I deal with media coverage of 19 May separately, below.

(6) The question of whether Ms Monroe suffered or did not suffer a torrent of abuse as a consequence of the tweets (the 'torrent' point). . . . My conclusion is that 'torrent' is probably something of an overstatement, and much of what is relied on cannot be shown to be causally linked to the tweets complained of. But I accept that there was some abuse resulting from the tweets complained of, and reflecting harm to reputation.

(7) The state of Ms Monroe's existing standing or reputation in the eyes of the publishees. As Mr Price accepts, a defendant who wishes to prove that a claimant had an existing bad reputation must plead and prove it. That has not been done. Instead, Mr Price relies on documentary evidence that the (as he would say) few who abused Ms Monroe in the aftermath of the tweets complained of were people who were 'already making the same or similar comments about her before the tweets'. That is what the analysis of Ms Harris tends to show. This is a tricky area. In principle, evidence of bad reputation, however it may come into a case, is relevant only if it goes to the same sector of the claimant's reputation. This evidence is not clearly of that nature. But even assuming this is a legitimate line to take (which may be debatable) I do not think this is a matter to which any great weight should be attached. It is not safe

to infer that a claimant's reputation has not been harmed by a specific defamatory allegation just because a person who makes rude remarks about the claimant after publication also made rude remarks about her before.

(8) Another variant of this point is put forward: that those who engaged with the tweets were users who were already strongly supportive of Ms Monroe or strongly opposed to her; in summary, people 'whose opinions of the parties can't be shifted.' This comes dangerously close to evidence of bad reputation by the back door. Besides, I am not convinced that this is how people actually think, at least not in the mass. A person can have a low opinion of another, and yet the other's reputation can be harmed by a fresh defamatory allegation. An example is provided by serious allegations made against a politician of a rival party. I have recently held that it does not follow from the fact that a publishee is a political opponent of the claimant, that they will think no worse of the claimant if told that he or she has covered up sexual abuse: *Barron v Collins* [2017] EWHC 162 (QB) [56]. The same line of reasoning is applicable to the different facts of this case. As Mr Bennett [counsel for the claimant] puts it, if someone is hated for their sexuality or their left-wing views, that does not mean they cannot be libelled by being accused of condoning the vandalisation of a war memorial. It can add to the list of reasons to revile her.

(9) Ms Monroe's own responses on Twitter. These are said to have mitigated harm by making her position clear. There are several difficulties with this contention. One is that denials are not at all the same thing as corrections, retractions or apologies. The response of the accused is inherently unlikely to undo the damage caused initially. A second, and probably more significant point, is that Ms Monroe had no access to the followers of Ms Hopkins. The fact that the overlap in their followers was so small tends to undermine this submission.

(10) National and international media coverage of the tweets complained of, Ms Monroe's reaction to them, 'and the matter generally' on 19 May 2015. Nine articles are relied on. Three are in mainstream English newspapers (Metro, The Mirror and The Independent). The others are in the Belfast Telegraph, the Huffington Post, and a range of lesser known outlets. All are said to have been published 'within hours'. I am invited to infer that their publication meant that anyone with an interest in either party will have become aware that Ms Hopkins had made a mistake, Ms Monroe denied having vandalised anything, and intended to sue, that there was no attempt to justify what had been said. It is also suggested, in mitigation, that readers of these media would have realised that 'the claimant considered that she could make £5,000 in damages because of the tweets' (sic). This last contention seems to me offensive in its formulation, implying that compensation would be some kind of gain for the claimant. Otherwise, I would not attach any great weight to this point. The majority of the media coverage was in publications of the left, and it is not likely there was a substantial overlap with the defendant's own readership. The coverage did not amount to an authoritative or comprehensive refutation of the original allegation. As Mr Bennett points out, there was a potentially harmful impact of this publication, as it brought the whole matter to the attention of a fresh audience.

(11) The defendant's tweet of 2 June 2015. This was several weeks later, early in the morning. It was not self-explanatory. It was inconspicuous and carried no apology. It was sent as a reply, and hence to the common followers only. . . .

74. In all the circumstances and for the reasons I have given, whilst the claimant may not have proved that her reputation suffered gravely, I am satisfied that she has established that the publications complained of caused serious harm to her reputation, and met the threshold set by s 1 of the 2013 Act.

Notes

1. In *Lachaux* v *Independent Print Ltd* [2019] UKSC 27 the reputation of the claimant, who was a French national living in the United Arab Emirates, was found to have suffered 'serious harm' as a result of a series of articles in the *Huffington Post* and other UK newspapers which suggested he had abused his (former) wife and falsely accused her of kidnapping their son. The Supreme Court unanimously dismissed the newspaper's appeal:

   > [S]ection 1 necessarily means that a statement which would previously have been regarded as defamatory, because of its inherent tendency to cause some harm to reputation, is not to be so regarded unless it 'has caused or is likely to cause' harm which is 'serious'. The reference to a situation where the statement 'has caused' serious harm is to the consequences of the publication, and not the publication itself. It points to some historic harm, which is shown to have actually occurred. This is a proposition of fact which can be established only by reference to the impact which the statement is shown actually to have had. It depends on a combination of the inherent tendency of the words and their actual impact on those to whom they were communicated. (Lord Sumption at [14])

   Lord Sumption continued:

   > Mr Lachaux must demonstrate as a fact that the harm caused by the publications complained of was serious, Warby J [the trial judge] held that it was. He heard evidence from Mr Lachaux himself and three other witnesses of fact, and received written evidence from his solicitor. He also received agreed figures, some of them estimates, of the print runs and estimated readership of the publications complained of and the user numbers for online publications. He based his finding of serious harm on (i) the scale of the publications; (ii) the fact that the statements complained of had come to the attention of at least one identifiable person in the United Kingdom who knew Mr Lachaux and (iii) that they were likely to have come to the attention of others who either knew him or would come to know him in future; and (iv) the gravity of the statements themselves, according to the meaning attributed to them . . . Mr Lachaux would have been entitled to produce evidence from those who had read the statements about its impact on them. But I do not accept, any more than the judge did, that his case must necessarily fail for want of such evidence. The judge's finding was based on a combination of the meaning of the words, the situation of Mr Lachaux, the circumstances of publication and the inherent probabilities. There is no reason why inferences of fact as to the seriousness of the harm done to Mr Lachaux's reputation should not be drawn from considerations of this kind. Warby J's task was to evaluate the material before him, and arrive at a conclusion on an issue on which precision will rarely be possible. A concurrent assessment of the facts was made by the Court of Appeal. Findings of this kind would only rarely be disturbed by this court, in the absence of some error of principle potentially critical to the outcome. (at [21])

2. While **Monroe v Hopkins** was not the first time defamation law has been used in the context of Twitter, it is the first time that the serious harm test has been applied to tweets. In addition, Warby J makes a number of interesting determinations and observations that the courts are likely to return to in the future—including notably judicial 'common knowledge' of how Twitter and Twitter analytics work:

   5. Twitter is an online news and social networking service, which is widely used and very well known. It allows people using the Twitter website or a mobile device app to post and interact with messages of not more than 140 characters, called 'tweets'. This much is common knowledge. But Twitter is still a relatively new medium, and not everyone knows all the details of how it works. Where something is not a matter of common knowledge a Judge is not entitled to bring his or her own knowledge to bear. The facts normally have to be proved. In this case, however, many of the relevant facts about Twitter have been agreed, and set out in a Schedule called 'How Twitter Works', which is attached to this judgment as an Appendix.

3. On the developing case law around the 'serious harm' requirement, see David Erdos 'Serious Harm to Reputation Rights? Defamation in the Supreme Court' [2019] CLJ 510; Tom Rudkin 'Defamation Act 2013: You cannot be serious' Inforrm's blog, 3 March 2016; Oliver Lock and Tom Rudkin 'A time to reflect: the serious harm test' Inforrm's blog, 31 July 2016; and Mathilde Groppo 'Case Preview: *Lachaux v Independent Print*, Supreme Court to hear "serious harm" appeal' Inforrm's blog, 6 November 2018.

15.5 What do the words used mean?

While in everyday life the meaning of a particular statement may be unclear, in defamation it is down to the judge to determine 'a single immutable meaning from a series of words which are capable of bearing more than one' (Lord Kerr, ***Stocker v Stocker*** [2019] UKSC 17 at [33]). But how ought she go about doing this?

Stocker v Stocker
Supreme Court [2019] UKSC 17

The defendant, Nicola Stocker, had posted a number of comments on the Facebook wall of her ex-husband's new partner in which she claimed her ex-husband, Ronald Stocker, had 'tried to strangle me'. Mr Stocker sued her in defamation. Held: giving due consideration to the context in which the message was posted, the interpretation that Mr Stocker had grasped his wife by the neck was 'the obvious, indeed the inescapable, choice of meaning' (at [47]) and one that could be met by the defendant by the defence of justification.

LORD KERR:

1. 'He tried to strangle me.' What would those words convey to the 'ordinary reasonable reader' of a Facebook post?

Background

2. The respondent to this appeal, Ronald Stocker, is the former husband of the appellant, Nicola Stocker. Their marriage ended in acrimony in 2012. Mr Stocker subsequently formed a relationship with Ms Deborah Bligh. On 23 December 2012 an exchange took place between Mrs Stocker and Ms Bligh on the Facebook website. In the course of that exchange, Mrs Stocker informed Ms Bligh that her former husband (now Ms Bligh's partner) had tried to strangle her. . . .

3. Mrs Stocker also said that her husband had been removed from the house following a number of threats that he had made; that there were some 'gun issues'; and that the police felt that he had broken the terms of a non-molestation order. These statements and the allegation that Mr Stocker had tried to strangle her were the basis on which he took proceedings against her for defamation.

4. The allegations about threats, gun issues and the breach of a non-molestation order are relevant to provide context to the statement that Mr Stocker had tried to strangle Mrs Stocker. They paint a picture of acute marital conflict and on that account set the scene for any reader of the Facebook post. That reader would know that Mrs Stocker's statement that her former husband had tried to strangle her was made against the background that this had been, towards the end of its life, a most disharmonious marriage.

The proceedings in the High Court

5. Mr Stocker issued proceedings against his former wife, claiming that the statement that he had tried to strangle her was defamatory of him. He claimed that the meaning to be given to the words 'tried to strangle me' was that he had tried to kill her. Mrs Stocker denied that the words bore that meaning. She claimed that, in the context of domestic violence, the words do not impute an intention to kill. What they would be understood to mean, she said, was that her husband had violently gripped her neck, inhibiting her breathing so as to put her in fear of being killed.

6. Mr Stocker also claimed that the statement that he had uttered threats and breached a non-molestation order was defamatory and was to be taken as implying that he was a dangerous and thoroughly disreputable man. Mrs Stocker refuted this. She said that it was not reasonable to infer that she had suggested that her husband was dangerous on account of his having been arrested a number of times. It is to be observed, however, that in the defence filed on her behalf, Mrs Stocker averred that the statement that her husband was dangerous and disreputable was justified. It seems likely that this was by way of alternative plea. In any event, for reasons that will later appear, this is immaterial because of the rule concerning the substantial truth of the statements made by the alleged defamer.

7. At the start of the defamation proceedings, Mitting J, the trial judge, suggested that the parties should refer to the Oxford English Dictionary's definition of the verb, 'strangle'. This provided two possible meanings: (a) to kill by external compression of the throat; and (b) to constrict the neck or throat painfully. The judge was asked by counsel for the appellant, Mr Price QC, to consider how the words, 'tried to strangle' had been used in different contexts. Mr Price also sought to introduce legal definitions of the word 'strangle'. These do not appear to have been taken into account by Mitting J and he did not refer to them in his judgment.

15. It is clear . . . that the trial judge [referring to the two dictionary definitions referred to in paragraph 7] had confined the possible meaning of the statement, 'he tried to strangle me' to two stark alternatives. Either Mr Stocker had tried to kill his wife, or he had constricted her neck or throat painfully. In the judge's estimation, the fact that Mrs Stocker had said that her husband 'tried' to strangle her precluded the possibility of her statement being taken to mean that he had constricted her neck painfully.

16. This approach produces an obviously anomalous result. If Mrs Stocker had said, 'he strangled me', she should be understood to have meant that her husband had constricted her neck or throat painfully, on account of her having survived to tell the tale. But, because she said that he had 'tried' to strangle her (in the normal order of things and in common experience a less serious accusation), she was fixed with the momentous allegation that her husband had tried to kill her. On this analysis, the use of the verb, 'to try' assumes a critical significance. The possible meaning of constricting the neck painfully was shut out by what might be regarded as the adventitious circumstance that Mrs Stocker had said that her husband had 'tried' to strangle her rather than that he had strangled her.

17. This anomalous result was the product of confining the meaning of the words exclusively to two dictionary definitions. If 'tried to strangle' did not fit with the notion of trying to constrict the neck or throat painfully (because of the prosaic fact that Mrs Stocker was still alive), the only possible meaning was that Mr Stocker had tried to kill.

The Court of Appeal

22. At para 17 of her judgment, Sharp LJ in the Court of Appeal said this about the use of dictionaries as a means of deciding the meaning to be given to a statement alleged to be defamatory:

The use of dictionaries does not form part of the process of determining the natural and ordinary meaning of words, because what matters is the impression conveyed by the words to the ordinary reader when they are read, and it is this that the judge must identify. As it happened however no harm was done in this case. The judge told counsel during the course of submissions that he had looked at the OED definitions and what they said, so the parties had the opportunity to address him about it; the judge, as he then said, merely used the dictionary definitions as a check, and no more; those definitions were in substance the rival ones contended for by the parties, and in the event, the judge's ultimate reasoning, not dependent on dictionaries, was sound.

23. The suggestion that the judge told counsel 'in the course of submissions' that he had looked at the dictionary definition may mislead. On the first day of the trial, before any evidence had been given, counsel for Mr Stocker, Mr Barca QC, had suggested to Mitting J that no time would be saved by asking him to deliver a preliminary ruling on meaning. The judge replied that he had 'a preliminary opinion about it' which he was willing to disclose. Shortly thereafter, he suggested that counsel should look at the Oxford English Dictionary definitions and said, 'You might from that gain the primary and secondary definition and fit it (sic) into the context of a message that he "tried" to do something'. All of this occurred before the judge heard any argument about meanings. This suggests that, contrary to Sharp LJ's view, the judge was not using the dictionary definitions as a cross-check. Plainly, he regarded those definitions as comprehensive of the possible meanings of the statement, 'he tried to strangle me'.

24. Sharp LJ's statement that Mitting J merely used the dictionary definitions as a check may have been based on his comment in para 36 of his judgment that the authorities do not 'prohibit reference to an authoritative English dictionary such as the Oxford English Dictionary to confirm the meaning in ordinary usage of a single English word'. I do not construe this statement as signifying that the judge was using the dictionary definitions as a cross-check and, indeed, neither in his judgment nor in his exchanges with counsel, does he ever use the expression, 'check'. Given that Mitting J had consulted the dictionary before the trial began and commended consideration of it to counsel, it seems to me plain that, far from using the definitions as a check, what the judge did was to regard the two definitions as the only possible meanings which he could consider or, at the very least, the starting point for his analysis, rather than a cross-check or confirmation of the correct approach.

25. Therein lies the danger of the use of dictionary definitions to provide a guide to the meaning of an alleged defamatory statement. That meaning is to be determined according to how it would be understood by the ordinary reasonable reader. It is not fixed by technical, linguistically precise dictionary definitions, divorced from the context in which the statement was made.

26. Moreover, once the verb, 'strangle' is removed from its context and given only two possible meanings before it is reconnected to the word, 'tried' the chances of a strained meaning are increased. The words must be taken together so as to determine what the ordinary reasonable reader would understand them to mean. Mitting J examined the word 'strangle' in conspicuous detail before considering it in conjunction with the word, 'tried'. Having determined that 'strangle' admitted of only two possible meanings, he then decided that 'tried' could be applied to only one of these. Underpinning his reasoning is the unarticulated premise that 'to try' is necessarily 'to try and fail'. Since Mr Stocker had not failed to constrict his wife's throat, the judge concluded that the only feasible meaning of the words was that he had tried (and failed) to kill her. But that is not how the words are used in common language. If I say, 'I tried to regain my breath', I would not be understood to have tried but failed to recover respiratory function.

The single meaning rule

32. Section 11 of the Defamation Act 2013 abolished the statutory right to trial by jury (in section 69(1) of the Senior Courts Act 1981). . . .

35. It is then for the judge to decide which meaning to plump for. Guidance as to how she or he should set about that mission was provided in Jeynes . . . At para 14, Sir Anthony Clarke MR set out the essential criteria:

(1) The governing principle is reasonableness. (2) The hypothetical reasonable reader is not naïve, but he is not unduly suspicious. He can read between the lines. He can read in an implication more readily than a lawyer and may indulge in a certain amount of loose thinking, but he must be treated as being a man who is not avid for scandal and someone who does not, and should not, select one bad meaning where other non-defamatory meanings are available. (3) Over-elaborate analysis is best avoided. (4) The intention of the publisher is irrelevant. (5) The article must be read as a whole, and any 'bane and antidote' taken together. (6) The hypothetical reader is taken to be representative of those who would read the publication in question. (7) In delimiting the range of permissible defamatory meanings, the court should rule out any meaning which, 'can only emerge as the produce of some strained, or forced, or utterly unreasonable interpretation . . .' (see Eady J in *Gillick v Brook Advisory Centres* approved by this court [2001] EWCA Civ 1263 at para 7 and Gatley on Libel and Slander (10th ed), para 30.6). (8) It follows that 'it is not enough to say that by some person or another the words might be understood in a defamatory sense.' *Neville v Fine Arts Co* [1897] AC 68 per Lord Halsbury LC at 73.

36. Sharp LJ added a rider to the second of these criteria in *Rufus v Elliott* [2015] EWCA Civ 121 when she said at para 11:

To this I would only add that the words 'should not select one bad meaning where other non-defamatory meanings are available' are apt to be misleading without fuller explanation. They obviously do not mean in a case such as this one, where it is open to a defendant to contend either on a capability application or indeed at trial that the words complained of are not defamatory of the claimant, that the tribunal adjudicating on the question must then select the non-defamatory meaning for which the defendant contends. Instead, those words are 'part of the description of the hypothetical reasonable reader, rather than (as) a prescription of how such a reader should attribute meanings to words complained of as defamatory': see *McAlpine v Bercow* [2013] EWHC 1342 (QB), paras 63 to 66.

37. Clearly, therefore, where a range of meanings is available and where it is possible to light on one meaning which is not defamatory among a series of meanings which are, the court is not obliged to select the non-defamatory meaning. The touchstone remains what would the ordinary reasonable reader consider the words to mean. Simply because it is theoretically possible to come up with a meaning which is not defamatory, the court is not impelled to select that meaning.

38. All of this, of course, emphasises that the primary role of the court is to focus on how the ordinary reasonable reader would construe the words. And this highlights the court's duty to step aside from a lawyerly analysis and to inhabit the world of the typical reader of a Facebook post. To fulfil that obligation, the court should be particularly conscious of the context in which the statement was made, and it is to that subject that I now turn.

Context

41. The fact that this was a Facebook post is critical. The advent of the 21st century has brought with it a new class of reader: the social media user. The judge tasked with deciding how a Facebook post or a tweet on Twitter would be interpreted by a social media user must keep in mind the way in which such postings and tweets are made and read.

43. . . . it is wrong to engage in elaborate analysis of a tweet; it is likewise unwise to parse a Facebook posting for its theoretically or logically deducible meaning. The imperative is to

ascertain how a typical (ie an ordinary reasonable) reader would interpret the message. That search should reflect the circumstance that this is a casual medium; it is in the nature of conversation rather than carefully chosen expression; and that it is pre-eminently one in which the reader reads and passes on.

Further discussion

47. It will be clear . . . that, in my view, Mitting J fell into legal error by relying upon the dictionary definition of the verb 'to strangle' as dictating the meaning of Mrs Stocker's Facebook post, rather than as (as Sharp LJ suggested) a check. In consequence, he failed to conduct a realistic exploration of how the ordinary reader of the post would have understood it. Readers of Facebook posts do not subject them to close analysis. They do not have someone by their side pointing out the possible meanings that might, theoretically, be given to the post. —Anyone reading this post would not break it down in the way that Mitting J did by saying, well, strangle means either killing someone by choking them to death or grasping them by the throat and since Mrs Stocker is not dead, she must have meant that her husband tried to kill her—no other meaning is conceivable.

48. In view of the judge's error of law, his decision as to the meaning of the Facebook post cannot stand, and this court must either determine the meaning for itself, or if that is not possible, remit the case for a rehearing. It is entirely appropriate in this case for us to take the former course, determining the meaning ourselves.

49. I return to the ordinary reader of the Facebook post. Such a reader does not splice the post into separate clauses, much less isolate individual words and contemplate their possible significance. Knowing that the author was alive, he or she would unquestionably have interpreted the post as meaning that Mr Stocker had grasped his wife by the throat and applied force to her neck rather than that he had tried deliberately to kill her.

50. Ironically, perhaps, this conclusion is reinforced by the consideration that only one meaning is to be attributed to the statement. Taking a broad, overarching view, and keeping in mind that only one meaning could be chosen, the choice to be made between the meaning of the words being that Mr Stocker grasped his wife by the neck or that he tried to kill her is, in my opinion, a clear one. If Mrs Stocker had meant to convey that her husband had attempted to kill her, why would she not say so explicitly? And, given that she made no such allegation, what would the ordinary reasonable reader, the casual viewer of this Facebook post, think that it meant? In my view, giving due consideration to the context in which the message was posted, the interpretation that Mr Stocker had grasped his wife by the neck is the obvious, indeed the inescapable, choice of meaning.

51. I emphasise again that it is a legal error on the part of the judge that has opened the door to a redetermination of the meaning of Mrs Stocker's words. This is not a case of the appellate court giving precedence to its view of meaning over that legitimately reached by the judge. To the contrary, it is the court's recognition that the meaning determined by the judge was reached via a route which was impermissible and having then to confront the question what meaning should properly be attributed to the relevant words.

Justification

61. In light of my conclusion as to the correct meaning to be given to the words, 'tried to strangle me', section 5 of the Defamation Act 1952 must occupy centre stage. It is beyond dispute that Mr Stocker grasped his wife by the throat so tightly as to leave red marks on her neck visible to police officers two hours after the attack on her took place. It is not disputed that he breached a non-molestation order. Nor has it been asserted that he did not utter threats to Mrs Stocker. Many would consider these to be sufficient to establish that he was a dangerous and disreputable man, which is the justification which Mrs Stocker sought to establish. Mitting J considered that the meaning of the statement that the claimant was arrested on numerous occasions, in the context of the other statements, was that he represented a danger to any woman with whom he might live. I see no warrant for adding that dimension to the actual words used by Mrs Stocker in her various Facebook postings.

62. Even if all her allegations were considered not to have been established to the letter, there is more than enough to satisfy the provision in section 5 of the 1952 Act that her defence of justification should not fail by reason only that the truth of every charge is not proved, having regard to the truth of what has been proved.

Wherever possible words should be construed in their ordinary and natural meaning, but there are times when words may also have a hidden meaning—the innuendo. Typically there are said to be two kinds of innuendo, rather confusingly called a 'true' (or legal) innuendo and a 'false' (or popular) innuendo. A true innuendo occurs where there are facts known to the recipient of the information which gives the apparently innocuous statement a different meaning; for example, 'to say of a man that he was seen entering a named house would contain a derogatory implication for anyone who knew that the house was a brothel but not for anyone who did not' (Lord Devlin, *Lewis v Daily Telegraph* [1964] AC 234). A false innuendo is where the statement itself carries with it an implied meaning.

> ### Lewis v Daily Telegraph
> House of Lords [1964] AC 234

The defendants published a story headed 'Inquiry on firm by City Police', which stated that the City of London Fraud Squad were inquiring into the affairs of Rubber Improvement Ltd, of which the claimant, John Lewis, was chairman. It was claimed that the story meant that the affairs of the company were conducted fraudulently or dishonestly, or in such a way that the police suspected that their affairs were so conducted. Held: the words could not mean that the claimant was actually guilty of fraud, and a new trial was ordered on the basis that the words were only capable of meaning that the police suspected fraud.

LORD REID: The essence of the controversy between the parties is that the appellants maintain that these passages are capable of meaning that they were guilty of fraud. The respondents deny this: they admit that the paragraphs are libellous but maintain that the juries ought to have been directed that they are not capable of the meaning which the appellants attribute to them. The learned judge directed the juries in such a way as to leave it open to them to accept the appellants' contention, and it is obvious from the amounts of the damages awarded that the juries must have done this.

The gist of the two paragraphs is that the police, the City Fraud Squad, were inquiring into the appellants' affairs. There is no doubt that in actions for libel the question is what the words would convey to the ordinary man: it is not one of construction in the legal sense. The ordinary man does not live in an ivory tower and he is not inhibited by a knowledge of the rules of construction. So he can and does read between the lines in the light of his general knowledge and experience of worldly affairs. . . .

What the ordinary man would infer without special knowledge has generally been called the natural and ordinary meaning of the words. But that expression is rather misleading in that it conceals the fact that there are two elements in it. Sometimes it is not necessary to go beyond the words themselves, as where the plaintiff has been called a thief or a murderer. But more often the sting is not so much in the words themselves as in what the ordinary man will infer from them, and that is also regarded as part of their natural and ordinary meaning. Here there would be nothing libellous in saying that an inquiry into the appellants' affairs was proceeding: the inquiry might be by a statistician or other expert. The sting is in inferences drawn from the fact that it is the fraud squad which is making the inquiry. What those inferences should be is ultimately a question for the jury, but the trial judge has an important duty to perform.

Generally the controversy is whether the words are capable of having a libellous meaning at all, and undoubtedly it is the judge's duty to rule on that. I shall have to deal later with the test which he must apply. Here the controversy is in a different form. The respondents admit that their words were libellous, although I am still in some doubt as to what is the admitted libellous meaning. But they sought and seek a ruling that these words are not capable of having the particular meaning which the appellants attribute to them. I think that they are entitled to such a ruling and that the test must be the same as that applied in deciding whether the words are capable of having any libellous meaning. I say that because it appears that when a particular meaning has been pleaded, either as a 'true' or a 'false' innuendo, it has not been doubted that the judge must rule on the innuendo. And the case surely cannot be different where a part of the natural and ordinary meaning is, and where it is not, expressly pleaded.

The leading case is *Capital and Counties Bank Ltd v Henry & Sons* (1882) 7 App Cas 741. In that case Lord Selborne LC said: 'The test, according to the authorities, is, whether under the circumstances in which the writing was published, reasonable men, to whom the publication was made, would be likely to understand it in a libellous sense'. Each of the four noble Lords who formed the majority stated the test in a different way, and the speeches of Lord Blackburn and Lord Watson could be read as imposing a heavier burden on the plaintiff. But I do not think that they should now be so read. In *Nevill v Fine Art & General Insurance Co Ltd* [1897] AC 68 Lord Halsbury said: '. . . what is the sense in which any ordinary reasonable man would understand the words of the communication so as to expose the plaintiff to hatred, or contempt or ridicule . . . it is not enough to say that by some person or another the words *might* be understood in a defamatory sense.' These statements of the law appear to have been generally accepted and I would not attempt to restate the general principle.

In this case it is, I think, sufficient to put the test in this way. Ordinary men and women have different temperaments and outlooks. Some are unusually suspicious and some are unusually naïve. One must try to envisage people between these two extremes and see what is the most damaging meaning they would put on the words in question. So let me suppose a number of ordinary people discussing one of these paragraphs which they had read in the newspaper. No doubt one of them might say—'Oh, if the fraud squad are after these people you can take it they are guilty.' But I would expect the others to turn on him, if he did say that, with such remarks as—'Be fair. This is not a police state. No doubt their affairs are in a mess or the police would not be interested. But that could be because Lewis or the cashier has been very stupid or careless. We really must not jump to conclusions. The police are fair and know their job and we shall know soon enough if there is anything in it. Wait till we see if they charge him. I wouldn't trust him until this is cleared up, but it is another thing to condemn him unheard.'

What the ordinary man, not avid for scandal, would read into the words complained of must be a matter of impression. I can only say that I do not think that he would infer guilt of fraud merely because an inquiry is on foot.

Notes

1. Inherent in the decision in **Lewis** is the so-called 'repetition' rule—that is, that it is no defence for the defendant to say that he was merely repeating what he has been told. In other words, it is still defamatory for A to say, 'I was told by X that Y is a thief'. It may be true that X said this but A would still need to prove that Y is a thief. In **Lewis** Lord Reid said, 'I can well understand that if you say there is a rumour that X is guilty you can only justify it by proving that he is guilty, because repeating someone else's libellous statement is just as bad as making the statement directly' (at 260).

2. In *Gillick* v *BBC* The Times, 20 October 1995, Neill LJ said that the court should give to the material the natural and ordinary meaning which it would have conveyed to the ordinary reasonable reader or viewer, and that the reasonable reader was not naïve but nor was he unduly suspicious, and he could read between the lines. He could read in an implication more readily than a lawyer and might indulge in a certain amount of loose thinking. But he must be treated as a man who was not avid for scandal and someone who did not select one bad meaning where other non-defamatory meanings were available. The court should be cautious of over-elaborate analysis of the material in issue and should not be too literal in its approach. Finally, a statement should be taken to be defamatory if it would tend to lower the claimant in the estimation of right-thinking members of society generally, or be likely to affect a person adversely in the estimation of reasonable people generally.

> ### McAlpine v Bercow
> Queen's Bench Division [2013] EWHC 1342 (QB)

The facts are set out in section 15.3.

TUGENDHAT J: . . .

. . .

HOW THE COURT MUST DECIDE AN ISSUE AS TO MEANING

Two different kinds of meaning

47. The meanings of words for the purposes of defamation are of two kinds. There may be a natural and ordinary meaning and there may be an innuendo meaning.

48. In *Jones v Skelton* [1963] 1 WLR 1362 at 1370–1 the court explained what is meant by a natural and ordinary meaning as follows:

> The ordinary and natural meaning of words may be either the literal meaning or it may be an implied or inferred or an indirect meaning: any meaning that does not require the support of extrinsic facts passing beyond general knowledge but is a meaning which is capable of being detected in the language used can be a part of the ordinary and natural meaning of words. . . .. The ordinary and natural meaning may therefore include any implication or inference which a reasonable reader guided not by any special but only by general knowledge and not fettered by any strict legal rules of construction would draw from the words.

49. An innuendo meaning (in the technical legal sense) is something more than a meaning that can be implied from the words complained. It is a meaning which can be implied from the words complained of, but only if the reader also knows other facts (which are not general knowledge). These are generally called extrinsic facts.

50. In respect of an innuendo meaning, a claimant must, in addition to identifying the meaning complained of, prove the extrinsic facts relied upon and prove that these facts were known to readers

(*Gatley on Libel & Slander* 11th ed §3.19). The claimant will have been defamed in the minds of those readers, but not in the minds of the readers who did not know the extrinsic facts.

51. There may be an issue between the parties whether the circumstances of a publication amount to extrinsic facts, which have to be proved as such to support an innuendo, or whether they are general knowledge, which can be relied on in support of its natural and ordinary meaning. Either way, the court must find that the facts are known to the reader.

52. In the present case there is no dispute about the truth of the fact that the Claimant was a prominent Conservative politician from the Thatcher years. The issue is as to whether any reader of the Tweet knew who the Claimant was.

55. In *Fullam v Newcastle Chronicle & Journal Ltd* [1977] 1 WLR 651 the plaintiff complained that an article in a local newspaper meant that he had fathered an illegitimate child. But the meaning in question could only be understood by readers of the newspaper who knew facts about the plaintiff's wife and child (the date of the marriage and the date of the birth) which were not set out in the article he complained of. At 659 Scarman LJ explained:

> There may well be cases in which it would not be necessary to plead more than the fact of publication by newspaper and the extrinsic circumstances, leaving it to be inferred that there would be readers with knowledge of the facts [about his wife and child].
>
> For instance, the facts may be very well known in the area of the newspaper's distribution —in which event I would think it would suffice to plead merely that the plaintiff will rely on inference that some of the newspaper's readers must have been aware of the facts [about his wife and child] which are said to give rise to the innuendo.

56. In the present case the Claimant's primary case is that his having been a politician, the gist of the *Newsnight* report, and the reporting of it by the media, were so well known to Twitter followers generally that these facts should be treated as part of their general knowledge. If he is wrong about that, his alternative case is that he relies on inference. He submits that the court should infer that there probably were some readers who knew these facts, as explained in the *Fullam* case.

The test of reasonableness

57. The legal principles to be applied when determining the question of meaning are in part derived from the *Rubber Improvements* case. They were summarised by Sir Anthony Clarke MR in *Jeynes v News Magazines Limited* [2008] EWCA Civ 130 at [14]–[15] (where 'he' means 'he or she'):

> The legal principles relevant to meaning have been summarised many times and are not in dispute. . .. They may be summarised in this way: (1) The governing principle is reasonableness. (2) The hypothetical reasonable reader is not naïve but he is not unduly suspicious. He can read between the lines. He can read in an implication more readily than a lawyer and may indulge in a certain amount of loose thinking but he must be treated as being a man who is not avid for scandal and someone who does not, and should not, select one bad meaning where other non-defamatory meanings are available. (3) Over-elaborate analysis is best avoided. (4) The intention of the publisher is irrelevant. (5) The article must be read as a whole, and any 'bane and antidote' taken together. (6) The hypothetical reader is taken to be representative of those who would read the publication in question.

58. It is important in this case to stress point (6). The Tweet was not a publication to the world at large, such as a daily newspaper or broadcast. It was a publication on Twitter. The hypothetical reader must be taken to be a reasonable representative of users of Twitter who follow the Defendant. What the characteristics of such people might be is in part agreed, and in part for submissions by the parties as to what I should infer from what is agreed.

62. The law is clear that words may be defamatory in whatever form they are used. A question, or a rhetorical question, or any other form of words may, in principle, be understood to convey a defamatory meaning. The meaning of a statement or question depends on the context. The extent to which a reader can draw defamatory inferences from neutral words depends on the context. The writer is not responsible for an inference unless it is one that a reasonable person would draw: *Gatley* para 3.17.

66. . . . If there are two possible meanings, one less derogatory than the other, whether it is the more or the less derogatory meaning that the court should adopt is to be determined by reference to what the hypothetical reasonable reader would understand in all the circumstances. It would be unreasonable for a reader to be avid for scandal, and always to adopt a bad meaning where a non-defamatory meaning was available. But always to adopt the less derogatory meaning would also be unreasonable: it would be naïve.

67. Sir Edward [counsel for the claimant] submits that the Tweet taken just by itself, consisting of its seven words, suggests that the Claimant has done something wrong. It is not neutral, even to a reader who knew none of the events of the preceding two days. The question is followed by the words 'innocent face'.

68. The parties differ as to what the words 'innocent face' should be understood to mean in this context. Sir Edward submits that the words 'innocent face' are to be read as irony, that is, as meaning the opposite of their literal meaning. People sometimes ask a question to which they already know the answer. They may do that as an indirect way of bringing out into the open something they already know, or believe to be, a fact. They sometimes seek to conceal what they are up to (or pretend to conceal what they are up to) by putting on an expression which suggests that they do not already know the answer to the question. Sir Edward submits that the reasonable explanation for the Defendant inserting the words 'innocent face' in the Tweet is to negate a neutral interpretation, and to hint, or nudge readers into understanding that the Claimant has been doing wrong.

75. Mr McCormick [counsel for the defendant] submits that the words 'innocent face' are to be read literally: that the expression which the reader is being invited to imagine on the Defendant's face in asking the question is 'deadpan'. It is an expression to convey that she is asking it in a neutral and straightforward manner. She has noticed that the Claimant is trending and all she is asking is that someone should tell her why.

Discussion

81. In my judgment followers of the Defendant on Twitter probably are very largely made up of people who share her interest in politics and current affairs. They probably are people who, by 4 November, knew these elements of the story told in the *Newsnight* report: that Mr Messham had been abused at a children's home in Wales some 20 years or so before, that the man he identified as his abuser was a leading Conservative politician from that time, and that the decision of the BBC not to name the person Mr Messham [the person who made the allegation in the *Newsnight* report] identified was the subject of public controversy.

82. In my judgment some followers of the Defendant probably did also have prior knowledge of the Claimant as a leading Conservative politician of those years. Some followers probably did remember him in that capacity, and some others probably had sufficient interest in politics to have read about him. 56,000 is a substantial number of people, although I do not find that all of those read the Tweet.

83. However, in my judgment it was not necessary for a reader of the Tweet to have had any prior knowledge of the Claimant as a leading politician of the Thatcher years in order for them reasonably to have linked the Tweet naming him with what I have found they knew about the allegations in the *Newsnight* report. This is because the Tweet identified him by his title, Lord McAlpine, that is to say,

as a peer of the realm. It is common knowledge that peers nowadays are generally people who have held prominent positions in public life, in many cases in politics, including as members of the House of Lords. The Tweet asked why the named Lord was trending, in circumstances where (1) he was not otherwise in the public eye on 4 November 2012 and (2) there was much speculation as to the identity of an unnamed politician who had been prominent some 20 years ago.

84. In my judgment the reasonable reader would understand the words 'innocent face' as being insincere and ironical. There is no sensible reason for including those words in the Tweet if they are to be taken as meaning that the Defendant simply wants to know the answer to a factual question.

85. The Defendant does not have any burden of proof in the issue I have to decide. She does not have to offer an alternative explanation of why a peer, whose name and career is known to few members of the public today, might have been trending on 4 November 2012 without her knowing why he was trending. But where the Defendant is telling her followers that she does not know why he is trending, and there is no alternative explanation for why this particular peer was being named in the tweets which produce the Trend, then it is reasonable to infer that he is trending because he fits the description of the unnamed abuser. I find the reader would infer that. The reader would reasonably infer that the Defendant had provided the last piece in the jigsaw.

86. That leads to the question: what is the level of seriousness of the allegation that the Claimant fits the description of the unnamed abuser?

87. The *Newsnight* report was not a report of an investigation by the police (or by anyone else). Nor do the media reports suggest that they were reporting on an investigation. The *Newsnight* report, and all the other reports are of the allegations of a man who complained he was sexually abused. It is true that some reports also included that the unnamed person who is accused of the crime has vehemently denied it. But what is reported is the accusation. The Tweet is linked to those reports, in that it adds a name that was not in the reports themselves. So it is by implication a repetition of the accusation with the addition of the name which had previously been omitted.

88. The effect of the repetition rule is that the Defendant, as the writer of the Tweet, is treated as if she had made, with the addition of the Claimant's name, the allegation in the *Newsnight* and other media reports which had previously been made without his name. It is an allegation of guilt. I see no room on these facts for any less serious meaning. The fact that the accused's denial was also reported in media (other than *Newsnight*) may be one of a number of factors that the Defendant can rely on in mitigation of damage, but it does not reduce the seriousness of the allegation. . . .

CONCLUSION

90. It follows that, for these reasons, I find that the Tweet meant, in its natural and ordinary defamatory meaning, that the Claimant was a paedophile who was guilty of sexually abusing boys living in care.

91. If I were wrong about that, I would find that the Tweet bore an innuendo meaning to the same effect. But if it is an innuendo meaning it is one that was understood by that small number of readers who, before reading the Tweet on 4 November, either remembered, or had learnt, that the Claimant had been a prominent Conservative politician in the Thatcher years.

15.6 Do the words refer to the claimant?

The defamatory statement must be reasonably capable of applying to the claimant, although it is not necessary for the claimant to be specifically referred to. It is sufficient if reasonable people who are aware of the special facts (which must be proved by the claimant) would believe that he was the person being referred to. For example, in *Hulton & Co v Jones* [1910] AC 20, the defendants published a humorous article about the behaviour in Dieppe of a fictitious character named Artemus Jones, referring to his being accompanied by a woman who was not his wife. A barrister named Artemus Jones successfully sued, even though the defendants had not intended to refer to him—not least because they did not know he existed! Liability in defamation is strict and so it is no defence that the defendant acted reasonably and never intended to identify the claimant.

> ### *Newstead* v *London Express Newspapers*
> Court of Appeal [1940] 1 KB 377

Under the heading 'Why do people commit bigamy?' the defendants published a story stating that 'Harold Newstead, a 30-year-old Camberwell man, who was jailed for nine months liked having two wives at once'. The allegation was true of a 30-year-old Camberwell bartender, but not true of the claimant of the same name, who was a hairdresser in Camberwell and of about the same age. Held: the article was defamatory of the hairdresser, even though the defendant had not intended to refer to him in any way.

SIR WILFRED GREENE MR: If the words used when read in the light of the relevant circumstances are understood by reasonable persons to refer to the plaintiff, refer to him they do for all relevant purposes. Their meaning cannot be affected by the recklessness or honesty of the writer.

I do not propose to refer to the authorities which establish this proposition, except to quote the words of Lord Loreburn LC in *E Hulton & Co v Jones* [1910] AC 20, where he said: 'What does the tort consist in? It consists in using language which others knowing the circumstances would reasonably think to be defamatory of the person complaining of and injured by it.' In the case of libel, once it is held that the words are capable of referring to the plaintiff, it is, of course, for the jury to say whether or not they do so refer. Subject to this, the principle is in truth an illustration of the rule that the author of a written document is to be taken as having intended his words to have the meaning which they convey when understood in the light of the relevant surrounding circumstances. In the case of libel, the same words may reasonably convey different meanings to a number of different persons or groups of persons, and so be held to be defamatory of more persons than one.

After giving careful consideration to the matter, I am unable to hold that the fact that defamatory words are true of A, makes it as a matter of law impossible for them to be defamatory of B, which was in substance the main argument on behalf of the appellants. At first sight this looks as though it would lead to great hardship. But the hardships are in practice not so serious as might appear, at any rate in the case of statements which are *ex facie* defamatory. Persons who make statements of this character may not unreasonably be expected, when describing the person of whom they are made, to identify that person so closely as to make it very unlikely that a judge would hold them to be reasonably capable of referring to someone else, or that a jury would hold that they did so refer. This is particularly so in the case of statements which purport to deal with actual facts. If there is a risk of coincidence it ought, I think, in reason to be borne not by the innocent party to whom the words are held to refer, but by the party who puts them into circulation. In matters of fiction, there is no doubt more room for hardship. Even in the case of matters of fact it is no doubt possible to construct imaginary facts which would lead to hardship. There may also be hardship if words, not on their faces defamatory, are true of A, but are reasonably understood by some as referring to B, and as applied to B are defamatory. But such cases must be rare. The law as I understand it is well settled, and can only be altered by legislation. . . .

MACKINNON LJ: If A publishes to another person, or persons, words which upon their reasonable meaning refer to B, if those words are defamatory as holding B up to hatred, ridicule, or contempt, and if the words so referring to B cannot be justified as true, A may be liable for damages to B.

Secondly, the reasonable meaning of the words, upon the question whether they refer to B must be tested objectively and not subjectively. The question is what do the words mean as words, not what did A in his own mind mean by them or intend them to mean.

Thirdly, A cannot plead as a defence that he was unaware of B's existence.

Fourthly, A cannot plead as a defence that the words are, in their reasonable meaning, equally capable of referring to C, and that when referring to C they are true.

Fifthly, there has been in some of the cases (notably by Farwell LJ in *Jones v Hulton & Co* [1909] 2 KB 444) reference to negligence or recklessness on the part of A in making the publication. If the words, on their reasonable meaning, do refer to B, I think it is immaterial whether A was either negligent or reckless in not ascertaining the existence of B, or guarding against the applicability to him of the words. If B establishes his claim, the jury in assessing his damages may take into account all the circumstances of the publication. The negligence or recklessness of A may well be among such circumstances. Further or otherwise negligence or recklessness on the part of A is immaterial.

It is hardly necessary to add, sixthly, the rule which is elementary, namely, that it is the primary duty of the judge to decide whether the words complained of are capable of a meaning that is defamatory of B, and only if he answers that question in the affirmative to leave to the jury the questions whether they are in fact defamatory of B, and, if so, what damages he shall be awarded.

In a case in which there is no question that the words are defamatory of him, if they refer to B, and the contest is only whether they do so refer, this preliminary question for the judge must be: 'Are these words on their reasonable meaning capable of referring to the plaintiff?' And if he answers that affirmatively I think that, properly, the first question to be left to the jury should be: 'Could the words used by the defendant be reasonably interpreted by those to whom they were published as referring to the plaintiff?'

Notes

1. The principle does not mean that any person with the same name as the person mentioned can sue, for the rule is that reasonable people must believe the story in fact refers to the claimant. Thus, in *Blennerhasset v Novelty Sales Service* (1933) 175 LTJo 393 the defendants advertised their yo-yo by saying that a Mr Blennerhasset had become obsessed by it and was under 'sympathetic surveillance' in the country. A stockbroker of the same name failed in his action for defamation because no reasonable person would think it applied to him.

2. The Faulks Committee Report on Defamation (Cmnd 5909, 1975) considered this principle, but ultimately decided that it should be retained. However, following *O'Shea v MGN* [2001] EMLR 40, a case involving the application of the strict liability principle to 'look-a-like' photographs, it appears that it might not survive an Article 10 challenge. The defendants published a pornographic advertisement for a website using the photograph of a model, which looked very much like a picture of the claimant. Rejecting the claim, Morland J held that to apply the common law to the strict liability principle would be an unjustifiable interference with the defendant's Article 10 right of freedom of expression and would be disproportionate to the legitimate aim of protecting the reputations of look-a-likes. He distinguished *Hulton* and **Newstead** on the ground that the real claimants involved there could have been discovered by the defendants, but it would be impossible to discover whether a look-a-like existed.

15.7 **Truth**

It has long been a common law defence—the defence of justification—to show that the words are true 'in substance and in fact'. This defence has now been replaced by the defence of truth in section 2 of the Defamation Act 2013. The new defence is intended to broadly reflect the common law defence and, as such, earlier case law is helpful, though not binding, in terms of how the new defence should be applied.

DEFAMATION ACT 2013

2. Truth

(1) It is a defence to an action for defamation for the defendant to show that the imputation conveyed by the statement complained of is substantially true.

(2) Subsection (3) applies in an action for defamation if the statement complained of conveys two or more distinct imputations.

(3) If one or more of the imputations is not shown to be substantially true, the defence under this section does not fail if, having regard to the imputations which are shown to be substantially true, the imputations which are not shown to be substantially true do not seriously harm the claimant's reputation.

(4) The common law defence of justification is abolished and, accordingly, section 5 of the Defamation Act 1952 (justification) is repealed.

Notes

1. It is not necessary for the defendant to demonstrate that *everything* they said was true (s 2(3)). This reflects the position at common law: 'the defendant does not have to prove that every word he/she published was true. He/she has to establish the "essential" or "substantial" truth of the sting of the libel' (Brooke LJ, *Chase v News Group Newspapers Ltd* [2002] EWCA Civ 1772 at [34]).

2. However, the 'sting' of the defamation can sometimes be unclear. In *Grobbelaar v News Group Newspapers Ltd* [2002] UKHL 40, for example, the claimant, a professional footballer, was filmed undercover confessing to match fixing and taking bribes. This was reported in the *Sun* newspaper. The question for the court was whether the 'sting' of the defamatory statement was the allegation that the claimant had conspired to throw matches (which, on the basis of the video evidence, the defendant could prove) or whether he had actually gone on to throw matches (which the defendant could not prove to be true). The House of Lords held that the question was one for the jury to decide and, as such, their decision—that the sting related to the allegation that the claimant threw a particular match (which could not have been shown to be true by the defendants)—was not perverse and should not have been overturned. Nevertheless, the law lords reduced Grobbelaar's damages from £85,000 to £1 on the basis that he had been proven to be corrupt.

15.8 **Honest opinion**

Section 3 of the Defamation Act 2013 replaces the common law defence of honest or fair comment with the statutory defence of honest opinion. This provides a defence, in certain circumstances, for statements of opinion (as opposed to fact). It differs from the common law defence in that the opinion need not be on a matter of public interest (this is now covered by the new defence of 'publication in a matter of public interest'; Defamation Act 2013, s 4) and it is not defeated by malice. Again, the earlier incarnations of the defence are abolished by the 2013 Act, and so the case law must be read with this in mind; nevertheless it remains a helpful guide as to how the new defence may be interpreted.

DEFAMATION ACT 2013

3. Honest opinion

(1) It is a defence to an action for defamation for the defendant to show that the following conditions are met.

(2) The first condition is that the statement complained of was a statement of opinion.

(3) The second condition is that the statement complained of indicated, whether in general or specific terms, the basis of the opinion.

(4) The third condition is that an honest person could have held the opinion on the basis of—

(a) any fact which existed at the time the statement complained of was published;

(b) anything asserted to be a fact in a privileged statement published before the statement complained of.

(5) The defence is defeated if the claimant shows that the defendant did not hold the opinion.

(6) Subsection (5) does not apply in a case where the statement complained of was published by the defendant but made by another person ('the author'); and in such a case the defence is defeated if the claimant shows that the defendant knew or ought to have known that the author did not hold the opinion.

(7) For the purposes of subsection (4)(b) a statement is a 'privileged statement' if the person responsible for its publication would have one or more of the following defences if an action for defamation were brought in respect of it—

(a) a defence under section 4 (publication on matter of public interest);

(b) a defence under section 6 (peer-reviewed statement in scientific or academic journal);

(c) a defence under section 14 of the Defamation Act 1996 (reports of court proceedings protected by absolute privilege);

(d) a defence under section 15 of that Act (other reports protected by qualified privilege).

(8) The common law defence of fair comment is abolished and, accordingly, section 6 of the Defamation Act 1952 (fair comment) is repealed.

Spiller v Joseph
Supreme Court [2010] UKSC 53

The claimants were members of musical acts 'The Gillettes' and 'Saturday Night at the Movies'. The defendants provided entertainment booking services, and advertised acts and performers on their website for weddings, etc. In 2007, the defendants posted a message on their website, which stated that 'Events is no longer able to accept bookings for this artist as the Gillettes c/o Craig Joseph are not professional enough to feature in our portfolio and have not been able to abide by the terms of their contract'. The claimants alleged that this meant that they were grossly unprofessional and untrustworthy. The defendants claimed that the facts were such that they were entitled to make this comment. The defence of fair comment was struck out by the Court of Appeal, but was reinstated by the Supreme Court.

LORD PHILLIPS:

3. Sitting in the Court of Final Appeal of Hong Kong in *Tse Wai Chun Paul v Albert Cheng* [2001] EMLR 777, [2000] HKCFA 35 Lord Nicholls of Birkenhead was concerned with the ingredients of malice that can defeat the defence of fair comment. Before considering that question he set out at paras 16–21, under the heading 'Fair Comment: The Objective Limits' what he optimistically described as five 'non-controversial matters', which were 'well established' in relation to the defence of fair comment:

16. . . . First, the comment must be on a matter of public interest. Public interest is not to be confined within narrow limits today: see Lord Denning in *London Artists Ltd v Littler* [1969] 2 QB 375, 391.

17. Second, the comment must be recognisable as comment, as distinct from an imputation of fact. If the imputation is one of fact, a ground of defence must be sought elsewhere, for example, justification or privilege. Much learning has grown up around the distinction between fact and comment. For present purposes it is sufficient to note that a statement may be one or the other, depending on the context. Ferguson J gave a simple example in the New South Wales case of *Myerson v Smith's Weekly* (1923) 24 SR (NSW) 20, 26:

To say that a man's conduct was dishonourable is not comment, it is a statement of fact. To say that he did certain specific things and that his conduct was dishonourable is a statement of fact coupled with a comment.

18. Third, the comment must be based on facts which are true or protected by privilege: see, for instance, *London Artists Ltd v Littler* [1969] 2 QB 375, 395. If the facts on which the comment purports to be founded are not proved to be true or published on a privilege occasion, the defence of fair comment is not available.

19. Next, the comment must explicitly or implicitly indicate, at least in general terms, what are the facts on which the comment is being made. The reader or hearer should be in a position to judge for himself how far the comment was well founded.

20. Finally, the comment must be one which could have been made by an honest person, however prejudiced he might be, and however exaggerated or obstinate his views: see Lord Porter in *Turner v Metro-Goldwyn-Mayer Pictures Ltd* [1950] 1 All ER 449, 461, commenting on an observation of Lord Esher MR in *Merivale v Carson* (1888) 20 QBD 275, 281. It must be germane to the subject-matter criticised. Dislike of an artist's style would not justify an attack upon his morals or manners. But a critic need not be mealy-mouthed in denouncing what he disagrees with. He is entitled to dip his pen in gall for the purposes of legitimate criticism: see Jordan CJ in *Gardiner v Fairfax* (1942) 42 SR (NSW) 171, 174.

21. These are the outer limits of the defence. The burden of establishing that a comment falls within these limits, and hence within the scope of the defence, lies upon the defendant who wishes to rely upon the defence.

4. These five propositions relate to elements of the defence of fair comment in respect of which the burden of proof is on the defendant. *Cheng* was primarily concerned with a sixth element—absence of malice. A defendant is not entitled to rely on the defence of fair comment if the comment was made maliciously. The onus of proving malice lies on the claimant.

5. *The second proposition.* This merits elaboration. Jurists have had difficulty in defining the difference between a statement of fact and a comment in the context of the defence of fair comment. The example in *Myerson* (1923) 24 SR (NSW) 20, 26 cited by Lord Nicholls is not wholly satisfactory. To say that a man's conduct was dishonourable is not a simple statement of fact. It is a comment coupled with an allegation of unspecified conduct upon which the comment is based. A defamatory

comment about a person will almost always be based, either expressly or inferentially, on conduct on the part of that person. Judges and commentators have, however, treated a comment that does not identify the conduct on which it is based as if it were a statement of fact. For such a comment the defence of fair comment does not run. The defendant must justify his comment. To do this he must prove the existence of facts which justify the comment.

6. *The fifth proposition.* The requirement to show that the comment is germane to the subject-matter criticised and is one that an honest person could have made, albeit that that person may have been prejudiced, or have had exaggerated or obstinate views, is one that is bizarre and elusive. I am not aware of any action in which this has actually been an issue. I shall describe this element as 'pertinence'.

7. *The fourth proposition.* It is this proposition that is directly in issue in this appeal. The facts on which the defendants wish to rely in support of their plea of fair comment include a fact to which they made no reference in the publication complained of. The claimants say that they cannot rely on this, for this would run foul of Lord Nicholls' fourth proposition. Mr Price submits that far from being well established, that proposition is contrary to authority and wrong. Mr Caldecott supports that submission. The important issue raised by this appeal is thus the extent to which, if at all, the defence of fair comment requires that the comment should identify the matter or matters to which it relates. . . .

The development of the defence of fair comment

70. Lord Nicholls' fourth proposition has come under attack before that launched in the present action. It is questioned in *Duncan & Neill* 3rd ed at para 13.20 and in *Gatley* at para 12.8. Eady J dissented from it at para 57 of his judgment in *Lowe v Associated Newspapers Ltd* [2006] EWHC 320 (QB); [2007] QB 580. That decision merits attention, for it contains the carefully considered views of a judge who has great experience of the law of defamation on the subject matter of the present appeal. The publication complained of in that case was a short paragraph about matters that will have been of interest to a large number of football supporters: the replacement of the Manager of Southampton Football Club and the claimant's acquisition of ownership of the Club by a reverse take-over. The defendant's primary case was that the paragraph complained of contained comment and was protected by the defence of fair comment. In the alternative, in case the publication should be held to consist of fact rather than comment, there was a plea of justification. The defendant pleaded some 19 pages of facts which were claimed to support both the plea of fair comment and the plea of justification. No less than 16 interlocutory applications were listed before the judge, but the issues to which his judgment was essentially directed were:

(i) To what extent is it necessary for a defendant relying upon fair comment to be able to demonstrate that the facts upon which the comment was based are to be found in the text of the words complained of?

(ii) How far must the author of the words complained of be aware at the time of publication of the facts sought to be relied upon to support the comment?

Eady J carried out a detailed analysis of many of the authorities to which I have referred and reached the following conclusions:

(1) Any fact pleaded to support fair comment must have existed at the time of publication.

(2) Any such facts must have been known, at least in general terms, at the time the comment was made, although it is not necessary that they should all have been in the forefront of the commentator's mind.

(3) A general fact within the commentator's knowledge (as opposed to the comment itself) may be supported by specific examples even if the commentator had not been aware of them (rather as examples of previously published material from Lord Kemsley's newspapers were allowed).

(4) Facts may not be pleaded of which the commentator was unaware (even in general terms) on the basis that the defamatory comment is one he would have made if he had known them.

(5) A commentator may rely upon a specific or a general fact (and, it follows, provide examples to illustrate it) even if he has forgotten it, because it may have contributed to the formation of his opinion.

(6) The purpose of the defence of fair comment is to protect honest expressions of opinion, or inferences honestly drawn from, specific facts.

(7) The ultimate test is the objective one of whether someone could have expressed the commentator's defamatory opinion (or drawn the inference) upon the facts known to the commentator, at least in general terms, and upon which he was purporting to comment.

71. I have some difficulty with propositions (3) and (5). I do not understand the nature of the 'support' for facts within the commentator's knowledge that can be derived from facts of which he was not aware. Nor is it easy to understand how a commentator can know that a fact is one that he has forgotten. . . .

Discussion

94. My reading of the position is as follows. The House [in *Kemsley* v *Foot* [1952] AC 345] had held that the defence of fair comment could be raised where the comment identified the subject matter of the comment generically as a class of material that was in the public domain. There was no need for the commentator to spell out the specific parts of that material that had given rise to the comment. The defendant none the less had quite naturally given particulars of these in order to support the comment. Lord Porter held that it was not necessary to prove that each of these facts was accurate provided that at least one was accurate and supported the comment.

95. This passage does not support the proposition that a defendant can rely in support of the defence of fair comment on a fact that does not form part of the subject matter identified generically by the comment. Even less does it support the proposition that a defendant can base a defence of fair comment on a fact that was not instrumental in his forming the opinion that he expressed by his comment. The last sentence of the passage that I have cited makes this plain.

96. I can summarise the position as follows. Where, expressly or by implication, general criticism is made of a play, a book, an organ of the press or a notorious course of conduct in the public domain, the defendant is likely to wish in his defence to identify particular aspects of the matter in question by way of explanation of precisely what it was that led him to make his comment. These particular aspects will be relevant to establishing the pertinence of his comment and to rebutting any question of malice, should this be in issue. Lord Porter's speech indicates that the comment does not have to refer to these particular aspects specifically and that it is not necessary that all that are pleaded should be accurate, provided that the comment is supported by at least one that is.

97. Can Lord Nicholls' fourth proposition in *Cheng* [2001] EMLR 777, [2000] HKCFA 35, para 19 be reconciled with these propositions? The passage in *Odgers*, 6th ed (1929), p 166 that was cited with approval by Lord Porter (see para 51 above) suggested that where conduct is identified by a clear reference the defendant thereby enables his readers to judge for themselves how far his opinion is well founded. As Lord Ackner pointed out, however, in *Telnikoff* [1992] 2 AC 343, 361, it is fallacious to suggest that readers will be able to form their own view of the validity of the criticism of a matter merely because in the past it was placed in the public domain. Readers of 'The Tribune' who did not read the Kemsley Press could no doubt have gained access to a representative sample of this, but this will not be possible where the criticism is of an ephemeral matter such as a concert, or the single performance of a play, or a football match, all of which can give rise to general criticism that is protected by the defence of fair comment.

98. For these reasons I do not consider that Lord Nicholls' fourth proposition in *Cheng* can be reconciled with *Kemsley v Foot*. Lord Nicholls' proposition echoed what Fletcher Moulton LJ had said in *Hunt v Star Newspaper Co Ltd* [1908] 2 KB 309—see para 39 above, but each observation was obiter. There is no case in which a defence of fair comment has failed on the ground that the comment did not identify the subject matter on which it was based with sufficient particularity to enable the reader to form his own view as to its validity. For these reasons, where adverse comment is made generally or generically on matters that are in the public domain I do not consider that it is a prerequisite of the defence of fair comment that the readers should be in a position to evaluate the comment for themselves.

99. What of a case where the subject matter of the comment is not within the public domain, but is known only to the commentator or to a small circle of which he is one? Today the internet has made it possible for the man in the street to make public comment about others in a manner that did not exist when the principles of the law of fair comment were developed, and millions take advantage of that opportunity. Where the comments that they make are derogatory it will often be impossible for other readers to evaluate them without detailed information about the facts that have given rise to the comments. Frequently these will not be set out. If Lord Nicholls' fourth proposition is to apply the defence of fair comment will be robbed of much of its efficacy.

100. The cases have none the less emphasised repeatedly the requirement that the comment should identify the subject matter on which it is based, as is demonstrated by the passages in the judgments that I have emphasised by placing them in italics. If the requirement that the comment should identify the subject matter on which it is based is not imposed in order to enable the reader of the comment to form his own view of its validity, what is the object of the requirement? Bingham LJ in *Brent Walker* [1991] 2 QB 33, 44 said that the true facts must be 'stated or sufficiently indicated'— sufficiently for what?

101. There are a number of reasons why the subject matter of the comment must be identified by the comment, at least in general terms. The underlying justification for the creation of the fair comment exception was the desirability that a person should be entitled to express his view freely about a matter of public interest. That remains a justification for the defence, albeit that the concept of public interest has been greatly widened. If the subject matter of the comment is not apparent from the comment this justification for the defence will be lacking. The defamatory comment will be wholly unfocussed.

102. It is a requirement of the defence that it should be based on facts that are true. This requirement is better enforced if the comment has to identify, at least in general terms, the matters on which it is based. The same is true of the requirement that the defendant's comment should be honestly founded on facts that are true.

103. More fundamentally, even if it is not practicable to require that those reading criticism should be able to evaluate the criticism, it may be thought desirable that the commentator should be required to identify at least the general nature of the facts that have led him to make the criticism. If he states that a barrister is 'a disgrace to his profession' he should make it clear whether this is because he does not deal honestly with the court, or does not read his papers thoroughly, or refuses to accept legally aided work, or is constantly late for court, or wears dirty collars and bands.

104. Such considerations are, I believe, what Mr Caldecott had in mind when submitting that a defendant's comments must have identified the subject matter of his criticism if he is to be able to advance a defence of fair comment. If so, it is a submission that I would endorse. I do not consider that Lord Nicholls was correct to require that the comment must identify the matters on which it is based with sufficient particularity to enable the reader to judge for himself whether it was well

founded. The comment must, however, identify at least in general terms what it is that has led the commentator to make the comment, so that the reader can understand what the comment is about and the commentator can, if challenged, explain by giving particulars of the subject matter of his comment why he expressed the views that he did. A fair balance must be struck between allowing a critic the freedom to express himself as he will and requiring him to identify to his readers why it is that he is making the criticism.

Conclusion

For the reasons that I have given I would endorse Lord Nicholls' summary of the elements of fair comment that I have set out at para 3 above, save that I would re-write the fourth proposition:

Next the comment must explicitly or implicitly indicate, at least in general terms, the facts on which it is based.

Notes

1. The second condition of the new defence, that 'the statement complained of indicated, whether in general or specific terms, the basis of the opinion' (s 3(3)), reflects the test approved in *Spiller*. Lord Phillips went on to consider whether the 'case for reform' of the common law (at [106]–[117]) including whether 'there may be a case for widening the scope of the defence of fair comment by removing the requirement that it must be on a matter of public interest' (at [113]) (public interest is not a requirement of the new defence) and whether 'the time [had] come to recognise that defamation is no longer a field in which trial by jury is desirable?' (at [116]) (the presumption in favour of jury trials has been abolished; Defamation Act 2013, s 11).

   However not all of Lord Phillips's suggestions were followed. While Lord Phillips remained unconvinced as to the extension of the defence of fair comment to inferences of fact—'Careful consideration needs to be given to Mr Caldecott's first proposition that the defence of fair comment should extend to inferences of fact . . . It is questionable whether this is satisfactory' (at [114])—the Act's Explanatory Notes state that 'as an inference of fact is a form of opinion, this would be encompassed by the defence' (at [21]).

2. It can sometimes be hard to draw a clear line between a statement of fact and a comment on a fact. This was at issue in *British Chiropractic Association v Singh* [2010] EWCA Civ 350 where the British Chiropractic Association (BCA) sued the author of an article published in a national newspaper in which he stated that there was 'not a jot of evidence' for the BCA's 'bogus claims' that its members could treat various listed conditions, including ear infections and asthma. The question for the Court of Appeal was whether this was a statement of fact or opinion. Though the words 'not a jot of evidence' may be thought to involve a question of fact—either such evidence exists or it does not—the court held that the words should be read as meaning there is 'no worthwhile or reliable evidence'. And whether evidence not only exists but is *worthwhile* is a value judgement, and so a matter of opinion. Hence, then, defence of fair comment could apply.

3. Though the defendant in *Singh* ultimately won, the case became something of a cause célèbre during discussions around changes to the law of defamation and led directly to the inclusion of section 6 in the Defamation Act 2013 which identifies a new category of privilege aimed at protecting defendants in the position of Singh (section 15.9).

4. More recently, in *Koutsogiannis v The Random House Group Ltd* [2019] EWHC 48 (QB), Nicklin J provides a useful summary of the guidance between fact and opinion:

   ### Fact and Opinion: The Law

   16. Again, there is no dispute as to the principles to be applied. Drawn from *Grech -v- Odhams Press* [1958] 2 QB 75; *Branson -v- Bower* [2001] EMLR 32; *Lowe -v- Associated Newspapers Ltd*

[2007] QB 580; *Joseph -v- Spiller* [2011] 1 AC 852; *British Chiropractic Association -v- Singh* [2011] 1 WLR 133; *Yeo -v- Times Newspapers Limited* [2015] 1 WLR 971 [88]-[89]; *Wasserman -v- Freilich* [2016] EWHC 312 (QB); *Morgan -v- Associated Newspapers Limited* [2018] EWHC 1850 (QB) [13]; and *Zarb-Cousin -v- Association of British Bookmakers* [2018] EWHC 2240 (QB), when determining whether the words complained of contain allegations of fact or opinion, the Court will be guided by the following points:

i) The statement must be recognisable as comment, as distinct from an imputation of fact.

ii) Opinion is something which is or can reasonably be inferred to be a deduction, inference, conclusion, criticism, remark, observation, etc.

iii) The ultimate question is how the word would strike the ordinary reasonable reader. The subject matter and context of the words may be an important indicator of whether they are fact or opinion.

iv) Some statements which are, by their nature and appearance opinion, are nevertheless treated as statements of fact where, for instance, the opinion implies that a claimant has done something but does not indicate what that something is, i.e. the statement is a bare comment.

v) Whether an allegation that someone has acted 'dishonestly' or 'criminally' is an allegation of fact or expression of opinion will very much depend upon context. There is no fixed rule that a statement that someone has been dishonest must be treated as an allegation of fact.

17. I would also note here what I said recently in *Tinkler -v- Ferguson* [2018] EWHC 3563 (QB) [37] about implied or inferred expression of opinion:

. . . a number of adjectives and adverbs have been inserted into the Claimant's meaning which are not part of the natural and ordinary meaning of the words. They are strained constructions of what is being said in the [publication]. For example, if an individual reader thought that the Claimant's alleged behaviour was 'selfish', that would be a personal judgment made by the individual reader. It is neither stated nor implied in the text. Such inferential meanings (that depend upon—and vary between—each individual reader's moral judgment) are not part of the natural and ordinary meaning of words: *Brown -v- Bower* [2017] 4 WLR 197 [54]. In context, a suggestion that the conduct of the Claimant was 'selfish' would be an expression of an opinion. If such an opinion is expressly stated by the author, then it can readily be identified as such by readers. I find the notion of an 'inferred opinion' conceptually difficult. I suppose it is conceivable that an article may not make express an author's view, but it nevertheless emerges clearly as a result of discernible indications in the text as to what his or her opinion actually is on the given facts. But this is very subjective; and it may be difficult to separate out those cases from cases where what is really happening is simply that the reader is supplying his or her own judgment on the stated facts rather than detecting the author's opinion by implication.

15.9 **Privilege**

The defence of privilege comes in two forms: absolute and qualified. It essentially allows people to speak without fear of defamation proceedings in circumstances where it is important that people are able to speak freely. Examples of situations in which the defence of absolute privilege applies include:

(1) parliamentary proceedings, including statements in Parliament and in reports published by Parliament;

(2) contemporaneous reports of judicial proceedings;

(3) court proceedings—including those before the UK and international domestic courts, the Court of Justice of the European Union, the European Court of Human Rights and UN international tribunals.

Qualified privilege is wider in scope than absolute privilege. It offers a defence where the person making the statement has an 'interest or duty, legal, social or moral, to make it to the person to whom it is made, and the person to whom it is made has a corresponding interest or duty to receive it' (Lord Atkinson, *Adam* v *Ward* [1917] AC 309 at 334). It only protects the maker of a defamatory statement who speaks honestly and without malice. Though the qualified privilege has, in recent years, been relied on by the media in cases where there has been a 'public interest' in a particular story being published, notwithstanding the fact that it cannot be proven to be true, in the form of the so-called *Reynolds* defence (now replaced by a new defence of 'publication in a matter of public interest'; Defamation Act 2013, s 4), it is not limited to such cases.

> ### *Watt v Longsdon*
> Court of Appeal [1930] 1 KB 130

Longsdon was the liquidator of the Scottish Petroleum Company, which carried on business in Morocco and elsewhere. Watt, a managing director, and Browne, a manager, were in Casablanca. Browne wrote a letter to Longsdon, the liquidator, stating that Watt had left Casablanca, leaving behind an unpaid bill for £88 for whisky, and that he had been 'in immoral relations' with his housemaid, who was described as an old woman, stone deaf, almost blind and with dyed hair. Longsdon gave a copy of the letter to Singer, the chairman of the board of directors, and to Mrs Watt. Longsdon also wrote a letter defamatory of Watt to Browne. The defendants claimed qualified privilege. Held: while the publication of the defamatory statement by Longsdon to Singer and Browne was privileged (there being a corresponding duty and interest in the information), its publication to Mrs Watt was not privileged. In any event, there was evidence of malice which ought to be left to a jury, and a new trial was ordered.

SCRUTTON LJ: Lord Esher MR says in *Pullman v Hill & Co* [1891] 1 QB 524: 'An occasion is privileged when the person who makes the communication has a moral duty to make it to the person to whom he does make it, and the person who receives it has an interest in hearing it. Both these conditions must exist in order that the occasion may be privileged.' Lord Atkinson in *Adam v Ward* [1917] AC 309 expresses it thus: 'It was not disputed, in this case on either side, that a privileged occasion is, in reference to qualified privilege, an occasion where the person who makes a communication has an interest or a duty, legal, social, or moral, to make it to the person to whom it is made, and the person to whom it is so made has a corresponding interest or duty to receive it. This reciprocity is essential.' With slight modifications in particular circumstances, this appears to me to be well established law, but, except in the case of communications based on common interest, the principle is that either there must be interest in the recipient and a duty to communicate in the speaker, or an interest to be protected in the speaker and a duty to protect it in the recipient. Except in the case of common interest justifying intercommunication, the correspondence must be between duty and interest. There may, in the common interest cases, be also a common or reciprocal duty. It is not every interest which will create a duty in a stranger or volunteer. This appears to fit in with the two statements of Parke B already referred to . . . that the communication was made in the discharge of some social or moral duty, or on the ground of an interest in the party making or receiving it. This is approved by Lindley LJ in *Stuart v Bell* [1891] 2 QB 341, but I think should be expanded into:

> either (1) a duty to communicate information believed to be true to a person who has a material interest in receiving the information, or (2) an interest in the speaker to be protected by communicating information, if true, relevant to that interest, to a person honestly believed to have a duty to protect that interest, or (3) a common interest in and reciprocal duty in respect of the subject matter of the communication between speaker and recipient.

. . . In my opinion Horridge J went too far in holding that there could be a privileged occasion on the ground of interest in the recipient without any duty to communicate on the part of the person making the communication. But that does not settle the question, for it is necessary to consider, in the present case, whether there was, as to each communication, a duty to communicate, and an interest in the recipient.

First as to the communication between Longsdon and Singer, I think the case must proceed on the admission that at all material times Watt, Longsdon and Browne were in the employment of the same company, and the evidence afforded by the answer to the interrogatory put in by the plaintiff that Longsdon believed the statements in Browne's letter. In my view on these facts there was a duty, both from a moral and a material point of view, on Longsdon to communicate the letter to Singer, the chairman of his company, who, apart from questions of present employment, might be asked by Watt for a testimonial to a future employer. Equally, I think Longsdon receiving the letter from Browne, might discuss the matter with him, and ask for further information, on the ground of a common interest in the affairs of the company, and to obtain further information for the chairman. . . .

The communication to Mrs Watt stands on a different footing. I have no intention of writing an exhaustive treatise on the circumstances when a stranger or a friend should communicate to husband or wife information he receives as to the conduct of the other party to the marriage. I am clear that it is impossible to say he is always under a moral or social duty to do so; it is equally impossible to say he is never under such a duty. It must depend on the circumstances of each case, the nature of the information, and the relation of speaker and recipient. . . .. Using the best judgment I can in this difficult matter, I have come to the conclusion that there was not a moral or social duty in Longsdon to make this communication to Mrs Watt such as to make the occasion privileged, and that there must be a new trial so far as it relates to the claim for publication of a libel to Mrs Watt.

Notes

1. The general principles adopted by Scrutton LJ in this case were applied in *Beach v Freeson* [1971] 2 All ER 860 in the area of communication to public bodies. Reg Freeson MP received a complaint from one of his constituents about the claimant solicitors, and the constituent asked him to write to the Law Society believing that the involvement of an MP would add weight to his complaint. The defendant did so, and added that he had received other complaints about the claimants in the past. He sent the letter to the Law Society, and also a copy to the Lord Chancellor. On the question of privilege, the Court of Appeal said that the defendant had a duty to pass on the complaint to the Law Society and to make additional comments which he thought should be investigated. The Law Society, as the relevant disciplinary body, had a reciprocal interest in receiving the complaint. That letter was therefore privileged. The same was true of the letter to the Lord Chancellor, who had an interest in the proper administration of justice. However, the court pointed out that the recipient must, as the Lord Chancellor did, have an actual interest in receiving the information, and it would not be enough merely for the sender mistakenly to believe that such an interest existed.

15.10 Publication on a matter of public interest

Section 4 of the Defamation Act introduces an entirely new defence of 'publication on a matter of public interest'. This replaces the so-called *Reynolds* defence (itself the application of qualified privilege) and provides a defence where the statement is on a matter of public interest and the defendant reasonably believes that its publication is in the public interest.

DEFAMATION ACT 2013

4. Publication on matter of public interest

(1) It is a defence to an action for defamation for the defendant to show that—

(a) the statement complained of was, or formed part of, a statement on a matter of public interest; and

(b) the defendant reasonably believed that publishing the statement complained of was in the public interest.

(2) Subject to subsections (3) and (4), in determining whether the defendant has shown the matters mentioned in subsection (1), the court must have regard to all the circumstances of the case.

(3) If the statement complained of was, or formed part of, an accurate and impartial account of a dispute to which the claimant was a party, the court must in determining whether it was reasonable for the defendant to believe that publishing the statement was in the public interest disregard any omission of the defendant to take steps to verify the truth of the imputation conveyed by it.

(4) In determining whether it was reasonable for the defendant to believe that publishing the statement complained of was in the public interest, the court must make such allowance for editorial judgement as it considers appropriate.

(5) For the avoidance of doubt, the defence under this section may be relied upon irrespective of whether the statement complained of is a statement of fact or a statement of opinion.

(6) The common law defence known as the Reynolds defence is abolished.

Reynolds v *Times Newspapers*
House of Lords [2001] 2 AC 127

The claimant was the Prime Minister of Ireland, and a few days after he resigned the *Sunday Times* published an article with the headline 'Goodbye gombeen man' with the sub-heading 'Why a fib too far proved fatal for the political career of Ireland's peacemaker and Mr Fixit'. The claimant claimed that the article meant that he had dishonestly misled the Dail by suppressing information. The jury found that the allegations were untrue and that there was no malice on the part of the defendants. The claimant was awarded damages of one penny. The defendants claimed qualified privilege on the ground that information of political significance attracted a special privilege. Held: by majority, the article was not privileged. The existing protection provided by the defences of privilege and honest comment was adequate when dealing with matters of public interest and it would be wrong to single out political debate from other matters of public importance.

LORD NICHOLLS: . . . As highlighted by the Court of Appeal judgment in the present case, the common law solution is for the court to have regard to all the circumstances when deciding whether the publication of particular material was privileged because of its value to the public. Its value to the public depends upon its quality as well as its subject matter. This solution has the merit of elasticity. As observed by the Court of Appeal, this principle can be applied appropriately to the particular circumstances of individual cases in their infinite variety. It can be applied appropriately to all information published by a newspaper, whatever its source or origin.

Hand in hand with this advantage goes the disadvantage of an element of unpredictability and uncertainty. The outcome of a court decision, it was suggested, cannot always be predicted with certainty when the newspaper is deciding whether to publish a story. To an extent this is a valid criticism. A degree of uncertainty in borderline cases is inevitable. This uncertainty, coupled with the expense of court proceedings, may 'chill' the publication of true statements of fact as well as those which are untrue. The chill factor is perhaps felt more keenly by the regional press, book publishers and broadcasters than the national press. However, the extent of this uncertainty should not be exaggerated. With the enunciation of some guidelines by the court, any practical problems should be manageable. The common law does not seek to set a higher standard than that of responsible journalism, a standard the media themselves espouse.

Conclusion

My conclusion is that the established common law approach to misstatements of fact remains essentially sound. The common law should not develop 'political information' as a new 'subject matter' category of qualified privilege, whereby the publication of all such information would attract qualified privilege, whatever the circumstances. That would not provide adequate protection for reputation. Moreover, it would be unsound in principle to distinguish political discussion from discussion of other matters of serious public concern. The elasticity of the common law principle enables interference with freedom of speech to be confined to what is necessary in the circumstances of the case. This elasticity enables the court to give appropriate weight, in today's conditions, to the importance of freedom of expression by the media on all matters of public concern.

Depending on the circumstances, the matters to be taken into account include the following. The comments are illustrative only. 1. The seriousness of the allegation. The more serious the charge, the more the public is misinformed and the individual harmed, if the allegation is not true. 2. The nature of the information, and the extent to which the subject matter is a matter of public concern. 3. The source of the information. Some informants have no direct knowledge of the events. Some have their own axes to grind, or are being paid for their stories. 4. The steps taken to verify the information. 5. The status of the information. The allegation may have already been the subject of an investigation which commands respect. 6. The urgency of the matter. News is often a perishable commodity. 7. Whether comment was sought from the plaintiff. He may have information others do not possess or have not disclosed. An approach to the plaintiff will not always be necessary. 8. Whether the article contained the gist of the plaintiff's side of the story. 9. The tone of the article. A newspaper can raise queries or call for an investigation. It need not adopt allegations as statements of fact. 10. The circumstances of the publication, including the timing.

This list is not exhaustive. The weight to be given to these and any other relevant factors will vary from case to case. Any disputes of primary fact will be a matter for the jury, if there is one. The decision on whether, having regard to the admitted or proved facts, the publication was subject to qualified privilege is a matter for the judge. This is the established practice and seems sound. A balancing operation is better carried out by a judge in a reasoned judgment than by a jury. Over time, a valuable corpus of case law will be built up.

In general, a newspaper's unwillingness to disclose the identity of its sources should not weigh against it. Further, it should always be remembered that journalists act without the benefit of the clear light of hindsight. Matters which are obvious in retrospect may have been far from clear in the heat of the moment. Above all, the court should have particular regard to the importance of freedom of expression. The press discharges vital functions as a bloodhound as well as a watchdog. The court should be slow to conclude that a publication was not in the public interest and, therefore, the public had no right to know, especially when the information is in the field of political discussion. Any lingering doubts should be resolved in favour of publication.

Notes

1. As the claimant was awarded only one penny in damages the dispute was wholly about who should pay the costs. The decision that the article was not privileged was based on the view that, although it was a matter of public concern, the paper had made serious allegations without mentioning the claimant's explanation.

2. The test in *Reynolds* was widely criticised. The general consensus was that it was being applied too cautiously in the lower courts and, as a result, it did little to give editors confidence in publishing a story. *Reynolds* was followed by a number of cases seeking to clarify and explain the defence's meaning (see e.g. *Loutchansky* v *The Times Newspapers (No 2)* [2001] EWCA Civ 1805; *Bonnick* v *Morris* [2002] UKPC 31; *Jameel* v *Wall Street Journal Europe* [2006] UKHL 44; *Flood* v *Times Newspapers* [2012] UKSC 11). By the time the Defamation Bill came to be debated in Parliament, it was ripe for reform. However, once again, Parliament's intension was to 'codify' and 'reflect' the current common law defence as developed from *Reynolds* and set out by the Supreme Court in *Flood* v *Times Newspapers*. Section 4(4) expressly recognises the importance of editorial judgement and discretion as affirmed in *Flood*.

3. Nevertheless, Parliament's strategy of abolishing a relatively new defence to replace it with a defence that is—at least in its view—exactly the same is a surprising one (and one that is repeated for the common law defences of justification and honest comment). While its purported rationale is to avoid the situations where defendants may tend to rely on the common law defence instead of or alongside the statutory defence, it may well create more problems than it solves. As Lord Hoffmann noted in a debate on an earlier incarnation of the Defamation Bill:

   But I am slightly puzzled by what . . . [the proposed public interest defence] does do—which is to take the public interest defence as laid down by your Lordships' House in *Reynolds* and *Jameel*, and restate it in its own language. I am always nervous, speaking as a former judge, about legislative attempts to restate the rules of common law. They lead to expensive litigation over whether or not Parliament intended to change things. As the *Jameel* case appeared to be generally welcomed by the press and has been followed by the Canadians [in *Grant* v *Torstar Corporation* [2009] SCC 61)], I should have thought that there was a case for leaving well alone. (HL Deb, 9 July 2010, col 432)

Economou v *de Freitas*
Court of Appeal [2018] EWCA Civ 2591

Economou was accused by his former girlfriend (Ms de Freitas) of rape. He was arrested but not charged. Eight months later, he brought a private prosecution (which the CPS subsequently took over) against Ms de Freitas. Four days before the trial started, she committed suicide. Her father (Mr de Freitas) subsequently authored (or authorized) seven articles in which he repeated his daughter's accusation. Economou sued in defamation. At first instance, Warby J held that only two of the seven articles were actionable (the others were either not defamatory or failed to reach the 'serious harm' threshold); however, the public interest defence was made out in relation to all of them. Held: the Court of Appeal rejected Economou's argument that Warby J had effectively conferred 'contributor immunity' on the defendant and reaffirmed the importance of *Reynolds* when assessing the reasonableness of the defendant's belief.

LADY JUSTICE SHARP:

The public interest defence: section 4 of the 2013 Act

75. The area of controversy. . . raises difficult issues: in particular, the extent to which contributors to media publications or 'citizen journalists' are subject to the same standard of 'responsible conduct' that might be required of professional journalists, and the organs in which they publish, if they are to take advantage of the public interest defence. These issues fall to be considered against the statutory language used in section 4 of the 2013 Act, the common law roots of that provision and the unusual and tragic facts of this case.

76. Section 4 of the 2013 Act as it says at subsection (6), abolished and replaced the common law defence identified by the House of Lords in *Reynolds v Times Newspapers and ors* [2001] 2 AC 127. However, the judge and the parties proceeded on the footing that the common law principles identified in *Reynolds* as interpreted or applied in subsequent cases, such as *Bonnick v Morris* [2002] UKPC 31, [2003] 1 AC 300, *Jameel (Mohammed) and anor v Wall Street Journal Europe Sprl* [2006] UKHL 44, [2007] 1 AC 359 and *Flood v Times Newspapers Ltd* [2012] UKSC 11, [2012] 2 AC 273, were of relevance to the interpretation of section 4. Though the point was uncontroversial before us, in my view, this is the correct approach.

77. As the judge noted, the Explanatory Notes to section 4 of the 2013 Act state that the intention is to create 'a new defence. . . of publication on a matter of public interest

> . . . based on the existing common law defence established in *Reynolds* . . . and . . . is intended to reflect the principles in that case and subsequent case law . . . [it] is intended essentially to codify the common law defence . . . [while] the current case law would constitute a helpful (albeit not binding) guide to interpreting how the new statutory defence should be applied.' See paras 29 and 35. The Explanatory Notes also say at para 29: '*Subsection (1)* provides for the defence to be available in circumstances where the defendant can show that the statement complained of was, or formed part of, a statement on a matter of public interest and that he reasonably believed that publishing the statement complained of was in the public interest. The intention is to reflect the existing common law as most recently set out in *Flood* . . . It reflects the fact that the common law test contained both a subjective element—what the defendant believed was in the public interest at the time of publication—and an objective element—whether the belief was a reasonable one for the defendant to hold in all the circumstances.'

The judge's analysis

87. There were three questions that had to be addressed in relation to each of the publications complained of. Was the statement complained of, or did it form part of, a statement on a matter of public interest? If so, did the defendant believe that publishing the statement complained of was in the public interest? If so, was that belief reasonable?

88. We are principally concerned with the third question. As I have said, it was accepted below that the statements complained of were or formed part of a statement on a matter of public interest, and no issue is taken in this appeal with the judge's conclusion that the defendant believed that publishing the statement complained of, was in the public interest. . . .

89. Before considering the third question, it is important to draw attention to the strength of the public interest considerations, carefully outlined by the judge at [142] to [150] of which there were a number of interrelated strands; and to a question of statutory interpretation that has arisen.

90. The principal matter of public interest was whether the CPS, a public authority, may have gone wrong in making a decision to prosecute because it had been mistaken in its assessment of the strength of the evidential basis for the prosecution and/or the public interest in pursuing a prosecution[.] This was in a context that was especially sensitive, because the person prosecuted was a rape complainant, she was a mentally disordered person and she had killed herself on the eve of her trial. The judge highlighted the enhanced public interest in considering whether to prosecute a person suffering from mental illness in these circumstances, and the possibility of a causal link between their death and the prosecution. An additional matter was the role of an inquest in examining such cases, and whether in this particular case, there were lessons to be learned, something to which the publications complained of directly related.

91. There was, more generally, a strong public interest in ensuring that victims of rape came forward and an obvious risk that they may be deterred from doing so by the risk of prosecution for perverting the course of justice. As the judge noted, it does not follow from the fact that an accused person is not prosecuted or charged, that an allegation made against them is false, still less that it is made with knowledge that it is false; and how decisions are made as to whether or not to prosecute those who complain of rape or other sexual crimes, for perverting the course of justice is a matter of considerable public importance. . . .

96. Against that background, I turn to the third question: was the defendant's belief that publishing the statement complained of was in the public interest, reasonable?

97. The judge decided that it was. . . .

103. The case put for the claimant was that the defendant's conduct fell short of the standard of responsibility comprised by the *Reynolds* factors. It followed therefore, as night follows day, that his conduct was not reasonable, and the public interest defence should fail. Specifically, there was no credible source of any evidence to support the defendant's condemnation of the evidential case against his daughter; no steps were taken by the defendant to verify the truth of the allegations before he made them; the defendant had no adequate reasons for taking issue with investigations that commanded respect (namely, the CPS's decision to continue the prosecution and the DPP's confirmation of the correctness of the decision); the defendant sought no comment from the claimant and ignored what the claimant had repeatedly told him; the defendant failed to include even the gist of the claimant's side of the story, and his purpose in going public was improper. See [238].

104. The judge gave very careful consideration to this aspect of the claimant's argument insofar as it was still a live one on the facts. He acknowledged that the case that the defendant's conduct had fallen far short of what the *Reynolds* approach required, would have had obvious force if the defendant had acted as a journalist, composing and publishing what purported to be investigative journalism. The critical point made by the judge however, was that it would not be appropriate to hold the defendant to the standard that might be required of a journalist because he was not one: his role was closer to that of a source or contributor. See [242].

105. The judge had correctly identified a number of considerations that were important when considering the outcome of a public interest defence, some of which were to be derived from the

Reynolds defence itself, viz. flexibility in the requirement to have regard to the circumstances of the particular case in section 4(2); the requirement to make allowance for editorial judgment in section 4(4) and the fact that there is little scope under article 10(2) of the Convention for restrictions on freedom of expression in relation to questions of public interest.

106. Building on his analysis of the case of *Hays Plc v Hartley* [2010] EWHC 1068 (QB) a decision of Tugendhat J, the judge then said this:

> 246. It seems to me wrong in principle to require an individual who contributes material for inclusion or use in an article or broadcast in the media to undertake all the enquiries which would be expected of the journalist, if they are to rely on a defence of public interest. The enquiries and checks that can reasonably be expected must be bespoke, depending on the precise role that the individual plays. It is hard to see how an individual could rely on the public interest defence to escape liability for a false factual statement about events within their own knowledge (see *Starr v Ward* [[2015] EWHC 1987 (QB)]). But I see no reason why the defence should not avail an individual source or contributor who passes to a journalist for publication information the truth or falsity of which is not within the knowledge of the contributor. The contributor may well be entitled to rely on the journalist to carry out at least some of the necessary investigation and to incorporate such additional material as is required, in order to ensure appropriate protection for the reputation of others.

> 247. Mr de Freitas accepted in his evidence that in contributing to, causing, authorising, and making the offending publications he did not focus on the impact these might have on Mr Economou's reputation. I am sure that is right. Mr de Freitas was at all times concentrating his thoughts on what to say about the CPS, and its decision-making. But I do not consider this to be as reprehensible as Mr Barnes [counsel for the claimant] contends. The defamatory meanings that I have found were conveyed by the publications complained of are all implied meanings. They are secondary to the principal messages of the articles and broadcasts, all of which are squarely aimed at the CPS. They are not only implied but, to a large extent, necessarily implied.

> 248. I raised with Mr Barnes the question of how Mr de Freitas could have expressed himself without unlawfully harming Mr Economou's reputation, by implication. His answer was that he could and should have refrained from attacking the CPS as he did. If it is not strictly true, it is not far from the truth to say that the options were stark: to say nothing adverse to the CPS, or to do so and impliedly defame Mr Economou. What Mr de Freitas did was to criticise or at least raise questions about the conduct of the CPS, but without naming Mr Economou or, for the most part, expressly referring to him in any other way. This limited room for manoeuvre seems to me a further factor to take into account when assessing the reasonableness of Mr de Freitas' belief.

107. Mr Browne QC [counsel for the claimant] submits this part of the judge's analysis was flawed for a number of reasons, principally, in his approach to the defendant's role, which he argues amounts to the creation of 'contributor immunity'. It left out of account, or failed to give sufficient weight to the seriousness of the allegations, it failed to take account of the fact that the defendant was closest to knowing the truth, or that there was no evidence that he had relied on the media to fill the gap left by his own inadequate compliance with the *Reynolds* factors. The judge also erred in giving any weight to the defendant's intentions with regard to meaning (since intention is irrelevant in determining meaning) and/or in having regard to his intention or not to refer to claimant, in circumstances where the test for identification is an objective binary one, which does not depend on what a defendant

knows or intends will happen. But principally, the judge was at fault in excusing the defendant's failure to include the gist of the claimant's case (which had been forcibly presented to him by the claimant over the material period) on the footing that it was someone else's (i.e. the media's) 'job' and/ or that it was difficult for him to do so. On the latter point, he submits it is not difficult to see how the claimant could have incorporated distancing wording, which, if not removing, would have substantially lessened the sting of the defamatory words.

108. The result of all this he submits is that someone who was setting the agenda, and pursuing a media strategy on inadequate and misleading information, is absolved from the consequences, and that the claimant has been defamed on the basis of information which was untrue, partial or misleading and never subject to the sort of responsibility filter, or journalistic inquiry or consideration that is required if a proper balance is to be struck between freedom of expression on matters of public interest, and reputation. In this connection he also draws attention to the wording of section 4(3) of the 2013 Act, which, in summary, requires the court to disregard a defendant's omission to verify the truth of the imputation when determining whether it was reasonable for the defendant to believe that publishing the statement was in the public interest, in relation to the (now) statutory defence of 'reportage'. The removal of verification in section 4(3), necessarily implies, Mr Browne QC submits, its presence as a component of what is required if a belief can be found to be reasonable for the purposes of section 4(2).

109. Looking at the matter generally, it seems to me the issue raises difficulties on both sides of the equation, free speech on one side, and reputation on the other, that must be acknowledged. And I readily accept that mediating between the rights engaged here is not an easy task. I have already referred to what Lord Nicholls said about the importance of reputation to the individual and to society more generally. The implications of the publication of false information are, if anything, more serious now than they were when *Reynolds* was decided. The fact that information is present on the Internet, gives it permanence and reach, which may have profound implications for the life and future prospects of the person defamed. A successful public interest defence leaves a claimant whose reputation is damaged without vindication, damages or the ability to obtain injunctive relief. We were not addressed on how these matters are affected by section 8 of the 2013 Act, which abrogates the single publication rule, and provides, in summary, that a cause of action is treated as having accrued on the date of first publication. On one view however, a limitation defence might prevent the removal of information from the Internet, even if the public interest justification for it, which might have formed the basis of a successful public interest defence when it was first published, no longer exists. It might also be said, that in an era of distrust and 'fake news', it is more important than ever that the public should, so far as possible, be put in the picture as to where the truth, or some approximation of it, lies: see for example, the observations of Lord Phillips in *Flood* [v *Times Newspapers Ltd* [2012] UKSC 11] at para 48.

110. Looking at the matter from the other perspective however, it is not necessary to expatiate on the importance of freedom of expression to a functioning democracy, and to the individuals within it, which concerns the freedom to receive information as well as to impart it, in particular, as the judge noted, on matters of public concern. The importance of the right in this arena is what led to the recognition of the *Reynolds* defence, and to the subsequent enactment of the public interest defence in section 4 of the 2013 Act. This defence is not confined to the media, which has resources and other support structures others do not have. Section 4 requires the court to have regard to all the circumstances of the case when determining the all-important question arising under section 4(1)(b): it says the court must have regard to all the circumstances of the case in determining whether the defendant has shown that he or she reasonably believed that publishing the statement complained

of was in the public interest. In my judgment, all the circumstances of the case must include the sort of factors carefully identified by the judge, including, importantly, the particular role of the defendant in question. The statute could have made reference to the *Reynolds* factors in this connection, but it did not do so. That is not to say however, that the matters identified in the non-exhaustive checklist may not be relevant to the outcome of a public interest defence, or that, on the facts of the individual case, the failure to comply with one or some of the factors, may not tell decisively against a defendant. However, even under the *Reynolds* regime, as Lord Nicholls made clear, the weight to be given to those factors, and any other relevant factors, would vary from case to case. As with *Reynolds* therefore, with its emphasis on practicality and flexibility, all will depend on the facts.

111. I quite accept that an appropriate balance between the rights engaged would not be struck if the bar of 'reasonable belief' was set too low, or if all those who took part in a particular publication were able to look to the other participants to fulfil what they would otherwise reasonably be expected to do, given their particular role in the process. But the principles applied by the judge do not lead to that result. . . .

112. . . . On the unusual facts of this case, the judge was entitled to conclude, and made no error of principle in concluding, first, that incorporating the 'claimant's side of the story' would have made little sense where the defamatory meanings were implied meanings, and secondary to the principal messages of the articles, squarely aimed at the CPS; and secondly, that the defendant had limited room for manoeuvre. It is true that the defendant could have added distancing words, as Mr Browne QC submits, but in my judgment it did not follow from this that the statutory criteria for the public interest defence were not satisfied.

Notes

1. Sharp LJ's analysis in **Economou v de Freitas** was approved by the Supreme Court in *Serafin v Malkiewicz and others* [2020] UKSC 23:

   . . . the [Defamation] Bill, as introduced, *did* in effect make reference to the **Reynolds** factors but later they were deliberately omitted. Subject to what some may regard as only a quibble, the observations of Sharp LJ are valid. The quibble, if such it be, relates to her use of the word 'checklist'. I suggest that a check list is a list of factors to which reference ought to be made, in particular in order to check whether a preliminary conclusion should be confirmed. . . . But, in removing the listed matters from the Bill and in proceeding to substitute a reference to all the circumstances, Parliament made clear its intention that the **Reynolds** factors, upon which the list had been based, were not to be used as a check list. Even if, at the time of the decision in the **Reynolds** case, it was appropriate to describe the factors identified by Lord Nicholls as a check list, it is clearly inappropriate so to regard them in the context of the statutory defence. But, as Sharp LJ proceeded to explain, that is not to deny that one or more of them may well be relevant to whether the defendant's belief was reasonable within the meaning of subsection (1)(b). (Lord Wilson at [69])

2. The facts of *Hourani v Thomson and others* [2017] EWHC 432 (QB) arose from a six-month campaign of street protest, online publication and sticker distribution targeting the claimant, a wealthy businessman (and two members of his family) and denouncing them as murderers responsible for the torture, drugging, beating and sexual assault of a young woman, Anastasiya Novikova, and her subsequent death in Beirut in 2004. Finding the defendants' actions to be both harassment and libellous, Warby J rejected the application of the public interest defence in the later. He continued:

   166. It is easy to accept that the question of whether an innocent young mother has been imprisoned, abused, and murdered is—speaking generally—a matter of public interest. It

does not seem to me that the fact that such events are alleged to have taken place in a foreign country would of itself defeat that conclusion. Nor, I dare say, would the fact that the alleged victim and perpetrators were all foreigners, and that there was no United Kingdom aspect to the matter. If those factors would defeat such a conclusion, then the fact that at the time of publication Mr Hourani was not only resident in London but also a British citizen means that the topic was clearly of legitimate interest and concern to the general public in England and Wales. But it is not by any means obvious that to parade in public holding a placard bearing a person's photograph under the single word 'murderer' is, or forms part of, 'a statement on a matter of public interest.' It looks more like a bare accusation, unexplained by any context. It is easier to regard the written statements published at the November Event as part of a statement on a matter of public interest, because of what was read out to accompany those statements. Even so, I have my doubts about whether demonstrations created in the way that these were can properly be described as involving statements on any matter of public interest. But if driven to reach a conclusion I would say that the statements did qualify, as they had to do with a matter which was one of public interest. I reject this defence, however, because I do not accept that the other requirements of s 4 are satisfied.

3. See further Jacob Rowbottom 'Citizen journalists, standards of care, and the public interest defence in defamation' Inforrm's blog, 18 December 2018.

15.11 Offer of amends

An offer of amends under the Defamation Act 1996 can either provide a complete defence or act to reduce the damages substantially.

DEFAMATION ACT 1996

2. —(1) A person who has published a statement alleged to be defamatory of another may offer to make amends under this section.

(2) The offer may be in relation to the statement generally or in relation to a specific defamatory meaning which the person making the offer accepts that the statement conveys ('a qualified offer').

(3) An offer to make amends—

(a) must be in writing,

(b) must be expressed to be an offer to make amends under section 2 of the Defamation Act 1996, and

(c) must state whether it is a qualified offer and, if so, set out the defamatory meaning in relation to which it is made.

(4) An offer to make amends under this section is an offer—

(a) to make a suitable correction of the statement complained of and a sufficient apology to the aggrieved party,

(b) to publish the correction and apology in a manner that is reasonable and practicable in the circumstances, and

(c) to pay to the aggrieved party such compensation (if any), and such costs, as may be agreed or determined to be payable.

The fact that the offer is accompanied by an offer to take specific steps does not affect the fact that an offer to make amends under this section is an offer to do all the things mentioned in paragraphs (a) to (c).

(5) An offer to make amends under this section may not be made by a person after serving a defence in defamation proceedings brought against him by the aggrieved party in respect of the publication in question.

(6) An offer to make amends under this section may be withdrawn before it is accepted; and a renewal of an offer which has been withdrawn shall be treated as a new offer.

3. —(1) If an offer to make amends under section 2 is accepted by the aggrieved party, the following provisions apply.

(2) The party accepting the offer may not bring or continue defamation proceedings in respect of the publication concerned against the person making the offer, but he is entitled to enforce the offer to make amends as follows.

(3) If the parties agree on the steps to be taken in fulfilment of the offer, the aggrieved party may apply to the court for an order that the other party fulfil his offer by taking the steps agreed.

(4) If the parties do not agree on the steps to be taken by way of correction, apology and publication, the party who made the offer may take such steps as he thinks appropriate, and may in particular—

    (a) make the correction and apology by a statement in open court in terms approved by the court, and

    (b) give an undertaking to the court as to the manner of their publication.

(5) If the parties do not agree on the amount to be paid by way of compensation, it shall be determined by the court on the same principles as damages in defamation proceedings.

The court shall take account of any steps taken in fulfilment of the offer and (so far as not agreed between the parties) of the suitability of the correction, the sufficiency of the apology and whether the manner of their publication was reasonable in the circumstances, and may reduce or increase the amount of compensation accordingly.

(6) If the parties do not agree on the amount to be paid by way of costs, it shall be determined by the court on the same principles as costs awarded in court proceedings.

(7) The acceptance of an offer by one person to make amends does not affect any cause of action against another person in respect of the same publication, subject as follows.

(8) In England and Wales or Northern Ireland, for the purposes of the Civil Liability (Contribution) Act 1978—

    (a) the amount of compensation paid under the offer shall be treated as paid in bona fide settlement or compromise of the claim; and

    (b) where another person is liable in respect of the same damage (whether jointly or otherwise), the person whose offer to make amends was accepted is not required to pay by virtue of any contribution under section 1 of that Act a greater amount than the amount of the compensation payable in pursuance of the offer.. . .

(10) Proceedings under this section shall be heard and determined without a jury.

4. —(1) If an offer to make amends under section 2, duly made and not withdrawn, is not accepted by the aggrieved party, the following provisions apply.

(2) The fact that the offer was made is a defence (subject to subsection (3)) to defamation proceedings in respect of the publication in question by that party against the person making the offer.

A qualified offer is only a defence in respect of the meaning to which the offer related.

(3) There is no such defence if the person by whom the offer was made knew or had reason to believe that the statement complained of—

    (a) referred to the aggrieved party or was likely to be understood as referring to him, and

    (b) was both false and defamatory of that party;

    but it shall be presumed until the contrary is shown that he did not know and had no reason to believe that was the case.

(4) The person who made the offer need not rely on it by way of defence, but if he does he may not rely on any other defence.

If the offer was a qualified offer, this applies only in respect of the meaning to which the offer related.

(5) The offer may be relied on in mitigation of damages whether or not it was relied on as a defence.

Notes

1. The effect of an offer of amends is illustrated by *Nail v News Group Newspapers* [2005] 1 All ER 1040 where the *News of the World* made a number of untrue allegations about the sexual history of the actor Jimmy Nail. The defendants accepted that the stories were untrue and made an offer of amends. The parties agreed the terms of an appropriate apology, but were unable to agree on compensation. Under section 3(5) of the Defamation Act 1996 the court may reduce the amount of compensation which would normally be payable. Here the court held that certain factors would reduce the damages by 50 per cent. These factors were: (a) an early offer of amends and an agreed apology; (b) an early offer to compensate; and (c) the claimant knows that his reputation has been repaired as far as possible and is relieved from the stress and anxiety of a court case.

2. Section 4 of the 1996 Act provides a complete defence if the offer of amends is rejected, except where the defendant 'knew or had reasonable grounds to believe' that the statement complained of was untrue. In *Milne v Express Newspapers* [2005] 1 All ER 1021 the Court of Appeal held that this meant recklessness in the sense that the defendant must know of a fact and then have reasonable grounds for positively believing that the words complained of were false. The phrase does not import negligence or constructive knowledge.

3. The suggestion that there might be an offer of amends does not always have to come from the defendant. In **Monroe v Hopkins**, Monroe tweeted 'Dear @KTHopkins, public apology +£5k to migrant rescue & I won't sue. It'll be cheaper for you and v. satisfying for me.' Hopkins did not take her up on this offer. Had she done, as Warby J noted,

> the case could easily have been resolved at an early stage. There was an open offer to settle for £5,000. It was a reasonable offer. There could have been an offer of amends under the Defamation Act 1996. Such an offer attracts a substantial discount: up to half if the offer is prompt and unqualified. Such an offer would have meant the compensation would have been modest. The costs would have been a fraction of those which I am sure these parties have incurred in the event. Those costs have largely been incurred in contesting the issue of whether a statement which on its face had a defamatory tendency had actually caused serious harm. (at [83])

Instead, Monroe was awarded £24,000 in damages. In September 2018, Hopkins, facing a reported £300,000 costs bill, filed for an insolvency agreement in order to avoid bankruptcy (Matthew Taylor 'Katie Hopkins "very likely" to challenge Jack Monroe libel ruling' *The Guardian* 15 March 2017; Jim Waterson 'Katie Hopkins applies for insolvency agreement to avoid bankruptcy' *The Guardian* 16 September 2018).

see online resources

15.12 Damages

Damages for defamation are 'at large', and there has been considerable concern at the high level of awards in some cases. The record to date is £1,500,000 in favour of Lord Aldington, awarded against Count Tolstoy and Mr Watts for allegations concerning the repatriation of Yugoslavs at the end of the Second World War. The size of this award was subsequently found by the European Commission of Human Rights to be in violation of the defendant's Article 10 rights (*Tolstoy Miloslavsky* v *UK* (Application no 18139/91) (1995) 20 EHRR 442) and the case was eventually settled for £100,000. Lord Aldington died in 2000 never having received a penny of his award. Now that the presumption of a jury trial has been abolished (Defamation Act 2013, s 11), the level of damages is a matter for the judge, which is—one would hope—likely to lead to more restraint in the award of damages.

Damages, with the exception of exemplary damages, are intended to be compensatory, but in the words of Windeyer J in *Uren* v *John Fairfax* (1967) 117 CLR 115:

> a man defamed does not get damages *for* his damaged reputation. He gets damages *because* he was injured in his reputation, that is simply because he was publicly defamed. For this reason, compensation by damages operates in two ways—as a vindication of the plaintiff to the public and as a consolation to him for a wrong done. Compensation is here a solatium rather than a monetary recompense for a harm measurable in money. (at 150)

Damages can include compensation for injury to feelings, and 'aggravated' damages can be awarded for the subsequent conduct of the defendant, including a failure to make a sufficient apology; a repetition of the libel; conduct calculated to deter the claimant from proceeding; persistence in a plea of justification which is bound to fail; and persecution of the claimant by other means. However, as *Flymenow Ltd v Quick Air Jet Charter GmbH* [2016] EWHC 3197 (QB) demonstrates, awards can also be reduced in light of the *claimant's* action.

> ## *Flymenow Ltd* v *Quick Air Jet Charter GmbH*
> Queen's Bench Division [2016] EWHC 3197 (QB)

The claimant, an aircraft charter company, and the defendant, a provider of private jets, entered into a contract to provide two air ambulance flights. When the claimant did not pay, the defendant sent an email to a mailing list which included 26 aviation companies titled: 'WARNING. Company you should not deal with! Pecuniary difficulties!' The text of the email stated the claimant was 'not able to pay' outstanding amounts due to the defendant. Despite finding for the claimant, the judge held they were not entitled to substantial damages due to their 'disgraceful' behaviour before and during the litigation.

WARBY J:

125. In my judgment, the appropriate way in which to reflect the fact that the claimant led the defendant to believe it was insolvent is to take this into account on the issue of damages. It is one of four factors that lead me to the conclusion that the appropriate course in this case is, as Mr Bennett [counsel for the defendant] submits, to award only minimal damages. The other three factors are (i) the significant extent to which the defendant has proved the truth of the defamatory meanings of the words complained of; (ii) the claimant's dishonest behaviour in 2013; and (iii) the claimant's disreputable and, ultimately, dishonest conduct of its case, including at this trial.

126. In a libel action brought by an individual, compensation is awarded for injury to reputation and to feelings. The award must provide appropriate vindication. A claimant is entitled to point to a sum of money which clears his reputation. A corporate claimant has no feelings, and can only suffer

in its 'pocket'. It is entitled to a sum in damages that properly reflects the financial loss that has been caused by the publication, and which will vindicate. In most cases special damage cannot be proved, and therefore is not alleged. This is such a case. That does not preclude a substantial award of general damages. The claimant has established that significant reputational harm resulted from the defendant's email, and no doubt that was reflected in financial harm. But this is not a large business. And where partial justification is established the claimant is only entitled to be compensated for damage which the court finds was probably caused by the libellous part of the publication. Here, the partial justification of the words complained of has the effect of substantially reducing what would otherwise be the award. The claimant falls to be compensated as a company that was not insolvent, but had failed to pay its debts to the defendant over many months, was perilously close to insolvency, and was financially risky to do business with.

127. The award would nonetheless have been in the modest five figure range but for the other three factors I have mentioned. A company that is falsely accused of being insolvent would not ordinarily have its damages reduced to a negligible level just because it was in some lesser form of financial difficulty, and had unjustifiably delayed payment of some of its debts. This case, however, is highly unusual. In the process of attempting to prove insolvency, and successfully proving the matters it has established, the defendant has incidentally proved that the claimant behaved disgracefully in fobbing it off with a series of dishonest excuses. Those are facts which are properly before the court, which ought to be taken into account in mitigation of damages, pursuant to the principle summarised in *Pamplin*. They also fall to be taken into account as directly relevant background context under the *Burstein* principle (*Burstein v Times Newspapers Ltd* [2001] 1 WLR 579 (CA)). These are facts which go to a relevant sector of the claimant's business reputation, and show that it is undeserving of a sum which would appear to the outside world to represent substantial vindication of its reputation.

128. So also do the facts that I have summarised about the way this action has been conducted by the claimant company. It has emerged that a central element of its case was false from the beginning and should have been recognised as such by the company's principal, Mr Whitney. He has given false evidence and, as I find, continued to stand by the original case after he realised that it was false. Those too are disreputable facts that are properly before the court, which logically affect the extent to which the claimant is entitled to the vindication of its reputation through an award of damages. The propriety of this approach appears to me to be supported by the decision at trial in *Joseph v Spiller* [2012] EWHC 2958 (QB).

129. Returning to the claimant's behaviour in causing the defendant to believe that the claimant was insolvent, it seems to me that this is properly considered as evidence of the claimant's own conduct which goes to mitigate or reduce damages. This category of evidence is discussed in the 12th edition of Gatley at paragraph 33.51 and following. The editors express the view that 'conduct' in this context 'relates in particular (but not exclusively) to activities which can be causally connected to the publication of the libel of which the claimant complains, such as direct provocation. . .' The present case is perhaps not easily categorised as one of 'provocation'. The cases cited in the textbook do not appear to include any involving facts akin to those of the present case, nor have any such been cited in argument; but that does not affect the principle. In my judgment, in this case, (a) the claimant's conduct can be properly said to have played a part in causing the publication complained of, and (b) the claimant's conduct in that regard is culpable to a degree that makes it just to reduce damages. This is conduct that is directly related to the sector of the claimant's reputation that was wrongfully damaged by the words complained of, and reduces damages on that account.

130. Bearing in mind all of these factors, I have concluded that the right sum to award is £10.

Notes

1. The Court of Appeal in *Cairns v Modi* [2012] EWCA Civ 1382 confirmed that the 'ceiling figure' for damages in defamation was around £275,000, corresponding to the current maximum level of damages for pain and suffering and loss of amenity in personal injury cases (at [25]). By way of example, recent awards include a 'six figure sum' awarded to Eurovision song contest winner Dana, who sued the *Sunday World* over false claims related to her brother ('Dana to receive six-figure sum after Sunday World settles libel case BBC News' 26 November 2018), £54,000 each to three Labour Party MPs defamed by a member of UKIP who suggested they were aware of the abuses in Rotherham and had chosen not to intervene (*Barron v Collins* [2017] EWHC 162 (QB)) and £140,000 for the publication of an allegation that the claimant was guilty of terrorism (*Harrath v Stand for Peace Ltd* [2017] EWHC 653 (QB)).

2. In *Shakil-Ur-Rahman v ARY Network Ltd* [2016] EWHC 3110 (QB) the claimant, a well-known Pakistani businessman, was awarded 'top bracket' damages of £185,000 against a UK broad-caster for a series of programmes (broadcast in Urdu in the UK) which, among other things, had portrayed the claimant as treasonous towards Pakistan. Explaining the award, Eady J noted the following:

> 102. Where there are multiple libels, as here, it is difficult sometimes for the court to find the right balance between fair compensation and proportionality. It is a matter for the judge's discretion whether to make a single award or fix upon separate sums for each of the publica-tions complained of: see e.g. *Hayward v Thompson* [1982] QB 47. Mr Nicklin [counsel for the claimant] suggested that it might be appropriate here to divide the offending broadcasts into groups depending on the allegations made (e.g. 'treachery', 'blasphemy', etc.). There might be cases where that would be a convenient method to adopt, but here it seems to me that there is too much overlap between the programmes. I think it would be better to find a single figure to cover the 24 programmes. It would be idle to pretend that the exercise is capable of more precise breakdown. . . .

> 104. . . . [T]he allegations complained of in these proceedings are quite distinctive and very serious. They go to 'the core attributes' of the Claimant's personality: *John v MGN Ltd* [1997] QB 586, at 607. They were published to tens of thousands of people within this jurisdiction. Despite the fact that in most cases no substantive defence has been put forward, there has been no withdrawal or apology. Mr Browne [counsel for the defendant] had a delicate path to tread in his conduct of the trial because, though he was entitled to ensure that his clients were not blamed for *all* the distress or *all* the damage to the Claimant's reputation at the ma-terial times, he made it clear that he was not suggesting that any of these allegations was true. Certainly, there was nothing in his conduct of the trial which in itself aggravated the harm done. On the other hand, there were defences of truth/justification on the record until they were struck out on 25 October. That was an aggravating element. There were also the many other broadcasts, relied upon to support the harassment claim, which clearly made things worse. There is on the other hand little, if anything, available to the Defendants by way of mitigation. . . .

> 106. I believe the right approach is to go towards the top of the bracket for general compensa-tory damages, while making only one award rather than attempting to calculate two dozen separate figures. I pay what I hope is due regard to the gravity and scale of these publications, and also to the persistence with which they were advanced and to the aggravating factors. Bearing in mind all that Mr Browne has said on the subject of causation, I consider that the appropriate award is £185,000. As was observed in *Cairns v Modi* [2013] 1 WLR 1015, most onlookers who are interested in the outcome of a libel action are only concerned to know the answer to the question 'How much did he get?' The sum I am awarding should be enough to convince any fair-minded observer of the baselessness of these serious charges and to afford some measure of solatium in respect of the hurt and distress undoubtedly caused.

107.   There are, I accept, a significant number of people whose attitude to the Claimant will be unaffected by the outcome of English libel proceedings. In particular, it is obvious that the Defendants, while having recognised the weakness of their position, will never withdraw the defamatory allegations, even though they know there is no evidence to support them. But to make an even higher award would make no difference. The court has to be concerned only with fair-minded (hypothetical) onlookers: they cannot but recognise that these seriously defamatory allegations simply had no foundation. The objective of vindicating the Claimant's reputation has thus been achieved. The compensation for injury to reputation and for distress may seem high to some people, and inadequate to others, but that is inevitable when courts are given the task of expressing non-monetary damage in monetary terms. All one can do is to work within the conventional tariffs.

The land torts

PART IV

16 Trespass to land and nuisance

   16.1 Trespass to land

   16.2 Private nuisance

17 Actions under *Rylands* v *Fletcher*

   17.1 Merging *Rylands*, nuisance and negligence?

Trespass to land and nuisance

16.1 Trespass to land

The tort of trespass to land protects those in possession of land against direct invasion of their property. (If the invasion is indirect, the appropriate tort would be private nuisance, covered in section 16.2.) The right to sue in trespass includes those with a proprietary interest in the land or property concerned, such as owners and tenants, as well as those who have exclusive occupation. In some cases, even a licensee may have sufficient exclusive occupation to be able to sue. For example, in *Monsanto v Tilly* [2000] Env LR 313, the claimants had permission to plant genetically modified crops on a farmer's land and the defendants entered and attacked the crops. The claimants were entitled to an injunction (this case is also the authority that there is no defence of public interest in trespass to land).

Like the trespass to the person torts, trespass to land is actionable per se. The fact that any invasion of land, however minute and whether it causes damage or not, is a trespass, indicates that the primary function of this tort is to protect rights in property (often achieved via an injunction), rather than simply to provide compensation.

Gregory v Piper
Court of King's Bench (1820) 9 B & C 591

The claimant owned the wall which separated the yard of his property from that of the defendant. In the course of a dispute about a right of way, the defendant ordered an employee, Stubbings, to dump rubbish so as to block the way but not to touch the wall. The rubbish was loose and as it dried out some of it rolled or settled against the wall. Held: the defendant was liable in trespass.

PARKE J: I think that the defendant is liable in this form of action. If a single stone had been put against the wall it would have been sufficient. Independently of Stubbings's evidence there was sufficient evidence to satisfy the jury that the rubbish was placed there by the defendant, for he expressed his determination not to remove it. It does not rest there. Stubbings says he was desired not to let the rubbish touch the wall. But it appeared to be of a loose kind, and it was therefore probable that some of it naturally might run against the wall. Stubbings said that some of it of course would go against the wall. Now the defendant must be taken to have contemplated all the probable consequences of the act which he had ordered to be done, and one of these probable consequences was, that the rubbish would touch the plaintiff's wall. If that was so, then the laying the rubbish against the wall was as much the defendant's act as if it had been done by his express command. The defendant, therefore, was the person who caused the act to be done, and for the necessary or natural consequence of his own act he is responsible as a trespasser.

Notes

1. Compare *Esso Petroleum* v *Southport Corporation* [1956] AC 218, where it was doubted, without deciding, whether it would be trespass to discharge oil at sea, which was then washed onto the foreshore. The oil was 'committed to the action of wind and wave, with no certainty . . . how, when or under what conditions it might come to shore' (at 242).

League Against Cruel Sports v Scott
Queen's Bench Division [1986] 1 QB 240

The claimants owned various areas of unfenced moorland around Exmoor for the purpose of establishing a deer sanctuary. Accordingly, they did not allow hunting on their land. The defendants were a hunting group, and on a number of occasions hounds belonging to the hunt entered the moorland. No material damage was caused. The claimants alleged trespass by the defendants, their servants or agents. Held: the defendants were liable. Damages were awarded and in respect of one property an injunction was granted.

PARK J: In my judgment the law as I take it to be may be stated thus: where a master of staghounds takes out a pack of hounds and deliberately sets them in pursuit of a stag or hind, knowing that there is a real risk that in the pursuit hounds may enter or cross prohibited land, the master will be liable for trespass if he intended to cause hounds to enter such land, or if by his failure to exercise proper control over them he caused them to enter such land.

In the present case, on each of the occasions on which the league alleges trespass by hounds the master (or on some occasions the masters) had taken out the pack and set hounds in pursuit of a stag or hind. On each occasion the master or masters knew that there was a real risk that one or more hounds might enter league land; on each occasion one or more hounds did, in fact, enter league land. The question is, therefore, whether on any, and if so which, of those occasions the trespass was caused either by the master intending that hounds should enter or by his failure to exercise proper control over them.

This is, in each case, a question of fact. The master's intention, or the intention of those servants or agents or followers of the hunt for whose conduct he is responsible, has to be inferred from his or their conduct in all the circumstances of the case. For example, whether he or they stood by and allowed hounds which were plainly about to enter prohibited land to do so, or allowed hounds which were plainly on the land to remain there; or whether, by making appropriate sounds vocally or on the horn, he encouraged hounds to go on to or to remain on such land.

Further, if it is virtually impossible, whatever precautions are taken, to prevent hounds from entering league land, such as Pitleigh for example, yet the master knowing that to be the case, nevertheless persists in hunting in its vicinity, with the result that hounds frequently trespass on the land, then the inference might well be drawn that his indifference to the risk of trespass amounted to an intention that hounds should trespass on the land.

The master's negligence, or the negligence of those servants or agents or followers of the hunt for whose conduct he is responsible, has also to be judged in the light of all the circumstances in which the trespass in question occurred.

It involves consideration of such questions as the stage in the chase at which it ought reasonably to have been foreseen that there was a risk that hounds might trespass on league land and what precautions, if any, were taken by the master at that stage to prevent trespass by heading off the hounds.

Notes

1. Trespass is a tort of intention and so there is no liability for involuntary acts. But according to **League Against Cruel Sports**, it seems that recklessness can equate to intention.

2. It is not always easy to determine which actions are voluntary (i.e. intentional) in this respect, and which are not. In *Smith* v *Stone* (1647) Sty 65 there was no liability in trespass for a man carried onto another's land, as his action in entering the land was involuntary. However, in *Gilbert* v *Stone* (1647) Sty 72, 82 ER 539 a man under duress entered the claimant's premises—he was found to be a trespasser as his act of entering the land was deliberate and intentional, even if not truly 'voluntary'.

3. In *Basely* v *Clarkson* (1682) 3 Lev 37, the defendant was liable because he intentionally did an act (albeit under a misapprehension) which in fact was an invasion of the claimant's land. He did not mean to cut the claimant's grass, but rather he made a mistake about where the boundary was. This illustrates how trespass can be used to determine disputes between neighbouring landowners about where the proper boundary lies. The question in *Basely* was whether a person could be liable if he intentionally entered land, believing the land was his.

Bernstein v Skyviews and General Ltd
Queen's Bench Division [1978] QB 479

The defendants flew above Bernstein's country house and took a photograph of it, which they then offered to sell to him. The claimant claimed damages for trespass by invasion of his air space. Held: the defendants were not liable.

GRIFFITHS J: The plaintiff claims that as owner of the land he is also owner of the air space above the land, or at least has the right to exclude any entry into the air space above his land. . . .. There are a number of cases in which the maxim has been used by English judges, but an examination of those cases shows that they have all been concerned with structures attached to the adjoining land, such as overhanging buildings, signs or telegraph wires, and for their solution it has not been necessary for the judge to cast his eyes towards the heavens; he has been concerned with the rights of the owner in the air space immediately adjacent to the surface of the land. . . .

I can find no support in authority for the view that a landowner's rights in the air space above his property extend to an unlimited height. In *Wandsworth Board of Works v United Telephone Co Ltd*, 13 QBD 904 Bowen LJ described the maxim, *usque ad coelum*, as a fanciful phrase, to which I would add that if applied literally it is a fanciful notion leading to the absurdity of a trespass at common law being committed by a satellite every time it passes over a suburban garden. The academic writers speak with one voice in rejecting the uncritical and literal application of the maxim . . . I accept their collective approach as correct. The problem is to balance the rights of an owner to enjoy the use of his land against the rights of the general public to take advantage of all that science now offers in the use of air space. This balance is in my judgment best struck in our present society by restricting the rights of an owner in the air space above his land to such height as is necessary for the ordinary use and enjoyment of his land and the structures upon it, and declaring that above that height he has no greater rights in the air space than any other member of the public.

Applying this test to the facts of this case, I find that the defendants' aircraft did not infringe any rights in the plaintiff's air space, and thus no trespass was committed. It was on any view of the evidence flying many hundreds of feet above the ground and it is not suggested that by its mere presence in the air space it caused any interference with any use to which the plaintiff put or might wish to put his land. The plaintiff's complaint is not that the aircraft interfered with the use of his land but that a photograph was taken from it. There is, however, no law against taking a photograph, and the mere taking of a photograph cannot turn an act which is not a trespass into the plaintiff's air space into one that is a trespass.

My finding that no trespass at common law has been established is sufficient to determine this case in the defendants' favour. I should, however, deal with a further defence under the Civil Aviation Act 1949, section 40(1) of which provides:

> No action shall lie in respect of trespass or in respect of nuisance, by reason only of the flight of an aircraft over any property at a height above the ground, which, having regard to wind, weather and all the circumstances of the case is reasonable, or the ordinary incidents of such flight so long as the provisions of Part II and this Part of this Act and any Order in Council or order made under Part II or this Part of this Act are duly complied with.

It is agreed that all the statutory provisions have been complied with by the defendants, nor is there any suggestion that the aircraft was not flying at a reasonable height; but it is submitted by the plaintiff that the protection given by the subsection is limited to a bare right of passage over land analogous to the limited right of a member of the public to pass over the surface of a highway, and my attention has been drawn to a passage in *Shawcross & Beaumont on Air Law*, 3rd ed (1966), p 561 in which the editors express this view. I see nothing in the language of the section to invite such a restricted reading which would withdraw from its protection many very beneficial activities carried on from aircraft. For example, we heard during this case that Granada Television, a company of which Lord Bernstein is chairman, made a series of educational films called 'The Land' for educational purposes. To make the films helicopters flew far and wide over the country and photographed the land below in all its various aspects. Of course they had not obtained the permission of every occupier whose land they photographed—it would have been an impossible task. According to the plaintiff's contention that innocent activity would not be protected even if the helicopters were flying at a reasonable height and complying with all statutory requirements, for they would not be mere birds of passage but making use of the air space for the purpose of aerial photography or survey. As I read the section its protection extends to all flights provided they are at a reasonable height and comply with the statutory requirements. And I adopt this construction the more readily because subsection (2) imposes upon the owner of the aircraft a strict liability to pay damages for any material loss or damage that may be caused by his aircraft.

It is, however, to be observed that the protection given is limited by the words 'by reason only of the flight,' so although an owner can found no action in trespass or nuisance if he relies solely upon the flight of the aircraft above his property as founding his cause of action, the section will not preclude him from bringing an action if he can point to some activity carried on by or from the aircraft that can properly be considered a trespass or nuisance, or some other tort. For example, the section would give no protection against the deliberate emission of vast quantities of smoke that polluted the atmosphere and seriously interfered with the plaintiff's use and enjoyment of his property; such behaviour remains an actionable nuisance. Nor would I wish this judgment to be understood as deciding that in no circumstances could a successful action be brought against an aerial photographer to restrain his activities. The present action is not founded in nuisance for no court would regard the taking of a single photograph as an actionable nuisance. But if the circumstances were such that a plaintiff was subjected to the harassment of constant surveillance of his house from the air, accompanied by the photographing of his every activity, I am far from saying that the court would not regard such a monstrous invasion of his privacy as an actionable nuisance for which they would give relief. However, that question does not fall for decision in this case and will be decided if and when it arises.

On the facts of this case even if contrary to my view the defendants' aircraft committed a trespass at common law in flying over the plaintiff's land, the plaintiff is prevented from bringing any action in respect of that trespass by the terms of section 40(1) of the Civil Aviation Act 1949.

Notes

1. The Civil Aviation Act 1949 has been replaced by the Civil Aviation Act 1982 (s 76(1) is the relevant section). The statute also imposes strict liability upon the owner of an aircraft for any material damage caused by any article, animal or person falling from an aircraft in flight.

2. A landowner may not 'own' everything up to the sky, but what about the earth below his property? In *Bocardo SA v Star Energy UK Onshore Ltd* [2010] UKSC 35, an oil company drilled pipelines at an angle into the earth around its property, which entered the neighbouring property at a depth of about 800 ft below the surface, and ran for about 0.5 and 0.7 km respectively, terminating about 2,800 ft beneath the surface. The claimants sued for trespass to land. Lord Hope said that the maxim 'whoever owns the soil also owns up to the sky and down to the depths':

> still has value in English law as encapsulating, in simple language, a proposition of law which has commanded general acceptance . . . The better view . . . is to hold that the owner of the surface is the owner of the strata beneath it, including the minerals that are to be found there, unless there has been an alienation of them by a conveyance, at common law or by statute to someone else . . . There must obviously be some stopping point, as one reaches the point at which physical features such as pressure and temperature render the concept of the strata belonging to anybody so absurd as to be not worth arguing about. But the wells that are at issue in this case, extending from about 800 feet to 2,800 feet below the surface, are far from being so deep as to reach the point of absurdity. Indeed the fact that the strata can be worked upon at those depths points to the opposite conclusion. (at [26])

Accordingly, the defendants were liable. However, the claimants received only £1,000 damages (not the much higher sum claimed—and awarded by the High Court at first instance—which reflected a proportion of the profits made from the drilling), to compensate the amenity loss caused by the trespass.

Anchor Brewhouse Developments Ltd v *Berkley House Ltd*
Chancery Division [1987] 2 EGLR 172

The defendants were using a tower crane in construction work. The jib of the tower crane swung over the claimants' property; this was held to be a trespass to the claimants' airspace. Another question was whether the claimants were limited to a remedy in damages or whether they could obtain an injunction and, if so, whether that injunction could be temporarily suspended to allow the defendants to complete their building. Held: it was a trespass to the airspace and an injunction was granted.

SCOTT J: . . . What is complained of in the present case is infringement of air space by a structure positioned upon a neighbour's land. The defendant has erected tower cranes on its land. Attached to each tower crane is a boom which swings over the plaintiffs' land. The booms invade the air space over the plaintiffs' land. Each boom is part of the structure on the defendant's land. The tort of trespass represents an interference with possession or with the right to possession. A landowner is entitled, as an attribute of his ownership of the land, to place structures on his land and thereby to reduce into actual possession the air space above his land. If an adjoining owner places a structure on his (the adjoining owner's) land that overhangs his neighbour's land, he thereby takes into his possession air space to which his neighbour is entitled. That, in my judgment, is trespass. It does not depend upon any balancing of rights.

The difficulties posed by overflying aircraft or balloons, bullets or missiles seem to me to be wholly separate from the problem which arises where there is invasion of air space by a structure placed or standing upon the land of a neighbour. One of the characteristics of the common law of trespass is, or ought to be, certainty. The extent of proprietary rights enjoyed by landowners ought to be clear. It may be that, where aircraft or overflying missiles are concerned, certainty cannot be achieved. I do not wish to dissent at all from Griffiths J's approach to that problem in the **Bernstein** case. But certainty is capable of being achieved where invasion of air space by tower cranes, advertising signs and other structures are concerned. In my judgment, if somebody erects on his own land a structure, part of which invades the air space above the land of another, the invasion is trespass. . .

Notes

1. The second aspect Scott J had to consider was whether, given the trespass, an injunction should be awarded. After some discussion, he regretfully came to the conclusion that he must grant one, on the basis that the defendants planned to continue using the cranes in any case. The problem of whether to award damages or to grant an injunction also arises in nuisance (discussed in section 16.2). As Scott J admitted in **Anchor Brewhouse**, the effect is to dramatically alter the bargaining power of the claimant who may be tempted to charge an exorbitant sum for permission to use the airspace. In the Australian case, *LJP Investments v Howard Chia Investments* (1991) 24 NSWLR 499, it was necessary to measure damages for trespass to airspace by scaffolding. Hodgson J held that, where the space used has peculiar value for a defendant, damages should reflect that value rather than the general market value. They should reflect the price which the claimant and defendant would reasonably have negotiated having regard to the claimant's position and the defendant's wish to develop the site.

2. In *Jaggard* v *Sawyer* [1995] 2 All ER 189, the Court of Appeal approved *Shelfer* v *City of London Electric Lighting* [1895] 1 Ch 287 which said that an injunction may be refused where: (a) the injury to the claimant's legal rights is small; (b) it is one which is capable of being estimated in money; (c) it can be adequately compensated by a small money payment; and (d) it would be oppressive to the defendant to grant an injunction. In deciding whether it would be oppressive in relation to a permanent invasion of land (e.g. by erecting a building on the claimant's land) the court would take into account whether the defendant knew he was committing a trespass and completed the work in the hope of presenting a court with a *fait accompli*. Note, however, the *Shelfer* criteria appear no longer to be the binding principle, following **Coventry v Lawrence** [2014] UKSC 13 (see section 16.2.5).

3. Part 55 of the Civil Procedure Rules provides an expeditious remedy for recovery of possession when land is being occupied by trespassers. Apart from speed, the main advantage is that an order can be obtained against trespassers without knowing their names.

4. Trespass is not generally a crime, but several statutes make it so in particular circumstances. For example, section 6 of the Criminal Law Act 1977 makes it a crime (except for a displaced residential occupier) to use force to enter premises. Section 61 of the Criminal Justice and Public Order Act 1994 deals with the case of two or more persons entering land with a view to residing there, and causing damage or using abusive language or bringing six or more vehicles onto the land and section 68 establishes an offence of aggravated trespass in relation to a person who trespasses on land in the open air and obstructs or disrupts a lawful activity on that or adjoining land. It is also a crime to trespass on specific kinds of land such as railways (British Transport Commission Act 1949, s 55) or airports (Civil Aviation Act 1982, s 39).

Burton v *Winters*
Court of Appeal [1993] 1 WLR 1077

The defendant built a garage which encroached by 4 inches onto the claimant's land. Having failed to obtain an injunction to have the garage removed, the claimant built a counter wall on the defendant's land which she refused to remove and was sentenced to 12 months' imprisonment for contempt. The claimant later damaged the garage and was sentenced to two years' imprisonment. On appeal from that order, one issue was whether the claimant was entitled to use 'self-help' (or exercise a right of abatement) in order to put an end to the trespass by the defendant's garage. Held: the claimant had no right of abatement and was limited to damages.

LLOYD LJ: There is a common law right of self-redress for trespass by encroachment, which was already regarded as an ancient remedy in the time of Bracton. It is similar to the common law right of abatement in the case of nuisance. But at an early stage of our history the right of abatement was supplemented by the assize of nuisance or '*quod permittat prosternere*'. The action lay to have the nuisance abated by the defendants and to recover damages: see *Baten's Case* (1610) 9 Co Rep 536. If the plaintiff abated the nuisance himself, he lost his right to recover damages.

With the coming of equity, the common law action for abatement was supplanted by the mandatory injunction. But the remedy by way of self-help was still available . . .

Ever since the assize of nuisance became available, the courts have confined the remedy by way of self-redress to simple cases such as an overhanging branch, or an encroaching root, which would not justify the expense of legal proceedings, and urgent cases which require an immediate remedy. Thus, it was Bracton's view that where there is resort to self-redress, the remedy should be taken without delay. In *Blackstone's Commentaries on the Laws of England*, Book III, chapter 1, we find:

> And the reason why the law allows this private and summary method of doing one's self justice, is because injuries of this kind, which obstruct or annoy such things as are of daily convenience and use, require an immediate remedy; and cannot wait for the slow progress of the ordinary forms of justice.

. . . In *Prosser & Keeton* we find:

> Consequently the privilege [of abatement] must be exercised within a reasonable time after knowledge of the nuisance is acquired or should have been acquired by the person entitled to abate; if there has been sufficient delay to allow resort to legal process, the reason for the privilege fails, and the privilege with it.

The authority cited for this proposition is *Moffett v Brewer* (1848) Iowa 1 Greene 348, 350, where Greene J said:

> This summary method of redressing a grievance, by the act of an injured party, should be regarded with great jealousy, and authorised only in cases of particular emergency, requiring a more speedy remedy than can be had by the ordinary proceedings at law.

Applying this stream of authority to the facts of the present case, it is obvious that it is now far too late for the plaintiff to have her remedy by way of abatement. The garage wall was built in 1975. Not only was there ample time for the plaintiff to 'wait for the slow progress of the ordinary forms of justice'; she actually did so.

But it is not only a question of delay. There is modern House of Lords authority for the proposition that the law does not favour the remedy of abatement: see *Lagan Navigation Co v Lambeg Bleaching, Dyeing and Finishing Co Ltd* [1927] AC 226, 244, *per* Lord Atkinson.

In my opinion, this never was an appropriate case for self-redress, even if the plaintiff had acted promptly. There was no emergency. There were difficult questions of law and fact to be considered and the remedy by way of self-redress, if it had resulted in the demolition of the garage wall, would have been out of all proportion to the damage suffered by the plaintiff.

But, even if there had ever been a right of self-redress, it ceased when Judge Main refused to grant a mandatory injunction. We are now in a position to answer the question left open by Chitty J in *Lane v Capsey* [1891] 3 Ch 411. Self-redress is a summary remedy, which is justified only in clear and simple cases, or in an emergency. Where a plaintiff has applied for a mandatory injunction and failed, the sole justification for a summary remedy has gone. The court has decided the very point in issue. This is so whether the complaint lies in trespass or nuisance. In the present case, the court has decided that the plaintiff is not entitled to have the wall on her side of the boundary removed. It follows that she has no right to remove it herself.

16.2 Private nuisance

Private nuisance is an ancient wrong designed as an action between neighbouring landowners to protect a person's interest in land being adversely affected by the activities of neighbours. The harm is usually indirect (whereas, as discussed in the previous section, trespass protects a person against direct intrusions). Nuisance protects a limited range of interests including physical harm to or interference with quiet enjoyment of land, and generally a defendant's activity must be unreasonable (but does not need to be careless). Two things must be determined: first, whether the claimant is *able* to sue in respect of the alleged violation of their interest in land (i.e. do they have the right to sue, or 'standing') and, secondly, if their interest has been interfered with, whether the level of the interference is unreasonable and has been caused by an unreasonable use of land.

Confusion is sometimes caused by the analogous wrong of public nuisance, which has entirely different antecedents, but covers similar subject matter. The distinction between public and private nuisance will be dealt with first, and public nuisance can then be left to one side.

16.2.1 Comparison with public nuisance

Whereas private nuisance deals with the rights between two landowners, and generally the harm must affect private land, public nuisance is a crime to which a civil remedy has been attached, and the harm need not emanate from or affect private land. A civil action will be allowed only where an individual has suffered harm over and above that experienced by a community or a section of it. The various heads of damage claimed in **Halsey v Esso Petroleum** [1961] 1 WLR 683 neatly illustrate which kinds of harm can be claimed in private and which in public nuisance.

Halsey v Esso Petroleum
Queen's Bench Division [1961] 1 WLR 683

The claimants owned a house in Fulham, opposite which the defendants operated an oil depot. The claimant complained of the following: (a) acid smuts from a boiler in the depot which damaged the claimant's washing; (b) the same acid smuts which damaged his car standing in the road outside; (c) the smell of oil, which was unpleasant but caused no damage to health; (d) noise from the boilers; (e) noise from lorries in the depot; and (f) noise from lorries on the road entering the depot. Held: the defendants were liable. Complaints (a), (c), (d) and (e) were private nuisance, and (b) and (f) were public nuisance.

VEALE J: So far as the present case is concerned, liability for nuisance by harmful deposits could be established by proving damage by the deposits to the property in question, provided of course that the injury was not merely trivial. Negligence is not an ingredient of the cause of action, and the character of the neighbourhood is not a matter to be taken into consideration. On the other hand, nuisance by smell or noise is something to which no absolute standard can be applied. It is always a question of degree whether the interference with comfort or convenience is sufficiently serious to constitute a nuisance. The character of the neighbourhood is very relevant and all the relevant circumstances have to be taken into account. What might be a nuisance in one area is by no means necessarily so in another. In an urban area, everyone must put up with a certain amount of discomfort and annoyance from the activities of neighbours, and the law must strike a fair and reasonable balance between the right of the plaintiff on the one hand to the undisturbed enjoyment of his property, and the right of the defendant on the other hand to use his property for his own lawful enjoyment. That is how I approach this case.

It may be possible in some cases to prove that noise or smell have in fact diminished the value of the plaintiff's property in the market. That consideration does not arise in this case, and no evidence has been called in regard to it. The standard in respect of discomfort and inconvenience from noise and smell which I have to apply is that of the ordinary reasonable and responsible person who lives in this particular area of Fulham. This is not necessarily the same as the standard which the plaintiff chooses to set up for himself. It is the standard of the ordinary man, and the ordinary man, who may well like peace and quiet, will not complain, for instance, of the noise of traffic if he chooses to live on a main street in an urban centre, nor of the reasonable noises of industry, if he chooses to live alongside a factory.

Nuisance is commonly regarded as a tort in respect of land. In *Read v J Lyons & Co Ltd* [1947] AC 156, Lord Simonds said: 'he alone has a lawful claim who has suffered an invasion of some proprietary or other interest in land.' In this connection the allegation of damage to the plaintiff's motor-car calls for special consideration, since the allegation is that when the offending smuts from the defendants' chimney alighted upon it, the motor-car was not actually upon land in the plaintiff's occupation, but was on the public highway outside his door. In my judgment the plaintiff is also right in saying that if the motor-car was damaged in this way while on the public highway, it is a public nuisance in respect of which he has suffered special damage. . . .

I approach this question [of the smell] with caution, as Mr Gardiner asked me to do, since there has been no injury to health, but injury to health is not a necessary ingredient in the cause of action for nuisance by smell, and authority for that proposition is to be found in the judgment of Lord Romilly MR in *Crump v Lambert* (1867) 3 Eq 409, 412. I reject the contention that the evidence for the plaintiff has been exaggerated by people who feel strongly against the defendants on other grounds. I accept the evidence for the plaintiff, and it is right to add that the description by the witnesses of the nature of the smell was confirmed by my own experience on the night of February 10. On that night, at half past eleven, there was in Rainville Road and Wingrave Road, clearly emanating from the defendants' depot, a nasty smell, which could properly be described, as the plaintiff has described it in his further and better particulars, namely, 'a pungent, rather nauseating smell of an oily character.' The defendants in my judgment are liable for nuisance by smell.

I turn now to the question of nuisance by noise. This question relates to two distinct matters: the noise of the plant and the noise of the vehicles, the latter complaint including the noise of the vehicles themselves and the attendant noises made by drivers shouting and slamming doors and banging pipes. It is in connection with noise that, in my judgment, the operations of the defendants at night are particularly important. After all, one of the main objects of living in a house or flat is to have a room with a bed in it where one can sleep at night. Night is the time when the ordinary man takes his rest. No real complaint is made by the plaintiff so far as the daytime is concerned; but he complains bitterly of the noise at night. . . .

I accept the evidence of the plaintiff as to noise and I hold it is a serious nuisance, going far beyond a triviality, and one in respect of which the plaintiff is entitled to complain. Because of the noise made by the boilers, I think that the plaintiff is not so much, certainly since the throbbing of the steam pumps ceased, troubled by the noise of the electric pumps. But that is because the noise of the pumps is largely drowned by the noise of the boilers, and even if the noise of the boilers stopped, it might be that the plaintiff could justifiably complain of the noise of the pumps.

. . . But bearing in mind, I hope, all the relevant considerations, in my judgment the defendants are liable in nuisance for the noise of their plant, though only at night. Applying and adapting the well-known words of Knight-Bruce V-C in *Walter v Selfe*, 64 ER 849, this inconvenience is, as I find to be the fact, more than fanciful, more than one of mere delicacy or fastidiousness. It is an inconvenience materially interfering with the ordinary comfort physically of human existence, not merely according to elegant or dainty modes of living, but according to plain and sober and simple notions among ordinary people living in this part of Fulham.

But the question of noise does not stop there. At intervals through the night tankers leave and come to the defendants' depot. It has been urged upon me that the public highway is for the use of all, and that is true. But it must be borne in mind that these tankers are not ordinary motor-cars; they are not ordinary lorries which make more noise than a motor-car; they are enormous vehicles, some when laden weighing 24 tons, which, apart from the loud noise of the engine, may rattle as they go, particularly when empty and especially if they hit something in the road like a grating. They all enter the depot almost opposite the plaintiff's house, which involves a sharp turn in order to do so, often changing down into low great at the same time. They leave by the exit gate which is also close to the plaintiff's house. The noise of a tanker was 83 decibels—in the 'very loud' category. . . .

It is said by the defendants that since the public highway is for the use of everyone, the plaintiff cannot complain if all the defendants do is to make use of their right to use the public highway. I agree, if that is all that the defendants have done. If a person makes an unreasonable use of the public highway, for instance, by parking stationary vehicles on it, a member of the public who suffers special damage has a cause of action against him for public nuisance. Similarly, in my view, if a person makes an unreasonable use of the public highway by concentrating in one small area of the highway vehicles in motion and a member of the public suffers special damage, he is equally entitled to complain, although in most cases concentration of moving as opposed to stationary vehicles will be more likely to be reasonable. . . .

Notes

1. The central characteristic of a claim in public nuisance is that the nuisance affects a sufficiently large number of people. An *individual* may bring a civil claim in public nuisance if they can show that they suffered harm over and above that suffered by everyone else. In *Attorney General* v *PYA Quarries Ltd* [1957] 2 QB 169, Romer LJ said that:

   [A]ny nuisance is 'public' which materially affects the reasonable comfort and convenience of life of a class of Her Majesty's subjects. The sphere of the nuisance may be described generally as 'the neighbourhood'; but the question whether the local community within that sphere comprises a sufficient number of persons to constitute a class of the public is a question of fact in every case. It is not necessary . . . to prove that every member of the class has been injuriously affected; it is sufficient to show that a representative cross-section of the class has been so affected . . . (at 184)

2. An example of a person suffering greater damage than that suffered by the public at large is *Tate and Lyle* v *Greater London Council* [1983] 2 AC 509. The claimants operated a sugar refinery which had a jetty in the River Thames. The defendants' predecessors had built a ferry terminal, which caused the channel to the claimants' jetty to silt up. It was held that the claimants did not have any *private* rights which enabled them to insist on a certain depth of water round their jetty, so there was no liability in *private* nuisance. However, in relation to *public* nuisance it was held that the siltation caused by the ferry terminals was an interference with the public right of navigation, and that the claimants had suffered particular damage over and above that caused to the public at large, and therefore the defendants were liable for public nuisance.

3. A recent claim in public nuisance was brought in relation to increasing anti-social behaviour occurring in London Fields in summer 2020, when some of the restrictions in place because of the Covid-19 pandemic began to be lifted. The claim related to, inter alia, 'organising, attending or participating in . . . raves', 'playing loud music', 'urinating and/or defecating other than when making use of toilet facilities', 'lighting fires, fireworks, stoves, barbeques and/or naked flames', 'consuming or selling of nitrous oxide (laughing gas)' and 'bringing vehicles, including any engine or generator, onto any part of the prescribed area' (*London Borough of Hackney* v *Persons Unknown In London Fields, Hackney (The 'prescribed Area')* [2020] EWHC 1900 (QB)).

16.2.2 Private nuisance: who can sue?

The traditional view was that the function of nuisance was to protect a person who has a legal interest in land in the enjoyment of their property. This included not only freeholders, but also lessees and even tenants at will, but excluded those with no proprietary interest from being able to claim. In *Malone* v *Laskey* [1907] 2 KB 141 it was said that a wife 'who had no interest in property, no right of occupation in the proper sense of the term' (at 151) could not sue in nuisance for personal injuries arising out of a neighbour's activities. In **Hunter v Canary Wharf** [1997] AC 655, the House of Lords confirmed this rule.

Even if the claimant does have sufficient standing, nuisance only protects certain interests of the claimant, and whether there is a protectable interest is a matter of law. Physical damage and interference with quiet enjoyment of land are covered, but it is not clear the extent to which the law protects recreational or aesthetic interests. Probably the tort does not protect the value of the property itself as opposed to an invasion of a protectable interest which causes a diminution in value, but *Thompson-Schwab* v *Costaki* [1956] 1 WLR 335 comes close to simply protecting property values. If the interest is not regarded as protectable, neither unreasonableness nor malice on the defendant's part can make it protectable.

Hunter v Canary Wharf
House of Lords [1997] AC 655

Several hundred people complained that their television reception had been impaired by the construction of the Canary Wharf Tower, which is nearly 250 metres high. Some of the claimants were householders but others, such as spouses, children or lodgers, had no property interest in the houses where they lived. The case raised two issues. (1) Is a proprietary interest necessary to be able to sue in private nuisance? (2) Is interference with television reception by a physical obstruction a nuisance? Held: the defendants were not liable.

LORD LLOYD: . . . Private nuisances are of three kinds. They are (1) nuisance by encroachment on a neighbour's land; (2) nuisance by direct physical injury to a neighbour's land; and (3) nuisance by interference with a neighbour's quiet enjoyment of his land. In cases (1) and (2) it is the owner, or the occupier with the right to exclusive possession, who is entitled to sue. It has never, so far as I know, been suggested that anyone else can sue, for example, a visitor or a lodger; and the reason is not far to seek. For the basis of the cause of action in cases (1) and (2) is damage to the land itself, whether by encroachment or by direct physical injury.

In the case of encroachment the plaintiff may have a remedy by way of abatement. In other cases he may be entitled to an injunction. But where he claims damages, the measure of damages in cases (1) and (2) will be the diminution in the value of the land. This will usually (though not always) be equal to the cost of reinstatement. The loss resulting from diminution in the value of the land is a loss suffered by the owner or occupier with the exclusive right to possession (as the case may be) or both, since it is they alone who have a proprietary interest, or stake, in the land. So it is they alone who can bring an action to recover the loss.

Mr Brennan [counsel for the claimants] argues that the position is quite different when one comes to the third category of private nuisance, namely, interference with a neighbour's quiet enjoyment of his land. He submits that here the right to bring an action for nuisance is not confined to those with a proprietary interest, but extends to all those who occupy the property as their home. This would include not only the wife and children of the owner, as has been held by the Court of Appeal, but also, as Mr Brennan argues, a lodger with a contractual right to remain in the house as licensee, or a living-in servant or an au pair girl.

One can see the attraction in this approach. The wife at least, if not the children, should surely be regarded nowadays as sharing the exclusive possession of the home which she occupies, so as to give her an independent right of action. There is also a superficial logic in the approach. Suppose there are two adjoining properties, affected by smoke from a neighbouring factory. One of the properties is occupied by a bachelor, the other is occupied by a married man with two children. If they are all equally affected by the smoke, it would seem to follow that the damages recoverable by the married man and his family should be four times the damages recovered by the bachelor. Many of the textbooks favour this approach. In the current edition of *Clerk & Lindsell On Torts*, 17th ed (1995), pp 910–911, para 18-39 it is said that such a conclusion would affect 'a degree of modernisation' in the law, 'while freeing it from undue reliance upon the technicalities of land law.'

Like, I imagine, all your Lordships, I would be in favour of modernising the law wherever this can be done. But it is one thing to modernise the law by ridding it of unnecessary technicalities; it is another thing to bring about a fundamental change in the nature and scope of a cause of action. It has been said that an actionable nuisance is incapable of exact definition. But the essence of private nuisance is easy enough to identify, and it is the same in all three classes of private nuisance, namely, interference with land or the enjoyment of land. In the case of nuisances within class (1) or (2) the measure of damages is, as I have said, the diminution in the value of the land. Exactly the same should be true of nuisances within class (3). There is no difference of principle. The effect of smoke from a neighbouring factory is to reduce the value of the land. There may be no diminution in the market value. But there will certainly be loss of amenity value so long as the nuisance lasts. If that be the right approach, then the reduction in amenity value is the same whether the land is occupied by the family man or the bachelor.

If the occupier of land suffers personal injury as a result of inhaling the smoke, he may have a cause of action in negligence. But he does not have a cause of action in nuisance for his *personal* injury, nor for interference with his *personal* enjoyment. It follows that the quantum of damages in private nuisance does not depend on the number of those enjoying the land in question. It also follows that the only persons entitled to sue for loss in amenity value of the land are the owner or the occupier with the right to exclusive possession.

Damages for loss of amenity value cannot be assessed mathematically. But this does not mean that such damages cannot be awarded. . . .

It was said that confining the right to sue would cause inconvenience. There might be a case, for example, where the owner was unwilling to bring proceedings because he was less sensitive to smoke than other members of his family. I find it difficult to visualise such a case in practice. In any event the inconvenience, such as it would be, does not justify a departure from principle.

As for authority, one need look no further than the dictum of Lord Simonds in *Read v J Lyons & Co Ltd* [1947] AC 156, 183:

> For if a man commits a legal nuisance it is no answer to his injured neighbour that he took the utmost care not to commit it. There the liability is strict, and there he alone has a lawful claim who has suffered an invasion of some proprietary or other interest in land.

No doubt Lord Simonds will have had in mind the decision of the Court of Appeal in *Malone v Laskey* [1907] 2 KB 141. There the plaintiff was injured by a falling bracket in the lavatory, caused by vibrations from the defendants' engine next door. The plaintiff occupied the house as her home, but neither she nor her husband had any proprietary interest in the house. They were mere licensees. The plaintiff sued in nuisance and negligence. As to nuisance, Sir Gorell Barnes P said, at p 151:

> The main question, however, on this part of the case is whether the plaintiff can maintain this action on the ground of vibration causing the damage complained of, and in my opinion the plaintiff has no cause of action upon that ground. Many cases were cited in the course of the argument in which it had been held that actions for nuisance could be maintained where a person's rights of property had been affected by the nuisance, but no authority was cited, nor in my opinion can any principle of law be formulated, to the effect that a person who has no interest in property, no right of occupation in the proper sense of the term, can maintain

an action for a nuisance arising from the vibration caused by the working of an engine in an adjoining house.

If *Malone v Laskey* was correctly decided, the decision below cannot stand.

LORD HOFFMANN: . . . *St Helen's Smelting Co* v *Tipping* was a landmark case. It drew the line beyond which rural and landed England did not have to accept external costs imposed upon it by industrial pollution. But there has been, I think, some inclination to treat it as having divided nuisance into two torts, one of causing 'material injury to the property,' such as flooding or depositing poisonous substances on crops, and the other of causing 'sensible personal discomfort' such as excessive noise or smells. In cases in the first category, there has never been any doubt that the remedy,

whether by way of injunction or damages, is for causing damage to the land. It is plain that in such a case only a person with an interest in the land can sue. But there has been a tendency to regard cases in the second category as actions in respect of the discomfort or even personal injury which the plaintiff has suffered or is likely to suffer. On this view, the plaintiff's interest in the land becomes no more than a qualifying condition or springboard which entitles him to sue for injury to himself.

If this were the case, the need for the plaintiff to have an interest in land would indeed be hard to justify. The passage I have quoted from Dillon LJ (*Khorasandjian v Bush* [1993] QB 727, 734) is an eloquent statement of the reasons. But the premise is quite mistaken. In the case of nuisances 'productive of sensible personal discomfort,' the action is not for causing discomfort to the person but, as in the case of the first category, for causing injury to the land. True it is that the land has not suffered 'sensible' injury, but its utility has been diminished by the existence of the nuisance. It is for an unlawful threat to the utility of his land that the possessor or occupier is entitled to an injunction and it is for the diminution in such utility that he is entitled to compensation.

. . .

It follows that damages for nuisance recoverable by the possessor or occupier may be affected by the size, commodiousness and value of his property but cannot be increased merely because more people are in occupation and therefore suffer greater collective discomfort. If more than one person has an interest in the property, the damages will have to be divided among them. If there are joint owners, they will be jointly entitled to the damages. If there is a reversioner and the nuisance has caused damage of a permanent character which affects the reversion, he will be entitled to damages according to his interest. But the damages cannot be increased by the fact that the interests in the land are divided; still less according to the number of persons residing on the premises. . . .

Once it is understood that nuisances 'productive of sensible personal discomfort' (*St Helen's Smelting Co v Tipping* 11 HL Cas 642, 650) do not constitute a separate tort of causing discomfort to people but are merely part of a single tort of causing injury to land, the rule that the plaintiff must have an interest in the land falls into place as logical and, indeed, inevitable.

Is there any reason of policy why the rule should be abandoned? Once nuisance has escaped the bounds of being a tort against land, there seems no logic in compromise limitations, such as that proposed by the Court of Appeal in this case, requiring the plaintiff to have been residing on land as his or her home. This was recognised by the Court of Appeal in *Khorasandjian v Bush* [1993] QB 727 where the injunction applied whether the plaintiff was at home or not. There is a good deal in this case and other writings about the need for the law to adapt to modern social conditions. But the development of the common law should be rational and coherent. It should not distort its principles and create anomalies merely as an expedient to fill a gap.

The perceived gap in *Khorasandjian v Bush* was the absence of a tort of intentional harassment causing distress without actual bodily or psychiatric illness. This limitation is thought to arise out of cases like *Wilkinson v Downton* [1897] 2 QB 57 and *Janvier v Sweeney* [1919] 2 KB 316. The law of harassment has now been put on a statutory basis (see the Protection from Harassment Act 1997) and it is unnecessary to consider how the common law might have developed. But as at present advised, I see no reason why a tort of intention should be subject to the rule which excludes compensation for mere distress, inconvenience or discomfort in actions based on negligence: see *Hicks v Chief Constable of the South Yorkshire Police* [1992] 2 All ER 65. The policy considerations are quite different. I do not therefore say that *Khorasandjian v Bush* was wrongly decided. But it must be seen as a case on *intentional* harassment, not nuisance.

So far as the claim is for personal injury, it seems to me that the only appropriate cause of action is negligence. It would be anomalous if the rules for recovery of damages under this head were different according as to whether, for example, the plaintiff was at home or at work. It is true, as I have said, that the law of negligence gives no remedy for discomfort or distress which does not result in bodily or psychiatric illness. But this is a matter of general policy and I can see no logic in making an exception for cases in which the discomfort or distress was suffered at home rather than somewhere else.

Finally there is the position of spouses. It is said to be contrary to modern ways of thinking that a wife should not be able to sue for interference with the enjoyment of the matrimonial home merely because she has no proprietary right in the property. To some extent, this argument is based upon the fallacy which I have already discussed, namely that the action in nuisance lies for inconvenience or annoyance caused to people who happen to be in possession or occupation of land. But so far as it is thought desirable that the wife should be able to sue for injury to a proprietary or possessory interest in the home, the answer in my view lies in the law of property, not the law of tort. The courts today will readily assume that a wife has acquired a beneficial interest in the matrimonial home. If so, she will be entitled to sue for damage to that interest. On the other hand, if she has no such interest, I think it would be wrong to create a quasi-proprietary interest only for the purposes of giving her locus standi to sue for nuisance. . . .

Interference with television

In the television action, the plaintiffs complain that Canary Wharf Tower has diminished the amenity of their houses by interfering with television reception. In *Bridlington Relay Ltd v Yorkshire Electricity Board* [1965] Ch 436, 447 Buckley J said, tentatively and *obiter*:

> For myself, however, I do not think that it can at present be said that the ability to receive television free from occasional, even recurrent and severe, electrical interference is so important a part of an ordinary householder's enjoyment of his property that such interference should be regarded as a legal nuisance, particularly, perhaps, if such interference affects only one of the available alternative programmes.

The judge was plainly not laying down a general rule that interference with television can never be an actionable nuisance. In principle I do not see why in an appropriate case it should not. *Bridlington Relay* was a case of alleged interference by electromagnetic radiation from high tension electric cables. The Court of Appeal left open the question of whether interference of such a kind could be actionable and so would I.

In this case, however, the defendants say that the type of interference alleged, namely by the erection of a building between the plaintiffs' homes and the Crystal Palace transmitter, cannot as a matter of law constitute an actionable nuisance. This is not by virtue of anything peculiar to television. It applies equally to interference with the passage of light or air or radio signals or to the obstruction of a view. The general principle is that at common law anyone may build whatever he likes upon his land. If the effect is to interfere with the light, air or view of his neighbour, that is his misfortune. The owner's right to build can be restrained only by covenant or the acquisition (by grant or prescription) of an easement of light or air for the benefit of windows or apertures on adjoining land.

That such has until now been the law of England seems to me indisputable. A right to an uninterrupted prospect cannot be acquired even by prescription: *Aldred's Case* 9 Co Rep 57b. The same is true of a right to the uninterrupted flow of undefined air to a chimney: *Bryant v Lefever* (1879) 4 CPD 172. In the absence of an easement, there is no right to light. . . .

In the absence of agreement, therefore, the English common law allows the rights of a landowner to build as he pleases to be restricted only in carefully limited cases and then only after the period of prescription has elapsed. In this case there is no claim to an easement of television by prescription. And in any event, on the reasoning in *Dalton v Angus* I do not think that such an easement can exist. The extent to which a building may interfere with television reception is far from obvious. Nor is its potential effect limited to immediate neighbours. The number of plaintiffs in the television action is itself enough to demonstrate how large a burden would be imposed on anyone wishing to erect a tall building.

Once again we must consider whether modern conditions require these well established principles to be modified. The common law freedom of an owner to build upon his land has been drastically curtailed by the Town and Country Planning Act 1947 and its successors. It is now in normal cases necessary to obtain planning permission. The power of the planning authority to grant or refuse permission, subject to such conditions as it thinks fit, provides a mechanism for control of the unrestricted right to build which can be used for the protection of people living in the vicinity of a development. In a case such as this, where the development is likely to have an impact upon many people over a large area, the planning system is, I think, a far more appropriate form of control, from the point of view of both the developer and the public, than enlarging the right to bring actions for nuisance at common law. It enables the issues to be debated before an expert forum at a planning inquiry and gives the developer the advantage of certainty as to what he is entitled to build.

In saying this, I am not suggesting that a grant of planning permission should be a defence to anything which is an actionable nuisance under the existing law. It would, I think, be wrong to allow the private rights of third parties to be taken away by a permission granted by the planning authority to the developer. The Court of Appeal rejected such an argument in this case and the point has not been pursued in your Lordships' House. But when your Lordships are invited to develop the common law by creating a new right of action against an owner who erects a building upon his land, it is relevant to take into account the existence of other methods by which the interests of the locality can be protected.

In this case, as I mentioned at the beginning of this speech, the normal protection offered to the community by the Act of 1971 was largely removed. Parliament authorised this to be done on the grounds that the national interest required the rapid regeneration of the Docklands urban development area. The plaintiffs may well feel that their personal convenience was temporarily sacrificed to the national interest. But this is not a good enough reason for changing the principles of the law of nuisance which apply throughout the country.

On the one hand, therefore, we have a rule of common law which, absent easements, entitles an owner of land to build what he likes upon his land. It has stood for many centuries. If an exception were to be created for large buildings which interfere with television reception, the developers would be exposed to legal action by an indeterminate number of plaintiffs, each claiming compensation in a relatively modest amount. Defending such actions, whatever their merits or demerits, would hardly be cost-effective. The compensation and legal fees would form an unpredictable additional cost of the building. On the other hand, the plaintiffs will ordinarily have been able to make their complaints at the planning stage of the development and, if necessary, secure whatever conditions were necessary to provide them with an alternative source of television signals. The interference in such a case is not likely to last very long because there is no technical difficulty about the solution. In my view the case for a change in the law is not made out.

Notes

1. **Hunter** confirmed that only invasions which affect a property owner or occupier as owner or occupier will found an action in nuisance; that is, damage to the land itself or interference with rights of property. Other people who might be affected lack the 'standing' to sue.

2. Personal injury is not actionable in private nuisance—such actions must be based on negligence or public nuisance. This also affects the interests that are protected by nuisance since damages can only be for injury to the amenity value of the land—for example, the interference with television reception as discussed in **Hunter**.

3. In *Corby Group Litigation v Corby Borough Council* [2008] EWCA Civ 463 (damage caused by toxic waste), the Court of Appeal decided that although damages for personal injury cannot be recovered in private nuisance, they can be awarded for a public nuisance. Dyson LJ found that anything said in **Hunter** about public nuisance was *obiter*, but admitted that the House may yet change the law. He said:

   > [I]n my judgment, therefore, the long-established principle that damages for personal injury can be recovered in public nuisance has not been impliedly reversed . . . The most that can be said is that **Hunter** has raised the serious possibility that the House of Lords may in the future . . . change the law. I readily accept that the House of Lords may decide to take that course. But it is not open to this court to do so. (at [22])

4. The mere fact that an interference with rights of enjoyment (the television reception in **Hunter**) reduces the value of a property should not by itself amount to a nuisance. The question is whether freedom from electronic interference is a right that adheres to rights of property, and it may be that in this modern digital age it should. **Hunter** did not say that it could never amount to a nuisance but only that if the interference is by physical obstruction there will be no nuisance because the right of a landowner to put up a building (subject to planning laws) overrides the interests of the neighbouring owner. This leaves open the question of whether interference with electronic reception by electrical means should be a nuisance. See *Bridlington Relay v Yorkshire Electricity Board* [1965] Ch 436 and *Network Rail Infrastructure Ltd v Morris* [2004] EWCA Civ 172 and compare the Canadian case of *Nor-Video Services v Ontario Hydro* (1978) 84 DLR (3d) 221.

5. The tension between what can be considered damage to property (which will be a nuisance) and 'lost enjoyment' of property (which can be) is illustrated in *Network Rail Infrastructure Ltd v Williams and another* [2018] EWCA Civ 1514, a case involving the encroachment of Japanese knotweed, a virulent and damaging weed, from the defendant's property to the claimant's. The presence of knotweed rhizomes in the claimant's soil lessened the resale value of the property, but had not caused any physical damage to the structure of it (though this would be potentially possible). The defendant argued that the claimant was merely 'worried' about what may happen in the future, and had suffered only economic loss (which could be rectified by removing the weed). However, Sir Terence Etherton MR in the Court of Appeal found that the presence of the rhizomes, and the activity that would be needed to rid the claimant's soil of them, was a 'classic example' of the interference with amenity interests in land (at [55]).

6. In *Fearn and others v The Board of Trustees of the Tate Gallery* [2019] EWHC 246 (Ch), a case involving neighbours of London's Tate Modern claiming nuisance in respect of their glass-walled apartments being looked into by the museum's customers on its external viewing gallery, Mann J found that non-emanation did not bar recovery (as was thought to be the case post-**Hunter**, but

cf *Thompson-Schwab* v *Costaki*) (at [174]). Despite this, however, the finding of nuisance was overturned by the Court of Appeal, which found that 'overlooking' was a privacy concept not one giving rise to private nuisance (*Fearn and others* v *The Board of Trustees of the Tate Gallery* [2020] EWCA Civ 104).

16.2.3 Reasonable user

The standard required of an occupier is that of reasonable use of land. This is quite different from reasonableness in negligence for it relates to a balance between what it is reasonable for a person to do on his land and what it is reasonable for his neighbour to put up with. This relates not only to the kind of activity but also to its intensity and both will be subject to society's view at the time as to what is reasonable. *Halsey v Esso Petroleum*, discussed in section 16.2.1, is a good example of this balancing process.

St Helen's Smelting Co v Tipping
House of Lords (1865) 11 ER 1483

The claimant owned property near the defendants' smelting works. He complained that noxious gases, vapours and other matter caused damage to hedges and trees on his land. Held: the defendants were liable.

LORD WESTBURY LC: My Lords, in matters of this description it appears to me that it is a very desirable thing to mark the difference between an action brought for a nuisance upon the ground that the alleged nuisance produces material injury to the property, and an action brought for a nuisance on the ground that the thing alleged to be a nuisance is productive of sensible personal discomfort. With regard to the latter, namely, the personal inconvenience and interference with one's enjoyment, one's quiet, one's personal freedom, anything that discomposes or injuriously affects the senses of the nerves, whether that may or may not be denominated a nuisance, must undoubtedly depend greatly on the circumstances of the place where the thing complained of actually occurs. If a man lives in a town, it is necessary that he should subject himself to the consequences of those operations of trade which may be carried on in his immediate locality, which are actually necessary for trade and commerce, and also for the enjoyment of property, and for the benefit of the inhabitants of the town and of the public at large. If a man lives in a street where there are numerous shops, and a shop is opened next door to him, which is carried on in a fair and reasonable way, he has no ground for complaint, because to himself individually there may arise much discomfort from the trade carried on in that shop. But when an occupation is carried on by one person in the neighbourhood of another, and the result of that trade, or occupation, or business, is a material injury to property, then there unquestionably arises a very different consideration. I think, my Lords, that in a case of that description, the submission which is required from persons living in society to that amount of discomfort which may be necessary for the legitimate and free exercise of the trade of their neighbours, would not apply to circumstances the immediate result of which is sensible injury to the value of the property.

Notes

1. In *Sturges* v *Bridgman* (1879) 11 ChD 852 at 865, Thesiger LJ said, 'What would be a nuisance in Belgrave Square would not necessarily be so in Bermondsey'. At the time, Belgravia was a very affluent area of London, while Bermondsey was well known for its tanneries, which emitted

unpleasant smells. Essentially, what this means is that the nature and character of the locality are relevant when assessing a claim in nuisance (when physical damage to property is not at issue) and whether a defendant is a reasonable user of their land or not. This was recently confirmed in *Fearn and others* v *The Board of Trustees of the Tate Gallery* [2019] EWHC 246 (Ch).

2. With regard to interference with enjoyment of land (the 'amenity interest'), Knight-Bruce LJ said in *Walter* v *Selfe* (1851) 64 ER 849 that the question is:

> ought this inconvenience to be considered in fact as more than fanciful, more than one of mere delicacy or fastidiousness, as an inconvenience materially interfering with the ordinary comfort physically of human existence, not merely according to elegant or dainty modes and habits of living, but according to plain and sober and simple notions among the English people?

3. Substantive liability in nuisance does not depend on fault: as we have seen the controlling factor is reasonable use of land. In ***Overseas Tankship (UK) Ltd* v *Miller Steamship Co Pty Ltd (The Wagon Mound) (No 2)*** [1967] 1 AC 617 Lord Reid said that 'negligence is not an essential element in nuisance' (at 369), but nevertheless went on to say that foreseeability is relevant in relation to remoteness of damage. This was later confirmed in *Cambridge Water Co* v *Eastern Counties Leather plc* [1994] 2 AC 264 (discussed in Chapter 17). Thus, an occupier who creates a nuisance will be liable if her acts are an unreasonable use of land, but will only be liable insofar as the kind of damage which occurred was foreseeable (see also *Network Rail Infrastructure Ltd* v *Morris* [2004] EWCA Civ 172). 'Fault' plays a different role in nuisance as it is only relevant at the remoteness stage and foreseeability for this purpose may be weaker than that required to establish a duty of care in negligence. Thus, it is probably premature to regard nuisance as being subsumed under negligence.

4. It was long thought that an 'extra-sensitive' claimant could sue only if a person of ordinary sensitivity could have sued. In other words, a person cannot impose a higher burden upon his neighbour by engaging in especially sensitive activities. In *Robinson* v *Kilvert* (1889) 41 ChD 88, the defendants manufactured paper boxes in the cellar of a building. This required considerable heat which damaged the claimant's stock of brown paper on the floor above. It was found that the heat would not have damaged normal paper, and therefore the defendant was not liable (though compare *McKinnon Industries Ltd* v *Walker* [1951] 3 DLR 577). However, this principle was disapproved by the Court of Appeal in *Network Rail Infrastructure* v *Morris* [2004] EWCA Civ 172 (at [35]). The claimant (Morris) operated a recording studio 80 metres from a railway line. In 1994 Network Rail installed new track circuits which interfered with his amplifiers, causing him to lose business. It was held that the defendants were not liable as it was not foreseeable that the track circuits would interfere with the amplifiers. Buxton LJ said that there was no longer any need for the principle of 'abnormal sensitiveness' in nuisance which was developed at a time when liability for nuisance was thought to be strict. What is now required is an 'analysis of the demands of reasonableness' which the court can assess in terms of foreseeability. Thus, the test of liability is still reasonable user, but foreseeability of harm now plays a major part in deciding this. Overall, this judgment is a part of the continuing process of 'generalisation' of the concepts of nuisance, which is bringing nuisance closer to negligence.

5. If the interest invaded is not regarded as one protected in law, not even intentional or malicious interference will ground an action. Malice cannot change an unprotected interest into a protected one. In *Mayor of Bradford* v *Pickles* [1895] AC 587, the defendant owned land through which water percolated, which ultimately was collected in the Corporation reservoirs. The defendant wanted the Corporation to buy his land, or at least his rights to the water, and deliberately obstructed the flow of water to the reservoir by sinking a shaft. It was held that as the claimants had no right to receive percolating water, the fact that the defendant was acting maliciously could not convert into a nuisance what would otherwise not be.

6. Malice can, however, deprive a defendant of the argument that his use of land was reasonable. In *Hollywood Silver Fox Farm* v *Emmett* [1936] 2 KB 468 the defendant objected to the claimant's development of his land as a mink farm, so deliberately fired shotguns near the claimant's mink

pens. Firing shotguns does not make an unreasonable noise and is a reasonable use of land in the country. However, when subjected to loud noises mink tend to devour their young. It was held that the defendant was liable. Intentionally causing harm is not a reasonable use of land, and if a person intends a consequence he cannot claim it is too remote or sensitive.

16.2.3.1 Statutory authority and planning permission

Statutory authority to engage in activities can be a defence to any tort, but most commonly arises in relation to nuisance. If Parliament has authorised the commission of a nuisance there can be no liability, but statutes are rarely explicit on the issue. The question is often whether an authorised act necessarily amounts to a nuisance. If it does, there is no liability, but where the interference with the claimant's interests is greater than or different from the necessary consequences of the authorised act, there will be no defence to nuisance.

Similar problems arise where the granting of planning permission might appear to authorise a nuisance, or at least seem to have the same effect as doing so (see *Gillingham Borough Council v Medway (Chatham) Dock Co Ltd* [1993] QB 343, discussed in **Wheeler v Saunders** later in this section. It appears that where 'zoning' or regeneration issues are involved it may do so if the nuisance is a strategic and inevitable consequence of a change in character of the locality brought about by planning permission, but in other cases activities authorised by planning permission must still be carried on in such a way as not to create a nuisance (see **Coventry v Lawrence** [2014] UKSC 13).

Allen v Gulf Oil Refining Ltd
House of Lords [1981] AC 1001

The claimants sued for nuisances caused by a Gulf Oil refinery in Wales. The Gulf Oil Refining Act 1965 authorised the company to compulsorily purchase land for the construction of a refinery, but said nothing about the use or operation of it. The House of Lords held that the power to purchase land for a refinery necessarily implied the operation of a refinery. Held: the defence of statutory authority applied and the defendants were not liable.

LORD WILBERFORCE: We are here in the well charted field of statutory authority. It is now well settled that where Parliament by express direction or by necessary implication has authorised the construction and use of an undertaking or works, that carries with it an authority to do what is authorised with immunity from any action based on nuisance. The right of action is taken away: *Hammersmith and City Railway Co v Brand* (1869) LR 4 HL 171, 215 *per* Lord Cairns. To this there is made the qualification, or condition, that the statutory powers are exercised without 'negligence'—that word here being used in a special sense so as to require the undertaker, as a condition of obtaining immunity from action, to carry out the work and conduct the operation with all reasonable regard and care for the interests of other persons: *Geddis v Proprietors of Bann Reservoir* (1878) 3 App Cas 430, 455 *per* Lord Blackburn. It is within the same principle that immunity from action is withheld where the terms of the statute are permissive only, in which case the powers conferred must be exercised in strict conformity with private rights: *Metropolitan Asylum District v Hill* (1881) 6 App Cas 193. . . .

My Lords, . . . Parliament considered it in the public interest that a *refinery*, not merely the works (jetties etc.), should be constructed, and constructed upon lands at Llandstadwell to be compulsorily acquired.

To show how this intention was to be carried out I need only quote section 5:

(1) Subject to the provisions of this Act, the company may enter upon, take and use such of the lands delineated on the deposited plans and described in the deposited book of reference as it may require for the purposes of the authorised works or *for the construction of a refinery* in the parish of Llandstadwell in the rural district of Haverfordwest in the county of Pembroke or for purposes ancillary thereto or connected therewith. (2) The powers of compulsory acquisition of land under this section shall cease after the expiration of three years from October 1, 1965.

. . .

I cannot but regard this as an authority—whether it should be called express or by necessary implication may be a matter of preference—but an authority to construct and operate *a refinery* upon the lands to be acquired—a refinery moreover which should be commensurate with the facilities for unloading offered by the jetties (for large tankers), with the size of the lands to be acquired, and with the discharging facilities to be provided by the railway lines. I emphasize the words *a refinery* by way of distinction from *the refinery* because no authority was given or sought except in the indefinite form. But that there was authority to construct and operate *a* refinery seems to me indisputable. . . .

If I am right upon this point, the position as regards the action would be as follows. The respondent alleges a nuisance, by smell, noise, vibration, etc. The facts regarding these matters are for her to prove. It is then for the appellants to show, if they can, that it was impossible to construct and operate a refinery upon the site, conforming with Parliament's intention, without creating the nuisance alleged, or at least a nuisance. Involved in this issue would be the point discussed by Cumming-Bruce LJ in the Court of Appeal, that the establishment of an oil refinery, etc. was bound to involve some alteration of the environment and so of the standard of amenity and comfort which neighbouring occupiers might expect. To the extent that the environment has been changed from that of a peaceful unpolluted countryside to an industrial complex (as to which different standards apply—*Sturges v Bridgman* (1879) 11 ChD 852) Parliament must be taken to have authorised it. So far, I venture to think, the matter is not open to doubt. But in my opinion the statutory authority extends beyond merely authorising a change in the environment and an alteration of standard. It confers immunity against proceedings for any nuisance which can be shown (the burden of so showing being upon the appellants) to be the inevitable result of erecting a refinery upon the site—not, I repeat, the existing refinery, but any refinery—however carefully and with however great a regard for the interest of adjoining occupiers it is sited, constructed and operated. To the extent and only to the extent that the actual nuisance (if any) caused by the actual refinery and its operation exceeds that for which immunity is conferred, the plaintiff has a remedy.

Notes

1. *Tate & Lyle* v *Greater London Council* [1983] 2 AC 509 is an example of a case where a defendant did have statutory authority, without it providing a defence (because the powers could have been exercised without causing a nuisance). Though the construction was authorised by statute, it was shown that the choice of design caused an additional siltation, which need not have occurred if a different design had been adopted. The House of Lords held that the statute did not absolve the defendants from the need to 'have all reasonable regard and care for the interests of other persons' (at 538).

> ### *Wheeler* v *Saunders*
> Court of Appeal [1996] Ch 19

The claimant owned a house and holiday cottages adjacent to the defendants' pig farm. The defendants obtained planning permission to increase the capacity of the pig farm. One of the new pig houses built under this permission was only 11 metres from the claimant's holiday cottage. The claimant sued for nuisance because of the smell; the defendants claimed that the planning permission meant they were not liable. Held: the defendants were liable.

STAUGHTON LJ: . . . What then was the effect of the planning permission for two Trowbridge houses? It was opposed by Dr and Mrs Wheeler, but nevertheless granted. Does that mean that they have lost any right which they had previously enjoyed to live their lives free from the smell of pigs on their doorstep? Surprisingly, there appears to have been no direct authority on the point until recently. There have however been cases dealing with the question of whether statutory authority is a defence to a claim in nuisance. One such was *Allen v Gulf Oil Refining Ltd* [1981] AC 1001, where Mrs Allen complained of nuisance from an oil refinery built with statutory authority. Lord Wilberforce said, at p 1011:

> It is now well settled that where Parliament by express direction or by necessary implication has authorised the construction and use of an undertaking or works, that carries with it an authority to do what is authorised with immunity from any action based on nuisance.

However, he added, at p 1114, that the immunity was confined to harm which was the inevitable result of what Parliament had authorised. The Gulf company had to show that it was impossible to construct the refinery without creating the nuisance complained of.

I do not consider that planning permission necessarily has the same effect as statutory authority. Parliament is sovereign and can abolish or limit the civil rights of individuals. As Sir John May [one of the other judges in the case] put it in the course of argument, Parliament cannot be irrational just as the Sovereign can do no wrong. The planning authority on the other hand has only the powers delegated to it by Parliament. It is not in my view self-evident that they include the power to abolish or limit civil rights in any or all circumstances. The process by which planning permission is obtained allows for objections by those who might be adversely affected, but they have no right of appeal if their objections are overruled. It is not for us to say whether the private bill procedure in Parliament is better or worse. It is enough that it is different.

In *Allen v Gulf Oil Refining Ltd* [1980] QB 156, before the Court of Appeal Cumming-Bruce LJ touched on the effect of planning permission on what would otherwise be a nuisance. He said, at p 174: 'the planning authority has no jurisdiction to authorise a nuisance save (if at all) in so far as it has statutory power to permit the change of the character of a neighbourhood.'

One can readily appreciate that planning permission will, quite frequently, have unpleasant consequences for some people. The man with a view over open fields from his window may well be displeased if a housing estate is authorised by the planners and built in front of his house; the character of the neighbourhood is changed. But there may be nothing which would qualify as a nuisance and no infringement of his civil rights. What if the development does inevitably create what would otherwise be a nuisance? Instead of a housing estate the planners may authorise a factory which would emit noise and smoke to the detriment of neighbouring residents. Does that come within the first proposition of Cumming-Bruce LJ that a planning authority has no jurisdiction to authorise a nuisance? Or is it within the second, that the authority may change the character of a neighbourhood? The problem arose directly in *Gillingham Borough Council v Medway (Chatham) Dock Co Ltd* [1993] QB 343. There planning permission had been granted for the development as a commercial port of part of the Bulmer Road dockyard in Chatham. This had the result that heavy goods vehicles in large numbers used roads in the neighbourhood for 24 hours a day, much to the harm of local residents. This was said to be an actionable public nuisance. Buckley J held that it was authorised by the grant of planning permission and so was not actionable. His reasoning closely followed the dictum of Cumming-Bruce LJ which I have quoted. He said, at p 359:

> It has been said, no doubt correctly, that planning permission is not a licence to commit nuisance and that a planning authority has no jurisdiction to authorise nuisance. However, a planning authority can, through its development plans and decisions, alter the character of a neighbourhood.

He concluded at p 361:

> In short, where planning consent is given for a development or change of use, the question of nuisance will thereafter fall to be decided by reference to a neighbourhood with that development or use and not as it was previously.

However, he did accept, at p 360: 'it is only a nuisance inevitably resulting from the authorised works on which immunity is conferred.' . . .

What may matter is whether the subsequent nuisance flowed inevitably from the activity which was authorised by the two planning permissions. In my opinion it did. The Trowbridge houses were to contain 800 pigs based on slurry within 36 feet of the nearest holiday cottage. There was bound to be nuisance by smell. True the nuisance would be greater when the pigs were fed on whey, but there would inevitably be nuisance even if they were not. It follows that if this were a case where the buildings were authorised by statute, there would be immunity from any action based on nuisance. But, as I have already said, I consider that the case may be different where one is concerned with planning permission rather than statute.

I accept what was said by Cumming-Bruce LJ: first, that a planning authority has in general no jurisdiction to authorise a nuisance, and secondly, if it can do so at all, that is only by the exercise of its power to permit a change in the character of a neighbourhood. To the extent that those two propositions feature in the judgment of Buckley J, I agree with his decision, but I would not for the present go any further than that.

It would in my opinion be a misuse of language to describe what has happened in the present case as a change in the character of a neighbourhood. It is a change of use of a very small piece of land, a little over 350 square metres according to the dimensions on the plan, for the benefit of the applicant and to the detriment of the objectors in the quiet enjoyment of their house. It is not a strategic planning decision affected by considerations of public interest. Unless one is prepared to accept that any planning decision authorises any nuisance which must inevitably come from it, the argument that the nuisance was authorised by planning permission in this case must fail. I am not prepared to accept that premise. It may be—I express no concluded opinion—that some planning decisions will authorise some nuisances. But that is as far as I am prepared to go. There is no immunity from liability for nuisance in the present case. I would dismiss the second part of this appeal.

Notes

1. As one of the other judges pointed out, the decision means that the defendants, having constructed the pig houses in accordance with planning permission, could not use them. But why should planning permission allow them to disregard other rules of law?

2. Sir John May said that apart from cases where the permission changes the character of the locality, even if the nuisance complained of was an inevitable consequence of the permission, that could not license the nuisance. Furthermore, he pointed out that permission which inevitably resulted in a nuisance would be able to be judicially reviewed on the ground of irrationality (at 36–9).

3. In *Coventry v Lawrence* [2014] UKSC 13 Lord Neuberger cast doubt on whether planning permission will be sufficient to change the nature of a locality and thought this would fall to be assessed on a case-by-case basis. He added 'the mere fact that the activity which is said to give rise to the nuisance has the benefit of a planning permission is normally of no assistance to the defendant in a claim brought by a neighbour who contends that the activity causes a nuisance' (at [94]). Lord Carnwath thought that planning permission might in 'exceptional cases' change the nature of a locality (at [223]).

4. In *Barr and others* v *Biffa Waste Services Ltd* [2012] EWCA Civ 312 the Court of Appeal held that environmental permits are not equivalent to statutory authority, nor will they change the nature of a locality.

16.2.4 The effect of the Human Rights Act 1998

As well as Article 8 (the right to family and private life), the First Protocol (on the protection of property) to the European Convention on Human Rights (ECHR) says 'every natural or legal person is entitled to the peaceful enjoyment of his possessions. No one shall be deprived of his possessions except in the public interest and subject to the conditions provided for by law and by the general principles of international law.' Both can be relied on in actions under the Human Rights Act (HRA) 1998 in relation to nuisance.

These provisions may affect nuisance in various ways. One way relates to the rule that only a person with an interest in the property can sue, as affirmed in **Hunter** (see *McKenna* v *British Aluminium* [2002] Env LR 30). Another relates to the balance between public and private interests, as discussed in **Marcic v Thames Water** [2003] UKHL 66. In *Hatton v UK* (Application no 36022/97) (2003) 37 EHRR 28, which concerned noise from Heathrow Airport, the Court reiterated the fundamentally subsidiary role of the Convention, saying that the national authorities have direct democratic legitimation and are better placed than an international court to evaluate local needs and conditions, thus the role of the domestic policy-maker should be given special weight. It was said that 'Article 8 may apply in environmental cases whether the pollution is directly caused by the State or whether State responsibility arises from the failure properly to regulate private industry. Whether the case is analysed in terms of a positive duty on the State to take reasonable and appropriate measures to secure the applicants' rights under paragraph 1 of Article 8 or in terms of an interference by a public authority to be justified in accordance with paragraph 2, the applicable principles are broadly similar. In both contexts regard must be had to the fair balance that has to be struck between the competing interests of the individual and of the community as a whole; and in both contexts the State enjoys a certain margin of appreciation in determining the steps to be taken to ensure compliance with the Convention' (at 98).

Marcic v Thames Water Utilities Ltd
House of Lords [2003] UKHL 66

The claimant suffered a number of incidents of flooding from two sewers near his house. The sewers were built in the 1930s but had become inadequate after later housing development. The Water Industry Act 1991 provides that the remedy for breach of a sewerage undertaker's obligations is an enforcement order issued by the Director General of Water Services and no direct statutory remedy is available to a member of the public affected by the breach. The claimant tried to sidestep this by asserting claims in nuisance and for breach of the HRA. The claim in nuisance was rejected because Thames Water was not an ordinary occupier of land but a provider of public utilities and this raised questions of public interest which courts are not equipped to resolve in ordinary litigation. It was also said that the common law should not impose obligations inconsistent with the 1991 Act. The HRA claim was also rejected. Held: the defendants were not liable.

LORD NICHOLLS:

The claim under the Human Rights Act 1998

37. I turn to Mr Marcic's claim under the Human Rights Act 1998. His claim is that as a public authority within the meaning of section 6 of the Human Rights Act 1998 Thames Water has acted unlawfully. Thames Water has conducted itself in a way which is incompatible with Mr Marcic's Convention rights under article 8 of the Convention and article 1 of the First Protocol to the Convention. His submission was to the following effect. The flooding of Mr Marcic's property falls within the first paragraph of article 8 and also within article 1 of the First Protocol. That was common ground between the parties. Direct and serious interference of this nature with a person's home is prima facie a violation of a person's right to respect for his private and family life (article 8) and of his entitlement to the peaceful enjoyment of his possessions (article 1 of the First Protocol). The burden of justifying this interference rests on Thames Water. At the trial of the preliminary issues Thames Water failed to discharge this burden. The trial judge found that the system of priorities used by Thames Water in deciding whether to carry out flood alleviation works might be entirely fair. The judge also said that on the limited evidence before him it was not possible to decide this issue, or to decide whether for all its apparent faults the system fell within the wide margin of discretion open to Thames Water and the Director: [2002] QB 929, 964, para 102.

38. To my mind the fatal weakness in this submission is the same as that afflicting Mr Marcic's claim in nuisance: it does not take sufficient account of the statutory scheme under which Thames Water is operating the offending sewers. The need to adopt some system of priorities for building more sewers is self-evident. So is the need for the system to be fair. A fair system of priorities necessarily involves balancing many intangible factors. Whether the system adopted by a sewerage undertaker is fair is a matter inherently more suited for decision by the industry regulator than by a court. And the statutory scheme so provides. Moreover, the statutory scheme provides a remedy where a system of priorities is not fair. An unfair system of priorities means that a sewerage undertaker is not properly discharging its statutory drainage obligation so far as those who are being treated unfairly are concerned. The statute provides what should happen in these circumstances. The Director is charged with deciding whether to make an enforcement order in respect of a sewerage undertaker's failure to drain property properly. Parliament entrusted this decision to the Director, not the courts.

39. What happens in practice accords with this statutory scheme. When people affected by sewer flooding complain to the Director he considers whether he should require the sewerage undertaker to take remedial action. Before doing so he considers, among other matters, the severity and history of the problem in the context of that undertaker's sewer flooding relief programme, as allowed for in its current price limits. In many cases the company agrees to take action, but sometimes he accepts that a solution is not possible in the short term.

40. So the claim based on the Human Rights Act 1998 raises a broader issue: is the statutory scheme as a whole, of which this enforcement procedure is part, Convention-compliant? Stated

more specifically and at the risk of over-simplification, is the statutory scheme unreasonable in its impact on Mr Marcic and other householders whose properties are periodically subjected to sewer flooding?

41. The recent decision of the European Court of Human Rights, sitting as a Grand Chamber, in *Hatton v United Kingdom* Application No 36022/97, (unreported) 8 July 2003 confirms how courts should approach questions such as these. In *Hatton's* case the applicants lived near Heathrow airport. They claimed that the government's policy on night flights at Heathrow violated their rights under article 8. The court emphasised 'the fundamentally subsidiary nature' of the Convention. National authorities have 'direct democratic legitimation' and are in principle better placed than an international court to evaluate local needs and conditions. In matters of general policy, on which opinions within a democratic society may reasonably differ widely, 'the role of the domestic policy maker should be given special weight': see paragraph 97. A fair balance must be struck between the interests of the individual and of the community as a whole.

42. In the present case the interests Parliament had to balance included, on the one hand, the interests of customers of a company whose properties are prone to sewer flooding and, on the other hand, all the other customers of the company whose properties are drained through the company's sewers. The interests of the first group conflict with the interests of the company's customers as a whole in that only a minority of customers suffer sewer flooding but the company's customers as a whole meet the cost of building more sewers. As already noted, the balance struck by the statutory scheme is to impose a general drainage obligation on a sewerage undertaker but to entrust enforcement of this obligation to an independent regulator who has regard to all the different interests involved. Decisions of the Director are of course subject to an appropriately penetrating degree of judicial review by the courts.

43. In principle this scheme seems to me to strike a reasonable balance. Parliament acted well within its bounds as policy maker. In Mr Marcic's case matters plainly went awry. It cannot be acceptable that in 2001, several years after Thames Water knew of Mr Marcic's serious problems, there was still no prospect of the necessary work being carried out for the foreseeable future. At times Thames Water handled Mr Marcic's complaint in a tardy and insensitive fashion. But the malfunctioning of the statutory scheme on this occasion does not cast doubt on its overall fairness as a scheme. A complaint by an individual about his particular case can, and should, be pursued with the Director pursuant to the statutory scheme, with the long stop availability of judicial review. That remedial avenue was not taken in this case.

44. I must add that one aspect of the statutory scheme as presently administered does cause concern. This is the uncertain position regarding payment of compensation to those who suffer flooding while waiting for flood alleviation works to be carried out. A modest statutory compensation scheme exists regarding internal flooding: see paragraph 7B of the Water Supply and Sewerage Services (Customer Service Standards) Regulations 1989, SI 1989/1159, as amended by SI 1993/500 and SI 2000/2301. There seems to be no statutory provision regarding external sewer flooding. Some sewerage undertakers make payments, others do not. They all provide a free clean up and disinfecting service, including removal of residual effluent.

45. It seems to me that, in principle, if it is not practicable for reasons of expense to carry out remedial works for the time being, those who enjoy the benefit of effective drainage should bear the cost of paying some compensation to those whose properties are situated lower down in the catchment area and who, in consequence, have to endure intolerable sewer flooding, whether internal or external. As the Court of Appeal noted, the flooding is the consequence of the benefit provided to those making use of the system: [2002] QB 929, 1001, para 113. The minority who suffer damage and disturbance as a consequence of the inadequacy of the sewerage system ought not to be required

to bear an unreasonable burden. This is a matter the Director and others should reconsider in the light of the facts in the present case.

46. For these reasons I consider the claim under the Human Rights Act 1998 is ill founded. The scheme set up by the 1991 Act is Convention-compliant. The scheme provides a remedy for persons in Mr Marcic's unhappy position, but Mr Marcic chose not to avail himself of this remedy.

Notes

1. In *Dennis* v *Ministry of Defence* [2003] EWHC 198 (QB) (decided before **Marcic**), the claimant complained of noise from RAF Wittering. The noise was at such a level as to constitute a nuisance, but the public interest required the training of pilots and, as the airfield was operated responsibly, the nuisance was justified. However, the effect of the HRA was to require compensation as even though the public interest was greater than the individual private interests of the claimants, it was not 'proportionate' to give effect to the public interest without compensating the individuals affected. In *Hatton* v *UK*, the issue was whether the system of limiting the number of night flights at Heathrow was fair, and the European Court accepted that national governments have a wide discretion on matters such as these and the scheme was held to be valid. In *Dennis*, the view was that the choice was not simply between allowing or not allowing the flights, but rather whether the flights should continue albeit with compensation being paid.

2. *McKenna* v *British Aluminium* [2002] Env LR 30 concerned pollution from a factory where some of the neighbouring claimants had no proprietary interest in the affected land (many were children). In a striking-out action Neuberger J thought there was a powerful case for saying that effect had not properly been given to Article 8 ECHR if a person with no interest in the home, but who has lived there for some time, is at the mercy of the person who owns the home as the only person who may bring proceedings. He also thought it questionable whether it would be Article 8 compliant if damages were limited. This latter point refers to the fact that damages are for interference with the land rather than for personal inconvenience. However, he also noted the argument that nuisance is a property-based wrong and that it may not be appropriate to test it by Article 8, as that relates to personal rights.

3. In *Dobson* v *Thames Water Utilities Ltd* [2008] EWCA Civ 473 the defendant caused nuisance (smells and mosquitoes) by negligent management of its sewage treatment works. A number of claimants (including some with no proprietary interests, including children) sued in nuisance, negligence and under the HRA. It was held that **Marcic** would prevent a successful claim in nuisance, but only in the *absence of negligence*. The claim under the HRA was also allowed to proceed. The question then became whether the claimants who had no proprietary interests had received 'just satisfaction' of their claim under the HRA—the Court of Appeal thought that this should be determined at a new trial and reversed the lower court decision on this point.

16.2.5 **Remedies**

Remedies for nuisance include abatement (self-help), injunctions and damages. Interim injunctions are commonly applied for in nuisance cases, and examples of the application of the principles in *American Cyanamid* v *Ethicon* [1975] AC 396 are *Hubbard* v *Pitt* [1975] ICR 308 and *Laws* v *Florinplace* [1981] 1 All ER 659. This section, however, focuses on whether a claimant should be awarded an injunction or be satisfied with damages. This is an area which has been subject to considerable analysis and raises wide questions of policy—for example, does the payment of damages essentially amount to the same as the purchase of a licence to commit an unlawful act (*Shelfer* v *City of London Lighting* [1895] 1 Ch 287)? While this has been a matter of debate for some time, the position now seems clearer following the decision in **Coventry v Lawrence** [2014] UKSC 13 which appears to move away from the *Shelfer* principles.

> ### *Regan* v *Paul Properties*
> Court of Appeal [2006] EWCA Civ 1319

The defendants were property developers whose project would affect the light in the claimant's living room, reducing the area of adequate light from 65 per cent to 45 per cent. The market value of his property would be reduced by £5,000. The cost to the developers to avoid the infringement would be £175,000. Held: an injunction was granted to prevent the nuisance.

MUMMERY LJ:

36. *Shelfer v City of London Lighting* [1895] 1 Ch 287 has, for over a century, been the leading case on the power of the court to award damages instead of an injunction. It is authority for the following propositions which I derive from the judgments of Lord Halsbury and Lindley and AL Smith LJJ:

(1) A claimant is prima facie entitled to an injunction against a person committing a wrongful act, such as continuing nuisance, which invades the claimant's legal right.

(2) The wrongdoer is not entitled to ask the court to sanction his wrongdoing by purchasing the claimant's rights on payment of damages assessed by the court.

(3) The court has jurisdiction to award damages instead of an injunction, even in cases of a continuing nuisance; but the jurisdiction does not mean that the court is 'a tribunal for legalising wrongful acts' by a defendant, who is able and willing to pay damages. (Lindley LJ at 315 and 316).

(4) The judicial discretion to award damages in lieu should pay attention to well settled principles and should not be exercised to deprive a claimant of his prima facie right 'except under very exceptional circumstances. (Lindley LJ at 315 and 316).

(5) Although it is not possible to specify all the circumstances relevant to the exercise of the discretion or to lay down rules for its exercise, the judgments indicated that it was relevant to consider the following factors: whether the injury to the claimant's legal rights was small; whether the injury could be estimated in money; whether it could be adequately compensated by a small money payment; whether it would be oppressive to the defendant to grant an injunction; whether the claimant had shown that he only wanted money; whether the conduct of the claimant rendered it unjust to give him more than pecuniary relief; and whether there were any other circumstances which justified the refusal of an injunction: see AL Smith LJ at 322 and 323 and Lindley LJ at 317.

37. In my judgment, none of the above propositions has been overruled by later decisions of any higher court or of this court. Only one case in the House of Lords was cited, *Colls v Home and Colonial Stores Limited* [1904] AC 179. The case is authority for the proposition that the test for infringement of the right to light is whether the obstruction complained of is a nuisance, that is whether there is a substantial loss of light so as to render the occupation of the house less fit for occupation and uncomfortable according to the ordinary notions of mankind. It is not enough for the claimant simply to prove that the light is less than it was.

38. As the House of Lords restored the decision of Joyce J dismissing the action, the issue of remedies did not arise for decision. Lord Lindley said (at 212) that, even if there was a cause of action, the case was not one for a mandatory injunction, as the damages that could properly be awarded were small and to grant a mandatory injunction would be unduly oppressive and not in accordance with the principles on which equitable relief has usually been granted. He cited a number of authorities including *Shelfer* to which he had been a party.

39. Lord Macnaghten was the only other member of the House who said anything about remedies for infringement of ancient lights: see 192–5. He prefaced what he described as 'practical suggestions' with the comment that he did not 'put them forward as carrying any authority'. This is important, as some later cases citing Lord Macnaghten's *obiter* 'practical suggestions' seem to have treated them as having an effect which they did not and were never intended to have. The weight attached to them is no doubt explicable by the very high judicial reputation enjoyed by him. Lord Macnaghten made no adverse comment on *Shelfer*.

40. He rightly described the giving of damages in addition to or substitution for an injunction as 'a delicate matter' of judicial discretion. He doubted whether the amount of damages which could be recovered was a satisfactory test. He recognised that in some cases an injunction is necessary to do justice to the plaintiff and as a warning to others. He commented at p 193:

> But if there is really a question as to whether the obstruction is legal or not, and if the defendant has acted fairly and not in an unneighbourly spirit, I am disposed to think that the court ought to incline to damages rather than to an injunction.

41. Lord Macnaghten agreed that a man ought not to be compelled to part with his property against his will or to have the value of his property diminished, but, in the following terms on the same page, warned against allowing the action for infringement of ancient lights being used as a means of extorting money:

> Often a person who is engaged in a large building scheme has to pay money right and left in order to avoid litigation, which will put him to even greater expense by delaying his proceedings. As far as my experience goes, there is quite as much oppression on the part of those who invoke the assistance of the Court to protect some ancient lights, which they have never before considered of any great value, as there is on the part of those who are improving the neighbourhood by the erection of buildings that must necessarily to some extent interfere with the light of adjoining premises.

69. I have reached the conclusion that the judge acted on a wrong principle of law in placing the burden on Mr Regan to show why damages should not be awarded and that, on the basis of the correct legal principles deduced from the authorities, the proper course is to grant an injunction against the defendants. I would make the following points.

70. First, the light in the living room would be reduced so that the area receiving adequate light would be 42–45 per cent in place of 67 per cent. I would not regard this obstruction as a 'small injury' to Mr Regan's right to light for the living room of his maisonette. In order to enjoy adequate light Mr Regan would now either have to use artificial light in the part of the living room where the natural light has become inadequate or he would have to move into the area of the living room into or close by the bay window, where he would be in full view of the occupants of the defendants' development. The deputy judge's comment (in paragraph 95(a) of his judgment) that the living room 'is certainly not rendered uninhabitable' by the obstruction to light is not a correct approach to the question whether the injury to the rights was small.

71. Secondly, although the injury is capable of being estimated in money, I would not regard this injury as adequately compensated by 'a small money payment'. So far as the diminution in the value of his maisonette is concerned it was more than a small amount. The valuers agreed that the loss of value of the maisonette, if Unit 16 were cut back so as to give 53 per cent adequate light, would be £5000–£5500. This is not a small figure. It is no doubt smaller than the cost to the defendants of having to comply with a mandatory injunction, but that is not, in my view, the correct approach to whether the injury to Mr Regan was small. Further, according to Mr Regan's valuer, the diminution in the value of the maisonette is twice that figure if a comparison is made between pre- and post-development situations.

72. Further on the evidence available I do not think that it can be said that the sum of equitable compensation which Mr Regan could reasonably ask the defendants to pay for the negotiated release or modification of his right to light for the future would, when linked to a proportion of the

net profit of the defendants from that part of the development of Unit 16 which infringes the light, be small.

73. Thirdly, as to whether an injunction would be oppressive to the defendants, it would obviously be serious in its effect on cutting back the defendants' plans for Unit 16 which would reduce the sale price, create extra costs in cutting back Unit 16 and possibly cause planning and building regulation difficulties. In total the defendants' losses would be substantial and would probably exceed Mr Regan's losses, but those things on their own are not determinative of the issue of oppressiveness and of the choice of remedy. It is necessary to consider all the surrounding circumstances of the dispute and the conduct of the parties.

Notes

1. If damages are awarded they will theoretically be based on the reduction in value of the claimant's property or his rights. In practice, in this situation, that will be the amount a reasonable person would negotiate for permission to commit the nuisance. In a case like *Regan* could this be an amount just below the potential loss to the defendant—for example, in this case around £150,000?

Kennaway v Thompson
Court of Appeal [1981] QB 88

In 1969 the claimant built a house near a lake, which for a number of years had been used for motor-boat racing. The defendants were held liable for the nuisance created by the noise. At first instance the claimant was awarded damages of £16,000. The claimant appealed, seeking an injunction. Held: the claimant was entitled to an injunction limiting the use of the lake to certain days and to certain noise limits.

LAWTON LJ: Mr Kempster based his submissions primarily on the decision of this court in *Shelfer v City of London Electric Lighting Co* [1895] 1 Ch 287. The opening paragraph of the headnote, which correctly summarises the judgment, is as follows:

Lord Cairns' Act 1858, in conferring upon courts of equity a jurisdiction to award damages instead of an injunction, has not altered the settled principles upon which those courts interfered by way of injunction; and in cases of continuing actionable nuisance the jurisdiction so conferred ought only to be exercised under very exceptional circumstances.

In a much-quoted passage, Lindley LJ said, at pp 315–316:

. . . ever since Lord Cairns' Act was passed the Court of Chancery has repudiated the notion that the legislature intended to turn that court into a tribunal for legalising wrongful acts; or in other words, the court has always protested against the notion that it ought to allow a wrong to continue simply because the wrongdoer is able and willing to pay for the injury he may inflict. Neither has the circumstance that the wrongdoer is in some sense a public benefactor (eg, a gas or water company or a sewer authority) ever been considered a sufficient reason for refusing to protect by injunction an individual whose rights are being persistently infringed.

AL Smith LJ, in his judgment, set out what he called a good working rule for the award of damages in substitution for an injunction. His working rule does not apply in this case. The injury to the plaintiff's legal rights is not small; it is not capable of being estimated in terms of money save in the way the judge tried to make an estimate, namely by fixing a figure for the diminution of the value of the plaintiff's house because of the prospect of a continuing nuisance—and the figure he fixed could not be described as small. The principles enunciated in *Shelfer's* case, which is binding on us, have been applied time and time again during the past 85 years. The only case which raises a doubt about the application of the *Shelfer* principles to all cases is *Miller v Jackson* [1977] QB 966, a decision of this court. The majority (Geoffrey Lane and Cumming-Bruce LJJ, Lord Denning MR dissenting) adjudged that the activities of an old-established cricket club which had been going for over 70 years, had been a nuisance to the plaintiffs by reason of cricket balls landing in their garden. The question then was whether the plaintiffs should be granted an injunction. Geoffrey Lane LJ was of the opinion that one should be granted. Lord Denning MR and Cumming-Bruce LJ thought otherwise. Lord Denning MR said that the public interest should prevail over the private interest. Cumming-Bruce LJ stated that a factor to be taken into account when exercising the judicial discretion whether to grant an injunction was that the plaintiffs had bought their house knowing that it was next to the cricket ground. He thought that there were special circumstances which should inhibit a court of equity from granting the injunction claimed. Lord Denning MR's statement that the public interest should prevail over the private interest runs counter to the principles enunciated in *Shelfer's* case and does not accord with Cumming-Bruce LJ's reason for refusing an injunction. We are of the opinion that there is nothing in *Miller v Jackson* [1977] QB 966 binding on us, which qualifies what was decided in *Shelfer's* case. Any decisions before *Shelfer's* case (and there were some at first instance, as Mr Gorman pointed out) which give support for the proposition that the public interest should prevail over the private interest must be read subject to the decision in *Shelfer's* case.

It follows that the plaintiff was entitled to an injunction and that the judge misdirected himself in law in adjudging that the appropriate remedy for her was an award of damages under Lord Cairns Act. But she was only entitled to an injunction restraining the club from activities which caused a nuisance, and not all of their activities did. As the judge pointed out, and the plaintiff, by her counsel, accepted in this court, an injunction in general terms would be unworkable.

Our task has been to decide on a form of order which will protect the plaintiff from the noise which the judge found to be intolerable but which will not stop the club from organising activities about which she cannot reasonably complain.

When she decided to build a house alongside Mallam Water she knew that some motor-boat racing and water skiing was done on the club's water and she thought that the noise which such activities created was tolerable. She cannot now complain about that kind of noise provided it does not increase in volume by reason of any increase in activities. The intolerable noise is mostly caused by the large boats; it is these which attract the public interest.

Now nearly all of us living in these islands have to put up with a certain amount of annoyance from our neighbours. Those living in towns may be irritated by their neighbours' noisy radios or incompetent playing of musical instruments; and they in turn may be inconvenienced by the noise caused by our guests slamming car doors and chattering after a late party. Even in the country the lowing of a sick cow or the early morning crowing of a farmyard cock may interfere with sleep and comfort. Intervention by injunction is only justified when the irritating noise causes inconvenience beyond what other occupiers in the neighbourhood can be expected to bear. The question is whether the neighbour is using his property reasonably, having regard to the fact that he has a neighbour. The neighbour who is complaining must remember, too, that the other man can use his property in a reasonable way and there must be a measure of give and take, live and let live.

Notes

1. In *Miller* v *Jackson* [1977] QB 966 Lord Denning clearly thought that cricket was 'a good thing' and should be allowed in the public interest despite the nuisance. **Kennaway** rejects that approach in line with *Shelfer*. Note, however, that in *Dennis* v *Ministry of Defence* [2003] EWHC 198 (QB), in effect the public interest did prevent an injunction because it justified the nuisance (see section 16.2.4).

2. **Kennaway** v **Thompson** also illustrates the principle that it is no defence that the claimant came to the nuisance (i.e. the nuisance was already there and the claimant knew of it when she built the house). The rule was established in *Sturges* v *Bridgman* (1879) 11 ChD 852, where a doctor built a consulting room near the premises of a confectioner which had been used for many years. The claimant succeeded in his claim for nuisance arising from noise and vibrations caused by the defendant. In *Miller* v *Jackson* [1977] QB 966, the claimant bought a house near a cricket ground which had been used since 1905. The cricket club was liable for the nuisance created by balls being hit out of the ground, and Geoffrey Lane LJ said he was bound by *Sturges* v *Bridgman*, but he also commented that 'it does not seem just that a long-established activity—in itself innocuous—should be brought to an end because someone chooses to build a house nearby and so turn an innocent pastime into an actionable nuisance' (at 986). The court in that case refused to grant an injunction.

> ### *Coventry v Lawrence*
> Supreme Court [2014] UKSC 13

The claimants bought a house near a speedway stadium, built with the necessary planning permissions in 1974. Banger racing had started at the stadium in 1984. A motocross track adjacent to the stadium also had planning permission. The claimants contended that the activities at the stadium and track amounted to a nuisance. At first instance an injunction was awarded. The Court of Appeal had found that there was no nuisance, as the planning permissions had changed the character of the area. Held: there was a nuisance and the injunction should be granted.

LORD NEUBERGER:

115. In *Watson* [2009] 3 All ER 249, the Court of Appeal reversed the trial judge's decision to award damages instead of an injunction in a case where the nuisance was very similar in nature and cause to that alleged in this case. At para 44, Sir Andrew Morritt C described 'the appropriate test' as having been 'clearly established by the decision of the Court of Appeal in *Shelfer*', namely 'that damages in lieu of an injunction should only be awarded under "very exceptional circumstances."' He also said that *Shelfer* 'established that the circumstance that the wrongdoer is in some sense a public benefactor is not a sufficient reason for refusing an injunction', although he accepted at para 51 that 'the effect on the public' could properly be taken into account in a case 'where the damage to the claimant is minimal'.

116. It seems to me that there are two problems about the current state of the authorities on this question of the proper approach for a court to adopt on the question whether to award damages instead of an injunction.

117. The first is what at best might be described as a tension, and at worst as an inconsistency, between two sets of judicial dicta since *Shelfer*. Observations in *Slack*, *Miller*, **Kennaway**, *Regan*, and *Watson* appear to support the notion that AL Smith LJ's approach in *Shelfer* is generally to be

adopted and that it requires an exceptional case before damages should be awarded in lieu of an injunction, whereas the approach adopted in *Colls, Kine*, and *Fishenden* seems to support a more open-minded approach, taking into account the conduct of the parties. In *Jaggard*, the Court of Appeal did not need to address the question, as even on the stricter approach it upheld the trial judge's award of damages in lieu, although Millett LJ seems to have tried to reconcile the two approaches.

118. The second problem is the unsatisfactory way in which it seems that the public interest is to be taken into account when considering the issue whether to grant an injunction or award damages. The notion that it can be relevant where the damages are minimal, but not otherwise, as stated in *Watson*, seems very strange. Either the public interest is capable of being relevant to the issue or it is not. As part of this second problem, there is a question as to the extent to which it is relevant that the activity giving rise to the nuisance has the benefit of a planning permission.

119. So far as the first problem is concerned, the approach to be adopted by a judge when being asked to award damages instead of an injunction should, in my view, be much more flexible than that suggested in the recent cases of **Regan** and **Watson**. It seems to me that (i) an almost mechanical application of AL Smith LJ's four tests, and (ii) an approach which involves damages being awarded only in 'very exceptional circumstances', are each simply wrong in principle, and give rise to a serious risk of going wrong in practice . . .

120. The court's power to award damages in lieu of an injunction involves a classic exercise of discretion, which should not, as a matter of principle, be fettered, particularly in the very constrained way in which the Court of Appeal has suggested in **Regan** and **Watson**. And, as a matter of practical fairness, each case is likely to be so fact-sensitive that any firm guidance is likely to do more harm than good. On this aspect, I would adopt the observation of Millett LJ in *Jaggard* [1995] 1 WLR 269, 288, where he said:

> Reported cases are merely illustrations of circumstances in which particular judges have exercised their discretion, in some cases by granting an injunction, and in others by awarding damages instead. Since they are all cases on the exercise of a discretion, none of them is a binding authority on how the discretion should be exercised. The most that any of them can demonstrate is that in similar circumstances it would not be wrong to exercise the discretion in the same way. But it does not follow that it would be wrong to exercise it differently.

121. Having approved that statement, it is only right to acknowledge that this does not prevent the courts from laying down rules as to what factors can, and cannot, be taken into account by a judge when deciding whether to exercise his discretion to award damages in lieu. Indeed, it is appropriate to give as much guidance as possible so as to ensure that, while the discretion is not fettered, its manner of exercise is as predictable as possible. I would accept that the *prima facie* position is that an injunction should be granted, so the legal burden is on the defendant to show why it should not. And, subject to one possible point, I would cautiously (in the light of the fact that each case turns on its facts) approve the observations of Lord Macnaghten in *Colls* [1904] AC 179, 193, where he said:

> In some cases, of course, an injunction is necessary—if, for instance, the injury cannot fairly be compensated by money—if the defendant has acted in a high-handed manner—if he has endeavoured to steal a march upon the plaintiff or to evade the jurisdiction of the Court. In all these cases an injunction is necessary, in order to do justice to the plaintiff and as a warning to others. But if there is really a question as to whether the obstruction is legal or not, and if the defendant has acted fairly and not in an unneighbourly spirit, I am disposed to think that the Court ought to incline to damages rather than to an injunction. It is quite true that a man

ought not to be compelled to part with his property against his will, or to have the value of his property diminished, without an Act of Parliament. On the other hand, the Court ought to be very careful not to allow an action for the protection of ancient lights to be used as a means of extorting money.

122. The one possible doubt that I have about this observation relates to the suggestion in the antepenultimate sentence that the court 'ought to incline to damages' in the event he describes. If, as I suspect, Lord Macnaghten was simply suggesting that, if there was no prejudice to a claimant other than the bare fact of an interference with her rights, and there was no other ground for granting an injunction, I agree with him. However, it is right to emphasise that, when a judge is called on to decide whether to award damages in lieu of an injunction, I do not think that there should be any inclination either way (subject to the legal burden discussed above): the outcome should depend on all the evidence and arguments. Further, the sentence should not be taken as suggesting that there could not be any other relevant factors: clearly there could be. (It is true that *Colls*, like a number of the cases on the issue of damages in lieu, was concerned with rights of light, but I do not see such cases as involving special rules when it comes to this issue. *Shelfer* itself was not a right to light case; nor were *Jaggard* and *Watson*. However, in many cases involving nuisance by noise, there may be more wide-ranging issues and more possible forms of relief than in cases concerned with infringements of a right to light.)

123. Where does that leave AL Smith LJ's four tests? While the application of any such series of tests cannot be mechanical, I would adopt a modified version of the view expressed by Romer LJ in *Fishenden* 153 LT 128, 141. First, the application of the four tests must not be such as 'to be a fetter on the exercise of the court's discretion'. Secondly, it would, in the absence of additional relevant circumstances pointing the other way, normally be right to refuse an injunction if those four tests were satisfied. Thirdly, the fact that those tests are not all satisfied does not mean that an injunction should be granted.

124. As for the second problem, that of public interest, I find it hard to see how there could be any circumstances in which it arose and could not, as a matter of law, be a relevant factor. Of course, it is very easy to think of circumstances in which it might arise but did not begin to justify the court refusing, or, as the case may be, deciding, to award an injunction if it was otherwise minded to do so. But that is not the point. The fact that a defendant's business may have to shut down if an injunction is granted should, it seems to me, obviously be a relevant fact, and it is hard to see why relevance should not extend to the fact that a number of the defendant's employees would lose their livelihood, although in many cases that may well not be sufficient to justify the refusal of an injunction. Equally, I do not see why the court should not be entitled to have regard to the fact that many other neighbours in addition to the claimant are badly affected by the nuisance as a factor in favour of granting an injunction.

Notes

1. Though the injunction was restored in this case, Lord Neuberger's judgment indicates that judges need no longer adhere rigidly to the *Shelfer* criteria. The discretion of the court should be 'unfettered' and a decision on whether or not to award damages in lieu of an injunction will be determined by consideration of all relevant facts. It seems like courts are still prepared to award injunctions (including partial injunctions) where the circumstances suggest this to be the most appropriate remedy: see *Peires* v *Bickerton's Aerodromes Ltd* [2016] EWHC 560 (Ch).

2. The parties in *Coventry* v *Lawrence* returned to the Supreme Court in July 2014 at which point Lord Neuberger held that the injunction against Coventry and others should be suspended until the claimant's property was fit to be occupied, subject to any party having liberty to apply at any time to vary or discharge the injunction (the claimant's property was unoccupied at the time of the trial due to a fire, and was still fire-damaged) (*Coventry and others* v *Lawrence and another (No 2)* [2014] UKSC 46).

3. In the Court of Appeal further issues arose from the costs the defendants would end up having to pay (about £640,000, including sums derived from a conditional fee agreement (CFA) success fee and before-the-event insurance premiums), which they claimed violated their rights under Article 6 ECHR. This particular issue was heard by a seven-member panel of the Supreme Court (*Coventry and others* v *Lawrence and another* [2015] UKSC 50). No violation of Article 6 was found (Lady Hale and Lord Clarke dissenting).

see online
resources

17

Actions under
Rylands v *Fletcher*

It has long been considered whether dangerous activities on land should attract a more stringent form of liability and there are various statutory examples of such activities being regulated, such as nuclear escapes (e.g. under the Nuclear Installation Act 1965). **Rylands v Fletcher** created a new action and brought a common law version of strict liability for the escape of dangerous things from land, although this tort has been strictly interpreted and has been rendered less effective than it might have been. That it was *capable* of transforming the law cannot be doubted and we might have had a tort of strict liability for hazardous activities had the rise of the fault principle not hampered the growth of the doctrine. The 'rule' has been restricted by its origins in trespass and nuisance, and now seems unlikely to be developed further.

> ### *Rylands* v *Fletcher*
> Court of Exchequer Chamber (1866) LR 1 Ex 265

Rylands owned a mill in Lancashire, and Fletcher owned a nearby colliery. In 1860, Rylands constructed a reservoir for his mill and employed engineers and contractors to build it. During construction they found a number of old shafts, but did not realise that these indirectly connected with the colliery. The contractors were negligent in not ensuring that the filled-in shafts could bear the weight of water in the reservoir above. The partially filled reservoir burst through the shafts into the claimant's colliery. Held: the defendant (Rylands) was liable.

BLACKBURN J: We think that the true rule of law is, that the person who for his own purposes brings on his lands and collects and keeps there anything likely to do mischief if it escapes, must keep it in at his peril, and, if he does not do so, is prima facie answerable for all the damage which is the natural consequence of its escape. He can excuse himself by shewing that the escape was owing to the plaintiff's default; or perhaps that the escape was the consequence of *vis major*, or the act of God; but as nothing of this sort exists here, it is unnecessary to inquire what excuse would be sufficient. The general rule, as above stated, seems on principle just. The person whose grass or corn is eaten down by the escaping cattle of his neighbour, or whose mine is flooded by the water from his neighbour's reservoir, or whose cellar is invaded by the filth of his neighbour's privy, or whose habitation is made unhealthy by the fumes and noisome vapours of his neighbour's alkali works, is damnified without any fault of his own; and it seems but reasonable and just that the neighbour, who has brought something on his own property which was not naturally there, harmless to others so long as it is confined to his own property, but which he knows to be mischievous if it gets on his neighbour's, should be obliged to make good the damage which ensues if he does not succeed in confining it to his own property. But for his act in bringing it there no mischief could have accrued, and it seems but just that he should at his peril keep it there so that no mischief may accrue, or answer for the natural and anticipated consequences. And upon authority, this we think is established to be the law whether the things so brought be beasts, or water, or filth, or stenches. . . .

The view which we take of the first point renders it unnecessary to consider whether the defendants would or would not be responsible for the want of care and skill in the persons employed by them, under the circumstances stated in the case.

> ### Rylands v Fletcher
> House of Lords (1868) LR 3 HL 330

LORD CAIRNS LC: My Lords, the principles on which this case must be determined appear to me to be extremely simple. The defendants, treating them as the owners or occupiers of the close on which the reservoir was constructed, might lawfully have used that close for any purpose for which it might in the ordinary course of the enjoyment of land be used; and if, in what I may term the natural user of that land, there had been any accumulation of water, either on the surface or underground, and if, by the operation of the laws of nature, that accumulation of water had passed off into the close occupied by the plaintiff, the plaintiff could not have complained that that result had taken place. If he had desired to guard himself against it, it would have lain upon him to have done so, by leaving or by interposing, some barrier between his close and the close of the defendants in order to have prevented that operation of the laws of nature. . . .

On the other hand if the defendants, not stopping at the natural use of their close, had desired to use it for any purpose which I may term a non-natural use, for the purpose of introducing into the close that which in its natural condition was not in or upon it, for the purpose of introducing water either above or below ground in quantities and in a manner not the result of any work or operation on or under the land,—and if in consequence of their doing so, or in consequence of any imperfection in the mode of their doing so, the water came to escape and to pass off into the close of the plaintiff, then it appears to me that that which the defendants were doing they were doing at their own peril; and, if in the course of their doing it, the evil arose to which I have referred, the evil, namely, of the escape of the water and its passing away to the close of the plaintiff and injuring the plaintiff, then for the consequence of that, in my opinion, the defendants would be liable. . . .

My Lords, these simple principles, if they are well founded, as it appears to me they are, really dispose of this case.

The same result is arrived at on the principles referred to by Mr Justice Blackburn in his judgment, in the Court of Exchequer Chamber . . .

LORD CRANWORTH: My Lords, I concur with my noble and learned friend in thinking that the rule of law was correctly stated by Mr Justice Blackburn in delivering the opinion of the Exchequer Chamber. If a person brings, or accumulates, on his land anything which, if it should escape, may cause damage to his neighbour, he does so at his peril. If it does escape, and cause damage, he is responsible, however careful he may have been, and whatever precautions he may have taken to prevent the damage.

Notes

1. It may be that Lord Cairns in the House of Lords thought he was saying the same thing as Blackburn J, but the difference between something 'which was not naturally there' in Blackburn J's formulation and Lord Cairns' 'non-natural use' has proved to be crucial and has enabled subsequent courts to substantially limit the scope of the action. It seems likely that the original point of the restriction was merely to exclude liability for natural lakes.

2. The facts of this case and the reasons for it have attracted enormous attention over the years. See, for example, AWB Simpson *Leading Cases in the Common Law* (OUP, 2001), Ch 8. For a discussion of the fact that only two law lords appear to have sat in the case (whereas the quorum is three), see RFV Heuston 'Who was the Third Law Lord in *Rylands v Fletcher*?' (1970) 86 LQR 160. For general studies see Allen M Linden 'Whatever Happened to *Rylands v Fletcher*?' in Lewis Klar (ed) *Studies in Canadian Tort Law* (Carswell, 1977); Kumaralingam Amirthalingam '*Rylands* Lives' [2004] CLJ 273 and Donal Nolan 'The Distinctiveness of *Rylands v Fletcher*' (2005) 121 LQR 421.

3. In *Cambridge Water Co v Eastern Counties Leather* [1994] 2 AC 264, chemical solvent had been spilt at the defendant's tannery and over the years small quantities had soaked into the ground and then dissolved in percolating groundwater. This eventually contaminated the claimant's water borehole over a mile away. It was not foreseeable that the chemical would create an environmental hazard. In finding the defendants not liable for the escape, Lord Goff added the requirement that the harm caused must be reasonably foreseeable—one of the limits on the scope of the action and a move away from the strict liability idea, aligning the action more closely with fault-based liability.

4. The 'reasonably foreseeable' requirement is important where a person knowingly does an unjustified act and can foresee that some damage will follow but not damage of the kind that occurred. Thus, in **The Wagon Mound (No 2)** the defendants could foresee that the oil they discharged would foul neighbouring slipways but not that it would cause a fire. This may limit common law liability for pollution, for example where a person unjustifiably discharges waste which he has no reason to believe is toxic but which is later found to have caused damage. See G Cross 'Does Only the Careless Polluter Pay?' (1994) 111 LQR 445.

Transco v *Stockport Metropolitan Borough Council*
House of Lords [2003] UKHL 61

The defendants owned an 11-storey tower block which was served by a high-pressure water pipe. This supplied large tanks in the basement which then pumped water to the flats. This pipe fractured and a considerable amount of water escaped before the break was discovered and repaired. The water had run into an old landfill and then along an old railway formation. Transco had laid a gas main under the old railway line and where it became an embankment the water washed away the formation leaving the gas pipe suspended. Repairs by the claimants cost £93,681. Held: the defendants were not liable for the damage caused by the escape of the water.

LORD HOFFMANN:

27. *Rylands v Fletcher* was therefore an innovation in being the first clear imposition of liability for damage caused by an escape which was not alleged to be either intended or reasonably foreseeable. I think that this is what Professor Newark meant when he said in his celebrated article ('The Boundaries of Nuisance' (1949) 65 LQR 480, 488) that the novelty in *Rylands v Fletcher* was the decision that 'an isolated escape is actionable'. That is not because a single deluge is less of a nuisance than a steady trickle, but because repeated escapes such as the discharge of water in the mining cases and the discharge of chemicals in the factory cases do not raise any question about whether the escape was reasonably foreseeable. If the defendant does not know what he is doing, the plaintiff will certainly tell him. It is the single escape which raises the question of whether or not it was reasonably foreseeable and, if not, whether the defendant should nevertheless be liable. *Rylands v Fletcher* decided that he should.

THE SOCIAL BACKGROUND TO THE RULE

28. Although the judgment of Blackburn J is constructed in the traditional common law style of deducing principle from precedent, without reference to questions of social policy, Professor Brian Simpson has demonstrated in his article 'Legal Liability for Bursting Reservoirs: The Historical Context of *Rylands v Fletcher*' (1984) 13 J Leg Stud 209 that the background to the case was public anxiety about the safety of reservoirs, caused in particular by the bursting of the Bradfield Reservoir near Sheffield on 12 March 1864, with the loss of about 250 lives. The judicial response was to impose strict liability upon the proprietors of reservoirs. But, since the common law deals in principles rather than ad hoc solutions, the rule had to be more widely formulated.

29. It is tempting to see, beneath the surface of the rule, a policy of requiring the costs of a commercial enterprise to be internalised; to require the entrepreneur to provide, by insurance or otherwise, for the risks to others which his enterprise creates. That was certainly the opinion of Bramwell B, who was in favour of liability when the case was before the Court of Exchequer: (1865) 3 H & C 774. He had a clear and consistent view on the matter: see *Bamford v Turnley* (1862) 3 B & S 62, 84–85 and *Hammersmith and City Railway Co v Brand* (1867) LR 2 QB 223, 230–231. But others thought differently. They considered that the public interest in promoting economic development made it unreasonable to hold an entrepreneur liable when he had not been negligent: see *Wildtree Hotels Ltd v Harrow London Borough Council* [2001] 2 AC 1, 8–9 for a discussion of this debate in the context of compensation for disturbance caused by the construction and operation of works authorised by statutory powers. On the whole, it was the latter view—no liability without fault—which gained the ascendancy. With hindsight, *Rylands v Fletcher* can be seen as an isolated victory for the internalisers. The following century saw a steady refusal to treat it as laying down any broad principle of liability. I shall briefly trace the various restrictions imposed on its scope.

RESTRICTIONS ON THE RULE

(a) Statutory authority

30. A statute which authorises the construction of works like a reservoir, involving risk to others, may deal expressly with the liability of the undertakers. It may provide that they are to be strictly liable, liable only for negligence or not liable at all. But what if it contains no express provision? If the principle of *Rylands v Fletcher* is that costs should be internalised, the undertakers should be liable in the same way as private entrepreneurs. The fact that Parliament considered the construction and operation of the works to be in the public interest should make no difference. As Bramwell B repeatedly explained, the risk should be borne by the public and not by the individual who happens to have been injured. But within a year of the decision of the House of Lords in *Rylands v Fletcher*, Blackburn J advised the House that, in the absence of negligence, damage caused by operations authorised by statute is not compensatable unless the statute expressly so provides: see *Hammersmith and City Railway Co v Brand* (1869) LR 4 HL 171, 196. The default position is that the owner of land injured by the operations 'suffers a private loss for the public benefit'. In *Geddis v Proprietors of Bann Reservoir* (1878) 3 App Cas 430, 455 Lord Blackburn summed up the law:

> It is now thoroughly well established that no action will lie for doing that which the legislature has authorised, if it be done without negligence, although it does occasion damage to anyone.

31. The effect of this principle was to exclude the application of the rule in *Rylands v Fletcher* to works constructed or conducted under statutory authority: see *Green v Chelsea Waterworks Co* (1894) 70 LT 547; *Dunne v North Western Gas Board* [1964] 2 QB 806.

(b) Acts of God and third parties

32. Escapes of water and the like are often the result of natural events—heavy rain or drains blocked by falling leaves—or the acts of third parties, like vandals who open taps or sluices. This form of causation does not usually make the damage any the less a consequence of the risk created by the presence of the water or other escaping substance. No serious principle of allocating risk to the enterprise would leave the injured third party to pursue his remedy against the vandal. But early cases on *Rylands v Fletcher* quickly established that natural events ('Acts of God') and acts of third parties excluded strict liability. In *Carstairs v Taylor* (1871) LR 6 Ex 217, 221 Kelly CB said that he thought a rat gnawing a hole in a wooden gutter box counted as an Act of God and in *Nichols v Marsland* (1876) 2 Ex D 1 Mellish LJ (who, as counsel, had lost *Rylands v Fletcher*) said that an exceptionally heavy rainstorm was a sufficient excuse. In *Rickards v Lothian* [1913] AC 263 the same was said of the act of a vandal who blocked a washbasin and turned on the tap. By contrast, acts of third parties and natural events are not defences to the strict criminal liability imposed by section 85(1) of the Water Resources Act 1991 for polluting controlled waters unless they are really exceptional events: *Environment Agency (formerly National Rivers Authority) v Empress Car Co (Abertillery) Ltd* [1999] 2 AC 22.

(c) Remoteness

33. *Rylands v Fletcher* established that, in a case to which the rule applies, the defendant will be liable even if he could not reasonably have foreseen that there would be an escape. But is he liable for all the consequences of the escape? In *Cambridge Water Co v Eastern Counties Leather plc* [1994] 2 AC 264 the House of Lords decided that liability was limited to damage which was what Blackburn J had called the 'natural', ie reasonably foreseeable, consequence of the escape. Lord Goff of Chieveley, in a speech which repays close attention, took the rule back to its origins in the law of nuisance and said that liability should be no more extensive than it would have been in nuisance if the discharge itself had been negligent or intentional. Adopting the opinion of Professor Newark, to which I have already referred, he said that the novel feature of *Rylands v Fletcher* was to create liability for an 'isolated' (ie unforeseeable) escape. But the rule was nevertheless founded on the principles of nuisance and should not otherwise impose liability for unforeseeable damage.

(d) Escape

34. In *Read v J Lyons & Co Ltd* [1947] AC 156 a radical attempt was made to persuade the House of Lords to develop the rule into a broad principle that an enterprise which created an unusual risk of

damage should bear that risk. Mrs Read had been drafted into the Ministry of Supply and directed to inspect the manufacture of munitions at a factory operated by J Lyons & Company Ltd. In August 1942 she was injured by the explosion of a shell. There was no allegation of negligence; the cause of action was said to be the hazardous nature of the activity. But the invitation to generalise the rule was comprehensively rejected. The House of Lords stressed that the rule was primarily concerned with the rights and duties of occupiers of land. Escape from the defendant's land or control is an essential element of the tort.

(e) Personal injury

35. In some cases in the first half of the 20th century plaintiffs recovered damages under the rule for personal injury: *Shiffman v St John of Jerusalem (Grand Priory in the British Realm of the Venerable Order of the Hospital)* [1936] 1 All ER 557; *Hale v Jennings Bros* [1938] 1 All ER 579 are examples. But dicta in *Read v J Lyons & Co Ltd* cast doubt upon whether the rule protected anything beyond interests in land. Lord Macmillan (at pp 170–171) was clear that it had no application to personal injury and Lord Simonds (at p 180) was doubtful. But I think that the point is now settled by two recent decisions of the House of Lords: *Cambridge Water Co v Eastern Counties Leather plc* [1994] AC 264, which decided that *Rylands v Fletcher* is a special form of nuisance and *Hunter v Canary Wharf Ltd* [1997] AC 655, which decided that nuisance is a tort against land. It must, I think, follow that damages for personal injuries are not recoverable under the rule.

(f) Non-natural user

36. The principle in *Rylands v Fletcher* was widely expressed; the essence was the escape of something which the defendant had brought upon his land. Not surprisingly, attempts were immediately made to apply the rule in all kinds of situations far removed from the specific social problem of bursting reservoirs which had produced it. Leaks caused by a rat gnawing a hole in a wooden gutter-box (*Carstairs v Taylor* LR 6 Ex 217) were not at all what Blackburn J and Lord Cairns had had in mind. In some cases the attempt to invoke the rule was repelled by relying on Blackburn J's statement that the defendant must have brought whatever escaped onto his land 'for his own purposes'. This excluded claims by tenants that they had been damaged by escapes of water from plumbing installed for the benefit of the premises as [a] whole. Another technique was to imply the claimant's consent to the existence of the accumulation. But the most generalized restriction was formulated by Lord Moulton in *Rickards v Lothian* [1913] AC 263, 280:

> It is not every use to which land is put that brings into play that principle. It must be some special use bringing with it increased danger to others, and must not merely be the ordinary use of the land or such a use as is proper for the general benefit of the community.

37. The context in which Lord Moulton made this statement was a claim under *Rylands v Fletcher* for damage caused by damage to stock in a shop caused by an overflow of water from a wash-basin in a lavatory on a floor above. To exclude domestic use is understandable if one thinks of the rule as a principle for the allocation of costs; there is no enterprise of which the risk can be regarded as a cost which should be internalised. That would at least provide a fairly rational distinction. But the rather vague reference to 'the ordinary use of the land' and in particular the reference to a use 'proper for the general benefit of the community' has resulted in the rule being applied to some commercial enterprises but not others, the distinctions being sometimes very hard to explain.

38. In the *Cambridge Water Co* case [1994] 2 AC 264, 308–309 Lord Goff of Chieveley noted these difficulties but expressed the hope that it would be possible to give the distinction 'a more recognisable basis of principle.' The facts of that case, involving the storage of substantial quantities of

chemicals on industrial premises, were in his opinion 'an almost classic case of non-natural use'. He thought that the restriction of liability to the foreseeable consequences of the escape would reduce the inclination of the courts to find other ways of limiting strict liability, such as extension of the concept of natural use.

WHERE STANDS THE RULE TODAY?

39. I pause at this point to summarise the very limited circumstances to which the rule has been confined. First, it is a remedy for damage to land or interests in land. As there can be few properties in the country, commercial or domestic, which are not insured against damage by flood and the like, this means that disputes over the application of the rule will tend to be between property insurers and liability insurers. Secondly, it does not apply to works or enterprises authorised by statute. That means that it will usually have no application to really high risk activities. As Professor Simpson points out ([1984] 13 J Leg Stud 225) the Bradfield Reservoir was built under statutory powers. In the absence of negligence, the occupiers whose lands had been inundated would have had no remedy. Thirdly, it is not particularly strict because it excludes liability when the escape is for the most common reasons, namely vandalism or unusual natural events. Fourthly, the cases in which there is an escape which is not attributable to an unusual natural event or the act of a third party will, by the same token, usually give rise to an inference of negligence. Fifthly, there is a broad and ill-defined exception for 'natural' uses of land. It is perhaps not surprising that counsel could not find a reported case since the second world war in which anyone had succeeded in a claim under the rule. It is hard to escape the conclusion that the intellectual effort devoted to the rule by judges and writers over many years has brought forth a mouse.

IS IT WORTH KEEPING?

40. In *Burnie Port Authority v General Jones Pty Ltd* (1994) 179 CLR 520 a majority of the High Court of Australia lost patience with the pretensions and uncertainties of the rule and decided that it had been 'absorbed' into the law of negligence. Your Lordships have been invited by the respondents to kill off the rule in England in similar fashion. It is said, first, that in its present attenuated form it serves little practical purpose; secondly, that its application is unacceptably vague ('an essentially unprincipled and ad hoc subjective determination' said the High Court (at p 540) in the *Burnie* case) and thirdly, that strict liability on social grounds is better left to statutory intervention.

43. But despite the strength of these arguments, I do not think it would be consistent with the judicial function of your Lordships' House to abolish the rule. It has been part of English law for nearly 150 years and despite a searching examination by Lord Goff of Chieveley in the *Cambridge Water* case [1994] 2 AC 264, 308, there was no suggestion in his speech that it could or should be abolished. I think that would be too radical a step to take.

44. It remains, however, if not to rationalise the law of England, at least to introduce greater certainty into the concept of natural user which is in issue in this case. In order to do so, I think it must be frankly acknowledged that little assistance can be obtained from the kinds of user which Lord Cairns must be assumed to have regarded as 'non-natural' in **Rylands v Fletcher** itself. They are, as Lord Goff of Chieveley said in the *Cambridge Water* case [1994] 2 AC 264, 308, 'redolent of a different age'. So nothing can be made of the anomaly that one of the illustrations of the rule given by Blackburn J is cattle trespass. Whatever Blackburn J and Lord Cairns may have meant by 'natural', the law was set on a different course by the opinion of Lord Moulton in *Rickards v Lothian* [1913] AC 263 and the question of what is a natural use of land or, (the converse) a use creating an increased risk, must be judged by contemporary standards.

45. Two features of contemporary society seem to me to be relevant. First, the extension of statutory regulation to a number of activities, such as discharge of water (section 209 of the Water Industry Act 1991) pollution by the escape of waste (section 73(6) of the Environmental Protection Act 1990) and radio-active matter (section 7 of the Nuclear Installations Act 1965). It may have to be considered whether these and similar provisions create an exhaustive code of liability for a particular form of escape which excludes the rule in *Rylands v Fletcher*.

46. Secondly, so far as the rule does have a residuary role to play, it must be borne in mind that it is concerned only with damage to property and that insurance against various forms of damage to property is extremely common. A useful guide in deciding whether the risk has been created by a 'non-natural' user of land is therefore to ask whether the damage which eventuated was something against which the occupier could reasonably be expected to have insured himself. Property insurance is relatively cheap and accessible; in my opinion people should be encouraged to insure their own property rather than seek to transfer the risk to others by means of litigation, with the heavy transactional costs which that involves. The present substantial litigation over £100,000 should be a warning to anyone seeking to rely on an esoteric cause of action to shift a commonplace insured risk.

47. In the present case, I am willing to assume that if the risk arose from a 'non-natural user' of the council's land, all the other elements of the tort were satisfied. Transco complains of expense having to be undertaken to avoid damage to its gas pipe; I am willing to assume that if damage to the pipe would have been actionable, the expense incurred in avoiding that damage would have been recoverable. I [am] also willing to assume that Transco's easement which entitled it to maintain its pipe in the embankment and receive support from the soil was a sufficient proprietary interest to enable it to sue in nuisance and therefore, by analogy, under the rule in *Rylands v Fletcher*. Although the council, as owner of Hollow End Towers, was no doubt under a statutory duty to provide its occupiers with water, it had no statutory duty or authority to build that particular tower block and it is therefore not suggested that the pipe was laid pursuant to statutory powers so as to exclude the rule. So the question is whether the risk came within the rule.

48. The damage which eventuated was subsidence beneath a gas main: a form of risk against which no rational owner of a gas main would fail to insure. The casualty was caused by the escape of water from the council's land. But the source was a perfectly normal item of plumbing. The pipe was, it is true, considerably larger than the ordinary domestic size. But it was smaller than a water main. It was installed to serve the occupiers of the council's high rise flats; not strictly speaking a commercial purpose, but not a private one either.

49. In my opinion the Court of Appeal was right to say that it was not a 'non-natural' user of land. I am influenced by two matters. First, there is no evidence that it created a greater risk than is normally associated with domestic or commercial plumbing. True, the pipe was larger. But whether that involved greater risk depends upon its specification. One cannot simply assume that the larger the pipe, the greater the risk of fracture or the greater the quantity of water likely to be discharged. I agree with my noble and learned friend Lord Bingham of Cornhill that the criterion of exceptional risk must be taken seriously and creates a high threshold for a claimant to surmount. Secondly, I think that the risk of damage to property caused by leaking water is one against which most people can and do commonly insure. This is, as I have said, particularly true of Transco, which can be expected to have insured against any form of damage to its pipe. It would be a very strange result if Transco were entitled to recover against the council when it would not have been entitled to recover against the Water Authority for similar damage emanating from its high pressure main.

Notes

1. This case is an important further restatement of the **Rylands** principle, but it is also important for what it does *not* do. The decision restricts any move towards a more general tort of strict liability for hazardous activities and closely limits **Rylands** to its historical origins. The Supreme Court of India took a very much wider view in *Mehta v Union of India* 1987 AIR (SC) 1086, where there was a discharge of toxic gas from a factory in Delhi. The court rejected many of the traditional limitations of **Rylands**, adopting a more general tort of strict liability for engaging in hazardous activities (see David Bergman 'The Sabotage Theory and the Legal Strategy of Union Carbide' (1988) 138 NLJ 420). This approach has been rejected by the Law Commission (Report No 32, 1970) and twice by the House of Lords, citing the uncertainties and practical difficulties of its application.

2. **Transco** also adopts a very strict interpretation of the elements of the tort, including the rules on escape from the premises, non-natural user and no liability for personal injuries. The concept of the 'non-natural user' has been much discussed and in **Transco** Lord Bingham said that 'ordinary user is a preferable test to natural user . . . [as it makes] clear that the rule in **Rylands v Fletcher** is engaged only where the defendant's use is shown to be extraordinary and unusual' (at [11]). It is not a question of reasonable user but rather whether the defendant has done something quite out of the ordinary in the place and time when he does it. The question is to what extent industrial activities might these days be considered to be an ordinary use of land, and later Lord Bingham refers to an occupier who has brought onto his land an 'exceptionally dangerous or mischievous thing in extraordinary or unusual circumstances'. This is a very narrow interpretation.

3. One particular problem with **Rylands** has been the issue of remoteness of damage, but this seems to have been resolved in **Transco**. In *Cambridge Water v Eastern Counties Leather* [1994] 2 AC 264, the House of Lords held that the use of the chemical was 'non-natural' but that the eventual damage was not a foreseeable kind of damage. It seems clear from **Transco** that the issue is whether, *assuming* there is an escape, the damage which has occurred is of a foreseeable kind (see Lord Hoffmann at [33]). There is no need to foresee the escape itself.

4. In *Burnie Port Authority v General Jones Pty Ltd* (1992) 179 CLR 520, the High Court of Australia rejected **Rylands v Fletcher** altogether, saying that the situations envisaged by that doctrine can be dealt with by negligence. It was said that proximity would exist because of the special vulnerability and dependence of the claimant arising out of the hazardous activities of the defendant, and that this would give rise to a non-delegable duty of care arising out of the defendant's control of the premises. It was also said that the standard of care would relate to the degree of danger and that it could even involve 'a degree of diligence so stringent as to amount practically to a guarantee of safety'. For a general discussion of the value of the tort, see Donal Nolan 'The Distinctiveness of *Rylands* v *Fletcher*' (2005) 121 LQR 421 who argues that the tort has become so emasculated that it no longer serves a useful function. Note, however, John Murphy 'The Merits of *Rylands* v *Fletcher*' (2004) 24 OJLS 643, which seeks to defend the rule, arguing that it provides a useful residual mechanism for securing environmental protection by individuals affected by harmful escapes from polluting heavyweight industrialists.

5. In *Stannard (t/a Wyvern Tyres) v Gore* [2012] EWCA Civ 1248, the defendant stored large quantities of tyres on his land. These caught fire, subsequently destroying both the claimant's and the defendant's premises. There was no liability under **Rylands** as the tyres themselves had not escaped and the fire was not something that had been 'brought onto land' by the defendant, nor was the storage of tyres a 'non-natural' use of land.

17.1 Merging *Rylands*, nuisance and negligence?

Just as the creator of a nuisance or a person who is 'responsible' for its continuance can be liable—an occupier can be liable for a nuisance created by a trespasser if they 'adopt' or 'continue' that nuisance—equally a person can be liable for a natural hazard on their land which they ought to have removed or done something about, for instance in order to prevent a one-off escape.

> ### Sedleigh-Denfield v O'Callaghan
> House of Lords [1940] AC 880

A council replaced a culvert with a pipe, the end of which projected about two feet onto the defendant's land (therefore the council were technically trespassing when they put the pipe there). The workmen placed a grating over the end of the pipe to prevent leaves blocking it, but this was done incorrectly, as the grating was placed directly onto the end of the pipe so leaves collected on the grating and blocked the pipe. After the pipe was in place, the defendant's workers regularly cleaned out the ditch and the end of the pipe. In 1937 a severe storm blocked the pipe causing flooding on the claimant's neighbouring land. Held: the defendant was liable for the nuisance.

LORD ATKIN: In this state of the facts the legal position is not I think difficult to discover. For the purposes of ascertaining whether as here the plaintiff can establish a private nuisance I think that nuisance is sufficiently defined as a wrongful interference with another's enjoyment of his land or premises by the use of land or premises either occupied or in some cases owned by oneself. The occupier or owner is not an insurer; there must be something more than the mere harm done to the neighbour's property to make the party responsible. Deliberate act or negligence is not an essential ingredient but some degree of personal responsibility is required, which is connoted in my definition by the word 'use.' This conception is implicit in all the decisions which impose liability only where the defendant has 'caused or continued' the nuisance. We may eliminate in this case 'caused.' What is the meaning of 'continued'? In the context in which it is used 'continued' must indicate mere passive continuance. If a man uses on premises something which he found there, and which itself causes a nuisance by noise, vibration, smell or fumes, he is himself in continuing to bring into existence the noise, vibration, etc, causing a nuisance. Continuing in this sense and causing are the same thing. It seems to me clear that if a man permits an offensive thing on his premises to continue to offend, that is, if he knows that it is operating offensively, is able to prevent it, and omits to prevent it, he is permitting the nuisance to continue; in other words he is continuing it. The liability of an occupier has been carried so far that it appears to have been decided that, if he comes to occupy, say as tenant, premises upon which a cause of nuisance exists, caused by a previous occupier, he is responsible even though he does not know that either the cause or the result is in existence. . . .

In the present case, however, there is as I have said sufficient proof of the knowledge of the defendants both of the cause and its probable effect. What is the legal result of the original cause being due to the act of a trespasser? In my opinion the defendants clearly continued the nuisance for they come clearly within the terms I have mentioned above, they knew the danger, they were able to prevent it and they omitted to prevent it. In this respect at least there seems to me to be no difference between the case of a public nuisance and a private nuisance, and the case of *Attorney-General v Tod-Heatley* [1897] 1 Ch 560, is conclusive to show that where the occupier has knowledge of a public nuisance, has the means of remedying it and fails to do so, he may be enjoined from allowing it to continue. I cannot think that the obligation not to 'continue' can have a different meaning in 'public' and in 'private' nuisances. . . .

LORD WRIGHT: Though the rule has not been laid down by this House, it has I think been rightly established in the Court of Appeal that an occupier is not prima facie responsible for a nuisance created without his knowledge and consent. If he is to be liable a further condition is necessary, namely, that he had knowledge or means of knowledge, that he knew or should have known of the nuisance in time to correct it and obviate its mischievous effects. The liability for a nuisance is not, at least in modern law, a strict or absolute liability. If the defendant by himself or those for whom he is responsible has created what constitutes a nuisance and if it causes damage, the difficulty now being considered does not arise. But he may have taken over the nuisance, ready made as it were, when he acquired the property, or the nuisance may be due to a latent defect or to the act of a trespasser, or stranger. Then he is not liable unless he continued or adopted the nuisance, or, more accurately, did not without undue delay remedy it when he became aware of it, or with ordinary and reasonable care should have become aware of it. This rule seems to be in accordance with good sense and convenience. The responsibility which attaches to the occupier because he has possession and control of the property cannot logically be limited to the mere creation of the nuisance. It should extend to his conduct if, with knowledge, he leaves the nuisance on his land. The same is true if the nuisance was such that with ordinary care in the management of his property he should have realised the risk of its existence.

Notes

1. A person can be liable even for natural phenomena which 'escapes' and causes harm. In *Leakey v National Trust* [1980] QB 485, the claimants owned houses next to a large mound in Somerset called Burrow Mump, which was owned by the defendants. Part of the mound collapsed and large quantities of earth landed on the claimants' houses, causing damage. The defendants were liable even though the mound was natural and the collapse was caused by the forces of nature. The Court of Appeal found that the defendant landowner's obligation is what it is reasonable for him as an individual to do, taking account, for example, of his means, and the practicality of taking preventative measures.

Holbeck Hall Hotel v *Scarborough Borough Council*
Court of Appeal [2000] QB 836

The Holbeck Hall Hotel stood 65 metres above sea level on South Cliff, Scarborough. The defendants owned the land between the hotel and the sea. In 1993 there was a massive landslip on the defendants' land. The hotel's gardens disappeared and the ground collapsed under part of the building, rendering it unsafe and needing to be demolished. Earlier, minor slips in 1982 and 1986 led to some rather ineffective remedial steps being taken, and it was said that the defendants knew that at some indeterminate time the slip might progress. However, no one could have foreseen the catastrophic slip that did occur without further extensive geological investigation. The trial judge held the defendants liable for the total loss. Held: the defendants were under a duty to the claimants but were liable only for part of the loss.

STUART-SMITH LJ:

31. In *Goldman v Hargrave* [1971] AC 645 the Privy Council extended the principle in *Sedleigh-Denfield's* case to a hazard caused on the Defendant's land by the operation of nature. In that case a tall redgum tree on the Defendant's land was struck by lightening [sic] and set on fire. The Defendant at first took reasonable steps to deal with the problem. He cleared and dampened the area round the tree and then cut it down. Having done so, however, the Defendant took no further steps to prevent the spread of fire, which he could readily have done by dousing it with water. Instead, he let the fire burn out. The wind got up and set light to the surrounding area from whence it spread to the Plaintiff's land and damaged his property. The Privy Council held the Defendant liable. There was no difference in principle between a nuisance created by a trespasser and one created by the forces of nature, provided the Defendant knew of the hazard. Lord Wilberforce, who delivered the advice of the Board, said in relation to the supposed distinction at p 661:

> The fallacy of this argument is that, as already explained, the basis of the occupier's liability lies not in the use of his land: in the absence of 'adoption' there is no such use; but in the neglect of action in the face of something which may damage his neighbour. To this, the suggested distinction is irrelevant.

32. In both *Sedleigh-Denfield's* case and *Goldman's* case the hazard arose entirely on the Defendant's land; the Plaintiff had no knowledge of it before the damage was done; the Defendant was liable for failing to take steps to stop the spread or escape to the Plaintiff's land, steps which he could reasonably take.

33. In *Leakey v National Trust* [1980] QB 485 the Court of Appeal held that the law, as laid down in *Goldman's* case, correctly stated the law of England. In that case the Plaintiffs' houses had been built at the foot of a large mound on the Defendant's land. Over the years soil and rubble had fallen from the Defendant's land onto the Plaintiffs'. The falls were due to natural weathering and the nature of the soil. By 1968 the Defendant knew that there was a threat to the Plaintiffs' properties. After a very dry summer and wet autumn a large crack opened in the mound above the Plaintiffs' house. They drew the Defendant's attention to the danger to their houses; but the Defendant said it had no responsibility. A few weeks later a large quantity of earth and some stumps fell onto the Plaintiffs' land. In interlocutory proceedings the Defendant was ordered to carry out the necessary work to abate the nuisance. The Court of Appeal upheld the judge's decision in the trial of the action to the effect that the Defendant was liable. . . .

The extent of the Defendant's knowledge

39. In order to give rise to a measured duty of care, the Defendant must know or be presumed to know of the defect or condition giving rise to the hazard and must, as a reasonable man, foresee that the defect or condition will, if not remedied, cause damage to the Claimant's land. In *Goldman* [and] *Leakey* . . . the Defendant had actual knowledge of the defect or condition giving rise to the hazard or alleged hazard. In *Sedleigh-Denfield* the Defendant's responsible servant knew. In each case it was reasonably foreseeable that damage would occur to the Plaintiff's land if nothing was done.

41. In *Leakey's* case Megaw LJ said at p 518D:

> So long as the defect remains 'latent' there is no duty on the occupier, whether the defect has been caused by a trespasser or by nature. Equally, once the latent becomes patent, a duty will arise, whether the causative agent of the defect is man or nature. But the mere fact that there is a duty does not necessarily mean that inaction constitutes a breach of the duty.

In that passage Megaw LJ referred to the defect. At p 522D he said:

> . . . the duty arising from a nuisance which is not brought about by human agency does not arise unless and until the defendant has, or ought to have had, knowledge of the existence of the defect and the danger thereby created.

Here the Lord Justice is referring both to the defect and the danger arising from it. And again at p 524G when discussing the scope of the duty he posed this question:

> Was there sufficient time for preventive action to have been taken, by persons acting reasonably in relation to the known risk, between the time when it became known to, or should have been realised by, the defendant, and the time when the damage occurred?

Here Megaw LJ refers to the risk or the danger.

46. But the present is a case of non-feasance: Scarborough have done nothing to create the danger which has arisen by the operation of nature. And it is clear that the scope of the duty is much more restricted. It is defined in the cases of *Goldman* and *Leakey* as a measured duty of care. In the former case Lord Wilberforce said at p 663A:

> So far it has been possible to consider the existence of a duty, in general terms. But the matter cannot be left there without some definition of the scope of his duty. How far does it go? What is the standard of the effort required? What is the position as regards expenditure? It is not enough to say merely that these must be 'reasonable,' since what is reasonable to one man may be very unreasonable, and indeed ruinous, to another: the law must take account of the fact that the occupier on whom the duty is cast has, *ex hypothesi*, had this hazard thrust upon him through no seeking or fault of his own. His interest, and his resources, whether physical or material, may be of a very modest character either in relation to the magnitude of the hazard, or as compared with those of his threatened neighbour. A rule which required of him in such unsought circumstances in his neighbour's interest a physical effort of which he is not capable, or an excessive expenditure of money, would be unenforceable or unjust. *One may say in general terms that the existence of a duty must be based upon knowledge of the hazard, ability to foresee the consequences of not checking or removing it, and the ability to abate it.* And in many cases, as, for example, in Scrutton LJ's hypothetical case of stamping out a fire, or the present case, where the hazard could have been removed with little effort and no expenditure, no problem arises. But other cases may not be so simple. In such situations the standard ought to be to require of the occupier what it is reasonable to expect of him in his individual circumstances. . . .

47. In the passage which I have [emphasized] Lord Wilberforce refers expressly only to the existence of the duty; but the passage occurs in the middle of that part of the judgment dealing with the scope of the duty. It seems to me that Lord Wilberforce could equally have said 'existence and scope of the duty', especially as ability to abate it is related to the subjective characteristics of the Defendant.

48. In *Leakey's* case Megaw LJ dealt with the scope of the duty at p 524E:

> The duty is a duty to do that which is reasonable in all the circumstances, and no more than what, if anything, is reasonable, to prevent or minimise the known risk of damage or injury to one's neighbour or to his property. The considerations with which the law is familiar are all to be taken into account in deciding whether there had been a breach of duty, and, if so, what that breach is, and whether it is causative of the damage in respect of which the

claim is made. Thus, there will fall to be considered the extent of the risk; what, so far as reasonably can be foreseen, are the chances that anything untoward will happen or that any damage will be caused? *What is to be foreseen as to the possible extent of the damage if the risk becomes a reality*? Is it practicable to prevent, or to minimise, the happening of any damage? If it is practicable, how simple or how difficult are the measures which could be taken, how much and how lengthy work do they involve, and what is the probable cost of such work? Was there sufficient time for preventive action to have been taken, by persons acting reasonably in relation to the known risk, between the time when it became known to, or should have been realised by, the defendant, and the time when the damage occurred? Factors such as these, so far as they apply in a particular case, fall to be weighed in deciding whether the defendant's duty of care requires, or required, him to do anything, and, if so, what.

49. In both these passages concentration tends to be upon the ease and expense of abatement and the ability of the Defendant to achieve it. But in the passage in Megaw LJ's judgment which I have [emphasized], the extent of the foreseen damage is said to be a relevant consideration. Moreover, I do not think either judge was purporting to give an exhaustive list of relevant considerations. While I agree with Megaw LJ (see p 524B) that it would be a grievous blot on our law if there was no liability on the Defendants in those cases, I do not think justice requires that a Defendant should be held liable for damage which, albeit of the same type, was vastly more extensive than that which was foreseen or could have been foreseen without extensive further geological investigation; and this is particularly so where the defect existed just as much on the Claimant's land as on their own. In considering the scope of the measured duty of care, the courts are still in relatively uncharted waters. But I can find nothing in the two cases where it has been considered, namely *Goldman* and *Leakey* to prevent the Court reaching a just result.

51. The cases of *Goldman* and *Leakey* were decided before the decision of the House of Lords in **Caparo Industries Ltd v Dickman** [1990] 2 AC 605, in which the three stage test for the existence of a duty of care was laid down, namely foreseeability, proximity and the need for it to be fair, just and reasonable. In **Marc Rich & Co v Bishop Rock Ltd** [1996] 1 AC 211 it was held that the three stage **Caparo** test was appropriate whatever the nature of the damage. (See per Lord Steyn at p 235 approving a dictum of Saville LJ.) The requirement that it must be fair, just and reasonable is a limiting condition where foreseeability and proximity are established. In my judgment very similar considerations arise whether the court is determining the scope of a measured duty of care or whether it is fair, just and reasonable to impose a duty or the extent of that duty. And for my part I do not think it is just and reasonable in a case like the present to impose liability for damage which is greater in extent than anything that was foreseen or foreseeable (without further geological investigation), especially where the defect and danger existed as much on the Claimants' land as the Defendants'.

54. For the reasons I have given I conclude that the scope of Scarborough's duty was confined to an obligation to take care to avoid damage to the Claimants' land which they ought to have foreseen without further geological investigation. It may also have been limited by other factors, as the passages from *Goldman* and *Leakey* cited in paragraphs 46 and 48 make clear, so that it is not necessarily incumbent on someone in Scarborough's position to carry out extensive and expensive remedial work to prevent the damage which they ought to have foreseen; the scope of the duty may be limited to warning claimants of such risk as they were aware of or ought to have foreseen and sharing such information as they had acquired relating to it.

Notes

1. In **Holbeck Hall Hotel**, Stuart-Smith LJ talks of a 'measured' duty in cases of omission by which the defendant will not be liable for all the damage even if it is of a type of damage that was foreseeable, where what actually happened was more extensive than expected. This is not a matter of remoteness of damage, but rather defines what it is that the defendant failed to do (the scope of the duty). Here the defendants were aware that the land was unstable and should have taken remedial steps to prevent that limited damage, or perhaps even only warn the claimants of the problem. The court said that the defendants were only liable for damage that might have been expected bearing in mind the previous minor slips, and held that this was limited to slips which would have affected the garden and some part of the lawn and did not extend to the collapse of the whole hotel.

2. An occupier of land can be liable for the acts of their licensees away from the land, either because they created the nuisance or because they have allowed it to continue. In *Lippiatt* v *South Gloucestershire Council* [1999] 4 All ER 149, a number of travellers occupied council land from 1991 until 1994. During that time they entered neighbouring land causing damage. It was held that the nuisance 'emanated' from the defendants' land and they were liable either because they had created the nuisance by allowing the travellers to occupy the land, or because they 'continued' or 'adopted' the nuisance. However, a landlord is not liable for the acts of their tenants unless they have authorised the nuisance (see *Hussain* v *Lancaster City Council* [1999] 4 All ER 125).

3. In *Delaware Mansions Ltd* v *Westminster City Council* [2001] UKHL 55, Lord Cooke said that the nuisance/negligence distinction in this kind of case 'is treated as of no real significance' (at [31]). See also *Bybrook Barn Centre Ltd* v *Kent County Council* [2001] BLR 55; *Lambert* v *Barratt Homes Ltd* [2010] EWCA Civ 681; and *Vernon Knight Associates* v *Cornwall Council* [2013] EWCA Civ 950.

Liability, damages and limitations

PART V

18 Vicarious liability
    18.1 A relationship of, or akin to, employment
    18.2 The course of employment
    18.3 Liability for independent contractors

19 Damages for death and personal injuries
    19.1 Types of action for damages
    19.2 Calculation of loss of earnings and other losses
    19.3 Intangible losses

Vicarious liability

Vicarious liability is a mechanism by which the defendant is held liable for a tort committed by someone else. Its principal application is in employment relationships: an employer is vicariously liable for torts committed by its employees in the course of their employment. It is not predicated on the wrongdoing of the employer, who may well be entirely blameless. As such, the principle of vicarious liability is at odds with the general approach of the common law whereby a person is responsible only for their own acts. One might expect, then, that there would be a clear and principled reason for imposing such liability. However, this has been largely unforthcoming. Instead, a number of policy reasons have been suggested.

JGE v *The Trustees of the Portsmouth Roman Catholic Diocesan Trust*
Court of Appeal [2012] EWCA Civ 938

The claimant, now 48 years old, alleged that she was sexually abused by Father Baldwin, a parish priest, when she was living in a children's home in the 1970s operated by a Roman Catholic order of nuns. The defendant denied liability on the basis that the priest was not an employee. Held: on a preliminary issue (the facts were disputed), the majority of the Court of Appeal held that, although the priest was not an employee as typically understood (e.g. he was not treated as an employee by the Inland Revenue), his relationship with the defendant was 'akin to that of an employee' and, as such, it was close enough in character to one of employer and employee that it was just and fair to hold the defendant vicariously liable.

WARD LJ:

The policy considerations which inform the doctrine of vicarious liability

50. The doctrine of vicarious liability does give rise to a clash of two broad policies upon which the law of torts is founded, one that there ought to be an effective remedy for the victim of another's wrongful act, and the other that the defendant should not generally be held liable unless he was at fault. Only policy considerations can explain the triumph of the former over the latter. Identifying the relevant strands of policy and evaluating their importance is not straightforward.

51. Longmore LJ observed in *Maga* [v *Archbishop of Birmingham* [2010] EWCA Civ 256] at [81]:

Since this case is not covered by previous authority, it may be necessary to have in mind the policy behind the imposition of vicarious liability. That is difficult because there is by no means universal agreement as to what that policy is. Is it that the law should impose liability on someone who can pay rather than someone who cannot? Or is it to encourage employers to be even more vigilant than they would be pursuant to a duty of care? Or is it just a weapon of distributive justice? Academic writers disagree and the House of Lords in *Lister's* case did not give any definitive guidance to lower courts.

52. There is of course much instructive academic debate about the subject but it is, unfortunately, not possible fully to deal with it in this judgement. In *A Theory of Vicarious Liability* 2005 Alberta LR 1 . . . JW Neyers conducts a perceptive analysis of the main rationales and examines the failures of the leading theories of control, compensation, deterrence, loss spreading and enterprise liability adequately to explain the doctrine of vicarious liability and its limits. It may be useful to summarise some of the main themes.

(a) Control is one of the traditional explanations of vicarious liability but as Atiyah points out, 'control cannot be treated either as a sufficient reason for always imposing liability or as a necessary reason without which there should never be vicarious liability.' A parent is not liable for the torts of his children though he controls them; absence of control is no longer a serious obstacle to liability.

(b) Compensation/deep pockets: this explanation is necessary to ensure that innocent claimants have a solvent defendant against whom they may recover as employers are likely to be wealthier and/or carry insurance. That does not adequately explain why the employer should not be liable for the wrongful acts of his independent contractor.

(c) Deterrence: in one form the theory argues that since larger economic units are in the best position to reduce accidents through efficient organisation and discipline of staff, the law is justified in making them vicariously liable. If this was the reason for the rule, then one would expect that the employer would be able to escape from 'vicarious' liability by proving he was without fault (as he would be able to do, for example, in Germany). The notion of deterrence does not work well in the case of sexual predators who are deterred neither by potential criminal sanctions nor by more efficient administration of a church's affairs, so the imposition of liability on the church—whatever its rationale—will bear little relationship to deterrence.

(d) Loss-spreading: the idea here is that by fixing liability on the employer, the burden of the injury will be spread among his customers and insurers. That does not help explain why the employer of a domestic servant is vicariously liable for his employee's torts when this cannot be spread through any customer base.

(e) Enterprise liability: one notion here is that a business enterprise cannot justly disclaim responsibility for accidents which may fairly be said to be characteristic of its activities. As suggested in [the Supreme Court of Canada case] Bazley [v Curry (1999) 174 DLR (4th) 45], it is fair that the employer pays because the employer's enterprise created or exacerbated the risk that the claimant would suffer the injury she did. This of course does not explain why charitable organisations should nonetheless be vicariously responsible.

53. It seems, therefore, that no single rationale provides a complete answer for the imposition of vicarious liability. I have to agree with the view expressed by, among others, Fleming in *Law of Torts*, 10th edition (2011) p 438 that: '. . . the modern doctrine of vicarious liability should be frankly recognised as having its basis in a combination of policy considerations'.

See also Lord Phillips in *Various Claimants v Catholic Child Welfare Society and others* [2012] UKSC 56 and Lord Reed in *Cox v Ministry of Justice* [2016] UKSC 10 extracted in section 18.1.

What is clear, however, is that an employee must have committed a tort or some other legal wrong. Most often the cases involve the tort of negligence, though vicarious liability is not limited to negligence or to common law torts. In *Majrowski v Guy's and St Thomas' NHS Trust* [2006] UKHL 34, the House of Lords held that an employer can be vicariously liable for an employee's breach of the Protection from Harassment Act 1997. Lord Nicholls said:

it is difficult to see a coherent basis for confining the common law principle of vicarious liability to common law wrongs. The rationale underlying the principle holds good for equitable wrongs. The rationale also holds good for a wrong comprising a breach of a statutory duty or prohibition which gives rise to civil liability, provided always the statute does not expressly or impliedly indicate otherwise. (at [10])

In order for vicarious liability to be established the following conditions must be met:

- there is a relationship of employment, or one akin to employment, between the defendant and the person for whose actions they are being held liable (stage 1);
- the employee committed the tortious act while acting in the course of their employment (stage 2).

18.1 A relationship of, or akin to, employment

Traditionally, workers have been divided into two categories: employees and independent contractors. This distinction was key to the operation of vicarious liability, for, while employers could be vicariously liable for the torts of their employees, there could be no such liability for torts committed by one's independent contractors. The question of which workers were employees was traditionally addressed by looking to the level of 'control' the employer exercised not only over what the potential employee did, but over *how* they did it as a way of determining employment status (*Stephenson Jordan & Harrison Ltd v McDonall & Evans* [1952] 1 TLR 101). However, as the nature of employment has changed—with more part-time, contract, agency and home workers as well as changing working practices encouraging independent working and innovation—so the 'control' test has come to be viewed as inadequate for determining whether such persons are employees for the purposes of vicarious liability. Thus, while control remains a factor that goes to whether an individual is an employee, it is not the only, nor indeed the most important, one.

More importantly, recent developments in the law of vicarious liability mean that the question of who exactly is an employee is no longer decisive. Instead the courts have held that what matters is whether the defendant's relationship with the tortfeasor is, if not strictly one of employment, at least 'akin to' employment, such as to justify the imposition of vicarious liability for the tortfeasor's actions. This approach was first set out by Ward LJ in *JGE v The Trustees of the Portsmouth Roman Catholic Diocesan Trust* [2012] EWCA Civ 938 (adopting the reasoning of the judge at first instance, MacDuff J) and then adopted in what is now the leading case, *Various Claimants v Catholic Child Welfare Society and others* [2012] UKSC 56 (also known as the *'Christian Brothers'* case).

> ### *Various Claimants v Catholic Child Welfare Society and others*
> Supreme Court [2012] UKSC 56

The case was brought by 170 men who had been sexually and physically abused by members ('the brothers') of a Catholic group—the Brothers of the Christian Schools ('the Institute')—who were employed as teachers at a residential school for children in local authority care attended by the claimants. The abuse was alleged to have taken place over a 40-year period. Held: the relationship between the brothers and the Institute and the connection between the acts of abuse and the brothers' employment was such as to justify holding the Institute (alongside the managers of the school) vicariously liable. (See also discussion in section 18.2.)

LORD PHILLIPS:

An overview of the issues

19. [In *JGE* v *The Trustees of the Portsmouth Roman Catholic Diocesan Trust* [2012] EWCA Civ 938] Ward LJ traces the origin of vicarious liability back to the middle ages, but rightly identifies that the law upon which he and I cut our teeth rendered the employer, D2, liable for the tortious act of the employee, D1, provided that the act in question was committed 'in the course of the employee's employment'. Thus, in a case about vicarious liability, the focus was on two stages: (1) was there a true relationship of employer/employee between D2 and D1? (2) was D1 acting in the course of his employment when he committed the tortious act?

20. Since Ward LJ and I cut our teeth the courts have developed the law of vicarious liability by establishing the following propositions:

    i)   It is possible for an unincorporated association to be vicariously liable for the tortious acts of one or more of its members: *Heaton's Transport (St Helens) Ltd v Transport and General Workers' Union* [1973] AC 15, 99; *Thomas v National Union of Mineworkers (South Wales Area)* [1986] Ch 20, 66–7; *Dubai Aluminium Co Ltd v Salaam* [2002] UKHL 48 . . .

    ii)   D2 may be vicariously liable for the tortious act of D1 even though the act in question constitutes a violation of the duty owed to D2 by D1 and even if the act in question is a criminal offence: *Morris v CW Martin & Sons Ltd* [1966] 1 QB 716; *Dubai Aluminium; Brink's Global Services v Igrox* [2010] EWCA Civ 1207 . . .

    iii)   Vicarious liability can even extend to liability for a criminal act of sexual assault: **Lister v Hesley Hall** [2001] UKHL 22 . . .

    iv)   It is possible for two different defendants, D2 and D3, each to be vicariously liable for the single tortious act of D1: *Viasystems (Tyneside) Ltd v Thermal Transfer (Northern) Ltd and others* [2005] EWCA Civ 1151 . . .

21. None of these developments of the law of vicarious liability has been challenged by Lord Faulks QC, who has represented the Institute. I consider that he was right not to challenge them, for they represent sound and logical incremental developments of the law. They have, however, made it more difficult to identify the criteria that must be demonstrated to establish vicarious liability than it was 50 years ago. At para 37 of his judgment in this case Hughes LJ rightly observed that the test requires a synthesis of two stages:

    i)   The first stage is to consider the relationship of D1 and D2 to see whether it is one that is capable of giving rise to vicarious liability.

    ii)   Hughes LJ identified the second stage as requiring examination of the connection between D2 and the act or omission of D1. This is not entirely correct. What is critical at the second stage is the connection that links *the relationship between D1 and D2* and the act or omission of D1, hence the synthesis of the two stages.

22. Both stages are in issue in the present case. There is an issue as to whether the relationship between the Institute and the brothers teaching at St William's was one that was capable of giving rise to vicarious liability. There is also an issue as to whether the acts, or alleged acts, of sexual abuse were connected to that relationship in such a way as to give rise to vicarious liability.

    . . .

Stage 1: the essential elements of the relationship

34. Vicarious liability is a longstanding and vitally important part of the common law of tort. A glance at the Table of Cases in *Clerk & Lindsell on Torts,* 20th ed (2010) shows that in the majority of modern cases the defendant is not an individual but a corporate entity. In most of them vicarious liability is likely to be the basis upon which the defendant was sued. The policy objective underlying vicarious liability is to ensure, insofar as it is fair, just and reasonable, that liability for tortious wrong is borne by a defendant with the means to compensate the victim. Such defendants can usually be expected to insure against the risk of such liability, so that this risk is more widely spread. It is for the court to identify the policy reasons why it is fair, just and reasonable to impose vicarious liability and to lay down the criteria that must be shown to be satisfied in order to establish vicarious liability. . . .

35. The relationship that gives rise to vicarious liability is in the vast majority of cases that of employer and employee under a contract of employment. The employer will be vicariously liable when the employee commits a tort in the course of his employment. There is no difficulty in identifying a number of policy reasons that usually make it fair, just and reasonable to impose vicarious liability on the employer when these criteria are satisfied:

   i)   The employer is more likely to have the means to compensate the victim than the employee and can be expected to have insured against that liability;
   ii) The tort will have been committed as a result of activity being taken by the employee on behalf of the employer;
   iii) The employee's activity is likely to be part of the business activity of the employer;
   iv) The employer, by employing the employee to carry on the activity will have created the risk of the tort committed by the employee;
   v)   The employee will, to a greater or lesser degree, have been under the control of the employer.. . . .

47. At paragraph 35 above I have identified those incidents of the relationship between employer and employee that make it fair, just and reasonable to impose vicarious liability on a defendant. Where the defendant and the tortfeasor are not bound by a contract of employment, but their relationship has the same incidents, that relationship can properly give rise to vicarious liability on the ground that it is 'akin to that between an employer and an employee'. That was the approach adopted by the Court of Appeal in *JGE*. . . .

56. In the context of vicarious liability the relationship between the teaching brothers and the Institute had many of the elements, and all the essential elements, of the relationship between employer and employees:

   i)   The institute was subdivided into a hierarchical structure and conducted its activities as if it were a corporate body.
   ii) The teaching activity of the brothers was undertaken because the Provincial directed the brothers to undertake it. True it is that the brothers entered into contracts of employment with the [school], but they did so because the Provincial required them to do so.
   iii) The teaching activity undertaken by the brothers was in furtherance of the objective, or mission, of the Institute.
   iv) The manner in which the brother teachers were obliged to conduct themselves as teachers was dictated by the Institute's rules.

57. The relationship between the teacher brothers and the Institute differed from that of the relationship between employer and employee in that:

   i)   The brothers were bound to the Institute not by contract, but by their vows.
   ii) Far from the Institute paying the brothers, the brothers entered into deeds under which they were obliged to transfer all their earnings to the Institute. The Institute catered for their needs from these funds.

58. Neither of these differences is material. Indeed they rendered the relationship between the brothers and the Institute closer than that of an employer and its employees.

59. Hughes LJ [in the Court of Appeal] held at para 54 that the brothers no more acted on behalf of the Institute 'than any member of a professional organisation who accepts employment with that status is acting on behalf of the organisation when he does his job'. I do not agree with this analysis. The business of the Institute was not to train teachers or to confer status on them. It was to provide Christian teaching for boys. All members of the Institute were united in that objective. The relationship between individual teacher brothers and the Institute was directed to achieving that objective.

60. For these reasons I consider that the relationship between the teaching brothers and the Institute was sufficiently akin to that of employer and employees to satisfy stage 1 of the test of vicarious liability.

61. There is a simpler analysis that leads to the conclusion that stage 1 was satisfied. Provided that a brother was acting for the common purpose of the brothers as an unincorporated association, the relationship between them would be sufficient to satisfy stage 1, just as in the case of the action of a member of a partnership. Had one of the brothers injured a pedestrian when negligently driving a vehicle owned by the Institute in order to collect groceries for the community few would question that the Institute was vicariously liable for his tort.

Cox v Ministry of Justice
Supreme Court [2016] UKSC 10

Cox, the catering manager at HM Prison Swansea, was negligently injured by a prisoner who was carrying out paid work under her supervision in the kitchen. In the process of transferring large sacks of rice to the kitchen stores, a bag had been dropped and had burst open. Cox was bending over attempting to stop the rice from spilling further when Inder (a prisoner) attempted to carry two sacks past her, lost his balance and dropped one of the sacks on to Cox's back, causing her injury. It is accepted that Inder was negligent. Held: Inder's activity in unloading supplies was 'akin to employment' even though his relationship to the prison was not voluntary.

LORD REED (with whom LORD NEUBERGER, LADY HALE, LORD DYSON and LORD TOULSON agreed):

1. 'The law of vicarious liability is on the move.' So Lord Phillips said, in the last judgment which he delivered as President of this court, in *Various Claimants v Catholic Child Welfare Society* [2012] UKSC 56; [2013] 2 AC 1 ('the *Christian Brothers* case'), para 19. It has not yet come to a stop. This appeal, and the companion appeal in *Mohamud v WM Morrison Supermarkets plc* [2016] UKSC 11, provide an opportunity to take stock of where it has got to so far.

2. The scope of vicarious liability depends upon the answers to two questions. First, what sort of relationship has to exist between an individual and a defendant before the defendant can be made vicariously liable in tort for the conduct of that individual? Secondly, in what manner does the conduct of that individual have to be related to that relationship, in order for vicarious liability to be imposed on the defendant? Although the answers to those questions are inter-connected, the present appeal is concerned with the first question, and approaches it principally in the light of the judgment in the *Christian Brothers* case, where the same issue was considered. The appeal in the case of *Mohamud* is concerned with the second question, and approaches it principally in the light of the historical development of this branch of the law. As will appear, the present judgment also seeks to relate the approach adopted to the first question to ideas which have long been present in the law. The two judgments are intended to be complementary.

3. Vicarious liability in tort is imposed upon a person in respect of the act or omission of another individual, because of his relationship with that individual, and the connection between that relationship and the act or omission in question. Leaving aside other areas of the law where vicarious liability can operate, such as partnership and agency (with which this judgment is not concerned), the relationship is classically one of employment, and the connection is that the employee committed the act or omission in the course of his employment: that is to say, within the field of activities assigned to him, as Lord Cullen put it in *Central Motors (Glasgow) Ltd v Cessnock Garage & Motor Co* 1925 SC 796, 802, or, adapting the words of Diplock LJ in *Ilkiw v Samuels* [1963] 1 WLR 991, 1004, in the course of his job, considered broadly. That aspect of vicarious liability is fully considered by Lord Toulson in the case of *Mohamud*.

4. It has however long been recognised that a relationship can give rise to vicarious liability even in the absence of a contract of employment. For example, where an employer lends his employee to a third party, the third party may be treated as the employer for the purposes of vicarious liability. In recent years, the courts have sought to explain more generally the basis on which vicarious liability can arise out of a relationship other than that of employer and employee.

5. The general approach to be adopted in deciding whether a relationship other than one of employment can give rise to vicarious liability, subject to there being a sufficient connection between that relationship and the tort in question, was explained by this court in the *Christian Brothers* case, in a judgment given by Lord Phillips with which the other members of the court agreed. That judgment was intended to bring greater clarity to an area of the law which had been unsettled by a number of recent decisions, including those of the House of Lords in *Lister v Hesley Hall Ltd* [2001] UKHL 22; [2002] 1 AC 215 and *Dubai Aluminium Co Ltd v Salaam* [2002] UKHL 48; [2003] 2 AC 366.

6. The case concerned the question whether the Institute of the Brothers of the Christian Schools, an international unincorporated association whose mission was to provide children with a Christian education, was vicariously liable for the sexual abuse of children by members of the institute, otherwise known as brothers, who taught at an approved school. Another organisation managed the school and employed the brothers as teachers. It had been held to be vicariously liable for the abuse. The issue was whether the institute was also vicariously liable. The Supreme Court held that it was. Vicarious liability was thus imposed on a body which did not employ the wrongdoers, in circumstances where another body did employ them and was also vicariously liable for the same tort.

[Lord Reed then cited [35] and [47] of Lord Phillips's judgment in the *Christian Brothers* case.]

7. The five factors which Lord Phillips mentioned in para 35 are not all equally significant. The first—that the defendant is more likely than the tortfeasor to have the means to compensate the victim, and can be expected to have insured against vicarious liability—did not feature in the remainder of the judgment, and is unlikely to be of independent significance in most cases. It is, of course, true that where an individual is employed under a contract of employment, his employer is likely to have a deeper pocket, and can in any event be expected to have insured against vicarious liability. Neither of these, however, is a principled justification for imposing vicarious liability. The mere possession of wealth is not in itself any ground for imposing liability. As for insurance, employers insure themselves because they are liable: they are not liable because they have insured themselves. On the other hand, given the infinite variety of circumstances in which the question of vicarious liability might arise, it cannot be ruled out that there might be circumstances in which the absence or unavailability of insurance, or other means of meeting a potential liability, might be a relevant consideration.

8. The fifth of the factors—that the tortfeasor will, to a greater or lesser degree, have been under the control of the defendant—no longer has the significance that it was sometimes considered to have in the past, as Lord Phillips immediately made clear. As he explained at para 36, the ability to direct how an individual did his work was sometimes regarded as an important test of the existence of a relationship of master and servant, and came to be treated at times as the test for the imposition of vicarious liability. But it is not realistic in modern life to look for a right to direct how an employee should perform his duties as a necessary element in the relationship between employer and employee; nor indeed was it in times gone by, if one thinks for example of the degree of control which the owner of a ship could have exercised over the master while the ship was at sea. Accordingly, as Lord Phillips stated, the significance of control is that the defendant can direct what the tortfeasor does, not how he does it. So understood, it is a factor which is unlikely to be of independent significance in most cases. On the other hand, the absence of even that vestigial degree of control would be liable to negative the imposition of vicarious liability.

9. The remaining factors listed by Lord Phillips were that (1) the tort will have been committed as a result of activity being taken by the tortfeasor on behalf of the defendant, (2) the tortfeasor's activity is likely to be part of the business activity of the defendant, and (3) the defendant, by employing the tortfeasor to carry on the activity, will have created the risk of the tort committed by the tortfeasor.

10. These three factors are inter-related. The first has been reflected historically in explanations of the vicarious liability of employers based on deemed authorisation or delegation, as for example in *Turberville v Stampe* (1698) 1 Ld Raym 264, 265 per Holt CJ and *Bartonshill Coal Co v McGuire* (1858) 3 Macq 300, [1858] UKHL 3 Macqueen 300, 306 per Lord Chelmsford LC. The second, that the tortfeasor's activity is likely to be an integral part of the business activity of the defendant, has long been regarded as a justification for the imposition of vicarious liability on employers, on the basis that, since the employee's activities are undertaken as part of the activities of the employer and for its benefit, it is appropriate that the employer should bear the cost of harm wrongfully done by the employee within the field of activities assigned to him: see, for example, *Duncan v Findlater* (1839) 6 Cl & Fin 894, 909–910; (1839) MacL & Rob 911, 940, [1839] UKHL MacRob 911, per Lord Brougham and *Broom v Morgan* [1953] 1 QB 597, 607–608 per Denning LJ. The third factor, that the defendant, by employing the tortfeasor to carry on the activities, will have created the risk of the tort committed by the tortfeasor, is very closely related to the second: since the risk of an individual behaving negligently, or indeed committing an intentional wrong, is a fact of life, anyone who employs others to carry out activities is likely to create the risk of their behaving tortiously within the field of activities assigned to them. The essential idea is that the defendant should be liable for torts that may fairly be regarded as risks of his business activities, whether they are committed for the purpose of furthering those activities or not. This idea has been emphasised in recent times in United States and Canadian authorities, sometimes in the context of an economic analysis, but has much older roots, as I have explained. It was reaffirmed in the cases of *Lister* and *Dubai Aluminium*. In the latter case, Lord Nicholls of Birkenhead said at para 21:

> The underlying legal policy is based on the recognition that carrying on a business enterprise necessarily involves risks to others. It involves the risk that others will be harmed by wrongful acts committed by the agents through whom the business is carried on. When those risks ripen into loss, it is just that the business should be responsible for compensating the person who has been wronged.

11. Lord Phillips's analysis in the **Christian Brothers** case wove together these related ideas so as to develop a modern theory of vicarious liability. The result of this approach is that a relationship other than one of employment is in principle capable of giving rise to vicarious liability where harm is wrongfully done by an individual who carries on activities as an integral part of the business activities carried on by a defendant and for its benefit (rather than his activities being entirely attributable to the conduct of a recognisably independent business of his own or of a third party), and where the commission of the wrongful act is a risk created by the defendant by assigning those activities to the individual in question.

12. . . . It may be said that the criteria are insufficiently precise to make their application to border-line cases plain and straightforward: a criticism which might, of course, also be made of other general principles of the law of tort. As Lord Nicholls observed in *Dubai Aluminium* at para 26, a lack of precision is inevitable, given the infinite range of circumstances where the issue arises. The court has to make a judgment, assisted by previous judicial decisions in the same or analogous contexts. Such decisions may enable the criteria to be refined in particular contexts, as Lord Phillips suggested in the *Christian Brothers* case at para 83.

13. It is important, however, to understand that the general approach which Lord Phillips described is not confined to some special category of cases, such as the sexual abuse of children. It is intended to provide a basis for identifying the circumstances in which vicarious liability may in principle be imposed outside relationships of employment. By focusing upon the business activities carried on by the defendant and their attendant risks, it directs attention to the issues which are likely to be relevant in the context of modern workplaces, where workers may in reality be part of the workforce of an organisation without having a contract of employment with it, and also reflects prevailing ideas about the responsibility of businesses for the risks which are created by their activities. It results in an extension of the scope of vicarious liability beyond the responsibility of an employer for the acts and omissions of its employees in the course of their employment, but not to the extent of imposing such liability where a tortfeasor's activities are entirely attributable to the conduct of a recognisably independent business of his own or of a third party. An important consequence of that extension is to enable the law to maintain previous levels of protection for the victims of torts, notwithstanding changes in the legal relationships between enterprises and members of their workforces which may be motivated by factors which have nothing to do with the nature of the enterprises' activities or the attendant risks.

14. It is also important not to be misled by a narrow focus on semantics: for example, by words such as 'business', 'benefit', and 'enterprise'. The defendant need not be carrying on activities of a commercial nature: that is apparent not only from the cases of *E* and the *Christian Brothers*, but also from the long-established application of vicarious liability to public authorities and hospitals. It need not therefore be a business or enterprise in any ordinary sense. Nor need the benefit which it derives from the tortfeasor's activities take the form of a profit. It is sufficient that there is a defendant which is carrying on activities in the furtherance of its own interests. The individual for whose conduct it may be vicariously liable must carry on activities assigned to him by the defendant as an integral part of its operation and for its benefit. The defendant must, by assigning those activities to him, have created a risk of his committing the tort. . . .

15. . . . [D]efendants cannot avoid vicarious liability on the basis of technical arguments about the employment status of the individual who committed the tort. As Professor John Bell noted in his article, 'The Basis of Vicarious Liability' [2013] CLJ 17, what weighed with the courts in *E* and the *Christian Brothers* case was that the abusers were placed by the organisations in question, as part of their mission, in a position in which they committed a tort whose commission was a risk inherent in the activities assigned to them.

The present case

32. In the present case, the requirements laid down in the *Christian Brothers* case are met. The prison service carries on activities in furtherance of its aims. The fact that those aims are not

commercially motivated, but serve the public interest, is no bar to the imposition of vicarious liability. Prisoners working in the prison kitchens, such as Mr Inder, are integrated into the operation of the prison, so that the activities assigned to them by the prison service form an integral part of the activities which it carries on in the furtherance of its aims: in particular, the activity of providing meals for prisoners. They are placed by the prison service in a position where there is a risk that they may commit a variety of negligent acts within the field of activities assigned to them. That is recognised by the health and safety training which they receive. Furthermore, they work under the direction of prison staff. Mrs Cox was injured as a result of negligence by Mr Inder in carrying on the activities assigned to him. The prison service is therefore vicariously liable to her.

40. . . . [I]t was argued that it was always necessary to ask the broader question whether it would be fair, just and reasonable to impose vicarious liability. In that regard, reliance was placed on the fact that the prison service acts for the benefit of the public, and on the fact that any liability would have to be met out of scarce public funds. It was also argued that there was no justification for imposing vicarious liability on the prison service in addition to its common law duty of care towards Mrs Cox, and its various statutory duties.

41. I do not consider that it is always necessary to ask the broader question. The criteria for the imposition of vicarious liability listed by Lord Phillips in the **Christian Brothers** case are designed, as he made clear at paras 34, 35 and 47, to ensure that it is imposed where it is fair, just and reasonable to do so. That was the whole point of seeking to align the criteria with the various policy justifications for its imposition. As I have explained, the criteria may be capable of refinement in particular contexts. But in cases where the criteria are satisfied, it should not generally be necessary to re-assess the fairness, justice and reasonableness of the result in the particular case. Such an exercise, if carried out routinely, would be liable to lead to uncertainty and inconsistency.

42. At the same time, the criteria are not to be applied mechanically or slavishly. . . . [T]he words used by judges are not to be treated as if they were the words of a statute. Where a case concerns circumstances which have not previously been the subject of an authoritative judicial decision, it may be valuable to stand back and consider whether the imposition of vicarious liability would be fair, just and reasonable. The present appeal is such a case. On considering the matter, however, I do not regard the conclusion which I have reached as unreasonable or unjust. . . .

43. Finally, like the Fat Boy in *The Pickwick Papers*, counsel sought to make our flesh creep. It was argued that, if the present claim succeeded, there would be similar claims arising from the other activities undertaken by prisoners with a view to their rehabilitation, such as educational classes or offending behaviour programmes. There was also a risk of fraudulent claims being made for prisoner on prisoner incidents. A finding of vicarious liability might lead the prison service to adopt an unduly cautious approach to the type of tasks which prisoners were given the opportunity to do, given the potential impact on scarce financial resources.

44. I am not persuaded by these apprehensions. It is true that prisoners who participate in educational classes or offending behaviour programmes contribute towards their own rehabilitation, and in that sense may be said to be acting in furtherance of one of the aims of the prison service. But there is an intelligible distinction between taking part in activities of that kind and working as an integral part of the operation of the prison and for its benefit. As for the risk of fraudulent claims, that risk is inherent in the law relating to compensation for personal injuries, and employers, insurers and the courts are all experienced in guarding against it. As for the risk of an unduly cautious approach being adopted by the prison service, that risk is entirely speculative, and is based on a consideration only of the costs potentially resulting from the imposition of vicarious liability, without taking account of the costs which would result from a decision to cease employing prisoners and instead to employ civilian staff or external contractors at market rates of pay.

Notes

1. The 'modern theory of vicarious liability', set out in the **Christian Brothers** case and endorsed in **Cox**, was applied by the Supreme Court once more in *Armes* v *Nottinghamshire County Council* [2017] UKSC 60. The case concerned abuses committed by foster parents on children put into their care by the local authority. The court held that the relationship between the local authority and the foster parents was akin to employment, and that the authority was, therefore, vicariously liable for the latter's torts. The court came to its decision by appealing to the five incidents identified in the **Christian Brothers** case, concluding that they were all present in the relationship between the authority and the foster parents. In particular, it held that the fact that the child was placed into a foster home in fulfilment of the authority's duty towards children in its care, and that the authority recruited and trained foster carers and paid them allowances, meant that the foster parents played an 'integral part of the local authority's organisation of its child care services' (at [60]). Moreover, while the authority did not micro-manage how the foster parents cared for the children, it nonetheless 'exercised powers of approval, inspection, supervision and removal', which gave it 'a significant degree of control over both what the foster parents did and how they did it' (at [62]).

2. Where a defendant is vicariously liable for another's torts, this supplements rather than replaces the tortfeasor's own liability. One of the justifications given for vicarious liability is that the employer will typically be better placed to compensate the claimant. As such, the claimant will typically have no reason to seek damages from the employee. However, there may be cases in which the employer is bankrupt or an exemption clause limits his liability and the claimant decides to sue the employee in tort. In *Lister* v *Romford Ice and Cold Storage Co* [1957] AC 555, the House of Lords went so far as to hold that an employee may even be required to indemnify an employer if he has had to pay damages, but companies which insure employers have refused to take advantage of so unfair a rule.

   This issue is now affected by the Contracts (Rights of Third Parties) Act 1999. The effect of section 1 is that where the contract between a customer and the employer contains an exemption clause which *specifically* states that it shall be extended to the employer's employees, the employees will gain the benefit of the exemption clause. However, this still leaves open the common problem of what happens if there is no specific extension of the exemption clause. The Law Commission, in its Report on *Privity of Contract* (Law Com No 242, 1996), left open the possibility of the doctrine of 'vicarious immunity' being adopted in England, specifically stating that the passing of the 1999 Act should not inhibit the courts from judicial development of third party rights and mentioning in particular the development of a form of vicarious immunity (at [5.10]).

3. In some instances, it is clear that the tortfeasor is an employee but not who their employer is. Take, for example, an office 'temp'—are they an employee of the agency to which they belong (and which allocates the work) or the company which hires them for a particular period of time (and who tells them what to do)? Historically, dual vicarious liability was not permitted: an employee 'is the servant of one or the other, but not the servant of one and the other; the law does not recognise several liability in two principals who are unconnected' (*Laugher* v *Pointer* (1826) 5 B & C 547) and complicated rules developed as to when employment transferred to another (usually temporary) employer (see *Mersey Docks and Harbour Board* v *Coggins & Griffith (Liverpool) Ltd* [1947] AC 1 and *Hawley* v *Luminar Leisure Ltd* [2006] EWCA Civ 18).

4. But why not just find *both* employers liable? The question of 'dual' vicarious liability was reconsidered in *Viasystems* v *Thermal Transfer Ltd* [2005] EWCA Civ 1151. The claimants engaged A Ltd to install air conditioning in its factory. A Ltd subcontracted the ducting work to B Ltd which then contracted with C Ltd to provide the labour. H (employed by B Ltd) and M (employed by C Ltd) were in charge of the work. S, an employee of C Ltd, negligently caused a flood and it was held that both H and M were entitled to control S (even though strictly speaking he was employed by C Ltd). Accordingly, *both* B Ltd and C Ltd (employers of H and M) were vicariously liable for the flood: 'what one is looking for is a situation where the employee in question . . . is so much part of the work, business or organisation of both employers that it is just to make both employers answer for his negligence' (Rix LJ at [79]). This was affirmed by the Supreme Court in the **Christian Brothers** case in which *both* the school *and* the Institute were vicariously liable for the abuse the brothers had committed.

18.2 The course of employment

An employer is only liable for the torts of his employee if the act is committed 'in the course of his employment'. Since *Lister v Hesley Hall* [2001] UKHL 22, the key question is whether there is a sufficiently 'close connection' between the employee's act and their employment. However, the 'close connection test' is easier to state than apply. As Lord Phillips in *Christian Brothers* notes, the 'test of "close connection" approved by all tells one nothing about the nature of the connection' (at [74]). It simply prompts a further question: how closely connected to their employment do the employee's actions need to be? (Paula Giliker 'Rough Justice in an Unjust World' (2002) 65 MLR 269.) Unsurprisingly, then, the question as to what precisely amounts to a sufficiently close connection to make it just for the employer to be held vicariously liable made its way back to the Supreme Court in *Mohamud v WM Morrison Supermarkets plc* [2016] UKSC 11 and, once more, in *Wm Morrison Supermarkets plc v Various Claimants* [2020] UKSC 12.

Lister v Hesley Hall
House of Lords [2001] UKHL 22

The claimants were residents at Axeholme House, a school boarding facility, owned by the defendants. The school specialised in teaching children with emotional and behavioural difficulties and the boarding house was intended to provide the children with a homely and caring setting in which to adjust to everyday living. The defendants employed a warden, Grain, to supervise the boys but over a period of four years he sexually abused a number of them. The claimants sued on the basis that the defendants were vicariously liable for the acts of their employee. Held: the warden's actions were 'so closely connected' with his employment that it would be fair and just to hold the employers vicariously liable.

LORD STEYN:

The perspective of principle

14. Vicarious liability is legal responsibility imposed on an employer, although he is himself free from blame, for a tort committed by his employee in the course of his employment. Fleming observed that this formula represented 'a compromise between two conflicting policies: on the one end, the social interest in furnishing an innocent tort victim with recourse against a financially responsible defendant; on the other, a hesitation to foist any undue burden on business enterprise': *The Law of Torts*, 9th ed (1998), pp 409–410.

15. For nearly a century English judges have adopted Salmond's statement of the applicable test as correct. Salmond said that a wrongful act is deemed to be done by a 'servant' in the course of his employment if 'it is either (a) a wrongful act authorised by the master, or (b) a wrongful and unauthorised *mode* of doing some act authorised by the master': *Salmond, Law of Torts*, 1st ed (1907), p 83; and *Salmond & Heuston on the Law of Torts*, 21st ed, p 443. Situation (a) causes no problems. The difficulty arises in respect of cases under (b). Salmond did, however, offer an explanation which has sometimes been overlooked. He said (*Salmond on Torts*, 1st ed, pp 83–84) that 'a master . . . is liable even for acts which he has not authorised, provided they are *so connected* with acts which he has authorised, that they may rightly *be regarded* as modes—although improper modes—of doing them' (my emphasis). . . .

16. It is not necessary to embark on a detailed examination of the development of the modern principle of vicarious liability. But it is necessary to face up to the way in which the law of vicarious liability sometimes may embrace intentional wrongdoing by an employee. If one mechanically applies *Salmond's* test, the result might at first glance be thought to be that a bank is not liable to a customer where a bank employee defrauds a customer by giving him only half the foreign exchange which he paid for, the employee pocketing the difference. A preoccupation with conceptualistic reasoning may lead to the absurd conclusion that there can only be vicarious liability if the bank carries on business in defrauding its customers. Ideas divorced from reality have never held much attraction for judges steeped in the tradition that their task is to deliver principled but practical justice. How the courts set the law on a sensible course is a matter to which I now turn.

17. It is easy to accept the idea that where an employee acts for the benefit of his employer, or intends to do so, that is strong evidence that he was acting in the course of his employment. But until the decision of the House of Lords in *Lloyd v Grace, Smith & Co* [1912] AC 716 it was thought that vicarious liability could only be established if such requirements were satisfied. This was an overly restrictive view and hardly in tune with the needs of society. In *Lloyd v Grace, Smith & Co* it was laid to rest by the House of Lords. A firm of solicitors were held liable for the dishonesty of their managing clerk who persuaded a client to transfer property to him and then disposed of it for his own advantage. The decisive factor was that the client had been invited by the firm to deal with their managing clerk. This decision was a breakthrough: it finally established that vicarious liability is not necessarily defeated if the employee acted for his own benefit. On the other hand, an intense focus on the connection between the nature of the employment and the tort of the employee became necessary. . . .

19. The classic example of vicarious liability for intentional wrongdoing is *Morris v CW Martin & Sons Ltd* [1966] 1 QB 716. A woman wanted her mink stole cleaned. With her permission it was delivered to the defendants for cleaning. An employee took charge of the fur and stole it. At first instance the judge held that the defendants were not liable because the theft was not committed in the course of employment. The Court of Appeal reversed the judge's decision and held the defendants liable. It is possible to read the case narrowly simply as a bailment case, the wrong being failure to redeliver. But two of the judgments are authority for the proposition that the employee converted the fur in the course of his employment. Diplock LJ observed, at pp 736–737:

> If the principle laid down in *Lloyd v Grace, Smith & Co* [1912] AC 716 is applied to the facts of the present case, the defendants cannot in my view escape liability for the conversion of the plaintiff's fur by their servant Morrissey. They accepted the fur as bailees for reward in order to clean it. They put Morrissey as their agent in their place to clean the fur and to take charge of it while doing so. The manner in which he conducted himself in doing that work was to convert it. What he was doing, albeit dishonestly, he was doing in the scope or course of his employment in the technical sense of that infelicitous but time-honoured phrase. The defendants as his masters are responsible for his tortious act.

Salmon LJ held, at p 738, that 'the defendants are liable for what amounted to negligence and conversion by their servant in the course of his employment'. The deciding factor was that the employee had been given custody of the fur. *Morris's* case has consistently been regarded as high authority on the principles of vicarious liability. *Atiyah, Vicarious Liability in the Law of Torts* (1967), p 271 described it as 'a striking and valuable extension of the law of vicarious liability'. *Palmer on Bailment*, 2nd ed (1991), pp 424–425 treats *Morris's* case as an authority on vicarious liability beyond bailment. He states that 'if a television repairman steals a television he is called in to repair, his employers would be liable, for the loss occurred whilst he was performing one of the class of acts in respect of which their duty lay'. And that does not involve bailment. Moreover, in *Port Swettenham Authority v TW Wu & Co (M) Sdn Bhd* [1979] AC 580 the Privy Council expressly approved *Morris's* case in respect of vicarious liability as explained by Diplock and Salmon LLJ [sic].

20. Our law no longer struggles with the concept of vicarious liability for intentional wrongdoing. . . . It remains, however, to consider how vicarious liability for intentional wrongdoing fits in with Salmond's formulation. The answer is that it does not cope ideally with such cases. It must, however, be remembered that the great tort writer did not attempt to enunciate precise propositions of law on vicarious liability. At most he propounded a broad test which deems as within the course of employment 'a wrongful and unauthorised mode of doing some *act* authorised by the master'. And he emphasised the connection between the authorised *acts* and the 'improper modes' of doing them. In reality it is simply a practical test serving as a dividing line between cases where it is or is not just to impose vicarious liability. The usefulness of the *Salmond* formulation is, however, crucially dependent on focusing on the right act of the employee. This point was explored in *Rose v Plenty* [1976] 1 WLR 141. The Court of Appeal held that a milkman who deliberately disobeyed his employers' order not to allow children to help on his rounds did not go beyond his course of employment in allowing a child to help him. The analysis in this decision shows how the pitfalls of terminology must be avoided. Scarman LJ said, at pp 147–148:

> The servant was, of course, employed at the time of the accident to do a whole number of operations. He was certainly not employed to give the boy a lift, and if one confines one's analysis of the facts to the incident of injury to the plaintiff, then no doubt one would say that carrying the boy on the float—giving him a lift—was not in the course of the servant's employment. But in *Ilkiw v Samuels* [1983] 1 WLR 991 Diplock LJ indicated that the proper approach to the nature of the servant's employment is a broad one. He says, at p 1004: 'As each of these nouns implies'—he is referring to the nouns used to describe course of employment, sphere, scope and so forth—'the matter must be looked at broadly, not dissecting the servant's task into its component activities—such as driving, loading, sheeting and the like—by asking: what was the job on which he was engaged for his employer? and answering that question as a jury would.'
>
> Applying those words to the employment of this servant, I think it is clear from the evidence that he was employed as a roundsman to drive his float round his round and to deliver milk, to collect empties and to obtain payment. That was his job. . . .. He chose to disregard the prohibition and to enlist the assistance of the plaintiff. As a matter of common sense, that does seem to me to be a mode, albeit a prohibited mode, of doing the job with which he was entrusted. Why was the plaintiff being carried on the float when the accident occurred? Because it was necessary to take him from point to point so that he could assist in delivering milk, collecting empties and, on occasions obtaining payment.

If this approach to the nature of employment is adopted, it is not necessary to ask the simplistic question whether in the cases under consideration the acts of sexual abuse were modes of doing authorised acts. It becomes possible to consider the question of vicarious liability on the basis that the employer undertook to care for the boys through the services of the warden and that there is a very close connection between the torts of the warden and his employment. After all, they were committed in the time and on the premises of the employers while the warden was also busy caring for the children. . . .

The application of the correct test

27. My Lords, I have been greatly assisted by the luminous and illuminating judgments of the Canadian Supreme Court in *Bazley v Curry* 174 DLR (4th) 45 and *Jacobi v Griffiths* 174 DLR (4th) 71.

Wherever such problems are considered in future in the common law world these judgments will be the starting point. On the other hand, it is unnecessary to express views on the full range of policy considerations examined in those decisions.

28. Employing the traditional methodology of English law, I am satisfied that in the case of the appeals under consideration the evidence showed that the employers entrusted the care of the children in Axeholme House to the warden. The question is whether the warden's torts were so closely connected with his employment that it would be fair and just to hold the employers vicariously liable. On the facts of the case the answer is yes. After all, the sexual abuse was inextricably interwoven with the carrying out by the warden of his duties in Axeholme House. Matters of degree arise. But the present cases clearly fall on the side of vicarious liability.

LORD HOBHOUSE:

59. The classic *Salmond* test for vicarious liability and scope of employment has two limbs. The first covers authorised acts which are tortious. These present no relevant problem and the present cases clearly do not fall within the first limb. The defendants did not authorise Mr Grain to abuse the children in his charge. The argument of the respondent (accepted by the Court of Appeal) is that Mr Grain's acts of abuse did not come within the second limb either: abusing children cannot properly be described as a mode of caring for children. The answer to this argument is provided by the analysis which I have set out in the preceding paragraphs. Whether or not some act comes within the scope of the servant's employment depends upon an identification of what duty the servant was employed by his employer to perform. . . .. If the act of the servant which gives rise to the servant's liability to the plaintiff amounted to a failure by the servant to perform that duty, the act comes within 'the scope of his employment' and the employer is vicariously liable. If, on the other hand, the servant's employment merely gave the servant the opportunity to do what he did without more, there will be no vicarious liability, hence the use by Salmond and in the Scottish and some other authorities of the word 'connection' to indicate something which is not a casual coincidence but has the requisite relationship to the employment of the tortfeasor (servant) by his employer: *Kirby v National Coal Board* 1958 SC 514; *Williams v A & W Hemphill Ltd* 1966 SC(HL) 31.

60. My Lords, the correct approach to answering the question whether the tortious act of the servant falls within or without the scope of the servant's employment for the purposes of the principle of vicarious liability is to ask what was the duty of the servant towards the plaintiff which was broken by the servant and what was the contractual duty of the servant towards his employer. The second limb of the classic *Salmond* test is a convenient rule of thumb which provides the answer in very many cases but does not represent the fundamental criterion which is the comparison of the duties respectively owed by the servant to the plaintiff and to his employer. Similarly, I do not believe that it is appropriate to follow the lead given by the Supreme Court of Canada in *Bazley v Curry* 174 DLR (4th) 45. The judgments contain a useful and impressive discussion of the social and economic reasons for having a principle of vicarious liability as part of the law of tort which extends to embrace acts of child abuse. But an exposition of the policy reasons for a rule (or even a description) is not the same as defining the criteria for its application. Legal rules have to have a greater degree of clarity and definition than is provided by simply explaining the reasons for the existence of the rule and the social need for it, instructive though that may be. In English law that clarity is provided by the application of the criterion to which I have referred derived from the English authorities.

61. It follows that the reasoning of the Court of Appeal in *Trotman v North Yorkshire County Council* [1999] LGR 584 and the present cases cannot be supported. On the undisputed facts, the present cases satisfy the criteria for demonstrating the vicarious liability of the defendants for the acts of Mr Grain.

> **Various Claimants v Catholic Child Welfare Society and others**
> Supreme Court [2012] UKSC 56

The facts are stated in section 18.1.

LORD PHILLIPS:

Stage 2: The connection between the brothers' acts of abuse and the relationship between the brothers and the Institute

62. Where an employee commits a tortious act the employer will be vicariously liable if the act was done 'in the course of the employment' of the employee. This plainly covers the situation where the employee does something that he is employed to do in a manner that is negligent. In that situation the necessary connection between his relationship with his employer and his tortious act will be established. Stage 2 of the test will be satisfied. The same is true where the relationship between the defendant and the tortfeasor is akin to that of an employer and employee. Where the tortfeasor does something that he is required or requested to do pursuant to his relationship with the defendant in a manner that is negligent, stage 2 of the test is likely to be satisfied. But sexual abuse can never be a negligent way of performing such a requirement. In what circumstances, then, can an act of sexual abuse give rise to vicarious liability?

68. In *Lister v Hesley Hall Ltd* [2002] 1 AC 215 the House of Lords, reversing previous authority, held the owners and managers of a school vicariously liable for sexual assaults committed by the warden of a boarding house, employed by them. Although the result was unanimous the reasoning of the House was not identical. Lord Steyn at para 27 referred to [Supreme Court of Canada decisions] *Bazley* and *Jacobi* [v *Griffiths* (1999) 174 DLR (4th) 71] as 'luminous and illuminating' judgments which would henceforth be the starting point for consideration of similar cases. He held, however, that it was not necessary to express views on the full range of policy considerations examined in those decisions. At para 10 he stated that those cases enunciated a principle of 'close connection' and at para 28 he said that the question was whether the warden's torts were so closely connected with his employment that it would be fair and just to hold the employers vicariously liable. He gave an affirmative answer to that question, observing that the sexual abuse was 'inextricably interwoven' with the carrying out by the warden of his duties at the school. . . .

74. It is not easy to deduce from *Lister* the precise criteria that will give rise to vicarious liability for sexual abuse. The test of 'close connection' approved by all tells one nothing about the nature of the connection. . . .

75. The reasoning in *Lister* was applied by the House of Lords in a commercial context. In *Dubai Aluminium Co Ltd v Salaam* [2002] UKHL 48 . . . the relevant issue was whether dishonest conduct by a solicitor could involve the firm in liability under section 10 of the Partnership Act 1890 as having been carried on 'in the ordinary course of the business of the firm'. Giving the leading speech Lord Nicholls held that it was necessary to apply the legal policy underlying vicarious liability, which he stated at para 21:

> is based on the recognition that carrying on a business enterprise necessarily involves risks to others. It involves the risk that others will be harmed by wrongful acts committed by the agents through whom the business is carried on. When those risks ripen into loss, it is just that the business should be responsible for compensating the person who has been wronged.

This has strong echoes of the 'enterprise risk' approach of the Canadian Supreme Court and, indeed, Lord Nicholls went on at para 23 to cite with approval from the judgment of McLachlin CJ in *Bazley*.

. . .

Discussion

83. Sexual abuse of children is now recognised as a widespread evil and the Criminal Records Bureau was established under Part V of the Police Act 1997 to reduce the risk of this by enabling screening of those seeking positions involving greater contact with young people and vulnerable adults. In *Lister* at para 48 Lord Clyde said that cases of sexual abuse by an employee should be approached in the same way as other cases in the context of vicarious liability. None the less the courts have been tailoring this area of the law by emphasising the importance of criteria that are particularly relevant to this form of wrong. In this way the courts have succeeded in developing the law of vicarious liability so as to ensure that a remedy for the harm caused by abuse is provided by those that should fairly bear that liability.

84. Where those who have abused children have been members of a particular church or religious order and have committed the abuse in the course of carrying out activities in that capacity claimants have had difficulty in establishing the conventional relationship of employer/employee. What has weighed with the courts has been the fact that the relationship has facilitated the commission of the abuse by placing the abusers in a position where they enjoyed both physical proximity to their victims and the influence of authority over them both as teachers and as men of god.

85. The precise criteria for imposing vicarious liability for sexual abuse are still in the course of refinement by judicial decision. Sexual abuse of children may be facilitated in a number of different circumstances. There is currently concern at the possibility that widespread sexual abuse of children may have occurred within the entertainment industry. This case is not concerned with that scenario. It is concerned with the liability of bodies that have, in pursuance of their own interests, caused their employees or persons in a relationship similar to that of employees, to have access to children in circumstances where abuse has been facilitated.

86. Starting with the Canadian authorities a common theme can be traced through most of the cases to which I have referred. Vicarious liability is imposed where a defendant, whose relationship with the abuser put it in a position to use the abuser to carry on its business or to further its own interests, has done so in a manner which has created or significantly enhanced the risk that the victim or victims would suffer the relevant abuse. The essential closeness of connection between the relationship between the defendant and the tortfeasor and the acts of abuse thus involves a strong causative link.

87. These are the criteria that establish the necessary 'close connection' between relationship and abuse. I do not think that it is right to say that creation of risk is simply a policy consideration and not one of the criteria. Creation of risk is not enough, of itself, to give rise to vicarious liability for abuse but it is always likely to be an important element in the facts that give rise to such liability.

This case

88. In this case both the necessary relationship between the brothers and the Institute and the close connection between that relationship and the abuse committed at the school have been made out.

89. The relationship between the brothers and the Institute was much closer to that of employment than the relationship between the priest and the bishop in *JGE*. The Institute was subdivided into a hierarchical structure and conducted its activities as if it were a corporate body. The brothers were subject to the directions as to their employment and the general supervision of the Provincial, their superior within that hierarchical structure. But the relationship was not simply one akin to that of employer and employee. The business and mission of the Institute was the common business and mission of every brother who was a member of it.

90. That business was the provision of a Christian education to boys. It was to achieve that mission that the brothers joined and remained members of the Institute. . . .

92. Living cloistered on the school premises were vulnerable boys. They were triply vulnerable. They were vulnerable because they were children in a school; they were vulnerable because they were virtually prisoners in the school; and they were vulnerable because their personal histories made it even less likely that if they attempted to disclose what was happening to them they would be believed. The brother teachers were placed in the school to care for the educational and religious needs of these pupils. Abusing the boys in their care was diametrically opposed to those objectives but, paradoxically, that very fact was one of the factors that provided the necessary close connection between the abuse and the relationship between the brothers and the Institute that gives rise to vicarious liability on the part of the latter.

93. There was a very close connection between the brother teachers' employment in the school and the sexual abuse that they committed, or must for present purposes be assumed to have committed. There was no Criminal Records Bureau at the time, but the risk of sexual abuse was recognised, as demonstrated by the prohibition on touching the children in the chapter in the Rule dealing with chastity. No doubt the status of a brother was treated by the managers as an assurance that children could safely be entrusted to his care. The placement of brother teachers in St William's, a residential school in the precincts of which they also resided, greatly enhanced the risk of abuse by them if they had a propensity for such misconduct.

94. This is not a borderline case. It is one where it is fair, just and reasonable, by reason of the satisfaction of the relevant criteria, for the Institute to share with the Middlesbrough Defendants vicarious liability for the abuse committed by the brothers. I would allow this appeal.

Mohamud v WM Morrison Supermarkets plc
Supreme Court [2016] UKSC 11

A petrol station attendant assaulted the claimant in a brutal and unprovoked attack while at work. The claimant, who was of Somali origin, entered the kiosk and asked the defendant's employee, Amjid Khan, if it was possible to print off some documents which were stored on a USB stick. Khan responded in an abusive fashion, including racist language. When the claimant left the kiosk he was immediately followed by Khan, who opened the front passenger door and partly entered the claimant's vehicle. The claimant was then subjected to a 'brutal and unprovoked' attack including punches and kicks while he was curled up on the petrol station forecourt. The Supreme Court unanimously held the employer vicariously liable for the employee's attack.

LORD TOULSON (with whom LORD NEUBERGER, LADY HALE, LORD DYSON and LORD REED agreed):

1. Vicarious liability in tort requires, first, a relationship between the defendant and the wrongdoer, and secondly, a connection between that relationship and the wrongdoer's act or default, such as to make it just that the defendant should be held legally responsible to the claimant for the consequences of the wrongdoer's conduct. In this case the wrongdoer was employed by the defendant, and so there is no issue about the first requirement. The issue in the appeal is whether there was sufficient connection between the wrongdoer's employment and his conduct towards the claimant to make the defendant legally responsible. By contrast, the case of *Cox v Ministry of Justice* [2016] UKSC 10, which was heard by the same division of the court at the same time, is concerned with the first requirement. The judgments are separate because the claims and issues are separate, but

they are intended to be complementary to each other in their legal analysis. In preparing this judgment I have had the benefit of Lord Reed's judgment in *Cox*, and I agree fully with his reasoning and
conclusion.

2. The question in this appeal concerns an employer's vicarious liability in tort for an assault carried
out by an employee. It is a subject which has troubled the courts on numerous occasions and the
case law is not entirely consistent. . . .

Origins and development of vicarious liability

10. The development of the doctrine of vicarious liability can be traced to a number of factors; in
part to legal theories, of which there have been several; in part to changes in the structure and size
of economic and other (eg charitable) enterprises; and in part to changes in social attitudes and the
courts' sense of justice and fairness, particularly when faced with new problems such as cases of
sexual abuse of children by people in a position of authority.

25. In 1907 Salmond published the first edition of his text book on the *Law of Torts*. He defined a
wrongful act by a servant in the course of his employment as 'either (a) a wrongful act authorised by
the master or (b) a wrongful and unauthorised *mode* of doing some act authorised by the master',
with the amplification that a master is liable for acts which he has not authorised if they are 'so connected with acts which he has authorised, that they may rightly be regarded as modes—although
improper modes—of doing them' (pp 83–84).

26. Salmond's formula, repeated in later editions, was cited and applied in many cases, sometimes
by stretching it artificially; but even with stretching, it was not universally satisfactory. The difficulties
in its application were particularly evident in cases of injury to persons or property caused by an
employee's deliberate act of misconduct.

Lister v Hesley Hall Ltd

39. In *Lister* the House of Lords was faced with the problem of the application of the doctrine of vicarious liability to the warden of a school boarding house who sexually abused the children in his care. The
Salmond formula was stretched to breaking point. Even on its most elastic interpretation, the sexual
abuse of the children could not be described as a mode, albeit an improper mode, of caring for them.
Drawing on Scarman LJ's approach, Lord Steyn (with whom Lords Hutton and Hobhouse agreed) spoke
of the pitfalls of terminology and said that it was not necessary to ask whether the acts of sexual abuse
were modes of doing authorised acts. He posed the broad question whether the warden's torts was so
closely connected with his employment that it would be just to hold the employers liable. He concluded
that the employers were vicariously liable because they undertook the care of the children through the
warden and he abused them. There was therefore a close connection between his employment and
his tortious acts. To similar effect, Lord Clyde said that the warden had a general duty to look after the
children, and the fact that he abused them did not sever the connection with his employment; his acts
had to be seen in the context that he was entrusted with responsibility for their care, and it was right that
his employers should be liable for the way in which he behaved towards them as warden of the house.

43. In the *Christian Brothers* case Lord Phillips of Worth Matravers said at para 74 that it is not easy
to deduce from *Lister* the precise criteria that will give rise to vicarious liability for sexual abuse (or,
he might have added, other abuse), and that the test of 'close connection' tells one nothing about the
nature of the connection. However, in *Lister* the court was mindful of the risk of over-concentration
on a particular form of terminology, and there is a similar risk in attempting to over-refine, or lay down
a list of criteria for determining, what precisely amounts to a sufficiently close connection to make
it just for the employer to be held vicariously liable. Simplification of the essence is more desirable.

The present law

44. In the simplest terms, the court has to consider two matters. The first question is what functions or 'field of activities' have been entrusted by the employer to the employee, or, in everyday language, what was the nature of his job. As has been emphasised in several cases, this question must be addressed broadly

45. Secondly, the court must decide whether there was sufficient connection between the position in which he was employed and his wrongful conduct to make it right for the employer to be held liable under the principle of social justice which goes back to Holt [CJ in *Boston v Sandford* (1691) 2 Salk 440 [17]]. To try to measure the closeness of connection, as it were, on a scale of 1 to 10, would be a forlorn exercise and, what is more, it would miss the point. The cases in which the necessary connection has been found for Holt's principle to be applied are cases in which the employee used or misused the position entrusted to him in a way which injured the third party. *Lloyd v Grace, Smith & Co*, *Peterson* and *Lister* were all cases in which the employee misused his position in a way which injured the claimant, and that is the reason why it was just that the employer who selected him and put him in that position should be held responsible. By contrast, in *Warren v Henlys Ltd* any misbehaviour by the petrol pump attendant, qua petrol pump attendant, was past history by the time that he assaulted the claimant. The claimant had in the meantime left the scene, and the context in which the assault occurred was that he had returned with the police officer to pursue a complaint against the attendant.

46. Contrary to the primary submission advanced on the claimant's behalf, I am not persuaded that there is anything wrong with the *Lister* approach as such. It has been affirmed many times and I do not see that the law would now be improved by a change of vocabulary. Indeed, the more the argument developed, the less clear it became whether the claimant was advocating a different approach as a matter of substance and, if so, what the difference of substance was.

The present case

47. In the present case it was Mr Khan's job to attend to customers and to respond to their inquiries. His conduct in answering the claimant's request in a foul mouthed way and ordering him to leave was inexcusable but within the 'field of activities' assigned to him. What happened thereafter was an unbroken sequence of events. It was argued by the respondent and accepted by the judge that there ceased to be any significant connection between Mr Khan's employment and his behaviour towards the claimant when he came out from behind the counter and followed the claimant onto the forecourt. I disagree for two reasons. First, I do not consider that it is right to regard him as having metaphorically taken off his uniform the moment he stepped from behind the counter. He was following up on what he had said to the claimant. It was a seamless episode. Secondly, when Mr Khan followed the claimant back to his car and opened the front passenger door, he again told the claimant in threatening words that he was never to come back to the petrol station. This was not something personal between them; it was an order to keep away from his employer's premises, which he reinforced by violence. In giving such an order he was purporting to act about his employer's business. It was a gross abuse of his position, but it was in connection with the business in which he was employed to serve customers. His employers entrusted him with that position and it is just that as between them and the claimant, they should be held responsible for their employee's abuse of it.

48. Mr Khan's motive is irrelevant. It looks obvious that he was motivated by personal racism rather than a desire to benefit his employer's business, but that is neither here nor there.

Notes

1. The House of Lords in **Lister** adopted the reasoning of the Supreme Court of Canada in *Bazley v Curry* [1999] 2 SCR 53. In this case the claimant, Bazley, was sexually abused by a worker in a children's home where he was living. In finding the employer's vicariously liable, the court held that their enterprise had created the risk that produced the tortious act. Accordingly, the court said that the fundamental question is whether the wrongful act is sufficiently related to conduct authorised by the employer to justify the imposition of vicarious liability, and that such liability is generally appropriate where there is sufficient connection between the creation or enhancement of risk and the wrong that accrues therefrom. In relation to intentional torts, the court said that significant linking factors would include: (a) the opportunity that the enterprise afforded the employee to abuse her power; (b) the extent to which the wrongful act may have furthered the employer's aims; (c) the extent to which the wrongful act was related to friction, confrontation or intimacy inherent in the employer's enterprise; (d) the extent of power conferred on the employee in relation to the victim; and (e) the vulnerability of potential victims to wrongful exercise of the employee's power.

2. The *Lister* approach was applied by the House of Lords in *Dubai Aluminium Co Ltd v Salaam* [2002] UKHL 48, a case of commercial fraud. In a judgment which has proved influential in the later cases, Lord Nicholls explained the approach in the following way:

   > 22. [I]t is a fact of life, and therefore to be expected by those who carry on businesses, that sometimes their agents may exceed the bounds of their authority or even defy express instructions. It is fair to allocate the risk of losses thus arising to the businesses rather than to leave those wronged with the sole remedy, of doubtful value, against the individual employee who committed the wrong. To this end, the law has given the concept of 'ordinary course of employment' an extended scope.
   >
   > 23. If, then, authority is not the touchstone, what is? . . . Perhaps the best general answer is that the wrongful conduct must be so closely connected with the acts the partner or employee was authorised to do that, for the purpose of the liability of the firm or the employer to third parties, the wrongful act *may fairly and properly be regarded* as done by the partner while acting in the ordinary course of the firm's business or the employee's employment.

   This was recently glossed by Lord Reed in *Wm Morrison Supermarkets plc v Various Claimants* [2020] UKSC 12:

   > 24. The general principle set out by Lord Nicholls in *Dubai Aluminium*, like many other principles of the law of tort, has to be applied with regard to the circumstances of the case before the court and the assistance provided by previous court decisions. The words 'fairly and properly' are not, therefore, intended as an invitation to judges to decide cases according to their personal sense of justice, but require them to consider how the guidance derived from decided cases furnishes a solution to the case before the court. Judges should therefore identify from the decided cases the factors or principles which point towards or away from vicarious liability in the case before the court, and which explain why it should or should not be imposed. Following that approach, cases can be decided on a basis which is principled and consistent.

3. In *Maga v Birmingham Archdiocese of the Roman Catholic Church* [2010] EWCA Civ 256 the claimant had been sexually abused by a priest as a young boy in the 1970s. The claimant was not a Roman Catholic (and so not a member of the priest's church), but had been befriended by the priest who had employed him to do odd jobs around the church and presbytery. Though acknowledging that the claim was weaker than that in **Lister**, the court unanimously held that abuse had occurred in the course of the priest's employment. There was a sufficiently close connection between the priest's employment at the church and his abuse of the claimant to make it fair, just and reasonable to make his employers vicariously liable (at [55]). In particular, Lord Neuberger MR noted that the priest, known as 'Father Chris' around the parish, was in a position

analogous to that of a parent or carer. He was always dressed in clerical garb and was therefore 'never off duty'. In particular, he had special responsibility for youth work at the church and he was able to develop his relationship with the claimant through activities taking place at the church, allowing him to 'draw the claimant further into his sexually abusive orbit by ostensibly respectable means connected with his employment' (at [48]). Moreover, the Court of Appeal noted that abuse was a known (however undesired) risk of the priest's employment (at [53]).

This case extends *Lister* into uncertain territory. Do you think it successfully avoids the principle in *Heasmans* v *Clarity Cleaning* that merely providing the opportunity to cause the damage does not bring about vicarious liability? See further Jonathan Morgan 'Distorting Vicarious Liability' (2011) 74 MLR 932, which criticises imposing vicarious liability simply on the status of the person who did the act, rather than upon what he is engaged to do.

4. If vicarious liability is 'on the move', Lord Dyson in a short concurring judgment in **Mohamud**, suggested this movement is only in relation to the *relationship* between individual and defendant, not in regard to the *circumstances* when an employer may be held vicariously liable:

> 53. The close connection test has now been repeatedly applied by our courts for some 13 years. In my view, it should only be abrogated or refined if a demonstrably better test can be devised. . . . The attraction of the close connection test is that it is firmly rooted in justice. It asks whether the employee's tort is so closely connected with his employment as to make it just to hold the employer liable.
>
> 54. It is true that the test is imprecise. But this is an area of the law in which, as Lord Nicholls said, imprecision is inevitable. To search for certainty and precision in vicarious liability is to undertake a quest for a chimaera. Many aspects of the law of torts are inherently imprecise. For example, the imprecise concepts of fairness, justice and reasonableness are central to the law of negligence. The test for the existence of a duty of care is whether it is fair, just and reasonable to impose such a duty. The test for remoteness of loss is one of reasonable foreseeability. Questions such as whether to impose a duty of care and whether loss is recoverable are not always easy to answer because they are imprecise. But these tests are now well established in our law. To adopt the words of Lord Nicholls, the court has to make an evaluative judgment in each case having regard to all the circumstances and having regard to the assistance provided by previous decisions on the facts of other cases.
>
> 55. In **Various Claimants v Catholic Child Welfare Society** [2012] UKSC 56; [2013] 2 AC 1 Lord Phillips said, at para 19, 'the law of vicarious liability is on the move'. It is true that there have been developments in the law as to the type of *relationship* that has to exist between an individual and a defendant for vicarious liability to be imposed on the defendant in respect of a tort committed by that individual. These developments have been a response to changes in the legal relationships between enterprises and members of their workforces and the increasing complexity and sophistication of the organisation of enterprises in the modern world. A good example is provided by the facts of the **Catholic Child Welfare Society** case itself.
>
> 56. But there is no need for the law governing the *circumstances* in which an employer should be held vicariously liable for a tort committed by his employee to be on the move. There have been no changes in societal conditions which require such a development. The changes in the case law relating to the definition of the circumstances in which an employer is vicariously liable for the tort of his employee have not been made in response to changing social conditions. Rather they have been prompted by the aim of producing a fairer and more workable test. Unsurprisingly, this basic aim has remained constant. . . . It is difficult to see how the close connection test might be further refined. It is sufficient to say that no satisfactory refinement of the test has been suggested in the present case.

See further Phillip Morgan 'Certainty in Vicarious Liability: A Quest for a Chimaera?' [2016] CLJ 202.

5. The close connection test was considered once more by the Supreme Court in *Wm Morrison Supermarkets plc* v *Various Claimants*. In so doing, the court distanced itself from certain comments in Lord Toulson's judgment in **Mohamud** and, more generally, might be seen as cautioning

against further expansion of the law of vicarious liability. The case concerned a Morrison's employee named Skelton who, in breach, inter alia, of section 4(4) of the Data Protection Act 1998, made publicly available confidential payroll data relating to other Morrison's employees. Though Skelton only had the opportunity to commit the tort as a result of his employment, the court held that Morrison were not vicariously liable for his actions. Vicarious liability is *not* established simply by showing a causal link between the tortfeasor's employment and the torts they then commit. Lord Toulson's description in **Mohamud** (at [47]) of there being 'an unbroken sequence of events' connecting the tortfeasor's employment and the tort they later committed was, so the court held, to be understood as referring not to the mere temporal or causal connection between the relevant events but rather to the 'capacity in which [the employee] was acting when those events took place' (at [28]). Moreover, Lord Toulson's statement that 'motive is irrelevant' (**Mohamud** at [48]) was potentially 'misleading': the question whether the employee 'was acting, albeit wrongly, on his employer's business, or was acting for personal reasons, [is] plainly important' (at [29]).

18.3 Liability for independent contractors

The law has long been that an employer would not be *vicariously* liable for the tortious actions of an independent contractor. As Widgery LJ noted in *Salsbury* v *Woodland and others* [1970] 1 QB 324:

> It is trite law that an employer who employs an independent contractor is not vicariously responsible for the negligence of that contractor. He is not able to control the way in which the independent contractor does the work, and the vicarious obligation of a master for the negligence of his servant does not arise under the relationship of employer and independent contractor. I think that it is entirely accepted that those cases—and there are some—in which an employer has been held liable for injury done by the negligence of an independent contractor are in truth cases where the employer owes a direct duty to the person injured, a duty which he cannot delegate to the contractor on his behalf. (at 336)

However, the development of the 'akin to employment' approach was thought to pose a challenge to this position. While the cases which first heralded this development concerned workers who were not in any contractual relationship with the defendant—and so who were neither employees nor independent contractors—the adoption of the 'akin to employment' approach suggested that the rule that there could be no vicarious liability for the acts of one's independent contractors may no longer hold good. Orthodoxy was, however, reaffirmed by the Supreme Court in *Barclays Bank* v *Various Claimants* [2020] UKSC 13.

The case concerned sexual assaults committed by a doctor whom Barclays had contracted to carry out medical examinations on present or potential Barclays employees. It was accepted that the doctor was an independent contractor and the question was whether Barclays was nonetheless vicariously liable for its doctor's actions. The Supreme Court, reversing the Court of Appeal, held that they were not. Lady Hale confirmed (at [27]):

> The question . . . is, as it has always been, whether the tortfeasor is carrying on business on his own account or whether he is in a relationship akin to employment by the defendant. In doubtful cases, the five 'incidents' identified by Lord Phillips may be helpful in identifying a relationship which is sufficiently

analogous to employment to make it fair, just and reasonable to impose vicarious liability. Although they were enunciated in the context of non-commercial enterprises, they may be relevant in deciding whether workers who may be technically self-employed or agency workers are effectively part and parcel of the employer's business. But the key, as it was in *Christian Brothers*, *Cox* and *Armes*, will usually lie in understanding the details of the relationship. Where it is clear that the tortfeasor is carrying out his own independent business it is not necessary to consider the five incidents.

An employer may also be *personally* liable for harms resulting from the actions of an independent contractor (and others), if the harms result from the breach of a non-delegable duty of care. Non-delegable duties arise in various situations. One example is an employer's duty of care towards their employees, established in *Wilsons & Clyde Coal Co Ltd v English* [1937] UKHL 2, which requires an employer to see that reasonable care is taken for their employees' safety. This duty is non-delegable in nature, which means that it is not enough for the employer themselves to take reasonable care to see that their employees are safe or to discharge their duty by entrusting—delegating—responsibility for the discharge of the duty to another. Rather, their duty is to ensure that reasonable care *is* taken. This means that if the employer delegates the job of seeing that their employees are safe to a third party, the employer will be personally liable if the delegate negligently fails to see that the employees are safe, even if the employer has taken reasonable care in appointing that delegate.

Non-delegable duties also arise in other contexts.

Woodland v Essex County Council
Supreme Court [2013] UKSC 66

The claimant, then aged 10, suffered a serious brain injury following an incident during a swimming lesson at a local pool, provided by professional swimming instructors employed by the school as independent contractors. Unable to rely on vicarious liability (the swimming instructors were not the school's employees) and/or occupier's liability (the school did not control the premises), it was argued (on a strike-out basis) that the school owed the claimant a non-delegable duty of care to ensure that reasonable care was taken of her not only by the school and its employees, but also by any third party with which the school contracted to perform its educational functions. Held: that the school owed the claimant a non-delegable duty of care.

LORD SUMPTION:

Non-delegable duties

3. In principle, liability in tort depends upon proof of a personal breach of duty. To that principle, there is at common law only one true exception, namely vicarious liability. Where a defendant is vicariously liable for the tort of another, he commits no tort himself and may not even owe the relevant duty, but is held liable as a matter of public policy for the tort of the other: *Majrowski v Guy's and St Thomas's NHS Hospital Trust* [2005] QB 848. The boundaries of vicarious liability have been expanded by recent decisions of the courts to embrace tortfeasors who are not employees of the defendant, but stand in a relationship which is sufficiently analogous to employment: *Various Claimants v Catholic Child Welfare Society and Others* [2013] 2 AC 1. But it has never extended to the negligence of those who are truly independent contractors . . .

In what circumstances will a non-delegable duty arise?

25. The courts should be sensitive about imposing unreasonable financial burdens on those providing critical public services. A non-delegable duty of care should be imputed to schools only so far as it would be fair, just and reasonable to do so. But I do not accept that any unreasonable burden would be cast on them by recognising the existence of a non-delegable duty . . . My reasons are as follows:

(1) The criteria themselves are consistent with the long-standing policy of the law, apparent notably in the employment cases, to protect those who are both inherently vulnerable and highly dependent on the observance of proper standards of care by those with a significant degree of control over their lives. Schools are employed to educate children, which they can do only if they are allowed authority over them. That authority confers on them a significant degree of control. When the school's own control is delegated to someone else for the purpose of performing part of the school's own educational function, it is wholly reasonable that the school should be answerable for the careful exercise of its control by the delegate.

(2) Parents are required by law to entrust their child to a school. They do so in reliance on the school's ability to look after them, and generally have no knowledge of or influence over the arrangements that the school may make to delegate specialised functions, or the basis on which they do so, or the competence of the delegates, all of which are matters about which only the school is in a position to satisfy itself.

(3) This is not an open-ended liability, for there are important limitations on the range of matters for which a school or education authority assumes non-delegable duties. They are liable for the negligence of independent contractors only if and so far as the latter are performing functions which the school has assumed for itself a duty to perform, generally in school hours and on school premises (or at other times or places where the school may carry out its educational functions). In the absence of negligence of their own, for example in the selection of contractors, they will not be liable for the negligence of independent contractors where on analysis their own duty is not to perform the relevant function but only to arrange for its performance. They will not be liable for the defaults of independent contractors providing extra-curricular activities outside school hours, such as school trips in the holidays. Nor will they be liable for the negligence of those to whom no control over the child has been delegated, such as bus drivers or the theatres, zoos or museums to which children may be taken by school staff in school hours . . .

(4) It is important to bear in mind that until relatively recently, most of the functions now routinely delegated by schools to independent contractors would have been performed by staff for whom the authority would have been vicariously liable. The recognition of limited non-delegable duties has become more significant as a result of the growing scale on which the educational and supervisory functions of schools are outsourced, but in a longer historical perspective, it does not significantly increase the potential liability of education authorities.

(5) The responsibilities of fee-paying schools are already non-delegable because they are contractual, and the possibility of contracting out of them is limited by legislation. In this particular context, there seems to be no rational reason why the mere absence of consideration should lead to an entirely different result when comparable services are provided by a public authority. A similar point can be made about the technical distinctions that would otherwise arise between privately funded and NHS hospital treatment.

(6) It can fairly be said that the recognition of a non-delegable duty of care owed by schools involves imputing to them a greater responsibility than any which the law presently recognises as being owed by parents. Parents would not normally incur personal liability for the

negligence of (say) a swimming instructor to whom they had handed custody of a child . . . The position of parents is very different to that of schools. Schools provide a service either by contract or pursuant to a statutory obligation, and while LEA schools do not receive fees, their staff and contractors are paid professionals. By comparison, the custody and control which parents exercise over their children is not only gratuitous, but based on an intimate relationship not readily analysable in legal terms. For this reason, the common law has always been extremely cautious about recognising legally enforceable duties owed by parents on the same basis as those owed by institutional carers: see . . . *Barrett v Enfield London Borough Council* [2001] 2 AC 550, 588.

26. In my opinion, on the limited facts pleaded or admitted, the respondent education authority assumed a duty to ensure that the Appellant's swimming lessons were carefully conducted and supervised, by whomever they might get to perform these functions. The Appellant was entrusted to the school for certain essential purposes, which included teaching and supervision. The swimming lessons were an integral part of the school's teaching function. They did not occur on school premises, but they occurred in school hours in a place where the school chose to carry out this part of its functions. The teaching and the supervisory functions of the school, and the control of the child that went with them, were delegated by the school to Mrs Stopford and through her to Ms Burlinson, and probably to Ms Maxwell as well, to the extent necessary to enable them to give swimming lessons. The alleged negligence occurred in the course of the very functions which the school assumed an obligation to perform and delegated to its contractors. It must follow that if the latter were negligent in performing those functions and the child was injured as a result, the educational authority is in breach of duty.

LADY HALE:

28. The common law is a dynamic instrument. It develops and adapts to meet new situations as they arise. Therein lies its strength. But therein also lies a danger, the danger of unbridled and unprincipled growth to match what the court perceives to be the merits of the particular case. So it must proceed with caution, incrementally by analogy with existing categories, and consistently with some underlying principle (see *Caparo Industries plc v Dickman* [1990] 2 AC 605). But the words used by judges in explaining why they are deciding as they do are not be treated as if they were the words of statute, setting the rules in stone and precluding further principled development should new situations arise . . .

29. It is also important, so far as possible, that the distinctions produced by this process make sense to ordinary people. They should not, as Lord Steyn observed in *White v Chief Constable of South Yorkshire Police* [1999] 2 AC 455, 495, produce 'an imbalance in the law of tort which might perplex the man on the underground'. . . . [T]he public might well be perplexed if one pupil could sue her school for injuries sustained during a negligently conducted swimming lesson but another could not.

30. Consider the cases of three 10-year-old children, Amelia, Belinda and Clara. Their parents are under a statutory duty to ensure that they receive efficient full-time education suitable to their age, ability and aptitude, and to any special needs they may have (Education Act 1996, section 7). Amelia's parents send her to a well-known and very expensive independent school. Swimming lessons are among the services offered and the school contracts with another school which has its own swimming pool to provide these. Belinda's parents send her to a large school run by a local education authority which employs a large sports staff to service its schools, including swimming teachers and life-guards.

Clara's parents send her to a small state-funded faith school which contracts with an independent service provider to provide swimming lessons and life-guards for its pupils. All three children are injured during a swimming lesson as a result (it must be assumed) of the carelessness either of the swimming teachers or of the life-guards or of both. Would the man on the underground be perplexed to learn that Amelia and Belinda can each sue their own school for compensation but Clara cannot? . . .

32. As lawyers, we know that the three girls fall into three different legal categories. Amelia (we will assume) has the benefit of a contractual obligation of the school to secure that care be taken for her safety. Belinda has the benefit of the rule which makes an employer vicariously liable for the negligence of its employees. Clara has the benefit of neither and can only succeed if the school has an obligation to secure that care be taken for her safety.

34. No-one in this case has seriously questioned that if a hospital patient is injured as a result of a nurse's carelessness it matters whether the nurse is employed by the hospital or by an agency; or if a pupil at school is injured by a teacher it matters whether the teacher is employed by the school or is self-employed. Yet these are not employees of the hospital or school, nor can it be said that their relationship with the school is 'akin to employment' in the sense in which the relationship of the individual Christian Brothers to their Order was akin to employment in the case of *Various Claimants v Catholic Child Welfare Society and Others* [2012] UKSC 56 . . . The reason why the hospital or school is liable is that the hospital has undertaken to care for the patient, and the school has undertaken to teach the pupil, and that responsibility is not discharged simply by choosing apparently competent people to do it. The hospital or school remains personally responsible to see that care is taken in doing it.

Notes

1. The parties in **Woodland** returned to court in February 2015, nearly 15 years after the accident, to determine the primary facts on which the negligence claim depended (*Woodland* v *Maxwell and Essex County Council* [2015] EWHC 273 (QB)). The court held that both the swimming teacher and lifeguard had fallen below the standard of care expected of them and that, following the Supreme Court's ruling, Essex County Council was, as a result, in breach of their non-delegable duty of care towards the claimant.

> BLAKE J:
>
> **52.** The question then is whether, on these primary findings of fact, the actions and omissions of either Ms Burlinson [the swimming teacher] or Ms Maxwell [the lifeguard] fell below that which could reasonably be expected of them as teacher and lifeguard responsible for the school swimming lesson of a group of 10 year olds?
>
> **53.** I accept the timing is tight and those supervising swimming lessons cannot be expected to spot every incident and respond instantly. The children did not enter the water until after 10.45 and Ms Burlinson may well be right in her original estimate of 10.48. I was unimpressed by her evidence that the timing of 10.48 was intended to refer to when the children were waiting for the lesson to begin at the shallow end of the pool. The note is clear that this was when the children were instructed to enter the water.
>
> **54.** Working backwards from when the ambulance was called at 10.54, it is likely that the rescue had begun and Annie [the claimant] was out of the water, two minutes or so earlier. It is possible that she was in the water for three to four minutes, and she could not have been in the water for longer than six minutes, even making due allowance for potential uncertainties in the assessment of the chronology. However, this time range can accommodate all the events described above: a 20 second swim, a 30 second period of taking in water and the onset of hypoxia, some seconds for an attempted child rescue, Ms Burlinson identifying Annie in the water, lifting her chin and then calling for help.

55. I am driven to the conclusion that for her to fail to notice a pupil in difficulties in the water for more than 30 seconds, falls below the standard of care reasonably to be expected of a teacher. Apart from possibly having to remonstrate with some pupils who exited the pool too early, she had no legitimate distractions to explain this period of time. Her estimate of how long Annie was in the water overall is seriously adrift of the realities of the situation. It is not possible to determine why her attention was deflected from her pupils who were in the water and the one pupil who was in difficulties there, but I am satisfied that it was deflected and the opportunity for an earlier response was missed.

56. Debbie Maxwell was considerably further away from Annie. If she was at the shallow end of the pool when Ms Burlinson's group entered the water, this is not the best place for a lifeguard to scan the entry into the water of the pupils. She then moved half way down the right side of the pool, which would be a better place to keep the pool under observation overall. Once Zoe Dean's class had started, as her pupils were the less strong swimmers, it would be reasonable for the lifeguard to be situated on that side of the pool and give those pupils particular attention.

57. However, the lifeguard is there to keep an eye on all pool users, and one might have expected the deep end of the pool to be the place where observation needed to be maintained. It was common ground that entry to the water is a particular time of danger for children. There was sufficient time available for her to have performed her functions effectively despite the distance away. There was some urgency in the situation when she realised that the children had entered the water before she climbed the lifeguard chair. A lifeguard needs to remain alert to dangers, focused on the users of the pool, and keeping constant observation and intervening if necessary. If a rescue is to be effected she is the person who is trained to undertake it and whose role it is to do so. I am satisfied that her failure to observe Annie until her attention was drawn to her by Mrs Beecham, either at the same time as or shortly before Zoe Dean reached Ms Burlinson, is indicative of a failure to perform her role to the reasonable standard to be expected. Although I cannot be sure that Ms Burlinson blew her whistle as she claims, she certainly shouted across the pool to Ms. Dean. This was not heard or noticed by Ms Maxwell. All in all, I conclude that she was not paying sufficient attention to users in the water on the other side of the pool at the material time.

58. If she had spotted Annie within seconds of her getting into difficulties, she could have raised the alarm and started the rescue process even if Ms Burlinson's attention was distracted elsewhere. The lifeguard's duties are an additional safety feature intended to be distinct from the responsibilities arising from taking a class. Her failure therefore significantly contributed to the passage of time before Annie was seen and rescue effected.

59. In the event I find that both Debbie Maxwell and Paula Burlinson were negligent and as a consequence the third defendant [the local education authority] is liable for their negligence. The claimant therefore succeeds on this trial of liability as these failures of the duty of care caused or materially contributed to Annie's injuries.

2. Damages had reportedly been assessed earlier at £3 million. A later judgment found the lifeguard should contribute one-third to the third defendant's liabilities to the claimant both in respect of damage and legal costs. Essex County Council did not seek a contribution from the swimming teacher, who was uninsured at the time of the accident (*Woodland* v *Maxwell and Essex County Council* [2015] EWHC 820 (QB)).

3. In *Armes* v *Nottinghamshire County Council* [2017] UKSC 60, discussed in section 18.1, the Supreme Court rejected an argument that the authority owed a non-delegable duty to the children in its care, such as would make the authority personally liable for the abuses carried out by the foster parents. The court concluded that such a duty would come into conflict with the authority's duty to act in the best interests of children in its care. The child's best interests would sometimes require allowing them to stay with their families or friends. Yet, if the authority was to be liable for the tortious acts of those family members and friends, its own interest in avoiding liability would steer it away from allowing the children to stay with them.

19

Damages for death and personal injuries

The law relating to damages for personal injuries is a large and complicated subject, and only a few of the topics contained within it can be dealt with here, and even then only in outline. The object of this chapter is to give some idea of what damages are awarded for in tort law and how they are calculated, as well as some of the criticisms and problems that such calculations often raise.

19.1 Types of action for damages

Where a living claimant sues, the award will usually be for a lump sum to compensate for such matters as loss of future income, medical and care costs, pain, suffering and loss of amenity (PSLA). This once and for all payment has the advantage of finality and continues to be preferred by many claimants, but there may be occasions where it is inappropriate. Accordingly, the court can in the alternative now order that the damages should be paid by way of periodic payments, and in cases where medical prognosis is uncertain there can be an interim payment. Furthermore, claimants may prefer to negotiate a structured settlement which essentially is a lump sum converted to an annuity. Apart from longer term stability and predictability, this has considerable tax advantages.

Where a person dies as the result of a tort there are two methods of claiming damages and their interrelationship can be complicated. First, there is an action for personal injuries by the deceased through their estate under the Law Reform (Miscellaneous Provisions) Act 1934. Secondly, there can be an action by the dependants of the deceased under section 1 of the Fatal Accidents Act 1976 for the extent to which they were dependent on the deceased. This is independent of the action by the estate (*Reader* v *Molesworths* [2007] 3 All ER 108): the dependants sue for their *own* loss, although their right to sue is conditional upon the deceased having had a right of action. There can be an action both by the estate and by the dependants for their separate losses. Note also that any damages received by the estate will be distributed according to the deceased's will (or on the deceased's intestacy), and the money may not have been left to the dependants. In addition, section 1A of the Fatal Accidents Act also allows a claim for 'bereavement' by certain closely related parties, currently set at £15,120.

DAMAGES ACT 1996

2. Periodical payments

(1) A court awarding damages for future pecuniary loss in respect of personal injury—

(a) may order that the damages are wholly or partly to take the form of periodical payments, and

(b) shall consider whether to make that order.

(2) A court awarding other damages in respect of personal injury may, if the parties consent, order that the damages are wholly or partly to take the form of periodical payments.

(3) A court may not make an order for periodical payments unless satisfied that the continuity of payment under the order is reasonably secure.

Notes

1. This section of the Damages Act 1996 was amended by the Courts Act 2003 and allows for a periodic payment order in relation to future income loss without the consent of the parties. An order is 'reasonably secure' if: (a) there is a Financial Services Compensation Scheme set up under section 213 of the Financial Services and Markets Act 2000; or (b) a minister has provided a guarantee in relation to a designated body under section 6 of the Damages Act 1996; or (c) the defendant is a government or health service body. The Damages (Variation of Periodical Payments) Order 2005, SI 2005/841, allows for an order to be varied at a later date under certain conditions, such as a later serious deterioration in the claimant's condition or the onset of disease connected to the original injury (or, conversely, improvement in the claimant's position).

2. A periodic payment includes a structured settlement which is an arrangement whereby a claimant purchases an annuity from an insurance company with the damages they have been awarded or are entitled to. It works in the same way as any insurance policy whereby the insurer agrees to make a regular payment to the insured. If the policy is to last for the life of the claimant, the insurance company will make the usual actuarial assessments of his life expectancy. The advantage of a structured settlement is the tax benefit, but in negotiations with the insurance company as to the amount of the annuity some of this benefit may well accrue to them rather than to the claimant. See generally the Law Commission *Structured Settlements and Interim and Provisional Damages* (Law Com No 224, 1994).

SENIOR COURTS ACT 1981

32A. Orders for provisional damages for personal injuries

(1) This section applies to an action for damages for personal injuries in which there is proved or admitted to be a chance that at some definite or indefinite time in the future the injured person will, as a result of the act or omission which gave rise to the cause of action, develop some serious disease or suffer some serious deterioration in his physical or mental condition.

(2) Subject to subsection (4) below, as regards any action for damages to which this section applies in which a judgment is given in the High Court, provision may be made by rules of court for enabling the court, in such circumstances as may be prescribed, to award the injured person—

(a) damages assessed on the assumption that the injured person will not develop the disease or suffer the deterioration in his condition; and

(b) further damages at a future date if he develops the disease or suffers the deterioration.. . .

(3) Nothing in this section shall be construed—

(a) as affecting the exercise of any power relating to costs, including any power to make rules of court relating to costs; or

(b) as prejudicing any duty of the court under any enactment or rule of law to reduce or limit the total damages which would have been recoverable apart from any such duty.

LAW REFORM (MISCELLANEOUS PROVISIONS) ACT 1934

1. Effect of death on certain causes of action

(1) Subject to the provisions of this section, on the death of any person after the commencement of this Act all causes of action subsisting against or vested in him shall survive against, or, as the case may be, for the benefit of, his estate. Provided that this subsection shall not apply to causes of action for defamation. . . .

(2) The right of a person to claim under section 1A of the Fatal Accidents Act 1976 (bereavement) shall not survive for the benefit of his estate on his death.

(3) Where a cause of action survives as aforesaid for the benefit of the estate of a deceased person, the damages recoverable for the benefit of the estate of that person—

    (a) shall not include:

        any exemplary damages;

        any damages for loss of income in respect of any period after that person's death.

    (b) [repealed]

    (c) where the death of that person has been caused by the act or omission which gives rise to the cause of action, shall be calculated without reference to any loss or gain to his estate consequent on his death, except that a sum in respect of funeral expenses may be included.

(4) [Repealed]

(5) Where damage has been suffered by reason of any act or omission in respect of which a cause of action would have subsisted against any person if that person had not died before or at the same time as the damage was suffered, there shall be deemed, for the purposes of this Act, to have been subsisting against him before his death such cause of action in respect of that act or omission as would have subsisted if he had died after the damage was suffered.

(6) The rights conferred by this Act for the benefit of the estates of deceased persons shall be in addition to and not in derogation of any rights conferred on the dependants of deceased persons by the Fatal Accidents Act 1976, and so much of this Act as relates to causes of action against the estates of deceased persons shall apply in relation to causes of action under the said Act as it applies in relation to other causes of action not expressly excepted from the operation of subsection (1) of this section.

(7) In the event of the insolvency of an estate against which proceedings are maintainable by virtue of this section, any liability in respect of the cause of action in respect of which the proceedings are maintainable shall be deemed to be a debt provable in the administration of the estate, notwithstanding that it is a demand in the nature of unliquidated damages arising otherwise than by a contract, promise or breach of trust.

Notes

1. The question of 'lost years' has caused considerable difficulty. This refers to the years the claimant would have lived but for the act of the defendant. If the claimant's estate sues under the 1934 Act, damages for those lost years are not recoverable. Instead, the dependants will have an action under the Fatal Accidents Act 1976 for the years they would have been supported by the deceased had they remained alive. However, if a victim sues while still alive they *are* able to recover for the lost years, because in those circumstances the dependants will not have an action and the damages for the lost years will be needed to support them after the claimant's death.

FATAL ACCIDENTS ACT 1976

1. Right of action for wrongful act causing death

(1) If death is caused by any wrongful act, neglect or default which is such as would (if death had not ensued) have entitled the person injured to maintain an action and recover damages in respect thereof, the person who would have been liable if death had not ensued shall be liable to an action for damages, notwithstanding the death of the person injured.

(2) Subject to section 1A(2) below, every such action shall be for the benefit of the dependants of the person ('the deceased') whose death has been so caused.

(3) In this Act 'dependant' means—

    (a)   the wife or husband or former wife or husband of the deceased;

    (aa) the civil partner or former civil partner of the deceased;

    (b)   any person who—

        (i)   was living with the deceased in the same household immediately before the date of the death; and

        (ii) had been living with the deceased in the same household for at least two years before that date; and

        (iii) was living during the whole of that period as the husband or wife or civil partner of the deceased;

    (c)   any parent or other ascendant of the deceased;

    (d)   any person who was treated by the deceased as his parent;

    (e)   any child or other descendant of the deceased;

    (f)   any person (not being a child of the deceased) who, in the case of any marriage to which the deceased was at any time a party, was treated by the deceased as a child of the family in relation to that marriage;

    (fa) any person (not being a child of the deceased) who, in the case of any civil partnership in which the deceased was at any time a civil partner, was treated by the deceased as a child of the family in relation to that civil partnership;

    (g)   any person who is, or is the issue of, a brother, sister, uncle or aunt of the deceased.

(4) The reference to the former wife or husband of the deceased in subsection (3)(a) above includes a reference to a person whose marriage to the deceased has been annulled or declared void as well as a person whose marriage to the deceased has been dissolved.

(4A) The reference to the former civil partner of the deceased in subsection (3)(aa) above includes a reference to a person whose civil partnership with the deceased has been annulled as well as a person whose civil partnership with the deceased has been dissolved.

(5) In deducing any relationship for the purposes of subsection (3) above—

    (a)   any relationship by marriage or civil partnership shall be treated as a relationship by consanguinity, any relationship of the half blood as a relationship of the whole blood, and the stepchild of any person as his child, and

    (b)   an illegitimate person shall be treated as—

        (i)   in the legitimate child of his mother and reputed father, or

        (ii) in the case of a person who has a female parent by virtue of section 43 of the Human Fertilisation and Embryology Act 2008, the legitimate child of his mother and that female parent.

(6) Any reference in this Act to injury includes any disease and any impairment of a person's physical or mental condition.

1A. Bereavement

(1) An action under this Act may consist of or include a claim for damages for bereavement.

(2) A claim for damages for bereavement shall only be for the benefit—

    (a)   of the wife or husband or civil partner of the deceased; and

    (aa) of the cohabiting partner of the deceased; and

    (b)   where the deceased was a minor who was never married or a civil partner—

        (i)   of his parents, if he was legitimate; and

        (ii) of his mother, if he was illegitimate.

(2A) In subsection (2) 'cohabiting partner' means any person who—

    (a)   was living with the deceased in the same household immediately before the date of the death; and

    (b)   had been living with the deceased in the same household for at least two years before that date; and

    (c)   was living during the whole of that period as the wife or husband or civil partner of the deceased.

(3) Subject to subsection (5) below, the sum to be awarded as damages under this section shall be £15,120.

(4) Where there is a claim for damages under subsection (2)(a) and (aa), or under subsection (2)(b) for the benefit of more than one person, the sum awarded shall be divided equally between them (subject to any deduction falling to be made in respect of costs not recovered from the defendant).

(5) The Lord Chancellor may by order made by statutory instrument, subject to annulment in pursuance of a resolution of either House of Parliament, amend this section by varying the sum for the time being specified in subsection (3) above.

2. Persons entitled to bring the action

(1) The action shall be brought by and in the name of the executor or administrator of the deceased.

(2) If—

    (a)   there is no executor or administrator of the deceased, or

    (b)   no action is brought within six months after the death by and in the name of an executor or administrator of the deceased,the action may be brought by and in the name of all or any of the persons for whose benefit an executor or administrator could have brought it.

(3) Not more than one action shall lie for and in respect of the same subject matter of complaint.

(4) The plaintiff in the action shall be required to deliver to the defendant or his solicitor full particulars of the persons for whom and on whose behalf the action is brought and of the nature of the claim in respect of which damages are sought to be recovered.

3. Assessment of damages

(1) In the action such damages, other than damages for bereavement, may be awarded as are proportioned to the injury resulting from the death to the dependants respectively.

(2) After deducting the costs not recovered from the defendant any amount recovered otherwise than as damages for bereavement shall be divided among the dependants in such shares as may be directed.

(3) In an action under this Act where there fall to be assessed damages payable to a widow in respect of the death of her husband there shall not be taken account the re-marriage of the widow or her prospects of re-marriage.

(4) In an action under this Act where there fall to be assessed damages payable to a person who is a dependant by virtue of section 1(3)(b) above in respect of the death of the person with whom the dependant was living as husband or wife or civil partner there shall be taken into account (together with any other matter that appears to the court to be relevant to the action) the fact that the dependant had no enforceable right to financial support by the deceased as a result of their living together.

(5) If the dependants have incurred funeral expenses in respect of the deceased, damages may be awarded in respect of those expenses.

(6) Money paid into court in satisfaction of a cause of action under this Act may be in one sum without specifying any person's share.

4. Assessment of damages: disregard of benefits

In assessing damages in respect of a person's death in an action under this Act, benefits which have accrued or will or may accrue to any person from his estate or otherwise as a result of his death shall be disregarded.

5. Contributory negligence

Where any person dies as the result partly of his own fault and partly of the fault of any other person or persons, and accordingly if an action were brought for the benefit of the estate under the Law Reform (Miscellaneous Provisions) Act 1934 the damages recoverable would be reduced under section 1(1) of the Law Reform (Contributory Negligence) Act 1945, any damages recoverable in an action under this Act shall be reduced to a proportionate extent.

Notes

1. Section 32A of the Senior Courts Act 1981 is intended for the cases where liability is clear but the medical prognosis is not. In that situation the claimant may apply for the loss known at the time of the trial and return to court for a further award if their condition deteriorates as a result of the tort. By rule 25.7 of the Civil Procedure Rules (CPR) 1998, the section only applies if: (a) the defendant has admitted liability; or (b) the claimant has obtained judgment for damages to be assessed; or (c) if the action proceeded to trial the claimant would obtain substantial damages. Furthermore, the defendant must either (a) be insured or (b) be a public authority. Where a claimant has been awarded provisional damages and subsequently dies within three years of the original cause of action arising, then the dependants may still claim under the Fatal Accidents Act 1976.

Notes

1. In 1999 the Law Commission proposed a number of reforms of the Fatal Accidents Act (*Claims for Wrongful Death*, Law Com No 263). It recommended that the present structure should remain, but with the following amendments.

   (a) *Who can claim?* The fixed list in section 1 would remain but with the addition of a general clause to cover anyone who 'was being wholly or partly maintained by the deceased immediately before the death or who would, but for the death, have been so maintained at a time beginning after the death'.

   (b) *Prospects of remarriage.* See note 2 below.

(c) *Collateral benefits.* A new section would specify that in addition to benefits accruing from the estate, insurance money, pensions and gifts should also not be deducted.

(d) *Bereavement.* See note 3 below.

2. *Prospects of remarriage.* Section 3(3) states that the chances of a widow remarrying are not to be taken into account in assessing damages. This rule was introduced because it was felt to be disparaging for a woman but not, it seems, a man to be judged with a view to her eligibility in the marriage market. This approach is both dated and paternalistic, and has led to some absurd consequences. In *Thompson* v *Price* [1973] 2 All ER 846, for example, the widow had already re-married before the trial, a fact ignored in assessing damages, which meant she received damages for the support she would have received from the deceased, even though her new husband was now legally obliged to support her. Moreover, a woman's chances of remarriage *can* be taken into account when assessing the children's damages as can the husband's chances of marrying again where the deceased is his wife. Finally, the Act, while including civil partners as dependants (s 1(3)), does not mention this in the same context.

The Law Commission recommended that prospects of remarriage should be taken into account only where at the time of the trial the dependant had actually remarried, or was engaged to marry or had entered into financially supportive cohabitation (at [4.53]). Equally, prospects of divorce or separation should not be taken into account unless at the time of the death the parties were not living in the same household, or one of the parties was petitioning for divorce, separation or nullity. An amendment was drafted to bring this recommendation into effect, though it was abandoned by the Coalition Government in January 2011.

A related problem is whether a widow's prospects of earning should be taken into account. Should a widow of 25 who has no children be provided with the equivalent of income for the rest of her life, even though she is able to earn for herself? In fact, such issues are ignored (see **Howitt v Heads** [1973] 1 QB 64).

3. *Bereavement.* The statute now provides for a fixed sum of £15,120 for bereavement (last updated 2020). One function of this is to provide damages where no other loss is apparent. Thus, in the case of the death of a young child this will be the only loss. There has been much criticism by parents in such cases that this grossly undervalues a life, but the fact remains that the purpose of damages is to compensate for a pecuniary loss, and such parents have in fact suffered no monetary loss.

The Law Commission found that the function of bereavement damages is 'to compensate, in so far as a standardised award of money can, grief, sorrow and the loss of non-pecuniary benefits of the deceased's care, guidance and society'. It suggested that the standard award should be index-linked. Those entitled to the payment would be a spouse (and presumably now civil partner), a parent, a child, a brother or sister, a person engaged to be married and cohabitants (including persons of the same sex) for at least two years. Where more than one person would be entitled the maximum payable by the defendant would be £30,000, index-linked. If there were more than three claimants they would share pro rata.

4. In *Swift* v *Secretary of State for Justice* [2013] EWCA Civ 193, the Court of Appeal held that the rule in section 1(3)(b) that a person must have cohabited with the deceased for at least two years in order to claim as a dependant is a valid provision and does not violate Article 8 European Convention on Human Rights (ECHR).

5. In *Smith* v *Lancashire Teaching Hospitals NHS Trust and another* [2016] EWHC 2208 (QB), the High Court was asked to consider whether the Article 8 ECHR rights (respect for private and family life) of cohabitees were engaged by their non-inclusion in the list of those entitled to claim bereavement damages. While deciding that Article 8 was not directly engaged, the court found no legal justification for maintaining the distinction (which seems particularly strange given that cohabitees may sue under other provisions of the legislation) and called for the law to be reviewed. Later, in *Smith* v *Lancashire Teaching Hospitals NHS Foundation Trust and others* [2017] EWCA Civ 1916, the Court of Appeal found that the exclusion of unmarried cohabiting couples

from bereavement claims is contrary to their rights under Articles 8 and 14 ECHR. As a response, the government published the Fatal Accidents Act 1976 (Remedial) Order 2020, SI 2020/1023, which inserted sections 1A(2)(aa) and 1A(2A) into the Act.

6. For a different perspective on bereavement damages, consider Atiyah's view that they are 'highly objectionable' in principle (Peter Cane *Atiyah's Accidents, Compensation and the Law* (7th edn, CUP, 2006), p 90).

7. Note that the range of potential claimants who may claim bereavement under the 1976 Act is narrower than the range of 'victims' who might claim for violation of Article 2 ECHR under the Human Rights Act 1998 (*Rabone* v *Pennine Care NHS Trust* [2012] UKSC 2).

8. Section 1(5)(b) was amended to include provision (ii) by the Marriage (Same Sex Couples) Act 2013 (Consequential and Contrary Provisions and Scotland) Order 2014, SI 2014/560.

9. The Court of Appeal has ruled (*Simmons* v *Castle* [2012] EWCA Civ 1039) that from 1 April 2013 all damages should be uplifted by 10 per cent, to take account of changes to legal aid and the rules relating to costs introduced by Part 2 of the Legal Aid, Sentencing and Punishment of Offenders Act (LASPO) 2012. The Lord Chief Justice said: '[we] declare that, with effect from 1 April 2013, the proper level of general damages for (i) pain, suffering and loss of amenity in respect of personal injury, (ii) nuisance, (iii) defamation and (iv) all other torts which cause suffering, inconvenience or distress to individuals, will be 10% higher than previously' (at [20]).

19.2 Calculation of loss of earnings and other losses

This is the most difficult part of the subject, as the principles involved are wholly unscientific, and assessments are made on the basis of assumptions which need to be explained. The problem is the need to calculate a future, permanent, income stream artificially as a lump sum, and the situation is the same in the case of both fatal accident cases and claims by living claimants.

The objective of an award of damages is to 'put the claimant in the position they would have been in had it not been for the tort of the defendant' so, in terms of lost earnings, to provide the equivalent of the income which would have been received by the claimant (whether for the victim or the dependants of a deceased victim) for the period during which they are unable to earn (or suffers a loss of earning capacity if still alive) due to the tort committed by the defendant. For living claimants, as well as lost income, additional ongoing costs (e.g. healthcare, specialist equipment, help in the home etc) incurred as a result of the tort can be claimed as part of the lump sum. There are three steps in the determination of this.

(1) Calculation of the length of time (in years) for which the earnings have been lost, or, in a fatal accident case, the period during which the dependants would have been supported by the deceased (the 'multiplier').

(2) Calculation of the amount of loss, or the dependency, in weekly, monthly or annual terms (the 'multiplicand').

(3) Calculation of the present capital lump-sum value of that future loss.

It is the third step which produces the problems: you do not simply multiply the amount of the loss by the number of years for which it will occur, because when you give the claimant (or their dependants) a lump sum they will be able to earn interest on that money, and that must be taken into account. Thus, if a claimant has lost £10,000 per year for ten years, they would be overcompensated if awarded £100,000, for they would be able to earn, say, £2,000 per year interest on this sum. What is needed is to work out a capital sum from which the person can, after investing it, withdraw £10,000 per year, and which will be exhausted at the end of the period of loss. What this sum will be will depend to a great extent on the assumed rate of interest gained on the capital sum, the 'discount rate', which was for many years set at 2.5 per cent on the basis that this is approximately what might be gained on top of inflation. In 2017, however, the Lord Chancellor announced a change to the discount rate in the wake of lower returns on investments as a result, in part, of the banking crisis and global financial downturn, which meant that without significant risk to investments, a return of 2.5 per cent had become difficult to achieve. In order that claimants receiving lump sum damages were not negatively affected in this financial climate, the discount rate was changed to –0.75 per cent. Responding to claims of over-compensation and increased pressure on public services (e.g. the NHS) with large personal injury liabilities, in August 2019 this was raised to –0.25 per cent.

In practice, judges use a 'multiplier'. This is the figure which, when multiplied by the amount of annual loss (the 'multiplicand'), will produce a capital sum from which the amount of the loss may be drawn (net of tax) for the period of loss. For example, in **Howitt v Heads** [1973] 1 QB 64 the loss was assessed at £936 per year for 40 years, and the judge awarded a capital sum of £16,848, that is 18 times the annual loss. The figure 18 was chosen because if the capital sum (18 × 936) was invested at about 5 per cent expected return (as might have been expected at that time), then £936 could be drawn out of the fund each year for 40 years. Another way to explain the multiplier is to say that if A gives B £18 he should be able to draw out £1 per year for 40 years, assuming that it is invested at about 5 per cent net of tax.

The actual multiplier selected will also be affected by other uncertainties about the future: for example, a slight reduction will be made for what are called 'the vicissitudes of life'; that is, the chance that the claimant will not survive for the period of the loss or that some other injury will occur to the claimant. In the past calculating these chances was often a matter of intuition and guesswork but now, by virtue of section 10 of the Civil Evidence Act 1995, actuarial tables prepared by the government's actuaries (the 'Ogden Tables') may be used in assessing the chance of future risks materialising.

Howitt v Heads is given as a simple example of the application of the Fatal Accidents Act and of the calculation of the multiplier.

Howitt v Heads
Queen's Bench Division [1973] 1 QB 64

The claimant was a widow aged 21 with a young son, who was suing under the Fatal Accidents Act 1976 for the loss of her husband. The dependency was calculated at £936 per year for a period of 40 years. Held: neither prospects of remarriage nor of the claimant being able to earn should be taken into account, and a multiplier of 18 should be applied, giving lump sum damages of £16,848.

CUMMING-BRUCE J: On the basis of that dependency [of £18 per week] I approach the next problem, which is the problem of the capital sum which fairly represents the injury to the wife occurring from the death. I have to do it with rather less guidance from authority than has for many years been possible in fatal accident cases, as a consequence of the new situation flowing from the effect of section 4(1) of the Law Reform (Miscellaneous Provisions) Act 1971. Here is a young lady now, I think, 21, with one child. Her prospects of remarriage are not to be taken into account. The situation as I see it is this: on the wife's evidence it is likely, being evidently a lady of ability, that when it is convenient for her to make suitable arrangements for their son, she probably will at some stage—perhaps when the boy starts going to school—resume employment, not only to have the advantage of the money, but also because obviously it is likely to make life more interesting for her. And so, peering into the future, I envisage a situation in which it is likely that after a period of years, probably not very far ahead, she will resume employment and make a good deal of money every week as a result. That, of course, is upon the contingency that she does not remarry with all the implications that that might have—implications which I have to leave out of account.

What is the correct approach in a Fatal Accidents Act case to the situation of a widow who has an earning capacity which she will probably use after a fairly short period of years? As far as I know there is no explicit authority in English cases, though there is a good deal of authority to the effect that a wife's private means are not to be taken into account. There is a useful discussion in the well known textbook of *Kemp and Kemp, The Quantum of Damages*, 2nd ed, vol 2 (1962), p 272, upon the relevance or otherwise of a widow's capacity to support herself, and there have been two cases in Australia, which were approved in the High Court of Australia, dealing with the matter: see *Carroll v Purcell* (1927) 35 ALJR 384. And in *Goodger v Knapman* [1924] SASR 347 (and I rely on the citation from that case given in the textbook to which I have referred) Murray CJ said, at p 358: 'Mr Thomson asked me to make a further reduction by reason of the widow being relieved from the heavier part of her domestic duties, and thereby set free to go out and earn something on her own account. I do not accede to the suggestion, as I am unable to see how liberty to work can reasonably be brought within the description of a pecuniary advantage she has derived from the death of her husband. Any money she might earn would be the result of her labour, not of his death.' The same decision was made by Wolff J in Western Australia in *Usher v Williams* (1955) 60 WALR 69, 80:

> The argument for the diminution of the claim by some allowance of the widow's earning potential proceeds on the theory that the husband's death has released a flood of earning capacity. . . .. In my opinion the plaintiff's ability to earn is not a gain resulting from the death of her husband within the principle established by *Davies v Powell Duffryn Collieries Ltd* [1942] AC 601. The widow's ability to work was always there and she could perhaps, as many women do—particularly in professions—have preferred to work after marriage. The same argument that is put forward for the defendants could be applied to any woman who goes out to work through necessity to support herself and her children following her husband's death; and if it can be applied to the widow there is no reason why it should not be used to diminish or extinguish the children's claims in a case where, by her efforts, she is able to support them as well as her husband did in his lifetime. . . .. I therefore hold that the widow's earning capacity is not to be taken into account in diminution of damages.

I agree with the principle enunciated in those cases and I follow them. I therefore make no deduction in respect of the widow's capacity to earn, even though I am satisfied as a matter of probability that she will fairly soon be obtaining a significant degree of financial independence. . . .

The exercise upon which I embark, in seeking to capitalise her loss therefore, has two elements of some artificiality, but by statute I consider that I am bound to postulate one artificiality and on principle, having regard to the approach of the court to the widow's own capacity to earn, I think it is my duty to introduce the second artificiality. Having regard to the age and good health of the husband, subject to what is commonly described as the changes and chances of life, he had a prospect of remunerative employment of not less than 40 years, and having regard to the lady's health and youth, her expectation of life is at least as good as his. And so, subject as I say to changes and chances of the unknown future, this widow has been deprived of the prospect of a settled and stable financial future afforded by her husband over a period of some 40 years.

Mr Cobb put in, as an aid to testing the effect of an award of £15,000 some tables showing what the effect would be if such a sum was invested to yield either 3 per cent or 4 per cent and I approach the case on the basis of the guidance given in the House of Lords in *Taylor v O'Connor* [1971] AC 115. I cite in particular a passage from the speech of Lord Pearson, which I think Mr Cobb had in mind when he caused to be prepared the tables that he put before me. Lord Pearson said, at p 143: 'The fund of damages is not expected to be preserved intact. It is expected to be used up gradually over the relevant period—15 or 18 years in this case—so as to be exhausted by the end of the period.' The case with which their Lordships were dealing was a case where the deceased was 53 at the time of death and the respondent 52. 'Therefore, what the widow received annually—£3,750 in this case—is made up partly of income and partly of capital. As the fund is used up, the income becomes less and less and the amounts withdrawn from the capital of the fund become greater and greater, because the total sum to be provided in each year—£3,750—is assumed (subject to what is said below) to remain constant throughout the relevant period. It is not difficult, though somewhat laborious, to work out without expert assistance how long a given fund will last with a given rate of interest and a given sum of money to be provided in each year.'

Then he gives the first few lines of such a calculation to show the method, which was the method Mr Cobb presented to me. And when one looks at Mr Cobb's figures showing the consequences of an award of £15,000 invested at 3 per cent on the basis that the loss of dependency was £1,000, so that that is the income one is seeking to afford the widow throughout the future, it appears that on that investment of 3 per cent the fund disappears altogether in the 20th year. And at 4 per cent it disappears in the 23rd year. . .. On an £18 a week dependency the annual loss of dependency is £936. So that I seek by my award to provide the widow with capital that will afford her and her son over the foreseeable future an income of £936, and I find in the speeches of the House of Lords in *Taylor v O'Connor*, an indication that it is by the management of the capital fund that the widow may reasonably expect to counteract the probable fall in the value of money as a consequence of inflation. I have looked at annuity tables and I have taken them into account as providing one test of the appropriateness of the calculations, but I accept unhesitatingly the view frequently expressed that the actual evidence of such computations (and there is no evidence in this case of an actuarial character), is of limited value in assistance in a fatal accidents case.

I hope that I have thus indicated the factors that have affected my mind, and I have decided that the capital value that should be placed on the loss of dependency by this widow is the sum of £16,848. If my arithmetic is correct it will be found that can be represented as a multiplier of 18.

Note

1. ***Howitt v Heads*** illustrates the traditional method of calculating damages and what is meant by a 'multiplier'. It also shows the relationship between the three elements in the calculation (period of loss, amount of loss and present capital value of future income) and how the total is arrived at.

> **Wells v Wells**
>
> House of Lords [1999] 1 AC 345

This case involved the assessment of damages in three personal injury cases. The particular point at issue was the amount of 'discount' to be applied in capitalising the loss of future earnings, and thus how future inflation should be dealt with. The traditional view was to ignore inflation but to apply a discount rate which would represent earnings on investments in times of stable currencies. This was taken to be 4–5 per cent. The alternative (adopted here) is to use the rate available for Index Linked Government Stock (ILGS) which pays approximately 1 per cent on top of inflation.

LORD LLOYD: . . . The starting-point is the multiplicand, that is to say the annual loss of earnings or the annual cost of care, as the case may be. . . .. The medical evidence may be that the need for care will increase or decrease as the years go by, in which case it may be necessary to take different multiplicands for different periods covered by the award. But to simplify the illustration one can take an average annual cost of care of £10,000 on a life expectancy of 20 years. If one assumes a constant value for money, then if the court were to award 20 times £10,000 it is obvious that the plaintiff would be over-compensated. For the £10,000 needed to purchase care in the twentieth year should have been earning interest for 19 years. The purpose of the discount is to eliminate this element of over-compensation. The objective is to arrive at a lump sum which by drawing down both interest and capital will provide exactly £10,000 a year for 20 years, and no more. This is known as the annuity approach. It is a simple enough matter to find the answer by reference to standard tables. The higher the assumed return on capital, net of tax, the lower the lump sum. If one assumes a net return of 5 per cent the discounted figure would be £124,600 instead of £200,000. If one assumes a net return of 3 per cent the figure would be £148,800.

The same point can be put the other way round. £200,000 invested at 5 per cent will produce £10,000 a year for 20 years. But there would still be £200,000 left at the end.

So far there is no problem. The difficulty arises because, contrary to the assumption made above, money does not retain its value. How is the court to ensure that the plaintiff receives the money he will need to purchase the care he needs as the years go by despite the impact of inflation? In the past the courts have solved this problem by assuming that the plaintiff can take care of future inflation in a rough and ready way by investing the lump sum sensibly in a mixed 'basket' of equities and gilts. But the advent of the index-linked government stock ('ILGS') (they were first issued in 1981) has provided an alternative. The return of income and capital on ILGS is fully protected against inflation. Thus the purchaser of £100 of ILGS with a maturity date of 2020 knows that his investment will then be worth £100 plus x per cent of £100, where x represents the percentage increase in the retail price index between the date of issue and the date of maturity (or, more accurately, eight months before the two dates). Of course if the plaintiff were to invest his £100 in equities it might then be worth much more. But it might also be worth less. The virtue of ILGS is that it provides a risk-free investment.

The first-instance judges in these appeals have broken with the past. They have each assumed for the purpose of the calculation that the plaintiffs will go into the market, and purchase the required amount of ILGS so as to provide for his or her future needs with the minimum risk of their damages being eroded by inflation. How the plaintiffs will in fact invest their damages is, of course, irrelevant. That is a question for them. It cannot affect the calculation. The question for decision therefore is whether the judges were right to assume that the plaintiffs would invest in ILGS with a low average net return of 2.5 per cent, instead of a mixed portfolio of equities and gilts. The Court of Appeal has held not. They have reverted to the traditional 4 to 5 per cent with the consequential reduction in the sums awarded.

Conclusion

My conclusion is that the judges in these three cases were right to assume for the purpose of their calculations that the plaintiffs would invest their damages in ILGS for the following reasons.

(1) Investment in ILGS is the most accurate way of calculating the present value of the loss which the plaintiffs will actually suffer in real terms.

(2) Although this will result in a heavier burden on these defendants, and, if the principle is applied across the board, on the insurance industry in general, I can see nothing unjust. It is true that insurance premiums may have been fixed on the basis of the 4 to 5 per cent discount rate indicated in *Cookson v Knowles* [1979] AC 556 and the earlier authorities. But this was only because there was then no better way of allowing for future inflation. The objective was always the same. No doubt insurance premiums will have to increase in order to take account of the new lower rate of discount. Whether this is something which the country can afford is not a subject on which your Lordships were addressed. So we are not in a position to form any view as to the wider consequences.

(3) The search for a prudent investment will always depend on the circumstances of the particular investor. Some are able to take a measure of risk, others are not. For a plaintiff who is not in a position to take risks, and who wishes to protect himself against inflation in the short term of up to 10 years, it is clearly prudent to invest in ILGS It cannot therefore be assumed that he will invest in equities and gilts. Still less is it his duty to invest in equities and gilts in order to mitigate his loss.

(4) Logically the same applies to a plaintiff investing for the long term. In any event it is desirable to have a single rate applying across the board, in order to facilitate settlements and to save the expense of expert evidence at the trial. I take this view even though it is open to the Lord Chancellor under section 1(3) of the Act of 1996 to prescribe different rates of return for different classes of case. Mr Leighton Williams conceded that it is not desirable in practice to distinguish between different classes of plaintiff when assessing the multiplier.

(5) How the plaintiff, or the majority of plaintiffs, in fact invest their money is irrelevant. The research carried out by the Law Commission suggests that the majority of plaintiffs do not in fact invest in equities and gilts but rather in a building society or a bank deposit.

(6) There was no agreement between the parties as to how much greater, if at all, the return on equities is likely to be in the short or long term. But it is at least clear that an investment in ILGS will save up to 1 per cent per annum by obviating the need for continuing investment advice.

(7) The practice of the Court of Protection when investing for the long term affords little guidance. In any event the policy may change when lump sums are calculated at a lower rate of return.

(8) The views of the Ogden Working Party, the Law Commission and the author of *Kemp & Kemp, The Quantum of Damages* in favour of an investment in ILGS are entitled to great weight.

(9) There is nothing in the previous decisions of the House which inhibits a new approach. It is therefore unnecessary to have resort to the *Practice Statement (Judicial Precedent)* [1966] 1 WLR 1234.

Notes

1. In the event, the House set the rate at 3 per cent, but this was superseded in 2001 by a statutory instrument setting the rate at 2.5 per cent. Nevertheless, the point is that rather than set a rate based on the total returns from investments (which would include sufficient return to cover inflation), the new method uses a return based on what might be gained over and above inflation. Note that the lower the rate of discount, the higher will be the damages. As described earlier, in 2017 the discount rate was reduced to –0.75 per cent, then raised again in 2019 to –0.25 per cent.

2. In *LMS v East Lancashire Hospitals NHS Trust* [2017] (unreported), the first case to show the effect of the Lord Chancellor's 2017 change to the discount rate (to –0.75 per cent), the High Court settled the claim of a 10-year-old girl who had been left with cerebral palsy. Under the old discount rate, the lump-sum value of her claim would have been around £3.77 million. When calculated using the new discount rate, she was awarded around £9.29 million.

3. Atiyah has criticised the full compensation principle, saying that it is very expensive and reduces the incentive to return to work (see now Peter Cane *Atiyah's Accidents, Compensation and the Law* (7th edn, CUP, 2006), pp 156–7).

DAMAGES ACT 1996

1. Assumed rate of return on investment of damages

(1) In determining the return to be expected from the investment of a sum awarded as damages for future pecuniary loss in an action for personal injury the court shall, subject to and in accordance with rules of court made for the purposes of this section, take into account such rate of return (if any) as may from time to time be prescribed by an order made by the Lord Chancellor.

(2) Subsection (1) above shall not however prevent the court taking a different rate of return into account if any party to the proceedings shows that it is more appropriate in the case in question.

(3) An order under subsection (1) above may prescribe different rates for different classes of case.

Notes

1. The discount rate to be applied under the 1996 Act was originally set at 2.5 per cent by the Damages (Personal Injury) Order 2001, SI 2001/230. As discussed, the rate has most recently been set at –0.25 per cent by the Damages (Personal Injury) Order 2019, SI 2019/1126.

   For a discussion of when the discount rate may be departed from, see *Warriner v Warriner* [2003] 3 All ER 447, where it was said that certainty was extremely important and a different rate could only be applied where there were special features material to the rate of return and it could be shown that these were factors which had not been taken into account by the Lord Chancellor when setting the rate. A long life expectancy would not justify a different rate. (The claimant had a life expectancy of 46 years and asked for a 2 per cent rate to be applied: this was refused.)

19.3 Intangible losses

Intangible losses include damages for pain and suffering and loss of amenity (PSLA), and the amounts awarded tend to be conventional and are arrived at on the basis of experience. *Kemp and Kemp: Quantum of Damages* (which publishes four practitioner volumes per year) lists awards under these heads, and these are used as guidelines in any given case. See also the Judicial College *Guidelines for the Assessment of General Damages in Personal Injury Cases* (15th edn, OUP, 2019).

'Loss of amenity' means loss by the claimant of the ability to enjoy life—or a particular aspect of it—to the full. However, one issue over which there has been disagreement is whether damages should be awarded under this head for a person who is unable to appreciate such a loss, such as someone in a coma. Are the damages for the deprivation or for the awareness of the deprivation?

> ### *West* v *Shepherd*
> House of Lords [1964] AC 326

The claimant, aged 41, was injured in a road accident and she suffered from 'post-traumatic spastic quadriplegia and intellectual deficit'. She may have been aware of her condition to a slight degree, but the House of Lords discussed the question of the basis of awards for loss of amenities. Held: a person would be entitled to damages even if unaware of the loss.

LORD PEARCE: My Lords, the appellants seek to use the plaintiff's condition as the foundation for two arguments in extinction or diminution of damages claimed in respect of her injuries and pain and loss of amenities.

First it is argued that such damages are given as compensation or consolation, and therefore, when the plaintiff's condition is so bad that they cannot be used by her to compensate or console they should either be greatly reduced or should not be awarded at all. No authority is cited in favour of such a proposition nor can I see any principle of common law that supports it.

The argument contains the assumption, which in my opinion is fallacious, that the court is concerned with what happens to the damages when they have been awarded. The court has to perform the difficult and artificial task of converting into monetary damages the physical injury and deprivation and pain and to give judgment for what it considers to be a reasonable sum. It does not look beyond the judgment to the spending of the damages. If it did so, many difficult problems would arise. Similar sums awarded for similar suffering may produce wholly different results. To a poor man who is thereby enabled to achieve some cherished object such as the education of his family the sum awarded may prove to be a more than adequate consolation. To a man who already has more money than he wants, it may be no consolation at all. But these are matters with which the court is not concerned. Whether the sum awarded is spent or how it is spent is entirely a matter for the plaintiff or the plaintiff's legal representatives. If the plaintiff's personal ability to use or enjoy the damages awarded for injury and pain and loss of amenity were a condition precedent to their award, it would be impossible for the executors of an injured person to obtain such damages. Yet they did so in *Rose v Ford* [1937] AC 826 and *Benham v Gambling* [1941] AC 157 and many other cases.

The second argument is founded on *Benham v Gambling* and would affect the whole basis of damages awarded for personal injury, apart, of course, from economic loss with which the argument is not concerned. Substantial damages are not awarded, it is said, for physical injury simpliciter, but only for the pain and suffering and general loss of happiness which it occasions. Therefore the deprivation of a limb can only command any substantial compensation in so far as it results in suffering or loss of happiness; and where there is little or no consciousness of deprivation there can be little or no damages. For this argument the appellants rely on *Benham v Gambling* and on the minority judgment of Diplock LJ in *Wise v Kaye* [1962] 1 QB 368.

The practice of the courts hitherto has been to treat bodily injury as a deprivation which in itself entitles a plaintiff to substantial damages according to its gravity. In *Phillips v London and South Western Railway Co* 4 QBD 406 Cockburn CJ in enumerating the heads of damage which the jury must take into account and in respect of which a plaintiff is entitled to compensation, said: 'These are the bodily injury sustained; the pain undergone; the effect on the health of the sufferer, according to its degree and its probable duration as likely to be temporary or permanent; the expenses incidental to attempts to effect a cure, or to lessen the amount of injury; the pecuniary loss.' In *Rose v Ford* Lord Roche said: 'I regard impaired health and vitality not merely as a cause of pain and suffering but as a loss of a good thing in itself.' If a plaintiff has lost a leg, the court approaches the matter on the basis that he has suffered a serious physical deprivation no matter what his condition or temperament or state of mind may be. That deprivation may also create future economic loss which is added to the assessment. Past and prospective pain and discomfort increase the assessment. If there is loss of amenity apart from the obvious and normal loss inherent in the deprivation of the limb—if, for instance, the plaintiff's main interest in life was some sport or hobby from which he will in future be debarred, that too increases the assessment. If there is a particular consequential injury to the nervous system, that also increases the assessment. So, too, with other personal and subjective matters that fall to be decided in the light of common sense in particular cases. These considerations are not dealt with as separate items but are taken into account by the court in fixing one inclusive sum for general damages. . . .

The loss of happiness of the individual plaintiffs is not, in my opinion, a practicable or correct guide to reasonable compensation in cases of personal injury to a living plaintiff. A man of fortitude is not made less happy because he loses a limb. It may alter the scope of his activities and force him to seek his happiness in other directions. The cripple by the fireside reading or talking with friends may achieve happiness as great as that which, but for the accident, he would have achieved playing golf in the fresh air of the links. To some ancient philosopher the former kind of happiness might even have seemed of a higher nature than the latter, provided that the book or the talk were such as they would approve. Some less robust persons, on the other hand, are prepared to attribute a great loss of happiness to a quite trivial event. It would be lamentable if the trial of a personal injury claim put a premium on protestations of misery and if a long face was the only safe passport to a large award. Under the present practice there is no call for a parade of personal unhappiness. A plaintiff who cheerfully admits that he is happy as ever he was, may yet receive a large award as reasonable compensation for the grave injury and loss of amenity over which he has managed to triumph.

Notes

1. The Pearson Commission disagreed with this view, saying that non-pecuniary damages should not be recoverable for permanent unconsciousness (at [398]). It took the view that damages should be paid under this head only where they can serve some useful purpose, such as providing some alternative source of satisfaction to replace one that has been lost. The High Court of Australia, in *Skelton v Collins* (1966) 39 AJLR 480, also, by a majority, took this view, saying that the subjective element could not be ignored, although some damages should be awarded for the objective elements.

2. A similar issue was considered in *Hicks v Chief Constable of South Yorkshire Police* [1992] 2 All ER 65. An action was brought on behalf of Sarah and Victoria Hicks, teenage sisters, killed by asphyxia in the Hillsborough Stadium disaster. Medical evidence showed that they would have been unconscious within a short while, and dead within five minutes after falling unconscious. The question was whether they could claim damages in respect of the pain and suffering they underwent during that short period (one of the girls had some superficial bruising but there was otherwise no evidence of any 'injury' other than the asphyxia itself), including suffering the fear of impending death. The claim was dismissed at first instance, in the Court of Appeal and by the House of Lords. The girls' estates therefore received nothing for the PSLA suffered between injury and death. (Also see *Rothwell v Chemical and Insulating Co Ltd* [2008] AC 281 but cf *Dryden and others v Johnson Matthey plc* [2018] UKSC 18.)

Index

A

abatement (self-help) 459–60, 464, 479
abuse *see* sexual and physical abuse
Acts of God 492
advice 148–61
aims of law of tort 4–9
airspace, trespass over 455–8
alternatives to tort system 7–8
ambulance service 19, 64, 114–15, 121, 179
asbestos exposure/mesothelioma 38, 70, 212–16,
    217–19, 323
assault 2, 327, 330–4 *see also* **sexual and physical**
    abuse
  battery 333–4
  contributory negligence 343
  ex turpi causa rule 342–3
  illegality 342–3
  provocation 342–3
  vicarious liability 522–5
  volenti non fit injuria 343
assumption of responsibility
  analogy 153
  children 100–2
  economic loss 132, 139, 141, 149–53, 161–4, 168
  omissions 51, 54–5
  police 121–2
  psychiatric harm 87
  public bodies 100–2, 104
  reliance 141, 150–1
  third parties 56–7, 61
  wills, liability to beneficiaries of 161–2

B

battery 2, 330–4
  assault 333–4
  consent 331, 333
  contributory negligence 343
  horseplay 330
  hostile intent 330–2
  imminency 334
    medical treatment, consent to 340–2
  police 331–3
  rape, civil claims for 327
  touching 328, 331–3
bereavement damages 78, 533, 537, 539–40
blood products, liability for infected 309–14
Bolam test 113–14, 179–83, 189
breach of confidence
  freedom of expression 360, 362, 364–7

Human Rights Act 1998 360, 366
misuse of private information 357, 378–9
privacy 118, 357–60, 362–7, 371–7
breach of statutory duty 316–24
  asbestos 323
  causation 205, 316
  claimant, whether duty owed to 316–23
  claims, whether statute gives rise to 316–23
  contributory negligence 250–1
  employers' liability 316–18, 319, 324
  motor cars, use and construction of 318–19
  policy 319, 322
  public rights, creation of 321–2
  sanctions 321–2
  scope of duty 323–4
  volenti non fit injuria 319
  whether duty has been breached 323–4
but for test 49, 203–4, 212–19, 224, 250

C

Caparo three-stage test 14, 23, 28–34, 141, 154–9,
    161–2
care and skill 173–93, 196–7
  children 173, 178
  clinical negligence 178–93
  common practice 179–93
  disclosure, duty of 186–91
  learner drivers 175–7, 178
  objectivity 173, 177
  professional negligence 178–9
  reasonable care and skill 106, 166,, 173–93
  special skills and common practice 179–93
  standard of care 173–93, 196–7
  under-skilled 175–9
causation 5, 203–19 *see also* **intervening acts**
  asbestos/mesothelioma 212–16, 217–19
  balance of probabilities 204, 207 , 209–12, 216
  breach of statutory duty 205, 316
  burden of proof 205–7, 218
  but for test 49, 203–4, 212–19, 224, 250
  cause in fact test 203
  clinical negligence 16–17, 20–3, 45, 203–12,
    216–19
  contributory negligence 244, 246–50, 253–6
  corrective justice 5
  defamation 409–10, 440
  doubling of risk test 212
  duty of care 22–3, 203–19
  foreseeability 206, 215, 246
  lost chance claims 216–19

causation (*Cont.*)
  material contribution approach 75, 205–16
  material increase in risk 205–8, 212–16
  multiple causes 2, 205–8, 212–16
  occupiers' liability 289–90
  policy 45–7, 203, 206, 213–15, 218
  privacy 386
  product liability 301
  psychiatric harm 75–6, 81–2, 95, 347
  remoteness 203, 222, 224, 226–7, 229
  Rylands v Fletcher, rule in 492
  vicarious liability 527
celebrities
  anonymised injunctions 387–90
  photographs 354, 357, 359, 362–74, 387, 425
  privacy 357, 362–74, 387–90
  super-injunctions 387
  children *see also* sexual and physical abuse
  allurements 226
  assumption of responsibility 100–2
  care and skill 173, 178
  chastisement 333
  contributory negligence 194, 246–9, 252–7
  foreseeability 194–5
  foster care 515, 532
  inhuman or degrading treatment 102–3
  occupiers' liability 261–2, 275–82
  privacy 364, 371–4
  private and family life, right to respect for 371–4
  private nuisance 464–5, 479
  psychiatric harm 34, 84–5, 96
  public bodies 56, 96–106, 120, 124
  remoteness 225–7
  standard of care 171–2, 194–5
  third parties 56, 58–9
  trespass to land 40, 58
  Wilkinson v Downton, rule in 346–50
chilling effect 116–17, 289, 367, 383–4, 386, 437
classification societies 41–4
clinical negligence 102–4, 126
  autonomy 127, 186, 192–3
  Bolam test 113–14, 179–83, 189
  care and skill 178–93
  causation 16–17, 20–3, 45, 203–12, 216–19
  consent to treatment 2, 182–92, 212, 333, 340–2
  delay in treatment 14–23, 33
  disclosure of risk 186–91
  duty of care 14–23, 33, 45–8
  emergencies 14–24, 33
  fair, just and reasonable test 16–20, 45, 47–9
  foreseeability 16–18, 21–3
  informed consent 182–92, 286, 293
  life, right to 126
  lost chance claims 216–19
  material risks, warnings of 191–2
  policy 45–9
  private and family life, right to respect for 188
  psychiatric harm 37, 70–6, 82–6
  responsible body of medical opinion 178–83, 193
  special skills and common practice 179–93
  standard of care 20, 179–93
  therapeutic exception 189–91
  waiting times in A&E 14–24, 33
  warn, failure to 182–92
  wrongful birth 45–9
compensation 4–5, 6–9 *see also* damages
  Compensation Act 2006 169–70
  compensation culture 3–4, 6–7, 169, 290–1, 293
  no-fault systems 7, 9, 158, 169
  vicarious liability 506
concurrent liability 149–53
confidentiality *see* breach of confidence
consent *see also* voluntary assumption of risk
      (*volenti non fit injuria*)
  battery 331, 333
  chastisement of children 333
  damages for death and personal injuries 534
  implied consent 332–3
  informed consent 182–92, 286, 293
  medical treatment, to 2, 182–92, 212, 333, 340–2
  occupiers' liability 277
  privacy 359, 369, 372–8, 383, 389
  Rylands v Fletcher, rule in 493, 498
  trespass to the person 331–3, 340–5
consumer protection *see* product liability
contractors *see* independent contractors
contractual relationships 26, 41–2, 94, 146, 291–4,
      338–9
contributory negligence 231, 243–57
  apportionment 244, 250–5, 257
  assault or battery 343
  blameworthiness 247–8, 250–7
  breach of statutory duty 250–1
  but for test 250
  causation 244, 246–50, 253–6
  children 194, 246–9, 252–7
  damages, reduction in 243–5, 248–57, 538
  deterrence 244
  exclusions 245
  fault 243–6, 249, 254
  foreseeability 245–6
  insurance 243–4
  intoxication 232–3
  Law Reform (Contributory Negligence) Act
      1945 244–7, 250, 252–6
  occupiers' liability 292, 294, 296–7
  omissions 55
  police 245
  prisoners 249–50
  privacy 386
  product liability 301
  proximity 257
  psychiatric harm 91
  reasonableness 244–9, 252–4, 257
  remoteness 223, 230
  rescuers 91
  road traffic accidents 2, 245–57
  seat belts 2, 244

standard of care 175–7, 194, 196
  suicide 245
  trespass to the person 343
  volenti non fit injuria 233, 245
corrective justice 3, 5, 6, 45–6
costs 367, 487, 533
crime
  defamation 391
  murder 56, 61, 116, 119–20, 235, 443–4
  rape, civil claims for 327
  trespass to land 459

D

damages 533–48 *see also* **compensation**
  aggravated damages 387, 447
  annuities 533–4, 543–4
  assessment of damages 537–48
  assumed rate of return on investment 546
  bereavement 78, 533, 537, 539–40
  capital sum 541–2
  causes of action, effect of death on 535
  children 539
  cohabitees 539–40
  collateral benefits 539
  compensatory damages 73, 343, 385–6, 397,
      447, 449
  contributory negligence 243–5, 248–57, 538
  Damages Act 1996 534, 546
  defamation 374–5, 381–3, 385–6, 446–50, 540
  dependency 533, 535, 540–3
  discount rate 541, 544–6
  disregard of benefits 538
  economic loss 132–68
  exemplary damages 343, 385–6, 447
  fatal accidents 78, 533, 535–43
  Financial Services Compensation Scheme
      (FSCS) 534
  fines 384
  full compensation principle 546
  harassment 351–4
  Index Linked Government Stock (ILGS) 544–5
  inflation 541, 543–6
  injury to feelings 447–8
  intangible losses 546–8
  interim payments 533
  Law Reform (Miscellaneous Provisions) Act
      1934 535
  legal aid 540
  loss of amenity 8, 449, 457, 465–9, 533, 540, 546–8
  loss of earnings 8, 234–7, 540–6
  loss of future income 533
  loss of profits 1, 133–8, 154
  lost years 535
  lump sums 533, 541
  medical and legal costs 533
  multipliers and multiplicands 540–6
  nuisance 479–86
  Ogden Tables 541, 545

pain and suffering 8, 45, 48, 66, 89, 449, 533,
      546, 548
  periodic payments 534
  personal injury 4, 514, 533–48
  persons entitled to bring action 537
  police 387
  privacy 374–5, 384–90
  private and family life, right to respect for 539–40
  proportionality 385
  provisional damages 534, 538
  psychiatric harm 63–79, 82, 86, 89–90, 93, 548
  remarriage, prospects of 539, 541
  structured settlements 533
  tax advantages 533
  types of action for damages 533–48
  uplift 540
  vicarious liability 493, 515
  vicissitudes of life 541
death *see* **deaths in custody; fatal accidents**
deaths in custody 53–4, 125–8, 130
defamation 391–450
  apologies 407, 411, 444–49
  chastity of women and contagious diseases, repeal
      of provisions on 391
  contributor immunity 439, 441
  costs, chilling effect of 367
  criminal conduct, imputation of 391
  damages 374–5, 381–3, 385–6, 446–50, 540
    aggravated 447
    injury to feelings 447–8
  Defamation Act 1996 395, 397–9, 444–6
  Defamation Act 2013 391–3, 398–402, 404, 426–7,
      432, 436
  defamatory, meaning of 403–4
  defences 391, 395, 425, 426–46
  economic loss 166–7
  fair comment 426–32
  Faulks Committee 425
  freedom of expression 391–4, 425, 437,
      447–8, 441–2
  grapevine effect 397, 409
  honest opinion 391, 426–33
  Human Rights Act 1998 391
  immunity 399, 439, 441
  injurious falsehood 166–7
  innocent dissemination 395, 399
  innuendo 418–23
  Internet and websites 395–404
    EU law 400–1
    jurisdiction 400–1
    operators of websites 401
    social media 395–7, 407–18, 420–3, 446
  judicial proceedings 434
  jurisdiction 397–8
  jury trials 391, 404, 426, 432, 447
  justification 391, 413, 417–18, 429, 431
  libel tourism 391
  limitation periods 402
  look-a-like photographs 425

defamation (*Cont.*)
malice 166–7, 394, 402, 427
malicious falsehood 166–7, 394, 402
margin of appreciation 393
natural and ordinary meaning 403, 414–15,
    418–23
offer of amends 444–6
parliamentary proceedings 433
political parties 394
privacy 385–6
privilege 433–5
    absolute 433, 434
    qualified 167, 433–43
    scientists and academics, protection of 391
public bodies/local authorities 392–4
public interest 391, 394, 426–44
publication 391, 394–5, 397–8
reasonableness 404, 416, 421–5, 439
references 166–7
repetition rule 420, 423
reporting court proceedings 433
reputation 391–450
Reynolds defence 391, 436–43
    scientists and academics, protection of 391
secondary publishers 391, 395
serious harm requirement 391, 404, 405–13
single meaning rule 415–16
single publication rule 391, 395, 402
slander 391–2
social media 395–7, 407–18, 420–3, 446
strict liability 424–5
third parties, communication to 394–5
truth 348, 391, 414, 418, 426, 436, 440–2, 447, 449
who can be liable 394–402
who can sue 392–4
words refer to claimant, whether 423–6
words used, meaning of 413–23
defective premises 141–8, 270
defective products *see* **product liability**
defences *see also* **contributory negligence;**
        voluntary assumption of risk (volenti non
        fit injuria)
defamation 391, 395, 425, 426–46
false imprisonment 340
negligence 231–57
occupiers' liability 294–7
trespass 340–3
defensive practices 5, 20, 101, 115–18, 286–7
deterrence 4, 5–6, 170, 327, 386, 506
disclaimers 138–61
disclosure 186–91
distributive justice 45–6, 49, 92, 506
doctors, liability of *see* **clinical negligence**
domestic violence 117–22
Donoghue v Stevenson
duty of care 24–36, 105
omissions 51
economic loss 140, 144–6, 152, 156
occupiers' liability 265

product liability 298–300
psychiatric harm 79
standard of care 190
drunk driving 176, 232–3
duty of care 13–49 *see also* **fair, just and reasonable**
        test; standard of care
analogy, development of law by 18–19, 28, 31,
    32, 41
Caparo three-stage test 14, 23, 28–34
carelessness 27–8
causation 22–3, 203–19
clinical negligence 14–23, 33, 45–8
    fair, just and reasonable test 16–20
    foreseeability 16–18, 21–3
    waiting times 14–24, 33
defences to negligence 231–57
economic loss 132–68
emergency services 111–24
foreseeability 25, 28, 34–40
incremental test 17, 19, 28, 31, 32
intervening acts 22
neighbour principle 24–34
novel duty cases 14–15, 17, 23, 31, 33–4
occupiers' liability 261–97
omissions 50–5
policy 23–4, 31, 40–9
product liability 298–315
proximity 25, 28–31, 43–4, 46
psychiatric harm 62–95
public bodies 96–131
remoteness 219–30
Rylands v Fletcher, rule in 488–502
skill of the defendant 169–202
third parties 42, 44, 55–60
trespass to land 40
trespass to the person 329–31
unforeseeable claimant problem 34
vicarious liability 505–32

E

economic loss 132–68
advice 148–61
assumption of responsibility 132, 139, 141,
    149–53, 161–4, 168
Caparo three-stage test 141, 154–9, 161–2
complex structure theory 145–6
concurrent liability 149–53
consequential loss 135–6
damages 132–68
defamation 166–7
defective premises 141–8
disclaimers in references 138–61
duty of care 132–68
fair, just and reasonable test 151–2
fiduciary relationship 148, 162–4, 168
floodgates argument 133
foreseeability 30, 133, 135, 137–8, 154–5, 163–4
Hedley Byrne exception 138–68

loss of profits 133–7
negligent misstatements 138–65
omissions 143, 150
physical damage 132–8, 141–8
policy 133, 135, 167
proximity 132, 137, 140, 144, 146, 148, 154, 158, 160–1, 167
public bodies 98
pure economic loss 13, 31, 98, 132–8, 146–8, 150, 163
references 138–61, 164–8
reliance 132, 139, 141, 146, 149–61, 163, 168
remoteness 133, 136
statements 148–61
third parties 148, 161–8
wills, liability to beneficiaries of 161–4, 168
education cases 1, 101–2, 528–32
effective remedy, right to an 122–4
egg shell skull rule 65, 212, 223–4
emergency services 111–24
ambulance service 19, 64, 114–15, 121, 179
assumption of responsibility 121
Bolam test 113–14
defensive practices 113
delays 114–15
duty of care 111–24
economic loss 114
fair, just and reasonable test 112
fire service 112–15
floodgates argument 114
immunity from suit 112–14
incremental development 114
insurance 114
police 115, 117–22
policy 112, 114
proximity 112, 114
resources 113, 114–15
rescuers 38–9, 80, 87–92
standard of care 113, 115
emotional distress *see* **psychiatric harm**
employers' liability *see also* **vicarious liability**
asbestos exposure/mesothelioma 38, 70, 212–16, 217–19, 323
breach of statutory duty 199, 316–18, 319, 324
employer-employee relationship 93–5, 164–8
occupiers' liability 278–9
references 1, 132, 138–61, 163, 167–8
stress 87, 95
environmental protection/degradation 476, 490, 492, 495–6
escape of dangerous things from land *see* **Rylands v Fletcher, rule in**
European Convention on Human Rights (ECHR) 357, 361–75, 378, 384 *see also* **private and family life, right to respect for**
peaceful enjoyment of possessions 476
public bodies 96, 102–6
ex turpi causa non oritur actio 234, 237–43, 342–3
exclusion of liability 138–61, 291–4, 305, 515

F

fair, just and reasonable test 28, 30–1, 40–9
Caparo three-stage test 14, 23, 28–34, 141, 154–9, 161–2
causation 45, 47–9
clinical negligence 16–20
economic loss 151–2
emergency services 112
occupiers' liability 267
omissions 52
police 32–3, 122–4, 130
policy 40–1, 43–5, 47–9
public bodies 98, 102–3, 104, 124, 130
Rylands v Fletcher, rule in 501
vicarious liability 509, 522, 526, 528–9
fair trial, right to 122–4, 130, 487
false imprisonment 2, 327, 330, 334–40
defences 340
escape, reasonable means of 336–7
intention 329
liberty and security, right to 334–6
MHA patients 337
prisoners 338–40
fatal accidents
bereavement damages 533, 537, 539–40
damages 78, 533, 535–43
product liability 302
fault 3, 5, 243–6. 249, 254, 261, 490
fiduciary relationships 148, 162–4, 168
fire service 112–15
floodgates argument 40, 68, 86, 114, 133
foreseeability
Caparo three-stage test 14, 23, 28–34, 141, 154–9, 161–2
causation 206, 215, 246
children 194–5
clinical negligence 16–18, 21–3
contributory negligence 245–6
duty of care 25, 28, 34–40
harassment 356
nuisance 471, 478
occupiers' liability 267, 277, 280–1, 284, 289
product liability 300
proximity 31, 46
psychiatric harm 62–3, 65–70, 74, 76–81, 87–91, 94
public bodies 98–9, 105, 107–9
reasonableness 31, 34–9, 68, 78–9, 89, 98, 222, 229, 526
remoteness 2, 219–30
Rylands v Fletcher, rule in 490–2, 496, 501
standard of care 197–8, 200, 202
third parties 55, 56–9
trespass to land 40, 58, 223
freedom of expression
breach of confidence 360, 362, 366
chilling effect 384
defamation 391–4, 425, 437, 447–8, 441–2

freedom of expression (*Cont.*)
    harassment 353–4
    privacy 2, 360–2, 364–8, 377, 379–84
    Wilkinson v Downton, rule in 347–8, 350

H

Hague Rules 40–1, 43–4
harassment 327, 350–6
    course of conduct 346, 352–5
    damages 351–4
    foreseeability 356
    freedom of expression 353–4
    injunctions 351–4
    intention 345, 466–7
    nuisance 466–7
    privacy 353, 358
    Protection from Harassment Act 1997 350–6, 358,
        506–7
    publication, by 351–4
    stalking 352, 355
    telephone calls 358
    trespass 350–6
    vicarious liability 506–7
    vulnerable children in housing from harassment
        and bullying, failure to protect 56, 96–106
    Wilkinson v Downton 327, 334, 345–6, 467
Hillsborough disaster 1, 46, 64, 77–82, 87–93, 548
horseplay 330
hospitals *see* **clinical negligence**
Human Rights Act 1998 *see also* **freedom of
    expression**
    breach of confidence 360, 366
    defamation 391
    effective remedy, right to 122–4
    European Convention on Human Rights 124
    fair trial, right to 122–4, 130, 487
    inhuman or degrading treatment 102–3, 119,
        122–4, 131
    life, right to 54, 119, 122, 125–8, 128–31
    margin of appreciation 368, 370, 380, 382–4, 393,
        476
    nuisance 476–9
    peaceful enjoyment of possessions 111, 476–7
    police 118–19, 124
    privacy 2, 357, 359–84
    public bodies 96, 102, 104–5, 111, 117–20, 122,
        124, 128, 130, 360–3

I

illegality 231, 234–43, 342–3
    ex turpi causa rule 234, 236–7
    policy 234, 237–43
    range of factors approach 234, 238–42
    reliance 238
    rule-based approach 234, 238–42
    trespass to the person 343

immunity
    defamation 399, 439, 441
    discretion 97
    emergency services 112–14
    nuisance 472–5
    police 32–4, 42, 117–23, 130
    standard of care 198
    vicarious immunity 515
imprisonment *see* **false imprisonment;
    prison/prisoners**
incremental development of law 17, 19, 28, 31, 32, 114
independent contractors
    occupiers' liability 262, 266
    vicarious liability 507, 527–32
inhuman or degrading treatment 102–3, 119,
    122–4, 131
injunctions
    anonymised 387–90
    harassment 351–4
    interim injunctions 379, 382, 388, 479
    interlocutory injunctions 359, 366, 386
    mandatory injunctions 459, 460, 480–1
    nuisance 479–87
    privacy 387–90
    super-injunctions 384, 387
    trespass to land 453–4, 458–9
injury to feelings, damages for 447–8
insurance 3, 5–7
    compulsory insurance 3, 7
    contributory negligence 243–4
    corrective justice 3
    damages 534, 545
    defences to negligence 234, 244
    deterrence 5–6
    duty of care 41–4
    economic loss 134
    emergency services 114
    employers' liability 3
    first-party 9
    loss-shifting 3, 6
    motor insurance 3, 5–6, 8, 234
    negligence 6
    public bodies 110, 114
    Rylands v Fletcher, rule in 491, 495
    standard of care 175–6
    vicarious liability 506, 511
intention
    conduct element 347–9
    false imprisonment 329
    interference with the person 2, 327–56
    physical harm or distress, intentional infliction
        of 344–56
Internet and websites
    defamation 395–404, 407–18, 420–3, 446
    EU law 400–1
    jurisdiction 400–1
    operators of websites, liability of 401
    social media 395–7, 407–18, 420–3, 446

intervening acts
  duty of care 22
  foreseeability 22, 224
  psychiatric harm 81, 91
  remoteness 203, 222, 224, 226, 229
  rescuers 91
  third parties 57
intoxication 54–5, 176, 232–3, 243, 250, 275–7, 296–7

L

land *see* occupiers' liability; private nuisance;
    Rylands v Fletcher, rule in; trespass to land
legitimate expectations 21, 178, 311–13, 369–71
libel *see* defamation
liberty and security, right to 334–6
life, right to 54, 119, 122, 125–8, 128–31
limitation periods 68, 146, 306, 329–30, 402
local authorities 28, 60, 97–102, 146, 287, 392–4
loss of amenity, damages for 8, 449, 457, 465–9,
    533, 540, 546–8
lost chance claims 216–19
loss of earnings, damages for 8, 234–7, 540–6
loss of profits 1, 133–8, 154
lost years, damages for 535

M

malice
  defamation 394, 402, 427
  malicious falsehood 166–7, 359, 394, 402
  nuisance 471–2
medical negligence *see* clinical negligence
medical treatment, consent to 2, 182–92, 212, 333,
    340–2
mental capacity/mental illness 54, 125–8, 130, 337,
    342, 382 *see also* psychiatric harm
mesothelioma/asbestos 38, 70, 212–16, 217–19, 323
misuse of private information 357, 360, 377–9
murder 56, 61, 116, 119–20, 235, 443–4

N

negligence 1–4, 13 *see also* causation; clinical
    negligence; contributory negligence; duty
    of care; economic loss; psychiatric harm;
    public bodies
  actionable 36, 42, 140, 245–6
  defamation 425
  defences 231–57
  insurance 6
  negligent misstatements 28, 114, 141, 149, 162–5
  occupiers' liability 265–7
  product liability 298–301
  professional negligence 178–9
  remoteness of damage 219–30
  Rylands v Fletcher, rule in 488, 491–502
  trespass 327–30

neighbour principle 24–36 *see also Donoghue v
    Stevenson*
  duty of care 24–34
  manufacturers 24–34
  omissions 51–2
  psychiatric harm 79
nervous shock *see* psychiatric harm
no-fault systems 7, 9, 158, 169
novel duty cases 14–15, 17, 23, 31, 33–4, 111
novus actus interveniens see intervening acts
nuisance *see also* private nuisance
  public nuisance 460–3, 469, 497
  Rylands v Fletcher, rule in 496–502

O

occupiers' liability 261–97
  access land, special considerations relating to 265
  activity and occupancy duties, difference
    between 266–7
  balancing risk, gravity of injury, cost and social
    value 281
  calling, visitors exercising a 278–9
  causation 289–90
  children 261–2, 275–82
  compensation culture 290–1, 293
  contractors, selection of competent and safe 267
  contributory negligence 292, 294, 296–7
  control test 268–70
  danger due to state of premises 261, 263–4,
    266–72, 275–6, 283–4
  dangerous activities 266, 283
  defective premises 141–8, 270
  defences 294–7
  Donoghue v Stevenson 265
  exclusions of liability and warnings 291–4
  extent of ordinary duty 262
  fair, just and reasonable test 267
  fault 261
  foreseeability 267, 277, 280–1, 284, 289
  implied terms 263
  independent contractors 262, 266
  invitees 261–3, 268–70, 276–8
  knowledge of danger 284, 296–7
  lawful visitors 261–3
  licensees 261–3, 270, 276–8
  negligence 265–7
  non-visitors 270–7, 282–91
  notices 271–2, 291
  occupancy duties 265–7
  occupier, who is an 268–70
  Occupiers' Liability Act 1957 261–73, 278–80,
    282–5, 288, 291–4
  Occupiers' Liability Act 1984 261, 264–5, 268–76,
    282–5, 294
  permission, scope of 261–2, 270–1
  property damage 282
  proximity 267

occupiers' liability (*Cont.*)
  reasonable to expect protection 284–5
  repair 262–3, 266, 269–70, 276
  rights of way 282
  skilled entrants 278–9
  social value of activities 285–6
  status of entrants 270–7
  third parties 263
  trespassers 2, 38–9, 57–9, 261, 263, 271–7, 282–91,
      294–5
  unfair contract terms and exclusion of
      liability 291
  unlawful visitors 261, 264–5
  visitors 261–97
  volenti non fit injuria 231, 296
  vulnerability of visitors 281, 290
  warnings 2, 267, 271–2, 278–9, 281, 291–4
Ogden Tables 541, 545
omissions 50–5
  assumption of responsibility 51, 54–5
  alcohol abuse, caring for someone with 54–5
  defective premises 143
  duty of care 50–5
  economic loss 143, 150
  exceptions to the rule 53–5
  fair, just and reasonable test 52
  neighbour principle 51–2
  police 53–4, 55, 120, 124
  positive acts, distinguishing 50, 51–3
  pre-tort relationships 52–3
  public bodies 107–11
  Rylands v Fletcher, rule in 502
  standard of care 170–2
  suicide in police custody 53–4

P

pain and suffering, damages for 8, 45, 48, 66, 89,
    449, 533, 546, 548
peaceful enjoyment of possessions 111, 476–7
Pearson Commission 548
personal injury *see also* **contributory negligence;**
    occupiers' liability; psychiatric harm; road
    traffic accidents (RTAs); trespass
  abolition of personal injuries law 7–9
  causation 229
  damages 4, 514, 533–48
  compensation culture 3–4, 6–7, 169, 290–1, 293
  egg shell skull rule 223–4
  insurance 114
  limitation periods 329
  no-fault systems 7, 9, 158, 169
  no-fault systems 7, 169, 290–1, 293
  police 105, 121
  private nuisance 463, 465–7, 469
  product liability 298, 303–6
  proximity 31
  reliance 109
  remoteness 229

Rylands v Fletcher 493, 496
  trespass to the person 331
  whiplash 7, 9
photographs
  aerial photos 456–7
  celebrities 354, 357, 359, 362–74, 387, 425
  children 371–4
  defamation
  look-a-likes 425
  privacy 362–74, 387
  sexual activity 374–7
physical harm or distress
  domestic violence 117–22
  economic loss 132–8, 141–8
  harassment 344–6
  intention 344–56
  nuisance 464
  psychiatric harm 62–70, 73–5, 78, 82, 88–90
  trespass 344–56
physical injury *see* **personal injury; physical harm**
    or distress, intentional infliction of
planning permission 468, 472–6, 484–7
police 115–22
  aid, duty to come to each other's 55
  assumption of responsibility 121–2
  battery 331–3
  bystanders, injury to 32–4, 116
  contributory negligence 245
  damages 387
  deaths in custody 53–4, 126–7
  defamation 417–19, 423
  defensive practices 115, 116–18
  domestic violence 117–22
  economic loss 153
  effective remedy, right to an 122–4
  emergency calls 115, 117–22
  fair hearing, right to a 122–4, 130
  fair, just and reasonable test 32–3, 122–4, 130
  Hillsborough disaster 1, 64, 77–82, 87–93, 548
  Human Rights Act 1998 118–19, 124
  immunity 32–4, 42, 117–23, 130
  informants 87
  inhuman or degrading treatment 119, 122–4, 131
  life, right to 54, 119, 122, 125, 128–31
  omissions 53–4, 55, 120, 124
  policy 112, 115, 122–4
  privacy 371, 387
  private and family life, right to respect for 118–19
  proximity 32, 112, 115, 120–1
  psychiatric harm 64, 87–94
  rescuers 39, 87–93
  witnesses, duty to 116, 128–31
policy
  breach of statutory duty 319, 322
  causation 45–7, 203, 206, 213–15, 218
  clinical negligence 45–9
    but for causation 49
    fair, just and reasonable test 45, 47–9
    wrongful birth 45–9

distributive justice 45–6, 49, 92, 506
duty of care 23–4, 31, 40–9
economic loss 133, 135, 167
emergency services 112, 114
fair, just and reasonable test 40–1, 43–5, 47–9
floodgates argument 40
illegality 234, 237–43
immunity 112–14
nuisance 466–7, 476, 478–9
occupiers' liability 287, 290
omissions 55
police 112, 115, 122–4
principle, contrasted with 44
privacy 379, 385
proximity 40–1, 44, 46–7
psychiatric harm 62–4, 73, 82
public bodies 96, 98, 101, 103, 108–9, 111
public interest 40–1
Rylands v Fletcher, rule in 491
standard of care 169, 175, 191
third parties 60
trespass to the person 342
vicarious liability 505–6, 512–14, 519–20, 528
wrongful birth 45–9
post-traumatic stress disorder (PTSD) 86, 116,
    234–5, 547
practical jokes 344, 345–6
prescription 468
prison/prisoners
    contributory negligence 249–50
    deaths in custody 126–7
    false imprisonment 338–40
    mentally ill patients 125–8
    omissions 53
    segregation 320
    strip-searches of visitors 344–6, 359, 364
    vicarious liability 510–15
privacy 357–90 *see also* **private and family life,
    right to respect for**
    breach of confidence 118, 357–60, 362–7, 371–7
        freedom of expression 360, 362, 364–7
        Human Rights Act 1998 360, 366
        misuse of private information 378–9
    Calcutt Committee 357, 359
    causation 386
    celebrities 357, 362–74, 387–90
    children 364, 371–4
    common law 357–9
    consent 359, 369, 372–8, 383, 389
    costs, chilling effect of 367
    damages 374–5, 384–90
    defamation 385–6
    deterrence 386
    European Convention on Human Rights
        (ECHR) 357, 361–75, 378, 384
    existence of tort 358–9
    freedom of expression 2, 360–2, 364–7
    harassment 358
    Human Rights Act 1998 2, 357, 359–84

Independent Press Standards Organisation (IPSO)
    Editors' Code 374, 381
injunctions 387–90
Internet usage 2
legitimate expectations 369–71
misuse of private information 357, 360, 377–9
open justice rule 388–9
personal information 357, 363–7
phone hacking scandal 367, 387
photographs 362–74, 387
police 371, 387
pre-notification rules for media 379–83
proportionality 375, 385
public interest 360, 362, 367–71, 374–8, 380–4,
    389–391
reasonable expectation of privacy 357, 359–84
remedies 374–5, 384–90
sexual activity on private property 374–7
strip searches of prison visitors 344–6, 359, 364
telephone harassment 355
private and family life, right to respect for 360–1,
    379–84
children 371–4
clinical negligence 188
damages 539–40
freedom of expression 365, 368, 377, 379–84
freedom of the press 367–71
harassment 353
horizontal claims 357
legitimate expectations 371
margin of appreciation 380, 382–4
nuisance 476–9
photographs 367–74
police 118–19
pre-notification requirement 379–84
proportionality 365, 381
public authorities 363
sexual activities and personal information 374–7
private nuisance 460–87
abatement (self-help) 459–60, 464, 479
character of a neighbourhood, change in 461–2,
    471–2, 474–6, 484
children 464–5, 479
continuance of nuisance 496–7, 502
damages 479–86
direct physical injury to neighbour's land 464
encroachment 2, 464, 469
enjoyment, interference with (amenity
    interest) 460–1, 463–71, 475, 489, 497
environment cases and pollution 476, 490, 492,
    495–6
flooding 476–9
foreseeability 471, 478
harassment 466–7
Human Rights Act 1998 476–9
immunity 472–5
injunctions 479–87
light, blocking 480–2
locality 461–2, 471–2, 474–6, 484

private nuisance (*Cont.*)
  malice 471–2
  material injury to property 466, 470
  noise 2, 461–2, 472, 482–7
  overlooking 469–70
  ownership rights 2
  peaceful enjoyment of possessions 476
  personal inconvenience 470, 479
  planning permission 472–6, 484–7
  policy 466–7, 476, 478–9
  prescription 468
  private and family life, right to respect for 476–9
  proprietary interests 462–4
  public interest 472, 475–7, 479, 483–6
  public nuisance, comparison with 460–3, 469
  quiet enjoyment 464, 469
  reasonable user 460, 462–4, 470–6
  remedies 479–87
  Rylands v Fletcher, rule in 496–502
  sensitivity of claimants 471
  sewerage 476–9
  smells 2, 461–2, 470–1, 474–5
  smoke 2
  statutory authority 472–6
  telephone calls 358
  television, interference with 2, 464–70
  who can sue 460, 463–70
product liability 298–315
  blood products, liability for infected 309–14
  causation 301
  computer software 307
  Consumer Protection Act 1987 298, 301–9, 313–14
  Consumer Rights Act 2015 298, 307
  contributory negligence 301
  defect, definition of 303
  design defects 301
  development risks/state of the art defence 303–4,
     307–8, 315
  Donoghue v Stevenson 298–300
  EU law 298, 302, 306–14
  exclusions from liability, prohibition on 305
  foreseeability 300
  intermediate examination 299
  knowledge of defect, actual or constructive 301,
     307–8
  limitation periods 306
  manufacturers 299–302, 307
  negligence 298–301
  non-standard products 310, 312–14
  producers 298
  remoteness 300
  repairers 301
  strict liability 298, 301–15
professional negligence 178–9
property rights 111, 476–7
proportionality 240, 395, 365, 375, 381, 385, 449
provocation 340, 342–3, 368, 448
proximity

Caparo three-stage test 14, 23, 28–34, 141,
   154–9, 161–2
  contributory negligence 257
  duty of care 25, 28–31, 43–4, 46
  economic loss 132, 137, 140, 144, 148, 154, 158,
     160–1, 167
  emergency services 112, 114–15
  foreseeability 31, 46
  occupiers' liability 267
  police 32, 112, 115, 120–1
  policy 40–1, 44, 46–7
  psychiatric harm 62, 69, 76–7, 79–83, 88, 92
  public bodies 98, 107, 111
  Rylands v Fletcher, rule in 496
  third parties 55, 60–1
psychiatric harm 10, 31, 35, 62–95
  anxiety 70, 76
  asbestos 70
  assumption of responsibility 87
  bystanders 62–3, 80, 92
  causation 75–6, 81–2, 95, 347
  children 34, 84–5, 96
  clinical negligence 37, 70–6, 82–6
  close family ties 80–1, 83, 93
  close ties of love and affection 80, 83, 88
  control mechanisms 67–8, 71, 75, 82–3, 87–9
  damages 63–79, 82, 86, 89–90, 93, 548
  eggshell skull rule 67
  expert evidence 63–4, 75
  foreseeability 30, 62–3, 65–70, 74, 76–81,
     87–91, 94
  floodgates argument 68, 86
  grief reaction 63, 77
  Hillsborough disaster 1, 64, 77–82, 87–93, 548
  immediate aftermath of events 70, 78, 80–2, 86,
     88, 90–2
  intervening acts 81, 91
  neighbour principle 79
  physical injury distinguished 62–70, 73–5, 78, 82,
     88–90
  police 64, 87–94
  policy 62–4, 73, 82
  post-traumatic stress disorder 86, 116, 234–5, 547
  primary victims 62, 65–76, 87–95
  proximity 62, 69, 76–7, 79–83, 88, 92
  pure psychiatric harm 62, 64, 75, 87, 91–2
  recognisable psychiatric illness requirement 64–5,
     68, 75
  remoteness 69, 70, 75
  rescuers 80, 87–8, 91–3
  road traffic accidents 65–70
  secondary victims 62, 65–8, 71, 73–95
  stress at work cases 87, 95
  sudden shocking events 84, 86
  television broadcasts 77, 81
  Wilkinson v Downton, tort in 345–50
  witnesses to shocking events 63–4, 66, 71, 73–7,
     83, 85–9, 92–5

public bodies 96–131 *see also* **clinical negligence; emergency services; police; prison/prisoners**
assumption of responsibility 100–2, 104
carelessness 97
children 56, 96–106, 120, 124
assumption of responsibility 100–2
inhuman or degrading treatment 102–3
common law 96–111
defamation 392–4
discretion 96
Donoghue v Stevenson 105
duty of care 96–131
economic loss 98
education-based cases 102
European Convention on Human Rights 96, 102–6, 123–30
fair, just and reasonable test 98, 102–3, 104, 124, 130
foreseeability 98–9, 105, 107–9
Human Rights Act 1998 96, 102, 104–5, 111, 117–20, 122, 124, 128, 130
immunity 97, 101
insurance 110, 114
judicial review 96
justiciability and policy/operational dichotomy 98
life, right to 125–8
local authorities 97–102
MHA patients, suicide by 125–8, 130
negligence 97–105
novel situations 111
omission to use statutory powers 107–11
policy 96, 98, 101, 103, 108–9, 111
powers and duties 96
private and family life, right to respect for 363
proximity 98, 107, 111
relationships 991–10, 111, 114, 118, 120–1
reliance, particular and general 109–11
standard of care 113
statutory power 97–111
systemic failures 129–31
vicarious liability 99, 101–2
vulnerable children in housing from harassment and bullying, failure to protect 56, 96–106
public interest
defamation 391, 394, 426–44
illegality 242
immunity 107
nuisance 472, 475–7, 479, 483–6
policy 40–1
privacy 360, 362, 367–71, 374–8, 380–4, 389–391
public nuisance 460–3, 469, 497

R

reasonableness *see* **fair, just and reasonable test**
recklessness 39–40, 329, 342, 348–9, 386, 424–5, 446
references 1, 132, 138–61, 163, 167–8
reliance 103–4, 109–11, 150, 238

remedies *see also* **compensation; damages; injunctions**
effective remedy, right to 122–4
privacy 374–5, 384–90
private nuisance 479–87
self-help 449, 479
remoteness 219–30
causation 203, 222, 224, 226–7, 229
children 225–7
contributory negligence 223, 230
economic loss 133, 136f
egg shell skull rule 223–4
foreseeability 2, 219–30
intervening acts 203, 222, 224, 226, 229
kind of damage 225–30
product liability 300
psychiatric harm 69, 70, 75
reasonableness 220–30
Rylands v Fletcher, rule in 492, 496
standard of care 198, 199
suicide 228–30
vicarious liability 526
rescuers 35, 38–9, 80, 87–93, 233–4
road traffic accidents (RTAs)
collision cases 35–6, 64–5, 196, 253
contributory negligence 2, 245–57
drunk driving 176, 232–3
learner drivers 175–7, 178
motor insurance 3, 5–6, 8, 234
no-fault systems 7
passengers, liability towards 176–7, 249
psychiatric harm 65–70
public bodies 107–10
seat belts 2, 6, 244
standard of care 175–7, 178
whiplash 7, 9
Rylands v Fletcher, **actions under** 488–502
Acts of God 492
Cambridge Water case 490, 492–4, 496
causation 492
consent 493, 498
escape, definition of 492–3, 498
fair, just and reasonable test 501
fault 490
foreseeability 490–2, 496, 501
hazardous activities 488, 493, 496
insurance 491, 495
knowledge 499–500
licensees 502
natural user 489, 492, 494
negligence 488, 491–502
non-natural user 489, 490, 493–6
nuisance 496–502
omissions 502
personal injuries 493, 496
policy 491
proximity 496
public interest 491–2

private nuisance (*Cont.*)
  reasonableness 489, 500–1
  remoteness 492, 496
  restrictions on the rule 491–4
  social background to rule 491
  statutory authority 491–2
  strict liability 488, 496, 498
  third parties 492
  trespass to land 496–9

S

schools (education cases) 1, 101–2, 528–32
seat belts 2, 6, 244
self-help 449, 479
sexual and physical abuse
  limitation periods 329–30
  public bodies 96–106, 122–4
  vicarious liability 505–25
  Wilkinson v Downton, rule in 346–9
sexual and physical abuse
  children in housing from harassment and bullying,
    failure to protect vulnerable 56, 96–106
  limitation periods 329–30
  psychiatric harm 96
  public bodies 96–106, 122–4
  vicarious liability 505–25
  Wilkinson v Downton, tort in 346–50
skill *see* **care and skill**
slander 391–2
social media 395–7, 407–18, 420–3, 446
social security 7, 538
solicitors 139, 149–51, 158, 161–4
special relationships
  economic loss 133, 137, 139–41, 144–56, 159–68
  psychiatric harm 80–1, 83, 88, 93
  pre-tort relationships 51–3, 55
special skills and common practice 179–83
standard of care 13, 169–202
  ambulance service 114–15
  children 171–2, 194–5
  clinical negligence 20, 179–93
  Compensation Act 2006 169, 170
  compensation culture 169
  contributory negligence 175–7, 194, 196
  cost of prevention 199–201
  deterrence 170
  emergency services 113, 115
  foreseeability 197–8, 200, 202
  Human Rights Act 1998 188
  immunity 198, 202
  individual responsibility 169
  insurance 175
  learner drivers 175–7
  objectivity 170–3
  omissions 170–2
  policy 169, 175, 191
  privacy 188

  probability and seriousness of injury 197–9
  psychiatric harm 113–15
  public bodies 113–15
  reasonableness 169, 170–3, 196–200
  remoteness 198, 199
  setting the standard of care 195–202
  social value of activity 201–2
  skill of defendants 173–93, 196–7
  social policy 169
  spectators 195–7
  strict liability 177
  subjectivity 172
  trespass to land 58
  volenti non fit injuria 196
statutory authority 472–6, 491–2
stress at work 87, 95
strict liability
  defamation 424–5
  limitation periods 306–7
  non-standard products 310, 312
  product liability 298, 301–15
  Rylands v Fletcher, rule in 488, 496, 498
  standard of care 177
  trespass to land 456–7
studying tort law and reading cases 9–10
suicide 53–4, 125–8, 130, 228–30, 233, 245
surveyors 159–61

T

television reception, interference with 2, 464–70
third parties 55–61
  assumption of responsibility 56–7, 61
  children 56, 58–9
  Contracts (Rights of Third Parties) Act 1999 515
  danger, failure to prevent creation of sources
    of 56–9
  defamation 394–5
  duty of care 42, 44, 55–60
  economic loss 148, 161–8
  foreseeability 55, 56–9
  intervening acts 57
  occupiers' liability 235, 263
  pre-tort relationships 55, 59
  privacy 366
  private nuisance 468
  proximity 55, 60–1
  psychiatric harm 79
  Rylands v Fletcher, rule in 492
  trespass 57–9
  vulnerable children in housing from harassment
    and bullying, failure to protect 56
  warn, duty to 56, 59–61
time limits 68, 146, 306, 329–30, 402
tipping off 390
trespass 327–34 *see also* **assault; battery; false
    imprisonment; trespass to land**
  consent 331–3, 340–5

defences 340–3
deterrence 327
direct and immediate harm 330
duty of care 329–31
goods, to 245
harassment 327, 350–6
loss, actionable without 330
negligence 327–30
person, trespass to the 2, 327, 328–56
physical harm or distress, intentional infliction
    of 344–56
privacy 345
psychiatric harm 91
third parties 57–8
Wilkinson v Downton, tort in 344–9
trespass to land 453–60
abatement, remedy of 459–60
aggravated trespass 469
air space 455–8
children 40, 58
crime, as a 459
duty of care 40
encroachment 459
exclusive occupation 453
foreseeability 40, 58, 223
injunctions 453–4, 458–9
intention 40
nuisance 496–9
occupiers' liability 2, 38–9, 57–9, 261, 263, 271–7,
    282–91, 294–5
proprietary interests 453
recklessness 454–5
rescuers 38, 91
Rylands v Fletcher, rule in 496–9
self-redress 460
standard of care 58
strict liability 456
third parties 57–9

v

vicarious liability 505–32
akin to employment, relationships which
    are 507–15, 527
assault 522–5
causation 527
close connection test 516, 519–27
compensation/deep pockets 506
Contracts (Rights of Third Parties) Act 1999 515
control test 506–7, 509, 512, 515, 527–30
course of employment 3, 505, 507, 509, 516–27
damages 493, 515
deterrence 506
distributive justice 506
dual vicarious liability 515

duty of care 505–32
employees, definition of 505–15
enterprise liability 506
essential elements of relationship 508–15
exemption clauses 515
fair, just and reasonable test 509, 522, 526, 528–9
harassment 506–7
immunity 515
independent contractors 507, 527–32
insurance 506, 511
loss-spreading 506, 525
non-delegable duties 528–32
policy 505–6, 512–14, 519–20, 528
prison/prisoners 510–15
public bodies 99, 101–2
remoteness 526
sexual and physical abuse 505–25
voluntary assumption of risk (*volenti non fit
    injuria*) 231–4 *see also* **consent**
assault 343
breach of statutory duty 319
contributory negligence 233, 245
occupiers' liability 231, 296
omissions 53
passengers and drunk driving 232–3
rescuers 91, 233–4
road traffic accidents and compulsory
    insurance 234
secondary victims 91
specific harm, consent to 232–4
standard of care 196
suicide 233, 245
trespass to the person 343

W

warnings
medical treatment, consent to 342
occupiers' liability 2, 267, 271–2, 278–9,
    281, 291–4
third parties 56, 59–61
websites *see* **Internet and websites**
whiplash claims 7, 9
Wilkinson v Downton, **rule in** 327, 344–50
freedom of expression 347–8, 350
harassment 327, 334, 345–6
indirect harm, causing 327, 334, 344–50
justification 347
practical jokes 344, 345–6
psychiatric harm 345–50
recklessness 348–9
strip-searching of prison visitors 344–5
trespass 344–9
wills, liability to beneficiaries of
    161–4, 168